THE
SNOWBALL

THE
SNOWBALL

Warren Buffett

and the

Business *of* Life

Updated and Condensed

ALICE SCHROEDER

BLOOMSBURY
LONDON · BERLIN · NEW YORK

First published in Great Britain 2008
This revised and updated paperback edition published 2009

Copyright © 2008, 2009 by Alice Schroeder

The moral right of the author has been asserted

Photo credits and permissions appear on p789

Chart on pages 352-353 by Daniel R. Lynch

Bloomsbury Publishing, London, New York and Berlin

36 Soho Square, London W1D 3QY

A CIP catalogue record for this book is available from the British Library

ISBN 978 0 7475 9649 3

10 9 8 7 6 5 4

Printed in Great Britain by Clays Ltd, St Ives plc

www.bloomsbury.com/aliceschroeder

FSC
Mixed Sources
Product group from well-managed
forests and other controlled sources
Cert no. SGS-COC-2061
www.fsc.org
© 1996 Forest Stewardship Council

Praise for THE SNOWBALL

"Even people who don't care a whit about business will be intrigued by this portrait.... Schroeder, a former insurance-industry analyst, spent years interviewing Buffett, and the result is a side of the Oracle of Omaha that has rarely been seen."

—*Time*

"Alice Schroeder's accumulation of detail, her vivid, artless descriptions of people and places, and the resulting narrative fluidity make this a compelling book. It has the bouncing vitality of an early Sinclair Lewis novel."

—*The Times Literary Supplement*

"*The Snowball* is likely to remain the most authoritative portrait of one of the most important American investors of our time."

—*Los Angeles Times*

"In this startlingly frank account of Buffett's life, Schroeder, a former managing director at Morgan Stanley—and hand picked by Buffett to be his biographer—strips away the mystery that has long cloaked the world's richest man to reveal a life and fortune erected around lucid and inspired business vision and unimaginable personal complexity."

—*Publishers Weekly*

"An instructive chronicle of financial success at a moment when financial failure is on everyone's mind...There are lessons to be learned....Most tellingly: The next time Warren Buffett warns of a crisis, we'd all better listen."

—*The Wall Street Journal*

"[I]f the replication of any great achievement first requires knowledge of how it was done, then *The Snowball*, the most detailed glimpse inside Warren Buffett and his world that we likely will ever get, should become a Bible for capitalists."

—*The Washington Post*

"A...penetrating and personal look at the Oracle of Omaha...[gets] deeply inside the head of the man who achieved such amazing long-term investment returns that some academics believe them to be a fluke."

—*BusinessWeek*

"[Schroeder] has sought to describe Buffett's psychological landscape as clearly as his financial one. For the reader, the results are pretty terrific.... In describing how Buffett's mind works, and why it is so well suited to his chosen career, Schroeder is particularly good.... Schroeder's brave book offers a close-up of [Buffett's] cellulite, but more fairly, in the context of a genuinely delightful character.... [H]istory's most legendary investor was not a cartoon but a real live human being. And still, somehow, deeply admirable."

—MICHAEL LEWIS, *The New Republic*

"An unvarnished and well-paced biography that is essential for all public and academic business collections."

—*Library Journal*

"The mandatory book to read in these treacherous times of financial crisis."
—*Forbes*

"Buffett has been ahead of the curve for most of the past fifty years, making him one of the world's richest people. Alice Schroeder's ... *The Snowball* provides some clues about how he's done it."

—*Financial Times*

"[Ms. Schroeder's] real contribution is her own investment expertise which enables her to make the convoluted financing schemes over the last fifty years understandable to lay readers and truly instructive to the business information junkie."

—*The Washington Times*

CELEBRATED AS ONE OF THE BEST BOOKS OF 2008 BY MANY PUBLICATIONS, INCLUDING

Time magazine Top 5 Non-Fiction Books of 2008
People magazine Top 10 Books of 2008
BusinessWeek Best Business Books of 2008
USA Today Best Business Books of 2008
The New York Times Janet Maslin's 10 Favorite Books of 2008
Publishers Weekly Staff Picks of 2008
Barnes and Noble Best Life Stories of 2008
Amazon.com Editors' Best of 2008

To David

It is the winter of Warren's ninth year. Outside in the yard, he and his little sister, Bertie, are playing in the snow.

Warren is catching snowflakes. One at a time at first. Then he is scooping them up by handfuls. He starts to pack them into a ball. As the snowball grows bigger, he places it on the ground. Slowly it begins to roll. He gives it a push, and it picks up more snow. He pushes the snowball across the lawn, piling snow on snow. Soon he reaches the edge of the yard. After a moment of hesitation, he heads off, rolling the snowball through the neighborhood.

And from there, Warren continues onward, casting his eye on a whole world full of snow.

Contents

PART SIX / Claim Checks   569

PART ONE

The Bubble

1

The Less Flattering Version

Omaha · June 2003

Warren Buffett rocks back in his chair, long legs crossed at the knee behind his father Howard's plain wooden desk. His expensive Zegna suit jacket bunches around his shoulders like an untailored version bought off the rack. The jacket stays on all day, every day, no matter how casually the other fifteen employees at Berkshire Hathaway headquarters are dressed. His predictable white shirt sits low on the neck, its undersize collar bulging away from his tie, looking left over from his days as a young businessman, as if he had forgotten to check his neck size for the last forty years.

His hands lace behind his head through strands of whitening hair. One particularly large and messy finger-combed chunk takes off over his skull like a ski jump, lofting upward at the knoll of his right ear. His shaggy right eyebrow wanders toward it above the tortoiseshell glasses. At various times this eyebrow gives him a skeptical, knowing, or beguiling look. Right now he wears a subtle smile, which lends the wayward eyebrow a captivating air. Nonetheless, his pale-blue eyes are focused and intent.

He sits surrounded by icons and mementos of fifty years. In the hallways outside his office, Nebraska Cornhuskers football photographs, his paycheck from an appearance on a soap opera, the offer letter (never accepted) to buy a hedge fund called Long-Term Capital Management, and Coca-Cola memorabilia everywhere. On the coffee table inside the office, a classic Coca-Cola bottle. A baseball glove encased in Lucite. Over the sofa, a certificate that he completed Dale Carnegie's public-speaking course in January 1952. The Wells Fargo stagecoach, westbound atop a bookcase. A Pulitzer Prize, won in 1973 by the *Sun*

Newspapers of Omaha, which his investment partnership owned. Scattered about the room are books and newspapers. Photographs of his family and friends cover the credenza and a side table, and sit under the hutch beside his desk in place of a computer. A large portrait of his father hangs above Buffett's head on the wall behind his desk. It faces every visitor who enters the room.

Although a late-spring Omaha morning beckons outside the windows, the brown wooden shutters are closed to block the view. The television beaming toward his desk is tuned to CNBC. The sound is muted, but the crawl at the bottom of the screen feeds him news all day long. Over the years, to his pleasure, the news has often been about him.

Only a few people, however, actually know him well. I have been acquainted with him for six years, originally as a financial analyst covering Berkshire Hathaway stock. Over time our relationship has turned friendly, and now I will get to know him better still. We are sitting in Warren's office because he is not going to write a book. The unruly eyebrows punctuate his words as he says repeatedly, "You'll do a better job than I would, Alice. I'm glad you're writing this book, not me." Why he would say that is something that will eventually become clear. In the meantime, we start with the matter closest to his heart.

"Where did it come from, Warren? Caring so much about making money?"

His eyes go distant for a few seconds, thoughts traveling inward: *flip flip flip* through the mental files. Warren begins to tell his story: "Balzac said that behind every great fortune lies a crime.[1] That's not true at Berkshire."

He leaps out of his chair to bring home the thought, crossing the room in a couple of strides. Landing on a mustardy-gold brocade armchair, he leans forward, more like a teenager bragging about his first romance than a seventy-two-year-old financier. How to interpret the story, who else to interview, what to write: The book is up to me. He talks at length about human nature and memory's frailty, then says, "Whenever my version is different from somebody else's, Alice, use the less flattering version."

Among the many lessons, some of the best come simply from observing him. Here is the first: Humility disarms.

In the end, there won't be too many reasons to choose the less flattering version—but when I do, human nature, not memory's frailty, is usually why. One of those occasions happened at Sun Valley in 1999.

2

Sun Valley

Idaho • July 1999

Warren Buffett stepped out of his car and pulled his suitcase from the trunk. He walked through the gate onto the airport's tarmac, where a gleaming white Gulfstream IV jet—the size of a regional commercial airliner and one of the largest private aircraft in the world in 1999—waited. One of the pilots grabbed the suitcase from him to stow in the cargo hold. Every new pilot who flew with Buffett was shocked to see him carrying his own luggage from a car he drove himself. He climbed the boarding stairs and headed to a seat next to a window, which he would not glance out of at any time during the flight. His mood was buoyant; he had been anticipating this trip for weeks.

Inside, his son Peter and daughter-in-law Jennifer, his daughter Susan and her boyfriend, and two of his grandchildren swiveled their seats away from the curved wall panels to give themselves more space as the flight attendant brought drinks from the galley, which was stocked with the family's favorite snacks and beverages. A pile of magazines lay nearby on the sofa. She brought Buffett an armload of newspapers instead, along with a basket of potato chips and a Cherry Coke that matched his red Nebraska sweater. He complimented her, chatted for a few minutes to ease her nervousness at flying for the first time with her boss, and told her that she could let the copilot know that they were ready to take off. Then he buried his head in a newspaper as the plane rolled down the runway and ascended to forty thousand feet. For the next two hours, six people hummed around him, watching videos, talking, and making phone calls, while the flight attendant set out linens and bud vases filled with orchids on the bird's-eye maple dining tables before returning to the galley to prepare lunch. Buffett never moved. He sat reading, hidden behind his newspapers, as if he were alone in his study at home.

They were flying in a $30 million airborne palace called a "fractional" jet. As many as eight owners shared it, but it served as part of a fleet, so all the owners could fly at once if they wished. The pilots in the cockpit, the crew that maintained it, the schedulers who got it to the gate on six hours' notice, and the flight attendant who served their lunch all worked for NetJets, which belonged to Warren Buffett's company, Berkshire Hathaway.

Sometime later, the G-IV crossed the Snake River Plain and approached the Sawtooth Mountains, baking in the summer sun. It sailed through the bright clear air into the Wood River Valley, descending to eight thousand feet, where it started to buck on the mountain wave of turbulence thrown into the sky by the brown foothills beneath. Buffett read on, unperturbed, as the plane rocked and his family jerked about in their seats. Brush dotted higher altitudes of a second ridge of hills and rows of pines began their march up the ridges between ravines on the leeward side. The family grinned with anticipation. As the aircraft descended through the narrowing slot between the rising mountain peaks ahead, the midday sun cast the plane's lengthening shadow over the old mining town of Hailey, Idaho.

A few seconds later, the wheels touched down on the Friedman Memorial Airport runway. By the time the Buffetts had bounded down the stairs onto the tarmac, squinting in the July sunshine, two SUVs had driven through the gate and pulled up alongside the jet, driven by men and women from Hertz. They all wore the company's gold-and-black shirts. Instead of Hertz, however, the logo said "Allen & Co."

The grandchildren bounced on their heels as the pilots unloaded the luggage and Buffett's red-and-white Coca-Cola golf bag. Then he and the others said good-bye and climbed into the SUVs. Bypassing Sun Valley Aviation—a pocket-size trailer at the runway's southern end—they swung through the gate onto the road that led to the peaks beyond. About two minutes had elapsed since the plane's wheels first touched the runway.

Right on schedule, eight minutes later, another jet followed theirs, headed to its own runway parking spot.

Throughout the golden afternoon, jet after jet cruised into Idaho from the south and east or swung around the peaks from the west and descended into Hailey. As the afternoon waned, dozens of huge, gleaming white aircraft lined the runway like a shop window full of tycoons' toys.

The Buffetts followed the trail blazed by earlier SUVs a few miles onward from the airport to the tiny town of Ketchum, near the turnoff to the Elkhorn Pass. A few miles later, they rounded Dollar Mountain, where a green oasis appeared, nestled among the brown slopes. Here amid the lacy pines and shimmering aspens lay Sun Valley, the mountains' most fabled resort.

The tide of families they were joining this Tuesday afternoon all had some connection to Allen & Co., a boutique investment bank that specialized in the media and communications industries. Allen & Co. had put together some of the biggest mergers in Hollywood, and for more than a decade had been hosting an annual series of discussions and seminars mingled with outdoor recreation at Sun Valley for its clients and friends. Herbert Allen, the firm's CEO, invited only people he liked, or those with whom he was at least willing to do business.

Thus the conference was always filled with faces both famous and rich: Hollywood folk like Candice Bergen, Tom Hanks, and Ron Howard; media moguls like Barry Diller, Rupert Murdoch, Robert Iger, and Michael Eisner; pedigreed journalists like Tom Brokaw, Diane Sawyer, and Charlie Rose; and technology titans like Bill Gates, Steve Jobs, and Andy Grove. A pack of reporters lay in wait for them every year outside the Sun Valley Lodge.

The reporters had traveled a day earlier to the Newark, New Jersey, airport or some similar embarkation point to board a commercial flight to Salt Lake City, then raced to Concourse E's bullpen to sit amid a crush of people waiting for flights to places like Sioux City, Iowa, until it was time to cram themselves into a prop plane for the one-hour bronco ride to Sun Valley. On arrival their plane was directed to the opposite end of the airport next to the tennis-court-size terminal, where they witnessed a crew of tanned young Allen & Co. employees dressed in pastel "SV99" polo shirts and white shorts welcoming the handful of Allen & Co. guests who were arriving early on commercial flights. These were instantly recognizable among the other passengers: men in Western boots and Paul Stuart shirts with jeans, women wearing goatskin-suede jackets and marble-size turquoise beads. The Allen staff had memorized the newcomers' faces from photographs supplied in advance. They hugged people they had gotten to know in years past as if they were old friends, whisked away the guests' bags, and led their charges off to the SUVs lined up steps away in the parking lot.

The reporters went to the rental-car desk, then drove to the Lodge, by now acutely conscious of their lowly status. For the next few days, many areas of Sun Valley would be marked as "private," blocked from prying eyes by closed doors, omnipresent security, hanging flower baskets, and large potted plants. The reporters would lurk around the fringes, noses pressed against the bushes.[1] Ever since Disney's Michael Eisner and Capital Cities/ABC's Tom Murphy had dreamed up a deal to merge their companies at Sun Valley '95 (the way the conference was often referred to—as if it had engulfed the entire resort, which, in a way, it had), the press coverage had grown until it took on the artificially giddy atmosphere of a business version of Cannes. Sun Valley was about more than making deals, though the deals garnered most of the press. Every year the rumors sizzled that a deal was hatching at the mysterious conclave in the Idaho mountains. Thus, as the SUVs rolled one by one into the porte cochere, the reporters peered through the front windows to see who was inside. When someone newsworthy arrived, they chased their prey into the lodge, brandishing cameras and microphones.

The press quickly recognized Warren Buffett as he stepped out of his SUV. "The DNA of the conference had him built into it," said his friend Don Keough, chairman of Allen & Co.[2] Most of the press people liked Buffett, who went out of his way not to be disliked by anyone. He also intrigued them. His public image was that of a simple man, and he seemed genuine. Yet he lived a complicated life. He owned five homes but occupied only two of them. Somehow he had wound up having, in effect, two wives. He spoke in homely aphorisms with a kindly twinkle in his eye and had a notably loyal group of friends, yet along the way he had earned a reputation as a tough, even icy dealmaker. He seemed to shun publicity yet managed to attract more of it than almost any other businessman on earth.[3] He jetted around the country in a G-IV, often attended celebrity events, and had many famous friends, yet said that he preferred Omaha, hamburgers, and thrift. He spoke of his success as being based on a few simple investing ideas and tap-dancing to work with enthusiasm every day, but if that was so, why had nobody else been able to replicate it?

Buffett, as always, gave the photographers a willing wave and a grandfatherly smile. They captured him on film, then began peering at the next car.

The Buffetts drove around to their condominium, one of the coveted Wildflower group, where Herbert Allen housed his VIPs. Inside, the usual loot awaited them: a pile of Allen & Co. SV99 logo jackets, baseball caps, zip fleeces, polo shirts—every year a different color—and a zippered notebook. Despite his fortune of more than $30 billion—enough to buy a thousand of those G-IVs parked out at the airport—Buffett liked few things more than getting a free golf shirt from a friend. He took the time to look carefully through this year's swag. Of even more interest to him, however, was the personal note that Herbert Allen sent to each guest—and the perfectly organized conference notebook that explained what Sun Valley had in store for him this year.

Timed to the second, organized to the hilt, crisp as Herbert Allen's French cuffs, Buffett's schedule was laid out hour by hour, day by day. The notebook spelled out the conference speakers and topics—until now a closely guarded secret—and the luncheons and dinners that he would attend. Unlike the other guests, Buffett knew much of this in advance, but still he wanted to see what the notebook had to say.

Herbert Allen, the so-called "Lord of Sun Valley" and the conference's quiet choreographer, set the tone of casual luxury that pervaded the event. People always cited him for high principles, brilliance, good advice, and generosity. "You'd like to die with the respect of somebody like Herbert Allen," a guest gushed. Afraid of being disinvited to the conference, attendees rarely went beyond vague hints that Herbert was "unusual," restless, impatient, and possessed of an oversize personality. Standing in the shadow of his tall, wiry frame, one had to strain to keep up with the words that crackled forth like machine-gun fire. He barked questions, then cut off respondents midsentence, lest they waste a second of his time. He specialized in saying the unsayable. "Ultimately Wall Street will be eliminated," he once told a reporter, although he ran a Wall Street bank. He referred to his competitors as "hot-dog vendors."[4]

Allen kept his firm small, and his bankers staked their own money on their deals. This unconventional approach made the firm a partner rather than a mere servant to its clients, who were the elite of Hollywood and the media world. Thus, when he played host, his guests felt privileged, rather than like captives pitched by salesmen at every turn. Allen & Co. arranged a detailed social agenda every year built around each guest's personal network of relationships—which the firm understood—and the new people that Allen's majordomos felt each should meet. Unspoken hierarchies dictated the distances of the guests' condominiums from the Inn (where meetings were held), which meals the guests were invited to attend, and with whom they would be seated.

Buffett's friend Tom Murphy referred to this kind of event as "elephant-bumping." *"Anytime a bunch of big shots get together,"* says Buffett, *"you can get people to come, because it reassures them if they're at an elephant-bumping that they're an elephant too."*[5]

Sun Valley was always very reassuring, because unlike most elephant-bumps, one could not buy one's way in. The result was a sort of faux democracy of the elite. Part of the thrill of coming was to see who was not invited, and, more thrilling still, who was disinvited. Yet within their stratum, people did develop genuine relationships. Allen & Co. fostered conviviality through lavish entertainment, beginning on the first evening, when the guests donned Western gear, climbed into old-fashioned horse-drawn wagons, and followed cowboys up a winding trail onto Trail Creek Cabin meadow. There, Herbert Allen or one of his two sons greeted the guests as the sun began to set. Cowboys entertained the children with rope tricks while the Sun Valley old guard reunited and welcomed new guests. The Buffetts usually ended the evening sitting with friends around the bonfire beneath the star-dappled western sky.

The frolicking continued on Wednesday afternoon with an optional and very mild white-water paddle down the Salmon River. Here, relationships blossomed, for Allen & Co. orchestrated who sat where on the bus to the embarkation point as well as on the rafts. The river guides steered through the mountain valley in silence, lest they interrupt conversations. Spotters hired from the local population and ambulances lined the route in case someone tumbled into the freezing water. The guests were handed warm towels as soon as they stepped out of the rafts, then served plates of barbecue.

Those not rafting could be found fly-fishing, horseback riding, shooting trap and skeet, mountain biking, playing bridge, studying nature photography, ice-skating on the outdoor rink, or golfing on immaculate greens, where they rode in carts stuffed full of Allen & Co. sunscreen, snacks, and bug spray.[6] All the entertainment flowed quietly, seamlessly, whatever was needed appearing unasked, supplied by a seemingly inexhaustible staff of almost-invisible yet ever-present Allenites in SV99 polo shirts.

It was the babysitters, however, a hundred-some good-looking, mostly blond, deeply tanned teenagers in these same polo shirts and matching Allen & Co. backpacks, who were Herbert Allen's secret weapon. As the parents and grandparents played, the sitters saw to it that each Joshua and Brittany was accompanied by his or her own playmate for whatever activity they chose—a tennis clinic, soccer, bicycling, kickball, a wagon ride, a horse show, ice-skating, relay races, rafting, fishing, an art project, or pizza and ice cream. Each babysitter was personally selected to ensure that every child always had such a wonderful time that they would beg to come back year after year—while at the same time delighting their parents with occasional glimpses of the very, very attractive young person who was allowing them to spend days of guilt-free time with other adults.

Buffett had always been one of the most appreciative of Allen's beneficiaries.

He loved Sun Valley as a family vacation, for left to his own devices at a mountain resort with his grandchildren, he would have been at a complete loss for what to do. He had no interest in outdoor activities other than golf. He never went skeet shooting or mountain biking, thought of water as "a prison of sorts," and would rather go around handcuffed than ride on a raft. Instead, he played a standing golf game with Jack Valenti, president of the Motion Picture Association of America, for a dollar bet, and a bridge game with Meredith Brokaw, and otherwise spent his time socializing with people like Playboy CEO Christie Hefner and computer hardware CEO Michael Dell.

Often he disappeared for long periods into his condo overlooking the golf course, where he read and watched business news in the living room seated next to an enormous stone fireplace.[7] He barely noticed the view of pine-covered Baldy, the mountain outside his window, or the bank of blossoms like a Persian palace rug. "The scenery is there, I guess," he said. He came for the warm atmosphere Herbert Allen had created.[8] He liked being with his closest friends: Kay Graham and her son Don; Bill and Melinda Gates; Mickie and Don Keough; Barry Diller and Diane von Furstenberg; Andy Grove and his wife, Eva.

But above all, for Buffett, Sun Valley was about reuniting with his family during one of the rare times most of the family spent together. His daughter, Susie Buffett Jr., lived in Omaha; her younger brother, Howie, and his wife, Devon—missing this year—lived in Decatur, Illinois; while their younger sibling, Peter, and his wife, Jennifer, lived in Milwaukee.

Buffett's wife of forty-seven years, Susan, who lived apart from him, had flown in to meet them from her home in San Francisco. And Astrid Menks, his companion for more than twenty years, remained at their home in Omaha.

On Friday night, Warren donned a Hawaiian shirt and escorted his wife to the traditional Pool Party on the tennis courts. Most of the guests knew and liked Susie. Always the star of the Pool Party, she sang old-fashioned standards by the light of tiki torches in front of the illuminated Olympic pool.

This year, as the cocktails and camaraderie flowed, the babble of a barely comprehensible new language—B2B, B2C, banner ads, bandwidth, broadband—competed with the sounds of Al Oehrle's band. All week long a vague sense of unease had drifted through the lunches and dinners and cocktails like a silent fog amid the handshakes, kisses, and hugs. A new group of recently minted technology executives, filled with an unusual swagger, introduced themselves to people who had never heard of them a year before.[9] Some displayed a hubris

that was at odds with Sun Valley's usual atmosphere, where a determined infor-
mality reigned and Herbert Allen enforced a sort of unwritten rule against pomposity, on penalty of banishment.

The cloud of arrogance hung heaviest over the presentations that were the
conference's centerpiece. Heads of companies, high government officials, and
other people of note gave talks unlike those they delivered anywhere else,
because hardly a word of what was said was ever whispered beyond the flower
boxes hanging by the doors of the Sun Valley Inn. Reporters were banned, and
the celebrity journalists and the media barons sat in the audience but honored a
code of silence. Thus freed to perform only for their peers, the speakers said
important and often true things that could never be articulated in front of the
press because they were too blunt, too nuanced, too alarming, too easily satirized, or too likely to be misinterpreted. The workaday journalists lurked outside, hoping for crumbs that were rarely thrown.

This year the new moguls of the Internet had been strutting, trumpeting
their latest mergers and looking to raise cash from the money managers sitting
in the audience. The money people, who stewarded other people's pensions and
savings, together commanded so much wealth that it could hardly be compre-
hended: more than a trillion dollars.[10] With a trillion dollars in 1999, you could
pay the income tax of every single individual in the United States. You could give
a brand-new Bentley automobile to every household in more than nine states.[11]
You could buy every single piece of real estate in Chicago, New York City, and Los
Angeles—combined. Some of the companies making presentations needed that
money, and they wanted this audience to give it to them.

Early in the week, Tom Brokaw's panel, called "The Internet and Our Lives,"
had drum-majored a procession of presentations about how the Internet would
reshape the communications business. One after another, executives laid out the
glittering prospects for their companies, filling the room with the intoxicating
vapor of a future unlimited by storage space and geography, so slick and visionary that while some were convinced that a whole new world was unfolding,
others were reminded of snake-oil salesmen. The folks who ran technology
companies saw themselves as Promethean geniuses bringing fire to lesser mor-
tals. Other businesses that grubbed in the ashes to make the dull necessities of
life—auto parts, lawn furniture—were now of interest mostly for how much
technology they could buy. Some Internet stocks traded at infinite multiples of
their nonexistent earnings, while "real companies" that made real things had
declined in value. As technology stocks overtook the "old economy," the Dow

Jones Industrial Average* had burst through the once-distant 10,000-point barrier only four months before, doubling in less than three and a half years.

Many of the recently enriched congregated between speeches at a cordoned-
off dining terrace by the Duck Pond, where a pair of captive swans paddled
around a pool. There, any guest—but not a reporter—could edge through the
masses of people in khaki pants and cashmere cable sweaters to ask a question
of Bill Gates or Andy Grove. Meanwhile, the journalists chased after the Internet
moguls as they moved between the Inn and their condos, amplifying the atmosphere of inflated self-importance that permeated Sun Valley this year.

Some of the Internet czars spent Friday afternoon lobbying Herbert Allen to
get them into celebrity photographer Annie Leibovitz's Saturday afternoon
shoot of the Media All-Star Team for *Vanity Fair*. They had been invited to Sun
Valley as the people of the moment, and they had trouble believing that
Leibovitz had made her own choices about who to photograph. Why, for example, would she include Buffett? His role in media had come mostly second-
hand—through board memberships, a large network of personal influence, and
a history of media investments large and small. Besides, he was old media. They
found it hard to believe that his face in a photograph still sold magazines.

These would-be all-stars also felt slighted because they knew perfectly well
that the balance in media had shifted toward the Internet. That was so even
though their banker host, Herbert Allen, thought the "new paradigm" for valuing technology stocks—based on clicks and eyeballs and projections of far-off
growth rather than a company's ability to earn cold hard cash—was bunk. "New
paradigm," he sniffed. "It's like new sex. There just isn't any such thing."[12]

The next morning, Buffett, emblem of the old paradigm, rose early, for he
would be the closing speaker of the year. Invariably, he turned down requests to
speak at conferences sponsored by other companies, but when Herbert Allen
asked him to speak at Sun Valley, he always said yes.[13] The Saturday morning
closing talk was the keynote event of the conference, so instead of heading
straight to the golf course, almost everyone went to the Sun Valley Inn, then settled into a seat. Today Buffett would be talking about the stock market.

In private, he had been critical of the gunslinging, promoter-driven market
that had sent technology stocks galloping toward delirious heights all year. The
stock of his company, Berkshire Hathaway, languished in their dust, and his

---

* A widely quoted U.S. stock measure.

rigid rule of not buying technology stocks seemed outmoded. But the criticism had no influence on how he invested, and to date, the only public statement he had made was that he never made market predictions. So his decision to do just that at Sun Valley was unprecedented. Perhaps it was the times. Buffett had a firm conviction and an overwhelming urge to preach.[14]

He had spent weeks preparing for this speech. He understood that the market was not just people trading stocks as though they were chips in a casino. The chips represented businesses. Buffett thought about the total value of the chips. What were they worth? Next he reviewed history, pulling from an exhaustive mental file. This was not the first time that world-changing new technologies had come along and shaken up the stock market. Business history was replete with new technologies—railroads, telegraph, telephone, automobiles, airplanes, television: all revolutionary ways to connect things faster—but how many had made investors rich? He was about to explain.

After the breakfast buffet, Clarke Keough walked to the podium. Buffett had known the Keough family for many years; they had been neighbors back in Omaha. It was through Clarke's father, Don, a Sioux City cattleman's son and former altar boy, that Buffett had made the connections that led him to Sun Valley. Don Keough, former president of Coca-Cola, had met Herbert Allen when he bought Columbia Pictures from Allen & Co. for Coca-Cola in 1982. Keough and his boss, Coca-Cola's CEO, Roberto Goizueta, had been so impressed by Herbert Allen's unsalesmanlike approach to selling that they had convinced him to join their board.

Keough had now technically retired from Coca-Cola to become vice chairman of Allen & Co., but he still lived and breathed the Real Thing, so powerful he was sometimes called the company's shadow chief executive.[15]

When the Keoughs were his neighbors in Omaha in the 1950s, Warren had asked Don how he was going to pay for his kids' college and suggested that he invest $10,000 in Buffett's partnership. But Don was putting six kids through parochial school on $200 a week as a Butter-Nut coffee salesman. "We didn't have the money," his son Clarke now told the audience. "This is part of my family's past that we will never forget."

Buffett joined Clarke at the podium, wearing his favorite Nebraska red sweater over a plaid shirt. He finished the story.[16]

"The Keoughs were wonderful neighbors," he said. *"It's true that occasionally Don would mention that, unlike me, he had a job, but the relationship was terrific. One time my wife, Susie, went over and did the proverbial Midwestern bit of asking*

to borrow a cup of sugar, and Don's wife, Mickie, gave her a whole sack. When I heard about that, I decided to go over to the Keoughs' that night myself. I said to Don, 'Why don't you give me twenty-five thousand dollars for the partnership to invest?' And the Keough family stiffened a little bit at that point, and I was rejected.

"*I came back sometime later and asked for the ten thousand dollars Clarke referred to and got a similar result. But I wasn't proud. So I returned at a later time and asked for five thousand dollars. And at that point, I got rejected again.*

"*So one night, in the summer of 1962, I started heading over to the Keough house. I don't know whether I would have dropped it to twenty-five hundred dollars or not, but by the time I got to the Keough household, the whole place was dark, silent. There wasn't a thing to see. But I knew what was going on. I knew that Don and Mickie were hiding upstairs, so I didn't leave.*

"*I rang that doorbell. I knocked. Nothing happened. But Don and Mickie were upstairs, and it was pitch-black.*

"*Too dark to read, and too early to go to sleep. And I remember that day as if it were yesterday. That was June twenty-first, 1962.*

"*Clarke, when were you born?*"

"*March twenty-first, 1963.*"

"*It's little things like that that history turns on. So you should be glad they didn't give me the ten thousand dollars.*"

Having charmed the audience with this little piece of give and take, Buffett turned to the matter at hand. "*Now, I'm going to attempt to multitask today. Herb told me to include a few slides. 'Show you're with it,' he said. When Herb says something, it's practically an order in the Buffett household.*" Speeding past exactly what comprised "the Buffett household"—for Buffett thought of his household as being like any other family's—he launched into a joke about Allen. The secretary to the President of the U.S. rushed into the Oval Office, apologizing for accidentally scheduling two meetings at once. The President had to choose between seeing the Pope and seeing Herbert Allen. Buffett paused for effect. "'*Send in the Pope,' said the President. 'At least I only have to kiss his ring.*'"

"*To all you fellow ring-kissers, I would like to talk today about the stock market,*" he said. "*I will be talking about pricing stocks, but I will not be talking about predicting their course of action next month or next year. Valuing is not the same as predicting.*

"*In the short run, the market is a voting machine. In the long run, it's a weighing machine.*

"*Weight counts eventually. But votes count in the short term. And it's a very undemocratic way of voting. Unfortunately, they have no literacy tests in terms of voting qualifications, as you've all learned."*

Buffett clicked a button, which illuminated a PowerPoint slide on a huge screen to his right.[17] Bill Gates, sitting in the audience, caught his breath until the notoriously fumble-fingered Buffett managed to get the first slide up.[18]

DOW JONES
INDUSTRIAL AVERAGE

| December 31, 1964 | 874.12 |
| December 31, 1981 | 875.00 |

He walked over to the screen and started explaining.

"During these seventeen years, the size of the economy grew fivefold. The sales of the Fortune five hundred companies grew more than fivefold.* Yet, during these seventeen years, the stock market went exactly nowhere."

He backed up a step or two. *"What you're doing when you invest is deferring consumption and laying money out now to get more money back at a later time. And there are really only two questions. One is how much you're going to get back, and the other is when.*

"Now, Aesop was not much of a finance major, because he said something like, 'A bird in the hand is worth two in the bush.' But he doesn't say when." Interest rates—the cost of borrowing—Buffett explained, are the price of "when." They are to finance as gravity is to physics. As interest rates vary, the value of all financial assets—houses, stocks, bonds—changes, as if the price of birds had fluctuated. *"And that's why sometimes a bird in the hand is better than two birds in the bush and sometimes two in the bush are better than one in the hand."*

In his flat, breathy twang, the words coming so fast that they sometimes ran over one another, Buffett related Aesop to the great bull market of the 1990s, which he described as baloney. Profits had grown much less than in that previous period, but birds in the bush were expensive because interest rates were low. Fewer people wanted cash—the bird in the hand—at such low rates. So

---

*Fortune magazine ranks the largest 500 companies based on sales and refers to them as the "Fortune 500." This group of companies can be used as a rough proxy for U.S.-based business.

investors were paying unheard-of prices for those birds in the bush. Casually, Buffett referred to this as the "greed factor."

The audience, full of technology gurus who were changing the world while getting rich off the great bull market, sat silent. They were perched atop portfolios that were jam-packed with stocks trading at extravagant valuations. They felt terrific about that. It was a new paradigm, this dawning of the Internet age. Their attitude was that Buffett had no right to call them greedy. Warren—who'd hoarded his money for years and given very little away, who was so cheap his license plate said "Thrifty," who spent most of his time thinking about how to make money, who had blown the technology boom and missed the boat—was spitting in their champagne.

Buffett continued. There were only three ways the stock market could keep rising at ten percent or more a year. One was if interest rates fell and remained below historic levels. The second was if the share of the economy that went to investors, as opposed to employees and government and other things, rose above its already historically high level.[19] Or, he said, the economy could start growing faster than normal.[20] He called it "wishful thinking" to use optimistic assumptions like these.

Some people, he said, were not thinking that the whole market would flourish. They just believed they could pick the winners from the rest. Swinging his arms like an orchestra conductor, he succeeded in putting up another slide while explaining that, although innovation might lift the world out of poverty, people who invest in innovation historically have not been glad afterward.

"*This is half of a page which comes from a list seventy pages long of all the auto companies in the United States.*" He waved the complete list in the air. "*There were two thousand auto companies: the most important invention, probably, of the first half of the twentieth century. It had an enormous impact on people's lives. If you had seen at the time of the first cars how this country would develop in connection with autos, you would have said, 'This is the place I must be.' But of the two thousand companies, as of a few years ago, only three car companies survived.*[21] *And, at one time or another, all three were selling for less than book value, which is the amount of money that had been put into the companies and left there. So autos had an enormous impact on America, but in the opposite direction on investors.*"

He put down the list to shove his hand in his pocket. "*Now, sometimes it's much easier to figure out the losers. There was, I think, one obvious decision back*

*then. And, of course, the thing you should have been doing was shorting horses."**
Click. A slide about horses popped up.

U.S. HORSE POPULATION

1900—17 million

1998—5 million

"Frankly, I'm kind of disappointed that the Buffett family was not shorting horses throughout this entire period. There are always losers."

Members of the audience chuckled, albeit faintly. Their companies might be losing money, but in their hearts beat a conviction that they were winners, supernovas blazing at the cusp of a momentous shift in the heavens.

Click. Another slide appeared.

"Now, the other great invention of the first half of the century was the airplane. In this period from 1919 to 1939, there were about two hundred companies. Imagine if you could have seen the future of the airline industry back there at Kitty Hawk. You would have seen a world undreamed of. But assume you had the insight, and you saw all of these people wishing to fly and to visit their relatives or run away from their relatives or whatever you do in an airplane, and you decided this was the place to be.

"As of a couple of years ago, there had been zero money made from the aggregate of all stock investments in the airline industry in history.

"So I submit to you: I really like to think that if I had been down there at Kitty Hawk, I would have been farsighted enough and public-spirited enough to have <u>shot Orville down.</u> I owed it to future capitalists."[22]

Another light chuckle. Some were getting tired of these musty old examples. But out of respect, they let Buffett get on with it.

Now he was talking about their businesses. *"It's wonderful to promote new industries, because they are very promotable. It's very hard to promote investment in a mundane product. It's much easier to promote an esoteric product, even particularly one with losses, because there's no quantitative guideline."* This was goring the audience directly, where it hurt. *"But people will keep coming back to invest,*

---

*A short-seller borrows a stock and sells it, betting it will go down. If so, the "short-seller" profits from buying the stock back cheaper. He loses if the price rises. Short-selling is normally risky: You are betting against the long-term trend of the market.

you know. It reminds me a little of that story of the oil prospector who died and went to heaven. And St. Peter said, 'Well, I checked you out, and you meet all of the qualifications. But there's one problem.' He said, 'We have some tough zoning laws up here, and we keep all of the oil prospectors over in that pen. And as you can see, it is absolutely chock-full. There is no room for you.'

"And the prospector said, 'Do you mind if I just say four words?'

"St. Peter said, 'No harm in that.'

"So the prospector cupped his hands and yells out, 'Oil discovered in hell!'

"And of course, the lock comes off the cage and all of the oil prospectors start heading right straight down.

"St. Peter said, 'That's a pretty slick trick. So,' he says, 'go on in, make yourself at home. All the room in the world.'

"The prospector paused for a minute, then said, 'No, I think I'll go along with the rest of the boys. There might be some truth to that rumor after all.' [23]

"Well, that's the way people feel with stocks. It's very easy to believe that there's some truth to that rumor after all."

This got a mild laugh for a half second, which choked off as soon as the audience caught on to Buffett's point, which was that, like the prospectors, they might be mindless enough to follow rumors and drill for oil in hell.

He closed by returning to the proverbial bird in the bush. There was no new paradigm, he said. Ultimately, the value of the stock market could only reflect the output of the economy.

He put up a slide to illustrate how, for several years, the market's valuation had outstripped the economy's growth by an enormous degree. This meant, Buffett said, that the next seventeen years might not look much better than that long stretch from 1964 to 1981 when the Dow had gone exactly nowhere—that is, unless the market plummeted. *"If I had to pick the most probable return over that period,"* he said, *"it would probably be six percent."* [24] Yet a recent PaineWebber-Gallup poll had shown that investors expected stocks to return thirteen to twenty-two percent. [25]

He walked over to the screen. Waggling his bushy eyebrows, he gestured at the cartoon of a naked man and woman, taken from a legendary book on the stock market, *Where Are the Customers' Yachts?* [26] *"The man said to the woman, 'There are certain things that cannot be adequately explained to a virgin either by words or pictures.'"* The audience took his point, which was that people who bought Internet stocks were about to get screwed. They sat in stony silence. Nobody laughed. Nobody chuckled or snickered or guffawed.

Seeming not to notice, Buffett moved back to the podium and told the audience about the goody bag he had brought for them from Berkshire Hathaway. *"I just bought a company that sells fractional jets, NetJets,"* he said. *"I thought about giving each of you a quarter share of a Gulfstream IV. But when I went to the airport, I realized that'd be a step down for most of you."* At that, they laughed. So, he continued, he was giving each of them a jeweler's loupe instead, which he said they should use to look at one another's wives' rings—the third wives' especially.

That hit its mark. The audience laughed and applauded. Then they stopped. A resentful undercurrent was washing through the room. Sermonizing on the stock market's excesses at Sun Valley in 1999 was like preaching chastity in a house of ill repute. The speech might rivet the audience to its chairs, but that didn't mean that they would go forth and abstain.

Yet some thought they were hearing something important. "This is great; it's the basic tutorial on the stock market, all in one lesson," thought Gates.[27] The money managers, many of whom were hunting for cheaper stocks, found it comforting and even cathartic.

Buffett waved a book in the air. *"This book was the intellectual underpinning of the 1929 stock-market mania. Edgar Lawrence Smith's* Common Stocks as Long Term Investments *proved that stocks always yielded more than bonds. Smith identified five reasons, but the most novel of these was the fact that companies retained some of their earnings, which they could reinvest at the same rate of return. That was the plowback—a novel idea in 1924! But as my mentor, Ben Graham, always used to say, 'You can get in way more trouble with a good idea than a bad idea,' because you forget that the good idea has limits. Lord Keynes, in his preface to this book, said, 'There is a danger of expecting the results of the future to be predicted from the past.'"*[28]

He had worked his way back around to the same subject: that one couldn't extrapolate from the past few years of accelerating stock prices. *"Now, is there anyone I haven't insulted?"*[29] He paused. The question was rhetorical; nobody raised a hand.

"Thank you," he said, and ended.

"Praise by name, criticize by category" was Buffett's rule. The speech was meant to be provocative, not off-putting—for he cared a great deal what they thought of him. He had named no culprits, and he assumed they would get over his jokes. His argument was so powerful, almost unassailable, that he thought even those who didn't like its message must acknowledge its force. And whatever unease the audience felt was not expressed aloud. He answered questions until the session ended. People began to stand, awarding him an ovation. No matter how they saw it—a masterful exposition on how to think about investing or the last roar of an old lion—the speech was by any standard a tour de force.

Buffett had stayed on top for forty-four years in a business where five years of good performance was a meaningful accomplishment. Still, as the record lengthened, the question always loomed: When would he falter? Would he declare an end to his reign, or would some seismic shift dethrone him? Now, it seemed to some, the time had come. It may have taken an invention as significant as the personal computer, coupled with a technology as pervasive as the Internet, to topple him, but he'd apparently overlooked information that was freely available and rejected the reality of the approaching millennium. As they muttered a polite "wonderful speech, Warren," the young lions prowled, restive. And so, even in the ladies' room at the break, sarcastic remarks were heard from the Silicon Valley wives.[30]

It was not just that Buffett was wrong, as some felt, but that even if he were eventually proved right—as others suspected he would be—his dour prediction of the investing future contrasted so sharply with Buffett's own legendary past. For in his early glory days, stocks were cheap, and Buffett had scooped them up in handfuls, almost alone in noticing the golden apples lying untouched on the path. As the years passed, barriers grew up that made it harder to invest, to get an edge, to figure out what others didn't know. So who was Buffett to preach at them, now that it was their turn? Who was he to say that they shouldn't make money while they could off this wonderful market?

Throughout the rest of the lazy afternoon, Herbert Allen's guests played one last game of tennis or golf or headed to the Duck Pond Lawn for a leisurely chat. Buffett's old friends congratulated him on his triumph of a speech. He believed he had done a convincing job of swaying the audience. He had not given a speech full of such commanding evidence simply to go on the record.

Buffett, who wanted to be liked, had registered the standing ovation, not the mutterings. But the less flattering version was how many were not convinced. They believed that Buffett was rationalizing having missed the technology boom, and they were startled to see him make such specific predictions, prophecies that surely would turn out to be wrong. Beyond his earshot, the rumbling went on: "Good ol' Warren. He missed the boat. How could he miss the tech boat? He's a friend of *Bill Gates*."[31]

A few miles away at the River Run Lodge later that evening, with the guests at the closing dinner again arranged according to some invisible plan, Herbert

Allen finally spoke, thanking various people and reflecting on the week. Then Susie Buffett took the stage beside the windows that overlooked the pebbly Big Wood River and once again sang the old standards. Later the guests returned to the Sun Valley Lodge terrace, where Olympic skaters axeled and arabesqued in the Saturday night ice show.

By the time fireworks exploded across the sky at evening's end, Sun Valley '99 had been declared another glorious five-day extravaganza. Yet what most people would remember was not the rafting or the skaters; it was Buffett's talk about the stock market—the first forecast he had made in exactly thirty years.

3

Creatures of Habit

Buffett's partner, Charles T. Munger, was nowhere to be seen at Sun Valley. The Allen & Co. organizers had never invited him. Which was fine with Munger, for Sun Valley was the kind of event he would almost pay not to attend. Its rituals required pleasing too many people.[1] Buffett was the one who enjoyed pleasing people. Even as he took his jabs at the audience, he made sure to remain personally well liked. Whereas Munger wanted only respect, and didn't care who thought he was a son of a bitch.

Yet the two, in many people's minds, were almost interchangeable. Buffett himself referred to them as "Siamese twins, practically." They walked with the same lurching, awkward gait. They wore the same sort of gray suits draped stiffly over their frames, the inflexible bodies of men who have spent decades reading books and newspapers rather than playing sports or working outdoors. They arranged their graying hair in the same comb-over, they wore similar Clark Kentish glasses, and the same intensity flickered through their eyes.

They thought alike and had the same fascination with business as a puzzle worth spending a lifetime to solve. Both regarded rationality and honesty as the highest virtues. Quickened pulses and self-delusion, in their view, were the major causes of mistakes. They liked to ponder the reasons for failure as a way of deducing the rules of success. "I had long looked for insight by inversion, in the intense manner counseled by the great algebraist Carl Jacobi," Munger said. "'Invert, always invert.'" He illustrated this with the story of a wise peasant who said, "Tell me where I'm going to die so I won't go there."[2] But while Munger meant this figuratively, Buffett took it more literally. He lacked Munger's subtle sense of fatalism, particularly when it came to the subject of his own mortality.

Both men, however, were infected by the urge to preach. Munger described himself as "didactic." He labored over occasional speeches on the art of success-ful living, which struck people as so insightful that they were passed from hand to hand until, finally, the Internet made them accessible to all. He grew so enthused delivering these speeches that, on a few occasions, he became "self-intoxicated," as Buffett put it, and had to be dragged from the stage.

But while he considered himself an amateur scientist and architect and did not hesitate to expound on Einstein, Darwin, rational habits of thinking, and the ideal distance between houses in a Santa Barbara subdivision, Munger was nonetheless wary of venturing very far from what he had spent some time to learn. He dreaded falling prey to what a Harvard Law School classmate of his had called "the Shoe Button Complex."

"His father commuted daily with the same group of men," Munger said. "One of them had managed to corner the market in shoe buttons—a really small market, but he had it all. He pontificated on every subject, all subjects imaginable. Cornering the market on shoe buttons made him an expert on everything. Warren and I have always sensed it would be a big mistake to behave that way."[3]

Buffett was in no danger of suffering from the Shoe Button Complex. He feared appearing obnoxious or, worse, sanctimonious. He believed in what he called the Circle of Competence, drew a line around himself, and stayed within the three subjects on which he would be recognized as absolutely expert: money, business, and his own life.

Yet, like Munger, he had his own form of self-intoxication. While Munger chose his speeches selectively but had trouble winding them up, Buffett could usually conclude a lecture, but found it hard not to start one.

He gave speeches; he wrote articles; he wrote editorials; he gathered people at parties and gave little lessons; he testified in lawsuits; he appeared in television documentaries and did television interviews and took journalists along with him on trips; he went around to colleges and taught classes; he got college stu-dents to come and visit him; he gave lessons at the openings of furniture stores, the inauguration of insurance telemarketing centers, and dinners for would-be customers of NetJets; he gave locker-room talks to football players; he spoke at lunches with Congressmen; he educated newspaper folk in editorial board meetings; he gave lessons to his own board of directors; and, above all, he put on the teacher's robes in his letters to and meetings with his shareholders. Berkshire Hathaway was his "Sistine Chapel"—not just a work of art, but an illustrated text of his beliefs, which Munger referred to as Buffett's "didactic enterprise."

The two men had been each other's best audience ever since they first met through mutual friends over lunch in 1959. After they talked their hosts into exhaustion, they wound up alone at the table, jabbering to each other. Since then, they had carried on an uninterrupted conversation for decades. Eventually, they could read each other's minds, stopped talking, and carried on by telepathy. But by then their other audiences had expanded to include their friends, business partners, shareholders—indeed, the whole world. People reeled out of Buffett's office or away from Munger's speeches, figuratively smacking their foreheads and saying, "My God!" at some insight one of them had about a seemingly intractable problem, which now, in hindsight, seemed obvious. No matter how much either talked, demand for their words only increased. Like most things in their lives, they found this role easy and comfortable, engraved in their beings by long habit.

But, accused of being a creature of habit, Buffett responded with a wounded look. "I'm not a creature of habit," he said. "Now, Charlie—*Charlie* is a creature of habit."

Munger rose in the morning and set his quarter-inch-thick, old-fashioned cataract glasses on the bridge of his nose. He climbed into his car at precisely the same time every day, carefully placed his father's briefcase on the seat next to him, and drove from Pasadena to downtown Los Angeles.[4] He changed lanes on his left side by counting the cars in his rearview mirror, then watching them pass in the front to sense when there would be a gap.[5] (For years he drove with a can of gasoline in his trunk in case he forgot to stop for gas, but was finally persuaded to give up this particular habit.) Once downtown, he often met someone for breakfast at the sandy-brick art deco California Club, one of the city's venerable institutions, where he strode automatically to the first table in the dining room after grabbing a clutch of newspapers from the console table by the third-floor elevator. He tore through the papers like gift wrap on Christmas morning, until they lay around him in a heap.

"Good morning, Mr. Munger." The members of the L.A. business establishment genuflected as they passed by on their way to lesser tables, pleased if he recognized them and chatted for a moment or two.

Munger regarded them through his right eye. His left had been destroyed in a failed cataract operation.[6] While he spoke, his left eyelid hung at half-mast as his head swiveled back and forth across the room, taking in the scene. The rotating half-gaze gave him an aspect of eternal vigilance and permanent disdain.

After finishing his blueberries, Munger repaired to the modest, cluttered office he rented from Munger, Tolles & Olson, the law firm he had founded in 1962 and retired from just three years later. His domain was watched over by his longtime secretary, the Teutonic Dorothe Obert. There, surrounded by science and history books, biographies of Benjamin Franklin, an enormous portrait of aphorist and lexicographer Samuel Johnson, plans and models of his latest real estate deal, and a hydrocephalic bust of Franklin next to the windows, he felt at home. Munger admired Franklin for espousing Protestant bourgeois values while living as he damn well pleased. He frequently cited Franklin, and spent his days studying his works and those of other "eminent dead," as he put it, like Cicero and Maimonides. He also administered Wesco Financial, a subsidiary of Berkshire, and the Daily Journal Corporation, a legal publishing company that he and a partner controlled. Would-be chatterers—except for family, close friends, or business associates—met with obscure ironic witticisms and discouragement from Dorothe.

Munger spent much of his time working on four causes. When he chose, he could pitch in with an almost stunning generosity. Lacking a soft spot for the people of what he called "Dregsville," however, his charity took the form of a Darwinian quest to boost the brightest. Good Samaritan Hospital, the Harvard-Westlake School, the Huntington Library, and the Stanford Law School were the beneficiaries. These organizations knew that Munger's money and effort would be accompanied by much lecturing and insistence that everyone do things Charlie's way. He would gladly pay for dormitories at Stanford Law School, as long as Stanford made each room exactly so many feet wide, with a window exactly here and the bedroom so many feet from the kitchen, and provided that the university locate the parking garage where he insisted. He embodied old-fashioned noblesse oblige, with all sorts of irritating strings attached to the money for the recipients' own good, because he knew best.

Even with all this overseeing of others' activities, Munger often left for the day in time to play a little golf with his cronies at the Los Angeles Country Club. Then he joined his wife, Nancy, for dinner, sometimes at the Pasadena house he'd designed himself or, more likely, with a longtime group of close-knit friends, once again either at the California Club or the L.A. Country Club. He concluded his day by burying his nose in a book. He vacationed regularly with his eight children and stepchildren and assorted grandchildren, usually at his cabin on Minnesota's Star Island, where, like his father, he was an avid fisherman. He hosted dozens of people on his enormous catamaran, the *Channel Cat* (described as a "floating restaurant" by one friend, and used mainly to entertain). In short, despite his idiosyncrasies, Munger was a straightforward family man who liked his friends, his clubs, and his charities.

Buffett liked his friends and his clubs, but had little to do with charities. His life was even simpler than Munger's, despite a personality that was far more complex. He spent the vast majority of his time in Omaha, but his schedule revolved around a series of board meetings and trips to visit friends, orchestrated with an unhurried regularity, like the phases of the moon. On the days he was in town, he drove 1.5 miles from the house he'd inhabited for four decades to the office at Kiewit Plaza that he'd occupied for almost as long, where he sat down behind his father's desk by eight-thirty a.m. There, he turned on the television to CNBC with the sound muted before picking up his pile of newspapers, keeping half an eye on the screen while plowing through a pile of publications on his desk: *American Banker, Editor & Publisher, Broadcasting, Beverage Digest, Furniture Today, A.M. Best's Property-Casualty Review,* the *New Yorker, Columbia Journalism Review,* the *New York Observer,* and newsletters from writers he admired on the stock and bond market.

After that he digested the monthly, weekly, and daily reports faxed, mailed, and e-mailed by the businesses that Berkshire owned, a list that grew longer year by year, telling him how many auto policies GEICO had sold last week and how many claims it had paid; how many pounds of See's Candies had sold yesterday; how many prison-guard uniforms had been ordered from Fechheimers; how many jet time-shares NetJets was selling in Europe and the United States; and all the rest—awnings, battery chargers, kilowatt hours, air compressors, engagement rings, leased trucks, encyclopedias, pilot training, home furnishings, cardiopulmonary equipment, pig stalls, boat loans, real estate listings, ice cream sundaes, winches and windlasses, cubic feet of gas, sump pumps, vacuum cleaners, newspaper advertising, egg counters, knives, furniture rentals, nurses' shoes, electromechanical components. All the numbers on their costs and sales poured into his office, and he knew many of them from memory.[7]

In his spare time, he pored over reports from the hundreds of companies he hadn't bought yet. Partly out of interest, and partly just in case.

If some dignitary made the pilgrimage to Omaha to meet him, he got in his steel-blue Lincoln Town Car and drove the 1.5 miles through downtown and out to the airport to pick him or her up personally. People were startled and charmed by the unaffected gesture, although he soon scraped their nerves raw by barely noticing stop signs, traffic lights, or other cars, weaving around the road while talking animatedly. He rationalized his distractedness by saying that he drove so slowly that, if he had an accident, the damage would be light.[8]

He always gave a tour of his office, showing off his totems, the memorabilia that told the story of his business life. Then he sat, leaning forward in a chair, hands clasped and eyebrows raised sympathetically as he listened to the visitor's questions and requests. To each of them Buffett offered off-the-cuff wit, quick decisions on business proposals, and warm advice. As they left, he might surprise a famous politician or the CEO of some huge company by dropping in for lunch at McDonald's before ferrying him back to the airport.

In between the reading, the research, and the occasional meetings, the phone rang all day long. First-time callers punching in Buffett's number were shocked to hear a hearty "Hello!" and often stumbled in confusion when they realized that he answered his own phone. His secretary, the amiable Debbie Bosanek, trotted in and out of his office with messages from the overflow calls. On his credenza, another phone rang from time to time. He took these calls instantly, for they were from his trader. "Yello ... mmm hmm ... yep ... how much ... mmm hmm ... go ahead," he would say, and hang up. Then he turned back to the other calls, or to his reading or CNBC, before leaving promptly at five-thirty p.m. for home.

The woman waiting for him there was not his wife. He was perfectly open about Astrid Menks, with whom he had lived in an unusual triangular arrangement since 1978. Susie Buffett approved of and in fact had arranged the relationship; yet he and Susie both made a great point of saying how very married they were, their routine as a couple as scheduled and orchestrated as everything else in Buffett's life. All the while, he offered no more explanation in public than "If you knew everybody well, you'd understand it quite well."[9] While this was true in its way, it did not help the curious, since almost nobody knew both Susie and Astrid well, or, for that matter, Buffett himself. He kept these relationships separate, as he kept many of his relationships separate. By all appearances, however, Astrid and Susie were friends.

Most nights, Buffett ate dinner—something like a hamburger or pork chop—at home with Astrid. After a couple of hours he turned his attention to his nightly bridge game on the Internet, to which he devoted about twelve hours a week. While he tapped away, glued to the screen with the background noise of the TV, Astrid mostly left him to his game, except when occasionally he said, "Astrid, get me a Coke!" Afterward, he usually talked to Sharon Osberg, his bridge partner and a close confidante, for a while on the phone as Astrid puttered around the house until ten, when Buffett had his nightly conference call with Ajit Jain, who ran his reinsurance business. Meanwhile, Astrid went to the market and picked up the early edition of the next day's newspaper. While he read it, she went to bed. And that, it seemed, was the simple, ordinary life of a megabillionaire.

4

Warren, What's Wrong?

Omaha and Atlanta · August–December 1999

Nearly all of Buffett's $30 billion plus—ninety-nine percent—was invested in the stock of Berkshire Hathaway. He had spoken at Sun Valley about how the market's weighing machine was more important than its voting machine. But it was the voting machine's opinion of his stock price that set the altitude from which he preached. People paid attention to him because he was rich. So when he predicted that the market could disappoint investors for seventeen years,[1] he was standing on the edge of a cliff, and he knew it. If he was wrong, not only would he be the laughingstock of Sun Valley; in the record books of the world's wealthiest men, his personal rank might drop. And Buffett paid close attention to that rank.

Through the late 1990s, BRK (Berkshire Hathaway's stock symbol) had boosted his profile by outpacing the market, until it peaked at $80,900 per share in June 1998. That a single share of Berkshire stock cost enough to buy a small condo was unique among American businesses. To Buffett, the stock price represented an uncomplicated measure of his success. It had grown in an ascending line since the day he first bought BRK for $7.50 a share. Even though the market had rocked through the late 1990s, until 1999 an investor who bought BRK and held on to it would have been better off.

Annual Stock Price Appreciation						
	1993	1994	1995	1996	1997	1998
BRK	39%	25%	57%	6%	35%	52%
S&P[2]	10%	1%	38%	23%	33%	29%

But now, Buffett found himself standing on the sinking platform of an unloved stock, watching the "T&T" (tech and telecommunications) stocks ascend. By August 1999, BRK had slumped to $65,000. How much should someone pay for a large, established business that returned $400 million to them in profits every year? How much for a small, new business that was losing money?

- Toys "R" Us was earning $400 million a year and had sales of $11 billion.
- eToys was losing $123 million a year and had sales of $100 million.

The market's voting machine said that eToys was worth $4.9 billion, and Toys "R" Us was worth about a billion less than that. The presumption was that eToys was going to crush Toys "R" Us through the Internet.[3]

The one cloud of doubt that hung over the market concerned the calendar. Experts were predicting that disaster might strike at midnight, December 31, 1999, because the world's computers were not programmed to handle dates beginning with a "2." Fearing panic, the Federal Reserve began to increase the supply of money rapidly to prevent cash shortages in case all the country's ATMs froze at once. Thus turbocharged, shortly after Sun Valley the market had spiraled upward like a Fourth of July firecracker. If you had invested a dollar in January in the NASDAQ, an index full of technology stocks, your bet was now worth a buck twenty-five. The same bet in BRK was worth only eighty cents. By December, the Dow Jones Industrial Average closed the year up twenty-five percent. The NASDAQ blasted through the 4,000-point level, up an incredible eighty-six percent. BRK fell to $56,100. In just a few months BRK's lead for the past five years had been tsunamied.

For more than a year, financial pundits had made sport of Buffett, a has-been, an emblem of the past. Now, on the eve of the millennium, *Barron's,* a weekly must-read on Wall Street, put Buffett on its cover with the headline "Warren, What's Wrong?" The accompanying article said Berkshire had "stumbled" badly. He was running a Pamplona of negative press like nothing he had ever experienced. "I know it's going to change," he repeated over and over, "I just don't know when."[4] His shrilling nerves were urging him to fight back. Instead, he did nothing. He did not respond.

Near the end of 1999, even many longtime "value investors" who followed Buffett's style had either shuttered their businesses or given in and bought technology stocks. Buffett did not. What he called his Inner Scorecard—a toughness about financial decisions that had infused him for as long as anyone could remember—kept him from wavering.

"*I feel like I'm on my back, and there's the Sistine Chapel, and I'm painting away. I like it when people say, 'Gee, that's a pretty good-looking painting.' But it's my painting, and when somebody says, 'Why don't you use more red instead of blue?' Good-bye. It's my painting. And I don't care what they sell it for. The painting itself will never be finished. That's one of the great things about it.*[5]

"*The big question about how people behave is whether they've got an Inner Scorecard or an Outer Scorecard. It helps if you can be satisfied with an Inner Scorecard. I always pose it this way. I say: 'Lookit. Would you rather be the world's greatest lover, but have everyone think you're the world's worst lover? Or would you rather be the world's worst lover but have everyone think you're the world's greatest lover?' Now, that's an interesting question.*

"*Here's another one. If the world couldn't see your results, would you rather be thought of as the world's greatest investor but in reality have the world's worst record? Or be thought of as the world's worst investor when you were actually the best?*

"*In teaching your kids, I think the lesson they're learning at a very, very early age is what their parents put the emphasis on. If all the emphasis is on what the world's going to think about you, forgetting about how you really behave, you'll wind up with an Outer Scorecard. Now, my dad: He was a hundred percent Inner Scorecard guy.*

"*He was <u>really</u> a maverick. But he wasn't a maverick for the sake of being a maverick. He just didn't care what other people thought. My dad taught me how life should be lived. I've never seen anybody quite like him.*"

PART TWO

The Inner Scorecard

5

The Urge to Preach

John Buffett, the first known Buffett in the New World, was a serge weaver believed to be of French Huguenot descent. He fled to America in the seventeenth century to escape religious persecution and settled in Huntington, Long Island, as a farmer.

Little else is known of the earliest Buffetts in the United States, except that they were farmers.[1] It is clear, however, that Warren Buffett's urge to preach is part of a family legacy. An early example was one of John Buffett's sons,[2] remembered for sailing north across the Long Island Sound to a coastal settlement in Connecticut, where he climbed a hill and commenced to preach religion to the heathens. But it is doubtful that the outcasts, scofflaws, and unbelievers of Greenwich repented on hearing his words, since history records that lightning promptly struck him down.

Several generations later, Zebulon Buffett, a farmer in Dix Hills, Long Island, left his trace on the family tree as the first recorded exemplar of another Buffett trait—treating one's own relatives with extreme tightfistedness—when his grandson, Sidney Homan Buffett, quit his job working on Zebulon's farm in disgust over the insultingly low pay.

A gangly teenager, Sidney went west to Omaha, Nebraska, to join his maternal grandfather George Homan in his livery-stable business.[3] The year was 1867; Omaha a settlement consisting mainly of a collection of wooden shacks. But with the end of the Civil War, it was about to be transformed. A grand transcontinental railroad would link the coasts of the newly reunited states for the first time; Omaha would be the railroad's headquarters. The coming of the Union

Pacific filled the town with a bustling commercial spirit, as well as a sense of destiny.

Sidney left the livery stable to open the first grocery store in a town with no paved streets. In this respectable but modest business, he sold fruit, vegetables, and game until eleven every night: prairie chickens for a quarter, jackrabbits for a dime.[4] His grandfather Zebulon feared for Sidney's prospects and pelted him with letters containing advice, all rules that—with one significant exception— his descendants still heed.

> "Try to be punctual in all your dealings. You will find it difficult to get along with some men, deal as little as possible with such. . . . Save your credit, for that is better than money. . . . If you go on in business, *be content with moderate gains.* Don't be too hasty to get too rich. . . . I want you to live so as to be fit to live and fit to die."[5]

Content with moderate gains in an upward-scrambling, freewheeling place, Sidney gradually built the store into a success.[6] He married Evelyn Ketchum and they had six children, several of whom died young. Two sons, Ernest and Frank, were among the survivors.[7]

It has been said, "No man was ever better named than Ernest Buffett."[8] Born in 1877, he ended his formal schooling in the eighth grade, and joined his father behind the counter during the Panic of 1893. Far more eccentric than his businesslike brother, Frank Buffett became a large, stove-bellied man, the heathen among the Puritans of the family, who even enjoyed the occasional drink.

One day, a stunning young woman appeared at the store looking for a job. Her name was Henrietta Duvall, and she had traveled to Omaha to escape an unfriendly stepmother.[9] Frank and Ernest were both immediately smitten, but it was the more handsome Ernest who won Henrietta as his wife in 1898. Ernest and Henrietta's first child, Clarence, was born within a year of their marriage, followed by three more sons and a daughter. Shortly after the quarrel, Ernest went into a partnership with his father, Sidney; eventually he left to set up another grocery store. Frank remained single for most of his life, and for the next twenty-five years, as long as Henrietta lived, he and Ernest apparently never spoke.

At Ernest's new store, the "hours were long, pay low, opinions cast in iron, and foolishness zero."[10] Always dressed in a dapper suit, he scowled from his desk on the mezzanine to stop his employees from idling, and penned letters demanding that suppliers "kindly speed up the celery."[11] He charmed his lady customers, but never hesitated to judge and carried a little black notebook to write down the names of people who irritated him—Democrats, and people who didn't pay their grocery bills.[12] Ernest was sure that the world needed his opinion and traveled to conferences around the country to bemoan the sorry state of the nation with like-minded businessmen.[13] *"Self-doubt was not his strong suit. He always spoke in exclamation points and expected you to acknowledge that he knew best,"* says Buffett.

In a letter to his son and daughter-in-law advising them to always have some ready cash, Ernest described the Buffetts as bourgeois incarnate:

> "I might mention that there has never been a Buffett who ever left a very large estate, but there has never been one that did not leave something. They never spent all they made, but always saved part of what they made, and it has all worked out pretty well."[14]

"Spend less than you make" could, in fact, have been the Buffett family motto, if accompanied by its corollary, "Don't go into debt."

Henrietta, also of French Huguenot extraction, was as thrifty, iron-willed, and teetotaling as her husband. While Ernest was at the store, she would gather her children to drive in the family's fringed surrey out into the countryside, where she knocked on farmhouse doors to hand out religious tracts.

The Buffetts were tradespeople, not members of the merchant or professional class, but as pioneer settlers of Omaha, they were exceedingly conscious of their place. Henrietta's hope was that her children, four sons and a daughter, would become the first in the family to graduate from college. All the boys toiled at the family store when they were young. Then Clarence went into the oil business, with a graduate degree in geology.[15] George, her second, got a PhD in chemistry and wound up on the East Coast. Her three youngest, Howard, Fred, and Alice, all graduated from the University of Nebraska. Fred took up duties at the family store, and Alice became a home-economics teacher.

Howard, the third son and Warren's father, was born in 1903. He had unhappy memories of feeling like an outsider during his years at Central High School in the early 1920s. Omaha was run by a handful of families who owned the stockyards, banks, department stores, and had inherited fortunes from the breweries now closed under Prohibition. "My clothes were pretty much hand-me-downs from my two older brothers," he said, "and I was a paperboy and the son of a grocery man. So the high school fraternities didn't look my way, and I was just one of the boys from what approximated outside of the tracks." He felt these snubs keenly; they marked him with a deep revulsion toward rank and privilege acquired by birth.[16]

At the University of Nebraska, Howard majored in journalism and worked at the college newspaper, the *Daily Nebraskan*, where he was able to combine the outsider's love of reporting on the activities of the powerful with the family fascination with politics. It would not be long before he met Leila Stahl, a girl whose background mingled the same interest in newspapers with self-consciousness about social class.

Leila's father, John Stahl, a sweet little dumpling of a man of German-American descent, had traveled Cuming County, Nebraska, in a horse and buggy with a buffalo robe on his lap as superintendent of schools.[17] The family history says he adored his wife, Stella, who gave him three daughters—Edith, Leila, and Bernice—and one son, Marion. Of English descent, Stella was unhappy living in West Point, Nebraska, a town of German-American hausfraus, where she never felt at ease. In 1909, Stella suffered a mental breakdown. This must have seemed an ominous recurrence of family history, for her mother, Susan Barber, who was described as "maniacal," had been an inmate of the Nebraska State Insane Asylum, where she died in 1899. After an incident in which, according to family lore, Stella went after Edie with the fireplace poker, John Stahl gave up his traveling job to care for their children. Increasingly, Stella retreated to her darkened room, where she sat twisting her hair, apparently depressed. This isolation was punctuated by occasional episodes of cruel behavior toward her husband and the girls.[18] Stahl, realizing that he could not leave the children alone with their mother, bought a newspaper, the *Cuming County Democrat*, so he could make a living working from home. From the time Leila was five, she and her sisters essentially ran the household and helped their father put out the paper. She learned to spell by setting type. By age eleven she could run a jackhammer of a Linotype press, and every Friday she missed school because of the headaches she suffered after having to get out the paper on Thursday night. Living above the business in a house infested by mice, the family pinned all their hopes for the future on Marion, the brilliant brother who was studying to be a lawyer.

During World War I the Stahls' difficulties grew. When the *Cuming County Democrat* came out against Germany in a German-American town, half their subscribers dropped the paper and switched to the *West Point Republican*—a financial catastrophe. John Stahl himself was an ardent supporter of the

Democratic political giant William Jennings Bryan. At the turn of the century, Bryan had been one of the most important politicians of his era, nearly becoming President of the United States. In his heyday, he stood for a kind of "populism" that he set forth in his most famous speech:

> "There are two ideas of government. There are those who believe that if you just legislate to make the well-to-do prosperous, that their prosperity will leak through on those below. The Democratic idea has been that if you legislate to make the masses prosperous their prosperity will find its way up and through every class that rests upon it."[19]

The Stahls viewed themselves as part of the masses, the class that the rest rested upon. Their ability to bear that load was not increasing. By 1918, Leila's sixteen-year-old sister, Bernice—considered the dullard of the sisters, with a tested IQ of 139—had apparently begun to give up on life. She was convinced she would end up mentally ill like her grandmother and mother, and die like her grandmother in the Nebraska State Insane Asylum.[20] During this time, Leila's educational schedule suggests a chaotic home life. She delayed going to college for two years to help her father. After a single semester at the University of Nebraska in Lincoln, she returned home for another year to help out again.[21] Energetic and considered the brightest of the girls, Leila later portrayed this episode in a different light, describing her family as perfect and saying that she stayed out of college three years to earn her tuition.

When she arrived at Lincoln in 1923, she had one clear and acknowledged ambition, which was to find a husband. She headed straight to the college newspaper and asked for a job.[22] A small-boned girl with a soft brown bob who bustled like the robin of spring, Leila wore a charming smile that softened the expression in her arrowhead-sharp eyes. Howard Buffett, who had started at the *Daily Nebraskan* as a sportswriter before rising to editor, hired her straightaway.

Good-looking in a dark-haired, professorish way, Howard was one of only thirteen in the entire student body who had been "tackled" for the Innocents, a society of outstanding men modeled after the honorary societies of Harvard and Yale. Named for the thirteen Popes Innocent of Rome, the Innocents declared themselves champions against evil. They also sponsored the prom and Homecoming.[23] Presented with such a big man on campus, Leila grabbed him instantly.

Howard, who was about to graduate, went to his father to discuss his choice of career. He had no real interest in money but, at Ernest's insistence, gave up the high-minded, low-paying business of journalism and the possibility of law school in favor of selling insurance.[24]

The newlyweds moved into a tiny white four-room bungalow in Omaha, which Ernest filled with groceries as their wedding gift. Leila furnished it top to bottom for $366—items bought, she noted, at "sort of wholesale prices."[25] She channeled her energy, ambition, and talent for math—which by all accounts exceeded her husband's—into boosting Howard's career.[26]

In early 1928, the Buffetts' first child, Doris Eleanor, was born.[27] Later that year, Leila's sister Bernice suffered a mental breakdown and quit her teaching job. But Leila seemed free of the moody listlessness that oppressed her mother and sister. A whirlwind of energy, she could talk nonstop for hours (although she litanied the same stories). Howard called her the "Cyclone."

As the Buffetts settled into the life of a young married couple, Leila got Howard to join her own First Christian Church, and noted proudly in her "day book" when he was made a deacon.[28] Still avidly interested in politics, Howard began to show signs of the family urge to preach. Leila had converted to her new husband's politics, and was now an enthusiastic Republican. The Buffetts applauded Calvin Coolidge, the man who proclaimed "The chief business of the American people is business,"[29] and shared his belief in small government with minimal regulation. Coolidge had lowered taxes and granted citizenship to American Indians, but mostly he shut up and stayed out of the way. In 1928, his Secretary of Commerce, Herbert Hoover, was elected as his successor, vowing to continue pro-business policies. The stock market had prospered under Coolidge, and the Buffetts felt Hoover was the man to keep it going.

"When I was a kid," Warren would later say, *"I got all kinds of good things. I had the advantage of a home where people talked about interesting things, and I had intelligent parents and I went to decent schools. I don't think I could have been raised with a better pair of parents. That was enormously important. I didn't get money from my parents, and I really didn't want it. But I was born at the right time and place. I won the 'Ovarian Lottery.'"*

Buffett always credited most of his success to luck. When it came to his recollections of his family, however, he was creating some of his own reality. Few would agree he couldn't have been raised with a better set of parents. When he talked about how important it is for parents to have an Inner Scorecard when raising their kids, he always used his father's Inner Scorecard as an example. He never mentioned his mother.

6

The Bathtub Steeplechase

Omaha · 1930s

In the 1920s, the champagne bubbles of a frothy stock market led ordinary people to invest for the first time.[1] By 1927, Howard Buffett decided to join them and got a job as a stockbroker with the Union State Bank.

The celebration ended two years later. On "Black Tuesday," October 29, 1929, the market dropped $14 billion in a single day.[2] Wealth worth four times the budget of the United States government evaporated in a few hours.[3]

Amid the bankruptcies and suicides that followed, people began to hoard money, and nobody wanted stocks.[4]

"It was four months before my dad made his next sale. His first commission was five bucks. My mother used to go out with him at night on the streetcar, waiting outside when he would call on somebody, just so he wouldn't feel so depressed when he came home."

Ten months after the crash, on August 30, 1930, the Buffetts' second child, Warren Edward, was born, five weeks before his due date.

An anxious Howard went to see his father, hoping to be hired on at the family grocery store. All the Buffetts, even those with other jobs, put in a stint at the store every week, but only his brother Fred worked there full-time, and that for meager pay. Now Ernest told Howard that he had no money to pay another son.[5]

In one sense, Howard felt relief. He'd "escaped" from working at the store and never wanted to go back.[6] But he worried that his family would starve. "Don't worry about food, Howard," Ernest told him. "I'll just let your bill run."

"That was my grandfather," Warren says. *"'I'll just let the bill run.'"* It wasn't that Ernest didn't love his family, *"you just wished he showed it a little more often."*

"I guess you'd better go back on home to West Point," Howard told his wife. "At least you'll have three meals a day." But Leila stayed. She walked to Robert's Dairy to pay the bill rather than pay a streetcar fare. She started skipping her church circle because she couldn't afford the twenty-nine cents for her turn at bringing coffee.[7] Rather than run up a tab at the family store, she sometimes went without to make sure Howard was fed.[8]

One Saturday, two weeks before Warren's first birthday, people stood on line downtown, dripping with sweat in the hundred-degree heat, waiting to reclaim their cash from the shaky custody of the local banks. They shuffled forward from early morning until ten p.m. and counted and recounted the people ahead in line, silently repeating a financial rosary: Please, God, let there be money left when it's my turn.[9]

Not every prayer was heard. Four state banks closed their doors that month, leaving their depositors unpaid. One of them was Howard Buffett's employer, the Union State Bank.[10] Warren repeats the family legend: *On August 15, 1931, he went down to the bank. It was two days after his birthday, and the bank was closed. He had no job, and his money was in the bank. He had two little kids to feed.[11] He didn't know what to do. There was not another job to find.*"

But within two weeks Howard and two partners, Carl Falk and George Sklenicka, filed the papers to start a stockbrokerage firm, Buffett, Sklenicka & Co.[12] It was a maverick decision—to open a stockbroking business at a time when no one wanted to buy stocks.

Three weeks later, England went off the "gold standard."* This meant that, to avoid bankruptcy, the country—which was deep in debt—would simply print more money to pay off its loans. It was as if the country with the most widely trusted and accepted currency of the age announced: "We are going to write bad checks, and you can take them or else." The announcement instantly exploded trust in formerly gilt-edged institutions. All over the world, financial markets plunged.

The already sputtering United States economy plummeted into free fall. A rush of banks was sucked into its trailing vacuum and collapsed.[13] But in the middle of this maelstrom, Howard's business was succeeding. His clients at first were mostly family friends. He sold them safe securities like utility stocks and

---

*In those days, the amount of gold held by government treasuries fixed the amount of dollars in circulation. The "gold standard" stopped the government from provoking inflation simply by printing money.

municipal bonds. In the firm's first month of operation, as financial panic spread around the world, he produced $400 of commissions and the firm was profitable.[14] Through the ensuing months, even as people's savings evaporated and faith in banks disappeared, Howard stuck to the same kind of conservative investments that had gotten him started, steadily adding customers and growing his business.[15]

The family's fortunes had turned around. Then, shortly before Warren's second birthday, twenty-month-old Charles Lindbergh Jr. was kidnapped and murdered in March 1932. The snatching of the "Lone Eagle's" baby was "the biggest story since the Resurrection," according to pundit H. L. Mencken. The country flew into a kidnapping paranoia in which parents conveyed their terror of abduction to their children, the Buffetts being no exception.[16] Around then, Howard suffered some kind of attack serious enough for Leila to call an ambulance. The Mayo Clinic eventually diagnosed him with a heart condition.[17] From that time on, he lived with restrictions: He wasn't supposed to lift things, run, swim. Leila, whose life now revolved entirely around Howard, the Prince Charming who had rescued her from the miserable fate of running a Linotype press, must have been terrified at the thought of anything happening to him.

Warren was already a cautious child, who had kept his knees bent and stayed close to the ground when he learned to walk. Now, when his mother took him to her church circle meetings, he was content to sit placidly at her feet. She diverted him with an improvised toy—a toothbrush. Warren gazed quietly at the toothbrush for two hours at a stretch.[18] What could he have been thinking as he stared at its columns and rows of bristles?

That November, with the country in crisis, Franklin Delano Roosevelt was elected President. Howard was certain this man of privilege who knew nothing of the common people would pollute the country's currency and drive it to ruination.[19] He stuck a big sack of sugar in the attic to prepare for the worst. By this time, Howard looked like a boyish Clark Kent in a business suit, nearsighted behind his wire-rimmed glasses, with receding dark hair, an earnest smile, and a genial manner. But he turned thunderous when it came to politics, reviewing the news of the day at top volume over dinner. After dinner, Doris and Warren watched their awe-inspiring father retire to his red leather armchair in the living room next to the radio and disappear for hours behind his nightly newspaper and magazines.

Politics, money, and philosophy were acceptable topics for dinner-table discussion at the Buffett house, but feelings were not.[20] Even in an era of undemonstrative parents, Howard and Leila were notable for their lack of warmth.

Nobody in the Buffett household said "I love you," and nobody tucked the children into bed with a kiss.

But to everyone outside the family, Leila appeared the perfect mother and wife. People called her peppy, upbeat, motherly, sweet, even "a gusher."[21] In repeating her history, as she was fond of doing, she painted out the awkward bits, describing herself as a fortunate person brought up by wonderful Christian parents. Her favorite stories told of her and Howard's sacrifices—the three years of school she had missed to earn her college money, the four months Howard had gone without making a sale when he first started his business. Leila referred often to bouts of "neuralgia" (sometimes mistaken for migraines), which she attributed to the childhood years spent alongside the pounding Linotype.[22] Nevertheless, she acted as though she must do everything and drove herself hard. She paid more visits, baked more cookies, and wrote more notes than anyone. When pregnant, she once cooked dinner by herself for the family while trying to quell her morning sickness by smelling a bar of soap.[23] Above all her attitude was: anything for Howard. "She crucified herself," said her sister-in-law Katie Buffett.[24]

But Leila's attitude of duty and sacrifice had another, darker, side: blame and shame. After Howard left on the streetcar for work in the morning, Doris and Warren would be playing or getting dressed and suddenly Leila might explode at them. Something in the tone of her voice might give a clue that the fuse was lit, but most of the time there was no warning.

"It was always something that we did or said, and there would be this flash, and then it didn't subside. All your past sins would be brought up. It was just endless. And my mother attributed it sometimes to having neuralgia, but she never showed that outwardly."

When in a rage, Leila would verbally lash the children over and over again, always the same: Their lives were easy compared to her sacrifices; they were worthless, ungrateful, and selfish, and should feel ashamed. She would pick at every real and imagined flaw; she nearly always aimed the tirade at Doris, and carried on saying the same things for at least an hour, sometimes as long as two. She never stopped until both children "just folded," says Warren, weeping helplessly. "She was not content until she reduced you to tears," says Doris. Warren was forced to watch her explosions, unable to protect his sister and desperate to avoid being targeted himself. While it was apparent that her attacks were deliberate and she had some degree of control over them, it isn't at all clear how she perceived her behavior as a parent. But no matter what she thought she was doing, by the time Warren was three years old and their sister Roberta, known as Bertie, was born, "it couldn't be put back together," he says, for him or for Doris. The damage to their souls was done.

The children never asked for help from their father, even though they knew that he was aware of Leila's eruptions. Howard might say to them, "Mom's on the warpath," a tipoff that a rage was coming, but he didn't intervene. Usually, Leila's explosions took place out of Howard's earshot, and they were never aimed at him. Even though he did not save them, Howard meant security, because when he was around, they were safe.

Outside the tidy white bungalow on Barker Avenue, Nebraska was sliding into lawlessness. Bootlegging flourished in Omaha until Warren was three years old.[25] Out in the countryside, farmers faced with foreclosure on mortgages backed by nearly worthless farmland rose up in civil disobedience.[26] Five thousand farmers marched on the state capitol in Lincoln until panicked lawmakers hastily passed a mortgage moratorium bill.[27]

As the cold winds scoured the parched western sand hills in November of 1933, they kicked up vast swirls of topsoil in towering black clouds that swept eastward as far as New York City at a clipper speed of sixty miles per hour. The *New York Times* compared it to the volcanic eruption of Krakatoa. The dust-storm years had begun.[28]

In the middle of the worst drought of the twentieth century, Leila swept red dust off the porch every morning. On Warren's fourth birthday, a cloud of ruddy dust buried the Buffetts' front porch and the wind blew the paper plates and napkins off the party table.[29]

Along with the dust came years of extraordinary heat. In summertime 1934 the thermometer in Omaha hit 118 degrees. After searching for days, a Nebraska farmer found his cow down a crack in a remote stubble field, trapped when the parched earth split apart.[30] People slept in their backyards, camped on the grounds of Central High School, and on the grassy lawn of Omaha's Joslyn Art Museum, so as not to roast in the ovens of their own homes. Warren tried in vain to sleep covered in bedsheets soaked with water, but nothing could cool the baked air that steamed up to his second-story room.

With the record drought and heat of 1934,[31] millions of grasshoppers arrived to devour the parched corn and wheat down to stubble.[32] Leila's father, John Stahl, suffered a stroke that year, and while visiting his grandfather in West Point, Warren could hear the background drone of the ravenous hoppers. At their worst, they consumed fence posts, the laundry on the clothesline, and finally one another, gumming up tractor engines and clouding the air, thick enough to obscure a car.[33]

In truth, the early 1930s brought many other things to fear than fear itself.[34] The economy worsened. Imitators of the era's most notorious gangsters—Al Capone, John Dillinger, and Baby Face Nelson—roamed the Midwest, pillaging the already vulnerable banks.[35] Parents worried about the dust-bowl drifters and gypsies who passed through town. Occasional "mad dog" rabies scares quarantined children at home. The public swimming pools closed in the summer out of fear of "infantile paralysis"—polio.[36] Yet Nebraskans were trained from birth to respond to calamity with teeth-gritted optimism. The three little Buffetts went to school, played with friends, and ran around with a dozen kids in hundred-degree weather at neighborhood potluck picnics, their fathers in suits and their mothers in dresses and stockings.

Many of their neighbors may have suffered, their standard of living in decline, but Howard, son of a grocery man, had elevated his family into the more comfortable half of the middle class. "We made steady progress even in those tough times," he was to recall, "in an extremely modest sort of way." He was being modest about the family's modesty. While fifty men stood in line for a $17-a-week job driving the orange Buffett & Son grocery trucks, Howard's persistence in knocking on doors had made his stockbroking business, now called Buffett & Co., a success.[37] Omaha was briefly under martial law during violent streetcar strikes and rioting in 1935, but Howard bought a brand-new Buick. He became active in local Republican politics. At age seven Doris, who had always worshipped her father, contemplated his future biography and wrote in the front of one of her notebooks, *Howard Buffett, A Statesman*.[38] A year later, still in the shadow of the Great Depression, Howard built the family a much larger two-story red-brick Tudor-revival house in Dundee, a suburb of Omaha.[39]

As the family prepared to move, Leila got word that her brother, Marion, now a successful lawyer in New York, had been stricken with incurable cancer at age thirty-seven. *"My uncle Marion was the pride and joy of my mother's family,"* says Buffett, as well as their principal hope to carry on the family name, unsullied by insanity.[40] His death that November, childless, devastated his family. The next piece of bad news arrived when Leila's father, John Stahl, suffered another stroke that year, this one debilitating. Her sister Bernice, who cared for him at home, seemed increasingly sunk in depression. Her other sister, Edie, a schoolteacher, the prettiest and most adventurous of the girls, had vowed to stay single until either her thirties or until Bernice wed, but Leila, sharp and aware, refused to be trapped by her family's woes. She was going to make it, no matter what; she was going to create a normal life with a normal family.[41] She planned the move and bought new furniture. In a major step up in the world, Leila could afford to hire a part-time housekeeper, Ethel Crump.

Now a more experienced mother of a more prosperous family, Leila formed a much healthier relationship with her youngest child, Bertie, as the intervals between her rages lessened. Bertie knew her mother had a temper but says she always felt loved. Warren and Doris never did. And Leila's obvious affection for Bertie did not help their sense of worthlessness.[42]

While the Buffetts' new house reflected their upward progress, Leila always bought her children thrifty, practical, forgettable gifts, clothing bought on sale that couldn't be returned, and necessities—nothing that answered a child's fantasies. Warren had a little single-oval HO-gauge train set and coveted a more elaborate version, the kind he saw at the Brandeis department store downtown, which had multiple engines twisting and turning past flashing lights and signals, rising over snow-covered hills and dropping into tunnels, racing past tiny villages and disappearing into pine forests. But the closest he came to owning it was buying the catalog that depicted it.

"If you were a little kid with one little oval track, looking at this thing, it was completely unbelievable. You'd gladly pay a dime for the model-train catalog and just sit there and fantasize."

An introverted child, Warren could lose himself for hours in a model-train catalog. Sometimes, however, as a preschooler, he "hid," as he put it, at his friend Jack Frost's house, developing a babyish "crush" on Jack's kindhearted mother, Hazel. As time passed, his habit grew of spending much time at neighbors' and relatives' houses.[43] His favorite relative was his father's sister Alice, a tall woman who had remained unmarried, lived at home with her father, and taught home economics. Surrounding Warren with warmth, she showed interest in everything he did and was thoughtful about how to motivate him.

By the time Warren entered kindergarten,[44] his hobbies and interests revolved around numbers. Around age six, he became fascinated by the precision of measuring time in seconds, and desperately wanted a stopwatch. Alice knew better than to offer such an important gift with no strings. *"She was nuts about me,"* Buffett says, *"but she still would attach a condition or two. I had to eat asparagus or something like that. That was what motivated me. But I got a stopwatch in the end."*

Warren would pick up his stopwatch and summon his sisters to join him in the bathroom they shared to watch the new game he had invented.[45] He filled the bathtub with water and picked up his marbles. Each had a name. He lined them up on the flat edge at the back of the tub. Then he clicked the stopwatch just as he swept the marbles into the water. They raced down the porcelain slope, clicking and rattling, jumping as they hit the waterline. The marbles chased each other toward the stopper. When the first one hit, Warren punched the stopwatch and declared the winner. His sisters watched him race the marbles over and over, trying to improve their times. The marbles never tired, the stopwatch never erred, and—unlike his audience—Warren never seemed bored by the repetition.

Warren thought about numbers all the time and everywhere, even in church. He liked the sermons, he was bored by the rest of the service; he passed the time by calculating the life span of hymn composers from their birth and death dates in the hymnals. In his mind, the religious should reap some reward for their faith. He assumed that hymn composers would live longer than average. Living longer than average seemed to him an important goal. But piety, he found, did nothing to improve longevity. Lacking any personal sense of grace, he began to feel skeptical about religion.

The bathtub steeplechase and the information he had collected about the hymn composers had taught him something else, however, something valuable. He was learning to calculate odds. Warren looked around him. There were opportunities to calculate odds everywhere. The key was to collect information, as much information as you could find.

7

Armistice Day

Omaha · 1936–1939

When Warren started first grade at Rosehill School in 1936,[1] he took to it right away. For one thing, it liberated him from spending part of the day at home with his mother. School opened up a whole new world for him, and right away he made two friends, Bob Russell and Stu Erickson. He and Bob, whom he called "Russ," began walking to school together, and on some days, he went over to the Russells' house after school. On other days, Stu, whose family lived in a modest frame house, went to the Buffetts' new brick home in the Happy Hollow country club neighborhood. Warren had something to do almost every day after school until his father returned from work. He had always gotten along with other children; now they kept him safe.

He and Russ would sit on the Russells' porch for hours, watching the traffic on Military Avenue. Scribbling in notebooks, they filled column after column with the license-plate numbers of passing cars. Their families found this hobby strange but attributed it to the boys' love of numbers. They knew Warren liked to calculate the frequency of letters and numbers on license plates. And he and Russ never explained their *real* reason. The street in front of the Russells' house was the only route out of a cul-de-sac neighborhood where the Douglas County Bank was located. Warren had convinced Russ that if someday that bank were robbed, the cops could nab the robbers using license-plate numbers. And only he and Russ would own the evidence that the cops would need to solve the crime.

Warren liked anything that involved collecting, counting, and memorizing numbers. He was already a keen stamp and coin collector. He counted how often letters recurred in the newspaper and in the Bible. He loved to read and spent many hours with books he checked out of the Benson Library.

But it was the crime-fighting and the theatrical potential of the license plates—which his family and the Russells never knew about—that brought out other aspects of his temperament. He loved to play cop, and he liked almost anything that brought him attention, including dressing up and playing at different roles. When Warren was a preschooler, Howard had returned from business trips to New York City with costumes for him and Doris, and he became an Indian chief, a cowboy, or a policeman. Once he started school, he began coming up with dramatic ideas of his own.

Warren's favorite games, however, were competitive, even if he was only competing with himself. He progressed from the bathtub steeplechase to a yo-yo, then to bolo, sending the bolo ball on its rubber string flying away from his wooden paddle a thousand times. On Saturday afternoons at the Benson Theater, in between movies—three films for a nickel, plus a serial—he stood on the stage with other kids, competing to see who could keep the ball going longest. In the end everyone else stepped down, exhausted, leaving him alone onstage, still smacking the ball.

He even played out his competitiveness in his special, teasing, warm relationship with Bertie. He called her "chubby" because it made her mad and tricked her into singing at the dinner table, which was against the family rules. He played games with her constantly but never let her win, even though she was three years younger. But he had a tender side too. Once when Bertie stuffed her treasured Dy-Dee doll in a wastebasket in a fit of anger at her mother, Warren rescued it and returned it to her in the sunroom. "I found this in the wastebasket," he said. "You wouldn't want this in the wastebasket, would you?"[2] Even as a child, Bertie recognized that her brother knew how to be tactful.

Bertie, on the other hand, was the self-confident, adventurous one, which Doris and Warren thought might explain why Leila rarely tore into her. Bertie had her own theory, seeing herself as someone who was able to keep up appearances in the way that their mother valued.

What mattered most to Leila was the esteem of others; she had what Warren would later come to call an Outer Scorecard. She was always worrying about what the neighbors would think, nagging her daughters to create the right appearance. "I was so careful to do the right things. I didn't want it to happen to me," Bertie says of Leila's tirades.

Doris was the rebellious one. Early on, she displayed a refined sense of taste and a high threshold for excitement, which put her at odds with the Buffetts' sedate routines and cheeseparing ways. The exotic, the stylish, and the novel attracted her, while her mother sheathed herself in a cloak of humility and preferred a self-conscious austerity to any kind of display. Thus Doris's very being seemed an affront to her mother, and the two clashed constantly. Leila's occasional rages were no less fierce than before. Doris had become a pretty child. And *"the prettier she got,"* says Buffett, *"the worse it was."*

Warren showed early signs of a knack with people, but was also the competitive, precocious child, intellectually aggressive yet physically retiring. When his parents got him boxing gloves at age eight, he took one lesson and never put them on again.[3] He tried skating, but his ankles wobbled.[4] He didn't join in the street games with the other boys, even though he loved sports and was well-coordinated. The only exception to his aversion to hand-to-hand combat was Ping-Pong. When the Buffetts got a Ping-Pong table, he slammed away at it night and day against anyone who would take him on—his parents' friends, kids from school—until he became a menace with the paddle. On the single occasion anyone remembers that called for fists, however, little Bertie went out and took care of things for him. He cried easily if anyone was mean to him; he worked hard to be liked and to get along well with others. Yet despite Warren's cheerful demeanor, something about him struck his friends as lonely.

The Buffetts took a photograph of the three children at Christmas in 1937. Bertie seems happy. Doris looks wretched. Warren, clutching his favorite possession, a nickel-plated money changer, a gift from his aunt Alice, looks far less happy than called for by the occasion.

Leila's determination that they appear to be the perfect Norman Rockwell family hardened when Warren was eight and new calamities befell the Stahls. Her mother, Stella, had deteriorated, and the family admitted her to the Norfolk State Hospital, formerly the Nebraska State Insane Asylum, where Leila's grandmother had died.[5] Her sister Edie spent three months in the hospital and nearly died of peritonitis after suffering a ruptured appendix. Afterward, she made up her mind to go ahead and get married, and wed a man of questionable background who made her laugh. This did not improve Leila's dim view of her sister, who had always seemed to her more interested in adventure than duty.

Meanwhile, Howard had been elected to the school board, a new role that became a point of pride in the family.[6] Amid this mixture of Buffett progress and Stahl backsliding, Warren spent most of his time away from home, out of his mother's way. He paid calls around the neighborhood, made friends with other people's parents, and listened to political talk at their houses.[7] As he roamed, he began collecting bottle caps. He went to filling stations all over town, scooping bottle caps out of the wells beneath the ice chests where they had fallen after customers popped their sodas open. Down in the Buffetts' basement, the piles of bottle caps grew: Pepsi, root beer, Coca-Cola, ginger ale. He became obsessed with collecting bottle caps. All this free information was lying around untouched—and no one wanted it! He found it amazing. After dinner, he spread his collection of bottle caps on newspapers all over the living-room floor, sorting and counting, sorting and counting.[8] The numbers told him which soft drinks were most popular. But he also enjoyed sorting and counting as a way of relaxing. When he wasn't working on his bottle caps, he liked sorting and counting his coin collection and his collection of stamps.

School for the most part bored him. In Miss Thickstun's fourth-grade class with Bob Russell and his other friend Stu Erickson, to pass the time, he played math games and counted in his head. He liked geography, however, and found spelling exciting.

But nothing motivated him like blackboard arithmetic. From the second grade on, students raced to the board, two at a time. First they competed at sums against the clock, then subtraction, finally multiplication and division, tallying their numbers down the board. Warren, Stu, and Russ were the brightest in the class. At first they scored about the same, but over time Warren pulled ahead a little. And then, with practice, a little more.[9]

Finally one day Miss Thickstun asked Warren and Stu to stay after school. Warren's heart pounded in his chest. "We wondered what the hell we had done," Stu says. Instead of a scolding, Miss Thickstun told Warren and Stu to move their books from the 4A section on one side of the room to the 4B section on the other.[10] They were skipping half a grade. Bob Russell was left behind.

Warren stayed friends with both, but kept his relationships with them separate: As before, although each was a friend of his, they were never really friends with each other.

Warren's fondness for minutiae continued to develop. His parents and their friends—who called him "Warreny"—got a kick out of his party trick of naming state capitals. By fifth grade he had immersed himself in the 1939 *World Almanac,* which quickly became his favorite book. He memorized the population of every city. He got a contest going with Stu over who could name the most world cities with populations over a million.[11]

One evening, however, Warren was distracted from his *Almanac* and his bottle caps by a terrible pain in his belly. The doctor made a house call, then went home to bed. But he couldn't get the house call out of his mind, so he returned and sent Warren to the hospital. Later that night, Warren underwent surgery for a ruptured appendix.

The doctor had almost been too late. Warren lay gravely ill in the Catholic-run hospital for several weeks. But cared for by the nursing sisters, he soon found the hospital was a comforting haven. As he began to recover, other plea-sures came his way. The *World Almanac* was brought for him to study. His teacher made all the girls in his class write him get-well letters.[12] His aunt Edie, who understood her nephew well, brought him a toy fingerprinting kit. He knew exactly what to do with it. He coaxed each of the sisters into stopping by his room. He inked all of their fingers, got a set of prints, and filed this collection away carefully upon returning home. His family found this behavior entertain-ing. Who would want a set of nuns' fingerprints? But Warren theorized that one of the sisters might eventually commit a crime. And if that happened, then only *he, Warren Buffett,* would own the clues to the culprit's identity.[13]

Not long after his hospitalization, on an exceptionally cold and windy day in May 1939, his parents told him to get dressed. Then his grandfather appeared. Clad in a dignified single-breasted suit, a handkerchief tucked neatly in his breast pocket, Ernest Peabody Buffett looked the picture of respectability, like the president of the Rotary that he was.

Ernest had a way with children, despite his stern air, and he liked to entertain his grandchildren. Bertie worshipped him. "We're going to Chicago today, Warren," he announced. They boarded a train and went to see the Cubs play the Brooklyn Dodgers in what turned out to be a marathon baseball game that went scoreless for ten extra innings, tied nine to nine, and was finally called on account of darkness. It had lasted for four hours and forty-one minutes.[14] After this exciting introduction to major-league baseball, Warren was thrilled when Ernest bought him a twenty-five-cent book about the 1938 baseball season. Warren memorized it. *"That was the most precious book to me,"* he says. *"I knew every player's history from every team and could have told you clearly every word in that book. I knew it in my sleep."*

His aunt Alice introduced him to another new interest when she gave him a book about bridge—probably Culbertson's *Contract Bridge Complete: The New Gold Book of Bidding and Play.*[15] Contract bridge—a social, psychological game in which figuring out the problem is as important as solving it—was sweeping the country at the time, and Warren found it suited him more than chess.[16]

Yet another of his many interests was music. For several years, he had been learning to play the cornet; among his heroes were the trumpet players Bunny Berigan and Harry James. Although music practice meant spending time at home with his mother, trying to please someone who could never be pleased, he persisted, and there came a time, after many painful hours of practice peppered with Leila's criticism, that he was rewarded by being chosen to participate in his school's Armistice Day ceremony.

Each year on November 11, the anniversary of the treaty that ended World War I, the entire Rosehill student body went down to the gym for a ceremony honoring the war's dead heroes. In what had become a school tradition, trumpet players stationed at doors on either side of the gym would alternate playing "Taps," one blowing the first *dum da dum* notes, and the other echoing *dum da DUM,* and so on.

That year, Warren's cornet skills had advanced enough for him to be given the part of the echo. He woke up the morning of the event, exhilarated at the prospect of performing in front of the entire school. When the big moment came, he was ready.

As Warren stood in the doorway with his cornet, the first trumpet player sounded, *Dum da DUM.*

But on the second *dum,* he hit a wrong note.

"My whole life flashed before my eyes, because I didn't know what to do with the echo. They hadn't prepared me for this. Paralyzed—my big moment."

Should he copy the other trumpet player's mistake or embarrass him by contradicting what he'd played? Warren was undone. The scene scalded itself permanently into his memory—except for what he did next. Years later, which course he followed—assuming he played any note at all—had become a blank.

He had learned a lesson: It might seem easier to go through life as the echo—but only until the other guy plays a wrong note.

8

A Thousand Ways

The first few cents Warren Buffett ever earned came from selling packs of
chewing gum. And from the day he started selling—at six years of age—
he showed an unyielding attitude toward his customers that revealed much
about his later style.

*"I had this little green tray, which had five different areas in it. I'm pretty sure
my aunt Edie gave me that. It had containers for five different brands of gum, Juicy
Fruit, Spearmint, Doublemint, and so on. I would buy packs of gum from my
grandfather and go around door to door in the neighborhood selling this stuff. I
used to do that in the evening, largely.*[1]

*"I remember a woman named Virginia Macoubrie saying, 'I'll take one stick of
Juicy Fruit.' I said, 'We don't break up packs of gum'—I mean, I've got my principles. I still, to this day, remember Mrs. Macoubrie saying she wanted one stick. No,
they were sold only in five-stick packs. They were a nickel, and she wanted to spend
a penny with me."*

Making a sale was tempting, but not tempting enough to change his mind. If
he sold one stick to Virginia Macoubrie, he would have four sticks left to sell to
somebody else, not worth the work or the risk. From each whole pack, he made
two cents profit. He could hold those pennies, weighty and solid, in his palm.
They became the first few snowflakes in a snowball of money to come.

What Warren *was* willing to break up were red cartons of Coca-Cola, which
he sold door to door on summer nights. He carried on selling them during family vacations, approaching sunbathers around the shores of Lake Okoboji in
Iowa. Soda pop was more profitable than chewing gum: He netted a nickel for

every six bottles, and stuffed these coins proudly into the ball-park-style nickel-plated money changer on his belt. He also wore it when he went door to door selling copies of the *Saturday Evening Post* and *Liberty* magazines.

The money changer made him feel professional. It emblemized the part of selling that Warren most enjoyed: collecting. Although he now collected bottle caps, coins, and stamps, mainly he collected cash. He kept his coins at home in a drawer, sometimes adding to the $20 his father had given him when he turned six, all recorded in a little maroon passbook—his first bank account.

By the time he was nine or ten, he and Stu Erickson were selling used golf balls at Elmwood Park golf course—until somebody reported them and they got kicked out by the cops. When the police talked to Warren's parents, however, Howard and Leila weren't concerned. They just considered their son ambitious. As the Buffetts' only—and precocious—son, Warren had a sort of "halo," according to his sisters, and got away with a hell of a lot.[2]

At age ten, he got a job selling peanuts and popcorn at the University of Omaha football games. He walked through the stands yelling, "Peanuts, popcorn, five cents, a nickel, half dime, fifth of a quarter, get your peanuts and popcorn here!" The 1940 presidential election campaign was under way, and he had collected dozens of different Willkie–McNary buttons, which he wore on his shirt. His favorite read: "Washington Wouldn't, Grant Couldn't, Roosevelt Shouldn't," which referred to FDR's outrageous—to the Buffetts—decision to run for a third term. While the U.S. had no constitutional term limit, the country had—so far—rebuffed the idea of an "imperial President."[3]

Though he found Wendell Willkie too liberal for his personal tastes, Howard felt, Anyone to get rid of Roosevelt. Warren, who followed along with his father's political views, enjoyed showing off his Willkie–McNary buttons at the stadium. Then his manager called him into the office and said, "Take those off. You'll get a reaction from the Roosevelt people."

Warren put the buttons in his apron, where some of the dimes and nickels got wedged inside the backs of the pins. When he reported in after the game, his manager told him to dump out the contents of the pocket, pins and all. Then he swept them off the counter and took them away. *"That was my introduction to Business 101,"* Buffett says. *"I was pretty sad."* And when Roosevelt won an unprecedented third term, the Buffetts were sadder still.

But while politics was Howard's main interest and money a sideline, for his son, those interests were reversed. Warren hung around his father's office at the grand old Omaha National Bank building every chance he got, reading "The

Trader" column in *Barron's* and the books on his father's bookshelf. He planted himself in the customers' room of Harris Upham & Co. At this regional stock-broking firm, down two flights of stairs from Howard's office, he found it the height of glamour to be allowed to "mark the board," chalking stock prices on a slow Depression-era Saturday morning. The market still traded for a two-hour session on weekends. Root-bound men with nothing better to do filled the semi-circle of chairs in the customers' room, listlessly watching numbers crawl by on the Trans-Lux, an electronic display of prices of major stocks.[4] Occasionally somebody would jump up and rip a handful of tape off the lazily clicking ticker machine. Warren arrived with his paternal great-uncle Frank Buffett—the family misanthrope who had been brokenhearted over losing Henrietta, now long dead, to his brother Ernest—and his maternal great-uncle John Barber.[5] Each man was enslaved by his long-standing habit of thinking in only one direction.

"Uncle Frank was a total bear on the world, and Uncle John was a total bull. I would sit between the two of them, and they'd sort of vie for my attention and try to sell me that they were right. They didn't like each other, so they wouldn't talk to each other, but they would talk to me in between. My great-uncle Frank thought everything in the world was going to go broke.

"And when somebody'd go up there to the counter behind the chairs and say, 'I want to buy a hundred shares of U.S. Steel at twenty-three,' my uncle Frank would always boom out and say, 'U.S. STEEL? IT'S GOING TO ZERO!'" That was not good for business. *"They couldn't throw him out, but they hated him around this place. It was not an office designed for short-sellers."*

Snug between his two great-uncles, Warren stared at the numbers, which were fuzzy. His trouble reading the Trans-Lux led to his family's discovery that he was nearsighted. After being fitted for glasses, Warren noticed that the numbers seemed to change according to some immutable law of their own. Although his great-uncles were both eager to sway him to their respective—and extreme—points of view, Warren noticed that their opinions appeared to have no connection whatsoever to the numbers passing overhead on the Trans-Lux. He was determined to figure out the pattern, but as yet did not know how.

"My uncle Frank and my uncle John would vie for who would take me to lunch, because that was sort of beating the other guy. With my uncle Frank, we'd go down to the old Paxton Hotel, where we could buy day-old food for a quarter."

Warren, who enjoyed spending time with adults, relished being vied over by his uncles. Actually, he enjoyed being vied over by anyone. He craved attention from his other relatives and his parents' friends, but especially from his father.

Howard gave each of his children an East Coast trip at age ten, an important event in their lives. Warren knew exactly what he wanted to do: "*I told my dad I wanted to see three things. I wanted to see the Scott Stamp and Coin Company. I wanted to see the Lionel Train Company. I wanted to see the New York Stock Exchange. Scott Stamp and Coin was at Forty-seventh Street, Lionel was down around Twenty-seventh, and the Stock Exchange was all the way downtown.*"

Wall Street in 1940 had begun to revive from the crash, yet remained a chastened place. The men of Wall Street were like a band of hardy mercenaries fighting on after most of their comrades had been felled in war. The way they made a living seemed vaguely disreputable with memories of the 1929 Crash so fresh in people's minds. Yet even though they did not brag about it outside the bunker walls, some of these mercenaries were doing very well indeed. Howard Buffett took his son down to lower Manhattan and dropped in on the top man at one of the largest brokerage firms. Little Warren Buffett was getting a peek inside the bunker's gold-plated doors.

"*That's when I met Sidney Weinberg, who was the most famous man on Wall Street. My dad had never met him. He had this little tiny firm out here in Omaha. But Mr. Weinberg let us in, maybe because a little kid was along or something. We talked for about thirty minutes.*"

As the senior partner of the investment bank Goldman Sachs, Weinberg had spent a decade painstakingly repairing the firm's reputation after its disgrace for misleading investors with a notorious pyramid scheme in the market crash of 1929.[6] Warren knew nothing about that, nor that Weinberg grew up an immigrant's child and had started as a porter's assistant at Goldman, emptying cuspidors and brushing the partners' silk hats.[7] But he certainly understood that he was in the presence of a big shot once he found himself in Sidney Weinberg's walnut-paneled office, its walls hung with original letters, documents, and portraits of Abraham Lincoln. And what Weinberg did at the end of their visit made a huge impression on him. "*As I went out, he put his arm around me and he said, 'What stock do you like, Warren?'*"

"*He'd forgotten it all the next day, but I remembered it forever.*"

Buffett would never forget that Weinberg, a big shot on Wall Street, had paid such attention to him and seemed to care about his opinion.[8]

From Goldman Sachs, Howard took Warren over to Broad Street and through a set of enormous Corinthian columns into the New York Stock Exchange. Here, in the temple of money, men in brightly colored jackets shouted and scribbled standing around wrought-iron trading posts while clerks darted back and forth, strewing the floor with paper scraps. Yet it was a scene from the Stock Exchange dining room that captured Warren's imagination.

"We had lunch at the Exchange with a fellow named At Mol, a Dutchman, a member of the Stock Exchange and a very impressive-looking man. After lunch, a guy came along with a tray that had all these different kinds of tobacco leaves on it. He made up a cigar for Mr. Mol, who picked out the leaves that he wanted. And I thought, This is it. It doesn't get any better than this. A custom-made cigar."

A custom-made cigar. The visions that cigar evoked in Warren's mathematical mind! He had exactly zero interest in *smoking* a cigar. But working backward, he saw what hiring a man for such a frivolous purpose implied. To justify the expense must mean that, even while most of the country was still mired in the Depression, the cigar man's employer was making a great deal of money. He grasped it right away. The Stock Exchange must pour forth streams of money: rivers, fountains, cascades, torrents of money, enough to hire a man for the pure frippery of rolling cigars—handmade, custom-made cigars—for the Stock Exchange members' own particular pleasure.

That day, as he beheld the cigar man, a vision of his future was planted.

He kept that vision when he went back to Omaha, old enough now to organize his quest and pursue it all the more systematically. Even as he followed the pastimes of an ordinary boy, playing basketball and Ping-Pong and collecting coins and stamps; even as his family mourned his small, sweet grandfather, John Stahl, who died that year at age seventy-three—the first loss in his life—he worked with a passion for the future he saw ahead of him, right there in sight. He wanted money.

"It could make me independent. Then I could do what I wanted to do with my life. And the biggest thing I wanted to do was work for myself. I didn't want other people directing me. The idea of doing what I wanted to do every day was important to me."

A tool that would help him soon fell into his hands. One day, down at the Benson Library, a book beckoned from the shelves. Its shiny silver cover gleamed like a heap of coins, hinting at the value of its contents. Captivated by the title, he opened it and was immediately hooked. *One Thousand Ways to Make $1,000*, it was called. A million dollars, in other words!

Inside the cover, in a photograph, a tiny man gazed up at an enormous pile of coins.

"Opportunity Knocks," read the first page of the text. "Never in the history of the United States has the time been so favorable for a man with small capital to start his own business as it is today."

What a message! "We have all heard a great deal about the opportunities of bygone years. . . . Why, the opportunities of yesterday are as nothing compared with the opportunities that await the courageous, resourceful man of today! There are fortunes to be made that will make those of Astor and Rockefeller seem picayune." These words rose like sweet visions of heaven to Warren Buffett's eyes. He turned the pages faster.

"But," the book cautioned, "you cannot possibly succeed *until you start*. The way to begin making money is to begin. . . . Hundreds of thousands of people in this country who would like to make a lot of money are not making it because they are waiting for this, that, or the other to happen." Begin it! the book admonished, and explained how. Crammed with practical business advice and ideas for making money, *One Thousand Ways to Make $1,000* started with "the story of money" and was written in a straightforward, friendly style, like someone sitting on the front stoop talking to a friend. Some of its ideas were limited—goat-dairying and running doll hospitals—but many were more practical. The idea that captivated Warren was pennyweight scales. If he had a weighing machine, he would weigh himself fifty times a day. He was sure that other people would pay money to do that too.

"The weighing machine was easy to understand. I'd buy a weighing machine and use the profits to buy more weighing machines. Pretty soon I'd have twenty weighing machines, and everybody would weigh themselves fifty times a day. I thought—that's where the money is.[9] *The compounding of it—what could be better than that?"*

This concept—compounding—struck him as critically important. The book said he could make a thousand dollars. If he started with a thousand dollars and grew it ten percent a year:

> In five years, $1,000 became more than $1,600.
> In ten years, it became almost $2,600.
> In twenty-five years, it became more than $10,800.

The way that numbers exploded as they grew at a constant rate over time was how a small sum could turn into a fortune. He could picture the numbers compounding as vividly as the way a snowball grew when he rolled it across the lawn. Warren began to think about time in a different way. Compounding married the present to the future. If a dollar today was going to be worth ten some years from now, then in his mind the two were the same.

Sitting on the stoop at his friend Stu Erickson's, Warren announced that he would be a millionaire by the time he reached age thirty-five.[10] That was an audacious, almost silly-sounding statement for a child to make in the depressed world of 1941. But his calculations—and the book—said it was possible. He had twenty-five years, and he needed more money. Still, he was sure he could do it. The more money he collected early on, the longer the money could compound, and the better his chances of achieving his goal.

A year later, he brought forth the kernel of his reality. To his family's amusement and surprise, by the spring of 1942, his hoard totaled $120.

Enlisting his sister Doris as a partner, he bought three shares of a stock for each of them, costing him $114.75 for his three shares of Cities Service Preferred.[11]

"*I didn't understand that stock very well when I bought it,*" he says; he knew only that it was a favorite stock that Howard had sold to his customers for years.[12]

The market hit a low that June, and Cities Service Preferred plunged from $38.25 to $27 a share. Doris, he says, "reminded" him every day on the way to school that her stock was going down. Warren says he felt terribly responsible. So when the stock finally recovered, he sold at $40, netting a $5 profit for the two of them. "That's when I knew that he knew what he was doing," Doris recalls. But Cities Service quickly soared to $202 a share. Warren learned three lessons and would call this episode one of the most important of his life. One lesson was not to overly fixate on what he had paid for a stock. The second was not to rush unthinkingly to grab a small profit. He learned these two lessons by brooding over the $492 he would have made had he been more patient. It had taken five years of work, since he was six years old, to save the $120 to buy this stock. Based on how much he currently made from selling golf balls or peddling popcorn and peanuts at the ballpark, he realized that it could take years to earn back the profit he had "lost." He would never, never, never forget this mistake.

And there was a third lesson, which was about investing other people's money. If he made a mistake, it might get somebody upset at him. So he didn't want to have responsibility for anyone else's money unless he was sure he could succeed.

9

Inky Fingers

Omaha and Washington, D.C. · 1941–1944

One December Sunday afternoon when Warren was eleven, the Buffetts were driving back from a visit to West Point after church. As they listened to the radio in the car, the announcer broke in to say that the Japanese had struck Pearl Harbor. Nobody explained exactly what had happened or how many were killed or injured, but from the commotion Warren quickly realized that the world was going to change.

His father's already reactionary political views quickly turned even more extreme. Howard and his friends considered Roosevelt a warmonger who lusted after dictatorship and was trying to achieve it by luring America into yet another European war.

Howard now came to believe that in a desperate gamble, Roosevelt and his army's chief of staff, General George C. Marshall, had decided that *"the only way to get us into the European war was to get the Japanese to attack us,"* says Warren, *"and not tip off the people at Pearl Harbor."* This belief was common among conservatives at the time, although Howard, as in most things, was strikingly firm in his convictions.

The following spring, the Nebraska Republican Party tapped Howard with the awkward job of finding a candidate to run for Congress against a popular incumbent, Charles F. McLaughlin. At the last minute, according to family lore, Howard entered his own name on the ballot, unable to find another sacrificial lamb willing to run against a heavily favored Democrat.

He found himself thrust into the role of campaigner. The Buffetts plastered simple flyers saying "Buffett for Congress" on telephone poles. They went to county fairs, where Howard and Leila handed out cards amid the livestock displays and entries in the best pickle competition. *"He was the most unlikely candidate. He hated to speak in public. My mother was a good campaigner, but my dad was introverted."* Leila, a talker, instinctively knew how to work a crowd and enjoyed approaching people. The kids circulated, saying, "Would you vote for my daddy?" Afterward they got to ride on the Ferris wheel.

"Then we made this little fifteen-minute radio program. My mother played the organ; my father introduced us: 'There's Doris, age fourteen. And there's Warren, age eleven.' And my line was 'Just a second, Pop, I'm reading the sports section.' Then, the three of us sang 'America the Beautiful.'" It was no stemwinder, but *"With that fifteen-minute radio program, everybody started volunteering. Still, the other guy had been in for four terms."*

Howard struggled against the political handicaps of his pessimism and his literal honesty. Thus, the Buffett political platform demanded that voters "buy one-way tickets out of Washington for all of the screwballs, stuffed shirts, stool pigeons, sleepwalkers, and society snobs."

This fire-breathing rhetoric belied a sweetness in him, a subtle wit, and a certain innocence. For years, Howard had carried in his pocket a handwritten piece of paper, softened and worn to the texture of linen, which said, "I am God's child. I am in His Hands. As for my body—it was never meant to be permanent. As for my soul—it is immortal. Why, then, should I be afraid of anything?"[1]

Unfortunately for his only son, when it came to the streets of Omaha, Howard meant this almost literally.

When campaigning, he would roust Warren, now twelve years old, out of bed long before dawn, to head down to the stockyards in South Omaha. Along with the railroads, these were Omaha's main business, employing almost twenty thousand people, mostly immigrants. More than eight million animals a year[2] lumbered into a metropolis of meat and rolled out as billions of pounds of packaged goods.[3] South Omaha once was a separate city, a short distance from downtown geographically but culturally a continent away. For decades it had served as the brewing ground for most of the city's ethnic and racial unrest.

Warren planted his sneakers at one end of the block, hands clenched and eyes fixed anxiously on his father. Howard limped from a childhood bout with polio, and the family worried about his heart condition. Warren's stomach churned as he watched his father down the street, approaching huge, cleaver-faced men in overalls on their way into the packinghouses for the five-thirty a.m. shift.

Many of them did not speak English at home. The least well off, the blacks and new immigrants, lived crammed into a buffer zone of boardinghouses and shanties next to the yards. Those with greater savvy and more means had worked their way out into the ethnic parishes nearby.

Men and women, black and white, these people were Democrats in every fiber of their being. The rest of Nebraska might be turning against the New Deal, the President's cure for the Great Depression, but Franklin Delano Roosevelt was still a hero in this part of town. Yet the leaflets that Howard Buffett politely pressed into their callused hands shrieked that FDR was the greatest danger to democracy that America had ever known. If given a moment to speak, he would calmly explain why, as their Congressman, he would always vote to enact laws that the stockyard workers would oppose.

Howard was a zealot, but he was neither stupid nor crazy. Even though he placed his trust in God's hands, he had a backup plan. Warren had not come for an education, nor to tag-team his father in a fight. His job was to run like hell for the cops if the stockyard workers started beating up his father.

Under the circumstances, a reasonable person might ask what Howard was doing there at all. His efforts might not be repaid by a single vote. But apparently he felt an obligation to appear before every potential voter in his district, however little of him they cared to see.

Warren always managed to return home intact; he never had to run for the cops. That may have been just luck or it may have been Howard's demeanor, which conveyed his basic decency. Still, the Buffetts had no reason to believe the voters saw that, nor that if they did, it would overcome his underdog status. On election day, November 3, 1942, "*My dad wrote out his concession statement. We all went to bed at eight-thirty or nine o'clock, because we never stayed up late. And he woke up the next morning to find out he'd won.*"

Howard's deep suspicion of foreign adventures was more than a quirk of his Quaker-like personality. It reflected a reservoir of conservative isolationism, which had once run deep and wide through the Midwest. Although that stream was drying up, Pearl Harbor had revived it for a little while. Despite Roosevelt's overwhelming popularity, labor's support for his foreign policies had wavered temporarily in Omaha, just long enough to get Howard elected against an opponent who had been, perhaps, overconfident.

The following January, the Buffetts rented out their house in Dundee and boarded a train to Virginia. They arrived at Washington's Union Station to find a provincial city grown packed and chaotic. Great crowds of people filled the town, most of them working at vast new wartime government agencies. The military had commandeered every building, office, chair, and pencil within reach in the effort to get itself organized in the newly finished Pentagon, the world's largest office building, which was outgrown by the time it was completed. By now, flimsy temporary office buildings lined every inch of the Mall.[4] Rickety nineteenth-century wooden trolleys packed with government workers crept their way along impassable streets. Hordes of new arrivals had doubled the population. Following in the dust of the respectable, impoverished, and naive came pickpockets, prostitutes, grifters, and drifters, turning Washington into the nation's crime capital.

The Buffetts had friends, the Reichels[5]—acquaintances of Howard's from his stockbroking days—who told them, don't live in Washington, it's terrible. They knew of an enormous house in Virginia that someone in the Marines had just vacated. The house had ten fireplaces and a greenhouse. Although its grandeur was far above the Buffetts' style, and it was located almost an hour from the city, they leased it temporarily. Howard rented a tiny apartment in the District of Columbia and commuted on the weekends. His time filled quickly as he started fitting in and learning the rules and procedures and unwritten customs of serving as a Congressman.

Leila soon began riding into Washington to look for a permanent place to live. She had been unusually irritable since their arrival and often spoke longingly of Omaha. The timing of the move had turned out to be inauspicious. Her sister Bernice had just insinuated that she would commit suicide, saying that she would not be responsible for what happened unless the family committed her to the Norfolk State Hospital, where their mother, Stella, was also housed. Edie, now in charge of her sister's care, consulted a doctor. They thought that Bernice wanted to live with her mother and was conceivably using melodramatic means to get her way. Nevertheless, they took the suicide threat seriously, and the family sent her off to Norfolk.

The details of the Stahl family's problems were rarely discussed in front of the children. Each adapted to Washington in his or her own way. Beautiful fifteen-year-old Doris felt like Dorothy, who had just left black-and-white Kansas and stepped into the Technicolor land of Oz. She became the belle of

Fredericksburg and fell in love with the town.[6] Leila began to treat her daughter as a social climber who had pretensions above her station, and still launched the occasional tirade against her. But by now, Doris's spirit resisted her mother's constraints, and she had begun to fight for her own identity.

Meanwhile, Warren, twelve years old, spent the first six weeks in an eighth-grade class that was *"way behind"* where he had been academically in Omaha. Naturally, his first instinct was to get a job, working at a bakery where he *"did damned near nothing. I wasn't baking and I wasn't selling."* At home, furious and miserable at being uprooted, he reported a mysterious "allergy" that disturbed his sleep so that he had to sleep standing up. *"I wrote my grandfather these pathetic letters, too, and he sort of said, 'You've got to send that boy back. You know, you're destroying my grandson.'"* Succumbing, the Buffetts put Warren on a train back to Nebraska for a few months' stay. To his delight, his companion on the train was Nebraska Senator Hugh Butler. He had always gotten along well with older people and chatted easily with Butler, in his precocious manner, all the way back to Omaha, his "allergy" forgotten.

Bertie, nine years old, felt close to her grandfather and thought she had a special bond with him. She was jealous. Trusting in her relationship with Ernest, she wrote him: "Don't tell my parents, but send for me too."

"When Bertie wrote the same kind of letters, I said, 'Don't pay any attention. She's a fake.'"[7]

Ernest wrote back, "A girl should be with her mother." Bertie sat in Fredericksburg, fuming that her brother always seemed to get his way.[8]

Warren returned to Rosehill School and reunited with his friends. Every day he showed up around noontime at the house of his father's former partner, Carl Falk, whose wife, Gladys, served him sandwiches and tomato soup and kindness for lunch. He "worshipped" Mrs. Falk[9] as if she were a surrogate mother, just as he had done with his friend Jack Frost's mother, Hazel, and with his aunts.

Though Warren was comfortable with all these middle-aged women, he was shy, hopelessly shy, and girls his own age terrified him. Even so, he soon developed a crush on Dorothy Hume, one of the girls in his new eighth-grade class. His friend Stu Erickson had a similar crush on Margie Lee Canaday, and his other friend Byron Swanson had a crush on Joan Fugate. After weeks of talk, they worked themselves up to ask the girls to go to the movies.[10]

On the appointed Saturday, Byron and Warren went together to pick up their dates because they were afraid to show up alone. Thus the afternoon started with a lengthy trudge from house to house to the streetcar stop, walking for blocks in uncomfortable silence. Margie Lee, who lived in the opposite direction, arrived at the stop with Stu and they all boarded the streetcar, where the boys stared red-faced at their shoes throughout the trip downtown as the girls chatted easily with one another. When they reached the theater, Margie Lee, Dorothy, and Joan strolled directly to a row of seats and sat down next to each other. The boys' plan to cuddle up with the girls during two horror films, *The Mummy's Tomb* and *Cat People,* instantly fell apart. Instead, they sat in their own group and watched the girls' brunette heads huddled together as they giggled and shrieked through the weekly serials, the cartoons, and both movies. After a painful trip to Walgreen's for after-movie treats, the boys retraced their trip on the streetcar in a dazed little group and began the long march back to the girls' houses before being dismissed by their dates. They had barely spoken a word the entire afternoon.[11] All three were so mortified that it took each of them years thereafter to summon the courage to ask another girl out on a date.[12]

But while Warren lost heart, he did not lose interest; he next developed a crush on another girl in his class, Clo-Ann Kaul, a striking blonde. Yet she was not interested in him either. His way of diverting himself from disappointment was, again, making money.

"My grandfather liked the idea that I was always thinking of ways to make money. I used to go around the neighborhood collecting wastepaper and magazines to sell for scrap. My aunt Alice would take me down to the collection drop-off, where you could get thirty-five cents for a hundred pounds, or something like that."

At Ernest's house, Warren read a shelf full of back issues of the *Progressive Grocer.* Subjects like "how to stock a meat department" fascinated him. On the weekends, Ernest put him to work at Buffett & Son, the empire over which he presided. About the size of a two-story garage, it had a Spanish-style tile roof that stood out in the pleasant upper-middle-class suburb of Dundee. The Buffetts had always sold on "credit and delivery." Ladies or their cooks would ring up Walnut 0761 on the telephone and read their lists to clerks who took down their orders.[13] Clerks rushed around the store, scrambling up and down a rolling wooden ladder that flew back and forth along the shelves, retrieving boxes, bags, and cans, and filling their baskets from the pyramids of vegetables and fruit. They ran down to the basement to fill orders for sauerkraut and pickles that lay cooling in barrels near crates of eggs and other perishables. All the goods went into baskets, which the clerks on the mezzanine raised on a pulley, priced and packaged, and sent back downstairs. Then the orange Buffett & Son delivery trucks with rolled-up rubber or leather panels on the side drove the packages off to Omaha's waiting housewives.

Ernest sat at a desk on the mezzanine and glared down at the clerks. Behind his back, the employees called him Old Man Ernie. *"He didn't do a damn thing. He just gave orders,"* says Warren. *"I mean, he was king. He could see everything. And if a customer walked in who wasn't waited on like that . . ."* Snap of the fingers and woe to the clerks. He believed in *"work, work, plenty of work."* Ernest felt so responsible for making sure that no one in his charge had foolish notions about there being any free lunch in this world that he had once made a lowly stock boy bring two pennies to work to pay his Social Security tax in cash. This handover had been accompanied by a half-hour lecture on the evils of socialism.[14]

The only time Ernest left the mezzanine was the minute he saw an important woman drive up with her chauffeur. He would tear down the stairs, grab an order slip, and wait on her himself, handing peppermint sticks to her children.[15] In the face of all this attention to rank, when her brother-in-law Fred once stopped waiting on Leila in order to attend to another customer, she stalked out in a huff and never shopped at the store again.[16] Howard bought the groceries from then on.

Warren now felt like one of these clerks, hustling around the store under Old Man Ernie's thumb. Working in his grandfather's store, he came as close to being a slave as he ever would be in his life.

"He had me do a lot of little lesser jobs. Sometimes I was on the floor. Sometimes he had me counting wartime rationing stamps—sugar stamps, coffee stamps, sitting up on the mezzanine with him. And sometimes I was hiding where he couldn't see me.

"The worst job was when he hired me and my friend John Pescal to shovel snow. We had this huge snowstorm, a foot of superwet snow. We had to shovel out the whole bank of snow, in front where the customers parked and in the alleyway behind the store, in the loading dock, and by the garage where we had the six trucks.

"We worked at this for about five hours—shoveling, shoveling, shoveling, shoveling. Eventually, we couldn't even straighten our hands. And then we went to my grandfather. He said, 'Well, how much should I pay you boys? A dime's too little and a dollar's too much!'

"I'll never forget—John and I looked at each other. . . ."

That worked out to—at most—twenty cents an hour for shoveling snow.

"Oh no! This was the amount we were supposed to split. That was my grandfather. . . ."

Well, a Buffett was a Buffett, but Warren had learned a valuable lesson: Know what the deal is in advance.[17]

Ernest had two other Buffett traits: an impulsive streak with women and perfectionism. He had entered into two short-lived marriages after Henrietta died, once coming back from a vacation in California newly wed to a woman he had just met. His perfectionism expressed itself at work. Buffett & Son was a direct descendant of the oldest grocery store in Omaha and Ernest's demanding ways were all in pursuit of an ideal vision of service to his customers. He felt certain the discount national chain stores that were encroaching on the neighborhoods were a fad that would disappear because they could never provide a comparable level of service. Sometime during this period, he wrote confidently to one of his relatives: "The day of the chain store is over."[18]

When Buffett & Son ran out of bread, rather than disappoint his customers, Ernest sent Warren trotting down the street to the nearby Hinky Dinky supermarket to buy bread at retail. Warren did not enjoy this errand because he was quickly recognized once inside. "*Hellooooooo*, Mr. Buffett!" the clerks would call out to him, loud enough for everyone to hear, as he slunk through the store, "*trying to look inconspicuous*," weighed down with armfuls of loaves. Ernest resented the Hinky Dinky, which, like Sommers, his other major competitor in Dundee, was run by a Jewish family. It rankled him to pay good money to a competitor, much less somebody Jewish. Like much of America before mid-century, Omaha practiced de facto segregation by both religion and race. Jews and Christians (and even Catholics and Protestants) lived essentially separate lives, with social clubs, civic groups, and many businesses refusing to accept Jews as members or hire them as employees. Ernest and Howard used the code name "Eskimos" to make offensive remarks about Jews when they were out in public. Since anti-Semitism was so much a matter of course in society at the time, Warren never gave their attitudes a thought.

Ernest, in fact, was an authority figure to Warren, and he only escaped that authority when he was at school, and for a few hours every Saturday when his grandfather put him to work on the delivery truck. Unloading groceries from the truck was exhausting work, and Warren started to figure out how much he disliked manual labor.

"*There was this driver, Eddie, that I thought was a hundred years old. He was probably about sixty-five, although he had driven a mule truck back when Buffett & Son delivered that way.*

"*He had the craziest delivery system that involved going first to Benson, then about five miles back to Dundee to drop somebody's groceries off, then back to Benson. All this during wartime gas rationing. Finally I asked why, and he gave me this disgusted look and said, 'If it's early enough, we may catch her when she's undressed.'"* Warren at first had no idea what this cryptic phrase meant. *"He took the groceries up to the house personally in the mornings while I carried twenty-four-bottle boxes of empty soda bottles that were being returned to the store. Eddie would be there ogling Mrs. Kaul, the best-looking customer, trying to catch her undressed."* Mrs. Kaul was Clo-Ann Kaul's mother, and while Warren was hauling empty soda bottles, Clo-Ann was ignoring him. *"I may have been the lowest-paid person to ever work in the grocery business. I didn't learn anything—except that I didn't like hard work."*

Warren took his battle for autonomy home to Ernest's Sunday dinner table. He had despised everything green from birth, except money. Now, broccoli, Brussels sprouts, and asparagus lined Warren's plate like foot soldiers in a battle of wills. With his parents, he had generally gotten his way. Ernest, however, brooked no nonsense. While Alice tried coaxing her nephew, his grandfather glared from his seat at one end of the table, waiting, waiting, waiting for Warren to finish his vegetables. *"You sat at the table for two hours to finish your asparagus, but he always won in the end."*

In most other ways, however, being at Ernest's brought Warren a large measure of freedom. In his grandfather's garage, he had spotted Doris's blue Schwinn bicycle with her initials on it—a gift from Ernest, left behind when they went to Washington. Warren had never owned a bicycle. *"A bicycle was a pretty big present in those days, you know,"* he says. He started riding Doris's. After a while he traded it in, using it as most of the down payment on a boy's bike.[19] Nobody said anything. Warren had that "halo."

His grandfather doted on him, in his way. At night he and Ernest listened with "reverential attention" to Ernest's favorite conservative radio host, Fulton Lewis Jr. Afterward, Ernest would gather his latest thoughts on the best seller he was writing. He had decided to call it *How to Run a Grocery Store and a Few Things I Learned About Fishing,* feeling these were *"the only two subjects about which mankind had any valid concern.*[20]

"I would sit there at night, or late afternoon, early evening, and my grandfather would dictate this to me. I'd write it on the back of old ledger sheets because we never wasted anything at Buffett and Son. He thought that it was the book all America was waiting for. I mean, there wasn't any sense writing another book. Not <u>Gone With the Wind</u> *or anything like that. Why would anybody want to read* <u>Gone</u>

<u>With the Wind</u> when they could be reading <u>How to Run a Grocery Store and a Few Things I Learned About Fishing</u>?"[21]

Warren loved it all, or almost all. He was so glad to be back in Omaha and reunited with his aunt, grandfather, and friends that he almost forgot about Washington for a while.

A few months later, the rest of the family made the three-day drive to Nebraska for the summer and moved into a rented house. Their finances were becoming stretched. Heretofore, the stockyards had simply been the home of some of Howard's constituents. But when their reek drifted through town every time the wind blew from the south, everybody in Omaha knew—that was the smell of money. Howard now bought the South Omaha Feed Company to supplement his Congressional salary. And Warren went to work for his father.

"*South Omaha Feed was a huge warehouse that seemed hundreds of feet long and had no air-conditioning. My job was to carry fifty-pound sacks of animal feed from a freight car into the warehouse. You can't imagine how big a freight car looks when you get inside and it is packed to the top. And a freight car in the summer, that is really something. There was a guy named Frankie Zick who was tossing these things around. He was a weight lifter. I had on a short-sleeved shirt because it was so hot, and struggling to sort of get these feed bags into my arms and drag them. By noon my arms were kind of a bloody mess. That job lasted for about three hours. I just walked over to the streetcar and went home. Manual labor is for the birds.*"

Before the summer ended, the family took a short vacation at Lake Okoboji. As they were leaving, Doris discovered that Warren had traded in her bicycle. But through some miscarriage of family justice, again he suffered no consequences. Indeed, when summer ended and his parents forced Warren, sullen and grim-faced, onto a train headed back to Washington, the new bicycle he had bought for himself with his filched funds went along. Doris was furious. But the theft of her bicycle only marked the beginning of her brother's descent into behavior that would ultimately force his parents to take action.

Back in Washington, the Buffetts moved into the Fitchous' house, an attractive two-story white colonial with a mimosa tree in the yard in the sophisticated Washington suburb of Spring Valley, right off Massachusetts Avenue. A restricted community* built in 1930 for the "socially and officially prominent," Spring

---

*"Restricted" meant Jews were not allowed to buy houses there.

Valley was designed as a little "colony of outstanding personages."[22] Leila had paid $17,500 for the house, including some furniture. Warren got the front bedroom. The families on either side had sons, all older than Warren. Across the street lived the Keavneys, and Warren, now thirteen years old, developed a crush on Mrs. Keavney, the nearest motherly middle-aged woman in sight. "*I was nuts about her,*" he says.

The neighborhood had an international feel; it teemed with diplomats. The Buffetts began adjusting to wartime life in Washington, a very different place from Omaha. The country had finally become prosperous, the Depression over, but with wartime rationing on, money mattered less and less. Everyday life was measured in points and coupons: 48 blue points a month for canned goods; 64 red points for perishables; coupons for meat, shoes, butter, sugar, gasoline, and stockings. No amount of money would buy meat without coupons; only chicken went unrationed. With butter rationed and scarce, everyone learned to squeeze yellow food coloring into containers of tasteless white oleomargarine. No one could buy a new car, because the carmakers devoted their plants to defense work. To take an automobile trip, you pooled the family's gas coupons.

Every morning, Howard took the streetcar that ran down Wisconsin Avenue to M Street in Georgetown, then turned down Pennsylvania Avenue. He got off near the old Executive Office Building and went to work in a Washington that heaved and roiled with thousands of new government workers and military personnel.

Leila disliked Washington from the day she arrived. She was homesick for Omaha, and lonely too. Immersed in his new job, Howard had become a more distant husband and father. He worked at the office all day, then read the *Congressional Record* and legislative materials all evening. He spent Saturdays at the office and often returned there on Sunday afternoons after church.

Doris now attended Woodrow Wilson High School, where again she fell in right away with the popular crowd. Bertie, too, made friends easily, finding a compatible group of girls in the neighborhood. Warren's experience was nothing like his sisters'. He enrolled at Alice Deal Junior High School,[23] which sat atop the highest hill in Washington, overlooking Spring Valley, the black school in the hollow behind it, and the rest of the city below.

The students in his class—many of them diplomats' kids—were a world more polished than Warren and his now-lost friends from Rosehill School. At first, he had difficulty making friends. He went out for basketball and football, but since he wore glasses and was timid in physical contact sports, neither was a success. "*I'd been pulled away from my friends and I wasn't making new friends.*

I was young for my class. I was not poised at all. I wasn't a terrible athlete, but I wasn't a great athlete in the least, so that was not an entry ticket. And Doris and Bertie were knockouts, so they did fine. A good-looking girl does not have trouble, because the world will adjust to her. So they both fit in better than I did, far better, which was a little irritating too."

His grades started out at Cs and Bs and improved to As, except in English. "*Mostly my grades related to how I felt about the teachers. I hated my English teacher, Miss Allwine.*[24] *Music class was also Cs all the way through.*" Miss Baum, the music teacher, was the best-looking teacher in the school. Most of the boys had crushes on her, but Warren had real difficulties with Miss Baum, who reported that he needed to improve in cooperation, courtesy, and self-reliance.

"*I was the youngest one in the class. I was interested in girls, and I wasn't avoiding them, but I felt I had less poise. The girls were way ahead of me socially. When I left Omaha, nobody in my class was dancing. When I moved to Washington, everybody had been dancing for a year or two. So I never caught up, in effect.*"

The Buffetts' move when Warren was twelve had deprived him of a crucial experience: Addie Fogg's dancing class. At the American Legion hall in Omaha on Friday nights, Addie Fogg, a short, stout woman of middle age, lined the boys and girls up by height and paired them off, boys in bow ties and girls in stiff petticoats. They practiced the fox-trot and box-step waltz. A boy learned how a "gentleman" behaves in public with a young lady, and struggled through elementary small talk to break a painful silence. He felt the touch of a girl's hand, learned to hold her by the waist, and sensed her face close to his own. He tasted for the first time the demands and potential pleasures of leading a partner as they moved in unison. With its many small but shared embarrassments and triumphs, this group rite of passage awakened in its graduates a sense of belonging. To miss it could be profoundly isolating. Already insecure, Warren had been left behind, a child among budding young men.

His classmates noticed he was friendly but seemed shy, especially around girls.[25] He was a year younger than most of them, born in August and having skipped a half grade at Rosehill. "*I was out of whack. I felt very inept with girls at that time, and socially in general. But with older people, I was fine.*"

Not long after the family's arrival in Spring Valley, Howard's friend Ed S. Miller—one of those older people—called from Omaha. He wanted to talk to Warren.

"'*Warren,*' he said, '*I'm in a terrible jam. The board of directors told me to get rid of our Washington, D.C., warehouse. This is a real problem for me. We have*

hundreds of pounds—cases—of stale cornflakes and cases of Barbecubes dog bis-
cuits. I'm in a real pickle. I'm twelve hundred miles away and you're the only busi-
nessman I know in Washington.'

"So he said, 'I know I can count on you. As a matter of fact, I told our warehouse
men to deliver these cornflakes and Barbecubes dog biscuits to your house.
Whatever you get for them, send me half; you keep the rest.'

"And all of a sudden, these huge trucks come up and fill our garage, fill our basement, everything! Now my dad couldn't get the car in or anything.

"And now I've got these things.

"Well, I just tried to figure out who it would be useful to, you know. And obviously the dog biscuits would be useful to a kennel. The cornflakes were not fit for
human consumption anymore, so I figured they might be good for some animal. I
sold the cornflakes to some poultry guy. I made probably a hundred bucks for the
merchandise.[26] When I sent the fifty percent to Mr. Miller, he wrote back and said,
'You saved my job.'

"There were some awfully nice people like that back in Omaha. I always liked to
hang around with adults when I was a kid. Always. I would walk over to church or
something, and then I would just drop in on people.

"My dad's friends were very nice too. They had this Bible class and various
things at the rectory, and they would come over to the house and play bridge afterward. All these guys were very, very nice to me; they all liked me and called me
Warreny. I'd learned Ping-Pong from taking out books from the library and practicing at the Y. They knew I enjoyed playing with them down in the basement, and
they'd take me on.

"I had all these things I was doing in Omaha. I had a nice niche there.

"When we moved to Washington, the Ping-Pong table disappeared. It was like
my cornet. And the Boy Scouts. I was doing all these different things, but they all
ended when we moved.

"So I was mad.

"But I didn't know exactly how to direct that. I just knew I was having a whole
lot less fun than I was having before my dad got elected."

After his father took him to watch a couple of sessions of Congress, Warren
decided he wanted to become a congressional page, but Howard was not in a
position to pull that off. Instead, Warren got a job caddying at the Chevy Chase
Club, but once again discovered that physical labor did not suit him. *"My
mother sewed towels inside my shirts because I was carrying these heavy bags
around. Sometimes the golfers—mainly women golfers—would feel sorry for me*

and practically carry the things themselves." He needed a job that better fit his skills and talents.

Almost from birth, like all the Buffetts, Warren had lived and breathed the news. He loved hearing it and now he would enter the business of delivering it and find he loved that too. He got himself hired to throw a paper route, delivering the *Washington Post* and two different routes for the *Times-Herald*.

Warren started delivering in Spring Valley, near his home. "*The first year, the houses were far apart, which I was not too keen on. You had to deliver it every day, including Christmas Day. On Christmas morning, the family had to wait until I had done my paper route. When I was sick, my mom delivered the papers, but I handled the money. I had these jars in my room with half dollars and quarters.*[27] Then he added an afternoon route to his workload.

"*The Evening Star, which was owned by this blue-blooded Washington family, was the dominant paper in town.*"

In the afternoons, he rolled down the streets on his bike, grabbing copies of the *Star* to throw from the huge basket on the front. Near the end of the route he had to steel himself. "*On Sedgwick was this terrible dog.*

"*I liked to work by myself, where I could spend my time thinking about things I wanted to think about. Washington was upsetting at first, but I was in my own world all the time. I could be sitting in a room thinking, or I could be riding around flinging things and thinking.*"

The thoughts he was thinking were angry thoughts. He spent his days acting them out at Alice Deal Junior High. Bertie Backus, Alice Deal's principal, prided herself on knowing each pupil by name. She soon had special reason to know Warren Buffett's.

"*I was kind of behind when I got there, and then I fell further behind. I was just mad at the world. I did a lot of daydreaming, and I was always charting things—I would bring stock charts to school and just wasn't paying attention to what was going on in class. Then I got to be friends with John McRae and Roger Bell. And I became disruptive.*"

The pleasing personality of his childhood all but disappeared. In one class, Warren enlisted John McRae to play chess with him while the teacher was talking, just to be obnoxious. In another class, he cut open a golf ball, which squirted some sort of liquid onto the ceiling.

The boys had started to golf. John McRae's father worked as a greenskeeper at Tregaron, a famous estate close to downtown Washington that belonged to heiress Marjorie Merriweather Post and her husband, Joseph E. Davies, who was ambassador to Russia. The family had dozens of servants and was almost never home, so the boys went over and played on the nine-hole golf course. Then Warren convinced Roger and John to run away with him to Hershey, Pennsylvania, where they were going to try to get jobs caddying at a well-known golf course.[28] "*We hitchhiked. And after we had successfully gone a hundred fifty miles or so, we made it to Hershey and stopped at this hotel and we made the mistake of bragging to the bellboy.*

"*The next morning, when we came down, there was this huge highway patrolman waiting for us, who took us down to the highway patrol headquarters.*

"*We just started lying. And we lied and lied and lied about having our parents' permission. All the while there was this Teletype machine spitting out alerts about this and that. I was sitting there thinking that pretty soon there was going to be an alert from Washington, D.C., and this guy will know we're lying. All I wanted to do was get out of there.*"

Somehow they lied convincingly enough that the patrolman let them go.[29] "*We started walking toward Gettysburg or someplace. We were having no luck hitchhiking, and then a trucker picked us up and stuffed all three of us into the cab.*" They were so scared by then, they only wanted to go home. "*The trucker stopped at a diner in Baltimore and divided us up with other truckers. It was getting dark and we felt like we'd never get out of there alive, but they took us back to Washington, separately. Roger Bell's mother was in the hospital. I mean, she had gone to the hospital over this, which made me feel terrible 'cause I had talked Roger into going. I was on my way to being a four-star delinquent.*"

He had made another friend by then, Lou Battistone; but, as in Omaha, he had kept his friendship with Lou separate from his relationship with Roger and John. Meanwhile, Warren was doing worse than ever at school. His grades dropped to Cs and Ds and even D minuses: in English, in history, in freehand drawing, in music, even Cs in mathematics.[30] "*Some of these grades were from the classes where I was supposedly good.*" Warren's teachers found him stubborn, rude, and lazy.[31] Some of the teachers gave him double black Xs, for extra bad. His behavior was shocking for the times. In the 1940s, children did what they were told and obeyed their teachers. "*I was going downhill fast. My parents were dying, they were dying.*"

He excelled in only one class, and that was typing. Washington was fighting the war on paper, and typing was considered a critical skill.

At Alice Deal, typing was taught by placing black covers over the keys so that the students were forced to type by touch.[32] It helped to be able to memorize, and it paid to have good hand-eye coordination. Warren was gifted at both. "*I made As every semester in typing. We all had these manual typewriters and, of course, you'd slam the carriage back to hear this 'ding!'*

"*I was—by far—the best in the class at typing out of twenty people in the room. When they'd have a speed test, I would just race through the first line so I could SLAM the carriage back. Everybody else would stop at that point, because they were still on the first word when they would hear my 'ding!' Then they'd panic, and they'd try to go faster, and they'd screw up. So I had a lot of fun in typing class.*"

Warren put this same ferocious energy into his three paper routes. He took to the paper-throwing as if he had been born with inky fingers. Next, says Lou Battistone, "he conned the route manager, with that personality of his, into giving him The Westchester" in historic Tenleytown. In this, Warren had pulled off a coup. The Westchester was the kind of route an adult news carrier would ordinarily manage.

"*It was a great opportunity. The Westchester was classy. The Westchester was just the crème de la crème. Queen Wilhelmina of the Netherlands owned it.*[33] *There were six U.S. Senators on that route, and colonels, and Supreme Court justices, all these biggies. There was Oveta Culp Hobby, and Leon Henderson, the head of the Office of Price Administration.*" Mrs. Hobby came from a famous Texas publishing family, and had moved to Washington to serve as director of the WACs, the Women's Army Corps.

"*So all of a sudden, I had this huge operation. I might have been thirteen or fourteen years old. I first got The Westchester just for the* Post. *I had to give up my other morning routes when I got The Westchester, and I felt badly.*" Warren had grown close to his *Times-Herald* manager. "*And when I told him that I had the chance to get the* Post *at The Westchester and that meant I had to give up his route in Spring Valley . . . he was terrific with me, but that was really kind of a sad moment.*"

By then Warren considered himself an experienced paper-route operator, but he was tackling a complex logistical challenge. The Westchester consisted of five buildings that sprawled over 27½ acres, four of them connected and one separate. The route included two more apartment buildings across Cathedral Avenue, the Marlin and the Warwick. He would also be covering a small route of single-family homes up to Wisconsin Avenue.

"*I started on a Sunday, and they handed me a book telling me the people and their apartment numbers. There was no training session and I didn't have the book in advance.*" He put on his tennis shoes and pulled out his bus pass, which cost three cents each way, and climbed sleepily aboard the Capital Transit bus. He did not stop for breakfast.

"*I got up there around four-thirty a.m. There were these bundles and bundles of papers. I didn't know what the hell I was doing. I didn't know how the numbering system worked or anything. I sat there for hours and hours sorting and bundling the papers. I was short papers in the end, because people just took them from the bundles as they left for church.*

"*The whole thing was a disaster. I thought, what the hell have I gotten into? It took until ten or eleven in the morning to finish up.*

"*But I stumbled my way through. And it got better and I got good very fast. It was easy.*"

Warren raced out of his house to catch the first N2 bus over to The Westchester at 3900 Cathedral Avenue every morning. Often he had bus pass number 001, the first person buying a bus pass each week.[34] The driver got used to looking out for him if he was running a little late. He would jump off the bus and run the couple of blocks over to The Westchester.

He had figured out the most efficient route and turned what could have been a boring and repetitive job delivering hundreds of newspapers each day into a competition with himself. "*See, the papers were a little thinner in those days, because of newsprint rationing. A thirty-six-page paper was a pretty good-size paper. I'd stand at one end of the hallway with a bundle and pull off a paper, fold it over flat, and tuck it to make a pancake, or roll it into a biscuit. Then I smacked it against my thigh. And I'd twist it against my wrist to put some spin on it and slide it down the hall. I could slide that thing fifty, even a hundred feet. It was kind of a test of skill, because the apartment doors were at different lengths down the hallway. I'd do the longest ones first. But the trick was to be able to do it in such a way that they'd all come to rest a few inches from the door. And sometimes people would have milk bottles, which made it more interesting.*"

He also sold calendars to his newspaper customers, and he developed another sideline too. He asked all his customers for their old magazines as scrap paper for the war effort.[35] Then he would check the labels on the magazines to figure out when the subscriptions were expiring, using a code book he had gotten from Moore-Cottrell, the publishing powerhouse that had hired him as an agent to sell magazines. He made a card file of subscribers, and before their subscriptions expired, Warren would be knocking at their door, selling them a new magazine.[36]

Because The Westchester had so much turnover in wartime, Warren's biggest dread was customers who skipped out and didn't pay, leaving him stuck with the cost of their papers. After a few people skipped out on him, he started tipping the elevator girls to let him know when people were about to move. Then the imperious Oveta Culp Hobby got behind. He thought that she should have a little more empathy for her paperboy, since she owned her own newspaper, the *Houston Post*. But he began to worry that she would skip out on him.

"I paid my own bills monthly, always on time, and I always showed up to deliver the papers. I was a responsible kid. I got presented with a war bond for perfect service. With the customers, I didn't want to let the receivables build up. I tried all kinds of things with Oveta Culp Hobby—leaving notes—and finally ended up knocking on her door at six in the morning to catch her before she could escape." Shy in other ways, Warren was never timid when it came to money. When Mrs. Hobby answered the door, *"I handed her an envelope, and she had to pay me."*

After school, Warren rode the bus back to Spring Valley and jumped on his bike to deliver the *Star*. On rainy winter afternoons, he would sometimes come off his paper route and appear on the doorstep of his friends' homes. He always wore battered canvas sneakers, so full of holes that his feet were swimming to the ankles; his skin would be pimply with cold inside a soaking-wet oversize plaid shirt. For some reason he never seemed to wear a coat. Motherly Mrs. Whoever would smile and shake her head at the pitiful sight, bundle him up, and towel him off while he basked in her warmth.[37]

At the end of 1944, Warren filed his first income tax return. He paid only seven dollars in taxes; to get it down to that, he deducted his wristwatch and bicycle as business expenses. He knew that was questionable. But at the time, he was not above cutting a few corners to get where he wanted to go.

At age fourteen, he had now fulfilled the promise laid out in his favorite book, *One Thousand Ways to Make $1,000*. His savings now totaled around a thousand dollars. He took great pride in that accomplishment. So far, he was ahead of the game, way ahead of the game, and getting ahead of the game, he knew, was the way to his goal.

10

True Crime Stories

Washington, D.C. • 1943–1945

Bad grades, tax evasion, and running away were the least of Warren's troubles in junior high. His parents didn't know it, but their son had turned to a life of crime.

"Well, I was antisocial, in eighth and ninth grade, after I moved there. I fell in with bad people and did things I shouldn't have. I was just rebelling. I was unhappy."

He started with minor schoolboy pranks.

"I loved print shop. I used to make calculations in print-shop class of the frequency of letters and numbers. That was something I could do by myself. I could set type, you know, and that sort of thing. I enjoyed printing up all kinds of things.

"I made up a letterhead from the American Temperance Union, Reverend A. W. Paul, President. I'd write letters to people on that letterhead saying that for years I'd lectured around the country on the evils of drink, and in these travels my appearances were always accompanied by my young apprentice, Harold. Harold was an example of what drink could do to men. He'd stand there on the stage with a pint, drooling, unable to comprehend what was going on around him, pathetic. Then I said that, unfortunately, young Harold died last week, and a mutual friend had suggested that you might be a replacement for him."[1]

The people with whom Warren felt most comfortable encouraged his antisocial impulses. He and a couple of new friends, Don Danly and Charlie Tron, took to hanging out at the new Sears store. Near Tenley Circle where Nebraska and Wisconsin Avenues intersected, the store was an eye-opening swoop of modern design dropped into the middle of Tenleytown, the second oldest neighborhood in Washington. Letters the height of a man spelled out SEARS on a curved metal deck several stories above sidewalk level.[2] On the roof behind the Sears sign was hidden a great novelty, an open-air parking garage, which quickly became popular with high school kids as a place to park and neck. The store had become the hangout for all the junior high kids too. Warren and his friends rode the H2 bus there at lunchtime or on Saturdays.

Most of the kids liked the dark little lunch counter Sears had installed in the basement, with its mesmerizing conveyer belt that spit out doughnuts all day long. But Warren, Don, and Charlie preferred Woolworth's across the street, even though the police station was on the opposite corner. Woolworth's sat kitty-corner from Sears. They could eat lunch and case the joint through the windows.

After their hamburgers, the boys would stroll down the stairs into Sears's lower level, bypassing the lunch counter and going straight to the sporting-goods section.

"*We'd just steal the place blind. We'd steal stuff for which we had no use. We'd steal golf bags and golf clubs. I walked out of the lower level where the sporting goods were, up the stairway to the street, carrying a golf bag and golf clubs, and the clubs were stolen, and so was the bag. I stole hundreds of golf balls.*" They referred to their theft as "hooking."

"*I don't know how we didn't get caught. We couldn't have looked innocent. A teenager who's doing something wrong does not look innocent.*[3]

"*I took the golf balls and filled up these orange sacks in my closet. As fast as Sears put them out, I was hooking them. I had no use for them, really. I wasn't selling them then. It's hard to think of a reason why you had this multiplying group of golf balls in the closet, this orange sack that's just getting bigger all the time. I should have diversified my theft. Instead, I made up this crazy story for my parents—and I know they didn't believe me, but—I told them I had this friend, and his father had died. He kept finding more of these golf balls that his father had bought. Who knows what my parents talked about at night.*"[4]

The Buffetts were aghast. Warren was their gifted child, but by the end of 1944, he had become the school delinquent. "*My grades were a quantification of my unhappiness. Math—Cs. English—C, D, D. Everything Xs for self-reliance, industry, courtesy. The less I interacted with teachers, the better it was. They actually put me in a room by myself there for a while where they would kind of shove my lessons under the door like Hannibal Lecter.*"[5]

When graduation day came and the students were told to show up in a suit and tie, Warren refused. With that his principal, Bertie Backus, had had enough.

"They wouldn't let me graduate with the class at Alice Deal, because I was so disruptive and I wouldn't wear clothes that were appropriate. It was major. It was unpleasant. I was really rebelling. Some of the teachers predicted that I was going to be a disastrous failure. I set the record for checks on deficiencies in deportment and all that.

"But my dad never gave up on me. And my mother didn't either, actually. Neither one. It's great to have parents that believe in you."

Yet by the spring of 1945, as Warren was starting high school, the Buffetts had had enough too. By now, it was no great mystery how to motivate Warren. Howard threatened to take away the source of his money.

"My dad, who was always supportive of me, said, 'I know what you're capable of. And I'm not asking you to perform one hundred percent, but you can either keep behaving this way or you can do something in relation to your potential. But if you don't do it, you have to give up the paper routes.' And that hit me. My dad was low-key, just sort of letting me know he was disappointed with me. And that killed me probably a lot more than his telling me I couldn't do this or that, you know."

11

Pudgy She Was Not

Washington, D.C. · 1944–1945

Howard Buffett quickly gained a reputation as perhaps the least-backslapping Congressman ever to represent his state. He stayed miles away from the "rubber chicken circuit" of campaign money and vote-getting events that occupied so many Congressmen, and made it known his vote was not for sale or barter. He turned down a raise because the people who elected him had voted him in at a lower salary. He went around with eyebrows lofted at the perks that came with being a Congressman. The subsidized restaurants, the payrolls padded with friends, relatives, and mistresses, the "stationery store" that sold, at wholesale prices, everything from tires to jewelry—Howard was shocked by all of it and let that be known.

Moreover, with the country at war and the government running at a deficit, Howard was obsessed with the quixotic goal of trying to return the country to the "gold standard," which the United States had dropped in 1933. Ever since, the Treasury had been printing money freely to finance first the New Deal and now the war. Howard feared that someday the United States might wind up like Germany in the 1920s, when people had to cart wheelbarrows of money down the street to buy a head of cabbage—the direct result of Germany being forced to deplete its gold stock to pay reparations after World War I.[1] The economic chaos that resulted was one of the major factors that had led to Hitler.

Certain that the government was going to spend the country into ruination, Howard bought a farm back in Nebraska to serve as a refuge for the family when everybody else starved. A distrust of government bonds was so well entrenched in the Buffett household that when the family held a powwow about giving a savings bond to somebody for a birthday present, young Bertie, nine years old, thought her parents were trying to put one over on the guy. "But won't he know they're *worthless*?"[2] she asked.

Howard's rigidity impeded him from doing his job, which was to legislate.

"He would lose these votes in the House, maybe 412 to 3. My dad would be among the three. And it just didn't get to him. He was very much at peace. It would have gotten to me—I get mad when I lose. I can't ever recall seeing him depressed or despondent. He just figured he was doing the best he could. He went his own way, and he knew why he was there—for us kids. He had a very pessimistic appraisal of where the country was going, but he was not a pessimist."

The way Howard invariably held aloft his principles—instead of working toward Republican Party goals by joining coalitions—strained relationships with his colleagues and took a toll on the family. Leila cared about fitting in; other people's opinions mattered to her. She was also competitive. "We believed in him," says Doris, "but it was hard to see him lose all the time." That was an understatement. All the Buffetts admired Howard's fortitude and credit their father for teaching them integrity. But each of the children absorbed in their own way a desire to belong that somehow muted or balanced the family streak of independence.

Her husband's stance as the lone wolf of the party exacerbated Leila's irritable mood. Still miserable about living in Washington, she tried to create a miniature Omaha and spent her free time with the women of the Nebraska delegation. She no longer had a cleaning lady, and felt put upon. "I gave it all up to marry Howard,"[3] she would say, adding this lament to her stories of how she and Howard had sacrificed for their ungrateful children's welfare. But rather than teaching those children to help around the house, she did everything, because "it was just easier to do it myself." Feelings of martyrdom made her angry at the kids a lot of the time, especially at Doris, who was having her own issues about fitting in.

Although strikingly pretty, Doris says she never felt that way, and was insecure about whether she was good enough for the sophisticated Washington crowd of which she longed to be a part. She was invited to the French Embassy for Margaret Truman's birthday party and began planning to debut as a Princess of Ak-Sar-Ben* with the crowd she would have been graduating with back in Omaha. Warren made fun of her for her pretensions.

---

*Nebraska spelled backward.

Leila, herself a determined striver who cared deeply about appearances, would pore over every bit of news about the Duchess of Windsor, a penniless commoner who had been rescued by a prince.[4] But, unlike the duchess, who spent the rest of her life amassing one of the world's most impressive collections of jewels, Leila's ambition and pride wrapped themselves in a self-conscious disdain for ostentation. She pictured the family as a middle-class Midwestern archetype, a *Saturday Evening Post* magazine cover, and berated Doris for being socially ambitious.

Still fourteen years old, Warren became a sophomore at Woodrow Wilson High School in February 1945, upon his graduation from Alice Deal.[5] He wanted to be both "special" and "normal" at the same time. Much less mature than his classmates, he was being carefully watched by his parents, who were determined to see him straighten out. His paper routes were the source of his autonomy, such autonomy as he now had. And he had been reading—as well as throwing—the papers.

"I read the comics, the sports section, and looked at the stock pages every morning before I delivered the newspapers. I read the cartoon <u>Li'l Abner</u> every morning. I had to know what Li'l Abner was doing every day. His appeal was that he made you feel so smart. You'd read this thing and think, 'If I was in that position . . . this guy is so dumb.' Because here was Daisy Mae, this incredible woman who was just nuts about him, and was always chasing after him, and he just kept passing her up and not noticing her. Every red-blooded American boy in those days would have been just waiting there for Daisy Mae to catch him."

Daisy Mae Scragg, the hillbilly heroine of the Appalachian cartoon hamlet of Dogpatch, was a bodacious blonde whose cleavage burst from an off-the-shoulder polka-dot blouse. The dim-witted strongman Li'l Abner Yokum spent most of his time trying to evade Daisy Mae's marital designs on him. The more he spurned her, the harder Daisy Mae chased him. Even though rich and powerful men wooed her, to Daisy Mae there was but one man on earth, Li'l Abner.[6]

Besides elusiveness, Li'l Abner's only apparent asset was his manly physique. Warren's poor record with girls so far suggested that if he ever wanted to attract the interest of a girl like Daisy Mae, he had better do something to make himself more attractive. Now he developed a new interest, which conveniently gave him an excuse as well for hiding away down in the basement. The way that Frankie Zick could clean-and-jerk fifty-pound bags of animal feed for hours at a time at South Omaha Feed had impressed him. He got his friend Lou Battistone interested and they embarked on a weight-lifting program. At the time, weight training was not the stuff of serious athletes, but it had many qualities that appealed to Warren: systems, measuring, counting, repetition, and competing with yourself. In search of technique, he had discovered Bob Hoffman and his magazine, *Strength and Health.*

Strength and Health was Hoffman's attempt to overcome the stigma against weight lifting through aggressive promotion. It was edited, published, and apparently written largely by Hoffman himself. Ads for his products appeared on nearly every page. "Uncle" Bob's technical knowledge, his razzle-dazzle, the man's unflagging ability to market himself, were striking.

"He was the coach of most of the Olympic team. He was the head of the York Barbell Company, and he was the author of the __Big Arms__ and the __Big Chest__ books. The basic thing he sold initially was barbell sets. If you went to a sporting-goods store then, everything was York barbells. You could buy all these different kinds of sets."

Warren got a set of dumbbells and a barbell with a set of plates in increments of one and a quarter pounds that slipped on and off the bar, which he tightened with a little screwdriver that came with the set. He kept the weights in the basement and was *"always down there clanking."*

But while Warren was clanking down in the basement, the Republicans were in hell. Franklin Roosevelt had managed to win a fourth term as President, ensuring the Democrats another four years in the White House. At the dinner table, the family listened to much ranting from Howard. Then, on April 12, Roosevelt died of a cerebral hemorrhage, and his Vice President, Harry Truman, succeeded him as President.

Roosevelt's death sent most of the country into deep mourning, tinged with fear. Three and a half years into the war, the country had lost the man who made it feel secure, and it had low expectations of Truman. He retained FDR's cabinet and sounded so humble that some thought he might be overwhelmed by the job. But to the Buffetts, no one could be worse than FDR. And to Warren, the death of a President meant another way to make money. Newspapers put out special editions, and he hustled himself out to the street corner, hawking papers while everybody mourned.

One month later, on May 8, 1945, came V-E Day, the formal end of the war in Europe, following Germany's unconditional surrender. Again there were special editions to sell, and Warren echoed his father's political convictions as a matter of course. But at the time, he was only passingly interested in these adult concerns, because his real obsession was weight lifting and Bob Hoffman.

But the most impressive celebrity in *Strength and Health*—apart from Uncle Bob himself—was not John Grimek, the greatest bodybuilder in the world. It was a woman.

"There were not a lot of women in <u>Strength and Health</u>. Pudgy Stockton's about the only one that ever made it. I liked Pudgy. She was impressive. We talked about her a lot at school."

That was more than a slight understatement. Warren and Lou were obsessed with Abbye "Pudgy" Stockton, a work of art in human flesh—taut thighs rippling as her chiseled arms lofted a huge barbell above her wind-whipped hair, bikini showing off her tiny waist and perky bosom to all the musclemen and gaping onlookers at Santa Monica's Muscle Beach. Five foot one and 115 pounds, she could lift a grown man in the air over her head and do it without sacrificing any of her femininity.[7]

"She had the muscle tone of Mitzi Gaynor and the mammary development of Sophia Loren," says Lou Battistone. "She was phenomenal. And we—I have to admit to you—we lusted for her."

Until now, Daisy Mae had been Warren's fantasy girl. He would always look for the qualities of Daisy Mae in a woman. But Pudgy—Pudgy was *real*.

It was not clear, however, exactly what you did if you had a girlfriend like Pudgy.[8] The boys puzzled over ads for "Bob Hoffman's guide to a successful happy marriage," which featured "Premarital examination. How to examine your wife before marriage to make sure she's 'intact,' as well as courtship, why people marry, and minor forms of lovemaking." Just what were the minor forms of lovemaking? they wondered. Even the major forms were largely a mystery to them; the ads in the back of *Strength and Health* were the best the 1940s could do in terms of sex education.

In the end, however, Warren's fascination with numbers won out.

"You know, you kept measuring that biceps to see if it'd gone from thirteen to thirteen and a quarter inches. And you were always worried whether you were loosening up the tape or anything. But I never improved from looking like the Charles Atlas 'before' picture. I think my biceps went from thirteen inches to thirteen and a quarter inches after thousands of curls.

"The <u>Big Arms</u> book didn't do me much good."

12

Silent Sales

That August, while the Buffetts were in Omaha, the United States dropped two atomic bombs on Hiroshima and Nagasaki; on September 2, Japan formally surrendered. The war was over. Americans celebrated in near hysteria.

A few weeks later, with the family back in Washington, Warren returned to finish tenth grade at Woodrow Wilson High School, at fifteen still a kid but now also a businessman. He was making so much money throwing papers that he had accumulated more than $2,000. Howard had let his son invest in Builders Supply Co., a hardware store that he and Carl Falk were opening next to the feed store back in Omaha.[1] Meanwhile, Warren himself had bought a forty-acre farm for $1,200 about seventy miles away, near Walthill, in Thurston County, Nebraska.[2] A tenant farmer worked the farm and they shared the profits—just the kind of arrangement Warren liked, with someone else doing the sweaty, boring work. Warren began introducing himself to people in high school as Warren Buffett from Nebraska, who owned a tenant farm back in the Midwest.[3]

He thought like a businessman but did not look like one. He fit uncomfortably into the high school crowd, showing up with the same tattered sneakers and droopy socks peeking out from under baggy trousers day after day, skinny neck and narrow shoulders swallowed inside his shirt. If forced into dress shoes, he wore startling yellow or white socks above the scuffed leather. He seemed to squirm in his seat all the time. Sometimes he looked shy, almost innocent. At others, he wore a sharp, tough expression.

Doris and Warren ignored each other if their paths crossed in the halls of high school. "*Doris, who was very popular, was particularly ashamed of me, because I dressed terribly. Sometimes your sister would help you get socialized but I rejected that, basically. It wasn't her fault; I was painfully aware of being socially maladjusted. I may just have felt so hopeless.*"

Warren's stone-faced, smart-aleck act covered up the feelings of inadequacy that had made his life so difficult since leaving Omaha. He desperately wanted to be normal, but still felt very much the outsider.

He was "hesitant," said classmate Norma Thurston, his friend Don Danly's girlfriend, "and he chose his words carefully and never made any commitment, however small, if he thought he might have to take it back."[4]

Many of his classmates plunged enthusiastically into teenage life, joining fraternities and sororities, getting pinned, and going to parties in their families' basements where they served soda pop, hot dogs, and ice cream and then turned the lights down while everybody necked. Instead of necking, Warren rubbernecked. He had a regular Saturday night reservation with Lou Battistone at Jimmy Lake's theater, a local burlesque joint, where they had a fantasy flirtation with one of the dancers, Kitty Lyne. Warren would roar with laughter when a comedian took a pratfall or the second banana in the balcony started heckling him.[5] He spent twenty-five dollars on a 1920s-style raccoon coat. When he wore it down to Jimmy Lake's, the bouncer told him, "No clowning around, you guys. Either take that coat off, or you can't come in."[6] He took it off.

The side of Warren that had robbed Sears blind was in transition: fading, but not gone. He and Danly still took the occasional five-finger discount at Sears. When his teachers told him they had most of their retirement savings in AT&T stock, he shorted it, then showed them the trade tickets to give them heartburn. "*I was a pain in the ass,*" he says.[7]

His exceptional powers of reasoning and smart-aleck tendencies combined into a talent for taking perverse stands. Somehow, probably because he was the son of a Congressman, he wound up appearing on a radio program on January 3, 1946. CBS "American School of the Air" brought its program to WTOP, the local station owned by the *Washington Post*. On that Saturday morning, Warren went down to the station, where he and four other kids sat around a microphone and debated as "Congress in Session."

The show's hostess assigned him the job of spicing up the debate. He argued convincingly in favor of absurdities—ideas on the order of eliminating income taxes or annexing Japan. "*When they wanted someone to take a crazy position,*" he says, "*I did it.*" But while he relished argument for its own sake, his clever retorts, lightning-fast counterarguments, and general contrariness hindered his quest to be liked by his peers.

Until now, Warren's efforts to get along with people had had mixed results. He charmed adults, except for his teachers. He felt ill at ease with his peers, but had always managed to make a few close friends. He desperately wanted people to like him and especially not to attack him personally. He wanted a system. In fact, he already had one, but he wasn't using the system to its full effect. Now, lacking any other resources, he began to work harder at it.

Warren had found this system at his grandfather's house, where he read everything he could get his hands on at a blazing pace, just as he did at home. Browsing the bookshelf in the back bedroom, he had consumed every issue of the *Progressive Grocer* and every single copy of the *Daily Nebraskan* that had been edited by his father, and worked his way like a boll weevil through all fifteen years of the *Reader's Digest* that Ernest had accumulated. This bookcase also held a series of small biographies, many of them on business leaders. Since a young age Warren had studied the lives of men like Jay Cooke, Daniel Drew, Jim Fisk, Cornelius Vanderbilt, Jay Gould, John D. Rockefeller, and Andrew Carnegie. Some of these books he read and reread. One of them was special— not a biography but a paperback written by former salesman Dale Carnegie,[8] enticingly titled *How to Win Friends and Influence People*. He had discovered it at age eight or nine.

Warren knew he needed to win friends, and he wanted to influence people. He opened the book. It hooked him from the first page. "If you want to gather honey," it began, "don't kick over the beehive."[9]

Criticism is futile, said Carnegie.

Rule number one: Don't criticize, condemn, or complain.

This idea riveted Warren. Criticism was something he knew everything about.

Criticism puts people on the defensive, Carnegie said, and makes them strive to justify themselves. It is dangerous, because it wounds people's precious pride, hurts their sense of importance, and arouses resentment. Carnegie advocated avoiding confrontation. "People don't want criticism. They want honest and sincere appreciation." I am not talking about flattery, Carnegie said. Flattery is insincere and selfish. Appreciation is sincere and comes from the heart. The deepest urge in human nature is "the desire to be important."[10]

Although "Don't criticize" was the most important, there were thirty rules in all.

Everybody wants attention and admiration. Nobody wants to be criticized.

The sweetest sound in the English language is the sound of a person's
   own name.

The only way to get the best of an argument is to avoid it.

If you are wrong, admit it quickly and emphatically.

Ask questions instead of giving direct orders.

Give the other person a fine reputation to live up to.

Call attention to people's mistakes indirectly. Let the other person save face.

I am talking about a new way of life, Carnegie said. *I am talking about a new
way of life.*

Warren's heart lifted. He thought he had found the truth. This was a system.
He felt so disadvantaged socially that he needed a system to sell himself to people, a system he could learn once and use without having to respond in a new
way to each changing situation.

But it took numbers to prove that it actually worked. He decided to do a statistical analysis of what happened if he did follow Dale Carnegie's rules, and
what happened if he didn't. He tried giving attention and appreciation, and he
tried doing nothing or being disagreeable. People around him did not know
he was performing experiments on them in the silence of his own head, but he
watched how they responded. He kept track of his results. Filled with a rising
joy, he saw what the numbers proved: The rules worked.

Now he had a system. He had a set of rules.

But it did you no good to *read* about the rules. You had to *live* them. *I am
talking about a new way of life,* said Carnegie.

Warren began to practice. He started at a very elementary level. Some of it
came naturally to him, but he found that this system could not be applied in an
automatic and easy manner. "Don't criticize" sounded simple, but there were
ways to criticize without even realizing it. It was hard not to show off, not to display annoyance and impatience. And admitting you were wrong was easy sometimes and very difficult at other times. Giving people attention and sincere
appreciation and admiration was one of the hardest. Someone sunk in misery
much of the time, as Warren was, found it hard to focus on others, not himself.

Nevertheless, he gradually worked out for himself that the dark years of junior high were living proof that ignoring Dale Carnegie's rules didn't work. As
he started to gain his footing in high school, he continued to practice the rules
in encounters with others.

Unlike most people who read Carnegie's book and thought, gee, that makes sense, then set the book aside and forgot about it, Warren worked at this project with unusual concentration; he kept coming back to these ideas and using them. Even when he failed and forgot and went for long stretches without applying himself to the system, he returned and resumed practicing in the end. By high school, he had accumulated a few more friends, joined the Woodrow Wilson golf team, and managed to make himself inoffensive if not popular. Dale Carnegie's system had honed his natural wit; above all, it enhanced his persuasiveness, his flair for salesmanship.

He seemed intense, yet with an impish side; even-tempered and congenial, yet somehow solitary. Certainly his passion for making money—which occupied most of his spare time—made him unique at Woodrow Wilson.

No one else in high school was a businessman. Just from pitching newspapers a couple of hours a day, he was earning $175 a month, more money than his teachers. In 1946, a grown man felt well paid if he made $3,000 a year for full-time work.[11] Warren kept his money in a chifforobe at home, which no one but he was allowed to touch. "I was in his house one day," says Lou Battistone, "and he opened up a drawer and said, 'This is what I've been saving.' And he had seven hundred dollars in small bills. That's a big stack, let me tell you."[12]

He had started several new businesses. Buffett's Golf Balls peddled refurbished golf balls for six bucks a dozen.[13] These he ordered from a fellow in Chicago named Witek, whom Warren couldn't resist nicknaming "Half-Witek." *"They were classy balls, really good golf balls too, Titleist and Spalding Dots and Maxflis, which I bought for three and a half bucks a dozen. They looked brand-new. He probably got them the way we first tried to get them, out of water traps, only he was better."* Nobody at school knew about Half-Witek. Even his family didn't seem to realize that he bought the used golf balls that he and his friend Don Danly were selling. Fellow members of the Wilson golf team thought he fished them out of water traps.[14]

Buffett's Approval Service sold sets of collectible stamps to collectors out of state. Buffett's Showroom Shine was a car-buffing business that he and Battistone ran out of Lou's father's used-car lot, until they abandoned this because it involved manual labor and turned out to be too damn much work.[15]

Then one day when Warren was seventeen and a senior, he raced to tell Don Danly about a new idea. It had the same exponential quality to it as the weighing machines from *One Thousand Ways to Make $1,000*—where one machine could pay for another and another. "I bought this old pinball machine for twenty-five bucks," he said, "and we can have a partnership. Your part of the deal is to fix it up.[16] And, lookit, we'll tell Frank Erico, the barber, 'We represent Wilson's Coin-Operated Machine Company, and we have a proposition from Mr. Wilson. It's at no risk to you. Let's put this nickel machine in the back, Mr. Erico, and your customers can play while they wait. And we'll split the money.' "[17]

Danly was game. Although no one had ever put pinball machines in barbershops before, they presented their proposition to Mr. Erico, who bit. The boys took the legs off the pinball machine, put it in Don's father's car, and hauled it over to Mr. Erico's barbershop. Sure enough, the very first evening, when Warren and Don came back to check, "Gee zip!" Warren said—four bucks' worth of nickels had found their way into the machine. Mr. Erico was delighted, and the pinball machine stayed.[18]

After a week, Warren emptied the machine and scooped the nickels into two piles. "Mr. Erico," he said, "let's not bother going one for you, one for me. Just pick the pile you want."[19] It was like the old-fashioned way of dividing cake: One child cuts, the other child chooses. After Mr. Erico swept one pile over toward his side of the table, Warren counted $25 in his pile. That was enough to buy another pinball machine. Pretty soon, seven or eight of "Mr. Wilson's" pinball machines were sitting in barbershops around town. Warren had discovered the miracle of capital: money that works for its owner, as if it had a job of its own.

"You had to get along with the barbers. That was crucial. I mean, these guys could all go buy these machines for twenty-five bucks themselves. So we would always convince them that it took someone with a four-hundred IQ to repair pinball machines.

"Now, there were some pretty unsavory characters in the pinball business, and they all hung out at a place called Silent Sales. That was our hunting ground. Silent Sales was in the 900 block of D Street, right near the Gayety burlesque house on the seedy side of downtown. These characters at Silent Sales were amused by us, sort of. Danly and I would go down there, and we'd look at these machines and buy whatever we could for twenty-five bucks. New machines cost about three hundred dollars. I used to subscribe to Billboard *magazine in those days to keep track of what was going on in pinball machines.*

"The guys at Silent Sales taught us some things. There were some illegal slot machines around. And they showed us how to pour beer into them to make a

fifty-cent piece get stuck in the mechanism, and you could just keep pulling the handle until it paid. They showed us how to disable the electric cutoff for the coin-operated soda machines at the movie theaters so if you stuck a nickel in, then immediately pulled the plug, you could empty the whole machine.

"These guys would explain all this stuff to us and we'd just eat it up.

"My dad probably suspected the kind of characters we were hanging out with. But he always felt I'd turn out okay."

Warren and Don were already making good money with single pinball machines in barbershops, but then they found a gold mine. *"Our home run of all time was down near Griffith Stadium, which is the old baseball park."* In the middle of Washington's worst slums, they found *"a seven-chair black barbershop. There were a lot of dudes down there. After we put a pinball machine in, we would come back to collect, and these guys had drilled holes in the bottom of the machine and rigged the tilt mechanism. It was a real contest of wills. But that was our mother lode, our best location by far. The guys who played at these barbershops were constantly imploring us to adjust the tilt mechanism so you could shove the machine harder without making it tilt.*

"Listen, we were not judgmental about our customers." If anything, they were probably trying to pick up more ideas like the scams the guys at Silent Sales had taught them, and those they were inventing on their own. *"One time we were down in Danly's basement playing with my coin collection. To make collecting on the paper route more interesting, I used to collect different kinds of coins. So I had these Whitman coin boards with slots for the coins. I said to Don, 'It looks to me like we could take these coin boards and use them as molds for casting slugs.'*

"Danly was the brains of the operation. And so, sure enough, he learned how to pour these molds for casting slugs, and I supplied the coin boards. We would try to use the slugs for vending machines for soda pop and things like that. Our basic formula was to have our income in currency and our outgo in slugs."

At school, however, Warren mostly liked to talk about his businesses—not his scams—and by the spring semester, near the end of high school, his raconteuring had turned him and Don into a minor legend around Woodrow Wilson.

"Everybody knew we had the pinball-machine business, and everybody kind of knew we were raking it in. We probably exaggerated too when we told them. And so people wanted in on it. It was like stocks."

One of them was a boy named Bob Kerlin—an intense kid who played on the golf team with Warren.[20] He and Don weren't open to letting anyone in on their pinball business, but they did have a plan for using Kerlin for their newest venture. *"We had given up stealing the golf balls from Sears, but we got this idea that we were going to retrieve lost golf balls from the lakes on golf courses around Washington. And now we saw a position for Kerlin, because neither one of us wanted to retrieve the golf balls."*

They created an elaborate scenario for how Kerlin would do this. It bordered on an evil prank, but school was out in a couple of months, so what the hell.

"We went down again to Ninth and D, where the Army surplus store was located, right by Silent Sales, and bought a gas mask. And then we got this garden hose and we hooked them up and tested this thing in a bathtub by putting our faces in three inches of water."

Doing what he called his Tom Sawyer routine, Warren said to Kerlin: *" 'This is your chance. We're going to deal you in.' We told him that we would go out at four in the morning to some golf course in Virginia, and that he would wear the gas mask in the lake and retrieve the balls, and we'd split the money three ways.*

"Kerlin said, 'How do I stay down on the bottom?' I said, 'Oh, I've got that all worked out. What we will do is, you'll strip, and you'll be nude, but you'll wear my <u>Washington Post</u> *newspaper bag, and we'll put barbell plates in the newspaper bag so that you'll stay on the bottom.'*

"So we went out to this golf course, and all the way Kerlin was expressing some doubt. And Danly and I said, 'Have we ever failed? I mean, you're looking at a couple of guys . . . if you want to quit now, okay, but, you know, you're not in any future deals.'

"So we got out there at the crack of dawn. Kerlin was stripped, and we were dressed warmly. He was totally nude with a <u>Washington Post</u> *newspaper bag on and all these barbell plates, and he started wading into the lake. Of course, he didn't know if he was stepping on snakes or golf balls or whatever. And then he got down and when he tugged on the rope, we pulled him back up. He said, 'I can't see anything.' We said, 'Don't worry about seeing anything, just grope around.' And he started to go back down.*

"But before his head went under, this truck came over the rise, carrying the guy that's going to fill up sand traps in the morning. He saw us and drove up, saying, 'What are you kids doing?' Danly and I were thinking fast. 'We're conducting an experiment for our high school physics class, sir.' Kerlin was nodding the whole time. So we had to get him out of the pond. The whole thing blew up on us."[21]

Whatever happened to poor Kerlin, and however nude he actually was, a watered-down version of this story got around. It would be the last great Tom Sawyering of Warren's high school career.

By now, however, he had made a small fortune: a glistening $5,000 heap, sticky with the newsprint from throwing more than five hundred thousand newspapers. Newsprint snowflakes made up more than half his snowball. Rich as he was, however, Warren meant to keep that snowball rolling.*

---

*Thanks to inflation, a sixteen-year-old with a similar pile as of 2007 would have roughly $53,000.

13

The Rules of the Racetrack

Omaha and Washington, D.C. • 1940s

Warren's Dale Carnegie tests of behavior were handicapping: a mathematical experiment on human nature. The data he collected gave him the odds that Carnegie was right.

This way of thinking was an extension of his childhood hobbies of racing marbles and collecting bottle caps. Warren's passion for handicapping, however, extended to many other subjects, especially his own lifespan. His interest in longevity was no mere abstraction. Ernest Buffett, to whom Warren was extremely attached, had died in September 1946 at age sixty-nine. Warren was sixteen. Of his four grandparents, only Stella, age seventy-three, remained alive, confined in the Norfolk State Hospital. Yet long before Ernest's death, since his days of calculating the odds on life expectancies of hymn composers, Warren had been preoccupied with his lifespan. The data points from these latest family events did nothing to ease his mind about either longevity or insanity.

The art of such handicapping is based on data. The key was having *more information than the other guy*—then analyzing it right and using it rationally. Warren had first put this into practical use as a child down at the Ak-Sar-Ben racetrack, when his friend Bob Russell's mother introduced the boys to the world of pari-mutuel betting.

Warren and Russ were too young to wager, but they quickly figured out how to make a buck. Amid the cigarette butts, beer slops, old programs, and hot-dog remnants in the grime and sawdust of the Ak-Sar-Ben floorboards were thousands of discarded tickets, peeping out like mushrooms on the forest floor. The boys turned themselves into truffle hounds.

"They call that 'stooping.' At the start of the racing season you get all these people who'd never seen a race except in the movies. And they'd think that if your horse came in second or third, you didn't get paid, because all the emphasis is on the winner, so they'd throw away place and show tickets. The other time you would hit it big was when there was a disputed race. That little light would go on that said 'contested' or 'protest.' By that time, some people had thrown away their tickets. Meanwhile, we were just gobbling them up. We wouldn't even look at them when we were working. At night we'd go through them. It was awful; people would spit on the floor. But we had great fun. If I found any winning tickets, my aunt Alice, who didn't care anything at all about races, would cash them in for us, because they wouldn't cash them for kids."

Warren wanted to go to the races all the time. When Mrs. Russell wasn't taking him, *"my dad would never go to the races,"* says Buffett. *"He did not believe in the races."* Instead, his parents let his great-uncle Frank, the oddball of the family, take him. Frank had long ago reconciled with his brother Ernest and had eventually married a woman whom the family referred to as "the gold-digger."[1] He had no particular interest in the horses, but he took Warren to Ak-Sar-Ben because his great-nephew wanted to go.

At Ak-Sar-Ben, Warren had learned something about how to read the tip sheet, and it opened up a whole new world. Handicapping horses combined two things he was very, very good at: collecting information and math. It was not unlike counting cards at blackjack, except that the winning hand had four legs and ran around a track. Soon, he and Russ knew enough to put out their own tip sheet, the cannily named *Stable-Boy Selections*.

"We got away with it for a while. They weren't the hottest sellers in the world. I mean, a couple of little kids selling this thing we typed up in my basement on an old Royal typewriter. The limiting factor was carbons in those days. You could probably only get in five or so carbons. But I got on the Royal and Bob Russell and I doped out the horses and then we typed up this thing.

"We were in the track, yelling, 'Get your <u>Stable-Boy Selections</u>!' But the Blue Sheet was the number-one tip sheet, and the racetrack was getting a commission on it. The Blue Sheet sold for a little more. At twenty-five cents, we were a cut-rate product. They shut down the <u>Stable-Boy Selections</u> fast because they were getting a cut on everything sold in the place except for us."

When the Buffetts moved to Washington, D.C., the only plus for Warren was the chance to upgrade his handicapping skills.

"The one thing I knew about Congress was that Congressmen had access to the

Library of Congress—and the Library of Congress had everything that had ever been written. So when we got to Washington, I said, 'Pop, there's just one thing I want. I want you to ask the Library of Congress for every book they have on horse handicapping.' And my dad said, 'Well, don't you think they're going to think it's a little strange if the first thing a new Congressman asks for is all the books on horse handicapping?' I said, 'Pop, who was out there at the county fairs stumping for your election? Who was down there at the packinghouses ready to get to the cops if something happened?' I said, 'And you're coming up for reelection in two more years. You're going to need me. So this is payoff time.' And he got me hundreds of books on horse handicapping.[2]

"Then what I would do is read all these books. I sent away to a place in Chicago on North Clark Street where you could get old racing forms, months of them, for very little. They were old, so who wanted them? I would go through them, using my handicapping techniques to handicap one day and see the next day how it worked out. I ran tests of my handicapping ability day after day, all these different systems I had in my mind.*

"There are two kinds of handicappers. There are speed handicappers and class handicappers. Speed handicappers figure out the horse with the best times in the past. The fastest horse will win. Class handicappers feel that the horse that's run against ten-thousand-dollar horses and done well and now is running against the five-thousand-dollar horses will beat them. Because, they say, the horse runs just fast enough to win.*

"In horse racing it pays to understand both types of handicapping. But back then I was basically a speed guy. I was a quantitative guy to start with."*

As he tested, thought, and observed, Warren discovered the Rules of the Racetrack:

1. Nobody ever goes home after the first race.
2. You don't have to make it back the way you lost it.

The racetrack counts on people to keep betting until they lose. Couldn't a good handicapper turn these rules around and win?

"The market is a racetrack too. But I was not developing elaborate theories in those days. I was just a little kid."*

Betting in Washington was ubiquitous.

"I would go down to my dad's office fairly often, and there was actually a bookie in what was then called the Old House Office Building. You could go to the elevator* *shaft and yell 'Sammy!' or something like that and this kid would come up and take bets.*

"Now, I used to do a little bookmaking too, for guys who wanted to bet on the Preakness or something like that. That's the end of the game I liked, the fifteen percent take with no risk. My dad, you know, was struggling somewhat to keep this under control. He was amused by it to some extent, but he could also see how it could veer off in the wrong direction."

During summer vacations, Warren returned to Omaha and went stooping at the Ak-Sar-Ben track, this time with his friend Stu Erickson.[3] Back in Washington, he found a new friend to go to the racetrack with, someone who could advance his handicapping skills. Bob Dwyer, his high school golf coach, a potbellied, enterprising young man, made far more than his teacher's stipend by selling life insurance and ice chests and other things during the summer when school was out.[4] The other members of the golf team viewed Dwyer as tough and crusty, but he took a shine to Warren, who had a way about him and played enthusiastically despite his glasses always fogging up.

One day Warren asked Dwyer to take him to the races. His coach said he needed permission. "The next morning," Dwyer says, "bright and early, he came prancing in with a note from his mother, saying it was all right to go to the races." So Dwyer wrote Warren some phony excuse to get out of class[5] and then they took the Chesapeake & Ohio from Silver Spring, Maryland, over to the racetrack in Charles Town, West Virginia. Going to the races with a teacher polished Warren's sophistication about handicapping. Dwyer taught Warren advanced skills in reading the most important tip sheet, the *Daily Racing Form*.

"I'd get the <u>Daily Racing Form</u> ahead of time and figure out the probability of each horse winning the race. Then I would compare those percentages to the odds. But I wouldn't look at the odds first, to avoid prejudicing myself. Sometimes you would find a horse where the odds were way, way off from the actual probability. You figure the horse has a ten percent chance of winning but it's going off at fifteen to one.*

"The less sophisticated the track, the better. You have people betting on the jockey's colors, and you have them betting on their birthdays, you have them betting on the horses' names. And the trick, of course, is to be in a group where practically

---

*That is, the horse would pay out as if its odds of winning were only 6.7 percent. Thus, if it won, the payout would be 50 percent bigger than the horse's track record suggested should occur. A handicapper would take this bet even on the worst horse in the field, because the expected payout is so high compared to the odds. This is an "overlay."

no one is analytical and you have a lot of data. So I would study the forms like crazy when I was a kid."

One grade behind Warren at Woodrow Wilson but slightly older, Bill Gray went to a few horse races with him. "He was very sharp with numbers. Very talkative.[6] Very outgoing. We would discuss baseball, batting averages, sports.[7]

"He knew which horses he was going to pick the minute he got off the train. He would go down to the track and say, well, this horse is too much weight, or this horse, where he's come in the last few races has not been good enough, or his times are not good enough. He knew how to judge the horses." Warren made six- to ten-dollar bets, sometimes on the nose.* He only bet big if the odds looked good, but he had a way of risking some of his hard-earned paper-route money on the right horse. "He might change his mind as the different races came forward," says Gray. "But for a sixteen-year-old, that's not so common, you know?"

Then one time, Warren went to Charles Town by himself. And he lost in the first race. But he didn't go home. He kept on betting and he kept on losing, until he had lost more than $175 and his pockets were stripped nearly bare.

"I came back. I went to the Hot Shoppe, and I treated myself to the biggest thing they offered—a giant fudge sundae or something—and there went all the rest of my money. While I ate, I figured out how many newspapers I had to deliver to make up what I had lost. I was going to have to work more than a week to make back the money. And I'd done it for dumb reasons.

"You're not supposed to bet every race. I'd committed the worst sin, which is that you get behind and you think you've got to break even that day. The first rule is that nobody goes home after the first race, and the second rule is that you don't have to make it back the way you lost it. That is so fundamental, you know."

Did he realize that he'd made an emotional decision?

"Oh, yeah. Oh, I was sick. It was the last time I ever did anything like that."

---

*Betting "on the nose" is betting to win.

14

The Elephant

Philadelphia · 1947–1949

Warren graduated sixteenth out of 350 in his high school class, putting "future stockbroker" under his picture in the yearbook.[1] The first thing he and Danly did with their freedom was to go in together and buy a used hearse. Warren parked the hearse in front of the house and used it to take a girl out on a date.[2] When Howard came home later, he asked, "Who put that hearse out here?" Then Leila said one of their neighbors was gravely ill, and she was *not* having a hearse in front of the house. That was the end of the hearse.

While he and Don were selling the hearse, Warren gave up his paper routes and got a summer job as a relief circulation manager for the *Times-Herald*. Whenever he had to substitute for his paper carriers, he rose at four a.m. and delivered the papers from a little Ford coupe he borrowed from David Brown, a young man from Fredericksburg who had a crush on Doris and who had gone into the Navy.[3] Standing on the running board of the car with the door open, he coasted at about fifteen miles an hour, one hand reaching inside the car to hold on to the wheel, the other hand grabbing the papers and pitching them onto the subscribers' lawns. He rationalized that at such an early hour of the morning, nothing too terrible was likely to result from driving the car that way.[4]

Afterward he stopped by the Toddle House to treat himself to a double order of hash browns with paprika for breakfast. Then he went on to his second job, distributing papers at Georgetown University Hospital.

"I had to give the priests and nuns about a half a dozen papers free, which always irritated me no end. I thought they weren't supposed to be interested in secular things. But this was part of the deal. And then I went room by room.

"After they had the baby, the women in the obstetrics ward would see me come in and say, 'Oh, Warren! I'm going to give you something more valuable than a cash tip. I'm going to tell you when my baby was born and how much it weighed. Eight thirty-one a.m., six pounds and eleven ounces.'" These "tips" were meant for betting on the "policy racket," the numbers game in Washington.[5]

Warren ground his teeth whenever he got useless information instead of a cash tip. The policy racket odds were terrible. *"The policy racket paid off six hundred to one, and the guy that was your runner got ten percent of it. So you have a five-hundred-forty-to-one payoff on what was a thousand-to-one shot, basically. People made penny bets and dime bets. If you put a penny up, you might win $5.40 net. And everybody in town played. Some of my newspaper delivery customers used to ask me, 'Do you run policy numbers?' I never did. My dad would not have approved if I'd become a policy runner."*

He was already a good enough oddsmaker to work in Vegas, but he probably would not have bet on the next thing his father did. Howard Buffett voted for a bill that actually *passed.* One of the most controversial pieces of legislation ever enacted in the United States, the 1947 Taft-Hartley Act severely restricted the tactics used by labor unions. It made it illegal for them to support one another through secondary strikes and authorized U.S. Presidents to declare a national emergency and force striking workers back to work. It was referred to as a "slave labor" bill.[6] Omaha was, of course, a union town, but it would never have occurred to Howard to vote according to his constituents' preferences; he always voted his principles.

So when the Buffetts went home to Omaha for a visit during the summer, and Warren went to a hometown baseball game with his father, he saw just how unpopular Howard had become among the blue-collar voters. *"They introduced the dignitaries in between the doubleheader. And he stood up and everybody in the place started booing. He just stood there and didn't say anything. He could handle things like that. But you just can't imagine the effect that has on a kid."*

Even the mildest forms of confrontation terrified him. But soon he would be standing on his own, out from under his father's wing.

In the fall, at seventeen, he was starting college. The Buffetts had long taken for granted that Warren would attend the University of Pennsylvania's Wharton business school.[7] Wharton was the nation's most important undergraduate business college. In theory, Penn and Warren were a perfect fit.

Warren would have just as soon skipped the whole thing. *"What was the point?"* he asked himself. *"I knew what I wanted to do. I was making enough money to live on. College was only going to slow me down.*" But he would never have defied his father on something so important, so he acquiesced.

Knowing their son's immaturity, the Buffetts arranged a roommate for him who was the son of some friends from Omaha. Five years older, Chuck Peterson had just returned from eighteen months' service in the war. He was a handsome young man-about-town, dating a different girl every night, and *drinking*. Naively, the Petersons supposed that Warren might settle Chuck down, while the Buffetts reckoned that an older boy might help Warren adjust to college.

In the fall of 1947, the entire family piled into the car and drove Warren to Philadelphia, where they deposited him and his raccoon coat in a little dormitory suite with a shared bathroom.

As the Buffetts drove away to return to Washington, they left their son at a campus filled with people much like Chuck. An army of World War II veterans marched across College Green and filled the Quad, the centers of Penn university life. Their worldliness widened by years the gap Warren had felt between himself and his classmates ever since moving to Washington. Penn was a football powerhouse; its fall social life revolved around football dates, followed by fraternity parties. Warren loved sports, but the social requirements were beyond him. He was used to spending much of his time honing ideas, counting his money, organizing his collections, and playing music in the privacy of his room. At Penn, his solitude battered by the sixteen hundred flirting, necking, jitterbugging, keg-tapping, football-tossing members of the Class of 1951,[8] he was a butterfly in a beehive.

The bees reacted much as expected to the butterfly that had flown into their midst. Chuck retained his military tidiness and the habit of constantly polishing his shoes. When he met his new roommate, Warren's disgraceful wardrobe shocked him. He soon discovered that the way Warren dressed symptomized something else. Just as Leila waited hand and foot on Howard and did all the work around the house, Warren had never been taught the most basic ways of taking care of himself.

Chuck woke late the first morning to find the bathroom in a mess and his new roommate gone to early classes. When he saw Warren that evening, he said, "Clean up after yourself, will you?" "Okay, Chas-o," Warren said. "I came in this morning and you left a razor lying at the bottom of the sink," Chuck went on. "You left soap all over the sink, the towels were on the floor, and it's sloppier than hell. I like things neat." Warren appeared to agree. "Okay, Chas-o, okay, Chas-o," he said.

The next morning, when Chuck got up, he stepped through sodden towels on the bathroom floor to find tiny damp hairs covering the sink, and a brand-new, soaking-wet electric razor lying in the basin, tethered to the outlet in the wall by its cord. "Warren, lookit," said Chuck that evening. "Unplug the damn thing. Somebody's going to get electrocuted. You're driving me nuts with your sloppiness." "Okay, okay, fine, Chas-o," said Warren.

The next day was exactly as before. Chuck realized that his words were bouncing off Warren's head. He lost his temper and unplugged the razor, filled the sink with water, and threw the razor in. The following morning, Warren had bought a new razor, plugged it in, and left the bathroom in the same state as before.

Chas-o gave up. He was living in a pigsty with a hyperactive teenager who hopped around in constant motion, drumming his hands, beating them on every nearby surface. Warren was obsessed with Al Jolson and played Jolson records day and night.[9] He sang, over and over, imitating Jolson: "Mammy, my little Mammy, I'd walk a million miles for one of your smiles, my Mammy!"[10]

Chuck needed to study, and he could not hear himself think inside the suite. Warren, on the other hand, had plenty of time to sing. He hadn't bought a lot of textbooks, but he had read the ones he bought at the beginning of the semester, before classes started, the way someone else might flip through a *Life* magazine. Then he threw them aside and never opened them again. This left him all night long to sing "Mammy" if he felt like it. Chuck thought he was going mad. Warren knew he was immature, but he couldn't help it.

"I probably wouldn't have fit in very well anyplace at that time. I was still out of sync with the world. But I was also younger than anybody else, and, on top of that, I was young for my age in many ways. I really didn't fit in socially."

That fall, Leila and Doris struggled to describe Warren's crew-cut, slightly bucktoothed appearance truthfully on a radio show in Washington called *Coffee with Congress.*

> Host: Incidentally, is Warren good-looking?
>
> Leila: He was good-looking as a small child. He's just boyish—I wouldn't call him good-looking, but he's not poor-looking either.
>
> Host: He's handsome-looking.
>
> Leila: No, not handsome, just friendly.
>
> Host: Let's take the girls' angle: Is he a cute boy?
>
> Doris (*diplomatically*): I think he has a rugged sort of look.[11]

Despite the drumming and the "Mammy" singing, Chuck came to be fond of Warren, viewing him as a sort of goofy kid brother, although he still could not believe his roommate continued to wear beat-up Keds throughout the winter, and even when dressed up was likely to wear one black shoe and one brown shoe without noticing.

Like many people who met Warren, Chuck began to feel the urge to take care of him. They had lunch together at the Student Union a couple of times a week. Warren always ordered the same thing: a minute steak, hash browns, and a Pepsi. One day after lunch Chuck took Warren over to the new Ping-Pong table that had just been installed in the Student Union. After four years in Washington, Warren was so rusty that Chuck got the impression he had never played Ping-Pong. Chuck won easily.

Within a day or two, Warren played like a demon. The first thing every morning, he got up, went straight over to the Student Union, found a hapless victim, and slaughtered him at the Ping-Pong table. Before long, he was playing Ping-Pong three or four hours at a stretch every afternoon. "I was his first victim at Penn," Chuck recalls. Ping-Pong kept Warren out of the suite and away from the record player while Chuck was studying.[12]

But Ping-Pong did not fulfill Penn's physical-education requirement. Rowing and sculling on the Schuylkill River were two of Penn's most popular sports. Gaily painted boathouses belonging to the school's many rowing clubs lined the riverbanks. Warren went out for the 150-pound freshman crew with the Vesper Boat Club. He rowed on a team of eight oarsmen guided by a coxswain. Rowing was repetitious and rhythmic, like weight lifting, basketball, and his game of bolo—but it was a team sport. Warren liked to shoot a basketball in his driveway because you could practice alone. He had never succeeded at team sports or learned to dance with a partner. He had been the leader of every stunt or business venture in which he had ever been involved. He couldn't play the part of the echo.

"It was miserable. The thing about crew is, you can't coast or fake it. You have to put your oar in the water at exactly the same time as everybody else. You can be unbelievably tired but you have to match the pace, and it must be done in unison. It's an incredibly grueling sport." He came back to the dorm every afternoon sweating, hands bloodied and blistered, and dropped crew as soon as he could.

Warren was looking for a different kind of team. He wanted Chuck to sell used golf balls with him, but Chuck was too busy. Warren also suggested that Chuck join him in a pinball business. He didn't need Chuck's money or labor, and it wasn't even clear what Chuck's role would be. But Warren, a one-man bandwagon, wanted someone to whom he could talk about his businesses, always and endlessly. If Chuck became a partner, it would make him part of Warren's world. He had always been good at this Tom Sawyering, but he failed with Chuck. Still, he wanted Chuck as a friend as well as a business partner. He invited Chuck to visit him in Washington. Leila was astonished when Chuck ate everything she offered him, even oatmeal. "Warren won't eat this, he won't eat that," she said. "He always makes me fix something special for him." Chuck, ignorant of Warren's history, saw only that Leila was well-trained, not that Warren calmed his fears by controlling his mother.

To Chuck, Warren seemed an odd mix of immature kid and brilliant prodigy. In many of his classes, he simply memorized what the professor said, not needing to look at a textbook.[13] He flaunted obnoxious feats of memory by quoting page numbers and passages back in class and correcting his teachers on their text citations.[14] "You forgot the comma," he said to one.[15]

Wharton was no picnic; a quarter of the class would flunk out. But Warren cruised through with no apparent effort, leaving him as much time as he wanted to drum his hands and sing Mammy, my little Mammy, all night long.

Chuck liked Warren well enough, but it all finally got to him.

"He moved out on me. One morning I woke up and Chuck was gone."[16]

At term's end that summer, Warren—who would never have thought he'd actually be glad to return to Washington—went home. Leila was in Omaha helping Howard campaign for reelection. So the Buffett kids, who had rarely gotten any relief from their parents' austere regimen, experienced a glorious summer of freedom. Bertie was a camp counselor. Doris had a job at Garfinkel's.

Warren returned that summer to his duties as relief circulation manager for the *Times-Herald.* He also reunited with his pal Don Danly. They thought about buying a fire engine together, but instead found a 1928 Springfield Rolls-Royce Phantom I Brewster coupe for $350 in a junkyard in Baltimore. It was gray, weighed more than a Lincoln Continental, and was adorned with little bud vases. The car had two sets of instruments, so the lady in back—the employer— could see how fast the chauffeur was driving. The starter was broken, so Don and Warren took turns cranking it until it finally started up; then they drove it the fifty miles or so back to Washington. It belched smoke, leaked oil, and lacked taillights and license plates, but when they were stopped by a cop, Warren kept "talking and talking and talking" until he wiggled their way out of a ticket.[17]

They put the Rolls in the garage underneath the Buffett house and started the motor. The house immediately filled with acrid smoke, so they pulled it back out and up the steep driveway onto the street. They worked on it Saturday after Saturday. "Danly did all the work," according to Doris, "and Warren watched admiringly and encouraged it along." Naturally, word had gotten around, so they rented it out, thirty-five bucks a pop.

Then Warren had an idea for a stunt. He wanted to be seen in the car. Danly dressed up like a chauffeur, Warren put on the raccoon coat, and the two cranked and cranked to start the car, then drove downtown with platinum-blond Norma. As Danly lunged about under the hood, pretending to fix the motor, Warren directed him with a cane and Norma draped herself over the hood like a movie star. "It was Warren's idea," says Norma. "He was the more theatrical one. We were going to see how many people would look at us."

Norma knew that Warren had never really dated in high school and needed help with girls, so she set him up with her cousin, Bobbie Worley. They dated chastely that summer, going to movies and playing bridge, Warren barraging her with an endless series of brainteasers and riddles.[18]

When fall came, he left Bobbie behind and returned to Penn as an eighteen-year-old sophomore. Warren had little interest in Greek life but had pledged his father's fraternity, Alpha Sigma Phi. He now had two roommates, his fraternity brother Clyde Reighard and a freshman who was assigned to them, George Oesmann. The year before, he had Tom Sawyered Clyde into acting as the front man for a business venture that went nowhere, but during their short-lived partnership, the two had become friends.

Warren had much more in common with Clyde than he had with Chuck Peterson. Clyde was amused by Warren's tennis shoes and T-shirts and dirty khaki pants, and he took it in stride when Warren needled and taunted him about his grades. While "he didn't make me any smarter," says Reighard, "he did make me use what I had more efficiently." Indeed, Warren was a master at using what he had efficiently, his own time especially. He rose early in the morning, ate chicken salad at the dorm for breakfast, then headed off to classes.[19] After sleep-walking through his freshman year, he had finally found one class he liked: Professor Hockenberry's Industry 101, which discussed different industries and the nuts and bolts of running a business. "*It was textiles, it was steel, it was petroleum. I can still remember that book. I got a lot of stuff from it. I can remember talking about the laws of capture in petroleum, and the Bessemer processes in steel. I devoured that book. That was really interesting to me.*" But his suitemate Harry

Beja, a grind who sweated through Hockenberry's class alongside Warren, resented the way he tobogganed ahead effortlessly.[20]

Helped by his prodigious memory, Warren was free to do as he pleased for much of the day. At lunchtime, he dropped by the Alpha Sig house, an old three-story mansion with a spiral staircase. A bridge game went on twenty-four hours a day in a corner alcove, and Warren would sit down and play a few hands.[21] His taste for practical jokes continued unabated. He occasionally enlisted one of his fraternity brothers, Lenny Farina, to pose for attention-getting photographs out on the street while he pretended to pick Lenny's pocket or shine his shoes.[22]

Meanwhile, in a scam reminiscent of sending poor old Kerlin into a water trap naked wearing a gas mask, he and Clyde had told their third roommate, George, that he looked "run-down and puny and would never attract girls unless he developed muscles." They finally maneuvered George into buying himself some barbells—so they could use them.[23]

By college, however, the evidence had become convincing. Warren had begun to give up on the idea of becoming a strongman. *"After a while, I decided my bones were wrong. My clavicles were not long enough. It's your clavicles that determine how broad-shouldered you'll be, and you can't do much about your clavicles. That's why I got disgusted and eventually quit. I decided that if I was going to have girl-like muscles anyway, then to hell with it."*

Girl-like muscles did not attract girls, and Warren had still not gone out on any dates since he arrived at Penn. Saturdays were big fraternity party days, with prefootball luncheons and postgame cocktail parties, dinners, and evening dances. Warren wrote a letter to Bobbie Worley, asking her to come up for a weekend and saying, in effect, that he had fallen in love. Bobbie liked him and was touched by his letter, but did not return his feelings. She would have enjoyed the weekend but said no because she felt it was wrong to lead him on.[24]

Warren had one date, with Ann Beck, a Bryn Mawr girl. He had worked at her father's bakery shortly after moving to Washington, when he was in eighth grade and she was "just a little girl with long blond hair." Ann had been voted the most bashful girl at her high school, and the day she and Warren spent together was like a shyness contest: They walked around Philadelphia in awkward silence.[25] *"We were probably the two shyest people in the whole United States."* Warren had no idea how to make small talk; when stressed, he emitted small grunts instead.[26]

Sometimes Warren and Clyde took the borrowed Ford coupe and drove off to the suburbs in search of movies about mummies, Frankenstein, vampires, or anything macabre.[27] Since hardly anybody had a car at that time, his fraternity brothers were impressed.[28] That was the irony: Warren was the only one with a car to make out in, but nobody to make out with. He passed on the Ivy Ball and the Inter-Fraternity Ball. He always skipped the Alpha Sig Sunday tea dances and never had a date at the fraternity house.[29] His face would flush and he would stare at his shoes if anyone talked about sex.[30] He was out of his element at such a hard-partying school, where the college fight song was "Drink a Highball."

"I tried drinking because I was in a fraternity where about half my dues were going to buy alcohol for these parties. I felt I was getting screwed. But I just didn't like the taste. I don't like beer. And I can behave silly enough without it."

But even without a date on his arm or a glass in his hand, Warren sometimes showed up at his fraternity's Saturday night parties. He was able to draw a little crowd by sitting in a corner and lecturing on the stock market. He had a wit and an arresting way of talking. His Alpha Sig brothers deferred to his opinion when it came to money and business; they respected his deep, if one-sided, knowledge of politics. They decided he had some "politician in him" and gave him a paddle with his nickname: the Senator.[31]

Warren had joined the Young Republicans as a freshman because he was attracted to a girl who was a member. But instead of becoming her boyfriend, he became the group's president when he was a sophomore. Warren took over at an exciting time—the fall of a presidential election year. In 1948, the Republicans were supporting Thomas E. Dewey against the weak incumbent Harry Truman, who had become President on FDR's death.

The Buffetts had grown to hate Truman, who had implemented the Marshall Plan, which sent eighteen million tons of food to Europe after World War II. Howard was one of seventy-four Congressmen who had voted against it. Convinced that the Marshall Plan was Operation Rat Hole and that the Democrats were wrecking the economy, Howard started buying gold chain bracelets for his daughters so they could feed themselves when the day came that the dollar was worthless.[32]

Howard was running for reelection to his fourth term that year. Even though Warren had been present when Howard was hissed and booed after he'd voted for passage of the Taft-Hartley "slave labor" bill, he, like the rest of the family, considered Howard's Congressional seat relatively safe. Nonetheless, Howard had placed his reelection in the hands of a campaign manager for the first time—family friend Dr. William Thompson. Well-known and admired in Omaha, Thompson knew the pulse of the town and was a psychologist to boot.

Day after day as the campaign progressed, people in Omaha would come up and say, "Congratulations, Howard," as if the election were over.

Dewey, too, appeared to be a shoo-in. The polls showed that Truman was trailing him badly. Truman ignored this, and for months had been traveling around the country speaking from the back of his train on a "whistle-stop" tour. He had whistle-stopped in Omaha, marched in a parade, and dedicated a park, looking as cheerful as if he hadn't read the newspapers predicting his defeat.[33]

As Election Day approached, in happy anticipation of his father's reelection and of Dewey's victory, Warren made arrangements with the Philadelphia Zoo to ride an elephant down Woodland Avenue on November 3. He envisioned it as a sort of triumphal march, like Hannibal entering Sardinia.

But on the morning after Election Day, Warren had to cancel his stunt. Not only had Truman won the 1948 election, but his father had lost. The voters had thrown Howard Buffett out of Congress. *"I'd never ridden an elephant before. When Truman beat Dewey, the elephant went down the tube. And my dad lost an election for the first time in four campaigns. That was a really lousy day."*

Two months later, just a few days before the Buffetts left Washington at the end of Howard's term, Warren's great-uncle Frank died. Frank had boomed "IT'S GOING TO ZERO!" about every stock down at Harris Upham when Warren was a boy, and when his will was read, the family discovered that he owned government bonds and nothing else.[34] He had outlived "the gold-digger," and the terms of his will placed the bonds in a restricted trust that required that, upon maturing, they could only be reinvested in more U.S. government bonds. As if to convince his nephew and trustee, Howard, Frank had also apparently left various family members subscriptions to *Baxter's Letter,* a doomsday sheet that preached that government bonds were the only safe investment. Frank meant to be at peace in the afterlife, the only Buffett (so far) to arrange that his opinions would resound from the grave.

But Howard, of course, dreaded inflation and believed that government bonds could turn into worthless paper. Overcoming his scruples, he went to work to break the terms of Frank's will and got a judge to approve some technical changes so the money could eventually be invested in stocks.[35]

These events took place during what Leila called the "worst winter in years." Blizzards buried the Midwest and hay had to be airlifted to Nebraska from surrounding states for weeks during the freeze to keep the snowbound livestock from dying on their feet.[36] The winter of the haylift became emblematic of the

Truman victory. Howard, who had never gotten rich, now had two kids in college and another about to start. He went back to work at his old firm, now known as Buffett-Falk, but his partner Carl Falk, who had been handling his clients during his absence in Washington, was not interested in sharing them now. Striding around downtown Omaha with the bitter snow pelting his face, Howard tried to drum up new clients. But his long absence meant that his writings were the way most people knew him now, and articles like "Human Freedom Rests on Gold Redeemable Money" had given him the reputation of an extremist.[37] In the spring of 1949, he went out into the countryside and knocked on farmhouse doors in search of a new clientele.[38]

As for Warren, his father's defeat left him heartsick, but also offered him an excuse for leaving the East Coast. He was bored at school and hated Philadelphia so much that he had nicknamed it "Filthy-delphia."[39]

At the end of the spring semester he headed back home for good, so relieved that he signed his letters "Ex-Wharton Buffett." He rationalized this by saying that enrolling at the University of Nebraska in Lincoln, where he would spend the last years of his college career, would be cheaper than Penn.[40] He gave the little Ford coupe back to David Brown, its tires threadbare. Warren wanted only one memento of Penn. On the way out the door, he and Clyde flipped a coin to see who got to keep their treasured copy of S. J. Simon's *Why You Lose at Bridge*. Warren won.

15

The Interview

Lincoln and Chicago • 1949–Summer 1950

The first thing Warren did on returning to Nebraska in that summer of 1949 was get a job managing country circulation for the *Lincoln Journal*. He and his friend Truman Wood, who was Doris's boyfriend, went halves on a car. Warren felt comfortable in Lincoln, going to university classes in the morning, then driving around managing his route in the afternoon. Supervising rural paperboys was a serious job, for he was now the boss. Fifty young boys in six rural counties reported to "Mr. Buffett." The challenges of management suddenly became clear when he hired a minister's daughter in the town of Beatrice, thinking she would be a responsible paper carrier. The three paperboys in Beatrice promptly quit: He'd turned it into a sissy job.

Warren spent part of his time that summer in Omaha, selling men's furnishings at JC Penney's. His spirits had begun to revive. He bought a ukulele to compete with the uke-playing boyfriend of a girl he was pursuing, but wound up holding only the ukulele instead of the girl.

Penney's, however, was a good place to work. The employees put on an unofficial pep rally in the basement every morning where Warren, clad in a cheap suit, played his new ukulele—off the clock—while everyone sang, before heading off to his seventy-five-cents-an-hour job in men's furnishings. Penney's called him back over the Christmas holidays, improbably putting him to work selling menswear and Towncraft shirts. Looking at racks filled with products about as comprehensible to him as a French restaurant menu, he asked his manager what to tell the customers about the clothes. "Just tell them it's a sort of worsted," Mr. Lanford said. "Nobody knows what a worsted is." Warren never did learn what a worsted was, but at JC Penney's he sold nothing but.*

In the fall, he started full time at the University of Nebraska. He liked the teachers better than at Penn and he enrolled with a heavy course load, studying accounting with Ray Dein, the best professor he had had thus far.

That year Warren revived his golf ball business, this time with a college friend from Penn, Jerry Orans, as a partner, and using his old supplier, Half-Witek.[1] Orans acted as his East Coast distributor. (Needless to say, in Warren's partnerships, he was always the senior partner.) He was also investing and got the idea of shorting stock in the automaker Kaiser-Frazer. This company saw its share of the auto market fall by ninety-five percent in less than a year. "Dear Pop," he wrote his father on Nebraska Cornhusker stationery. "If there isn't a trend line apparent in those percentages, I'm no statistician." Kaiser-Frazer had lost $8 million during the first six months, "so even with phony bookkeeping the loss will probably run more."[2]

Back at school, he went down to the broker Cruttenden-Podesta's office and asked a stockbroker, Bob Soener, where the stock was trading. Soener looked at the chalkboard and said, "Five bucks." Warren explained that he and his father had shorted the stock, borrowing shares to sell. If the price dropped, as he expected, he could buy the stock back, return the shares, and keep the difference. Since Warren thought Kaiser-Frazer was going bust, he could buy the shares back for pennies and make nearly five dollars on each share.

I'll show this young whippersnapper, thought Soener. "You're not old enough to short a stock legally," he said. "Oh yes," Warren said, "I did it in my older sister Doris's name." He laid out the evidence for shorting Kaiser-Frazer.[3] "And he cut my feet right out from under me," says Soener. "I had no retort whatsoever."

Warren waited for the Kaiser-Frazer idea to work. And waited. He started hanging around Cruttenden-Podesta while he waited. Meanwhile, he and Soener became friends.

In the spring of 1950, after three years of study, Warren needed only a few summer school classes to graduate. And then he made a decision that reversed his path to date. After high school he had felt fully qualified to achieve his goal of becoming a millionaire by age thirty-five with no further education. But now

---

*Worsted, commonly used in men's suiting, is a high-quality, tightly woven wool fabric made of long-staple fibers.

that he was close to graduating, Warren prepared to put work aside. He had fixed his ambitions on attending the Harvard Business School. Throughout his entire educational history he had shown little interest in formal schooling—as opposed to learning—and considered himself largely self-taught. Harvard, however, offered him two important things: prestige and a network of future connections. He had just seen his father thrown out of Congress and his career as a stockbroker crushed, in part because he had tended to isolate himself by sacrificing relationships for the sake of rigid ideals. So perhaps it was not surprising that Warren chose Harvard.

He was so certain that Harvard would accept him that he was already urging his friend "Big Jerry" Orans to "Join me at Harvard."[4] Furthermore, he wasn't even going to have to pay for all of his tuition.

"One day I read in the Daily Nebraskan *a little item that said, 'The John E. Miller Scholarship will be awarded today.[5] Applicants should go to Room 300 at the Business Administration building.' And it provided five hundred dollars* to go to the accredited school of your choice.*

"I went to Room 300, and I was the only guy who showed up. The three professors there kept wanting to wait. I said, 'No, no. It was three o'clock.' So I won the scholarship without doing anything."

Enriched with this nugget mined from the college newspaper, Warren rose in the middle of the night to catch the train to Chicago, where his Harvard interview would take place. He was nineteen, two years younger than the average college graduate, and younger still than the average business-school student. His grades were good but not stellar. Despite being the son of a U.S. Congressman, he was using no connections to try to get into Harvard. Since Howard Buffett scratched no backs, his own back went unscratched, and his son's as well.

Warren was relying on his knowledge of stocks to make a good impression in the interview. So far his experience had been that whenever he started talking about stocks, people could not help but listen. His relatives, his teachers, his fellow students—all wanted to hear him discourse on this subject.

But he had misunderstood Harvard's mission, which was to turn out leaders. When he arrived in Chicago and introduced himself to the interviewer, the man saw past his confidence as a prodigy in a single subject straight through to his self-consciousness, his shaky inner core. *"I looked about sixteen and emotionally*

---

*Five hundred dollars was not chicken feed. It would have been equivalent to about $4,300 in 2007.

was about nine. I spent ten minutes with the Harvard alumnus who was doing the interview, and he assessed my capabilities and turned me down."

Warren never got the chance to show off his knowledge of stocks. The man from Harvard told him gently that he would have a better chance in a few years. Warren was naive; it did not quite sink in what this meant. When the letter arrived from Harvard refusing him admission, he was shocked. His first thought, he says, was, "What am I going to tell my dad?"

Awkward and stiff-necked he might be, but Howard was undemanding of his children. The Harvard dream was Warren's, not his father's. Howard was accustomed to failure and resolute in defeat. The real question must have been: What am I going to tell my mom?

And yet Warren would later come to consider his rejection by Harvard the pivotal episode of his life.

Almost immediately, he started investigating other graduate schools. While leafing through the Columbia catalog one day, he came across two names that were familiar to him: Benjamin Graham and David Dodd.

"These were big names to me. I'd just read Graham's book, but I had no idea he was teaching at Columbia."

"Graham's book" was *The Intelligent Investor,* published in 1949.[6] This book of "practical counsel" for all types of investors—the cautious (or "defensive") and speculative (or "enterprising")—blew apart the conventions of Wall Street, overturning what had heretofore been largely uninformed speculation in stocks. It explained for the first time in a way that ordinary people could understand that the stock market does not operate through black magic. Through examples of real stocks such as the Northern Pacific Railway and the American-Hawaiian Steamship Company, Graham illustrated a rational, mathematical approach to valuing stocks. Investing, he said, should be *systematic.*

The book had mesmerized Warren. For years, he had been going downtown to the library and checking out every book available on stocks and investing. Many of the books dealt with stock-picking systems based on models and patterns; Warren wanted a system, something that would work reliably. He had been fascinated by numerical patterns—technical analysis.

"I read all of them over and over. The book that probably had the most influence on me was Garfield Drew, who wrote an important book about odd-lot stock trading.[7] I read that about three times. I read Edwards and McGee, which is the bible of technical analysis.[8] I would go down to the library and just clean them out." But when he found *The Intelligent Investor,* he read and reread it. "It was almost like

he found a god," said Truman Wood, his housemate.[9] After careful study, he had gone ahead and made a "value" investment on his own. Through a connection of his father's, he had heard of a company called Parkersburg Rig & Reel, which he researched according to Graham's rules. He bought two hundred shares.[10]

According to the catalog Warren had now picked up, the man who had become his favorite author, Ben Graham, was lecturing in finance at Columbia University. And David Dodd was there too. Dodd was associate dean of the Graduate School of Business, and head of the department of finance. In 1934 Graham and Dodd had coauthored the seminal text on investing, *Security Analysis*. *The Intelligent Investor* was the layman's version of *Security Analysis*. Enrolling at Columbia would mean he could study with Graham and Dodd. And as Columbia's catalog pointed out: "No other city in the world offers as many opportunities to become acquainted at firsthand with the actual conduct of business. Here a student may come into personal contact with the outstanding leaders of American business. . . . Business establishments of the city cheerfully welcome groups of students as visitors."[11] Even Harvard could not offer this.

Warren now determined that he would go to Columbia. But it was almost too late.

"I wrote in August, about a month before school started, way past when you were supposed to do it. Who knows what I wrote? I probably wrote that I just found this catalog at the University of Omaha, and it said that you and Ben Graham taught, whereas I thought you guys were on Mount Olympus someplace just smiling down on the rest of us. And if I can get in, I'd love to come. I'm sure it was not a very conventional application. It was probably fairly personal."

But in a written application, Warren could shape the impression he made more successfully than in a personal interview. The application wound up on the desk of David Dodd, who as associate dean was in charge of admissions. By 1950, after teaching at Columbia for twenty-seven years, Dodd had effectively become the junior partner of the famous Benjamin Graham.

A thin, frail, balding man who cared for a disabled wife at home, Dodd was the son of a Presbyterian minister and eight years older than Warren's father. While Dodd may have been touched in some way by the personal nature of the application, it was also true that at Columbia, he and Graham were more interested in their students' aptitude for business and investing than their emotional maturity. Graham and Dodd were not trying to create leaders. They taught a specialized craft.

Whatever the reason, after the deadline, and without an interview, Warren was accepted by Columbia.

16

Strike One

Warren had applied to Columbia too late to get into a university dorm, so he found the cheapest lodgings available: joining the YMCA for a dime a day and paying a dollar a day for a room at the Y's Sloane House on West 34th Street, down near Penn Station.[1] He was far from broke, enriched by $500 from the Miller scholarship and $2,000 from Howard, a graduation gift and part of a deal not to start smoking.[2] He also had $9,803.70 saved, some of it placed in stocks.[3] His net worth included $44 in cash, his half interest in the car, and $334 invested in his Half-Witek golf ball business. But since Warren looked at every dollar as ten dollars someday, he wasn't going to hand over a dollar more than he needed to spend. Every penny was another snowflake for his snowball.

On his first day in David Dodd's class, "Finance 111–112: Investment management and security analysis," he recalls that Dodd broke his customary reserve and greeted him personally and warmly. Warren had already more or less memorized the course textbook, *Security Analysis,* Graham and Dodd's seminal book on investing.[4] As the principal drafter and organizer of *Security Analysis,* Dodd was of course intimately familiar with its contents. Yet when it came to the text itself, Buffett says, *"The truth was that I knew the book even better than Dodd. I could quote from any part of it. At that time, literally, almost in those whole seven or eight hundred pages, I knew every example. I had just sopped it up. And you can imagine the effect that would have on the guy, that somebody was that keen on his book."*

Published in 1934, *Security Analysis* was a mammoth textbook for serious students of the market, laying out in much more detail the innovative concepts that were later summarized for a popular audience in *The Intelligent Investor*. Dodd had taken meticulous notes at Ben Graham's lectures and seminars for four years, organizing them and enriching the examples with his own knowledge of corporate finance and accounting.[5]

Dodd's class focused on valuing defaulted railroad bonds. Since childhood, Warren had been slightly obsessed with trains, and thanks to the checkered history of the Union Pacific, Omaha was practically the center of the universe when it came to bankrupt railroads.[6] Warren had read his favorite book on bonds, Townsend's *Bond Salesmanship,* for the first time at the age of seven after making a special plea to Santa Claus for this tome.[7] Now he took to the subject of bankrupt railroad bonds like a duck to the warm spring rain. Dodd showed an unusual interest in him, introducing him to his family and taking him to dinner. Warren soaked up the fatherly attention and also felt sympathy for Dodd, who cared for his mentally ill wife.

In class, Dodd would ask a question and Warren's arm would shoot into the air before anyone else's, waving for attention. He knew the answer every time, wanted to give it, was not afraid of attention, and did not mind looking silly. Nor did he seem to be showing off, as a classmate recalled; he was simply young, eager, and immature.[8]

Unlike Warren, most of his Columbia classmates had little interest in stocks and bonds and were probably bored by this mandatory class. They were a remarkably homogenous group of men,[9] mostly headed to General Motors, IBM, or U.S. Steel after they got their degrees.

One of them, Bob Dunn, was on his way to becoming the academic star of the class of 1951. Warren admired his presence and intelligence and often went over to the dorm to visit him. One afternoon, in the other room of Dunn's two-room suite, Fred Stanback found himself wakened from a nap by a loud voice. Half asleep, he began to realize that the voice was saying such interesting things that he didn't want to doze off again. Rising from his bunk, he wandered into the next room. There he found a crew-cut, badly dressed kid, rattling a mile a minute, who leaned forward in his seat as if a starting gun were poised behind his head. Stanback plopped down in a chair and began to listen to Warren, who was declaiming with great authority about some undervalued stocks he'd found.

Warren talked about a clutch of tiny companies, including Tyer Rubber Company, Sargent & Co., and a somewhat larger business, hardware wholesaler Marshall-Wells.[10] Listening, Stanback became an instant disciple. He went out straightaway and bought stocks for the first time in his life.

Stanback grew up, analytical and reserved, on Confederate Avenue in the tiny hamlet of Salisbury, North Carolina. He was a born audience for Warren. The two started spending time together—a fast-talking, scrawny-looking kid and a sandy-blond handsome young man with a molasses voice. One day Warren had an idea. He asked Professor Dodd's permission to cut class to attend the annual meeting of Marshall-Wells. A few months before starting at Columbia, he and Howard had jointly bought twenty-five shares of this stock.

"That was the first annual meeting I ever attended. They held their meeting in Jersey City, New Jersey, probably so fewer shareholders would attend."

Warren's vision of shareholder meetings rose from his conception of the nature of a business. He had recently sold his tenant farm, doubling his money over five years. During the time he had owned it, he and his tenant farmer had shared the profits on the crop. But his tenant didn't share the profits from selling the land. As the capitalist, Warren put up the money and took the risk, and then he got the gain, if there was any.

Warren thought of all businesses this way. The employees who managed the business shared in the earnings that their labors produced. But they were accountable to their owners, and it was the owners who got the gains as the value of the business increased. Of course, if the employees bought stock themselves, they became owners, too, and partners with the other capitalists. But no matter how much stock they owned, as employees their job required them to report to the owners on how well they had done. Thus, Warren saw a shareholder meeting as a time of accounting for the stewardship of the managers.

This vision was rarely shared by company managements, however.

Warren and his new friend Stanback took the train to Jersey City. Arriving in a drab meeting room, they found half a dozen people awaiting a session in which the company planned to shuffle through an agenda of legal obligations in a perfunctory fashion.

One of those present was Walter Schloss, a thirty-four-year-old man who was working for the pittance of fifty dollars a week as one of four employees of Ben Graham's company, the Graham-Newman Corporation.[11] As the meeting began, Schloss starting asking pointed questions of management. He was a bantamweight, mild-mannered, dark-haired man from a family of New York Jewish immigrants, but he probably struck the Marshall-Wells crowd as abrupt by the standards of Duluth. "They were a little upset," says Stanback, "that these outsiders were barging in on their meeting. They'd never had anybody come to their meeting before, and they didn't like that."[12]

Warren was immediately taken with Schloss's approach, and when Schloss identified himself as working for Graham-Newman, he reacted as though at a family reunion. As soon as the meeting ended, Warren approached Schloss and they began to talk. He found him a man after his own heart, a believer that wealth is hard to accumulate and easy to lose. Along with other financial setbacks, when Walter was thirteen, his mother had lost her inheritance in the crash of 1929.

The Schloss family got by through perspiration and determination. Fresh out of high school in 1934, Walter worked as a Wall Street runner—a member of the Pony Express of the brokerage firms—carrying messages up and down the street. Next, working in the company's "cage" handling securities, he had asked his boss if he could analyze stocks. The answer was no—but he was told, "There's a fellow named Ben Graham who's just written a book called *Security Analysis*. Read that book and you won't need anything else."[13]

Schloss read Graham's book cover to cover and wanted more. Two nights a week from five to seven, he started going to the New York Institute of Finance, where Graham taught investing. Graham had begun these seminars in 1927 as trial runs for a college course he was thinking of teaching at Columbia. At the time, the public couldn't get enough of stocks, and the class was packed.

Graham mentioned names of stocks he was currently buying as teaching examples. People like Gustave Levy, the head trader at Goldman Sachs, scurried back to act on these ideas and make their firms and themselves rich. Schloss was so captivated that he wound up as one of a couple of employees working for his idol, Ben Graham, and his partner, Jerry Newman. Warren found himself instinctively drawn to Walter, not just for his enviable job but also because of the story of his gritty, disadvantaged background. At the Marshall-Wells meeting, Warren also recognized another shareholder by his barrel-shouldered, cigar-smoking profile. This was Louis Green, a well-known investor who was a partner in a small but respected securities firm, Stryker & Brown, and an ally of Ben Graham's.[14]

Warren was mightily impressed by Lou Green and wanted to make a good impression, so he struck up a conversation with him, and he and Stanback and Green rode back together on the train from New Jersey. Green offered to take the two young men to lunch.

That was like hitting the jackpot. Warren discovered Green was tightfisted, a man after his own heart. *"This guy was enormously wealthy, and we went to some cafeteria or something like that."*

At lunch Green began explaining what it was like to be pursued by women who were after his money. As he was somewhat past middle age, his technique for dealing with this was to confront the woman's motives directly: "You like these false teeth? How about my bald head? Or the potbelly?" Warren was enjoying the conversation, until Green suddenly changed the subject and put him on the spot.

"He said to me, 'Why did you buy Marshall-Wells?'

"And I said, 'Because Ben Graham bought it.' "

True, Graham was already his hero, even though the two had never met. And since the inspiration for buying Marshall-Wells had indeed come from *Security Analysis,* Warren may have felt he had to be scrupulous about how he had learned of it.[15] But, in fact, he had good reason to own Marshall-Wells beyond its mention in *Security Analysis.*

Reputedly the largest hardware wholesaler in North America, Marshall-Wells was earning so much money that if it had paid out those earnings to shareholders as a dividend, they would have gotten $62 a share. The stock traded at around $200 a share. Owning a Marshall-Wells share was something like owning a bond, one that paid thirty-one percent interest (the $62 earnings on a $200 share). At that rate, in three years, Warren would have nearly two dollars of value for every dollar he had invested in Marshall-Wells. Even if the company didn't pay the money out, the stock would have to rise eventually.

But Warren did not explain any of this to Lou Green. Instead, he said, *" 'Because Ben Graham bought it.'*

"Lou looked at me and said, 'Strike one!'

"I'll never forget the way he looked at me when he said it."

It dawned on him: "Warren, think for yourself." He felt foolish.

"We're sitting in this little cafeteria, I'm with this impressive character, and all of a sudden I'm striking out."

He did not want to make any more mistakes like this, and he did want to find more stocks like Marshall-Wells, so as Graham's seminar approached, Warren started memorizing everything he could find out about Ben Graham's method, his books, his specific investments, and Graham himself. He had learned that Graham was chairman of the board of a company called Government Employees Insurance Company, or GEICO.[16] This stock was not mentioned in *Security Analysis.* When he looked in the *Moody's Manual,* he found that the Graham-Newman Corporation had owned fifty-five percent of it but had recently given out the stock to its shareholders.[17]

What was this GEICO? Warren was curious. So on a cold, wintry Saturday morning a few weeks later, he jumped on the earliest train to Washington, D.C., and showed up at GEICO's door. No one was about, but a guard answered his knock. As he recalls, Warren asked in his humblest manner whether anyone was there who might explain GEICO's business to him. He made sure to mention that he was a student of Ben Graham's.

The guard trotted upstairs to the office where GEICO's financial vice president, Lorimer Davidson, sat working. Faced with this request, Davidson thought to himself that "being a pupil of Ben's, I would give him five minutes and thank him, find a polite way of sending him on his way."[18] He told the guard to show Warren in.

Warren introduced himself to Davidson with precise but flattering sincerity: " '*My name is Warren Buffett. I'm a student at Columbia. Ben Graham is going to be, probably, my professor. I read his book, and I think he's wonderful. And I noticed that he's the chairman of Government Employees Insurance. I don't know anything about it, but I wanted to come here and learn.*' "

Davidson started talking to Warren about the arcane business of auto insurance, thinking that out of kindness to a pupil of Graham's, he would waste a few minutes of his valuable time. But, he said, "After about ten to twelve minutes of his questions, I realized that I was talking to a highly unusual young man. The questions he was asking me were the questions that would have been asked by an experienced insurance-stock analyst. His follow-up questions were professional. He was young, and he looked young. He described himself as a student, but he was talking like a man who had been around a long time, and he knew a great deal. When my opinion of Warren changed, I began asking *him* questions. And I found out that he had been a successful businessman at age sixteen. That he had filed his own income tax at age fourteen and every year since then. That he had had a number of small businesses."

Lorimer Davidson had accomplished so much himself that he was hard to impress. "Davy," as he was universally known, had been pocketing an incredible $100,000 a year in commissions before the 1929 crash.[19] Afterward, he found a job making about $100 a week selling bonds.

One day, Davy happened to call on the Government Employees Insurance Company. When he found out how GEICO worked, he was instantly captivated.

GEICO sought to make auto insurance cheaper by marketing through the mail without an agent.[20] That was a revolutionary concept at the time. Borrowing an idea from a company called USAA that sold only to military officers,

GEICO's founders, Leo Goodwin and Cleves Rhea, had decided to sell its insurance only to government employees because they were responsible individuals who were accustomed to following the law. Thus, the Government Employees Insurance Company was born.

Later, the founding Rhea family had hired Davidson to sell their stock. While putting together a syndicate of buyers, he approached Graham-Newman Corporation in New York. Ben Graham was interested but deferred to his gruff partner, Jerry Newman. "Jerry thought that to buy something at the offering price was illegal. He said, 'I never bought anything at the offering price before; I'm not going to start now,'" Davidson said.

They dickered. Davidson brought Jerry Newman around to investing $1 million for fifty-five percent of the company, with some modest concessions. Ben Graham became chairman of GEICO, and Newman joined its board. Six or seven months later, Lorimer Davidson told GEICO's CEO Leo Goodwin that he would take a pay cut to work for GEICO, managing its investments. Goodwin consulted with Ben Graham, who agreed.

Hearing this story from Davidson, Warren was fascinated. *"I just kept asking questions about insurance and GEICO. He didn't go to lunch that day—he just sat there and talked to me for four hours like I was the most important person in the world. When he opened that door to me, he opened the door to the insurance world."*

Warren had studied insurance at Penn, and there was an aspect of it a little like gambling that intrigued the oddsmaker in him. He had become interested in an insurance scheme called a tontine, in which people pool their money and the last survivor gets the whole pot. But tontines were now illegal.[21]

Warren had even considered actuarial science—the mathematics of insurance—as a career. He could have spent decades toiling over tables of mortality statistics, handicapping people's life expectancies. Besides the obvious ways this suited his personality—which tended toward specialization; relished memorizing, collecting, and manipulating numbers; and preferred solitude—working as a life actuary would have let him spend his time pondering one of his two favorite preoccupations: life expectancy.

However, his other favorite, collecting money, had won out.

Warren was starting to grapple with the fundamental concept of business: How do companies *make money*? A company was much like a person. It had to go out and find a way to keep a roof over its employees' and shareholders' heads.

He grasped that because GEICO sold insurance at the cheapest price, the only way it could make money would be to have the lowest possible costs. He also learned that insurance companies take their customers' premiums and invest them long before the claims are paid. That sounded to him like getting to use somebody else's money for free, just the kind of idea that appealed to him.

GEICO seemed to Warren a no-lose proposition.

That Monday, less than forty-eight hours after he arrived back in New York, Warren dumped stocks worth three-quarters of his growing portfolio and used the cash to buy 350 shares of GEICO. It was an extraordinary move for the normally cautious young man.

That was especially true because, at its current price, GEICO was an investment that Ben Graham would not have approved of, even though Graham-Newman had only recently become its largest shareholder. Graham's idea was to buy stocks trading for less than the value of their assets, and he did not believe in concentrating in just a few stocks. But GEICO was growing so fast that Warren felt confident of being able to predict what it would be worth in a few years. On that basis, it was cheap. He wrote a report about it for his father's stockbrokerage firm, saying that GEICO was trading at $42 per share, a multiple of about eight times its recent earnings per share. Other insurance companies, he noted, were selling at much higher multiples of their earnings. Yet GEICO was a small company in a large field, whereas its competitors were companies "whose growth possibilities have largely been exhausted." Warren then made a conservative projection of the company's value in five years. He thought the stock would be worth between $80 and $90 per share.[22]

In April, he wrote to Geyer & Co. and Blythe and Company, the most prominent brokerage firms specializing in insurance stocks, asking for their research. Next he visited these experts to talk to them about GEICO. After he heard their views, he explained his own theory.

They told Warren he was nuts.

GEICO, they said, could not succeed over the larger, more established companies that used agents. It was a tiny company, with a market share of less than one percent. Huge insurance companies with thousands of agents dominated the industry, and so it would ever be. Yet here was GEICO, growing like a dandelion in June and printing money like the U.S. Mint.

Warren didn't understand why they couldn't see what was right before their eyes.

17

Mount Everest

As his second semester began at Columbia, Warren hummed with excitement. His father had just been reelected to Congress for a fourth time—by the largest majority yet—and he was finally going to meet his hero.

In his memoir, Ben Graham describes himself as a loner who never had an intimate friend after high school: "I was cut out to be everybody's friend but no one's bosom pal or crony."[1] *"Nobody cracked his shell. Men all admired him, they all liked him, and they all wanted to be his friend more than he wanted them to be. You came away feeling terrific about him, but you never got to be his pal."* Buffett would later call this Graham's "protective coating." Even his partner David Dodd never became an intimate. People found him almost painful to talk to—so cerebral, so erudite, so clever. They had to keep their wits about them all the time in his company. While he was always kind, he quickly tired of conversing with his fellow human beings; the "real friends and intimates" of his life were his favorite authors—Gibbon, Virgil, Milton, Lessing—and their subjects, which, he said, "had far more significance for me and left a greater impression on my memory than the living people around me."

Born Benjamin Grossbaum,[2] Graham passed his first twenty-five years in a period when the country experienced four financial panics and three depressions.[3] His family's fortune dwindled after his father's death when Ben was nine; his worldly, ambitious mother lost most of her own small stake in the stock-market panic of 1907, and she wound up having to pawn her jewelry. During this time, Graham recalled, the family was saved through the charity of relatives "from misery, though not from humiliation."[4]

Nonetheless, Ben excelled throughout his education in the New York City public schools, where he read Victor Hugo in French, Goethe in German, Homer in Greek, and Virgil in Latin. Upon graduation, he wanted to attend Columbia University but needed financial aid. When the scholarship examiner visited the Grossbaums, he turned Ben down. Ben was sure the examiner had detected a "secret deformity" in his soul: "For years I had been struggling against something the French call *mauvaises habitudes* [bad habits, a euphemism for masturbation], and which a combination of innate puritanism on my part and the hair-raising health tracts prevalent in those days had raised to a moral and physical issue of enormous proportions."[5]

Graham and his bad habits wound up at tuition-free City College, bereft and broke, convinced that a degree from this school would not advance him in the snobbish, cultivated world to which he aspired. He dropped out, got a job assembling doorbells, and recited the *Aeneid* and the *Rubáiyát* to himself as he worked. Eventually, he reapplied to Columbia and this time was given the scholarship that had earlier been denied him—through a clerical error, it turned out. At Columbia, he became an academic star, even while working at a variety of menial jobs. Checking waybills, he would mentally compose sonnets for distraction. On graduation, he turned down a scholarship to law school as well as offers to teach philosophy, mathematics, and English—in order to follow his dean's advice and go into the advertising business.[6]

Graham's sense of humor always tended toward irony. His first effort at writing a jingle for the nonflammable cleaning fluid Carbona was rejected as too frightening to customers when he produced this limerick:

> There was a young girl from Winona
> Who never had heard of Carbona
> She started to clean
> With a can of benzene
> And now her poor parents bemoan her.

After this episode, Columbia's Dean Keppel recommended Graham for a job at the brokerage house Newburger, Henderson & Loeb.

He started in 1914 on the bottom rung of the Wall Street ladder, as a runner, then worked as an assistant board boy, changing stock prices on a chalkboard. Graham parlayed these jobs into a career through a classic Wall Street maneuver: He did research on the side, until one day a floor broker gave a report he had written on the Missouri Pacific Railroad to a partner at Bache & Company, which hired him as a statistician.[7] Later, he returned to Newburger, Henderson & Loeb as a partner until 1923, when a group of financial backers, including members of the Rosenwald family (early partners in Sears), lured him away by providing him with starting capital of $250,000, which enabled him to go out on his own.

Graham closed this business in 1925 when he and his backers disagreed over his compensation, and established the "Benjamin Graham Joint Account" with $450,000 from clients and his own money. Shortly afterward, Jerome Newman, the brother of one of his clients, offered to invest in the firm and join Graham as a partner at no salary until he learned the business and added value. Graham insisted on paying him, and Newman brought to the partnership a broad general knowledge of business as well as management skills.

In 1932, Graham wrote a series of articles in *Forbes*, "Is American Business Worth More Dead Than Alive?" in which he chastised company managements for sitting on troves of cash and investments, and investors for overlooking this value, which was not reflected in the prices of stocks. Graham knew how to dislodge the value, but his problem was capital. Through its stock-market losses, the firm's account was down from $2.5 million to $375,000.* Graham felt responsible for recouping his partners' losses, but that meant he would have to more than triple their money. It would take some doing even to keep the Joint Account alive. Jerry Newman's father-in-law saved it by putting in $50,000. And by December 1935, Graham did triple the money, and earned the losses back.

For tax reasons, in 1936 Graham and Newman reorganized the Joint Account into two businesses—Graham-Newman Corporation, and Newman & Graham.[8] Graham-Newman charged a fixed fee and had issued shares to the public which now traded on an exchange. Newman & Graham was a "hedge fund," or private partnership with a limited number of sophisticated partners, that paid Graham and Newman based on their performance as managers.

The two men remained partners for thirty years, although in his memoir, Graham cited Jerry Newman's "lack of amiability," his demanding, impatient, and fault-finding personality, and his inclination to be "too tough" in negotiation. He and Graham got along because other people's behavior never seemed to disturb Graham's equanimity.

---

*Including distributions, withdrawals, and losses.

The one exception to this was Graham's penchant for taking on established business figures in a fight. The most famous episode in Graham's business career consisted of forcing the Northern Pipeline to distribute valuable bonds to shareholders.

Graham went down to the shareholders' meeting in remote Oil City, Pennsylvania, where he made a motion about the railroad bonds. But the management refused to recognize him because he had brought no one along to second the motion. In its dealings with him, the management also made what he felt were some anti-Semitic innuendos, which hardly inclined him to give up the fight. By the time of the next shareholders' meeting, he had assembled enough votes to get two additional directors elected to the board, which tilted the balance in favor of distributing the bonds. The company submitted and ended up handing out the equivalent of $110 per share in cash and stock to its shareholders.

The battle became a famous incident on Wall Street, and Graham went on to build the Graham-Newman Corporation into one of the best-known, although far from the largest, investment firms in the business.

He did it even while inflicting a handicap on his own performance. Every time he mentioned a stock Graham-Newman was buying in the classroom, the students ran out and bought it too, pushing up the price and making it more expensive. This drove Jerry Newman crazy. Why let other people in on what they were doing? To make money on Wall Street meant keeping your ideas to yourself. But, as Buffett said, *"Ben didn't really care how much money he had. He wanted to have enough, and he went through that period in '29 to '33 that was very rough. But if he had as much money as he felt he needed, anything else was totally immaterial to him."*

Over the twenty-year life of Graham-Newman Corporation, its performance had beaten the stock market's performance by an average of 2.5 percent a year—a record exceeded by only a handful of people in the history of Wall Street. That percent might sound trifling, but compounded for two decades, it meant that an investor in Graham-Newman wound up with almost sixty-five percent more in his pocket than someone who earned the market's average result. *Much* more important, Graham had achieved this superior performance while taking considerably less risk than someone who simply invested in the stock market as a whole.

And Graham did it mainly through his skill at analyzing numbers. Before him, assessments of a security's value were largely guesswork. Graham developed the first thorough, systematic way of analyzing the value of a stock. He preferred to work by studying only publicly available information—usually a company's financial statements—and rarely attended even public meetings with a company's management.[9] Although his associate Walter Schloss had been at the Marshall-Wells meeting, it was his own idea to go, not Graham's.

Ben's third wife, Estey, drove her husband up to Columbia from the Graham-Newman Corporation's office at 55 Wall Street every Thursday afternoon after the market closed to teach his "seminar on common stock valuation." This course was the culmination of the Columbia finance curriculum, so highly regarded that men who were already working in money management signed up for it, sometimes more than once.

Warren, of course, looked up to Graham with worshipful awe. He had read the Northern Pipeline story over and over when he was ten years old, well before he understood who Benjamin Graham was in the investing world. Now he hoped to bond with his teacher. But outside the classroom, he and Ben had few hobbies in common. Graham dabbled in the arts and sciences in a quest for knowledge, writing poetry, failing spectacularly as a Broadway playwright, and puttering around filling notebooks with ideas for clumsy inventions. He also devoted himself to ballroom dancing, clumping around for years at the Arthur Murray studio, where he counted the steps out loud. During dinner parties, Graham often disappeared in the middle of a course to work on mathematical formulas, read Proust (in French), or listen to the opera, rather than suffer the dull company of his fellow man.[10] "I remember the things I learn," he wrote in his memoir, "rather than the things I live." The one exception where living took precedence over learning was his assignations.

About the only way a human being could compete with the classic authors for Graham's attention was to be female and beddable. He was short and physically unimposing. There was something elfish-looking about him, and he was not a handsome man. Nonetheless, Graham seemed to be a Mount Everest for women who liked a challenge: They met him and wanted to climb on top.

In his three wives, Graham's taste had ranged wide: from the passionate, strong-willed Hazel Mazur to Broadway showgirl Carol Wade—eighteen years his junior—to his third wife and former secretary, the intelligent, lighthearted Estelle "Estey" Messing. Complicating all these marriages was his complete indifference to monogamy. Graham later wrote a memoir[11] in which he begins, "Let me describe my first extramarital affair in the soberest fashion," a sobriety he giddily abandons six sentences later as he explains the recipe for his liaison with the sharp-tongued, "by no means beautiful" Jenny: "one part attraction and four parts opportunity." If more attraction was present, he needed less opportunity, making him shameless, even annoying, in his sexual advances toward women. Combining two of his hobbies, Graham might dash off a seductive little poem to a woman he fancied on the subway. Yet he was so cerebral that it must have been a challenge for his lovers to hold his attention. The darting from amour to business in the following passage of the memoir is pure Graham:[12]

> I have a sentimental memory of the last hour we spent together in the cabin
> of her Ward Line steamer. (Little did I think then that my firm was later to
> control that old-established steamship company.)

But Warren at the time knew nothing about Graham's personal life and was focused only on what he could learn from the brilliant teacher. On the first day of Graham's seminar in January 1951, Warren walked into a classroom containing a long rectangular table. In the middle sat Graham, surrounded by eighteen or twenty men. Most of the other students were older, some of them war veterans. Half were businessmen who were auditing the course. Once again, Warren was the youngest—yet also the most knowledgeable. When Graham asked a question, inevitably he "would be the first one to have his hand up and immediately start talking," recalls a classmate, Jack Alexander.[13] The rest of the class became the audience to a duet.

In 1951, many American businesses were still worth more dead than alive. Graham encouraged his students to use real-life examples from the stock market to illustrate this, down-and-dirty companies such as Greif Bros. Cooperage, a barrel maker whose stock Warren owned. Its main business was slowly disappearing but its stock was trading at a substantial discount to the cash that could be netted if its properties and inventory were simply sold off and its debts repaid. Eventually, Graham reasoned, that "intrinsic" value would surface the way a river-tossed barrel, trapped under winter ice, pops to the surface in a spring thaw. You had only to interpret the balance sheet, decoding the numbers that proved there was a barrel of money trapped under the ice.

Graham said that a company is no different than a person, who might think that her net worth was $7,000, comprising her house, worth $50,000, less her mortgage of $45,000, plus her other savings of $2,000. Just like people, companies have assets that they own, such as the products they make and sell, and debts—or liabilities—that they owe. If you sold all the assets to pay off the debts, what would be left was the company's equity, or net worth. If someone could buy the stock at a price that valued the company cheaper than its net worth, Graham said, eventually—a tricky word, "eventually"—the stock's price would rise to reflect this *intrinsic value*.[14]

It sounded simple, but the art of security analysis lay in the details—playing detective, probing for what assets were really worth, excavating hidden assets and liabilities, considering what the company could earn—or not earn—and stripping apart the fine print to lay bare the rights of shareholders. Graham's students learned that stocks were not abstract pieces of paper, and their value could be analyzed by figuring what the whole pie of a business was worth, then dividing it into slices.

Complicating matters was that word "eventually." Stocks often traded at odds with their *intrinsic value* for long periods of time. Even if an analyst figured everything right, he could still appear wrong in the eyes of the market for the investing equivalent of a lifetime. You had to build in what Graham and Dodd called a MARGIN OF SAFETY—that is, plenty of room for error.

Graham's method struck people who studied it in one of two ways. Some grasped it immediately as a fascinating, all-consuming treasure hunt and others recoiled from it as a dreary homework assignment. Warren's reaction was that of a man emerging from the cave in which he had been living all his life, blinking in the sunlight as he perceived reality for the first time.[15] His former concept of a "stock" was derived from the patterns formed by the prices at which pieces of paper traded. Now he instantly grasped that the patterns formed by trading these pieces of paper did not signify a "stock" any more than those childhood piles of bottle caps had signified the effervescent, sweet-sour-spicy taste of soda pop that made people crave it. His old notions dissolved in an instant, conquered by Graham's ideas and illuminated by the way he taught.

Graham used all kinds of nifty, effective tricks in his class. He would ask paired questions, one at a time. His students thought they knew the answer to the first, but when the second came along, it made them realize that maybe they didn't. He would put up descriptions of two companies, one in terrible shape, practically bankrupt, another in fine form. After asking the class to analyze them, he would reveal that they were the same company at different times. Everyone was surprised.

Along with his Company A and Company B teaching method, Graham used to talk about Class 1 and Class 2 truths. Class 1 truths were absolutes. Class 2 truths became truths by conviction. If enough people thought a company's stock was worth X, it became worth X until enough people thought otherwise. Yet that did not affect the stock's intrinsic value—which was a Class 1 truth. Thus, Graham's investing method was not simply about buying stocks cheap. As much as anything it was rooted in an understanding of psychology, enabling its followers to keep their emotions from influencing their decision-making.

From Graham's class, Warren took away three main principles:

- *A stock is the right to own a little piece of a business.* A stock is worth a certain fraction of what you would be willing to pay for the whole business.
- *Use a margin of safety.* Investing is built on estimates and uncertainty. A wide margin of safety ensures that the effects of good decisions are not wiped out by errors. The way to advance, above all, is by not retreating.
- *Mr. Market is your servant, not your master.* Graham postulated a moody character called Mr. Market, who offers to buy and sell stocks every day, often at prices that don't make sense. Mr. Market's moods should not influence *your* view of price. However, from time to time he does offer the chance to buy low and sell high.

Of these points, the margin of safety was most important. A stock might be the right to own a piece of a business, and the intrinsic value of the stock was something you could estimate, but with a margin of safety, you could sleep at night. Graham built in his margin of safety in various ways. He never forgot the danger of using debt. And although the 1950s had become one of the most prosperous eras in American history, his early experiences had given him the habit of assuming the worst. He looked at business through the lens of his 1932 *Forbes* articles—as worth more dead than alive—thinking of a stock's value mostly in terms of what the company would be worth if dead—that is, shut down and liquidated. Implicitly, Graham was always looking over his shoulder at the 1930s, when so many businesses went into bankruptcy. He kept his firm small in part because he was so risk-averse. And he rarely bought more than a tiny position in any company's stock, no matter how sound the business.[16] This meant the firm owned a large array of stocks that required much tending. While plenty of stocks did sell at prices below the businesses' liquidation value, which made Warren an enthusiastic follower of Graham, he disagreed with his teacher about the need to buy so many stocks. He had cast his lot with one stock: *"Ben would always tell me GEICO was too high. By his standards, it wasn't the right kind of stock to buy. Still, by the end of 1951, I had three-quarters of my net worth or close to it invested in GEICO."* And yet Warren "worshipped" his teacher, even though he had strayed so far from one of Graham's ideas.

As the spring semester wore on, Warren's classmates gradually accepted the routine of the classroom duet. Warren "was a very focused person. He could focus like a spotlight, twenty-four hours a day almost, seven days a week almost. I don't know when he slept," says Jack Alexander.[17] He could quote Graham's examples and come up with examples of his own. He haunted the Columbia library, reading old newspapers for hours on end.

"I would get these papers from 1929. I couldn't get enough of it. I read every-thing—not just the business and stock-market stories. History is interesting, and there is something about history in a newspaper, just seeing a place, the stories, even the ads, everything. It takes you into a different world, told by somebody who was an eyewitness, and you are really living in that time."

Warren spent hours reading the *Moody's* and *Standard & Poor's* manuals, looking for stocks. But it was the weekly Graham seminar that he looked forward to more than anything else.

While the chemistry between Warren and his teacher was obvious to everyone else in the class, one student in particular had taken note of him. Bill Ruane, a stockbroker at Kidder, Peabody, had found his way to Graham through his alma mater, Harvard Business School, after reading two important and memorable books—*Where Are the Customers' Yachts?* and *Security Analysis.*[18] He and Warren had connected immediately. But neither Ruane, nor any other of Graham's students, nor Warren himself, ever had the temerity to try to see Graham outside the seminar room. Warren did manage to find reasons, however, to drop in on his new acquaintance, Walter Schloss, down at the Graham-Newman Corporation.[19] He got to know Schloss better and learned he was caring for a wife who had been suffering from depression throughout most of their marriage.[20] Schloss, like David Dodd, appeared to be remarkably loyal and steadfast, qualities that Buffett sought out in people. He also envied Schloss his job; he would have cleaned the washrooms for free in exchange for one of those gray laboratory-style jackets, made of thin cotton, that everyone at Graham-Newman wore to keep from dirtying their shirtsleeves while they filled out the forms that Graham used to test stocks against his investing criteria.[21] Above all, Warren wanted to work for Graham.

As the semester neared an end, the rest of the class was busy finding their futures. Bob Dunn would be heading off to U.S. Steel, possibly the most prestigious corporate job in the United States. Almost every young businessman saw the route to success as working his way up the ladder in a great industrial corporation. In Eisenhower's postwar, post-Depression America, finding one's cell inside the institutional beehive and learning how to fit in was the normal and expected thing to do.

"I don't think there was one guy in the class that thought about whether U.S. Steel was a good business. I mean, it was a <u>big</u> business, but they weren't thinking about what <u>kind</u> of train they were getting on."

Warren had one goal in mind. He knew he would excel if Graham would hire him. While lacking self-confidence in many things, he had always felt sure-footed in the specialized area of stocks. He proposed himself to Graham for a job at Graham-Newman Corporation. It took audacity to even dream of working for the great man himself, but Warren was audacious. He was, after all, Ben Graham's star student, the only one to earn an A+ in his class. If Walter Schloss could work there, why couldn't he? To clinch the deal, he offered to work for free. He went in and asked for the job with far more confidence than he had felt riding up to Chicago for his interview with the Harvard Business School.

Graham turned him down.

"He was terrific. He just said, 'Lookit, Warren. In Wall Street still, the "white-shoe" firms, the big investment banks, they don't hire Jews. We only have the ability to hire a very few people here. And, therefore, we only hire Jews.' That was true of the two gals in the office and everybody. It was sort of like his version of affirmative action. And the truth is, there was a lot of prejudice against Jews in the fifties. I understood."

Buffett found it impossible to say anything that could be interpreted as criticism, even decades later. Of course, it must have been incredibly disappointing. Couldn't Graham have made an exception for his star student? Someone it wouldn't cost him anything to employ?

Warren, who idolized his teacher, had to accept that Graham viewed him impersonally, so much so that he would not overrule a principle even for the best student who had ever taken his class. There was no appeal—at least for now. Chagrined, he stayed through graduation, then once again he pulled himself together and stepped aboard a train.

He had two consolations. He would be back in Omaha, where he felt he belonged. And it would be much easier to pursue his love life there, for he had met an Omaha girl and was now smitten. As usual, the girl he wanted was not smitten with him. But this time, he was determined to change her mind.

18

Miss Nebraska

New York City and Omaha · 1950–1952

Warren had always been a washout with girls. He longed to have a girl-friend, but the very things that made him different hindered his quest. *"Nobody was more shy than I was with girls,"* he says. *"But my reaction to that was probably to turn into a talking machine."* His attitude was, "Why would they want to go out with me?" Thus he didn't go on many dates during high school or college. And when he did, something always seemed to go wrong.

On a date to a baseball game with a girl named Jackie Gillian, the high point was hitting a cow with his car on the way home. Driving a hearse to pick up Barbara Weigand, he says, was "sort of desperate," not a stunt. After that ice-breaker, what was there to say? On a date with a shy girl like Ann Beck, he was struck mute. Girls didn't want to hear about Ben Graham and the margin of safety. If he couldn't get to first base with Bobbie Worley, who had dated him all one summer, what hope did he have? Very little, he thought, and maybe the girls could sense it.

Finally, the summer of 1950 before he went to Columbia, his sister Bertie set him up on a date with her roommate from Northwestern. A round-cheeked kewpie of a brunette named Susan Thompson,[1] she had quickly impressed Bertie, who was a year and a half younger, as a special girl with a knack for understanding people.[2] As soon as Warren met Susie, he was fascinated, but suspected she was too good to be true: *"I bet she was a fake at first. I was intrigued by her and I was pursuing her, but I was determined to find the hole in the dike. I just couldn't believe anybody was really like her."* Susie was not interested in him. She was in love with somebody else.

After Warren went off to Columbia, he read in Earl Wilson's gossip column[3] in the *New York Post* that Miss Nebraska 1949, Vanita Mae Brown, was living at the Webster women's residence[4] and performing with the singer and teen idol Eddie Fisher on a television show. Something about the situation overcame his shyness. Since the glamorous Miss Nebraska was living in New York, he telephoned her at the Webster.

Vanita took the bait. Before long, she and Mr. Omaha had a date. He learned that her upbringing had been nothing like his. She grew up in South Omaha near the stockyards, cleaning chickens at Omaha Cold Storage after school. Her pinup body and girl-next-door face had been her ticket out. She got a job in Omaha as an usherette at the Paramount Theater, then parlayed her love of putting herself on display into victory in a local beauty pageant. *"I think her talent was bedazzling the judges,"* Buffett says. After winning the Miss Nebraska title, she represented the state as Princess Nebraska in the Washington, D.C., Cherry Blossom Festival. From there she moved to New York City, where she was now desperately trying to make it in show business.

Although Warren was not the kind of guy to take a girl to dinner at the Stork Club or a show at the Copacabana, she must have welcomed a hometown face. Soon the two of them were exploring the streets of New York together. Looking to upgrade themselves, they went to Marble Collegiate Church to hear Dr. Norman Vincent Peale, a famous self-improvement writer and speaker. Warren serenaded her with "Sweet Georgia Brown" by ukulele on the bank of the Hudson, toting along cheese sandwiches as riverside picnic fare.

Even though Vanita hated cheese sandwiches,[5] she seemed willing to keep seeing him. He found her so entertaining and quick-witted that talking to her was like playing verbal Ping-Pong.[6] The aura of Technicolor that surrounded her made her magnetizing. Vanita's interest did not delude him, however, about his woefully lacking social skills. With each passing year, he had become more desperate to improve them. He'd seen an ad for a public-speaking course in the Dale Carnegie method. Warren trusted Dale Carnegie, who had already helped him to get along better with people. He went to a Carnegie course in New York with a $100 check in his pocket.

"I went to Dale Carnegie because I was painfully aware of being socially maladjusted. And I went and gave them a check, but then I stopped payment on it because I lost my nerve."

Nor did Warren's social deficiencies augur well for his prospects with Susan Thompson, to whom he had been writing all fall. She was not encouraging, but neither did she tell him outright to stop bothering her. Warren quickly hit on the strategy of befriending Susie's parents as a gateway to their daughter. Over Thanksgiving, he went to Evanston with them for a Northwestern football game. Afterward, the three of them had dinner with Susie, but she ditched them early to go out on a date.[7]

Warren returned to New York after the holiday, discouraged but no less intrigued. He continued to see Vanita. *"She had one of the most imaginative minds I've ever run into,"* he says.

In fact, dating her began to take on an edge of unpredictability and risk. At various times she threatened to go down to Washington when Howard was speaking on the floor of Congress and throw herself at his feet, shrieking, "Your son is the father of my unborn child!" Warren thought she might actually do it. Another time, she created such a scene as they left a movie theater that, unable to listen to it any longer, he hoisted her up and stuffed her, jackknifed, into a wire-mesh trash basket on the street corner. She hung there, suspended and screaming, as he stalked away.[8]

Vanita was beautiful, she was smart, and she was entertaining. She was also dangerous, and Warren knew it was risky to get more involved with her. But there must have been some sort of thrill to it. Dating Vanita was like walking a leopard on a leash to see if it would make a good pet. Yet, *"Vanita could handle herself fine. She had no problem carrying it off. The only question was whether she was going to want to carry it off. You didn't have to worry about her embarrassing you unless she wanted to."*

Finally, Warren realized that *"the truth was that she would always want to embarrass me. She preferred acting that way with me,"* he says, and she did so regularly. Vanita had a fascination about her, however, and had he not had an alternative, there is no telling what would have happened next.[9]

Every time Warren went home to Nebraska, he saw Susan Thompson as much as she allowed. To him she seemed immensely sophisticated, even authoritative, and generous with her emotions. *"Susie was way, way, way more mature than I was,"* he says. He started falling hard for her and disentangling himself from Vanita, even though *"it was obvious I wasn't Number One"*[10] with Susie. *"My intentions were clear,"* he says, *"they just weren't having any effect on her."*

Susan Thompson's family was well known to the Buffetts—in fact it was her father, "Doc Thompson," who had managed Howard's only failed reelection campaign—but in most respects they were as different as could be from Warren's. Susie's mother, Dorothy Thompson, a sweet, tiny woman, warm, genuine, and wise to the world, was known in the family as the "wife who went along." She made sure dinner was on the table at six p.m. sharp and supported the many lives her husband, Dr. William Thompson, led. A smallish, silver-haired peacock of a man who wore bow ties and dressed in three-piece wool suits in lavender or cotton-candy pink or chartreuse, he cut a striking figure and carried himself with the posture of someone who was confident that he was being admired. He came, he said, "from a long line of teachers and preachers," and seemed to want to replicate all their labors at once.[11]

As dean of the College of Arts and Sciences at the University of Omaha, he ran the college while at the same time teaching psychology. As assistant athletic director, he controlled the university athletic programs and directed them with all the gusto of a former football player and sports fanatic. This role made him so prominent that *"every cop in town knew him,"* says Buffett, *"which was a good thing, because of the way he drove."* He also designed IQ tests and psychology tests, and supervised the testing of all the city's schoolchildren.[12] Not content to enjoy a day of rest from bossing people around and testing their children, on Sundays he donned the vestments of an ordained minister and preached v-e-r-y s-l-o-w-l-y in a deep, booming voice at the tiny Irvington Christian Church, where his daughters made up the two-person choir.[13] The rest of the time, he broadcast his political beliefs, which were similar to Howard Buffett's, to anyone who came within the sound of his voice.

Doc Thompson expressed his wishes with a jovial smile while insisting that they be obeyed at once. He talked of the importance of women while expecting them to wait on him. His work revolved around the inner self, but he was noticeably vain. He clung to those he loved, growing nervous when they were out of his sight. A chronically anxious hypochondriac, he often predicted that some sort of disaster would befall anyone he cared about. He lavished affection on those who satisfied his demanding ways.

The Thompsons' older daughter, Dorothy, known as Dottie, was not one of those. According to family lore, during the first few years of Dottie's life, when her father was especially displeased with her, he locked her in a closet.[14] A charitable interpretation would be that the pressure of trying to finish his PhD with a toddler underfoot unhinged him.

Seven years after Dottie's arrival, their second daughter, Susie, was born. Dorothy Thompson, seeing how badly Dottie was responding to her husband's harsh child-rearing methods, supposedly asserted herself to tell him "that one was yours, I'm raising the next."

Susie was sickly from birth. She had allergies and chronic ear infections and endured a dozen ear lancings during her first eighteen months. She suffered through long bouts of rheumatic fever, and her illnesses confined her to the house for four to five months at a time from kindergarten through second grade. She later recalled watching her friends playing outside her window during these periods, while she longed to join them.[15]

Through her many illnesses, the Thompsons constantly comforted, cuddled, and rocked their daughter. Her father doted on her. *"There was nothing in his life remotely approaching her,"* says Warren. *"Susie could do no wrong, but everything that Dottie did was wrong. They were always critical of her."*

A family home movie shows Susie, about age four, shouting, "No!" and ordering around Dottie, age eleven, as they played with a tea set.[16]

When at last Susie was well and no longer a prisoner of her bedroom, she never chose to play sports or games outdoors but was always eager to make friends.[17] It was people she had missed during those long days of illness.

As Susie grew older, she retained her girlish round cheeks and a breathy, deceptively childlike voice. During her teens she went to Omaha's Central High, an integrated school with a student body of different faiths and colors, unusual in the 1940s. Even though she was part of a crowd that some considered snobbish, her classmates recall her as having friends among all these groups.[18] Her exuberant warmth and her ethereal way of speaking could come across as "a little phony," even "a little loopy,"[19] but her friends said there wasn't anything phony about her. Her interests ran to speech and performing arts rather than academics. She argued with passion and persuasiveness on the Central High debate team, where people noticed that her politics had strayed far from her father's. She acted charmingly in school plays and sang in a smooth contralto in school operettas and as a mainstay of the choir. Her performance as the sweetly harebrained lead in *Our Hearts Were Young and Gay* so sparkled that her teachers recalled it for years afterward.[20] Indeed, her charm and strength of personality made her "Most Popular," a "lady in waiting" to the school sweetheart, Miss Central, and led her classmates to elect her senior class president.

Susie's first boyfriend was John Gillmore, a quiet, bland boy whom she openly adored. By the time he became her steady at Central High, Gillmore towered over her by almost a foot, but despite her "kittenish" demeanor, she dominated him.[21]

During those years, she also began dating a friendly, intelligent boy she had met at a freshman debate competition. A student at Thomas Jefferson High

School in Council Bluffs, Iowa, across the Missouri River from Omaha, Milton Brown was a tall, dark-haired young man with a warm, wide smile. They saw each other several times a week throughout high school.[22] While her close friends were aware of Milt, it was Gillmore who continued to be her steady date for parties and school events.

Susie's father did not approve of Brown, who was the son of an unschooled Russian-Jewish immigrant worker on the Union Pacific Railroad. The three or four times that she dared to bring him to the house, he was made to feel unwelcome by Doc Thompson, who lectured him about FDR and Truman. Susie's father made no secret of his determination to pry his daughter loose from dating a Jew.[23] Like the Buffetts, Doc Thompson had all the prejudices typical of Omaha, where different ethnic and religious groups kept to themselves, and life for a couple of mixed religion would be taxing at best. Yet Susie dared to cross these social lines—while at the same time managing to maintain another life as a conventional, popular high school girl.

Susie navigated these choppy waters until she went to college, when she and Milt headed off to freedom—together—at Northwestern University in Evanston, Illinois. There she roomed with Bertie Buffett, and both pledged sororities. Susie, a journalism major, had arranged her schedule so that she could see Milt nearly every day.

The two joined the Wildcat Council together and met at the library after he got off one of the several jobs he held after school to pay his tuition.[24] Susie's unconventional choice to openly date a Jewish boy clashed with her life as a typical coed, and members of her sorority forbade her to bring Brown to a dance because he had pledged a Jewish fraternity. Susie, although hurt, did not depledge.[25] But she and Milt began to study Zen Buddhism, looking for a faith that could reflect their common spiritual beliefs.[26]

Knowing nothing of this, Warren made his futile Thanksgiving trip to Evanston, then visited Susie in Omaha over the winter holidays. By then he had made up his mind to pursue her seriously. She had the qualities he'd always looked for in a woman. But the person she wanted to give her love to was Milt Brown.

That spring of 1951, Milt was elected sophomore class president and Bertie its vice president. Susie cried every time she opened a letter from home demanding that she break off her relationship with Brown. Bertie could see what was going on, but Susie never confided in her, even though they had grown to be friends.[27] She seemed to have a way of never letting anyone get inside her head. Then, one day as the semester neared an end, the two were sitting in their dorm room when the phone rang. It was Doc Thompson. "Come home *now*," he commanded. He wanted her away from Milt and he let her know she would not be going back to Northwestern in the fall. Susie collapsed, sobbing, but there was never any appeal of her father's decisions.

After graduating from Columbia that spring, Warren, too, returned to Omaha. He would be living in his parents' home since they were away in Washington, but he would have to spend part of that first summer after his return fulfilling his obligation to the National Guard. Though he wasn't particularly well suited to the Guard, it was better than the alternative—going off to fight in Korea. The Guard required him to attend training camp in La Crosse, Wisconsin, for several weeks every year, however. Training camp did nothing to help him mature.

"It's a very democratic organization. I mean, what you do outside doesn't mean much. To fit in, all you had to do was be willing to read comic books. About an hour after I got there, I was reading comic books. Everybody else was reading comic books, why shouldn't I? My vocabulary shrank to about four words, and you can guess what they were.

"I learned that it pays to hang around with people better than you are, because you will float upward a little bit. And if you hang around with people that behave worse than you, pretty soon you'll start sliding down the pole. It just works that way."

The experience gave Warren incentive to make good on another vow just as soon as he got back from National Guard camp. *"I was terrified of public speaking. You can't believe what I was like if I had to give a talk. I was so terrified that I just couldn't do it. I would throw up. In fact, I arranged my life so that I never had to get up in front of anybody. When I came out here to Omaha after graduating, I saw another ad. And I knew I was going to have to speak in public sometimes. The agony was such that just to get rid of the pain I signed up for the course again."* That was not his only mission: To win the heart of Susan Thompson, he knew he would have to be able to converse with her as well. The odds against succeeding with Susie were long, but he would do anything to improve them, and this summer might be his last chance.

The Dale Carnegie class met down at the Rome Hotel, a favorite of the cattlemen. *"I took a hundred bucks in cash and gave it to Wally Keenan, the instructor, and said, 'Take it before I change my mind.'*

"There were about twenty-five or thirty of us in there. We were all just terrified. We couldn't say our own names. We all stood there and wouldn't talk to each other.

Meanwhile, one thing that impressed me was that, after meeting all those people once, Wally could rattle off all our names from memory. He was a good teacher, and he tried to teach us the memory association trick, but I never learned that part.

"They gave us this book of speeches—keynote speech, election speech, lieutenant governor's speech—and we were supposed to deliver these things every week. The way it works is that you learn to get out of yourself. I mean, why should you be able to talk alone with somebody five minutes before and then freeze in front of a group? So they teach you the psychological tricks to overcome this. Some of it is just practice—just doing it and practicing. We really helped each other through. And it worked. That's the most important degree that I have."

Yet Warren could not try out his new skills on Susie, who made herself scarce. Mindful of Doc Thompson's influence over his daughter, Warren showed up every night, ukulele in tow, to romance her father in her stead. *"She would go out with other guys,"* says Buffett, *"and I didn't have anything to do when I would go over there. So I would flirt with him instead, and he and I would talk about things."* Doc Thompson, who loved the summer heat, sat outside on the screened porch on the boiling July nights, dressed in his three-piece pastel wool suit, while Susie was secretly out with Milt. Doc Thompson played the mandolin while Warren sweated and sang, accompanying him on the ukulele.

Warren felt comfortable with Doc Thompson, whose style reminded him of his father's way of holding forth on how the world was going to hell because of the Democrats. Whittaker Chambers's autobiography, *Witness,* describing his conversion from Communist spy to ardent Cold War anti-Communist, had just been released. Warren had read this book with great interest. This was the kind of fodder that Doc Thompson could chew on endlessly. Unlike Howard, however, he also talked about sports. He had no sons, and he thought Warren was the best thing since bubble gum.[28] Warren was smart, Warren was Protestant, Warren was Republican, and, above all, Warren was not Milt Brown.

The support of Bill Thompson was not as much of a plus as it might have seemed. Warren was up against stiff odds in winning Susie's heart. She could overlook his baggy socks and cheap suits; it was the rest that worked against him. He came across to her as a Congressman's son, somebody considered "special," a boy who had every advantage—a graduate degree and a good bit of money—and who was obviously headed for success. He talked about stocks all the time, a subject she cared nothing about. His way of entertaining a date was telling rehearsed jokes, riddles, and brainteasers. That her father liked Warren so much made her think of Warren as an extension of her father's control. Doc

Thompson "practically threw Susie at Warren."[29] *"It was two against one,"* says Buffett.

Milt, who needed her, suffered the injustice of being a Jew from literally the wrong side of the tracks. He was all the more attractive because he was the guy her father couldn't stand.

Susie was enrolling that fall at the University of Omaha, and by then, she and Milt had to acknowledge that, because of her father, they were "off and on." She spent the summer in tears.

Meanwhile, despite her initial lack of interest in Warren, Susie could never spend time with anyone without wanting to learn all about him. She soon started to realize that her first impression had been wrong. He was not the privileged, cocky, self-confident guy she thought. *"I was a wreck,"* he recalls; he was jittering on the brink of a nervous breakdown. *"I felt odd, I was socially inept, but beyond that, I hadn't found a cruising speed in life."* Even her friends noticed the vulnerability that lay beneath his veneer of self-assurance. Susie gradually recognized how worthless he felt inside.[30] All that confident chatter about stocks, the aura of a prodigy, the tinny twang of the ukulele, were wrapped around a fragile, needy core: a boy who was stumbling through his days in a shroud of desolation. *"I was a mess,"* he says. *"It was incredible the way Susie saw through to some of that."* Indeed, somebody who felt like a wreck and a mess was catnip to Susie. Warren would later say of her need to turn him into a cause that he *"was Jewish enough for Susie, but not too Jewish"* for her dad. And so she started coming around.

Warren, who was nearly blind to the way others dressed—even women— was so in love with Susie by now that he actually noticed her clothes. He would never forget the blue dress she wore on their dates or the black-and-white print outfit he called the "newspaper dress."[31] Amid the summer fireflies at the Peony Park pavilion, they stumbled around the dance floor to the sounds of a Glenn Miller tune. Warren had still never learned to dance and tried as hard as he could. He was about as cozy on the dance floor as a sixth grader at a sorority social. But *"I would have done anything she asked,"* he says. *"I would have let her put worms down the back of my shirt."*

By Labor Day, when Warren took her to the state fair, they were a couple. Warren wrote his aunt Dorothy Stahl in October 1951 in his best smart-alecky style: "Things in the girl department are at an all-time peak...the hooks have been sunk pretty deep into me by one of the local gals. As soon as I get the go-ahead from [my uncle] Fred and you, I may proceed further. This girl has only one drawback; she knows nothing about stocks. Otherwise she is unbeatable and I guess I can overlook her Achilles' heel."[32]

Cautiously "proceeding further" was putting it right. Warren worked up his nerve. Instead of proposing marriage, he "just sort of assumed it, and kept talking." Susie, for her part, "realized she had been chosen," although "she wasn't sure how."[33]

Triumphant, Warren went to his Dale Carnegie class on schedule. *"That's the week I won the pencil. They gave a pencil award for doing something difficult and doing the most with the training. The week I won the pencil was the week that I proposed."*

Afterward, Susie wrote a long, sad letter to Milton Brown, telling him the news. He was shocked. He knew she had been out on some dates with Warren but had no idea it was anything serious.[34]

Warren went to talk to Susie's father to get his blessing. This, he already knew, would be easily had. But Doc Thompson took a while—quite a while—to get to the point. The government was downright ineffectual—or worse—when it came to dealing with Communism. Truman had lost China for democracy. The Communists were taking over the world, and stocks were going to be nothing but valueless bits of paper. So Warren's plan to work in the stock market was going to fail. But Doc Thompson would never blame Warren when his daughter starved. He was a smart young man. If not for the Democrats ruining the country, he would probably do all right. The miserable future that awaited Susie wouldn't be Warren's fault.

Long used to this kind of talk, from both his own father and Susie's, Warren waited patiently for the crucial word "yes." Three hours later, Doc Thompson wound his way to a conclusion and gave his consent.[35]

By Thanksgiving, Susie and Warren were planning their April wedding.

19

Stage Fright

Omaha • Summer 1951–Spring 1952

Warren understood Doc Thompson's concern about how he would support a family, even though he had no such doubts himself. Since he couldn't work for Graham-Newman, he had decided to become a stockbroker, and to do it in Omaha, far from the canyons of Wall Street. If you wanted to make money in the stock market, went the common wisdom, the place to do it was New York, so his decision was an unusual one. But he felt free from the conventions of Wall Street; he wanted to work with his father; Susie was in Omaha; and he was never happy far from home.

At almost twenty-one, Warren was supremely confident in his own investing abilities. By the end of 1951, he had already boosted his capital from $9,804 to $19,738. He had earned seventy-five percent in a single year.[1] As a matter of course, however, he consulted his father and Ben Graham. To his surprise, both said, "Maybe you should wait a few years." Graham—as always—thought the market was too high. Howard, pessimistic, favored mining stocks and gold stocks and other investments designed to protect against inflation. He didn't think any other kind of business would be a good investment, and he worried about his son's future.

That didn't make sense to Warren. Since 1929, the value of businesses had grown substantially.

"It was absolutely the reverse effect of what you saw in other times, when the market was staggeringly overvalued. I had looked at companies. I just couldn't see why you wouldn't want to own them. It was on a micro level, not an assessment of the growth of the economy or anything like that, and I was working with micro

money. But it just seemed to me that it was crazy not to own them. On the other hand, here's Ben, with his two hundred IQ, telling me to wait. And my dad, who, if he told me to walk out a window, I would have done it." To make this decision to defy the advice of his two great authorities—his father and Ben Graham—was an enormous step for Warren. It required him to consider the possibility that his judgment might be superior to theirs. Yet he was certain he was right. He might have walked out a window if his father told him to—but not if it meant leaving a *Moody's Manual* full of cheap stocks behind.

In fact, the opportunities he saw were so plentiful that they justified borrowing money for the first time. He was willing to take on debt equal to a quarter of his net worth. "*I was already running short of money to invest. If I was enthused about a stock I would have to sell something else to buy it. I had an aversion to borrowing money, but I got a loan for five thousand dollars or so from the Omaha National Bank. I was under twenty-one and my dad had to cosign the loan.*"

Howard probably felt both proud and a little silly cosigning a loan for his son, who had been a full-fledged businessman for at least a dozen years. Since Warren had made up his mind, Howard was also willing to take him on at his own firm, Buffett-Falk—though only after suggesting that he interview at a prominent local firm, Kirkpatrick Pettis Co., to see what the best of Omaha stockbroking had to offer.

"*I went to see Stewart Kirkpatrick and said during the interview that I wanted intelligent customers. I was going to try to look for people who could understand things. And Kirkpatrick said, in effect, don't worry about whether they're intelligent, worry about whether they're rich. Which is okay, you can't knock him for that. But I wouldn't have wanted to work anyplace but at my dad's firm.*"

At Buffett-Falk, Warren was installed in one of its four private unairconditioned offices, next to the "cage," a glassed-in area where a clerk handled the money and securities. He started out selling his favorite stock to the safest people he knew, his aunt and his college friends, including his first roommate at Wharton, Chuck Peterson, who was now in the real estate business in Omaha and with whom he'd reconnected.

"*My aunt Alice was the first call I made, and I sold her a hundred shares of GEICO. She made me feel good about myself. She was interested in me. And after that Fred Stanback, Chuck Peterson, and anybody I could get to buy it. But mostly I got myself to buy it, because when other people didn't buy it, I'd just figure out a way to buy five more shares myself. I had this big ambition. I was going to own one-tenth of one percent of the company. It had 175,000 shares outstanding, and I figured if the company would become worth one billion dollars someday and I owned that much, I would be worth a million dollars. So I needed 175 shares."*[2]

Yet in the meantime, his job was to sell on commission, and beyond this narrow circle, Warren found that almost insurmountably difficult. He got a taste of the obstacles his father had faced to build his brokerage business back when the grand old families of Omaha peered down their noses at the grandson of a grocer. Alone in Omaha now, with his parents back in Washington, Warren felt that he got no respect.

These were the days when all stocks were sold by full-service stockbrokers, and most people bought individual stocks rather than mutual funds. Everybody paid fixed commissions of six cents a share. Transactions took place as part of a relationship. Every trade was preceded by a few minutes of chat with "your broker," part salesman, part adviser, part friend. Your broker might live in your neighborhood, and you saw him at parties, you golfed with him at your country club, and he came to your daughter's wedding. General Motors brought out new models of its cars every year, and a businessman might trade his car more often than his stocks. That is, if he owned any stocks.

Important accounts didn't take Warren seriously. *"I was twenty-one. And I'd go around to all these people to sell them stocks, and when I'd get all through they'd say, 'What does your dad think?' I got that all the time."* Warren, who looked like a "dork," struggled to make sales.[3] He didn't know how to read people, couldn't make small talk, and his mode of conversation was to broadcast rather than receive. When nervous, he sprayed forth information about his favorite stocks like a fire hose. Some potential clients listened to his pitch, checked with other sources, and used his ideas, but bought the stocks through other brokers, so he didn't get the commission. He was shocked at this perfidy from people he'd spoken to face-to-face and would be seeing again around town. He felt cheated.

"Generally speaking, I was not getting reinforcement. When I first started selling GEICO to people, Buffett-Falk had this little office downtown, and the stock certificates would come in and Jerome Newman's name would be on those certificates. He was the seller I was buying from. And the guys at Buffett-Falk said, 'What the hell. If you think you're smarter than Jerry Newman…'"

In fact, Graham-Newman was forming a new partnership, and some of the investors had given the firm GEICO shares to fund money into the partnership. So in effect, it was they who were selling, not Graham-Newman. Warren didn't know that.[4] But when it came to GEICO, he didn't care who was selling. It did not occur to him to ask anyone at the firm why they were selling. He was unshakeably certain of his own opinion. Nor did he hide that fact.

"I was sort of a wise guy, with this graduate degree, among people who hadn't gone to college. One time an insurance agent, Ralph Campbell, came in to see Mr. Falk and said, 'What's this kid doing going around promoting this company?' GEICO was a company that didn't use insurance agents. And I said, like a wise guy, 'Mr. Campbell, you better buy this stock for unemployment insurance.' "

The full import of Dale Carnegie's first rule, don't criticize, hadn't sunk in. Warren used what would later become the trademark Buffett wit to show that he knew more than everybody else, but why would anyone have been willing to believe that of a twenty-one-year-old? And yet he did. It must have stunned people at Buffett-Falk to watch him, morning through night, ripping through the manuals, adding to his file cabinets of knowledge.

"I went through the <u>Moody's Manuals</u> page by page. Ten thousand pages in the <u>Moody's Industrial, Transportation, Banks</u> and <u>Finance Manuals</u>—twice. I actually looked at every business—although I didn't look very hard at some."

And Warren wanted to be more than an investor, more than a salesman. He wanted to be a teacher, to emulate Ben Graham. He signed up to teach a night course at the University of Omaha.

At first he partnered with his stockbroker friend Bob Soener, who taught the first four weeks of "Profitable Investing in Stocks." While Soener explained to the class basics such as how to read the *Wall Street Journal,* Warren stood in the hallway listening for any good investment ideas. Then he took over for the next six weeks.[5] Eventually he taught the whole course and gave it the more cautious name of "Sound Investing in Stocks." In front of his classroom, he lit up, pacing the floor as if he couldn't get the words out fast enough, even though the students had to struggle not to drown in the flood of information he threw at them. But despite his deep vein of knowledge, he never promised the class they would get rich or that taking his class would give them any particular result. Nor did he brag about his own success at investing.

His students ranged from stock-market professionals to people who had no head for business—housewives, doctors, retirees. They symbolized a subtle shift: Long-absent investors were starting to come back for the first time since the 1920s—part of why Graham thought the market was overvalued. Warren adapted his teaching to the range of their knowledge and skills. He modeled his teaching style after Graham's, using the "Company A, Company B" method and some of his mentor's other little teaching tricks. He handed out grades with the strictest fairness. His aunt Alice took the course and sat in the classroom gazing at him with adoring eyes.[6] He gave her a C.

People were always throwing out the names of stocks, asking him whether to buy or sell. He could speak from memory for five or even ten minutes about any stock they named: its financial data, its price/earnings ratio, the volume of shares that traded—and from all appearances, he could do this for hundreds of stocks, as if he were quoting baseball statistics.[7] The students remarked on his unusual conservatism when responding to their questions about how to invest.

Meanwhile, Warren was going to be taking care of a family soon, which would divide his income into two streams. Part of what he made—his stream—would go back into the mill and continue to grow. And part he would spend for him and Susie to live, a significant change in his circumstances. Until now, he had been able to pare his expenses by living in the maid's room at Columbia, eating cheese sandwiches, and taking his dates to lectures or playing the ukulele for them instead of escorting them to the posh "21" Club. Now that he was back in Nebraska, he was able to cut his costs even further by living in his parents' house, even though it meant occasional contact with Leila when they came back from Washington.

He had never needed motivation to try to work his capital as hard as possible, and now he sat in the office at Buffett-Falk with his feet on his desk, searching systematically through the Graham and Dodd book for more ideas.[8] He found a stock, Philadelphia and Reading Coal & Iron Company. He bought Philadelphia and Reading Coal & Iron shares himself and sold them to his aunt Alice and Chuck Peterson. When the stock immediately dropped to $9 a share, he saw that as a reason to buy even more.

He bought a textile company called Cleveland Worsted Mills. It had current assets* of $146 per share, and the stock was selling for less than that. He felt the price did not reflect the value of "several well-equipped mills."

Warren wrote a short report on the stock. He liked the fact that the company was paying out a lot of what it earned to shareholders—giving them a bird in the hand. He thought Cleveland Worsted Mills had enough earnings to cover its dividend. That proved less than prescient.

---

* Current assets are a measure of liquidity—how fast a company can raise cash. They include cash, easily saleable investments, inventory, and money due from others. They exclude items like real estate, equipment, debt, and pensions, which cannot be readily liquidated or are owed to others.

"*I called it Cleveland's Worst Mill after they cut off paying the dividend.*" Warren was so mad that he decided to spend some money to find out what was wrong. "*I went to an annual meeting of Cleveland's Worst Mill, and I flew all the way to Cleveland. I got there about five minutes late, and the meeting had been adjourned. And here I was, this kid from Omaha, twenty-two years old, with my own money in the stock. The chairman said, 'Sorry, too late.' But then their sales agent, who was on the board of directors, actually took pity on me, and so he got me off on the side and talked to me and answered some questions.*" The answers, however, changed nothing. Warren felt awful; he had gotten other people to buy Cleveland's Worst Mill too.

There was nothing he hated more than selling people investments that lost them money. He couldn't stand disappointing people. This was what it had been like back in the sixth grade when the Cities Service Preferred stock he'd gotten Doris to invest in was clobbered. She hadn't hesitated to "remind" him about it, and he'd felt responsible. Now he would do anything to avoid the feeling of letting someone down.

Warren began looking for any way to make himself less dependent on the job he was starting to hate. He had always enjoyed owning businesses, and decided to buy a gas station with a friend from the National Guard, Jim Schaeffer. They bought a Sinclair station that was next to a Texaco station "*that consistently outsold us, which drove us crazy.*" Warren and his brother-in-law Truman Wood, who had married Doris, even worked at the station themselves on weekends. They washed windshields "*with a smile*"—despite Warren's aversion to manual labor—and did everything they could to attract new customers, but instead drivers continued to pull in to the Texaco station across the street. Its owner "*was very well established and very well liked. He beat us every month. That's when I learned the power of customer loyalty. The guy had been in business forever and had a clientele. Nothing we could do was going to change that.*

"*My service station was the dumbest thing—I lost two thousand dollars, and that was a lot of money for me at the time. I'd never had real damage in a loss. It was painful.*"

It seemed to Warren that nearly everything he did in Omaha reinforced his sense of youth and inexperience. He was no longer a precocious boy who was acting like a man, but a young man—about to get married—who looked and sometimes acted like a boy. Kaiser-Frazer, the stock he had shorted two years before in Bob Soener's office, still hung stubbornly around five dollars a share instead of going to zero as he had expected. Carl Falk was always giving him funny looks and questioning his judgment. And Warren felt more and more queasy about the very nature of his job. He started to think of himself as being like "a prescriptionist." *"I had to explain to people who didn't know enough about whether they should take aspirin or Anacin,"* and people would do anything the "guy in the white coat"—the stockbroker—told them to do. The stockbroker got paid based on turnover instead of advice. In other words, *"he's getting paid based on how many pills he sells. He gets paid more for some pills than others. You wouldn't go to a doctor whose pay was totally contingent on how many pills you took."* But that's how the business of being a stockbroker worked at the time.

Warren felt there was a conflict of interest inherent in the business. He'd recommend a stock like GEICO to his friends and family, and tell them that the best thing to do was to hold it for twenty years. That meant he didn't get any more commissions from them. *"You can't make a living that way. The system pits your interests against your clients."*

Nevertheless, he had begun to develop a small clientele of his own through his network of graduate school friends. But he still felt conflicted. He had turned Buffett-Falk into a "market maker," a firm that acted as a middleman, buying and selling stocks as a dealer.[9] The firm made a profit by selling a stock to clients at a slightly higher price than it paid, and buying stock from clients at a lower price than it sold the stock for. The difference, or "spread," was its profit. The spread was invisible to the customers. Acting as a market maker lifted a brokerage firm from being a mere order taker to being a player in the Wall Street game. While Warren was proud that he had the know-how to set Buffett-Falk up as a market maker, the conflict bothered him.

"I don't want to be on the other side of the table from the customer. I never was selling anything I didn't believe in myself or own myself. On the other hand, there was a markup that was undisclosed. If anybody asked me about it, I told them. But I don't like anything like that. I want to be on the same side of the table with the people who are my partners, everybody knowing what's going on. And a promoter, by his nature, doesn't do that."

No matter how Warren thought about his job as a stockbroker, there was always a potential conflict of interest, and always the possibility that he would lose money for his clients and open himself up to disappointing them. He would much rather manage people's money instead of selling them stocks, with his interest on the same side as the customer's. The problem was, there were no such opportunities in Omaha. But in the spring of 1952, he wrote an article about GEICO that attracted the attention of a powerful man, and with that, his luck seemed about to change. The article, "The Security I Like Best," which appeared in the *Commercial and Financial Chronicle,* was not just an advertisement for Warren's favorite stock, but an explanation of his ideas about investing. It caught the attention of Bill Rosenwald, who was a son of Julius Rosenwald, a philanthropist and the longtime chairman of Sears, Roebuck & Co. The younger Rosenwald ran American Securities, a money management firm launched with family stock in Sears[10] that sought high returns while minimizing risk and preserving capital. After contacting Ben Graham, who gave Warren a strong recommendation, Rosenwald offered Warren a job. Few jobs in money management were as prestigious, and Warren was dying to accept it, even though that meant moving back to New York City. To do so, however, he had to get permission from the National Guard to leave Omaha.

"I asked my commanding officer whether it would be possible to transfer to New York to take this job. He said, 'You'll have to go down and see the commanding general.' So I went down to Lincoln, sat there in the state capitol, waited awhile, went in to see General Henninger, and said, 'Corporal Buffett reporting.' I'd written him ahead of time explaining and asking permission.

"And right away he said, 'Permission denied.'

"That was the end of it. That meant I was in Omaha as long as he wanted to keep me captive."

Thus Warren was stuck at Buffett-Falk, writing prescriptions for a living. The main comfort he had during the challenges of his first year back in Omaha was his fiancée. He had begun to lean on Susie. All the while, she was working at figuring Warren out. She began to understand the damage Leila Buffett's rages had done to her son's self-worth, and she started trying to repair it. She knew that the main thing he needed was to feel loved and never criticized. He also needed to feel that he could succeed socially. *"People accepted me more when I was with her,"* he says. Even though she was still at the University of Omaha while he had been working, he was like a toddler gazing up at a parent when it came to his relationship with his future wife. Both were still living in their parents' homes. Over time, Warren had developed a way of dealing with his mother, which was to avoid being alone with her, while making use of her dutiful nature when in her presence by besieging her with demands and requests. Yet the long stretches that he had spent away from her while attending college had lowered his tolerance for

Leila's company instead of raising it. When she and Howard came back from Washington for Warren and Susie's wedding, Susie noticed that her fiancé avoided his mother as much as he could. When forced to be in her company, he would turn his face away from her and clench his teeth.

It was time for Warren to move out. He called Chuck Peterson, saying "Chas-o, I haven't got a place for us to live," and Chas-o rented him a tiny apartment a couple of miles from downtown. When Warren gave Susie, who had a strong sense of self-expression, an allowance of $1,500 to furnish their first apartment, she and her future sister-in-law Doris took off for Chicago to shop for furniture in the colorful modern style she liked.[11]

As the wedding date, April 19, 1952, approached, the question arose whether the ceremony would take place at all. The week before, the Missouri River flooded upstream of Omaha. With the waters heading south, officials predicted they would crest above the riverbank and flood the city during the weekend. This made it likely that the National Guard would be called out.

"The whole town turned out with sandbags. I had all these buddies coming in for the wedding—Fred Stanback was going to be best man, and various ushers and guests. They were all kidding me because I was in the National Guard. They said, 'Well, don't worry about it, because we'll substitute for you on the honeymoon.' Jokes like that. This was going on all week.

"Saturday came, and we were getting married about three in the afternoon. Around noon, the phone rang. My mother said, 'It's for you.' I picked up the phone. The guy at the other end said, 'C-C-C-Corporal Buffett?' I had a commanding officer who had a really distinctive stutter. 'This is C-C-C-Captain Murphy,' he said.

"If he hadn't stuttered, I'd have said something that'd probably have gotten me court-martialed, because I would have thought it was the guys pulling a trick on me. But as it was, he said, 'We've been activated. What time c-c-c-can you show up at the Armory?' And I said, 'Well, I'm getting married at three o'clock.' I said, 'I could probably be there by five.' He said, 'Report for d-d-d-duty. We're going to be p-p-p-patrolling East Omaha d-d-down by the river.' I said, 'Yes, sir.'

"I got off the phone totally depressed. Then I get a call an hour later. And this guy had a perfectly normal voice. He says, 'Corporal Buffett?' I said, 'Yes, sir.' He said, 'This is General Wood.'[12] That was the commanding general of the Thirty-fourth Division, who lived way out in west Nebraska. General Wood said, 'I'm countermanding Captain Murphy's order. Have a good time.'"

He had two hours left before the biggest event of his life. Warren showed up at the soaring Gothic sanctuary of Dundee Presbyterian Church well before three o'clock. The wedding of a Congressman's son and Doc Thompson's daughter was a major event in Omaha. Several hundred guests, including many of Omaha's top-drawer people, were expected.[13]

"I was so nervous that I just figured—well, I didn't wear my glasses so that I wouldn't be able to see all those people out there." Warren also asked Fred Stanback to distract him by talking so he wouldn't have to focus on what was happening.[14]

After the ceremony, the guests drank nonalcoholic punch and ate wedding cake downstairs in the linoleum-floored church basement. Susie smiled wide as an ivory fan. Warren glowed, incandescent, and wrapped his arm around her waist as if trying to keep them both from sailing off into the air. After photographs, they changed into their going-away clothes and ran through the crowd of cheering guests to duck into Alice Buffett's car, which she had lent them for the honeymoon. Warren had already loaded the backseat with *Moody's Manuals* and ledgers. All of a sudden, Susie saw the writing on the wall.[15] And from Omaha, the newlyweds set off on their honeymoon—a cross-country automobile trip.

"On my wedding night, I had chicken fried steak at the Wigwam Café in Wahoo, Nebraska," Buffett says.[16] The Wigwam was a tiny hole-in-the-wall less than an hour from Omaha, with a few booths and cowboy decor. From there, Warren and Susie drove thirty miles to the Cornhusker Hotel in Lincoln to spend the night, *"and that's all I'll say on that subject,"* Buffett says.

"The next day I bought a copy of the Omaha World-Herald *and it had run an article that said, 'Only love can stop the Guard.' "*[17] The 1952 flood was the worst in modern times in Omaha, the effort spent to avert it Herculean. "*The other guys were sandbagging for days, patrolling in the flood, with the snakes and rats. I was the only guy that didn't get called out."*

The newlyweds traveled all over the western and southwestern United States. But, *"We did not stop to visit companies and look at investments, as has been reported,"* Buffett insists. On the way back they stopped in Las Vegas, which was full of ex–Omaha people who had moved there shortly before and bought into the Flamingo Hotel and casinos from the Flamingo to the Barbary Coast. All these characters had shopped at the Buffett grocery store; Vegas felt almost homey, carrying echoes of the racetrack and full of people who knew his family. So he was not afraid of the house. *"Susie won a jackpot on the slot machine. She was only nineteen. They wouldn't pay her because she was underage. I said, 'Lookit, you took her nickels.' And they paid her."*

After Vegas, the Buffetts headed back to Omaha. Warren could not stop chortling over his luckless colleagues in the Guard. *"Oh, the honeymoon was great. It was great. Three weeks. And all the time, these guys in the Guard were sloshing it up."*

PART THREE

The Racetrack

20

Graham-Newman

Omaha and New York City · 1952–1955

A few months after the wedding, Susie went to Chicago with her parents and new in-laws for the Republican convention in July of 1952. They were on a crusade to reclaim the White House for the Republicans after twenty agonizing years under the Democrats.[1] Warren, of course, stayed in Omaha, grinding away. Politics fascinated him, but not like money. Nonetheless, when the convention was covered on television for the first time in history, Warren watched eagerly, struck by the power of this medium to magnify and influence events.

The front-runner going into the convention was Senator Robert Taft of Ohio.[2] Known as "Mr. Integrity," Taft headed a minority wing of the Republican Party that wanted the government to be small, to stay out of everybody's business, and above all to go after Communism more aggressively than Truman had done.[3] Taft made his friend Howard Buffett head of his Nebraska presidential campaign and also head of his speakers' bureau. Taft's opponent, retired General Dwight D. Eisenhower—a moderate who had served as the Supreme Commander of Allied Forces in Europe during World War II and was the first Supreme Commander of NATO forces—was a popular figure viewed by many as a war hero. As the convention approached, "Ike" began to catch up in the polls.

What would prove to be the most controversial Republican convention in history unfolded in Chicago as Eisenhower backers pushed through an amendment to the convention rules, passed on a contentious vote, that handed him the nomination on the first ballot. Taft's outraged supporters felt robbed. But Eisenhower soon made peace with them by promising to combat "creeping socialism." Taft insisted that his followers swallow their outrage and vote for Eisenhower for the sake of regaining the White House. The Republicans united behind him and his running mate, Richard Nixon; "I Like Ike" buttons sprouted everywhere.[4] Everywhere, that is, except on Howard Buffett's chest. He broke with the party by refusing to endorse Eisenhower.[5]

This was an act of political suicide. His support within the party evaporated overnight. He was left standing on principle—alone. Warren recognized that his father had "painted himself into a corner."[6] From his earliest childhood, Warren had always tried to avoid broken promises, burned bridges, and confrontation. Now Howard's struggles branded three principles even deeper into his son: that allies are essential; that commitments are so sacred that by nature they should be rare; and that grandstanding rarely gets anything done.

Eisenhower defeated Adlai Stevenson in the November election, and in January Warren's parents dragged themselves back to Washington to finish out the rest of Howard's lame-duck term. Warren, who had for some time recognized obsessive qualities in Howard and Leila that disadvantaged them in various ways, had begun to absorb something of his in-laws' style. Dorothy Thompson was easygoing, and her husband, though autocratic, was more personable and astute at human relations than Howard Buffett. The more time Warren spent with Susie and her family, the more they influenced him.

"Warren," said Doc Thompson, who handed down advice with the authority of the Sermon on the Mount, "always surround yourself with women. They're more loyal and they work harder."[7] His son-in-law hardly needed to be told that. Indeed, Warren had always craved being taken care of by women, as long as they didn't try to order him around. Susie could see that he was eager for her to assume a motherly role. So she wrapped herself around her husband as she worked on "fixing" him, the wreck, the mess. "Oh, my God," she said, "he was a case."[8] When they met, she recalled, "I had never seen anyone in so much pain."

Warren may not have been aware of the depths or dimensions of his pain, but describes the powerful role she played in his life. *"Susie was as big an influence on me as my dad, or bigger probably, in a different way. I had all these defense mechanisms that she could explain, but I can't. She probably saw things in me that other people couldn't see. But she knew it would take time and a lot of nourishment to bring it out. She made me feel that I had somebody with a little sprinkling can who was going to make sure that the flowers grew."*

Susie recognized Warren's vulnerability, his need to be soothed and comforted and reassured. More and more, she could see the effect his mother had

had on her children. Doris was the more badly damaged, but Leila had convinced both Warren and Doris that deep down they were worthless. In every area of life except business, Susie was discovering, her husband was riddled with self-doubt. He had never felt loved, and she saw that he did not feel lovable.[9]

"*I needed her like crazy,*" he says. "*I was happy in my work, but I wasn't happy with myself. She literally saved my life. She resurrected me.*[10] *She put me together. It was the same kind of unconditional love you would get from a parent.*"

Warren wanted a lot of things from his wife that you would ordinarily get from a parent. Not only that, he had grown up with a mother who did everything for him. Now Susie took over. Although their basic model of wedded life was typical of the time—he made the money, she took care of him and covered the domestic front—their arrangement was extreme. Everything in the Buffett household revolved around Warren and his business. Susie understood her husband was special; she willingly became the cocoon for his embryonic ambitions. He spent his days working and his nights hunched over the *Moody's Manual.* He also arranged his schedule to give himself leisure time to play golf and Ping-Pong, even signing up as a junior member of the Omaha Country Club.

Susie, barely twenty years old, was no Betty Crocker, but she had taken up rudimentary cooking and basic housekeeping like any 1950s wife—at a time when Omaha women were auditioning to appear on the show *Typical Housewife* on local television station KTMV. She devoted herself to fulfilling her husband's few but specific requirements: Pepsi in the refrigerator, a lightbulb in his reading lamp, some indifferently cooked version of meat and potatoes for dinner, a shaker full of salt, popcorn in the cupboard, ice cream in the freezer. He also needed help getting dressed, tenderness, head rubs, cuddling, hugs, and assistance in dealing with people. She even cut his hair, because he claimed he was afraid to go to the barber.[11]

Warren was "*nuts about Susie, and she felt things*" that were inside him, he says. He describes her role as the giver, his as the receiver. "*She was absorbing more about me and sensing much more about me than I was sensing about her.*" They were always seen kissing and cuddling, Susie often in Warren's lap; she frequently said this reminded her of her father.

Six months after the wedding, Susie was pregnant and had dropped out of the University of Omaha. Her sister, Dottie, was pregnant, too, with her second baby. She and Susie had remained particularly close. A dark-haired beauty, Dottie resembled her father in intelligence, and, according to family lore, she had possessed the highest IQ in the school when she attended Central High. But in both looks and domesticity, she was more like her mother.[12] She had married Homer Rogers, a pilot and war hero with a big baritone voice whom everybody called Buck Rogers, although he was modest about his war exploits. Homer was a convivial, energetic cattleman, as beefy as the oversize steers he bought and sold. The Rogerses always had a crowd at their house, Dottie playing piano while Homer sang something like "Katie, Katie, get off the table, the money's for the beer." Susie and Warren did not take part in the Rogerses' active social life, since they tended to be more serious-minded and they did not drink, but the sisters spent a lot of time together on their own. Dottie had always had difficulty making decisions, and since having her first son, Billy, she seemed dazed at the demands of motherhood. Susie, naturally, took charge and helped her.

Susie had also become close to her sister-in-law Doris, who was working in Omaha as a schoolteacher now that she was married. Her husband, Truman Wood, was a handsome man with a pleasant personality who came from a prominent Omaha family, but Doris was starting to wonder if she was a racing filly hitched to a Clydesdale. A girl of action, Doris told Truman to giddyup. He ambled along a little faster, but not much.

Susie's protectiveness toward Warren and his sister ticked up a notch in January 1953 after Eisenhower was sworn in, when Howard's final congressional term ended and he and Leila returned to Nebraska for good. Doris and Warren felt the strain of having Leila back in town. Warren could hardly bear to be in the same room with his mother, and she still turned on Doris periodically.

Howard was at loose ends back in Omaha. Warren set up a partnership, Buffett & Buffett, that formalized the way they had occasionally bought stocks together. Howard contributed some capital, and Warren's contribution was a token amount of money, but mostly ideas and labor. But Howard looked at going back into the stockbroking business for the third time with dismay. Warren had been tending his old accounts while he served in Congress, but Howard knew that Warren hated it, had never stopped trying to get Ben Graham to hire him, and would leave in an instant if he could go to New York. For his part, Howard missed his true love, politics. He harbored a desire to enter the Senate, especially now that there was a Republican in the White House. Yet his ambitions conflicted with his extreme political views.

On July 30, 1953—Alice Buffett's birthday—Susie and Warren's first child, a daughter, was born. They named her Susan Alice and called her Little Susie, sometimes Little Sooz. And Susie became a passionate, playful, and devoted mother.

Little Susie was Howard and Leila's first grandchild. A week later, Susie's sister, Dottie, gave birth to her second son, Tommy. Within months, Doris became pregnant with her first child, a daughter, Robin Wood. By the spring of 1954, Susie was pregnant with her second child. Now the Buffetts and Thompsons had a new focus—grandchildren.

A few months later, a moment came when it looked as though Howard's time might have arrived. On the morning of July 1, 1954, news came from Washington that Nebraska's senior Senator, Hugh Butler, had been rushed to the hospital with a stroke and was not expected to live. The deadline for entering the primary election that would fill his Senate seat was that very night. Howard's sense of propriety was such that he refused to file the papers to run until Butler had actually died, so the Buffetts waited anxiously all day for news. Howard's local name recognition meant that if he ran in a special election without having to go through the party nominating process, even though the party bigwigs were disenchanted with him, the odds were excellent that he could win.

Word of Butler's death came in the early evening, after Secretary of State Frank Marsh's office had closed at its usual five p.m. Howard threw his candidacy filing in the car and he and Leila drove to Lincoln, assuming that they had plenty of time because the deadline was midnight. They tried to file the papers at Marsh's home, but he refused them, even though Howard had paid the filing fee earlier in the day. Infuriated, they returned to Omaha.

The state Republican convention was in session at the time, and on the news of Butler's death, delegates on the floor elected a temporary successor to serve out his term.[13] Anyone serving would more or less automatically be elected to Butler's job in November. As the ranking Republican in the state, Howard was an obvious choice. But he was seen as a zealot, as a guy who tilted at windmills, unyielding on trivial ethical matters and disloyal to his own party for not supporting Eisenhower. Instead, the convention elected Roman Hruska, the well-liked Congressman who had taken Howard's seat when he retired. Howard and Leila sped back to Lincoln and quickly filed suit with the State Supreme Court to force the party to accept his nomination. But twenty-four hours later, they gave up the futile fight and dropped the lawsuit.

Warren was furious when he heard the news about Hruska. "They slit Daddy's throat from ear to ear," he said. How dare the party repay Howard's decades of loyalty this way?

At fifty-one years of age, Howard had just seen his future disappear. As his anger ebbed, his depression grew. He had been shut out of the arena that was the center of his life, that made him feel useful in the world. He ended up going back to work at Buffett-Falk.

Leila dissolved in a pool of misery. Through the reflected glory it bestowed on her, Howard's position in the world may have meant even more to her than it did to him. Her sister Edie was now living in Brazil, Bertie lived in Chicago, and her relationships with Doris and Warren were unsettled at best, so she had only twenty-two-year-old Susie to lean on. But Susie was a busy, pregnant young mother, who had her hands full caring for Warren as well.

And soon, Susie would no longer be in Omaha. For two years, Warren had kept corresponding with Ben Graham. He suggested stock ideas like Greif Bros. Cooperage, a company he and his father had bought for their partnership. He traveled to New York periodically and dropped in on Graham-Newman.

"I would always try to see Mr. Graham."

Surely it wasn't typical for former students to hang about at Graham-Newman.

"No, well, I was persistent."

By the time the local Republican Party slammed the door to the Senate nomination in his father's face, Warren was already on his way to New York. *"Ben wrote and said, 'Come on back.' His partner, Jerry Newman, explained it by saying, 'You know, we just checked you out a little further.' I felt I'd struck the mother lode."* Whether he would accept the position was never in question. And this time, the National Guard said yes.

Warren was so excited about being hired that he arrived in New York on August 1, 1954, and showed up at his new job at Graham-Newman on August 2, a month before his official starting date. There, he discovered that a week earlier, tragedy had struck Ben Graham. Four weeks shy of his own twenty-fourth birthday, Warren wrote his father: "Ben Graham's son Newton (26) who was in the Army in France committed suicide last week. He had always been a little unbalanced. However Graham didn't know it had been a suicide til he read it in the *New York Times* on an Army release, which of course is really tough."[14] When he went to France to collect his son's remains, Ben met Newton's girlfriend, Marie Louise Amingues, known as Malou, who was several years older than Newton. He returned a few weeks later but was never quite the same afterward. He also began to correspond with Malou and made periodic visits back to France. But in those days Warren knew nothing of his idol's personal life.

Instead, he had to attend to his own, for one of his first tasks was to find his family a place to live. Susie and Little Susie had remained in Omaha during his first month in New York City.

Warren searched far and wide for a cheap apartment. He finally settled on a three-bedroom apartment in a white-brick building in the middle-class suburb of White Plains, about thirty miles away in Westchester County, New York. When Susie and Little Susie arrived a few weeks later, the apartment was still not ready, so the family moved into a room in a house in Westchester that was so cramped they had to devise a makeshift crib from a dresser drawer. The Buffetts stayed there only a day or two.

But such were the tales that would later be told about Warren's frugal habits that this story grew into the legend that he was too cheap to buy Little Susie a crib, and she therefore slept in a drawer throughout much of her White Plains infancy.[15]

As the pregnant Susie unpacked and arranged her new household while taking care of their baby and getting to know the neighbors, Warren rose every morning and took the New York Central train to Grand Central. In that first month, he had parked himself in the file room at Graham-Newman and begun to read through every single piece of paper in every single drawer in an entire room filled with big wooden files.

Only eight people worked there: Ben Graham; Jerry Newman; his son Mickey; Bernie, the treasurer; Walter Schloss; two women secretaries; and now Warren. The thin gray laboratory-style jacket Warren had coveted was at last his. *"It was a big moment when they gave me my jacket. We all wore them. Ben wore it, Jerry Newman wore it. We were all equal in our jackets."*

Well, not quite. Warren and Walter sat at desks in a windowless room that contained the ticker machine, the direct lines to the brokerage houses, some reference books and files. Ben, Mickey Newman, or, most commonly, Jerry Newman appeared periodically from their private offices to check a quote on the ticker machine. "We would look up stuff and read. We would go through *Standard & Poor's* or a *Moody's Manual* and look at companies selling below working capital. There were a lot then," recalls Schloss.

These companies were what Graham called "cigar butts": cheap and unloved stocks that had been cast aside like the sticky, mashed stub of a stogie one might find on the sidewalk. Graham specialized in spotting these unappetizing remnants that everyone else overlooked. He coaxed them alight and sucked out one last free puff.

Graham knew that a certain number of cigar butts would turn out foul, and thought it futile to spend time examining any individual cigar butt's quality. The law of averages said most of them were good for a puff. He was always thinking in terms of how much companies would be worth dead—what their assets would be worth if liquidated. Buying at a discount to that value was his "margin of safety"—his backstop against the percentage that presumably would go bankrupt. As a further backstop, he bought tiny positions in a huge number of stocks—the principle of diversification. Graham's idea of diversification was extreme; some of his positions were as small as $1,000.

Warren, who had such confidence in his own judgment, saw no reason to hedge his bets this way and inwardly rolled his eyes at diversification. He and Walter collected numbers from the *Moody's Manuals* and filled out hundreds of the simple forms that Graham-Newman used to make decisions. Once Warren had looked over the field, he narrowed it down to a handful of stocks worth even more careful study, then concentrated his money on what he considered the best bets. He was willing to put *most* of his eggs in one basket, as he had done with GEICO. By that time, however, he had sold his GEICO shares, because he never seemed to have enough money to invest. Every decision had an *opportunity cost*—he had to compare each investing opportunity with the next best one. As much as he liked GEICO, he had made the wrenching decision to sell it after finding another stock that he coveted even more, called Western Insurance. This company was earning $29 a share, and its stock was selling for as little as three bucks.

This was like finding a slot machine that would come up cherries every time you played. If you put in twenty-five cents and pulled the handle, the Western Insurance machine was virtually guaranteed to pay at least two bucks.[16] Anyone sane would play that slot as long as she could stay awake. It was the cheapest stock with the highest margin of safety he'd ever seen in his life. He bought as much of it as he could, and he cut his friends in on the deal.[17]

Warren was a bloodhound for anything free or cheap. With his prodigious ability to absorb numbers and to analyze them, he quickly became the fair-haired boy of Graham-Newman. It came so naturally to him; Ben Graham's cigar butts resembled his old hobby of stooping at the racetrack for cast-off winning tickets.

He paid close attention to what was going on in the back where the partners—Ben, Jerry, and Mickey—worked. Ben Graham was on the board of Philadelphia and Reading Coal & Iron Company, and Graham-Newman controlled the company. Warren had discovered this stock on his own, and by the end of 1954 he had put $35,000 into it. Warren eavesdropped with fascination.[18] Philadelphia and Reading actually wasn't worth much as a business. But it was throwing off extra cash, which it could use to transform itself into a better business by buying another company.

"I was just a peon sitting in the outer office. They bought the Union Underwear Company for Philadelphia and Reading Coal and Iron, creating what became Philadelphia and Reading Corporation.[19] That was the beginning of the company's transformation into something more diversified. I was not in the inner circle, but I was terribly interested, knowing something was going on."

What Warren was learning about by keeping his ears open was the art of capital allocation—placing money where it would earn the highest return. In this case, Graham-Newman was using money from one business to buy a more profitable business. Over time, it could mean the difference between bankruptcy and success.

Transactions like this made Warren feel that he was sitting on the windowsill looking in at high finance as it was taking place. Yet, as he soon found, Graham did not behave like anyone else on Wall Street. He was always mentally reciting poetry or quoting Virgil and was apt to lose packages on the subway. Like Warren, he was indifferent to how he looked. When someone observed, "That's an interesting pair of shoes," Graham looked down at the brown oxford on one foot and the black one on the other and said, without blinking, "Yes, as a matter of fact, I've got another pair just like them at home."[20] Unlike Warren, however, he cared nothing about money for its own sake, nor was he interested in trading as a competitive game. To him, stock-picking was an intellectual exercise.

"One time, we were waiting for an elevator. We were going to eat in the cafeteria down at the bottom of the Chanin Building at Forty-second and Lex. And Ben said to me, 'Remember one thing, Warren: Money isn't making that much difference in how you and I live. We're both going down to the cafeteria for lunch and working every day and having a good time. So don't worry too much about money, because it won't make much difference in how you live.'"

Warren was in awe of Ben Graham, but nonetheless he *was* preoccupied with money. He wanted to amass a lot of it, and saw it as a competitive game. If asked to give up some of his money, Warren responded like a dog fiercely guarding its bone, or even as though he had been attacked. His struggle to let go of the smallest amounts of money was so apparent that it was as if the money possessed him, rather than the other way around.

Susie had learned this only too well. Even within their apartment building,

Warren had quickly earned a reputation for tightfistedness and eccentricity. It was only after he was embarrassed by the state of his shirts at work—for Susie never ironed more than the collar, front placket, and cuffs—that he allowed her to send the shirts to a laundry.[21] He made a deal with a local newsstand to buy week-old magazines at a discount as they were about to be thrown away. He had no car, and when he borrowed that of a neighbor, he never filled up the tank. (When he finally got a car, he washed it only when it was raining, so the rain could do the manual labor of rinsing.)[22]

For Warren, holding on to every penny this way, since he had sold that first pack of chewing gum, was one of the two things that had made him comparatively rich at age twenty-five. The other was collecting more cash. Since Columbia, he had started making money at an accelerating rate. Now, much of his time Warren spent in a reverie, statistics about businesses and their stock prices swirling in his head. When he wasn't studying something, he was teaching it. To keep his Dale Carnegie skills limber so he would not freeze in front of an audience, he got a gig teaching investing for the Scarsdale Adult School at the high school in a nearby suburb. Meanwhile, the Buffetts' social set consisted of couples whose breadwinners were mainly interested in stocks.

Now and then he and Susie were invited to a country club or to dinner parties with other young Wall Street couples. Bill Ruane had introduced him to several new acquaintances, like Henry Brandt, a stockbroker who looked like a disheveled Jerry Lewis and had graduated at the top of his class from Harvard Business School, and his wife, Roxanne. Among the Wall Street set, Warren struck people as the "hickiest person you ever saw," as one of them put it. But when he started holding forth about stocks, the others sat transfixed at his feet, like "Jesus and the apostles," said Roxanne Brandt.[23]

The wives sat by themselves, and while Warren wove his financial spells, Susie charmed the wives with her engaging simplicity. She wanted to know all about their children, or their plans to have children. She knew how to get people to open up to her. She would ask about some big life decision, then, with a soulful look, say, "Any regrets?" Out would come pouring the other person's most intimate feelings. Soon someone she had met half an hour before felt she had a new best friend, even though Susie never confided intimacies in return. People loved her for being so interested in them.

But mostly Susie was on her own as she waited for their second child to be born, her days filled with laundry, shopping, cleaning, and cooking, as well as feeding, changing, and playing with Little Susie. She fed Warren dinner; she supported him at his work as if it were a daily sacrament; she recognized the reverence he felt for Mr. Graham. Warren didn't share the details of his job, which in any case didn't interest her. All the while she continued the patient work of bolstering his confidence, and of "putting him together" by showering him with affection and teaching him about people. One thing she was firm about, however, was the importance of his bonding with their daughter. Warren was not the type to play peekaboo or take over the diaper changing, but he would sing to Little Susie every night.

"I sang 'Over the Rainbow' all the time. It got to be hypnotic, almost like Pavlov's dogs. I don't know whether it was too boring or what—but she'd fall asleep as soon as I started. I'd put her up on my shoulder, and, basically, she would just sort of melt in my arms."

Having hit on a reliable system, Warren never messed with it. While singing, he could easily be off rummaging around in his mental files. So "Over the Rainbow" it was, night after night.

On December 15, 1954, Warren had come home from work because Susie's labor was beginning, and then came a ring at the door. Susie answered it and found a door-to-door missionary who had come to call. She politely invited him to sit down in the living room. And she listened.

So did Warren, who was thinking to himself that only Susie would have let the man inside. Warren began to encourage the conversation to wind down. Agnostic for a number of years, he had no interest in being converted, and his wife was in labor. They needed to get to the hospital.

Susie continued listening. "Tell me more," she said. Now and then she pulsed and moaned slightly as the missionary kept talking.[24] She ignored Warren's signals, obviously feeling it more important to be polite to the visitor and make him feel understood than to get to the hospital. The caller seemed oblivious to the fact that she was in labor. Warren sat there, helpless and increasingly agitated, until the preacher ran out of steam. "I wanted to kill the guy," he says. But they made it to the hospital in ample time, and Howard Graham Buffett arrived early the next morning.

21

The Side to Play

Howie was a "difficult" baby. Whereas Little Sooz had been quiet and placid, Howie was like an alarm clock you couldn't turn off. His parents kept waiting for the clamor to lessen, but it only increased. The apartment suddenly seemed full and noisy all the time.

Of course, it was Big Susie who jumped to the sound of the alarm clock. Not even Howie's howling nights distracted Warren much. In his little office in the apartment's third bedroom, he could lose himself for hours in his thoughts.

At work he had become absorbed in a complicated new project that would become a seminal event in his career. Shortly after Warren joined Graham-Newman, the price of cocoa suddenly spiked from a nickel to more than fifty cents a pound. Over in Brooklyn, Rockwood & Co., a chocolate maker "of limited profitability,"[1] faced a dilemma. Its number one product was Rockwood chocolate bits, the kind of nuggets used in chocolate chip cookies, and the company couldn't raise its prices much on this grocery item, so it began running a huge loss. However, with cocoa-bean prices so high, Rockwood also had a chance to unload the cocoa beans it already owned to reap a windfall profit. Unfortunately, the ensuing tax bill would eat up more than half those profits.[2]

Rockwood's owners approached Graham-Newman as a possible buyer of the company, but Graham-Newman wouldn't pay the asking price. So they turned instead to the investor Jay Pritzker, who had spotted a way to avoid the huge tax bill.[3] What he realized was that the 1954 U.S. Tax Code said that if a company was reducing the scope of its business, it could pay no tax on such a "partial liquidation" of its inventory. So Pritzker bought enough stock to take control of Rockwood, choosing to keep the company going as a maker of chocolate bits, and to get out of the cocoa-butter business. He attributed thirteen million pounds of cocoa beans to the cocoa-butter side of the business, the amount of beans that would be "liquidated."

Rather than sell the beans for cash, however, Pritzker offered them to the other shareholders in exchange for stock. He did so because he wanted their shares to increase his ownership of the company. So he offered them a good deal as an incentive—$36 worth of beans[4] for shares that were trading at $34.[5]

Graham spotted a way to make money from this offer—Graham-Newman could buy Rockwood stock and swap it to Pritzker for cocoa beans it could sell to make a $2 profit on every share. This was arbitrage: two nearly identical things trading at a different price, which enabled a canny trader to simultaneously buy one and sell the other and profit on the difference, with virtually *no* risk. "In Wall Street the old proverb has been reworded," as Buffett wrote later. "Give a man a fish and you feed him for a day. Teach a man to arbitrage and you feed him forever."[6] Pritzker would give Graham-Newman a warehouse certificate, which is just what it sounds like: a piece of paper that says the holder owns so many cocoa beans. It could be traded like a stock. By selling the warehouse certificate, Graham-Newman would make its money.

$34 (G-N's cost for a share of Rockwood—which it turns in to Pritzker)
<u>$36</u> (Pritzker gives G-N a warehouse receipt—which it sells at this price)
$ 2 (Profit on each share of Rockwood stock)

Virtually no risk, however, means there is at least *some* risk. What if the price of cocoa beans dropped, and the warehouse receipt was suddenly worth only $30? Instead of making two dollars, Graham-Newman would lose four bucks for every share of stock. To lock in its profit and eliminate that risk, Graham-Newman sold cocoa "futures." It was a good thing, too—for cocoa prices were about to drop.

The "futures" market lets buyers and sellers agree to exchange commodities like cocoa or gold or bananas in the future at a price agreed upon today. In exchange for a small fee, Graham-Newman could arrange to sell its cocoa beans at a known price for a specified period of time, thus eliminating the risk that the market price would drop. The person on the other side of the trade—who was acquiring the risk that the price would drop—was speculating.[7] If cocoa beans got cheaper, Graham-Newman was protected, because the speculator would have to buy Graham-Newman's cocoa beans for more than they were worth.[8] The speculator's role, from Graham-Newman's perspective, was to sell what amounted to insurance against the risk of the price dropping. At the time, of course, neither knew which way cocoa prices would move.

Thus, the goal of the arbitrage was to buy as many Rockwood shares as possible while at the same time selling an equivalent amount of futures.

Graham-Newman assigned Warren to the Rockwood deal. He was made for it; he had been arbitraging stocks for several years, buying convertible preferred stock and shorting common stock issued by the same company.[9] For several weeks, Warren spent his days shuttling back and forth to Brooklyn on the subway, exchanging stock for warehouse certificates at Schroder Trust. He spent his evenings studying the situation, sunk in thought while singing "Over the Rainbow" to Little Sooz and shutting out the screams as Big Susie struggled to give Howie a bottle.

On the surface, Rockwood was a simple transaction for Graham-Newman: Its only cost was subway tokens, thought, and time. But Warren recognized the potential for even more "financial fireworks" than Graham-Newman had.[10] Unlike Ben Graham, he did *not* do the arbitrage. Thus he did not need to sell cocoa futures either. Instead, he bought 222 shares of Rockwood stock for himself and simply kept it.

Warren had thought through Pritzker's offer carefully. When he divided all the beans Rockwood owned—not just the beans attributed to the cocoa-butter business—by the number of Rockwood shares, it amounted to more than the eighty pounds per share that Pritzker was offering. So people who did *not* turn in their shares would end up with stock worth more cocoa beans per share. Not only that—all the extra beans left on the table by those who did turn in their stock would bump up the number of beans per share even more.

Those who kept their stock would also profit because they wound up with a share of the company's plant, its equipment, money due from customers, and the rest of the Rockwood business that was not being shut down.

Warren had inverted the situation, thinking about it from Pritzker's point of view. If Pritzker was buying, he wondered, *why did it make sense to sell?* And after doing the math, he could see that it didn't make sense. The side to play on was Pritzker's. Warren had looked at the stock as a little slice of the business.

With fewer shares outstanding, his slice was worth more. He was taking more risk than had he simply done the arbitrage—but he was also making a calculated bet with odds heavily in his favor. The $2 profit from the arbitrage was easy to earn, however, and riskless. When the price of cocoa beans dropped, the futures contracts protected Graham-Newman. They, and a significant percentage of other shareholders, accepted Pritzker's offer and left a lot of cocoa beans on the table.

Hanging on to the stock, however, turned out to be a brilliant call. Those who played the arbitrage, like Graham-Newman, made their $2 a share. But Rockwood stock, which had traded for $15 before Pritzker's offer, shot up to $85 after it was over. So instead of making $444 from his 222 shares, as he would have from the arbitrage, Warren's calculated bet earned him an extraordinary sum—around $13,000.[11]

In the process, he had also made a point of getting to know Jay Pritzker. He figured anybody smart enough to have figured out that deal "was going to do more smart things later." He went to a shareholders' meeting and asked some questions, and that was his introduction to Pritzker.[12] Warren was then twenty-five, Pritzker thirty-two.

Even working with a relatively small amount of capital—less than $100,000—Warren saw that by using this kind of thinking he could open up a world of possibilities for himself. His only constraints were the money, energy, and time he had available. It was lumberjack labor, but he loved doing it. This was nothing like the way most people invested: sitting in an office and reading reports that described research performed by other people. Warren was a detective, and he naturally did his own research, just as he had collected bottle caps and thought about fingerprinting nuns.

To do his detective work he used the *Moody's Manuals—Industrial, Banks and Finance,* and *Public Utility.* Often he went down in person to Moody's or Standard & Poor's. "*I was the only one who ever showed up at those places. They never even asked if I was a customer. I would get these files that dated back forty or fifty years. They didn't have copy machines, so I'd sit there and scribble all these little notes, this figure and that figure. They had a library, but you couldn't select from it yourself. You had to request things. So I would name all these companies— Jersey Mortgage, Bankers Commercial, all these things that nobody'd ever requested, ever. They'd bring them out, and I'd sit there taking notes. If you wanted to look at SEC documents, as I often did, I went down to the SEC. That was the only way to get them. Then, if the company was nearby, I might very well go see the management. I didn't make appointments ahead of time. But I got a lot done.*"

One of his favorite sources was the Pink Sheets, a weekly printed on pink paper, which gave information about the stocks of companies so small that they were not traded on a stock exchange. Another was the National Quotation book, which came out only every six months and described stocks of companies so minuscule that they never even made it into the Pink Sheets. No company was too small, no detail too obscure. *"I would pore through volumes of businesses and I'd find one or two that I could put ten or fifteen thousand dollars into that were just <u>ridiculously</u> cheap."*

Warren was not proud; he also felt honored to borrow ideas from Graham, Pritzker, or any useful source. He called that riding coattails and did not care whether the idea was glamorous or mundane. One day he followed up on a lead of Graham's, the Union Street Railway.[13] This was a bus company in New Bedford, Massachusetts, selling at a big discount to its net assets. Through some legwork and a visit to the company's management,[14] he made about $20,000 profit on this one stock in just a few weeks.

Nobody in the history of the Buffett family had ever made $20,000 on one idea. In 1955, that was several times more than the average person earned for a whole year's work. Doubling your money and then some for a few weeks' work was spectacular. And yet, what was more important to him was doing it without taking any significant risk.

Susie and Warren did not talk about the details of cocoa-bean arbitrage and bus-company stocks. She wasn't interested in money, except as something to be spent. And what she knew was that even though waves of money were rolling in to the little apartment in White Plains, Warren gave her only a small household allowance. She hadn't grown up keeping track of every tiny expense, so being married to a man who saved money by making deals with newsstands to buy week-old magazines meant a whole new way of life. She did her best to manage the household herself, but the disparity between what Warren was making and what he gave his wife had become stunning. One day she telephoned her neighbor Madeleine O'Sullivan in a panic.

" Madeleine, something terrible has happened," she said. "You've got to come down here!" Madeleine rushed down to the Buffett apartment and found Susie distraught. She had accidentally thrown a batch of dividend checks that had been sitting on Warren's desk into the apartment's incinerator chute, which led straight down to the building's furnace.[15]

"Maybe the incinerator isn't running," Madeleine said, so they called the building superintendent, who let them into the basement. Sure enough, the incinerator was cold. They rooted through the garbage looking for the checks, with Susie all the while wringing her hands and saying, "I can't face Warren." When they found the checks, Madeleine's eyes grew wide. They were for as much as thousands of dollars, not $25 or $10 as she had assumed.[16] The Buffetts, living in the little apartment in White Plains, were getting truly rich.

Warren's brilliant performance at Graham-Newman had made him the golden boy of the firm. Ben Graham took a personal interest in Warren, and in his warmly outgoing and beleaguered wife. Graham had given them a movie camera and projector as a baby gift when Howie was born, and even showed up at their apartment with a teddy bear for the little boy.[17] On one or two occasions when he and his wife, Estey, had the Buffetts over for dinner, he noticed that Warren gazed googly-eyed at Susie, and that the two of them held hands a lot. But he could also see that Warren did not woo his wife, and that Susie might have liked the occasional romantic gesture.[18] When Susie mentioned with longing that Warren did not dance, Graham dropped by Warren's desk with a gift certificate to the Arthur Murray dance studio in White Plains, where Graham clumped around the dance floor during his own lessons. Graham checked with the studio a little later and found that his protégé had never used the gift certificate. He mentioned this to Warren and encouraged him to go ahead. Now on the hook, Warren stumbled through three lessons with Susie, then dropped out. He never did learn to dance.[19]

This didn't get in the way of his rapid ascent at Graham-Newman. Within eighteen months of his starting there, both Ben Graham and Jerry Newman seemed to be treating Warren as a potential partner, which meant a certain amount of family socializing. In mid-1955, even the dyspeptic Jerry Newman extended an invitation to the Buffetts to what they thought was to be a "picnic" at Meadowpond, the Newmans' mansion in Lewisboro, New York. Susie arrived wearing something suitable for a hayride, only to find the other women in dresses and pearls. Though they felt like a couple of hillbillies, the faux pas did nothing to hurt Warren's golden boy status.

Walter Schloss was not invited to events like these. He had been pigeonholed as a journeyman employee who would never rise to partnership. Jerry Newman, who rarely bothered to be kind to anyone, treated Schloss with more than his usual contempt, so Schloss, married with two young children, decided to strike out on his own. It took him a while to get up the nerve to tell Graham,[20] but by the end of 1955 he had started his own investment partnership, funded with $100,000 raised from a group of partners whose names, as Buffett later put it, "were straight from a roll call at Ellis Island."[21]

Buffett was certain that Schloss could apply Graham's methods successfully and admired him for having the guts to set up his own firm. Though he worried that "Big Walter" was starting out with so little capital that he would not be able to feed his family,[22] Buffett put not a dime of his own money into Schloss's partnership, just as he had not invested in Graham-Newman. It would be unthinkable for Warren Buffett to let someone else invest his money.

He did find someone to replace Schloss, however. Buffett had met Tom Knapp at a luncheon at Blythe and Company down on Wall Street.[23] Ten years older than Warren, tall, handsome, dark-haired, blessed with a wicked sense of humor, Knapp had taken one of David Dodd's night courses and gotten hooked; he changed his major from chemistry to business on the spot. Graham hired Knapp as the second gentile in the firm. "*I told Jerry Newman, 'It's the old story— you hire one gentile, they take over the place,'* " Buffett says.

By the time Knapp was sitting at Walter Schloss's old desk next to Buffett, Warren had begun to be aware of the private side of Graham's life. Knapp himself got initiated when Graham invited him to watch a speech at the New School for Social Research, where, he says, he found himself seated at a table with six women. "As Ben spoke," Knapp says, "I became aware that each one of those women was in love with him. And they didn't seem to be jealous of each other, and they all seemed to know him very, very well."[24]

Indeed, by early 1956, Graham was bored by investing: His outside interests— women, the classics, and fine arts—tugged at him so strongly that he had a foot out the door. One day when Knapp was out, the receptionist directed a gangly young man into the windowless lair where Warren was filling out forms. Looming over him was Ed Anderson, who explained that he was a chemist, like Knapp, not a professional investor. He worked at the Livermore Laboratory of the Atomic Energy Commission in California, but followed the market in his spare time. He had read *The Intelligent Investor,* with its copious examples of cheap stocks like Easy Washing Machine, and was wildly impressed. My God! he thought. That can't be true. How could you buy these companies for less money than they had cash in the bank?[25]

Intrigued, Anderson had been riding Graham's coattails. After buying a single share of Graham-Newman, he used its quarterly statements to figure out what Graham was doing, then bought those stocks. Graham never discouraged this; he liked other people to learn from and emulate him.

Anderson had come in because he was thinking about buying another share of Graham-Newman, but he had noticed an oddity and he wanted to ask about it. Graham had loaded up on shares of American Telephone & Telegraph. It was the least Graham-like stock imaginable—owned, studied, and followed by all, valued fairly, with as little potential as it had risk. Was something going on? he asked Warren.

Warren thought for a second. It was impressive that this man with no business background—a chemist—had the perception to see that AT&T was out of pattern. Too many people thought that "business" was some sort of priesthood practiced only by those with special training. He said to Anderson, "This might not be the best time to buy another share."[26] They chatted a bit longer and then parted in a friendly way, intending to keep up the acquaintance. Warren was very glad that his friend Schloss had gone out on his own. From watching the firm's trading patterns and keeping his ears open, he had already figured out that Graham was going to shut down his partnership.

Ben Graham's career was coming to an end. He was sixty-two years old, and the market had surpassed the peak of 1929.[27] Its priciness made him nervous. He had beaten the market by 2.5 percent for more than twenty years.[28] He wanted to retire and move out to California to enjoy life. Jerry Newman was also retiring, but Mickey, Jerry's son, would stay on. In the spring of 1956 Graham gave notice to his partners. But first he offered Warren the opportunity to become a general partner in the firm. That he would choose someone of Warren's age and experience shows how valuable he had made himself in such a short time. Nevertheless: *"If I had stayed I would have been sort of the Ben Graham of it, and Mickey would have been the Jerry Newman of it—but Mickey would have been the senior partner by miles. It would have been called Newman-Buffett."*

Even though Warren was flattered, he had gone to Graham-Newman to work for Ben. Without Ben there, it wasn't worth it to him to stay, not even to be thought of as Graham's intellectual heir. Moreover, all the while that he was carrying out the bus bell-ringer and the cocoa-bean caper he was thinking, "I don't like living in New York. I'm on the train back and forth all the time." Above all, he was not cut out to work with a partner—least of all as someone's junior partner. He turned the offer down.

22

Hidden Splendor

Omaha · 1956–1958

I had about $174,000, and I was going to retire. I rented a house at 5202 Underwood in Omaha for $175 a month. We'd live on $12,000 a year. My capital would grow."

In retrospect, it would strike people as odd that at the age of twenty-six, Warren used the term "retire."

True, mathematically speaking, Warren could retire on his own money and still reach his goal of being a millionaire by age thirty-five.* Since entering Columbia with $9,800, he had grown his money by more than sixty-one percent a year. But he was in a hurry, and it would require a very aggressive compounding rate to meet his goal.[1] Therefore he had decided to start a partnership like Graham-Newman's sister hedge fund, Newman & Graham.[2] He would have no boss, could invest from his house, and could put friends and relatives into the same stocks that he would have bought for himself. If he took a quarter of every dollar he earned for these partners as a fee and then reinvested that in the partnership, he could be a millionaire much faster. Armed with Ben Graham's method of buying stocks and a Graham-like hedge fund, he had every reason to think of himself as a rich man.

There was only one problem with his idea. He couldn't tolerate it if his partners criticized him because the stocks went down. But Warren planned to invite only his family and friends—people he was sure trusted him—into the

* A million dollars in those days would be worth closer to eight million in 2007.

partnership. On May 1, 1956, he started Buffett Associates, Ltd., a partnership based on the Newman & Graham model,[3] with seven partners.

Doc Thompson invested $25,000. *"Doc Thompson was the kind of guy, he gave me every penny he had, basically. I was his boy."* Warren's sister Doris, with her husband, Truman Wood, put in $10,000. His aunt Alice Buffett put in $35,000. *"I had sold securities to other people before that, but now I became a fiduciary, and for people who were enormously important to me. These were the people who believed in me. There's no way in the world I would have taken my aunt Alice's or my sister's or my father-in-law's money if I had thought that I'd lose it. At that point I didn't think I could lose money over time."*

His Wharton roommate Chuck Peterson, who put in $5,000, became his fourth partner. Chuck had been one of the first to let Warren dispense him scrips as a prescriptionist, buying stocks from him before he went to New York City. Peterson's mother, Elizabeth, invested $25,000 of the money she had inherited when her husband died the year before.

The sixth partner, Dan Monen, was a quiet, stocky, dark-haired young man who used to play with Warren as a child, digging up dandelions in Ernest Buffett's backyard. Now Warren's lawyer, he put in what he could: $5,000.

Warren was the seventh. He put in only $100. The rest of his share would come from future fees he earned by managing the partnership. *"In effect, I got my leverage from managing the partnership. I was brimming with ideas, but I was not brimming with capital."* Actually, by most of the country's standards, Warren *was* brimming with capital. But he viewed the partnership as a compounding machine—once money went into it, he did not intend to make withdrawals. So he needed to earn the $12,000 a year his family would live on from the rest of his funds. He invested that money separately.

He devised a formula to charge his new partners. *"I got half the upside above a four percent threshold, and I took a quarter of the downside myself. So if I broke even, I lost money. And my obligation to pay back losses was not limited to my capital. It was unlimited."*[4]

At the time, Warren was already managing money for Anne Gottschaldt and Catherine Elberfeld, the mother and aunt of Fred Kuhlken, a friend from Columbia. When Fred left for Europe the year before, he had asked Warren to look after part of his aunt's and mother's money.[5] Ever since, Warren had been investing it with utmost caution in government bonds under a different, more modest fee arrangement.

He could have invited Gottschaldt and Elberfeld into the partnership, but he felt that it was unfair to charge them a higher fee than they were already paying. Of course, if the partnership was the sure thing he thought it was, that meant he was depriving them of a golden opportunity. If something went wrong with the investments, however, his aunt and his sister and Doc Thompson would never condemn him. He wasn't so sure about anybody else.

Acting as a "fiduciary" meant to Warren that any responsibility he took on would be unlimited. To lay out the ground rules for his partners, he called the first official meeting of Buffett Associates on the very day he founded the partnership. Chuck got them a reservation for dinner at the Omaha Club, the best place in town if you wanted a private room. Warren meant to carefully define and limit his responsibilities; one responsibility he was not assuming was picking up the check for dinner. He told Chuck to pass the word that everyone was going dutch.[6] He then used the dinner as an opportunity to talk not just about the partnership's ground rules, but about the stock market. Already he viewed the partnership as a teaching exercise.

The partners quickly split into two camps: the teetotalers and the rest. From his end of the table, Doc Thompson suggested, in a paternal way, that the other faction was going to hell. It was Warren, however, who was the preacher that night; they were there for him to hold forth.

"I started with an agreement with the investors, which has not needed to be changed much as we've evolved. All kinds of good things have flowed out of that, you know. It is the least complicated thing I can imagine.

"I gave them a little summary of the ground rules: Here's what I can do. Here's what I can't do. And here are some things I don't know whether I can do or not. Here's how I'll judge myself. It was fairly short. If you don't feel this way you shouldn't join, because I don't want you unhappy while I'm happy or vice versa."[7]

After Warren launched the partnership, the Buffetts returned to New York for their final summer. Mickey Newman was now the CEO of Philadelphia & Reading, a full-time job. With neither he nor Warren available to serve as general partner, Graham had decided to shut down the firm.[8] Warren was helping Graham wind the partnership down. He rented a rustic seaside cottage on Long Island for his family from his friend Tom Knapp. The house, part of a group built for people fleeing an influenza epidemic many years before, sat on West Meadow Beach, near Stony Brook on Long Island's North Shore, and faced Connecticut, across Long Island Sound.

During the week, Warren saved money by bunking in the city with his stockbroker friend Henry Brandt, whose wife and children were also summering on Long Island. On the weekends he joined his family at the shore and worked in a tiny bedroom in the house. The neighbors told the Knapps they never saw him.[9] While Warren worked, Susie, who was afraid of the water and never swam, beachcombed with the kids along the bluffs near the water's edge. Since the cottage had minimal plumbing facilities, the Buffetts fetched drinking water from a spring across the street, and Susie bathed Little Susie, now almost three, Howie, eighteen months old, and herself in the unheated outdoor shower.

That summer brought them two pieces of shocking news. The father of Warren's boyhood friend Bob Russell had committed suicide. And Anne Gottschaldt and Catherine Elberfeld, the mother and aunt of Fred Kuhlken, Warren's friend from Columbia, called to say that Fred had been killed in Portugal after his car skidded eighty feet and rammed into a cork tree.[10]

As the summer ended, the Buffetts made their plans to return to Omaha. The extreme caution Warren displayed in trying never to disappoint anyone stood in sharp contrast with his risky decision to pursue an investing career working on his own outside of New York City. The market was composed of relationships, people who lunched together at the Stock Exchange or played poker once a week. It hummed along on tips and rumors, gossip passed on by personal contacts and connections made at investor luncheons, in bars, on squash courts, at chance meetings at university-club coat checks. While every small regional city had its little brokerage firms—like Buffett-Falk—these were not important players. The hinterlands were staffed by stockbrokers—prescriptionists who filled the scrips written by the Manhattan money doctors. At that time, no serious American money man worked anywhere but New York City. To leave all this, to go it alone, to think of getting really rich anywhere farther than a limo ride from Wall and Broad, was a truly bold and venturesome stroke.

Indeed, for a college graduate to become self-employed, to work at home, to work alone, was strikingly unusual in the 1950s. The Man in the Gray Flannel Suit was the guy who got ahead.[11] Businessmen joined a big organization—the bigger the better—then competed with polished ferocity for the best-paying job on the steady climb up the ladder of success, trying not to break a sweat or a golf club along the way. They competed to amass not riches but power—or at the very least to buy the right kind of house in a good suburban neighborhood, to get a new-model car every year, and to pave the way for a lifetime of security.

Well aware of her husband's unusual qualities—if not of the apparent riskiness of the course he was charting—Susie flew to Omaha with Little Susie and Howie and moved them all into the house on Underwood Avenue Warren had rented from Chuck Peterson. He had chosen an inviting gray two-story Tudor with picturesque half-beams, a big stone chimney, and a cathedral ceiling. Even the decision to rent a home had been unconventional; owning a home was the quintessence of what most young Americans aspired to in the mid-1950s. The hopelessness of the Depression and the dreary wartime days of making do were fading into memory. Americans stocked their new houses with all the exciting new features and appliances that were suddenly available: washer-dryers, freezers, dishwashers, electric mixers. The Buffetts had plenty of money to buy all these things. But Warren had other plans for his capital, so they rented. And the house they were renting, while attractive, was just barely big enough for them. Howie at almost two would have to sleep in a largish closet.

As Susie began to settle her family in Omaha, Warren closed out his affairs in New York. He sent out notices to the companies whose stocks he owned to ensure that the dividend checks followed him to Omaha. Then he got in his car and started driving back to Nebraska, visiting companies along the way.

"I did this zigzag across the country. I just thought it was a great time to hit these companies. I drove through Hazleton, Pennsylvania, and visited the Jeddo-Highland Coal Company. I went through Kalamazoo, and saw the Kalamazoo Stove and Furnace Company. This little odyssey went through Delaware, Ohio, and I visited Greif Bros. Cooperage. That was a company selling at a ridiculously cheap price"— a company he had first discovered in 1951 by flipping through the Moody's Manuals. He and his father had each bought two hundred shares and put them in their little partnership.

Warren arrived in Omaha toward the end of the summer and found that he was needed at home. Little Sooz, calm and timid, sat watching while her brother's inexhaustible demands vacuumed up her mother's energies.[12] But in the evenings she wanted her father; she was now afraid to go to bed. When they arrived at the house on Underwood, a moving-company man wearing glasses had spoken to her, and though she did not remember his saying anything untoward, she was now convinced that the "glasses man" lurked just outside her bedroom, next to a wrought-iron balcony that overlooked the living room. Warren had to inspect the balcony every night and reassure her that it was safe to go to sleep.

After he had taken care of the "glasses man," he went down the hall to the tiny sunporch off his and Susie's bedroom and got down to business, either partnership work or preparing his lessons—for the first thing he had done when he returned to Omaha, besides forming a partnership, was to take on two classes for the fall semester at the University of Omaha: Investment Analysis for Men Only, and Intelligent Investing. Before long he would add a third course, Investing for Women. The terrified boy who so recently couldn't even strike up a conversation in a Dale Carnegie class had vanished. In his place was a still-awkward young man who nonetheless made a striking impression as he moved restlessly around the room, exhorting the students and spouting an inexhaustible series of facts and figures. Dressed as usual in a cheap suit that looked a couple of sizes too large, he seemed more like a youngish preacher from some missionary sect than a college lecturer.

Despite his brilliance, Warren was still very immature. For Susie, his helplessness at home meant that he was like having a third child to care for. His personality and interests also shaped their social life. In Omaha, a midsize Midwestern city with relatively few important cultural institutions, weekends were filled with weddings, parties, teas, and charity events. The Buffetts lived a much quieter life than most young married couples of their class and era. Most of their social life took place at dinner with other couples or at occasional dinner parties where Warren could talk about stocks. It was always the same: Warren entertained, either holding forth to an audience on stocks or playing the ukulele. Under Susie's tutelage, he could now exchange remarks about other subjects more easily than before, but his mind remained fixated on making money. During meals and parties at home, he often fled small talk by leaving the table to go upstairs. But unlike Ben Graham, he was not upstairs reading Proust; he was working.

All Warren's recreations remained repetitive, competitive, or, better yet, both. He found playing bridge with Susie unendurable because she wanted the other side to win, and soon sought other partners.[13] His mind was like a restless monkey; to relax, he needed an active form of concentration that could keep the monkey occupied. Ping-Pong, bridge, poker, golf all absorbed him and took his mind off money temporarily. But he never lazed around a swimming pool, stargazed, or simply went for a walk in the woods. A stargazing Warren would have looked at the Big Dipper and seen a dollar sign.

All of this, plus his nonconformist streak, meant that Warren was not a "joiner," sitting through committee and board meetings. Family loyalty did lead him to say yes when his uncle Fred Buffett came over to the house and asked him to join the Rotary Club. On the other hand, when asked to join the Knights of Ak-Sar-Ben, a more important group of civic leaders that combined philanthropy, business, boosterism, and social activities, he said no. For a budding money manager who needed to raise funds for his business, that was like thumbing his nose in the faces of the men who ran Omaha—an act of cocky self-assurance, even arrogance, which set him apart from much of his social set. His sister Doris had made her debut as a Princess of Ak-Sar-Ben. Friends like Chuck Peterson were regulars on its social circuit. As a Congressman, Howard had been obliged to join. But Warren disdained the smoke-filled backroom clubbiness and conformity of the Ak-Sar-Ben crowd. These were the people who had looked down on his father as the "son of a grocer man." Warren reveled in the chance to spurn Ak-Sar-Ben, and disparaged it with withering comments.

Susie had her own brand of nonconformity. Since high school, she had prided herself on her openness and her commitment to inclusiveness at a time when most people chose friends who were religious, cultural, ethnic, and economic clones. Many of her friends—and by this time many of Warren's—were Jewish. In segregated Omaha, choosing to cross these social lines was a bold, even defiant act. Susie was aware of this, just as she had been aware in high school and college that dating a Jew was considered shocking, especially to her own family. Her social status had value to her mostly as a way to make her friends feel more included. Warren, the anti-elitist, found this aspect of Susie highly attractive. And the Jewish friends he'd made at Columbia and while working for Graham-Newman had opened his eyes to anti-Semitism.

In contrast to Susie, Warren's mother had always been obsessed with fitting in. Leila had researched her ancestry and joined the Daughters of the American Revolution and the Huguenot Society, perhaps searching the past for a stability that she could not find in the present, and certainly not in her immediate family. She had recently received word from Norfolk State Hospital that her sister Bernice had thrown herself into the river in an apparent suicide attempt. Leila, now responsible for Bernice and their mother, handled their affairs in businesslike fashion, striving to be a dutiful daughter while keeping some distance from the family's problems. The Stahl family's history of mental illness was a threatening and shameful topic in the Buffett family, just as it was in society as a whole at the time. The Buffetts' perception of the family history was further muddied by uncertainty over Stella's and Bernice's diagnoses. The doctors could give only vague descriptions of what were clearly serious problems. Obviously, however, the mental illness was inherited, and it manifested in adulthood. Warren and Doris, who were close to their aunt Edie, knew that their mother had grown apart from her as Edie, too, had become more impulsive and moody. They had some suspicions that Leila's own behavior and personality might be at least partly related to the family lineage. The ticking clock hung over them, and they examined themselves for any signs of abnormality.

Warren, who desperately wanted to be but had never felt "normal," assuaged his anxiety with statistics, reasoning that the mysterious disorder seemed to affect only the family's women. He never dwelled on the unpleasant. He would later come to think of his memory as functioning like a bathtub. The tub filled with ideas and experiences and matters that interested him. When he had no more use for information, *whoosh*—the plug popped up, and the memory drained away. If new information about a subject appeared, it would replace the old version. If he didn't want to think about something at all, down the drain it went. Certain events, facts, memories, and even people appeared to vanish. Painful memories were the first to be flushed. The bathtub memory's efficiency freed up enormous amounts of space for the new and the productive. Buffett thought of the bathtub memory as a helper that allowed him to "look forward," rather than "looking backward" all the time like his mother. And it allowed him, at the age of twenty-six, to ruminate in depth on business to the exclusion of almost everything else—in pursuit of his goal of becoming a millionaire.

The fastest way to that goal was to raise more money to manage. In August, he went back to New York to attend the final shareholders' meeting of the Graham-Newman Corporation. Everyone important on Wall Street seemed to be present at Graham-Newman's wake. Investor Lou Green, his head wreathed in clouds of foul-smelling smoke from an enormous stogie, towered over them from his six-foot-four height.[14] Why had Graham and Newman not developed talent? he asked. "They'd been working here for thirty years building up this business," he declared to everyone standing nearby. "And all they would have had to run it was this kid named Warren Buffett. He's the best they could come up with. And who'd want to ride with him?"[15]

Warren's long-ago mistake of telling Lou Green that he bought Marshall-Wells "because Ben Graham bought it" had now come back to dilute Graham's endorsement of him in front of an important audience. Yet Graham's imprimatur had already paid him one important dividend. Homer Dodge, a Harvard-educated physics professor who was the president of Norwich University in Northfield, Vermont, until 1951, and a longtime investor in Graham-Newman, had gone to Graham and asked him what he should do with his money now that Graham-Newman was shutting down. *And Ben said, 'Well, I've got this fellow who used to work with us that might be a possibility.'*

So one hot Midwestern day that July, Dodge had stopped in Omaha on his way to a vacation out west, a blue canoe strapped to the roof of his woody wagon. *"He talked to me for a while and said, 'Would you handle my money?' And I set up a separate partnership for him."*

Dodge gave him $120,000 to manage in the Buffett Fund, Ltd., on September 1, 1956.[16] That was more money than the original Buffett Associates partnership—an enormous step* that made Warren a professional money manager, not just a former stockbroker running a little money for his family and friends. Now he had invested for someone recommended by *Ben Graham*.[17]

With the formation of a third partnership, B-C, seeded by his father's former associate John Cleary,[18] by October 1, 1956, Warren was now managing more than half a million dollars, including his own money, which was not in any of the partnerships. He operated out of a tiny study at home that could be entered only by passing through the bedroom. He worked odd hours, a night owl like Susie, reading annual reports in his pajamas, drinking Pepsi-Cola and eating Kitty Clover potato chips, enjoying the freedom and solitude. He pored over the *Moody's Manuals* looking for ideas, absorbing statistics on company after company. During the day, he went to the library and read newspapers and industry trade magazines. He typed his own letters on an IBM typewriter, carefully lining up his letterhead sheet on the carriage. To make copies he slid sheets of blue carbon paper and tissue-thin onionskin behind the first page. He did all his own filing. He did the bookkeeping himself and prepared his own tax returns. With its numbers, accuracy, and the measuring of results, the record-keeping aspect of the job pleased him.

Every stock certificate was delivered directly to him, made out in the partnerships' names, rather than left on deposit with a broker as was the usual practice. When they arrived, he carried them—smooth cream-colored diplomas in investing, engraved with finely etched drawings of railroads and bald eagles, sea beasts and toga-clad women—down to the Omaha National Bank in his own hands and placed them in a safe-deposit box. Whenever he sold a stock, he went to the bank, riffled through the collection of certificates, and mailed off the correct ones from the post office on 38th Street. The bank would call to let him

---

* Suppose Warren earned 15% for the Buffett Associates partnership. His fee would be $5,781 after each partner got their set 4% interest. With Homer Dodge's money he would earn fees of $9,081 in total. He would invest his fees back into the partnerships. The next year, he would get 100% of the earnings on that $9,081, plus another round of fees on the others' capital. And so on.

know when a dividend check came in to be deposited, and he would go there, examine the check, and endorse it personally.

He tied up the family's single telephone line with his daily calls to the handful of brokers he used. His expenses were as close to zero as he could get. He listed them by hand on a lined sheet of yellow paper: 31¢ for postage, $15.32 for a *Moody's Manual,* $4.00 for the *Oil & Gas Journal,* $3.08 for telephone calls.[19] Except for more meticulous accounting and a great deal more thought, he ran the business much as though he were just anybody trading stocks through a broker for a personal account.

At the end of 1956, Warren wrote a letter to the partners outlining the partnership's results at year-end. He reported that it had earned a total income of slightly more than $4,500, beating the market by about four percent.[20] By then, Dan Monen, his lawyer, had joined Warren on a personal side project that he had been pursuing for some time: buying the stock of an Omaha-based insurer, National American Fire Insurance. This company's worthless stock had been sold to farmers all over Nebraska in 1919 by unscrupulous promoters in exchange for the Liberty Bonds issued during World War I.[21] Since then, its certificates had lain crumbling in drawers, while their owners gradually lost hope of ever seeing their money again.

Warren had discovered National American while working at Buffett-Falk, flipping through the *Moody's Manual.*[22] The company was headquartered only a block away from his father's office. William Ahmanson, a prominent Omaha insurance agent, had originally been sucked into it unawares, set up as a local front man for what had started out as a fraud. But the Ahmanson family had gradually turned it into a legitimate company. Now Howard Ahmanson, William's son, was feeding top-drawer insurance business into National American through Home Savings of America, a company he had founded in California, which was becoming one of the largest and most successful savings-and-loan companies in the United States.[23]

The defrauded farmers had no idea that their moldering paper was now worth something. Howard had been quietly buying the stock back from them on the cheap for years through his younger brother Hayden, who ran National American. By now the Ahmansons owned seventy percent of the company.

Warren admired Howard Ahmanson. *"Nobody else was quite as audacious at managing capital as Howard Ahmanson. He was very shrewd in a lot of ways. Formerly, a lot of people came in to Home Savings and paid their mortgages in person. Howard put the mortgage at the farthest branch away from where you lived so that you paid by mail and didn't spend half an hour of one of his guys' time telling them about your kids. Everybody else had been to see* It's a Wonderful Life *and felt that you should do this Jimmy Stewart stuff, but Howard didn't want to see his customers. His operating costs were way under anybody else's."*

National American was earning $29 per share, and Howard's brother Hayden was buying its stock for around $30 per share. Thus, as with the rarest and most attractive of the cheap stocks that Warren stalked, the Ahmansons could pay virtually the entire cost of buying a share of stock out of one year's profits from that single share. National American was one of the cheapest stocks Warren had ever seen. And it was a nice little company, too, not a soggy cigar butt.

"I tried to buy the stock for a long time. But none of it was getting to me, because there was a security dealer in town and Hayden had given this guy the shareholders list. This stockbroker—he regarded me as a punk kid. But he had the list. And I didn't have the list. So he was buying the stock at thirty for Hayden's account."

Cash on the barrel from Hayden Ahmanson sounded good to some of the farmers compared to their worthless certificates. Though they had paid around $100 per share many years before and were only receiving $30, many of them had gradually convinced themselves that they were better off without the stock.

Warren was determined. *"I looked it up in some insurance book or something. If you went back to the twenties you could see who were the directors. They made some of these bigger stockholders the directors from the towns they worked the hardest for sales. There was a town called Ewing, Nebraska, which has got no population at all. But somebody sold a lot of stock out there. And that's how they probably got the local banker on the board thirty-five years earlier."*

So Dan Monen, Warren's partner and proxy, went off to the countryside carrying wads of Warren's money and some of his own. He cruised around the state in a red-and-white Chevrolet, showing up in rural county courthouses and banks, casually asking who might own shares of National American.[24] He sat on front porches, drinking iced tea, eating pie with farmers and their wives, and offering cash for their stock certificates.[25]

"I didn't want Howard to know because I was topping his price. He had been picking it off at thirty bucks, and I'd had to raise the price some. The shareholders had been listening for probably ten years at thirty bucks, so it was the first time the price moved.

"Finally, toward the end, I paid a hundred. That was the magic number, because it was what they'd paid in the first place. A hundred bucks, I knew, would

bring out all the stock. And sure enough, one guy came in when Dan Monen was doing this and he said, 'We bought this like sheep, and we're selling it like sheep.'"[26]

That they were. Many had sold at less than three times the $29 a year the company was earning. Monen eventually accumulated ten percent of National American's stock. Warren kept it in the original shareholders' names, with a power of attorney attached that gave him control, rather than transferring it into his name. *"That would have tipped Howard off to the fact that I was out there competing with him. He didn't know. Or, if he did, he had insufficient information. I just kept collecting shares. Then, the day I walked into Hayden's office, I plopped them all down and said I wanted to transfer them to my name. And he said, 'My brother's going to kill me.' But in the end, he transferred the stock."*[27]

The brainstorm behind Warren's National American coup had been more than just the price. He had learned the value of gathering as much as possible of something scarce. From license plates to nuns' fingerprints to coins and stamps, to the Union Street Railway, and National American, he had always thought this way, a born collector.[28]

Alas, this voracious instinct could steer him awry on occasion. Tom Knapp, who had gone to work for a small broker, Tweedy, Browne and Reilly, after helping Jerry Newman close down the remnants of Graham-Newman, came out to visit Warren and to go hear Ben Graham give a speech in Beloit, Wisconsin. Driving through the Iowa cornfields on the way, Knapp mentioned that the U.S. government was about to take the four-cent Blue Eagle stamp out of circulation. The cash register *dinged!* in Warren's head. "Let's stop at a few post offices and see if they have any four-cent stamps," he said on the way back. Knapp went into the first post office and returned to say that it had twenty-eight stamps. "Go buy them," said Buffett. They talked about it some more and decided to write to post offices after they returned home, to offer to buy their stamp inventory. The stamps started coming in a few thousand at a time. Then Denver replied and said they had twenty pads. A pad is a hundred sheets of a hundred stamps. That meant Denver had two hundred thousand stamps.

"We might as well control the issue," Warren said. They spent $8,000 and bought the pads.

"And that was our mistake," says Knapp. "We should have let the Denver post office send them back to Washington to reduce the supply."

Through expending enormous effort to become virtual post offices themselves—with most of the work done by Knapp—they gathered more than six hundred thousand Blue Eagle stamps, collectively spending roughly $25,000. For Warren that was a lot, considering his attitude about money and his net worth. They stored the piles of stamps in their basements. And then they realized what they had done. They had laboriously acquired basements full of stamps that would never be worth more than four cents apiece. "When you have so many stamps," Knapp explains, "there are not many collectors."

So the next task became disposing of the stamps. Warren expertly delegated the problem of getting rid of $25,000 worth of four-cent stamps to Tom. Then he simply put it out of his mind, except for the funny story, and instead turned back to what was actually important: raising money for the partnerships.

In the summer of 1957, Buffett got a call from Dr. Edwin Davis, a prominent urologist in town. He had been referred to Buffett by one of his patients, Arthur Wiesenberger of New York City, one of the most famous money managers of the era. Buffett was familiar with Wiesenberger because he published *Investment Companies*, an annual "bible" on closed-end investment funds, which were like publicly traded mutual funds, except that they did not accept new investors. Since they nearly always sold at a discount to the value of their assets, they were like mutual-fund cigar butts. Wiesenberger was a proponent of buying them.[29] The summer before graduate school, Warren had sat in a chair at Buffett-Falk's office, reading Wiesenberger's bible while Howard worked. While at Graham-Newman, he also managed to meet Wiesenberger, who had been impressed by Buffett, *"even though I wasn't very impressive in those days."*

In 1957, Wiesenberger referred Buffett to Davis as a money manager. "I tried to hire him myself," said Wiesenberger, "but he was forming a partnership and so I couldn't."[30] He urged Davis to consider investing with Buffett.

Shortly after Davis called him, Warren scheduled a meeting with the Davis family on a Sunday afternoon. *"I went down to their place and sat in their living room and talked to them for about an hour. I said, 'Here's how I manage money and the arrangement I have.' I was probably twenty-six. I looked about twenty years old at the time."* Actually, he looked more like eighteen, according to Eddie Davis: "His collar was open; his coat was too big. He talked so very fast." At the time, Warren went around Omaha wearing a mangy sweater—which one person observed probably should have been given to Goodwill—an old pair of pants, and scuffed shoes. *"I acted immature for my age,"* Buffett recalls. *"The kind of things I talked about were what you would expect from a much younger person."* In fact, there was still more than a trace of the hand-drumming, "Mammy"-singing boy from Penn. *"You had to overlook a lot back then."*

But Warren was not there to sell the Davises. He laid out his ground rules. He wanted absolute control over the money and would tell his partners nothing about how it was invested. That was the sticking point. Not for him was Ben Graham's handicap of people riding on his coattails. They would get an annual summary of his performance, and they could put money in or withdraw it only on December 31. The rest of the year, their money would be locked into the partnership.

"All the while, Eddie paid no attention to me. Dorothy Davis listened very intently, asking good questions. Eddie was over in the corner doing nothing. He seemed like a very old guy to me, but he was not yet seventy. When we got all the way through, Dorothy turned to Eddie and said, 'What do you think?' Eddie said, 'Let's give him a hundred thousand dollars.' In a much more polite way, I said, 'Dr. Davis, you know, I'm delighted to get this money. But you weren't really paying a lot of attention to me while I was talking. How come you're doing it?'

"And he said, 'Well, you remind me of Charlie Munger.'[31]

"I said, 'Well, I don't know who Charlie Munger is, but I really like him.'"

But the other reason the Davises were so willing to invest with Warren was because, to their surprise, he "knew more about Arthur Wiesenberger than they did."[32] They also liked the way he laid out his terms—clear and transparent, so they knew whose side he was on. He would win or lose along with them. As Dorothy Davis put it, "He's smart, he's bright, and I can tell he's honest. I like everything about this young man." On August 5, 1957, the money from the Davises and their three children seeded the Dacee partnership with $100,000.[33]

With Dacee, Warren's business jumped another leg upward. He could now land bigger positions in larger stocks. In his personal portfolio, he still played with things like the "penny" uranium stocks that had been in vogue a few years earlier when the government was buying uranium. These were now fantastically cheap.[34] Warren bought companies like Hidden Splendor, Stanrock, Northspan. *"There were some attractive issues—it was shooting fish in a barrel. They weren't huge fish, but you were shooting them in a barrel. You knew you were going to make good money. It was minor. The bigger stuff I was putting in the partnerships."*

Having new partners meant more money, of course, but it also meant that the number of stock certificates and amount of paperwork managing the five partnerships plus Buffett & Buffett increased substantially. He had to hustle, but it felt good. The shortfall, as always, was money—he never seemed to have enough. The kind of companies he was researching often had market values of one to ten million dollars, so he wanted as much as $100,000 to get a significant position in their stocks. Getting more money to manage was key.

At the time, Warren Buffett probably understood the potential of money management to beget more money better than anyone on Wall Street. Every dollar added to a partnership would net him a share of what he earned for his partners.[35] Each of those dollars, reinvested, would generate earnings of its own.[36] Those earnings, reinvested, would beget still more earnings. The better his performance, the more he would earn, and the larger his share of the partnerships would grow, enabling him to earn even more. His talent for investing could exploit that potential of managing money to the hilt. And despite Warren's apparent awkwardness, he was indisputably successful at merchandising himself. In short order, he had formed two more partnerships: Underwood, with $85,000 more from Elizabeth Peterson, and Mo-Buff, with $70,000 from Dan Monen and his wife, Mary Ellen, thanks to the money Monen had made from the National American shares. Even though Warren was nearly invisible in the investing world, the snowball was starting to roll.

With momentum behind him, Warren realized it was time to leave a house where there was barely room for a family with two young children—one an unusually energetic three-and-a-half-year-old—and a third on the way. The Buffetts bought their first house. While the largest house on the block, it had an unpretentious and charming air, with dormers set into the sloping shingled roof and an eyebrow window.[37] Warren paid $31,500 to Sam Reynolds, a local businessman, and promptly named it "Buffett's Folly."[38] In his mind $31,500 was a million dollars after compounding for a dozen years or so, because he could invest it at such an impressive rate of return. Thus, he felt as though he were spending an outrageous million dollars on the house.

Just before the moving van left the house on Underwood Avenue, Warren took five-year-old Little Susie back up the stairs to the wrought-iron balcony. "The glasses man is staying here," he said. "You need to say good-bye to him." Susie Jr. said good-bye, and, indeed, the glasses man remained behind.[39]

Big Susie's job was to oversee the move and lasso Howie while more than eight months pregnant with her third child. As longtime friends observed, Howie was a "hell-raiser." The inexhaustible Buffett energy poured from him in such a whirlwind that he was nicknamed the Tornado, a cousin to Warren's childhood nickname, Firebolt—but with a very different connotation. As soon as Howie could walk, he became peripatetic. He dug up the garden with his Tonka toys; when Susie took them away, he tore the house apart to find them. When Susie snatched away the front-loader, the battle was repeated.[40]

A week after arriving at Farnam Street and just a day before the Mo-Buff partnership was born, the Buffetts' second son, Peter, arrived. From the start he was a quiet, easy baby. But shortly after his birth, Susie came down with a kidney infection.[41] Since her rheumatic fever and ear infections as a child, she had always considered herself healthy. The kidney infection did not concern her as much as shielding Warren from dealing with it; his discomfort around illness was so great that she had trained the family to pay attention to him whenever somebody got sick, as if he, too, were ill and required care.

Her real focus was on having a home of her own at last. Even illness and the demands of caring for a new baby and two small children could not suppress her urge to decorate. As it sprang to life, she redid the house in cheery contemporary style, with chrome-and-leather furniture and huge, bright modern paintings covering the white walls. The $15,000 decorating bill totaled almost half of what the house itself had cost, which "just about killed Warren," according to Bob Billig, a golfing pal.[42] Since he was indifferent to visual aesthetics, all he saw was the outrageous bill.

"Do I really want to spend $300,000 for this haircut?" was his attitude.[43] But since Susie wanted to spend money that he wanted to withhold, and since he wanted Susie to be happy and she wanted to please him, their personalities were gradually meshing into a system of bargaining and trades.

Susie was considered a flexible, easygoing, but attentive mother by her friends and relatives. Now that the Buffetts lived closer to both their parents, the children spent more time with their grandparents. The atmosphere at the Thompsons', a block and a half away, was relaxed and enjoyable; they didn't care if Howie broke a window or the kids made a mess. Dorothy Thompson got into the spirit of things, playing games, organizing Easter egg hunts, and making elaborate multilayered ice-cream cones. The children loved Doc Thompson, despite his sober self-importance and the way he pontificated. Once he sat Howie on his knee. "Don't drink alcohol," he said, over and over. "It will kill your brain cells, and you don't have any to waste."[44]

On Sundays, Doc Thompson sometimes came over and preached in a jelly-bean-colored suit right in Warren and Susie's living room. Otherwise, Howie and Susie Jr. went to the Buffetts', where Leila towed them off to church. Compared to the Thompsons, she and Howard seemed stiff and straitlaced. Howard remained such a Victorian throwback that when he called Doris and Warren with news about their sister Bertie, he could only choke out, "All hell's broken loose!" They finally managed to discover, from someone else, that she had lost her baby. Howard couldn't bring himself to say the word "miscarriage."

With their large new house, Warren and Susie began to play host for the families. But at family gatherings when his mother was present, as soon as he could get away with it, Warren disappeared upstairs to work.

Susie had covered Warren's new little office off the master bedroom with greenback-patterned wallpaper. Comfortably surrounded by money, he now set about buying cheap stocks as fast as his fingers could fly through the *Moody's Manuals*: businesses that sold basic items or commodities that could be easily valued, like Davenport Hosiery, Meadow River Coal & Land, Westpan Hydrocarbon, and Maracaibo Oil Exploration. For the partnership, for himself, for Susie, or for all of these whenever he had money, he put it to work as fast as he could bring it through the door.

Often he needed secrecy to execute his ideas and he used intelligent, willing people like Dan Monen to act as his proxies. Another of these proxies was Daniel Cowin, who worked for the small brokerage firm Hettleman & Co. in New York. Warren had met Dan through their late friend from Columbia, Fred Kuhlken.[45]

Cowin was nine years older, with deep-set eyes and a penetrating gaze. When the two of them were together, it seemed, on the surface, like a grown man hobnobbing with a college boy, but they had much in common. As a teenager Cowin had supported his family. He put the money he got for a thirteenth-birthday gift into stocks.[46] What attracted Buffett to him was that Cowin traded well and worked his own ideas.[47] Cowin had also endeared himself to Warren early on, when he was at Graham-Newman, by lending him $50,000 for a week so that Warren could buy some mutual-fund shares to achieve a thousand-dollar tax saving.[48] Over time, they collaborated, with Dan the balding senior partner: more experienced and with more money to invest, but sharing information and ideas.

Buffett and Cowin used to call each other weekly when the Pink Sheets that listed small stocks came out, and compare notes. "Did you get that one?" "Yes! I bought that, that's mine!"—both feeling like winners when they had picked the same ones. "It was like picking a horse," says Dan's wife, Joyce.[49]

Once, Buffett says, they had even tried to buy a Maryland "town" that the Federal Housing Authority was auctioning off for peanuts: It consisted of the post office, the town hall, and a large number of rental properties that were charging below-market rents. The town had been built during the Depression. Buffett recalls that the ad for the town made them salivate with Snidely Whiplash dreams of quickly raising the rents to a market rate. But even for "peanuts," the town was expensive and they couldn't get together enough cash.[50]

Warren could never get enough cash. But the Graham connection was about to pay off again. Bernie Sarnat—a pioneer in plastic and reconstructive surgery—went to have a chat one day with Ben Graham, his wife's first cousin. Ben had moved across the street from the Sarnats when he and Estey retired to California. Sarnat says he asked Graham what he should do with his money now. "Well," recalls Sarnat, "he said, 'Oh, buy AT&T,' and he handed me shares in three closed-end funds and some stock. And then he very casually mentioned, 'One of my former students is doing some investing. Warren Buffett.' And that was it. So casually that I didn't even pick it up."

Hardly anybody knew Warren Buffett. He might as well have been a patch of moss hidden under a rock in Omaha. Sarnat's wife, Rhoda, took a walk every day with her cousin-in-law Estey. "One day not long after," she recalls, "Estey said to me, 'Listen, Rhoda, people are always approaching us to invest in their partnerships, because if they can tell people that Ben Graham invests in them, they have it made. We say no to everybody. But that Warren Buffett—he has potential. We're investing with him, and you'd better do it too.'

" 'Estey, I know you think he's bright,' " said Rhoda, " 'but I'm more interested in whether he's honest.' Estey said, 'Absolutely. Totally. I trust him a hundred percent.' " The Sarnats and Estey Graham put $10,000 and $15,000, respectively, into Mo-Buff.

Some of the students in Warren's investing classes had also joined the partnerships, as had Wally Keenan, his former Dale Carnegie instructor. In fact, by 1959, he was getting somewhat of a name around town. No longer hidden, his qualities—good and bad—had begun to be recognized in Omaha. The side of him that had taken the counterposition in the teenage radio show *American School of the Air* came across in Omaha as brash, a know-it-all. "*I used to love to take the opposite side of any argument,*" he says, "*no matter what. I could turn in a second.*" People thought it was nervy of him to ask for money to invest without telling them what he would be buying. "*There were people in Omaha who thought what I was doing was some sort of Ponzi scheme,*" he recalls. It had repercussions. When Warren had reapplied for full membership in the Omaha Country Club, he was blackballed. To be blackballed from the country club was a serious matter; someone disliked him enough to show it in a tangible and embarrassing way. It was one thing to identify with outsiders, but he also wanted to belong. Through connections, he worked at it until he got off the blacklist.

But his talents shone through to many more people now, and brought him partners of increasing prominence. In February 1959, Casper Offutt and his son, Cap Jr., members of one of Omaha's most prominent families, approached him about a partnership of their own. When Warren explained that they would not know what he was buying, Cap Sr. bowed out. But Cap Jr., together with his brother John and William Glenn, a businessman for whom Chuck Peterson managed real estate properties, invested anyway. They put $50,000 into Glenoff, the seventh partnership.

And all the while that Warren was investing during these early years of the partnerships, he never deviated from the principles of Ben Graham. Everything he bought was extraordinarily cheap, cigar butts all, soggy stogies containing one free puff. But that was before he met Charlie Munger.

23

The Omaha Club

Omaha · 1959

Like a steel bank vault door, the arched portals of the Omaha Club swung closed behind the bankers and insurance men and railroad executives of the city as George, the black doorman, welcomed them inside. The men loitered by the tiled fireplace in the front hall, chatting until the women entered through a separate side door in the building's Italian Renaissance facade to join them. The assembled parties ascended the curving mahogany staircase to the second floor, passing on the way the life-size painting of a Scotsman catching a trout in a stream. The Omaha Club was where the town came to dance, to raise money, to get married, and to celebrate anniversaries. But above all, it was where the town came to do business, for at its tables you were left to talk in peace.

One summer Friday in 1959, Buffett strode through the club's entrance to have lunch with two of his partners, Neal Davis and his brother-in-law Lee Seeman, who had arranged for him to meet Davis's best friend since childhood. It was Neal's father, Dr. Eddie Davis, who had said to Warren, "You remind me of Charlie Munger" when the Davises had joined the partnership. Now Munger was in town to settle his father's estate.[1]

Munger knew only a few facts about the crew-cut Buffett kid, six years his junior.[2] But, consistent with his expectations of life in general, his expectations of this meeting were not high. He had developed the habit of expecting little so as never to be disappointed. And rarely did Charles T. Munger meet anyone to whom he enjoyed listening as much as himself.

The Mungers had started in poverty, but by the latter part of the nineteenth century, T. C. Munger, Charlie's grandfather, a federal judge, had brought the family to prominence, welcome in every drawing room in Omaha—rather than only at the back door, delivering groceries, like the Buffetts. Judge Munger, an iron disciplinarian, had forced the whole family to read *Robinson Crusoe* to absorb the book's portrayal of the conquest of nature through discipline. He was known for giving longer jury instructions than any judge in the middle west.[3] He liked to lecture his relatives on the virtue of saving and the vices of gambling and saloons.

Judge Munger's son Al followed his father into the law, becoming a respectable but not rich attorney who counted among his clients the *Omaha World-Herald* and other important local institutions. Lighthearted, unlike his father, he was often seen enjoying a pipe, hunting, or catching a fish. His son later said of him that Al Munger "achieved exactly what he wished to achieve, no more or less… with less fuss than either his father or his son, each of whom spent considerable time foreseeing troubles that never happened."[4]

Al's wife, the beautiful, witty Florence "Toody" Russell, came from another clan raised on duty and moral rectitude, an enterprising family of New England intellectuals known for what Charlie referred to as "plenty of plain living and high thinking."

Al and Toody Munger had three children: Charles, Carol, and Mary. A photograph of Charlie as an infant shows him already wearing the petulant expression so typical of him later in life. At Dundee Elementary School, his most prominent features were a pair of huge elfin ears and, when he chose to reveal it, a broad smile. He was recognized as intelligent, "lively," and "too independent-minded to bow down to meet certain teachers' expectations," according to his sister Carol Estabrook.[5] "Smart, and a smarty," is how the Mungers' neighbor Dorothy Davis recalls Charlie from his earliest childhood.[6] Mrs. Davis tried to control Charlie's influence on her son, Neal, but nothing tamed Charlie's mouth, not even the sight of her with a switch in her hand, coming after the boys to lash their bare calves.

Warren had borne the indignities of childhood with only brief rebellion before learning to hide his misery and adopt artful strategies to cope. Too proud to submit, Charlie suffered through the woes of youth by employing his talent for wounding sarcasm. At Central High School, he gained the nickname "Brains" and a reputation for hyperactiveness—and for being aloof.[7]

From a family that treasured learning, he grew up intellectually ambitious and enrolled in the University of Michigan at seventeen, majoring in mathematics. He enlisted in the Army a year after Pearl Harbor, halfway through his sophomore year. While in the service he attended the University of New Mexico and California Institute of Technology for credits in meteorology, though he never actually graduated. After more coursework he worked in Nome, Alaska, as an Army meteorologist. Later, Munger would make a point of saying that he never saw active duty and would emphasize his luck in having been stationed out of harm's way. The main risk that he took was financial: He augmented his Army pay by playing poker. He found he was good at it. It turned out to be his version of the racetrack. He said he learned to fold fast when odds were bad and bet heavily when they were good, lessons he would use to advantage later in life.

With the help of well-oiled family connections, he brazened his way into Harvard Law School after the war without ever having finished his undergraduate degree.[8] By then he was married to Nancy Huggins, an impulsive match entered into when he was twenty-one and she nineteen. He had sprouted into a medium-height, well-dressed young man whose close-cut dark hair and alert eyes gave him a polished look. But his most prominent feature—apart from his ears, now only slightly winged from his skull—was a hallmark skeptical expression. He wore it often while racing through Harvard—without learning anything, he says.[9]

Nancy was "willful, indulged," says her daughter Molly, not exactly ideal traits given her new husband's temperament.[10] Within a few years their marriage was in trouble. Nonetheless, after Harvard they hightailed it back to her hometown with their son, Teddy, and settled in Pasadena, California, where Charlie became a successful lawyer.

By 1953, after three children and eight years of incompatibility, fighting, and misery, Munger found himself divorcing at a time when divorce was a disgrace. Despite their problems, he and Nancy worked out a civilized arrangement regarding their son and two daughters. Munger moved into a room at the University Club, bought a dented yellow Pontiac with a bad paint job "to discourage gold diggers," and became a devoted Saturday father.[11] Then, within a year of the separation, Teddy, now eight years old, was diagnosed with leukemia. Munger and his ex-wife scoured the medical community but quickly discovered the disease was incurable. They sat in the leukemia ward with the other parents and grandparents in different stages of watching their children waste away.[12]

Teddy was in and out of the hospital often. Charlie would visit, hold him in his arms, then walk the streets of Pasadena, weeping. He found the combination of his failed marriage and his son's terminal illness almost unbearable. The loneliness of living as a divorced single father also chafed at him. He felt a failure without an intact family, and wanted to live surrounded by children.

When things went wrong, Munger would set out toward new goals rather than let himself dwell on the negative.[13] That could come across as pragmatic, or even callous, but he viewed it as keeping the horizon in sight. "You should never, when facing some unbelievable tragedy, let one tragedy increase into two or three through your failure of will," he would later say.[14]

So even as he cared for his dying son, Munger decided to marry again. His analysis of the odds of a successful match made him pessimistic, however.

"Charlie was despairing over whether he would ever meet anyone else. 'How can I find somebody? Out of twenty million people in California, half are women. Of these ten million, only two million are of an appropriate age. From that group, a million and a half would be married, leaving five hundred thousand. Three hundred thousand of them are too dumb, fifty thousand are too smart, and of the remaining hundred fifty thousand, the number I would want to marry would fit on a basketball court. I've got to find one of those. And then I've got to be on her basketball court.'"

Munger's mental habit of setting low expectations was well established. He equated this with the route to happiness, since he felt that high expectations led to fault-finding. Low expectations made it harder to be disappointed. Paradoxically, however, they could also confound success.

Out of desperation, Munger started reviewing divorce and death notices to find newly single women. That got his friends' attention. Thinking this pathetic, they began to intervene. One of his law partners came up with another Nancy, a divorcée with two young boys. Nancy Barry Borthwick, a petite brunette, played tennis avidly, skied, and golfed. She was also a Phi Beta Kappa economics graduate of Stanford.

On their first date he warned her, "I'm didactic." The thought of a man infected by the urge to preach failed to put Nancy off, which augured well for their relationship. They started taking their children on outings. At first Teddy went along with them, but he soon became too ill. Later, thirty-one-year-old Charlie spent much of his son's final weeks sitting by Teddy's bedside. By the time Teddy died in 1955 at age nine, Charlie had lost between ten and fifteen pounds. "I can't imagine any experience in life worse than losing a child inch by inch," he said later.[15]

Charlie married Nancy Borthwick in January 1956. She quickly became his ballast. Nancy had moxie, pricking Charlie's balloon without hesitation when it inflated with too much hot air. She was an excellent manager, observant, calm, reasonable, and practical. Nancy curbed his caprices when Charlie took off on occasional bolts of impulsiveness. In time, they added three sons and a daughter to his two girls and her two boys. She set about raising eight children while keeping house and taking care of Charlie.[16] He became known to his children as a "book with legs," constantly studying science and the achievements of great men. Meanwhile, he continued seeking his fortune at the law firm of Musick, Peeler & Garrett, but realized that the law would not make him rich. He began to develop some profitable sidelines. *"Charlie, as a very young lawyer, was probably getting $20 an hour. He thought to himself, 'Who's my most valuable client?' And he decided it was himself. So he decided to sell himself an hour each day. He did it early in the morning, working on these construction projects and real estate deals. Everybody should do this, be the client, and then work for other people, too, and sell yourself an hour a day."*

"I had a considerable passion to get rich," Munger said. "Not because I wanted Ferraris—I wanted the independence. I desperately wanted it. I thought it was undignified to have to send invoices to other people. I don't know where I got that notion from, but I had it."[17] He saw himself as the gentleman squire. Money wasn't a competition to him. He wanted to join the right clubs but he didn't care whether the other members were richer than him. Beneath the surface arrogance, his deep respect for authentic achievement gave him a genuine humility that would be crucial in forming a relationship with the man he was about to meet.

That man who sat across from him in a private room of the Omaha Club and started to talk was dressed like a youngish salesman come to sell insurance to the gentleman squire. The worldly Munger by now was well ensconced in Los Angeles business and society, and looked the part. As soon as the Davises and Seemans had made the introductions, however, the two fell into a tête-à-tête. Charlie allowed that he had actually "slaved" a short stint at the Buffett grocery store, where "you were just goddamn busy from the first hour of morning until night."[18] Ernest had let the sons of favored customers like Toody Munger loaf, however, at least compared to the rest of the beleaguered clerks.[19] After the pleasantries, the conversation picked up speed and the rest of the party listened, rapt, as Warren began to talk about investing and Ben Graham. Charlie grasped the concepts right away. *"He had spent plenty of time thinking about investing and business by then,"* Buffett says.

He told Charlie the story of National American insurance. Munger had gone to Central High with Howard and Hayden Ahmanson. He was amazed that someone like Buffett, who was not from California, could know so much about the Ahmansons and their savings and loan. Before long, the two men were talking simultaneously, yet they seemed to understand each other perfectly.[20] After a while, Charlie asked, "Warren, what do you do specifically?"

Well, I've got these partnerships, Buffett explained, and I do this, and this, and that. In 1957, he said, his partnerships had earned over ten percent in a year when the market had declined over eight percent. The next year the partnerships' investments had risen more than forty percent in value.[21] Buffett's fees so far from managing the partnerships, reinvested, came to $83,085. These fees had mushroomed his initial contribution of only $700—$100 contributed to each of the seven partnerships[22]—into a stake worth 9.5 percent of the combined value of all the partnerships. Moreover, his performance was well on its way to beating the Dow again in 1959, which would make him richer still and raise his stake again. Meanwhile, his investors were thrilled; new partners kept joining. Charlie listened. Eventually he asked, "Do you think that *I* could do something like that out in California?" Warren paused for a moment and looked at him. This was an unconventional question coming from a successful Los Angeles lawyer. "Yeah," he said, "I'm quite sure you could do it."[23] As the luncheon wound its way to an end, the Seemans and the Davises decided it was time to go. When they got on the elevator, their last sight was of Buffett and Munger, still sitting at the table, engrossed.[24]

A few nights later, the two men took their wives to Johnny's Café, a red-velvet steak joint, where Munger became so self-intoxicated at one of his own jokes that he slipped out of the booth and began rolling on the floor with laughter. When the Mungers returned to Los Angeles, the conversation continued in installments, the two men talking on the phone for an hour or two with increasing frequency. Buffett, once obsessed with Ping-Pong, had found something *far* more interesting.

"Why are you paying so much attention to him?" Nancy asked her husband.

"You don't understand," said Charlie. "That is no ordinary human being."[25]

24

The Locomotive

New York City and Omaha · 1958–1962

Warren and Susie seemed like ordinary people. They kept a low profile. Their house was large but not ostentatious. It had a log cabin in the backyard for the kids. The back door was never locked; neighborhood children wandered in and out. Inside the house, the Buffetts clickety-clacked on their different tracks at gathering speed. As Susie added stop after stop to her local schedule, Warren headed out on a nonstop trip to Dollar Mountain.

Until 1958, his straightforward route was to buy a stock and wait for the cigar butt to light. Then he usually sold the stock, sometimes with regret, to buy another he wanted more, his ambitions limited by his partnerships' capital.

Now, however, he was managing more than $1 million in seven partnerships plus Buffett & Buffett and his personal money,[1] which let him operate on a different scale. His network of business pals like Stanback, Knapp, Brandt, Cowin, Munger, Schloss, and Ruane had grown by the addition of Roy Tolles, a lanky former Marine fighter pilot who wore a constant placid smile and kept the thoughts inside his quick mind to himself—except for the occasional barbed zingers he had a way of throwing out, which made people "want to keep a few Band-Aids around," as one friend put it. Buffett could parry and riposte with the best, and added Tolles to his collection. This knack for signing up volunteers to his cause had created a large, if loosely organized, support structure. Warren more or less automatically Tom-Sawyered these supporters, hived off into several cells, into helping his interests, which had grown so fast that he could no longer carry out every detail of them by himself.

The days when Warren simply sat in his study at home, picking stocks out of

Security Analysis or the *Moody's Manuals*, were gone. Increasingly, he began to work on large-scale, lucrative projects that required time and planning to execute—even more so than buying up the shares of National American insurance. These projects would sometimes evolve into complicated, even dramatic episodes that would absorb his attention for months, or occasionally years, at a stretch. Sometimes several of these investing projects operated simultaneously. Already preoccupied to the point that he was barely present to his family much of the time, this expansion of scale would exacerbate that tendency, while binding him more tightly to his friends.

The first of these complicated episodes involved a company called Sanborn Map. It published minutely detailed maps of power lines, water mains, building engineering, and emergency stairwells for all the cities of the United States, maps that were mainly bought by insurance companies.[2] Its customer base was slowly shrinking as insurers merged. But its stock was cheap at $45 per share, since Sanborn's investment portfolio alone was worth $65 per share. To get hold of that investment portfolio, however, Warren needed not just money from his partnerships but also help from other people.

Beginning in November 1958, he put more than one-third of the partnerships' assets into Sanborn. He bought the stock for himself and for Susie. He had his aunt Alice, his father, his mother, his sisters, all buy it. He passed the Sanborn idea along to Cowin, to Stanback, to Knapp, and to Schloss. Some people got in on it as a favor from him. He took an override—a percentage of the profits—from others as a way of leveraging his capital. Eventually he controlled enough of Sanborn's shares to be elected to the board.

In March 1959, Warren took one of his regular trips to New York, staying out on Long Island at Anne Gottschaldt's little white colonial house. By now she and her sister had adopted him as a sort of surrogate son, as if to replace the long-dead Fred. Warren kept spare sets of underwear and pajamas at her house, and Gottschaldt made him hamburgers for breakfast. On these journeys, he always set out with a list of between ten and thirty things he wanted to accomplish. He would go to the Standard & Poor's library to look up some information. He would visit some companies, visit some brokers, and always spend time with Brandt, Cowin, Schloss, Knapp, and Ruane, his New York City network.

This particular trip was lengthy, about ten days. He had sit-downs with prospects for the partnership and another important appointment: his first meeting as a board member at Sanborn Map.

Sanborn's board consisted almost entirely of insurance-company representatives—its biggest customers—so it operated more like a club than a business. None of the board members owned more than token amounts of stock.[3] At the meeting, Warren proposed that the company distribute the investments to the shareholders. But since the Depression and World War II, American businesses treated money as a scarce commodity to be hoarded and husbanded. This way of thinking had become automatic even though the economic justification for it had long disappeared. The board responded to the idea of separating the investment portfolio from the map business as preposterous. Then, toward the end of the meeting, the board broke out the humidor and passed around cigars. Warren sat fuming. "That's my money paying for those cigars," he thought. On the way back to the airport, he took pictures of his children out of his wallet and looked at them to bring his blood pressure down.

Frustrated, Warren decided that he would take the company away from Sanborn's undeserving board on behalf of the other shareholders. They deserved it more. Therefore, Buffett's group kept buying. Warren also used new money coming into the partnerships. He had Howard put a number of his brokerage clients into Sanborn. Warren was probably doing his father a financial favor, even as he tightened his grip on the company.

Before long, people friendly to Warren, including the famous money manager Phil Carret, had corralled about 24,000 shares. Once they had effective control, Warren decided it was time to act.[4]

Another board meeting took place at which nothing happened except for more of the investors' money going up in cigar smoke. For a second time Buffett rode back to the airport looking at pictures of his kids to calm himself down. Three days later, he threatened to call a special meeting and take control of the company unless the directors took action by October 31.[5] His patience had run out.

In the end, the board capitulated. Thus, through force of energy, organization, and will, early in 1960 Warren won the fight. Sanborn made a Rockwood-type offer to shareholders, exchanging a portion of the investment portfolio for stock.[6]

The Sanborn deal set a new high-water mark: Buffett could use his brains and his partnerships' money to alter the course of even a stubborn and unwilling company.

During this episode, as Buffett traveled back and forth to New York and worked on the Sanborn project, figuring out where to get the stock he needed for control and how to make the board fall in line, all the while looking for other investment ideas, his mind whirled with the thousands of numbers that clicked and spun inside his head. At home, he would disappear upstairs to do his reading and thinking.

Susie understood his work as a sort of holy mission. Still, she tried to get him out of his study and into the family's world: scheduled outings, vacations, dinners in restaurants. She had a saying: "Anyone can be a father, but you have to be a daddy too."[7] Yet she was talking to someone who'd never had the kind of daddy to which she was referring. "Let's go to Bronco's," she would say, and stuff a gang of neighborhood kids into the car for a burger run. At the table, Warren would laugh when something funny happened and would appear engaged, but he rarely spoke. His mind could have been anywhere.[8] On vacation once in California, he took a bunch of kids to Disneyland one night and sat on a bench reading while the kids ran wild and had a grand time.[9]

Peter was now almost two, Howie five, and Little Sooz—who occupied her own pink checked-gingham kingdom with a canopy bed up a separate flight of stairs—six and a half. Howie tested his parents with destruction to see how much it took to get a reaction from them. He picked on Peter, who was slow to start talking, prodding him as if he were a science experiment to see how he would respond.[10] Little Susie policed them both to keep things under control. Warren simply turned to Susie to cope with their son's explosive energy. And Howie remembers that his mother almost "never got angry, and was always supportive."[11]

Susie juggled all this while playing the part of the standard-issue upper-middle-class wife circa 1960: appearing every day in her trademark look, a tailored dress or pantsuit, often in sunshine yellow, and a lacquered bouffant wig; taking perfect care of her husband and family; becoming a community leader; and gracefully entertaining her husband's business associates as if this required no more effort than tossing a Swanson TV Dinner into the oven. Soon a series of au pairs took up residence in an airy, light-filled room with its own bath on the second floor. Letha Clark, the new housekeeper, assumed some of the burden. Susie would always describe herself as a simple person, but she steadily added layers of complexity to her life. She was setting up a group called the Volunteer Bureau[12] to do office work and teach swimming at the University of Omaha. "You, too, can be a Paul Revere" was its motto, invoking an image of one individual saving an entire nation through his (or her) daring and self-sacrificing deeds.

Susie—like Paul Revere—was impatient to mount and ride;[13] she dashed back and forth between family obligations and the growing number of people who wanted her attention. Many of these were disadvantaged or traumatized in some way.

Her closest friend, Bella Eisenberg, was an Auschwitz survivor who had made her way to America and Omaha after the camp was liberated. Another, Eunice Denenberg, was only a child when her father committed suicide. The Buffetts also had black friends, including the most intimidating pitcher in baseball, Bob Gibson, and his wife, Charlene. Being a star athlete meant little in 1960 if you were black. "Those were the days when white people wouldn't be seen with black people in Omaha," says Buffett's childhood friend Byron Swanson.[14]

Susie reached out to everyone; in fact, the more troubled the person, the more willingly she helped. She took a deep interest in the personal lives of people she barely knew. Almost everyone she met glowed under her attention and felt touched by the encounter. But even with her closest friends, Susie nearly always took care not to share her own problems.

She played the same role of ministering angel with her own family, above all with her sister. Dottie remained the beauty of the family, but seemed vacant and, as one person put it, "valiantly unhappy." She maintained a pleasant surface but told Susie that she never cried because if she ever started, she would never stop. Homer, her husband, appeared frustrated that he could not penetrate his wife's cocoon. Still, the Rogerses kept up their vigorous social schedule, and at night, amid the drinks and merriment, their two young sons, Billy and Tommy, roamed underfoot. At times, Homer punished them harshly or Dottie teased Billy cruelly—so Susie mothered her nephews along with her own children.

She also helped the senior Buffetts, who were saddled with both Howard's health issues and his ideology. Just as the rest of America had caught up to his level of paranoia about Communism, Howard leapfrogged ahead. He joined a newly formed group, the John Birch Society, which combined paranoia about Communism with what he described as concern for the "moral and spiritual problem of America, which would be with us even if Communism were stopped tomorrow."[15] He covered his office walls with maps showing the menacing red advance of Communism. Howard was respected as a philosophical purist among the libertarian-leaning wing of the Republican Party, but anyone associated with the Birchers attracted both alarm and ridicule. After he went to the local press to defend his Birch membership, people increasingly wrote him off as an eccentric. That Omaha snickered at his revered father was painful to Warren.

But anxiety about Howard had even more to do with eighteen months of mysterious symptoms that doctors could not seem to diagnose despite a trip to the Mayo Clinic in Rochester, Minnesota.[16] Finally, in May of 1958, Howard had been told he had colon cancer that required immediate surgery.[17] Warren had been upset by the diagnosis and angered by what he considered its inexcusable tardiness. Since then, Susie had shielded him from the details of his father's illness.[18] She gave him head rubs and kept up the household schedule. She also devoted herself to propping up Leila during Howard's surgery and long recuperation. She did all of this cheerfully; she seemed to thrive as the calm, soothing presence on whom everyone could depend in this crisis. She helped her older children understand the illness and saw that all of them, including little Peter, visited their grandfather regularly. Howie watched college football in the afternoons with Howard, who would sit in his recliner and switch sides repeatedly during games, cheering for whichever team was losing. When Howie asked him why, he said, "They're the underdogs now." [19]

Throughout his father's ordeal, Warren used business as a distraction. He kept his head buried in *American Banker* or the *Oil & Gas Journal*.

And he began to radiate a presence in public, no matter what was going on at home. He displayed an authority, an almost electric charge of energy, that radiated to an audience. "He just used to ooze that stuff wherever he went," says Chuck Peterson.[20] The man who had so impressed Charlie Munger talked constantly and convincingly about investing and the partnerships; he raised money as fast as he could talk—but not as fast as he could invest.

Munger listened to Buffett's investing and money-raising exploits on their almost-daily phone calls, wondering at the natural salesmanship that enabled Buffett to promote himself so well. His trips to New York became more frequent now that Henry Brandt prospected for him. Cash poured into the partnerships' coffers, making 1960 a watershed year.

Buffett made a presentation to a group of doctors headed by Carol and Bill Angle, Peterson's neighbors from across the street, and wound up managing the Emdee partnership of $110,000 for eleven of the doctors. A twelfth doctor, who worried about losing all his money, did not join.

There were other skeptics. Not everyone in Omaha liked what they heard about Warren Buffett. His secretiveness put people off. Some thought the young hotshot wouldn't amount to anything, and believed the authority he radiated was unearned arrogance. One member of a prominent Omaha family was lunching with half a dozen people at the Blackstone Hotel when Buffett's name came up. "He'll be broke in a year," the man said. "Just give him a year and he's gone."[21] A partner at Kirkpatrick Pettis, which Howard's firm had merged with in 1957, said time after time, "The jury's still out on him."[22]

That fall, the already frothy stock market took off on a tear. The economy had been slogging along in a mild recession, and the country's mood was dark because the Soviets seemed to be winning the arms and space races. But when John F. Kennedy won the presidency in a squeaker of an election, the pending change in administrations to a man from a vigorous young generation uplifted the nation. The market shot up, and once again comparisons were made to 1929. Warren had never ridden out a speculative market, yet he remained unruffled. It was as if he had been waiting for this moment. Instead of pulling back, as Graham might have done, he did something remarkable. He went into overdrive raising money for the partnerships.

He put Bertie and her husband, his uncle George from Albuquerque, and his cousin Bill into Buffett Associates, the original partnership. Wayne Eves, his friend John Cleary's partner, got on board too. And he finally put Fred Kulhken's mother and aunt, Anne Gottschaldt and Catherine Elberfeld, into the partnership. Their presence suggested that he felt the timing was not just highly propitious but also safe.

Warren set up Ann Investments, his ninth partnership, for a member of another prominent Omaha family, Elizabeth Storz. He put Mattie Topp, who owned the fanciest dress shop in town, along with her two daughters and sons-in-law and $250,000, into the tenth, Buffett-TD. Meanwhile, many new partners joined Buffett Associates and Underwood.

Legally, he could take on only a hundred partners without having to register with the SEC as an investment adviser. As the partnerships burgeoned, he started encouraging people to team up informally and come in as a single partner. Eventually he would put people into pools, combining their money himself.[23] He later described the tactic as questionable—but it worked. His compulsion to get more money, to make more money, drove him on. Warren was on fire, shuttling back and forth to New York at a frantic pace. He began to suffer from stress-related back pain. It often worsened when he was on an airplane, and he tried all sorts of things to alleviate it—everything but staying home.

By now his name was passed along like a secret. *Invest with Warren Buffett to get rich.* But the routine had changed. By 1960 it took at least $8,000 to get in the door. And he no longer asked people to invest with him. They had to bring it up.

It had to be their idea. People not only would have no inkling what he was doing, they had to put *themselves* in this position.* It converted them into enthusiasts for Buffett, and reduced the odds of their complaining about anything he did. Instead of asking a favor, he was granting one; people felt indebted to him for taking their money. Making people ask put him psychologically in charge. He would come to use this technique often, in many contexts, for the rest of his life. Along with getting him what he wanted, it seemed to soothe his persisting fears of being responsible for other people's fates.

Though his insecurity was rampant as ever, his success and Susie's care and tutoring had given him a bit of polish and flair. He was starting to appear powerful, not vulnerable. Plenty of people were happy to ask him to invest for them. Buffett formed the eleventh and last of his partnerships, Buffett-Holland, on May 16, 1961, for his friends Dick and Mary Holland. When Dick Holland decided to invest in the partnership, members of his family pressured him not to do it. Buffett's abilities were apparent to him, Holland says, even though in Omaha people were still "laughing up their sleeves" at Warren's ambitions.[24] Yet in 1959 the partnerships had outperformed the market by six percent. In 1960 they leaped to nearly $1.9 million in assets by beating the market by twenty-nine percent. Even more impressive than any single year's profits was the compounding power of repeated growth. A thousand dollars invested in Buffett Fund, the second partnership, was now worth $2,407 four years later. Invested in the Dow Jones Industrial Average, it would have been worth just $1,426.[25] And he accomplished this higher return while taking less risk than the market as a whole.

And Buffett's fees, reinvested, had by the end of 1960 earned him $243,494. More than thirteen percent of the partnerships' assets now belonged to him alone. Yet even as his share of the partnerships increased, he had made the partners so much money that they were no longer simply happy; many regarded him with awe.

Bill Angle, his partner in Emdee, was foremost among them. He Tom-Sawyered himself into becoming Warren's "partner" in building a gigantic model train set with an HO gauge track on the third floor of the Buffetts' house, which had been a ballroom in a former life and was now the family attic. Warreny, the boy who had lingered at the Brandeis store every Christmas, longing for the huge, magical model train that he couldn't have, awoke inside the

---

* Although Dan Monen, or some other helpful proxy, would often clue the aspirant in to what was required.

grown man. He "supervised" as Angle did all the work to create Warren's child-hood fantasy.

Warren also tried to Tom-Sawyer Chuck Peterson into investing in it. "Warren, you must be out of your mind," Peterson said. "Why would I want to go fifty-fifty with you on a train that *you* possess?" But Warren didn't get this, so carried away was he by enthusiasm for the train and its accoutrements. "You can come over and use it," he said.[26] Shining with the reflected glow of a delayed childhood, burnished with the patina of Omaha's railroading history, the train was Warren's totem. His children were forbidden to go near it.

By now, Warren's relentless obsession with money and obliviousness to his family were a running joke among his friends. "Warren, those are your chil-dren—you recognize them, don't you?" people said.[27] When he was not travel-ing, he could be found wandering through the house, nose buried in an annual report. The family swirled around him and his holy pursuit—the disengaged, silent presence, feet up in his stringy bathrobe, eyes fixed on the *Wall Street Journal* at the breakfast table.

The bookkeeping and banking and safe-depositing and post-officing required for his complicated empire, which had grown to almost four million dollars, eleven partnerships, and well over a hundred investors, now became almost overwhelming. Amazingly, Warren was still handling all the money and doing all the clerical work himself: filing the tax returns, typing the letters, depositing the dividend and capital checks, stopping for a meal at the Spare Time Café along the way, stuffing the stock certificates in the safe-deposit box.

On January 1, 1962, Buffett dissolved all of the partnerships into a single entity, Buffett Partnership, Ltd.—or BPL. The partnerships had produced a stel-lar forty-six percent return in 1961, compared with the Dow's twenty-two per-cent. After the partners invested more money that January 1, the new Buffett Partnership, Ltd., started the year with net assets of $7.2 million. In just six years, his partnerships had grown bigger than Graham-Newman. Yet when Peat, Marwick, Mitchell audited it, the auditor, Verne McKenzie, pored over the BPL files not in a conference room on Wall Street but in the alcove off Warren's bed-room upstairs, where the two of them worked side by side.

Including his outside investments—which totaled well over half a million dollars by now—Warren had become a millionaire at age thirty.[28] He rented office space in Kiewit Plaza, a new white granite building a straight shot down Farnam Street about twenty blocks from his house and less than two miles from downtown. He and his father now shared space, a longtime goal of Warren's.

But Howard was clearly very ill. He soldiered gamely into the office with a stiff gait, making the effort. Warren's face would shadow when he learned some new piece of ominous news about his father's health, but mostly he tried to avoid knowing the details.

Just before moving into Kiewit Plaza, he had hired Bill Scott, a trust officer from the U.S. National Bank who had read an article in the *Commercial & Financial Chronicle* that Warren had written about an obscure insurance company. Scott signed up for Buffett's investing course, and then, he says, "I set out to suck up to him until I got a job."[29] Scott began to help Buffett as he herded money into the partnership as fast as the two of them could open the mail. Buffett had his mother join for the first time, along with Scott, Don Danly, and Marge Loring, the widow of Warren's bridge partner Russ Loring, and even Fred Stanback, who had a family business and heretofore had worked with Warren only on specific ideas.[30] And for the first time, Warren put his own money—all of it, almost $450,000—into the partnership.[31] With that, his and Susie's share of the partnership rose to more than a million dollars after his six years of work; together they owned fourteen percent of BPL.

The timing was stupendous. In mid-March 1962, the market finally broke. It continued its slide until the end of June. Stocks were suddenly cheaper than they had been in many years. Buffett was now sitting on a single partnership with a huge pile of cash to invest. Its portfolio was relatively unscathed in the down-turn—"Compared to more conventional (often termed *conservative*, which is not synonymous) methods of common stock investing, it would appear that our method involved considerably less risk," he wrote in a letter to his partners.[32] He went racing through the stock tables. He often paraphrased Graham, saying: "Be fearful when others are greedy, and greedy when others are fearful." This was the time to be greedy.[33]

25

The Windmill War

In the late 1950s and the early 1960s, while Buffett wrestled with Sanborn, consolidated the partnerships, and moved into the office with his father, he embarked on another project, again some distance from Omaha. The second major orchestration of his supporting group, this was the first in which he actually took control of a company. And it would consume far more of his time and energy than had Sanborn Map.

Dempster Mill Manufacturing was a family-run company in the worst sense of the word. It made windmills and water irrigation systems in Beatrice,* Nebraska, a windswept prairie town that depended on Dempster as its sole important employer. This episode of Buffett's career had started like putting a quarter in yet another slot machine to get a dollar back—or so it seemed. The stock sold for $18 a share and the company had a steadily growing book value of $72 a share. ("Book value" is the stated value of a company's assets less what it owes—like a house less the mortgage, or cash in the bank less a credit-card balance.) Dempster's assets were windmills, irrigation equipment, and its manufacturing plant.

Since Dempster was just another cigar butt, Warren applied his cigar-butt technique, which was to keep buying a stock as long as it continued to sell below book value. If the price rose for any reason, he could sell out at a profit. If it didn't, and he ended up buying until he owned so much stock that he controlled the company, he could sell off—that is, liquidate—its assets at a profit.[1]

---

* Pronounced "bee-*A*-triss."

Over several years, Buffett, Walter Schloss, and Tom Knapp got hold of eleven percent of the stock—second only to the Dempster family—and Warren joined the board. In early 1960, the board hired Lee Dimon, formerly purchasing manager of Minneapolis Molding Co., as Dempster's general manager, over Buffett's reservations.[2] Buffett maneuvered the chairman, Clyde Dempster, into a figurehead role and continued buying stock.[3] He wanted every share that he could lay his hands on. He rang up Schloss in New York and said, "Walter, I want to buy your stock."

"Gee, I don't want to sell it to you," said Schloss. "You know, it's a nice little company."

"Look, I'm doing all the work on this idea. I'd like your stock," said Buffett.

"Warren, you're a friend of mine. If you want it—take it," said Schloss.[4]

In the adult version of absconding with Doris's bicycle, Buffett took it. He had a weakness: If he felt he needed something, he *needed* it, and that need must be satisfied. He did this, however, without any apparent malice or arrogance. If anything, it was the opposite; he was just so terribly needy. People like Schloss generally gave in to him because they liked him, and besides, whatever it was he wanted, he obviously seemed to feel he needed it more than they did.

As he gained more stock, Buffett also bought out the Dempster family. With that transaction, he achieved control, eased out Clyde Dempster, and made an offer to all other shareholders on the same terms.[5]

Here Buffett was treading on tricky ground. As chairman, he felt he could not rightly urge other investors to sell when he was buying. He even bent over backward to warn them that he thought Dempster stock would do well. Nevertheless, money and human nature could be counted on to do their job. People convinced themselves that they would rather have the cash than a thinly traded stock of dubious value. Soon, therefore, Dempster made up twenty-one percent of the partnership's assets.

In July 1961, Warren wrote his partners that the partnership had invested in a nameless company that might prove to be *"a deterrent to short-range performance, but it gives strong promise of superior results over a several-year period."*[6] He named Dempster, which the partnership now controlled, and wrote a little sermon about it in his January 1962 letter.[7] The "deterrent to short-range performance" part would prove more prescient than he expected.

During 1962, Buffett coached Lee Dimon and tried to explain to him how to manage inventory. But as a former purchasing manager, Dimon knew how to purchase—so he did. The warehouse bulged with windmill parts[8] as Dempster sucked up cash. By early 1962, the company's bank grew alarmed enough to make noises about shutting Dempster down.

Buffett was looking at only a few months before it all caved in and he would have to report to the partners that a business into which he had sunk a million dollars of their money was broke. He rarely asked advice, but finally that April he took the situation up with his friend Munger. Munger referred him to a turnaround specialist, Harry Bottle.

Six days later, lured by a $50,000 sign-on bonus, Harry Bottle was in Beatrice. This meant that Buffett had to fire someone. Not only that, someone at Dempster, the only major business in town.

Buffett dreaded confrontation. His first instinct was to avoid it, and he ran like a singed cat if anyone threatened to explode at him the way his mother had. But he had also learned to shut down emotionally in the face of a possible eruption. The trick, he felt, was *"to create a shell around yourself with respect to that, without creating a shell that extends beyond"* the situation, to keep from becoming a hardened person.

Whatever happened when he fired Lee Dimon, his wife, Harriett, afterward wrote Warren a letter in which she accused him of being "abrupt and unethical," and, through his coldness, of destroying her husband's confidence. Buffett, at almost thirty-two, had not yet learned to fire people with empathy.

Within days he sent his new employee Bill Scott over to Beatrice to help Harry Bottle rummage around the parts department and decide what to toss out and what to reprice.[9] They swept through the place like a swarm of boll weevils and slashed inventory, sold off equipment, closed five branches, raised prices for repair parts, and shut down unprofitable product lines. They laid off a hundred people. This extensive shrinkage of the business by its new out-of-town management on the heels of the firing prompted the townspeople of Beatrice to eye Buffett with increasing distrust, suspecting that he was a ruthless liquidator.

By year-end 1962, Bottle had pulled Dempster into the black. In his letter to partners, Buffett called Dempster the high point of the year, and named Harry Bottle the man of the year.[10] The bank was happy. Buffett tried to sell Dempster privately but found no takers at his price, so in August he notified the shareholders that the company was for sale, and ran an ad in the *Wall Street Journal*.

He gave buyers a month to get their bids in before the public auction. He had already been talking to most of the obvious candidates.

Beatrice went berserk at the thought of another new owner that might impose layoffs or a plant closing on its biggest and virtually only employer. In the postwar boom, plants opened, they didn't close. Less than a quarter century after the end of the Great Depression, the prospect of mass unemployment brought back haunting memories of gray-faced men in soup lines, a quarter of the nation unemployed, and demeaning government make-work jobs.

The people of Beatrice pulled out the pitchforks.[11] Buffett was shocked. He had saved a dying company. Didn't they understand that without him, Dempster would have gone under?[12] He had not expected the ferocity, the personal vitriol.

The townspeople launched a crusade to foil Buffett by raising nearly $3 million to keep the ownership in Beatrice.[13] Day by day the *Beatrice Daily Sun* breathlessly counted down to the deadline as the town fought to save its only factory. The day of the deadline, fire sirens sounded and bells rang out as the mayor stepped to a microphone and announced that Buffett had been defeated; Charles B. Dempster, grandson of the company's founder, headed an investor group that pledged to keep the plant open.[14] Cash in hand, Buffett handed out more than $2 million to his shareholders.[15] But the experience scarred him. Instead of becoming toughened against animosity, he vowed never to let it happen again. He couldn't take a whole town hating him.

One day not long after, Buffett called Walter Schloss, saying, "You know, Walter, I have these small positions in five different companies, and I'll sell them to you." "Well, what price would you want, Warren?" Schloss asked. "I'll sell them to you at the price that I'm carrying them at," Buffett said. "Okay, I'll buy them from you," said Schloss immediately.

"I didn't say, 'Well, you know, you have to look up each one and check what it's worth,'" Schloss says. "I trusted Warren. If I had said, 'Well, I can buy it for ninety percent of what you're carrying it at,' Warren would have said—'Forget it!' I did him a favor, so he wanted to do me one too. If he had also made a profit, then that was fine. And they all worked out brilliantly. I felt that it was his way of saying, 'Thank you for selling me your Dempster stock.' I don't say that's the reason, but that's what I mean by being an honest guy."

26

Haystacks of Gold

Omaha and California · 1963–1964

W arren may have said he wanted to become a millionaire, but he never said that he would stop there. Later he would describe himself during this period as "a lousy sport at doing anything I didn't want to do." What he wanted to do was invest. His children now ranged from five to ten years old, and one friend described Susie as "sort of a single mother." Warren would show up at school events or toss around a football if asked, but he never initiated a game. Susie taught the children that his special mission must be respected; she told them, "He can only be so much, so don't expect any more from him." That applied to her too; Warren was obviously devoted to his wife, and showed that in public, caressing "Susan-o" affectionately. At the same time he was so used to her attention and remained so undomesticated that once, when she was nauseous and asked him to bring her a basin, he came back with a colander. She pointed out the holes; he rattled around in the kitchen and returned triumphantly bearing the colander on a cookie sheet. After that, she knew it was hopeless.

Yet the predictability of Warren's habits gave a certain stability to the Buffett household, as Susie's come-on-in, take-a-number atmosphere unfolded around them. In the evenings he reenacted his own father's routine, arriving at the same time every night, slamming the door from the garage, and yelling, "I'm home!" before heading to the living room to read the newspaper. He wasn't uncaring, and he was often available. But in conversation his words often had a subtly prepared, even rehearsed quality. Whatever went on inside his mind took place between the lines; it came through in the silences, the flashes of wit, the tremulous flight from certain topics of conversation. His feelings danced behind so many veils that even he seemed unaware of them most of the time.

Susie herself was less available these days. Like her father, she stayed busy and surrounded by people; she avoided being alone and unoccupied. She was vice president of the theater guild, was involved with United Community Services, and spent far more time with those in the Jewish and black communities than among white socialites.

Susie was becoming prominent among a group of Omaha women who were passionate civil-rights supporters. She helped organize the Omaha branch of the Panel of Americans, a speakers' bureau that sent one Jew, one Catholic, one white Protestant, and one black Protestant to talk to civic groups, churches, and other organizations about their experiences. One of Susie's friends satirized her role on it as "to apologize for being a WASP." But at a time when "Negroes" could not use public "white only" restrooms throughout much of the South, the sight of a black woman sitting as an equal on the same stage as white women stirred the audiences.[1]

In the afternoons, often with Susie Jr. in tow, Susie shot back and forth to meetings and committees on the north side of town, trying to tackle the city's worst problem: abysmal living conditions in the ghetto.[2] The police stopped her several times. "Why are you in this neighborhood?" they'd ask.

"Honey," the fretful Doc Thompson told Susie Jr., "your mother is going to get killed." He made her carry a police whistle when she rode with her mother. "Honey, you're going to get kidnapped," he said.[3]

Susie's role as problem-solver and emotional carpet-sweeper meant that people thought of calling her whenever there was trouble, of any kind. She had referred to Warren as her "first patient,"[4] and there were others. She stepped in more often now to manage Dottie's life as her sister's ability to cope declined and her drinking increased. She counseled Doris through her divorce from Truman and gave her a copy of a book, Viktor Frankl's *Man's Search for Meaning,* that Doris turned to again and again looking for hope amid misery.[5]

Outside of Warren's study, the Buffetts' home was never a refuge from the world, and opportunities for solitude were rare. Yet the children were growing up with a balance of freedom and discipline, strong ethical principles instilled by both parents, an excellent education, and an emphasis on enriching experiences. Warren and Susie had many long conversations about how to bring up children in a rich family so that they became self-sufficient rather than feeling entitled.

What the children lacked was attention from their parents. They responded to this upbringing in their different ways. The older Little Susie got, the fewer overtures she made for her mother's attention and the more authority she assumed over her brothers. Howie, the tornado, tunneled through the backyard, leaped off the banisters, hung from the curtains, and tore through the house. He dumped a bucket of water from the roof onto Phyllis the babysitter. Everybody knew not to drink a glass of anything he handed them. But he was also easily wounded. Tenderhearted like his mother, he craved more attention than she could supply. When Susie reached her limit, she sometimes locked Howie in his room.[6]

Peter, who was naturally quiet, felt rewarded for staying in the background as his siblings ruled through squabbles, with bossy Little Susie striving to contain Howie's whirlwind.[7] When the energy around Peter grew too intense, he retreated inside his head. Rather than express his feelings in words, he played "Yankee Doodle" on the piano in a minor key whenever he was unhappy.[8]

Warren approved of his wife's sprawling interests and was proud of her generosity and her leadership role in Omaha, which freed him to focus on his work. He, too, was always adding one more thing to his list, but unlike her he never overextended himself. When something new came into his life, something else went out. The two exceptions were money and friends.

Thanks to both, by 1963 the word had spread that this Buffett fellow out in Omaha knew what he was doing. He no longer had to charm, much less prospect; he simply laid down the terms on which he would take people's money.

Those outside Omaha often knew more about him than his own neighbors. A friend of Little Susie's was in the family car on the way to the 1964 New York World's Fair when her parents stopped for gas. They struck up a conversation with the woman at the next pump, who turned out to be the mother's former high school teacher. The woman was traveling from Elmira, New York, to Omaha, carrying with her $10,000 to invest with Warren Buffett. Do you know him? she asked. Should I invest with him? He's our neighbor, the family said. Yes, you should. They got back in the car and headed onward to the World's Fair, thinking no more of it. With five kids and a new house, it didn't occur to them to invest for themselves.[9]

Another would-be partner, Laurence Tisch, one of two brothers who were building a New York hotel empire, sent in a check for $30,000 made out to

Charlie Munger. Buffett called him and said he was glad to have Tisch join the partnership, but next time, "make the check out to me."

Munger could have used the money. Whatever Laurence Tisch may have thought, in 1963 he and Buffett were not partners. Munger had just opened a partnership of his own after waiting until he had accumulated a fair amount of money—around $300,000—by investing in real estate. But this was peanuts by Buffett's standards, a fraction of Warren and Susie's wealth.

"Charlie had a lot of children early on. That hindered him a lot in getting independent. Starting early with no encumbrances is a big advantage."

Ever since they first met, Buffett would say to Munger, It's nice to be a lawyer and to do real estate on the side, but if you want to make some real money, you ought to start something like my partnerships.[10] In 1962, Munger had gone into partnership with his poker buddy Jack Wheeler, a trader on the Pacific Coast Stock Exchange who owned an investing partnership, Wheeler, Cruttenden & Company, which included two "specialist posts" on the exchange, where traders took orders from brokers to trade stocks on the floor. They renamed the business Wheeler, Munger & Co., and sold the trading operation.

Munger had continued his law practice but bolted from his old firm together with several other lawyers, among them Roy Tolles and Rod Hills. They founded a new firm, Munger, Tolles, Hills & Wood.[11] All along, Munger had naturally resisted following the rules of a law firm run by anyone but himself.

At their new firm, Munger and Hills imposed an elitist, Darwinian ethos designed to attract the brightest and most ambitious. Within three years, when he was forty-one, Munger abandoned the law altogether to work full-time at investing. But he still consulted to the firm and kept an office there, where he remained an important, almost spiritual presence. Tolles, too, shifted most of his attention to investing.

In his new role as a money manager, Munger had to raise money to manage. Buffett had always hustled for investors in an understated way, often using others as his promoters—people like Bill Angle and Henry Brandt, who found and prepared prospects—so that he could show off his impressive track record with a pleasing modesty. But however gracefully he'd hustled, he'd still done it. Munger felt this was demeaning. He managed to parlay his law practice into an investing partnership, albeit one smaller than Buffett's, by raising funds from his powerful Los Angeles business connections.

Jack Wheeler had explained to him that, as a member of the exchange, under its rules he could borrow an additional ninety-five cents for every dollar invested.[12] If the investment earned a profit of twenty-five percent, the profit on Munger's capital would be nearly double that.[13] This borrowing likewise nearly doubled his risk. If he lost twenty-five percent, he would lose nearly half his capital. But Munger, more than Buffett—*far* more than Buffett—was willing to take on some debt if he was positive the odds were right.

He and Wheeler set themselves up at the exchange in a "crude, cheap" office festooned with radiator pipes and stuck their secretary, Vivian, in the tiny private back office overlooking an alley.[14] Wheeler, a big spender who liked to live large, had just had a hip replacement and soon started showing up for work on the golf course most mornings.[15] Munger fell into a routine, arriving at five a.m., before the market opened on the East Coast, and checking the quotation board.[16] Buffett had connected him with Ed Anderson, the Graham-Newman investor who had worked for the Atomic Energy Commission and seemed so smart; Munger hired him as his assistant.

Most of the traders at the stock exchange had ignored Munger's arrival on the scene, but one of them, J. Patrick Guerin, took note. Guerin had bought the trading part of Wheeler's partnership. A rough-and-tumble guy who was scrambling like mad to better himself, Guerin had worked as a salesman for IBM, then became a stockbroker at a couple of small firms that peddled third-class stocks. This was a part of stockbroking Buffett had detested; Guerin, too, found it a relief to escape life as a "prescriptionist."

By the time Munger met him, the lean, handsome Guerin had learned to roll his crisp shirt cuff down over his tanned forearm to cover his tattoo. He did the trading for Wheeler, Munger, and says he immediately recognized that Munger had a money mind and began to emulate Munger and Buffett, with the goal of forming his own investing partnership.[17]

Munger bought cigar butts, did arbitrage, even acquired small businesses—much of this in Buffett's style—but he seemed to be heading in a slightly different direction than Buffett. Periodically, he said to Ed Anderson, "I just like the great businesses." He told Anderson to write up companies like Allergan, the contact-lens-solution maker. Anderson misunderstood and wrote a Grahamian report emphasizing the company's balance sheet. Munger dressed him down for it; he wanted to hear about the intangibles: the strength of its management, the durability of its brand, how someone else could compete with it.

Munger had a Caterpillar tractor dealership as a client. To grow, the business had to buy more tractors, gobbling up more money. Munger wanted to own a business that did not require continual investment, and spat out more cash than it consumed. But what were the qualities of such a business? And what gave such a business an enduring *competitive advantage*? Munger was always asking people, "What's the best business you've ever heard of?" But he was a man of no great patience, and inclined to think that people could read his mind.[18]

His impatience stood out more than any theory that was emerging inside his head. He wanted to get really rich, really fast. He and Roy Tolles made bets on whose portfolio would be up more than one hundred percent in a year. And he was willing to borrow money to make money, whereas Buffett had never borrowed a significant sum in his life. "I need three million dollars," Munger would say, on one of his frequent visits to the Union Bank of California. "Sign here," the bank would reply.[19] Munger did enormous trades like British Columbia Power, which was selling at around $19 and being taken over by the Canadian government at a little more than $22. Munger put not just his whole partnership, but *all the money he had, and all that he could borrow* into an arbitrage on this single stock[20]—but only because there was *almost* no chance that this deal would fall apart. When the transaction went through, the deal paid off handsomely.

Yet despite their different approaches, Munger regarded Buffett as the king of investing, and saw himself as merely a friendly pretender to the throne.[21] "Vivian, get me Warren!" he shouted several times a day to whichever secretary had come to occupy Vivian's desk.[22] He cultivated Buffett like a garden he was tending. Buffett explained his philosophy: "You've got to coattail," he said.[23] But he did not want his friends to coattail *him* and considered it unethical when they did. Hence, while Munger, cultivating Buffett, was open about his trades—he got Buffett into his British Columbia Power deal, for example—Buffett always kept his trades to himself unless he was working an idea with a partner.

By the early 1960s, the Buffetts had begun to vacation in California, so that Warren could spend more time with Graham and Munger. Once Warren and Susie took the kids on a long trip up and down the coast, but usually when they came to visit, they'd settle into a motel on Santa Monica Boulevard, and he and Munger would talk stocks for hours. The differences in their philosophies made for long conversations. Buffett would forgo the chance of profits any day to avoid too much risk, and viewed preserving his capital as an almost holy imperative. Munger had the attitude that if you weren't already rich, you could afford to take some risk—if the odds were right—to get rich. His audacity put him in a different category from all the others who cultivated Buffett, for his deference to Buffett was limited by his high opinion of himself.

In his quest for the great businesses, Munger did not understand Buffett's fascination with Ben Graham. "Because he is good at explaining Ben Graham," Munger later wrote, Buffett was "behaving like the old Civil War veteran who after a few minutes of ordinary conversation always interjected: 'Boom Boom, that reminds me of the battle of Gettysburg.' "[24]

Graham's flaw, Munger felt, was that he considered the future "more fraught with hazard than ripe with opportunity."[25] Munger began trying to wean Buffett away from Graham's dreary pessimism, which underlay the drudgery of stooping for cigar butts and sucking out their last puff.

Buffett had a buoyant optimism about the long-term economic future of American business, which had enabled him to invest in the market against his father's and Graham's advice. Yet his investing style still reflected Graham's doom-laden habits of looking at businesses based on what they were worth dead, not alive. Munger wanted Buffett to define the margin of safety in other than purely statistical terms. In doing so, Munger was working against a subtle tendency toward catastrophism in Buffett's outlook that sometimes cropped up when solving theoretical problems. His father, Howard, had always prepared for the day the currency became worthless, as if that day were imminent. Warren was far more realistic. Nonetheless, he tended to extrapolate mathematical probabilities over time to the inevitable (and often correct) conclusion that if something can go wrong, it eventually will. This style of thinking was the proverbial double-edged sword: It made Buffett a gifted visionary whose thoughts oriented toward doomsday. He would come to use this sword often to slice through knotty problems, sometimes in a very public way.

A few years earlier, another friend of Buffett's, Herb Wolf of New York Hanseatic, an over-the-counter trading house, had helped Buffett tame another personality trait that was hindering his financial quest. Wolf, an investor in the water utility American Water Works, had sought Buffett out in the early 1950s after reading an article that Warren had written on IDS Corporation in the *Commercial & Financial Chronicle.*[26]

"Herb Wolf could tell the effect on American Water Works' earnings if somebody took a bath in Hackensack, New Jersey. One day Herb said to me, 'Warren, if you're looking for a <u>gold needle</u> in a <u>haystack of gold</u>, it's <u>not</u> better to find the gold <u>needle</u>.' I had this thing that the more obscure something was, the better I liked it. I thought it was a treasure hunt. Herb got me out of that way of thinking."

By 1962, Buffett had shaken off the treasure-hunt way of thinking. But he still had Wolf's passion for detail, and his operations had expanded so much that he now needed another employee to assist him. He managed to keep this one off his own payroll; Buffett would forever go to extremes to control his overhead by paying for expenses in ways that could be shut off as needed, or, better yet—as in this case—could be covered in ways that made them effectively free.

Henry Brandt, Buffett's stockbroker friend who worked at Wood, Struthers & Winthrop, had been doing part-time research for the BPL partnership. Buffett had been paying Wood, Struthers for Brandt's time through the brokerage commissions he paid for trading stocks through it. He would be paying commissions to somebody anyway, so Brandt effectively worked for him for free.[27]

Now Brandt worked for Buffett almost one hundred percent of the time. Buffett paid Brandt by waiving his partnership fee and beginning to cut him in on outside deals without an override. The two men shared an interest in knowing the minutest details about a company. Brandt was fearless about asking questions. Unlike Buffett, he never thought twice about making himself obnoxious if this was what it took. He gladly did enormous amounts of meticulous research by gumshoeing and pestering people. Brandt, however, was incapable of stopping before he found the gold needle. Therefore, Buffett set the agenda and steered the process to keep it from turning into a treasure hunt. Brandt produced foot-high stacks of notes and reports.[28]

Part of Brandt's job for Buffett was finding scuttlebutt, a term used by investment writer Phil Fisher, who said that qualitative factors like the ability to maintain sales growth, good management, and research and development characterized a good investment.[29] These were the qualities that Munger was searching for in the great businesses. Fisher's proof that these factors could be used to assess a stock's long-term potential was beginning to creep into Buffett's thinking, and would eventually take hold.

Buffett now had Brandt digging into an idea that would have pleased Munger, had he known about it. The episode that resulted would become one of the high points of Buffett's career. This opportunity had its roots in the machinations of a big-time commodities trader, Anthony "Tino" De Angelis, who arguably was the world's most important and legitimate dealer in soybean oil. De Angelis had become convinced in the late 1950s that he'd found a shortcut to making money in soybean oil.

De Angelis was using the oil as collateral to borrow from fifty-one banks.[30] It apparently struck him that as long as nobody knew how much soybean oil was in the tanks, why not goose up the numbers a little bit so he could borrow more money?

The tanks sat in a warehouse in Bayonne, New Jersey, which was managed by a tiny subsidiary that was an almost invisible part of the gigantic empire of American Express. This arm of the business issued warehouse receipts: documents that certified how much oil was in a tank and could be bought and sold. American Express stood as guarantor of the quantity of oil behind those receipts.

The tanks were connected by a system of pipes and valves, and De Angelis found that the soybean oil could be sloshed and shunted around from one tank to another. Thus, a gallon of oil could pull double or triple or quadruple duty as collateral for a loan. Pretty soon, the loans guaranteed by warehouse receipts were secured by a smaller and smaller amount of soybean oil.

Eventually, it occurred to De Angelis that, in fact, very little oil was needed. Indeed, just enough to fool the inspectors would do the trick. So the tanks were filled with seawater, and oil was placed inside a little tube that the inspectors used to guide their measuring sticks. They did not notice the difference or think to test a sample from outside the tube.[31]

In September 1963, De Angelis saw a chance to make a further killing. The Soviet sunflower crop had failed, and rumors spread that the Russians would have to turn to soybeans for oil. De Angelis decided to corner the soybean market, forcing the Communists to buy from him at an inflated price. He began to trade in the futures market. Futures contracts give someone the right to buy soybean oil at a later date, betting on the price of oil in the future versus the price today. There was no particular limit to how many soybean futures he could buy. In fact, he could and did control more soybean oil than actually existed on the planet[32] by borrowing heavily from his broker. Then, suddenly, it appeared that the U.S. government might not let the Soviet deal go through. The price of soybean oil collapsed. De Angelis's lenders, holding the now-worthless warehouse receipts, hired investigators and turned to American Express, issuer of the receipts, to recoup their $150 to $175 million in losses. And American Express—caught holding tanks full of nothing but worthless seawater—saw its stock plummet. The story began to hit the newspapers.

Two days later, on Friday, November 22, 1963, President John F. Kennedy was assassinated while riding in a Dallas motorcade.

Buffett was downstairs eating lunch in the Kiewit Plaza cafeteria when somebody came in with the news that Kennedy had been shot. He went back upstairs to his office and found that stocks were plunging on heavy trading. Then the exchange closed, its first emergency closing during trading since the Great Depression.[33]

As a stunned country erupted in sorrow, anger, and shame, Buffett went home to sit, along with the rest of the country, and watch the nonstop television coverage throughout the weekend. He characteristically displayed no powerful surge of emotion, rather a detached gravity. For the first time, shock and sorrow united the world through the medium of television. For a brief while America stopped thinking about anything but the assassination.

The newspapers, of course, relegated the American Express scandal to their back inside pages for days as the dramatic headlines took precedence.[34] But Buffett went looking for it. The stock never recovered from the blow it took on Friday when the market closed, and afterward it continued to slide downhill. Investors were fleeing from the stock of one of America's most prestigious financial institutions.[35] It wasn't clear whether American Express would survive.

But the company was an emerging financial powerhouse. Half a billion dollars of its Travelers Cheques floated around the world. Its credit card, launched five years earlier, was a huge success. The company's value was its brand name. American Express sold *trust*. Had the taint to its reputation so leaked into customers' consciousness that they no longer trusted the name? Buffett started dropping in on Omaha restaurants and visiting places that took American Express cards and Travelers Cheques.[36] He put Henry Brandt on the case.

Brandt scouted Travelers Cheque users, bank tellers, restaurants, and credit-card holders to gauge how American Express was doing versus its competitors.[37] Back came the usual foot-high stack of material. Buffett's verdict after sorting through it was that customers were still happy to be associated with the name American Express. The tarnish on Wall Street had not spread to Main Street.[38]

During the months that Buffett was investigating American Express, his father's health declined precipitously. Despite having undergone several surgeries, Howard's cancer had spread throughout his body. In early 1964, Warren took charge as the de facto leader of the family. While time remained, he had Howard remove him from his will to increase the share left to Doris and Bertie in a trust. The amount—$180,000—was a fraction of his and Susie's net worth; he felt it made no sense for him to share it when he could so easily earn money himself. He set up another trust for his children so that Howard could leave them the farm to which the Buffett family had planned to flee when the dollar became worthless. Warren would be trustee of these trusts. Howard's previous will had specified an ordinary wood casket and an economical funeral, and the family convinced him to delete that part.[39] One of the most difficult things Warren felt he had to do was to level with his father that he was no longer a Republican at heart.[40] The reason, he said, was civil rights.[41] Amazingly, however, he could not bring himself to change his voter registration as long as Howard was alive.[42]

"I wouldn't throw that in his face. In fact if he had lived, it would have really constrained my life. I would not have come out against my father politically in public. I can envision his friends wondering why Warren was behaving that way. I couldn't have done it."

Although the family did not talk about Howard's impending death at home,[43] Susie took over much of his care from Leila. She arranged for the children to stand outside his hospital window with a sign that said, "We Love You, Grandpa." Susie also made sure that Warren—who had trouble facing illness under any circumstances—went to the hospital every day to see his father.

As Howard worsened, Warren poured his attention into American Express. He had the largest cache of money with which to work that the partnership had ever seen: BPL's capital at the beginning of 1964 stood at just under $17.5 million. His own money had exploded: He was now worth $1.8 million. During Howard's last weeks, Warren began to invest in American Express, working tirelessly and methodically to get as many shares as he could without running up the price. Only five years before, he had had to scrape and scrounge to find a few tens of thousands for National American. Never had he put to work anything approaching this much money, and so fast, in his life.

Through most of Howard's final few days, Susie was alone with him, often for hours at a time. She both feared and understood pain, but she was unafraid of death and had the strength to sit with Howard even when those around her were falling apart. Leila, devastated, let her take charge. In such close proximity to death, Susie found that the boundaries between herself and the other dissolved. "Many people kind of flee, but for me it was natural," she said. "It was a beautiful experience to be that physically and emotionally intimate with someone you loved, because I knew exactly what his needs were. You know when they need to turn their head, or you know when they need a little ice chip. You know. You feel it. I loved him very much. And he gave me that gift for myself of knowing, of having that experience, and realizing how I felt about it."[44]

Susie Jr., Howie, and Peter were sitting at the kitchen table one evening when their father came in, looking more depressed than they had ever seen him. "I'm going to Grandma's house," he said. "Why?" they asked. "Aren't you going to the hospital?" "Grandpa died today," Warren said, and walked out the back door without another word.

Big Susie planned the funeral, while Warren sat at home, stunned into silence. Leila was distraught, but she anticipated her reunion with her husband in heaven. Though Susie tried to get Warren to explore his feelings about his father's death, he literally could not think about it, fending it off with anything else available. Falling back upon his core of financial conservatism, he argued with Susie that she had been conned into spending too much money on Howard's coffin.

Warren sat in silence at the funeral as five hundred people mourned his father. No matter how controversial Howard Buffett's views were during his life, people came out to show respect for him in the end. Afterward, Warren stayed home for a few days.[45] He parried unwelcome thoughts by watching Congress debate landmark civil-rights legislation on television. When he returned to the office, he continued buying American Express at a hectic pace. By the end of June 1964, two months after Howard's death, he had put almost $3 million into the stock; it was now the partnership's largest investment. Although he never did show any visible sign of grief,[46] eventually he placed a large portrait of his father on the wall across from his desk. And weeks after the funeral, two bald patches appeared on the sides of his head. His hair had fallen out from the shock.

27

Folly

Omaha and New Bedford, Massachusetts • 1964–1966

Six weeks after Howard died, Warren did something unexpected. It was not just about money anymore. American Express had done wrong, and he thought that the company should make amends. The company had offered the banks $60 million to settle their demands, saying the company felt morally bound. A group of shareholders sued, arguing that American Express should defend itself rather than pay. Buffett offered to testify on behalf of the management's plan to settle, at his own expense.

But American Express wasn't offering the money to be an example; it just wanted to get rid of a lawsuit that was shadowing its stock. Nor did its customers care; the salad-oil scandal hadn't registered with them in the first place.

Buffett wrote that an American Express that paid the $60 million to the banks would be "worth very substantially more than American Express disclaiming responsibility for its subsidiary's acts."[1] He described the $60 million payment as inconsequential in the long run, like a dividend check that got "lost in the mail."

Susie, who had thrown the dividend checks down the incinerator and had never had the nerve to tell her husband about the incident, might have been shocked to hear him so cavalierly dismiss a $60 million dividend check lost in the mail, had she known.[2] And why should Buffett now be interested in whether American Express had, as he put it, "standards for financial integrity and responsibility... beyond those of the normal commercial enterprise"? From whence had come the notion that a reputation for integrity would translate into a business "worth substantially more"? Why did Warren want to testify? While he had always shared his father's commitment to honesty, now he seemed to have inherited Howard's penchant for pontificating on matters of principle.

Buffett had always wanted to influence the managements of companies in which he invested. But in the past he had not attempted to turn his investments into a church, where he could preach while passing around the collection plate.

As if to confirm Buffett's sense that moral rectitude had financial value, American Express paid the settlement and worked through its travails, and the stock, which had plunged below $35, rose to more than $49 per share. By November 1964, the partnership owned more than $4.3 million of American Express stock. It had made other huge bets: $4.6 million in Texas Gulf Producing and another $3.5 million in Pure Oil. Together, the three made up more than half the portfolio.[3] By 1965, American Express alone was almost one-third of the partnership's portfolio.

Buffett, fearless in concentrating his bets, would keep buying into 1966 until he had spent $13 million on American Express. He felt the partners ought to know a new "ground rule" and told them he might invest as much as forty per-cent of the assets in a single stock.[4]

Warren had ventured far from the worldview of his mentor, Ben Graham. The hard-nosed "quantitative" approach espoused by Graham was the world of the speed handicapper, of the cigar-butt stooper who worked from pure statistics. Come to work in the morning, flip through the *Moody's Manual* or the Standard & Poor's weekly report, look for cheap stocks based on a handful of numbers, call Tom Knapp at Tweedy, Browne & Knapp and buy them, go home when the market closed, and sleep well at night. As Buffett said of this, his favorite approach, "The more sure money tends to be made on the obvious quantitative decisions." But the method had a couple of drawbacks. The number of statistical bargains had shrunk to virtually nil, and since cigar butts tended to be small companies, it did not work when large sums of money were involved.

While still working this approach, Buffett had had what he would later call a "high-probability insight" about American Express that confounded Ben Graham's core idea. American Express's main asset was its customers' goodwill. He had bet his partners' money—his family's, his friends'—on the competitive advantage that Charlie Munger had been talking about when he spoke of the "great businesses." This was the method of the class handicapper, of Phil Fisher, and it involved qualitative, as opposed to quantitative, assessments.

Buffett would later write to the partners that buying *"the right company (with the right prospects, inherent industry conditions, management, etc.)" means "the price will take care of itself.... This is what causes the cash register to really sing. However, it is an infrequent occurrence, as insights usually are, and of course, no insight is required on the quantitative side—the figures should hit you over the head with a baseball bat. So the really big money tends to be made by investors who are right on qualitative decisions."*[5]

This new emphasis on a qualitative approach paid off in the stupendous results Buffett was able to announce to his partners at the end of 1965. When Buffett made his annual report to them, he compared the huge gain to an earlier prediction that he could beat the Dow by ten percent a year—and referred to the dazzling performance by saying, *"Naturally no writer likes to be publicly humiliated by such a mistake. It is unlikely to be repeated."*[6] Despite the irony, he had begun a tradition of hedging against his partners' high expectations. As his record of outstanding results lengthened, his letters also began to display a preoccupation with measuring success and failure. As readers began to recognize this pattern, some assumed he was manipulating them, while others accused him of false modesty. Hardly anybody knew how deep his sense of insecurity ran.

In the year following Howard's death, Warren began to think of memorializing him in some way—for example, through endowing a university chair. But he could never seem to find the perfect vehicle. He and Susie did set up the Buffett Foundation, which made small grants to educational causes. But this wasn't what he had in mind for his father. And he had no intention of becoming a philanthropist; it was Susie who liked to dispense money and she who ran the foundation. Instead, Warren worked with no slacking of intensity. After his incredible home run on American Express, he hired John Harding from the Omaha National Bank trust department in April 1965, to handle administration. And yet, when Harding took the job, Buffett warned him: "I don't know if I'll necessarily be doing this forever, and if I quit, you'll be out of a job."[7]

But there was no sign of his quitting. Harding had hoped to learn investing, but that ambition was soon destroyed. "Any idea that I wanted to handle investments on my own disappeared when I saw how good Warren was," he says. Instead, Harding simply put most of his money into the partnership.

Besides shoveling millions of dollars' worth of American Express stock into BPL, Warren now chased bigger deals that required travel and coordination, both giant cigar butts and "qualitative" class handicapping deals that were a far cry from flipping through the *Moody's Manual* in his bathrobe at home. His next target, another cigar butt, lay far from Omaha.

Each of the Grahamites in Buffett's network was always looking for ideas, and Dan Cowin had brought Buffett a textile maker in New Bedford, Massachusetts, that was selling at a discount to the value of its assets.[8] His idea was to buy it and liquidate it, to sell it off piecemeal, and to shut it down. Its name was Berkshire Hathaway. By the time the hair had grown back on Warren's head from the shock of his father's loss, he was in full pursuit of this new idea.

Buffett began by circling over the company and observing it. He started leisurely accumulating stock in Berkshire Hathaway. This time, for better or worse, he had chosen a business run by a personality the size of Massachusetts.

Seabury Stanton, president of Berkshire Hathaway, had reluctantly closed more than a dozen mills, one by one, over the past decade. The remnants sprawled along the rivers of the gently moldering towns of coastal New England like empty red-brick temples of a long-lost faith.

He was the second Stanton to oversee the company, and was filled with a sense of destiny. A New England version of *American Gothic* come to life, Seabury peered coldly down on visitors from his six-foot two-inch height— peered down if, that is, they managed to find him. He sat tucked away in a remote penthouse office at the top of a long, narrow staircase, protected by his secretary's secretary, far from the din of the looms.

New Bedford, the town that was his headquarters, once shone as the diamond in New England's crown. For a while the ships that sailed from its harbor to hunt sperm whales made New Bedford North America's richest city.[9] Stanton's grandfather, a whaling captain, had been head of one of the ruling families of the city, capital of the world's most swashbuckling business. But as sperm whales grew scarce, Horatio Hathaway, whose family had roots in the China tea trade,[10] and Joseph Knowles, his treasurer, organized a group of partners to follow what they saw as the next business trend. They formed a pair of textile mills, Acushnet Mill Corporation and Hathaway Manufacturing Company.[11] One of their partners was Hetty Green, the notorious "Witch of Wall Street," a shipping heiress raised in New Bedford who rode the ferry to New York City from her tenement apartment in Hoboken to make loans and investments. She stalked through lower Manhattan in an ancient black alpaca gown, swirling cape, and rusty veiled hat like an elderly bat. By the time of her death in 1916, Green would be the richest woman in the world.[12]

Financed by such investors, mill after mill sprang up to comb, spin, weave, and dye the deep stacks of cotton bales unloaded from Southern ships onto the wharves of New Bedford. Congressman William McKinley, chairman of the

House Ways and Means Committee, who passed through the region from time to time to christen new mills, sponsored a tariff to protect the textile mills from foreign trade, for it was already cheaper to make fabric elsewhere.[13] Thus, even from the beginning, the textile mills of the North needed political help to survive. Early in the twentieth century, a new technology—air-conditioning— revolutionized factories by allowing precise control of humidity as well as particulate matter in the air, and it was no longer economically justifiable to ship cotton out of the South, where labor was cheaper, to the chilly shores of New England. Knowles's successor, James E. Stanton Jr., watched half his competitors' mills melt away to the South.[14] James Stanton "hesitated to spend stockholders' money on new equipment when business was so bad and the prospects were so uncertain," recalled his son.[15] He pulled capital out of the business by paying dividends.

By the time Stanton's son Seabury, a Harvard graduate, took over in 1934, the aged, rickety Hathaway plant still rattled out a few bolts of cotton cloth each day. Seabury became seized with a vision of himself as the hero who saved the textile mills. He and his brother Otis conceived a five-year plan to modernize.[16] They shifted from cotton to rayon, the poor man's silk, and made rayon parachute cloth during the war, enjoying a temporary boom. Year by year the tides lapping at his shore—cheaper foreign fabric, better-automated competition, and lower labor costs in the South—presented a rising threat to Seabury's mills.

In 1954, Hurricane Carol's fourteen-foot storm surge poured into Hathaway's Cove Street headquarters. Rather than rebuild the mill, the obvious response would have been to join the march southward. Instead, Seabury Stanton merged Hathaway with another mill, Berkshire Fine Spinning, trying in effect to build a levee against a tidal wave.[17]

Malcolm Chace, Berkshire's master, steadfastly refused to sink a nickel into modernization. Chace naturally opposed Seabury Stanton's plans, but the new Berkshire Hathaway was governed by Stanton's sense of destiny. He simplified the product line, focusing on rayon, turning out more than half the men's suit linings in the United States.[18] He continued his "relentless" modernizing, pouring another million dollars into the mills.

By this time, his brother Otis had begun to have doubts about the feasibility of remaining in New Bedford, but Seabury thought the time for a textile mill to move south had passed,[19] and refused to give up his dream of reviving the mills.[20]

When Dan Cowin approached Buffett about Berkshire in 1962, Buffett was already aware of it, just as he was of any U.S. business of a meaningful size.

Berkshire was worth—according to its accountants—$22 million as a business, or $19.46 per share.[21] And yet, after nine years of losses, anyone could acquire the stock for just seven and a half bucks. Buffett started buying it.[22]

Seabury had been buying Berkshire's stock as well, making a tender offer for shares every couple of years. Buffett's theory was that Seabury would continue, and he could time his own transactions, buying whenever the stock got cheap and selling it back to the company whenever the price rose.

He and Cowin set about buying stock. Had anyone known Buffett was buying, it might have pushed up the price, so he bought through Howard Browne of Tweedy, Browne. The broker was a favorite of Buffett's because everyone there was closemouthed, of utmost importance to him. Tweedy, Browne had code-named the Buffett partnership's account BWX.[23]

When Buffett arrived at Tweedy, Browne, which maintained a tiny office at 52 Wall Street—the same Art Deco building where Ben Graham had once worked—it felt like entering an old-fashioned barbershop, with its black-and-white ceramic tile floor. Along the center of the trading room ran a twenty-foot wooden table, which the firm had acquired somewhere on its way to a garbage dump. Its surface bore the marks of generations of schoolchildren armed with penknives. To write down figures, a tablet had to be placed underneath the paper; otherwise, "Todd loves Mary" would be embossed into the text.

On one side of the child-scarred table, Howard Browne ruled with benign authority. He and his partners faced the firm's trader, who—like all traders—sat, jumpy and restless, waiting for the phone to ring so that he could trade. Next to him, an empty space at the table served as the "visitors' desk." The cheapest of wooden filing cabinets lined the walls.

Past the trading room, in a small rented alcove half filled with a water cooler and a coatrack—in effect a sort of closet—sat Walter Schloss, running his partnership from a battered desk. Using Graham's method without the slightest variation, he had been averaging returns of better than twenty percent a year since leaving Graham-Newman. To pay his rent to Tweedy, Browne, in lieu of cash he gave the firm commissions by trading stocks. His trades were few, and he was getting a great bargain on the rent. He limited his other expenses to the cost of a subscription to *Value Line Investment Survey,* some paper and pencils, subway tokens, and nothing else.

Nowhere else in New York did Buffett feel so at home as sitting at the Tweedy, Browne visitors' desk. The firm had branched out into arbitrage, workouts (all-but-completed turnaround situations where a little money remained to be made), and "stubs" (companies being acquired and broken up)—all the sorts of things he liked. It traded securities such as fifteen-year Jamaica (Queens) Water warrants—rights to buy the water company's stock, which rose whenever there was speculation that New York City would someday take over the waterworks. They fell again when speculation lulled. Tweedy, Browne bought them every time they dropped and sold them every time they rose, over and over and over again.

The firm also made a specialty of fencing with the managements of these obscure, undervalued businesses, trying to force out hidden value, as with Sanborn Map. "We were always in court suing," one partner says.[24] All of it reeked of the old Graham-Newman days and bore little similarity to the gargantuan American Express deal, but Buffett loved the atmosphere. Tom Knapp had commandeered a huge storage closet, filling it with the four-cent Blue Eagle stamps he and Buffett had made the mistake of buying and topographical maps of the Maine coastline. The pile of maps continually grew, for Knapp was funneling the cash he made from stocks into buying up the coast of Maine.[25] The pile of Blue Eagles slowly shrank as Tweedy, Browne pasted forty stamps onto each batch of the Pink Sheets they sent to Buffett once a week, every week.

The Pink Sheet quotations for stocks not listed on the New York Stock Exchange were stale the moment they went to print. Buffett used them merely as a starting point for the telephonic bazaar in which calls to numerous brokers might be required to make a trade. He was a master at working this system through his brokers. The lack of a publicly posted price reduced competition. Someone who was willing to call every market maker and squeeze them mercilessly had a meaningful advantage over the less energetic or the more fainthearted.

Browne would call Buffett to let him know they had XYZ stock on offer at $5 a share.

"Hmmm, $4¾ bid," Buffett would say, without hesitation. This maneuver, Casting the Line, would fish out how hungry the seller was.

After calling the client to see if he would take a lower price, Browne would call Buffett with the response: "Sorry. Can't take less than five bucks."

"Unthinkable," Buffett would answer.

A few days later, Browne would call Buffett again. "We got the stock at $4¾. We'll go along with $4¾ bid."

"Sorry," Buffett would now say instantly. "$4½ bid."

Browne would go back to the seller, who would say, "What the hell? What happened to the $4¾?"

"We're just passing along the message. $4½ bid."

More calls would go back and forth until a week later, Browne came back to Buffett: "Okay. $4½ bid," he'd say.

"Sorry," Buffett would say, and drop it another eighth. "$4⅜."

Thus he Buffetted the price ever lower. And rarely—almost never—did he want a stock badly enough to raise his bid.[26]

He placed his first order for Berkshire Hathaway through Tweedy on December 12, 1962, for two thousand shares at $7.50 a share, paying the broker a $20 commission.[27] He told Tweedy to keep buying.

Cowin got the scuttlebutt on Berkshire from board member Stanley Rubin, Berkshire's top salesman, who happened to be a friend of Otis Stanton, another member of the board. Otis felt his brother was out of touch. Protected by his secretaries in his ivory tower, Seabury was doing more and more drinking as the clash between his lofty vision and reality worsened.[28] The brothers were by now sharply at odds.[29] Otis felt his brother should have taken a strike rather than giving in to demands for higher wages.[30] He also disapproved of Seabury's choice of a successor, his son, Jack. Otis had his own idea about who should succeed Seabury—Ken Chace, the vice president of manufacturing.

Seabury Stanton responded to Buffett's purchases as though a takeover threat was imminent, and made several tender offers for the stock. This was exactly what Buffett wanted, for his purchases were predicated on the theory that, eventually, Seabury would buy him out. He wanted the Berkshire stock not to keep it but to sell it. Nevertheless, in every trade there is a buyer and a seller. Seabury Stanton had so far withstood the forces of cheap foreign fabric and Hurricane Carol. Instead of Seabury getting Buffetted, there was a chance that Buffett could get Seaburied.

Eventually, Warren drove up to New Bedford to see the place for himself. For once, he was not just dropping in. Miss Tabor, who was fiercely loyal to Seabury, decided which callers would be allowed through the glass doors and up the narrow stairs to Stanton's penthouse office.

The two men seated themselves at the glass conference table in a corner, and Buffett asked where Stanton stood on the next tender offer. Stanton looked at him through the wire-rimmed glasses perched on the tip of his nose. *"He was reasonably cordial. But then he said, 'We'll probably have a tender one of these days, and what price would you sell at, Mr. Buffett?' or words to that effect. The stock at the time was selling at something like $9 or $10 a share.*

"I said I'd sell at $11.50 a share on a tender offer, if they had one. And he said, 'Well, will you promise me that if we have a tender offer you'll tender?'

"I said, 'Well, you know, if it's in the reasonably near future, but not if it's twenty years from now.' But I said, 'Fine.'

"So now I was frozen. I felt that I couldn't buy any more stock because I knew too much about what he might do. So I went home, and not too long after, a letter comes from the Old Colony Trust Company, which was part of First National of Boston, offering $11⅜ per share to anyone who would tender their Berkshire." That was 12½ cents less per share than agreed.

Buffett was furious. "It really burned me up. You know, this guy was trying to chisel an eighth of a point from having, in effect, shaken my hand saying this was the deal."

Warren was used to doing the Buffetting, and now Stanton had tried to chisel him. He sent Dan Cowin to New Bedford to try to reason with Stanton not to renege on the deal. The two men argued, and Stanton denied that he had made a deal with Buffett; he told Cowin that it was his company and he would do as he pleased. That was a mistake. For trying to chisel Warren Buffett, Seabury Stanton was going to be sorry, very sorry. Buffett decided that—instead of selling—now he would *buy.*

He vowed that he would have Berkshire; he would buy it all. He would own it lock, stock, loom, and spindle. That Berkshire Hathaway was a failing, futile enterprise daunted him not. It was cheap, and he craved it. Above all, he wanted Seabury Stanton not to have it. Buffett and the other shareholders deserved it more. In his determination, he ignored all the lessons learned from the experience at Dempster—save one. And that was the one he should have ignored.

Buffett sent his scouts out, looking for more chunks of the closely held stock. Cowin got hold of enough to join Berkshire's board. But other people began to take notice too. Jack Alexander, Buffett's old friend from Columbia, had an investment partnership with his classmate Buddy Fox. "One day we saw that Warren was buying this Berkshire Hathaway," he says. "And we started to buy." On a trip to New York from their office in Connecticut they told him they were following him in the stock. "He got very upset. 'Look,' he said, 'you're riding on my coattails. That's not right. Cut it out.'"

Fox and Alexander were taken aback. What were they doing wrong? Buffett gave them to understand that he was seeking control. Yet coattail-riding, even in control situations, was a popular pastime among the Graham crowd. It was considered sporting conduct. In effect, Buffett took their stock. I need it more than you, he said. They agreed to sell their stock to him at the then-market price, because it clearly mattered to him so much. He appeared to have some sort of mysterious attachment to Berkshire Hathaway. "It wasn't that important to us. It was obviously very important to him," Alexander says.

Like Fox and Alexander, a few others had also become Buffett-watchers, tracking Warren's trail like the spoor of Bigfoot. This created competition for the stock. He made it understood among the Grahamites that they were to keep their mitts off Berkshire. The only exception was Henry Brandt; he let Brandt— in recompense for his services—buy it below $8.00. He had begun to carry himself with a bit of swagger, which some people found irritating. Yet his surefootedness, the way he always seemed to be so *right,* kept them fascinated. Even his cheapskate qualities were part of the aura. For years he had been possibly the only person doing business regularly in New York who managed to get by with not only free lodging (by staying with Fred Kuhlken's mother, Anne Gottschaldt, on Long Island), but free office space to boot (at Tweedy, Browne).

Now that Susie accompanied him on some of these trips, however, at her behest he had upgraded from hosteling with his deceased college friend's mother to taking a room at the Plaza Hotel. Not only was the Plaza more convenient for business, but from Susie's perspective, it put department stores like Bergdorf Goodman, Best & Company, and Henri Bendel close at hand. Then a rumor circulated among Buffett's friends—the kinds of rumors that always swirled around Buffett, like the one that had him stashing his daughter in a dresser drawer rather than buying her a crib—a rumor that he had found the Plaza's cheapest room, a tiny windowless cubicle like his old maid's room at Columbia, and cut a deal to stay there at a beggarly price whenever he came alone to New York.[31] Regardless of the rumor's truth, each time he checked in to the Plaza he doubtless felt a pang of regret, for he no longer stayed in New York scot-free.

The trips to Bergdorf's were another aspect of how much the New York routine had changed. Susie spent her days going to lunch and shopping; in the evenings they went to dinner, then Broadway or cabaret shows. He liked to see her enjoy herself, and she had become used to shopping at the better stores. Nevertheless, while she now had the power to loosen the purse strings, their game was to tussle over how much money she got to spend. Her way of justifying spending was to do it on someone else's behalf. Susie Jr. was often a beneficiary; her closets filled with clothes from Bergdorf's. One time Susie came back from New York with an ermine jacket. They had met a friend of Warren's who took them to a furrier. "I felt like I had to buy something," she said. "They were being so nice to me." She had done it for the furrier's sake.

Now, all this protecting Berkshire from coattailing would be for naught unless Buffett figured out how to run it well enough to keep Susie in ermine jackets. He made another visit to New Bedford, going by the mill to see Jack Stanton, the heir apparent. Somebody was going to have to run the place once it was wrested from Seabury's hands, and Warren needed to know who that would be.

But Stanton claimed to be very busy, and sent Ken Chace to escort Buffett around the mill.* Stanton had no idea that his uncle had already suggested Chace as a possible replacement for Seabury.

Ken Chace was a chemical engineer by training, forty-seven, quiet, controlled, and sincere. He did not know that he was a contender to run the company; nonetheless, he spent two days teaching Buffett the textile business while Buffett asked question after question and Chace explained the mills' problems. Buffett was impressed by his candor and equally impressed by his attitude. Chace made it clear that he thought the Stantons foolish for pouring money into a business that was on its way down the drain.[32] When the tour was over, Buffett told Chace he would "be in touch."[33]

A month or so later, Stanley Rubin had to be called into service to persuade Chace not to take a job at a competing textile mill. Meanwhile, Buffett was scrambling to buy more stock, including shares that belonged to various members of the Chace family.

Buffett's final target was Otis Stanton, who wanted his brother to retire. He had no confidence in Seabury's son, Jack, and doubted Seabury would ever let go of the reins.

Otis and his wife, Mary, agreed to meet Buffett at the Wamsutta Club in New Bedford.[34] Over lunch at the graceful Italianate mansion, a relic of New Bedford's onetime grandeur, Otis acknowledged that he would sell, on the condition that Buffett make an equivalent offer to Seabury. Warren agreed. Then Mary Stanton asked if they could keep just a couple of shares out of the two thousand they were selling, out of family sentiment. Just a couple of shares.

Buffett said no. It was all or nothing.[35]

Otis Stanton's two thousand shares pushed Warren's ownership to forty-nine percent of Berkshire Hathaway—enough to give him effective control. With the prize within his grasp, he met Ken Chace one April afternoon in New York and walked him out to the teeming plaza at Fifth Avenue and Central Park South,

---

*No relation to Malcolm Chace, who had become chairman of the board when Berkshire Fine Spinning merged with Hathaway Manufacturing.

where he sprang for two bars of ice cream on a stick. Within a bite or two he got to the point, saying, "Ken, I'd like to have you become president of Berkshire Hathaway. How do you feel about that?" Now that he controlled the company, he said, he could change the management at the next directors' meeting.[36] Chace, who was stunned to be selected despite the hints Rubin had given him when he convinced him not to take another job, agreed to keep quiet until the board meeting.

Not realizing that his fate had been decided, Jack Stanton and his wife raced down from New Bedford to meet Warren and Susie at the Plaza Hotel for breakfast. Kitty Stanton, more aggressive than her husband, pled Jack's case. Reaching for an argument that would appeal to the Buffetts, Kitty threw in what she must have thought was the clincher. Buffett surely would not overturn New England's hereditary mill aristocracy, who had overseen the business for generations, to put a mill rat like Ken Chace in charge. She and Jack fit in at the Wamsutta Club. Kitty, after all, was a Junior Leaguer, like Susie.[37]

Poor Kitty, making this pitch to the man who had refused to join Ak-Sar-Ben and had thumbed his nose at the establishment of Omaha.

It was too late for Jack. It was too late for Seabury, who ruled by autocracy and had no friends on the board. Even his own chairman, Malcolm Chace, did not like him. Thus, when backers of Buffett arranged for him to be nominated to the board at a special meeting, on April 14, 1965, he was swiftly elected a director with much of the board's support.[38]

A few weeks later, Buffett flew into New Bedford, where he was greeted by a headline in the *New Bedford Standard-Times* about "outside interests" taking over the company.[39] The planted story infuriated him. The one lesson that had stuck with him from Dempster was to never, ever let himself be branded a liquidator—and wind up with a whole town hating him. Buffett vowed to the press that he would carry on business as usual. He denied that mill closings would result from the takeover—and saddled himself publicly with this commitment.

On May 10, 1965, the board convened at Berkshire's headquarters in New Bedford. It presented a silver tray to the retiring vice president of sales, approved the minutes of the last meeting, and agreed to increase wages five percent. Then the meeting turned surreal.

Seabury, his nearly bald seventy-year-old head speckled with age spots, claimed that he had planned to retire in December to let Jack succeed him. But, he said, he could not continue as president "of an organization over which he would not have complete authority."[40] With as much hauteur as his character allowed him—which was considerable, despite the mutineers having taken over the ship—Seabury made a little speech, commending himself for his accomplishments. Then he tendered his resignation. Jack Stanton added a bitter little coda, saying that, had he become president in December, he was certain that it would have meant "continued success and profitable operations." The board listened patiently, then accepted his resignation as well. At that point, Jack Stanton put down his pen and stopped taking the minutes in which these two speeches had been recorded, and the two Stantons stalked out of the room.

Moving quickly on, the board elected Buffett chairman and confirmed Ken Chace in his new job running the doomed company that Buffett—in a moment of folly—had exerted such strenuous effort to acquire. A few days later, he explained his thinking on textiles in a newspaper interview. *"We're neither pro nor con. It's a business decision. We try to assess a business. Price is the big factor in investment.... We bought Berkshire Hathaway at a good price."*[41]

He would later come to revise that opinion.

"So I bought my own cigar butt, and I tried to smoke it. You walk down the street and you see a cigar butt, and it's kind of soggy and disgusting and repels you, but it's free ... and there may be one puff left in it. Berkshire didn't have any more puffs. So all you had was a soggy cigar butt in your mouth. That was Berkshire Hathaway in 1965. I had a lot of money tied up in the cigar butt.[42]

"I would have been better off if I'd never heard of Berkshire Hathaway."

28

Dry Tinder

The dynamics changed one hundred percent when my father died," says Doris. "Everything went flying into space. My father was the linchpin of our family. The center was gone."

Leila had endured multiple losses over recent years. Her mother, Stella, had died in 1960 in Norfolk State Hospital, and her sister Bernice had died a year later of bone cancer. Without Howard, she became dependent on Warren and Susie and their family. The grandchildren went to her house on Sundays, where she gave them bags of candy to eat during church, then took them to lunch afterward and gave them money if they could add up the bill correctly. In the afternoons, she took them to Woolworth's to buy a toy to play with at her house. Like Howard, who had once paid his children to go to church, she found a Buffettesque solution to the problem of her loneliness—making deals with the grandchildren so that they would stay with her as long as possible.

Howard's presence was what had always made being with Leila tolerable to Doris and Warren. Without him, both found visits with their mother unbearable. Warren trembled when forced to be in proximity to her. At Thanksgiving, he took a plate upstairs and ate dinner by himself. Leila continued to erupt in occasional fits of rage. For decades, her bizarre behavior had been aimed mainly at family members, though once she leaped out of the car in a parking lot and spent an hour screaming at an acquaintance over some trivial matter, as Big Susie and Howie looked on in astonishment. But Doris, who had idolized her father even more than her brother had, was still her main victim. Doris had always felt she had let the whole family down with her divorce from Truman.

The contrast between Warren and Susie's successes and her own life as a divorcée at a time when divorce was still rare only reinforced her lingering feelings of worthlessness. Shortly before his death, Howard had told her that she must remarry to provide a father for her children. So she did.[1] But even though her husband was a lovable man, Doris felt coerced into remarrying, which augured poorly for the union's prospects.

Bertie, always the least troubled by her mother's behavior and the least dependent on her father, now found her life the least changed by Howard's death. Like Warren, however, her relationship with money both triggered her anxieties and gave her a sense of control. She kept records of every dollar she spent, and when she felt stressed, she paid bills to relax.

All of the Buffetts had "issues" with money that ran so deep none of them really noticed what an unusual family they were. After Howard's death, Warren and Susie naturally assumed leadership of the family—partly because of their money, but also through the force of their personalities. Perhaps it was not surprising, therefore, that Warren's aunt Alice, his favorite relative since childhood, had grown to trust Susie more than anyone else in the family except him.

So it was Susie, not Leila, whom Alice tracked down one Monday in late 1965. Susie was at the beauty parlor with Doris when the call came. She got out from under the dryer to go to the phone at the front desk; Alice explained that she was concerned about Leila's sister Edie, who had called her on Sunday to say she was feeling extremely depressed. Alice, a fellow teacher, had taken Edie for a drive and talked to her, and they had stopped for ice cream. Edie idolized Warren and Susie and Alice, indeed all the Buffetts; she confided that she felt she had disgraced the perfect family with her imperfect life.[2] Her impulsive, high-spirited marriage had not worked out; the husband she had followed to Brazil had turned out to be a philandering embezzler who left her there for someone else. Since returning from Brazil, she had found it hard adjusting to life as a divorced single mother of two daughters in Omaha.

Alice told Susie that today Edie hadn't shown up at Technical High School to teach her home economics classes. Worried, Alice had gone over to Edie's apartment. Nobody answered when she rang and knocked. Alice told Susie that she feared that something had happened.

So Susie raced out the door to her gold Cadillac convertible, with her rollers still in her hair, drove over to the garage apartment where Edie lived, and started knocking and ringing herself. When nobody answered, she got inside somehow and began to search. She found no sign of anybody; the place was immaculate.

There were no notes or messages and Edie's car was there. Susie continued searching until she reached the basement of the house, and there she found Edie. She had slit her wrists, and was already dead.[3]

Susie called an ambulance, then had to break the news to the family. Nobody had known Edie was this depressed, and nobody had seriously considered her a possible victim of the Stahl family's history of mental instability until now. There is no telling what Leila, sixty-two years old, felt at her sister's death. At the very least, Edie's death meant that Leila was the last remaining member of her immediate family. And yet another of the Stahls had embarrassed the Buffetts, this time by stigmatizing the family with suicide. Whatever Leila did feel, less than a month later she abruptly married Roy Ralph, a pleasant man twenty years her senior who had been pursuing her since Howard's death. Until now she had refused his proposals. Her relatives had listened with numb boredom through-out her widowhood as she ceaselessly invoked the past and the 38½ wonderful years with Howard. Thus she stunned them all when she remarried—and changed her name to Leila Ralph.

Susie, meanwhile, was taking on more obligations than ever, not just in the family but in the community. She began to press Warren to call a halt to his continuing obsession. The Buffett Partnership was stuffed like a Thanksgiving turkey by American Express. It ended 1965 with assets of $37 million, including more than $3.5 million in profit on this one stock, bringing Warren and Susie's stake in the partnership to $6.8 million. He was thirty-five years old. The Buffetts were among the very rich by the standards of 1966. How much money did they need? Now that they were so rich, Susie thought they should do more for Omaha.

In 1966 she glowed with the fire of a woman who had found her cause in life. She had become close to leaders of the black community and was all over Omaha, brainstorming, coordinating, cajoling, publicizing, working on behind-the-scenes relationships in a town where racial tensions were reaching the point of violence. Every summer now in the nation's major cities, race riots flared after minor incidents involving the police. During a fifteen-day heat wave in July 1966, riots erupted in Omaha; the governor called out the National Guard, blaming the riots on "an environment unfit for human habitation."[4] Susie now made the elimination of segregated housing in Omaha—an idea that terrified many whites—her central cause. She tried to involve Warren in some of her community and civil-rights work, and he complied, but he was not much for committees.

Committee meetings gave Warren a "splitting headache," according to Munger; his way, therefore, was to let other people sit on the committees while he fed them ideas. Warren was far from indifferent to social and political causes, however. He had become deeply concerned about the potential for nuclear warfare—a vivid and seemingly imminent threat after the Cuban missile crisis of 1962, when the standoff between Kennedy and Khrushchev over the removal of Soviet missiles from Cuba had nearly resulted in nuclear war. When Buffett discovered philosopher Bertrand Russell's 1962 antinuclear treatise, *Has Man a Future?*, it affected him powerfully.[5] He identified with Russell, admired his philosophical rigor, and frequently cited his opinions and aphorisms. He even kept a small plaque on his desk quoting a phrase from an influential antinuclear "manifesto" on which Russell had collaborated with Albert Einstein: "Remember your humanity, and forget the rest."[6]

The antiwar movement took on more urgency in Buffett's mind after Congress passed the Gulf of Tonkin Resolution in 1964, authorizing President Johnson to use military force in Southeast Asia without formally declaring war. He started asking speakers over to the house to talk to his friends about it. Once he brought an antiwar speaker from as far away as Pennsylvania.[7] He himself, however, was not going to march against the war.

Warren had strong views about specialization; he defined his special skills as thinking and making money. When asked to donate, his first choice, always, was to donate ideas, including ideas that would get other people to give money. But he would also give money himself—not a lot, but some—to politicians and to Susie's causes. He never labored in the trenches stuffing envelopes; volunteering directly for causes, no matter how urgent and important, would consume time he felt was more efficiently spent thinking of ideas and making more money to write bigger checks.

Many people in the 1960s felt a burning desire to tear down the Establishment that had created the war and operated the "military-industrial complex"—a desire to avoid "selling out" to "The Man." For some, therefore, social consciousness clashed with the need to make a living. Warren, however, saw himself as working for his partners, not for "The Man," and as someone whose business acumen and money helped the civil-rights and antiwar causes. So he could focus on his business with a sense of dual purpose, and felt no inner conflict about how he spent his time.

The conflict he *was* beginning to feel was a struggle to find investments for the partnership. He had managed to find some of the few undervalued stocks that still paraded through the Standard & Poor's weekly report: Employers Reinsurance, F. W. Woolworth, and First Lincoln Financial. He'd also bought some stock in Disney after meeting Walt Disney and seeing the entertainment showman's singular focus, his love of his work, and the way these had translated into a priceless catalog of entertainment. But the concept of "great businesses" had not entirely sunk in, and he didn't load up. Instead, he bought more Berkshire, and built a $7 million "short" position in stocks like Alcoa, Montgomery Ward, Travelers Insurance, and Caterpillar Tractor—borrowing the shares and selling them against the risk that the market would plunge.[8]

In January 1966, another $6.8 million had rolled in from his partners; Buffett found himself with a $44 million partnership and too few cigar butts to light with his cash. Thus, for the first time, he had set aside some money and left it unused—an extraordinary decision.[9] Ever since the day he left Columbia Business School, his problem had always been getting his hands on enough money to pump into a seemingly endless supply of investment ideas.

Then, on February 9, 1966, the Dow had briefly streaked across the mythical one thousand mark before closing just a few points below. The chant began: Dow one thousand! Dow one thousand! The market would not break through the barrier again that year, but the euphoria carried on anyway.

Buffett had been worrying all year about disappointing his partners. Although he started his latest letter to them cheerily with the news about the huge profits on American Express—"Our War on Poverty was successful in 1965," he wrote, alluding to President Johnson's program to bring about a "Great Society" through a vast array of new social-welfare programs—he then delivered the real news in what would be the first of many similar warnings: "I now feel that we are much closer to the point where increased size may prove disadvantageous." And with that he announced that he would be shutting the door to the partnership, locking it, and putting away the key.

There would be no more new partners. He made a joke of it. Susie couldn't have any more kids, he wrote, because they wouldn't be allowed in. This joke was not particularly apt, since none of their children had ever actually been partners—or would be. He was determined to manage their expectations about money, in order to ensure that they would find their own way in life. From an early age, each of the kids knew not to expect financial help from him except to pay for their education. He could have brought the children into the partnership as a learning exercise—to teach them about money, about investing, and about how he spent his time. Certainly he used it that way with those who were members of the partnership. But Warren rarely—if ever—"taught" those he saw day to day. For him, teaching was a performance, a conscious act that took place before an audience. His kids got no lessons.

Instead, he bought them stock in the benighted Berkshire Hathaway. As trustee of the trust left to his children by his father, he sold the farm that Howard had bought as a refuge for the family and used the money to buy the stock. Given that Warren didn't approve of unearned wealth—which was how he viewed inheritance—he might have left the farm alone. A small farm in Nebraska would never be worth much, and the kids would never become rich from their grandfather's inheritance. But by investing the proceeds in his floundering textile business, he increased his hold on Berkshire by another two thousand shares. Why he cared so much about it was a mystery to observers, but ever since Buffetting his way to control of Berkshire, he seemed obsessed by it.

The Buffett kids were not expecting to get rich. They did not even really know that their family was rich.[10] Their parents wanted them to be raised unspoiled, and they were. Like children everywhere, they had to do chores to get their allowances. But when it came to money, their family's odd disconnection meant that Susie and Warren tussled over her allowance as if the Buffetts were broke; then she got the money anyway and used it to give them an upper-middle-class life. The children went on nice vacations, enjoyed themselves at the country club, wore good clothes, and saw their mother's Cadillac and fur coats. But they never got to take money for granted. Their father niggled over small amounts of money all the time and surprised them by denying little requests. If he took them to a movie, he might not pay for popcorn. If one of the kids asked for something, his answer might well be no: If I did it for you, I'd have to do it for everyone.

Whatever message he and Susie were trying to give the children about money, one unvarying theme came through: Money was important. They were growing up in a household where it was routinely used as a tool of control. Warren would take Big Susie to a store for her birthday and give her ninety minutes to race through and buy whatever she could grab. The Buffett side of the family had always been about making deals. Although Susie felt that Warren's obsession with making money was unworthy, she still angled to get more of it from him. Now she was struggling with her weight and this too became a money deal. Warren's childhood obsession with weighing machines—he would have weighed himself fifty times a day—had been no passing phase; he was obsessed with his family's weight and preoccupied with keeping them all thin.

The family's eating habits helped neither his cause nor their health. Susie, who had suffered from a mysterious and excruciating abdominal adhesion two years before, cooked unenthusiastically. She and Warren both willingly ate the same thing day after day: mostly meat and potatoes.

Finally, Susie asked him to make a deal to pay her to keep her weight at 118 pounds. Since she cared less about money than her husband did, however, motivation was a problem for her. All month long she picked and snacked; but then, as the weigh-in date approached, she would get on the scale. If the news was bad and she had to take the pounds off fast, "Uh-oh," she'd say to one of Susie Jr.'s friends: "Kelsey, I've got to call your mom for her diuretic pills."[11]

Warren disciplined himself to maintain his own weight by dangling money in front of his kids. When they were younger, he made out unsigned checks to them for $10,000 and said that if he didn't weigh 173 pounds on such-and-such a date, he would sign the checks. Little Susie and Howie went crazy trying to tempt him with ice cream and chocolate cake. But the prospect of giving up money pained Warren far more than giving up a treat. He made out those checks over and over, but he never had to sign a single one.[12]

Instead of his children, one of the last new partners Warren allowed to join his partnership was Marshall Weinberg, a stockbroker friend of Walter Schloss who had taken Graham's seminar twice. A cultivated man with a bent for the arts and philosophy, Weinberg had met Buffett at one of Graham's lectures at the New School in New York. Lunching together a few times and talking of stocks, they had become friends. Weinberg soon gave up on interesting Buffett in music, art, philosophy, or travel, but Buffett traded through him at times and Weinberg became interested in joining the partnership. So on one of the Buffetts' frequent trips to New York, Warren agreed to meet with him to discuss it.

Loping downstairs from his room at the Plaza, Warren met Weinberg in the lobby. Then Susie glided in, and Warren lit up. She sidled over to him and gave him a hug, then put her hand behind him as if he were a child and gazed at Weinberg with her large brown eyes. "How *are* you?" she asked, beaming at him. She wanted to know everything about him. He felt he was being welcomed into a family and went away thinking that he had made a new friend in Susie. He also intuited that he had just met Buffett's most powerful asset.[13]

Weinberg had squeaked through the door just in time. Through 1966, the urban riots continued, the war in Vietnam escalated, and antiwar protesters rallied in New York, Boston, Philadelphia, Chicago, Washington, and San

Francisco. The stock market began to decline, down ten percent from the beginning of the year. Buffett had never stopped looking for things to buy, no matter how uphill the climb, but despite the market's easing, the days of cigar butts scattered everywhere were gone. He became seriously worried about how to keep up his performance. He thought more often of buying entire businesses now. In fact, he had gotten started on an entirely new venture, one that consumed large amounts of his time.

29

What a Worsted Is

Buffett ran a $50 million partnership that owned a textile business, yet he had never stopped looking like the Raggedy Man.[1] He never varied his skinny striped ties and white shirt, though the shirt's collar had grown tighter, and the jacket of the old gray suit he wore day after day bunched around his shoulders and gapped at the neckline. He refused to part with his favorite camel-colored V-neck sweater, although its elbows had grown thin. His shoes had holes in the soles. His only concession to the sideburns and long hair that other men wore was a little patch of fine dark hairs that he occasionally let sprout from his crew cut like baby grass over his domed forehead. When Chuck Peterson tried to introduce him to a potential investor at a party, the man's reaction had been "You're kidding!" He didn't even want to talk to Buffett, based purely on the way Warren dressed.[2] Susie had no influence; her husband's taste had formed back in 1949 when he was selling suits at JC Penney's, and Mr. Lanford told him that "nobody knows what a worsted is."

He now bought his suits at Parsow's, downstairs in the lobby of Kiewit Plaza, where Sol Parsow was always trying to upgrade his taste. Buffett considered Parsow a *"very wild dresser"* and paid no attention to his suggestions. Warren's idea of a proper suit was one *"that you could bury a ninety-year-old banker from a small town in western Nebraska in."*[3] Parsow prided himself on giving Buffett good advice about stocks, however. He had steered Buffett away from hatter Byer-Rolnick, warning that hats were going out of style. He had also kept him from investing in Oxxford Clothes, delivering the news that suits were not a growth business in the 1960s.[4] Buffett had ignored Parsow's warning not to buy suit-lining maker Berkshire Hathaway.[5]

Since he knew nothing about clothing, why the next episode of his career would consist of buying a department store remains somewhat mysterious. It took a whopper of an idea to crack open his wallet these days. But in 1966 he was having trouble finding things to buy for the partnership.

It was one of his newer friends, David "Sandy" Gottesman, who brought him this latest idea. The ever-handy Ruane had connected them at a lunch in New York City. Gottesman, a fellow Harvard graduate from a different year, worked for a small investment bank and sometimes found the odd cigar butt or two.[6] The quintessential New Yorker, Gottesman valued his time with Buffett so highly, he traveled to Omaha often. He stayed up late talking stocks with Buffett every Sunday evening for about ninety minutes. "I was looking forward to that conversation all week," says Gottesman. "No matter what I talked to him about, he knew as much as I did about them, most of the time. After I hung up, I couldn't go to sleep for a couple of hours, I was so charged up." Buffett considered him a shrewd, disciplined, hard-nosed, opinionated, unabashed capitalist. Naturally, they hit it off.

"From then on," says Gottesman, "every time I had a good idea, I would call Warren. It was like vetting. If you could get Warren interested in something, you knew that you had the right idea."

In January 1966, Gottesman brought Buffett an idea: Hochschild-Kohn, a venerable department store headquartered in a building a city block in size that sat at an intersection in downtown Baltimore.

Martin Kohn, the company's CEO, had called Gottesman to tell him that several branches of the family were thinking of selling and would probably accept a discount price. Buffet and Munger flew into Baltimore, and liked the Kohns immediately. Louis Kohn, who had a financial background, was going to run the business for them. Buffett had become confident of his ability to assess people quickly after experience bringing in three hundred partners and meeting countless business executives over the years. He and Munger looked at the balance sheet and made a $12 million bid on the spot.

On January 30, 1966, Buffett, Munger, and Gottesman formed a holding company, Diversified Retailing Company, Inc., to "acquire diversified businesses, especially in the retail field."[7] Buffett owned eighty percent of DRC. Gottesman and Munger each took ten percent. Buffett and Munger then went to the Maryland National Bank and asked for a loan to make the purchase. The lending officer looked at them goggle-eyed and exclaimed, *"Six million dollars for little old Hochschild-Kohn?"*[8] Even after hearing this, Buffett and Munger—characteristically—did not question their own judgment and run screaming out the door.

"We thought we were buying a second-class department store at a third-class price" is how Buffett describes little old Hochschild-Kohn.

He had never borrowed any significant money to buy a company. But they figured the margin of safety reduced their risk, and interest rates were cheap at the time. Profits in department stores were thin, but as those profits grew over the years, the interest on the debt would stay the same and any increase in the profits would flow to themselves. *If* the profits grew over the years.

"Buying Hochschild-Kohn was like the story of a man who buys a yacht," says Munger. "The two happy days are the day he buys it and the day he sells it."[9]

Buffett began to grow concerned on his next trip to Baltimore, when Kohn showed him a plan the company had been developing for some time to build two new stores, one in York, Pennsylvania, the other in Maryland. The idea was to capitalize on the exodus from city to suburb that was sending people to suburban shopping malls.

"They'd been planning those two stores for a couple of years. The guy that had the men's furnishings department had his section laid out. He knew exactly how he was going to decorate it. The woman who ran the high-priced dress department had hers all planned too." Buffett didn't like confrontation and dreaded disappointing people, but he and Munger agreed that neither of these locations made sense. He spiked the York store and the Hochschild-Kohn employees and management resisted. Lacking the stomach for a fight, Buffett gave in. But he drew the line at the Columbia, Maryland, store. *"I ended up killing that. And everybody died. They just died."*

Still, for the first time, Buffett and Munger had found something they could partner on. Through Diversified Retailing, they and Gottesman had, in effect, created a separate company specifically to own retailers. But Hochschild-Kohn was the beginning of a pattern that would recur more than once in frothy markets: Buffett had lowered his standards to justify an investment. That he had done it at a time when he was having more and more trouble finding what he considered to be good investments in the stock market was no coincidence.

In this case, "we were enough influenced by the Graham ethos," says Munger, "that we thought if you just got enough assets for your dollars, somehow you could make it work out. And we didn't weigh heavily enough the intense competition between four different department stores in Baltimore at a time when department stores no longer had an automatic edge."

Within the first couple of years at Hochschild-Kohn, Buffett had figured out that the essential skill in retailing was merchandising, not finance. He and his partners also had learned enough about retailing to understand that it was a lot like the restaurant business: a wearying marathon in which, every mile, fresh, aggressive competition could leap in and race ahead of you. When the three had the opportunity to acquire another retailer through DRC—this one very different and run by a true merchandiser—they went ahead, however. This retailer came to them through Will Felstiner, the lawyer who had also worked on the Hochschild-Kohn deal, who called to say, "If you're interested in retailing, here's the numbers on Associated Cotton Shops." The Cotton Shops sold women's dresses. Here Buffett was headed even further afield from his basic "circle of competence," although this next episode would bring into his fold one of the all-time greatest managers and characters he would ever meet in his life.

"A cheap little scroungey" is how Munger described Associated Retail Stores, the parent of the Cotton Shops.[10] Seeing a set of third-class stores for a fourth-class price, he and Buffett were immediately interested. Associated owned eighty stores with $44 million of sales and earned a couple of million dollars a year. Benjamin Rosner, its sixty-three-year-old proprietor, ran discount dress shops, in tough neighborhoods in cities such as Chicago, Buffalo, New York, and Gary, Indiana, under names like Fashion Outlet, Gaytime, and York. Sometimes he installed several tiny stores carrying the same goods under different names on the same city block. Rosner kept the overhead microscopic and sold only for cash. Running these outlets required unusual skills. In Chicago, a manager at the Milwaukee Avenue store, a big, hard-boiled woman, *"blew a whistle every time she saw somebody come in that she knew was a shoplifter type. All the employees would look over and watch the guy from then on. She knew them all and had the lowest 'shrinkage' rate of practically any store you could ever find in the toughest neighborhood you could imagine."*

Born in 1904 to Austro-Hungarian immigrants, Ben Rosner dropped out of school in the fourth grade. In 1931, the downdraft of the Great Depression, he started with one little store on the North Side of Chicago, $3,200 in capital, a

---

*Inventory "shrinkage" is just what it sounds like: inventory that is unaccounted for, usually because of shoplifting or employee theft.

partner, Leo Simon, and a batch of dresses they sold for $2.88 apiece.[11] When Simon died in the mid-1960s, more than three decades later, Rosner continued to pay his widow, Aye Simon* (daughter of communications mogul Moses Annenberg), Leo's salary in exchange for the nominal task of signing the rent checks for their eighty stores.

"This went on for about six months, and then she started complaining and second-guessing and criticizing. And that really got to Ben. She was a spoiled, spoiled, spoiled woman. Now, Ben was a guy whose principle, as he later explained to me, was to screw everybody except his partner. And in his mind, she's no longer his partner. So he decided that he had to end this whole thing.

"So as the switch flips in his mind, he's going to screw her. He decided that he was going to sell the business to me too cheap, even though he owns half of it, because it'll show her. When we met with him, he started talking and I got the picture very quickly."

Buffett had been there before with people who were talking themselves into thinking they were better off without something, and he knew not to do anything that would interfere. *"He's talking about selling his business that he's built up all his life, and he's going crazy because he can't stand it and he can't stand her. He's just a total mess. So Charlie goes back in the room with me. And after about half an hour, Ben was jumping up and down, and he said, 'They told me you were the fastest gun in the West! Draw!' And I said, 'I'll draw on you before I leave this afternoon.'"*

Buffett needed a manager, but Rosner told him that he would stay only until the end of the year. Buffett could see, however, that, just as the business couldn't carry on without Rosner, fortunately, Rosner couldn't carry on without the business.

"He loved it too much to quit. He kept a duplicate set of store records in the bathroom so that he could look at them while he was sitting on the can. He had this rival, Milton Petrie of Petrie Stores. One time, Ben went to a big bash at the Waldorf. Milton's there. They immediately started talking business. Ben said, 'How much do you pay for lightbulbs? How much do you mark up . . . ?' And that's all Ben could talk about. Finally, he said to Milton, 'How much are you paying for toilet paper?' And Milton said so much. Ben was buying his quite a bit cheaper, and he knew that you want to be not just cheaper but right. Milton said, 'Yeah, that's the best I can get.' And Ben said, 'Excuse me,' and he got up, left the black-tie benefit,

---

*Her name was pronounced "A" like the letter of the alphabet.

drove out to his warehouse in Long Island, and started tearing open cartons of toilet paper and counting the sheets, because he was suspicious. He knew that Milton could not be paying too much by that wide a margin, and therefore that he must be getting screwed himself somehow on toilet paper.

"And, sure enough, the vendors were saying there were five hundred sheets per roll in one of these things. And there weren't. He <u>was</u> getting screwed on toilet paper."

Buffett knew that he wanted to be in business with the kind of guy who would leave a black-tie party to count sheets of toilet paper; a guy who might screw the guy across the table but never his own partner. He made a deal with Rosner for $6 million. To make sure that Rosner would stay on the job after he bought the business, he flattered Rosner, made certain he got the numbers to evaluate its performance, and otherwise left him alone.[12]

Buffett felt at one with the Ben Rosners of the world—he saw in their relentlessness the spirit of success. He was sick of problem companies like Hochschild-Kohn and was looking for more Ben Rosners, people who had built excellent businesses that he could buy. He and Rosner shared a mutual obsession. As Buffett liked to put it, "Intensity is the price of excellence."

30

Jet Jack

As late as 1967, Susie seemed to think that Warren would be more attentive to her and the family if he quit working. In her mind, the two of them had an understanding that they would scale back their lives once he made $8 or $10 million. His 1966 fees and capital gains brought the family's net worth to over $9 million.[1] She badgered him that the time had come. But Warren's pace never slackened. Sometimes his back seized up when he got on a plane, and occasionally Susie had to nurse him for several days while he was bedridden with pain. His doctor couldn't find any specific cause, suggesting that work or stress might have something to do with it. But Warren was about as likely to stop working for the sake of his back as he was to fork down a big plate of broccoli for the sake of his health.

He was always sitting hunched over something, a book, the phone, a bridge or poker game with friends like Dick Holland and Nick Newman, a prominent businessman who owned Hinky Dinky, the same grocery chain from which Warren had slunk, humiliated, as a boy after his grandfather sent him to buy loaves of bread. Newman and his wife were active in the community and in civil-rights circles, and, like the low-key Hollands, they were typical of the Buffetts' friends. Warren and Susie stayed away from the Omaha social circuit. Their joint social life was evolving into a series of recurring events that followed the rhythm of Warren's work and often took place when they were traveling to see Warren's friends. In town, Susie stayed on call; she shuttled between her own friends, family, needy cases, and community work. A sign now hung on the Buffetts' unlocked back door that read: "The Doctor Is In." One or another of

Susie's "patients" could often be found wandering around the house. Her clientele came from all different ages and stations in life, and some were demanding. They asked and Susie gave, and when they asked for more, she gave more.

When Susie asked, Warren gave. Unyielding about how he spent his time, he gave in to her on almost everything else. This was the year they remodeled the house. Already the biggest on the block, under Susie's direction a new wing replaced the old garage, giving the neighborhood kids a place to gather in a new family room. Warren was excited at having his own racquetball court in the basement underneath—like Ping-Pong on a human-size scale—where he took his friends and business colleagues to play.

But even though Warren was like a kid in many ways, and Susie wished he were a more attentive father, he was loyal and committed: He showed up at school events and took the children on vacations. The year of "White Rabbit" and *Sgt. Pepper's Lonely Hearts Club Band,* 1967, marked the apex of the rock-and-roll drug culture, but with Susie Jr. in eighth grade, Howie in sixth, and Peter in third, the Buffetts were blessedly free of worries faced by many other parents.

Susie Jr. had developed from a timid child to a self-sufficient teen and the undisputed boss of her siblings. A rock-and-roll girl, she introduced her brothers to groups like the Byrds and the Kinks. She was a straight kid, however, not sucked into the druggy element at school. Howie, now twelve, was still young enough to try to scare his sister and her friends by looming from the crabapple tree outside her window in a gorilla costume. But his pranks were getting more sophisticated, and more dangerous. He put Scout the dog on the roof, went downstairs, and called him to see if he would come. Scout did, and wound up at the vet with a broken leg. "Well, I just wanted to see if he would come," Howie protested.[2] To foil his mother from periodically locking him in his room out of frustration, he bought a lock at a hardware store and started locking *her* out. Peter spent hours at the piano, playing by himself or with his friend Lars Erickson. He was winning talent shows and seemed as absorbed in his music as his father was in making money.

The one person in the family who was seduced by the dark side of the psychedelic sixties was seventeen-year-old Billy Rogers, son of Susie's sister, Dottie, now a budding jazz guitarist who was experimenting with drugs. His mother did some volunteer work and was an expert seamstress, but she also slept until noon, seemed paralyzed by making decisions, and at times was so distant and vague that it was literally impossible to carry on a coherent conversation with her. Dottie was drinking more and not paying attention to her kids. Susie often took Billy to watch Calvin Keys, a local jazz guitar player—so that Billy could learn technique from him, but also to try to straighten Billy out.[3]

She faced a daunting task in an era when the drug culture of pot and LSD was ubiquitous and Timothy Leary invited America to "Turn on, tune in, drop out." The youth-led counterculture was rebelling against all forms of authority, everything for which the prior decades had stood. "This ain't Eisenhower's America no more," said one of the hundred thousand hippies milling about San Francisco's Haight-Ashbury that summer, as if that were explanation enough.[4]

Warren still lived in Eisenhower's America. He had never suffered from Beatlemania. His state of consciousness remained unaltered. His mind was deep in rigorous philosophical inquiry, torn between the cigar-butt philosophy of Ben Graham and the "great businesses" of Phil Fisher and Charlie Munger.

"I was in this Charlie Munger–influenced type transition—sort of back and forth. It was kind of like during the Protestant Reformation. And I would listen to Martin Luther one day and the Pope the next. Ben Graham, of course, being the Pope."

While Munger was nailing his theses on the door of the Cigar Butt Cathedral, the market itself had abandoned all authorities past and present; as the 1960s progressed, chatter about stocks enlivened cocktail parties, and housewives called their brokers from the beauty parlor. Trading volumes were up by one-third.[5] Buffett, at thirty-six, felt like a grizzled old man in a world that craved Transitron, Polaroid, Xerox, Electronic Data Systems—companies whose technology he did not understand. He told his partners that he was slowing down. "We simply don't have that many good ideas," he wrote.[6]

Yet he did not relax his rules in search of ways to keep the money at work. Instead, he laid out two new restrictions that would make it even harder for him to invest. These personal preferences now became part of the official canon.

> 1. *We will not go into businesses where technology which is way over my head is crucial to the investment decision. I know about as much about semiconductors or integrated circuits as I do of the mating habits of the chrzaszcz.*
> 2. *[W]e will not seek out activity in investment operations, even if offering splendid profit expectations, where major human problems appear to have a substantial chance of developing.*

By "major human problems" he meant layoffs, plant closings—and union businesses that couldn't take a strike. This also meant he would think once, twice, three times, before smoking any more cigar butts.

The cigar butts he owned were problem enough. Berkshire Hathaway was now "on life support." Buffett had recently hired his Peat, Marwick auditor, Verne McKenzie, and sent him off to New Bedford to oversee the wretched textile mill. He had been regretting a mistake he had made at a recent Berkshire Hathaway board meeting. Feeling flush during what would turn out to be a brief moment of financial success, Buffett had let himself get talked into a ten-cent-per-share dividend. Either while daydreaming or simply in a moment of weakness, Buffett went along with the distribution; a dime a share sounded measly; it somehow took him twenty-four hours to wake up. By then it was too late and his uncharacteristic agreeableness had showered on the partners and shareholders $101,733 that he knew he could have turned into millions someday.[7] He would never make a mistake like that again.

Eight months later, Buffett offered the Berkshire shareholders a swap. Anyone who wanted an income-producing security could have a 7½ percent debenture in exchange for stock. A total of 32,000 shares were turned in. With this move Buffett washed out of the mix a group of shareholders who wanted income, ensuring that the rest were more likely to care about growth instead of dividends. And, of course, with fewer shares outstanding, he was able to tighten his grip on Berkshire that much more—curiously, even as the magnitude of his original error in buying the place was clearer. Ken Chace stoically followed Buffett's orders to shrink the business. Rather than precipitate a hateful backlash like that at Dempster, Buffett listened to Chace's recommendations that the unions be treated well, and tolerated losses to keep some remnant of the company operational and New Bedford content.

By 1967 Chace and McKenzie had managed to pull the hapless maker of men's suit linings back to breakeven. But the term "inflation"—moribund since the Second World War—was again on everyone's lips. The costs of wages and raw materials were rising like silt in a river, and both foreign and southern textile mills with cheaper labor were drying up Berkshire's sales.

Buffett tried to pull money out of the textile business as fast as possible. He became intimately involved in the most ordinary decisions of the mills, on the phone almost daily with Chace and McKenzie.[8] Chace had had to shut down the Box Loom division for a week back in October 1966 because of competition from imports; less than six months later Buffett told him to permanently shut down the King Philip D division in Rhode Island, which made fine lawn cotton, about one-tenth of Berkshire's output. The loss of 450 jobs marked the end of Rhode Island's cotton industry.[9] *"The tide continues to be far more important than the swimmers"* was the bottom line, as Buffett saw it.[10]

It wasn't enough. As the numbers came in, Buffett realized that the Apparel Fabrics and Box Loom divisions were losing so much money that the only way to salvage them was to modernize the equipment. But throwing good money after bad had been Seabury Stanton's mistake. Buffett refused to invest in the business; it would be like trying to irrigate the desert with a garden hose. Still, closing the plants down would throw hundreds of people out of work. He sat behind his desk and swiveled his chair and thought about it, then thought about it some more.

The irony was that the partnership was swimming in a sea of money.[11] And on Wall Street, brokers in pinstripes were getting high on cash. A new breed of men, who had come of age after World War II without the lessons of the Crash and the Great Depression seared into their brains, had risen on the Street. As they pushed stocks to never-before-seen values, Buffett began selling down his American Express position, which by now was worth $28 million compared to the $13 million that it had cost, accounting for two-thirds of the partnership's gain. But he didn't want to plow that money back into Berkshire Hathaway.

Rather, his most important task that year was to find something new to which he could hitch the broken-down nag of Berkshire before its "substantial drag" on his performance became intolerable. In Omaha, he had long had his eye on a company, National Indemnity, headquartered just a few blocks away from his Kiewit Plaza office. Buffett first met its founder, Jack Ringwalt, in the early 1950s, in the boardroom at the broker Cruttenden and Company. Ringwalt was one of the smartest, most enterprising men in town. At one point he had declined to invest in the Buffett Partnership—in Ringwalt's version, because Buffett had demanded a minimum investment of $50,000 (although he was taking far less from nearly everyone at the time). Ringwalt considered himself an investing expert; perhaps Buffett's penchant for secrecy put him off.[12]

Buffett kept an eye on National Indemnity. A nonstop learning machine, he wanted to know everything there was to know about the insurance business. He checked out armloads of books from the library and came to understand Ringwalt's strategy, which was to insure the most difficult customers. Ringwalt, Buffett saw, was the mix-up player of insurance—the cautious risk-taker and the penny-pinching, aggressive underwriter who went around the office every night and turned off all the lights.[13] For a fancy price, he insured the unusual: circus performers, lion tamers, the body parts of burlesque stars.[14] "There's no such thing as a bad risk," Ringwalt liked to say, "only bad rates." He soon became the fastest-moving, most swashbuckling, energetic businessman in Omaha. His daughter referred to him by the racy-sounding nickname Jet Jack. He managed National Indemnity's investments himself, buying tiny positions in hundreds of stocks, scribbled almost illegibly on ledger sheets: fifty shares of National Distillers, 2,500 of Shaver Food Marts. He carried around hundreds of stock certificates in an old gym bag.

In the early 1960s, Buffett asked his friend Charlie Heider, who was on the board of National Indemnity, whether Ringwalt had any interest in selling. Heider's answer was intriguing.

"For fifteen minutes every year, Jack would want to sell National Indemnity. Something would make him mad. Some claim would come in that irritated him, or something of that sort. So Charlie Heider and I discussed this phenomenon of Jack being in heat once a year for fifteen minutes. And I told him if he ever caught him in this particular phase to let me know."

One gray and gloomy February Omaha day in 1967, Heider was having lunch with Ringwalt, who said, "I don't like this weather." The conversation wound around to the fact that he wanted to sell National Indemnity. The fifteen-minute window had appeared. Heider set up a meeting with Buffett that very afternoon.[15] When Ringwalt went to see Buffett in his office, however, he started laying down conditions. He said he wanted to keep the company in Omaha. Sensing that the fifteen-minute window was about to disappear, Buffett agreed he wouldn't move the company. Ringwalt said he didn't want any employees fired. Buffett said that was okay. Ringwalt said all the other offers had been too low. "How much do you want?" Buffett asked. Fifty dollars a share, said Ringwalt, fifteen dollars more than Warren thought it was worth. "I'll take it," Buffett said.

"So we made a deal in that fifteen-minute zone. Then, Jack, having made the deal, really didn't want to do it. But he was an honest guy and wouldn't back out of a deal. However, he said to me after we'd shaken hands, 'Well, I suppose you'll want audited financial statements.' And if I'd have said yes, he would've said, 'Well, that's too bad, then, we don't have a deal.' So I just responded, 'I wouldn't dream of looking at audited financial statements—they're the worst kind.' We went through about three or four iterations like this. And finally Jack gave up and sold me the business, though I don't think he really wanted to do it."

Since Buffett knew that Ringwalt would be having second thoughts, he moved fast to seal the deal before Ringwalt could change his mind. Both men wanted a contract no more than one page long.[16] Buffett had final papers drawn up quickly and the funds deposited in the U.S. National Bank.[17]

When Ringwalt returned from a vacation in Florida a week later, Buffett freight-trained him with a deal ready to close. Ringwalt showed up to the closing meeting ten minutes late. Buffett and Heider would later explain this by saying that Ringwalt was driving around the block looking for a parking meter with time left on it.[18] Ringwalt always said he was just late. But maybe he was dragging his feet, sorry at losing National Indemnity.

Buffett, of course, knew full well that National Indemnity was the chance to give his fortunes a gigantic push. A short time later, he wrote a paper on the subject under the dull title "Thoughts Regarding Capital Requirements for Insurance Companies."

The word "capital"—money—was an important hint at what Buffett was thinking when he acquired National Indemnity, for capital was his partnership's lifeblood. He was pulling capital from Berkshire and it needed to be put to work. "By most standards," he wrote, "National Indemnity is pushing its capital quite hard. It is the availability of additional resources in Berkshire Hathaway that enables us to follow the policy of aggressively using our capital which, on a long-range basis, should result in the greatest profitability within National Indemnity.... Berkshire Hathaway could put additional capital into National Indemnity, should the underwriting turn sour."[19]

Buffett had figured out a whole new type of business. If National Indemnity made money, he could send those profits out to buy other businesses and stocks, instead of leaving them to hibernate in National Indemnity's vault. But if the lion ate the lion tamer, National Indemnity might need money to pay the lion tamer's weeping family. Then the money could come back home to National Indemnity from the other businesses.

Grafting the insurance business onto Berkshire Hathaway, the mess of a textile mill, made its capital homeostatic. It could respond internally to the environment at Buffett's command, rather than hibernating like a lizard when it got cold or running out when the sun shone to find a rock on which to sun itself.

The key was to price the risks right. As with Ben Rosner and Associated Cotton Shops, he had bought an excellent business run by an able manager. Thus he needed Jack Ringwalt to stick around. Buffett paid Ringwalt handsomely and cultivated him as a friend.

The two men often played tennis in California. Ringwalt, whose taste in clothes resembled Buffett's, would show up in a grimy old sweatshirt that his daughter had made for him. His racy nickname, Jet Jack, stretched in huge letters over his bay window of a gut. Once when he and Buffett were having lunch at a Jolly Roger restaurant, a little kid came up to him. "Can I have your autograph, Jet Jack?" he asked. Ringwalt swelled with pride. The kid thought he was a celebrity: an astronaut or a movie star. He may not have looked the part except to a little kid, but in his heart, he still felt like Jet Jack.

And rightly so, because the swashbuckle came from inside, not from the way he looked. Ringwalt may have sold his company, but he had gotten back a bit of his own—for what he did with some of the money he got from selling National Indemnity was to buy stock in Berkshire Hathaway.[20]

31

The Scaffold Sways the Future

Omaha · 1967–1968

The greatest wave of riots, lootings, and burnings since the Civil War swept the country during the summer of 1967. Omaha's nonviolent activists counted the Buffetts—both of whom were now influential in town—among their informal network. Rackie Newman, the wife of Warren's best friend in Omaha, Nick Newman, was working with Susie to pressure the YMCA and the boards of other organizations to give a fairer share of money to their branches in impoverished areas. Through the United Methodist Community Center, run by an African-American friend, Rodney Wead,[1] Susie and Rackie sent black kids to summer camp and set up an interracial dialogue group for local high school students.[2] Wead had become a frequent presence in the Buffett house. Nick Newman helped bring Warren directly into the struggle by sponsoring his participation in various local civil-rights groups. Warren's role was not to labor, but to speak: He testified before the legislature in Lincoln on open housing. For her part, Susie went out and at least a few times actually bought houses, fronting for blacks who wanted to move into white neighborhoods.[3]

Recently, Warren had been introduced to Joe Rosenfield, who ran the Younkers chain of department stores based in nearby Des Moines.[4] Rosenfield was well connected in both local and national politics and shared the Buffetts' political views. He was also a trustee of Grinnell College, which sat like a tiny radical island in the middle of the farming hamlet of Grinnell, Iowa.[5] Eighty-some years after its founding in 1846, Grinnell had nearly gone broke, but in the quarter century since Rosenfield had taken over the endowment, he had built it to nearly $10 million.[6] He had a keen wit, as well as an edge of sadness about him, having lost his only son in a tragic accident; Susie Buffett quickly developed a special relationship with him. Given all their shared interests, Rosenfield naturally wanted to involve the Buffetts with Grinnell, his most important cause.

In October 1967, the college was presenting a three-day fund-raising convocation on "the liberal arts college in a world of change" and had assembled a brilliant panoply of a speakers' roster—including author Ralph Ellison, whose novel *Invisible Man* had won a National Book Award, and communications theorist Marshall McLuhan, who had popularized the idea of a media-driven "global village." But the speaker they were all waiting for was Dr. Martin Luther King Jr.[7] Nobel Peace Prize winners were not everyday visitors to Iowa. Rosenfield had invited the Buffetts to the convocation; they were among the five thousand people who packed themselves into Darby Gymnasium for that Sunday morning's program.

King had chosen the theme of "Remaining Awake During a Revolution," and his resonant voice rang out with a quote from poet James Russell Lowell's "The Present Crisis," the anthem of the civil-rights movement.

> Truth forever on the scaffold,
> Wrong forever on the throne:
> Yet that scaffold sways the future,
> And behind the dim unknown,
> Standeth God within the shadow
> Keeping watch above His own.[8]

He spoke of the meaning of suffering. Inspired to nonviolent resistance by Gandhi, King invoked the lessons of the Sermon on the Mount. Blessed are the persecuted, it said, for theirs is the kingdom of heaven. Blessed are the meek, for they shall inherit the earth.

As touched as she was by Dr. King's powerful words, Susie must also have been deeply moved by the way he transfixed her husband.[9] Buffett had always responded to powerful, charismatic orators. Now he saw King standing before him: moral courage in the flesh, a man who had been beaten and imprisoned, put in shackles and sentenced to hard labor, stabbed and clubbed for his beliefs, a man who had carried a movement on the strength of his ideas for nearly a decade despite enraged opposition, violence, and limited success.

King was a prophet, a man who saw a vision of glory, of evil exposed through visible suffering, of people roused from sleep by the sight of horrors. He called his followers to nail themselves to his vision, to lift it up behind them and drag it through the streets. Christianity, he said, has always insisted that the cross we bear precedes the crown we wear. "If an individual has not discovered something that he will die for, he isn't fit to live," King said.[10] One of his lines, which he repeated in many of his speeches, struck Buffett's heart and pierced his reason.[11]

"The laws are not to change the heart," he said, "but to restrain the heartless."

"With that great voice of his, he just rumbled that out, and then went on and used that as a theme."

Susie had often told her husband that there was more to life than sitting in a room making money. That October 1967, in the throes of the civil-rights struggle, he had written a special letter to the partners, which showed that something in his thoughts had changed. It laid out his strategy without revealing the year's pending results. After describing the *"hyper-reactive pattern of market behavior,"* he went on to say: *"My own personal interests dictate a less compulsive approach to superior investment results than when I was younger and leaner....I am out of step with present conditions. On one point, however, I am clear. I will not abandon a previous approach whose logic I understand (although I find it difficult to apply) even though it may mean forgoing large, and apparently easy, profits to embrace an approach which I don't fully understand, have not practiced successfully, and which, possibly, could lead to substantial permanent loss of capital."*

Personal goals, he said, had begun to intrude: *"I would like to have an economic goal which allows for considerable noneconomic activity....I am likely to limit myself to things which are reasonably easy, safe, profitable, and pleasant."*

Buffett then stunned his partners by dropping his stated goal of beating the market by *ten* points a year to beating it by just *five* points a year—or to earning nine percent, whichever was *less*. If they could find better results elsewhere, he said, they should go, and he wouldn't blame them.

He knew that this was taking a risk. Some of the hot new mutual funds were doing much better than the partnership, doubling their money in a year. Each January, the partners could add money to the partnership—or take it out. Many other skippers were forecasting sunnier skies.

Yet his timing worked in his favor. The Dow produced an unusually poor year in 1966.[12] Some of the partners, shaken by the market's roiling, had advised him to sell stocks. He paid attention neither to the market nor to advice, and the partnership beat the Dow by thirty-six points, the best record in its ten-year history. *"If you can't join 'em, lick 'em,"* he wrote.[13] So, it was not a bad time to be offering his partners the chance to take their money elsewhere.

One side effect of this strategy would be to test their trust in him. Only he knew that for 1967 he was about to report his second stellar year in a row. If they stayed in, it would be because of that trust and because they were willing to accept his more modest goal. Even Ben Graham had beaten the market by just 2.5 percent a year. Buffett's revised goal of nine percent put a floor on their results that was still two percent or more better than owning an average bond. Beating the market by five points a year, year after year, *and not losing* money, would lead to a stunning result.* Sticking with him, an investor could achieve these extraordinary returns, and do so *safely*. Nevertheless, by lowering his target, Buffett had just taken his partners down a peg psychologically, and the results reflected that.

For the first time, instead of investors rushing to put more money into the partnership, they pulled out a net $1.6 million of capital in January 1968. Yet it was a fraction of what might have been. Less than one in thirty dollars had gone elsewhere. And when he reported his 1967 results a few weeks later, Buffett Partnership, Ltd. had advanced thirty-six percent—versus the nineteen percent rise in the Dow. Thus, in two years, a dollar in Buffett's stewardship had grown more than sixty cents, while a dollar in the Dow was still a measly dollar.

He wished the departing partners Godspeed with what might be perceived as the subtlest trace of irony: *"This makes good sense for them, since most of them have the ability and motivation to surpass our objectives and I am relieved from pushing for results that I probably can't attain under present conditions."*[14]

"Financial genius is a rising market," as Kenneth Galbraith would later say.[15]

Now Buffett had more time to pursue the personal interests he had spoken about, and less pressure—at least in theory. After King's speech, Rosenfield easily recruited Buffett to become a Grinnell trustee. Given Buffett's dislike of committees and meetings, this signified how much he had been touched by the convocation—as well as how close he had grown to Rosenfield. Naturally, he went straight onto the finance committee, where he found the trustees to be a group

---

*Assuming the Dow averaged four percent a year, a partner's thousand-dollar investment in BPL would turn into $5,604 after twenty years at nine percent—$3,413 more than the $2,191 that an owner of the Dow would have.

of like-minded men. Bob Noyce, who ran a company called Fairchild Semi-conductor, which made electronic circuits—something about which Buffett knew little and had even less interest—was chairman. Like Buffett, he had an overarching hatred of hierarchy and a love of the underdog, in keeping with the guiding spirit of Grinnell.

Buffett seemed to feel a sense of urgency to do something more for civil rights too. He felt he could best serve the cause by using his brains and financial savvy behind the scenes. Rosenfield began to introduce Buffett around the Democratic Party power network. Buffett started to get involved with Iowa's Democratic Senator Harold Hughes and with Gene Glenn, who was running for the Senate.

In March 1968, riots broke out after a visit to Omaha by former Alabama Governor George Wallace, the most controversial man in America. A segregationist who was running an independent campaign for President, Wallace lit the match for days of confrontation between police and blacks, including Omaha's Black Panthers.[16] The racial violence continued all that summer. Susie never stopped going to the North Side. She trusted in her excellent relations with the community and discounted the personal danger; Warren was not always aware of the details of what she was doing but did feel that at times she went too far in putting others' interests before her own. His own horror of violence and fear of mob rule had roots that went back a generation.

Howard Buffett had recounted over and over to his children a scene he had witnessed at age sixteen—a day when thousands of people converged on the Douglas County Courthouse, broke in and attempted to lynch the mayor of Omaha, and beat, castrated, and lynched an elderly black man who had been accused of rape. Afterward they dragged his body through the streets, shot bullets into it, lynched it again, and set it afire. The Courthouse Riot became the most shameful episode in Omaha's history. Howard missed seeing much of the violence, but witnessed the lynch mob turning a streetlamp into an improvised scaffold, and the mayor of Omaha hanging by a noose around his neck before being rescued in the nick of time.[17] The memory haunted him for the rest of his life.[18] He saw with his own eyes the speed with which ordinary people, formed into a mob, could act out the lowest depths of human nature.

King had warned earlier that year that mass social unrest could potentially lead to fascism. This required no explanation to Warren Buffett. His own commitment to siding with the underdog went beyond instinct and rested partly on this train of logic. Many people thought such a thing was inconceivable in the

United States, but the seemingly impossible happened time and again. The law is not to change the heart, King said, but to restrain the heartless. And who are they, the heartless? That he did not say.

A few weeks later, King flew to Memphis to speak at the Masonic temple. The next day, April 4, as he stood on the balcony of the Lorraine Motel preparing to lead a march of sanitation workers, he was fatally shot in the neck.

Grief, rage, and frustration poured out of black communities across America, turning urban centers into fiery combat zones. At the same time, tens of thousands of students were demonstrating against the Vietnam War on college campuses. The U.S. government had just eliminated most draft deferments, finally putting the sons of the upper middle class at risk of being drafted. Public sentiment turned decisively against the war. There was such turbulence in the air that the country felt as though revolution could erupt at any moment.

In their various ways, many people decided they were fed up, and done with being put down. Buffett's friend Nick Newman abruptly announced that he would no longer attend meetings at clubs that discriminated against Jews as members.[19] Warren, too, was moved to take action. Since his Graham-Newman days, he had broken away from the segregated 1950s culture and the anti-Semitism of his family's elder generation to forge friendships and business connections with a wide circle of Jewish people. He even seemed to feel a sense of personal identification with Jews, some thought; their status as outsiders fit with his own sense of maladjustment and his alignment with the underdog. Some time before, Buffett had quietly resigned from the Rotary Club, repelled by the bigotry he saw as a member of its membership committee. But he never told anyone the reason. Now he made it his personal project to sponsor a Jew—his friend Herman Goldstein—for membership in the Omaha Club.

Since one of the rationales that institutions like the Omaha Club used to defend their exclusionary policies was that "they have their own clubs that don't admit us," Buffett decided to ask Nick Newman to nominate him for the all-Jewish Highland Country Club.[20] Some of its members objected, using the same logic employed by the Omaha Club: Why take in gentiles when we had to establish our club because their clubs wouldn't have us?[21] But a couple of rabbis got involved and an Anti-Defamation League spokesman appeared on Buffett's behalf.[22] Once accepted, Buffett quietly stormed the Omaha Club, armed with his Jewish country-club membership. Herman Goldstein was voted in, and the long-standing religious barrier to membership there finally toppled.

Buffett had devised a clever solution, a way to get the club to do the right thing without confronting anyone. It avoided the thing he dreaded, but it also reflected his reasoning—probably correct—that marching and demonstrations would not change the minds of well-off businessmen.

It also worked because he was now a well-known figure in Omaha. He was no longer an upstart; he had clout. The man who had once had to work to get off the blacklist of the Omaha Country Club had singlehandedly effected what was perhaps the most significant organizational change since its founding in one of Omaha's most elite institutions.

Yet Buffett wanted to play more than just a local role. With his money, he knew he could have an impact at the national level. 1968 was an election year, and it would take a lot of money to try to unseat an incumbent President— Lyndon Johnson—in favor of an antiwar candidate.

Vietnam was the central issue of the campaign, and Eugene McCarthy, the liberal Senator from Minnesota, was initially the only Democrat willing to run in the primaries against Johnson.

The campaign had started in New Hampshire, where McCarthy won forty-two percent of the vote, a strikingly strong showing against an incumbent President. Many students, blue-collar workers, and antiwar voters considered McCarthy a hero. Buffett became treasurer of his Nebraska campaign, and he and Susie attended a campaign event, she smiling broadly in an eye-catching dress and mob cap that she had had made out of fabric striped with McCarthy's name.

Then Johnson announced that he would not run again and John F. Kennedy's brother Robert Kennedy entered the race. He and McCarthy raced through a bitter primary battle until Kennedy won the California primary. But on the night of his victory, he was shot by an assassin, dying twenty-four hours later, and Johnson's Vice President, Hubert Humphrey, announced his candidacy. He captured the nomination at a tumultuous Democratic convention in Chicago marked by battles between police equipped with nightsticks and Mace and rioting antiwar protesters. Buffett then supported Humphrey against the Republican Richard Nixon, who won the election.

Although Buffett regretted and downplayed his association with McCarthy, his involvement in politics during that tumultuous year signaled a sea change in his life. For the first time he had made room for something besides investing, a "non-economic activity" with roots in his family's past and branches that stretched toward the unknowable future.

32

Easy, Safe, Profitable, and Pleasant

Omaha · 1968–1969

In January 1968, Buffett had issued a call to his fellow Grahamites, summoning them together for the first time as a meeting of the faithful in the middle of a stock market gone mad. He invited *"about all that is left of the old guard,"* Graham's former students Bill Ruane, Walter Schloss, Marshall Weinberg, Jack Alexander, and Tom Knapp.[1] He also invited Charlie Munger, whom he had introduced to Graham, as well as Munger's partner, Roy Tolles, and Jack Alexander's partner, Buddy Fox. Ed Anderson, who had left Munger's partnership to become a partner in Tweedy, Browne, was on the guest list, too, as were Sandy Gottesman and Henry Brandt.

Fred Stanback, Buffett's partner in deals like Sanborn Map and the best man at his wedding, was too busy to attend. A few years after Warren had finished at Columbia, he and Miss Nebraska 1949, Vanita Mae Brown, had reunited for dinner in New York with Susie and Fred, who had met Vanita at least once before through Warren. After the dinner, Fred, Warren's most introverted friend, became, as another friend put it, "putty in Vanita's hands." Initially, their marriage probably seemed like a sort of charming postscript to Warren's career at Columbia: a couple brought into the Buffetts' circle from that era. He did have a tendency to arrange his friends' lives, putting them on his companies' boards, and in general wrapping them into his life through ties of various kinds. Two friends married may have felt almost like a compliment to him, but it turned out to be the worst decision Fred ever made in his life.

He and Vanita had been living in Salisbury, North Carolina, where Fred grew up. Now Fred was extracting himself from this pulse-pounding marriage. Thus, unlike the rest of the Grahamites, Fred's interest in the stock market had been temporarily diverted. It was at a time when the market was growing less attractive anyway: More than fifty new investment funds had come to market, with nearly sixty-five more waiting in the wings.[2] For the first time in U.S. history, it became fashionable for a broad group of individuals to own stocks.[3] Buffett would describe this phase as resembling "an ever-widening circle of chain letters," even a "mania," populated mostly by "the hopeful, credulous, and greedy, grasping for an excuse to believe."[4]

In a business that was still transacted through paper trade tickets and physical delivery of stock certificates, trading volume had reached such a level that the market was nearly crushed under the weight of paperwork. All sorts of reforms pushed through in 1967 and 1968 automated and computerized the trading systems in a desperate effort to catch up. One of the most important would shut down the old "under-the-counter" market. The National Association of Securities Dealers announced that it was about to bring online a new system called NASDAQ that would quote prices for smaller stocks.[5] Instead of appearing on Pink Sheets that were stale the moment they were printed, the prices of most companies not listed on the stock exchanges would now be posted electronically as they changed. Market makers had to show their hands and stand by the quotes they posted. Any trader who was very knowledgeable, good at haggling, and strong of backbone was not going to like the new system. In the middle of an already difficult market, it was going to make Buffett's job harder.

To each of the Grahamites coming to La Jolla, Warren sent out instructions. "Please do not bring anything more current than a 1934 edition of *Security Analysis* along with you," he wrote.[6] Wives, too, would remain at home.

In his letter, Buffett reminded them that they were there to listen to Graham, the Great Man, not one another. At age thirty-seven, Buffett had finally attained peerage and was able to call his former teacher "Ben," but sometimes he still slipped and said "Mr. Graham." So he must have been at least partly reminding himself not to try to take over as the best student in the class.

The dozen Graham-worshippers convened at the Hotel del Coronado, across the bay from San Diego. Warren had wanted to meet at a much cheaper venue such as a Holiday Inn; he made sure the group knew that the extravagance of this pink-and-white Victorian confection of a resort was Graham's idea.

By the time the dozen arrived in San Diego, a huge storm with lashing rain and churning seas had hit, but no one cared; they were there to talk about stocks. Buffett was bursting with pride at having engineered a tribute to his teacher and a chance to show off the wisdom of Ben Graham to his new friends. Graham arrived at the Coronado late. Ever the teacher, as soon as he got there, he immediately gave them an exam.

Graham was almost painful to listen to under any circumstances. Every sentence was complex and larded with classical allusions. The exam he gave them was much the same. *"They were not terribly complicated questions, although they were a little—you know, some were French history, or something like that. But you thought you knew some of the answers,"* says Buffett.

They didn't. Only Roy Tolles got more than half. By answering everything "true" except a couple that he knew for certain were not, he scored eleven out of twenty. The "little exam" turned out to be one of Graham's teaching tricks, designed to show that even an easy-looking game can be rigged. Buffett would later have a saying: Knowing that a clever guy is stacking the deck is not necessarily protection.

During the rest of the meeting, Graham tolerated the discussions of stocks with bemusement.[7] Instead, he wanted to tell riddles and joined with enthusiasm in brainteasers and word and numbers games.

Buffett, however, was as much engaged as ever, notwithstanding the tenor of his letter to his partners in October 1967, when he had written that from now on he would limit himself to activities that were "easy, safe, profitable, and pleasant." When he returned to Omaha from San Diego he focused intensely on the problems of the partnership. All was not well at some of the businesses it owned; his next two letters contained subtle hints. After having described the travails of textiles eloquently in 1967, he made no further mention of the business in 1968. Earnings at DRC were falling because of Hochschild-Kohn.[8] Still, Buffett did not take the logical next step, which would have been to sell the laggards.

Here, his commercial instincts chafed against some of his other traits: the urge to collect, the need to be liked, the fear of confrontation. In an intricate minuet of rationalization, he explained his thinking in his January 1968 letter to the partners: *"When I am dealing with people I like in businesses I find stimulating (what business isn't?), and achieving worthwhile overall returns on capital employed (say, ten to twelve percent), it seems foolish to rush from situation to situation to earn a few more percentage points. It also does not seem sensible to me to trade known pleasant personal relationships with high-grade people, at a decent rate of return, for possible irritation, aggravation, or worse at potentially higher returns."[9]*

Some of the growing crowd of Buffett-watchers read these words with surprise. Measuring by "overall" returns allowed for some businesses to do considerably worse than the average. To witness Buffett—who squeezed the last tenth
of a percentage point from a buck like a miser gripping a toothpaste tube—dis-
missively waving away "a few more percentage points" was astonishing.

Yet his performance stopped complaints, for even as he lowered expectations, he continued to surpass himself. Despite the deadweights, the partnership
had averaged more than a thirty-one percent return over the dozen years of its
existence, while the Dow had produced nine percent. The margin of safety
Buffett always insisted on had skewed the odds sharply in his favor.[10] Along with
his talent for investing, its cumulative impact on his batting average meant that
$1,000 put in the Dow was now worth $2,857, whereas he had turned it into
nearly ten times that, $27,106. Buffett's partners by now trusted him to always
deliver more than he promised. He manifested predictability in 1968, the
tumultuous year in which students would take over and close Columbia
University and activists would nominate a pig for President.[11]

But by mid-1968, Buffett had made a decision to try to jettison the
intractable Berkshire Hathaway. He tried to sell the company to Munger and
Gottesman. After three days of discussion in Omaha, however, neither man
wanted to buy something that Buffett thought he was better off without. He was
stuck with Berkshire Hathaway.

Buffett was now forced to act. Deploying capital with no hope of a return was
a cardinal sin to him. He told Ken Chace what to do. Chace was upset, but, in typically stoic fashion, he followed orders and shut two divisions down.[12] Still, Buffett
could not bring himself to put a spike through the whole thing and bury it.

What he was left with, therefore, was a partnership that owned two businesses, one thriving—National Indemnity—and one failing—Berkshire
Hathaway—plus eighty percent of DRC, the retail holding company, and, of
course, shares in a wide range of other companies. As 1968 waned, stocks on the
fringes of the market began to slide; investors concentrated on the biggest, safest
names. Buffett himself started buying the blandest, most popular stocks that
remained reasonably priced: AT&T, BF Goodrich, Jones & Laughlin Steel. But
above all, he kept accumulating more Berkshire Hathaway—despite his
restriction against buying any more bad businesses and even though the textile
business was sinking into the mud. Now that he could not sell it, he seemed to
want as much of the stock as he could get.

He and Munger had also discovered another promising company and were buying as much stock of it as they could. This was Blue Chip Stamps. They would buy it separately and together, and over the course of time Blue Chip would dramatically reshape the course of both men's careers.

The trading stamp was a marketing giveaway. Retailers handed stamps to their customers with their change. Customers pasted them into little booklets. When redeemed, enough of the booklets bought them anything from a toaster oven to a tetherball set. The small thrill of saving stamps fit neatly into a disappearing world: a world of thrift, a world that feared debt, that viewed these "free gifts" as the reward for taking the trouble to collect and save those stamps.[13]

But the stamps were not really free.[14] The stores paid for them and marked up the merchandise accordingly. The national leader in trading stamps was Sperry & Hutchinson, except in California. There, a group of chains had shut out the S&H Green Stamp by starting their own trading stamp, Blue Chip, and selling it to themselves at a discount.[15] Blue Chip had a classic monopoly.

"When you had all the major oil companies and grocers giving out a single stamp, it became like money. People would leave their change behind and take the stamps. Morticians gave out stamps. Prostitutes gave them. It was ubiquitous. People even counterfeited them."

In 1963, the Department of Justice had filed suit against Blue Chip for restraint of trade and monopolizing the trading-stamp business in California.[16] S&H also sued it. With the stock in a slump, Rick Guerin, who had founded his own partnership, Pacific Partners, noticed Blue Chip and took it to Munger. Buffett had noticed it too. "Blue Chip did not have an immaculate conception," Charlie Munger concedes, but they all decided to make a calculated bet that Blue Chip could work its way out of its woes.

They wanted it because Blue Chip had something called "float." The stamps were paid for in advance; the prizes got redeemed later. In between, Blue Chip had use of the money, sometimes for years. Buffett had first encountered this tantalizing concept with GEICO, and it was part of why he had wanted to own National Indemnity. Insurers, too, got paid premiums before the claims came in. All kinds of businesses had float. Deposits in banks also created float. Customers often thought of banks as doing them a kind of favor by holding their cash in a safe place. But the banks invested the deposits in loans at the highest interest they could charge. That was "float." To someone like Buffett, having other people's money to invest, on which he kept the profit, was catnip.

Buffett and his friends understood how to invert every financial situation. If someone offered them trading stamps, they thought, "Hmm, it's probably better to own the trading-stamp *company*." Even Buffett—a boyhood stamp collector who still dreamed occasionally about counting stamps, and had a sentimental stash of Blue Eagle stamps in his basement—would rather own Blue Chip stock than collect Blue Chip stamps.

In 1968, Blue Chip began settling the lawsuits filed against it by competitors.[17] It entered into a "consent decree" with the Justice Department, under which the grocery chains that owned it would sell forty-five percent of the company to the retailers who gave away the stamps.[18] To remove even more control from the grocers, the Justice Department required the company to find another buyer for one-third of its stamp business. Still, it looked as though Blue Chip had survived this part of the legal fight.[19]

Munger's partnership had bought 20,000 shares, and Guerin bought a similar amount. In the process, Munger developed the proprietary attitude about Blue Chip that Buffett displayed about Berkshire Hathaway. He warned others away from it. "We don't want anyone buying Blue Chip," he told people. "We don't want anyone buying this."[20]

As the market rose, Buffett increased the partnership's temporary cash position to the tens of millions. His partnership also took over large blocks of Blue Chip stock from grocers, and would continue to buy until the partnership had acquired more than 70,000 shares. Fortunately they were betting mainly on the S&H lawsuit settling—otherwise, the timing would have been awful.

Just as he and Munger and Guerin were making large commitments to Blue Chip, its steadily growing sales apexed. The burgeoning women's liberation movement meant that women had better things to do with their time, more money, and with that a sense of entitlement that meant that if they wanted an electric blender or a fondue set, they went out and bought it, rather than fussing over books of stamps to trade in for it. Social roles and conventions had gone topsy-turvy, the Establishment culture so reviled that young people said categorically, "Don't trust anyone over thirty." Buffett, at thirty-eight, did not feel old personally—he would never feel old personally—but "I am in the geriatric ward, philosophically," he wrote to the partners.[21] He was out of step with modern culture and finance.

In 1968, the prospect of Vietnam peace talks in Paris set off another boisterous rally in the market. Having husbanded, tended, and compounded his partnership, with minimal risk, to more than three hundred partners and $105 million, Buffett was seemingly eclipsed by young barnstormers who could joyride new investors into giving them $500 million nearly overnight.

He seemed especially—and comfortably—antiquated when it came to all the new technology companies that were forming. At Grinnell College, he showed up for a meeting to find his fellow trustee Bob Noyce itching to leave Fairchild Semiconductor. Noyce, Gordon Moore (its research director), and its assistant director of research and development, Andy Grove, had decided to start a nameless new company in Mountain View, California, based on a vague plan to extend the technology of circuits to "higher levels of integration."[22] Joe Rosenfield and the college endowment fund each said they would put in $100,000, joining dozens who were helping to raise $2.5 million for the new company—which was soon to be named Intel, for *Inte*grated *El*ectronics.

Buffett had a long-standing bias against technology investments, which he felt had no margin of safety. Years ago, in 1957, Katie Buffett, wife of his uncle Fred Buffett, had arrived at Warren's back door one day with a question. Should she and Fred invest in her brother Bill's new company? Bill Norris was leaving Remington Rand's* UNIVAC computer division to start a company called Control Data Corporation to compete with IBM.

Warren was horrified. *"Bill thought that Remington Rand was falling behind IBM. I thought he was out of his mind. Aunt Katie and Uncle Fred wanted to put a few bucks in Control Data there right at the start. Bill didn't have any money. Nobody had any money, in a sense."* Well, except Warren and Susie. *"I could have financed half the thing if I'd wanted. I was very negative on it. I told them, 'It doesn't sound like much to me. Who needs another computer company?' "*[23]

But since Bill was Katie's brother, for once she and Fred had ignored Warren's advice and invested $400 anyway, buying the stock at sixteen cents a share.[24]

Control Data's success hadn't changed Buffett's opinion about technology. Many of the other technology companies that had started at the same time had failed. As much out of regard for Rosenfield as for any other reason, however, Buffett signed off on a technology investment for Grinnell.[25] Rosenfield provided the margin of safety by guaranteeing the college's investment. And as much as Buffett admired Noyce, he did not buy Intel for the partnership, thus passing on one of the greatest investing opportunities of his life. While he had lowered his investing standards in difficult environments—and would do so again—one compromise he would never make was to give up his margin of safety. This particular quality—to pass up possible riches if he couldn't limit his risk—was what made him Warren Buffett.

---

*Later, through mergers, Unisys.

Now the whole market was starting to look like Intel to him. His 1968 year-end letter said that investing ideas were at an all-time low.[26]

That attitude was remarkably different from 1962, when the market was similarly soaring. Both times he bemoaned it. But then he had raised money with an energy that belied his inability to put it to work.

The partners were dumbfounded by the contrast between his dour words and the wing-walk way he seemed to be earning money for them. Some began to impart an almost supernatural level of confidence to him. The more he surpassed his own gloomy predictions, the more the legend seemed to grow. But he knew it wasn't going to last.

33

The Unwinding

In the outer office on Kiewit Plaza's eighth floor, Gladys Kaiser sat guarding Warren Buffett's doorway. Rail-thin, perfectly made up, chain-smoke drifting through her platinum hair, Gladys dispatched paperwork, phone calls, bills, and nonsense with brisk efficiency.[1] She kept Buffett off-limits to everyone—including, at times, his family. It made Susie seethe, but there was nothing she could do.

Susie blamed Gladys. Warren, of course, would never give Gladys an actual order to keep Susie out. But no one at his office would so much as cough if they thought he would disapprove. People had to follow hints and signals simply to work at the Buffett Partnership. Beetled brows and "hmmmf" meant "Don't even consider it." "Really?" meant "I disagree." An averted head, crinkled eyes, and backpedaling meant "Help me, I can't." Gladys brooked no nonsense in following these unarticulated requests and orders, and sometimes people's feelings got hurt. But her job was to protect her boss, and she had to be tough enough to take the blame.

On the dingy walls above her head hung some framed newspaper clippings, reminders of the 1929 Crash. Dented metal furniture, along with an old ticker machine, furnished the offices. Down the linoleum hallway beyond Gladys sat the other people who knew how to interpret Buffett's signals and signs. To the left was Bill Scott's little office, where he barked "Hurry up, I'm busy!" at the brokers to execute Buffett's trades. In a file room, by the small refrigerator Gladys kept filled with Pepsi bottles, part-time bookkeeper Donna Walters kept the partnership's records and prepared its tax returns.[2] Just past Walters sat John

Harding, managing the partnership's affairs. Behind Gladys was Buffett's sparsely furnished realm. Its most prominent feature was the large portrait of Howard Buffett on the wall across from his desk.

Warren arrived every morning, hung up his hat, and disappeared into his sanctuary to read the papers. After a while he emerged and told Gladys, "Get me Charlie." Then he shut the door, got on the phone, and spent the rest of the day swiveling between the phone and his reading. Once in a while he would reappear and tell Bill Scott about a trade.

With the stock market high, Scott was less busy these days. Buffett, his pockets full of the money that National Indemnity produced, was delving for entire businesses, since their prices were less subject to the whim of investors. He had discovered the Illinois National Bank & Trust, one of the most profitable banks he had ever seen, run by seventy-one-year-old Eugene Abegg in Rockford, Illinois. Buffett wanted the crusty Abegg as part of the deal. Abegg resembled Ben Rosner, who had counted sheets of toilet paper.

"He carried around thousands of dollars of cash in his pocket, and he cashed checks for people on the weekends. He carried a list of the numbers of unrented safe-deposit boxes with him everywhere and would try to rent you a safe-deposit box at a cocktail party. Mind you, this is the biggest bank in the second-largest city in Illinois at the time. He set every salary and paid every employee in cash, so the head of the trust department did not know how much his own secretaries made.

"Gene had already made a deal to sell the bank to somebody else. But the buyer had started criticizing it, or they wanted an audit and he'd never been audited and he wanted out. So I went out there, and I named a number that turned out to be about a million dollars less than the other guy. And Gene, who owned a quarter of the stock, called up his biggest shareholder, who owned more than half the stock, and said, 'This young guy from Omaha's come here and offered this. I'm tired of those guys at XYZ Company. If you want to sell to them, then you come run this bank, because I won't.'"

Sure enough, Abegg accepted his offer. And doing business with him cinched Buffett's instinct that strong-willed and ethical entrepreneurs often cared more about how they and the companies they had built were going to be treated by the new owners than about grabbing the last nickel in a sale.

The Illinois National Bank, which Buffett soon came to refer to by its colloquial name of Rockford Bank, had been chartered in the days before the U.S. Treasury assumed the exclusive right to coin money. Buffett was fascinated to discover that it still issued its own currency. The ten-dollar bills featured Abegg's picture. Buffett, whose net worth was now more than $26 million, could have bought almost anything he wanted, but not this.[3] The idea of legal tender with your own picture on it captivated him. He began carrying a Rockford bill in his wallet.

Heretofore, Buffett had not wanted his picture on a bill or anywhere else. He had more or less shunned the spotlight while managing the partnership. True, a few more stories and photographs of his family had found their way into the local paper than might be expected of someone who wanted privacy.[4] Nevertheless, except for his letters to the partners, he tiptoed through the "Go-Go" years of the sixties with his lips sealed—he didn't want anyone coattailing him.

Even when the opportunity to promote himself arrived on his doorstep, he hadn't used it. A few years earlier, John Loomis, a securities salesman, visited Buffett at Kiewit Plaza. Loomis's wife, Carol, wrote the investing column for *Fortune* magazine. She had once interviewed a money manager named Bill Ruane, who told her that the smartest investor in the United States lived in Omaha. Some time later, her husband arrived at Kiewit Plaza and made his way upstairs to the 227½-square-foot space that looked nothing like the office of one of the richest men in town.

Buffett took him over to the Blackstone Hotel, where he downed a strawberry malt and told Loomis what he did. Loomis talked about his wife's job as a journalist. Buffett said that if he had not become a money manager, he would have pursued journalism as a career.[5]

Warren and Susie met with the Loomises when they were in New York not long after. The well-connected young money manager from Omaha with the stellar track record and the ambitious reporter for *Fortune* found they shared many attributes: a zeal for unmasking flimflam, a magpie obsession with minutiae, and a streak of competitiveness. Carol Loomis was a tall, no-nonsense woman with short brown hair who tolerated shoddy journalism about as well as Buffett tolerated losing money. They began to correspond and she ushered him into the world of big-league journalism. He began helping her with her story ideas. "Carol very quickly became my best friend other than Charlie," he says.[6] At first she did not publish anything about Buffett.

By the late 1960s, however, the rising market had made investing in stocks less viable. The advantage of celebrity when trying to buy entire businesses began to outweigh the benefit of secrecy in buying stocks. And thus it was in the late 1960s that Buffett's longtime interest in newspapers and publishing came together with his newly recast investing goals and his desire for personal attention in a way that would fundamentally change his world.

Before long, Buffett was immersed in the black-and-white world of journalism. Page by page, newspapers fell to cover financial reports from newspapers and magazines that lay scattered on his desk. When he slept, more newspapers— pulled from a bundle and folded into tidy packets—flew through his dreams. On his most restless nights, he dreamed of oversleeping his childhood paper route.[7]

Buffett's fortune had grown large enough for him to afford the purchase of a newspaper or a magazine, or both. His dream was to be not just an investor but a *publisher*—to have the influence that went with owning the means through which the public learned the news. Around 1968, he and some friends tried unsuccessfully to buy the entertainment newspaper *Variety*.[8] Then another acquaintanceship bore fruit. Stanford Lipsey, a friend of Susie's, showed up in Warren's office and said he wanted to sell the *Omaha Sun* Newspapers. Buffett was immediately interested.

The *Sun* was a chain of weekly neighborhood newspapers that published seven editions in the Omaha suburbs. Its meat-and-potatoes stories were neighborhood doings; the *Sun*'s editor, Paul Williams, also competed by publishing stories that the leading paper, the *Omaha World-Herald*, missed, often stories that exposed the follies and misdeeds of city bigwigs.

Despite his own elevation to the Omaha establishment, Buffett took a particular interest in the muckraking aspect of the *Sun*. Ever since collecting license-plate numbers to catch bank robbers, he had wanted to play the cop. And "I recognized intuitively that Warren understood the role of newspapers in our society," Lipsey says. "I didn't like the *Sun*'s business prospects, but I knew that Warren had enough money that the journalism wouldn't suffer because of the economics. In twenty minutes, it was done."

"*I figured we'd pay a million and a quarter for it and take out a hundred thousand a year,*" Buffett says. This return was eight percent, about as much as a bond would provide—less, far less, than he expected to earn on a business or a stock, and the long-term outlook suggested that return would decline, not increase. But the partnership's money was lying fallow, and he really wanted to be a publisher. Buffett wanted the *Sun* so much that he agreed to make Lipsey a partner even though he was beginning to consider shutting the partnership down.

Berkshire Hathaway became owner of the *Omaha Sun* Newspapers on

January 1, 1969. But it was only a beginning; Buffett wanted to be a publisher on a national scale. Buffett was introduced through a political connection, West Virginia's Secretary of State Jay Rockefeller, to Charles Peters, an idealist whose start-up magazine, the *Washington Monthly*, seemed like the right national voice to express viewpoints on important ideas.

Buffett brought Fred Stanback and Rosenfield in as partners on the *Washington Monthly*, warning them not to expect big profits. In fact, he thought the financial prospects might vary in inverse proportion to the magazine's journalistic success. But the scandals it might uncover—the ideas it could promote—the exposés it could expose! They put in a little money.[9]

In short order, the *Washington Monthly* ran through its initial capital stake. Buffett held out the possibility of another $50,000. He and Peters had a fifty-minute phone conversation, in which Buffett's hard-nosed business instincts and his good-citizen journalist side went to war. "As an investment it reeked of the potential for failure," says Peters. "He was worried about his business reputation.... Warren kept finding new plausible escape routes, and I tried to block the exits."[10] Buffett said that the editors had to put in some of their own money, and raise some outside, which Buffett said he would match eighty percent.[11]

Peters was a better journalist than an accountant. They raised the money; the checks went out; then nobody heard from the *Washington Monthly*. "*They just vanished*," says Buffett.[12] Although the *Washington Monthly* was indeed putting out strong stories, it wasn't enough. He had known from the beginning that it would not make money, but he thought it ought to be accountable for the money that it had. He was embarrassed at having drawn in Stanback and Rosenfield. Buffett wanted to be a partner in journalism, not just the guy who bankrolled idealism.

Yet even with mixed results, Buffett was now pursuing the personal concerns of which he had spoken in his October 1967 letter to his partners. Meanwhile, the market continued to dry up. Spending part of his time as a publishing magnate was no help in adjusting to that reality. Whatever else occupied him, he remained wholly committed to the partnership, too, and it turned out that a "less compulsive approach" to investing was not in his nature. He says he received offers from a couple of people to buy the management firm, which would have meant the opportunity to sell at a large profit, but he thought this was not right. So far, Buffett had shown no inclination to avoid getting richer, but he had always stayed on the same side as his partners, harnessing his avarice to their benefit as well as his own. So he started to figure out the best way to wind down the partnership. Around Memorial Day 1969, Buffett wrote the partners to tell them that simply lowering his goal hadn't lessened his intensity:

"*If I am going to participate publicly, I can't help being competitive. I know I don't want to be totally occupied with outpacing an investment rabbit all my life. The only way to slow down is to stop.*"[13] And then he delivered his bombshell: He gave notice of closing down the partnership in early 1970. "*I am not attuned to this market environment, and I don't want to spoil a decent record by trying to play a game I don't understand just so I can go out a hero.*"[14]

What would he do now?

"*I don't have an answer to that question,*" he wrote. "*I do know that when I am sixty, I should be attempting to achieve different personal goals than those which had priority at age twenty.*"[15]

The partners howled with disappointment, and a few with fear. Many were naïfs, like his aunt Alice. They were ministers, rabbis, schoolteachers, grand-mothers, and mothers-in-law. His announcement amounted to a market call on stocks. He had taught even the inexperienced to be wary of an overheated mar-ket. Some trusted no one other than him.

Susie Buffett was happy that Warren was shutting down the partnership, at least for the kids' sake. They cared desperately what their father thought of them. Susie Jr. had always gotten most of what little attention Warren provided, and Peter felt rewarded for being quiet and staying in the background. But fourteen-year-old Howie, who had always sought some emotional connection to his father that was never forthcoming, had grown wilder as he grew up. Howie climbed on the roof in the gorilla costume to spy on Susie Jr. when she came home from dates and drenched her with the sprayer from the kitchen sink when she appeared in her prom dress. When their parents were in New York City, Howie seized the chance for an experiment in anarchy.[16] Warren assumed Susie would take care of everything. But by now, Susie herself had stopped trying to control her children. And she had long since let go of any idealistic expectations regarding her marriage. Her attention was increasingly taken up by an expand-ing number of "vagrants," as one friend put it, who wandered through the house, sought her help, and occupied her time.[17]

Since she almost always accepted people unconditionally, some of those "clients" had pasts as felons, con men, addicts, or, in one case, as the purported proprietor of a bawdy house. Some even conned her out of money and she didn't really mind. Buffett was infuriated at the thought of being cheated himself, but he had eventually come to think of her attitude as part of Susie's charm.

Her large group of women friends, which included Bella Eisenberg, Eunice Denenberg, Jeannie Lipsey, Rackie Newman, and others, continued to expand. Though Warren recognized most of them, this was Susie's circle, not his. Other ties of hers came from the activist community; another set of friends centered around the tennis courts at Dewey Park. And there was always the family.

Even though Susie was a fountainhead of generosity to her many fans, friends, and dependents, she was starting to need a little attention too. It wouldn't have taken much, according to her friends. She disagreed that making money was life's purpose. She felt impoverished denying herself travel, museums, theater, and other forms of culture because of Warren's lack of interest. He praised her effusively in public but when at home, lapsed into his normal preoccupied state. If he would make an effort to go to an art gallery with her now and then, or take her on a trip just because she wanted to go, it would make a difference, she said. But while he did sometimes show up when asked, if she had to ask, it was a favor, not a gift.

Now that Susie realized that Warren was never going to take off to Italy for weeks on end, she began to travel on her own or with friends, sometimes to visit family and sometimes to attend personal-growth seminars.

One day at the Chicago airport, a man stopped in front of her as she sat on a bench. "Are you Susie Thompson?" he asked. She looked up, embarrassed to have been caught with a mouth full of hot dog. It was Milt Brown, her high school sweetheart, whom she had not seen in years. He sat down and they began to get reacquainted.[18]

Susie, who was always reaching out for emotional connections, would later say that her husband wasn't lacking in emotion, he was just cut off from his own feelings. And it certainly seemed as though his strongest emotional bonds were with his friends and partners, to whom he felt an intense obligation, and with whom he had created a de facto family. The other Buffetts could not help but notice the way he lit up in their company, in contrast to the dutiful but preoccupied manner he displayed while attending his own family events.

Thus, even now that he was preparing to close the partnership, he seemed a little reluctant to let go of his connection to his partners. He wrote them another letter describing their options in meticulous detail.

This was unusual behavior for a money manager, to say the least. Even Ben

Graham had only said, "Oh, buy AT&T," when asked, and mentioned Buffett offhandedly to a few people. But Buffett made elaborate efforts to shepherd his partners on to their future investing life. Some of them were already in the Munger partnership; Buffett sent a few more to him. But Munger was queasy about the market.

"I recommended two people to the partners whom I knew were exceptionally good and exceptionally honest: Sandy Gottesman and Bill Ruane.... I not only knew their results, but I knew how they'd accomplished their results, which was terribly important."[19]

The richer partners would go to Gottesman at First Manhattan, but Sandy didn't want the small-fry. Buffett sent the rest to Ruane, who was leaving Kidder, Peabody to set up his own investment advisory firm, Ruane, Cunniff & Stires, with two partners, Rick Cunniff and Sidney Stires, and creating the Sequoia Fund specifically to take on the smaller accounts. He hired John Harding, who would be out of a job when the partnership dissolved, to run an Omaha office for the new company. John Loomis, Carol Loomis's husband, and Buffett's trusty researcher Henry Brandt also went to Ruane, Cunniff—giving it in effect a full staff. These connections also kept Harding, Loomis, and Brandt in Buffett's extended "family."

Buffett brought Ruane to Omaha and promoted the Sequoia Fund to the partners. He endorsed Ruane in typically mathematical terms. Unremarkably, even though he had known Ruane for years, he still felt it necessary to leave a small escape hatch, fearing blame in case things didn't work out, and wrote: *"There is no way to eliminate the possibility of error when judging humans... [but] I consider Bill to be an exceptionally high-probability decision on character and a high-probability one on investment performance."*[20]

Yet while Buffett made arrangements to close the partnership, the first signs appeared that the market's sparks were going to cool. By July 1969, when U.S. troops began withdrawing from Vietnam, the Dow had dropped nineteen percent. Exotic stocks like National Student Marketing and Minnie Pearl's Chicken System, Inc. were starting to collapse.[21]

Blue Chip Stamps, the trading-stamp stock painstakingly accumulated by Buffett, Munger, and Guerin, now became a striking exception to the general trend. The three of them had been betting on whether the company could settle its antitrust lawsuit with Sperry & Hutchinson. When a settlement was reached, this stock—which the Buffett partners didn't know they owned—showered nearly $7 million in profit on them in return for a $2 million investment less than a year ago.[22] Now Blue Chip decided to have a public offering, and Buffett elected to sell the partnership's shares as part of that deal.[23] It seemed that the partners were going to have a splendid final year in 1969.

That October, Buffett called another meeting of the Grahamites from San Diego the year before, sans Ben Graham himself. This time the wives were also invited, and although they did not join the meetings in which the men talked about stocks, their presence made the atmosphere more festive, like a vacation. Buffett delegated the planning to Marshall Weinberg, who lived in New York City and liked to travel. But Weinberg, who also liked to shave a dime and had no more experience of the jet-set life than Buffett, asked around and then made the unfortunate choice of the Colony Club, a Palm Beach, Florida, resort, where they were treated like rubes. Ruane reported at the first night's dinner that the bellhop had handed back his five-dollar tip, saying, "You need it more than I do."

For the next five days, as the group enjoyed bad food, small rooms, high winds, and lashing rains, the men sat classroom style, with Buffett most often in his usual place at the front. They batted thoughts back and forth in an encoded shorthand derived from many years of conversation and a closely shared set of concepts and values.[24]

Buffett posed the Desert Island Challenge. If you were stranded on a desert island for ten years, he asked, in what stock would you invest? The trick was to find the company least subject to the corroding forces of competition and time: Munger's idea of the great business. Buffett delivered his own choice: Dow Jones, owner of the *Wall Street Journal.* His interest in newspapers was growing and would only become more intense, yet curiously he did not actually own this stock.

The gathering ended much as it had begun, with more displays of rudeness from the hotel staff, who had no idea they were hosting anything other than a third-rate group of stockbrokers at a time when the market was falling.[25]

Buffett would go on to describe the Colony Club as *"a friendly family hotel— that is, friendly if you were the Kennedy family."*[26] Later, when a Fort Lauderdale businessman who held the mortgage on the Colony Club asked Buffett to advise him on a financing deal, Buffett told the man he would be happy to do it without taking a fee, but "if you ever have a chance to foreclose on them, do it."[27]

One of those Buffett had invited to the Colony Club was Hochschild-Kohn's Louis Kohn. Buffett had grown fond of Kohn and his wife, and he and Susie had even vacationed with the Kohns in Cozumel. But no sooner had the meeting been planned than Buffett and Munger started to realize that Hochschild-Kohn was not going to work out for them.

"Retail is a very tough business," says Charlie Munger. "Practically every great chain-store operation that has been around long enough eventually gets in trouble and is hard to fix." Their experience had given them a deep wariness of retailing—one that would only grow, not lessen, over time.

They wanted businesses that would marmalade them with money, businesses that had some sort of sustainable competitive advantage and could outwit the natural cycle of capital creation and destruction as long as possible. Not long after the meeting in Florida, Munger and Buffett sold Hochschild-Kohn to Supermarkets General for about what it had cost them.[28] Buffett wanted to act fast in order to unload the company before winding down the partnership. And along with the company, the Kohns disappeared from the Buffetts' lives.[29]

Diversified Retailing had issued unsecured debt ("debentures") to finance the Hochschild-Kohn purchase. Buffett had taken special care with this, his first public financing.

"That was the first bond issue I ever sold, and I put a few things in there that the underwriters had no interest in whatsoever. But I had thought a lot about bond issues over the years. And I had thought about how bondholders got taken."

Bondholders historically earned less than stockholders because they gave up the potentially unlimited opportunity of a shareholder in favor of lower risk. But Buffett knew that in the real world this was not necessarily true.

"One of the things I put in was that if we didn't pay the interest on the bond for any reason, the bondholders took over voting control of the company, so they didn't have to get Mickey-Moused by bankruptcy and all that kind of stuff." Ben Graham had written about this in *Security Analysis*, with as much passion as he mustered on any subject, describing how courts rarely allow bondholders to seize the assets that back those bonds unless the assets are nearly worthless. Unsecured bondholders' interests were worked over in receivership through a strangling process that delayed payment almost to the point of irrelevance. Thus, DRC's debenture also provided that the company could not pay dividends while interest on the bonds was in arrears.

The second unusual provision was that, depending on the company's earnings, the debentures could pay up to an extra one percent on top of eight percent.

Buffett added a third provision. The bonds would be redeemable if he sold enough stock in DRC that he was no longer the largest shareholder.[30]

"Nobody had ever stuck anything like this in a covenant. I said, 'You know,

they're entitled to have this in there. . . . They lent money to me, basically.'" When his banker, Nelson Wilder, protested that such clauses were unprecedented and unnecessary, Buffett overruled him.[31]

Now that interest rates had risen, and banks were newly reluctant to lend, the debentures suddenly became a valuable form of cheap financing, a powerful consolation prize. Nonetheless, since Buffett thought of a dollar today as the fifty or hundred dollars that it could become someday, it was as if he had lost many millions on Hochschild-Kohn because of the forgone opportunity to use the money more effectively. He drew a conclusion that he would later state as:

> Time is the friend of the wonderful business, the enemy of the mediocre. . . .
> It's far better to buy a wonderful company at a fair price than a fair company
> at a wonderful price. Charlie understood this early; I was a slow learner. But
> now, when buying companies or common stocks, we look for first-class busi-
> nesses accompanied by first-class managements. That leads right into a
> related lesson: Good jockeys will do well on good horses but not on broken-
> down nags.[32]

Even as Buffett and Munger were working on the sale of Hochschild-Kohn in the fall of 1969, *Forbes* hit the newsstand with a story about Buffett titled "How Omaha Beats Wall Street." The article opened in such an arresting manner that other writers covering Buffett would copy it for decades afterward.[33]

"$10,000 invested in his Buffett Partnership in 1957," *Forbes* said, "is now worth $260,000." The partnership, which now had assets of $100 million, had grown at an annual compounded rate of thirty-one percent without a single losing year. The anonymous columnist for *Forbes* then wrote one of the more insightful statements ever made about Buffett:

"Buffett is not a simple person, but he has simple tastes."

This not-simple Buffett with simple tastes had insisted on total secrecy in his stock dealings when he ran his partnership, and was never once profiled in an interview. Now, however, when secrecy was no longer important, he had coop-erated with a high-profile article about himself.

The article did not print, or even whisper, his net worth. The reporter did not know that since Buffett closed the partnership to new partners in 1966, his fees, reinvested, had quadrupled his net worth to $26.5 million in just three years—nor that, with no money coming in from new partners, his share of the partner-ship's assets had risen from nineteen percent to twenty-six percent. Instead, the story focused on his "rambling old Omaha house"[34] and the lack of computers and the minimal staff in his unimpressive office. And it was true that the man with simple tastes still chugged four or five bottles of Pepsi a day, asked for it instead of wine at dinner parties, and ate only the dinner rolls if anything more complicated than a steak or hamburger was served. A helpless captive of whoever happened to be doing the laundry at home, he still sometimes turned up in public looking little better than a hobo. He would have been happy in a two-room garage apartment; the money was just his scorecard.

Nonetheless, the Buffetts had for some time lived the life of a well-to-do couple—though not, of course, a life as luxurious as they could have afforded. It was Susie who cared about living well, and it was she who thought that money was pointless unless used for some purpose. Susie had even upgraded Warren to a Cadillac like her own, but only the most stripped-down version with no extra features, and only after she had called every dealer within miles to get the cheapest deal. People found the contrast between his homespun tastes and his ever-growing fortune refreshing. His genial manner, self-deprecating wit, and air of calm put them at ease. He had shed some of his earlier gracelessness and most of his arrogance along with the more obvious signs of insecurity—though his tolerance for criticism had not increased. He was learning to hide his impatience. Even though he worried constantly about how associating with others reflected on him, he showed great loyalty to longtime friends. People were especially struck by his fundamental honesty.

Those who spent long periods in his presence, however, found the unleashed whirlwind of his energy exhausting. "Insatiable," they whispered, and sometimes felt a guilty relief when his attention lapsed. He was prone to deluging his friends with mountains of clippings and reading material that he thought would interest them. Even apparently casual conversations were less casual than they seemed. They always seemed to have a purpose, however obscure, which sometimes involved his testing people. Buffett vibrated with an inner tension that belied his outwardly casual style.

It was hard to imagine what he was going to do with all that energy and intensity without the partnership. Many of the partners found it hard to imagine what they were going to do without him. Many of them were reluctant to let go. Their reluctance struck an ironic note next to the fate of the other Buffett family business. Concurrent with its centennial, Fred Buffett threw his hands in the air and gave up on the Buffett grocery store. Even though it had a half million dollars a year in sales, when he tried to find a buyer, there were no takers. The grinding wheel of capitalism had spoken.

The Buffetts were not socialites and had never thrown a really large party. But with both the store and the partnership closing, they celebrated with a bash one night in late September 1969. Nearly two hundred people of all ages and races poured into their house. Businessmen, society matrons, friends and poor adopted "clients" of Susie's, teenagers, partners, assorted priests, rabbis, and ministers, and local politicians made their way through a string of flashing lights, past the three-foot Pepsi bottles in the windows. Susie had chosen a New York theme—Stage Door Deli food and decor—and told people to dress in "casual kosher." They showed up in everything from culottes to cocktail dresses. A half-cut beer barrel burst with chrysanthemums in her favorite color, sunshine yellow. A table set up like a deli cart, hung with sausages and a real plucked chicken, offered pastrami sandwiches and cheeses. Next to the beer keg in the sunroom, a piano player encouraged guests to sing along. The racquetball court became an impromptu basement movie theater, its ceiling bobbing with giant helium balloons; films with W. C. Fields, Mae West, and Laurel and Hardy ran all evening long. In the solarium, the elderly Fred Buffett "protected" two bikini-clad models as the guests covered them with body paint.

"I had such a good time that I hate to think it's over," Susie said afterward.[35]

PART FOUR

Susie Sings

34

Candy Harry

Three months after the Stage Door Deli party, in January 1970, Buffett's friend Carol Loomis highlighted his spectacular performance—and his dour view of the prospects for stocks—in an article in *Fortune*.[1] Shortly before the article appeared, he sent the partners a letter explaining what they owned.

- Berkshire Hathaway, which he said was worth about $45 per share.[2] About $16 was tied up in textiles, a business that he said was not satisfactory and had an even smaller chance of being so in the future. But he would not liquidate it. Berkshire also owned the much more profitable insurer National Indemnity.
- Diversified Retailing, worth $11.50 to $12 per share. DRC consisted of only the scroungy Associated Cotton Shops and proceeds from the sale of Hochschild-Kohn, which he planned to use "for reinvestment in [unspecified] other operating businesses"—implicitly requiring the departing partners to continue to trust his judgment.
- Blue Chip Stamps, which Buffett said he would probably cash them out of because the company was planning a sale of stock around the end of the year.
- The Rockford Bank, also owned by Berkshire Hathaway.
- *Sun* Newspapers, which he described as "not financially significant."[3]

The departing partners were floored to find that they owned a trading-stamp company, a bank, and an insignificant newspaper.[4] Now they had to decide whether to hold their cards or trade them, because they could have all cash instead.

"He would cut the pie and you would be able to get the first choice on the pieces," says John Harding. Buffett, of course, wanted them to choose the cash, leaving the Berkshire Hathaway and Diversified Retailing stocks for himself. Nevertheless, he was honest with them. In a letter of October 9, 1969, he made a market forecast, which he had previously declined to do. With the market at such heights, *"... [f]or the first time in my professional life,"* he wrote, *"I now believe there is little choice for the average investor between professionally managed money in stocks and passive investment in bonds"*[5]—although he did allow as how the very best money managers might be able to squeeze out a few percentage points over the earnings of bonds.

Two months later, on December 5, he gave a prediction about how these two stocks would do. *"My personal opinion is that the intrinsic value of DRC and B-H will grow substantially over the years.... I would be disappointed if such growth wasn't at a rate of approximately ten percent per annum."* That was an important forecast that Berkshire and Diversified would not only do better than bonds, but better than he had said in October the partners could expect from even the very best money managers.

"I think both securities should be very decent long-term holdings and I am happy to have a substantial portion of my net worth invested in them.... I think there is a very high probability that I will maintain my investment in DRC and B-H for a very long period."[6]

Separately, Buffett wrote the partners a dissertation on how to invest in bonds, again extending himself considerably more than a typical money manager would ever do. Even so, *"I had four people panic when I closed down, all divorced women. They trusted me, they had had bad experiences with men, and they didn't feel they could make it again if they lost what money they'd gotten. They would call me in the middle of the night and say, 'You've got to keep earning me money.'"*[7]

But he refused to act as what he considered to be a fiduciary if he could not perform to his high standards. *"Basically, if I'm the guarantor, I just can't do it, knowing how hard it was on me once,"* he says, harkening back to what he had felt at age eleven when Cities Service Preferred had disappointed his sister.

He continued working on the partnership dissolution over Christmas in Laguna Beach. He had bought his Christmas gifts with his usual efficiency. As with most things, he had a system: He went to Topps, the best dress shop in Omaha, and gave them a list of the different sizes for all the women in his life.

"I would go over, and they'd wheel out the dresses. I'd make a variety of decisions and buy presents for my sisters, Susie, Gladys, and so forth. I kind of enjoyed it.

"You know, clothing holds its value better than jewelry."

On December 26, after the exchange of Christmas gifts, he sent the partners another long letter, going out of his way to answer at length a number of their questions.[8] A few of the partners had been challenging him. If it was such a lousy business, *why not get rid of the Berkshire Hathaway textile mill?*

"I have no desire to trade severe human dislocations for a few percentage points additional return per annum," he wrote. But since the whole point of his business was to eke out a few additional percentage points per annum, this kind of rationalization would have been unthinkable earlier in his career.

What is Sun Newspapers? they asked. It's worth a buck a share, he replied, kind of skipping the rest of the economics. Adding some famous last words, "We have no particular plans to expand in the communication field," he wrote.[9]

Why didn't you register the Berkshire Hathaway and Diversified stock so that it could be freely traded? Berkshire was so closely held that it traded "by appointment"—which made it hard for anyone to know what the stock was actually worth. Diversified did not trade at all.

A long, complicated explanation followed, in which Buffett argued that a freely traded and liquid public market for these stocks would be less efficient and less fair and "the more sophisticated partners might have an important edge over the less sophisticated partners." And it was certainly true that the more naive of his departing partners would be kept from the clutches of the manic-depressive Mr. Market, who might at times have valued the stock at a severely discounted price. It lowered the odds that a pack of brokers would talk them into selling just to buy IBM or AT&T. But it also meant that Buffett was limiting his partners' options—making it harder for them to buy and harder for them to sell—and, if they did sell, making it more likely that they would sell to him.

As general partner of the partnership, he was used to having total control of these two companies. Letting go and giving up control to the anonymous Mr. Market—he just couldn't do it. Moreover, as soon as he handed these stocks to his departing partners, for the first time his own self-interest and theirs might be at odds. This complicated rationale to justify keeping the stocks unregistered danced a little do-si-do around the fact that Buffett was the most sophisticated partner of all. It was he who would have the most important edge over his former partners. No matter how honest his intentions, the decision widened the potential conflict between his interests and theirs. The painfully earnest tone of

Buffett's letter sounds like someone who has had to talk himself into thinking that he is doing the right thing. But the conflict was guaranteed to cause hard feelings. Anyone who sold to him and was later sorry could look back with hindsight and think: He had an edge on me.

Still, the Howard in Warren demanded that he present their options with scrupulous honesty. The way he answered the next question told the departing partners exactly what to expect.

Should I hold my stock? they asked.

Buffett gave as clear and direct advice as he would ever give in public about a stock.

"All I can say is that I'm going to do so," he said, "and *I plan to buy more.*"[10]

The departing partners were also going to have a third stock to deal with. In this same letter of December 26, Buffett told them that the Blue Chip stock sale had fallen through.[11] The stock had plunged in a short time from a high of $25 to $13 a share because Safeway Stores had dropped Blue Chip stamps, its customer base was eroding, and no buyer was in sight for one-third of the business that the Justice Department had mandated it sell to break up its monopoly. Civil antitrust lawsuits seeking damages had been filed against it, one by Douglas Oil Company and another by a group of filling stations.[12]

Yet even as Blue Chip's problems multiplied and the price fell, Buffett had been *buying* the stock instead of selling. He had bought it for Diversified Retailing and for National Indemnity. He had bought it for Cornhusker Casualty and National Fire & Marine, two little insurance companies that Berkshire had acquired. He had also bought it for himself and for Susie.

Now the partners knew that Buffett wouldn't sell, and indeed planned to hoover up more of all these stocks. They would get whichever they wanted— stock or cash. If they took the money, he would get the stock. If they kept their stock, they would still be his partners, in a sense.

In his anxiety over whether people liked and accepted him, Buffett valued loyalty more than almost anything. The dissolution of the partnership had elements of a loyalty test, as his behavior afterward would make clear.

When the partnership unwound at the end of 1969, he and Susie had hauled home roughly $16 million in cash. During the ensuing year, the shares of Berkshire and Diversified quickly began to change hands. As he had promised— but on a scale that might have staggered his partners, had they known—Buffett used the cash he got from the partnership to buy still more Berkshire and Diversified for his own account. He also used Berkshire's cash to buy its own stock, and for DRC, offered to buy the company's stock from some people in exchange for a DRC note that paid interest at nine percent.[13] He bought from people ranging from his former brother-in-law Truman Wood to his first investor, Homer Dodge, and his son Norton.[14] Those who rejected these offers had to be willing to ride along and let Buffett reinvest the earnings without ever paying out a dime—a show of trust that was important to him.[15]

Forever after, he would feel a loyalty to those who kept the stock—a loyalty of such depth and strength that the standard-model modern CEO would find it completely incomprehensible. Berkshire, he would later reflect, is still *"like a partnership. You basically have the closest thing to a private business with share-holders who identify with you and who like to come to Omaha."* He thought of partners as people who had come together out of a complex set of shared values and interests, not out of short-term economic convenience. He often said that he tried to treat his partners the way he would his family. His partners were peo-ple to whom he owed a special duty. In return, he expected loyalty from them.

Yet people made their decisions for all sorts of reasons. Some needed money. Others simply invested in the Sequoia Fund after listening to Bill Ruane. Many people's brokers urged them to sell the stock of a money-gobbling textile mill. Some listened, some didn't. Some professional investors had other options and thought they were better off without these humdrum stocks. When Warren went to the West Coast in person and offered the DRC note, Estey Graham's sis-ter Betty sold her stock; Estey didn't. Rhoda Sarnat, Ben Graham's cousin, and her husband, Bernie, decided not to sell, telling themselves, Warren's buying, and if it's good enough for him, it's good enough for us.[16] When he offered the note to his sister Doris, she refused it, thinking, If he's buying, why would I sell?

A few partners quizzed Buffett more closely in person for his opinion of how the stocks would do. He said, carefully, that he thought they would do well, but it could take a long time. People like Jack Alexander and Marshall Weinberg parsed those words, considered the fact that they were good investors them-selves, and sold him part of their stock.

Munger would later call Buffett an "implacable acquirer," like John D. Rockefeller in the early days of assembling his empire, who let nobody and nothing get in his way.[17] With hindsight, some people felt hard done by, enticed, or even misled. Others said to themselves, in effect, Well, that's just Warren. I should have known.

By the end of 1970, many of the former partners had cashed out while Warren continued buying more stock. His and Susie's ownership of Berkshire had shot from eighteen percent to almost thirty-six percent. Their ownership of DRC had nearly doubled, to thirty-nine percent. As a practical matter, Buffett now controlled both.[18] He had also bought more Blue Chip, taking him from two percent to over thirteen percent ownership of its stock.

But it was clear to Susie Buffett that Warren's gyrations to get control of Diversified and Berkshire Hathaway meant that her husband's second "retirement" would be similar to his first. One reason was that Blue Chip was in the same sort of trouble as Berkshire Hathaway.[19] The business was no longer just shrinking, it was dying.

By 1971, with the country off the gold standard, prices of everything leapfrogged day by day because of inflation. The classic retailing method of enticing customers into a store through a panoply of services and giveaways was thrown overboard. Retailers headed to a discount model.[20] Any chance that housewives would plan their shopping to collect enough books of trading stamps to get an electric frying pan evaporated. Buffett and Munger needed something to replace Blue Chip's earnings.

Then one day Buffett got a call from Bill Ramsey, Blue Chip's president, saying that a local Los Angeles company, See's Candies, was for sale. Buffett had carved out a tiny subspecialty of studying candy companies.[21] But candy companies were *expensive*. So far, he had never bitten. "Call Charlie," he said.[22] Munger was in charge of Blue Chip, their West Coast business.

See's, founded in 1921, competed by using the finest quality butter, cream, chocolate, fruits, and nuts, painstakingly prepared to "See's Quality," which was better than "top quality." The company was a California institution.

"See's has a name that nobody can get near in California," Munger told Buffett. "We can get it at a reasonable price. It's impossible to compete with that brand without spending all kinds of money." Munger was overflowing with enthusiasm, although his assistant Ed Anderson believed the price was expensive.[23]

See's had a tentative deal on the table already and wanted $30 million for assets worth $5 million.[24] The difference was See's brand, reputation, and trademarks— and most of all, its customer goodwill.

They decided that See's was like a bond—worth paying $25 million for. If the company had paid out its earnings as "interest," the interest would average about nine percent. That was not enough—owning a business was riskier than owning a bond, and the "interest rate" was not guaranteed. But the earnings were growing, on average twelve percent a year. So See's was like a bond whose interest payments grew.[25] Furthermore:

"We thought it had uncapped pricing power. See's was selling candy for about the price of Russell Stover at the time, and the big question in my mind was, if you got another fifteen cents a pound, that was two and a half million dollars on top of four million dollars of earnings. So you really were buying something that perhaps could earn six and a half or seven million dollars at the time."

They had to negotiate to buy the company from two people: first, Charles B. See—or "Candy Harry," as Buffett, Munger, and Guerin called him.

"Candy Harry really didn't want to run See's. He was interested in wine and girls. He wanted to chase after girls. But, of course, he got cold feet about selling at the last minute. Rick and Charlie went to see him, and Charlie gave one of the great lectures of all time on the advantages of grapes and girls, how the highest and best use of Candy Harry's time was chasing after women."

At the price Blue Chip offered, $25 million, the $4 million it was earning pretax would give Buffett and Munger payback of nine percent after-tax on their investment from the first day they bought it—not factoring in future growth. Adding in the $2 to $3 million of price increases they thought See's could institute, the return on their capital would rise to fourteen percent—a decent return; the key was whether the earnings would continue to grow. Buffett and Munger came close to walking. The pickings had been so easy until now, and they had such an ingrained habit of underbidding, that it was like swallowing live guppies for them to pay the asking price.

"In the end," says Munger, "they came to the exact dollar limit of what we were willing to pay."[26]

While the deal was being struck, Buffett discovered that Tweedy, Browne already owned a thousand shares of See's. Buffett ordered the firm to tender its stock to him. The Tweedy, Browne partners knew how valuable See's was and thought the price was too *low*. They resisted and debated the issue briefly with Buffett. They did not see why they should give him their See's stock. He insisted he needed the stock more than Tweedy, Browne did. Buffett won. They gave him the stock.[27]

The instant that the deal was inked and the trio of Buffett, Munger, and Guerin joined the board, Buffett threw himself into the candy business with an enthusiasm he had never displayed before. Within days, he wrote a detailed letter to Chuck Huggins, executive vice president, about opening new See's stores in locations like Colorado Springs, Fayetteville, and Galveston. He suggested that Huggins avoid Iowa, because he had heard that "Iowans are generally not candy enthusiasts."[28] He gave Huggins permission to stop sending monthly boxes of candy to the long list of women whom Candy Harry had designated as his special friends. He started following sugar futures and cocoa futures, which at 58 cents a pound were approaching prices unheard of since the year of the Rockwood cocoa caper.[29]

Buffett suggested that Huggins "play around with" advertising slogans and try to come up with one along the lines of Coca-Cola's "pause that refreshes." It was as if, over his breakfast cornflakes, Huggins could dream up an advertising slogan that compelling.[30] One longtime employee described Buffett's management style this way: "He'd always praise you while he gave you more to do."[31]

Deceived by Buffett's initial eagerness to involve himself in the details of the business, Huggins signed him up for several candy-industry trade magazines. Eventually, Buffett, turning his attention to some newer interest, asked for a cease-and-desist. "Charlie may have visions of becoming a candymaker someday," he wrote, "but I will continue to just read the statements."[32] He had discovered that he liked *owning* a candy company, not *running* one.

It was much the same at home. Buffett would tell someone with great sincerity, "Please come visit, I really want to see you," then bury his head in a newspaper when they arrived, apparently satisfied with their presence. But there was also the odd chance that he wanted to talk and talk, and they might go away exhausted. Susie had seen his enthusiasms come and go.

Warren was still besotted with his wife, praised her constantly in public, and cuddled her on his lap. But at home, as always, he withdrew into his private pursuits and wanted to be taken care of. Susie referred to him as an "iceberg" to one of her friends. However, nothing had really changed in their relationship since the beginning—except her feelings. He was content. He reasoned that because she loved to give, by receiving he served her. Based on their past and her behavior, there was no reason for him to think otherwise. But Susie's own desires were changing. She, the emotional vending machine, was now developing a yearning to be taken care of herself.

Thus, while her husband pursued his new businesses away from Omaha or sat sunk in thought in his office, Susie spent less and less time at home. She now had a number of new friends much younger than she. They admired her and returned her generosity and tenderness with openly expressed feelings that ranged from warmhearted affection to outright adoration. But they were less like adopted children and more like genuine friends, albeit friends who, like all her friends, needed her. Meanwhile, Susie had begun treating Peter, her quiet son, in a different way, using him as friend, confidant, and source of emotional support, now that he was growing up and about to enter high school.

Susie Jr. was living in Lincoln, having enrolled at the University of Nebraska. Howie was in his junior year of high school and Susie now devoted herself to launching him into college. Warren, as usual, was happy to delegate all these responsibilities to her.

Susie did succeed in enticing Warren to really pitch in and get involved— rather than simply write checks—whenever business intersected with a cause to which he could lend his expertise. Her friend Rodney Wead and other leaders in the black community had gotten the idea of starting a minority-owned bank to enhance economic development on the North Side. Promoting "black capitalism," they came to Buffett and his friend Nick Newman, the man who had sponsored Warren in local civil-rights activities.[33]

Wead was a respected figure in Omaha, and Buffett liked banks. He had just joined the board of Omaha National Corporation, the biggest bank in town, a long-held ambition.[34] He had an automatic—and rational—predisposition toward any business where people gave money to the business faster than the company disbursed it. The hope was that Community Bank would attract a diverse group of customers. He hired Peter and one of his friends to sit outside another minority bank to count how many people went inside and to classify them by race.[35] Peter's tally made Warren optimistic, so he joined an advisory board of directors for the bank and also got John Harding from Ruane, Cunniff on the board.[36] Buffett told the founders that if they could raise $250,000 in stock from the black community, the advisory board would raise money to match it.[37]

Most of the managers and the board of directors—which included Buffett's baseball player friend Bob Gibson—were black, and most were financial tenderfoots. To stave off disaster, Buffett went into his teaching mode and tried to educate the founders on the need for strong lending standards. The bank, he stressed, was not a charity or social-services agency. He attended monthly board meetings that stretched late into the night, but, as with the companies Berkshire owned, he was never involved in the day-to-day management.[38] Asked for more money to cover bad loans, Buffett said no. Wead felt Buffett "never understood his role as a wealthy man in our beleaguered community."[39] But Buffett knew the bank wouldn't help anyone by relaxing its lending standards and making uncollectible loans, which would only teach the wrong financial lesson. So the bank limped along for years without growing.

He got a chance to help in another way when Hallie Smith, a friend of Susie's, began to bring her the names of black kids who needed money because they couldn't pay for college. Susie started giving a thousand dollars here and there. "I've got to ask Warren," she said over and over. "Susie, you have money; why don't you just pay for it?" Smith asked in amazement. "No, I can't," Susie always said. "It has to go through Warren." Smith found it incredible that someone as rich as Susie allowed her husband to make every decision involving money.[40]

Thus, while Susie was in charge of the family foundation, they worked together on funding and donations. She would have given away huge sums had Warren not put on the brakes. The foundation made small grants to education, and it didn't have professional management. To do a proper job of managing it required thinking forward: What was going to happen to all that money someday when it ended up in the foundation? Warren felt that someday was far away. Susie had a passionate desire to help in the here and now, but someone needed to strategize for the future.

A year before, Warren had had what for many forty-year-olds would have been a wake-up call. During a dinner at the Sarnats' in California, one of his fingers started to swell. He had taken a double dose of delayed-action penicillin earlier that day for a minor infection. Bernie Sarnat, a surgeon, suspected an allergic reaction. He gave Warren antihistamines and advised him to get to a hospital.[41]

Buffett didn't want to go to the hospital. He had already had enough of sickness in 1971, after a recent bout of salmonella.[42] He had Susie drive him back to the house they were renting for the summer. But as he continued ballooning and grew dizzy and sick, she began an urgent search for a doctor who could see Warren in a hurry. The one she finally reached insisted that they go to an emergency room immediately. By then Buffett was barely conscious, and the emergency room team started working to save his life. Three days later, he was still in the hospital. He was lucky, the doctors told him. His penicillin allergy was so severe that if he took it again, he would be dead.

Yet even after this encounter with his own mortality, he remained as fixated on business as ever. Retirement, in Buffett's special sense, meant no longer acting as a fiduciary. He would be investing as long as he was breathing. He could not help but be competitive—so much so that recently, when six-year-old Jonathan Brandt, son of his friends Henry and Roxanne Brandt, had taken him on in chess, Warren couldn't bear it when it looked as though he was losing. As the game neared its conclusion, he began Buffetting little Jonny until he won.[43]

By then, Susie had cultivated an attitude of ironic detachment about Warren's stubbornness. "Whatever Warren wants, Warren gets," was her way of describing the man who, as his little sister Bertie had observed all those years ago, always got his way.[44] On a visit to Des Moines with a friend to hear the writer and Holocaust survivor Elie Wiesel speak at one of the local synagogues, Susie had spent hours talking to Milt Brown, who now lived there, at a dessert party at somebody's house.[45] For some time she had been filled with feelings of regret about that interrupted relationship; she now wondered openly to close friends whether it was too late to go down a different path. While she rarely talked about her problems or showed self-pity, she acknowledged being depressed about the state of her marriage. But despite her unhappiness, she made no move to address her issues directly or to leave. Rather, she rekindled her relationship with Milt. And increasingly she seemed drawn to California. She had "fallen in love" with the place they had been renting at Emerald Bay in Laguna Beach, perched fifty feet above the ocean among a group of other luxury vacation homes.[46]

Warren particularly disliked buying houses, considering money spent on them as lying fallow. Susie needled him. "If we were rich," she said, "you would just go up to that house, and ask the owner how much she wants for it, and pay however much she asked. But I know we're not rich." In their perpetual tug-of-war, Susie was usually able to dislodge the cash from him in the end. Buffett delegated the task of buying the house to the Tolleses, who dickered the owner down to $150,000.[47] When Roy Tolles called to tell Warren, he said, "I have bad news. You bought it."

35

The *Sun*

S usie decorated the place in Emerald Bay with casual rattan furniture. She installed a separate telephone line for Warren, who spent most of his time there watching business news on television and talking on the phone.

His "personal concerns" and Joe Rosenfield were drawing her husband in the opposite direction—toward Washington, and politics. The Buffetts hosted a dinner in Omaha for Senator George McGovern, the 1972 Democratic candidate for President. Warren gave money to Allard Lowenstein, a former Congressman known as the "pied piper" of liberals, who had Gene McCarthy's power to galvanize young people into activism over civil rights. He backed John Tunney, the "Kennedyesque" son of heavyweight boxer Gene Tunney, in his successful California Senate run.[1] Tunney's golden-boy political career inspired the movie *The Candidate*, about a charismatic politician who is "too young, too handsome, too liberal, too perfect" to win, so can afford to tweak the Establishment. Buffett consistently fell for politicians like "The Candidate"— men with the ineffable magnetism of Hollywood stars, men whose presence stirred voters' emotions—except that he wanted his candidates to *win*.

Buffett became engrossed in an abortive attempt to nominate Iowa Senator Harold Hughes for president in 1972; then he supported George McGovern, who lost to Nixon. The 1972 elections would prove the end of Buffett as would-be kingmaker. His fascination with the intensity of backroom politics was satisfied; his attention now waned. Yet throughout, Buffett paid careful attention to the overwhelming influence of media in politics; he wanted some of that. A childhood throwing newspapers, his friendship with *Fortune* reporter Carol

Loomis, the purchase of the *Sun,* a search for other newspapers to buy, and his investment in the *Washington Monthly*—Buffett's interest in publishing had grown. He had seen the overwhelming power of television to capture attention throughout the tumultuous 1960s, from the JFK assassination to the Vietnam War to the civil-rights movement. Now, as the profitability of television became apparent, he wanted a piece of that business too.

Then Bill Ruane set him up at a dinner in New York with an acquaintance, Tom Murphy, who ran Capital Cities Communications, a company that owned broadcasting stations.

Murphy, the son of a Brooklyn judge, had grown up in the spicy chowder of New York politics before joining the Harvard Business School class of '49. Jowly, balding, easygoing, Murphy had started by managing a bankrupt TV station in Albany so frugally that he painted only the sides of the building that faced the road. Then he started to buy broadcasters, cable companies, and publishers, creating a media empire.

After their dinner, Murphy strategized with Ruane about how to get Buffett on his board of directors. Ruane said the way to Buffett's heart was to visit him in Omaha. Murphy promptly made the pilgrimage. Buffett plied him with a steak dinner, then drove him home to meet Susie. She must have known by now what to expect: Her husband had met another new object of infatuation. Buffett liked to show new people his totems: the office, Susie, and sometimes the train set. After the tour he and Murphy played a couple of games of racquetball in the Buffetts' basement court, Murphy running around in his oxford dress shoes. Buffett saw where he was headed. "You know, Tom," he said, "I couldn't become a director because I'd have to have a major position in your company, and your stock is too high."[2] Even though the rest of the market was stumbling downhill, investors were excited about television stocks. Cable television was new, and local franchises were consolidating into newly visible public companies. "Lookit," he said, "you can have me for nothing, you don't need me on the board."[3]

So Murphy started calling Buffett every time he made a deal. Buffett, just over forty, was flattered and made unlimited time for Murphy, then in his mid-to-late forties, even though he thought, "This guy is *old*." But "*he understands the whole world,*" and "*I was in awe of Murph,*" Buffett says. "*I thought he was the ultimate businessman.*" One evening, Murphy phoned him at home and offered him first shot at a Fort Worth TV station that was for sale.[4] Buffett was interested but, for reasons he doesn't recall, turned Murphy down—which he later called one of his greater business mistakes.[5]

What Buffett really wanted was to be a publisher. In fact, he thought he had a scoop, but when he gave the editors at the *Washington Monthly* the idea, they pooh-poohed it, probably disdaining a story idea that came from an investor. Then Buffett turned to the Omaha *Sun,* which might not have a national platform but was better than no newspaper at all. As matters turned out, says Peters, "I could have shot everybody on my staff."

What Buffett had heard was that Boys Town, one of Omaha's sacred cows, had turned into a hog. A refuge for homeless boys, Boys Town was founded in an old mansion near downtown in 1917 by Father Edward Flanagan, an Irish priest who wanted to save orphans and rejected children from wasted lives as drifters, criminals, or addicts. *"Father Flanagan was famous around town for getting five bucks at a time,"* says Buffett, *"and as soon as he got it, he spent it on a kid. Then he got ninety dollars and he put twenty-five kids in a house."*[6] By 1934 it occupied a 160-acre campus ten miles west of Omaha complete with a school and athletic facilities. With help from Howard Buffett, Boys Town set up its own post office in 1934 to assist in fund-raising.[7] It became an incorporated village in 1936. Then a 1938 Oscar-winning film starring Spencer Tracy and Mickey Rooney brought it national fame.

When Ted Miller, a professional fund-raiser, saw the movie, he recognized how to transform Boys Town's fund-raising appeals into a huge national campaign. Every year at Christmastime, Boys Town, which now called itself "The City of Little Men," sent out millions of letters that began, "There will be no joyous Christmas season this year for many homeless and forgotten boys...." and bore the picture the movie made famous of a street urchin carrying a tot with the legend "He ain't heavy, Father... He's m'brother."

People sent in as little as a dollar, but the take from tens of millions of letters that had been sent out added up to a lot of money.[8] Boys Town, then awash in contributions, expanded to a 1,300-acre campus. Father Flanagan died in 1948, but the money kept rolling in under his successor, Monsignor Nicholas Wegner. It was now a virtual shrine that was the state's biggest tourist attraction.

"I used to hear these stories about how the U.S. National Bank put on extra people for weeks and weeks before Christmas just to handle the Boys Town money that was coming in. Meanwhile, of course, I saw the boy count coming down."

In its early years, Flanagan had searched court records and taken in some hard-core delinquents, even a few murderers. But by 1971, the home screened out the emotionally disturbed, mentally retarded, and serious juvenile offenders; it wanted "homeless" boys who had no other significant problems.[9] Built to house a thousand, Boys Town now employed some six hundred people to care for its six hundred and sixty-five boys.[10] Its gigantic institutional approach of housing boys in isolation from the surrounding community, with a custodial, even prisonlike atmosphere, had begun to seem out of date.[11] The boys moved to the signal of bells. Their mail was censored and they were allowed only one visitor a month, chosen by the staff, not themselves. They had little recreation and no contact with girls. Boys Town emphasized menial jobs and low-grade vocational training: picking beans and making birdhouses.

So one evening in July 1971, at a meeting at the Buffetts' house, Warren and *Sun* editor Paul Williams discussed the Boys Town rumors and decided to commission a story on how the institution raised and spent its money.[12] Williams took three city reporters, Wes Iverson, Doug Smith, and Mick Rood, and set them to work on an elaborate investigative reporting project.[13] Having noticed that the Boys Town marketing material said it got no money from any church or from the state or federal government, reporter Mick Rood pawed through records at the Nebraska state capitol in Lincoln and found out that this was false.[14] That made them suspicious of Boys Town's other claims.

They got the institution's property-tax records, educational records, and articles of incorporation and found out that Boys Town had a history of strained relations with the state welfare department.[15] Williams got a report on the Boys Town post office and learned that it sent between thirty-four and fifty million pieces of fund-raising mail a year. This was a staggering number; fund-raisers for other organizations told them that Boys Town must be taking in at least $10 million a year. Buffett figured out that its operating costs could be no more than half of that.[16] Boys Town was accumulating money faster than it could possibly spend it. Assuming it had piled up $5 million a year ever since a major expansion in 1948, Buffett thought it must have at least $100 million in excess funds. But so far, there was no proof.

Buffett had joined the board of the local Urban League, and from that connection knew Dr. Claude Organ, a local surgeon, the only black man on the Boys Town board. Buffett thought the doctor was a decent guy.

"We had breakfast over at the Blackstone Hotel right across the street. And I talked and talked and I tried to get him to tell me. He wouldn't give me details, but he also told me I wasn't wrong. He did even better than that. He let me know there was a story there, although I couldn't get any numbers from him."

Dr. Organ began quietly steering the reporting team, helping them stay on track without disclosing confidential information.[17] Most of the Boys Town employees were too afraid to talk. Buffett, playing newshound, roamed Omaha in his beat-up old tennis shoes, moth-eaten sweater, and pants covered with streaks of chalk.[18] *"It was a high,"* he says. *"Whatever was the male equivalent of Brenda Starr, Girl Reporter, well, that was me."* By now Warren had also adopted a friend of Susie's, *Sun* publisher Stan Lipsey, as one of his new people, going jogging with him and playing racquetball in the Buffetts' basement.

Then Warren had a brainstorm. Congress had passed a law that, among other things, required nonprofit organizations to file a tax return with the IRS. *"I was sitting there in the family room doing the Form 990 for the Buffett Foundation, and it just hit me—if I had to file a return, maybe they did too."*[19]

The reporters tracked down the Form 990 to the IRS in Philadelphia and waited impatiently for twenty days for the IRS to dig it out of its files.[20]

Paul Williams had hired Randy Brown, a new assistant managing editor, in part to help coordinate the Boys Town story. "My first day at work, this 990 plopped down on my desk," says Brown.[21] Buffett, who had just bought See's and was still mailing out boxes of candy to friends all over North America, nonetheless was so enthralled by Boys Town that he threw himself into helping Brown figure it out. Sure enough, Boys Town had a net worth of $209 million, which was growing by about $18 million a year, four times more than it spent to fund its operations. Buffett was elated. All his life, he had been waiting for a nun to commit a crime so he could expose the culprit by whipping out her fingerprints. Now he had used a tax return to nab a monsignor red-handed.

They moved desks, file cabinets, and phones into Williams's basement recreation room. In the end, "we tracked everything," says Lipsey, "except, I think, two accounts in Switzerland. We couldn't break through those." The *Sun*'s reporters were stunned to find that Boys Town had an endowment three times the size of the University of Notre Dame. Conservatively stated, it was worth more than $200,000 per boy. Mick Rood took to calling it the "City of Little Men with a Large Portfolio."[22] The money machine was bringing in $25 million a year and could easily cover its costs out of investment income without raising another nickel.[23] The intrigue heightened as they worked on the obvious questions: What was Boys Town going to do with all that money? Why did it need to keep raising more? The last phase of the investigation meant to find that out.

As administrator of Boys Town, seventy-four-year-old Reverend Monsignor Nicholas H. Wegner knew by then that the *Sun* was asking questions; Boys Town had already started putting together a hasty program of reforms. But the reporters were confident that as yet he had no idea they had obtained Boys

Town's tax return. Their fear was losing the story to the *Omaha World-Herald*, which might swoop down with its greater resources once it realized that a juicy bit of news was waiting to be served up to the readership. An even greater risk was that Boys Town might work cooperatively and exclusively with the *World-Herald* to launch a preemptive strike with a friendlier story.[24]

The reporters plotted how to get to Wegner and to Archbishop Sheehan, his superior in the archdiocese. Rood, a thirtyish badass with shoulder-length wavy hair and a handlebar mustache, went to see Wegner. His first reaction was pity for Wegner, whose bald, wrinkled skull craned from his cassock like the head of an ancient tortoise. The monsignor was obviously frail, the survivor of fifteen surgeries, some of them major. As the interview proceeded, however, he rambled on incautiously and also denied receiving state funds. Asked to justify the exhaustive fund-raising, he said, "We're so deep in debt all the time." Knowing that nothing of the sort was true, Rood went straight back to Williams's basement with the tape of the interview. After it was transcribed, Williams put it in a safe-deposit box.

While Rood was interviewing Wegner, Williams was trying to nail the archbishop. Sheehan—possibly cued in at that point—confirmed statements Wegner had made but declined to add anything more. With confirmation in hand, however, the team showed up at the fund-raising office, which was a separate operation located in an Omaha building marked "Wells Fargo." They walked in the door uninvited and snapped photos of long rows of women typing solicitation letters and thank-you notes to donors. They also managed to talk to some of the fund-raisers, who said, "Please don't mention the fund-raising operation in your article. It's easy for the public to get the wrong idea. People will think we're rich," and "We want people to think the boys send out the letters."[25]

Meanwhile, the other reporters descended on the board of directors. It was made up mostly of people with little incentive to tip over the sacred cow. They included the banker who ran the Boys Town investment portfolio, the son of the architect who built the place and who ran the firm that stood in line to do any current building work, the retailer who supplied all the boys' clothing, and the lawyer who handled Boys Town's legal affairs. Apart from the financial interests many of them had in it, all the directors enjoyed the prestige of sitting on the board of Nebraska's most respected institution while doing very little work on its behalf. Wegner considered them a nuisance and had told Rood, "They've never been of much help," and "They don't know anything about social welfare . . . they don't know anything about education."[26] According to Williams, whatever they may have actually known, the board's reactions to the reporters' questions ranged from "dismay to innocence or downright ignorance."[27] Another Boys Town official would later put it this way with hindsight: "The board has not been all that good in serving Father Wegner.... The board could have advised him about slowing down on the fund-raising."[28]

That was indeed the irony. It was Boys Town's background of Depression-era poverty that had probably led Wegner to accumulate money as if the "wolf was at the door," as Randy Brown put it.[29] This same background had very likely lulled the board into overseeing Wegner's activities without questioning whether they made sense. And Warren Buffett, a product of the very same environment, who had the very same impulses, was going to bust them for it. The crime, in his eyes, was not just accumulating the money. It was piling it up mindlessly without a plan to use it. Boys Town didn't even have a *budget*.[30] The sin to Buffett was an abdication of fiduciary responsibility, the failure to manage money responsibly on others' behalf.

The reporters worked feverishly on the story all weekend, Buffett and Lipsey reading copy as it progressed. *"We were this little nothing weekly paper,"* says Buffett, but they intended to meet the journalistic standard of a top national daily. Finally they all trooped over to Paul Williams's living room, spread everything out on the floor, and tried to figure out headlines and captions. The story's banner lead asked: "Boys Town: America's Wealthiest City?" An eight-page special section with sidebars, it led off with a kicker in the form of a Bible verse, Luke 16:2—"Give an account of thy stewardship."

On the Wednesday afternoon before publication, Williams sent the story to the Associated Press, UPI, the *Omaha World-Herald,* and television stations. The next day, March 30, 1972, would be recalled by Buffett as one of the greatest of his life. The story not only fulfilled his wish to run a business as a church, but the section opened with a Bible-quoting headline about a favorite concept, stewardship—the lens through which he now viewed duty, moral obligation, and the responsibility that went along with a position of trust. By the end of that week, the wire services had broken the Boys Town story across the country and exposed a national scandal.[31] On Saturday, the Boys Town board held an emergency meeting and decided to cancel all fund-raising, including the spring mailing for which envelopes had already been partly stuffed.[32] In a new era of investigative reporting, the drama was of such magnitude that it gave an immediate push to reforms in the way nonprofits were governed all over the United

States. The story was picked up by *Time, Newsweek, Editor & Publisher,* and the *LA Times,* among others.[33] An informal survey of twenty-six boys' homes showed that immediately after the exposé, more than a third of them said that their fund-raising efforts were affected.[34]

But Monsignor Francis Schmitt, an understudy of Wegner's who had begun assuming some of his duties, quickly circulated a letter to Boys Town supporters that said, "There can only have been yellow journalism, prejudice, jealousy, and, for all I know, bigotry involved in the story," suggesting that the motive was anti-Catholic bias. In fact, the reporters had bent over backward to avoid such a bias. Moreover, Schmitt said, the story was full of "snide innuendos" that cut into his vitals all "because of a cheap editor of a cheap paper, whose owner is himself a millionaire many times over."[35] Wegner also remained unrepentant. "Boys Town," he said, "will still be here when that yellow rag, what's it called"—the *Sun*—"is forgotten."[36] To people who wrote asking about the Boys Town story, Wegner was sending out a form letter saying that while at the present time, Boys Town was not seeking donations, as "our properties and facilities have multiplied in value... SO HAVE OUR COSTS."[37] The letter was printed on the usual stationery, with "your contribution is an allowable income tax deduction" and "we employ no solicitors or fund-raising organization—we pay no commissions" at the bottom.

Buffett, who had never had so much fun reading a tax return, wanted to make sure that, contrary to the monsignor's prediction, the *Sun* would not be forgotten. The thought of a Pulitzer, the grandest prize in journalism, "started my adrenaline flowing," he said.[38] He got Paul Williams to prepare a detailed outline for the paper's submission for the prize. Buffett had some strategic thoughts of his own, drawn from a long history with the newspaper business. "*In a country where economics inevitably lead to one-daily towns,*" Buffett wrote, the *Sun*'s submission should stress "*the necessity for another printing press.*" Another paper, even a weekly suburban, adds "*value in terms of worrying Goliaths*"—whereas the dominant paper may fear to do so, because it "*may look silly.*"[39]

Mick Rood wrote a follow-up piece about Boys Town—a good story that was also meant to keep worrying the Goliath—that drew on some racially bigoted comments Father Wegner had made in his interview, as well as certain disclosures he had made about the boys growing marijuana at Boys Town down by the lake. Paul Williams spiked it, saying the *Sun* must take the high road, in part not to jeopardize future stories and in part to avoid looking anti-Catholic. Also, the Pulitzer was pending. "Too bad," wrote Rood in a note to himself.[40]

The *Sun* team knew it had strong competition for the Pulitzer. It would be up against the series of articles penned by *Washington Post* investigative journalists Carl Bernstein and Bob Woodward, who had followed what appeared to be a minor burglary inside the Watergate offices of the Democratic National Committee during the 1972 election campaign, and uncovered what turned out to be an enormous political spying and sabotage operation. But the *Sun* would fare very well in the prizes awarded for 1972 journalism.

In March 1973, Sigma Delta Chi, the national journalism society, gave the *Sun* its highest award for public service; the *Washington Post* won for investigative reporting. A few weeks later came the phone call. The *Sun* had won a Pulitzer for local investigative specialized reporting.[41] This time it had swapped awards with the *Washington Post,* which won the Pulitzer for public service. Susie Buffett threw a party to celebrate, fixing an oversize pretzel that spelled out "Sun Pulitzer" to the paneling in the family room. In part they were also celebrating some tangible results. Boys Town had started throwing money at projects and quickly announced a center for the study and treatment of children's hearing and speech defects. It was *something,* and it would do some good. Boys Town from now on would have a budget and would disclose its financial status publicly.

Instead of the annual Christmas fund-raising letter that year, there was only a Christmas card expressing thanks, as well as a letter from Archbishop Sheehan, announcing with "deep regret" that Monsignor Wegner would retire "due to his failing health." While he was genuinely frail and ill, some cynic at the *Sun* circled this before filing it and added, "due to something he read."[42]

The following Easter, 1974, Father (no longer Monsignor) Wegner sent out a letter to the Boys Town mailing list. Instead of whining that there would be no joyous Christmas for the homeless, abandoned boys, the letter talked at length of the costly new projects that Boys Town had just built and was going to build.[43] While down from previous highs, the contributions that rolled in after the letter was sent came to $3.6 million, never mind the scandal.

Thus, the story ended as such things usually do: a mixed triumph with a certain amount of ass-covering and reforms that came about because of public embarrassment rather than an institutional change of heart. While Boys Town eventually turned over its board of trustees and management, it did not happen easily or overnight, and the conflicts of interest on the board also did not disappear, at least not immediately.

And even the *Sun*'s glory proved short-lived. It was failing financially, and its muckraking editor, Paul Williams, retired not long after the Pulitzer. One by one the investigative reporters dispersed to other papers and the wire services. Unless Buffett was willing to run it as a money-losing hobby, the economics of the *Sun* couldn't support a future like its past. And the *Washington Monthly* had already proven that—even for great journalism—Buffett would not do that. In a sense, the *Sun* was one of his cigar butts, from which he had been able to enjoy one huge personal puff.

In another sense, the temporary boost of fame he had gotten from the *Sun* was a sidebar compared to something else. Buffett had recently exploded in investors' minds for a different reason. Under the pen name Adam Smith, a writer named George Goodman had published *Supermoney,* a fire-and-brimstone critique of the 1960s stock-market bubble, which sold more than a million copies.[44] It demonized the fund managers who had ascended to the stratosphere almost overnight and then crashed. They were featured as devil-horned, pitchfork-bearing tempters of the ordinary Joe Investor. But when it came to Ben Graham and his protégé Buffett, Goodman knew he had met a couple of very different characters, and he devoted an entire chapter to the two of them, in which he captured them brilliantly.

Goodman respected the Latin- and French-spouting Graham and had been highly entertained by him, but when Graham was quoted in *Supermoney,* he sounded painfully affected, speaking in a style that bordered on self-satire. Buffett, however, appeared as a blue-ribbon, All-American, Pepsi-quaffing, investing fundamentalist, one who plied his trade in glorious solitude, far from the Lucifers of Wall Street. Presented alongside Graham this way, Buffett came across like a two-inch-thick T-bone next to a dab of goose liver pâté on a plate. Everyone went for the steak.

One hundred percent of the book's reviewers mentioned Buffett. John Brooks, dean of the Wall Street writers, described him as a "Puritan in Babylon" among the "greedy, sideburned young portfolio wizards."[45] Overnight, he was a star.

Even in Omaha, *Supermoney* created a minor sensation. Buffett had been crowned as the king of investors in a best-selling book. After fifteen years, the jury had come in. He was now "*the* Warren Buffett."

36

Two Drowned Rats

Omaha and Washington, D.C. • 1971

Buffett had craved a niche in the publishing big leagues for quite some time. Newspapers, which were mostly family-owned businesses, had recently gone through a spasm of selling themselves. He and Charlie Munger had worked ceaselessly and unsuccessfully to buy everything from the *Cincinnati Enquirer*[1] to the *Albuquerque Tribune.*[2]

In 1971, Buffett called Charles Peters, publisher of the *Washington Monthly*, asking him for an introduction to *Washington Post* publisher Katharine Graham. Buffett said that he and Munger had bought some stock in the *New Yorker* and wanted to buy the whole magazine.[3] They wanted a partner in the purchase and thought the *Washington Post* might be the right choice.

Peters wasn't surprised to get the call. Aha, he thought, Buffett must be interested in the *Post* stock now that the Graham family is taking the company public. Perhaps Buffett thought that if the *Washington Monthly* turned into an entry point to making a killing on the *Post*, then the failed investment could be justified financially.

Buffett had never bought public offerings, which he felt were overhyped and overpromoted.[4] So he had no plans to buy *Post* stock—at least for now—but Peters set up the meeting and Buffett and Munger flew to Washington to see Kay Graham at the *Washington Post* headquarters.

When Graham took over the newspaper eight years earlier, at age forty-six, she was a widow with four children and had never worked in a business. Now she found herself preparing for the challenge of running a public company under the unremitting scrutiny of investors and the press.

"Charlie and I met her very, very briefly, for twenty minutes. I had no idea what she was like. The idea that she'd be frightened of her own business—I didn't know any of that. It was raining like hell, so we came in looking like a couple of drowned rats, and you know how we dress anyway."

At the time, Graham had no interest in the *New Yorker* purchase that had prompted the visit—and there was nothing in the meeting to suggest that she and Buffett would one day be great friends. He made no impression on her whatsoever. For his part, he did not find her particularly attractive—even though she was a handsome woman—for she lacked the soft femininity and caretaking qualities of his ideal, Daisy Mae. Moreover, their backgrounds were worlds apart.

Katharine Graham, born just before the twenties started to roar, was the daughter of a rich father, investor and *Post* publisher Eugene Meyer, and a self-absorbed mother, Agnes—"Big Ag," as the family called her behind her back because of her imposing stature and, as the years passed, increasing girth. Agnes, who had married her Jewish husband at least in part for his money, was passionate about Chinese art, music, literature, and other cultural interests, but indifferent to her husband and their five children. The family shuttled among their mansion in Mount Kisco, their full-floor apartment on Fifth Avenue in New York City, and a large, dark, red-brick Victorian house in Washington, D.C.

Katharine spent her early years under the rule of Agnes at the Mount Kisco estate, which the family referred to as the "farm." Every vegetable and piece of fruit on the dining table came from the surrounding fields and orchards. Kay ate meat from the farm's own pigs and chickens and drank milk from its Jersey cows. The Westchester mansion's walls were covered with magnificent Chinese paintings; it boasted every status symbol of the era: an indoor swimming pool, a bowling alley, tennis courts, a massive pipe organ. Kay was taken on incredible vacations, once visiting Albert Einstein himself in Germany. When Agnes took the children camping to teach them independence, they roughed it accompanied by five ranch hands, eleven saddle horses, and seventeen packhorses.

But the children had to make an appointment to see their own mother. They gobbled down their meals because Agnes, served first at the long dining-room table, began eating as the footmen moved around serving everyone else—and had the others' plates snatched away the instant that she herself had finished. By her own admission, she did not love her children. She left them to be raised by nannies, governesses, and riding instructors; she sent them off to summer camps, boarding schools, and dancing class. Their only playmates were one another and the servants' children. Agnes drank heavily, pursued flirtatious and obsessive (although apparently platonic) relationships with a number of famous men, and treated all other women as inferior, her own daughters among them. She compared Kay unfavorably to America's sweetheart, Shirley Temple, the singing, dancing, smiling child star with golden blond ringlets.[5] "If I said I loved *The Three Musketeers*," Graham recalled, "she responded by saying I couldn't really appreciate it unless I had read it in French as she had."[6] Kay was trained like a hybrid orchid, beautifully pampered, savagely critiqued for her show potential, and otherwise largely ignored. Still, by the time she reached the Madeira School in Washington, D.C., she had somehow managed to learn the skills of popularity and was elected head of her class—most surprising at that time and in that place because she was half Jewish.

In Protestant Mount Kisco, the family was socially shunned. At Agnes's insistence the children were raised as Protestants—albeit nonobservant ones—and were not even aware that their father was Jewish, leaving Graham ignorant of the reason for their isolation. She would later be stunned at Vassar when a friend apologized because someone had made a bigoted remark about Jews in front of her. She reflected with hindsight that this clash in her bloodlines "leaves you either a good survival capacity or a total mess."[7] Or, perhaps, both.

From her mother, Kay learned to be ungenerous about small things, fearful of being cheated, unable to give things away, and certain that people were trying to take advantage of her. By her own description, she also grew up inclined to be bossy.[8] Yet others saw in her qualities of naiveté, candor, generosity, and open-heartedness that she herself seemed unable to acknowledge.

She felt closer to her awkward, distant, yet supportive father. To Eugene Meyer, she attributed her zeal for tiny economies—compulsively turning out lights, never wasting anything. Her father's talent for such economies, along with great infusions of time, money, and energy, had been crucial in keeping the ailing *Washington Post* alive while Kay was growing up, when the paper ranked fifth in a field of five in the capital area, far behind the dominant paper, the *Washington Evening Star*.[9] When Meyer began thinking of retiring in 1942, Kay's brother, Bill, a doctor, had no interest in running an unprofitable newspaper, so the duty fell to Kay and her new husband, Philip Graham. Kay was besotted with Phil, and so convinced of her own lowliness that she accepted as a matter of course her father's decision to sell Phil nearly two-thirds of the *Post*'s voting stock, giving him absolute control. Meyer did it because, he said, no man should have to work for his wife. Kay got the remainder.[10]

When Phil Graham took it over, matters were out of hand. The newsroom and the circulation department stayed busy playing the horses and drinking. When Meyer was out of town, the office boy started every morning by bringing one man a half pint of booze and the *Daily Racing Form*.[11]

Phil Graham got the place shipshape, gave it an identity by fostering vigorous political coverage, and stamped its editorial page with a strong liberal voice. He bought *Newsweek* magazine and several television stations, and proved to be a brilliant publisher. But over time, drinking binges, a violent temper, unstable moods, and a cruel sense of humor showed themselves, with particularly devastating effects on his wife. When Katharine gained weight, he called her "Porky" and bought her a porcelain pig. She thought so little of herself that she found the joke funny and put the pig on the porch for display.

"I was very shy," she said. "I was afraid to be left alone with anybody because I'd bore them. I didn't speak when we went out; I let him speak. . . . He was really brilliant and funny. Marvelous combination."[12]

Her husband played on her fears. When they were out with friends, Phil would look at her in a certain way when she was talking; it told her that he thought she was going on too long and boring people. She was convinced that she occupied some lesser sphere and could never meet the expected—but impossible—standard of living up to Shirley Temple. Over time, she ceased speaking in public.[13] She grew so insecure that she vomited before parties. And by some accounts, the way Phil treated her in private was even worse.[14] Phil would drink and build up to a violent rage; then she froze and shut down.

She never confronted Phil, even when he embarked on a series of affairs with other women that supposedly included swapping mistresses with Jack Kennedy.[15] Instead, she defended him, swept away by the force of his personality, wit, and brains. The more cruelly he behaved, the more she seemed to want to please him.[16] "I thought that Phil literally created me," she said. "My interests were better. I was surer of myself."[17] He thought she was lucky to have him, and she did too. When he finally left her for *Newsweek* staffer Robin Webb, she was stunned by the response of one of her friends, who said, "Good!" It had never occurred to her that she might be better off without Phil. But then he began trying to take the paper away from her, since he controlled two-thirds of the stock. Kay was terrified that she would lose her family's newspaper.

In 1963, in the midst of her battle to keep the paper, Phil Graham suffered a spectacular public breakdown, was diagnosed with manic depression, and committed himself to a mental institution. Six weeks later, he talked his way out of the hospital for a weekend leave. He came home to Glen Welby, the Grahams' sprawling rural Virginia farm retreat. On Saturday, after eating lunch with Kay, he shot himself in a downstairs bathroom while she was upstairs taking a nap. He was forty-eight.

His suicide left Kay with the paper, no longer threatened with its loss. She dreaded being in charge, but even though some suggested that she sell, she was absolutely determined to keep it; she saw her stewardship as a holding action until the next generation was ready to take over. "I didn't know anything about management," she said. "I didn't know anything about complicated editorial issues. I didn't know how to use a secretary. I didn't know big things and small things and, worse still, I couldn't tell them apart."[18]

While Graham could project a determined confidence at times, she began to rely on other people as she constantly rethought and questioned her own decisions. "I just kept trying to learn the issues from the men who were running things," she wrote. "And of course, they were all men." She never trusted them or anyone else—but, of course, no one close to her had ever treated her in a trustworthy way. She would tentatively extend her confidence to someone, then second-guess herself and pull back. Alternately enthused, then disenchanted with her executives, she gained a fearsome reputation in the office. And all the while, she never stopped seeking advice.

"As decisions would come along in the course of a day where she was very uncertain how to proceed," says her son Don, "she was literally reinventing the wheel. She would be called upon to be a top manager of a company when she'd never been a bottom manager of a company. She hadn't watched people who were CEOs, except the way you watch your husband or your dad.

"And so she had the great habit, when she faced what she thought of as a difficult decision—it usually *was* a difficult decision—she would call directors, she would call friends whom she thought might have a relevant experience. It was partly getting advice to help her handle the problem. And it was partly trying out the friends as advisers to see who seemed to make sense and whom she'd call the next time."[19]

Early on, Graham began to lean on Fritz Beebe, a lawyer and the chairman of the Washington Post Company.[20] By then, the *Post* was the smallest of three remaining Washington newspapers, with $85 million in yearly revenues and $4 million in profits.

Gradually she grew into her role. She and her managing editor, Ben Bradlee, had a vision of a national paper that would set a standard to rival the *New York Times*. Bradlee, a Harvard graduate who had worked closely with intelligence agencies before turning to journalism, was funny, brilliant, had an unexpected saltiness that belied his background. He brought out the best in Graham and encouraged reporters to thrive. Before long, the *Post* had developed a reputation for solid journalism. Three years after taking over the paper, Graham made Bradlee executive editor.

In 1970 Kay was freed from the tyranny of her mother, Agnes, who died in bed while Kay was visiting Mount Kisco on Labor Day weekend. While the death of Agnes Meyer relieved Graham of a burden, it did not cure her insecurities. But she would soon find she had grown into her job at the *Post*.

In March 1971, amid continuing protests of the Vietnam War, the *New York Times* was leaked a copy of the Pentagon Papers—a top-secret and ruthlessly honest history of the decision-making that led the country into and through Vietnam.[21] The Pentagon Papers showed conclusively that the government had perpetrated a vast deception on the American public. The *Times* published its account of the scheme on Sunday, June 13.

On June 15, about two weeks after Buffett and Munger had gone down to Washington to meet Graham in her office, a federal district court enjoined the *Times* from publishing most of the Pentagon Papers. It was the first time in history that a U.S. judge had restrained publication by a newspaper, raising a major constitutional question.

The *Post,* mortified at having been scooped, was determined to get its hands on the Pentagon Papers. Through informed guesswork and contacts, an editor tracked down their source, Daniel Ellsberg, an expert on the Vietnam War. The editor flew to Boston with an empty suitcase and brought the Pentagon Papers back to Washington.

By then Graham had mastered some of the basics of being a publisher, though she remained deferential and ill at ease. Further, "we were in the middle of going public [but] we hadn't sold the stock," she recalled. "It was a terribly sensitive time for the company, and we could have been very badly hurt if we'd been to court or criminally enjoined. . . . The business people were all saying either don't do it or wait a day, and the lawyers were saying don't do it. And the editors were on the other phone saying you've got to do it."

"I would have had to quit if we hadn't published it," says Ben Bradlee. "A lot of people would have quit."

"Everybody knew we had those papers," Graham wrote later. "It was terribly important to maintain the momentum after the *Times* had been stopped," with a Constitutional issue at stake. "And I felt what Ben said, that the editors would really be demoralized, that the news floor would be demoralized, that a great deal depended on our doing it."

Notified on the terrace of her Georgetown mansion that beautiful June afternoon that she had a call, Graham went into her library and sat down on a small sofa to pick up the phone. *Post* chairman Fritz Beebe was on the line. He told her, "I'm afraid you are going to have to decide." Graham asked Beebe what he would do, and he said that he guessed he wouldn't.

"Why can't we wait a day?" said Graham. "The *Times* discussed this for three months." Now Bradlee and other editors joined the call. The grapevine, they said, knows we've got the papers, journalists inside and out are watching us. We've got to go, and we've got to go tonight.

Meanwhile, in the library, Paul Ignatius, president of the *Post*, was standing at Graham's side, saying, "each time more insistently—'Wait a day, wait a day.' I had about a minute to decide."

So she parsed Fritz Beebe's words and his lukewarm tone when he said that he guessed he wouldn't and concluded that he would back her if she chose a different course.

"I said, 'Go ahead, go ahead, go ahead. Let's go. Let's publish.' And I hung up."[22]

In that moment the woman who reached for the advice of others on every decision realized that only she could choose; when forced to reach inside to form her own opinion, she found that she did know what to do.

Before the afternoon was out, the government filed suit against the *Post*. The following day, June 21, Judge Gerhard Gesell ruled in the newspaper's favor. Less than two weeks later, the Supreme Court upheld him, saying the government had not met "the heavy burden" required to justify, on the grounds of national security, restraining publication.

With the Pentagon Papers, the *Post* transcended its status as a decently run business that produced good local journalism and began its transformation into a great paper of national importance.

"Her skill," wrote reporter Bob Woodward, "was to raise the bar, gently but relentlessly."[23]

37

Newshound

Nearly two years later, while the *Post* was deep into reporting the Watergate story, in Omaha, the *Sun*'s reporters were basking in the glow of the Boys Town exposé. Reporting on Watergate, which began in June 1972, had gradually picked up steam. The scandal unfolded over many months. Nixon was re-elected by a huge majority that fall, having vehemently denied any knowledge of or involvement in the break-in. The Nixon White House, which was already actively hostile to the *Post* because of the Pentagon Papers episode, dismissed Watergate as "a third-rate burglary attempt." Attorney General John Mitchell, who had managed Nixon's election campaign, told Woodward and Bernstein that "Katie Graham's gonna get her tit caught in a big fat wringer" if the *Post* continued to report the story. A Wall Street friend with administration contacts advised her "not to be alone."

In early 1973, a Republican fund-raiser friend of Nixon's challenged the renewal of the *Post*'s two Florida television licenses. The challenge threatened half of the company's earnings, an attack on the heart of the business.[1] In response, WPO stock plunged from a high of $38 to as low as $16 a share.

Most of Graham's time and attention now went to fighting these fires.[2] Her chairman, Fritz Beebe, was ill with cancer and declining rapidly.[3] Still in need of an authority figure, she increasingly turned toward another of her board members, André Meyer, senior partner of the investment bank Lazard Frères.

Vindictive, ruthless, secretive, snobbish, and sadistic, Meyer "crushed other people's personalities." He was known as "the Picasso of Banking" and a man with "an almost erotic attachment to money," and called the greatest investment banker of the twentieth century.[4] He was also the well-connected man who had warned Graham during Watergate not to be alone, and he soon took up Graham socially as well.

Beebe died in May 1973, and a week later his lawyer, George Gillespie, who was also Graham's personal lawyer, began settling his estate. Gillespie got wind that a big investor out in Omaha had been buying *Post* stock, so he called Buffett and offered a block of fifty thousand of Beebe's shares. Buffett snapped it up.

If he could, at the right price, Buffett would have bought almost any newspaper in sight for Berkshire Hathaway. He grabbed stock in Affiliated Publications, parent of the *Boston Globe,* in Booth Newspapers, in Scripps Howard, and in Harte-Hanks Communications, a San Antonio–based chain. The *Sun's* elevated status as a Pulitzer Prize winner enabled him to network his way through the newspaper world, talking with publishers as one of their peers. He chatted up the owners of the *Wilmington News Journal,* hoping to buy the paper. Alas, while newspaper stocks were cheap because investors failed to see their value, newspaper owners were not so blind. Competing with them, Buffett and Munger's efforts to buy whole newspapers had all come to naught.

Still, by late spring 1973 Buffett had accumulated more than five percent of the *Washington Post* stock.[5] He now sent a letter to Graham. She had never lost her terror that her company would be taken away from her, even though Beebe and Gillespie had structured the *Washington Post*'s stock in two classes to prevent that.[6] Buffett's letter told her that he owned 230,000 shares and meant to buy more. But instead of legalistic boilerplate, he wrote a highly flattering, personal missive that linked their common interest in journalism and stressed the *Sun's* Pulitzer.

Nonetheless, Graham panicked. She reached out for advice. While she instinctively pursued women's equality—she had given the seed money to Gloria Steinem for *Ms.* magazine—deep inside she still thought that only men knew anything about business. Thus, when she asked André Meyer his opinion and he became "irate" and told her that Buffett meant her no good, she took him seriously.[7]

"André Meyer really wanted to think he controlled everything. And it was easy when he got a woman like Kay—he would make her feel like she'd better not go to the bathroom without checking with him. He had that style. André kept referring to me as her new boss because I bought this stock.

"She was very sensitive to the idea that anyone would manipulate her, for political purposes or for the paper, which is understandable. She was used to every-

body in the world trying to use her. But what you could do with Kay is you could play on her fears. If you wanted to work her over, you could make her feel so insecure. And she knew you were doing it to her, but she couldn't resist it."

"She would fall in and out of love with people," says fellow *Post* board member Arjay Miller. "She could be bullied. She would meet somebody and be sort of dazzled with them for a little while and think they knew all the answers. She thought men knew all about business and women didn't know anything. At the bottom, that was the real problem. Her mother told her that and her husband told her that, over and over and over and over again."[8]

Graham barely remembered Buffett from their earlier encounter.[9] She and her colleagues bought copies of *Supermoney* and devoured the chapter on him, wondering what the man from Nebraska had in store for them. Those unfriendly to Buffett made sure she also saw a recent unsigned article in *Forbes* about a stock purchase of Buffett's, which cast a shadow on the sunny portrait that *Supermoney* had painted of him.

This *Forbes* piece described a San Jose Water Works shareholder who wanted to unload his stock. A company director sent him to Buffett. The article insinuated that Buffett must have known that a deal was brewing for the city to take over the water works at a higher price. He had connections, so he must have known something—right?

But there was nothing illegal about a director referring a seller of stock to a buyer.[10] Indeed, no deal ever took place. Yet to anyone checking him out, this would be the most prominent, public, recent mention of his name apart from *Supermoney*.[11] Buffett felt like a cat's scratching post. If this cascaded into a series of expanding stories, it could wreck his newly gilded reputation. Buffett was not the type to storm and shout, but to brood and plan. He wanted retribution and vindication. Too clever to confront the magazine and denounce its nameless reporter, however, he used the opportunity to bring himself to the attention of magazine publisher Malcolm Forbes, writing him an artfully worded letter in which he mentioned the *Sun*'s Pulitzer.[12] He also wrote to the *Forbes* editor, directly stating the facts to support his innocence.

Sure enough, *Forbes* ran a correction. Buffett knew, however, that corrections were rarely read and had no impact as compared to the initial story. So he also sent one of his proxies, the loyal Bill Ruane, to position Buffett with the *Forbes* editors as an expert who could write an article about investing.[13] This attempt failed, at least initially. He now had a new cause—outrage at bias in news reporting—which wound itself around his sense of justice and his interest in journalism in general. That a reporter could lie by inference and omission without any accountability drove him wild. He knew that even well-intentioned news publications flew into a state of high dudgeon and defended their reporters' dubious behavior on the premises of newsroom morale and press independence—a stance known as the "defensive crouch."[14]

Eventually, he would end up helping to fund the National News Council, a nonprofit organization that arbitrated complaints of journalistic malpractice. The council's position was that lack of media competition gave publishers "power without responsibility." The council offered redress to victims who had been "traduced, misquoted, libeled, held up to unjustified ridicule, or whose legitimate views have been ignored in a one-sided report." Unfortunately, those very monopolies and the few publishers who dominated the media had no interest in publishing the News Council's rulings, which exposed their biases and the carelessness of their reporters. The News Council eventually folded after its findings were spiked, time and time again, by the free and independent press that was supposed to publish them.[15]

The National News Council was a worthy crusade, indeed perhaps ahead of its time, like many of the causes on which Buffett spent his energy. But by 1973, Susie Buffett had seen him expend a tidal wave of energy on each new obsession, sometimes changing entire coastlines in his wake. From his childhood hobby of collecting license-plate numbers to reforming the jiggery-pokery of journalism, three roles invariably interested him. The first was the relentless collector, expanding his empire of money, people, and influence. The second was the preacher, sprinkling idealism from the lectern. The third was the cop, foiling the bad guys. The perfect business would allow him to do all of these at once: preach, play cop, and ring the cash register. The perfect business was a newspaper. That was why the *Sun* had been a sliver of something that he wanted more of, much, much more.

But he and Munger had struck out at trying to buy major city newspapers. Now here was Katharine Graham, unsteady on her feet when it came to business and seeking a lifesaver ring from anyone she could find. Yet despite her position at the helm of the *Washington Post,* which made her one of the most powerful people in the Western Hemisphere, Graham was afraid of Buffett. She asked George Gillespie whether he was crooked. She could not afford to make a mistake. For several years the Nixon administration had been waging an all-out war to discredit the *Post.* A set of newly discovered tapes implicated the President. Graham labored every day over the Watergate story. In a sense, she had staked the *Post*'s franchise on it.

She relied heavily on the opinion of the devoutly religious, utterly respectable Gillespie. He had served the Graham family ever since, as a twenty-eight-year-old trust lawyer, he had drafted Eugene Meyer's final will, witnessing the signature of the fading old man. "He's going to take over the *Washington Post*," she said about Buffett. "Forget it," Gillespie said. "It's not possible. It doesn't make any difference how much B stock he owns. He has no rights. All he could do would be to elect himself to the board if he owned the majority of the B stock."

Gillespie had called a San Jose Water Works director and was convinced that Buffett had had no inside information. He made it clear that he disagreed with the powerful André Meyer, going out on a limb, given Meyer's position and connections. He told her to talk to Buffett, that he would be good for her to know.[16]

Graham wrote Buffett, quaking as she dictated the letter, suggesting that they get together in California, where she would be late that summer on business. He agreed eagerly, and when she arrived at an office borrowed from the *Los Angeles Times*, she looked exactly as she had two years before: impeccably tailored shirtdress, her pageboy hairdo lacquered into place, lips pursed in a small smile. When she saw Buffett, Graham said, his "very appearance surprised" her.

"The great blessing and curse in my mother's life," says her son Don, "was she had very high standards when it came to taste. She was used to traveling in highfalutin circles. She thought there was one right way to dress and eat and one circle of people to be paid attention. Warren violated all her standards when it came to these things, yet he didn't care."[17] Wearing a suit that looked tailored for some other man, the hair no longer crew-cut and beginning to float up slightly at the ends, "he resembled no Wall Street figure or business tycoon I'd ever met," she later wrote. "Rather, he came across as corn-fed and Midwestern, but with that extraordinary combination of qualities that has appealed to me throughout my life—brains and humor. I liked him from the start."[18]

But at the time, that certainly didn't show.

"When I first met with Kay, she was wary and scared. She was terrified by me, and she was intrigued by me. And one thing about Kay was that you could tell. She was not a poker-face type."

Buffett told her he thought Wall Street did not see the value of the *Post*. Graham relaxed her guard slightly. In her patrician accent, she invited him to meet with her in Washington a few weeks later.

Warren and Susie arrived November 4, the evening before the meeting, drove up in a taxi to the Madison Hotel, directly across the street from the *Post* headquarters, and, as they were checking in, found that the newspaper was in the middle of a printers' union work stoppage. Federal marshals were evicting the mutinous printers amid rumors of pressmen carrying guns. Commotion, glaring lights, and television cameras carried on until dawn. Given what was happening in the political sphere, it would be hard to find a worse time to shut down a newspaper, which of course was exactly what the union intended. Vice President Spiro Agnew had suddenly pleaded "no contest" less than a month ago to a tax-evasion charge, then resigned. The Watergate scandal had reached an explosive crisis. Nixon had fired Special Prosecutor Archibald Cox in what became known as the "Saturday Night Massacre."[19] The President's interference in the supposedly independent judiciary branch of government shifted public opinion suddenly and decisively against him. Pressure was mounting rapidly on Congress to impeach.

The morning after the Buffetts' arrival, Graham, exhausted from working with most of her managers until six a.m. to get the paper out, was embarrassed at the introduction her new shareholder had received to her paper and nervous about how the day's meeting would proceed. But she had arranged lunch for Buffett with Ben Bradlee, Meg Greenfield, Howard Simons, and herself.

Graham considered editorial-page editor Meg Greenfield her closest friend, yet referred to her as "a lone fortress...no one ever really got to know Meg." Howard Simons, the *Post*'s managing editor, was known for his sharp-witted way of twitting Graham. *"Howard Simons used to say that you don't have to be dead to write obituaries. ... He was wicked. He used to tease Kay so much.*[20]

*"We were eating lunch, talking about acquisitions and media properties. I could see that even though she had all the A stock, she was afraid of me. ... So I said something about how the amortization of intangibles made it harder for the media companies, because they paid so much for goodwill."** Buffett was trying to reassure Graham that it was hard to take over media companies because the accounting made it burdensome to would-be acquirers. *"And Kay was showing off. She said, 'Yes, the amortization of intangibles caused us a problem' or something like that. Howard looked her right in the eye, and he said, 'Kay, what _is_ the amortization of intangibles?'*

"And at that moment, I mean, I loved it. She was just frozen. She was paralyzed. Howard was enjoying it. So I jumped in and explained what amortization of

---

*If a company's book value is $1 million and a buyer pays $3 million, the remaining $2 million is for intangible assets—some specifically identifiable, like trademarks and patents, the rest unidentifiable customer "goodwill." Accounting rules used to require sellers to gradually charge off, or amortize, these costs over time.

intangibles was to Howard. And when I got through with this description, Kay said, 'Exactly!'"

Buffett loved outthinking Simons, short-circuiting the game, and coming—indirectly and subtly—to Graham's defense. Graham's tight little smile began to ease. *"From that point forward, we were the best of friends. I was Sir Lancelot. That was one of the greatest moments of my life. Turning defeat into triumph for her."*[21]

After lunch, Buffett met with Graham for about an hour, then he reassured her in writing. *"I said, 'I'm telling you that even though these teeth look like Little Red Riding Hood's wolf fangs to you, they really are baby teeth. But we'll just take them out.'"*

That afternoon, Buffett—who had spent $10,627,605 to buy twelve percent of the company—signed an agreement with Graham not to buy any more of the *Post* stock without her permission. *"I knew that was the only way that she would ever be comfortable."*

In the evening, the Buffetts were due at Graham's for one of her famous dinners, this one for forty guests honoring Warren and Susie. Despite Graham's personal insecurity, she was considered Washington's greatest hostess, above all because she knew how to help people relax and enjoy themselves.

"She traveled widely in the world, so found occasions to give dinners," says Don Graham. "If she had gone to Malaysia, when the prime minister came to town she'd give a dinner for him. The ambassador would look up what they did last time, and there was always a meal at Mrs. Graham's house. Someone would publish a book, someone would have a birthday, and she'd give a dinner because she loved to give a dinner."[22] Graham used the dinners as a way of making new friends and as a way of getting people to know one another. She wanted to get to know Buffett, her new investor.

This evening, despite her exhaustion and the temptation to cancel, *"She had a little party for me. That was her way of reciprocating. And when she had a party, she could get anybody she wanted. Anybody—the President of the United States, anybody.*

"So all of a sudden I'm at the Madison Hotel with Susie, and about five o'clock somebody slips something under the door and it describes the party, which I had been invited to weeks before. At the bottom it says 'black tie.' Well, I didn't have that, needless to say. . . . So I called her secretary, panicked.

"Her secretary is a very nice gal. She says, well, let's put on our thinking cap." Graham's assistant, Liz Hylton, called a local store and found something suitable.[23]

The Buffetts left the Madison Hotel and were driven past mansion after mansion on Embassy Row. The taxi turned onto Q Street, past the historic Oak Hill
Cemetery where Phil Graham was buried. Around the corner, they passed a row
of historic nineteenth-century town houses with tiny manicured gardens. It was
early November; the leaves glowed with traces of russet, amber, and gold. The
taxi's passage into Georgetown was like crossing a border into a Colonial-era
town. Tucked into the corner of the cemetery and sprawling down its tree-
swagged hill stood Dumbarton Oaks, the ten-acre Federal estate where the conference at which the United Nations had been planned took place.[24]

The taxi swiveled left between a pair of stone gateposts. The sight ahead was
breathtaking. As the taxi crunched its way up the white-pebbled drive, the
Buffetts saw in the distance a three-story cream-colored Georgian mansion with
a green mansard roof. The broad lawns that surrounded it lapped all the way to
the top of Georgetown's Rock of Dumbarton, so that the house looked down
on the cemetery. To the right, down the hill past a deep colonnade of trees, were
the nearby neighborhoods leading to the old Buffett house in Spring Valley, and
just beyond them, Tenleytown, where Warren had delivered papers at The
Westchester and stolen golf balls from Sears.

The Buffetts were ushered through Graham's front door to join the other
guests, who were having cocktails in the living room. Asian art from her
mother's collection hung everywhere on eggshell-white walls swagged with blue
velvet curtains, along with a Renoir painting and Albrecht Dürer engravings.
Graham began to introduce the Buffetts to her other guests. "*She told them nice
things about me,*" Buffett says. "*Kay was doing everything in the world to make me
comfortable.* [Yet] *I was so uncomfortable.*"

He had never attended a gathering of such formality or grandeur. When the
cocktail hour ended, crossing the hallway to the huge dining room where
Graham held her famous parties, its paneled walls lit by the glow of tapered candles in bronze sconces, did nothing to make Buffett feel more at home. Crystal
candlesticks and armorial porcelain gleamed on the round walnut dining tables,
although the guests whom Graham had invited outshone the splendor of the
surroundings. The room at any given time could be filled with a selection of
U.S. Presidents, foreign leaders, diplomats, administration officials, Congressional members, senior lawyers in town, and people chosen from her group of
prominent friends.

Buffett found himself seated next to Edmund Muskie's wife, Jane, an obvious
dinner partner, since the Buffetts had entertained her husband in Omaha. On

his other side was Barbara Bush, whose husband was the U.S. Ambassador to the United Nations but would soon become the Chief of the U.S. Liaison Office in Peking, with the important role of steering the United States through the delicate process of renewing its diplomatic ties with China. Graham pressed a button to signal the kitchen, and waiters began to move around the antique Georgian tables and serve. Warren tried not to gape at the protocol. *"Susie's over there sitting next to some senator. And he's trying to make out with her, he's got his hand on her leg and all these things. But me, I'm dying, because I don't know what to talk to these people about. Barbara Bush could not have been nicer. She could see how ill at ease I was."*

The waiters began to follow an American version of service à la russe, serving the first course followed by a fish course, then the main course, all borne on trays from which the diners served themselves. On and on the courses went as wine was poured to the sound of Washington chatter. The waiters added and removed unfamiliar sterling implements like fish knives. As they offered him food that he would never eat and wines that he would never drink, he found the meal increasingly more complex and intimidating. Graham's other guests were relaxed and comfortable, but by the time dessert was served, Buffett was thoroughly cowed. Then came coffee he did not drink. His discomfort increased to terror when, as at the end of every evening, Graham stood up and read an articulate, witty, polished, personal, and original toast to her guest of honor that she had obviously put considerable thought into writing, however lacking in confidence her delivery. The guest of honor was supposed to stand and toast his hostess in kind.

"I didn't have the nerve to stand up and offer a toast, which you're supposed to do. I blew it totally. I was so uncomfortable. I even thought I might throw up, actually. I could not stand up there in front of half the cabinet and talk. I wasn't up to it." Afterward, as he and Susie made their good-byes, they had the feeling that the hicks from Nebraska would be the talk of Georgetown long after they left.

"This Senator was still trying to score with Susie and was so concentrating on explaining how she should come down to the Senate and see his offices as we were leaving that he opened the door to a closet and walked in. That was my introduction to Washington."

Yet while it was true that the formal, glittering society that surrounded the powerful Mrs. Graham may have unnerved Buffett and made him ill at ease, he had never been one to hide his enthusiasms. And so it must have soon become obvious to Susie Buffett that her husband wanted more of this world.

38

Spaghetti Western

Omaha · 1973–1974

By the time he dined with Katharine Graham in 1973, Buffett was no longer just an investor who was buying newspaper stocks. He was becoming a business mogul on a small scale. Berkshire Hathaway and Diversified were his bailiwick. Charlie Munger was the czar of Blue Chip Stamps.

The interlocking ownership of these three companies had tightened the business relationship between Buffett and Munger, and resembled the embryo of an empire built by an investor whom Buffett admired, Gurdon W. Wattles.[1] His company was like a Russian doll; open it and inside find another company, and another, and another. Wattles controlled them, although he did not own one hundred percent of any of them. From early in his career, Buffett admired the Wattles model. He talked about Wattles all the time to his friends. "The only way to go is coattail-riding," he would say.[2]

"*Wattles had this little closed-end investment company called Century Investors. He did this chain thing where he would be buying stock in a company at a discount, which would be buying stock in another company at a discount. . . . The big company at the end of the thing was Mergenthaler Linotype, which was two-thirds owned by American Manufacturing. In those days, you didn't have to file with the SEC to publicly reveal that you were buying, so nobody knew and he just would keep buying until he got control. He bought control of Electric Auto-Lite, partly through Mergenthaler, and he was doing the same thing with Crane Co. Somewhere in the chain was Webster Tobacco. . . . Everything sold at a discount, and you could just keep buying all of them and make more money every time you made a purchase. . . . I owned Mergenthaler, I owned Electric Auto-Lite, I owned*

American Manufacturing.[3] *What would cause the value to come out, that was always the question. But you just had a feeling you were with a smart guy and eventually it would.*

"For ten or fifteen years I followed him. He was very Graham-like. Nobody paid any attention to him except me. He was sort of my model as to what I hoped to do for a while. It was so understandable and so obvious and such a sure way of making money. Although it didn't make you huge money necessarily, you knew you were going to make money."[4] What interested Warren about the Wattles model: the way one company could legitimately buy cheap stock in another.

Eventually Wattles had merged his empire into one company, Eltra Corporation. This stock was now a favorite of Bill Ruane's, because the company's earnings were compounding at fifteen percent a year.[5]

The Buffett-Munger companies were beginning to look a little like Eltra before its combination: Berkshire was Diversified's largest shareholder and also owned Blue Chip stock. Each of them also owned businesses that were not traded publicly. See's Candies was so profitable that it more than offset the losses from Blue Chip's trading-stamp business. Munger now took the step of buying twenty percent of a near-defunct investment firm, Source Capital, for Blue Chip. "We bought it at a discount from its asset value," says Munger. "And there were two assholes who were the sellers. We had a no-asshole rule very early. Our basic rule has always been that we won't deal with assholes. And so Warren, when he heard about Source Capital, said, 'Now I understand the two-asshole exception to the no-asshole rule.'"[6]

Source Capital was small change. Buffett and Munger were always on the lookout for anything new they could acquire, especially something bigger that would give Blue Chip the kind of boost that See's Candies had. They had found a sleepy West Coast savings-and-loan company, Wesco Financial. They bought some cheap Wesco shares for Blue Chip Stamps.[7] Then Wesco announced that it was going to merge with Financial Corporation of Santa Barbara, a hot stock, with an aggressive approach that Wall Street liked. Analysts thought Santa Barbara was paying too much for Wesco.[8] Yet Buffett and Munger saw the opposite: They thought Wesco was handing over its stock too cheap.[9]

Founded by the Casper family, Wesco owned Mutual Savings, a savings and loan that had prospered when the GIs came home during the post-WWII building boom. Even so, Wesco had never exploited its opportunities for growth. But it was extremely profitable because it kept its costs so low.[10]

Betty Casper Peters, the only member of the founding family both interested and able to serve on the board, felt that Wesco's managers condescended to her, dismissed her suggestions that they should grow the company, and used her family's legacy only as a ticket to ride at the head of the Rose Bowl parade.[11] Peters, an elegantly dressed, high-cheekboned former art history student, had school-age kids, no business background, and spent much of her time tending the family vineyard in Napa. Now she drove back and forth to Pasadena on Wednesdays to attend board meetings. Running a savings and loan, she found, was hardly a black art. She subscribed to everything relevant she could get her hands on and sat down and read and figured it out.

As Peters's frustration grew, she pushed for a merger. She knew the Santa Barbara offer wasn't great. But although the company's executives hung around the country club too much for her taste, they were aggressive, acquiring branches and doing things that she thought should be done.

Munger thought that he and Buffett should keep buying Wesco stock. If Blue Chip kept adding to the eight percent of Wesco it already owned, it could accumulate enough stock to defeat the Santa Barbara deal. But then he discovered that it would take fifty percent of the stock, a much higher obstacle. Munger had a greater incentive than Buffett to keep going, since Blue Chip was his partnership's most important investment. He urged going ahead; Buffett thought the threshold too high and held back.[12]

Soon thereafter, Munger went to see Wesco's CEO, Louis Vincenti, and tried to persuade him to abandon the Santa Barbara deal.[13] And Vincenti brushed Munger off like a flake of dandruff—not an easy thing to do.

After being rebuffed, Munger and Buffett had no intention of launching a competing hostile bid. Further, Munger could not imagine that such a thing might be necessary. He wrote Vincenti, appealing to his higher values.[14] It was *wrong* that Wesco should sell itself too cheap; Vincenti should simply *see* that. Munger told Vincenti that he was Buffett and Munger's sort of fellow. He told Vincenti something like, "You're engaged to this other girl, so we can't talk to you, but if you were free, you're the kind of man we would like."[15]

Munger's old-fashioned, Ben Franklinesque sense of ethics and his noblesse oblige notion that gentlemen should agree upon the right conduct among themselves must have sounded like Sanskrit to Vincenti. But at least Vincenti did let slip that Betty Peters was the shareholder pushing for the merger.

Munger sent Don Koeppel, CEO of Blue Chip, to see Peters. She dismissed him as a minion.[16] So it was time for the big gun. Within ten minutes of Koeppel's departure, Buffett called her. Peters had just finished reading the chapter on him in Jerry Goodman's *Supermoney*, which her husband had given her for Christmas. "Are you the same Warren Buffett that's in *Supermoney*?" she asked. Buffett admitted that he was the man who, according to Jerry Goodman, represented the triumph of straight thinking and high standards over flapdoodle, folly, and flimflam. They agreed to meet twenty-four hours later.

At the TWA Ambassador Lounge at the San Francisco airport, Buffett, with Pepsi in hand, underplayed his talent and record while asking questions in a warm, unthreatening manner. They talked for three hours, mostly about Omaha, where Peters's mother had grown up. They talked about politics. Peters, a lifelong Democrat, was pleased by Buffett's views. Finally he said, with considerable understatement, "Betty, I think I can do better with Wesco than this merger. Inasmuch as you're giving up the company, why don't we give it a try?"

Peters was taken with Buffett. In fact, her concern now became that something might happen to him if she swung her vote to him. He told her he had a partner, someone who would be in charge of Berkshire and the Buffett family's stockholdings if the proverbial truck mowed him down.

On her next trip to Pasadena, Peters sat down to breakfast with Buffett and Munger at the grand old Huntington Hotel so that she could get to know this mysterious partner. They asked her for a meeting with the Wesco board. Peters then did something brave, allowing herself to look capricious in front of the board rather than let the company make a serious mistake. At the next board meeting she asked the board to reverse course and meet with Buffett and Munger. The board waved her off and voted at a special meeting to "use every effort to complete the merger with Financial Corporation of Santa Barbara."[17]

Forgetting who actually owned the company was their mistake. Peters brought her whole family around to voting against the Santa Barbara deal.

"And then my task," says Peters, "was to go back into that little hermetically sealed Pasadena boardroom and tell all these buttoned-down gentlemen, including the management, that we're not going forward with the Santa Barbara savings deal." When she returned to the Spanish-style building, she was thinking about the plaza outside the boardroom windows, with its tile-lined fountain. "If the windows had been open," she says, "they would have thrown me out of them. I knew that what was going on in everyone's mind was 'My God, is this what happens when you let a hormonal woman on the board?' "[18]

Wall Street thought so; it sent Wesco stock nosediving from a high of above

$18 to $11 on the news. An analyst claimed Santa Barbara was paying too much for Wesco, a "sleeping company for years, with old management." Another referred to it as "garbage."[19]

For her courage, Buffett and Munger now felt indebted to Peters.[20] They had also decided they wanted to own Wesco themselves and felt it would be possible to win Vincenti's cooperation. But, by then it must have been apparent that Lou Vincenti would not gambol along behind them like a lamb after its mother. Accordingly, they loosened the purse strings and told their brokers, for once, to bid liberally on the stock. Blue Chip paid $17 for Wesco shares—the price at which it had traded before the deal fell through.

"I will admit we were eccentric," says Munger. "We deliberately paid more than we had to, but we felt we'd scuttled the damn merger and we didn't like taking advantage of it by buying at the market price. We thought it was kind of the right thing to do. Well, nobody could understand that. They thought something must have been dishonorable about doing that. We really thought we'd make a better impression on Louie Vincenti. . . . [W]e wanted Louie to be our partner for the long term. We were trying to behave well."[21]

By March 1973, Blue Chip owned a quarter of the Wesco stock. And Buffett, who had never stopped buying Blue Chip, continued his drive to get hold of more. Including the thirteen percent of Blue Chip he owned outright as well as his share of the stock owned by Berkshire and Diversified, Buffett was now effectively the largest Blue Chip shareholder. Blue Chip began to formally tender for Wesco's shares, this time paying $15 a share in cash, until it owned more than half.[22] Within weeks, Munger outlined for Lou Vincenti a vision for the company[23] that, not surprisingly, resembled the way Buffett thought about Berkshire Hathaway and Diversified. Wesco, residing inside Blue Chip and with Munger as chairman, would be another new doll among the rest.[24]

Then, no sooner had Blue Chip bought the majority of Wesco than the whole stock market fell apart.[25] Buffett's stake in the *Washington Post* lost a quarter of its value.[26] Ordinarily he would have bought more, but he had promised Graham that he wouldn't. Instead, he recommended it to his friends, and looked for new opportunities.[27] He bought National Presto, maker of pressure cookers and popcorn poppers,[28] and Vornado Realty Trust, which put him on its board.[29]

Buffett had a set of legacy shareholders at Berkshire Hathaway who understood his investing approach and would never question his judgment. Thus he had earned the luxury of ignoring Mr. Market, which had marked down the value of his portfolio to a fire-sale price. Others were not so lucky. Bill Ruane's Sequoia Fund was headed for a terrible year, and Ruane's main financial backer and friend, Bob Malott, was unhappy and sold on Buffett's approach and track record instead. He asked for Buffett's help with the pension fund of FMC Corporation, the company he now headed. So Buffett went to San Diego and spent several days interviewing investment managers and explaining his thinking to FMC's investment people. At first he said no to the request of managing the portfolio himself—then eventually agreed to manage a portion.[30] Along with his acceptance, he gave a warning: FMC would come last among his priorities, after Berkshire and Diversified, and Warren and Susie Buffett. The canny Malott jumped at the opportunity anyway, not mistaking the larger point: That Buffett was willing to do it *at all* meant that he would do it *well*.[31]

Between his duties at FMC, Vornado, Blue Chip, and Wesco, and regular trips to New York, Buffett was now traveling much of the time. He was also busy courting Katharine Graham and had made such a good impression on her that she began to call him for advice. Susie made the rounds of Omaha, busy with the board of the Urban League, still giving out her scholarships and taking on other crusades.

As 1973 progressed, even Hamilton the dog must have noticed the silence and emptiness descending on the Buffetts' crazy, noisy home.[32] Howie was two hundred and seventy-five miles away from Omaha at Augustana College. Susie Jr., unhappy with Lincoln, had transferred to the University of California, Irvine, where she was majoring in criminal justice.[33] Susie had taken her confidante, Peter, a high school sophomore, to look at schools in Orange County. Instead of moving, they stayed in Omaha. Susie had gotten Peter interested in photography, and now he spent much of his time in the basement, where his mother had built him a darkroom.[34]

Often now Susie stayed up late at night alone, listening to music that transported her to some different place.[35] She loved the jazz guitar of Wes Montgomery and great soul music, like the Temptations, who sang of a world in which it was men who felt all the longing.[36] She read books like *I Know Why the Caged Bird Sings*, Maya Angelou's autobiographical account of overcoming the forces of racism, sexual abuse, and repression that made her early years a prison. "The idea of being confined in a place not of your choosing ran deep for her," Peter says—not surprising after her childhood shut away in a sickroom, and growing up with a sister who was disciplined by being locked in a closet. Susie longed for romance, but now understood that she and Milt were never going to get married. Nevertheless, she could not bring herself to give up her relationship with him.

She was also spending more time with her tennis crowd of younger people at Dewey Park. One, John McCabe, a coach with a subdued personality, a sadness somewhat like her own, and a certain fragility, resembled most of her other lonelyhearts, but she seemed particularly drawn to him.[37] Susie now had reasons to be away from the house most of the time. The rhythm of the house slowed from its all-day carnival atmosphere. Peter, never much attuned to his parents' lives, noticed only the growing silence, not its cause. When he got home from school, he petted Hamilton, made something for himself for dinner, and headed downstairs to the darkroom.[38]

Warren's conception of his marriage had never changed, even though the marriage itself was changing inexorably. When he was home, Susie still seemed just as devoted to him as ever. He saw how active and busy she was and wanted her to be fulfilled, as long as she continued to take care of him—which he assumed was fulfilling to her. As far as he knew, the balancing act that had always worked for them still did.

The "retired" Warren was investing at full throttle ahead in late 1973, in the midst of a market swoon. Between Cap Cities and the *Washington Post* and his growing friendship with Kay Graham, his interest in media over the past few years had permutated into a deep understanding of the subject at all levels. One night at dinner in Laguna Beach, he and Carol Loomis started strafing Buffett's friend Dick Holland, who worked in advertising, with questions about the advertising business. "Whenever he did that," Holland recalls, "I always knew something was cooking." Sure enough, as a secondary way to play media, Buffett plunked down a huge amount—almost $3 million—for the stocks of advertising agencies Interpublic, J. Walter Thompson, and Ogilvy & Mather, stocks so distressed he paid less than three times their earnings.

As 1974 began, stocks for which he had recently paid $50 million lost a quarter of their value. Berkshire, too, slid down to $64 per share. Some of the former partners began to fear it had been a mistake to keep the stock.

Buffett saw it just the opposite way. He wanted to buy more Berkshire and Blue Chip. But *"I'd run out of gas. I had used all the $16 million of cash I got out of the partnership to buy stock in Berkshire and Blue Chip. So all of a sudden I woke up one day and had no money at all. I was getting $50,000 a year salary from*

Berkshire Hathaway and some fees from FMC.[39] But I had to start my personal net worth over again from zero."

He was very, very rich but cash-poor. Yet the companies he controlled, especially Berkshire Hathaway, had cash to buy stocks. To move some of Berkshire's money to Diversified, Buffett sent a pipeline into Berkshire. He set up a reinsurance company—a company that insures other insurers[40]—in Diversified. This company, Reinsurance Corp. of Nebraska, agreed to take part of National Indemnity's business, receiving premiums and covering losses. Because National Indemnity was so profitable and generated so much "float"—premiums paid ahead of claims, i.e., cash—as time passed, the pipeline would give Diversified millions more dollars to invest.[41]

With this money, Buffett began to buy stocks for Diversified. Principally he bought stock in Blue Chip and Berkshire Hathaway. Soon, Diversified owned ten percent of Berkshire. It was almost as though Berkshire was buying back its own stock—but not quite. Diversified's owners and Berkshire's weren't the same. Buffett still forbade his friends to buy Berkshire—whereas he, Munger, and Gottesman were partners in Diversified.[42]

At the time, even though the three did one another business favors and swapped stock ideas on occasion, their interests didn't necessarily align. Asked later under oath if he was Buffett's "alter ego," Munger said no. He acknowledged similar mannerisms and ways of speech. But "I've never chosen a role of being a junior partner," he said. "I like the idea of having a sphere of activity" of my own.[43] On one occasion, Munger said, he had found a block of Blue Chip stock that he and Gottesman wanted to buy for Diversified. Buffett wanted to take the block away from them and buy it for Berkshire Hathaway. After "a discussion"—clearly about who needed it more—the combined strength of Munger and Gottesman had somehow overpowered Buffett, and Diversified got the stock.[44] At least that way they kept a little share.

Still, Buffett did own forty-three percent of Diversified, so its purchases of Berkshire had added almost five percent to his personal ownership. Buying through Diversified was particularly attractive in that it tended not to ratchet up Berkshire's stock price. Hardly anybody was paying attention.[45]

But why did he want it at all?

"Berkshire was not worth more than forty bucks as a business. You couldn't have sold the textile mills and insurance business for more. And half the money was in a lousy business, I mean a really lousy business: twenty bucks a share of the forty bucks. And I didn't know what I was going to do, I literally didn't. I mean, I was rich

enough already. But in effect, I was betting that I could do something. I was betting on myself."

He didn't know what he was going to do, except invest. Verne McKenzie, who had returned from New Bedford to become Berkshire's controller, thought that to Buffett, it simply "looked like an interesting game. All he was doing was solidifying his control." That he was, and doing so in the manner in which he always approached investing—as a collector, one who bought in secrecy to avoid tipping off other bargain hunters. But as the chairman of Berkshire Hathaway and Diversified, he was once again mostly buying from sellers who had been his former partners. Although perfectly legal, it was not exactly sporting conduct. But their willingness to sell, in his mind, ended his special obligation to them.

Buffett had also been buying Blue Chip Stamps all along, though so far, Blue Chip had remained primarily Munger's province. It owned the best of the businesses, however, namely See's. Now Buffett began to pursue Blue Chip stock like a great white shark after a well-fed seal. Buffett's ownership of Blue Chip quickly surpassed the combined interest of his partners in that stock, Munger and Rick Guerin—Munger's associate from the Pacific Coast Stock Exchange, who now ran an investment partnership of his own.

Buffett's accumulation of all these stocks, however, differed from his buying in the era of cheap cigar butts. Two large question marks hung over Blue Chip, Diversified, and Berkshire. All that money pouring in to both Berkshire and Diversified from the insurance business would have to be put to good use. And the bet on Blue Chip's legal problems would have to work out.

By year-end 1973, Blue Chip had settled eleven lawsuits.[46] All that remained was the Justice Department's ruling that it divest one-third of its business to cure its monopoly. That would not be easy because inflation had run rampant, President Nixon had frozen prices on commodities to try to halt it, and commerce had entered a new era of trying to match rising costs to frozen consumer prices.

The stamp business was dead, but Buffett, the implacable acquirer, had his stock. After this series of trading gyrations, Blue Chip had Wattled its way into the set of Russian dolls. *"It was the same principle,"* Buffett says. Including all the pockets in which he had bought shares indirectly, he owned more than forty percent of Berkshire and more than twenty-five percent of Blue Chip Stamps. Even though these stocks traded at depressed prices, he could fund more deals and buy more stocks because all of the dolls had their own self-charging batteries, "float," cash that could be invested in advance of paying claims. This innovation dramatically improved the deal.

The businesses themselves had also improved since the dismal days of windmills and fire maps. Berkshire owned not only the whopping float-generator National Indemnity but also a clutch of little insurance companies that Buffett hoped would eventually turn into small powerhouses, even though he was struggling to whip them into shape. Meanwhile, the deadweight of Hochschild-Kohn had disappeared and Buffett kept shrinking the textile mills.

But in the bigger picture, what Berkshire, Diversified, and Blue Chip really possessed were two things. The first was the homeostatic business model—the idea of grafting float onto a holding company so that it could respond internally to the changing environment. The second was the power of compounding, as float and investments doubled and redoubled over time.

The novelty and strength of Buffett's model cannot be overstated. Nothing else like it existed, or would for years to come. *"That was the golden period of textbook capital allocation,"* he says.

The timing was stupendous. Capital from the insurance companies was pouring into Berkshire and DRC at the same time that the market was collapsing, the environment that Buffett liked best. While he had not yet decided exactly what to do with the collective enterprise he had built by the end of 1974, of two things he was certain. One was the business model's power, and the other his skill in using it. Above all, he had confidence in himself.

"Always," he says. *"Always."*

39

The Giant

Howard Buffett was one of those rare people who prospered in the aftermath of the 1929 stock market crash.[1] Now his son's star was rising during the second great crash of the century. But the world had changed; stardom, even in business, now meant fame. Buffett had closed his partnership during a media explosion in the United States in which cable had transformed television, newspaper companies were going public, and advertising was still in a golden age of selling to a monolithic audience in which virtually the whole nation sat down together on Tuesday nights and watched *Happy Days*.

Buffett had entered the media world as an investor drawn to the business by a natural affinity. But as he embarked on a new, post-partnership phase of life, he began to enjoy the fruit of the discreet use of profile-raising press. Now he was a subject of media interest, not just a media investor; and no less a personage than Katharine Graham was paying him attention, which had brought him into the orbit of one of the most important newspapers in the United States.

As was her habit with powerful men, Graham reached out to him for help. Buffett needed little encouragement.

"*The first time she was going to speak to the New York Society of Security Analysts, I went over there to her apartment in New York on a Sunday morning to help her write her speech. She was a basket case. She was terrified that all these men were going to be there and she was going to have to stand up in front of them. Public speaking was something that was very hard for her always. The funny thing is, she had a great sense of humor, she was smart, but she tended to freeze in front of a crowd. Particularly if she thought they were going to question her about numbers.*"

As Robert Redford had said in an interview after first meeting her to discuss the Watergate movie *All the President's Men*, Graham had a "tight-jawed, blue-blooded" quality that demanded that her privacy not be invaded. Why, therefore, Redford asked himself, "did she keep making speeches and accepting awards?"[2]—particularly since it terrified her to do it.

Buffett sat down in the living room of Graham's apartment in the UN Plaza, overlooking New York City's East River. Surrounded by Asian art and antiques from Agnes Meyer's collection, they started to work.

"*She kept imagining these questions they were going to ask, like how much are you paying for your newsprint per ton? She thought it was a quiz. . . . I kept trying to get her away from trying to remember facts. Just have a theme.*" Graham wanted to say that good journalism makes good profits. Buffett snorted to himself over this notion and refocused her. "*You know, good journalism is not inconsistent with good profits, or something like that. The hell with all the other stuff. I just tried to convince her that she was a hell of a lot smarter than all those dumb males that were out there. That's what really sort of bonded us initially.*"

In an ironic turnabout, Buffett became Kay Graham's personal Dale Carnegie instructor. He, of all people, could sympathize with someone who tended to freeze in front of a crowd. Moreover, thanks to Susie's gentle tutelage over the years, he had learned a subtler way of dealing with people. He knew how to anticipate their reactions and to phrase things in a nonthreatening way. His letters, which had always been self-conscious, were now more deftly worded and empathetic. He had learned to listen and show interest in other people. It helped that he was genuinely fascinated by Graham.

Buffett returned to Omaha having seen a new side of Graham. As he continued getting to know her on a personal level, he saw her as a bundle of paradoxes. "*Fearful but willful. Patrician but democratic. Wounded by the people she cared most about.*" He was surprised how much she still talked about her former husband a decade after his suicide.

"*When you first met her, she would often get off on the subject of Phil very quickly, almost like Charlie getting off on a subject. And she described him in terms that were sort of hard to believe, considering how badly he treated her. But after I got to know her better, she told me everything about him and the relationship. . . . She felt she was a fraud, almost, even pretending to be in the same room with him. . . . Anything he said was funny, anything he did was right. When he used to chop up the children right in front of her, she wouldn't stop him.*"

That he and Graham—who showed the aftereffects of an upbringing by a cruel, neglectful mother and years of abuse by a sadistic husband with untreated bipolar disorder—would be mutually attracted seems almost a foregone conclusion given Buffett's own childhood experiences. By the spring of 1974, she began to switch her allegiance from her other advisers to him. He seized the chance to tutor the CEO of the Washington Post Company about business as if he had been waiting to play Pygmalion all his life: his very own Eliza Doolittle. More patient than Henry Higgins, he coached her gently and sent helpful, interesting articles to Kay and to her son Don.

As Buffett's influence grew stronger, Graham noticed that the words "Warren says" brought shudders from some of her board members.[3] And Buffett himself was hoping to be invited onto that board. When Tom Murphy had approached him to join the Cap Cities board, Buffett told him no, he was holding out for the *Post*.[4] Murphy dutifully spilled this news to Graham, who "felt dense" for not having figured it out herself.[5]

Susie thought that instead of taking on more business responsibilities, her husband should use their wealth for a higher cause. Riding with him in a taxi in Washington, D.C., she pointed out philanthropist Stewart Mott, who was running the Stewart R. Mott Charitable Trust, which gave money to peace, arms control, and population and family-planning causes. The Buffetts were now richer than Mott, who had started with $25 million. "Why don't you quit?" Susie said. "Stewart Mott is doing all these other things now and he doesn't have to work every day." But Warren was incapable of quitting; he fell back on his philosophy that $50 million today would be worth $500 million someday. Nonetheless, he had picked up some vibrations from Susie, a sense that she wanted more from her life. With Peter moving along in high school, Warren told her, "Susie, you're like someone who has lost his job after twenty-three years. Now what are you going to do?"

The answer, she said, was sing. Her nephew Billy Rogers had made her some instrumental guitar tracks so that she could practice. Rogers had been playing jazz guitar at clubs in Omaha, and along with him, Susie was now a familiar face in the local music scene. But when she first started practicing, "I was scared, really scared," she said. "I was bad." She got coaching and worked on contemporary love songs and ballads. Susie first debuted as a chanteuse that July, before a friendly audience at a private party at Emerald Bay. It thrilled her husband to see his friends applauding his wife's talent.

While the Buffetts were in Emerald Bay that summer, Warren invited Graham for a visit. Sensing that Graham was going to talk to him about joining the *Post* board, Buffett had been dancing around his office at Kiewit Plaza for days ahead of time, happy and excited as a kid on Christmas Eve.[6]

Apparently, he must have impressed upon his wife that they would have to make an unusual effort for Graham. The first morning after Kay arrived, Susie rose at an unheard-of hour and cooked a full breakfast, which both of the Buffetts pretended to eat. Her husband spent the rest of the day wrapped up in Graham, talking to her about newspapers, journalism, politics, and bringing up every opportunity for her to invite him on the board.

At some point, he donned a bathing suit purchased for the occasion, picked up a beach umbrella bought in Graham's honor, and walked the hundred or so yards to the shore to join the family. Previously, his attitude toward the ocean had been: "*I think having the ocean nearby is an attractive feature, and fun to listen to at night, and all that kind of stuff. But actually getting _in_ it—I feel I'll save that for my old age.*" But now, after sitting on the sand for a bit, looking at the water, he waded gamely into the Pacific. By all reports, Susie and the Buffett kids "went into convulsions of laughter" at the odd sight.

What Susie thought about this extraordinary gesture is not known. But Warren's explanation of it is on record: "Only for Kay," he says. "Only for Kay."

On Sunday morning, they dropped their company manners and Susie sleep-walked through cooking bacon and eggs for Graham, eating nothing herself, while Warren sat nearby spooning chocolate Ovaltine from a jar.[7] After breakfast, he and Graham resumed their tête-à-tête. At some point, Graham told him that she wanted him to join her board but was waiting for the right time. She knew that some of her board members, such as André Meyer, would not welcome Buffett. But he asked, "When *is* the right time?" thus forcing her to make up her mind. And so in short order it was done; they agreed that Buffett would join the board of the Washington Post Company. He was elated.

That afternoon, Buffett left his family at Emerald Bay and drove Graham to the Los Angeles airport. "*On the way, all of a sudden, she looked at me like a three-year-old kid. Her voice changed, and her eyes, and she said, basically pleading, 'Just be gentle with me, please don't ever assault me.' I learned later that Phil and some people at the paper, to get their own ends or for sheer enjoyment, would push her buttons just to watch her fall apart.*"

At summer's end, on September 11, 1974, Buffett officially joined the board, which catapulted him from a star investment manager from Omaha to official adviser at one of the most important media companies in the world. Even at that first meeting he could see that Graham had a habit of pleading with the board for help. Buffett thought, This won't do. You can't put yourself in that position as a CEO. But he didn't yet know her well enough to say anything. Instead, he educated himself about the *Post* board, which was full of many prominent and influential people, and began to tiptoe his way through the powerful, jockeying men who were used to dominating Graham. He was a quiet board member, however, and used his skills behind the scenes.

Buffett at the time was preoccupied with far more than just Kay Graham and the *Washington Post*. The market, expected to rally in 1974, instead was in the full throes of collapse. Pension fund managers had cut back their stock purchases by more than eighty percent. Berkshire's portfolio looked as though someone had given it a severe hedge trimming, shearing off nearly one-third in the second Great Crash, the kind that comes along only a few times in a century.

Munger had kept his partnership open after Buffett had shuttered his. Now its value was plunging, his partners losing nearly half of their money.[8] Like Ben Graham half a century earlier, he felt obliged to make their money back.

"Certainly the quoted value of my capital went down," says Munger. "I didn't like it, but just think about how many years could go by—what difference does it make at the end whether I have X dollars, or X minus Y? The only thing that bothered me was that I knew how hard it was on the partners. That was what killed me—the fiduciary aspect of my position."[9]

To earn back losses of half his capital, Munger would have to more than double the remaining stake. The value of Blue Chip Stamps would have a significant bearing on whether he could accomplish that.

Bill Ruane's Sequoia Fund was also in trouble. It had started with $50 million from Buffett's former partners and invested its money well by taking large positions in undervalued stocks like Tom Murphy's Capital Cities Communications.

"In this business," Ruane said, "you have the innovators, the imitators, and the swarming incompetents." The swarming incompetents were now at the wheel, and the stocks that Ruane and his partner Rick Cunniff had bought in 1970 had been cut in half. The fund's worst year yet was 1973 and it was on its way to another terrible year in 1974. The timing of Sequoia's opening was obviously inauspicious—Ruane had agreed to start up just as Buffett was shutting down due to lack of opportunities. Sequoia had underperformed the market every year—cumulatively by a dramatic amount.[10] Ruane's largest backer, Bob Malott, was incensed. He was already known as a "ballbuster" around the halls of Ruane, Cunniff for his habit of calling to complain about minor discrepancies in his family's accounts. Now he berated Ruane for buying a seat on the exchange before the crash, and for his poor performance with such persistence that Ruane feared he would pull his capital out of the firm.[11] Buffett, however, remained serene in the knowledge that Mr. Market's opinion of a stock's price at any time had no bearing on its intrinsic value.

If not exactly an ego booster, because of the snooty staff, Buffett's 1969 meeting of the Grahamites at the Colony Club had at least provided mutual support in a challenging market. Since then Buffett had named them the Graham Group; in 1971, Buffett made the meetings biennial. Out of loyalty, he let Ruane invite Malott—a favor normally verboten—for the meeting in Sun Valley in 1973.

Malott, mightily impressed by the whole affair, stayed in Ruane's fold, even though his complaints continued at a frequency and volume that still made Ruane fear his defection. By the end of 1974, however, the Sequoia Fund had at least managed to produce a smaller loss than the market's.

Nonetheless, the market's cumulative toll on the Sequoia Fund was such that Henry Brandt and John Loomis, Carol's husband, both of whom had gone to work there, feared the worst and cast off from what seemed a sinking ship.[12]

Forbes captured Buffett's attitude in an interview that November, which opened with a juicy quote: Asked how he felt about the market, "Like an oversexed man in a harem," Buffett replied. "This is the time to start investing."[13] He went on to say, "This is the first time I can remember that you could buy Phil Fisher [growth] stocks at Ben Graham [cigar butt] prices." He felt this was the most significant statement that he could make, but *Forbes* didn't include it; a general audience wouldn't understand the references to Fisher and Graham.[14]

But despite his enthusiasm for the market so far in 1974, he had invested at a trickle, and mostly moved money around. He had also bought 100,000 shares of Blue Chip from Rick Guerin. *"He sold me at five bucks because he was getting squeezed,"* Buffett says. *"That was a brutal period."*

The "harem" comment had a double meaning: Buffett, for the most part, could look but not touch. One of National Indemnity's business partners, an aviation broker, had run amok, selling money-losing aviation-insurance policies. The company had tried to stop the agent by revoking its authority but for several months was unable to shut it down.[15] The accounting records were a shambles and the losses were unclear. National Indemnity had no idea how high the bill for the "Omni affair" would run, but worst-case estimates ran as high as tens of millions of dollars. The hope was that they were much less, because National Indemnity did not have tens of millions. Buffett was sweating.[16]

Within a couple of months—by early 1975—his problems compounded monumentally. Chuck Rickershauser, a partner from Munger's law firm, now renamed Munger, Tolles & Rickershauser, called him and Munger to say that the Securities and Exchange Commission was considering pressing charges against them for violating securities laws. What had seemed like a brewing but manageable problem had now exploded into a full-scale emergency.

Rickershauser had first started doing legal work for Buffett during the See's transaction. More recently he had been fighting a rear-guard action, ever since an SEC staff lawyer had called him with some questions. Assuming the matter was routine, Rickershauser had directed the man to Verne McKenzie, Berkshire's controller.

When McKenzie's phone rang in Nebraska, he picked it up to find the head of the SEC's Enforcement Division, Stanley Sporkin, the much-feared "tough cop" of the business world, on the other end of the line. Sporkin looked as though he spent his evenings hunched droopy-eyed under a desk lamp, personally drafting the charges against large corporations that for the first time in American history had frightened a remarkable number of them into settling with the SEC without ever setting foot in court.[17] In a practical sense he had more power than his boss, the chairman of the SEC. Sporkin interrogated McKenzie on a wide range of subjects, from Wesco to Blue Chip to Berkshire and beyond. His tone was not friendly, but this, McKenzie had assumed, was simply his modus operandi. On the other hand, McKenzie did get the impression that Sporkin thought if you were rich, you must have done something wrong.[18]

What seemed to have drawn the SEC's attention was a project of nearly two years in which Buffett and Munger were trying to delicately untangle the many strands of spaghetti that connected the several companies they owned. Their first step had been to try to merge Diversified, the least essential piece, into Berkshire Hathaway. By 1973, Diversified had become little more than a vehicle for buying Berkshire and Blue Chip stock. But the Securities and Exchange Commission—whose approval was required—had delayed the Diversified deal. Munger had told Buffett that this was not anything serious.

Instead, over the next eighteen months, the SEC staff seemed to have nosed around looking at Blue Chip Stamps and other investments; it concluded that Buffett and Munger had smashed up the Wesco–Santa Barbara deal deliberately by offering a high price for a quarter of the stock for the purpose of taking over the rest. At least, that must have been how it looked to Santa Barbara, for it had apparently turned in Blue Chip to the SEC.[19]

For the first time they all realized that Blue Chip was in trouble.[20] No sooner had Buffett achieved the glory of joining the *Post* board than his and Munger's need for legal services was about to grow with stunning rapidity. Rickershauser, who already knew what it was like to work with Buffett, had once explained to a colleague that "the sun is nice and warm, but you don't want to get too close to it."[21] He would spend the next couple of years testing what could be called Rickershauser's Law of Thermodynamics.

In February 1975, the SEC issued subpoenas and launched a full-blown fraud investigation of Blue Chip's purchase of Wesco: *"In the Matter of Blue Chip Stamps, Berkshire Hathaway Incorporated, Warren Buffet [sic], HO-784."* The commission staff speculated that Buffett and Munger had committed fraud: *"Blue Chip, Berkshire, Buffet [sic], singly or in concert with others . . . may have engaged in acts which have, directly or indirectly, operated as a device, scheme, or artifice to defraud; or included an untrue statement of a material fact or omitted . . ."*

The commission's lawyers zeroed in on a theory that Blue Chip had secretly planned from the beginning to take over Wesco Financial but had not disclosed that fact, and that Blue Chip's purchases of stock after the Santa Barbara deal dissolved were "tender offers" that were never registered with the SEC.[22] This latter charge was most serious—the SEC might even file, with great fanfare and publicity, civil fraud charges not only against Blue Chip but also against Buffett and Munger personally.

In considering action against a target, Sporkin had a choice. He could prosecute or settle. A settlement let the target say sorry and accept a penalty without officially admitting guilt. And in agreeing to a settlement, the SEC could also make a deal with the company itself without naming anybody. Being named in a settlement might not be the literal end of someone's career, but there would be no elephant-bumping afterward. Having so recently been elevated into the high and mighty through *Supermoney* and *Forbes* and the board of the *Washington Post,* Buffett began to fight desperately to save his reputation.

Instead, the investigation widened. Under subpoena, Buffett had to open his files—which, naturally, represented a huge and comprehensive collection of documents, just as huge and comprehensive as everything he had ever collected.

Lawyers from Munger, Tolles sifted out trade tickets for recent stock purchases, memos to bankers, letters to See's Candies, notes to Verne McKenzie at the textile mill, and the like and shipped them off to investigators in Washington, D.C. Buffett felt persecuted. He and Munger were being chased in a nightmare by a huge, lumbering giant. To survive, they would have to outrun it.

Letters flew back and forth like shuttlecocks between Munger, Tolles and the SEC. Buffett maintained a veneer of calm, but his back problems were plaguing him. Munger did not hide his agitation.

By March 1975, the investigation had wound its way to a command performance at the SEC. Betty Peters was hauled in and came without a lawyer, surprising the SEC staff. "Don't you just want to know what happened?" she asked. They interviewed Peters without a lawyer.

Munger was summoned. For two days—also unaccompanied, for what additional legal counsel could Charles T. Munger possibly need?—he tried to defend Blue Chip against the charges. Yes, Blue Chip had thought about getting control, he said, but those plans were only "remote and contingent" until the Santa Barbara merger blew up. This discussion became somewhat circular given his and Buffett's role in talking to Vincenti and their admitted "wooing" of Betty Peters and the Casper family's votes. Munger had a regrettable tendency to interrupt and lecture the SEC staff lawyer, Larry Seidman. "We wanted to look very fair and equitable to Lou Vincenti and Betty Peters," he said.[23] What about your Blue Chip shareholders? Seidman asked. Seidman saw no reason for Blue Chip to be so generous to Wesco shareholders; Wesco's stock by then was largely in the hands of arbitrageurs.

These people had bought Wesco's stock knowing that once the deal closed it would rise to the price that Santa Barbara had offered. They hedged their bets by shorting Santa Barbara's stock. When the Wesco deal blew up, Wesco's price collapsed.[24] Why do the arbs a favor by propping up the price?

Munger reached for his ultimate weapon—Benjamin Franklin. "We didn't feel our obligation to the shareholders was inconsistent with leaning over backward to be fair. We have that Ben Franklin idea that the honest policy is the best policy. It had a sort of shoddy mental image to us to try to reduce the price."[25]

Seidman seemed a little baffled by this argument, and even Munger admitted that the details of what had been done did not look good. He begged Seidman to look at the big picture. "As you look at the overall records, we go way beyond any legal requirement in trying to be fair with people to observe the niceties of fair-dealing. . . . If there's any defect at all, it's not intentional."

When Buffett appeared, they asked him why he and Munger hadn't let Wesco go into the tank so they could buy it cheap. *"I think the general business reputation of Blue Chip would not have been as good,"* Buffett said. *"I think someone might have been sore about it."* But why should he care? Because, said Buffett, *"Lou Vincenti doesn't really need to work for us.... If he felt that we were, you know, slobs or something, it just wouldn't work."*

Now Buffett—who, like Munger, startled the enforcement lawyers by showing up alone—made himself helpful, venturing back to Washington several times, patiently explaining how Blue Chip worked, expounding on his investment philosophies, and talking about his childhood years in Washington. He made a favorable impression on Seidman, but not on the senior SEC staff lawyer who was in charge of the investigation, a "tiger" of a prosecutor whose motto was "They shall not pass." He found these arguments unconvincing.[26] The senior investigator's attitude was that nobody who did anything close to the line would ever get by him.[27]

The SEC staff seemed fascinated by the intricacies and complications of Buffett's empire. It even started looking into whether he had traded on inside information about San Jose Water Works.[28] The staff started kicking around Source Capital, the closed-end investment fund that Munger had bought a twenty percent interest in as a cigar butt. By then, the stock market had recovered. Ruane's Sequoia Fund had made a huge comeback in 1975. Munger had just about made back his partners' money, with a seventy-three percent gain in 1975. He took no fees for himself, and was winding his partnership down. Explaining why their convoluted empire made sense based on the cheap prices paid for stocks at the time grew harder as the market recovered.

Rickershauser had been studying a chart that showed Buffett and Munger's complex financial interests. Buffett sat at the center, buying Blue Chip, Diversified, and Berkshire, Wattling them into so many pockets that it made Rickershauser shudder.[29] Everyone knew Buffett, the great white shark, was virtually helpless to stop himself from acquiring these stocks. After he and Munger had bought the first twenty-five percent of Wesco, Rickershauser had finally advised Buffett to buy stock only through formal tender offers to avoid the appearance of impropriety.[30] The complex cross-holdings that Buffett had created looked suspicious. Rickershauser stared at the crazy diagram and fretted, "There's got to be an indictment in there somewhere."[31] He didn't think the SEC would have enough evidence to convict, but it would be awfully easy to accuse.

Munger was a two-bit player, his financial stake minute compared with

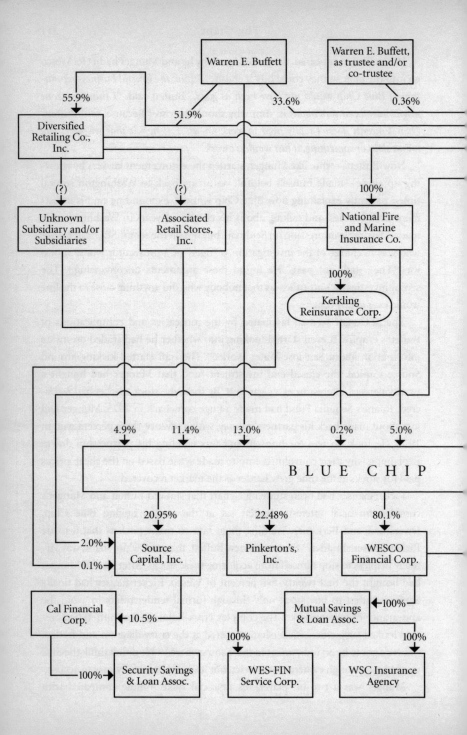

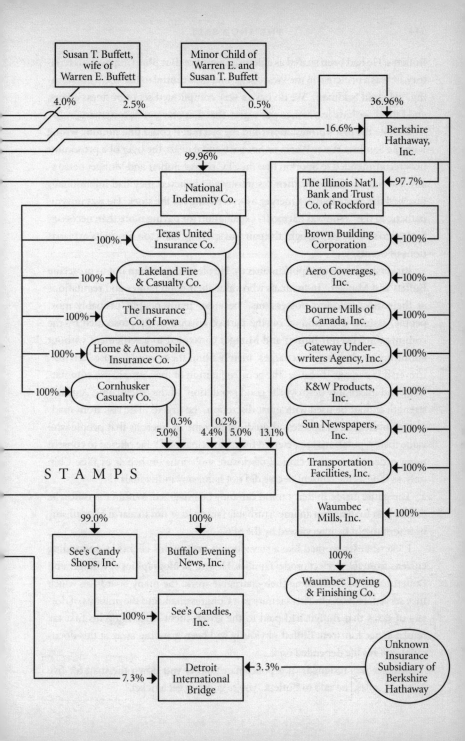

Buffett's. He had been snared as a petty accomplice. But Blue Chip was his territory, he was a principal in the Wesco saga, and thus central to the SEC's questioning.[32] He told Seidman, "We do have a very complicated set of business affairs, and I think we have learned, to our regret, that that may not be too smart."

Despite the pair's protestations and the fact that it could find nothing wrong with the San Jose Water Works or Source Capital deals, the tiger of a prosecutor now recommended to Sporkin that the SEC charge Buffett and Munger personally. He was unswayed by their testimony and believed they had intentionally quashed the Santa Barbara merger by overpaying for the stock. He was unsympathetic to the "Who was harmed?" explanation for paying more than necessary for Wesco's stock. He thought the pair was splitting hairs too fine in its explanations of events.[33]

Rickershauser wrote Sporkin directly. He pleaded with him not to prosecute Buffett and Munger, "individuals who value their good names and reputations as their most priceless possessions," because "many people, probably most people, assume evil conduct on the part of anyone civilly prosecuted by the commission." Even if Buffett and Munger consented to a settlement without admitting or denying the charges, merely filing them would cause "terrible, irreversible damage" because "the good reputation of the commission automatically and inexorably destroys the good reputation" of the defendants. "A giant's strength should be used with great discretion," he urged. "The risk from inadvertent oversights in business should not become so onerous that people who value their reputations are deterred from participation."[34] He offered to consent to an order on minor, technical disclosure violations on behalf of Blue Chip only, as long as the consent decree did not name any individuals.

The panic inside Buffett's mind can only be imagined. Within the office, he did his best to maintain an imperturbable facade so as not to alarm his staff, any of whom might be interviewed by the SEC.

Rickershauser worked like a stevedore to portray his clients as upstanding citizens from the perfect model families. He sent in biographies of Munger and Buffett to the SEC, stressing their charitable work, the many boards on which they served, Howard Buffett's tenure as a Congressman, and the millions of dollars of taxes that Buffett had paid to the government since filing his first tax return at age fourteen. Buffett obviously had been grinding away at this document as if his life depended on it.

Munger was resigned. "If a policeman follows you down the road for five hundred miles," he said to Buffett, "you're going to get a ticket."

Then Rickershauser made a further proffer to Sporkin, put delicately: "The complex financial interests of Mr. Buffett and Mr. Munger...have apparently raised the impression that compliance with various legal requirements is becoming difficult," he wrote, noting the pair had tried to comply with both the spirit and the letter of the law. "They now wish to simplify their holdings as rapidly as they can."[35]

In their interviews, the SEC lawyers had already explored what simplifying would mean. Buffett had acknowledged that he might merge Blue Chip with Berkshire, but until Blue Chip's legal problems were resolved, it would be hard to put a fair value on the company. "*I don't really like these complications,*" he said. "*It may look like I like these complications. I don't have a great staff to handle it all. It seemed fairly simple while we were doing it,*" he said, "*but not simple now.*"[36]

Asked by an SEC investigator if Buffett had "contingency plans" to simplify things, "Oh, does he ever," said Munger. "He has about twice as big a contingency plan as before this investigation started."[37]

In considering the proffer, says Sporkin today, much depended on Rickershauser. He "was one of those few lawyers that I've met in life that, whatever he told you, you could go to the bank on." Rickershauser told Sporkin that Buffett was "going to be the greatest person that Wall Street has ever seen" and that "he was the most decent, honorable person you would ever meet." Coming from almost anyone else, Sporkin says he would have dismissed this as rhetoric, but coming from Rickershauser, he took these statements to be both sincere and probably well-judged.[38] Sporkin felt he had as great a duty to absolve as to convict. He thought that a prosecutor had to differentiate between a fundamentally honest person who had made a misstep and a crook. His view of Buffett and Munger was that they had certainly misstepped, but that they were not crooks.[39]

And so the giant tapped Blue Chip gently on the wrist.[40]

The company consented to an SEC finding that named no individuals.[41] The publicity over the event had been trivial and would fade. Buffett's and Munger's records and reputations stayed clean.

Two weeks later, the SEC named Buffett to a blue-ribbon panel to study corporate disclosure practices. It was forgiveness and, above all, a fresh start.[42]

40

How Not to Run a Public Library

One day in early 1975, Susie Buffett's friend Eunice Denenberg came over to the house and sat on the dog-hair-covered sofa in the family room. Susie turned her back and clicked on the tape deck. Then she sang. Denenberg pronounced approval. They talked about Susie's dream of singing professionally, which she was too diffident to pursue. Denenberg went home; then she called back the next day and said, "This is your agent." She enlisted a backup band and got Susie a gig at a nightclub in Irvington, the tiny town on Omaha's outskirts where she and Dottie had once formed the choir in her father's church. Susie was nervous, but the rest of the family was enthusiastic. Only Doc Thompson, who said, "I don't know why you want to sing in bars," had any doubts.

The night of Susie's first public performance, before a crowd made up of about thirty-five friends, she was so anxious that she asked Warren not to come. Talking and greeting people in a long sequined dress, she stalled until Denenberg pushed her out onto the stage. From Aretha Franklin's "Call Me," to what she said was one of her favorites, Roberta Flack's "The First Time Ever I Saw Your Face," her choice of music was soulful, passionate, and romantic. The audience responded to and returned her warmth.[1] The same pulse and flow Susie got from connecting with people individually came through in a wave when she sang to a group in an intimate space. This was her special gift, transmuted and magnified. She wanted to become a cabaret singer.

Warren at the time had many distractions. He was closing the SEC investigation. He was so fascinated with Kay Graham that he literally could not get enough of her. When Warren got obsessed with something—especially someone new—he could not stop thinking about it or them; this came across to a new person as a wholehearted, flattering, and even overwhelming attentiveness. When business arose, however, he snapped back to it in a split second with all the fierce intensity his steely mind could muster. As Munger put it, Buffett "never let his minor obsessions interfere with his major obsession."[2] Katharine Graham, however, was no minor obsession.

Warren was also taking Kay to business school in a serious way. *"Kay had had me trying to explain accounting to her on the side. I'd bring these annual reports to Washington. And she'd say, 'Oh, Warren, lessons.' There I was, teaching again."* He considered her son Don "unbelievably smart," with "as close to a photographic memory as anyone I've ever run into." As a sign of reassurance to the family, Warren had signed the voting proxy on his shares over to Don. He now stayed at Kay's house when he came to Washington for monthly board meetings.

Buffett felt that Kay was *"very, very smart, and in many ways wise, as long as you didn't go into those areas where the wounds were."* As they grew more intimate, he felt he could say something to her about the way she presented herself to her board. He knew she was less needy than she herself realized. One day he took her aside and said, "You can't plead for help anymore from the board. It's just not the position you want to be in." And so, he says, she quit.

The business and personal ties between the Grahams and Buffett had become close enough that Warren invited Katharine and Don to join the Graham Group at their 1975 meeting, at Hilton Head. Don made an immediate impression with his unpretentious manner, while raising its already high average IQ. Many people quickly saw beneath Kay's brittle, patrician veneer to the vulnerability and humility that had endeared her to Warren. Thus she fit easily with most of the group despite her queenly presence, worldliness, and connections. She made a sincere effort to get along with everyone—although her deep belief that men were far superior to women wasn't lost on the women at the meeting. The beautifully dressed, perfectly coiffed Graham, an icon among them, would slide casually into a chair amid the men with a cocktail in her hand; somebody would utter a political opinion, and she would respond "Henry thinks thus-and-so"—speaking of Kissinger. It was impossible not to be impressed.

Henry Brandt pulled Buffett into a separate room and asked him to promise that Berkshire stock wouldn't drop below $40. By October 1975, the stock had been cut in half after trading at $93 just two years before. "Look, I love you," Buffett recalls saying, "but I can't promise you that." "The world is ending," said Brandt, or words to that effect. "I've got every dollar I own in this stock."

The world continued to end. Even though the rest of the stock market was recovering, Berkshire was not. Brandt panicked and called Buffett, who offered him $40 a share. Then Brandt called Walter Schloss and said, "Warren will pay me forty dollars and I want fifty. What should I do?"

Schloss was the last champion of cigar butts. At the meetings, the others razzed him about his "buggy-whip" portfolio of bankrupt steel companies and destitute auto-parts makers. "So what," said Schloss. "I don't like stress and I sleep well at night." He filled out his checklists, applying Graham's philosophy in its purest form. He went home from his desk in the closet at Tweedy, Browne at five o'clock every evening, and his results were phenomenal.

Now Schloss was dismayed to hear Brandt telling himself he was better off without Berkshire stock in a way that contravened this whole cigar-butt philosophy. Schloss worked on him for two hours, saying, You've got the smartest guy in the world managing your money, in effect, at no fee, you're making a big mistake to sell. "I thought I convinced him," says Schloss. But the U. S. economy by then was in so much trouble that New York City was nearly bankrupt; the country was in a mood of such profound pessimism that it affected people's judgment. "On Monday he called his broker," says Schloss, and began selling until half his family's shares were gone.[3]

Immediately afterward, President Ford refused a bailout of the New York City economy; the *New York Daily News* captured the feeling of the times in a huge headline: "Ford to City: Drop Dead."[4]

The partners who took Berkshire stock in 1970 when it traded around $40 seemed no better off five years later. "It looked like not much was happening favorably for a long, long time," says Munger. "And that was not the way our partners, by and large, had previously experienced things. The paper record looked terrible, yet the future, what you might call the intrinsic record, the real business momentum, was gaining all the while."

Buffett's own net worth, based on where the stock was trading, had been sliced correspondingly. Yet despite this apparent destruction of wealth—which would have frightened almost anyone else—his pulse never seemed to flutter. He just had the companies he controlled keep buying, and buying, and buying. In 1974, before the SEC investigation began, Berkshire had owned twenty-six percent of Blue Chip. When all was said and done, Berkshire would own more than forty-one percent of Blue Chip—so much that he and Susie owned, personally and through Berkshire Hathaway, thirty-seven percent of the stock all by themselves.

He thought of another way to capitalize on the situation, getting his mother, *"who cared nothing about money,"* to sell her 5,272 shares of Berkshire to Doris and Bertie. For $5,440 plus a $100,000 note, they each got 2,636 shares of Berkshire—paying the equivalent of $2 a share in cash.[5] Buffett, who viewed debt as almost sinful, thought Berkshire so cheap at $40 a share that he had his sisters borrow ninety-five percent of the purchase price to buy it. At the rate he obviously thought he could compound the stock's value, buying on these terms would make his sisters rich (and avoid an enormous estate tax bill).[6]

"That was probably the greatest move of all time. It will never happen again. That was a once-in-a-lifetime situation."

Valuable properties were being sold everywhere for a pittance. Around the same time, Tom Murphy came to Warren with the chance to buy a television station. Buffett realized it would be a terrific deal, but he couldn't buy it because the Washington Post Company also owned television stations. Since he sat on the *Post* board, it would put the *Post* over the limit the FCC allowed.[7] "What am I involved with that I don't own?" he asked himself. He actually had to think about it to find something. Then he remembered that he didn't own Grinnell College. At Buffett's recommendation, Grinnell eventually bought a Dayton, Ohio, station for $13 million, putting down only $2 million. Sandy Gottesman arranged debt financing for the rest. The broker who sold it to Grinnell called it the best deal he had seen in the past twenty years.[8]

There were some good reasons, however, why stocks were cheap and cities like New York were close to bankruptcy. Along with rampant inflation, out-of-control labor costs and unstable labor relations were strangling the economy. Newspapers were among the most severely affected businesses. Right after the Hilton Head meeting, the *Washington Post*'s union contracts expired, and the pressmen sabotaged the pressroom at four a.m. on their way out the door to go on strike.

Most of the unions other than the pressmen stayed at work, especially the all-important Newspaper Guild of journalists. Using helicopters to move key people past picket lines, the *Post* started getting out an attenuated paper after only one day's disruption. But as the strike ground on, Graham became paralyzed with fears that her paper was committing suicide. The *Post* could produce only half the number of papers at a quarter of their normal size, and advertisers marched steadily over to the *Post*'s archrival, the *Evening Star*.

"We crossed the picket line together. Kay was gutsy about that. But I saw her burst into tears when she picked up the Star," which was copying the *Post*'s format and stealing its advertisers.

When she felt threatened, the woman that her editor Howard Simons called the "Bad Katharine" flew down the chimney.

"It wasn't really the Bad Kay. It was the Insecure Kay. If she got feeling insecure, she could get pretty shrill. Occasionally some incident would set her off, and then she would react like an animal. It was as if she felt nobody was on her side. She felt cornered. And nobody would quite know what to do. That's when they would call for me. Phil hadn't been on her side, and her mother hadn't been on her side. The executives at the company hadn't always been on her side. And so she always had this sense in the back of her mind that she was in an unfriendly environment and it could be triggered by some incident.

"But she always knew that I was on her side. That didn't mean I agreed with her on everything or ate everything she wanted me to eat. But I was on her side. And I always would be."

The Bad Katharine bore some similarities to Leila Buffett. And Warren took an obvious pride in being the one person who could win Kay's trust and keep the Bad Katharine at bay.

For the next six months, the *Post* would continue to publish while navigating fruitless negotiations, threats, violence, a logistical war of nerves, and a constant struggle to keep the torn Newspaper Guild from striking in sympathy.

"She had people telling her, including some of the people she respected most, 'You've got to give in or you're going to lose.' They were afraid, they hated not publishing and seeing the Star gain on the Post.

"So I was the countervailing force. I said to her, 'I will tell you before the tipping point is reached.' The tipping point is the point at which the other guy becomes dominant, and after you go back, he is still dominant. At what point does it become more of a habit for them to buy the other paper?"

While "Warren encouraged her, it was her backbone, not his," stresses George Gillespie, Graham's lawyer.[9]

Two months into the strike, the *Post* had made a final offer to the pressmen, who rejected it.[10] Graham began to hire replacement workers, breaking the strike. Over the next few months, the paper gradually won back the remaining unions, readers, and advertisers, even though the picketing and bad publicity continued through the spring.

Just as Graham was slowly rescuing her company,[11] Buffett and Munger had finally reached their settlement with the SEC. Now Buffett invited Munger for a steak dinner down at Johnny's Café near the stockyards to finalize their "simpli-fication" plan. He had decided to stop managing money for FMC on the side.

Blue Chip would sell its interest in Source Capital,[12] and Berkshire and Diversified would merge. At Betty Peters's request, Wesco, owned only eighty percent by Blue Chip, would remain a public company, with Munger also chairman. They deferred merging Blue Chip into Berkshire Hathaway until they could more easily agree on the relative values of the companies.

With both Berkshire and the *Post* emerging from the tumultuous times that had consumed his attention for so long, Buffett's business routine began to normalize. The *Post* board meetings lost their edge of emergency, and Graham began thinking of expanding her empire.

Newspapers at the time were being snapped up left and right. *"Kay really wanted to buy newspapers. But above all, she didn't want other people to buy them instead of her,"* Buffett says. "Tell me what to do," she would beg. *"I would just make her make the damn decision,"* he says. He helped her understand that it was always a mistake to pay too much for something you wanted. Impatience was the enemy. For a long time, the *Post* did very little and grew slowly. Buffett taught the Grahams the immense value of buying their company's own stock when it was cheap to reduce the shares outstanding. That increased the size of each slice of the pie. Meanwhile, the *Post* avoided making expensive mistakes and became much more profitable as a result.[13]

Buffett, used to doing the taking, for the first time found himself in the giving role and discovered that, with Graham, he liked it. He began to be seen out with Graham more and more. She made it her job to try to give him some polish.[14]

Munger wrote to Graham about Buffett, "I can see damn well whose ways, predominantly, are actually being mended."

"Kay tried to upgrade me a little. It was just very gradual and not so I would notice. It was very funny. She worked so hard to sort of remold me, but it didn't work. She was a hell of a lot more sophisticated than I was, that's for sure." Buffett learned that Graham thought it was uncouth and disgusting to eat out in restaurants. *"Around Washington your cook was a big point of pride. The highest compliment you could pay somebody at a party was, 'I'm going to try and hire away your cook,' or 'You must have brought your cook over from France.' Kay cared about that, like everybody in Washington. So her dinners tended to be quite fancy, except that she would make exceptions for me."*

Graham's chef found the restrictions imposed by cooking for Warren a challenge. *"Broccoli, asparagus, and Brussels sprouts look to me like Chinese food crawling around on a plate. Cauliflower almost makes me sick. I eat carrots reluctantly.*

I don't like sweet potatoes. I don't even want to be close to a rhubarb, it makes me retch."

His idea of a feast was a half gallon of chocolate chip ice cream. He ate his foods in sequence, one at a time, and did not like the individual foods to touch. If a stalk of broccoli brushed his steak, he recoiled in horror. "*I like eating the same thing over and over and over again. I could eat a ham sandwich every day for fifty days in a row for breakfast. At dinner at her farm retreat, Glen Welby, Kay served lobster. I was attacking the shellfish through the wrong side, attacking the shell, and not having much luck. She told me to turn it over.*" Confronted with a nine-course dinner—each course accompanied by the appropriate wines and destined for a dinner table filled with dignitaries and celebrities and journalism's star reporters—"it threw him," says his former secretary, Gladys Kaiser. He never grew accustomed to life on this grand scale.

Yet Buffett became a regular guest at Graham's famous dinners, which he called her "Kay Parties." He enjoyed his status as the hayseed who was flummoxed by a lobster. His childlike tastes conveyed an air of authenticity and innocence. But his social naiveté was also genuine—mostly because he went around with blinders on. When "sightseeing" with Graham, he was focused like a laser on who was there, not on which fork to use. He had no desire to broaden this aspect of his horizons. Graham was amazed that Buffett continued to eat nothing but hamburgers and ice cream.[15]

"*She always talked to the cook in French, always, totally in French. So I would hear 'hamburger' among the French words and tease her and say, 'No, no, it's hambur-zhay.' Then I would just say, 'Order me a hambur-zhay,' and it would come out of the kitchen very fancy. The chef at Kay's wanted so much to be able to make hamburgers and french fries—and I ate them, but they were not even close to as good as you could get at McDonald's or Wendy's. The french fries were always mushy. And he wanted so hard to please.*

"*But at her big parties, she didn't make exceptions for me as much.*"

At the Kay Parties, Buffett's role was not to eat but, of course, to talk. As a star investor, he was like a bald eagle in a town where birds of any kind were scarce. Even the most hidebound of Georgetown "cave dwellers"—blue bloods who rarely emerged to socialize with anyone except others of their kind, many of whom were Graham's friends, such as the columnists Joe and Stewart Alsop, cousins of Eleanor Roosevelt—enjoyed having the charming Buffett around. Dinner guests pelted him with questions about investments, and he fell into his most comfortable role: the teacher.

By now he was in Washington so much that he began keeping a spare set of clothes in Graham's guest room: usually a fraying blue suede jacket and gray flannel slacks that looked like a rumpled bedspread.[16] Graham tried to improve his sartorial sense. "She was appalled by Warren's clothes," according to her son Don, "although my mother just hated the way that I dressed. And at one point she said, referring to her employees, 'Why am I of all people surrounded by the worst-dressed executive staff of anyone in America?' Her scorn for people's clothes was widespread, and not confined to Warren."[17] She took him to meet Halston, the tony designer whom she preferred and who had made over her own sense of style. Buffett's take on Halston: *"He was from Des Moines, you know."*

By June 1976, Buffett had occasion to invite Graham to an event of his own: Susie Jr.'s wedding. In every way this event would be the antithesis of a Kay Party—held in Newport Beach, California, a mix of the formal and the casual, with a Buffettish zoo of a guest list, to celebrate a marriage that everybody knew was a mistake from the start.

The spring semester of her senior year of college, Susie Jr. had dropped out of UC Irvine for a secretarial job at Century 21, a real estate company, that didn't require typing skills.[18] Though they were wise enough not to interfere, her parents knew that Susie Jr.'s marriage to blond surfer Dennis Westergard wasn't going to work out. On some level, Susie Jr. herself knew this, but she was caught up in the fantasy.[19] Her wedding was an important affair. Warren had asked that Kay be invited; Big Susie had reserved a special place for her at the church, right behind the family. For a few minutes she sat with Dick and Mary Holland, who had escorted her to the service. Then, not surprisingly, Kay said to them, "I feel uncomfortable. I don't know why, but it'd be better if I sat in back." She removed herself to the rear of the church, where she sat for the rest of the wedding.[20]

The traditional ceremony proceeded without incident. Then the reception at the Newport Beach Marriott turned wild. The Buffetts had let their music-groupie daughter hire any band she liked. Susie Jr. chose her favorite, Quicksilver Messenger Service, a psychedelic rock band that had been among the groups launched at San Francisco's Fillmore Auditorium in the 1960s. As the twenty-something men with white-boy afros and nipple-length uncombed hair mounted the stage and tuned up their instruments, Buffett looked on with inner horror. When Quicksilver Messenger Service hit it with the drums and electric guitars, Susie Jr. danced in ecstasy at her rock-and-roll wedding while her father managed to keep his composure, even though he was squirming inside. "*I was not wild about their music*," he says in an understatement. "*They played awfully loud.*" He longed for something like his wife's sweet Doris Day style of singing, or Florence Henderson or Sammy Davis Jr. After ninety minutes, the musicians flabbergasted him again when they stopped playing and put away their instruments. Then their manager compounded his astonishment by asking Buffett to fork over the staggering sum of $4,000—in cash.[21]

Now Susie Jr. had settled permanently in Los Angeles. Howie had already dropped out of Augustana College after having trouble adjusting and connecting with his roommate. He tried a couple of other schools, but had lost his support system and never graduated. "I was so close to my mom," he says, "and everything in my life revolved around our family and our home. In college I just could not get any traction."[22] Neither had their father's ambition, but both had money for the first time. The trust left by Howard to his grandchildren had distributed a little over six hundred shares of Berkshire Hathaway stock to them. Warren gave them no advice on what to do with it. He had never sold a share himself; why would they sell theirs? Susie Jr. sold most of hers to buy a Porsche and a condo. Howie sold some of his to start Buffett Excavating. In a grown-up version of his childhood love of Tonka Toys, he was now digging basements for a living.

Peter, just finishing his senior year in high school, had been accepted at Stanford and would be headed to California in the fall. More and more during the summer of 1976, the house in Omaha was simply empty. Most days after school Peter went to Arby's by himself to get something for dinner, then headed to the darkroom to work on his photography. Even the dog was decamping. Peter's friends had started calling to report "Hamilton's over here."[23]

Big Susie, who was rarely home these days, admitted to feeling depressed about the state of her marriage. She felt that Kay was an interloper who was pursuing her husband;[24] Kay had such a territorial way with men that it would have been surprising if Susie had felt otherwise. Yet despite—or perhaps because of—her sadness and anger at Warren, Susie herself was "running around like a teenager," as one person put it, in the hot rush of a midlife romance. She got careless, letting herself be seen with John McCabe, her tennis coach, around Omaha. She still called Milt from time to time as well, and when he agreed to see her they, too, were spotted out in public. She seemed to be living in different worlds, with no plan to proceed in any direction. She could not conceive of abandoning Warren. She described him as an "extraordinary man."[25] However much she joked and nagged about his rigidity and his preoccupation with money, he gave her security, stability, strength. "It mattered to her that he was honest and had a good value system," says Doris. "If I ever let down someone who needed me," Susie said, that would be the biggest failure she could imagine.[26] Susie had a natural confidence in her ability to manage complex relationships with multiple people, using her emotions as her guide. But somebody would have to be let down eventually.

While Susie was off on her various unknown pursuits, and his three children were headed in their respective directions—Peter taking off for Palo Alto in his little yellow Triumph convertible; Howie driving a backhoe, gorilla costume in tow; and Susie Jr. embarking on married life with her good-looking surfer— Warren was on a journey of his own. Katharine Graham was dragging the man of simple tastes who thought of his life as something out of *Leave It to Beaver* into elephant territory as fast as she could.

"She didn't change my behavior as much as changing what I knew and saw. Everywhere she went, she was treated just like royalty. I saw a whole lot of interesting things that I wouldn't have seen in the world. I had a lot of things explained to me. I picked up a lot around her. Kay knew so damned much about everybody that she would give me insights on people in the political arena.

"It bothered her that she thought I was teaching her all these things and she wasn't doing anything for me. She was constantly laboring in terms of trying to think of something she could do to help me out, whether it was inviting me to fancy dinners or something else. You could call all these events glamorous or exotic. I found them quite interesting. I'm not knocking these things. There were probably people who were way more dying to do them, particularly in her presence, than I would be. But I had a good time doing it, you know."

There undoubtedly were people who were "way more dying" to go. Nevertheless, Buffett did go, over and over again, no matter how ridiculous or awkward for him the events turned out to be.

One night Graham took him to a black-tie state dinner at the Iranian Embassy. She wore a golden gown to match the embassy's decor. Reza Pahlavi, the Shah of Iran, was an important U.S. strategic ally and a charming host. His embassy sat at the apex of the Embassy Row Washington social scene, and its doings glittered with a fin de siècle magnificence.

After the cocktail hour, Buffett sat down at his assigned table and found himself between one of Empress Farah Pahlavi's ladies-in-waiting and Illinois

Senator Charles Percy's wife. He turned toward Loraine Percy and found her locked in a tête-à-tête with her other dinner partner, Paul Newman. Seeing that it might be a while before she turned toward him, Buffett revolved toward his right and said something to the empress's lady-in-waiting. She smiled politely. He said something else. She smiled again, then went blank. Ted Kennedy, seated on her other side, leaned over and uttered some *bon mot* in French. Her face brightened and they began conversing animatedly in French. Buffett sat stranded in the middle. He turned back to Loraine Percy and found that she was still engrossed in Paul Newman. He realized with a dull feeling that with Paul Newman sitting on her left, it might become a very long evening.

Kay had been seated next to the Shah, at another table. Among these circles, Kay was the queen and he was some hayseed investor from Nebraska whom Kay had towed along. Forget *Supermoney;* this was old money. After a while, Ted Kennedy noticed his plight and asked, "Don't you speak *any* French?" Buffett felt like a poseur. He had landed in Bora-Bora with only a snowsuit to wear. The meal went on until one o'clock in the morning, and then the band began to play. One of the gentlemen began to waltz the empress round the floor. Buffett grabbed Graham's hand and escaped.

And yet, if she had asked him again, he would have gone. Because he was for sure not knocking it. The sightseeing was too good.

As he knew all too well by now, despite the fame from *Supermoney* and the articles in *Forbes,* many prominent people had never heard of him. In May 1976, Buffett was visiting Kay Graham in Washington when she said, I have someone I want you to meet. Jack Byrne, the person in question, was reluctant, however. When Graham called to arrange a meeting, he said, "Who's Buffett?"

"Well, he's a friend of mine," Graham said. "He's just bought a piece of the *Washington Post.*" Neither knowing nor caring, Byrne turned down the meeting. Then Buffett's old friend Lorimer "Davy" Davidson, who had retired from GEICO in 1970, called Byrne. "God, what kind of ninny are you to pass up a meeting with Warren Buffett?" he asked.[27]

Byrne had been hired in 1976 to try to pull GEICO—on the brink of bankruptcy—out of the ditch. Once an insurer only of government employees, GEICO had taken on John Q. Public. "Growth, growth, growth, the emphasis was all growth," says a longtime executive.[28] Fueled by growth, GEICO stock had traded as high as $61—far too rich for Buffett, but he had never stopped following it for the past twenty years.

In 1975, "*I looked again at GEICO and was startled by what I saw. It was clear in a sixty-second examination that the company was far underreserved [for claims] and the situation was getting worse. I went in to see [the CEO] Norm Gidden on one of my Washington Post trips. I had known and liked Norm for twenty years on a casual basis. He was friendly, but he had no interest at all in listening to my comments. They were in deep denial. He really sort of hustled me out of the office.*"[29]

That Buffett, who did not own the stock, was trying to help GEICO's management says something about how attached he still was to the company from which Lorimer Davidson had recently retired, the stock that had been his first really big idea, the investment that had made so much money for him and for his friends and family.

In early 1976, GEICO announced its worst year in history, a $190 million loss from underwriting operations during 1975.[30] The company stopped paying dividends, a move that conveys to shareholders that the till is empty. Gidden cast about frantically to bolster the mere $25 million in capital that GEICO had in its coffers.[31] That April, at Washington's Statler Hilton, four hundred angry stockholders stormed the shareholder meeting, armed with questions and accusations. Shortly afterward, the insurance commissioners arrived in a squadron at GEICO's offices. The board realized, a bit belatedly, that it had to fire the management.[32] The board itself was in disarray, several of its members having lost their personal fortunes in the debacle. Without a capable CEO to steer the company, Sam Butler, a steady-handed lawyer from Cravath, Swaine & Moore, took charge as the lead board member—in effect, a temporary CEO.

Butler knew that Byrne had quit Travelers on impulse, bitter at having just been passed over for the job of CEO. A former actuary who became a millionaire at age twenty-nine through a start-up insurance company, Byrne had been instrumental in turning around the Travelers' flailing home- and auto-insurance lines two years earlier. Butler called him in Hartford and played on his ego, explaining that if he took the job at GEICO it would prevent a national emergency that would throw the whole United States economy into jeopardy. Byrne was easily recruited to audition for CEO in Washington in early May.[33] "I came in and gave a sort of off-the-cuff five-hour blah, blah, blah, here's five points, here's what we have to do, boom boom boom speech,"[34] he says. The desperate board had no trouble deciding to hire this ruddy, round-faced cannonball.

Byrne's first task when he took over as CEO was to run straight to the dusty Chinatown offices of the District of Columbia's Insurance Superintendent Max

Wallach. An old-school German who spoke with a thick accent, Wallach was "stubborn as hell, and he had this enormous interest in serving the public," Byrne recalls. He was disgusted with GEICO's former management and had refused to deal with them. Byrne perceived that Wallach was not wild about him either. Nevertheless, the two men began talking daily, sometimes hourly.[35] Wallach insisted that the company put a deal in place by late June to raise money while simultaneously getting other insurance companies to take over some of its policies—that is, to "reinsure" GEICO.[36] The idea was to increase the resources GEICO had available to pay claims and to cut the risk it was carrying so that they were more in balance. Thus, Byrne had to sell other insurers on the idea of putting up money to save a competitor.

Byrne's prior experience was that he could sell anything. At first he was confident.

"My pitch was that if GEICO failed," says Byrne, "the regulators would just send the bill for GEICO's unpaid claims to its competitors. So they would end up bailing it out. But Ed Rust, Senior, who ran State Farm, he was a cooney old bastard. He concluded—and he was probably pretty smart—'I'll pay a hundred million to cover any of their unpaid claims if it puts GEICO out of business. . . . Killing GEICO will save us money in the long run.'" So State Farm backed out of the reinsurance deal.

"In the end," Byrne says, "a couple of really good friends reneged. The Travelers just said, 'We're not going to help.' They didn't have any principled idea behind this. Travelers was just wussy about it."

Three weeks after he joined GEICO, "I was racing around, thinking I had made the biggest mistake of my life. My wife, Dorothy, was up in Hartford, crying and crying." The market was suggesting GEICO might not survive; its stock had crashed from $61 to $2 a share. Somebody who owned, say, twenty-five thousand shares had just seen their fortune dwindle by almost ninety-seven percent—from more than $1.5 million to $50,000—from enough to live on for the rest of your life to enough to buy a very good sports car.

The reaction of the company's investors and shareholders to the calamity would, in not a few cases, literally determine their fate.

Many longtime shareholders had panicked and talked themselves into selling, which is how the stock got to $2 in the first place. Whoever was buying from them took a gamble on GEICO's fate.

Ben Graham, now age eighty-two, did nothing and kept his stock. Graham's cousin Rhoda and her husband, Bernie Sarnat, talked to the dean of the

University of Chicago business school. He told them to sell it, since stocks that cheap rarely recover. They decided—au contraire—a stock that had sunk so low was too cheap to sell. They had little to lose by keeping it. So they did nothing.[37] Likewise, Lorimer Davidson never sold a share.[38]

Leo Goodwin Jr., the son of GEICO's founder, sold and destituted himself. Shortly thereafter, his son, Leo Goodwin III, died of a drug overdose, a presumed suicide.[39]

As for Buffett, he had sniffed out another situation like American Express. Here, however, the company didn't have a franchise strong enough to pull it out of the ditch. GEICO needed a tow truck. Buffett felt that only a brilliant, energetic manager had any chance of turning the situation around. He wanted to size up Byrne before committing any money to the stock. He had Katharine Graham call Byrne; after overcoming Byrne's initial resistance, she set up the meeting.

Buffett waited at Graham's Georgetown house after a *Post* board dinner for Byrne to arrive. "This is risky," he told Don Graham. "It could go completely out of business. But in insurance it's very hard to get an edge, and they have an edge. If they got the right person in to run it, I think he could turn it around."[40]

In came Byrne like a firecracker exploding. The two men sat down by the fireplace in Graham's library. Buffett questioned Byrne for a couple of hours. Of all the Irish-Americans who would ever swing through Buffett's orbit, Byrne had the greatest gift of blarney, and *"by a wide margin,"* Buffett says. "I was excited and babbling on and on and on," says Byrne.

Despite the babbling, Buffett decided that Byrne *"understood insurance very well and had the analytical abilities. And he was a leader and a promoter. GEICO needed an analytical leader to figure out how to solve its problem and it needed a promoter to make that sale to all the constituencies that were involved."*[41]

The next morning, Buffett met up with George Gillespie, the lawyer who had sold him the *Post* stock, because they had a board meeting to attend at Pinkerton's, the detective company.[42] "George," he said, "it's pretty uncharacteristic of me, but today I bought some stock that really might be worthless tomorrow." He had just called Bill Scott back in the office. Scott put together a huge block trade, buying $4 million worth of GEICO for him.[43]

Buffett had waited years for the chance to buy GEICO at the right price. But GEICO still did not have reinsurance, it needed capital, and both depended on the goodwill of Max Wallach, the regulator.[44] Yet now a new phenomenon took hold. Buffett's margin of safety was his mere presence as a backer—a now-legendary investor whose company already owned a successful insurer. This gave Byrne a powerful card to play with the regulators.[45] In addition, "General McDermott, the head of USAA, wrote a letter" to other insurers, says Byrne. The United Services Automobile Association sold insurance only to military officers and behaved accordingly. Within the insurance industry, it was fabled, General Robert McDermott almost revered. He supposedly wrote that "in the military we never leave people behind; we have a fallen eagle here."[46]

Buffett went to see Wallach to do what he could to convince the crusty old public servant to ease up on the June deadline. But assembling the reinsurance deal was like convincing two dozen shivering children to hold hands and jump into a lake.[47] To pull it off, the story Byrne was selling was that the former management, befoulers of GEICO, had been tossed out; that what was left of the house was now clean; that Jack Byrne, rescuer of Travelers, had helicoptered in to restore the damage; and so confident was the infallible Warren Buffett in Jack Byrne that he had plunked down a whopping $4 million on the stock.

Nonetheless, when Byrne started hitting the banks on Wall Street, "people were walking out in the middle of lunch," he says. Then Sam Butler took him down to Salomon Inc. An old, respected specialist bond house, Salomon had never done an equity deal but craved to enter the lucrative business of underwriting stocks. John Gutfreund, an influential Salomon executive, sent a junior research analyst, Michael Frinquelli, and his sidekick, Joe Barone, to Washington to check GEICO out. "I kept them waiting for an hour and a half, so they were furious," says Byrne. "But I talked till the sun came up. And they were very blank-faced, but on the way to the airport, the company driver heard them talking, and he told me they were very, very enthused on the way back."[48]

"The insurance industry can't afford to let these guys go down," Frinquelli told Gutfreund. "It would be a terrible black eye on the industry, and these assholes will not tolerate that."[49] But when Byrne and Butler arrived at Salomon's offices for his last-ditch attempt to raise the money, Gutfreund opened with a bruising remark: "I don't know who'd ever buy that fucking reinsurance treaty you're trying to sell."

"You don't know any fucking thing you're talking about," said Byrne right back.[50]

Displays of testosterone out of the way, Byrne made a passionate speech, citing "God and the national interest" among reasons why Salomon should raise the money, and referring to Buffett's investment. As Byrne waxed about

GEICO's prospects and approached liftoff, Gutfreund fiddled with a long, expensive cigar. Finally, wrung out and crestfallen, Byrne ground to a halt. Then Butler said his piece. Byrne thought, from Gutfreund's demeanor, that they had failed. Then Gutfreund pointed at Byrne and said to Butler, "I will do this underwriting. I feel you've got the right guy, but you've got to keep him quiet."[51]

Salomon agreed to underwrite a $76 million convertible stock offering by itself. No other investment bank would participate and share the risk. GEICO had to consent to an SEC decree in which it neither admitted nor denied the SEC's conclusion that it had failed to disclose its losses to the shareholders—the mere description of which in a public offering prospectus would tend to poison the deal.[52] To get the financing done, Salomon had to convince investors that GEICO would survive, yet the financing was what would enable GEICO to survive. The deal reeked of desperation, and investors could smell it. GEICO was getting such bad press, Byrne said, that if he had walked across the Potomac River, the headlines would have screamed, "Byrne Can't Swim."[53]

Buffett, the ace in the hole, was unperturbed by these events. When the offering looked dicey, he simply went to New York and met with Gutfreund, saying he stood ready as a backup buyer for the whole deal. He strengthened Salomon's hand, but Gutfreund also got the impression that Buffett wouldn't mind if the deal failed and he ended up buying all the stock.[54] For Buffett, this was the ultimate no-risk deal. Naturally, the backup price he insisted on was low. Salomon told Byrne unequivocally that, given Buffett's ceiling, the convertible offering would sell no higher than $9.20 per share, not $10.50 as Byrne wanted.

Indeed, once the self-fulfilling prophecy of the sage of Omaha took hold, the deal became oversubscribed.[55] Buffett got only a quarter of the stock. Within a few weeks, after a total of twenty-seven reinsurers came forward to provide the required reinsurance, the stock had quadrupled to around $8 a share. And GEICO's savior, John Gutfreund, became one of a tiny handful of modern Wall Street figures whom Buffett genuinely admired.

But GEICO was still not fixed. Byrne needed a thirty-five percent rate increase in New York—and speedily got it.[56] In New Jersey, he went to plead with Commissioner James Sheeran, an ex-Marine who prided himself on being tough. Byrne marched into Sheeran's office with a copy of the company's license in his pocket and told him that GEICO must have a rate increase.

"He had a sour-ass, little wizened actuary at his side who had been fired by some insurance company and had a bone to pick," says Byrne. Sheeran said his numbers didn't justify a rate increase. "I did all the arm-waving and stuff that I could, and Mr. Sheeran was intractable." Byrne threw the license on Sheeran's desk, saying, "I have no choice but to turn in the license," or something to that effect but containing more four-letter words.[57] He then drove back to the office with tires screeching, sent out telegrams to thirty thousand policyholders canceling their insurance, and fired two thousand employees in a single afternoon, before Sheeran could go to court and get an injunction to stop him.[58]

"It showed everybody, all audiences, I was serious about this," recalls Byrne. "And that I was going to fight for the life of this company no matter what, including walking out of a state, which wasn't done back then." Byrne's impalement of New Jersey had exactly that effect. Everybody knew he was serious.

"It was like he had trained all his life for that position. It was like he'd been genetically designed for that particular period of time. If you'd searched the country, you could not have found a better battlefield commander.... It was a Herculean job. Nobody could have done it better than Jack."

Byrne walked through GEICO's door each morning, sailed his hat fifty feet up to the upper floor of the atrium, and hollered hello to the secretaries.[59] "If I don't whistle by the graveyard, who is going to?" he asked. "If I don't dance, who's going to dance?" He had a way of making people feel *tah*-riffic about the place where they went to work every morning, despite the career-threatening status of their employer. He chopped forty percent of the company's customers, sold half of its profitable life-insurance affiliate to raise cash, and withdrew from all but seven states plus the District of Columbia. Byrne seemed to run on rocket fuel. His attitude was: "You're not running a public library here, you're trying to save a company."[60]

"Jack was unmerciful on me," says Tony Nicely, who had worked for GEICO since he was eighteen years old. "He liked picking on young, aggressive people. But he taught me a lot and I will always be indebted to him. He taught me to think of the business as a whole, not separate functions like underwriting or investing. I learned the importance of a disciplined balance sheet."[61]

Byrne told his workers if they couldn't meet a certain sales figure, they would have to hoist his 240 pounds on their shoulders into a sedan chair like a Roman emperor and bear him into company meetings for a year.[62] They made the numbers. Wearing a huge chef's hat and a giant shamrock, "I cooked Irish dinners for them," he says. "Colcannon, which is turnips and potatoes and sour milk. It tastes terrible. I'd have these big kettles, and I'd pound these turnips, saying, 'Oh, this is going to be wonderful!'"

Buffett grabbed Byrne and his wife, Dorothy, and immediately pulled them into his circle of friends. Now, between GEICO, *Washington Post* meetings, West Coast trips for Blue Chip and Wesco, business trips to New York, meetings for Munsingwear, a board he had joined in 1974, and Kay Parties, he was traveling much of the time. Buffett decided that he needed help in the office. Pushed by Big Susie, one of her tennis friends approached Warren about a job. Dan Grossman, a bright Yale graduate with a Stanford business degree, even offered to work for free. Buffett didn't take him up on that, but latched on to Grossman with his usual intensity. Some thought that since neither of his sons wanted to work in the business, he saw in Grossman the chance at a surrogate son, someone who could potentially succeed him.

Buffett remodeled the office in order to install Grossman next door to himself. Gladys ran interference while Buffett spent hour after hour with him, explaining float, reviewing financial models of insurance companies, outlining regulatory filings, telling Grossman his stories, and leafing through the old *Moody's Manuals.* He played hours of tennis and handball with Grossman and added him to the Graham Group, where Grossman became friendly with many people.[63] Warren had found yet another object of obsession.

41

And Then What?

Susie's friends would say that she created a separate life for herself within her marriage as a way to accommodate Warren's obsessions. As one put it, Warren's "real marriage was to Berkshire Hathaway." There was no getting around that fact. However uneasily, however, their routine had worked for them. At least, that is, it worked for them until another of Buffett's obsessions—with Katharine Graham—reached the point that it began to push Susie offstage. That was when she finally took action.

Warren now spent much of his time elephant-bumping at black-tie events in New York and Washington with Graham, or staying at her house for her Kay Parties. Despite his residual awkwardness and cackling laugh, he was meeting a circle of powerful, celebrated friends and acquaintances of Kay's that opened his eyes to a new world.

"*I met Truman Capote,*" he says about the author of *Breakfast at Tiffany's* and *In Cold Blood,* who had thrown the legendary Black and White Ball in Graham's honor at the Plaza Hotel in New York; the event became known as the "party of the century." Capote had been a confidant of many rich international society women.

"*The one person he really liked was Kay. Unlike the rest, he just didn't feel she was a phony, I think.*"

Buffett had even been summoned by former ambassador to Great Britain Walter Annenberg, who owned Triangle Publications, which held, among other lucrative properties, the *Philadelphia Inquirer* and Buffett's childhood favorite, the *Daily Racing Form.*

"Walter read about me in the <u>Wall Street Journal</u> in 1977. I got this letter that read, 'Dear Mr. Buffett,' and he invited me to Sunnylands," his California estate. Having heard stories about the famously thin-skinned ambassador, Buffett was intrigued. Annenberg's father featured in many of the stories. Besides the publishing interests that he had bequeathed to his son, Moe Annenberg had also left him a legacy of scandal and shame. He ran a racing wire that telegraphed horse-race results to bookies all over the country. Of dubious legality, it was linked to organized crime. Reportedly to save his son from prosecution for tax evasion along with him, Moe Annenberg copped a plea and was led into jail wearing a homburg hat and chains. Walter was later to say that his gaunt, pain-racked father, dying of a brain tumor, whispered as his last few words, "My suffering is all for the purpose of making a man out of you."[1] Whether this scene was real or imagined, Walter would later act as though he believed it.

Consumed by a drive to redeem his family's honor, Walter learned the publishing business through trial by fire and proved a gifted entrepreneur. He dreamed up *Seventeen* magazine, then a booklet-size magazine called *TV Guide*, a brilliant conception that fed the public's appetite for information about television schedules, shows, and stars. By the time he met Buffett, he had not only become a great business success story but had reached the pinnacle of social respectability after Richard Nixon appointed him ambassador to England's Court of St. James's. Yet even though he restored the family name, he never overcame the personal scars of his legacy.

Buffett arrived at Sunnylands filled with curiosity to meet Annenberg. The two already had a connection; Annenberg was the brother of Aye Simon, the "spoiled, spoiled" widow whom Ben Rosner had decided to screw when he sold the Associated Cotton Shoppes to Buffett. On the one occasion that Buffett had met her, Aye Simon had entertained him in her vast art-filled apartment in New York City. Maids tiptoed back and forth carrying silver trays of sandwiches; Aye explained to Buffett that her "Pop," Moe Annenberg, once had his goons, known as "the boys," "take a few shots at" her husband, Leo Simon, to improve his attitude toward Moe. You can still see the bullet holes on a certain corner of Michigan Avenue in Chicago, she said. Aye then asked for her son to join the Buffett partnership. Warren, *"envisioning bullets"* if he turned in a year of bad results, had *"tap-danced"* his way out of the situation.

Her brother, Walter, had spent decades establishing a reputation for propriety about as different from the image of bullets on Michigan Avenue as could be imagined. Annenberg had entertained Prince Charles, hosted Frank Sinatra's fourth wedding, and given his friend Richard Nixon peace and quiet to write his last State of the Union address.

"*He had a courtly way about him and was very formal. We went outside in back by the pool, and Walter sat down. He was beautifully dressed and looked as though everything he was wearing had been bought that morning. He was about seventy at the time, and I was about forty-seven. And he said, in a nice, kind manner, as if he were talking to a young man he was trying to help, 'Mr. Buffett, the first thing you should understand is, nobody likes to be criticized.' That was setting the ground rules for getting along.*"

Nothing could be easier for Buffett. "*I said, 'Yes, Mr. Ambassador. I've got it. Don't worry about that one.'*

"*And then he started in on 'Essentiality.'*

"*'There are three properties in the world,' he said, 'that have the quality of 'Essentiality.' They are the Daily Racing Form, the TV Guide, and the Wall Street Journal. And I own two out of three.'*

"*What he meant by 'Essentiality' was that, even during the Depression, he saw the Racing Form being sold for two and a half bucks down in Cuba.*"

The *Racing Form* had that quality because there was no source of better or more complete information about handicapping horses.

"*It sold a hundred fifty thousand copies a day, and it had for about fifty years. It cost more than two bucks, and it was essential. If you were headed to the racetrack and were a serious racing handicapper, you wanted the Racing Form. He could charge whatever he wanted, and people were going to pay it. It's like selling needles to addicts, basically.*

"*So every year, Walter would go in and say, 'Mirror, mirror, on the wall, how much should I raise the price of the Racing Form this fall?'*

"*And the mirror would always say, 'Walter, charge another quarter!'*"

This was when you could buy the *New York Times* or *Washington Post* for a quarter. And yet, thought Buffett, the *Times* and the *Post* were great businesses! That meant the *Daily Racing Form* was an *incredible* business.

Annenberg wanted to own all three of the Essentialities. The visit to Sunnylands was the beginning of a reel that he and Buffett would dance from time to time: talking about whether and how they could buy the *Wall Street Journal* together.

But "*the real reason that he had me out there was to send a message to Kay.*"

The Annenbergs and the Grahams had once been friends.[2] Then, in 1969, during the confirmation hearing for Annenberg's appointment as ambassador to Great Britain, he had taken offense at columns written by the *Post*'s muckraking Drew Pearson, which described at length Annenberg's editorial vindictiveness at the *Philadelphia Inquirer,* said that his fortune "was built up by gang warfare," and repeated an unsubstantiated rumor that his father had paid $1 million a year in protection money to mob boss Al Capone.[3] Annenberg, enraged, accused Graham of using her paper as a political weapon against President Nixon, the man who had restored his family to respectability by taking the risk of nominating him for the ambassadorship. He called Graham to ask for a retraction. She tried to soothe his feelings, but said she never interfered with the editorial page.

After his Senate hearing, Annenberg stalked out of a Kay Party in his honor over what he felt were major, and others felt were unintentional, social slights.

"*Kay was distraught about it. She wanted enormously to get along with Walter. Kay was not looking to have fights with anybody. That was not her style.... She liked big shots, and she liked big-shot guys, particularly.... But she also wanted Walter to understand that she wasn't going to tell Ben Bradlee what to write about in the paper.*

"*So by the time I went out to see him, he was thinking about having a book commissioned about Phil Graham, and how Phil's teeth were in a funny way.*"

Phil Graham's teeth.

"*Walter had a theory that if you were gap-toothed, that was a sign of mental instability. And if Walter had a theory, you didn't argue with it. Walter liked me, but one reason that he liked me was that I never disagreed. If Walter said to me, black was white, I just wouldn't say anything.*

"*So I became the go-between with Kay.*" Annenberg expected Buffett to deliver the message that if he published the book about Phil Graham's teeth, well, that's show business.

"*Meanwhile, he couldn't have been nicer to me. He put me in this super-fancy guest room. And he took me into his office, where he had a little display in a glass case of a Prussian coin, a pocketknife, and one other thing. It was all that his grandfather had in his pocket when he landed in this country from Prussia. And he said, 'Everything you see here is a product of that.' In a period of not that many years, Walter had rehabilitated his family. He did his father proud. And that was his number one goal in life, to do his father proud.*"

Buffett understood Annenberg, yet never seemed to notice certain resemblances between the ambassador and himself. Probably this was because they were so different in other ways. Annenberg's humorlessness, his fondness for opulence and formality, and his enmity toward the Grahams set him strikingly apart from Buffett, and they were at opposite poles politically. Nonetheless, beneath their similarly paper-thin skins, these two shrewd businessmen shared a deep drive to prove themselves—both in business and socially—and a reverence for fathers whom they felt the world had treated unjustly.

They struck up a correspondence. Annenberg would come to think of himself, in an avuncular sort of way, as training Buffett in philanthropy. He thought rich people should give it all away before they died lest their appointed stewards dishonor their obligations.[4] Mistrustful by nature and always testing people— again, like Buffett in both respects—Annenberg had made a close study of failed foundations and the perfidy of foundation trustees. He sent Buffett examples, along with chitchat about stocks and courtly correspondence. Buffett—a budding philanthropist and a publisher whose paper had won a Pulitzer Prize for exposing the failed stewardship of a major charity—read this material with interest. Annenberg conveyed to him his dread of an imperial administrator for his money, one who would conduct what he referred to as "foundation rapings" after he was gone.

"Dear Warren," he wrote, thanking Buffett for sending an article about Mac Bundy, who ran the Ford Foundation in a way that Annenberg deemed abhorrent,[5] "Henry [Ford II] once described McGeorge Bundy as 'the most arrogant son of a bitch in the country, who developed the lifestyle of an Arabian prince on Ford Foundation money.'"[6]

Annenberg spent immense amounts of time scheming to avoid being double-crossed after he was dead. He told Buffett about the Donner Foundation, whose executive director had changed the name of the foundation to the Independence Fund, obliterating the founding donor.[7] "I respectfully suggest you make sure that no one can tamper with the name of your foundation after you're gone," he wrote. "Remember Mr. Donner."[8]

Buffett thought otherwise about the foundation he and Susie had set up. *"It should not have been named the Buffett Foundation,"* he said later. *"It was dumb to name it the Buffett Foundation. But it would also be dumb to change it now, because it would be too obvious."*[9]

He and Annenberg shared a fascination for media and publishing. *TV Guide* was Annenberg's greatest asset. Once Buffett got the idea that Annenberg was going to sell *TV Guide;* he and Tom Murphy flew out to Los Angeles to see if the imperious ambassador would sell it to them fifty-fifty. But Annenberg wanted to be paid in stock, not cash. Neither Buffett nor Murphy believed in giving away stock if they could possibly help it. "You don't get rich that way," says Murphy. So they didn't buy *TV Guide.*

As his relationship with Buffett developed, the proper, traditional Annenberg seemed to take at face value Buffett's relationship with Graham. He continued to use Buffett, in his role as a *Post* board member, as emissary to Graham. All the while, Graham was calling Buffett constantly about the smallest details of her personal life. Buffett visited her rambling shingle mansion on Martha's Vineyard, and they went, on a lark, to Niagara Falls. He took her to see one of his totems, the Berkshire textile mills. As the flirtatious, fifty-nine-year-old Kay was spotted tossing the forty-six-year-old Warren her house key at charity benefits and the two were seen together ever more often in public, by early 1977 the gossip columns had taken note, and, as Graham put it, "eyebrows shot up."[10]

Friends observed, as one put it, that the pair had "zero chemistry." Yet Graham presented their relationship as an affair to her friends.[11] She was obviously sexually insecure but tried to project the opposite, as illustrated in her memoir.[12] Whatever genuinely romantic elements the relationship with Kay may have had initially, at heart theirs was a friendship. But the publicity upset the delicate equilibrium between Susie and Warren. Whatever else was going on in her life, she still cared very much about her husband. Moreover, Susie needed the people in her life to need her, even to be dependent on her. Now she felt discounted and trivialized. Yet she would never allow herself to look like the spurned Daisy Mae in public. She continued to stay at Kay's house when she traveled to Washington and smiled benevolently no matter how often her husband was seen with Kay.

Some of Susie's friends believed that she was, in fact, indifferent. Others felt that she needed to be in control or that Warren's relationship with Kay gave her cover to live her own separate life in peace. Nevertheless, she made it plain to several friends that she was furious and humiliated. Her way of dealing with the situation was to send Graham a letter granting her leave to pursue a relationship with Warren—as if Kay had been waiting for any such permission.[13] Kay showed the letter to people as though it let her off the hook.[14]

Susie was now working hard on a serious singing career. In 1976, she had approached the owners of Omaha's French Café, a formal restaurant located in the quaint, cobblestoned Old Market district downtown, and suggested that she sing in their lounge. They were astonished but gladly agreed. Ads went up verifying the rumors that Susan Buffett would become a chanteuse. "This is very scary, but I've always wanted to live to the hilt,"[15] she had told a reporter before her first performance.

She "lacked self-confidence," said a reviewer, but her "Ann-Margret youthfulness," "stylized jazz," and desire to please won over the crowd. The audience was described as being made up of "uncritical friends" and people who attended out of curiosity to see a rich man's wife.[16] Within weeks, Bill Ruane had lined up auditions in New York. She did a three-week gig as an opening act at Yellow Brick Road, See Saw, Tramps, and The Ballroom. Afterward she said, "I've been asked back, but I'm going to be loose about the timing. Maybe after the first of the year. First I plan to find a musical director and put a package together. Now I know how hard it is, but I'm hooked on it, and when I go back, I want to do six months without stopping."[17] She signed up with the William Morris talent agency.

That summer had taken both Buffetts to New York. Warren played bridge in Kay's apartment, and on other evenings Susie sang while he gazed at her rapturously from the audience. Her musical career bound them together—he was thrilled for her success. They considered buying an apartment in a landmarked building just off Fifth Avenue in New York City, which would have given them a permanent base in New York—but decided to pass.[18]

Susie was indeed loose about the timing, and by the fall of 1976 had made no plans to go back to New York. She still spent more time at Laguna than Warren. Moreover, her "clientele" around Omaha was a distraction. From Leila, who besieged Susie with hours of stories about the 38½ wonderful years with Howard; to Howie, who was running a backhoe outside Omaha; to Dottie, who seemed to be sleepwalking through her life, so passive that one day when she called and reported that there was a big fire at her house, Susie had no sooner hung up the phone than she wondered whether Dottie had called the fire department. Susie phoned her sister back. Dottie said no, she had thought only of calling Susie.[19] And all these responsibilities came only from the family; outnumbering them by miles were Susie's "vagrants," lonelyhearts, and local relationships.

Instead of setting up commitments to sing in New York, therefore, she scheduled another round of performances for the spring of 1977 at the French Café in Omaha. With that, a magazine published by the *Omaha World-Herald* decided to do a cover piece on the millionaire's wife who set out to become a cabaret singer in midlife. The reporter, Al "Bud" Pagel, started out with a routine story, approaching Susie's friends and asking them simple questions about her life. What makes Susie sing? he wanted to know. Like many people in Omaha, of course, he had heard the rumors about Susie's extracurricular activities.[20] Susie's friends were "defensive" and "protective."

Eunice Denenberg "bristled" and declared, "Susie is one of those old-fashioned GOOD people that lots of folks today don't think exist. So they attribute some of their own baser behavior to her because it bothers them."[21] The worshippers circled to protect the saint. Pagel admitted that, faced with such an aggressive pack of defenders, yes, it did bring out a subconscious urge in him to toss a handful of mud at Susie's best white party dress.[22]

For her interview, Susie sat down with Pagel on the couch by the fireplace in the Buffetts' family room, with its Ping-Pong table and the posters on the wall. She struck him as vulnerable.

"Being a performer is kind of the opposite of being a mother," she told him in her interview. "I'm not used to the care and feeding of Susan Buffett. Maybe I am a reinforcement for someone who is on the verge of thinking, 'I want to try something but I'm afraid to do it.' I'm just one more person who tried something but was afraid to do it." She paused. "That's the only story I have."[23]

The reporter gave some indication he was looking for more of a story than that. His curiosity had been piqued rather than muzzled by her pit-bull defenders. Susie opened up and talked about herself for five hours, without getting into her personal relationships. Still, by the end, she said she was astonished at what she had done: The woman whose lips were sealed like a mollusk's when people tried to pry her open at dinner parties had given herself to Pagel. In the process she managed to win him over as a friend.

When the story was published, the cover of the magazine read, *What Makes Susie Sing?* and featured a photo of her with a "who knows?" expression, tentative smile, eyes tilted up, avoiding the camera. Inside, Susie faced away from the camera in the photographs. Something inward, an uncertain dream, had replaced the open-jawed grin that nearly always appeared in pictures of her.

The morning the story came out, Susie showed up on Pagel's doorstep with a huge box of See's Candies, excited as a child at the portrait he had drawn of her. She put him on the guest list to her opening at the French Café and sent him an invitation.[24] He and other guests remember her as looking young and radiant that night, wearing a brunette shag wig and a sequined dress that hugged her newly svelte figure. Raven-feather eyelashes fluttered around her beaming eyes. The look on her face suggested that she was discovering that the care and feeding of Susan Buffett was not so bad. By now she had developed some polish as a performer, and smiled seductively while the crowd hooted and hollered in between songs.[25] Her guests saw the glow of a woman emerging from behind her role as a wife and mother onto the stage of her own life. The audience found her tender delivery and smooth liquid styling of pop standards and sentimental favorites engaging and sweet. Her repertoire of medleys—"Daddy" songs like "My Heart Belongs to Daddy"; cabaret classics like "What Are You Doing the Rest of Your Life?"; and her personal favorite, Sondheim's "Send in the Clowns"[26]—moistened eyes. When she sang, Susie's torchy side came to life and she opened up emotionally. Standing in the back with his arms crossed, watching his wife vamping and flirting and romancing her audience, Buffett, in good humor, remarked, "This is pretty good of me to let her do this."

Yet by the summer of 1977, Susie still had not followed up on her New York opportunities. Warren thought it was because his spontaneous wife resisted the structured time commitments required of a professional singer. Some of the Buffetts' friends questioned whether Susie's pretty warble and her appealing stage presence could compete with established singers of greater artistry. While Susie loved to perform, it was Warren's dream that his wife might become a singing star with a recording career. Her ambitions had always been harnessed on behalf of others, not herself. Meanwhile, the care and feeding of Susan Buffett was something separate, a more private matter.

There was the rub. Being a rich man's wife opened doors that would have helped her pursue a serious singing career. But it also opened doors that invited others to peer into her personal life, doors that she would prefer remained shut. Warren could stay at Kay Graham's house and be seen as her date in public in perfect freedom, while the gossip columns did no more than wink. Yet as a married woman, Susie had no such liberty. The women's movement had changed many things, but not that. With her privacy eroding, the question of how to deal with her increasingly divided feelings was beginning to tear her apart.

Stan Lipsey, their *Sun* publisher friend, was also having some issues with his marriage, and he and Susie sat on park benches in the mornings, sharing confidences. Both of them were interested in Eastern thought and the human-potential movement.[27] They somehow convinced Warren, as well as Stan's wife, Jeannie, and Susie's sister, Dottie, to join them at a weekend workshop in a Lincoln hotel. The idea was to get in touch with yourself. The workshop started with an exercise to get people to open up to one another nonjudgmentally, a skill of Susie's. Warren's reaction to such an outpouring was nothing like his wife's.

"There were five hundred people who had come from as much as a thousand miles away. And they started doing all these crazy things. First we had to get a part-

ner. And one of them was to start talking, and the other person, no matter what, just keeps saying, 'And then what?'

"*So I paired up with this nice woman from Oklahoma, and she starts talking. Then she pauses and I say, 'And then what?' In ten minutes, she's sobbing uncontrollably. I've destroyed her, just by saying, 'And then what?' It was like I was boring into her. I felt like I was running a torture chamber or something.*"

After having misinterpreted this exercise in every possible way, Buffett left his tear-drenched companion, eager to move on. The leader told the participants to find another partner. "Now, when I hear the leader say, 'I want you to choose a partner of the opposite sex,' Lipsey says, "*I'm* looking for someone attractive." Buffett stood looking around like someone who didn't quite know what to do. "The next thing you know," says Lipsey, "he's paired with this very heavy woman."

"*She was wearing a muumuu and weighed about four hundred pounds. My job was to get down on the floor. And then the leader said this woman was to give me the 'gift of her weight.' Which meant she flopped right down on top of me. There was this whale coming right at me. I was just—ack! It turned out to be the gift that never stopped giving.*

"*Meanwhile, in the other room, they were having people bark like dogs. I could hear Dottie—who was so uptight she could hardly say hello to somebody—trying desperately to bark.*"

Following a session of being blindfolded and led through the streets of Lincoln to experience sensory deprivation, Susie and Stan gave up and they all ran away to a movie theater to watch *Annie Hall*—"a nervous romance"—and "spent the rest of the weekend gorging ourselves on fried food and ice-cream sundaes," says Lipsey.

The summer of 1977, while Buffett again played bridge marathons at Kay Graham's apartment in New York, Susie stayed away from home at all hours of the day and night.

Howie got married that August to Marcia Sue Duncan, despite her father's warnings that she would not be happy with a guy who dug basements for a living and drove a pickup with a couple of big shaggy dogs in its cargo bed.

Over Labor Day weekend, Susie gave her final performance in Omaha, appearing at the Orpheum Theater as the opening act for singer/songwriter Paul Williams. In a pink chiffon gown, she smiled and beguiled as her smooth contralto oozed romantic jazzy ballads, "languorous and sensual." She come-hithered the audience with "Let's feel like we're in love, okay?"[28] But in a small, gossipy city like Omaha, that announcement probably could have been left unmade.

That fall, Susie apparently began to realize what a mess her life had become. She went out until four o'clock in the morning, driving all the way to Wahoo—where she had spent her wedding night—playing music at top volume on the radio of her Porsche before returning at dawn to her lonely home.[29]

At her best Susie gave people part of her soul. Now panicked, she reached out to people and hoped they would reciprocate. Friends listened to her agonize in parks, on walks, on long drives. She stockpiled little sums of money and gave them to friends to hold, as if planning an escape. She appeared at Berkshire Hathaway's office in her tennis pal Dan Grossman's doorway, sobbing and asking for advice, while her husband sat in his office next door.

Susie seemed to realize on some level that she was compromising numerous people by letting them know more than her husband did about his troubled marriage and the secret yearnings of his disillusioned wife. You can't tell Warren, she said to one person. If you love him, you won't hurt him that way. If he ever found out, he would kill himself.[30]

So powerful was Susie, so beloved, so apparent was Warren's devotion to his wife, and so thoroughly had Susie trained everyone to think that he was helpless without her, that people accepted this burden. Some did it automatically, some did it out of loyalty, some did it uneasily, half aware of the flaws in her logic. But they all now felt responsible for keeping her secrets on the pretext of Warren's vulnerability.

Yet nothing appeared amiss at Gardiner's Tennis Ranch in Arizona, where the Graham Group was meeting that fall. Most of the group—now usually referred to as the Buffett Group—had long ago accepted the idea of "Warren-o" and "Susan-o" as an affectionate couple who lived separate lives. This year proceeded like any other, with Susie in attendance along with the rest of the wives. Bill Ruane presented Warren's *Fortune* article "How Inflation Swindles the Equity Investor."[31] Buffett explained that stocks, especially stocks of companies that can raise prices as their costs increase, are the best protection against inflation—but their value is still eroded by severe inflation, a problem that he referred to as a "giant corporate tapeworm."[32] At a social break, Marshall Weinberg told Warren and Susie about his niece, who was living and working on a reservation with Native Americans. "Oh!" gushed Susie. "I would love to do that! It would be so wonderful to live so simply and help those poor people on a reservation that way." Warren looked at her. "Sooz, I'll buy you one," he said, deadpan.[33]

At age forty-seven, Warren had already accomplished everything he had ever imagined he could want. He was worth $72 million. He ran a company that was worth $135 million.[34] His newspaper had won the two highest prizes in journalism. He was one of the most important men in Omaha and increasingly prominent at a national level. He was serving on the boards of the largest local bank, the *Washington Post,* and a number of other companies. He had been CEO of three companies and had bought and sold successfully more stocks than most people could name in a lifetime. Most of his original partners were now enormously rich.

All he wanted was to keep on making money for the thrill of it without changing anything else about his life. He knew Susie thought he was obsessed with money, just as she always had, yet they had managed to lead their lives in such a way so as to honor their differences while staying a united team for twenty-five years. Or so it seemed to him.

Later that fall, after the Buffett Group meeting, Susie went to visit a high school friend who lived in San Francisco. She stayed for four or five weeks. One relationship after another seemed to bind her to California. Her nephew Billy Rogers had moved to the West Coast to join the music scene. Susie had told him she would give him any help he needed to kick his heroin addiction, but she worried about him on his own in California. Bertie Buffett, who was now remarried, to Hilton Bialek, lived in San Francisco. The Lipseys were thinking of moving to San Francisco. Susie's widowed friend Rackie Newman now lived there. Susie Jr. and her husband were living in Los Angeles. Peter was now a sophomore at Stanford in Palo Alto. And she and Warren already had their own foothold in California—their vacation home in Emerald Bay, just south of Los Angeles. Fewer and fewer ties pulled her back to Nebraska. The house in Omaha was spooky empty: As soon as Peter left for college, Hamilton the dog ran away and went to live with one of Peter's friends.[35]

Spending this extended time in San Francisco, Susie found it a beautiful, creative, spirited city. At every angle from its rising hills, the bay and ocean and bridges and sunsets and rickrack rows of Victorian houses beckoned, Come look at me. A delirious mosaic of people, neighborhoods, architecture, culture, art, and music said, You'll never be bored in San Francisco. The thermometer never registered 110 degrees in San Francisco. The city's air raced through your lungs, clean and liberating. In the spontaneous, hot, do-anything-with-anyone mood of the 1970s, San Francisco was the capital of mind-expanding, hedonistic spirituality, a magnet of tolerance where people didn't judge one another.

Susie looked at some apartments. She came back to Omaha and went to the French Café, where she had been singing, and talked to Astrid Menks, who was the maître d' there on Monday nights as well as a sommelier and sometime chef. She and Menks were friendly; Astrid served her tea between sets at the French Café, and had catered a dinner at the Buffetts' earlier that year when Peter Jay, the new British ambassador to the United States, had visited Omaha. Knowing the Buffetts' tastes, Menks had sludged Jay with Warren's favorite meal: fried chicken, mashed potatoes, gravy, corn on the cob, and hot-fudge sundaes.

Now Susie asked Astrid to look in on Warren and cook an occasional meal for him. Then she had a talk with him and said she wanted to rent a funky little cubbyhole on Nob Hill so she could have a base in San Francisco.

Warren's tendency not to listen, to hear only what he wanted to hear, worked in Susie's favor as she explained that she was not leaving him. They were not "separating." They would stay married. Nothing would really change if she had a room of her own, a place where she could be herself in San Francisco. She simply wanted to surround herself with a city full of art and music and theater, she reassured him. Their lives were already on such different courses, and they both traveled so much anyway, he would barely notice the difference. With the children grown, it was time for her to tend to her needs. She told him, over and over, "We both—we *both*—have needs." That part was for sure true.

"*Susie wasn't totally leaving, either, that was the thing. She just wanted a change.*"

In all of Susie's travels, in her talk of buying this place or that place, it had never occurred to him that she would leave, because it would never occur to him to leave her. "Wanting a change" and "not totally leaving" were the kind of ambiguous Buffettesque statements they both tended to make to avoid feeling as though they were disappointing anyone.

And then she left.

Susie went off to Europe for a few weeks with her friend Bella Eisenberg. She returned to Emerald Bay for Christmas with the family but left to go back to Europe again. Increasingly, it was clear that for Susie, having a place of her own in San Francisco did not mean renting a pied-à-terre that she would escape to for a week every now and then. Warren was hopeless at taking care of himself and Susie Jr. came back to Omaha for a couple of weeks to lend a hand. Susie Jr. tried to explain to her father that, given how much time he and her mother had been spending apart, his life was not going to be that different from before. But Warren had not previously thought of himself and Susie as living virtually separate lives. In his mind, Susie lived for him. She certainly acted as if she did when they were together. So it was a hard concept to grasp, that Susie wanted her own life and would not be there for him all the time.

Susie and Warren talked for hours and hours on the phone. Now that he understood, Warren would have done anything she asked to get her back, submitted to any conditions, met any demands—move to California, learn to dance. But it was too late. He could not give her what she wanted, whatever that was. She explained it in terms of her freedom, her need to be separate and to fulfill her needs and find her own identity. She could not do that while spending all her time taking care of him. So he wandered aimlessly around the house, barely able to feed and clothe himself. He came to the office most days with a raging headache. In front of the staff, he maintained his self-control, although he did look as though he was not sleeping well at night. He was calling Susie every day, weeping. "It was as if they couldn't live together and they couldn't live without each other," one person said.

Seeing her husband helpless and destroyed, Susie wavered. She told a friend, "I might have to go back." But she didn't. They both had needs. One of her needs was for her tennis coach to move to San Francisco. She installed him in a tiny separate apartment down the street from her own. His understanding was that this was temporary and that when Susie got divorced, they would marry.[36]

While Susie waffled, she made no move to get divorced. "Warren and I don't want to lose anything," she told a friend who inquired about her plans. It wasn't the money she was talking about; she had enough Berkshire stock of her own. Susie was the type of person who never subtracted from but only added to her life, and she didn't consider acting differently now.

Meanwhile, she phoned Astrid Menks at the French Café over and over. "Have you called him yet? Have you called him yet?"[37]

Susie knew her target well. Born in West Germany in 1946 as Astrid Beaté Menks after her parents walked out of Latvia after the war, Menks had emigrated to the United States at age five with her parents and five siblings on a converted, broken-down battleship. Her first sight of America as they pulled into the harbor was a huge object approaching through a fog bank—the Statue of Liberty.

The Menks family was assigned to sponsors in Verdell, Nebraska, where they lived on a farm with a potbellied stove and no electricity or indoor plumbing. When Astrid was six, the family moved to Omaha. Shortly afterward, when their mother was diagnosed with breast cancer, Astrid and her two younger brothers entered the Immanuel Deaconess Institute of Omaha, an all-purpose facility operated by Lutheran sisters. Her father, who spoke little English, worked as a maintenance man on the grounds while the children lived at the orphanage.

Astrid's mother died in 1954. When Astrid was thirteen, she was sent to a succession of three foster homes. "I can't say I had wonderful experiences in foster care," she says. "I felt more secure at the children's home."

After high school, Menks attended the University of Nebraska, until she ran out of money. For a while she worked at Mutual of Omaha and as a buyer and manager for a women's clothing store, although she dressed herself in thrift-store finds. Eventually she wound up working as a garde-manger in restaurants, slicing fifty pounds of zucchini and preparing cold foods. She lived in a little apartment downtown in the Old Market close to work, which was convenient because the rusted-out floor of her Chevy Vega had holes through to the street.[38]

She was always broke but knew everybody in the perpetually gentrifying warehouse district, and was one of a restaurant crowd that would help organize the area's would-be artists, stray singles, and gay men to put on a meal or a holiday feast. Small-boned, fair-skinned with ice-blonde hair and refined features, Astrid had a Nordic beauty with a subtle hard-knocks edge to it. At times she looked even younger than her thirty-one years. She always made light of her life struggles, but when Susie Buffett got to know her, Astrid was depressed, empty, and unfulfilled. Nonetheless, when it came to caretaking people in need,[39] she could out-Susie Susie any day.

Faced with all this badgering about calling Warren, Menks wasn't exactly sure what Susie intended, so she was terrified. But finally she made the call.[40] Arriving at the door to cook a homemade meal, she found a cave filled with books, newspapers, and annual reports. Warren, who was incapable of functioning without female companionship, was desperate for affection; he had been trying to fill the void by taking Dottie to the movies and spending time with Ruthie Muchemore, a divorcée and family friend. Yet he was obviously still a lonely, miserable man who had been reduced emotionally to an eleven-year-old boy. He needed feeding. His clothes were a wreck. Astrid was the least pushy woman imaginable. But—as Susie had known would happen—when faced with a problem, she knew what to do.

Warren would eventually come to explain *"whatever he did"* to make Susie leave was his *"biggest mistake"*:

"Parts of it are sort of not understandable. It was definitely ninety-five percent my fault—no question about that. It may even have been ninety-nine percent. I just wasn't attuned enough to her, and she'd always been perfectly attuned to me. It had always been all in my direction, almost. You know, my job was getting more interesting and more interesting and more interesting as I went along. When Susie

left, she felt less needed than I should have made her feel. Your spouse starts coming second. She kept me together for a lot of years, and she contributed ninety percent to raising the kids. Although, strangely enough, I think I had about as much influence. It just wasn't proportional to the time spent. And then she lost her job, in effect, when the kids were raised.

"*In a sense, it was time for her to do what she liked to do. She did a lot of volunteer things along the way, but in the end, that never really works that well. She didn't want to be Mrs. Big the way a lot of wives of prominent guys in town do. She didn't like being a prominent woman because she's the wife of a prominent guy. She loves connecting with people, and everybody connects with her.*

"*She loved me, and she still loves me, and we have an incredible relationship. But still . . . it shouldn't have happened. And it's totally my fault.*"

No matter how huge the wound or its reasons, as each day passed Warren discovered that he was still alive. And so eventually he fell back on the one role that suited him best: the teacher, the preacher. As long as he had his brains and his reputation, people would listen to him.

In the winter of 1978, Buffett turned with renewed intensity to writing his annual letter. The previous letter had been a brief report on how the businesses were doing. Now he started drafting lessons on how managements' performance should be measured, why short-term earnings are a poor criterion for investment decisions, a dissertation on insurance, and a paean to his friend Tom Murphy's Cap Cities. His neediness at the time was of an almost unfathomable depth. He reached out to Carol Loomis for companionship, partly on the pretext of making her the letter's official editor. She filled the hours on trips to New York as together they put a great deal of thought into how he wanted to convey these lessons to the people who had stayed with him throughout, those who had placed their faith in him: the shareholders of Berkshire Hathaway.[41]

42

Blue Ribbon

By early 1978, with encouragement from Susie, Astrid Menks was coming to Farnam Street from time to time, cooking and caretaking. Susie was calling Astrid to cheer her on, saying, "Thank you so much for taking care of him." Gradually, however, the relationship with Menks became something more.

At first, he and Astrid spent time at her tiny place down in the old warehouse district. In May she moved in with him. By the time Peter came home from Stanford that summer, she was growing tomatoes in the yard on Farnam Street and searching for Pepsi at thirty cents off a gallon. After so many months, "I never gave it a thought," Astrid says. "It just happened naturally."[1]

Meeting Astrid, Buffett's friends were taken aback at the match. She was sixteen years younger, a blue-collar girl. Nonetheless, she knew everything that Buffett didn't about haute cuisine and fine wines, shellfish forks and chef's knives. In contrast to Susie's spending habits and preference for all things modern, Astrid haunted junk shops looking for bargain antiques. So parsimonious was Astrid that she made Buffett look like a wastrel. Her interests—cooking, gardening—were narrow compared to Susie's constantly expanding and evolving tastes. Although modest, Astrid had a blunt-spoken, provocative wit that bore no resemblance to Susie's sly sense of humor; Astrid's down-to-earth manner was as unlike Kay Graham's patrician refinement as could possibly be.

Their differences magnified Susie's shock. This wasn't what she had had in mind when she stressed to her husband that they *both* had needs. To her it seemed impossible that Warren could need a relationship with anyone else. But it might have been predicted. Warren had searched his whole life for the perfect Daisy

Mae, and whatever he wanted, Astrid did: buy the Pepsi, do the laundry, take care of the house, give him head rubs, cook the meals, answer the telephone, and provide all the companionship he needed. Astrid never told him what to do and asked for nothing in return except to be with him. Susie had fled Omaha partly to escape this endless well of neediness. As she adjusted to the shock, she came to accept the relationship, which did make her new life easier. But she was possessive by nature. No matter how she divided her own attention, she did not want Warren to divide his. And thus it was Susie's expectations—not Warren's—that came to define all of their roles.

The pieces of Buffett's life began to come back together into some sort of coherent whole. But he had been shocked into realizing the truth of Susie's insistence that sitting in a room making money was no way to spend a life; he began to see what he had missed. While he was friendly enough with his kids, he hadn't really gotten to know them. The reality behind the jokes ("Who is that? That's your son."[2]) meant that he would spend the next few decades trying to repair these relationships. Much of the damage could not be undone. At age forty-seven, he was just beginning to take stock of his losses.[3]

Warren, who placed a high value on honesty, was perfectly open about living with Astrid. Everybody knew (except Doc Thompson). Both Susie and Astrid remained closemouthed, saying merely that they liked each other. Warren made only one public statement: *"If you knew the people involved, you'd see that it suited all of us quite well."* That was true, as far as it went. Oddly, the situation resembled the life of Warren's idol, Ben Graham.

In the mid-1960s, Graham had proposed a novel arrangement to his wife, Estey, in which he would live half the year with his deceased son Newton's former girlfriend, Marie Louise Amingues, or Malou—ML, as she was called by the family—and half with Estey. But Estey had her limits, and had reached them. Ever since she said no, the Grahams had been separated but they never divorced. Ben felt perfectly friendly toward Estey, and ML was content to live without marriage.[4]

Buffett was not trying to emulate Graham; he did not want two wives. At first it was a real strain for him to explain the relationships. Much later he would describe it this way: *"Susie put me together, and Astrid keeps me together. They both need to give, and I'm a great receiver, so it works for them."*[5] Explanations like this and statements that the arrangement suited all of them glided past the fundamental inequality of all love triangles.

The imbalance of this particular triangle was multiplied because in fact it involved two triangles—but only one of them knew that. In a state of ignorance, Warren thought of Susie as the one who had been wronged. He tried to square things by placating her in private and showering her with lavish attentiveness in public, which left Astrid exposed and vulnerable. In a similar state of ignorance, Astrid—who practically worshipped Susie—accepted that Warren would never marry her, ceded Susie the turf of all social and business events outside Omaha, and unhappily tolerated being called Buffett's housekeeper and mistress so that his marriage to Susie would appear as intact as possible. Buffett would come to rationalize this: *"Astrid knows where she fits with me. She knows she's needed. That's not a bad place to be."* And her role, however narrowly defined, did give Astrid a security that she had always lacked.

It had taken a literal change in geography for Susie to maintain her aura of the selfless Mrs. Warren Buffett while simultaneously seeking fulfillment in a life completely outside that role. Yet it was Warren who looked as though he were getting the best of it, even though the new relationship didn't compensate for his loss. He couldn't defend himself against the impression that he had driven his wife to move out through his relationship with Katharine Graham or—when people got the time line wrong—his relationship with Astrid.

He wanted desperately to hold the remaining pieces together, and would try for the rest of Susie's life to make up for what he had done. But of course that didn't mean he would stop seeing Kay. Buffett invited Graham to Omaha to visit the Strategic Air Command, probably as a pretext to introduce her to Astrid. On meeting an attractive woman like Astrid, Buffett says, *"Kay's first thought would be how to get her out of the room."*

Buffett took them to dinner with Stan Lipsey at the Omaha Club. Kay carried on a spirited conversation with Warren; her friend Meg Greenfield, editorial page editor of the *Post,* who had come along, and Stan occasionally joined in. The conversation left Astrid, who was not the type to put herself forward, entirely on her own. Except for ordering, she sat in silence for the entire meal. Buffett did nothing to help. A couple of dozen people at a huge table nearby carried on with a raucous birthday celebration, then started doing the Chicken Dance. Ever Miss Proper, Graham sat staring with a "priceless" look on her face.[6] From then on, Buffett almost always saw Graham outside of Omaha. When she called the house and Astrid answered the phone, Kay had nothing to say.[7] She handled the situation mostly by acting as if she believed that Astrid didn't exist.

Susie and Astrid were on a wholly different footing; Astrid even went to San Francisco to visit Susie. Susie was grateful to Astrid for making her life easier, as long as Astrid accepted the limited public role that Susie had defined for her. Moving to San Francisco had been difficult enough because she had had to leave behind so many friends and causes she cared about. Her departure had left shock waves in its wake. Local civic organizations regrouped, but felt a huge hole had been ripped from their center. Her friends and her hangers-on had coped in varying ways. A few felt abandoned, others simply missed her. Some began going back and forth to San Francisco, considering it a sort of second home. A couple of them even followed her to San Francisco and relocated there.[8]

To many of the Buffetts' friends, the explanation that Susie needed to live in San Francisco because it offered her a richer palette that she couldn't find in Omaha conveyed a vague impression of time spent visiting art galleries, jazz clubs, and the symphony. But by the late 1970s, San Francisco was not the Paris of America. A wave of returning war veterans had washed up on the Bay Area's shores, many of them injured physically, mentally, and spiritually. Those still drawn to San Francisco for its hedonism stepped through a growing mass of homeless on the streets. The gays had burst from the closet earlier in the decade, making San Francisco the de facto capital for an era of gay-bashing.

Among the first of Susie's new friends were a gay couple. She added others—musicians, artists, people she met in stores, at church, while getting her nails done, at the theater. She soon had a large circle, many if not most of whom were gay men. The rebel in Susie blossomed and the former hostess of charity luncheons now threw parties that felt like being backstage at a rock concert. But, true to form, she also took up a cause, once again defying convention. As she worked the soup kitchen lines, she became the accepting mother that many of her gay friends had never had.

The part of her life that Warren still controlled was the money. She had plenty of Berkshire stock, but under the deal they had worked out, she wasn't to sell a share. She fell in love with a Marc Chagall painting and wanted to buy it for her tiny new apartment. But she told a friend that she couldn't do it. "It would ruin everything," she said. Warren was equally clear: "I don't want you selling Berkshire shares." He still covered all her expenses. Gladys monitored her spending and paid all her bills.

Similarly, it was Warren whom Susie got to lend her friend Charles Washington $24,900. He was an Omaha activist whom she had championed through thick and thin. Buffett thought the loan was a terrible idea, and probably wouldn't have agreed to it were he not now so eager to please his wife. Sure enough, seven months later, Washington missed a couple of payments. Rarely did anything pierce Buffett's pleasant demeanor, but if he felt someone was trying to cheat him out of money, his eyes would flash pain and rage and revenge all at once. Within seconds, the emotion would subside while he considered a businesslike response. This time, he promptly filed suit against Washington and won a judgment of $24,450.

The Washington episode symbolized the reality of Warren and Susie's new relationship; if Susie was to keep all her stock, his grip on the checkbook had to loosen. Warren gave her an allowance, besides covering all her bills: This was her giveaway budget. When the children had needs, she took care of expenses that Warren wouldn't. Howie had sold some of his Berkshire stock to build a tree house for him and Marcia to live in. They were struggling with their finances as well as their marriage. "It's just terrible that Warren won't pay for it," Susie grumbled. "He was going to let the ceiling fall in. He was going to let them lose the house." But this was part of their game: Warren knew that Susie would take care of it for them, as she had taken care of Little Sooz when she was unhappy in her marriage, as she always took care of everything.

Everything, that is, except the money. Making that was Warren's job, and all these changes and complexities and mounting bills had come at a time when the family fortunes were declining. Just as Susie was leaving for San Francisco, Warren had been dragged into court in Buffalo, New York, for a costly battle between two newspapers. Normally he was competitive enough to roll up his sleeves and relish something like this. But now, since he was facing a personal crisis, it became an absorbing episode that helped shut out the rest and blunted the pain. The *Buffalo Evening News* drama would be a protracted battle, one that would threaten Blue Chip's value and rank among the most unpleasant of his career. It bore a vivid resemblance to the conflict he had faced in Beatrice many years before, one he had sworn to himself never to repeat.

In the spring of 1977, he and Munger had finally bought the daily newspaper for which they had been searching these many years. At $35.5 million this was their biggest purchase ever.[9] Rusting, icebound Buffalo wasn't the growing one-newspaper town of their dreams, but it was still a good place to own a newspaper. Buffalo's citizens left for their factory jobs before dawn and read the paper in the evenings. The *Buffalo Evening News* dominated its nearest competitor, the *Courier-Express,* which was weak financially. Buffett had developed a well-founded theory of competition in the newspaper industry.

"Kay was always saying how competition made them better and all that stuff. I

said, 'Lookit. The economics in the business is inevitably leading to one newspaper in a town. Survival of the fattest is what I call it. And you win. There is no second place. There's no red ribbon. In the end, there isn't going to be any competition because that isn't the way it works.' "

The *Courier-Express*'s staff and publisher had also figured out that there was no red ribbon in newspapers. By 1977, the number of cities in the United States that had two major newspapers was down to not quite fifty, from seven hundred in 1920. On weekdays, the *Evening News* sold twice as many papers as the *Courier-Express*. The *Courier-Express* clung to survival through having the only Sunday paper in town.

The *Evening News* had been offered to the *Washington Post*, which had turned it down. Kay Graham could not stomach another paper with a strong labor union. Buffett was not afraid of that. He and Munger told the unions that if they went on an extended strike, the paper would fold. The unions seemed to understand.

Buffett and Munger's empire now had assets of over half a billion dollars,[10] and controlled more than half of Berkshire Hathaway and sixty-five percent of Blue Chip. These two companies owned National Indemnity, the Rockford Bank, See's, Wesco, ten percent of the *Washington Post*, a quarter of Pinkerton's detective agency, fifteen percent of GEICO, and a bushel of other stocks—and finally the daily city newspaper he had sought for so long.[11]

Murray Light, the managing editor of the *Evening News*, quickly discussed a plan with Buffett to start a weekend edition, a plan that the imperious former owner, the aristocratic heiress Kate Robinson Butler, had never liked. The late Mrs. Butler, a diminutive tyrant with bouffant white hair, had growled at her employees, pounded her fist on the leather surface of her imported French desk, and seen no need to change with the times.[12]

The *News*'s publisher, Henry Urban, had gotten on well with Mrs. Butler, a large part of his job being to calm her on the many occasions when she took issue with the paper's editorials. Mrs. Butler's focus was not on profits, and neither was Urban's. The *News* was paying ten percent more for newsprint than other papers just across the bridge in Canada paid. Buffett immediately negotiated $1.2 million savings in shipping costs.

But lower shipping costs alone would not cure the *Evening News*'s blues. Buffalo's newspapers existed in an odd sort of equilibrium. One controlled weekdays, another weekends.[13] Buffett and Munger agreed with Murray Light that the *News* had no choice but to extend its weekday advantage by expanding.[14]

"We had to do what we did if we were going to compete effectively," says Munger. "One side or the other was going to win."

Two weeks before the *Evening News* launched its new Sunday edition, the *Courier-Express* filed suit on grounds of antitrust, saying the *News*'s plan to give away free papers on Sunday for five weeks, then to sell at a discount, amounted to an illegal monopoly that was trying to run it out of business.[15] The *Courier-Express*'s lawyer, Frederick Furth, hit upon an ingenious strategy to spin Buffett's views about no red ribbons into a story about monopolists from out of town.

The *Courier-Express* launched an all-out public-relations war, portraying itself as a tiny neighborhood David fighting ruthless Goliaths from out of state. This message found eager ears in Buffalo, where jobs fell like rust flakes from the once-proud city's oxidizing employment rolls.

No sooner had Buffett been released from the hell of the Wesco investigation than he found himself embroiled in another bitter legal fight, one that would require his presence in the frigid, unfriendly locale of Buffalo, New York.

The *News* began to drain Blue Chip's coffers. Buffett's lawyer on this case, Ron Olson,[16] filed an affidavit that spoke of his client's love of newspapers beginning with his inky-fingered childhood, and his role in the *Sun*'s Pulitzer Prize. Fortune favored the *Courier-Express* in the assignment of federal judge Charles Brieant of the Southern District of New York. The *Courier-Express*'s lawyer, Furth, accused Buffett of having discussed whether the *News* would put the *Courier-Express* out of business, which Buffett denied. Furth approached the witness stand waving a copy of a recent, glowing *Wall Street Journal* profile of Buffett. His growing fame was about to be used against him as a weapon for the first time.[17] Buffett had told the reporter how glad he was to be out of money management, his ego no longer on the line. But, in fact, with his newly heightened profile, his ego was now more on the line than ever before. In this story, his friend Sandy Gottesman had been quoted by the reporter as saying, "Warren likens owning a monopoly or market-dominant newspaper to owning an unregulated toll bridge. You have relative freedom to increase rates when and as much as you want."[18]

Had he said this? Furth demanded in court.

No, well, Buffett responded, "whether it is like a toll bridge I don't remember, but it is a great business. It may be better than a toll bridge in Fremont, Nebraska. I know a lot of honest people, but when they start giving quotes they don't necessarily get them—"

Furth bore down. Did he believe it or not?

"I won't quarrel with that characterization.... I would like to own one.... I have said in an inflationary world that a toll bridge would be a great thing to own if it was unregulated."

"Why?" asked Furth.

Buffett looked at the judge, to whom he was trying to teach economics. "Because you have laid out the capital costs. You build the bridge in old dollars, and when there is inflation, you don't have to keep replacing it—a bridge you build only once."

"And you used the term 'unregulated' so that you can raise prices; is that right?"

"That is true."[19]

Buffett now hung twisting in a net of his own weaving. A toll bridge, the Douglas Street Bridge over the Missouri River, was, in fact, a prominent feature of his youth.[20] During Buffett's childhood, Omaha had been torn for more than a decade over how to liberate the only route to Iowa from the toll-taker's grasp. He and Munger later *tried* to buy the Detroit International Bridge Company, which owned the bridge that connected Detroit and Windsor, Ontario, but wound up with only twenty-four percent of the company.[21]

"It was one hell of a bridge. A thousand square feet, and it made more money ... I was terribly disappointed when we didn't get it. Charlie kept telling me how well off we were that we didn't get it. Because, he said, what could be worse for your image than a guy who raised the prices on a toll bridge?"

Indeed.

"The judge didn't like me. For one reason or another, he just didn't like me. He didn't like our lawyers either. Most people like Ron Olson, but the judge did not like Ron."

Judge Brieant's ruling on a preliminary injunction, which was issued in November 1977, said that the *Evening News* was perfectly within its rights to start a Sunday paper and it was in the public interest that it should do so. But Brieant, apparently taken with Furth's exploitation of the toll-bridge theme, took off with it on a flight to the land of metaphor, lamenting that the "readers and advertisers of Greater Buffalo [might] conclude that they can get along with only one newspaper as their unregulated toll bridge to the events of the outside world."[22] He deemed the *News*'s plan predatory and hamstrung its ability to promote the new edition. The *Courier-Express* fired a prepared publishing barrage crowing about its victory over an out-of-town bully that was trying to drive a small-fry local business into the ground. The *Evening News* could say nothing in response.

"Now we were going to lose or win, and we had a judge who didn't like us, and we were operating with our hands tied and under threat of contempt."

Five weeks later, advertisers had rallied behind the *Courier-Express*, and the new Sunday edition of the *News* could boast of only a quarter of the *Courier-Express*'s ad lineage.[23] The *Evening News* swung from a modest profit to a whopping $1.4 million loss.[24] Buffett was chilled by the news. No business he had ever owned had lost so much money so fast.

On a miserable, rain-driven day the week before Christmas 1977, Judge Brieant called the court into session for the beginning of a trial that would determine the terms of a final injunction. Buffett had spent the latter part of the fall sleepless and in tears, trying to digest what it meant that Susie was gone and yet not really leaving him. His idea of a distraction from his personal woes had been to cling like a junebug to Carol Loomis, Astrid, and Kay Graham in turn as he flew back and forth between New York, Omaha, and Washington. Certainly he had not wanted a distraction like this. The trial went into recess as he flew to Emerald Bay for the annual holiday family gathering, the first under the new arrangement with Susie, during which she would continue to reassure him that their lives would go on much as before. As soon as the Buffetts' New Year's Day party was over, Warren and Susie went their separate ways, Judge Brieant reconvened the litigants, and Olson and Munger began calling Buffett with updates on the trial as he returned to work in Omaha.

Judge Brieant's final opinion, issued in July 1978, a masterpiece of judicial unrestraint carrying the subtitle "Mr. Buffett Comes to Buffalo," kept in place restrictions against the *Evening News.* Munger and Olson planned to appeal. Characteristically, Buffett did not want to lengthen the fight with the judge. Munger had always kidded Buffett that his management technique was to take out all the cash from a company and raise prices. If that failed, Buffett didn't have any more arrows in his quiver. This technique wouldn't solve the problems of the *Evening News.* Buffett was so beaten down and wanted so badly not to get into a confrontation with the judge that he was willing to let $35.5 million go down the drain. A remnant of his last big legal battle was only now ending: The SEC had finally, at long last, approved the merger of Berkshire and Diversified. Buffett wanted desperately to be done with lawyers, depositions, subpoenas, and fighting. *"I didn't want to appeal. I just felt it would take so damned long, it would irritate the judge, and that we had more to lose by irritating him as he enforced this injunction and as the <u>Courier</u> came up with all these furious attacks, and he could just keep extending it. I declared, We're not going to appeal because in a year or year* *and a half we'll be dead anyway. And Ron and Charlie told me I was wrong, and I was wrong."*

In the end, he decided to go along with them. *"We had to appeal. I wasn't going to give in to a set of conditions which were going to make us noncompetitive. So basically I had no choice. We don't bluff. It's not my style anyway. Over a lifetime, you'll get a reputation for either bluffing or not bluffing. And therefore, I want it to be understood that I don't do it."*

The *Buffalo Evening News* was Buffett's single largest investment, and by a wide margin. It was tying up a third of Blue Chip's capital, losing money under Judge Brieant's restrictions, and vulnerable to any strike that would weaken it further at a time when the stock market was falling and Buffett needed it to produce cash to buy stocks at the bargain-basement prices he always favored. The potential failure of the *Buffalo Evening News* risked more than setting him and Munger back their $35 million; for the man who begrudged spending $31,500 on a house because that money could ultimately turn into a million, the lost compounding potential of their investment in the newspaper made the situation much graver than it appeared superficially. So Buffett not only decided to appeal the decision, but he Tom-Sawyered Stan Lipsey, who was thinking of moving to San Francisco, into trying to turn the paper around. "What would you think about going up to Buffalo?" Buffett asked. "My heart sank," Lipsey says, "but I couldn't turn Warren down on anything."[25]

Lipsey started spending one week a month in Buffalo. On one of his weeks in Omaha, he joined Warren and Astrid to take the temperature of Buffett's current life. Warren was clearly relaxed in his new relationship. He let Astrid take them all to a drag show.[26]

By 1979, Lipsey had straightened out the paper's management, and victory was approaching in the battle of the legal briefs with the *Courier-Express*. In April 1979, nearly a year and a half after Brieant's preliminary injunction, the Second Circuit Court of Appeals unanimously reversed him, saying his opinion was "infected with legal and factual error.... Courts must be on guard against efforts of plaintiffs to use the antitrust laws to insulate themselves from the impact of competition."[27]

But the reversal of Judge Brieant's order was a victory that came almost too late. The *Courier-Express* immediately appealed the ruling, seeking to reinstate the injunction. The *News*'s lawyers wearily took up their swords to continue the ludicrous fight. The battle had cost so much in legal fees and lost advertising lineage while the *News* operated under all the judge's restrictions for the better part of two years that it was losing millions—a $5 million operating loss before tax in 1979—multiples more than Buffett or Munger had ever experienced in any of their businesses. It was going to take heroic work to make the money back.

"How about moving to Buffalo?" Buffett asked Lipsey. "I don't really want to do that," Lipsey replied. Buffett said nothing, and Lipsey continued commuting.

By mid-1979, the stock market was sunk in gloom, and orders for stocks, Buffett said, were placed "with an eyedropper."[28] The Dow had languished for a decade, bucking and stalling in snorts and gasps, like a beat-up car with a faulty carburetor. Its latest stall-out took it back down to the familiar territory of the mid-800s. Inflation galloped at double digits; and lines formed at the gas pumps. *BusinessWeek* declared "The Death of Equities," as if no one would ever buy stocks again. Investors piled into gold, diamonds, platinum, art, real estate, rare coins, mining stocks, feedlot cattle, and oil; "cash is trash" was the watchword of the day.

In *Forbes,* Buffett wrote that it was time for investors to buy stocks. "The future is *never* clear," he wrote; "you pay a very high price in the stock market for a cheery consensus. Uncertainty actually is the friend of the buyer of long-term values."[29] *He* was the buyer of long-term values—except that he had no cash. Periodically, cash had showered on Buffett since the beginning of the decade— $16 million from distributing the partnership assets, then millions more from the sale of Data Documents stock, a private investment. But he had poured it all into Berkshire Hathaway. Buffett had always paid himself only $50,000 a year, a number that he now raised to a still-modest $100,000. He borrowed some money from banks and started to invest again.

And finally, Stan Lipsey made the move Warren had been hoping for. One day in 1980 Lipsey showed up at Warren's unlocked back door in Omaha to say that his wife, Jeannie, wanted a divorce and that her lawyer was, from Stan's perspective, raising hell. Buffett reminded Lipsey of something Tom Murphy had taught him. "You can always tell them to go to hell tomorrow, Stan," he said. He invited the sparring lawyers to his office and helped mediate the end of a marriage between his friends—the second time he had done so. Not long before, Buffett had brokered peace between his friend Ed Anderson and his wife, Shirley Smith Anderson, an old friend of Warren and Susie's. He was experienced at easing his friends through difficult transitions. He began talking to Lipsey about the need to make changes in his life. Maybe it's time, Stan thought. As the conversation progressed, Buffett helped Lipsey talk himself into moving to Buffalo. "It was typical Warren. He wanted me to come up here in the worst way," but in the end, just as with people investing in the partnership, it had to be Lipsey's idea.

Lipsey went to Buffalo, and stayed. By the end of 1980, the losses had mounted to $10 million. Munger's 1980 Blue Chip annual report repeated a warning Munger had first given in the 1978 report: "If any extended strike shuts down the *Buffalo Evening News,* it will probably be forced to cease operations and liquidate."[30]

Munger's viewpoint as he wrote these words and steered Blue Chip through the legal maze of the *Buffalo Evening News* could not have been helped by the dire and dark condition of his health. For several years he had stoically tolerated growing cataracts, until they reached the point at which his eyesight was seriously impaired. When he had cataract surgery on his left eye, it resulted in an extremely rare complication called an epithelial downgrowth: A specialized type of primary body tissue from outside the eye (probably corneal cells) got inside his eye and started growing like a cancer. The pressure and destruction of the optic nerve caused severe, disabling pain.[31] When he could no longer tolerate the agony of his slowly exploding eye, Munger arranged to have it eviscerated and replaced with a glass eye. But afterward, "I was like a wounded animal for several days."[32] He could not stand up to be bathed by the nurses because he was so nauseated from the pain. He told Buffett that he wanted to die. Terrified of going through another such ordeal and facing the possibility of blindness, he decided to have the remaining cataract in his right eye scraped off without replacing the lens. Instead, he wore old-fashioned cataract glasses, thick as a jellyfish, over his "good" eye.

During Munger's ordeal, the *Buffalo Evening News*'s drivers' union—perhaps emboldened after three years with new management running the place under duress—demanded overtime for work not performed. Then in December 1980, the Teamsters, figuring that Buffett couldn't take a strike while the battle with the *Courier-Express* dragged on, walked out at six a.m. after an all-night mediation attempt failed. Working with other unions, who crossed the picket line, Lipsey, Henry Urban, and Murray Light worked feverishly to get out the evening paper. Then, at the last minute, the pressmen walked off the job, pulling the page plates off the presses as they went.

Buffett figured he was sunk. From his background in newspaper circulation, he knew that, even more than the pressmen, the tiny drivers' union—all of thirty-eight employees—had the power to shut the paper down. Other unions and volunteers could run the presses, but without the drivers to distribute the newspapers, the paper was dead. Buffett would not use nonunion replacements. *"I was not going to send our people out in December, in the dark, dropping papers in some rural area where some guy can hit them with a tire iron."*

The *Evening News* closed its doors.

Buffett told the union, *"We're going to reopen only if there is a reasonable prospect of a viable operation."*[33] That tipping point could quickly be reached.[34]

This time, the unions blinked. Within forty-eight hours, the *Evening News* was back on the streets. By then, the *News,* though still trailing on Sundays, had gained some ground and was crawling toward the lead while maintaining its weekday advantage.[35] By the end of 1981, Lipsey and Buffett had cut the losses to $1.5 million a year, half of what the *Courier-Express* was suffering.[36] In a war of "survival of the fattest," it was almost certain to win—albeit at a staggering price. The *Courier-Express* had never given up the lawsuit trying to reinstate Judge Brieant's injunction, but its owners saw another judge, the judge of the marketplace, heading with the blue ribbon toward the *Buffalo Evening News.* The *Courier-Express* now tried to sell itself to press lord Rupert Murdoch, but the unions wouldn't cave in to Murdoch's demand that they give up seniority. And with that, the *Courier-Express* laid down its last card in September 1982. Its next move was to fold.

The *Buffalo Evening News* immediately rolled out a morning edition and changed its name to the *Buffalo News.* With victory in hand, Buffett and Munger went to a meeting of employees at the Statler Hilton downtown. Somebody asked about profit sharing. "There is nothing that anybody on the third floor"—where the newsroom sat—"can do that affects profits," Buffett said. Capital took the risk and reaped the rewards. He and Munger had staked $35 million on a series of decisions. They might have lost every dime; to them went all the profits that followed. The workers got a paycheck for the time and effort they put in—no more, no less. A deal's a deal. But after everything they had all been through, the staff was stunned at his lack of empathy.

As Buffett and Munger left the office, Munger walked past publisher Henry Urban, who was "waiting for at least a small accolade," said Ron Olson. Munger was famous for getting into cabs while people were talking to him as if he did not hear them and for disappearing through doors the second he finished talking without waiting for a response. Nonetheless Urban stood open-mouthed. Buffett followed along right after Munger without looking at anyone. Nobody said thanks. Olson, following in their wake, moved around the room shaking hands in an effort to make up for it.[37]

A year later, with higher ad rates and soaring circulation, the *News* was earning $19 million pretax, more than all the previous years' losses combined. About half of that went straight to Buffett. And as the excitement ended, his attention waned. While he still spoke well of the *Buffalo News* in his annual report, his interests had moved on to the next new thing.

PART FIVE

The King of Wall Street

43

Pharaoh

F ive hundred of the grateful rich, wearing black tie and ball gowns, walked up the red carpet and into New York's swanky Metropolitan Club for Buffett's fiftieth birthday party. With Berkshire Hathaway trading at $375 a share, the Buffetts' net worth had more than doubled in the past year and a half.[1] They could easily afford to rent the place. Dotted among the Buffett Group members were semi-demi-celebrities like the actor Gary Cooper's daughter. Susie had ordered a cake shaped like a six-pack of Warren's beloved Pepsi-Cola. He had asked his old pinball partner Don Danly to bring him the balance sheet for Wilson's Coin-Operated Machine Company.[2] Buffett was beginning to gather materials from his early business efforts—treating these objects like totems and showing them to people with a slight tinge of reverence. They seemed like tangible evidence of himself, reassuring artifacts.

Susie brought her band from San Francisco and took center stage to sing verse after verse of a version of "Shuffle Off to Buffalo" on the theme of Buffett's latest caper: packing up his duffel and shuffling off to Buffalo to buy an under-valued paper.

The man himself, with eyebrows sprouting like ivy tendrils over the frames of his glasses, now looked less awkward in black tie. Buffett's hunt for things to buy had become more ambitious, free of the cigar butts and lawsuits of the decades before. The great engine of compounding worked as a servant on his behalf, at exponential speed and under the gathering approval of a public gaze. The method was the same: Estimate an investment's intrinsic value, handicap its risk, buy using margin of safety, concentrate, stay in the circle of competence, let it roll as compounding did the work. Anyone could understand these simple ideas, but even though Buffett made the process look effortless, the technique and discipline underlying it involved an enormous amount of work for him and his employees. As his business empire had expanded, from the shores of Lake Erie to the suburbs of Los Angeles, Kiewit Plaza remained at the center—a quiet but endlessly busy temple of commerce, furnished with dinged, scuffed steel-frame furniture and linoleum floors. With every new investment, there was more to do; but the number of people at headquarters barely changed. Buffett still remained behind closed doors, guarded by Gladys. The very rich Bill Scott now worked part-time and spent the rest of his days playing with his polka band. A new manager, Mike Goldberg, now augmented the headquarters staff. Verne McKenzie managed the finances. The employees rarely left their tiny offices except for the occasional conclave in the conference room, which seated only four people. No chats took place around the watercooler. As for a period of ease following the scuffle at the *Buffalo Evening News,* McKenzie put it this way: "There was never such a time."[3] Those who tested Rickershauser's Law of Thermodynamics found that the sun was indeed nice and warm, but Buffett was so focused and his mind worked at such speed that extended conversations with him left them sunburned. "My mind was so tired," said one friend. "I had to recuperate from seeing him," said another. "It was like being pounded on the head all day long," said a onetime employee.

Buffett had the energy and enthusiasm of a restless teenager; he seemed to remember every fact and figure he had ever read; he finagled people into volunteering for tough jobs, then assumed they could accomplish miracles; and while remarkably tolerant of others' quirks and flaws, he was less so of quirks and flaws that cost him money. So eager for results was he, so confident of others' skills, so unaware of how far short of his own they fell, that he chronically underestimated people's workloads. Buffett, the sun around whom everyone revolved, was oblivious to the effects of Rickershauser's Law himself.

"People tell me I put pressure on them. I never intend to. Some people like to apply pressure. I never do. It's actually the last thing I like to do. I don't think I'm ever doing it, but I've had enough people tell me that I do it that it must be true."

The managers out in the hinterlands who ran the businesses that Berkshire and Blue Chip owned were lucky because Buffett largely left them alone, his trick of management being to find obsessed perfectionists like himself who worked incessantly; then ignore them except for a "Carnegizing"—attention, admiration, and Dale Carnegie's other techniques—every now and then. Most would not have had it any other way.

The decisions Buffett had made about stocks in the 1970s were defiant bets against pessimism in the great bear market, plagued by rampant unemployment and consumer prices that rose at an intolerable fifteen percent a year. Now that bet suddenly paid off, thanks to a desperate President Carter, who had appointed a new Federal Reserve Chairman, Paul Volcker, in 1979. Volcker ratcheted up the central bank discount rate to fourteen percent to get inflation under control. In 1981, new President Ronald Reagan began to cut taxes sharply, started deregulating business—and supported Volcker despite the howls of pain his policies were causing. In late 1982, the bull market of the 1980s began its stampede as the prices of stocks started catching up with the growth in corporate earnings.[4]

Much of the money used for Buffett's late-seventies spending spree came from a bonanza of float from insurance and trading stamps. National Indemnity prospered while at Blue Chip stamp sales continued to shrink.[5]

The turnaround of the *Buffalo Evening News* meant that Buffett and Munger no longer had to debate whether Blue Chip's largest asset was worth more dead than alive. The *News* would live; it now threw off a steady stream of profits. In 1983, they finally agreed on a value for Blue Chip, and Berkshire swallowed it whole—the last step of the great untangling.[6] Buffett and Munger were now full partners for the first time—although Munger was the junior partner by miles.

Buffett made Munger, who now owned two percent of Berkshire, the company's vice chairman. Munger also now took over as president and chairman of Wesco, a wee thing compared to the now-swollen Berkshire, but Munger's own. It dangled like a tiny strand of spaghetti from the corner of Berkshire Hathaway's mouth, the only morsel that Buffett had yet failed to swallow. Wesco's shareholders eventually figured out that he would get to it someday, and inevitably they began to value Wesco's stock at a forbidding price.

Munger's influence on Buffett's thinking had always far outweighed his financial clout. The main difference between their behavior in business was that Munger on occasion would veto deals that the more easily enraptured Buffett might have struck. Their attitude toward their shareholders was identical. With the merger done, in the 1983 annual report the two men spelled out to Berkshire's shareholders a set of principles from which they would operate. They called them the "owner-oriented principles." No other management told its company's owners these things.

"Although our form is corporate, our attitude is partnership," they wrote. "We do not view the company as the ultimate owner of our business assets, but, instead, view the company as a conduit through which our shareholders own the assets."[7]

This statement—deceptively simple—amounted to a throwback to a former generation of corporate governance. The modern-day corporate chief viewed the shareholders as a nuisance, a group to be either appeased or ignored.

We don't play accounting games, Buffett and Munger said. We don't like a lot of debt. We run the business to achieve the best long-term results. All of these sounded like simple truisms—except that so few managements could honestly make all of these statements.

Incidentally, Buffett also wrote that year, "[r]egardless of price, we have no interest at all in selling any good businesses that Berkshire owns, and are very reluctant to sell sub-par businesses as long as we expect them to generate at least some cash and as long as we feel good about their managers and labor relations."[8] That was a reference to Berkshire, the textile mill.

"The textile business would make money for about ten minutes each year. We made half the men's suit linings in the country, but nobody ever went to a tailor and said, 'I'd like a pin-striped gray suit with a Hathaway lining.' A square yard of cloth that came out of our mill cost more than a square yard from somewhere else, and capitalism's frugal that way."

And yet he clung to the beleaguered mills. Thus, it had been even harder, like having a root canal without novocaine, for him to sell one of the company's most profitable businesses, the Rockford Bank. But he had had to do it; the Bank Holding Company Act required it in order for Berkshire to carry on its nonbanking interests (especially in insurance).[9] Even so, he still carried money with Gene Abegg's picture on it in his wallet afterward.

He was equally loath to lose Ben Rosner, who had finally retired from Associated Cotton Shops. Rosner's underlings had made fun of his toilet-paper-pickin' ways. Sure enough, as soon as they took charge, Associated fell into the tank. For months, Verne McKenzie slogged back and forth to New York's garment district, peddling its soggy carcass.[10] Finally, he found some buyer willing to pay half a million dollars to haul away the remains of a business that only recently had earned Berkshire as much as $2 million a year.

A few of the Berkshire companies were so self-steering that it was hard to tell the difference between a well-run business and one guided by the wind alone. At Wesco, Lou Vincenti, who resisted being managed, succeeded in concealing his Alzheimer's from Buffett and Munger for several years.

"We didn't see him that often," says Buffett, *"and he would sort of get himself*

psyched up to try and get past that. Plus, we didn't want to see it. Charlie and I loved him so much we didn't want to face it."

"Lou Vincenti was decisive, he was intelligent, and he was honest and shrewd," says Munger. "He was cranky and independent and a very good human being. And we loved him so much that even after we found out, we kept him in his job until the week that he went off to the Alzheimer's home. He liked coming in, and he wasn't doing us any harm."[11]

Buffett and Munger turned this story into a jokey parable, saying that they wanted more businesses that could be run successfully by a manager with Alzheimer's.

Buffett was sensitive to the subject of Alzheimer's. He took great pride in his powerful memory; now his mother grew forgetful. Her state of mind could be obscured by the way that Leila had always tended to live in the past, and to create her own ideal reality—her version of Buffett's bathtub memory, in which—whoosh—the plug popped up, and bad memories drained away. Warren still trembled if he had to spend time with her. The old rages still flared up occasionally, and by now, virtually every member of the family had had the experience of picking up the phone and hearing her wrath come scorching over the line. Her victims all ran for comfort to Susie.

Peter was one grandchild whom Leila had always left alone. She sometimes commented that he resembled Howard, so possibly that was why. The resemblance was only in appearance, however. Peter had dropped out of Stanford not long before graduation and married Mary Lullo, a recently divorced woman six years his senior who had four-year-old twin girls, Nicole and Erica. Peter treated them as his own daughters, they began using the name Buffett, and they became great favorites of Big Susie's. Warren had been trying to interest Peter in Berkshire for some time and sent his protégé, Susie's former tennis buddy, Dan Grossman, to talk to him about working in the business, but Peter had no interest; his future lay in music.[12] He cashed in $30,000 of his Berkshire stock to finance a recording and music production company, Independent Sound, scoring commercials out of his apartment in San Francisco with Mary as his business manager and promoter.[13]

Susie stayed close to Peter through his music, while she continued to toy with the idea of reviving her own career, working with a pair of producers, Marvin Laird and Joel Paley. At last they settled on an act that Susie would perform at Delmonico's in New York at a benefit for New York University. The act she wanted them to create would reflect her personality—a bohemian, gypsy soul and a wicked, sly sense of humor. In the end, however, she sang a conventional medley, replacing the soulful, passionate songs of 1977 with standards: "String of Pearls," "I'll Be Seeing You," "The Way You Look Tonight."

At the benefit, Warren beamed as he watched his wife work the audience. Laird and Paley realized that showing off his talented, beautiful wife made Buffett proud and happy.[14] The two producers, who referred to themselves jokingly as "musical gigolos," became part of Susie's singing life, working with her for the next few years on her music as she considered whether she could make a viable career out of it.

Susie Jr., who had divorced the surfer, moved to Washington, where Katharine Graham took an interest and arranged for her to work as an editorial assistant, first at the *New Republic* and then at *U.S. News & World Report.* In November 1983, in a huge wedding at New York's Metropolitan Club, she married again, this time to Allen Greenberg, a public-interest lawyer for Ralph Nader. Greenberg had her father's cool analytical bent and looked like someone who lived in a library. Both Susie's parents took to their new son-in-law immediately, and people remarked on how much Allen resembled Susie's father— rational, dispassionate, good at saying no. The newlyweds moved into a Washington town house but rented most of it out to other tenants and lived in a tiny apartment. By this time Susie Jr. had sold all her Berkshire stock—when it was trading for less than $1,000 per share.

Howie's first marriage, like his sister's, had not lasted. Despondent, he spoke to his father, who had told him a change of geography would do him good and suggested that he work at one of Berkshire's businesses. Attracted to California, Howie took a job at See's Candies in Los Angeles. Big Susie sent him to live with Dan Grossman, whom Buffett had installed at one of Berkshire's little insurers in Los Angeles when it ran into trouble. Howie started mopping floors and doing maintenance and worked his way up to ordering boxes, while getting into adrenaline-charged scrapes of various types. Buffett told him he had to stay at See's for two years. Howie prepared to wait it out in resignation, and moved into the house at Laguna.[15]

By chance, he was partnered in doubles tennis at Emerald Bay with Devon Morse, a sweet, unhappily married blonde with four daughters. To impress her, he shimmied up a post to change the time on a clock by the tennis court, fell off, and broke his foot. She helped him get home, then they started to talk and he learned she was trying to leave her rich husband. The marriage that eventually resulted from their relationship followed a series of Howie-type adventures;

the couple removed the children from the home of Devon's husband, a gun collector whose house was filled with hundreds of weapons. In 1982, Howie had convinced Devon to relocate to Nebraska, where they were married by a judge, with Buffett and Gladys Kaiser as witnesses.[16]

Buffett now had six step-grandchildren, and soon added a grandson when Howie and Devon had a child of their own, Howard Graham Buffett Jr., who would become known as Howie B. Buffett liked children well enough but was awkward and stiff around them and had no idea how to play with or engage a child. So he did as he had done with his own children—left them to Susie, who took up the role of grandmother with zest at family gatherings, and quickly added visits to grandchildren in Nebraska to her already extensive travels.

Buffett involved himself more actively when it came to Howie's career. At first Howie had gotten a job in real estate, but what he really wanted to be was a farmer. Since he had no capital, Buffett agreed to buy a farm, which he would rent to his son—an arrangement rather like the one he had had with his sharecropper back when he was still in high school. Howie trudged through Nebraska, looking at over a hundred farms and making offers on behalf of his father, who was determined that a farm be a cigar butt. Finally, somebody bit in Tekamah, and Buffett plunked down the necessary $300,000.[17]

Although he took Howie's rent checks, he didn't set foot on the farm. As with Susie's art gallery, he had no interest in the experience, only the money. He compared the farm, as a commodity business, to men's suit linings. *"No one goes to the supermarket to buy Howie Buffett's corn,"* he said.[18]

That Buffett tried to control his children with money yet never spent any time teaching them about money might seem odd, but it was the same story as with his employees: He felt any smart person could figure it out. He handed the kids their Berkshire stock without stressing how important it might be to them someday, explaining compounding, or mentioning that they could borrow against the stock without selling it. By now, his shareholder letters, polished to a fine sheen by Carol Loomis, had tackled most financial subjects, and he undoubtedly thought that these, along with the example of his life, served as adequate lessons for his children.

Buffett did care very much about what they did with their stock, however, because he and Berkshire were as one. To sell the stock was to sell him too. Even so, he did not want his childen to live on Easy Street because of Berkshire Hathaway. Rather, he thought the future of his children and the future of Berkshire Hathaway would ultimately be joined not through ownership of the company, but by an act of philanthropy—their stewardship of the stock in the Buffett Foundation.

Buffett expressed his feelings on the subject of inheritance and philanthropy through a tribute he wrote in the *Omaha World-Herald* upon the death of Peter Kiewit, a near-mythical figure in Omaha. Kiewit's company, Peter Kiewit Sons', Inc., was reportedly the most profitable construction company in the world.[19] Buffett and Kiewit never had business dealings, but Kiewit owned the *Omaha World-Herald* and Buffett sat on its board.

The childless, workaholic Kiewit had lived in a penthouse apartment in Kiewit Plaza, where Berkshire was headquartered, and he commuted to work by elevator. Buffett envied him this arrangement.[20] Kiewit was another Buffett prototype, a hard taskmaster and penny-pincher in the office who instilled his values through pithy little sayings. The company was his labor of love, and he was often "pleased, but never satisfied." "A reputation is like fine china," he said, "expensive to acquire, and easily broken." In making ethical decisions, therefore, "If you're not sure if something is right or wrong, consider whether you'd want it reported in the morning paper."[21] Also like Buffett, Kiewit was obsessed with managing other people's weight.

In many ways, Peter Kiewit exemplified Warren Buffett's ideas about how a life should be lived. When Kiewit died, Buffett's tribute not only honored the man, it expressed—as much as anything that Buffett ever wrote—how he would like to be remembered himself. [22]

"Starting from scratch," he wrote, Kiewit "built one of the great construction companies of the world.... Although not the largest, it may well be the most profitable business of its type in the country, an achievement possible only because Kiewit was able to transmit, throughout an organization of thousands of employees, an unremitting insistence on excellence and efficiency.

"Kiewit was overwhelmingly a producer, not a consumer," he went on. "Profits went to build the capacity of the organization, not to provide opulence to the owner.

"In essence, one who spends less than he earns is accumulating 'claim checks' for future use. At some later date he may reverse the procedure and consume more than he earns by cashing some of the accumulated claim checks. Or he may pass them on to others—either during his lifetime by gifts, or upon his death by bequest."

William Randolph Hearst, Buffett wrote, used up many of his claim checks by building and maintaining his castle in San Simeon. He arranged to have ice hauled daily to the bears in his private zoo, much the way pharaohs used their claim checks to build the pyramids. Buffett had meditated on the economics of the pyramids. If he hired a thousand people to build a pyramid dedicated to himself, he says: *"It would all go into the economy. Every dime. And a lot of forms of giving and spending are just a form of that. It's crazy, and it's probably somewhat morally wrong too. But there are people who would think it's great that you're giving employment to the people who are tugging the slabs for the pyramid. And they're making a mistake. It isn't productive. They're thinking in terms of input, not output.*

"If you want to build pyramids to yourself, and take a lot of resources out of society, you ought to pay like hell for it. You ought to pay a perfectly appropriate tax. I would force you to give back a huge chunk to society, so that hospitals get built and kids get educated too."

Instead, he noted in this article, some who earned the claim checks passed them along to their heirs, enabling hundreds of descendants to *"consume far more than they personally have produced; in effect, their whole lifetimes have been spent at the withdrawal window of the bank of societal resources."* Buffett found the results ironic.

"I love it," he says, *"when I'm around the country club, and I hear people talk about the debilitating aspects of a welfare cycle, where some woman had a child at seventeen, and she gets food stamps, and we're perpetuating a cycle of dependency. And these same people are leaving their kids a lifetime supply of food stamps and beyond. But instead of having a welfare officer, they have a trust fund officer. And instead of having food stamps, they have stocks and bonds that pay dividends."*

Peter Kiewit, he wrote, "made major deposits in society's bank...but his withdrawals have been few." He left about five percent of his wealth to his family. The rest went to a charitable foundation.

Among philanthropists, Buffett also admired Andrew Carnegie and John D. Rockefeller as original thinkers. Carnegie had built public libraries in poor neighborhoods all across the United States. The Carnegie Foundation had sent Abraham Flexner to study medical education in the United States.[23] After his 1910 paper revealed the shocking condition of medical schools, Flexner convinced the Rockefeller Foundation to donate enough money to revolutionize medical education. Rockefeller also wanted to tackle problems that lacked a natural funding constituency. He found that poor black colleges, lacking rich alumni, had no way to improve themselves. *"In effect, John D. Rockefeller became their alumnus,"* Buffett says. *"He tackled problems without concern of which among them was most popular, and he backed them up big-time."*

At this point, the Buffett Foundation had a token $725,000 and gave away less than $40,000 a year, nearly all to education.[24] Susie ran the Buffett Foundation, which reflected their joint philosophy that money should go back to society. If she'd had access to them, Susie would have given away large amounts quickly. But Buffett was in no rush. He felt that by allowing the money to compound over time, there would be more to give away in the end—after he was gone. Certainly by 1983 he had a good argument in favor of this idea. Between 1978 and the end of 1983, the Buffetts' net worth had increased by a stunning amount, from $89 million to $680 million.

As he became richer, requests for money from friends, strangers, and charities poured in to Kiewit Plaza. Some were heartfelt pleas from the genuinely needy. Other people seemed to feel entitled to his money. To all, the answer was the same: If I did it for you, I would have to do it for everybody. Some of his friends agreed with him, while others were perplexed that a man so generous with his time, advice, and wisdom was such a tightwad with his cash. It's not like it would kill him to peel off a few bucks, they said. Why didn't he find the *joy* in giving?

But as long as Buffett was still amassing the snowball, promising to give it all away after he died was like the "jam tomorrow" of *Alice in Wonderland*'s White Queen. "After he died" was the same as never; another hedge against mortality, one of Buffett's great preoccupations. The "White Queen" form of denial was self-reinforcing in a peculiar way. By now, the Buffetts had at least nine friends or relatives who had, or whose family members had, attempted or committed suicide. Most recently, one of his friends' sons had driven his car off a cliff on Christmas Eve. Then, Rick Guerin's wife, Ann, had shot and killed herself a few days before their son's eighth birthday. Buffett had a queasy preoccupation with suicide that was perfectly reasonable under the circumstances. Yet he himself was determined to live as long as possible—and to make money until the very end.

As his wealth grew, Buffett's often articulated and unwavering determination to keep making money at a furious rate while withholding it from his family and his foundation finally sparked a rebellion among his friends. Rick Guerin had written to Joe Rosenfield about the possibility of Buffett becoming the world's richest man: "What will Warren do when he becomes No. 1 sled dog and sees that there's more to the world than hair and a small target? (He thinks it's a bull's-eye, but we know better.)"[25]

When the Buffett Group met in Lyford Cay, Bahamas, between the snorkeling and deep-sea fishing George Gillespie sparked a hot debate by organizing a talk on "The Children (and Charity) Will Have to Wait." Years earlier Buffett had said he gave his kids a few thousand dollars for Christmas each year and told them to expect half a million dollars when he died.[26] That, he thought, was "enough money so that they would feel they could do anything, but not so much that they could do nothing."[27] This phrase would become one of his mantras, repeated over the years. "Warren, that's *wrong*," said Larry Tisch, one of his former partners. "If they aren't spoiled by age twelve, they won't be spoiled."[28] Kay Graham, tears streaming down her face, asked, Don't you *love* your children, Warren?

Prompted by Carol Loomis, *Fortune* took up the issue in a cover story: "Should You Leave It All to the Children?" Family comes first, many people said. "My kids are going to carve out their own place in the world and they know that I'm for them, whatever they want to do," Buffett said. But "just because they came out of the right womb," setting them up with a trust fund—which he considered "a lifetime supply of food stamps"—could be "harmful" and an "antisocial act."[29]

Nevertheless, Buffett had made a decision that demonstrated newfound—if slight—flexibility. In 1981, he set up an innovative program in which Berkshire Hathaway would contribute $2 per share to a charity of the shareholder's choice. Berkshire did not pay a dividend, but this program allowed the shareholders to direct how the company spent its charitable dollars rather than letting top management donate to its pet causes. The program was minuscule, but for Buffett to do it at all was a loosening of the fist. And the shareholders loved it. The participation rate was always close to one hundred percent.

To Buffett, the collector of information, the contributions program also turned out to be a tiny gold mine. It gave him an insight into the philanthropic interests of each shareholder, which he could never have gotten any other way. Collecting this information had no purpose whatsoever—even less than collecting nuns' fingerprints. Buffett, however, was insatiably curious and had a deep interest in knowing about his shareholders as individuals, as if they were part of an extended family, which was how he thought of them.

At fifty-three, Buffett—who had already "retired" twice—was thinking through issues of philanthropy and inheritance. The subject that visibly unnerved him was retirement. He joked about working after he was dead and made a point of highlighting elderly managers like Gene Abegg and Ben Rosner. But now they had retired, and Lou Vincenti had Alzheimer's. Perhaps it was not surprising, therefore, that Warren's next move would be to strike a deal with an eighty-nine-year-old woman, one who would outlast anyone he had ever met.

44

Rose

Omaha · 1983

Rose Gorelick Blumkin came to Omaha from the tiny village of Shchedrin, in the region of Minsk. Born in 1893, she and her seven brothers slept on straw on the bare floor of a two-room log house because her rabbi father couldn't afford to buy them a mattress.

"I dreamed all my life, since I was six years old," she said. "The first dream of mine was to go to America.

"In Russia, they used to have pogroms against the Jews. They'd cut up the pregnant women and take out the kids. . . . I was six years old when I found out about that. I said, I'm going to America when I grow up."[1]

At thirteen, Rose walked barefoot for eighteen miles to the nearest train station to save the leather soles of her brand-new shoes. She hid under a train seat for three hundred miles to save her money, until she reached the closest town, Gomel. There she knocked on twenty-six doors until the owner of a dry-goods store responded to her proposition. "I'm not a beggar," the four-foot-ten-inch girl said. "I've got four cents in my pocket. Let me sleep in your house and I'll show you how good I am." The next morning, "I waited on customer. I rolled out the material and I added it up before anybody picked up a pencil. And at twelve o'clock he asked me if I was going to stay."[2]

By age sixteen, she was a manager, supervising six married men. "Don't worry about the men, Mamma!" she wrote her mother. "They all mind me!"[3] Four years later she married Isadore Blumkin, a shoe salesman in Gomel.[4] That same year, World War I broke out, vigilantes ran amok in Russia, and Rose made up her mind. She sent her husband to America and started saving to go herself.

Two years later, the czarist monk Rasputin was killed by revolutionaries in December 1916. Fearing the chaos that would ensue, Rose began her journey to America two weeks later, boarding the Trans-Siberian Railway on a train headed for China.

After seven days a Russian guard stopped her at the border town of Zabaykai'sk. She told the man she was buying leather for the army and promised him a bottle of slivovitz on her return. Either naive or lenient, he let her through the border. She rode through Manchuria to Tientsin, China, on another train. By then Rose had journeyed over nine thousand miles across almost the entire continent of Asia.[5] From Tientsin she took a boat to Yokohama, Japan. There she found the *Ava Maru,* a cargo boat carrying peanuts. As the *Ava Maru* crossed the Pacific on its way to Seattle, she was so sick for most of the six-week journey that she couldn't eat.[6]

Landing in Seattle after almost three months of travel with a face swollen from illness, Rose was met at the dock by the Hebrew Immigrant Aid Society. The HIAS put a tag around her neck with her name and "Ft. Dodge, Iowa," and sent her to join her husband, who was working there as a junk peddler. Rose got pregnant right away and gave birth to a daughter, Frances. She didn't know a word of English.

Two years later, she still spoke hardly any English. Feeling isolated, the Blumkins decided they had to live in a place where Rose could converse in Russian and Yiddish, so they moved to Omaha, a town filled with 32,000 immigrants drawn by the railroads and packinghouses.[7]

Isadore rented a pawnshop. "You never hear of a pawnshop going broke," he said.[8] Rose had three more children, Louis, Cynthia, and Sylvia. Sending fifty dollars at a time back to Russia, she brought ten of her relatives to America. Unlike her husband, she still didn't speak much English. "I was too dumb," she said. "They couldn't drill it in me with a nail. The kids teached me. When my Frances started kindergarten, she says, 'I'll show you what an apple is, what a tablecloth, what a knife.' "[9] But the store struggled and almost did go broke during the Depression. Then Rose took charge. I know what to do, undersell the big shots, she told her husband. "You buy an item for three dollars and sell it for $3.30. Ten percent over cost!" When the old-fashioned suits they carried weren't selling, Rose handed out ten thousand circulars all over Omaha, offering to outfit a man for five dollars—underwear, suit, tie, shoes, and straw hat. They took in $800 in a single day, more than they had made the entire year before.[10] The store branched into jewelry, fur coats, and furniture. Rose drove the department stores crazy when she started underselling them on new fur coats on consignment.[11] But she had a philosophy: "It's better to have them hate you than to feel sorry for you."

Soon customers started asking her for more furniture. She saw that, unlike pawnbroking, selling furniture was a "happy business," so in 1937 she borrowed $500 from a brother to open a store called Blumkin's in a basement near her husband's pawnshop. But the furniture wholesalers didn't want her as a customer, because their dealers complained that she was underselling them. So Rose went to Chicago, found one sympathetic man, and ordered $2,000 worth of merchandise from him on thirty days' credit. The time came due and she was short, so she sold her own house furnishings cheap to pay off the debt. "When my kids came home, they cried like somebody will die," she recalled. "Why I took away the beds and the refrigerator? The whole house, an empty house? I told them, they were so nice to me I can't stand it not to keep my promise."[12] That night she took a couple of mattresses from the store for the family to sleep on. "The next day I brought in a refrigerator and stove," she said, "and the kids quit crying."[13]

Louie worked in the store after school, and became an all-American diver at Tech High while delivering sofas until midnight. His mother by now had established the Nebraska Furniture Mart and moved to larger quarters. In a side business, she sold and rented out Browning automatic shotguns during hunting season. Louie's favorite job was testing the guns by firing them into cinder blocks in the family's basement.[14]

Louie dropped out of college to enlist in the service during World War II. During the war, he and his mother wrote each other every day. Rose was discouraged, and he urged her not to quit.[15] Because the big wholesalers refused to sell to the Nebraska Furniture Mart, Rose had become a furniture "bootlegger," traveling on trains all over the Midwest to buy overstock merchandise at five percent over wholesale from stores like Macy's and Marshall Field's. "The more [the wholesalers] boycotted me, the harder I worked," she said.[16] She developed a lasting hatred of big shots. Her slogan was "Sell cheap and tell the truth, don't cheat nobody, and don't take no kickbacks."[17]

Louie won a Purple Heart at the Battle of the Bulge. After the war, he came straight home to Omaha in 1946 and went back to work. He learned everything about merchandising: buying, pricing, inventories, accounting, delivery, display. To Rose, nobody was as good as Louie. Ruthless with her employees, she screamed at them at the top of her lungs: "You worthless golem! You dummy!" But after his mother fired them, Louie would hire them back.

Four years later, the store was prospering, but then the Korean War began, and sales started to sink. Rose decided to give the business a boost by adding carpet to her line. She went to Marshall Field's in Chicago and told them she was buying carpet for an apartment building; they sold her three thousand yards of Mohawk carpet for $3.00 a yard. She retailed it for $3.95, half the standard price, although the fact that she had lied to Marshall Field's seemed to bother her for years afterward.[18]

Rose had managed to launch a successful carpet business by giving her customers a better price than the other carpet dealers. But carpet maker Mohawk filed a lawsuit to enforce their minimum-pricing policies—under which manufacturers required all their retailers to charge a minimum price—and sent three lawyers to court. Rose showed up alone. "I say to the judge, 'I don't have any money for a lawyer because nobody would sell to me. Judge, I sell everything ten percent above cost, what's wrong? I don't rob my customers."[19] The trial lasted only an hour before the judge threw the case out. The next day, he went out to the Furniture Mart and bought $1,400 worth of carpet.

But selling carpet wasn't enough; Rose still couldn't pay her suppliers. Finally an Omaha banker loaned her $50,000 for ninety days; Rose couldn't sleep worrying about how she was going to pay it back. She hit upon the idea of renting the Omaha City Auditorium and cramming it with sofas and dinettes and coffee tables and TV sets. Master merchandisers, she and Louie took out an ad in the paper that played on wartime scarcity.

> This is It! The Sale of Sales! . . . We can't eat 'em! We must sell 'em! We've been shipped so much merchandise this past 60 days, we have no warehouse room.[20]

The Furniture Mart sold a quarter of a million dollars' worth of furniture in three days. Omaha now knew that Rose Blumkin and the Furniture Mart meant discount furniture, and "From that day, I never owed anybody a penny," she said.[21]

That same year, Isadore died of a heart attack. Rose and Louie kept on going. Gradually, "Mrs. B" was becoming a name that everybody knew in Omaha. People came into the store at every stage of their lives: when they got married, when they bought their first house, when they had a baby. A tornado tore the roof off their huge new West Side suburban store in 1975, and she and Louie moved everything to their remaining downtown store without hesitation. "If you have the lowest price, they will find you at the bottom of a river," she said. They did. When a fire burned down the store, she gave the firefighters free TV sets.[22]

"Everything Mrs. B knew how to do, she would do fast. She didn't hesitate and there was no second-guessing. She'd buy five thousand tables or sign a thirty-year lease or buy real estate or hire people. There was no looking back. She just swung. You got about two inches outside the perimeter of her circle of competence, she didn't even want to talk to you about it. She knew exactly what she was good at, and she had no desire to kid herself about those things."

By the early 1980s, Rose and Louie Blumkin had built the largest furniture store in North America. Its three acres sold over $100 million of furniture a year under one roof, ten times the volume of stores of similar size.[23] The home furnishing retailers in Omaha who had been her competitors when she started vanished. Other retailers came into the city and tried to compete with the Mart. Rose and Louie created discount campaigns that broke them financially and drove them away. Customers began to arrive from Iowa, Kansas, and the Dakotas.

Rose became known as Mrs. B, even to her family. She awoke at five a.m., ate only fruits and vegetables, and never touched liquor. A few gray hairs appeared around the edges of her lacquered black bun, but it stayed firmly in place as she raced around the store with the energy of a young woman. As her bargaining position grew stronger, she brooked no sympathy for her suppliers. "Seven dollars? We go bankruptcy tomorrow should we pay that," she sniffed at one's demand.[24] The wholesalers who had formerly snubbed her now kneeled at her feet. She loved it. *"If you want to sell her twenty-three hundred end tables, she will know in a minute what she can pay, how fast she can move them . . . and she'll buy them from you. She'll wait until just before your plane is going to leave in some blizzard when you have to get the hell out of Omaha and can't afford to miss your flight."*[25]

She was hard at it six and a half days a week. "It's mine habit," she said. In her mind, the showroom was her home. Her daughter, Cynthia Schneider, who decorated her mother's house, had arranged the furniture "just as you would find in the store" because "it's the only way we could be sure she would be comfortable."[26] The lamp shades remained covered in plastic. Price tags dangled from some of the furniture. "I only use the kitchen and bedroom," said Mrs. B. "I can't wait until it gets daylight, so I can get back to the business."

On Sunday afternoons—her only time off—she drove around town with Louie. "I go shop the windows," she said. "I plan an attack on the shopkeepers, thinking, 'How much hell can I give them?'"[27] All her work, she said, was inspired by her "diamond mother," who had run a grocery in Russia. She never forgot waking in the night to find her mother doing laundry and baking bread at three a.m. And so, Rose's soft spot was refugees and immigrants. She sometimes put them to work in the bookkeeping department, telling them, "You don't need English to count."[28]

In 1982, the *Omaha World-Herald* interviewed her. She said that over the years the family had rejected several offers to buy her company. "Who could afford to buy a store this big?" One of the offers was Berkshire's. She'd told Buffett: "You'll try to steal it."[29]

In 1983, Buffett heard that the Blumkins were negotiating with a company in Hamburg, Germany, that operated the largest furniture store in the world. The Blumkins were selling!

Maybe this time they were serious. Twenty-some-odd years before, on yet another occasion, Rose had summoned Buffett to her store downtown, indicating that she was thinking of selling. He really wanted to buy the Furniture Mart for Berkshire. He had walked in to find a short, squat woman lecturing a group of men lined up against the wall: her grandsons and sons-in-law and nephews. She turned to Buffett. " *'See all these guys next to me?' she said. 'If I sell it to you, you can fire them. These people are a bunch of bums, and they are all related to me and I can't fire them. But you can fire them. They're bums, bums, bums.'*

"She went on like this for an hour, literally. The word 'bums' recurred many, many times. She thought the only one who was worth anything was Louie, and he was perfect." The other relatives, long used to Rose, stood, impassive. *"Then she dismissed me. I had served my purpose."*[30]

If the Blumkins had talked themselves into selling, now was the time. Mrs. B had had two knee replacements, ceding most of the day-to-day operations to Louie. But she was still running the carpet department. "Something about carpet fascinated her," said Louie.[31] Nevertheless, it was Louie to whom Buffett talked. Louie said, "You should meet my sons Ron and Irv, who'll be running the store someday."

Buffett invited Ron and Irv to come to his office for a visit, and struck up a relationship with them. He sent Louie a letter, explaining his thoughts on the pros and cons of their selling to Berkshire.

They could sell to another furniture company, he wrote, or to somebody in a similar business. But *"such a buyer—no matter what promises are made—usually will have managers who feel they know how to run your business operations, and sooner or later, will want to get into hands-on activity."*

Then there is *"the financial maneuverer, usually operating on large amounts of borrowed money, who plans to resell either to the public or to another corporation as soon as the time is favorable,"* he wrote. *"If the sellers' business represents the creative work of a lifetime and remains an integral part of their personality and sense of being, both of these types of buyers have serious flaws.*

"Any buyer will tell you that he needs you and, if he has any brains, he most certainly does need you. But a great many, for the reasons mentioned above, don't subsequently behave in that manner. We will behave exactly as promised, both because we have so promised, and because we need to."

Buffett explained that he wanted the Blumkins to stay on as partners. He told Louie that he would get involved in only two things: capital allocation and selecting and compensating the "top man."

Buffett had something else to offer. He was not German. The German company had offered well over $90 million, but to Mrs. B, selling to a German company was anathema. The Blumkins agreed to sell the company to Berkshire. To seal the deal, Buffett drove out to the Mart. There he found the eighty-nine-year-old Rose gunning the motor of her three-wheeled golf cart and racing around the store, roaring at her employees, "You're all good for nothing! I wouldn't give a nickel for all of you!" while Louie and her three sons-in-law looked on.[32]

"I don't even want to take inventory," said Buffett. "I'll take your word, Mrs. B, whatever you say you got."

Mrs. B looked at her sons-in-law, who stood against a wall. One of them was taller than her by at least a foot. Her daughters owned twenty percent of the stock and had sent their husbands to sign off on the deal. The sons-in-law were not dumb and knew that they'd get far more money from the Germans. *"And she snarled at them, Just tell me how much more you think you're going to get and I'll give it to you. She wanted to divide up the money and get them out of there so it would be Louie's company. And then she said the price was fifty-five million dollars for ninety percent of the company."* She wanted cash.

"She really liked and trusted me. She would make up her mind about people and that was that." Buffett knew she made decisions about everything once and for all and in the blink of an eye, so he wasn't taking much risk when, after she signed, *"I said, 'If you change your mind on this it's okay with me.' I would never*

say that to any other seller in the world, but I just felt that this was just such a part of her, if there was any reason she decided she didn't want to do it after—I didn't want her to feel bound. And she said, 'I don't change my mind.'

"*After the deal was done, I said, 'Mrs. B, I've got to tell you something. It's my birthday today.'*" Buffett was fifty-three. "*And she said, 'You bought an oil well on your birthday.'*"

The Blumkins had never had an audit, and Buffett did not ask for one. He did not take inventory or look at the detailed accounts. They shook hands. "*We gave Mrs. B a check for fifty-five million dollars and she gave us her word,*" he said.[33] Her word was as good as "*the Bank of England.*" To announce the deal, he held a press conference and showed a video on the company's history. Mrs. B dabbed at her eyes as the film was shown.[34]

Buffett had not only found another unusual specimen to add to his collection of interesting personalities. Something about Mrs. B's indomitable will, history of hardship, and strength of character inspired awe in him.[35] "Dear Mrs. B," he wrote to her. "I have promised Louie and his boys that all members of the family are going to feel good about this transaction five, ten, and twenty years from now. I make you the same promise."[36]

Buffett had promised more than that. Mrs. B was used to operating in total control and privacy; she did not want Buffett to throw her financial dress up in the air and show her knickers to the world. He agreed that the accounts of the Mart would not be separately reported when Berkshire Hathaway filed its financial statements with the SEC, as of course was legally required.

Buffett had no worries about getting a waiver from the SEC—or rather getting one of his employees to get the waiver. He was a likable boss who never lost his temper, never changed his mind capriciously, never said a rude word to anyone, never berated or criticized his employees, didn't second-guess people on their work, and let them do their jobs without interference. He also operated on the assumption that if somebody was smart, they could do anything. Charlie Munger said of him, "Warren doesn't have stress, he causes it." Dale Carnegie said to give people a fine reputation to live up to, and Buffett had learned that lesson well. He knew how to Carnegize heroic accomplishments out of his people.

The gist of what he told his employees was something like: "*You're so good, this won't take you any time at all, and it won't cost anything to do. And, of course, you'll have it back to me in the next mail. Because you're just so damn great at what you do. It would take three people to replace you.*"[37]

Verne McKenzie, who had only just finished mopping up the Blue Chip mess, was assigned the thankless task of convincing the SEC to grant an exception to its rules so that Mrs. B would not suffer the pains of having to unveil her financial secrets to the shareholders of Berkshire Hathaway. He began to go through torture navigating the government's unsympathetic maze while Buffett offered blithe assurances that he could easily get this done.[38] Buffett, meanwhile, had the happy job of diving into a new business and a new collection of people. He grew fond of Louie and "the boys"; he started driving out to 72nd Street at eight-thirty in the evening when the store closed to go out to dinner with them, talking for hours about furniture and merchandising.

Buffett's affection and admiration for Rose Blumkin ran deep.[39] He had plans for her and enlisted Buffett Group member Larry Tisch in his behind-the-scenes machinations. In a virtuoso display of gratitude and showmanship, he had decided to turn the geriatric Rose into Cinderella.

With the help of Tisch, who was a trustee of New York University, he arranged it so that both Creighton University and NYU gave Rose honorary degrees.[40] At Creighton, the tiny Mrs. B was so overcome that she cried on the stage, saying, "Oy, oy, oy, I never even believe it."[41] Then she spoke of America, the country that made her dream come true. Her advice to the graduating seniors: "First, honesty," she said. "Second, hard work. Next, if you don't get the job you want right away, tell them you'll take anything. If you're good, they'll keep you."[42]

In the city for the NYU ceremony, the family took care to keep her from seeing the price of her hotel room, for she had been to New York before and thought anything more than $75 for a hotel room was outrageous.[43] She had Louie take her to see Ellis Island and Delancey Street, but getting around the city was a struggle, for she felt cheated by the price of a taxi.[44] On the morning of commencement, Mrs. B was "robed" with great pomp and circumstance and received her degree alongside Senator Daniel Patrick Moynihan and the poet Octavio Paz.

Despite the august company of the NYU ceremony, when asked which of the two honorary degrees she preferred, Rose did not hesitate. It was Creighton's. They had bought carpet from her.

Soon after, Berkshire's auditors conducted the Nebraska Furniture Mart's first inventory. The store was worth $85 million. Mrs. B, seized with a severe case of remorse after she had sold it for a total value of $60 million, including the share retained by the family, told *Regardie's* magazine, "I wouldn't go back on my word, but I was surprised. . . . He never thought a minute [before agreeing to the price], but he studies. I bet you he knew."[45] Buffett, of course, could not have "known," not literally. But he had certainly known there was a whopping margin of safety in the price.

Within two years, however, this fairy tale of a story turned ugly. Tired of being yelled at in front of customers and of being called bums, Mrs. B's grandsons Ron and Irv gradually stopped speaking to her.

Finally, when Mrs. B was ninety-five, "the boys" overruled her on a carpet purchase and she exploded. It was the last straw. "I was the boss. They never told me nothing,"[46] she said, and quit. She also demanded $96,000 in unused vacation pay on her way out the door.[47]

But sitting at home alone, she acknowledged, was "awful lonely, not to do nothing. I go nuts."[48] In ominous newspaper interviews she referred to her grandsons as "dummies" and, shockingly, "Nazis."[49] She hinted at solo trips to the North Carolina High Point Market, the furniture industry's largest trade show. She suddenly arranged to have a warehouse she owned right across the street from the Furniture Mart refurbished. She held a "garage sale" in it, and cleared $18,000 in one day, selling "some of her own things."[50] A few months later, "Mrs. B's Warehouse" was grossing $3,000 a day before it officially opened.

Asked about the impending battle for customers, she snarled to the local paper, "I'll give it to them." She put up a sign: "Their price $104, our price $80."[51] When Bob Brown on ABC's *20/20* program asked her about the Furniture Mart, she said, "I would it should go up in smoke. I like they should go down to hell...."[52]

Some time earlier, Buffett had created a saying. *"I would rather wrestle grizzlies than compete with Mrs. B and her progeny."*[53] Now Buffett acted as he always did when any of his friends' relationships broke down. He refused to take sides. Mrs. B thought that was disloyal. "Warren Buffett is not my friend," she told a reporter. "I made him fifteen million dollars every year, and when I disagreed with my grandkids, he didn't stand up for me."[54] This was torture to Buffett, who couldn't bear conflict and broken relationships.

Louie, who could do no wrong in his mother's eyes, made no headway with Rose. "She figured she lost control of this place, and she blew her top," he says.

After two years, Mrs. B's Warehouse, while still small, was growing at such a rate that pound for pound, it was trouncing the Mart. Finally Louie intervened again. "Mother," he said, "you've got to sell this thing back to us. There's no sense competing one against the other."[55] And so Rose called Buffett. She missed the Mart. She missed her family. She was lonely in her house, separated from her family. "I was wrong," she said. Mrs. B told Buffett that she wanted to come back. With a box of See's Candies under his arm and holding a huge bouquet of pink roses, Buffett went out to see her. He offered her $5 million simply for the use of her name and her lease.

He added one catch: She must sign a noncompete agreement, a contract designed so that she could never again compete with him. This was something he wished he'd done before. The absurdity of imposing a noncompete agreement on a ninety-nine-year-old woman was far from lost on him. Nevertheless, Buffett was taking no chances. The agreement was cunningly written to outlast Mrs. B. If she retired, or quit in a rage or for any other reason, no matter how old she was, for five years afterward she could not compete with Buffett and her relatives. *"I thought she might go on forever,"* he says. *"I needed five years beyond forever with her."*

Mrs. B still could not read or write English. Nevertheless, she signed the noncompete, which had been explained to her, with her characteristic mark. The truce made headlines. *"And then I made sure she never got mad,"* Buffett says. He set about flattering his new employee unctuously to make her so happy that she would never, ever quit and start the clock running on her noncompete.

On April 7, 1993, the Greater Omaha Chamber of Commerce put her in the inaugural class of its business hall of fame, alongside Buffett. Then Buffett, knees trembling slightly, got up on a stage at the Highland Club and sang in public, for the first time in his life, to Mrs. B on her hundredth birthday. He also donated a million dollars to a local theater she was renovating.

Nobody could believe it. Warren Buffett had given away a million dollars.

Rose felt she owed everything, all her good fortune, to this country for the opportunities it had given her. At family events, she insisted that her favorite song, "God Bless America," be played every time, sometimes even more than once.

And through all of the hosannas, none of it ever went to Rose Blumkin's head. "I don't think I deserve it," she said, over and over, of the accolades.[56] But she did.

45

Call the Tow Truck

S usie Buffett generally listened to her husband's tales of Mrs. B from a distance. She and Warren talked nearly every day on a special "hotline" installed in her apartment. When the phone rang, she jumped up instantly. "That's Warren!" she would say, and run away from whatever conversation she was having with a friend to answer it. He was still her number one obligation. But unless he needed her, her life was under her own control.

Susie had moved into another cubbyhole on the Washington Street cable-car line with a splendid view over the bay. She chose the building because Peter was living there with his wife, Mary, and her two daughters. He was still pursuing his musical career.

In the past few years, Susie had lost both of her parents. Doc Thompson had died in July 1981; Dorothy Thompson followed only thirteen months later. Afterward, her hyperkinetic tendencies did not abate; if anything, they increased. Warren had stopped taking her for granted, and his greater-than-ever desire to please found expression partly through the money he gave her. In her younger days, Susie's idea of a shopping spree had been buying a basketful of greeting cards.[1] That had gradually expanded to an annual attack on Bergdorf's shoe department. Warren's tightfistedness began to let up in light of the unspoken but inexorable reality that he now controlled the money by Susie's grace and favor. At any time she could take it back and use the money herself. Torn between two fur coats, she wanted to know, "Why do I have to choose?" The answer was, she didn't.

But mostly the looser purse strings fueled Susie's penchant for generosity to a ragtag collection of colorful friends that grew and grew. Nobody ever left the beguiling Buffetts. The rising tide of Susie's entourage would have overwhelmed almost anyone, but Susie Buffett was not just anyone. Unleashed from the confines of Omaha, with buckets of money at her disposal, she sprang to life as if powered by magic, like the Sorcerer's Apprentice's broom. How much do you need for Christmas? Warren said. Oh, seventy-five thousand would do it, Susie replied.[2] He wrote the check.

Her special cause was artists, creative types whose talents she felt were not being recognized. But of all the people she aided, her nephew Billy Rogers was her greatest challenge. A brilliant jazz guitarist, Rogers had played with different groups, backing up B. B. King and achieving his greatest success performing as one of the Crusaders. He was married, with a son, and living in Los Angeles. But he had bounced around the West Coast for several years, never staying clean for long before relapsing. Susie remained an optimist and refused to give up on him. No matter how squalid his life when he acted out his addiction, she always treated him like another son.

By 1984, when AIDS had claimed over two thousand American victims and infected two thousand more, Susie had found her next great cause among the gay men of San Francisco. With the disease's transmission poorly understood and badly communicated, gay-bashing turned to hysteria.[3] Already a mother figure to many men whose families had rejected them, Susie now once again dared to cross a social line, as a rich married woman who acted as a refuge for gay men during the early years of the AIDS crisis.[4]

Susie's own life in San Francisco was something of a high-wire act, requiring a sure sense of balance. She had remained Mrs. Warren Buffett publicly for six years now while privately teetering on the fence of divorce and remarriage. Some who were aware of her situation thought Susie chose to stay in this limbo as a way to please everyone else and avoid having to figure out what she herself wanted. Susie, they thought, was a woman who could never speak her own truth. Yet her life history suggests otherwise: that she preferred never to give all of herself to anyone. Susie—who had reason to be confident in her ability to manage people—on occasion could be overconfident. As the circle of those who knew Susie's secrets grew, it became harder for her to control what the two main men in her life knew about the state of their relationships with her.

Susie and her former tennis coach spent part of 1983 and early 1984 traveling in Europe, where she ran into some people she knew from Omaha. Suddenly, her two lives had collided on the Continent. In March 1984, she came to Omaha for Leila's eightieth birthday party; during her visit she admitted to Warren for the first time that part of the reason she had moved to San Francisco involved another man. Somehow, however, Warren wound up with the impression that this relationship was in the past, and that it involved someone she had met after she left Omaha.[5] Even while confessing, therefore, Susie kept her secrets. Yet she had finally committed herself to one course. By telling Warren, she had chosen his side of the fence. She would never leave him. They would stay married.

And Warren did not kill himself when he found out—as if that had ever been likely. But he did lose what appeared to be ten pounds almost overnight. Among the several shocks he had to absorb, he now knew that Susie had been spending some of the money he had dispensed to her with such a liberal hand in ways he would never have approved—had he known.

At Leila's birthday party, he looked thin, but behaved as he always did with the family gathered around. At home, there was no change in his relationship with Astrid, who knew nothing of what had transpired. At Berkshire headquarters, he sealed himself inside his office, protected by Gladys, and immersed himself in work. He never told anyone what he felt about the end of the beautiful illusion that had been his marriage. Instead, the bathtub memory went to work.

The dream of sustaining some remnant of Berkshire Hathaway was also dying, even though the ancient spinning frames still puffed and wheezed. Looms that looked like they were made from salvaged scrap metal creaked wearily in the weaving room. Only four hundred workers remained. Most were of Portuguese descent, many in their fifties or older, some speaking limited English, some deaf from the roar of the machines. Buffett could not squeeze another ounce of rayon out of the equipment without buying new spinning frames and looms. That was the end; in 1985 he pulled the plug on Berkshire's life support.[6] The equipment would have cost as much as $50 million to replace. Put to the auction block, it sold for $163,122.[7]

The workers asked for severance above their contract guarantee and got a couple of months' extra pay. They wanted to see Buffett to discuss it with him. He said no. They thought he was heartless. Probably, he couldn't face them.

"Through no fault of their own, they were in a position of being a horse when the tractor arrived. The free market did them in. . . . And there wasn't any answer. When you talk about retraining people—it's not like they'll all go become computer technicians by taking junior-college courses or something like that.

"But you've also got to deal with the people that are displaced. The free market

does all kinds of good things in this country, but we need a safety net. Society is get-
ting the benefits, and it should pick up the tab." Warren, of course, was not going
to pick up the tab because society lacked a proper safety net. Whatever pension
the workers were entitled to under their terms of employment, that was exactly
what they would get.

By the time he shut it down, the textile business had become a flyspeck on
the holding company that bore the Berkshire Hathaway name. Buffett's plan
was that insurance would drive that Berkshire Hathaway—the one that swallowed up whole businesses like the Nebraska Furniture Mart. During the 1970s,
he had cobbled together a diverse group of insurance companies and loaded
them onto the back of National Indemnity to give it an extra kick. It was a brilliant strategy, but for a number of years, they had mostly been going wrong.

First, Jet Jack Ringwalt had retired. Then, the "Omni affair," when National
Indemnity was swindled by a crooked agent, had threatened to explode into
losses that could have cost the company $10 million or more. Although the final
tab had settled into a couple of miserable millions, this was only the first of a
series of problems with the insurance companies. Buffett had bought a small
home- and auto-insurance company in the early 1970s that promptly skidded
into a ditch, until a new manager towed it out. That was to be the pattern with
all the rest of Buffett's insurance investments—straight into the ditch, then call
the tow truck. Berkshire had gotten involved in California workers' compensation insurance—coverage that pays for lost wages and health benefits when
people are injured on the job. By 1977, one of its two workers' comp companies
was in a full-blown "disaster," with its manager taking kickbacks from brokers.[8]
Buffett's protégé Dan Grossman, sent to L.A. to save it, quickly realized that he
did not understand insurance, a complex business that is rougher than it
sounds. (Verne McKenzie, for example, had once led a trip to personally repos-
sess an agent's house and car.[9]) Turning your controller into a repo man was not
the typical CEO's style, but in Buffett's world, after all, a smart person could do
anything. Grossman's solution was to hire an experienced manager, Frank
DeNardo, who began to straighten things out. Buffett larded praise on DeNardo
in Berkshire's annual report.

Buffett had also started a reinsurer—a company that insures other insurers—
as a sort of experiment. He hired George Young, a gentle, professorial man, to
run it. Money came in the door, but too many losses flowed back out. Buffett
Hail-Maryed Grossman to New York on a rescue mission. It was "kind of
vague," says Grossman. "He said, go talk to Lloyd's of London, go find some

reinsurance deals that you can do." Given no instructions and an impossible task, Grossman camped out at Ruane, Cunniff and started to learn investing.

Another of Buffett's ideas was the creation of the Homestate Companies—a batch of little insurers scattered among different states. But in 1978, Buffett wrote that these companies had done a "disappointing" job. Buffett had no plans to solve this problem himself. Nor did his standard management technique of taking out all the cash and raising prices release a flood of profits in insurance (although it was a good starting point). His friend Tom Murphy liked to tell him that he "delegated to the point of abdication."[10] Now he put Verne McKenzie in charge of one of these companies, until McKenzie, recognizing that he did not understand insurance either, threw up his hands and backed out.[11] Meanwhile Frank DeNardo, at age thirty-seven, had died tragically from a heart attack. Now the workers' compensation business in California was rudderless again. Buffett snatched Grossman back from New York to run it.

Grossman found himself a company president at age twenty-six, in a business where fraud prevention is more important than sales. He faced customers with decades of experience cheating insurers. His calls for help only splattered against Buffett's Teflon pleasantries. Bright and hardworking, Grossman felt "totally unqualified" to run an insurer at his age and level of experience, and explained that he was in over his head. Buffett said he was sure that he could rise to the occasion. Instead, the stress overwhelmed him, and his marriage fell apart. Finally, he told Buffett he simply couldn't handle it, and quit.[12]

Buffett, who hated to let anyone go, urged him to remain in the Buffett Group. Various friends in the group called to try to dissuade him from leaving. But he felt he was not strong enough to maintain his autonomy within the entanglements that bound people to the Buffetts—Susie with her crowd of dependent worshippers, Warren with his network of supportive protectors. Knowing what he was giving up, he cut everyone off. "He divorced the Buffetts," said one former friend, who understood why but thought it was too bad.

Now headquarters had one fewer person to support the growing insurance empire. During Grossman's peripatetics, Buffett had installed Mike Goldberg, a former McKinsey consultant, in Grossman's onetime office. A wiry Brooklynite of sardonic intensity and the subtlest humor, Goldberg turned out to have the so-called insurance gene, which is made up of one part knack for handicapping mixed with two parts dark skepticism about human nature. Thus he was able to teach himself the business—just as well, since it had been out of character for Buffett to mentor one protégé, let alone two.

With Goldberg's arrival, the polite, restrained Midwestern tone at headquarters changed abruptly. Managers that Goldberg decided were only ninety percent of grade were swiftly sent packing. As the packing cases flew out the doors of the failing Homestate Companies, Goldberg gained a fearsome reputation.

Goldberg's method was to call his managers and talk to them at length every day, quizzing them mercilessly. The value of Goldberg's hands-on approach in an atmosphere of chaos was hard to overstate. One former manager referred to it as working in a "Socratic wind tunnel." He was the type, an ex-employee said, who "yelled when hailing a cab."

Throughout the early 1980s, Goldberg worked against the tide to right the ship. Unlike the disappointing Hochschild-Kohn or the pathetic Berkshire Hathaway—businesses that Buffett simply should not have bought—for the first time, perfectly decent businesses were unaccountably floundering on Buffett's watch. He had confidence in Goldberg. However, the pleasant but unskeptical George Young, who ran the reinsurance division, had been taken by unscrupulous brokers, a problem endemic to the industry.[13] Buffett by now had a clear-cut pattern: He rationalized to avoid firing losing managers. He criticized his managers indirectly, often by withholding resources or praise. As the number of things he owned expanded, he used that technique ever more frequently. Trying to parse his shareholder letters for news about the insurance companies, one had to be Sherlock Holmes attending to the curious incident of the dog in the nighttime—the dog that didn't bark. Having lavished individual insurance managers with praise in the 1970s, Buffett gradually ceased to name any of the insurers or their managers, except the superbly performing GEICO and National Indemnity.

Buffett did not stop writing about the insurance industry, however. In fact, in the 1984 letter he wrote about it more than ever. But he lumped all of Berkshire's insurance companies together and took the blame for their poor performance himself, without naming a single company or a single manager who had been responsible for the hemorrhage of losses. He went on like this for an excruciating seven pages, citing the "walking dead" competition and the losses coming back to haunt him like bill collections for the man who was "buried in a rented suit." Although it was appropriate for him, as CEO, to feel accountable, he seemed almost to be trying to forestall criticism through self-flagellation.

And he was writing these things even as he knew that, underlying the terrible numbers, substantial improvements were already taking place. By the next year, the insurers began coming together into the powerful engine that Buffett had envisioned. They started to produce the cash flows that would be the raw material to fuel the rest of his career.

By 1985 the unique business model that Buffett had designed began rising to its potential. No other business resembled it, and this structure would enable the dramatic compounding effect that propelled the shareholders' wealth.

Then there came the moment when Goldberg found the capstone to the structure. One day, says Buffett, "*I was down here on a Saturday, and Mike Goldberg walked in with Ajit.*"

Ajit Jain, born in 1951, had an engineering degree from the prestigious Indian Institute of Technology in Kharagpur and a business degree from Harvard. Ajit was skeptical and hard-nosed like Buffett and Munger. Nobody would ever put one over on Ajit. Buffett saw himself in Ajit, who quickly rose in his esteem to share Mrs. B's pinnacle. "*He had no background in insurance. I just liked the guy. I would love to glue myself to Ajit. You can argue that Ajit was when we discovered the electric light. It was huge. It was huge compared to anything we'd ever done at Berkshire.*"

Buffett claimed that he "added nothing" to the quality of Ajit's decisions. But he was far from a passive participant in Ajit's deals, and if there was any job at Berkshire Hathaway he would have liked to do himself, it was Jain's. He loved the handicapping aspect, the tough negotiating in which temperament mattered and huge sums of money were won or lost based on pure intellect and will. This business in which psychology gave the right person an edge drew together all of Buffett's skills. Buffetting by proxy through Ajit was as close to the old "under-the-counter" market way of trading as he could get these days, and he loved doing it.

With Buffett glued to Ajit, and the chaos sorted out, Goldberg's job was done; he moved over to start Berkshire's credit and real estate business.

Ajit did not seem to need much sleep; when he got up around five or six a.m., he roused his colleagues for lengthy predawn talks about reinsurance deals, even on Saturdays and Sundays. He and Buffett established a routine of nightly ten o'clock phone calls, which Ajit maintained in every time zone throughout a ceaseless routine of globe-trotting.

Ajit had arrived at an opportune time. Insurance prices were peaking. He took an ad in *Business Insurance* magazine: "We are looking for more—more casualty risks where the premium exceeds one million." The ad combined the showmanship and sharp thinking that were Buffett hallmarks. "We didn't have a reputation, we didn't have the distribution system," says Buffett. But business came pouring in the door after that ad, and Ajit did deals, deals, deals.[14]

46

Rubicon

The 1980s would be an era of deals—most financed with debt. The Dow hadn't budged in seventeen years.[1] Grinding inflation had decimated corporate profits, yet companies dribbled away their earnings in sloppy operations and unthinking bureaucracy.[2] By the early 1980s, stocks were on sale like polyester suits. Then, under Federal Reserve Chairman Paul Volcker, interest rates, recently an astronomical fifteen percent, started to fall as inflation came under control. With debt now cheap, would-be buyers of a company could use the company's own soon-to-be-gutted assets as collateral to finance its purchase—like getting a hundred percent mortgage on a house. It cost no more to buy a huge company than to set up a lemonade stand.[3] The merger boom had begun.

In 1984, the burner under managements turned up another notch when "junk bonds" became respectable. More politely called "fallen angels," these were the bonds of companies like the Penn Central Railroad that were climbing out of the bankruptcy dustbin or teetering on its edge.[4] Only occasionally did a company issue junk bonds on purpose, paying a high interest rate because it was considered a dicey credit risk. Junk bonds were sort of shady, a little desperate.

Everything changed when Michael Milken, of the upstart investment bank Drexel Burnham Lambert, rose to become the most influential man on Wall Street through a simple proposition: that while individual "fallen angel" junk bonds were risky, through the law of averages, buying a bushel of them was *not.*

Soon, money managers felt at ease putting high-paying junk bonds in their portfolios. Indeed, it quickly became more respectable to issue *new* junk bonds—quite a different thing. Another short hop and takeovers of strong, well-financed companies could be financed with junk. Corporate raiders intent on "hostile takeovers" whose goal was to pluck a company clean suddenly stalked companies that had been waddling along complacently. Their targets lunged toward any buyer who might conceivably be more friendly; in the end the target company was usually sold to someone or another and financially gutted. This orgy of mergers that often took place with the consent of only one party riveted the public; clashes of titanic egos filled the daily papers. Michael Milken's annual junk-bond conference, the Predators' Ball,[5] lent its name to the entire era.

Buffett scorned the way these deals transferred riches from shareholders to managers and corporate raiders, helped by a long, long line of toll-taking bankers, brokers, and lawyers.[6] The deals of the 1980s repelled him above all because they were loaded with debt. To him, debt was something to be used only with a careful eye for the worst-case scenario. In the 1980s, however, debt became mere "leverage," a way of boosting profits using borrowed money. "Leverage" arrived at the same time that the U.S. government began running large deficits courtesy of "Reaganomics"—the "supply-side" idea that cutting taxes would ultimately increase tax revenues by stoking the economy. Fierce debates raged among economists over whether tax cuts could actually pay for themselves and, if so, by how much. The economy was heating up at the time from consumer spending, also fueled by debt; John and Jane Q. Public had gradually been accustoming themselves to buying everything with credit cards, building up a balance that they would never pay off until from their plastic death did them part. The Depression-era culture of hoarding and saving had turned turtle, into a culture of buy now, pay later.

Buffett still paid cash and chose the role of the white knight in takeovers. Early one morning in February 1985, while he was in Washington, Tom Murphy called and woke him to say he had just bought the ABC television network. ABC, caught in the crosshairs of the corporate raiders, had hung a lure out to see whether Murphy would save it by doing a friendly deal—and Murphy bit.[7]

"Think about how it will change your life," Buffett said. Buffett may well have been thinking about the incongruity between the modest, retiring Murphy, a devout Catholic, and the glamorous world of television, as Murphy believed[8]—but Buffett's next move signaled that he wouldn't mind such a change himself. Or so it seemed, since he recommended to Murphy that Cap Cities/ABC recruit a "gorilla" investor who could protect it from the raiders' attentions. To no one's surprise, Murphy suggested that this investor should be Buffett himself.

Likewise, Buffett had no trouble quickly agreeing to spend $517 million of Berkshire's money for fifteen percent of Cap Cities.[9]

Buffett now became a player in the biggest media deal in history. At a total of $3.5 billion, he and Murphy had paid a fancy price for ABC.[10] "The network business is no lollapalooza," Buffett would later say.[11] Yet he had watched the awesome ascendance of television from its infancy and knew well both its power to shape public opinion and its business potential. Buffett wanted Cap Cities/ABC so much that he was willing to leave the board of the *Washington Post* to comply with FCC regulations limiting the two companies' television interests through related entities.[12]

The year 1985 would be a humdinger. During the same week that Buffett's investing yielded Berkshire $332 million *from a single stock*—General Foods, when it was taken over by Philip Morris—*Forbes* caught on to how rich he was and added him to its list of America's 400 richest people. At the time, it took $150 million to make that list. But Buffett, at age fifty-five, was now a billionaire, one of only fourteen ranked by *Forbes*.

Berkshire Hathaway, its first few shares originally bought for $7.50, was now trading at more than *$2,000 a share*. But Buffett refused to "split"* the stock into smaller pieces, citing the way brokerage fees would multiply needlessly along with the number of shares. This policy made Berkshire more like a partnership—or even a club—and the high stock price drew attention to Berkshire like nothing else.

His fame ascended with Berkshire's stock price. Now when he entered a room of investors, an energy filled the air as attention gravitated toward him. The purchase of ABC by Cap Cities did indeed begin to change his life. Meeting soap opera impresario Agnes Nixon, he got invited to do a gig on the show *Loving*. A lot of CEOs would have feigned a mortal illness before doing something so undignified, but Buffett loved doing his cameo on *Loving* so much that he showed off the paycheck from his show-business debut. It was all of a piece with the Buffett who loved to play dress-up and would soon be appearing costumed as Elvis at his friends' parties. This same Buffett reveled in putting on black tie to take Susie Jr. to a state dinner at the Reagan White House. Jetting off to the Academy Awards with Astrid—who made a rare public appearance, proudly wearing a thrift-shop gown—he dined with Dolly Parton. But Buffett,

---

*A stock "split" carves a single share of stock into a certain number of pieces, each trading at the equivalent fraction of the former price.

who found Parton likable as well as hugely attractive, failed to make the lasting impression on her that he managed with most other women.

At the Kay Parties, where Graham always seated him between the two most important or interesting women, he did better. Yet he had never grown to love small talk, and found it challenging—or just plain tiresome.

"The truth is, you're sitting next to two people that you've never seen before and you're never going to see again. It's kind of strained, no matter what. Whether it was Babe Paley, or Marella Agnelli, or Princess Di, Kay always saw in these women what she aspired to be. I didn't have the faintest idea what to talk about. Princess Di was not as easy to talk to as Dolly Parton. What do you say to Princess Di—'How's Chuck? Anything new at the castle?'"

Still, by 1987 a billionaire commanded a certain cool respect; Buffett had become something of an elephant himself, no longer so dependent on Graham. And Graham no longer needed him so much as a regular escort, for their mutual obsession had cooled. Now her attraction to powerful men had heated up her longtime friendship with the recently widowed, paper-dry, encyclopedically brilliant, alpha-squared Robert McNamara, who had been defense secretary during the Kennedy and Johnson administrations. Before long, McNamara became Graham's "Husband Number Three," as one of her board members referred to him. True to form, she put him on the *Post* board. From the beginning, McNamara and Buffett "were not the best of friends," though over time, their relationship resolved into a sort of mutually respectful truce.

Buffett could handle people like McNamara through diplomacy; a greater problem was the physical danger that accompanied his fame. Two men arrived at Kiewit Plaza, one waving a chrome-plated replica of a .45, intending to kidnap Buffett and hold him for $100,000 ransom.[13] The building security and police handled it. Afterward, Buffett would not hear of hiring a bodyguard, for that would restrict his cherished privacy and freedom, but he did have a security camera installed, along with a three-hundred-pound security door to shield the office.[14]

Strangers called often now, insistent, wanting to speak with him. Gladys told them in crisp tones to write a letter spelling out their requests.[15] A lot of letters said, I've gotten in over my head with credit cards or gambling debt.[16]

Buffett the collector kept the letters; they began to fill up his files. Many of them confirmed the way he thought of himself, as a role model, as a teacher. Occasionally, he wrote a debtor or gambler back with firm but kind insistence that they take responsibility for their problems. As if they were his kids, he suggested they buy time to bail themselves out by telling their creditors how broke they were and negotiating easier payment terms. He always added a little soliloquy about the perils of too much debt—especially debt from credit cards, the junk bonds of the personal-finance world.

His own kids had received little such training about how to handle money—and their father remained inflexible about requests for money from them. He was still willing, however, to make financial deals with family members to manage their weight.

The thirty-something Susie Jr. struggled with a few extra pounds. Her father made a deal in which, for losing a certain amount of weight, she could shop for clothes for a month, no limit. The only catch was that she had to pay him back if she regained the weight in a year. This deal was better than the proverbial win/win: It was a no-risk deal in which Buffett won either way. He was out the money only if Susie Jr. did as he wanted and kept the weight off. So Susie Jr. dieted, and when she got down to the goal weight, Big Susie mailed credit cards to her daughter with a note—*"Have fun!"*

Susie Jr. dared not spend a dime at first, frightened by the thought of asking her father to pay the bills. Bit by bit she worked herself up, until finally she shopped in the blind daze induced by having unlimited money for the first time in her life, tossing the receipts unread each day on the dining-room table, too afraid to add the total. "Oh, my God!" said her husband, Allen, each night as he returned home to his wife's mounting pile of sales slips. After thirty days, she added them up. She had spent $47,000.

"I thought he was going to die over how much it was," she says of her father. Susie Jr. went for reinforcement. Her mother was powerful, but she knew who had even more leverage with Warren when it came to money. While Kay Graham barely knew Peter and was an "unreachable" figure to Howie—he was always afraid he would sit in the wrong place or break something in her house—Susie Jr. had developed a warm, close relationship with her.[17] She called Graham, who agreed to parachute in as backup if needed. But since a deal was a deal, Buffett paid the bill without strong-arming.

The rent that Buffett charged Howie for his farm similarly rose and fell with his son's poundage. Warren thought Howie should weigh 182.5 pounds. When Howie was over the limit, he had to pay twenty-six percent of the farm's gross receipts to his father. When he was under, he paid twenty-two percent. "I don't mind it, really," Howie said. "He's showing he's concerned about my health. But what I do mind is that, even at twenty-two percent, he's getting a bigger paycheck than almost anybody around."[18] So Warren couldn't lose on this deal either. He got either more money or a thinner son.[19] All of this was classic Buffett. As one of his friends put it, "He's the master of win/win... but he never does anything that isn't a win for him."

Peter and his family had moved from their apartment on Washington Street, in the building where his mother now lived, to a house on Scott Street. Peter got a gig writing music for some fifteen-second animated spots for a new cable channel, MTV. Success led to a business scoring commercials. Even though Peter was the least financially savvy of the Buffett kids, he had managed to tether his Berkshire stock to his musical talent and thus establish a career that freed him from the money games. He realized that if he wanted to pursue his own art, he needed to free himself from corporate lackeyship. While he continued doing commercial work, he cut a demo record and signed with the New Age label Narada to do an album.[20]

His mother, who still dabbled in music, was often at Peter's studio, but in 1984 she had some more health problems, including a painful abscess between the spleen and pancreas, and was hospitalized for exploratory surgery. Her doctors could find no cause, and she recovered without incident. She then continued her work as a "mobile Red Cross unit," as one family member put it, at her usual frenetic pace. Her self-image was as the healthy person whose role was to care for others. She threw masquerade parties in her tiny place on Washington Street, tried to learn to ride a bicycle, and gathered her impromptu family of gays and strays at large dinner parties and Thanksgiving celebrations. She wore jeans and sweatsuits and put away the wigs she had once worn, her hair now a lighter brown, released into a corona around her beaming face.

Warren—who would give his wife almost anything she asked for these days—let her expand and redecorate the Laguna house. She met Kathleen Cole, an interior designer, and together they began to give it the bright-colored contemporary look that Susie favored.[21] Susie and Warren continued to spar over money, but these spats had become almost scripted: Susie's allowance expanded at an accelerating pace—although never at the rate she wanted. She could afford Cole's services and those of a full-time secretary to manage her schedule, which freed her to extend herself further while also spending more time with the family. Howie remained the magnet who drew more of her support and energy than anyone else. She commuted back and forth to Nebraska to help with this and that and to lavish affection on Howie's children, her adopted granddaughters Erin, Heather, Chelsea, and Megan, and grandson Howie B.

When Susie Jr., who lived in Washington, D.C., became pregnant with her first child, Big Susie began making more trips to the East Coast. Susie and Allen needed to remodel their little house. It would cost $30,000. She considered how to pay for it, since she and Allen didn't have the money; she knew better than to ask her billionaire father to give it to her. Fortunately, her pregnancy had activated the one loophole in her weight deal with her father. Buffett was not getting his $47,000 back. Nevertheless—despite her father's belief that clothing holds its value better than jewelry—she and Allen could not hock her new wardrobe to pay for the kitchen. So she asked her father for a loan.

"Why not go to the bank?" he asked, and turned her down. Unearned position, inherited wealth drove Buffett crazy, offended his sense of justice, and disturbed his sense of the universe's symmetry. But applying such strictly rational rules to his own children was a chilly way to look at the world. "He won't give it to us on principle," said Susie. "All my life, my father has been teaching us. Well, I feel I've learned the lesson. At a certain point, you can stop."[22]

Before long, her doctor confined Susie Jr. to bed rest for a tedious six months. She lay in a tiny bedroom watching a small black-and-white television set. An appalled Kay Graham brought over meals prepared by her chef, then shamed Buffett into buying his daughter a larger color TV. When Big Susie caught wind of what was happening, she dropped everything and flew in to care for her daughter, spending months in Washington. As soon as she saw the condition of the place, she turned it upside down and renovated it. "It's just terrible that Warren won't pay for this," she complained. But everything she was spending had been dunned out of him. Their endless money game enhanced Warren's reputation for thriftiness, and Susie's reputation for generosity. Since they had both signed up for this arrangement, obviously they both wanted it this way.

With the birth of Emily in September 1986, the Buffetts now had eight grandchildren and stepgrandchildren in three cities: San Francisco, Omaha, and Washington, D.C. As the Emerald Bay house renovation reached habitability, Susie slowed the pace to a steady tinkering and began to use it as a base to entertain friends and, especially, her grandchildren. In San Francisco, she hopscotched into an apartment in Pacific Heights, close to Peter's new home on Scott Street. This large condominium sat at the top of four dizzying flights of stairs and had a glorious view over the bay from the Golden Gate Bridge to Alcatraz.

Now she hired her decorator, Kathleen Cole, as a personal assistant to help manage her life. "You can just work part-time," she told Cole, "and you'll have all this time for your two kids." The next thing Cole knew, she was working for the Buffett Foundation, planning Susie's travel arrangements, overseeing entertainment, hiring and managing a staff that included housekeepers, errand-runners, and friends employed partly as a favor, and buying gifts for Susie's ever-expanding list of beneficiaries.[23] She found herself managing two houses, including the ongoing renovation of the Laguna house and the two-year renovation project that Susie had launched on her new place. Cole's husband, Jim, a firefighter, stepped in as a favor to work as Susie's part-time handyman. Another friend, Ron Parks, a CPA Susie had met while traveling in Europe, managed the disbursements and taxes—out of kindness and without pay—for what he jokingly called "STB Enterprises," or, as another friend put it, Susie's "payroll and give-away roll."[24] Parks was the partner of Tom Newman, her friend Rackie's son; Susie had become close friends with the couple. Newman, a chef, occasionally helped out with her parties, but mostly tried unsuccessfully to improve her eating habits. By now, Susie's paid and unpaid staff had far outgrown that at Berkshire Hathaway headquarters.

Warren admired his wife's desire to rescue people and her skill in helping those in need. As "Mama Susie," she made it her mission to help people one on one. But the emotional opening-up of this work was beyond Warren. His way of helping people was to leverage his brains and money from a distance to affect as many lives as possible; and he connected to people as a teacher.

Buffett's earliest teachings had been preserved in the letters he had written to his former partners in the 1960s, letters that were photocopied and passed hand to hand around Wall Street. Ever since 1977, with the help of Carol Loomis, his unusual chairman's letters to his shareholders in the Berkshire annual reports—carefully crafted, enlightening, eye-opening letters—had grown more personal and entertaining by the year; they amounted to a crash course in business, written in clear language that ranged from biblical quotations to references to Alice in Wonderland and princesses kissing toads. Much of their acreage was devoted to discussions of matters other than Berkshire Hathaway's financial results—how to think about investing, the harm the dismal economy was doing to business, how businesses should measure results. These letters brought out both the preacher and the cop in Buffett, giving people a sense of him as a man. And the man was charming, he was attractive; his investors wanted more of him. So he gave it to them at the shareholder meetings.

The earliest meetings had taken place in Seabury Stanton's old loft above the New Bedford mill. Two or three people with Ben Graham connections came because of Buffett. One was Conrad Taff, who had taken Graham's class. Buffett wanted his shareholder meetings to be open and democratic, as unlike the old Marshall-Wells meeting as possible. Taff peppered Buffett with questions, and Buffett enjoyed it, as if he were sitting in an armchair at a party with people gathered round listening to his wisdom.

The meetings carried on like this for years, with only a sprinkling of people showing up to ask questions, even after the meetings moved to Nebraska and took place in the National Indemnity cafeteria. Buffett still enjoyed them, despite the sparse attendance. As recently as 1981, only twenty-two people attended. Jack Ringwalt actually had to recruit employees to stand in back of the National Indemnity cafeteria so as not to embarrass his boss with an empty room.[25]

Then in July 1983, coincident with the Blue Chip merger, a little crowd of people suddenly showed up at the cafeteria to hear Buffett talk. He answered them in his plainspoken, unpretentious style: He was teaching, and he came across as democratic, Midwestern, and refreshing, just as he did in his letters to the shareholders.

Buffett spoke in metaphors the audience understood—the emperor's new clothes, the bird in the hand versus the two in the bush. He told plainspoken truths that other businessmen would not acknowledge, and routinely burst the bubble of corporate double-speak. He developed a memorable way of fabulizing life and businesses into instructive tales that rang true. The meetings took on a quality associated with almost everything that Buffett touched. They began to snowball.

In 1986, Buffett moved the meeting to the Joslyn Art Museum. Four hundred people came, then five hundred the next year. Many of them worshipped Buffett, who had made them rich. In between questions, some people read poems of praise from the balcony.[26]

Buffett's anomalous success, and the fame it had brought him, was putting him on the road to becoming a brand just as surely as Skippy peanut butter. Inevitably, therefore, he became the target of a group of finance professors who were at that very moment attempting to prove that someone like Buffett was a mere accident who should not be paid attention, much less worshipped.

These academics believed that the modern-day market was "efficient," and no one was expert enough to beat it. The many who scrambled to beat the average would, in fact, become the average. Their very efforts to beat the market made the work self-defeating and futile, said Eugene Fama, a professor from the University of Chicago. Yet an army of professionals had sprung up who charged everything from modest fees to the soon-to-be-legendary hedge-fund cut of "two-and-twenty" (two percent of assets and twenty percent of returns) for the privilege of processing trades, managing an investor's money, and trying to predict the future behavior of stocks. Every year, the sum of all these people's labors added up to exactly what the market did (less the fees).

Charles Ellis, a consultant to professional money managers, published a book saying that the best way to make money in the market was to simply buy an index of the market itself without paying the high fees that the toll-takers charged.[27] Investors would receive the payback from the entire economy's growth. So far, so good.

The professors who had discovered this efficient-market hypothesis (EMH) kept hacking away at their computers over the years, however, to turn these ideas into an even tighter version. They concluded that *nobody* could beat the average, that the market was so efficient that the price of a stock at any time must reflect every piece of public information about a company. Thus, studying balance sheets, listening to scuttlebutt, digging in libraries, reading newspapers, studying a company's competitors—all of it was futile. The price of a stock at any time was "right." Anybody who beat the average was just lucky—or trading on inside information.

It was certainly true that exceptions to the efficient market had grown rarer. Yet the proponents of EMH denied all exceptions, and to them Buffett—the most visible exception of all—and his lengthening and increasingly acclaimed record became an inconvenient fact. Economists like Paul Samuelson at MIT, Fama at the University of Chicago, Michael Jensen at the University of Rochester, William Sharpe at Stanford, who believed in the "random walk" theory about market behavior, kicked around the Buffett conundrum. Was he a one-off genius or a freak statistical event? A certain amount of derision was heaped on him, as if such an anomalous stunt were not worthy of study. Burton Malkiel, a Princeton economist, summed the whole thing up by saying that anyone who outperformed the stock market consistently was no different from a lucky monkey that had a winning streak at picking stocks by throwing darts at the *Wall Street Journal* stock listings.[28]

Buffett loved the *Wall Street Journal*; he loved it so much that he had made a special deal with the local distributor of the paper. When the batches of *Journals* arrived in Omaha every night, a copy was pulled out and placed in his driveway before midnight. He sat up waiting to read tomorrow's news before everybody else got to see it. It was what he did with the information the *Wall Street Journal* gave him, however, that made him a superior investor. If a monkey got the *Wall Street Journal* in its driveway every night just before midnight, the monkey still could not match Buffett's investing record by throwing darts.

Buffett made sport of the controversy by playing with a *Wall Street Journal* dartboard in his office. The efficient-market hypothesis invalidated him, however. Furthermore, it invalidated Ben Graham. That would not do. He and Munger saw these academics as holders of witch doctorates.[29] Their theory offended Buffett's reverence for rationality and for the profession of teaching.

Columbia held a seminar in 1984 to celebrate the fiftieth anniversary of *Security Analysis* and invited Buffett to represent the Grahamian point of view at the seminar, which was actually more of a debate over EMH. His opponent on the panel, Michael Jensen, stood up and said he felt like "a turkey must feel at the beginning of a turkey shoot."[30] His role in the morality play was to cast withering comments at the antediluvian views of the Grahamian value investors. Some people could do better than the market for long periods, he said. In effect, if enough people flip coins, a few of them will flip heads over and over. That was how randomness worked.

Buffett had spent weeks preparing for this event. He'd anticipated the coin-flipping argument. When he got up for his turn, he said that while this might be so, the row of heads would not be random if all the successful coin-flippers came from the same town. For example, if all the coin-flippers who kept flipping heads came from the tiny village of Graham-and-Doddsville, something specific that they were doing must be making those coins flip heads.

He then pulled out a chart with the track record of nine money managers from Graham-and-Doddsville—Bill Ruane; Charlie Munger; Walter Schloss; Rick Guerin; Tom Knapp and Ed Anderson at Tweedy, Browne; the FMC pension fund; himself; and two others.[31] Their portfolios were not similar; despite a certain amount of coattailing in the early years, they had largely invested on their own. All of them, he said, had been flipping straight heads for more than twenty years, and for the most part had not retired and were still doing it. Such a concentration proved statistically that their success could not have come by random luck.

Since what Buffett said was obviously true on its face, the audience broke into applause and lobbed questions at him, which he answered gladly and at length. The random-walk theory was based on statistics and Greek-letter formulas. The existence of people like Buffett had been waved away using bafflemath. Now, to the Grahamites' relief, Buffett had used numbers to disprove the absolutist version of the efficient-market hypothesis.

That fall, he wrote up "The Superinvestors of Graham-and-Doddsville" as an article for *Hermes,* the magazine of the Columbia Business School. Firing a flamethrower at the edifice of the EMH, this article did much to cement his reputation among investors. And over time, the random walkers revised their argument into "semi-strong" and "weak" forms that allowed for exceptions.[32] The one great service EMH would have performed, if anybody had listened, was to discourage average people from believing they could outwit the market. Nobody except the toll-takers could object to that. But the tendencies of humankind being what they are, the market went on as before. Thus the main effect of "The Superinvestors of Graham-and-Doddsville" was to add to the growing legend, even the cult, that was building around Warren Buffett.

Meanwhile, EMH and its underpinning, the capital asset pricing model, drove extraordinary and deep roots into the investing world; it launched a view of the stock market as an efficient statistical machine. In a reliably efficient market, a stock was risky not based on where it was trading versus its intrinsic value, but based on "volatility"—how likely it was to deviate from the market average. Using that information and newly unleashed computing power, economists and mathematicians started going to Wall Street to make more money than they ever could in academia.

Knowing a stock's volatility allowed portfolio managers to pair up stocks and arbitrage them. But to make big money on arbitrage—buying and selling two nearly identical things to profit from their difference in price—required scaffoldings of debt, in which more and more assets were sold short to buy more and more assets on the "long" side.[33] This expansion of leverage from hedge funds and arbitrage was related to the rise of junk bonds and takeovers occurring at the same time. The models that supported the argument for leveraged buyouts using junk bonds were, like the models used by arbitrageurs, variations of the efficient-market hypothesis. Leverage, however, was like gasoline. In a rising market, a car used more of it to go faster. In a crash, it was what made the car blow up.

Buffett and Munger defined risk as not losing money. To them, risk was "inextricably bound up in your time horizon for holding an asset."[34] Someone who can hold an asset for years can afford to ignore its volatility. Someone who is leveraged does not have that luxury—the investor may not be able to wait out a volatile market. She is burdened by the "carry" (that is, the cost) and she depends on the lender's goodwill.

But betting on volatility seemed to make sense when the market rose as predicted. When enough time passes and nothing bad happens, people who are making a lot of money tend to think it is because they are smart, not because they are taking a lot of risk.[35]

Throughout these profound changes in Wall Street's ways, Buffett's own habits had changed little.[36] What still made his pulse race was buying a company like Fechheimer, which made prison-guard uniforms. People like Tom Murphy had to worry about whether they would be targeted by corporate raiders wielding junk bonds, but Berkshire Hathaway was impregnable because Buffett and friends of Buffett owned so much of its stock; his reputation made Berkshire a fortress where others could shelter. Berkshire had made $120 million on Cap Cities/ABC in the first twelve months it owned the stock; now the very mention that Buffett had bought a stock could, all by itself, move its price and revalue a company by hundreds of millions of dollars.

Ralph Schey, the head of Scott Fetzer, an Ohio conglomerate, got his company into a jam by trying to take it private in a leveraged buyout. With its stable of profitable businesses, from Kirby vacuums to the World Book encyclopedia, Scott Fetzer made appealing prey, and corporate raider Ivan Boesky quickly intervened to make a bid of his own.

Buffett sent Schey a simple letter saying, "We don't do unfriendly deals. If you want to pursue a merger, call me." Schey leaped at the proffer, and $410 million later, Berkshire Hathaway owned Scott Fetzer.[37]

The next to recognize the power of Buffett's reputation was Jamie Dimon, who worked for Sanford Weill, the CEO of the brokerage firm Shearson Lehman, an American Express subsidiary.[38] American Express wanted to sell its insurance arm, Fireman's Fund, to Weill in a management buyout. Weill had already recruited Jack Byrne to leave GEICO and run Fireman's Fund. Dimon approached Buffett to invest his money—and his reputation—in the deal.

Despite their friendship, Buffett was not sorry to lose Byrne. After repairing GEICO's woes, the perpetually itchy Byrne had embarked on a series of acquisitions and entered into new business lines. Buffett wanted GEICO to concentrate on a sure thing, its core business. Furthermore, he had hired a new chief investment officer for GEICO, Lou Simpson, a retiring Chicagoan who had a distaste for rapid trading and expensive growth stocks. Buffett had added Simpson to the Buffett Group right away, and by now Simpson had become the only person besides himself whom Buffett trusted to invest in other stocks—he allowed Simpson to manage all of GEICO's investments. But Simpson and Byrne acted like brothers who fought and made up. Periodically, Simpson tried to bolt; Buffett lured him back. Without Byrne, keeping Simpson would be easier.

"Never let go of a meal ticket" was Buffett's verdict when asked to invest in the Fireman's Fund deal—and Byrne. American Express decided to cut Weill out of the deal, however, and unload Fireman's Fund in a public offering, with Byrne as CEO. To keep Buffett on the menu to attract investors, it offered Berkshire a sweetheart reinsurance deal. Buffett took the deal; Weill, feeling double-crossed, blamed Buffett. By some accounts he carried a grudge against Buffett from then on.

From American Express to Sandy Weill, however, the financial world now understood the power of Buffett's name. At this point, Buffett was tending to so many major investments and advising so many managements that he was either an actual or de facto board member of Cap Cities, Fireman's Fund, the Washington Post Company, GEICO, and Omaha National Corp. And now he reached a turning point, the moment when he had to consider whether to cross the Rubicon.

Buffett had for some time played a dual role. He ran Berkshire Hathaway as if he still managed money for his "partners"—albeit without collecting any fee. He wrote them letters explaining that he made decisions based on personal criteria; he set up the shareholder contribution program, a personal solution to the problem of corporate giving; he refused to split the stock, had never listed it on the New York Stock Exchange, and considered the shareholders tantamount to members of a club. "Although our form is corporate, our attitude is partnership," he had written—and meant it. At the same time, he enjoyed living the life of a major-company CEO. Above all, he was now so attached to Berkshire that it had become a virtual extension of himself.

The loosely defined dual role he was playing had so far suited him and his shareholders. Now, however, a decision faced him that required him to choose— he could either run a de facto partnership or continue his role as a major-company CEO. But he could no longer do both.

The reason was taxes. Berkshire was already burdened with corporate income taxes, a cost the partnership had not faced. On the other hand, Buffett charged his Berkshire partners no "fee" to manage their money. That was a good deal (for everyone but Buffett) or at least the shareholders' loyalty suggests they saw it that way. Now, however, in 1986, Congress passed a major tax-reform act that, among other things, repealed what was called the General Utilities Doctrine. Formerly, a corporation could sell its assets without paying any taxes as long as it was liquidating and distributing the assets to the shareholders. The shareholders would be taxed on their gain, but the gain would not be taxed twice.

Once the General Utilities Doctrine was repealed, any liquidation of a corporation and distribution of its assets would result in a tax on the corporation's profits and another tax on the shareholders upon distribution. Since the double tax added up to a staggering amount of money, closely held and family corporations all over the country rushed to liquidate themselves before the act went into effect. Buffett, who regularly said in his shareholder letters that Berkshire had gotten so large that its money was a barrier to investing success, could have distributed its assets, then raised a more manageable sum—still in the billions—set up a new partnership, and started over investing within weeks (collecting his fee again, to boot). With $1.2 billion of unrealized profits on Berkshire's balance sheet, had Buffett liquidated Berkshire, he could have given his shareholders a total tax avoidance of more than $400 million and the chance to start over in a partnership free of the corporate double tax.[39] But he didn't.

Buffett wrote a lengthy dissertation on taxes in his annual letter, in which he addressed this topic and dismissed the idea of liquidating out of hand: *"If Berkshire, for example, were to be liquidated—which it most certainly won't be— shareholders would, under the new law, receive far less from the sales of our properties than they would have if the properties had been sold in the past."*[40]

The Warren Buffett of old would not have sneered at an extra $185 million in his own bank account and the chance to start over earning fees without the corporate income tax—which is what his decision not to liquidate Berkshire Hathaway in 1986 cost him personally. But ordinary greed no longer drove his decisions—for this cost him far more than any other shareholder. His long-standing attachment to Berkshire held him so firmly in its grip that he gave up the option of keeping Berkshire as a virtual partnership. Otherwise, he would have liquidated without a second's hesitation.

Instead he had crossed the Rubicon and chosen the role of being the CEO of a major corporation, like Procter & Gamble or Colgate-Palmolive, one that would continue to exist after he was gone.

This company, Berkshire, with its disparate parts, was hard to value. Munger liked to joke that Berkshire was the "Frozen Corporation,"[41] since it would grow endlessly but never pay a penny in dividends to its owners. If the owners couldn't extract any money from their money-making machine, how much was that company really worth?

But Buffett was growing Berkshire's book value far faster than his shareholders could have accumulated such wealth themselves, and he had the scorecard to prove it. Moreover, it was a long-term scorecard, far more comfortable for him than the year-to-year pressure of beating the market's bogey. By shutting down the partnership, he had freed himself from that tyranny; in fact he no longer presented numbers in a fashion that allowed someone to calculate his investing performance from inception.[42]

Yet even though Buffett had now officially joined the CEO club, he had no desire to acquire most of their habits—collecting wine or art, buying a yacht.

There was one exception. One day in 1986, he called his friend Walter Scott Jr., a down-to-earth hometown boy who had worked for Peter Kiewit Sons', Inc. all his life, just like his father before him. Scott had succeeded Peter Kiewit, then made his reputation during a federal highway bid-rigging scandal that threatened Kiewit's existence. By forthrightness, "groveling," and thorough reforms, Scott led the company through a long restoration—a model for dealing with the government in a corporate life-or-death situation.[43] He was such a trusted friend of Buffett that Katharine Graham stayed in the Scotts' apartment on the few occasions that she visited Omaha.

"Walter," Buffett asked, "how do you justify buying a private airplane?" Buffett knew that Kiewit had a fleet of private jets because it was always having to ferry its employees to remote construction sites.

"Warren," said Scott, "you don't justify it. You rationalize it."

Two days later, Buffett called back. "Walter, I've rationalized it," he said. "Now, how do you hire a pilot and maintain a plane?"

Scott offered to let Buffett piggyback the maintenance of his proposed new jet on Kiewit's fleet, and Buffett went off and sheepishly bought a used Falcon 20—the same type of plane that Kiewit employees flew—as Berkshire's corporate jet.[44]

Of course, buying a private jet conflicted with another of the things he cared most about: not wasting money. Buffett had never lived down an incident in an airport in which Kay Graham had asked him for a dime to make a phone call. He pulled out the only coin he had, a quarter, started to bolt off to get change, but Graham had stopped him by teasing him into letting her waste fifteen cents. So, for Buffett, it was like leaping in one bound over Mount Kilimanjaro to go from justifying twenty-five cents for a phone call to rationalizing two pilots and an entire airplane to carry him around like a pharaoh on a litter. But he was doing a fair amount of rationalizing this year, having just rationalized giving up $185 million in tax avoidance as well.

Still, it bothered him—the jet so plainly contradicted his upbringing and self-image. He started to make fun of himself to the shareholders, saying, "I work cheap and travel expensive."

The plane ushered in a new phase of his life. Buffett clung tenaciously to his corn belt—even while wearing black tie—yet fraternized ever more often with hoity-toity sosoity, as CEO of the Frozen Corporation. In 1987, Ambassador Walter Annenberg had invited Warren and Susie out to Palm Springs for a weekend with their friends Ronald and Nancy Reagan. Buffett had dined at the White House and already knew both the Reagans from visiting Kay Graham's house on Martha's Vineyard, but he had never spent a whole weekend with a sitting President. Nor had he ever played golf with one.

"*Walter had his own private nine-hole golf course at Sunnylands. He had his own driving range with ten tees lined up and all these golf balls piled in perfect little neat pyramids. And there wasn't anybody there. The course was immaculate. If he had four foursomes, Walter would say, 'That's too much play for my course,' and send one of them off to play at Thunderbird Country Club. I'd go out there and hit four golf balls, and somebody'd run out and replace the pyramids. And that was the day at Sunnylands. It was as fancy as living gets.*"

Annenberg paired Buffett that weekend with Reagan as a golf partner, so Secret Service agents trailed them—but refused to fetch golf balls out of water traps as Buffett had hoped.

Buffett had a mixed view of Reagan as President. He admired Reagan's handling of geopolitics. However, under Reagan the United States went from being the world's largest lender to its largest borrower. Just as junk bonds and leverage were ballooning on Wall Street, the government had been running up mountains of debt—which Buffett considered the Wimpy style of economics: I will gladly pay you Tuesday for a hamburger today.[45] Buffett's style was to own the cattle ranch—and he had the balance sheet to prove it.

Armored by Berkshire Hathaway's balance sheet—and a golf scorecard signed by the President of the United States—Buffett was now a fortress of power. Every financial statistic pertaining to him and his company rang with exclamation points. Berkshire Hathaway's book value per share had grown by more than twenty-three percent a year for twenty-three years! Buffett's first group of partners had reaped $1.1 million for each $1,000 put into the partnership!

Berkshire was trading at the dizzying price of $2,950 per share! Buffett himself had a net worth of $2.1 billion! A Wall Street money manager—an investor— was the ninth-richest man in the U.S.! Never had anyone climbed from the ranks of those who managed other people's wealth to join the celebrated few on top of the feeding chain of riches. For the first time, the money from a partner- ship of investors had been used to grow an enormous business enterprise through a chess-game series of decisions to buy whole businesses as well as stocks. Inevitably, more people were going to call him for help.

The next person to pick up the phone was John Gutfreund, the man who ran Salomon Brothers and had endeared himself to Buffett by helping to save GEICO in 1976.

That he had done so showed both the strength and weakness of Salomon. The GEICO stock underwriting had been based on the opinion of one equity research analyst. If the firm had any stature in the marketplace of selling stocks, it would have passed on the deal as far too small to be worth the legal liability if it failed—as all the other firms had done. But Salomon, bold and decisive rather than bureaucratic, dared the risk because it needed the business. Buffett had always taken a liking to people who extended themselves and helped him make money. And Gutfreund's reserved, intellectual prep-school personality, coupled with a domineering brutality, seems to have added to Buffett's trust in him as overseer of an unruly-by-nature investment bank.

Gutfreund had grown up the son of a well-to-do meat-truck company owner in Scarsdale, New York, a golf-course-ringed suburb close to New York City. He'd majored in literature at Oberlin College, but was drawn to the trad- ing floor by a golfing friend of his father's, Billy Salomon, a descendant of one of the firm's three founding brothers.

Salomon Brothers was born in 1910. Less than a decade later, the U.S. gov- ernment became the tiny firm's client by adding Salomon to its list of registered dealers of government securities. With this endorsement, Salomon, a game little terrier, scrapped its way to respectable size over the next three decades by stick- ing to its core business of trading bonds using its wits, nerve, and fidelity to clients.[46] Meanwhile, dozens of other small brokers closed shop or were swal- lowed up by larger ones.

Joining a roomful of men who spent their days buying and selling bonds for clients on the phone, Gutfreund, like the rest, carved off a little slice of everything for Salomon in return for his labors. He proved a deft trader and made partner in 1963 at the age of thirty-four.

In 1978 Billy Salomon promoted Gutfreund to head of the firm, then retired. Three years later, Gutfreund showed up on his friend and mentor's beachfront porch in East Hampton to say that he was selling Salomon to Phibro, a giant commodities dealer, to create Phibro-Salomon Inc. Gutfreund and his partners walked away with an average of nearly $8 million apiece in profit from the sale, while those who had built the firm and were now retired—like Billy Salomon— got zero, zilch.[47] One former partner thought it a Greek tragedy: the story of Oedipus, who had killed his own father.

Gutfreund became co-CEO with Phibro's David Tendler. Running a firm with a co-CEO is like trying to balance two ends of a seesaw in the air. When Phibro's business slumped after the sale just as Salomon's was soaring, Gutfreund wasted no time. He slammed his end of the seesaw to the ground and sent Tendler flying.

Gutfreund added a foreign-currency business, broadened into equity trad- ing and underwriting, and expanded the bond business into Japan, Switzerland, and Germany. For the next few years, the witch doctors from academia with their computers and formulas filtered onto Wall Street, and Phibro-Salomon's floor became populated with PhDs who unlocked the mathematical secrets of stripping, slicing, packaging, and trading mortgages. By inventing a whole new segment of the bond market, Salomon (for the Phibro-Salomon name never quite replaced "Solly" in people's minds and was dumped in 1986) grew in a few short years from a second-tier firm to the top of the Street, with a swagger to match.

They ruled from "The Room," Solly's trading floor, a smoky palace about a third the size of an airplane hangar, filled with long double rows of desks where the traders, salespeople, and assistants crouched in front of banks of screens with a slice of pizza in one hand and a telephone receiver in the other. The daily battle took place as a symphony of groans and curses and farts and screams punctuating the background babble. Eccentrics were welcome, as long as they produced. Gutfreund walked the aisles glaring through horn-rimmed specta- cles, chomping his stogie, and shredding screwups into piles of mulch on the trading floor.

The characters on the trading floor so dominated the bond-underwriting market that *BusinessWeek* crowned Salomon "The King of Wall Street."[48] The story also said it was the kind of place where the "long knives" could come out if things went south—in other words, that Gutfreund would purge anyone sus- pected of dissent in order to still a revolt.[49]

Salomon's profits peaked in 1985, when the firm made $557 million after tax. But the new businesses—principally equities—didn't earn their keep; thus, internal competition started to get out of hand. The star traders started to leave, enticed by million-dollar offers from other firms. Gutfreund ratcheted the pay upward to stem the tide. But he did not crack down on the new departments when they failed to produce, then came in with new five-year plans to fix their failures. His intimidating personality covered a soft underbelly: He shrank from hard decisions and substantive confrontations. As time passed, he spent less time in The Room and presided with a somewhat distracted air over a kingdom in which the threat of poison hung in the air. "My problem is that I am too deliberate on people issues,"[50] he would later say. Somewhat unfairly, observers blamed not him but his wife, Susan.

Tied to her husband by a long, long leash, all through the 1980s Susan Gutfreund had raced headlong up Fifth Avenue, dragging the once-retiring CEO of Salomon behind her into international society. Gutfreund came to tolerate and even enjoy it because, he said, she expanded his horizons.

"It's so expensive to be rich," the former flight attendant complained—perhaps facetiously but nonetheless famously—to Malcolm Forbes.[51] Susan's party guests received chauffeur-delivered invitations tied with yellow roses for events that featured four types of caviar. She chilled her perfume in a refrigerator next to her bathtub. She yanked up her Chicago roots to become such a Francophile that her butler answered the phone in French. And she redid Salomon's executive meeting room, drenching it with so much passementerie and ormolu that it "looked like a French bordello."[52] Thus did Susan Gutfreund become 1980s Nouvelle Society's most beloved object of parody. Susan's friends defended her, but nobody, not even her husband, denied that this outpouring of opulence had diverted his attention, at least a little bit.[53]

A corporate history published around this time included a telling remark. Instead of making a decision and expecting others to follow, it said Gutfreund "liked to involve the people who would be affected" and "would bend over backward to make them comfortable with what was to be done." Nevertheless, wrote the author, protesting a bit too heartily, Gutfreund "is in ultimate control" and "his decisions after consultations are final."[54] In fact, some of Gutfreund's former partners, now retitled "managing directors," were mounting a major challenge to his authority. Having kept their commitment to grow, they now blamed him for the bloated costs and vied with one another for territory.

By the end of 1986, when earnings had begun to sink from the burden of the payroll—newly swollen by a forty percent staff increase—the managing directors nearly dethroned Gutfreund in a coup. The firm's largest shareholder, the South African company Minorco, grew impatient and told Gutfreund it wanted to sell its block of stock. But when nothing happened and Salomon's stock languished as the Dow rose forty-four percent, Minorco found its own buyer: Ron Perelman, the feared corporate raider who had taken over Revlon.

The executives did not want to work for Perelman and his designee.[55] Gutfreund pushed the panic button and called Buffett, asking him to invest in Salomon as "white knight" to save Salomon from Perelman.[56]

Owning a company that sold vacuum cleaners was one thing. Even though Salomon was dominated by trading, which Buffett liked, the firm was muscling its way into investment banking and had belatedly caved to market pressure and set up a merchant banking business to finance takeovers using junk bonds, a technique he despised.

Yet Salomon's expertise in reshaping the bond market appealed to Buffett at a time when good stock ideas had become scarce.[57] While he denigrated junk bonds, he opportunistically arbitraged the takeovers that were done using them—shorting the stock of the acquirer and buying the stock of the acquiree. Since Salomon's bond arbitrage unit made most of the firm's profits, the firm in fact was an arbitrage machine, and he had a deep affinity and respect for this corner of Wall Street.

Moreover, Buffett's nostrils had caught the rich warm scent of money, for Gutfreund had the air of desperation. So he said that Berkshire would buy $700 million of Salomon preferred stock, as long as it made fifteen percent.[58] Gutfreund ordered his horrified employees to design a security that would deliver to Buffett the kind of returns normally earned only on a junk bond. Over the weekend of a Jewish holiday, when Gutfreund knew the observant Perelman would be neutralized, Buffett flew to New York, and he and Gutfreund met at Salomon's lawyers' offices. Buffett walked in by himself, without a briefcase or even a pad of paper in his hand. Over a handshake, he agreed to buy a preferred stock with a nine percent coupon that would convert to common stock at the price of $38.[59]

The nine percent yield gave Buffett a premium return until the stock went to $38, when he had the right to convert to equity. So the upside was unlimited. But if the stock went down, he had the right to "put" the security back to Salomon and get his money back.[60] The deal worked out to an expected fifteen percent profit, on an investment that carried very little risk.[61]

Inside Salomon, people were outraged.[62] For his huge fifteen percent return, Buffett was, as writer Michael Lewis would later explain, making "only the safe bet that Salomon would not go bankrupt."[63]

What the firm had bought with all this money was Buffett's reputation, which came partly at the expense of Gutfreund's power. Along with the deal, Buffett and Munger each got board seats. Before signing the papers, Buffett climbed aboard his new jet and flew to New York. He met Munger at One New York Plaza to inspect Salomon.

Standing outside Gutfreund's office next to the trading floor, he beheld The Room for the first time. Hundreds of disheveled people sweated in front of tiny green screens. Most had phones glued to each ear as they jostled, spat, puffed, and spun their way through multimillion-dollar deals. Curses and screams cut through the low roar that filled the air. Above the scene hung a hazy fog. So many traders calmed their nerves with tobacco, why bother to abstain? Everyone's lungs were always filled with nicotine anyway.

Munger crossed his arms and turned to Buffett. "So, Warren," he said. "You really want to invest in this, huh?"

Buffett stood, gazing out through the haze over the pandemonium that he was about to buy. "Mmmm-hmmmm," he said, after a long pause.[64]

47

White Nights

Observers stood slack-jawed that the Midas from Omaha had gilded Salomon Brothers with his touch. Buffett—the burger-chomping billionaire next door—had put his money behind a Wall Street bank.

He routinely railed against the Wall Street of which he was now very much a part. He wrote the Berkshire shareholders excoriating the junk bonds used to finance takeovers—including Salomon's—which, he said, were "sold by those who didn't care to those who didn't think."[1] *"Wall Street is the only place people ride to in a Rolls-Royce to get advice from people who take the subway,"* he said.[2] On the pages of the *Washington Post*, he had decried the "casino society" that was making the corporate raiders rich. Why not tax one hundred percent of the speculators' profits?[3] There was certainly a lot to tax. From 1982 to 1987, the Dow Jones Industrial Average had streaked from 777 to 2,722. If you want to make money, he told business-school students, "hold your nose and go to Wall Street." But he was already there.

The image of Wall Street seducing a Midwestern populist into bed was too good to leave alone. Asked by a reporter why he owned the largest single chunk of Salomon when Wall Street was such a sinkhole, Buffett did not hesitate. He had placed his faith in one man. John Gutfreund, he said, "is an outstanding, honorable man of integrity."[4]

Buffett always did fall in love with people, and observers said he was noticeably in love with Gutfreund—at first. Yet the man who once quit his job as a "prescriptionist" to escape the inherent conflict of interest with his customers couldn't allow his affection for John Gutfreund to shield him from the basic fact that he owned part of an investment bank. How had he gotten himself into the— at best, awkward—position of sitting on the board of such a company?[5] It was as if, during a dry spell, Buffett's urge to make money had once again overwhelmed his high hopes, high aspirations, and high principles. And as had been true throughout his life, whenever his avarice got the upper hand, trouble followed.

At the time that Buffett invested in Salomon, the market was near a breaking point. Unlike the 1960s, he didn't have a partnership to dissolve, but over the next few months he started dumping stocks. Part of what was driving the market upward was a new invention, the "S&P 500 future." Salomon, like all major banks, now traded these derivative contracts that were a way of betting how high or low the index of S&P 500 stocks would be on a certain date.[6] Derivative contracts work like this: In the Rockwood Chocolate deal, the value of the futures contract was "derived from" the price of cocoa beans on a certain date. If the beans turned out to be worth less than the price agreed to by the contract (including the insurance premium), the person who had bought the futures contract as insurance "won." Her losses were covered. If the beans were worth more, the person who had sold the futures contract as insurance "won." He got the insurance premium, plus the contract entitled him to buy the beans below the then-current market price.

Suppose that in the weight deal Buffett had made with Howie for the rent on his farm, he didn't want to risk Howie's actually losing weight, which would drop the rent. Since this was under Howie's control, Warren might want to buy insurance from someone else. He could say to Susie, "Lookit, I'll pay you a hundred bucks today. If Howie loses twenty pounds and keeps it off for the next six months, you'll pay me the two thousand dollars of rent that I'll lose. If he doesn't keep it off for the whole six months, you don't have to pay me the rent and you get to keep the hundred bucks." The index that determined the gain or loss was "derived" from Howie's weight, and whether or not Buffett would make such a deal was based on a handicap of the odds that Howie would be able to lose the weight and keep it off.

The S&P "equity index futures" that money managers were buying as insurance in 1987 paid them back if the stock market fell below a certain level. People who assumed the market would keep going up were often "gambling" by "selling" the insurance. They wanted income from the premiums.

Equity index futures were swarming like gnats in July. If stocks started to fall, all the bills would be presented to the sellers of insurance at once. They would have to dump stocks to meet their claims. The buyers of the index futures, meanwhile, were often using them to insure "program trades" that would sell automatically as the market fell, triggering a cascade of sales.

By the early fall the market got nervous, and began to stutter and stall. On Black Monday, October 19, 1987, stocks plunged a record-breaking 508 points as everybody tried to squeeze through the keyhole at once. The market came close to a trading halt, as it did in 1929, and suffered its largest one-day percentage drop in history.[7]

The Buffett Group happened to be meeting on the third day of the avalanche, this time in Colonial Williamsburg. The topic planned for discussion as stocks were peaking had been "Is the Group finished with the market?" Instead, with the market crashing around their ears, for three days Buffett and the others glowed like fireflies, checking stock prices and phoning their traders with controlled excitement. Unlike the many people devastated by losses, they were *buying* stocks.[8]

When the avalanche victims were dug out of the snow, however, Warren's sister Doris turned out to be one of them. She had sold what were called "naked puts," a type of derivative peddled by a Falls Church, Virginia, broker. Naked puts were promises to cover somebody else's losses if the market fell—"naked" because they were unclothed by collateral and thus unprotected against loss.[9] The broker had emphasized that the naked puts would provide Doris with a steady stream of income, which she needed. It is hard to imagine that the broker gave her any kind of realistic description of the risk she was taking, especially using a scary term like "naked put." Doris was unsophisticated about investing but highly intelligent, with a hard-nosed common sense. She had not talked to Warren about the investment, however. He was famous for recommending only extremely safe, low-return investments, like Treasury or municipal bonds, especially when counseling divorced women. These were investments that he would never make himself. Doris had trusted him enough to become one of his first partners; she trusted him implicitly when it came to investing for Berkshire. But that long-ago childhood episode when Cities Service Preferred went down after he bought it for himself and Doris might have loomed large in both their minds, had she asked him for advice. She didn't ask.

Now, acting on her own, Doris had incurred losses so large that they wiped out her Berkshire stock and threatened her with bankruptcy.

Doris idealized her brother, viewed him as a protective figure, and kept a little shrine to him, featuring miniature golf clubs, Pepsi bottles, and other symbolic accoutrements of his life. But when she had a problem, instead of going to Warren, she called Susie as a go-between, as everyone in the family did. By this time Doris had been married and divorced three times. She felt she had rushed into her first marriage out of insecurity; her second had failed in part because she had felt coerced into it and thus hadn't fought hard enough to save it. Her third marriage had been a terrible misjudgment. By now, Doris had experienced a great deal of mistreatment in her life, but rather than letting it cow her, she fought back. This time, however, she didn't know what to do.

"You don't ever need to worry," Susie had told her about her brother after her third divorce. "He'll always take care of you."

After she confessed to Susie what she had done and asked for help, Warren called her early on a Saturday morning. He said that if he gave her the money to pay her creditors, it would only help the businesses to whom she owed money—the counterparties whom she had insured. His logic was that they were specula-tors; therefore he would not bail them out. As she realized that this meant he was not going to help her, she broke out in a cold sweat and her legs started shaking. She was sure this meant that her brother despised her. He felt that his decision was simply rational.

"I could have given a couple million dollars to her creditors if I'd wanted. But, you know, the hell with them. I mean, this broker woman who sold this stuff to Doris—she'd busted everybody in that particular branch."

Doris hoped that Susie would save her. Susie had so much money of her own, and Warren gave her so much money, most of which she gave away. However, she did nothing now to help Doris financially.

The story hit the *Washington Post* that the sister of "a highly successful investor" had done something extremely dumb. Damaging Warren's reputation was a serious transgression in the Buffett family, and Doris's timing was terrible. The Buffetts were still trying to recover from a tragic event several months before. Susie's nephew Billy Rogers had died of a fatal overdose in a rooming house in San Francisco. Susie, Peter, and Mary discovered his body when they did not hear from him for several days. Losing Billy had been Susie's greatest failure as a rescuer of people, and the greatest sorrow she had ever known. His death had publicly bared the imperfections beneath the family's wholesome surface. Now, Warren may have known—on some level—that he was rationaliz-ing about not helping his sister. Certainly he feared Doris's ire; when she felt threatened—like Kay Graham—Doris defended herself as if cornered. Warren could not tolerate shrill behavior from anyone, not even her. So he stopped calling, and nobody else in the family contacted her either. Frightened at being abandoned and deeply wounded, Doris browbeat her mother for money and loans to prevent her from losing her home.[10] Ironically, the Federal Reserve had lowered interest rates, companies were buying their own stocks, and the market was recovering quickly from the debacle, leaving only victims like Doris behind in its wake.

But behind the scenes, Warren was arranging to advance his sister $10,000 a month from the trust left by Howard's will. "That was more money than I have ever spent in my whole life," she says. The tension deescalated; they were able to speak. She was almost prostrate with gratitude—until she realized that this was her own money, which she was simply being paid early. At the time, her share of the trust, having grown from a little over 2,000 shares of Berkshire that were worth $30,000 in 1964, was valued at about $10 million. The trust was not structured to pay out until Leila died, when Doris and Bertie would receive the money in four installments. As a further olive branch, however, her brother set up the Sherwood Foundation, which paid out $500,000 a year in charitable gifts. Doris, Warren's children, and Astrid could each allocate $100,000 to any causes they chose. The annual income produced was as if her brother had put around $7 million into a trust for the five of them. Doris's share, therefore, was almost as much as if Warren had given her the money after all, but in a different form.

Of course, it was not in a form she could use to pay her debts or save her house—Warren never gave money outright, only in a manner that he controlled. Still, as the storm subsided, Doris regained perspective. She was acutely aware that without him she would have had nothing in the first place. As she scraped together the money to pay her debts, their relationship gradually returned to normal, and the shrine stayed in place on her wall.

The other victim of the crash that Buffett had to deal with was Salomon. Only three months after Berkshire's investment, he and Munger attended their first board meeting. The topic of the day was the $75 million that Black Monday had cost the firm.[11] Salomon faced the cleanup from Black Monday weakened by the fact that, only days before the crash, Gutfreund, his moon-shaped face impassive, had laid off eight hundred people and discontinued marginally profitable businesses such as commercial paper trading (a backwater of the bond business) so abruptly that the disruption hurt relationships with some important clients almost beyond repair.[12] These and the losses from Black Monday were going to gouge a deep hole in the shareholders' pockets that year. And with that, Salomon's stock fell into the tank.

The shareholders were suffering, yet the compensation committee—which Buffett had joined—began to discuss lowering the price at which the employees' stock options could be exercised.

Buffett felt this was morally wrong. The others outvoted him two to one. He was outraged.[13] But his role on the Salomon board was mostly titular. His advice was rarely sought and less often taken. Even though Salomon stock by then was starting to recover, the repricing of the stock options, he says, made his investment in Salomon *way less attractive financially than it had been.*

"I could have fought harder and been more vocal. I might have felt better about myself if I did. But it wouldn't have changed the course of history. Unless you sort of enjoy combat, it doesn't make sense." Buffett's willingness to do combat—even in a roundabout way—had diminished markedly since the days of Sanborn Map, Dempster, and the Buffetting of Seabury Stanton.

"I don't enjoy battles. I won't run from them if I need to do it, but I don't enjoy them at all. When it came to the board, Charlie and I didn't even vote against it. We voted yes. We didn't even abstain, because abstaining is the same thing as throwing down the gauntlet. And there were other things at Salomon. One thing after another would come up that I thought was nutty, but they didn't want me to say anything. And then the question is, do you say anything? I don't get in fights just to get in fights."

Buffett had been originally attracted to Gutfreund, the reserved, thoughtful man in love with his work, who arrived every day at seven a.m., lit up the first of his huge Temple Hall Jamaican cigars, and wandered among the shirtsleeved traders to tell them, "You've got to be ready to bite the ass off a bear every morning."[14] Indeed, it appeared to employees who made presentations in board meetings that Buffett was a "relatively passive" board member.[15] He seemed to understand little of the details of how the business was run, and adjusting to a business that wasn't literally made of bricks-and-mortar or run like an assembly line was not easy for him.[16] Since he didn't like the way the investment was working out, he always had another choice, which was to sell it and resign from the board.[17] Wall Street boiled with rumors that Buffett and Gutfreund had had a falling out; that Buffett was either going to sell or to fire Gutfreund and bring in someone else to run the firm.[18] But it hadn't come to that. Someone as prominent as Buffett selling and resigning from the board as a major investor would be a shocking gesture that would drive down Salomon's stock price and cost his own shareholders. By now his reputation had become part of Berkshire's value. Moreover, he hadn't given up on Gutfreund. His whole reason for investing was

Gutfreund, and when Buffett threw his arms around someone, it took an ax to split them apart. Thus, as the holidays approached, he and Gutfreund struggled uneasily to work out their differences.

Buffett did have a merry Christmas that year. His present to himself was Coca-Cola. It would make up for a great deal of the unhappiness from Salomon. At a White House dinner some time earlier, he had reconnected with his old friend Don Keough, who was now president and chief operating officer of the company; Keough had convinced him to switch from his own concoction of Pepsi dosed with cherry syrup to the newly introduced Cherry Coke. Buffett tried it and liked it. His family and friends were gobsmacked when the man so famously loyal performed this turnaround. For years, KO (Coca-Cola) stock had been too expensive for Buffett to consider. Now the company had gotten into trouble, its bottlers locked in a fierce price war with Pepsi that had taken the price of Coke down to around $38 a share. Although still expensive, it had the same quality of a great brand under duress as American Express had had earlier. The way Warren looked at it, Coca-Cola was pouring forth a waterfall of cash, and spending only a small portion of that to operate.

When Coca-Cola products turned up at Buffett's shareholder meeting in 1988, Berkshire shareholders began swigging Coke in imitation of him. They had no idea that, through Berkshire, they also owned the stock. The meeting took on a whole new tenor that year when a thousand people showed up at the Joslyn Art Museum auditorium. This was the year that the Frozen Corporation, no longer a quasi-partnership, officially joined big-time corporate America and listed itself on the New York Stock Exchange. The Berkshire meeting had to be delayed because so many people came that shareholders were having trouble finding parking spots. Buffett had an inspiration. He rented two school buses and persuaded a few hundred shareholders to follow him after the meeting, like the Pied Piper of commerce, to the Nebraska Furniture Mart. Part of the appeal was the chance to meet the indomitable Mrs. B, about whom Buffett had been writing and talking for five years. The shareholders were so charmed by the tiny tank of a woman perched on her electric cart in the carpet department—and by her prices—that they spent $57,000.[19]

By year's end, the shareholders still did not know that Berkshire had purchased more than fourteen million shares of KO at a cost of almost $600 million.[20] Because his every action now moved markets, Buffett had gotten special dispensation from the SEC not to disclose his trades for a year. Berkshire soon owned more than six percent of the company, worth $1.2 billion.[21] In March

1989, when his position was revealed, the resulting hullaballoo caused so much demand that the New York Stock Exchange had to stop trading the stock to keep the price from skyrocketing out of control.

Coca-Cola's CEO, Roberto Goizueta, glowed with delight at the famous investor's endorsement. He asked Buffett to join his board, possibly the most prestigious in North America. Buffett accepted with alacrity, steeped himself in all things Coca-Cola, and met a number of new people who were fellow board members, including Herbert Allen, the blunt-spoken, straight-shooting chairman of Allen & Co. The two became allies. Allen invited the Buffetts to his Sun Valley conference, which was emerging as the quintessential elephant bump for corporate CEOs. At Sun Valley, investors, Hollywood, and media moguls met to mingle and play every July.

Buffett knew this meant adding a new annual event to his calendar, but Sun Valley was important and he wanted to attend. Moreover, he now had the means to arrive in style. In keeping with his rising stature as a member of the CEO Club, he had just swapped the used Falcon for a fancy new Challenger jet that cost nearly $7 million. He revealed the airplane—which he had dubbed the *Indefensible*—in his shareholder letter, making sport of himself with St. Augustine's prayer: "Help me, oh Lord, to become chaste—but not yet." He would soon write his shareholders that he wanted to be buried in the jet.

On his way to the airport to fly to Sun Valley, Buffett visited his sister-in-law, Dottie, in the hospital. Frail, twig-thin, a longtime alcoholic, Dottie had contracted a severe case of Guillain-Barré syndrome, an autoimmune disorder that can completely paralyze the nervous system. She was in a coma, and Susie had moved back to Omaha temporarily to care for her. While there, she was helping Howie campaign for Douglas County Commissioner as a Republican. Warren, naturally, had chosen not to back his son financially. But Susie was seen everywhere fund-raising for him; she put the family imprimatur behind her son.[22]

When Howie won the race, it meant that he would be spending more time in Omaha. Susie Jr. had also recently moved back, so that her husband, Allen, could take over as executive director of the Buffett Foundation.

Having his daughter around pleased Warren. Susie Jr. shared her mother's caretaking quality, although packaged in a more businesslike style. He would now have two women in Omaha to look after him. More women to look after him was something that he had always rationalized. *"Women don't mind taking care of themselves,"* he said. *"Men mind taking care of themselves. I think women understand men better than men understand women. I'll eat asparagus before I give up women.*" His desire to be taken care of by women was so overwhelming that he mostly left it up to the women to settle any differences in their hell-bent desire to do what, in each of their opinions, was in his best interest. Susie Jr. and Astrid began to work out their respective roles.

The network of connections he had forged now brought Buffett a business that would certainly put him in favor with all his women—Borsheim's, an Omaha jewelry store. Louis Friedman, the brother-in-law of Mrs. B, had founded this company, which carried high- and mid-range merchandise at discount prices. Buffett had learned how strongly women preferred jewelry to clothes, no matter how well clothing "held its value." The person most likely to be pleased by this purchase was Big Susie, who had been assembling an impressive collection of jewelry given by her contrite husband. Susie Jr. also appreciated jewelry, as did Warren's sisters and Kay Graham. The only one not that interested in jewelry was Astrid, who was uncomfortable with expensive things, though if he gave her jewelry, she certainly wouldn't turn it down.

So Warren's Christmas shopping for the women in his life was simplified in 1989. He worked out a system: earrings, pearls, watches, everybody would get a variation on some theme each year. But he himself got nothing to equal the hefty chunk of Coca-Cola that he'd bought so happily the year before. Worse still, he got a lump of coal in his stocking in the form of a new book, *Liar's Poker,* written by former Salomon bond salesman Michael Lewis. Named after a bluffing game that traders played using the serial numbers on dollar bills, the book captured Salomon's swaggering, innovative, energetic culture and how it had begun to break down in 1986 and 1987. *Liar's Poker* turned into a whopping bestseller; it depicted the firm's eccentricities so memorably that Salomon would never again live down its reputation as a sort of zoo for the most aggressive and uncouth people on Wall Street.[23] The end of the 1980s takeover boom was another problem for Buffett, for while he was still arbitraging announced deals, his usual feeding territory was empty. With no great businesses to buy, Buffett once again lowered his standards as he had when buying Hochschild-Kohn.

The lure this time was other CEOs, who, fearing for their jobs or their autonomy, began to offer him more special deals to invest. For Berkshire, he bought three apparently lucrative "convertible preferred" stocks, all structured along the lines of the Salomon deal, paying him on average nine percent, which gave him a floor on his return while also giving him the right to convert in case the companies did well. Each of these companies was quite different. Champion, a poorly managed paper business, was thought to be "in play" among takeover artists.[24] Gillette, a business with a huge "moat" around its brand—like See's Candies, invulnerable to competition—was being temporarily shunned by investors. And Pittsburgh-based US Air, formerly called Allegheny Airlines, a weak regional player in a newly deregulated industry, was also "in play."

Like the Salomon preferred stock, the terms of these special deals meant that critics suddenly viewed Buffett as protecting the interests of entrenched CEOs. It was of course in the interest of his own shareholders to maximize their returns while protecting them from risk, but Buffett now looked like one of those boardroom insiders who depended on special deals to get ahead.

In the age of the buyout funds and corporate raiders, this level of greed was chump change. Buffett could have easily been a buyout king himself. But what his determination to stay friendly and on the side of management did make clear was that he was now one of the guys at the country club. Ben Graham had always felt that if someone traded in stocks, this necessarily made him an outsider—because he had to be willing to displease a company's management. Buffett, who wanted to be liked by everyone, had been trying to bridge that gap since his earliest investing days when he became friends with Lorimer Davidson at GEICO. Now "Many Wall Street investors say Mr. Buffett's special deals amount to a kind of gentlemanly protection game," said one news story.[25]

In the end, what looked like sweetheart deals turned out to be no more than finely handicapped bets. Only Gillette turned into a winner, ultimately earning Berkshire $5.5 billion. US Air was the worst. Buffett had made a number of remarks over the years about the stupidity of investing in things with wings. Then the company suspended its dividend and, like Cleveland's Worst Mill, the stock plunged. "That was the dumbest fucking thing, going into that deal!" one friend exploded. "What the hell are you guys doing? You violated every one of your principles!"[26] Buffett would later agree, saying, *"As soon as the check cleared, the company went into the red and never came out. I have an 800 number I call and say, 'My name is Warren Buffett and I'm an Air-aholic.'"*[27] Charlie Munger's dry comment was, "Warren didn't call me on that one."

Salomon, the model for these deals, was also not doing well. After the crash and the near-escape from Perelman, the merger business had been slow to get back on its feet, and talented bankers left for elsewhere. Gutfreund had restructured the firm once again in another round of layoffs. But the managing directors no longer feared him. "People kept threatening John and he would try to buy them," said one vice chairman.

Already fragmented into disparate power bases, Salomon now evolved into a system of warlords: a corporate-bond warlord, a government-bond warlord, a mortgage-bond warlord, an equities warlord.[28]

One ruled above them all: the warlord of bond arbitrage, a soft-spoken, brilliant mathematician, forty-year-old John Meriwether. The shy, self-effacing "J.M." expressed his outsize ambitions through a team of professors he had lured with Wall Street salaries from schools like Harvard and MIT. These "arb boys," an oasis of intellect amid the belching, sweating traders, hunched protectively over their computers, fiddling with mathematical models portraying the bond universe. The arbs were launching a revolution in the bond business, and the edge their computer tip sheet gave them against the rest of the suckers produced most of Salomon's profits. They lived inside Meriwether's little bubble on the trading floor and felt they had earned their arrogance. J.M. was enormously forgiving of mistakes but relentless toward anyone he considered stupid, and the arbs were his personally chosen elite. He had a deeply complex personal relationship with his team, and spent nearly all his time with them, engaging in one of his three obsessions: work, gambling, and golf. Many an evening after the markets closed the arbs sat together, playing liar's poker to hone their handicapping skills.[29] The boyish-looking, blank-faced Meriwether usually won.

Despite his passivity and limited influence as a board member, Buffett certainly understood arbitrage. But the board's knowledge of Salomon's business details went only so far, and Buffett did not understand computers, which were becoming important to every business and intrinsic to the new Wall Street. He did know, however, that he was now a director of a corporation that was utterly dependent on computers, and he had certainly figured out that computers could increase risk.

To Buffett, it was obvious that the combination of fallible human beings and judgment-free computers in a completely unmonitored, unsupervised environment meant an almost unlimited potential for things to go wildly out of control. But as a board member, he lacked authority to make changes and could only try persuasion. By now he and Munger had wrangled repeatedly—and unsuccessfully—with Salomon's management. Munger had taken over the audit committee—which had not formerly been a bastion of zealous oversight—and put it through six- and seven-hour dissections of the firm and its accountants. Munger discovered that Salomon's derivatives business had grown immensely, using trades for which no ready market existed. The trades would not settle for long periods, sometimes years. With minimal cash changing hands, the derivatives were valued on Salomon's books using a model.[30] Since the model was created by those whose bonuses it would determine, not surprisingly the models usually showed the trades were quite profitable. As much as $20 million of profits had been overstated through such accounting mismarks.[31] The audit committee, however, addressed only trades and deals already approved, and usually completed. The real oversight took place before the fact.

There, in the one area in which Buffett and Munger unequivocally had more skill than anyone else—making investments—they weighed in loudest of all—and were ignored. Their protestations only alienated them from the employees. In one example, Salomon's Phibro unit had formed a joint venture with a Houston company, Anglo-Suisse, to build oil fields in West Siberia that would supposedly revolutionize oil production in Russia.

"Anglo-Suisse," Munger said when the idea was floated. "This is an idiotic idea. There are no Anglos and no Swiss involved in this company. The name alone is reason not to get involved."

But Salomon put $116 million into the joint venture anyway, thinking that oil was going to be integral to Russia's future and that Western capital was needed to extract the oil. But, while "the country isn't going to go away," as Buffett said, and "the oil isn't going to go away," the Russian political system could go away. No margin of safety could cover that.[32]

Sure enough, as soon as the White Nights joint venture got going, the Russian government began toying with a tax on oil exports. The tax nearly wiped out White Nights's profit. Then the volume of oil production proved disappointing. Russian nabobs flew to the United States and expected to be entertained with prostitutes. The Russian government was unpredictable and uncooperative, resulting in setbacks from start to finish. Somebody was going to make a lot of money from oil in Russia, but it wasn't going to be Salomon Inc.

Russia was merely a sideshow at the time. In 1989, the United States had become obsessed with the possibility that the whole country would be eclipsed by the rising sun of Japan. Salomon had invested large sums in Japan and was doing well in its start-up business there, which had grown rapidly to hundreds of employees and was making money under its head, Deryck Maughan, who had wisely given local talent the reins. Buffett, who generally did not buy foreign stocks and who believed Japanese stocks in particular to be outrageously expensive, had shown little interest in anything related to Japan.

Katharine Graham, however, had developed a fascination with Akio Morita, one of the world's most brilliant businessmen. Morita was chairman of Sony, one of the world's most successful corporations. Graham brought the two men together at one of her dinners, but they did not click. Finally, during one of Buffett's trips to New York, Morita-san held a small dinner for Graham, Buffett, and Graham's friend Meg Greenfield at his Fifth Avenue apartment overlooking the Metropolitan Museum. Buffett, who seemed slightly mystified by Graham's interest in this powerful, visionary man—observing grudgingly that Graham "was sort of enchanted by Morita"—agreed to go.

Buffett had never eaten Japanese food but knew it might be problematic. He went to plenty of events where he touched nothing more than the dinner rolls. He could easily go seven or eight hours at a time without eating. He disliked offending his hosts, however, and as his reputation had grown, he found that there was no way to fake eating by cutting things up and moving them around. People noticed.

One side of the Moritas' apartment had a sweeping view of Central Park, the other a view of the sushi kitchen. A highlight for guests was the opportunity to watch the four chefs preparing the elaborate meal behind a glass window.

As they were seated for dinner, Buffett looked at the chefs. What was this going to be like? he wondered. As guest of honor, he was seated facing the kitchen. There were chopsticks on a little stand and tiny cruets and miniature bowls of soy sauce. He already knew he didn't like soy sauce. The first course was brought out. Everyone slurped it down. Buffett mumbled an excuse. He motioned for his full plate to be taken away. The next course arrived. Buffett could not identify it but looked at it with dread. He saw that Meg Greenfield, who had eating habits similar to his, also was having difficulties. Mrs. Morita, seated next to him, smiled politely and barely spoke. Buffett gurgled another excuse. He nodded again for the waiter to remove his plate. As his untouched dishes returned to the kitchen, he was sure the chefs noticed.

The waiter brought out another unidentifiable course of something that looked rubbery and raw to him. Kay and the Moritas tucked in with enthusiasm. Mrs. Morita smiled politely once again when he offered a third excuse. Buffett squirmed. He liked his steaks bloody but did not eat raw fish. The waiter cleared the plates. The chefs kept their heads down. Buffett was sweating. He was running out of excuses. The chefs looked busy, but he was sure they must be peeking sideways from behind the glass to see what he would do. Course after course arrived, and each of his plates went back, untouched. He imagined that he heard a slight buzz from the kitchen. How many more courses could there possibly be? He had not realized there were this many things on the planet that could be eaten raw. Mrs. Morita seemed slightly embarrassed for him, but he wasn't sure, because she smiled politely all the time and said so little. Time crawled more slowly with each course. He had been counting, and the number of courses now exceeded ten. He tried to make up for his culinary lapses with witty, self-deprecating conversation about business with Morita-san, but he knew he was disgracing himself. Even in the middle of his bonfire of embarrassment, he could not help but think longingly of hamburgers. By the end of fifteen courses, he had still not eaten a bite. The Moritas could not have been more polite, which added to his humiliation. He was desperate to escape back to Kay's apartment, where popcorn and peanuts and strawberry ice cream awaited him.

"It was the worst," he says about the meal he did not eat. *"I've had others like that, but it was by far the worst. I will never eat Japanese food again."*

Meanwhile, hundreds of Salomon employees who would have crawled up Fifth Avenue on their knees blindfolded to eat this same dinner with the Moritas were instead dining at high-priced Japanese restaurants and mutinying over the size of their huge bonus checks. The hugeness of their checks was not the point. It was the hugeness of their checks compared with others' huge checks that mattered. Buffett and Munger knew little of the trouble fomenting at Salomon. Meriwether's arbs had been agitating for more money. The former college professors, hired away from salaries of $29,000, felt they were subsidizing money-losing departments like equity investment banking. They viewed sharing their profits as "socialist."[33] The arbs could have made more on their own. They wanted a cut of the hundreds of millions they earned for the firm.[34] Although he was so shy that he had trouble maintaining eye contact, Meriwether now became the world's most aggressive and successful bonus-pimp. Gutfreund caved and gave the arbs fifteen percent of what they made,[35] which meant they had the potential to come away with much more money than the traders, who shared their bonus pool. The deal was made in secret between Gutfreund and Salomon's president, Tom Strauss; the board never knew, nor did other employees at Salomon—yet.

By 1991, Buffett and Munger had been through a series of disappointments and setbacks at Salomon. The financial results they got were not always up-to-date. Staff demands for bonuses continued to spiral. They disagreed with much of what went on in the boardroom. The stock price had not moved for eight years. Earnings were down $167 million, mostly because of employees' pay.

Buffett, having so far let Munger be the Appointed Bad Guy, now roused himself, met with the executive committee, and told them to cut back. Yet when the final bonus pool number came through, it was $7 million *higher* than before. Under the new formula that Meriwether, as bonus-pimp, had procured for his arb boys, one of them, Larry Hilibrand, got a raise from $3 to $23 million.[36] When word of Hilibrand's bonus leaked to the press, some of his colleagues went crazy with envy and felt cheated—the millions they were making forgotten.

Buffett himself had no problem with the arbs' bonuses. *"I believe in paying talent,"* he says, *"but not, as Charlie would say, as a royalty on time."* The arrangement was like a hedge fund's fee structure and bore some resemblance to his old partnership.[37] It would put more pressure on the rest of the firm to perform. What he objected to was not being told. He objected even more to the fact that other people did not get haircuts for their lack of performance. Gutfreund had showed a better sense of proportion than most of his traders, opting to take a thirty-five percent pay cut, in line with the decline in earnings.[38] This helped him with Buffett, who thought Gutfreund had more class than his employees. But Buffett's sense of decency was so offended by the employees' greed that he overcame his natural inertia and voted against the bonuses for the traders. He was overruled. When word of Buffett's "no" vote raced through the hallways of Salomon, people were outraged. A billionaire who loved money had called them greedy.

Buffett considered Salomon a casino with a restaurant out front.[39] The restaurant was a loss-leader. The traders—especially Meriwether's people— were the casino: the purity of risk-taking done without conflicts of interest. That was the part of the business Buffett liked, and the new pay system was designed to keep the arbs from bolting.[40] But by trying to operate the firm under two distinct pay systems, as if it really were a casino with a restaurant out front, Gutfreund had driven a rift through Salomon's heart.

Now Meriwether and Hilibrand asked Gutfreund for permission to approach Buffett to buy back his convertible preferred stock. The terms were so rich that it was costing Salomon too much. They were no longer under threat of a takeover. Why pay for Buffett's protection? Gutfreund said they could talk to Buffett and try to convince him he was better off without the preferred stock. When approached, Buffett said that he was amenable. But having Buffett as an investor must have made Gutfreund feel more secure, for in the end he got cold feet.[41]

Thus, Buffett was held to his original deal. Having invested both Berkshire's $700 million and his own reputation in John Gutfreund, by 1991 it was too late to back out.

48

Thumb-Sucking, and Its
Hollow-Cheeked Result

New York City · 1991

On Thursday afternoon, August 8, 1991, Buffett was driving during his annual weekend with Astrid and the Blumkin boys in Lake Tahoe. He always looked forward to this trip and was in a relaxed and jovial mood. John Gutfreund's office had called him that morning. Where will you be tonight between nine p.m. E.S.T. and midnight? they asked. We want to talk to you.

Thinking this was really unusual, he said he was going to a show. They told him to call Wachtell, Lipton, Rosen & Katz, the law firm that represented Salomon, at seven-thirty p.m. Hmm, he thought. Maybe they're going to sell the firm. It sounded like good news to him. The stock was trading around $37, close to $38, the price at which his preferred stock would convert to common, and he could take his profits and be done with Salomon. Gutfreund, who had a long-standing habit of calling him for advice, might need help in negotiating terms.

At seven-thirty p.m., *"We got to the hotel and the rest of them went into the dining room of the steak house. I told them, 'This may take a while.' I found a pay phone outside on the wall and dialed in to the number they gave me."* Buffett expected to be connected with Gutfreund, but Gutfreund was on a plane from London. His flight had been delayed, and Buffett sat on hold for quite a while. Finally Tom Strauss and Don Feuerstein got on the phone to tell Buffett what was going on—or a version of it, anyway.

Tom Strauss, forty-nine years old, was there to protect Gutfreund's flank. He had been appointed Salomon's president five years earlier, during the Great Purge of 1987.[1] As recent history showed, however, management was not a skill cultivated at Salomon. The warlords reported to Gutfreund, to the extent that they reported to anyone at all. Their clout came from their groups' production of revenues. Strauss might be technically president of Salomon, but he had been promoted so high that he now floated distantly above the trading floor like a helium balloon. Periodically, the warlords batted him out of the way.

Don Feuerstein, the head of Salomon's legal department, had once played an important role at the SEC and was regarded as an excellent technical lawyer.[2] He was Gutfreund's consigliere, nicknamed POD, the "Prince of Darkness,"[3] for the behind-the-scenes dirty work he did. The warlord structure made the legal department both powerful and weak; it stewarded the firm's franchise in much the way that everything happened at Salomon: by catering to factions and reacting to events. Salomon's trading culture had embedded itself so strongly that even Feuerstein was a trader, lovingly operating a wine syndicate on behalf of several managing directors. His fax machine constantly spewed forth notices of wine auctions that were a profitable sideline for the syndicate's participants, its product more traded and collected than drunk.[4]

This evening no one was toasting anything, however. Feuerstein knew that Buffett and Gutfreund were friends. He felt awkward giving sensitive information to Buffett when Gutfreund should have been in on the call. A set of "talking papers" in hand, he and Strauss told Buffett that "a problem" had arisen. A Wachtell, Lipton investigation had uncovered the fact that Paul Mozer, who ran Salomon's government-bond department, had broken the Treasury Department's auction-bidding rules several times in 1990 and 1991. Mozer and his deputy, who was complicit, were now suspended, and the firm was notifying the regulators.

Who the hell is Paul Mozer? Buffett wondered.

Paul Mozer, thirty-six years old, had been swooped up by New York from the Chicago office. He was as intense as a laser beam and started his day before the sun came up, parked in front of a trading screen in his bedroom taking a call from London, then galloped a couple of blocks from his tiny apartment in Battery Park City over to Salomon's enormous new trading room, housed in the gleaming pink-granite space of 7 World Trade Center. There he stared at another set of screens until past sunset, and oversaw twenty traders, most of whom towered over his short, wiry frame. Mozer was smart and hyperaggressive, but he also struck people as frustrated and insecure, an odd duck. Although he'd grown up on Long Island, he seemed like a greenhorn from the Midwest among the slick New Yorkers. He had been one of Meriwether's arbitrage boys until the head of the government desk resigned and he was asked to take over. He still worked for Meriwether, but was now on the outside looking in at his former gang. Gutfreund, who was under pressure from Buffett and the board to improve the numbers, had added the foreign-exchange department to Mozer's duties; in a few months he had turned a "black hole" around and made it profitable.[5] So Gutfreund had reason to be grateful to Mozer.

While Mozer could be abrasive and condescending, as though he considered other people morons compared to himself, those who worked closely with him were fond of him. Unlike people on Salomon's infamous mortgage desk, he did not abuse trainees by hurling food at them or sending them racing out the door to buy twelve pizzas at a time. Sometimes he even talked to the trainees.

For his labors, Mozer had been paid $4.75 million that year. It was a lot of money, but it was not enough. Mozer was World Cup–competitive, and Mozer was pissed. Something had snapped in him when he found out that his former colleague, Larry Hilibrand, had gotten 23 million bucks from a secret pay deal. He used to earn more than the arb boys,[6] and he now went "ape-shit."[7] He copped such an attitude that he demanded that his department not be audited—as if, somehow, oversight did not apply to him.[8]

Mozer was one of a few dozen men who communed regularly with the U.S. government on its financing needs, talking to the Federal Reserve staff nearly every day. Representing Salomon as a "primary dealer," he offered the government market chatter and advice and, in turn, stood first in line as its largest customer whenever the government wanted to sell debt, like a member of the College of Cardinals who sat at the right hand of the Pope.

Only the primary dealers could buy bonds from the government. Everyone else had to do it by submitting bids through the primary dealers, who acted as brokers. This gave the dealers the clout that goes with access and enormous market share. Knowing the needs of both their clients and the government, the dealers clipped off a profit from the gap that lay between the supply and the demand. But with that position of power went a commensurate dose of trust. The government expected primary dealers to behave like cardinals who were celebrating Mass. Yes, they drank first from the communion cup, but they must not get loaded and embarrass the Church.

As an auction neared, the primary dealers would work the phones, polling customers to gauge their appetite for bonds. Mozer's sense of how hot the market was running translated into Salomon's bid.

The inherent tension of the market lay in the opposing interests of the Treasury and the dealers regarding pricing and amounts. The Treasury auctioned only a certain amount of bonds and wanted the highest price, while the dealers wanted to pay just enough in the auction to win a larger share than any-one else yet no more than necessary, for that would hurt their profit on resale. So finely calibrated were these bids that the traders used increments of 1/1,000th of a dollar. That sounds like almost nothing, but clipping off 1/1,000th of enough dollars amounted to a fortune. On $100 million, it was worth $100,000. On a billion dollars, it was worth $1 million. Because government bonds were less profitable than mortgages and corporate bonds, Treasury bonds had to be traded in blocks this size in order for the dealers and money managers to make enough money for it to be worth their while.

Dovetailing with the need for such large trades was the government's need to work with large dealers—those who knew the market well and had the power to distribute a lot of bonds. Salomon was the largest dealer by far. In the early 1980s, the Treasury had allowed any individual firm to buy up to half of a given bond issue for its own account. Salomon commonly "couped" an auction this way, then held on to the bonds long enough to "squeeze" anybody who was "short" Treasuries—having bet that prices would fall—because there were no bonds available for short-sellers to buy to cover their positions. Prices shot up, the short-sellers screamed, the trading floor erupted in cheers, and Salomon gloated over its huge profits and swung a big stick as the King of Wall Street. Couping the auctions fattened the usually thin profits on government bonds and sent a heady mist of testosterone drifting above the formerly stodgy section where the humdrum government-bond traders sat at their desks.

In response to grumbling, the Treasury lowered the limit and said no indi-vidual dealer could buy more than thirty-five percent, which made it harder to coup the auction. Smaller squeezes still occurred, but Salomon no longer owned the market unchallenged. Naturally, the new rule was unpopular at Salomon. Since the total of bids exceeded all the bonds on offer, the Treasury also prorated everyone, which meant a firm that wanted thirty-five percent had to bid more than thirty-five percent, a juggling act.

Thus in various ways the clampdown made it harder to profit at the govern-ment desk at Salomon. The mist of testosterone did not dissipate, however. Mozer tested the Treasury's patience twice in 1990, bidding more than one hun-dred percent of all the bonds to be issued. Michael Basham, who ran the auc-tions, told him not to do it again. Mozer was sent to an "apology breakfast" with Bob Glauber, an undersecretary of the Treasury. He squeaked out some words but did not exactly apologize. He claimed that overbidding was in the government's best interest because it increased demand for bonds.[9] Not mollified, Basham changed the rules so that no individual firm could even *bid* more than thirty-five percent for its own account. The limit on bids meant Salomon might not even get its full thirty-five percent limit of bonds.

Now Feuerstein read Buffett a copy of a Salomon press release to be issued the next morning, which was being explained to all board members that night. It described how Mozer had responded to this stare-down with Basham. He had proceeded to submit unauthorized bids in excess of the government's bidding limit in the December 1990 and February 1991 auctions.

Feuerstein gave Buffett a scripted version of events and told him that he had already spoken at length with Munger, who was at his cabin in Minnesota.[10] Munger had said to him something about thumb-sucking and added, "People do that all the time."[11] Buffett recognized the term "thumb-sucking" as a Mungerism for procrastination but wasn't terribly concerned. Feuerstein did not mention anything else discussed in the lengthy conversation with Munger, and Buffett did not ponder whose thumb was being sucked. Seven or eight minutes later he got off the phone, recognizing that this wasn't the good news for which he had been hoping but not feeling alarmed enough to call Munger immediately. He'd check in with Munger over the weekend, he decided, but for now he was going to enjoy Lake Tahoe. Then he wandered back to join Astrid and the Blumkins in the dining room, where they were having a steak before seeing Joan Rivers and Neil Sedaka perform.

While Buffett was watching the show, John Gutfreund's plane from London finally landed. Gutfreund and Strauss had a conversation late that evening with Richard Breeden and Bill McLucas, top officials at the SEC. They also placed a call to Gerald Corrigan, the beefy six-foot-four president of the New York branch of the Federal Reserve.

Using a different set of talking papers, Gutfreund and Strauss told Breeden, McLucas, and Corrigan more of the story than Salomon's board had just heard. Mozer had not just overbid. To get around the thirty-five percent limit, at the February 1991 Treasury auction he had entered a fake bid in the name of a customer and stashed the bonds he got in Salomon's account. In fact, he had placed more than one false bid in that auction. As to why these had not been reported earlier, they explained the delay as an oversight. Yet the SEC and the Treasury were in the midst of investigating Mozer, for he had pulled a huge squeeze in the May two-year-note auction. His actions were under intense scrutiny by regulators. That should have been true at Salomon as well. How could the delay have been an oversight? Now the regulators had to consider whether this confession indicated some major systemic problem at Salomon.

No matter what, these admissions were going to be highly embarrassing to the Treasury and the Federal Reserve. Corrigan was shocked that the firm had not already fired Mozer and created a remedial program that involved instituting all sorts of new controls. But he expected something like that to be announced within twenty-four or forty-eight hours, after which he could "keep them on probation for a while and hope that would be the end of it." He told Gutfreund and Strauss that they had an immediate obligation to release this information to the public. Based on what he knew, he surmised that the incident could blow up into a "very, very, very significant problem."[12] It seemed to him, however, that Strauss and Gutfreund did not fully grasp this. Indeed, with hindsight, the fact that Gutfreund had gone off to London, thus placing his ability to participate in the calls with Buffett, Munger, and the other directors in the hands of an airline, was itself a telling sign.

The next day, Friday, August 9, Buffett was enjoying himself with Astrid and the Blumkins, walking along the board sidewalks of Virginia City, the old Western gold-rush town. He called in to his office. Nothing urgent was happening. Nobody at Salomon had called him. Salomon had put out the press release describing the events in fairly bland terms. The stock had fallen five percent, however, to $34.75.

Buffett called Munger on Saturday. Munger flatly told him a much more detailed and alarming story. Feuerstein had said that "one part of the problem has been known since last April." While these same words had been read to the other directors, including Buffett, they had the effect of technically informing without really enlightening.[13] But Munger picked up instantly on bullshit legalese and the passive voice, which irritated him. What did that mean, "has been known"? What exactly had been known? And by whom?[14] When pressed, Feuerstein gave Munger a much fuller description of events, similar to what Corrigan had been told.[15]

As Feuerstein recounted, Mozer had gotten a letter from the Treasury Department in April saying they were investigating one of his bids.[16] Realizing that the game was up, on April 25 he had gone to his boss, John Meriwether, and made a confession of sorts. In February, to get around the thirty-five percent limit, he had not only bid in Salomon's name, he had also submitted phony bids under real customers' names.[17] Mozer swore to Meriwether that this was the only time, and he would never do it again.

Meriwether had recognized immediately that this was "career-threatening," had said so to Mozer, and had reported the situation to Feuerstein and Strauss. On April 29, the three of them went to Gutfreund and told him what Mozer had confessed. Gutfreund, they said later, had been red-faced and pissed off when he heard the news.

Therefore, in April, Gutfreund knew. Strauss knew. Meriwether knew. Feuerstein, the general counsel, knew. They all knew.

Feuerstein had said at the time that Mozer's actions appeared criminal. He didn't believe that the firm technically had a legal reporting requirement. Still, Feuerstein was sure that Salomon would run seriously afoul of the regulators unless the Federal Reserve was told. Gutfreund said it would be taken care of. Curiously, however, no specific plans were made to march down to the Federal Reserve and give Jerry Corrigan the news. Moreover, having concluded that the phony bid was a "one-time, aberrant act," they had left Mozer in charge of the government desk. Hearing this, "Well, that's just thumb-sucking," Munger had said. "People do that all the time." He later explained that by thumb-sucking he meant "sitting there thinking and doggling, musing, and consulting, when you should be acting."[18]

Munger told Buffett that he had challenged the press release: Shouldn't management's prior knowledge be disclosed? Feuerstein had said that, yes, it should be, but the decision had been made not to because Salomon's management thought that disclosure would threaten the company's funding. Salomon had tens of billions of short-term commercial paper debt that rolled over day by day. If the word got out, lenders would refuse to renew. To Munger, "funding difficulties" was shorthand for "financial panic."[19] Lacking the leverage to insist, he had given in, but he and Buffett now agreed that more disclosure was required. They mentally braced themselves for what would follow.

Two days later, on Monday morning, August 12, the *Wall Street Journal* reported the alleged details, with a blaring headline: "The Big Squeeze: Salomon's Admission of T-Note Infractions Gives Market a Jolt—Firm's Share of One Auction May Have Reached 85%; Investigations Under Way—How Much Did Bosses Know?" It mentioned the possibility of "civil charges of market manipulation, violations of the antifraud provisions of securities law, misrepresentations to federal authorities," "books and records violations," and "criminal charges" for committing "both wire and mail fraud."[20]

Gutfreund called Buffett, sounding calm. Buffett thought that he seemed to believe the whole situation meant "a few points on the stock." In light of the disastrous article, Buffett thought this attitude was unrealistic, a sign that Gutfreund believed the whole affair could somehow be finessed.[21] It seemed of a piece with Gutfreund's unwarranted composure the previous week. Buffett pressed for more disclosure. Salomon's Treasury division was beginning to have trouble rolling over its commercial paper, meaning the firm's lenders were starting to show signs of nervousness.[22]

Meanwhile, Munger was trying to get in touch with Wachtell, Lipton's Marty Lipton, who was John Gutfreund's indispensable best friend as well as Salomon's outside counsel. So entwined with Salomon was Lipton that the speed-dial buttons on Donald Feuerstein's phone rang his wife, the Sotheby's and Christie's auction houses, and Marty Lipton, not necessarily in that order.[23] Lipton and his telephone were as inseparable as Buffett and his Wall Street Journal. Cell phones still being so rare, however, that even name partners of major law firms did not use them, Munger had to rely on Wachtell, Lipton's office, which seemed to have a miraculous ability to track Lipton down, as Munger put it, "even in the middle of intercourse."[24]

When reached, Lipton—who was presumably vertical at the time—was badgered by Munger for a follow-up press release, saying the first had been inadequate. Lipton agreed that the board would hold a telephone meeting to discuss it on Wednesday.

Not surprisingly, Jerry Corrigan at the Federal Reserve was even less satisfied than Munger with Salomon's muted response. On Monday, August 12, he decided to have Peter Sternlight, one of his executive vice presidents, draft a letter to Salomon Inc. stating that the firm's actions had called into question its "continuing business relationship" with the Fed, which was "deeply troubled" by the failure to make a timely disclosure of what the firm had learned. Salomon would have ten days to report on all "irregularities, violations, and oversights" that it had discovered.

In light of Corrigan's earlier conversation with Strauss and Gutfreund, this letter would be a death threat. If the Fed cut off Salomon's business relationship with the government, customers and lenders would desert in droves. The consequences would be huge and immediate.

Salomon had the United States' second-largest balance sheet—larger than Merrill Lynch, Bank of America, or American Express. Nearly all of its loans consisted of short-term debt that was callable by lenders in days or at most weeks. Only $4 billion of equity supported $146 billion of debt. Dangling off the side of the balance sheet on any given day were tens more billions, perhaps as many as $50 billion a day, of uncleared trades—transactions executed, but not yet settled. These would stall midair. Salomon also had many hundreds of billions of derivative obligations not recorded anywhere on its balance sheet— interest-rate swaps, foreign-exchange swaps, futures contracts—a massive and intricate daisy chain of obligations with counterparties all over the world, many of whom in turn had other interrelated contracts outstanding, all part of a vast entangled global financial web. If the funding disappeared, Salomon's assets had to be sold—but while the funding could disappear in a few days, the assets would take time to liquidate. The government had no national policy to provide loans to teetering investment banks because they were "too big to fail." The firm could melt into a puddle overnight.[25]

Corrigan sat back in his chair, confident that once Salomon received Sternlight's letter, management would understand the loaded gun cocked at its head, and would respond accordingly.

Within Salomon, after the press release and the *Wall Street Journal* story, rumors were running wild. Late Monday afternoon, it held an all-hands-on-deck meeting in its huge auditorium on its lowest floor. Nearly five hundred people crowded in, while hundreds, maybe more, from upstairs and from Salomon offices around the world, watched on television screens. Gutfreund and Strauss walked the audience through a baked-Alaska version of events, a crisp well-done meringue of a surface that hid the chilly surprise. Afterward, Bill McIntosh, the head of the bond department, was summoned upstairs to Gutfreund's office, where he found Gutfreund, Strauss, and Marty Lipton, "three very scared men." Earlier in the day he had been calling for Gutfreund's head, but unexpectedly, they asked what he thought of the situation. McIntosh demanded more explanation; he felt the all-hands version and the press release had been misleading.[26] He and assistant general counsel Zachary Snow ended up getting drafted to write another press release.

The next morning, McIntosh and Snow began drafting. Around midday, McIntosh went to tell Deryck Maughan, the vice chairman of investment banking, who had just come back from running the firm's Asian operations, what was going on. Maughan knew he was hearing the harbinger of a disaster. He went to find Snow and pounced on him, saying you'd better be telling the whole truth to a vice chairman.

But Snow, who was in charge of legal matters for trading, had no intention of hiding anything from Maughan. He started talking, and a tale unfolded of what had transpired behind the scenes. He explained that in April, after Mozer made his first confession about the February auction, Meriwether had pleaded that Mozer not be fired, even though Feuerstein had said he believed Mozer's actions were criminal in nature. Snow had been told—in confidence—about the situation. A month later, Mozer still ran the government desk; Feuerstein was nagging Gutfreund to come clean; Gutfreund was telling him that he would. But in fact no one had told the government. Meanwhile, Meriwether was charged with keeping an eye on Mozer, who had supposedly reformed.

Then Mozer had asked for funding to bid on more than one hundred percent of the two-year-note auction in late May. Even though some of the funding was supposedly to put in bids for customers, John Macfarlane, Salomon's treasurer, had become alarmed. He thought it an obvious red flag and called a meeting with Snow and Meriwether. Snow had gone to Feuerstein, his boss, who agreed that it was an outrageous request. They had decided not to give Mozer the funds.[27]

But Mozer had secretly juggled the bids and money anyway.[28] Managing to evade his overseers, he put in one suspicious bid and pulled off an enormous auction coup. Salomon wound up with eighty-seven percent of the Treasury bonds, and it and a small group of customers controlled the two-year notes afterward. The price shot up.[29] Others' losses from the "squeeze" topped $100 million, and several small firms suffered so severely that they filed for bankruptcy.[30]

Within Salomon, the squeeze had caused considerable angst. In the press, the firm was painted by its competitors as the pirate of Wall Street. The board members, including Buffett, had expressed outrage at a meeting that Salomon had cornered the market for two-year notes. Feuerstein had had Snow commence an internal investigation of the squeeze in June. As it turned out, Mozer had held a dinner with two hedge-fund customers right before the auction, and these customers had placed bids involved in the squeeze. With hindsight, the dinner pointed to possible collusion and market manipulation. But in the absence of proof, Mozer explained it away.[31] Gutfreund had set up a meeting to see his overlords at the Treasury and the Fed to mend fences over the squeeze. When he went to see Glauber in mid-June, he sat on the sofa puffing a cigar. He offered a *mea culpa* to Glauber for the aftereffects of the squeeze and offered to cooperate with the Treasury—but defended Mozer against allegations of intentionally rigging the May auction. And he made no mention of what else he knew, leaving out anything about Mozer's false bids in the earlier auction. In response to the squeeze and to the earlier run-ins with Mozer, however, unbeknownst to anyone at Salomon, the SEC and the Antitrust Division of the Justice Department began investigating the firm anyway.

About a week after the Glauber meeting, Gutfreund, Strauss, and Meriwether met to consider whether the firm should now come clean with the Treasury about the February auction. Because the hue and cry over the squeeze had not abated, they decided to keep silent. They felt the time was not right. Days later, the SEC sent Salomon a letter asking for information about the May auction. This was the first indication that the problem of the two-year-note auction might be escalating instead of fading away. Anyone receiving this inquiry letter might reasonably have gotten nervous about the SEC's sudden interest in the operations of the government-bond trading desk.

Two days later, Gutfreund had flown to Omaha to visit Buffett, while on his way to Las Vegas to see some property that Salomon had financed. In telling the backstory to Maughan, Snow, who did not know about this trip, left it out. Buffett would later fill in these details.

"I picked him up at the airport. John was in the office for about an hour and a half. He spent about an hour making some calls, then we talked for about half an hour. He was sort of pacing around. We didn't talk about anything in the end. It's a pain in the neck to stop in Omaha, yet he really had nothing to say."

Somewhat baffled as to the purpose of the visit, Buffett took Gutfreund to a quick lunch, then for a visit to the recently acquired Borsheim's jewelry store, near the Furniture Mart. The proprietor, Ike Friedman, Mrs. B's nephew, was cast in the same mold and, like her, somewhat larger than life.

Friedman took Gutfreund to Borsheim's "center island," where the really expensive goods were displayed. Gutfreund picked out a $60,000 item for Susan. It mattered to Buffett, Gutfreund said later, that he had made a purchase.[32] Then he glanced at the expensive watches strategically displayed just behind the center island, and strolled over to look at the merchandise. Friedman preferred selling very expensive jewelry to timepieces. "Oh, watches," he said to Gutfreund. "You lose them, you break them. Why pay a lot of money for a watch?" He looked at the fancy wristwatch on Gutfreund's wrist and asked Gutfreund what he paid for it. Gutfreund told him.

"$1,995,"[33] Friedman repeated. "Well. You got taken, John."

"And you should have seen the look on John's face."

Wearing the watch on which he got taken, Gutfreund returned to New York at the end of June to present the satin-lined Borsheim's box to Susan.

Within days—by early July—the Antitrust Division of the Justice Department formally notified Salomon that it was investigating the squeeze in the May two-year-note auction, which the letter from the SEC had inquired about. Gutfreund now got serious, said Snow, and hired Marty Lipton's firm Wachtell, Lipton, Salomon's outside counsel, to begin its own investigation, on behalf of Salomon, of the circumstances surrounding the May squeeze.[34] People within Salomon had mixed views about the squeeze. Some said the Treasury market was inherently designed to be collusive. The job of a dealer was to work with its customers to distribute huge blocks of bonds into the market. Little squeezes happened all the time. This one was big. So what? The Treasury was picking on Salomon. It was the years of hubris, the wildness depicted in *Liar's Poker,* the gradual erosion of power, that had made Salomon a punching bag.[35]

But others were furious that Mozer had once again defied the Treasury, and were baffled that he would pull a huge squeeze when it was well known that he and Basham were already at loggerheads. Later, these questions would increase. Why did Mozer—on probation, told his behavior had been "probably criminal"—taunt the Treasury so outlandishly that his coup splashed headlines all over the press, in a way guaranteed to draw even more attention to himself?[36]

A few days after beginning their work, the Wachtell, Lipton investigators were told that senior management had known since April that Mozer had submitted an unauthorized bid in the February auction.

With hindsight, Salomon's actions looked far worse. After learning of Mozer's false bid in February, which Feuerstein had said was criminal in nature, management had taken Meriwether's vouching for Mozer and Mozer's word that he had never done it before, without investigating further or disciplining Mozer in any way. They had left him in place, which allowed the May squeeze to occur. Once it did occur, telling the government Salomon knew about Mozer's previous phony bids but had only now reported them would have caused more trouble by conveying the sense that they were a gang of thieves. Worst of all, Gutfreund had met with Bob Glauber in mid-June about the May squeeze, but had said nothing about all these earlier events. Now, as Snow explained to Maughan, when things started blowing up, everyone involved started excusing the original delay by saying the matter was a single minor event that caused no customer any harm, cost the government nothing, and didn't make sense, even from the standpoint of the trader involved.[37] Given the pressure of business, Gutfreund said, he simply hadn't deemed it that important.[38]

Unfortunately, he was wrong about that. The Wachtell investigators had discovered that the February auction was not the only one that Mozer had rigged. They now knew that five auctions had been compromised.[39] Two of these false bids had only just been unearthed. Snow concluded by telling Maughan about the previous evening's meeting with all the inside and outside lawyers that had followed the half-baked explanation given to all employees. Snow had argued that management's prior knowledge had to be disclosed. He was batted down. "I'm going to take a lot of heat for this," Gutfreund told him. "I don't see why you can't do your part."[40]

Maughan had been deeply concerned even before hearing all this new information from Snow. Seven days had passed since the first press release—seven days that included a salvo of stories in the media, the firm's falling stock price, trouble rolling over the commercial paper, and the discovery of new false bids. By the time Snow finished telling him all of this additional history of what Mozer had done and what others had not done, Maughan blew up and started pounding Snow to make sure there was nothing else. Then he went down to the trading floor and confronted Meriwether, Mozer's boss. "What the hell is going on, John?" he asked.

Meriwether hung his head. "It's too late," he said. He refused to talk further.[41]

Too late or not, Snow and McIntosh had to spend the evening drafting a second press release to try to explain things. That same night, Strauss and Gutfreund called Corrigan to respond in some fashion to the Sternlight "cocked gun" letter. The conversation started out with Corrigan being told that the firm had done an investigation and that "industry practice" of other firms was to pad their bids for new issuances of municipals and agency securities to get a bigger share. Corrigan viewed this opener as "a diversion, or worse." It had nothing to do with the squeeze, nor with the more serious issue of phony bids—in fact, nothing to do with the Treasury market. His Irish temper ignited. He yelled into the phone at Strauss and Gutfreund: "This is your last chance. Is there anything else you have to tell me?" They began to describe the other violations.

Corrigan meant to put an end to the obfuscations and rationalizations. "Well, goddammit," he said, "get yourselves together and release all of this information to the public immediately. I don't want to hear anything else from you, just get that goddamn press release out."[42]

Late that evening, the lawyers met with senior management to go over the press release. Gutfreund and Strauss arrived. McIntosh said there needed to be heads on a plate. This idea was quickly dismissed, but other people, including a board member, Gedale Horowitz, and Steve Bell, who ran Salomon's Washington office, pressed for fuller disclosure. Nobody could get hold of Buffett, but they reached Munger on the phone, who said, Look, you can't put this second press release out without names. Gutfreund's name went in automatically. Everyone knew that Strauss was not in charge and had not made any of these decisions; he had simply been present in the room. But he had gone along with his boss. His name went in. Feuerstein had tried to get Gutfreund to report it. Munger said that his name should stay out.

Meriwether was known as a brilliant, careful manager who was unusually close to his team and rarely left the desk. He had reported the matter exactly as he should.[43] On the other hand, he had vouched for Mozer, pleaded his cause, then left Mozer's responsibilities unchanged. When Munger said Meriwether's name should go in, says McIntosh, Meriwether, listening and seeing the lawyers write down his name, said, "Oh, my God, I'm doomed."[44]

The next day, Wednesday, August 14, a telephone meeting took place in which the board heard some of the story that was given to Corrigan the night before. Two board members called in from Europe, one from Alaska, Buffett from Omaha, and Munger from Minnesota to hear the first "orderly and half-way complete description" of the Mozer affair. Inside Salomon, a palace coup was well under way, with senior managers talking to one another on the assumption that Gutfreund and Strauss would have to resign.[45] The arbs wanted Meriwether as CEO, which was clearly unacceptable to many people. Meanwhile, on its conference call the board merely debated the wording of the new press release, which contained three pages of details and added the two additional violations that had been discovered by the investigators.

The draft release admitted that management had known about the February bids as far back as April but said that "the press of business" kept Salomon from reporting Mozer's actions to the authorities. Buffett called this ridiculous, and as the board debated, Munger became incensed. Eventually, the press release was rewritten to say that the failure occurred due to "lack of sufficient attention to the matter." Arrangements were made to put out the release that night.

As the meeting concluded, the board thought it had the full story. A number of things had not been mentioned, however. One was the "cocked gun" letter just received from Peter Sternlight at the Fed. Another was the June meeting with Bob Glauber at the Treasury Department, at which Gutfreund had failed to mention Mozer's earlier activities.

That afternoon, Salomon held another all-hands-on-deck meeting in the auditorium. Bill McIntosh, who ran the daily sales meeting, stood at the front as usual and had the unenviable job of reading the new press release to the employees. With Gutfreund and Strauss in the front row, directly opposite him, McIntosh said, This is what happened. If customers call and want to know what's going on, just tell them. Make no excuses for senior management, don't apologize for them, they did what they did.

The morning after the press release appeared, Thursday, August 15, rumors floated that the long knives were out and McIntosh was a goner. He stayed on the floor all day, figuring that Gutfreund and Strauss wouldn't fire him for insubordination in front of the whole trading floor. Meanwhile, market confidence in Salomon cracked. The stock, which had been sinking all week from the previous Thursday's close of almost $37, slumped to $27. It was trading down because shareholders were beginning to suspect a bigger problem than Mozer's misdeeds: a "run on the bank." And, indeed, one was beginning to take place.

The pyramided nature of the balance sheet of any investment bank was well understood by investors. Salomon was almost uniquely large, bigger than the biggest life insurer, second only to Citicorp in assets. As a major firm, Salomon's debt desk had always acted as a broker to buy and sell the firm's own medium-term notes. Suddenly, on Thursday, a long queue of sellers and no buyers appeared. In order to honor the sell orders, the traders had to buy the notes with Salomon's own cash. Since nobody else wanted to buy the notes, they now amounted to merely pieces of paper that said that Salomon would pay Salomon in the future from Salomon's own vault. As the vault emptied, in order to conserve cash, the traders tried to deter sellers by offering a lower price.[46] Sellers quickly figured out what was going on. The line of sellers grew longer and longer.

By the end of the day, Salomon's traders had reluctantly bought $700 million of the firm's own notes. Then they put up the "closed for business" sign, like a Depression bank snapping shut the teller's window.[47] No other firm would buy Solly's debt either. And with that, Salomon was teetering precariously close to the edge of bankruptcy.

The next morning, Friday, August 16, the New York Times front page ran the headline "Wall Street Sees a Serious Threat to Salomon Bros.—ILLEGAL BIDDING FALLOUT—High-Level Resignations and Client Defections Feared—Firm's Stock Drops."[48] The story featured prominent photographs of Gutfreund and Strauss. The two of them and Marty Lipton called Corrigan's office in New York and were patched through to Federal Reserve Chairman Alan Greenspan's office in Washington, where Corrigan and Greenspan had been on a conference call with Treasury Secretary Nick Brady since dawn "trying to figure out who the hell we're going to get to come in and run the firm."[49] The irate Federal Reserve Bank president, assuming that the board knew about the Sternlight death-threat

letter, had been shocked by the latest press release they had issued. He interpreted their failure to take any action—such as firing senior management—as a
sign that Salomon's board was defying him.[50]

Gutfreund said that he was going to resign. "What about Strauss?" asked
Corrigan. With this, it became clear that, as far as the New York Federal Reserve
was concerned, resigning was not optional, it was mandatory.[51]

Gutfreund then called Buffett. Buffett was still asleep when the phone rang,
but he came to consciousness rapidly as Gutfreund, with Marty Lipton and Tom
Strauss on the line, laid out the problem. "I just read my own obituary,"
Gutfreund said, referring to the *New York Times*. His picture on the front page
had done what the sequence of events—until then—had not. A freighted pause
ensued, as Buffett understood what they were really asking him. He told them
that he would consider taking over the job of chairman on an interim basis but
needed to see the *Times* story first. He wanted a few minutes to think but was
pretty sure he needed to go to New York. Marty Lipton said that it was unthinkable for Meriwether not to be fired immediately. Buffett insisted that they do
nothing until he could at least talk to Meriwether.

He hung up, called Gladys Kaiser at home, and told her to cancel all his plans
and put the pilot on alert that he might be going to New York. By the time he
arrived less than an hour later at the office, still empty of staff, to read the "obituary" on the fax machine, he had made up his mind.

Meanwhile, Gutfreund and Strauss had told Corrigan that Buffett was considering becoming interim chairman. "As far as I was concerned, they were both
being less than candid with me," Corrigan says. "I want to talk directly to Warren
Buffett immediately," he told them.[52] "I didn't know him personally, but I certainly knew his reputation."

When Corrigan talked to Buffett, he said something about his willingness to
be a little more lenient about the "ten-day schedule" if Buffett took the job.
Though Buffett did not grasp what Corrigan meant, he gathered that the
Federal Reserve must have been asking for information about something.
Corrigan sounded angry. He said that he would make no promises about anything if Buffett did take the job, and insisted that Buffett see him personally to
talk about the role of interim chairman in New York that very night.

At Salomon, all that the trading floor knew was that Buffett was supposedly
flying in to rescue the firm and that Salomon's stock was not trading, which told
investors that major news was pending. People speculated that he was considering Meriwether as a possible replacement for Gutfreund. The arb boys were cry-

ing, "We can't lose John." J.M. himself was nowhere to be seen. The trading floor stewed and seethed, but the stock was in limbo. News stories poured out on television that itemized Salomon's problems and speculated what would come next.

By early afternoon, Buffett had appeared. He hit the button on the press release announcing that Gutfreund was prepared to resign and Buffett was temporarily taking over as chairman, and the traders opened Salomon's stock.[53] It traded furiously for the final part of the day, closing up a dollar to almost $28.

After the market closed, Buffett went down to the amphitheater for a meeting with the managing directors. Gutfreund and Strauss took the stage and Gutfreund said that they were prepared to resign.[54] His face remained impassive, as usual. Strauss, noted Buffett, seemed shaken. Afterward, the senior management retired to the enormous conference room on the executive floor. Eric Rosenfeld and Larry Hilibrand, the key members of Meriwether's team, bullied their way into the meeting.[55] There, next to the wall of glass overlooking the two-story football-field-size trading floor where the trouble had begun, the top brass of Salomon began to thrash out what to do next.

People holding different viewpoints started kicking Meriwether around like a soccer ball. Nobody disputed that he had done the right thing by reporting Mozer's actions. The debate was whether he should have done more. Some people felt, as McIntosh articulated, that he was simply too close to the flame.[56] Meriwether had a reputation as a tight manager; in his areas, as one said, "no sparrow fell that Meriwether didn't see it." Meriwether had not been involved in the false bids, but how could Salomon expect clemency while keeping him on? It seemed obvious to them that the government would treat the firm more harshly if he stayed. Although Strauss and Gutfreund were not present, they, too, had told Buffett that they thought Meriwether should resign along with them.[57]

With uncanny timing, Meriwether himself arrived and leaned silently against a wall, watching as most of his peers demanded his head. Buffett had told Marty Lipton earlier that day that, unlike Strauss and Gutfreund, Meriwether must not be forced to resign. Buffett wanted time to deliberate. He did not agree with those who thought Meriwether had to go. Meriwether had not sucked his thumb; he had reported Mozer to Gutfreund and Strauss. It was not so much that they thought Meriwether had done anything wrong, Buffett decided. Rather, they were panicked. Their lives were simply going to be so much easier the next morning if Meriwether was gone.

After the meeting, he climbed into a waiting black Town Car with Gutfreund and Strauss and they wove their way through downtown rush-hour traffic to Corrigan's office.

Corrigan had felt it necessary to maintain his previous schedule in the interest of secrecy. He arrived directly from playing in the Federal Reserve's annual officers-versus-employees softball game, his tall frame clad in jeans, sneakers, and a Liberty Street Blues T-shirt.[58] But the chill in the air was such that "he could have been wearing black tie and I wouldn't have noticed, given my state of mind," Tom Strauss later said. Buffett opened disarmingly: "Look, the only thing I owe personally is $70,000 on a second home I have in California because the interest rate is cheap." He promised complete cooperation with the regulators. Corrigan refused to be charmed. Interim chairmanships usually didn't work very well, he said. Buffett had better not seek help for Salomon from his "Washington friends."

Corrigan demanded a thorough housecleaning. Buffett agreed to all sorts of fundamental changes to strengthen Salomon's policies, controls, and documentation. "His verbal commitment to me was absolute," says Corrigan, "and I trusted him."

Nevertheless, Corrigan made no promises. Giving Buffett a steely look, he said, "Prepare for all eventualities."

"It was a Dutch-uncle type of talk. It was cordial enough, but the Dutch-uncle aspect was there. We owed more money than virtually anybody in the country, and we owed it on very short terms. I tried once or twice to suggest how worried I was about the funding problem, hoping he might figuratively put his arm around me a little bit, but he didn't do it. Prepare for all eventualities—that was something I didn't know quite how to do. I certainly thought of strychnine or something of the sort."

Then Corrigan sent Buffett out of the room so he could talk to Gutfreund and Strauss. "You have a problem with an employee in your firm," he said, "that's his problem. You've got a problem with an employee in your firm and you fail to do something about it, that's your problem."[59] Then, with tears in his eyes, he told them how much he regretted ending their careers.

On the way out, while "Tom was in much more of a state of shock," Gutfreund again seemed "quite composed."[60] He seemed to be blaming Corrigan for forcing him to resign. "I'll be damned if I'm going to grant him absolution," Gutfreund said.[61] They rode back across downtown to Salomon, then went off to have a steak in a back room at Joe & Rose's steak house on 49th Street. Strauss and Gutfreund insisted again that Meriwether had to go.[62] They talked about the candidates for chief operating officer. Close to midnight, Buffett stumbled back to Katharine Graham's apartment at the UN Plaza, and tried to sleep.

Later, many people wrote many things about why Buffett took the job. Some said it was his $700 million, and some said it was his duty to the other shareholders. "Somebody had to take the job," he said shortly afterward. "I was the logical person."[63] Other than the people who were resigning, no one had more at stake. But it was not just the money, it was what he cared about just as much: his reputation. When he invested in Salomon and gave John Gutfreund his imprimatur, it was like nailing that reputation to Salomon's door like a shield.

Buffett had told his children, "It takes a lifetime to build a reputation and five minutes to ruin it." He thought of that risk primarily in terms of his own actions. Yet the people he had endorsed had put his reputation at risk. If he had made a mistake, it was to invest in Wall Street yet distance himself from it by relying on someone else; his judgment about Gutfreund's ability to oversee the runaway culture of Salomon was flawed.

By this time Buffett was the second richest man in the United States.[64] Berkshire's per-share book value had grown by more than twenty-three percent a year for twenty-six years. His first group of partners had an incredible $3 million for each $1,000 they had put in. Berkshire Hathaway was trading at $8,000 per share. Buffett had a net worth of $3.8 billion. He was one of the most respected businessmen in the world.

At some point during that long, horrible Friday, he recognized with a sickening jolt that investing in Salomon, a business with problems over which he had essentially no control, had from the beginning put all that at risk.

He did not want to become interim chairman of Salomon. That way lay greater peril. If Salomon went down afterward, he would be even more closely associated with shame and disaster. But if there was anybody who could get himself and the other shareholders out of this mess, he was that person.

To do so he would have to extend the umbrella of his reputation, already at risk, even further to protect the firm. There was no way to avoid this challenge. Deryck Maughan and John Meriwether could not do it. He could not send Charlie Munger, or Tom Murphy, or Bill Ruane. He could not solve it by passing an idea along to Carol Loomis for an incisive article in *Fortune.* Even Big Susie could not solve this. For once, nobody could be his proxy. Only he could save Salomon. And if he walked away, the odds were high that Salomon would implode.

At eight o'clock on Saturday morning, August 17, he arrived to a surreal scene at Wachtell, Lipton's offices. Gutfreund was not there; despite miserable weather he had decided to fly up to his Nantucket house, where Susan was staying. All the warlords—theoretically, candidates for CEO—had begun to gather outside an "interview room." Only a few of them made sense or actually wanted the job, but he had to interview every one. Meanwhile, a pair of "plenty smart," tough investigative lawyers from Wachtell, Lipton—Larry Pedowitz and Allen Martin—gave "a masterful presentation" to Buffett and Munger, who had flown in to participate in person. For the first time—to their outrage—they learned that the Treasury Department had investigated Mozer's earlier trades.[65]

Next, Buffett had to make what he considered the most important hire of his life: to decide who would lead the firm. If he made a mistake, he could not reverse the decision later. Before starting the fifteen-minute interviews, he told the group, "J.M. is not coming back."[66]

With that, he began to interview the candidates one by one. He asked them all the same question: Who should be the next CEO of Salomon?

"I was going into a foxhole with this guy, and he had to be the right choice. The question was, who would have all the qualities that would provide leadership to the firm, cause me not to worry for a second about whether anything was going on that was going to subsequently embarrass the firm or even put us out of business? As I talked to these people, what was really going through my mind was essentially the same questions that would go through your mind if you were deciding who you wanted to be a trustee under your will, or who you wanted to have marry your daughter. I wanted the kind of person who was going to be able to make decisions as to what should get to me and what could get solved below the line—who would tell me all the bad news, because good news always takes care of itself in business. I wanted to hear every bit of bad news as soon as it happened, so we could do something about it. I wanted someone who was ethical, who wouldn't stick a gun to my head later on knowing that I couldn't fire him."[67]

Buffett found that all but one of the other candidates thought it should be Deryck Maughan, who had returned three weeks earlier from running Salomon's Asian operations.[68] Maughan, forty-three years old, now headed the investment-banking group. He was not a trader, and he was English, not American. He had the least resemblance to Mozer or any of Salomon's frat-house trading boys of anyone that could be found. He was viewed as both ethical and possessed of common sense. Thanks to *Liar's Poker,* the public thought of Salomon as a place full of people who stuffed their faces with onion cheeseburgers for breakfast and dangled strippers' panties from their trading screens.[69] Salomon, after all, was the firm where, as Lewis had written, a vice chairman was more like a chairman of vice.[70] Maughan, however, was the very portrait of a dignified, impeccably tailored Englishman. Since he had spent the past several years in Tokyo, the chance that he was tainted by the Treasury auction scandal was remote.

Of all Maughan's qualifications, possibly the most valuable was his distance from the crime. Within Salomon, land of the long knives, all of the other candidates had enemies. Maughan was a question mark, like the token black guy in the movie *Putney Swope*, who gets elected to the job of CEO of a backstabbing advertising agency when the old CEO croaks during a boardroom meeting. The other executives try to sabotage one another's chances of getting his job by voting for Putney Swope, who ends up being elected by a huge majority.[71] Maughan was respected, but no one knew him all that well. As one of the other warlords put it, they all voted for Maughan because it's "better to choose someone you don't know than someone you think is bad."

In the movie, Putney Swope had had the sense to vote for himself. When Buffett asked Maughan who should run Salomon, Maughan replied adroitly: "I'm afraid you're going to find out that it's me."[72]

Two other things got Buffett's attention. Maughan did not ask him for protection against being sued. And Buffett—who, as much as he hated admitting it, did not enjoy paying people—was mightily impressed that Maughan did not ask how much the job would pay.

Maughan and two others were told to come to the office for the board meeting the next day. That afternoon, Buffett taxied back uptown to Graham's UN Plaza apartment, where the arb boys met him to plead "with passion and logic" for Meriwether's job. If J.M. left, Buffett knew, there was a risk that the arb boys would eventually join him.[73] Without Meriwether, the main source of Salomon's profits would drain away. Buffett's investment in Salomon could become worth far less. Then Meriwether himself arrived, shaken. He did not want to resign, and he talked to Buffett at length. Buffett began to waver. He focused on Meriwether's straightforwardness in reporting the problem.

"After listening to all of this, my reaction was not to ask for his resignation. As best I knew at the time, and this is still my belief, when he had heard of his subordinate's misdeeds, he had gone straight upstairs to his superiors and the general counsel and had reported it. It seemed to me that it was the job of his superiors and the general counsel of the firm to then take action. No one, at this point, was suggesting that the general counsel should resign."

Then Gutfreund called. His flight to Nantucket had been thwarted by

Hurricane Bob and he was headed back to New York. "I have no future," he said, agitated.[74] They made plans to go to dinner. Gutfreund insisted that first they talk to his newly hired lawyer, Philip Howard, about severance pay.

Buffett and Munger called Howard, with Munger doing most of the talking. Gutfreund felt the firm owed him $35 million.

"As he was laying all this out, I was listening like the Japanese, saying, 'Yes, I understand your position.' Not 'Yes, I agree with you.' We had no interest whatsoever in trying to arrange a compensation agreement with anyone who was in the middle of a scandal of this proportion without knowing the full facts."

Buffett then said that they could not agree upon an overall number, because no matter what the figure was, "Salomon Gives $XX Severance Package to Gutfreund" would "be the headline," rather than the break with former management.[75] They laid on praise of Gutfreund's character, however; they told Howard that Gutfreund would be treated fairly, that they had the power to make it happen and had never broken a promise before. Buffett said, "The only way this won't happen is if both Charlie and I die." He later explained that this was a way of avoiding confrontation; that is, "deflecting Mr. Howard and getting him off this kick" because it would be a "little abrupt" to say they didn't want to reach a settlement because "we don't know the full facts" yet.

Buffett and Munger then went out for a steak with Gutfreund at Christ Cella. Gutfreund offered to stay on as a consultant at no charge in the days ahead. "I'm going to need all the help I can get," Buffett said fervently. They talked about the problems of the firm, and Gutfreund said he thought Deryck Maughan was the right guy to run Salomon.

At one point, however, Gutfreund—who still knew a number of facts of which Buffett was not yet aware—said something that contradicted the warm and cozy scene of a few minutes before. "You guys are smarter than I am," he told them. "You guys are going to fuck me."[76]

It was with relief that Buffett and Munger escaped and went back to Kay Graham's apartment. A large suite filled with Asian art, it had many happy associations for Buffett. He, Carol Loomis, and George Gillespie often got together there for a bridge game, ordering in deli sandwiches on the side. But he was not having nearly as much fun tonight.

Almost as soon as they arrived, Philip Howard showed up, carrying a sheaf of papers about Gutfreund's severance, which he wanted Munger to sign.[77] He talked to both of them for a while, until Buffett left them alone and went off to make some phone calls. Munger started getting irritable. They discussed the matter for perhaps an hour or more.

Munger had already made up his mind that he was going to say no to this deal. As he recalled later, "I was deliberately not listening. I was being polite, but I wasn't paying much attention.... I sort of turned off my mind.... I was just sitting there politely with my head turned off."

When Howard reached the end of his lengthy list of demands, Munger refused to sign the papers, but stressed that Gutfreund would eventually be treated fairly.[78] On the way out the door, Howard hesitated. It bothered him that he still had nothing in writing. "You can't get paid after the divorce," he said. Munger reassured him: "Phil, you have to practice law the way my father did, by trusting in a man's word."[79]

While Howard and Munger were talking, Meriwether and his lawyer, Ted Levine, arrived. Meriwether had changed his mind. He said that he was in an impossible position and had to leave Salomon.

He "at least partially understood the seriousness of the company's situation. He was pacing back and forth, and he was smoking cigarettes as fast as he could light them. He said that the best thing for him to do was to resign."

Munger would later express feelings of guilt over agreeing to put Meriwether's name in the press release, which he viewed as a mistake he had made under pressure.[80] Both he and Buffett thought Meriwether could stay and fight it out, but they accepted his resignation.

"We talked for a considerable length of time. They stayed until midnight."

Finally, it was just Buffett and Munger. Buffett went to bed, feeling that matters were, if not under control, at least starting to be straightened out.

The next day, Sunday, August 18, no one would rest.

Early in the morning, Buffett, Gutfreund, and Strauss met in one of the many conference rooms on the forty-fifth floor of Salomon's office downtown before the meeting at which the board would ratify Buffett's role as interim chairman. Suddenly, a lawyer appeared, waving a message from the Treasury Department. It was going to announce in a few minutes that Salomon was barred from bidding at Treasury auctions, both for customers and for its own account. All of them understood that in minutes, Salomon would be shot in the head. "We immediately saw that this would put us out of business—not because of the economic loss, but because the message that would go out to the rest of the world in headlines in the papers on Monday would be 'Treasury to Salomon: Drop Dead.' In *effect, the response to installation of new management and banishment of the old would be an extraordinary censure delivered at an equally extraordinary time exactly coincident with the first actions of the new management."*

Buffett went off to another conference room to call the Treasury, seeking a stay of execution. The phone was busy. He got the phone company to agree to interrupt the call. They called back and said it was not a working phone. After many minutes of confusion, problems, and delays, Buffett finally spoke to someone in the Treasury Department. It was too late, he was told; the announcement had already gone out. The world now knew that Salomon was banned from doing business with the government.

Many of the board members were seeing their net worth evaporate in front of their eyes. Another slew of lawsuits, on top of those they already anticipated, would arrive on Salomon's doorstep. Buffett appeared calm but determined. He had come to a realization. Gutfreund was being drummed out for having created a nightmare. Now he, Warren Buffett, was actually on the brink—not of overseeing the salvation of a business—but of steering a zombie Salomon through the night of the living dead. Buffett balked.

He said to the board that he was going to tell Treasury Secretary Brady he would not serve as interim chairman; he had come to save the firm, not to oversee its dismemberment. His reputation would be shot either way, he thought, and the fallout from resigning would be less than the grief from staying on. The board understood and agreed. It was the only card that Buffett had to play with Brady. Meanwhile, the board decided to pursue two other courses simultaneously. Buffett turned to Marty Lipton. "Do you know a bankruptcy lawyer?" he asked. Everyone sat frozen for a split second. Then Feuerstein and Lipton began to set in motion the wheels of filing for bankruptcy. If necessary, the firm would fail in an orderly manner, rather than a rout.

Four and a half hours remained to try to reverse the Treasury's decision before a press conference that Salomon had already called for two-thirty p.m. to announce that Buffett would officially become interim chairman. Less than seven hours remained until the Japanese markets would begin to open for the week's business, and London seven hours after that. When Tokyo opened, the landslide would begin.[81] Lenders would start pulling their credits immediately. To plead for clemency had become immeasurably harder. They had not only to change the Treasury's mind but to convince it to reverse itself in public.

John Macfarlane, Salomon's treasurer, came in wearing a warm-up suit, directly from competing in a triathlon. He talked to the board about what the Treasury's action meant to the firm.[82] Banks had already started notifying Salomon they were pulling the firm's commercial paper lines. Solly was careening toward what would almost certainly be the largest failure of a financial firm in history. If the government withdrew its endorsement of Salomon and the firm lost its funding, it would have to liquidate assets at fire-sale prices. That would be followed by severe consequences in the world markets, as some of Salomon's creditors and counterparties, themselves unpaid, also began to fail. It was all going down the tubes. Buffett feared the regulators were going to regret their uncompromising stance.

"We were going to find a judge someplace in Manhattan, walk in on him while he's watching baseball probably and eating popcorn at two in the afternoon, and tell him, we're handing you the keys. You're running the place now. By the way, what do you know about Japanese law, because we owe ten or twelve billion dollars in Japan? We owe ten or twelve billion in Europe. London will open at two in the morning. And as of this very moment, you're running the place."

Corrigan was hard to reach. Asking to speak directly to Treasury Secretary Nick Brady, Buffett found that he was not available either.

Brady was the patrician former CEO of brokerage firm Dillon, Read & Co., and Malcolm Chace Jr.'s nephew, thus a member of the family that had sold Berkshire Fine Spinning to Hathaway Manufacturing. He had written his college thesis on Berkshire, which depressed him so much that he had decided to sell his stock. Through Malcolm Chace, Buffett had once gone to visit Brady at Dillon, Read. The two weren't close friends, but they had a "fine feeling about each other," Buffett says. There was no particular reason, however, why the blue-blooded Brady, who hailed from the old-line firm Dillon, Read, would have a fine feeling about a social parvenu like John Gutfreund—or a fine feeling about an arrogant upstart firm like Salomon.

Nonetheless, Brady called Buffett back. He expressed empathy but made it clear that reversing the decision was an enormous problem.

"They were going to look silly. And I felt they looked silly, too, but they would look a whole lot sillier a few days later when financial carnage was spread from this act."[83]

Brady said he thought Buffett was overreacting but agreed to call back again. He needed to consult with SEC Chairman Breeden, with Corrigan, and with Federal Reserve Chairman Alan Greenspan.

Buffett sat and waited for Brady's call. The phone system on the conference floor didn't ring on Sundays. To keep from missing an incoming call, someone had to stare continually at the phone to see whether a little green light lit up. For a while, Buffett stared at the phone, "as depressed as I have ever been." Finally, someone enlisted a hastily-called-in secretary to stare at the light.

Behind the scenes, the regulators were talking. Corrigan had contacted Paul Volcker, former chairman of the Federal Reserve Board and now chairman at a prestigious investment-banking firm. Volcker, like Breeden, was incensed at Salomon. None of the regulators believed that Buffett would walk; they felt he had too much money and reputation at stake. They knew the decision would have an adverse impact on Salomon and they thought that was appropriate. They didn't believe that Salomon would fail even if the Treasury pulled its imprimatur. The markets had so much confidence in Buffett that they assumed that simply by standing over Salomon holding his umbrella, he could save the firm. But they could not be certain of that. They considered whether the financial markets could survive a meltdown of one of its largest firms. The Federal Reserve would have to pump huge sums of money into the market to keep other banks afloat after Salomon failed to pay them. No rescue on this order of magnitude had ever been attempted. They were well aware of the likely second-order effects. The global financial market could potentially collapse. Did they think the Federal Reserve could handle it? "I was always an optimist," Corrigan says. "I always said to myself, 'You do what you have to do.'"[84]

Hours passed while Buffett waited for the phone to ring. Alan Greenspan called once, saying, no matter what, he wanted Buffett to stay. *"It was a plea to just sort of stand there at the bridge regardless of what happened."*

Little by little, the trading floor began to fill with people, as if summoned by some invisible jungle drum. They lit their cigarettes and their cigars, sat around The Room, and waited. The arbs huddled, mourning Meriwether. Nobody knew what was going on upstairs. Slowly, the clock ticked toward the hour when trading would begin in Tokyo, sounding the firm's death knell.

Upstairs, the board milled around uselessly, waiting while the regulators talked. Brady called Buffett back periodically but had nothing meaningful to say. Several times Buffett repeated his case in the gravelly voice that always betrayed him when under stress. He told Brady that Salomon's attorneys were working on a bankruptcy filing. He invoked Salomon's importance to the markets. He told Brady of the domino effect that the firm's failure could cause.

"I said to Nick, I'd talked to Jerry Corrigan. This thing was going to implode. Tokyo was going to open, and we weren't going to buy back our paper. It was over. Hour after hour, from ten o'clock, I kept telling the consequences of all these things, and it didn't mean anything to him."

Brady went back to his fellow regulators and talked. Most of them felt that this was special pleading. Buffett was asking for some kind of gold-star treatment for Salomon, and the firm did not deserve it.[85]

Salomon's board couldn't understand why Buffett's arguments weren't getting through to the regulators. They ran the financial markets. Why wasn't it obvious to them that Salomon was going down?

As the afternoon wore on, Buffett's logic failed, on this most critical occasion, to win over a key ally.

He had only one choice left. Of all avenues open to him, of all resources on which he could draw, this one was the most precious, the huge pool of crystal essence that he was most reluctant to tap. Buffett would undertake almost any item from his short list of most-loathed tasks—get into an angry, critical confrontation; fire someone; cut off a long friendship carefully cultivated; eat Japanese food; give away a vast sum of money; almost *anything*—rather than make a withdrawal from the Bank of Reputation. For all these many decades, he had brooded over, nurtured, cultivated, and stored that priceless commodity in its vault. Never had he withdrawn so much as a drop except when the odds hugely favored getting back even more in return.

Now the debacle at Salomon had exposed him utterly, putting the entirety at stake. And the only remaining hope was to ask, to literally beg as a personal favor, drawn purely on his own credibility, for help.

He would be putting himself eternally in Brady's debt. He was staking his entire reputation—the reputation that takes a lifetime to build and five minutes to lose—on whatever happened afterward.[86] He had to summon more courage than he knew he had.

Buffett's voice cracked. "Nick," he said, anguished, "this is the most important day of my life."

Brady had his own problems to deal with. He didn't think Buffett's arguments were any good. But he heard the feelings behind the words. He could hear in Buffett's voice that the man thought Salomon had thrown him over Niagara Falls in a barrel.

"Don't worry, Warren," Brady finally said. "We'll get through this." He hung up the phone and went off to consult.

But as the clock crawled toward two-thirty p.m., when the press conference was scheduled to begin, Brady had not called back.

Buffett decided to play the one card he could use with Corrigan. He picked up a phone. "Jerry," he said, "I haven't taken the job yet as interim chairman. We did not hold our meeting this morning because of what the Treasury did. So I am not the chairman of Salomon now. I could become the chairman in thirty seconds, but I am not going to spend the rest of my life shepherding the greatest financial disaster in history. I'm going to get sued either way by fifty people, but I don't want to spend my life trying to mop up a total disaster on Wall Street. However, I don't mind spending some of my life trying to save this damned place."

Corrigan took Buffett's threat to leave more seriously than the other regulators had, however. "I'll call you back," he said.

Buffett sat and waited, envisioning his next move. He pictured himself getting on an elevator, riding down six floors, walking onto the stage at the press conference all alone, and opening with the words "We've just declared bankruptcy."

Downstairs, in the August heat, more than a hundred reporters and photographers who had been pulled away unexpectedly from their baseball games and swimming pools and family picnics swarmed into Salomon's auditorium for the press conference. The only thing they had to fill their interrupted Sunday afternoon was the sight of Salomon's blood-drenched gladiators, gutted before their eyes on the sand of the Colosseum.

As the minutes passed, a white and shaken Meriwether arrived. He had gone, as instructed, to see Dick Breeden, chairman of the SEC, asking for help. Meriwether reported that Breeden had turned them down flat. Twice in the conversation, Breeden had said Salomon was "rotten to the core."

"Rotten to the core," Meriwether repeated in shock, "rotten to the core." All of them suddenly realized that the Treasury's move had been a joint decision among the Federal Reserve, the Treasury, and the SEC, their condemnation a sudden reversal of the world's opinion of Salomon, a dramatic payback for years of pride and arrogance.

The hour of the press conference came and went, while the reporters fidgeted and grew more irritable downstairs. Brady did not call. The phone sat unblinking.

Finally, Jerome Powell, assistant secretary of the Treasury, called. The Treasury would not fully reverse itself, he said. Salomon could not bid in Treasury auctions for customers. Yet it would compromise on Salomon's most important point: The firm could bid for its own accounts.

"Will that do?" Powell asked.

"I think it will," Buffett said.

He loped back into the boardroom and told them. The room erupted with relief and joy. As rapidly as he could talk, Buffett oversaw the election of himself as interim chairman and Deryck Maughan as director and operating head of Salomon Brothers. At about a quarter to three, he walked outside and had somebody call downstairs to the trading floor.

Maughan was sitting with the traders, watching the clock. At a nearby desk, John Macfarlane's team was working on a contingency plan to dump the firm's assets in Japan as fast as they could work the phones. Somebody called from upstairs and told Maughan to meet Buffett at the elevator bank for a talk. Maughan was uncertain whether he was about to be made the boss—or told he had a new one. He walked over to the elevator. The door opened, and he saw Buffett standing inside. "You've been tagged," Buffett said, and motioned for Maughan to get in. Instead of riding back up to the boardroom, they descended two more floors into the jaws of the waiting press.[87]

"The press was unruly. They were like animals. Every question was a trick question. It was a big story, and they wouldn't have minded if it had gotten bigger. It was their chance to shine. The TV people were particularly obnoxious. They wanted us to hurry up for the five o'clock news, or the six o' clock news, and I wouldn't cooperate with them. And I could just feel it. I could just tell it. I had to fall on my face. I had to be found a phony. They wanted it to develop that way. There were all kinds of book contracts floating around that room, but only if somehow Salomon failed."

Sitting on the dais, Buffett crossed his arms; he looked weary. Maughan, his light brown hair brushed into a neat pouf, stared wide-eyed at the crowd like the proverbial deer caught in the headlights. Both were clad in navy suits, white shirts, and funereal ties. "I had no preparation, zero," Maughan says. "'You're tagged' was my complete set of instructions." He did not know a single detail of what had transpired upstairs. They began.

What happened? the reporters wanted to know.

Buffett, suit jacket bunched up around his ears, explained: "The failure to report is, in my view, inexplicable and inexcusable. I have seen similar dumb things happen in other operations that I am more intimately involved in but not with such consequences."

Had the culture contributed to the scandal? "I don't think the same thing would have happened in a monastery," Buffett said.

Somebody asked him what he would get paid. "I'm going to do this for a dollar," he said. The board, sitting in the audience, was dumbfounded. This was the first they had heard of it.

The reporters declined to be soothed. Were records altered? Who altered them? Was there a cover-up? Who participated in the cover-up?

Yes, some records had been altered. There had been something resembling a cover-up. At that, the pack grew excited, throwing questions hard and fast. Here, perhaps, was the stumbling prey they were hunting, close to capture, ready to be torn apart by their sharp teeth. Alas, the trail grew cold when the cover-up included no one significant beyond those who had already been sacked.

Someone came out to the stage and told Buffett he had a phone call from the Treasury. He hurried from the dais, leaving Maughan, astonished, twisting in the wind alone. Nevertheless, Maughan managed to answer some questions in the perfectly articulated monotones of a BBC announcer narrating a documentary about the mating habits of the wildebeest.

Buffett returned with a press release from the Treasury Department, announcing that Salomon had part of its credibility back. The journalists were not mollified. They pressed on.

After well over an hour, one of the directors who was sitting next to Munger nudged him and said, "Isn't Warren ever going to end this thing?"

"Maybe he doesn't really want to," Munger said. "Warren knows what he's doing."[88]

How much did the phony trades cost the government? How many customers had told Salomon they wouldn't do business with the firm? What severance would be paid to the ex-executives? Why didn't Wachtell, Lipton take the situation more seriously? What were the details of the strange fraudulent trade the investigators had discovered, the one referred to in the press release as the "billion-dollar practical joke"?

"It is not a joke. I suppose if you had to characterize it in some way—" began Buffett.

"Those were your words in the release," retorted the reporter, sharply.

"Those were not my words. It was in the release. My name is not on the bottom of the release. You can characterize it as a bizarre incident. My definition of a practical joke is one you can laugh at after hearing it. I don't see it as the least bit funny."

The reporters, most of whom had read *Liar's Poker*, waited for an explanation. Salomon, they knew, was famous for its "goofs." Traders were constantly stealing the clothes out of each other's suitcases and replacing them with wet paper towels or lacy pink panties. The most famous goof at Salomon concerned the game of liar's poker itself, which Gutfreund once allegedly offered to play Meriwether for a million dollars on a single bet, no tears. Meriwether supposedly countered with ten million, causing Gutfreund to stand down. While even this story was thought to be a sort of goof, containing apocryphal elements, until now ten million dollars was the outside limit that anyone had ever imagined for a Salomon goof.

But for a billion dollars, you could fill New York Harbor with rubber chickens as high as the Statue of Liberty's thighs. What, then, could have been the "billion-dollar practical joke"?

"Apparently a woman was leaving the department after many, many years— retiring, I guess," Buffett said. "An order was worked out with somebody, to give her a very large order. A billion dollars. A billion-dollar order on a new offering of thirty-year Treasury bonds. Then—and this gets vague—I guess the plan was to maybe convince her somehow that the order was not submitted and have the client question the fact that it was not submitted. It was to try to scare the hell out of her or something. I don't know."

"The bid actually did get submitted."

A hundred fifty reporters sat in silence. Salomon had bought a billion dollars' worth of bonds in a practical joke gone wrong. Buffett was not kidding that the culture of Salomon was going to have to change.

"It should have been crossed out. My guess is that whoever did it did intend to cross it out. It has to be the dumbest joke ever attempted to be perpetrated."

No one said a word.

Maughan: "Any more questions?"

The hot air had been let out of the room. After this bit of truth-telling, what could anyone ask? Only a few more mild questions followed.

The press conference ended. Buffett looked at his watch as they walked off the stage. "I've got to get back to Omaha," he said.

"Warren, what's happening here?" asked Maughan. He had never spoken to any of the angry government officials, had never attended a Salomon board meeting, and the ship was sinking. "Do you have any views on who should form the management? Is there any direction you want to give me as a strategy?"

"If you have to ask me questions like that, I picked the wrong guy," Buffett said. He walked away without another word, leaving his $700 million and his reputation in the hands of a man he had met thirty hours before.[89]

On Monday morning, Maughan went out to The Room to shore up the staff's devastated morale. He took off his jacket and rolled up his sleeves. The firm, he said, had faced three tests. The first was character. By firing Mozer and his number two, Thomas Murphy, and accepting the others' resignations, the firm had passed that test.

The second was confidence. By regaining at least partially the Treasury Department's good graces, Salomon had passed that test.

The third was will. "This is not the same firm," said Maughan, "but we must keep aspects of the old culture while we bring in a new one."[90]

Some of the traders stirred uneasily. What did that mean, a new culture?

But at least Salomon had gotten one lucky break. Overnight, news had flashed over the wire that Soviet Premier Mikhail Gorbachev had been ousted in a coup. The stock market immediately dropped 107 points. Business coverage, which had been drilling on Salomon all day Friday, suddenly shifted focus as the world turned its attention toward Gorbachev, held under house arrest by eight of his own military and state officials. With tanks rolling into Moscow, customers got on the phones, and the bond desk did a brisk business that morning.

"There are lots of ways of getting off the front page," said a salesman, "but sending in the Red Army has got to be the most creative."[91]

49

The Angry Gods

The regulators' confidence that Salomon could survive on Buffett's reputation alone was almost certainly misplaced. Salomon barely survived even after the Treasury partially reversed itself. Some of its biggest customers simply felt revulsion toward the firm. First the huge and influential California Public Employees' Retirement System, then the World Bank, washed their hands of Salomon. Buffett fell asleep each night with visions of the hundreds of billions of dollars of Salomon debt that would fall due over the next few weeks staggering through his dreams like sickly sheep. *"Events could do me in, and I couldn't get off the train. I didn't know where the train was going to go."*

Buffett had to return to New York the following week. Senator Daniel Patrick Moynihan wanted to see him about Salomon, and there were many other matters that required his presence. He and Munger took Moynihan up to a private dining room on Salomon's forty-seventh floor, where the chef prepared a proper Wall Street meal for Moynihan, including the correct wines. Moynihan looked at Buffett and Munger, who had ordered sandwiches, in disgust. The aftermath of Hurricane Bob was still pounding the East Coast. Suddenly, cascades of rain began pouring in through a leak in the windows. "The gods are angry with Salomon," Buffett remarked.[1]

Later that week, he and Munger went down to Washington to see Bill McLucas and Dick Breeden at the SEC. They came into the office looking like "two guys you would see at the Greyhound bus station," according to McLucas. Then they started talking and laying out their plan to save Salomon; McLucas then understood, he says, why one person he was talking to was considered a legend and the other could finish the legend's sentences.[2]

Afterward, Buffett visited the Treasury Department himself to see Nick Brady, who told him that he had thought Buffett was bluffing. "Warren," he said, "I knew you were going to take the job no matter what we did."[3] It was only the sincerity of Buffett's plea that had touched him. Wind up the job as fast as you can, Brady said, and get out of there.

Buffett was determined that whatever was wrong at Salomon be found, confessed, and fixed right away. "Get it right, get it fast, get it out," he said. When he said fast, he meant fast; he talked to his new secretary, who had worked for Gutfreund and knew everybody well. Paula, he suggested, why don't you start talking to the board members and ask them questions about what they knew and when.[4] Bob Denham, the cautious, thorough Munger, Tolles lawyer who had been airlifted in from Los Angeles to head the investigation, got wind of this plan and put a stop to it. The investigating would be done by lawyers.

The first thing Denham did was interview Don Feuerstein. Afterward, Feuerstein was fired summarily. He asked to talk to Buffett, who told him only "You could have done more." Since Buffett had known that from the beginning, Feuerstein couldn't understand the about-face.[5] Buffett, however, had gradually focused on Feuerstein's loyalty to Gutfreund; Feuerstein had put his boss's interests ahead of Salomon's. Now Denham got the job of general counsel. As Buffett began to assume control, he discovered how much the board had been subjected to what he called adroit "information rationing" by Salomon's management. He and Munger now learned that when Mozer had first admitted in April to submitting an unauthorized bid, the firm had also discovered that he had tried to cover it up, and had misled the customer whose name he had used by claiming the bid was a clerical error.

Buffett had no doubt what he would have done. *"When you hear about an action like that, it is very obvious in ten seconds that you pick up the phone and say, Mozer, you're fired."*[6]

Of course, it wouldn't be obvious in ten seconds to many people. Mozer was so valuable to the firm—might it be possible to rehabilitate him? But Buffett thought in probabilities; he extrapolated right away to whether a catastrophic outcome was possible—then worked out very fast what it would take to get to the lowest probability of catastrophe. Here, it was firing Mozer and confessing right away. Buffett also thought in black-and-white terms about honesty; he had no tolerance for liars and cheaters. So that was that.

Now he found that the situation unfortunately involved more lying and cheating than he had previously been told. The investigators reported to him that Feuerstein had said at the time that Mozer's actions were "criminal in nature"—a startling contrast to the firm's agreeable response to later legal advice that no disclosure was required. And nobody had ever told the firm's compliance department—which was charged with overseeing regulatory conduct—of Mozer's behavior. True, Salomon had an attitude toward compliance that was best described as loose. There would later even be an argument over who should be considered a member of the compliance committee.[7] Nevertheless, the head of compliance had been disturbed when he found out that he was out of the loop and was angry that such procedures as did exist had been ignored.

Buffett and Munger also learned about Gutfreund's meeting in early June with Treasury Undersecretary Bob Glauber, after which Salomon's management had decided that the time was not right to disclose Mozer's actions. Glauber later said he felt that he was played for a sucker. Nothing had inflamed relations with the government and compromised Salomon's credibility more than this meeting with Glauber. It smacked of an outright cover-up.

The second press release that the board had approved, saying that the delay occurred thanks to "a lack of sufficient attention to the matter," had made the board look like part of the cover-up. But of course the board itself had been ignorant of the Glauber meeting.

Buffett was especially angry that he had known nothing of these matters during the entire weekend of the crisis when he had been negotiating with the government. Everybody whose number one job was to protect the firm's franchise had failed to do so. Yet even with all of this to outrage him, Buffett still did not know about one last thing: the "cocked gun" Sternlight letter that had been sent and ignored.

A few days later, the board met, and Buffett explained his thinking based on what he had learned. The board took away the former executives' secretaries and got rid of chauffeurs and limousines. They were barred from entering Salomon's offices. It tried to cancel their health insurance. Wachtell, Lipton offered to step aside as counsel, and Buffett accepted.

To augment the legal team, Buffett brought in Ron Olson, the most recent name partner of Munger, Tolles & Olson, who had worked on the *Buffalo Evening News* case and now represented Berkshire Hathaway.[8] Buffett told Olson that he wanted to pursue a novel strategy.[9] Salomon could not, in his view, survive a criminal indictment.[10] And he believed Salomon's best hope of

avoiding a criminal indictment was to show extreme contrition; he would surgi-
cally dig out every last cell of the cancer and, with scorching radiation, cleanse
the firm and burn out any trace of a recurrence.

On Olson's first day on the job, he was sent to see Otto Obermaier, the U.S.
Attorney for the Southern District of New York, who would make the decision
whether to criminally indict Salomon.

*"The argument we made to Otto Obermaier was that we would set an example.
This was going to be an example of the most extraordinary cooperation that a target has ever given, and the outcome would have an effect on the behavior of future
defendants and how the justice system worked."*

Olson had to make an extraordinary pledge. On the spot, he waived
Salomon's attorney-client privilege, which shielded communications between
the firm and its lawyers from prosecutors. He said that whatever MTO found in
its investigation, Obermaier would know it as soon as MTO knew it.[11] In plain
English, this meant that MTO, on behalf of Salomon, had volunteered to act as
an arm of the government.

Obermaier was "incredulous," Olson says. "He thought we were some Midwest
aw-shucks group, come to sell him a bill of goods."[12] He could not believe that
any company would make an offer voluntarily that was so against its own best
interest.

Initially, it was not clear what waiving the privilege meant. Frank Barron, an
attorney from Cravath, Swaine & Moore, one of Salomon's other law firms, was
put in charge of negotiating what this extraordinary gift would mean to the
Justice Department. Salomon had little leverage. The Justice Department
pressed hard for a broad interpretation of the commitment and largely got its
way.[13] The agreement put the firm in a peculiar and paradoxical situation of
prosecuting its own employees. The more evidence that MTO found that
employees were guilty, the more proof it could show that Salomon had cooperated and cleansed itself. The employees, meanwhile, must cooperate or be fired,
their statements to investigators unprotected by the normal attorney-client
privilege.[14]

Asked to help Buffett prepare for upcoming congressional testimony,
Gutfreund and his lawyer met with Olson a few days later. Gutfreund had volunteered to cooperate, but when his lawyers tried to lay down ground rules
for the conversation, Olson refused to accept them. Gutfreund and his lawyers
walked out.[15] Olson reported back to Buffett that he had been "stonewalled."[16]

Everything at Salomon was turned topsy-turvy as the new culture of openness went into effect. A couple of days after meeting with Obermaier, Olson and Buffett walked into a room at 7 World Trade Center for a meeting. Around a large square table, two dozen public-relations people sat waiting for them. Buffett listened for fifteen minutes as they described how they wanted to manage the crisis. Then he stood up. "I'm sorry, but I've got to excuse myself," he said. He leaned over, whispered in Olson's ear, "Tell them they won't be needed," and walked out of the room.[17]

"It isn't that we're misunderstood, for Christ's sake," said Buffett afterward. "We don't have a public-relations problem. We have a problem with what we *did*."

On his birthday, August 30, Buffett went down to Washington. He, Deryck Maughan, and Bob Denham went to testify before Congress. Buffett made a striking impression, seated alone at the subcommittee table and pledging extraordinary cooperation with Congress and the regulators.[18] *"I want to find out exactly what happened in the past so that this stain is borne by the guilty few,"* he said, *"and removed from the innocent."*

The Congressmen excoriated Salomon, postured as saviors of investors, and demanded a total break with the past. Nonetheless, they appeared slightly awed by Buffett. When he spoke, "The Red Sea parted, and the Oracle appeared," says Maughan.[19] Salomon, Buffett said, was going to have different priorities from now on.

"Lose money for the firm, and I will be understanding. Lose a shred of reputation for the firm, and I will be ruthless."

Those words have since been parsed and dissected in classrooms and case studies as the model of corporate nobility. Buffett's unflinching display of principle summed up much about the man. In this statement, many of his personal proclivities—rectitude, the urge to preach, his love of simple rules of behavior—had merged. Openness, integrity, extreme honesty, all the things that he meant to stand for: Buffett meant for Salomon to stand for them too.

Buffett headed back to 7 World Trade Center and put out a one-page letter to employees, insisting they report all legal violations and moral failures to him. He exempted petty moral failures like minor expense-account abuses, but, "when in doubt, call me," he told them. He put his home phone number on the letter. We are going to do "first-class business in a first-class way," he wrote.[20]

He wanted to run things by what he called the "front-page test."

I want employees to ask themselves whether they are willing to have any contemplated act appear the next day on the front page of their local paper, to be read by their spouses, children, and friends, with the reporting done by an informed and critical reporter.[21]

Employees at the time were frantically trying to keep from losing the firm. They called customers and begged them not to desert Salomon. John Macfarlane and the repo desk, which sold and bought batches of bonds, managed an intricate runoff of assets while negotiating tensely with numerous lenders, some of whom were refusing to advance money to the firm.[22]

The balance sheet dwindled at the rate of about a billion dollars a day. Macfarlane's team concentrated on stabilizing Salomon's balance sheet and customer relationships, gradually raising the firm's interest allocation charge and letting economics do the rest.[23] They restructured the debt toward medium-term notes and longer-term capital. The firm's traders tiptoed through the market to disguise the giant fire sale they were putting on. If other brokers recognized the pattern of their sales, it could set off a raid.[24]

Under threat of indictment, it was far from certain that Salomon would survive. The employees understood the message of Buffett's letter. Absolutely nothing else could go wrong in this atmosphere. "I want every employee to be his or her own compliance officer," Buffett said. This meant that to save the firm, they had to spy on each other. As the customers fled, the trades shrank, and the fear spread, the firm's long-standing culture of swashbuckling risk-taking began to fade.

Within days, Buffett was called back, this time to testify before the Senate. Corrigan, Breeden, and the federal prosecutors remained disgusted with Salomon. As he waited to be called, Buffett heard Senator Chris Dodd question Corrigan about whether the Federal Reserve had been asleep at the switch.[25] Corrigan said no, and that the Sternlight letter delivered on August 13 had been designed to produce a change in management but had been ignored.

Buffett sat figuratively scratching his head. He knew there was some kind of major problem here, but he didn't know what Corrigan was talking about.[26]

When it came time for him to testify, he was asked: Why hadn't a board filled with smart people been more aware and alert? Without betraying the fact that he was steaming inside about the Sternlight letter—whatever that might be—Buffett said that management had withheld information.[27]

He was not about to defend Salomon. Defending the firm of *Liar's Poker* was not likely to win friends. No, Salomon was a financial Gomorrah that must be investigated and purged of its ticket-forging, bonus-pimping, pizza-tossing ways.

This bold, arresting stance stopped a brewing witch hunt in its tracks. The pitchforks went back into the barns.

When Buffett got back to Salomon, he went after the details of the Sternlight letter; "he was livid," according to board member Gedale Horowitz. "It compounded the felony." Other than the Glauber meeting, the Sternlight letter was the most serious act of "information rationing." Buffett's and Munger's attitudes toward prior management hardened. Now the real import of Munger's term "thumb-sucking" became absolutely clear. "Thumb-sucking" meant ignoring the obvious until your diaper was full. As far as Gutfreund was concerned, "we had no option of forgiveness,"[28] Buffett said.

Through these revelations, Buffett led Salomon with apparent equanimity and poise. But beneath his eggshell-smooth demeanor, he was roiling in turmoil. He hated being away from Omaha. Gladys Kaiser noticed the lift in his step when he returned and the drag in his feet when he had to leave.[29] New York did not suit him any more than it had when he was young and working at Graham-Newman. He remained aloof, never appeared on the trading floor, and even a glimpse of him in the hallways at Salomon was a rare sighting. Before long, he had set up a regular bridge game with Carol Loomis, George Gillespie, and Ace Greenberg, the CEO of Bear Stearns. Bridge helped him relax because when he played bridge, he couldn't think about anything else. A couple of miles uptown, in his enormous Park Avenue apartment filled with a painstakingly assembled collection of art, his old friend Dan Cowin lay dying of cancer.

Buffett wasn't sleeping. When in New York, he would call home at twelve-thirty a.m., since he had the special deal to get the *Wall Street Journal* early in Omaha, and have tomorrow's news read to him over the phone.[30] He listened on tenterhooks, fearing that something horrible would be published about Salomon. Often there was, but at least he knew it before the rest of the employees. They were working fourteen or more hours a day to hold the firm together in the face of repeated obstacles and humiliations. Salomon's salesmen called clients, trying to convince them that the firm was not going under. Investment-banking clients were canceling previously committed deals as fast as they could run out the door. Competitors used the firm's precarious status against it when Salomon vied against them in banking "bake-offs."[31]

Other employees got field promotions of daunting magnitude. Maughan elevated one of the arbs, Eric Rosenfeld, to head trader. Rosenfeld, a former college professor who had never worked with a team of more than five people, suddenly found himself managing six hundred.

He did not want this promotion; he and the other arbs wanted J.M. back. Meriwether's office remained exactly as he had left it. The golf clubs, his ceremonial instruments of power, leaned in the corner. The cleaning crew kept the shrine well-dusted. The arbs gathered to consult the oracles of trading. They prayed for J.M.'s return. Salomon's stock continued to slump toward the low $20s.

By now, Salomon's investigators had discovered that Mozer had bid more than thirty-five percent on eight separate occasions, submitting false customer bids or jacking up customer bids and taking the extra bonds into Salomon's own account without informing the clients whose names had been used. On four occasions he had managed to acquire more than three-quarters of all the debt issued.[32] As the witch-hunt atmosphere heightened, Buffett upped the ante. At the next board meeting, he led a discussion. Why should Salomon be paying the attorneys of John Gutfreund to stonewall us? was the thrust of his questioning.[33] The directors voted, almost unanimously, to make two surprising moves. No severance pay, they said. And the firm cut off payment of legal fees for the former executives.[34]

The drama now revolved around two things: the Federal Reserve's deliberations over whether to keep Salomon as a primary dealer, and the criminal case.

The U.S. Attorney's prosecutors thought they had enough evidence to indict. The criminal law makes it very difficult to defend corporations against the acts of their employees. Gary Naftalis, Salomon's criminal lawyer, advised the firm that "Salomon plainly could be convicted" if it was indicted. For obvious reasons, everyone at the firm was desperate to get the criminal matter resolved.

After some three months of work dedicated to reforming the firm, Denham led Buffett, Olson, Naftalis, and Frank Barron to a secret location, chosen at U.S. Attorney Otto Obermaier's insistence. It was a last-ditch attempt to persuade Obermaier and his lawyers not to indict.[35]

A Teutonic old-school prosecutor with a love of the law and a deep respect for the history and traditions of the U.S. Attorney's office, Obermaier had been trying to figure out what to do with the fiasco that had landed in his lap. He recognized its unique nature. "This is no assault case on the New York subways," he said. Indeed, he had been calling Jerry Corrigan "alarmingly often" to learn the ins and outs of the Treasury bond market.[36]

Sitting in a little conference room facing Obermaier, Buffett did most of the talking. He worked very hard to convey what he had said so many times, that if the firm were indicted, it could not survive. Obermaier made comparisons to a case involving Chrysler, which had survived prosecution.[37] The difference between a firm that sold hard assets and a firm that bought and sold nothing more than promises on pieces of paper was initially not clear. Buffett tried to get past the image of onion-burger-tossing slobs inspired by *Liar's Poker* and invoked the innocent rank and file who would lose their jobs if Salomon went down. He promised that he would not sell his Salomon stock anytime soon and that his people would continue to run the place. He conveyed the sweeping nature of the cultural changes taking place inside the firm. This made an impression on Obermaier, but he kept a poker face. He had many other factors to consider.[38] The Salomon team went back across town with no idea whether they had succeeded or failed.

By midwinter, Salomon's status as a primary dealer remained unresolved. Under threat of corporate criminal indictment, Buffett and Maughan labored to prove the firm worthy of saving. Buffett had run a full-page ad in the *Wall Street Journal* explaining the firm's new standards.[39]

"I said that we would have people to match our principles, rather than the reverse. But I found out that wasn't so easy."

Day after day, Buffett bore down, shocked by the lavish lifestyle that was taken for granted on Wall Street. The executive dining room's kitchen, as large as that of any restaurant in New York, was run by a head chef trained at the Culinary Institute of America. Employees could order "anything on earth they wanted" for lunch.[40] In his first days in New York, Buffett received a letter from the head of another bank, inviting him to lunch so their chefs could do battle. "I follow a very simple rule when it comes to food," said Buffett, however. "If a three-year-old doesn't eat it, I don't eat it."[41]

For Buffett, the dining room symbolized the culture of Wall Street, which he found abhorrent. He had been born in an age where money was scarce and life was lived at a walking pace, and he'd arranged his own life to keep things that way. On Wall Street, money was plentiful and life was lived at whatever speed bandwidth could currently supply. People left their homes at five a.m. daily and returned at nine or ten at night. Their employers showered them with money for doing that but in return wanted every waking second of their time and supplied certain services to keep them working at a treadmill pace. Buffett as a child had been impressed by the Stock Exchange employee who rolled custom-made cigars, but now found all of this astonishing.

"They had a barbershop downstairs, and they didn't even tell me about it. They were afraid of what would happen when I found out. And they had a guy who came around and shined your shoes, and you didn't pay him."

But it was the battle over pay that became the watershed. Early in the fall,

Buffett had told the staff that he would be slashing $110 million from the year-end bonus pool. "Employees producing mediocre returns for their owners should expect their pay to reflect this shortfall," he wrote.[42] That seemed simple and obvious to him. Maughan agreed with Buffett that the culture of entitlement had to go.[43] But for once Buffett had miscalculated the limits of human nature. The formerly enriched employees, used to being showered with money on bonus day, now knew that they were about to be gouged.

Buffett's reasoning that employees should not take home all the spoils and the shareholders none was lost on them. Indeed, they believed the opposite, since they had been taking home the spoils for years. They felt that Buffett was trying to transfer some of the guilt from Mozer's misdeeds to them by making an issue out of the bonuses. They had not caused Salomon's woes. Rather, they had stayed out of loyalty and were enduring humiliation and misery in its aftermath. They were sweeping up behind the elephant. They felt that they deserved combat pay. It wasn't their fault that their businesses weren't performing. How could they sell an investment-banking deal while the firm was under threat of indictment? Didn't Buffett understand that? They were up against the fact that everybody on Wall Street knew that Buffett thought investment bankers were nothing but useless stuffed shirts with fancy cuff links. Meanwhile, despite its problems, Salomon was actually having a decent year financially. They resented being called greedy once again by an avaricious billionaire.

The deprived traders, sales force, and bankers had to hang around until year-end, the traditional time for quitting, after individual bonuses were paid and the smaller but nevertheless multimillion-dollar deferred bonus pool was scheduled to cash out.

When the bonus pool was divvied up around the holidays, the battle over pay reached epic scale. The top thirteen executives saw their bonuses slashed by half. As soon as the numbers were announced, Salomon's hallways and trading floor erupted in open revolt. With budgets and bonuses gutted, traders and bankers fled. Half the equity department—home of the investment bankers—ran out the door. The rest of the trading floor went on a temporary strike.

"They took the money and ran. Everybody just peeled off. It was just so apparent that the whole thing was being run for the employees."[44]

He had just saved Salomon and had thought that that would matter to the employees. But no, "We were grateful for about five minutes," was the verdict of one ex-employee. The fact that they wouldn't have a job without Buffett was forgotten in the grim shadow of the Bad Bonus Day. "Warren didn't understand how to run a people business" became the refrain among ex-employees. Buffett viewed the new pay deal as a cultural litmus test: Those who left were mercenaries whom the firm could do without, and those who stayed had signed on to the kind of firm he wanted.

Wall Street being a mercenary kind of place, little by little many of the top employees continued to drift away, carrying books of business to competitors as they departed. Buffett couldn't sleep. "*I couldn't turn off my mind,*" he says. He had spent his whole life avoiding commitments to anything where there was no escape hatch and he didn't have total control. "*I've always been leery of getting sucked into things. At Salomon I found myself defending things I didn't want to defend; and then I found myself being critical of my own organization.*"

Months had passed and Obermaier was still pondering whether Salomon's conduct was bad enough to indict.[45] In considering the phony bids, he thought it important that Mozer's actions were motivated more by rebellion against the Treasury rules than simply to enrich Salomon. Likewise, no serious financial losses had occurred.[46] He also weighed Buffett's promises and the new culture.

Together with Breeden at the SEC, he began to work on settlement talks with Salomon that would allow the firm to escape indictment. Frank Barron, the lawyer from Cravath, went down to the SEC to negotiate its share of the settlement in a meeting with Bill McLucas, Breeden's deputy, who informed Barron the fine from the Department of Justice and the Treasury Department would be $190 million plus a $100 million restitution fund. Barron was shocked—the fine was huge. Why? he asked. "Well, Frank," said McLucas, "you have to understand that it's going to be $190 million because that's what Richard Breeden says it's going to be."[47]

The moment when John Meriwether had rushed into the conference room that Sunday morning, white and shaken, quoting Dick Breeden, who had called Salomon "rotten to the core, rotten to the core," came to mind. There would be no appealing this decision. Salomon agreed to pay the extraordinary fine.

Buffett was trying to undo the "rotten to the core" image as fast as he could. Dubbed "Jimmy Stewart" by the staff, he nixed deal after deal that he thought was too close to the line, despite the resulting internal backlash.

On May 20, Obermaier's office called Olson to say that the government was not going to indict and had dropped all charges. The U.S. Attorney and the SEC announced a settlement with Salomon over fraud and record-keeping charges; including a $100 million restitution fund, it was in total the second largest fine in history. The settlement found no evidence of wrongdoing other than Mozer's illegal bidding, which had been discovered by Salomon itself. Mozer was going to prison for four months, and would pay a $1.1 million fine. He was barred from the industry for life.[48] Gutfreund, Meriwether, and Strauss were reprimanded for failing to supervise him, given small fines, and suspended for a few months from working in the industry.[49]

Most observers were dumbstruck at the size of the fine for what amounted to technical violations by one employee. In fact, by acknowledging its guilt to the government so freely, some thought Salomon had given up its negotiating leverage. But what the large fine really reflected was that the firm had bungled its reporting responsibilities so badly, and had made the regulators look asleep at the switch in front of Congress. Thus it was, as the well-exercised saying goes, the cover-up, not the crime.

Three days after the announcement, Dan Cowin died of cancer. Buffett wrote out a heartfelt eulogy, meaning to deliver it himself, and asked his secretary, Paula Orlowski, to stop by his hotel room and pick it up to have it typed. But when she arrived, he met her at the door and said, with an agonized look, that he could not bring himself to speak at Cowin's service. Instead, Susie was going to read it for him.[50] Buffett went to the service. *"I sat through it shaking all over the whole time,"* he says.

Then he went back to work. Salomon estimated that the $4 million profit Mozer had made from his trades had cost the firm $800 million in lost business, fines, penalties, and legal fees. The firm's status as a primary dealer remained unresolved, although it now seemed a foregone conclusion that this would be resolved in Salomon's favor.[51] Employee defections had slowed to a trickle, and the rating agencies were starting to upgrade Salomon's debt. Customers started coming back. As Salomon stock crept above $33, Buffett announced that he was stepping down. Deryck Maughan took over as permanent CEO, and Buffett appointed MTO lawyer Bob Denham as chairman.

In that mournful spring of 1992, as Salomon staggered to its feet, the question of how to deal with those who had nearly brought it down remained open. Second only to Mozer in the public's assessment of culpability was John Gutfreund. In the end it was he who was responsible, despite all the legal advice that reporting was not required.

When the time came for Gutfreund to discuss what money he would receive from the firm, he asked for the "fair treatment" he had been promised as long as Buffett and Munger were alive. Now, however, it turned out that the parties' opinions of what was fair differed dramatically.

Gutfreund's lawyer thought that he had made a deal with Charlie Munger on that fateful weekend in August of the previous year, and that Munger had accepted a resignation letter conditioned on the lengthy list of severance terms. Gutfreund felt that he had fallen on his sword to save the firm and believed he was owed $35 million in back pay, stock, and severance. Salomon took the position that Charlie Munger had made no deal at all. The board interpreted Gutfreund's employee-benefit plans strictly and also took back the stock options he had earned, even though the stock-option plan contained no provisions allowing for forfeiture under this or any circumstances. It countered with $8.6 million.

Insulted and outraged, Gutfreund turned it down. "It seemed wrong," he said. "As a matter of principle, I fought."[52] His lawyers interpreted the offer not as meant to inspire negotiation but as so insultingly low that it must be dismissed. In 1993, Gutfreund took Salomon to arbitration.

In arbitration, a panel of neutral parties listens to both sides and reaches a binding decision to resolve a dispute. Arbitration is a throw of the dice, for its very nature cuts off negotiation forever once a decision is reached.

John Gutfreund had been reduced to sitting in a small three-room office, where he answered his own phone when his part-time secretary was away. He and Susan, now dubbed "Marie Antoinette" by the press, had been cast out of the New York social set. The press had turned on him savagely, in a way he had never imagined could happen, comparing him to felons like Boesky and Milken.[53] Many of his former friends had abandoned him. Unassisted by Salomon, he was running up huge bills to defend himself in civil lawsuits.

Gutfreund wanted vindication through the arbitration. But a public raking and digging over the whole Salomon mess, which might have salved his wounded pride, was guaranteed to alienate Buffett and make him less likely to compromise. After Buffett had staked much of his image on Salomon, Gutfreund had let him down. Now that he and Gutfreund were no longer partners, in Buffett's special sense of the word, transgressions he might once have eventually forgiven became larger with hindsight. They were many, and even without benefit of hindsight they were large:

• The stock-option repricing in 1987, which had cost Buffett so much money.

• The Sternlight "cocked gun" letter from the Fed, which Buffett had not learned about until it was too late.

• The meeting with Bob Glauber at the Treasury, when Gutfreund had kept silent, which had also been kept from Buffett and the other board members.

Although he normally avoided conflict, if forced into battle Buffett made sure that his proxies fought for him like cornered hyenas. Charlie Munger, who was inclined to say things such as that Gutfreund made Napoleon look like a shrinking violet, was the appointed bad guy in the arbitration.[54] His testimony would be crucial, because he was the one who had negotiated with Gutfreund's lawyer, Philip Howard.

It was the young president of the New York Stock Exchange, Dick Grasso, who chose the three graying arbitrators who would decide Gutfreund's fate in a dingy conference room at the Exchange.[55] A team of lawyers from Cravath—backed by testimony from Salomon board members, employees, ex-employees, Buffett, and Munger—began to pulverize Gutfreund in a process that took more than sixty sessions and several months before the arbitrators.

Over and over, the arbitrators heard about the meeting between Munger and Philip Howard in which Howard reviewed the list of compensations Gutfreund wanted and Munger listened in some fashion or another. All agreed that Howard left without a signature on Gutfreund's severance papers, but there was no agreement about how to interpret the rest of the events of that evening. Howard was certain that Munger had made a deal with him.

Gutfreund's lawyers called Charlie Munger as a witness. Frank Barron of Cravath, Swaine & Moore had attempted to prepare Munger, who was utterly impatient with the process. Although Barron had prepared Munger by himself, Munger, a lawyer who disliked paying legal bills, extemporized to the arbitrators that, in preparing him for testimony, Cravath had employed an excessive number of expensive paralegals and "aspirin-carriers."[56] When he began to testify, every word that came out of his mouth "had nothing to do with what we had gone over," says Barron. "Putting Charlie Munger on the witness stand was the most nerve-racking, hair-raising experience I ever had as a lawyer."[57]

Munger's confidence as a witness was unmatched. A number of times the lead abitrator, growing irritated, admonished him: "Mr. Munger, would you please listen to the questions before you answer them."

Munger insisted that on the night when he had met with Philip Howard, he was "deliberately not listening... being polite, but I wasn't paying much attention... I sort of turned off my mind.... I was just sitting there politely with my head turned off."

Gutfreund's lawyers asked him whether he had made a conscious decision not to talk as well as not to listen.

"No," said Munger, "when the time came to talk, I talked. One of my faults—I am fairly outspoken. I may well have discussed some individual things that got through my band of indifference. This is one of my most irritating conversational habits. It followed me through the course of my life.

"So every time something would get through and I would see a counterargument," he said, he would give it. Howard had asked for an indemnification for Gutfreund against lawsuits. Being a legal matter, this had gotten through Munger's band of indifference.

"I think I said to him, You don't even know what you are going to need. God knows there will be litigation, there will be a big mess, who knows how things are going to work out. You are misrepresenting your own client if you think it makes sense to get into any of those issues at this time."

Was that also a conversation in which you were tuning out? asked Gutfreund's lawyer.

"No, I tend to tune in when I am speaking myself," said Munger, under oath. "I tend to remember what I say."

Was this also a conversation in which you were deliberately not listening at various times?

"What did you say?" said Munger. "I just tuned out again, and I wasn't doing it on purpose."

Was this also a conversation in which at various times you were deliberately not listening?

"I am ashamed to say I have done it again. Will you please do it one more time? This time I will use an effort."

Gutfreund's lawyer repeated the question for the third time.

"You bet," said Munger. "I was going through the motions."

In what mental state the arbitrators, the lawyers, and Gutfreund heard these words can only be imagined. Regrettably, much of the misunderstanding seems to have stemmed from Philip Howard's unfamiliarity with the outward signs of the workings of Charlie Munger's mind. He had labored that night under the illusion that he and Munger were having a conversation. He did not recognize Munger's occasional replies as intermittent thought-bursts ignited by some random mite that had pierced Munger's band of indifference. Whenever Munger objected, Howard assumed they were negotiating, not that he was simply being lectured. When Munger said nothing or emitted a grunt to move the conversation along, Howard inferred that Munger agreed, or at least that he had no objection to whatever had just been said. Nobody had explained to him that Munger's head was turned off.

Gutfreund's lawyer reminded Munger of Buffett's testimony, in which he had acknowledged saying to Gutfreund that he had the power to make all this happen. Did Mr. Munger recall Mr. Buffett saying that?

"I don't remember Mr. Buffett's words as well as I remember my own," said Munger. "But certainly the gist of the thing was that you can count on us to be fair."[58]

The issue was what was meant by "fair." Salomon never disputed that the money was Gutfreund's and that he had already earned it. The argument boiled down to whether Gutfreund would have been terminated had all the facts been known. Thus, the case became an exercise in proving that Gutfreund should have been terminated. Even Donald Feuerstein agreed that in concealing what he knew from Glauber, Gutfreund had been dishonest with the government. Although everyone thought this bizarre and out-of-character behavior, nonetheless, it had happened.

In fairness to Salomon, Gutfreund understood why the firm was expending so much effort to prove he should have been fired. He knew it was in everybody's interest to vilify him, but the lack of proportion bothered him. At some point it should have ended, he thought.

Everyone, even Buffett, felt that Gutfreund was entitled to some of the money. Buffett had Sam Butler, a fellow GEICO board member and friend of Gutfreund's, call him twice and offer $14 million. Butler whispered, "I can probably get you a little more." Buffett would have gone to $18 million.[59] But Gutfreund had been humiliated by the process. He considered Charlie Munger mean-spirited and self-righteous. He turned the offer down indignantly. The arbitrators would decide.

After months of testimony, lasting until spring 1994, the arbitrators were showing their impatience at the endless, circular, and conflicting arguments, one side professing complete innocence and the other portraying Gutfreund as an archfiend. Then, at the closing statements, Gutfreund's lawyers showed up with a chart, raising the demand to $56.3 million by adding interest, penalties, stock appreciation, and other items.

The lawyers and people involved at Salomon had set up a betting pool as the arbitration crawled at an agonizingly slow pace toward its conclusion. How much money would the arbitrators give Gutfreund? The lowest bet was $12 million. The highest was $22 million.[60]

No one will ever know what factors the arbitrators weighed in their decision. When the decision was announced, they awarded Gutfreund nothing, not a dime.

50

The Lottery

B uffett's testimony in Congress as the reformer and savior of Salomon had turned him from a rich investor into a hero. The success of his open and principled approach to scandal touched the yearning for nobility in many people's hearts: the dream that honesty is rewarded; that the besmirched can be redeemed through honor. Even as the furor from the crisis died, Buffett's star rose. Berkshire stock took off on a meteoric streak, bursting past $10,000 a share. Buffett was now worth $4.4 billion. Susie's stock alone was worth $500 million. His original partners would now have $3.5 million for every $1,000 they had laid out in 1957.

When Buffett walked into a room, the electricity was palpable. In his presence people felt brushed by greatness. They wanted to *touch* him. They became dumbstruck before him, or babbled inane remarks. No matter what he said, people listened uncritically.

"I was at my best at giving financial advice when I was twenty-one years old and people weren't listening to me. I could have gotten up there and said the most brilliant things and not very much attention would have been paid to me. And now I can say the dumbest things in the world and a fair number of people will think there's some great hidden meaning to it or something."

He went about surrounded by a little haze of fame. Reporters called all the time now. As writers began working on books about Buffett, people who saw him every day found the frenzy incomprehensible. A woman showed up at Berkshire's office and began bowing to him. Gladys Kaiser was overcome with annoyance. "Don't bow to him!" she said.

Many Salomon employees and ex-employees were not bowing. He had reined in their freewheeling culture, ruined their bonus day; he disdained their business and they knew it. Plenty of employees had unhappy stories to tell. Soon enough, the contrast between Buffett's aw-shucks image and his coldly rational side hit the radar screen of the national press. How to explain the dichotomy between Buffett figuratively sitting on a front porch with a glass of lemonade, telling folksy stories, and his long history of sophisticated business feats? What was he doing as interim chairman of an investment bank while describing Wall Street as a gang of con men, sharpies, and cheats?

By 1991, the *Wall Street Journal* and the *New Republic*[1] took note of his straddling of two worlds, and both ran stories pointing out the mismatch between Buffett's representation of himself as a middle-class Midwesterner who had woken up in Oz and the elephant-bumping in which he routinely engaged. The *Wall Street Journal* story ran a sidebar to its article, "Buffett's Circle Includes the Moneyed and Powerful," name-dropping people like Walter Annenberg.[2] But one of those mentioned in the story would go on to forge a relationship with Buffett that eclipsed all the rest, even though he had known Buffett for only five months at the time of the story's publication.

Buffett had met Bill Gates that summer over the Fourth of July holiday, when Kay Graham had dragged Buffett to her friend Meg Greenfield's house on Bainbridge Island, near Seattle, for a long holiday weekend. Greenfield had also recruited him for an all-day visit at the nearby compound that Bill Gates had built for his family. Gates, twenty-five years Buffett's junior, was appealing to Buffett mainly because he was known to be brilliant and because the two of them were neck-and-neck in the *Forbes* race. But computers looked like Brussels sprouts to Buffett; no, he did not want to try them this once. Greenfield, however, had assured him that he would like Gates's parents, Bill Sr. and Mary. With some reluctance, Buffett had agreed to go.

Gates had similar reservations. He was interested in meeting Graham, now a seventy-four-year-old legend, but, "I told my mom, 'I don't know about a guy who just invests money and picks stocks.' . . . But she insisted." The day of the visit, Gates flew in on a helicopter so he could make a quick getaway.[3]

Observers kept a weather eye on his introduction to Buffett. Gates was well-known for unleashing his impatience on things that didn't interest him. Buffett no longer walked off to read a book when he was bored but had a way of disentangling himself very quickly from conversations he wanted to exit.

Buffett skipped the small talk; he immediately asked Gates whether IBM was going to do well in the future and whether it was a competitor of Microsoft. Computer companies seemed to come and go, and why was that? Gates started explaining. He told Buffett to buy two stocks, Intel and Microsoft. Then he asked Buffett about the economics of newspapers, and Buffett told him that they had gotten worse, because of other media. Within minutes the two were deeply immersed in conversation.

"We talked and talked and talked and talked and paid no attention to anybody else. I started asking him a whole bunch of questions about his business, not expecting to understand any of it. He's a great teacher, and we couldn't stop talking."

The day started to go by; the croquet games began. Gates and Buffett talked on, even as many of Seattle's best-known people circulated around them. They took a walk on the pebbly beach. They were starting to attract attention. *"We were sort of ignoring all these important people, and Bill's father finally said, gently, that he'd prefer that we join in with the rest of the people a little more.*

"Bill started trying to convince me to get a computer. I said, I don't know what it's going to do for me. I don't care how my stock portfolio is doing every five minutes. And I can do my income taxes in my head. Gates said he would pick out the best-looking gal at Microsoft and send her to teach me how to use the computer. He would make it totally painless and pleasant. I told him, 'You've made me an offer I almost can't refuse, but I will refuse it.' "

As the sun descended toward the water during the cocktail hour, Buffett and Gates kept talking. At sunset the helicopter had to leave. Gates did not go with it.[4]

"Then at dinner, Bill Gates Sr. posed the question to the table: What factor did people feel was the most important in getting to where they'd gotten in life? And I said, 'Focus.' And Bill said the same thing."

It is unclear how many people at the table understood "focus" as Buffett lived that word. This kind of innate focus couldn't be emulated. It meant the intensity that is the price of excellence. It meant the discipline and passionate perfectionism that made Thomas Edison the quintessential American inventor, Walt Disney the king of family entertainment, and James Brown the Godfather of Soul. It meant single-minded obsession with an ideal.

A day later, Buffett escaped the island and returned to Omaha. He could see that Gates was brilliant and that he understood business very well. But since the days when he had passed on the chance to invest in the start-up of Intel, Buffett had never trusted technology companies as investments. Technology companies came and went, their products often made obsolete. Now, his interest piqued, he bought a hundred shares of Microsoft, which, to him, was like eating a single Cheerio. He still couldn't bring himself to buy any Intel, even though he sometimes bought a hundred shares of a stock just to keep track of a company.[5] But he did invite Gates to the next Buffett Group meeting. Soon thereafter he had gotten the phone call from Don Feuerstein and Tom Strauss and for the next two months had thought of nothing but the miseries of Salomon.

In October, released from the conference rooms of 7 World Trade Center and the browbeatings of Congressmen and regulators for a few days, he went to Vancouver, British Columbia, for the latest meeting of the Buffett Group.

Bill Gates was coming to the meeting for the one particular session that interested him. The Buffett Group was going to review the ten most valuable companies in 1950, 1960, 1970, 1980, 1990—and how the list had changed.

Arriving late because his new seaplane had been delayed by fog, Bill and his girlfriend, Melinda French, slipped into the room unobtrusively from the rear. Melinda had thought that they were going to leave early. However, after about the fourth slide, she realized that maybe they were going to stay.[6] Tom Murphy and Dan Burke, who both served on IBM's board, started talking about why IBM, the leader in hardware, hadn't gone on to become the leader in software. Buffett said, "I think we've got somebody here who can add a little something to this discussion." Everybody turned around and saw Bill Gates.[7] The conversation continued. If you were Sears in 1960, why couldn't you keep getting the smartest employees and selling at the best prices? What was it you couldn't see that prevented you from remaining the leader? Most of the proposed answers, regardless of the company, revolved around arrogance, complacency, and what Buffett called the "Institutional Imperative"—the tendency for companies to engage in activity for its own sake and to copy their peers instead of trying to stay ahead of them. Some companies didn't bring in young people with fresh ideas. Sometimes managements weren't attuned to tectonic shifts in their industry. Nobody suggested these problems were easy to cure. After a while Buffett asked everyone to pick their favorite stock.

What about Kodak? asked Bill Ruane. He looked back at Gates to see what he would say.

"Kodak is toast," said Gates.[8]

Nobody else in the Buffett Group knew that digital technology would make film cameras toast. In 1991, even Kodak didn't know that it was toast.[9]

"Bill probably thinks all the television networks are going to get killed," said Larry Tisch, whose company, Loews Corp., owned a stake in the CBS network.

"No, it's not that simple," said Gates. "The way networks create and expose shows is different than camera film, and nothing is going to come in and fundamentally change that. You'll see some falloff as people move toward variety, but the networks own the content and they can repurpose it. The networks face an interesting challenge as we move the transport of TV onto the Internet. But it's not like photography, where you get rid of film so knowing how to make film becomes absolutely irrelevant."[10]

Now everybody wanted to talk to Gates, who could explain the new digital world and what it meant to them. "The next thing we knew, we were going on the boat that afternoon," says Gates. "And Kay was making sure that I didn't just talk to Warren." That was fortunate, because Buffett—who liked to glue himself to certain people—would have liked to become Bill Gates's Siamese twin. They headed out on Walter and Suzanne Scott's enormous boat, the *Ice Bear*. Graham introduced Gates to Tisch and Murphy and Keough and the rest.[11] In half a day, he and Melinda had become de facto members of the Buffett Group.

Thanks partly to the salvation of Salomon, Berkshire stock had nearly doubled by the time Warren was starting to Buffett his way through the arbitration with John Gutfreund, bursting through $18,000 a share. Buffett was now worth $8.5 billion, and Susie's stock was worth $700 million. The original partners now had $6 million for every $1,000 they'd invested in 1957. Buffett was now the richest man in the United States.

Over the holidays, he and Carol Loomis turned to the annual ritual of writing and editing his chairman's letter, this time with the awareness of a much larger national—even international—audience. In May 1994, the same month that Gutfreund's arbitrators awarded him zero, Buffett held his annual shareholder meeting; more than 2,700 people arrived at the Orpheum Theater. Buffett told See's, the shoe companies, and World Book encyclopedia, which the company also owned, to set up booths in the lobby. See's sold eight hundred pounds of candy, and more than five hundred pairs of shoes walked out the door.[12] World Book sold well, too, although Buffett did not know that it, like Kodak, would soon be toasted by the Internet. Delighted with his shareholders' purchases, Buffett drove over to Borsheim's and made an appearance, then showed up at the Furniture Mart. "He goes out to where we have the mattresses displayed," said Louie Blumkin, "and he's selling, man."[13] Buffett started to think harder about the idea of hawking products at the shareholder meetings. He vowed to move the meeting to the Holiday Inn, which had more space for sales booths. And next year, he decided, he would also sell Ginsu knives.[14]

His rising fame swept most of the family along with it. Now that Buffett was worth more than $8 billion, his charitable foundation would be one of the five largest in the world, and it would be Berkshire's largest shareholder after he died. He had recently added Susie, who was president of the Buffett Foundation but knew nothing about business, to the Berkshire Hathaway board. The foundation had been giving away about $3.5 million a year, which had doubled by 1994—still small by the standards of families of similar wealth. Its future riches, however, were well-known. The Buffett Foundation and its president were suddenly in the public eye.

When Susie had moved to San Francisco and made the decision to stay married to Warren while going her own way, she envisioned being able to keep the two halves of her life separate, quiet, and in balance. She was caught by surprise when her husband became an icon of the business world, carrying her along with him. On the one hand, she wanted her privacy and freedom. On the other hand, she wanted to please Warren, enjoyed running the foundation, and also gravitated toward the elephant-bumping aspects of public life. To maintain her privacy, she had to juggle deftly, keeping a low profile in San Francisco and declining opportunities that went with her husband's rising stature. Susie expressed resentment of Warren from time to time to various people, as if it were his fault that her life was now so fraught.

Moreover, her pace had been slowed by painful bouts of adhesions in 1987 and more adhesions and a hysterectomy in 1993. Kathleen Cole found herself shuttling her friend and boss to the emergency room distressingly often. The family seemed strangely unperturbed each time Cole called Nebraska to say that Susie had been hospitalized, as if they had adopted her serene attitude.[15] "Thank God I have my health," she often remarked, and continued to view herself as the well person who ministered to the ill, rather than the other way around.

By now she was running a hospice in her apartment. Her first patient was an artist friend who was dying of AIDS, whom she invited to move in and spend his final weeks there. Cole, a former nurse, found herself administering IV drips to a terminal patient while Susie's other employees strolled in and out of the room, questioning her about foundation matters or the renovations and redecoration of the Laguna Beach house, still metamorphosing after a decade.[16] After that, whenever one of Susie's gay friends who was dying of AIDS neared the end, she invited him to come live with her. She and Cole took some of her dying friends on dream trips, one to Japan, another to Dharamsala for a personal audience with the Dalai Lama. She kept her friends' ashes on her mantel to make sure that someone would remember them. Peter took to calling his mother the Dalai Mama.

Howie, who had always absorbed so much of his mother's energy, now stepped out from under her wing at the same time that his father's growing fame began to have an impact on his life. During 1989, he had become chairman of the Nebraska Ethanol Authority & Development Board. Through this role, he became friendly with Marty Andreas, an executive at Archer Daniels Midland, a large Illinois-based agricultural company that was heavily involved in ethanol. Marty Andreas was nephew of ADM's CEO, Dwayne Andreas, who served on the Salomon board with Warren. Two years later, thirty-six-year-old Howie was asked to become the youngest member of the ADM board.

Dwayne Andreas had been charged, but acquitted, of making illegal political campaign contributions during Watergate; he also made huge and sometimes controversial donations to politicians of both parties while Congress was repeatedly passing the tax subsidies for ethanol that benefited ADM. Buffett's view that rich people and powerful business interests were far too able to buy access and influence with politicians conflicted sharply with the way that ADM did business in politics.

Six months after Howie joined the board, Andreas hired him for a job in public affairs. Howie had no public-relations or financial experience, and agreed to move to Decatur, Illinois, where ADM was headquartered. The company put him in charge of working with analysts.[17] Howie would not have accepted the offer if he thought it had something to do with his surname or his father's recently burnished reputation as a paragon of corporate ethics. His expertise in ethanol seemed to him to make it plausible. However, while Howie had many years of experience with people trying to use him for his father's wealth, he was naive about large corporations, and he saw nothing remarkable in a major company hiring a member of its board of directors to work as a public-affairs spokesperson.

Buffett, who would never invest in a company like ADM or hire a person who mixed business and politics the way Andreas did, said nothing to dissuade his son from serving on a board and working for a company so dependent on largesse from the government. This uncharacteristic reticence speaks volumes about his longing for his son to gain some business experience.

Andreas was tough and demanding, according to Howie, and gave him assignments like buying flour mills in Mexico and working on the North American Free Trade Agreement. But Howie remained the same person as before—driven by adrenaline, energetic, almost painfully honest, and vulnerable. At family trips and gatherings, he still surprised his relatives by jumping out of closets in his gorilla costume.[18] Nevertheless, Howie felt that he was getting years of business education compressed into a short time.

In 1992, Buffett had invited Howie to join the board of Berkshire Hathaway, saying that his son would become nonexecutive chairman after he died. Howie's business experience was still light, he had never finished college, and he was more interested in agriculture than investing. He now had the beginnings of a credible résumé, however. Since Buffett was the largest shareholder of what amounted to a family corporation, he was within his rights to do this. His reasoning was that Howie would steward the culture after he was gone.

Buffett now had to do some mental backflips, however, to reconcile all the statements he had made over the years—denunciations of the evils of the "divine right of the womb," dynastic wealth, and advantages based on parentage rather than merit—with his decision to make his relatively untested son the chairman of Berkshire Hathaway after he was gone. And it was not clear how Howie's role would complement that of the next CEO of Berkshire. That may have been the point. Every sign now indicated that Buffett would see to it that power would not be concentrated in any one individual after his death. This might inhibit Berkshire's potential or it might not, but it would fend off the grisly menace of the Institutional Imperative, which he viewed as the greatest danger that Berkshire faced. Buffett wanted a degree of control from beyond the grave, and this was his first step in getting it.

In a second step, he had put Susie Jr., then Peter, on the board of the Buffett Foundation, with the understanding that Susie Jr. would run the foundation after her mother died. This, by the assumption of all concerned, would not occur until after Warren himself was gone. Buffett's view of the foundation, as of so many other things, was that "Big Susie will take care of it." Susie Jr.'s shouldering of foundation responsibilities was presumably many years in the future. A philanthropist in training, she played an active role in her father's civic and social life in Omaha. As her father's fame increased, Susie Jr. was also becoming his most frequent elephant-bumping escort, now that Kay Graham, in her seventies, was not getting out as much. Astrid, who only occasionally attended events with him, did volunteer work at the zoo and had no interest in serving on committees or chairing events. Her life was less changed than almost anyone's by Buffett's new-found fame, interrupted only by the occasional gawker in the driveway.

Peter had moved to Milwaukee, headquarters of his record label. After a stressful marriage, he had separated from Mary in May 1991, and ever since had been going through a messy divorce. Afterward, Peter formally adopted his twin stepdaughters, Erica and Nicole. While Big Susie had always embraced them as her granddaughters, Warren was more reserved. Later—with hindsight—it would become clear that he viewed the adoption as a new postmarital link forged between Peter and his ex-wife—a link that Warren did not feel bound by himself.

Peter used this traumatic period in his personal life as a catalyst for personal growth. Meanwhile, his career had progressed. His music had begun to reflect Native American elements, which resonated strongly with him. That had led to a job scoring the Fire Dance scene in *Dances with Wolves*. He was now working on a movie score for *The Scarlet Letter* and a CBS miniseries.

Peter was respected but not famous, a working musician but not a star. In the music world, the Buffett name meant nothing. His father was proud of his son's work. But artistry divorced from fame or commercial success flew past Warren just the way his investing and business passion flew past Peter; their worlds did not connect. Yet, oddly, Warren and Peter were the most alike; both shared a passionate commitment to a vocation for which they had been destined from early childhood; both got wrapped up so obsessively in their work that they expected their wives to become their conduit to the outside world.

Buffett also now had, in effect, a third son—Bill Gates.

At first it was what Gates calls "a tiny bit of 'Warren's the adult and I'm the child.'" Gradually this evolved into "Hey, we're both in this learning at the same time."[19] Munger often attributed much of Buffett's success to the fact that he was a "learning machine." Their common intellect, interests, and way of thinking gave them considerable common ground. They shared the same intensity. Buffett taught Gates about investing and acted as the sounding board for Gates's ruminations about his business. It was the way Buffett had learned to think in models that impressed Gates most. Buffett was as eager to share his thoughts about what makes a great business with Gates as Gates was eager to hear them.

If Buffett could have found more great businesses, he would have bought them all. He never stopped looking for them. The town where the Superinvestors of Graham-and-Doddsville lived was getting crowded, however. Wall Street had been overrun; there were fewer and fewer pockets of overlooked opportunity. While Buffett's focus on business never lessened, as the nineties progressed, the deals became larger—but more sporadic. Meanwhile, a new interest took hold. It would not reduce his zeal for Berkshire, but it would alter his social priorities, his travel itineraries, and even his friendships.

What Buffett now wanted to do in his spare time was to play bridge. He had been playing a casual social game for nearly fifty years, and while in New York to handle Salomon, he had started playing a more serious and competitive game. One day in 1993, he was playing in a tournament with George Gillespie and met Sharon Osberg, who was partnered with Carol Loomis.

A former computer programmer, Osberg had grown up with a deck of cards in her hand. By the time she was running Wells Fargo's start-up Internet business, she had won two world team championships. It didn't hurt that she was a petite, sweet-faced brunette in her mid-forties.

"The next time she's going cross-country," Buffett told Loomis, "have her stop in Omaha. Have her call me."

"Where's Omaha?" Osberg said. It took her three days to build up the courage to pick up the phone. "I'd never talked to a living legend before."[20]

Osberg, who lived in San Francisco, was on her way to Omaha a week or so later. Buffett took her to dinner at his now-favorite steak house, Gorat's. Seated in a room full of families eating at Formica tables, Osberg decided to play it safe and declared, "I'm going to have whatever you're having." A few minutes later she found herself looking at "a piece of raw meat the size of a baseball mitt." Afraid of offending a living legend, she ate it. Then they went to the local bridge club to play, after which, at ten o'clock, Buffett took her on a driving tour of Omaha so he could show off his collection. She saw the Nebraska Furniture Mart parking lot, she saw his house, she saw the house he grew up in, she saw Borsheim's, all from a moving car in the dark. Then he dropped her off at her hotel. Both were leaving early the following day.

The next morning, when Osberg was checking out, the front desk clerk told her, "Someone came in and left a package for you." Buffett had come to the hotel at four-thirty in the morning and left her a compilation of his annual reports to shareholders, which he had had privately printed and bound into a book.[21] She had just become one of Buffett's people.

Not long after, Buffett sent Osberg to meet Kay Graham when she was in Washington on a business trip. She filled in as a fourth at bridge with Graham and her friends. Soon, Osberg was staying at Graham's house and playing bridge in Washington on a regular basis with people like Sandra Day O'Connor. She called Buffett from the guest bedroom. "Oh, my God!" she said. "There's a real Picasso in the bathroom!"

I never noticed it and I've stayed there for thirty years," Buffett later said of the Picasso sketch. *"All I know is she leaves shampoo out."*[22]

Buffett began to time his trips to coincide with Osberg's business trips to New York. Before long, the two had become fast friends. Osberg thought it was a shame that the only time Buffett got to play was when he was in a room with other bridge players. He needed a computer. They went round and round about this for several months. Finally Osberg said, "Warren, you really should just *try* it." "Okay, okay," he said. "You come to Omaha and set up the computer, you stay at the house."

Bridge and Osberg accomplished what even Bill Gates had not. Buffett had the Blumkins send someone over from the Furniture Mart to hook up a computer. Osberg arrived at the house, she got acquainted with Astrid, then taught Buffett how to navigate the Internet and use a mouse. "And he was fearless, just fearless," Osberg says. "He wanted to play bridge." And only bridge. "Just write down the things I need to know to get in to play bridge," he told her. "I don't want to know anything about anything else. Don't try to explain to me what this thing is doing."[23] Buffett adopted the moniker "tbone" and began playing on the Internet four or five nights a week with Osberg and other partners. Astrid would fix him an early dinner before he logged on to his bridge game.

Before long, Buffett was so engrossed in Internet bridge that nothing could disturb him. When a bat got into the house and flapped around the TV room, banging into the walls and entangling itself in the curtains, Astrid shrieked, "Warren, there's a bat in here!" Sitting across the room in his frayed terry-cloth bathrobe, staring at his bridge hand, he never moved his eyes from the screen as he said, "It's not bothering me any."[24] Astrid called the pest-control people and they removed the bat, all without disturbing his bridge game.

Buffett felt his skills had improved so much under Osberg's tutelage that he wanted to play in a serious tournament. "Why not start at the top?" she said. They signed up for the mixed pairs at the World Bridge Championships. The Albuquerque convention center was filled with hundreds of people sitting around bridge tables and kibitzers wandering around watching the players. Murmurs and stares flew through the room when the richest man in the United States and two-time world champion Sharon Osberg strolled into the World Bridge Championships together. By now, enough people recognized Buffett's

lanky frame and thatch of gray hair that he caused a stir. For an unranked amateur to show up at the world championships as his first tournament was an
unusual thing. For Warren Buffett to do it was shocking.

Osberg expected that they would lose in short order, so the point was to have
fun and get some experience. Instead, Buffett sat down at the table and seemed
to shut out everything. It was as if there was nobody else in the room. His bridge
skills were not close to the level of most other players, but he was able to focus as
calmly as if he were playing in his living room. Somehow his intensity overcame the weakness of his game. Osberg was amazed when they qualified for the
finals. "We were just good enough," she says.

But after a day and a half of playing to get to this point, Buffett was exhausted
and wrung out. The only breaks had been an hour here and there to slip out for
a hamburger. He looked like he had run a marathon. In the break before the
finals he told Osberg, "I can't do it."

"What?!" she said.

"I can't do it. Tell them we're not going to play in the finals. Tell them I had a
business emergency," he said. Now Osberg had the job of explaining this to the
World Bridge Federation.

Nobody who qualified for the finals had ever decided not to play. The representatives of the World Bridge Federation were outraged that Warren Buffett
would come to their tournament, endorse it by his famous and important presence, qualify for the finals, then try to leave. "You can't do that!" they said. When
Osberg insisted, they threatened to strip her of her ranking and credentials. "I'm
not the one who won't play!" she insisted, repeating that he had a business
emergency. Finally, they accepted that she was only Buffett's proxy, relented, and
allowed the two of them to leave without punishing her.

Naturally, Buffett had encouraged Bill Gates, who had fooled around with
the game a bit, to become a more serious bridge player. He also sent Osberg to
Seattle to set up Bill Gates Sr. on the computer to play bridge, thus beginning to
inject her into the Gates family.

Buffett's relationship with Gates was gradually becoming much closer. On
Easter weekend 1993, Bill and Melinda got engaged. On the way back from San
Diego, Bill had the pilot give fake weather reports from Seattle to fool Melinda
into thinking they were flying home. She was shocked when the aircraft door
opened after they landed and Warren and Astrid were waiting on the red carpet at
the bottom of the stairs. Warren drove them to Borsheim's, where they picked out
an engagement ring.

Nine months later, Buffett flew to Hawaii for their New Year's Day wedding. Even though his sister Bertie owned a house on the Big Island of Hawaii, Buffett had never been to Hawaii before. He was as excited about the Gates wedding as if one of his own children were getting married. Bill and Melinda's wedding conflicted with Charlie Munger's seventieth birthday party, which was taking place the same weekend. The famously loyal Buffett never dropped his old friends but sometimes had to play Twister to manage his relationships. If a conflict arose, he tended to resolve it by appeasing whoever he thought was most likely to get upset at him—which generally meant that he slighted the most loyal of his friends, the ones he could count on not to criticize or get angry at him. This left the rejected person the paradoxical consolation that he was the one Buffett most trusted and felt closest to. People understood this, so they put up with it. Munger, the long-standing friend, would tolerate almost anything of Buffett, even missing his seventieth birthday party.

So he opted for the wedding and brought along Kay Graham, now seventy-six, who still attended occasions of state like this. Warren, meanwhile, had sent Susie to Los Angeles for Munger's party, where she sang.[25]

Susie was used to this sort of thing. She had her own definition of what he needed from the women in his life, and pigeonholed each of them into a utilitarian category. One night when she was at dinner at Gorat's with Warren, Astrid, and Sharon Osberg, she looked around the table and surveyed the company. Only Kay and Carol Loomis were missing from the harem. She laughed and shook her head. "Someone for everything," she said.

But before long, Buffett was talking to Osberg several times a day on the phone, taking her along as a traveling companion on his trips, and making her one of his closest confidantes. Much like Astrid, however, she stayed in the background rather than upset the perceived order of all his other relationships, which Buffett had always tended to separate. By the mid-1990s, the public perception of how he spent his time and the way he actually spent it had long diverged. As always, conflicts were resolved to appease whomever might erupt on him. The shrieking wheel got the grease.

Another group of Buffett's loyal friends joined him for their biennial ritual when the Buffett Group held their meeting at the Kildare Club and in nearby Dublin in September 1995. Because Bill Gates was present (for Gates straddled all of Buffett's worlds, since Buffett would have liked to become his Siamese twin), the government of Ireland treated them like emperors. Filled with incredible artwork and antiques, the K Club raised all of its own food on-site and prepared it with a European staff and chefs.

The gloss and glamour of the surroundings belied the fact that the Buffett Group members, many of them fabulously wealthy by now, were largely unchanged. Warren saw some of these people only once a year or so; yet he remained utterly devoted to them.

Amid the K Club's luxury, Buffett handed out copies of a booklet, *The Gospel of Wealth* by turn-of-the-century industrialist and philanthropist Andrew Carnegie. As he celebrated his sixty-fifth birthday, and took stock of his life to date, he had been rereading Carnegie. Now he led the group in a debate of Carnegie's premise that "He who dies rich dies disgraced." Carnegie had honored that philosophy, spending nearly his whole fortune, one of the greatest in history at the time, to establish libraries in towns and cities all over the United States.[26] Buffett had always planned to die rich and disgraced. He insisted that the best use of his talents was to keep making more money until he died. He wanted to hear what other people thought and obviously was giving some consideration to this question.

Most of the Buffett Group members were heavily involved in philanthropy, and for years had begged Buffett to loosen his tightfisted ways. They welcomed the dialogue as a sign he might be rethinking his rigid position. When his turn in the conversation came, Bill Gates said, Shouldn't the measure of accomplishment be how many lives you can save with a given amount of money? He agreed with Buffett that you had to make the money first in order to have the money to give away. But as soon as he had made a certain amount, Gates said, he was going to use it to save more lives in the present, by giving most of it away.[27]

The Buffett Foundation had chosen two main philanthropic issues, overpopulation and nuclear proliferation, problems that are almost unimaginably hard to solve. Nuclear proliferation didn't lend itself well to financial solutions, although Buffett would have given as much money as he could to his highest priority, any plausible way of reducing the probability of nuclear war. His analysis of the problem was, characteristically, statistical.

"A nuclear attack is inevitable. It's the ultimate problem of mankind. If there's a ten percent probability that something will happen in a year, there's a 99.5 percent probability that it will happen in fifty years. But if you can get that probability down to three percent, that reduces the probability to only seventy-eight percent in fifty years. And if you can get it down to one percent, there is only a forty percent

probability in fifty years. That's a truly worthwhile goal—it could literally make all the difference in the world."

The other great problem, in Buffett's view, was the strain placed on the over-burdened planet by too many people. Population control was where the Buffett Foundation had spent most of its money since the mid-1980s. This, too, he approached from a mathematical perspective. In 1950, the world's population had been about 2.5 billion. By 1990 the world's population had passed the five-billion mark. The debate over how much this mattered essentially centered over whether technology could outpace population growth, species extinction, and global warming. Buffett looked at the problem of expanding population and diminishing resources in terms of a "margin of safety."

"There is a carrying capacity to the earth. It's far, far, far, far, far greater than [Thomas] Malthus ever dreamed. On the other hand, there is some carrying capacity, and the one thing about carrying capacity is that you want to err on the low side. If you were provisioning a huge rocket ship to the moon and had enough for two hundred people and didn't know how long the journey would take, you probably wouldn't put more than a hundred fifty people on the ship. And we have a spaceship of sorts, and we don't know how much the provisions are good for. It's very hard to argue that the earth would be better off in terms of average happiness or livelihood with twelve billion people instead of six.[28] There is a limit, and if you don't know what that limit is, you're better off erring on the safe side. It's a margin of safety approach for the survival of the earth."

Since the 1970s, Buffett had focused on giving women access to contraception and abortion—issues that were close to Susie's heart—as the answer to out-of-control population growth. This was a standard point of view among humanist organizations at the time.[29]

Buffett had been especially moved by the logic of Garrett Hardin, a leader of the population control movement, whose 1968 article "The Tragedy of the Commons" laid out the way that people who have no ownership stake in common goods—the air, the seas—overuse and destroy them.[30] While Buffett adopted many of Hardin's principles, he rejected solutions favored by Hardin, a social Darwinist who espoused authoritarian ideas and had written that the meek not only would inherit, but already had inherited the earth. He considered this "genetic suicide": "Look around you. How many heroes do you number among your neighbors? Or your colleagues?... Where are the heroes of yesteryear? Where is Sparta now?"[31]

Buffett thought that the idea of bringing back Sparta had already been tried. The man who had tried it was Adolf Hitler. The Spartans had groomed themselves genetically by abandoning weak or "undesirable" babies on a mountainside. Modern eugenics (social Darwinism) was a philosophy formulated by Sir Francis Galton, who drew on the work of his cousin Charles Darwin and theorized that selective breeding of the human race could improve the quality of the population. This notion had received extremely widespread support in the early twentieth century, until discredited by the experiments of Nazi Germany.[32] There was no safe way to think along lines like those Hardin was pursuing, which led to a deadly division of humanity into competing groups.[33] Buffett had renounced this view in favor of a civil-rights-based approach to the problems of spaceship Earth.

Accordingly, by 1994, Buffett's emphasis had shifted from "population control" to reproductive rights.[34] This change corresponded with a worldwide evolution in thinking among the population control movement. Women "were no longer to be treated as a convenient means toward the 'end' of population control."[35] Buffett had always felt that any means of solving the population problem that involved coercion was out of the question.[36] Now he went a step further. "*I wouldn't in any way limit a woman's right to bear children even if the world were extremely overpopulated, and I wouldn't ban the right to choose even if there were only two people on the planet and fertility was critical. I think the world should be limited to wanted people first. I don't think that the numbers should determine how many people are wanted. Even if everybody had seven children, I wouldn't do as Garrett Hardin said and link the right to the numbers.*" So the Buffett Foundation supported reproductive rights.

Increasingly, the complexities and nuances of reproductive rights, civil rights, and population control had all gotten lost in the controversy over abortion. Buffett's giving ultimately was based on what he called the Ovarian Lottery.[37] The idea had great resonance for Buffett.[38]

"*I've had it so good in this world, you know. The odds were fifty-to-one against me being born in the United States in 1930. I won the lottery the day I emerged from the womb by being in the United States instead of in some other country where my chances would have been way different.*

"*Imagine there are two identical twins in the womb, both equally bright and energetic. And the genie says to them, 'One of you is going to be born in the United States, and one of you is going to be born in Bangladesh. And if you wind up in Bangladesh, you will pay no taxes. What percentage of your income would you bid to be the one that is born in the United States?' It says something about the fact that society has something to do with your fate and not just your innate qualities. The people who say, 'I did it all myself,' and think of themselves as Horatio Alger— believe me, they'd bid more to be in the United States than in Bangladesh. That's the Ovarian Lottery."*

The Ovarian Lottery had come to shape all of his opinions about politics and philanthropy; Buffett's ideal was a world in which winners were free to strive, but obliged to narrow the gap by helping the losers. He had grown up with the lynchings and beatings of the civil-rights years; and had heard over and over of the Court House Riot, authority shoved onto a scaffold with a noose around its neck. Perhaps without being aware of it, Buffett had many years ago abandoned the libertarian leanings of his father[39] and spiritually circled back toward the democratic idealism of Nebraska's William Jennings Bryan, who had written of "the class that the rest rested upon."

Buffett, one of the least peripatetic people imaginable in both philosophy and geography, could make the occasional tectonic shift if enough conviction piled up. Now, after he and Susie returned from Ireland, they met in Vancouver to embark on a seventeen-day trip to China, "Across Cathay." Buffett's motivation for this round-the-world jaunt was the Gateses. Bill and Melinda had gone to considerable trouble to make the trip enjoyable for him. Ahead of time, they sent him and the other guests a questionnaire asking what they liked to eat. Buffett was not taking any chances on an experience like the one he'd had at the Moritas'. "I don't eat any Chinese food," he responded. "If necessary, serve me rice and I'll just move it around on my plate, and I'll go back to my room afterward and eat peanuts. Please get me a *Journal* every day; it's really hard if I don't have my *Journal*."[40]

And so Buffett went to China.

After checking in to Beijing's grand old Palace Hotel on Goldfish Lane, they ate a magnificent Sichuanese dinner in the hotel's Emerald Room. The Gateses had arranged for the tour company, Abercrombie & Kent, to send people ahead to teach the chefs to make hamburgers and french fries for Buffett. The first evening, to his delight he was served course after course of his french fries— even for dessert.

In Beijing, the group met the Premier of China. On the third day, they climbed to the top of the Great Wall, where the group found champagne awaiting them—and Cherry Coke for Buffett. Looking down at the world's largest structure, which represented eleven centuries of innovative engineering, human

labor, and Chinese history, everyone waited for Buffett to say something profound. Surely he would be moved by the sight.

"Boy, I sure would have liked to have been the company that got the brick
contract for this thing," he quipped.

The following morning, he skipped the martial-arts lesson in favor of a tour
of the local Coca-Cola plant. The next day, the group flew to Ürümqi to board a
train—no ordinary train, for the Gateses had arranged for the group to be the
first Westerners to rent Chairman Mao's personal train—for a journey across
northwest China. The train followed the Old Silk Road route, making stops
along the way so that the group could ride camels in the desert, visit ancient
cities and caves, see the giant pandas in Xi'an, and tour the archaeological dig of
the imperial Terra Cotta Warriors and Horses. The trip allowed for hours and
hours of conversation, during which Buffett and Gates continued their discussions of why some banks are better than other banks, why retailing is such a
tough business, the value of Microsoft stock, and the like.[41]

On the tenth day they visited the site of the Three Gorges Dam project, then
boarded the *M.S. East Queen,* a huge, five-deck cruise ship. The boat passed into
the first of the three gorges, the Shennong Xi, where many of those on board
donned orange life vests and climbed into longboats that were poled and pulled
by river trackers along an upstream tributary of the river. A group of ten men
using ropes dragged each boat against the current, while young, supposedly vir-
ginal girls sang to encourage the men at their grueling work.

Buffett cracked jokes about the virgins. But that night during the Cantonese
dinner, his mind obviously flashing to the implications of the Ovarian Lottery,
he said, "There could have been another Bill Gates among those men pulling
our boat. They were born here, and they were destined to spend their lives tugging those boats the way they did ours. They didn't have a chance. It was pure
luck that we had a shot at the brass ring."

From Shennong Xi, the boat steamed on to Outang Gorge, passing villages
where schoolchildren came out to bow at the strange Americans. Past a silk-
reeling mill, between sheer, mist-shrouded peaks, alongside a traditional cob-
blestone village, the boat slowly wound its way down the Yangtze. Finally, they
arrived in Guilin for a private Li River barge cruise through one of the most
scenically beautiful spots on earth, a pristine river lined with thousands of lime-
stone pinnacles covered in a mantle of green, "like jade hairpins," according to
the Tang poet Han Yu. Many of the Gates party bicycled along the riverbank to
experience the long waterside parade of two- and three-hundred-foot-high

untouched prehistoric stone shafts. Warren, Bill Sr., and Bill Jr. had obtained permission from their wives to have an hours-long bridge orgy on the boat as the barge floated through the magnificent pine-forested landscape.

When they finally arrived in Hong Kong at the end of the trip, Buffett towed the Gateses straight to McDonald's to buy hamburgers in the middle of the night. *"And all the way back from Hong Kong to San Francisco and then on to Omaha, I just read newspapers."*

But long after that journey through China, for years afterward in fact, Buffett's mind kept returning over and over to one of its moments. It was not the scenery, which he had barely noticed, or the camel ride, memorialized in a photograph. It was not the endless meals of french fries during the Chinese banquets that everyone else had enjoyed. He was thinking about the Three Gorges Dam project and the longboats on the Shennong Xi. But it was not the singing virgins that had beguiled him. It was the fate of the men who spent their lives ceaselessly dragging the longboats upstream that stayed with him, haunting his thoughts about individual destiny and fate.

51

To Hell with the Bear

Omaha and Greenwich, Connecticut • 1994–1998

Through the bridge, through Ireland, through China, as late as 1994, Buffett devoted every day to looking for stock to buy for Berkshire Hathaway. But it was growing steadily more difficult to find a wonderful business at a fair price. He was still putting money into Coca-Cola, until he had spent a total of $1.3 billion. He bought another shoe company, Dexter. Here he was a little outside his "circle of competence," making a bet that demand for imported shoes would wane.[1] Buffett was also buying American Express stock again.

He wanted the rest of GEICO.

Buffett negotiated furiously with Sam Butler, GEICO's chairman, and its new CEO, Tony Nicely, to buy the fifty-two percent of GEICO that Berkshire didn't already own. In the end, he wanted GEICO so badly that he paid $2.3 billion in stock. Despite having fought so hard, Buffett actually regarded the price as reasonable, considering that he'd gotten the first forty-eight percent for only $46 million.

The GEICO deal marked a turning point. The stock market was on a tear, with new technology offerings unexpectedly popular in 1994.[2] Buffett's knowledge of technology was spotty. Despite his sense of the Internet's importance, honed during his friendship with Bill Gates and his many games of bridge, it had not yet occurred to Buffett to tell GEICO to hurry up and exploit the Internet to sell insurance. To Buffett, computers were just tunnels that enabled him to reach other people who could play bridge. As investments, he still considered technology stocks risky bets.

Even had he been of the temperament to do so, Buffett didn't need to make risky bets. Decisions made years ago were still compounding for him. The hiring of Ajit Jain had meant that when Hurricane Andrew blew South Florida off the map in 1992, Buffett was able to start a new business, "catastrophe reinsurance," which charged a premium price to stand by as insurer of the unthinkable. Then the Northridge earthquake hit. Almost no one else had the capital to put up billions on a risk like that. But Berkshire Hathaway did.

The old days of scouring the *Moody's Manuals* for teensy companies were long gone. Most of the ideas for buying whole companies were now brought to him.

Some may have thought, If he'll buy Dexter Shoe, Buffett will buy *anything*. He was starting to regret that deal. Dexter was getting killed by foreign competition; people had not lost their interest in buying imported shoes. But the mistakes were few and the home runs many: Cap Cities/ABC negotiated a deal to sell itself to Disney for $19 billion, and Berkshire made $2 billion, almost four times its original investment. Tom Murphy went on the board of Disney, and Buffett became linked to Disney through Murphy. At Sun Valley, the Buffetts now mingled easily with a crowd that ranged from Coca-Cola executives to movie stars. He also went back on the board of the *Washington Post*, which was now being run by Don Graham, one of his favorite people, enabling him to rejoin his favorite company in his favorite milieu—newspapers.

In early 1996, Berkshire stock suddenly rocketed to $34,000 a share, valuing Berkshire as a company at $41 billion. An original partner who invested $1,000 in 1957 and left it untouched would now have $12 million stashed away—double the amount of just a couple of years before. Buffett himself was worth $16 billion. Susie now had $1.5 billion worth of Berkshire stock—which she had promised not to touch.[3] Both she and Charlie Munger were now on the *Forbes* 400 list—as billionaires. Once invisible, Berkshire was noticed by people who had never heard of it before. That year, five thousand people from all fifty states came to the shareholder meeting–cum–discount mall.

Now it cost so much to buy a share of BRK that copycats set up investment trusts. Their idea was to mimic Berkshire Hathaway's stock portfolio and let people buy in smaller units, as if it were a mutual fund. But Berkshire was not a mutual fund; it was a perpetual-motion vacuum cleaner that sucked up businesses and stocks and spit out cash to buy more businesses and stocks. That couldn't be replicated by buying the stocks it owned. Among other things, you didn't get Buffett.

Moreover, the copycat funds were buying the stocks that Berkshire owned at prices far higher than Berkshire had paid, and charging fat fees to do it. They were cheating investors. Now the cop in Buffett came out. To foil the putative copycats, he decided to issue a new class of shares. Each B share—or "Baby B"— was equal to 3.33 percent, or ⅓₀, of a pricy A share.

He had great fun with the B shares, writing: *"Neither Mr. Buffett nor Mr. Munger would currently buy Berkshire shares at that price, nor would they recommend that their families or friends do so."*[4]

He decided to sell an unlimited amount of stock to ensure that the price would not rise because of more demand than supply.

The inverted logic of selling stock that you wouldn't buy yourself, and explicitly saying so, pleased Buffett enormously. Moreover, issuing the B shares fulfilled a duty to his shareholder "partners." All that cash pouring in from the B shares would be a pretty good deal for them.

No CEO had ever done such a thing before. A small forest of trees was felled in media coverage of Buffett's honesty. Yet investors gobbled up the B shares anyway. Buffett thought them foolish and said so privately and often. Yet there was no denying it was enormously flattering that they did, for they were clearly buying only because of him. He would have been secretly disappointed had the B share offering been a flop. The B shares were a Buffett no-risk deal: His shareholders won, and Buffett won, no matter how the offering turned out.

The Baby Bs forever changed the character of Buffett's "club." After May 1996, forty thousand new owners could call themselves shareholders. At the next meeting, 7,500 people showed up and spent $5 million at the Nebraska Furniture Mart. The meeting turned into Woodstock for Capitalists. In 1998, ten thousand people came. Yet as the money and the people and the fame came rolling in, an underlying shift took place in the world in which Buffett worked that would have profound effects on him and everybody else.

There really was no such thing as "Wall Street" anymore. Now financial markets were a string of blinking terminals connected by computers hooked up to the Internet that reached every corner of the world. A guy named Mike Bloomberg, whom Salomon had been dumb enough to fire back in the eighties, had created a special computer that captured every piece of financial information that anyone could possibly want. It made graphs, it made tables, it did calculations, it gave news, it gave quotes; it could do historic comparisons and set up competitions between companies and bonds and currencies and commodities and industries for whoever was lucky enough to have a Bloomberg terminal on his or her desk.

By the early 1990s, the Bloomberg terminal was becoming ubiquitous. The Bloomberg saleswoman had called Berkshire Hathaway for three years in a row. "Nope" was the answer every time. Buffett felt that following the market minute to minute by computer was not the way to invest. Finally it became obvious even to Buffett that to trade bonds you had to have a Bloomberg terminal. But the Bloomberg sat some distance from Buffett's office and he never looked at it; that was the job of Mark Millard, the bond trader.[5]

The advent of the Bloomberg terminal mirrored the ongoing struggle over Salomon's identity, which continued within the firm. Its laggard businesses had never gotten back on their feet. In 1994, Maughan had tried to realign pay at Salomon on the theory that employees should suffer with the shareholders when times were bad. There were people inside the firm who agreed with him.[6] But that was not the standard anywhere else on Wall Street, so thirty-five senior people walked out the door. Buffett was disgusted with the employees' unwillingness to share the risk.

Deprived of Meriwether to bonus-pimp for them, the arbs fought for their share. Buffett was willing to pay them for results—the firm still made most of its money from arbitrage—but increasing competition made it harder for them to produce.

Arbitrageurs make a bet that a temporary gap of prices between similar or related assets will eventually tighten. For example, the bet may be whether two nearly identical bonds will trade at a closer price.[7] With so much new competition, the easy trades had become scarcer. In response, the arbs took larger positions with more risk, often using debt to finance their bets.

The rules of the racetrack said not to do so. The reason is the math of losing money, which works like this: If someone has a dollar and she loses fifty cents, she has to double her money to make back what she's lost. That's difficult to do. It is tempting to borrow another fifty cents for the next bet. That way you only have to make fifty percent (plus the interest you owe on the loan) to get back whole—much easier to do. But borrowing the money doubles your risk. If you lose fifty percent again, you're history. The loss has wiped out all your capital. Hence Buffett's sayings: Rule number one, don't lose money. Rule number two, don't forget rule number one. Rule number three, don't go into debt.

The arbs' strategy, however, assumed that their estimate of value was right. Therefore, when the market moved against them, they only had to wait to make the money back. But "risk" defined this way—in terms of volatility—presumes the investor *can* be patient and wait. Anyone who borrows to invest may not have that luxury of time. Moreover, to enlarge a losing trade required extra capital stashed somewhere that could be forked over on a moment's notice if the need arose.

Larry Hilibrand lost $400 million—an enormous sum—arbitraging the difference in interest rates on mortgage-backed bonds. He was convinced that he could make back the loss on the mortgage arbitrage if the firm would double his bet. Buffett agreed with Hilibrand in this instance and gave him the money for the trade—which in fact reversed to become profitable.

What the arbs really wanted, however, was J.M. During Salomon's recovery, Meriwether waited on the sidelines at first while the arbs begged to bring him back. While Deryck Maughan made polite noises, everybody knew he did not want Meriwether. Nevertheless, Buffett and Munger had given a thumbs-up, with some conditions. Meriwether could return to his old position but would have to report to Maughan, with less freedom to run his operation. Unwilling to work under a shorter leash, Meriwether had broken off negotiations and in 1994 went off to found his own hedge fund, Long-Term Capital Management. It would operate the same way as the bond arbitrage unit at Salomon, except that Meriwether and his partners got to keep the profits.

One by one, Meriwether's key lieutenants left Salomon to join him at the new harbor-front offices of Long-Term Capital Management in Greenwich, Connecticut. Deprived of his biggest moneymakers, Deryck Maughan saw the "for sale" sign heading for Buffett's block of stock and began planning for the day when Buffett would wash his hands of Salomon.[8]

In his 1996 shareholder letter, Buffett said that "virtually all stocks" were overvalued. Whenever the market ran hot it was because Wall Street was in vogue. That year, Maughan thought it timely to pitch the restaurant in front of Salomon's casino to Sandy Weill, CEO of Travelers Insurance, as the anchor tenant in a global financial shopping mall that could compete with Merrill Lynch. Weill supposedly still resented Buffett for the sweet deal Berkshire got after Weill's squeeze-out in the Fireman's Fund sale more than a decade earlier. He distrusted the arbitrage casino, but he saw an opportunity for the restaurant chain on a global scale. When he bought Salomon for Travelers, some observers felt that since Solly hadn't done well under Buffett, Weill saw it as a chance to beat Buffett at his own game. Buffett hailed Weill for the decision as a genius at building shareholder value.[9] And Travelers paid $9 billion for Salomon, bailing Buffett out of his problem-child investment.[10]

Meriwether, who knew that Buffett liked owning casinos, had gone to Omaha with one of his partners to try to raise money for Long-Term Capital for its February 1994 launch. They ate the now-obligatory dinner at Gorat's, where J.M. pulled out a schedule over his steak to show Buffett different probabilities of results and how much money Long-Term could make or lose. The strategy involved earning tiny profits on many thousands of trades, leveraged by at least twenty-five times the firm's capital. The highest loss that Long-Term contemplated was twenty percent of its assets, the odds of which it estimated at no more than one in a hundred.[11] Nobody estimated the odds of losses bigger than that; the numbers wouldn't make sense.

The name Long-Term came from the fact that investors were locked in. Meriwether knew that if he started losing money, he needed the investors to stay until the losses turned around. But so much leverage, combined with no way to cap the risk completely, made Buffett and Munger uncomfortable.

"We thought they were very smart people," says Munger. "But we were a little leery of the complexity and leverage. We were very leery of being used as a sales lead. We knew others would follow if we got in." Munger thought Long-Term wanted Berkshire as a "Judas goat." "The Judas goat led the animals to slaughter in the stockyards," he says, recalling Omaha. "The goat would live for fifteen years, and of course the animals that followed it would die every day as it betrayed them. Not that we didn't admire the intellect of the people at Long-Term."[12]

Long-Term charged its clients two cents off every dollar under management every year that they invested, plus a quarter of any profits it earned. Clients signed up for the prestige. It raised $1.25 billion, the largest hedge-fund start-up in history. The old arb team at Salomon now worked together in secrecy, with no outside interference and no more sharing of the profits with other parasitic Salomon departments. The fund smoked in its first three years, quadrupling its investors' money. By the end of 1997, Long-Term had amassed $7 billion of capital. Then competition from start-up hedge funds depressed returns. Meriwether sent $2.3 billion of money back to investors; the rest was all the market could digest. The hedge fund in Greenwich was now running more than $129 billion in assets—and a like amount of debt—on only $4.7 billion of capital. In a near-instant replication of Buffett's steady accumulation of wealth, through the magic of fees earned on borrowed money, nearly half of the capital belonged to the partners themselves.[13] Despite the fifty-year-old Meriwether's difficulty making eye contact, he and his firm had a swagger to match their brilliant reputations, and the partners took full advantage of the fund's position to dictate terms to its clients, to the fifty-something banks from which it borrowed, and to its brokers (in many cases these parties were one and the same).

Beating Buffett's record was now the goal of most money managers in worldwide finance. Some thought Meriwether had at least an unconscious grudge against Buffett for failing to protect him at Salomon, then subsequently not hiring him back.[14] Unbeknownst to anyone, Long-Term Capital was shorting Berkshire Hathaway, on the theory that BRK was overpriced relative to the value of the stocks that it owned.[15] Not only that, Long-Term set up a Bermuda reinsurance company, Osprey Re, named after the copper osprey that sank its talons into helpless prey in the fountain outside Long-Term's building. Osprey Re was going to insure earthquakes, hurricanes, and similar natural disasters—it was, in other words, entering Ajit Jain catastrophe reinsurance territory. The ditches on the roadside of the insurance highway were filled with wreckage. Buffett had barely escaped himself once or twice in his younger days. Whenever a novice came along, better find the keys to the tow truck.

Gradually, as Long-Term's coffers swelled and imitators followed for the next several years, through early summer of 1998, lenders collectively began to realize that, as periodically happens, they had gotten too euphoric about the prospects that all these people to whom they had lent money would pay them back. Long-Term's competitors started dumping their dodgier positions as interest rates rose. That pushed down prices and set off a cycle of selling. But Long-Term had bet the opposite way, selling the safest assets and buying the riskiest, which were relatively cheaper. Its intricate models basically said that over time the financial markets were becoming more efficient, so the prices of risky assets would converge toward the prices of safer assets. Its biggest trades were a formulaic guess that the market would become less volatile, meaning that as the market bounced around, it would oscillate in smaller arcs. And historically that had been so. But as history had also shown, generally did not mean always. Long-Term knew that. It had made investors lock in their capital long enough to be safe—or so it thought.

On August 17, 1998, Russia suddenly defaulted on its ruble debt, meaning it would not pay its bills. Investors began dumping everything in sight. A money manager had warned Long-Term, early on, that its strategy of eking out teensy profits on a zillion trades was like "picking up nickels in front of a bulldozer."[16] Now—surprise—the bulldozer turned out to have a Ferrari engine, and it was racing toward them at eighty miles an hour.

On Sunday, August 23, *I was playing bridge on the computer. I picked up the phone, and it was Eric Rosenfeld at Long-Term.* Buffett liked Rosenfeld, who had once gotten a field promotion to head trader at Salomon. Now he had been deputized by Meriwether to cut back the portfolio's size by selling the firm's merger arbitrage positions. *"I hadn't heard from him for years. With fear in his voice, Eric started to talk about me taking out their whole big stock arbitrage position, six billion dollars' worth. They thought stock arbitrage was mathematical."*[17] Responding reflexively, Warren Buffetted Rosenfeld. *"I just said to Eric, I would take certain ones but not all of them."*

By a few days later, the market's gyrations had cost Long-Term half its capital. The partners had spent a week talking to everybody in their well-connected database, trying to raise money before they had to report this dire news to their investors on August 31. No dice. Now they agreed that Larry Hilibrand—the superrationalist whose sobriquet on Wall Street was still "the $23 million man," for the outsize bonus that had set Mozer off on his tear—would make a pilgrimage to Omaha and reveal what Long-Term owned.

The next day the Dow dropped four percent in what the *Wall Street Journal* referred to as a "global margin call," with investors panicking and selling. Buffett picked up Hilibrand at the airport and drove him back to Kiewit Plaza.

Hilibrand had gone deep into debt to pump up his personal investment in the firm, leveraging the leverage with which Long-Term had already leveraged itself. He spent the day going over every position the firm owned and stressing the incredible opportunity he was offering to Buffett.[18] *"He wanted me to put in capital. He described the seven or eight big fundamental positions. I knew what was happening with relationships and on prices in these areas. I was getting more interested as time went along, because they were crazy relationships and spreads. But he was proposing a deal to me that didn't make any sense. They thought they had time to play the hand out. But I said no, so that was that."* Buffett told him, *"I am not an investor in other people's funds."*[19] He was only interested as an owner.

Long-Term didn't want an owner, only an investor. It came close to finding somebody else, but then he backed out.[20] By month-end, when it had to report to its investors, the fund had lost $1.9 billion—almost half of its capital—through a historically unusual combination of stock-market declines and almost hysterical aversion to risk in the bond markets.[21] Since the model had contemplated losses of twenty percent as being a one-in-one-hundred-year event—like a moderate West Coast earthquake—this was somewhat like a Category 4 hurricane hitting New York City. Meriwether wrote his investors a letter saying "The opportunity set in these trades at this time is believed to be among the best that LTCM has ever seen.... The Fund is offering you the opportunity to invest in the Fund on special terms related to LTCM fees."[22] Long-Term was behaving as though it could raise capital to wait out the crisis and profit from its turnaround. But with the kind of leverage it had taken on, it didn't have that option. The firm's insular culture and years of getting its way had blinded the partners to the reality that no investor would put in money to save it without also taking control.

The day he read this, Buffett wrote a letter to a colleague and forwarded Meriwether's entreaty, saying:

> Attached is an extraordinary example of what happens when you get 1) a dozen people with an average IQ of 160; 2) working in a field in which they collectively have 250 years of experience; 3) operating with a huge percentage of their net worth in the business; 4) employing a ton of leverage.[23]

Anything times zero is zero, Buffett said. A total loss is a "zero." No matter how small the likelihood of a total loss on any given day, if you kept betting and betting, the risk kept stacking up and multiplying. If you kept betting long enough, sooner or later, as long as a zero was not *impossible,* someday a zero was one hundred percent certain to show up.[24] Long-Term, however, had not even tried to estimate the risk of a loss greater than twenty percent—much less a zero.

In September, Long-Term searched desperately for money, having now lost sixty percent of its capital. Other traders had started putting the squeeze on the fund, shorting positions they knew Long-Term owned because they knew Long-Term needed to sell, which would force prices lower. Investors were fleeing anything risky in favor of anything safe, to a point that Long-Term's models had never considered possible because it made no economic sense to them. Long-Term hired Goldman Sachs, which came in as a partner to buy half the firm. It needed $4 billion, an almost unimaginable sum for a hedge fund in distress to raise.

Goldman Sachs got in touch with Buffett to see if he was interested in a bailout. He wasn't. However, he would consider teaming with Goldman to buy the entire portfolio of assets and debt. Together they would be strong enough to wait the crisis out and trade the positions deftly for a profit. But Buffett had a condition: no Meriwether.

Long-Term owed money to a subsidiary of Berkshire. It owed money to people who owed money to Berkshire. It owed money to people who owed money to people who owed money to Berkshire. "Derivatives are like sex," Buffett said. "It's not who *we're* sleeping with, it's who *they're* sleeping with that's the problem." As Buffett headed to Seattle that Friday to meet the Gateses and embark on a thirteen-day "Gold Rush" trip from Alaska to California, he called a manager and told him, "Accept no excuses from anyone who doesn't post collateral or make a margin call. Accept no excuses."[25] He meant that if the Howie-equivalents out there paid the rent one day late, then seize their farms.

The next morning he, Susie, the Gateses, and three other couples flew to Juneau to helicopter over the ice fields. They cruised up the fjords to view huge blue icebergs and waterfalls cascading over three-thousand-foot cliffs. But as Buffett sat politely through a slide presentation on glaciology on board the ship that evening, his mind wandered to whether Goldman Sachs would be able to put together a bid for Long-Term. Predatory sellers had pushed prices so far down that Long-Term was a cigar butt. An opportunity to buy such a large bundle of distressed assets had never arisen so quickly in his career.

The next day, the Gates party went ashore at low tide to view the hundreds of brown grizzly bears that frequented Pack Creek. Jon Corzine, the head of Goldman Sachs, called Buffett on his satellite phone but kept being cut off. "*The phone didn't work because of these half-mile-high rock walls on either side of the boat. The captain would point out, Look, there's a bear. I was saying, To hell with the bear. Let's get back where I can hear the satellite phone.*"

Two or three hours went by with Buffett held incommunicado as the party spent the afternoon crossing Frederick Sound so they could view the humpback whales. Corzine stewed in New York before he regained brief—and final—contact with Buffett. By the time Buffett resignedly trudged off to view a slide show on Alaskan marine wildlife that evening, Corzine had gathered that he could make a bid, as long as the investment had nothing to do with, and was not managed by, John Meriwether.

On Monday, Buffett remained out of touch and Corzine grew pessimistic about working out a bid. He had begun to talk with Peter Fisher at the Federal Reserve, who was drawing together Long-Term's creditors to negotiate a joint bailout. Hope began to stir that the Fed would cut interest rates.

Long-Term lost another half billion dollars; the banks picking over its books were using what they learned against it.[26] The fund now had less than a billion dollars of capital left. The irony was the $2.3 billion it had paid out to its own investors a year before in order to increase the share of the fund owned by its partners. If it had that money now, Long-Term might have been in a position to survive on its own. Instead, it had a hundred dollars of debt for every dollar of capital—a ratio no sane lender would ever entertain.

Buffett was en route to Bozeman, Montana, with the Gates party, but Corzine had reached him earlier that morning and gained permission to enlist a large insurer, AIG, which owned a derivatives business, to join the bid. Its chairman, Hank Greenberg, was on friendly terms with Buffett. AIG had the experience and the team to replace Meriwether as manager, and Greenberg's powerful presence would balance out Buffett's—and it might make Buffett's bid more palatable to Meriwether.

The next morning, forty-five bankers arrived at the Fed, as summoned, to discuss a bailout of the customer that had bullied them so relentlessly for the past four years. Long-Term had them over a figurative barrel once again, for if it went down, other hedge funds would go down with it. As one domino fell after another, a global financial meltdown was a real possibility—a repeat of Salomon. This was the warning that Buffett and Munger had been repeating at their shareholder meetings since 1993. Some of the banks now feared for their survival unless they helped save the fund. They were reluctantly contemplating putting more money into Long-Term—money that would only go to pay Long-Term's debts—on top of money they had already invested in the fund and lost. When Corzine told them Buffett was also bidding, the idea that he was going to come in and buy it to make a killing went down poorly, even though he would be bailing everybody out. Somehow, Buffett always won. People found it irksome. New York Federal Reserve Bank President William McDonough called Buffett to find out if he was serious. About to board a bus for Yellowstone National Park, Buffett told McDonough that, yes, indeed, he was ready to make a bid and could do so on short notice. He couldn't see why the Federal Reserve would be orchestrating a bailout when Berkshire, AIG, and Goldman Sachs, a group of private buyers, stood ready to solve the whole problem without government assistance. He called Long-Term around eleven o'clock New York time on a crackly satellite phone to say he was going to bid through Goldman for the whole portfolio.

"I didn't want to hold the bus up, so I went along. It was killing me."

An hour later, Goldman faxed a single page to Meriwether offering to buy the fund for $250 million. As part of the deal, Meriwether and his partners would be fired. If Meriwether accepted, AIG, Berkshire, and Goldman would put another $3.75 billion into Long-Term, with Berkshire funding most of that. To minimize the chance of Long-Term shopping the bid to gin up a higher offer, Buffett had given them only an hour to decide.

By then, Long-Term had just over $500 million left, and Buffett was bidding just under half that. After paying off debt and losses, Meriwether and his partners would be wiped out, their nearly $2 billion of capital gone. But the document had been drafted by Goldman with a mistake in it. It offered to buy LTCM, the management company, instead of its assets, which Meriwether knew was what Buffett wanted. Meriwether's lawyer said he needed his partners' consent to sell the entire portfolio rather than the management company.[27] Long-Term asked for a temporary emergency investment pending receipt of the approvals. But they couldn't reach Buffett on his phone. If they'd reached him, he said later, he would have taken that deal. Buffett was dialing and redialing the satellite phone in Yellowstone, trying to call Corzine at Goldman and Hank Greenberg at AIG. The phone didn't work. He had no idea what was going on back in New York.

In the room with the bankers, McDonough was in a quandary. He had an offer from the Berkshire-Goldman-AIG consortium but no deal. It was hard to justify government involvement in orchestrating a bailout when there was a viable private bid on the table. Finally, he told the assembled bankers that the other bid had failed for "structural reasons." Buffett was not there to make a counterargument. The Federal Reserve brokered a deal in which fourteen banks put up a total of $3.6 billion. Only one bank, Bear Stearns, refused to participate, earning the long-lasting enmity of the rest. Meriwether's crew negotiated an arrangement for themselves that they considered slightly better than "indentured servitude."[28]

That night at the Lake Hotel, Buffett found out what had happened. He felt that Meriwether didn't want to sell to him; otherwise, he would have found a way. Perhaps it had weighed on Meriwether's mind that, as one of the fund's partners said, "Buffett cares about one thing. His reputation. Because of the Salomon scandal he couldn't be seen to be in business with J.M."[29] In the end, financially, the bailout was a much better deal than Buffett's.

The next day, Buffett was still turning over in his mind whether there was some way to undo it. Gates had a treat in store. When they arrived in Livingston, Montana, in early afternoon to board a nine-car private train fitted out with burnished wood and polished leather that Gates had rented, Sharon Osberg was waiting along with Fred Gitelman, a low-key computer programmer and bridge player. Gates had flown them in. While everyone else was admiring the cliffs and waterfalls of the Wind River Canyon, the foursome retired to an upstairs lounge with a transparent dome for a twelve-hour bridge marathon. Periodically, Buffett's phone rang and he talked with someone in New York about Long-Term as the spectacular scenery rolled past. It still might not be too late to unwind the impending bailout and resurrect a private deal. But it wasn't working out.[30] At least the bridge distracted him.

The next morning, after a final round of bridge, the train rolled to a halt and dropped Osberg and Gitelman off in Denver. Over the next few days, as the train wound its leisurely way to the Napa Valley via the Grand Canyon, Buffett read about the rescue in the newspapers and gradually lost hope of participating.

Only seven years after the regulators had contemplated letting Salomon fail—with all the consequences that that potentially entailed—the Federal Reserve had now engineered the bailout of a private investment firm, an unprecedented intervention in the market to avoid a similar event. Afterward, the Fed slashed interest rates three times in seven weeks to help keep the financial stumble from paralyzing the economy. It was by no means certain that any such paralysis would occur, but the stock market took off like a screaming banshee.[31] Long-Term's partners and most of the staff worked for a year for $250,000—pauper's wages by their standards—to unwind the fund's positions and pay back most of the emergency creditors.[32] Hilibrand, in debt for $24 million, signed the employment contract with tears streaming down his cheeks.[33] Most of them got good jobs afterward. Meriwether made a comeback to start a smaller, less leveraged fund, taking some of his team. People thought the partners had gotten off light, considering that they had nearly sent the whole financial world into a seizure. And Buffett considered it one of the great missed opportunities of his life.

Eric Rosenfeld had an insight. Maybe models didn't work when the world went mad. For that you needed a lot of capital, the kind that Berkshire Hathaway offered. After all, if you were going to bet by a hundred billion or more in favor of risk, you needed a partner, even a parent, one with so much capital that it essentially undid the leverage, somebody to provide a big umbrella in a storm.[34] By implication, maybe they would have been better off being owned by somebody like Berkshire Hathaway. But that would have meant giving up their ownership.... You couldn't have it both ways. If you wanted Berkshire to take the risk and put up the money, to it went the gains.

To think otherwise was unrealistic—that one could lay off risk to someone else while keeping the rewards. But that point of view was beginning to dominate the financial markets and would have profound consequences over time.

It is hard to overstate the significance of a central-bank-led rescue of a private money manager. If a hedge fund, however large, was too big to fail, then what large financial institution would ever be allowed to collapse? The government risked becoming the margin of safety.[35] No serious consequences had followed the derivatives near-meltdown. The market afterward seemed to behave as if no serious consequences ever could. This threat, the so-called "moral hazard," was a chronic worry of regulators. But the world would always be full of people who loved risk. When it came to business, Buffett's veins were filled with ice, but plenty of other people's pulsed with adrenaline. Some of them had even been members of his own family.

52

Chickenfeed

Decatur, Illinois, and Atlanta · 1995–1999

Howie had been pacing the floor for ten days, ever since Mark Whitacre, an excitable manager he knew at ADM, suddenly confessed to him that he was acting as an FBI mole. Whitacre told him that the FBI was going to arrive at Howie's house at six o'clock on Tuesday night for an interview.

Howie was terrified, but had made up his mind to be completely forthcoming with the FBI. Three hundred agents were at that time fanning out across the country, interviewing people about price-fixing of an ADM product called lysine, which was used in chicken feed. When the agent charged with speaking to Howie showed up at his house, Howie said he didn't trust ADM's CEO, Dwayne Andreas.[1] The previous fall Andreas had rebuked him when he raised ethical questions about providing entertainment to a Congressman. Howie didn't know anything about price-fixing, however.

The second the FBI agents left, Howie called his father, flailing, saying, I don't know what to do, how do I know if these allegations are true? My name is on every press release. What should I do, should I resign?

Buffett refrained from the obvious response, which was that, of his three children, only Howie could have wound up with an FBI agent in his living room after taking his first job in the corporate world. He told Howie that it was his decision whether to stay at ADM. He gave only one piece of advice: to decide within the next twenty-four hours. If you stay in longer than that, he said, you'll become one of them. No matter what happens, it will be too late to get out.

The next day Howie went in, resigned, and told the general counsel that he would take legal action against the company if they put his name on any more press releases. Resigning from the board was a major event. For a director to resign was like sending up a smoke signal that said the company was guilty, guilty, guilty. People at ADM did not make it easy for Howie. They pushed for reprieve, they asked how he could in effect convict them without a trial. Howie held firm, however, and got out.[2]

Howie had just saved himself from being associated with a disaster in which three top executives, including the vice chairman Michael Andreas, would go to prison in the biggest price-fixing case in American history.[3] ADM paid an enormous fine to settle with the government, and its reputation took a hit that would shadow it for years.

Now, however, the contretemps had left Howie out of a job. Big Susie, who was concerned about him and also about Susie Jr., who was getting divorced from Allen, swung into action and convinced Warren to begin a tradition of giving each of the kids a million dollars once every five years on their birthdays, starting then. Buffett not only went along but bragged on himself for beginning this tradition. He had begun to loosen up significantly when it came to money. Susie's allowance had expanded dramatically. At her behest, Buffett bought another house in Laguna next to the first, known as the "dormitory," to house all the children and grandchildren and visitors.[4] Susie's Pacific Heights apartment had been transformed to feature white lacquered walls and carpeting in her trademark sunny yellow. Almost every inch of space was covered with things she had purchased, collected from her travels, or been given by friends. They filled her walls, cabinets, closets, and drawers to overflowing.

The effect struck observers, depending on their perspective, as colorful, beautiful, and a wonderful reflection of Susie's personality, or a chaotic magpie's nest of things. Susie was always lobbying for more space; along with a second apartment she had convinced Warren to buy her on the ground floor of her building, unknown to him, she had also begun to rent storage rooms around San Francisco to house her ever-expanding collections.

Susie's ministry to the sick and dying seemed to compound as rapidly as her collections. She had carried on her work with AIDS sufferers through the 1990s. Then her sister, Dottie, began a battle with terminal cancer. Susie stayed in Omaha to nurse her sister through her last months and days. When Dottie finally died, another person Susie had not, in the end, been able to save, it was the greatest loss she had suffered since her nephew's terrible death by overdose.

In summer 1996, she had to help Warren deal with the death of his ninety-two-year-old mother. Even in her later years, Leila had never stopped berating the family. She could still work Doris over on the phone or during a visit for an hour or more, sending Doris into tears and ending with "I'm glad we had this little talk." Warren had relegated most of her caretaking to Susie Jr. He spoke much more often and more fondly of Rose Blumkin than he ever did of his mother. When Astrid and Sharon Osberg took him out to visit Leila, he was a "wreck," and the two women would talk to Warren's mother while he sat by anxiously, not participating in the conversation. As Leila's memory faded, her story mostly wound down to the 38½ wonderful years with Howard and one other topic that seemed to have lodged itself in her mind during Warren's infancy: "Isn't it a shame about the little Lindbergh baby?" she would ask. "Isn't it a shame?"

After Leila died—on Warren's sixty-sixth birthday—the family assembled for a funeral, their grieving complicated by a cauldron of mixed emotions. She went to rest as the person she had been; any hopes of what she could have become had things been different went to the grave along with her.

"I cried a lot when my mother died. It wasn't because I was sad and missed her. It was because of the waste. She had her good parts, but the bad parts kept me from having a relationship with her. My dad and I never talked about it. But I really regret the waste of what could have been."

With both his parents gone, Warren was the senior member of his family, the watchkeeper at that thin boundary between life and death. It was his sisters, however, whose lives were most affected by Leila's death. They were surprised to find themselves inheriting a sizable amount of Berkshire stock from their mother, more than they had originally owned themselves, along with the first distribution from their father's trust set up by their brother years before.

Warren's sisters were now rich. Two of his children also had a little money, thanks to Susie's persuasiveness about the million-dollar birthday gifts. Buffett had never demanded an accounting of the huge amounts it took to fund Susie's largesse, although he scratched his head and wondered what on earth she did with all the money. The tax complication of the large gifts to their children, however, required that she give Warren a history of her gift-giving. He had always been proud of her generosity, although not always pleased about those who benefited from it. He was now particularly displeased by some of her larger gifts, which flew in the face of what he had understood about the nature of their marriage. His impression that she had ended her other relationship stood corrected. Despite the parallel between his own complicated personal life and Susie's, he was upset.

A discussion of Susie's will ensued. They had sharply differing opinions about who among her friends should receive bequests. In the end, his decision ruled. Afterward, the Buffett bathtub memory went to work. Anything negative that had transpired between them simply vanished, and Susie was restored as his ideal, because he needed her to be.

Warren had stood firm on the question of Susie's bequests to her friends. But she had gentled him enough on issues of money when it came to their children that he was not only comfortable giving them a million dollars every few years while he was alive, he was going to leave them a reasonable amount of money after his death.[5]

Howie had used his first million-dollar birthday gift to buy a nine-hundred-acre farm in Decatur, Illinois, where he still lived. This meant he had two farms, one of which he owned outright. After the ADM lawsuits settled down, Don Keough suggested that he become a professional director by going on the board of another high-profile business, Coca-Cola Enterprises (CCE).

A giant cola bottler, CCE had been smashed together out of smaller bottlers that were Coca-Cola's customers. They bought the syrup concentrate that Coke made, mixed it with fizzy water, and sold it, acting as middlemen, so their relationship with Coke was critical. Neither could live without the other.

Don Keough, Buffett's old Omaha friend, was now president of Coca-Cola. His boss, the CEO of Coca-Cola, the aristocratic Cuban-born Roberto Goizueta, was revered in the business world for creating the world's best-known brand through slogans like "Coke Is It" and "I'd like to buy the world a Coke." Buffett felt that Coca-Cola had by now become a self-sustaining enterprise—and he admired Goizueta for having gotten it to this stage.

In 1997, Gates joined Buffett and Goizueta on a panel discussion at Sun Valley that was moderated by Keough.

"I used to talk to Bill all the time, and I'd always use this expression that a ham sandwich could run Coca-Cola. And Bill wasn't quite housebroken then. So we were sitting on this panel, up in front of the audience, and Bill said something to the effect that it's pretty easy to run Coke."

"I was trying to make a point about how Coke is such a wonderful business," says Gates, "and I said something about how I'm going to step down from Microsoft before I'm sixty because it's a tough business and a young person may need to be in there to handle turns in the road. But it came across that I thought of Microsoft as exciting and I must have said something like, 'Unlike Coca-Cola...'

"Goizueta thought I was an uppity, arrogant kid who was painting some kind of picture that I was engaged in some masterful act on a daily basis whereas anybody could leave at noon and go golfing if they ran Coca-Cola."[6]

"And Roberto hated Bill from that point forward."

Buffett avoided technology stocks partly because these fast-moving businesses could never be run by a ham sandwich. He wanted to get Berkshire Hathaway to the point that it could be run by a ham sandwich too—though not until after he was gone.

But by 1997, Coca-Cola had started to set goals for itself that were so ambitious that it took a lot of financial engineering to achieve them.

"Roberto did a lot of things operationally that were terrific, and I loved the guy. But Roberto got tangled up in promising numbers that eventually couldn't be delivered. He talked about high-teens growth, eighteen percent. Big companies are not going to increase their earnings in the high teens over long periods of time. For a while you can do it, but it just isn't in the cards to keep it up forever....

"The prices they paid for bottling companies were just nuts. I asked the chief financial officer all these questions. But Roberto started the board meetings at ten o'clock and finished at noon; the atmosphere was such that it didn't lend itself to questioning. You just had a feeling when it got to be noon that it would not be at all polite to keep raising subjects or talking about things that would cause the meeting to last until one o'clock. He was just not a guy you questioned. Some people have that bearing about them, and when the bearing is backed up by a very good record, the combination of the two is pretty overpowering." Buffett was more than simply nonconfrontational; he was of an age and from an era that viewed serving on boards as a quasisocial activity in which deference and politeness held sway. In 1998, that was the boardroom culture throughout America. This culture reflected the reality that the structure of corporate boards gave directors very little leeway with management.

"As a director, you can't remotely tell management what to do. All this stuff you read in the press about the board setting strategy is baloney. As a board member, you can do practically nothing. If a CEO thinks a director is smart and on his side, he'll listen to some degree, but ninety-eight percent of the time, he'll do what he wants to anyway. Listen, that's the way I run Berkshire. I think Roberto liked me, but he was not looking for a lot of ideas from me."

But Buffett never knew of anything seriously enough awry at Coca-Cola to make him consider the drastic step of resigning from the board.

By the mid-1990s, Goizueta and his finance chief, Doug Ivester, were dosing Coke with even larger amounts of bottler profits to maintain the illusion of the company's rapid earnings flow. Then in 1997, Goizueta died unexpectedly, only a few months after announcing he had lung cancer. The board and the company and investors were shocked. The board had deferred to Goizueta so absolutely that nobody ever seemed to have thought of any alternative to his handpicked successor, the burly, table-pounding Ivester.[7]

Buffett liked Ivester and wanted him to succeed. Of course, under Goizueta he had enriched Buffett enormously. He had an underdog grit that Buffett liked. Moreover, Buffett laid responsibility for the accounting gimmickry at Goizueta's door, not Ivester's.

Juicing the earnings had certainly worked. Coca-Cola was trading at $70 per share. BRK itself, priced at $48,000 in June 1997, flew to $67,000 over the next nine months. The higher the market went, the tougher it got for Buffett to invest, and yet the higher BRK rose. It made no sense for BRK to follow the stocks that it owned—its past successes—instead of its future prospects. At the shareholder meeting, Buffett told investors, "Our idea of tough times is periods like now."[8]

Without calling the Air-a-holic hotline, Buffett now bought a company for Berkshire called NetJets.[9] This company sold time-shares in jets; its planes all had tail numbers that started with QS, or Quebec Sierra. Susie had gotten Warren to buy her a quarter share in a "fractional" jet from NetJets in 1995, worth two hundred hours a year of flight time, which she referred to as *The Richly Deserved*.[10] She joked that QS stood for Queen Susie. Buffett took to NetJets so much that he had appeared in an ad and endorsed it even before he bought it. He sold the *Indefensible* and became one of NetJets's customers. Still, on the surface, buying NetJets was an atypical decision for a man who would, one year later, tell the moguls at Sun Valley that somebody should "have shot Orville down."

The reasoning behind the purchase seemed sound, though. NetJets was dominant in its market. Buffett figured that it was not unlike the newspaper business, where there were no red ribbons. Eventually, the competitors would fall away.[11] Buffett was also intrigued with its CEO, Richard Santulli, an entrepreneurial mathematician from Goldman Sachs. Now he used his mathematical skills to schedule plane flights on six hours' notice for a database full of celebrity clients. Buffett met a whole new set of famous people, including Arnold Schwarzenegger and Tiger Woods.

Investors cheered Buffett's purchase of NetJets but were shocked when he almost simultaneously announced that Berkshire was buying General Re, a huge insurance wholesaler, or "reinsurer," which bought excess risk from other insurers. At $22 billion, this deal was almost thirty times larger than NetJets. It dwarfed by multiples his largest deal ever, GEICO.[12]

When he met with the Gen Re management team, Buffett told them, "I'm strictly hands-off. You guys run your own business. I won't interfere." Then he suddenly started spouting numbers from GEICO. "Last week their numbers were..." Holy cow! thought Tad Montross, General Re's chief underwriter. This is hands-off? He knows more about GEICO than we know about General Re.[13]

Buffett did not know much about the inner workings of General Re. He had made the decision to buy based on studying the company's results, and he liked its reputation. Still...given the pattern of Buffett's purchases of insurers—in almost every case they plunged straight into the ditch shortly after he bought them—and given the size of this deal, the distant rumble of the tow truck's engine warming up could be heard, barely audible, over the next hill.

But it was the high price paid for General Re that attracted most of the attention, and the fact that Buffett had paid in stock, not cash—in effect, swapping twenty percent of Berkshire Hathaway for General Re in a deal announced on the day that Berkshire hit its then-all-time high of $80,900 per share. People wondered if Buffett's willingness to give away his stock when it was trading at such an unheard-of price meant that he, too, thought BRK was overvalued.[14] Buffett had spent his career tightening his stranglehold on Berkshire. Giving stock to General Re's shareholders diluted his own personal voting interest in Berkshire from forty-three percent to less than thirty-eight percent.

The price of BRK swung up and down based partly on the prices of the stocks that Berkshire owned. So, if Buffett was subtly signaling through his purchase of General Re that BRK was overvalued, did that mean that its underlying stocks—like Coca-Cola—were overpriced? If so, this could have implications for the entire market. It might mean the whole market was overpriced.

Buffett's stake in KO had multiplied fourteenfold over a decade, to $13 billion, and he had gone so far as to declare the company an "inevitable" to his shareholders, as if it were a stock he would never sell.[15] He reasoned that Coca-Cola would send more swallows down more throats in each passing decade "for an investing lifetime." Berkshire now owned more than eight percent of the company. Coca-Cola stock was trading as high as forty times its estimated 2000 earnings—a multiple that said investors believed the stock would keep rising by at least twenty percent a year. But to do that, it would have to increase earnings twenty-five percent a year for five years—impossible. It would have to almost triple sales—again impossible.[16] Buffett knew it. Nevertheless, he did not sell his Coca-Cola stock.

Buffett carefully sidestepped these questions about the market and Coca-Cola when he used Berkshire stock to buy General Re, saying, "It is not a market call whatsoever."[17] BRK, he said, was "fairly valued" before the merger, and the combined companies would create "synergy." When Charlie Munger was asked, he stated that Buffett had consulted him about this deal very late in the game. In effect, he disowned the deal.[18] Not unexpectedly, investors began to reprice BRK as if either Berkshire and its holdings in stocks like Coca-Cola were overpriced or the deal's synergies would prove illusory.[19] Or both.

Buffett's explanation later that summer at Sun Valley was that *we wanted to buy Gen Re, but coming with Gen Re was $22 billion of investments.* Many were stocks; Buffett promptly sold them. Adding $22 billion of bonds *"changed the bond/stock ratio at Berkshire, which I was not unhappy with. It <u>did</u> have the effect of a portfolio allocation change."*

So Buffett—who sat on the Coca-Cola board with Herbert Allen—was "not unhappy with" swamping BRK's stocks, including Coca-Cola, in an ocean of General Re's bonds. He accompanied his "not unhappy with" remark with the warnings that interest rates must stay well below average and the economy stay unusually hot for the market to meet investors' expectations. This was the same Sun Valley speech where Buffett had explained that investing is laying out money today to get money back tomorrow, like Aesop's bird in the hand versus the birds in the bush; that interest rates are the price of waiting for the birds in the bush; that for periods sometimes as long as seventeen years the market had gone exactly nowhere; and that at other times—such as the present—the value of stocks grows much faster than the economy. And, of course, he had closed this speech by comparing investors to a bunch of oil prospectors who were going to hell.

Thus, if Buffett was reshuffling his portfolio and focusing on bonds, perhaps it meant that he thought that it was now easier to make a living in bonds than stocks, and it was going to get easier still.[20]

The following October, he made another move that was strikingly conservative by the standards of the market. He bought MidAmerican Energy Holding Company, an Iowa-based utility company with some international operations and a presence in alternative energy. He bought just over seventy-five percent of MidAmerican for about $2 billion plus $7 billion of assumed debt, with the other twenty-five percent owned by his friend Walter Scott; MidAmerican's CEO, Scott's protégé David Sokol; and Sokol's number two, Greg Abel.

Investors were mystified. Why would Buffett want to buy a regulated electric company? Admittedly, the business was growing moderately, was well-managed, and had attractive embedded returns that were relatively certain and would be so for as long as could reasonably be imagined.

Buffett saw this as a second cornerstone for Berkshire alongside the insurance business. He said he was working with excellent managers who could potentially put a lot of money to work in utilities and energy at predictable rates of return, which compensated for the limited growth. However, Buffett was already being ridiculed for his refusal to buy technology stocks. Now he had bought the light company. How dull!

But this was not how he thought. When it came to investing, the kind of electricity he sought was not the thrill of trading, but rather, kilowatts.

Buying MidAmerican and General Re significantly diluted the impact of Coca-Cola on Berkshire's shareholders, but Berkshire still owned 200 million shares of Coke. Buffett never stopped thinking about Coca-Cola, where matters continued to go awry. By late 1999, the value of his KO stock was down to $9.5 billion, dragging down the price of BRK with it. Thanks in large part to Coca-Cola, one share of BRK stock could no longer buy a top-of-the-line luxury sports car. Buffett kept turning over and over in his mind an incident back in June. Reports had trickled in that Coke products were poisoning children in Belgium and France. It was not hard to figure out what to do. The late Goizueta would have let "Mr. Coca-Cola," Don Keough, handle it: Fly over right away, visit the kids, shower the parents with free soft drinks. Instead, Ivester—who was actually in France at the time—returned to the U.S. without comment, leaving the local bottlers to deal with the mess.

As the episode blew up into a public-relations disaster, Ivester showed up in Europe weeks later and apologized in finely crafted legalese that never actually said, "We're sorry." The headlines died, and the Coke machines were plugged back in all over the continent. But the incident cost more than a hundred million dollars and impossible-to-measure damage to Coke's reputation. Buffett stewed.

Herbert Allen was stewing as well. Closer to the day-to-day management of the company, he questioned whether Coca-Cola was running off the rails. Despite the declining sales, at least 3,500 new employees had marched into Coca-Cola Plaza in Atlanta in the last two years. Allen looked at the burgeoning payroll and saw "a cancerous growth on the company."[21] Quarter after quarter,

Ivester promised to improve growth rates; quarter after quarter, Coca-Cola fell short. One day in Ivester's office, Allen asked him, What are you going to do? And Ivester said he didn't know; had no solution.[22]

Through Keough, Buffett also heard that Ivester had been dictating terms to the bottlers in an unheard-of way.[23] Keough had become a sort of "father confessor to the disaffected" among the bottlers.[24] They were in open revolt. Meanwhile, Ivester had snatched away Keough's official role, a dumb move since Ivester needed Keough on his side. He might be King Arthur, but Keough was Coca-Cola's Merlin and must be paid due respect.

Still, Buffett was pretty sure that these problems were not so obvious to the whole board. As he ticked off marks against Ivester, Buffett spent the whole fall in a wrung-out state of anxiety. By Thanksgiving, he had almost reached a breaking point.[25]

Then *Fortune* magazine, which had labeled Ivester "the 21st-century CEO" not two years earlier, published a highly critical piece blaming him for the company's problems.[26] That was a bad sign. Fortune rarely smiled on CEOs whom *Fortune* smacked around this way, especially if the CEO had previously been featured in a flattering profile on the cover of the magazine. Being knocked off one's pedestal in public signaled that the powerful people whom *Fortune*'s reporters used as sources were displeased, and on the brink of tossing away the teddy bear they had once embraced.

Right after Thanksgiving, Herbert Allen put in a call to Buffett. "I think we have a problem with Ivester," he said. "We picked the wrong guy," Buffett agreed.[27] They began to lay their plans. They both estimated that it would take more than a year for the board to come around to their point of view that Ivester had to go—and that, says Allen, "would have been devastating to the company. So I think we decided, just as two individuals, to tell him the truth about how we felt."

Allen called Ivester and said he and Buffett wanted a meeting. They agreed to get together in Chicago, where Ivester would be stopping following a meeting with McDonald's.

On a cool, cloudy Wednesday, the first day of December 1999, Buffett and Allen flew into Chicago. Ivester's well-known obstreperousness kindled Buffett's dread of confrontation. He lashed down his anxiety, turtling into his shell. Later, it was reported that he appeared cold. The three men got down to business without preamble.[28] Impersonally, Buffett and Allen told Ivester that they appreciated his efforts on behalf of Coca-Cola, but he no longer had their confidence.

Still, Ivester was not actually fired. Buffett and Allen lacked the authority to fire Ivester. *"He might have won a board vote, and he knew that,"* Buffett says.

Ivester took the news stoically. He rushed back to Atlanta to call an emergency telephone board meeting for four days later, leaving the mystified board to wait in suspense.

On Sunday, Ivester told the board members that he had concluded that he was not the right person to run the company. He would step down immediately. This was exactly as Buffett and Allen had hoped. But he also said there would be no transition; he was leaving as of that day. As the board listened in stunned silence, he described it as a voluntary decision, and that was true—in the sense that it is voluntary to avoid the firing squad by walking the plank.[29]

Board members began asking what had happened. Was he sick? Was something terribly wrong at Coca-Cola? Why didn't they have any warning? Must the transition be so sudden? Ivester never wavered from his script.[30]

A while back the board had insisted, against some resistance, that Ivester put a name in an envelope that said who should succeed him if he were hit by a truck. The envelope was now opened to reveal the name of Doug Daft, head of Coca-Cola's Middle and Far Eastern divisions. Daft was halfway out the door to retirement, but—just as it had done after Goizueta died—the board, among them Buffett and Allen, instantly made him Ivester's successor, with apparently no serious discussion of any alternative.

The recriminations began as the market took a hatchet to the stock.[31] Investors had figured out that Ivester was walking the plank. In private conversations with a few board members, he let out the truth. The board now realized with varying degrees of outrage how much their role had been usurped.

With the media howling, it became clear that the company needed to be more forthcoming. *Fortune* wrote an exclusive piece revealing details of the secret Chicago meeting.[32] Ivester had negotiated a staggering $115 million consolation package, which angered both his detractors and his supporters; it gave the impression that he was either paid off or wronged. And observers now realized that an inner circle ruled the Coke board.

But by year-end, Buffett's reputation was suffering in an even more overt way, because the biggest, most profitable feat of stock selection that he had ever made, Coca-Cola, was down by one-third after Ivester's departure. That Buffett had felt forced to intervene in a particularly graceless way, which had backfired in public on both the company and himself, left the impression not that he had ridden to the rescue—as with Salomon—but that what he and Herbert Allen had done was the meddling of a couple of old men.

That impression compounded the worries raised when the biggest acquisition he had ever made, General Re, coughed up a nasty surprise within days after Berkshire closed the purchase. Ron Ferguson, the CEO, had called to say that the company had been duped out of $275 million in an enormous, elaborately designed fraud called Unicover. Investors had been surprised, to say the least, when the first report Buffett gave them about General Re was an apology for this foolish thing, as well as an expression of confidence in Ferguson and the prediction that affairs would be righted. Since there had been concerns from the beginning about whether Buffett had bought General Re only to dilute his large positions in stocks like Coca-Cola, decades of blissful confidence in his judgment about buying businesses suddenly began to waver.

Even some of his most devoted believers were questioning his wisdom, as the stock market's repudiation of Buffett's Sun Valley manifesto grew even louder in the last few months of 1999. That December, he continued to look not just wrong about technology stocks but dead wrong and, at last, stubbornly blind to the obvious. The Dow closed the year up twenty-five percent, the NASDAQ an incredible eighty-six percent. The market valued Berkshire, with its burgeoning coffers of cash, at only $56,100 per share now, for a total market capitalization of $85 billion. That compared poorly to a little online media company called Yahoo!, which had quadrupled in the last year. Yahoo!, which captured the spirit of the times in its name, was now valued at $115 billion.

As 1999 spun to a close, there was no doubt who was important and influential at the turn of the millennium, and even less doubt who was not. Buffett's personal ranking had dropped on the annual taking-stock lists, which multiplied a thousandfold that year with the millennial summings-up and retrospectives. He was now only the fourth-richest man in the world. Technophiles reveled in pointing out the great investor's feet of clay, saying that "if Buffett headed a mutual fund, he'd be looking at a second career."[33] Barron's, a Wall Street weekly, put him on its cover with the accompanying headline "Warren, What's Wrong?" and the comment that Berkshire stock had "stumbled" badly.[34] He might as well have had a bull's-eye painted on his brow.

In public, Buffett repeated—in almost unvarying terms—the ideas that had made him famous: the margin of safety, the circle of competence, Mr. Market's vagaries. He still maintained that a stock is a piece of a business, not a bunch of numbers on a screen. All through the market's dizzy rise, he refrained from arguing or disputing any of the madness, except for making his now-famous speech at Sun Valley. People thought, from the way he disciplined every syllable that exited his mouth, that he was above the criticism. *"Nothing bothers me like that,"* he said, when asked if it bothered him when people called him a has-been. *"You can't do well in investing unless you think independently. And the truth is, you are neither right nor wrong because people agree with you. You're right because your facts and reasoning are right. In the end, that's what counts."*[35]

But these were separate issues. While he had no problem thinking independently, he was indeed miserable over being called a has-been. Asked around then if being in the public eye for decades helped keep the criticism in perspective, Buffett paused for a long while. *"No. It never gets easier,"* he said soberly. *"It always hurts just as much as the first time."* But he could not do a thing about it.

Buffett had spent his whole career competing in a contest that was impossible to win. Sooner or later he would have a bad year or the momentum would slow down. He knew that; over and over he had warned investors that trees don't grow to the sky. But that had never stopped him from climbing as fast as he could. And while he had loved the climb, somewhat to his surprise, there was no blue ribbon waiting at the top.

His life was fascinating, his business accomplishments important, the principles through which he had succeeded worthy of study. Everyone who knew him personally liked the man. His kaleidoscope personality perpetually revealed new facets, yet remained faithful at its core to his Inner Scorecard. The one thing that he would always be the best at was being himself.

As he did every year, Buffett spent the holidays with Susie and the family at their vacation home in Emerald Bay.[36] His work life may have been particularly challenging then, but Christmas of 1999 was a good one for his family. Warren was satisfied with the way his kids were maturing. Howie had settled down into life as a middle-aged farmer and businessman. Big Susie had gotten him interested in photography. Now he lived on an airplane half the time, photographing dangerous wild animals, his love of living on the edge channeled into getting bitten by a cheetah and chased by a polar bear.

A full-time mother of two children and unpaid part-time assistant to her father, Susie Jr. had followed in her mother's footsteps to become a force in Omaha philanthropy. Her ex-husband Allen ran the Buffett Foundation, and the two lived a few blocks apart and shared parenting.[37]

After his divorce, Peter had married Jennifer Heil and was still living in Milwaukee and writing music. In the early 1990s, he had gotten the opportunity to move to Hollywood and work in the entertainment industry. But "I realized if I moved to L.A.," he says, "I'd be one of thousands of me's out there trying to get work. My father was always into the movie *The Glenn Miller Story*. Glenn Miller searched and searched to find his sound; my father used to always talk about 'finding your sound.'" Peter stayed in Milwaukee; he felt that his father understood that this was analogous to his own choice to come back to Omaha to do things his way rather than staying in New York. Soon after Peter decided not to go to L.A., he was hired to compose and produce the soundtrack for a PBS documentary, the eight-part *500 Nations*.[38]

Howie had been working on Big Susie, saying, "Give us a chance, the money is there, give us the chance to do something with it."[39] That Christmas, Susie Jr., Howie, and Peter were shocked to receive five hundred shares of Berkshire stock in foundations that each could manage and give to any causes they chose. The kids were elated.[40]

The family settled in for New Year's Eve. You could follow the progress of the millennium's arrival on television, starting in the Kiribati Islands. From Sydney to Beijing to London, millions of people celebrated on streets and beaches as a chain of fireworks shot around the globe. As the hours ticked by, nothing disastrous happened anywhere, even at General Re and Coca-Cola. There was a mathematical neatness to the progression of time zones, locations, hours, that Buffett liked. After the stressful fall he had just spent, the change of millennium was not exciting to him—it was relaxing, and he needed that.

PART SIX

Claim Checks

53

The Genie

B uffett was always wary of falling into what Munger called the Shoe Button Complex, pontificating on any and all subjects merely because he was an expert on business. But by the mid-1990s, both he and Munger were starting to receive—and answer—more and more questions about the business of life. He often treated the athletes and college students to whom he periodically spoke to the fable of the Genie.

"*When I was sixteen, I had just two things on my mind—girls and cars,*" Buffett would say, taking a little poetic license here by leaving out the part about the money. "*I wasn't very good with girls. So I thought about cars. I thought about girls, too, but I had more luck with cars.*

"*Let's say that when I turned sixteen, a genie had appeared to me. And that genie said, 'Warren, I'm going to give you the car of your choice. It'll be here tomorrow morning with a big bow tied on it. Brand-new. And it's all yours.'*

"*Having heard all the genie stories, I would say, 'What's the catch?' And the genie would answer, 'There's only one catch. This is the last car you're ever going to get in your life. So it's got to last a lifetime.'*

"*If that had happened, I would have picked out that car. But, can you imagine, knowing it had to last a lifetime, what I would do with it?*

"*I would read the manual about five times. I would always keep it garaged. If there was the least little dent or scratch, I'd have it fixed right away because I wouldn't want it rusting. I would baby that car, because it would have to last a lifetime.*

"*That's exactly the position you are in concerning your mind and body. You only* get one mind and one body. And it's got to last a lifetime. Now, it's very easy to let them ride for many years. But if you don't take care of that mind and that body, they'll be a wreck forty years later, just like the car would be.

"It's what you do right now, today, that determines how your mind and body will operate ten, twenty, and thirty years from now."

54

Semicolon

O ne of the first pieces of correspondence Buffett received in the new millennium was an e-mail from Ron Ferguson, CEO of General Re.

Buffett was already bracing himself. General Re had so far brought him nothing but deplorable news. A year earlier, after the company had admitted being duped in the Unicover fraud mere weeks after Berkshire bought it, Ferguson had made a new confession. General Re had lost millions guaranteeing ticket sales on Hollywood films without knowing what scripts would be filmed or who would star in them. Buffett had been incredulous when he found out. It could have gone without saying that his *favorite* manager, the brilliant Ajit Jain, would never have guaranteed any dumb movie deals. Although it did get said.

Then Ferguson engaged him in a nitpicking match over how to underwrite an Internet lottery called Grab.com that Ajit was reinsuring. Buffett now realized that Ferguson had a philosophy that was sharply different from his. Buffett always liked to talk about how he would rather step over one-foot bars than look for seven-foot bars to hurdle. The Grab.com lottery deal offered an easy profit— a one-foot bar to step over.[1] Ferguson didn't want to do it because it was such a layup. General Re, he said, only did deals where it had an underwriting edge.

Buffett roundhoused the match to an end, then decided that he needed a change in management. Yet he did not act. The business needed mending, not a purge. Firing Ferguson so soon after he had bought Gen Re would mean a public hullabaloo. He hated firing people.

Two months after the Grab.com deal, come the millennium, Ferguson was confessing that General Re had lost another $273 million from bad insurance pricing. In its first twelve months as part of Berkshire, General Re—formerly a paragon of discipline—had run straight into the ditch and had lost nearly $1.5 billion dollars. No company that Buffett had ever owned had lost money approaching a fraction of this magnitude.

When the news was published, investors rapidly readjusted their thinking once again. Had paying $22 billion for General Re been a mistake? Buffett's reputation took another hit.

Meanwhile, at Coca-Cola, all was not well.[2] Its new CEO, Doug Daft, had laid off six thousand people in January as his opening act. Investors reacted with shock. Coca-Cola stock got socked, and along with it, BRK, already cheap at $56,100 on January 1, started to plummet.

Two weeks later, on February 9, in the early-morning sanctuary of his office, Buffett sat with half an eye fixed on CNBC, sorting through his reading. The hotline on the credenza behind his desk rang. Only Buffett answered this phone. He picked it up instantly. Jim Maguire, who traded BRK on the floor of the New York Stock Exchange, was calling to tell him that sell orders were pouring in for BRK. While Buffett had been playing bridge online the previous evening, an Internet bulletin-board writer on Yahoo! had posted, "Warren in Hospital—Critical." Over the next few hours, the rumor spread virally from posters like "hyperpumperfulofcrap," who said over and over "BUFFETT OLD AND WEAK, SELL," and "SELL, SELL, SELL, SELL, SELL." With the rumors filtering through Wall Street and convincing people that Buffett was in the hospital in critical condition, BRK was trading heavily and getting hammered.[3]

Buffett's personal phone line started ringing. He answered it himself, as usual, lighting up with a big grinning "Oh, hiiiiii!" to show he was happy to hear from the caller.

"How are you?" the caller inquired, with a slight tone of urgency.

"Well . . . never better!"

If a tornado were barreling straight toward Kiewit Plaza, Buffett would say that things were "never better" before mentioning the twister. People knew to read his tone of voice; today it sounded stressed. All morning, callers wanted to know—how was he, *really*?

I'm fine, Buffett explained, everything is fine. Really. But from the way BRK was trading, people were listening to hyperpumperfulofcrap.

CNBC broadcast the rumors about Buffett's possible demise, flambéing the story with word of his reassurances. Skepticism grew. If he was saying he was fine, he must not be. A second rumor began to circulate that he was taking advantage of the situation to buy Berkshire's own stock cheap. That hit him on the tender spot where his reputation for personal integrity collided with his reputation for ruthless rapacity.

For two days the siege continued while BRK traded down more than five percent. By presuming his indispensability, the rumor paid Buffett a sort of inverted compliment. But he was outraged that anyone would think he would cheat his own shareholders by buying back stock at their expense under false pretenses. And he hated being a dog on anyone's leash. He was appalled at the thought that responding to manipulation would reward and encourage more rumors—and thereby set a precedent.

Eventually, he reasoned, the rumors would die under their own demonstrated falsity. But a new reality had dawned: The Internet meant that he had less and less control over public perception of him. Finally, he capitulated and issued an extraordinary press release denying the rumors.

The announcement was useless. BRK plunged eleven percent that week and didn't recover.

On March 9, *Newsday* hit the stands quoting Harry Newton, publisher of *Technology Investor Magazine*: "I'll tell you what Warren Buffett should say when he releases his statement to shareholders: 'I'm sorry!' that's what." The next day, BRK hit a low of $41,300 per share, trading at scarcely more than the value at which its pieces were carried on its books. The legendary "Buffett premium"— the high price the stock supposedly traded at just because of Buffett—was gone. The NASDAQ index had just reached 5,000. Since January 1999 it had doubled, its component stocks increasing more than $3 trillion in value.

The contrast was too sharp to leave alone. A money manager wrote that investors like Buffett were "made obsolete in 1999 by mavericks who say the old laws of investing have been repealed and backed up their theories with eye-popping numbers."[4]

Buffett was miserable about the bad publicity, though he never considered changing his investment strategy. Owners of BRK apparently would have been better off investing in an index of the market over the past five years—the most prolonged drought in Berkshire's history. Buffett understood the basics of computers perfectly well. But he would not consider buying a technology stock at *any* price. "*When it comes to Microsoft and Intel,*" he said, "*I don't know what that world will look like ten years from now. And I don't want to play in a game where the other guy has an advantage.*"[5]

In February 2000, the SEC had denied Berkshire Hathaway's request to keep some of its stockholdings confidential. It weighed the various interests of investors in a stable market versus the right to know, and ruled in favor of the right to know. He would only have time to tweezer up stocks in little bits before people could ride his coattails. The SEC had turned him into Ben Graham, who opened up his books for the whole world to see. That stung at a time when the media referred to Buffett as "*formerly* the world's greatest investor."[6]

The *Wall Street Journal* compared his performance to a retired AT&T employee whose portfolio was up thirty-five percent, saying that this technology-stock dabbler "isn't exactly Warren Buffett—thank goodness."[7]

Never in Buffett's career had resolution and clear thinking been put to the kind of test that he had endured for the past three years. Every indication in the market said that he was wrong. He had only his inner conviction to steer him straight. And this was the needy man who was so sensitive to public criticism that he ran from anything that would expose him to it; who had sculpted his life around managing his reputation; and who fought like a tiger against anything that could sully it.

Yet, even under siege to his reputation, this time, Buffett never fought back. He neither wrote editorials, nor dueled in the press, nor gave television interviews to defend himself. He and Munger carried on their regular dialogue with Berkshire's shareholders, saying that while the market was overvalued, they could not predict how long it would last. Finally, not for the record but as a warning and a way of teaching, Buffett explained his views once and for all and predicted that the market would fall far short of investors' hopes for two decades in a tour de force of a speech at Sun Valley that he shortly afterward turned into a *Fortune* article.

It had taken one great surge of courage to burst past his fears and beg for help from Nick Brady to save Salomon. But to show such restraint, then commit himself to such a forecast in the face of years of criticism and ridicule, took a different kind of courage, making the Internet bubble one of the greatest personal challenges of his career.

On March 11, Berkshire Hathaway issued its annual report, and Buffett graded himself a "D" for failing to invest Berkshire's capital. He did not say, however, that he considered avoiding technology stocks to have been a mistake.

Separately, Buffett announced that BRK was so cheap that Berkshire would now entertain offers from investors to buy its *own* stock. To do so—to give money back to shareholders to whom he hadn't paid a dividend in decades—was extraordinary.

And for the second time, Buffett was publicly announcing what he wanted to buy in advance. Not since the Great Unwinding of the partnership in 1970 had he said, "I will buy Berkshire Hathaway." Once again, investors had to ask themselves which side to play. This time, many people understood the message. Before he could buy a single share, BRK rose twenty-four percent.

The following week, the NASDAQ, full of technology stocks, sent up a warning plume of ash.[8] By late April, it had cratered thirty-one percent, among the largest losses in historic terms.

By Easter, Buffett did not care; he was doubled over in pain. He could not believe it. Right before his all-important shareholder meeting, the critical performance of his year, the rumors about his health had come true. Susie Jr. rushed him to the hospital at three o'clock in the morning, where he spent the next several days trying to pass a kidney stone. He phoned Big Susie repeatedly in panic. She was away in Grand Lake, Colorado; there was nothing she could do.[9]

He sat up all night drinking tumblers of water until, finally, the water torture worked and he passed the stone. But from then on he had to worry about a part of his anatomy that had not previously concerned him, because kidney stones recur. *"The plumbing thing—I hate it. Basically that's what goes wrong as you get older,"* he said.

He took inventory of his problems. The stock was in such disrepute that only his offer to buy it himself had saved it. General Re, his largest deal, seemed cursed. Coca-Cola was nagging at his thoughts. How could so much damage have happened so quickly in a business with such a bulletproof brand? Could it really all be poor old Ivester's fault? And now a problem with his health had reared up to stare him in the face.

The fact of mortality dwelled beneath the surface of Buffett's bathtub memory, periodically sliding its way back up into the tub.[10] He had still never come to terms with his father's death. He had never decided on a suitable memorial to Howard. He had moved the large portrait of Howard so that it hung on the wall behind his desk, floating above his own head. Howard's papers sat in the basement of his house, untouched. Warren could not bring himself to go through them. He teared up if he even thought about it, obviously terrified to let the emotions that had been held back all these thirty-five years erupt.

He'd warned that trees don't grow to the sky; someday everything must end. Yet he himself couldn't face the day he would have to draw the line under his career and say: "This is it. I'm done. The Sistine Chapel is finished. No further brushstroke will improve it—any further effort will produce an ordinary result."

He was sixty-nine years old. He couldn't believe that he was sixty-nine years old; he still felt like a young man. He comforted himself with the knowledge that decades remained until he reached the age at which his mother had died. General Re would be fixed, and Coca-Cola, as he knew, could be run by a ham sandwich. The kidney stone...Whoosh! The bathtub memory went to work. He returned to preparing for his shareholder meeting, which had become the happiest week of his year.

For several days at the end of April, the airport grew busier than usual, and a rivulet, then a stream of people arrived in Omaha. People wearing Berkshire Hathaway meeting credentials strolled through town as if identifying them-selves as members of a club.

The shareholder meeting itself—which had multiplied to include thousands of staff, vendors, and volunteer employees; acres of exhibits, flowers, and dis-plays; truckloads of turkey sandwiches, hot dogs, and Coke; signage, exhibits, security, media, sound, video, lighting, and private parties for the vendors and helpers—was designed, choreographed, and overseen by just one employee, Kelly Muchemore, whom Buffett called the "Flo Ziegfeld" of Berkshire Hathaway. Kelly did not even have a secretary. Technically, she *was* a secretary. It would take four people to replace Kelly, Buffett pointed out with pride. (One side effect of this kind of praise was that it sometimes caused people to wonder whether they were getting paid a quarter of what they were worth.[11] Buffett, however, was skilled at paying people with more praise than cash.)

By four o'clock in the morning on Saturday, several hundred restless people wearing laminated meeting credentials on lanyards around their necks lined up outside the Civic Auditorium, waiting for the doors to open. Three hours later, people stampeded past the guards who checked their credentials to claim the prime seats on the floor. By eight o'clock it became clear that they needn't have bothered to show up before dawn. Half the seats in the house were empty. Thirty minutes later, the auditorium held nine thousand people.[12] Attendance was down by forty percent from the fifteen thousand who had come the year before.

Around nine-thirty Buffett and Munger walked onto the stage and looked out over the shrunken crowd of the faithful, clad in everything from business garb to shorts. After a five-minute business meeting, the question-and-answer session opened as usual, with shareholders lined up at microphones positioned around the auditorium, lobbing questions. Somebody asked about technology stocks. "I don't want to speculate about high-tech," Buffett said. "Anytime there have been real bursts of speculation, it eventually gets corrected." He compared the market to the phony riches of chain letters and Ponzi schemes. "Investors may feel richer, but they're not." Pause. "Charlie?"

Munger opened his mouth. The audience perked up slightly. Munger often said, "Nothing to add." But whenever Buffett handed the microphone to him, the auditorium hummed with the subtlest sensation of danger. It was like watching an experienced lion tamer working with a chair and a whip.

"The reason we use the phrase 'wretched excess,' " Munger said, "is because it produces wretched consequences. It's irrational. If you mix raisins with turds, they're still turds."

The crowd gasped. Did he say turds? Did Charlie just compare Internet stocks to turds in front of children who had come with their parents, not to mention in front of the press? He said turds! It took some time for the meeting to settle back into its normal rhythm.

The questions droned on as Buffett and Munger listened, unwrapping Dilly Bars with much rustling. Shareholders began to voice complaints. They didn't like the stock price.[13] One said she was going to look into correspondence schools, since her Berkshire stock would no longer pay for college.[14] Gaylord Hanson of Santa Barbara, California, stood at the microphone to harangue that he had bought BRK near its highs in 1998 because of Buffett's track record and had come out okay only because the money he'd lost had been made up by four technology stocks.[15] He urged Buffett to invest at least ten percent of Berkshire's assets in technology, "the only game in town. Isn't there enough left in your brain power to maybe pick a few?"

It was worse than humiliating. Looking out into the audience, Buffett saw that, for the first time, some of them assumed that he was letting them down: the effort of nearly fifty years rolled backward, undone, his own shareholders turned against him. His age suddenly signified not experience but obsolescence. In the press, people now referred to him as an old man.

Afterward, Buffett guzzled Cherry Coke while signing autographs, then made a round of parties with Astrid, Dilly Bars dripping in his wake. He held court at Gorat's with the family on Sunday night, then oversaw the board meeting—another teaching exercise—on Monday morning. Afterward, he, Susie, and the kids and their families flew to New York. By the time he was catching up with friends, eating out and seeing shows with the family, and dutifully checking off his list the unloved annual chore of buying suits at Bergdorf's, the bathtub memory had done its work.

Saturday morning he summoned three members of General Re's management to his suite at the Plaza Hotel. Ron Ferguson brought a series of PowerPoint handouts and began to pace through General Re's string of terrible results. Buffett listened for a few minutes, frowning and fidgeting. Finally he said, Why don't we just jump to the end. Results had to improve. The lines of authority must be reinforced. Clients were dictating terms to General Re, not the other way around. This must end. Somebody had to be accountable.[16]

He stopped short of telling Ferguson to retire, betrayed by his weakness for older managers. He sympathized with Ferguson, who'd suffered a subarachnoid hemorrhage in late 1999. Ferguson, who had seemed slightly off-kilter for some time afterward, had offered to step down then. Buffett had told him no. He didn't believe in putting people out to pasture; some of his best managers were elderly, including Mrs. B, who had worked until age 103 and died a year later. He missed her caustic little soul, and bragged all the time about Berkshire's geriatric crew. His board of directors was beginning to resemble the elderly U.S. Supreme Court. His own goal was to outlive Mrs. B.

Imagine, therefore, if Buffett's genie had been watching over his shoulder a few weeks later, as he played bridge after dinner at Bill and Melinda Gates's house. He was answering questions in the raspy voice that meant he hadn't been sleeping, repeating that he was "just fine," but Sharon Osberg, who knew how to read the signs that meant Buffett was in real distress, conferred with the Gateses, who immediately summoned a doctor over Buffett's protests.[17] The doctor was surprised that Buffett had never had a colonoscopy. He gave him a painkiller to get him home in comfort. But, he said, you really should go in and have a complete examination and a colonoscopy when you get back to Omaha.

The genie would have been less tactful. Howard Buffett had had colon cancer and died of complications from it. What was Buffett *thinking*, at age sixty-nine, never having had a colonoscopy? *This* was certainly not treating your body like the only car you'd ever own.

A month later, BRK had recovered by nearly $5,000 a share to $60,000. *Fortune* magazine noticed that even though he "lost his heavenly touch" in 1999, Berkshire's recent forty-seven percent recovery from its March low made him a "good revivalist."[18] He would need some reviving in other ways, however.

Buffett had scheduled the dread procedure at last.[19] So much medical attention at once—only a month after the kidney stone. But a colonoscopy could be considered "routine." He distracted himself by talking on the phone and playing bridge. He played helicopter on the computer. When people asked him about the upcoming procedure, he said, "I'm not the least bit worried."

But he woke up from the colonoscopy to a nasty shock. A sizable benign polyp was nesting in his gut. The polyp had taken over so much real estate that removing it would require demolishing a good chunk of the surrounding neighborhood. It had a few small friends nearby as well. This was not something to trifle with. Buffett decided to have surgery in late July, after Sun Valley. "Oh, I'm not worried at all," he said, making jokes and stressing the good results from his cardiology tests. "I never worry about my health. Unless you'd brought it up, I never would have even thought about it."

But Buffett now seemed cornered into issuing a press release about his health. The statement blared the details of his surgery, describing it as routine.[20]

The surgery took several hours, during which fifteen inches of Buffett's innards were removed, and left him marked with a seven-inch scar. During the week he spent recovering at home, he grew a beard for the first time in his life. Deprived of Berkshire, he talked a lot on the phone. He sounded weak.

"Oh, no, I'm not tired at all, I'm perfectly fine," he said. *"I've lost a few pounds I needed to lose. Astrid's taking good care of me. The doctor says I can eat anything I want. By the way, did I tell you that I went into the hospital with a colon, but I came out with a semicolon?"* Asked if he was concerned about a recurrence: *"Oh, no, I'm not worried at all about that. I never worry about anything, you know. Incidentally, did I tell you that the anesthesiologist used to be my caddy at the country club? I told him before he put me under that I sure hope I tipped him well."*

Berkshire Hathaway's press release simply noted that the polyp was confirmed benign and no further treatment was required. Despite the announcement, rumors raced over the Internet and around Wall Street again. Some insisted that Buffett must have had cancer; polyps did not require surgery. But Warren was not sick and certainly did not feel old. He still felt like the "Firebolt."

Yet after tolerating cavalier treatment all his life, his health was beginning to set limits. Someday, his wrestling match with infinity would end; the questions he was avoiding must be faced. Since Berkshire and Buffett were interchangeable in his mind, everything in his nature rebelled against this task. Many of the questions hinged on Big Susie, who he was sure was going to outlive him. He told people that she would take care of everything.

55

The Last Kay Party

By the time Buffett got his semicolon, the Internet boom had boomeranged. The dotcoms were dying at the pace of one a day.[1] The NASDAQ was trading at less than half the value of its peak; the old economy stocks were still swooning too. Buffett's reputation, however, began to revive.

Berkshire dipped its soup ladle into a huge stockpot of capital for Buffett to buy private companies, bankrupt companies, under-the-radar companies—everything from Ben Bridge jewelers to Benjamin Moore paint. Even so, by the end of 2000 Berkshire still had billions of unused capital: a baled-in-the-basement, thatched-to-the-rooftop mass of money that continued to pour out from the self-perpetuating cash-spinning machine.[2]

Buffett's foreboding prediction about the market in his 1999 Sun Valley speech had proven right. Now he sermonized in his letter—which had become a global media event, released on the Internet and awaited by so many thousands of people that the Berkshire Web site nearly crashed on the appointed Saturday morning—that the birth of the Internet had offered a chance for cynical financiers to "monetize the hopes" of the credulous. The resulting "wealth transfer on a massive scale" was going to benefit only the very few.

"Promoters have in recent years moved billions of dollars from the pockets of the public to their own purses (and to those of their friends and associates).... Speculation is most dangerous when it looks easiest."[3] The audience listened, and at the 2001 shareholder meeting, the crowds started coming back.

Buffett's return to Sun Valley in 2001 was another opportunity to table-thump—and, of course, to see old friends. On Friday afternoon, after playing bridge, Katharine Graham, who was now left in relative peace at age eighty-four, rode back to her condo in the little golf cart she used to get around in Sun Valley. Tall and still on the slender side, she had had both hips replaced, and one worked better than the other. People noticed that she seemed worn out and "fading," but she had been saying what a marvelous time she was having this year. The company that she and her son Don had created, with much help from Buffett's advice, was now regarded almost as iconic for its financial and journalistic success at a time when newspaper profits were slipping badly. Graham took obvious pleasure in the way the Allen conference brought together so many of the people she enjoyed. She had been assigned an assistant to escort her everywhere, but she had the grit to resist handling, so for much of the conference she was seen on the arm of either Don or Barry Diller, chairman of USA Networks and a close friend. At the moment, however, she was alone.

Susie Buffett Jr. and her mother, in their car, spotted Graham and drove into an unobtrusive parking lot so that they could watch her climb the four steps to her condominium. She was taking the anticoagulant Coumadin, which greatly increased the risk of serious hemorrhage should she fall. She clung to the handrail and looked shaky but made it inside without incident.[4]

Later, outside on the deck of the Wildflower condos, overlooking the golf course and mountains, where Graham often sat reading the *Washington Post* in the afternoons, fashion designer Diane von Furstenberg threw her annual women's cocktail party for Kay, a Sun Valley tradition.[5]

Saturday dawned. The audience settled into its chairs to hear Andy Grove, head of Intel, kick off the morning with "Internet Interrupted." Then Diane Sawyer moderated a panel, "Pulse of America: How Do You Find It?" After Diane Sawyer, Buffett was scheduled to speak. Since the market's peak in March 2000, over $4 trillion of stock-market value had evaporated.[6] The surviving Internet businesses were entering their adolescence. The audience hoped he would relent from his previous bearishness.

Yet Buffett showed them a graph indicating that the value of the market was still one-third larger than the economy. That was far higher than the level at which Buffett said he would buy stocks. It was considerably higher than the market had ever stood in modern history—higher, even, than the peak of the Great Bubble of 1929. In fact, the graph suggested that the economy would have to nearly double, or the value of the market would have to fall by nearly half, before he would get *really* excited about it.[7] He told them that despite two years of keelhauling, even with the NASDAQ down by more than half, he would *still* not buy. He expected the stock market (with dividends included) to grow at no better than about seven percent a year, on average, for possibly as long as the next twenty years.[8] That was only about one percent higher than he had said two years before. It was a dispiriting message.

"That shouldn't be the way markets work," he said, "but that *is* the way markets work. And in the end, that's what you should remember."

Many in the audience were shocked and sobered—but impressed. Buffett enjoyed congratulations for his speech at lunch under a tent on the deck behind Herbert Allen's condo, where a group of about a hundred people, including the Grahams, had gathered. He sat with President Vicente Fox of Mexico—whom he thought of as "an old Coca-Cola guy"—and kicked around the economy.[9] Then he went off to play golf.

Kay Graham rode over to the bridge room to play cards. After a while she said she was not feeling well and had decided to go back to her room. She called to alert her assistant, who was waiting for her at Herbert Allen's condo next door to her own, then drove back to her condo alone.

The assistant had started to check out the window for her every couple of minutes. She looked and saw that Kay's golf cart had already arrived, but it was empty. She sprinted outside and saw Kay lying at the top of the steps on the porch in front of her door. Running over, she bent and spoke to Graham, who didn't respond. She started screaming for Herbert Allen to come out.[10] By the time the emergency medical technicians arrived a few minutes later, Don Graham had rushed back from the golf course. He was going to need someone to help him make decisions, and asked Buffett whether he wanted to come along. But Buffett could not do it.[11] Griffith Harsh, a prominent neurosurgeon who was married to eBay CEO Meg Whitman, went with Don to look at the CAT scan at St. Luke's hospital in Ketchum, about ten minutes away.[12]

Susie Jr. drove off to meet Don and Herbert Allen at the hospital. She knew very well that no one could expect her father to deal with any kind of medical crisis. Big Susie had had a cardiac catheterization in 1997, and Warren got on a plane to go to San Francisco to be with her. When Kathleen Cole called to say that Susie was going to be okay, he turned the plane around in midair and went back to Omaha. Since then, Susie had been in the emergency room repeatedly with excruciating abdominal adhesions and intestinal blockages. In 1999 she had her gallbladder removed. Throughout all of her medical problems over the years, Warren had never once been able to endure the emotional distress of going to the hospital to be with his wife.[13]

After seeing the CAT scan, Dr. Harsh had Kay helicoptered to St. Alphonsus Regional Medical Center in Boise; Don and Susie flew after her in a private plane.

While all of this was transpiring, Warren retreated to his condo. Big Susie had left earlier that day for a wedding in Greece and knew nothing of what was going on. Peter and Jennifer, Howie and Devon were still at Sun Valley; Peter and Howie came by briefly, but even at such a time it was unnatural for Warren to tune the unfamiliar instrument of his emotions to make an openhearted connection with his sons. Bill and Melinda Gates, Ron and Jane Olson, and Susie Jr.'s boyfriend sat with him while he waited for news, and distracted him by talking of anything but Kay. Susie Jr. had called from Boise to say that she was going into surgery, but that was all.[14]

Kay was taken into the operating room, then brought out. Around two o'clock in the morning, since there had been no further word from Boise, Buffett decided to go to bed. Everybody left.

Ninety minutes or so later, after a second CAT scan, the doctors moved Kay to intensive care. "We're really not sure what's going to happen," they told Susie Jr. She called her father, woke him up, and told him to get the family on the plane.

A couple of hours later, when the NetJets plane taxied into Boise, Warren called Susie Jr. and said he didn't feel he could come to the hospital. She told him that he had to come; Don was distraught and needed him to be there. Even if Kay was not conscious and couldn't see him, she would be able to sense his presence. Reluctantly, he acquiesced.

When he got to the hospital, his daughter met him downstairs in the lobby. She knew he was so frightened that he would have to be coaxed. "You have to come upstairs," she insisted. "You have to come." She led him to intensive care, where Don Graham, red-faced from weeping, was sitting alone with his mother. Kay, drained of color and unconscious, lay connected to monitoring devices that blinked little lights and made tiny noises. Warren and Don clung to each other, sobbing. Lally Weymouth, Kay's oldest child and only daughter, arrived. Eventually, Susie Jr. took her father downstairs. There was nothing more they could do. As the rest of Kay's children gathered in Boise, the Buffetts boarded a plane for a sad ride back to Omaha.[15]

Two days later, the call came that Kay had died. Warren had already told Lally that he wasn't going to be able to speak at Kay's service. He would be an usher along with Bill Gates. Astrid took care of him at home, and work consumed him at the office. When he wasn't working, Sharon played bridge with him or he played helicopter, anything to distract himself from the horror of Kay's death.

And yet, the day after Graham died, Buffett arrived, as scheduled, to speak to an audience of college students at the Terry College of Business at the University of Georgia. He climbed onto the stage wearing his stiff gray suit and looking only a little more awkward than usual, his breathy voice grating slightly. *"Testing, one million, two million, three million,"* he said at the microphone. This line could always be counted on to get a laugh, and it did. He then launched into a couple of Nebraska football jokes but, out of character, rushed the punch line and got only chuckles from the audience.

Then he seemed to catch his rhythm. *"People ask me where they should go to work, and I always tell them to go to work for whom they admire the most,"* he said. He urged them not to waste their time and their life. *"It's crazy to take little in-between jobs just because they look good on your résumé. That's like saving sex for your old age. Do what you love and work for whom you admire the most, and you've given yourself the best chance in life you can."*

They asked him what mistakes he had made. Number one was Berkshire Hathaway, he said—spending twenty years trying to revive a failing textile mill. Second, US Air. Buffett spoke of his failure to call the Air-aholic hotline before-hand. Third, he said, had been buying the Sinclair gas station as a young man. That mistake, he reckoned, had cost him about $6 billion compared to what he could have earned on the money invested.

But his mistakes of omission—things he could have done and didn't do—had plagued him most, he said. He mentioned only one—failing to buy FNMA stock, the Federal National Mortgage Association. That, he said, had cost about $5 billion as of that date. There were others: passing on the television station that Tom Murphy had tried to sell him; not investing in Wal-Mart. The reason that he had made mostly mistakes of omission instead of commission, he explained, was his cautious approach to life.

Buffett had talked many times before about mistakes. But when he spoke, as he often did, of his mistakes of omission, he never ventured beyond business mistakes. The errors of omission in his personal life—inattention, neglect, missed chances—were always there, the side effects of intensity; but they were shadow presences visible only to those who knew him well. He spoke of them only in private, if at all.

To the students, he explained his "Twenty Punches" approach to investing. *"You'd get very rich,"* he said, *"if you thought of yourself as having a card with only twenty punches in a lifetime, and every financial decision used up one punch. You'd resist the temptation to dabble. You'd make more good decisions and you'd make more big decisions."*

He ran his life on Twenty Punches, too, with as little flitting as he could arrange. Same house, same wife for fifty years, same Astrid on Farnam Street; no desire to buy and sell real estate, art, cars, tokens of wealth; no jumping from city to city or career to career. Some of that was easy for a man so certain of himself; some of it came with being a creature of habit; some of it was a natural tendency to let things compound; and some of it was the wisdom of inertia. When he gave somebody a punch on his card, they became a part of him and that decision was permanent. Any crack in the facade of permanence was extraordinarily difficult for him to face.

A few days later, police arrived early in the morning to close nearby streets for the crowd they expected at the Washington National Cathedral, its gargoyle-bedecked flying buttresses silhouetted against a bright blue sky.[16] Television crews began to set up for an elaborately orchestrated event that had all the trappings of a funeral for a head of state. By late morning, buses bearing *Washington Post* employees pulled up one by one. A blue-and-white-striped bus carrying members of the Senate arrived, and people began streaming in from cars and limousines. Gradually the front pews filled with dignitaries like Bill and Hillary Clinton and Lynne and Dick Cheney. Famous faces were everywhere.[17] Hundreds, then thousands, of people filed in through the enormous bronze doors to the sound of the National Symphony Orchestra, gradually assembling into what looked like the largest crowd the cathedral had ever held.[18]

As the service began, Buffett and Bill Gates slipped into a pew next to Melinda. The music started. Historian Arthur Schlesinger spoke; Henry Kissinger spoke; Ben Bradlee spoke; Graham's children spoke. Near the end, former Senator John Danforth gave the homily. Graham, he thought, never said much about religion, but she lived the way a believer is supposed to live. "She dismissed out of hand the notion that she was the most powerful woman in the world," he said. "In Washington, especially, a lot of people strut, and Kay did not strut.... We do not attain the victory of life by selfishness. Victory is for those who give themselves to causes beyond themselves. It is very biblical and very true that everyone who exalts themselves will be humbled and he who humbles himself will be exalted. That is a text for all of us. It was lived by Katharine Graham."

Melinda Gates reached up and wiped away tears while Buffett sat next to her husband with a grief-stricken face. The two cathedral choirs, dressed in black and white robes, sang Mozart. Carefully, the pallbearers lifted the casket to their shoulders and bore it down the aisle while the congregation sang "America the Beautiful." The family followed the procession out of the cathedral to the Oak Hill Cemetery across the street from Graham's house, where she would be interred next to her late husband.

Early that afternoon, more than four hundred people swept up the circular driveway to Graham's house and walked around to the rear garden, where her children and grandchildren stood about, chatting with guests. At a buffet inside the tent, people ate finger sandwiches and sliced ham and tenderloin. They wandered around past the swimming pool, and found their way into the house to gather the collection of memories that it held. They stood in the living room where President Reagan had gotten down on his hands and knees to pick up ice cubes he'd spilled on the floor, and gazed for one last time at the books and knickknacks in the library where Mrs. Graham had pondered whether to print the Pentagon Papers. They paused by Napoleon's china on the walls next to the round dining tables in the golden room where American Presidents from Kennedy to Clinton had dined. From Jacqueline Onassis to Princess Diana, if Katharine Graham invited them, they all came.[19] The house itself was a kind of history.

Warren walked through Kay's house for one last time to remember, but he did not linger. He left early and would never return.[20]

As the afternoon wore on, the rest of Katharine Graham's friends and admirers told her good-bye. They withdrew down the long hallway gallery past the rooms where she had entertained them so often and slipped past the garden outside. Then slowly, sometimes reluctantly, they left the last Kay Party, and began their final trip down the pebbled drive.

By the Rich, for the Rich

Buffett flew back to Nebraska alone. He knotted every waking minute into a web of distractions. He read financial reports and newspapers. He watched CNBC. He talked to people on the phone. He played bridge in the evenings after work. He surfed the Internet for news online. In between, he played helicopter on the computer.

A week later he was crying on the phone, great gulping sobs, choking, gasping cries that left him out of breath. The convulsion broke through the dam that had kept his grief contained.

A moment later, after the torrent of grief had poured out of him, he was recovered enough to speak. He regretted not being able to eulogize Kay at her funeral, he said. It shamed him. The man who had worked so hard to become comfortable on a stage felt that he should have been able to do that for Kay. And there would be more regrets, more second thoughts.

"If I'd been playing bridge with her that day she might not have fallen," he reflected later, sadly. *"I would have taken her back in her golf cart myself. She might not have died."*

But Kay probably would have walked up the steps by herself anyway. And nobody knew whether she died from the fall or whether she had fallen because she had a stroke.

Still, Warren was plagued by a sense of lost opportunities. He felt at times that, had he been with her, he could somehow have kept Kay safe.

As weeks passed, if her death was mentioned, his eyes teared and the conversation would come to a stop while he collected himself. Then, like a motor turning over and restarting, he would brighten and shift to other subjects.

Buffett's birthday would be arriving in a few weeks, something to which he feigned indifference but actually dreaded. This year he was turning seventy-one. He could not believe he was seventy-one. He could not believe it, either, when he'd turned forty, and fifty, and sixty, and seventy. But this year, especially, he did not want to think about his birthday, because he did not want any reminders of mortality so soon after Kay's death.

Within ten days, he would have a new distraction to fully consume his time and attention. The morning of the Omaha Classic—Buffett's annual charity golf tournament, which attracted CEOs, celebrities, friends, and relatives— Buffet turned on the television to see that two planes had crashed into the World Trade Center. Almost everyone in Omaha at the golf tournament was affected in some way or another, however remotely. Many had friends, relatives, neighbors, or business acquaintances who worked in the towers. Berkshire, of course, had employees in businesses scattered all across the country. In the end Buffett would find that Berkshire had lost no employees—only money.

Some people decided to leave the golf tournament immediately, although with all airports closed this was not easy. Others stayed, some because they didn't want to insult Buffett, many because they had no choice.[1]

While these momentous events were occurring, Buffett proceeded with his schedule, compartmentalizing as he did under stress even in extreme situations. He arranged to complete the acquisition of a small business that was already in process. Then he went ahead with a meeting that had been scheduled with the head of Home Depot, Bob Nardelli.[2] Afterward he showed up at the Omaha Country Club, where about a hundred guests were milling around. Buffett said that things would go on as planned but people should do whatever they needed or wanted to do. As the tournament got rolling in a surreal atmosphere, Buffett rode a golf cart through a planned circuit of stops at different tees so guests could have their picture taken with him.[3] A strange calm hung over the event, which was like a celebrity golf tournament the day Pearl Harbor was attacked. And in fact, like Buffett, more than a few of the golfers could remember Pearl Harbor and its aftermath. This was not an excitable crowd. Most of them were prominent businessmen accustomed to stress and pressure, from a generation of men that considered poise and equanimity in the face of disaster as essential as the suits and ties they wore every day to work.

Buffett was even more prepared for this than most because he had already been thinking about terrorism risk. In May, he had told General Re and Berkshire Re to cut back on insuring buildings and clients that represented a concentration of exposure to terrorism risk, his mind working as it always did to extrapolate toward potential catastrophes. He had actually cited the World Trade Center as an example of such a risk.[4] While the rising threat of terrorism in the late 1990s and early-millennium years was no secret, Buffett's attempt to protect Berkshire against the danger had been unusually prescient, and probably unique among insurers.[5]

Over the next few days, as airports gradually began to allow flights to resume on a limited schedule, the Buffetts organized dinners, tennis, and golf for the remaining guests until everyone was able to straggle home from Omaha.[6] The stock market was about to reopen after its longest recess since the Great Depression. Buffett agreed to go on *60 Minutes* with former Treasury Secretary Robert Rubin and Jack Welch, the recently retired CEO of General Electric. He was the country's most trusted expert on investing and the stock market. On the show that Sunday evening, Buffett said that he would not be selling stocks—he might be a buyer if they declined enough—and explained that he had confidence in the ability of the United States economy to surmount the ripples from the terrorist attack. By now, when he said something, people knew he meant it. At Sun Valley, of course, Buffett had said the value of the market would need to fall by half before he would get *really* excited. So the savvy knew that "enough" meant "a hell of a lot."

The next day, the Dow fell 684 points, or seven percent, its largest point decline ever in a single day. The Federal Reserve began to take action after the market plunged on its reopening, cutting interest rates fifty basis points (half a percent). By the end of the week, the Dow had fallen more than fourteen percent, its largest one-week drop in history. Yet the drop as a percent of investors' wealth was less than half that of 1987, when the market plunged by one-third.

Within days, Buffett talked to Berkshire's insurers and tried to assess the damage to Berkshire Hathaway. The initial estimates indicated that Berkshire had lost $2.3 billion.[7] This was many times its largest loss from any earthquake, hurricane, or other natural disaster to date. Of the total, $1.7 billion came from General Re.

Buffett had had enough. He went to work writing a special letter that he posted on his Web site, excoriating General Re for having broken the "basic rules of underwriting." Since he had never, in the history of Berkshire Hathaway, publicly dressed down the management of one of his companies, the effect was to brand General Re with a red-ink scarlet letter, which remained posted on the Web site for all to see. It was now in a precarious situation. Having publicly embarrassed Buffett in such a dramatic way, it risked becoming the next Salomon—a business that he could never embrace, that would instead become only another cautionary tale.

To prevent panic, the Fed took interest rates down to historically low levels. The Fed's role was to maintain the banking system's liquidity. This time, however, the Fed would keep interest rates artifically low for three years.[8] One month after the attacks, stocks completed a full recovery, restoring $1.38 trillion in market value. But the market remained in a nervous mood, partly due to uncertainty over the outcome of the invasion of Afghanistan a few weeks after 9/11. Then, in November, an energy trading company called Enron stuck a pin in the remains of the late 1990s stock-market bubble, which had shrunk but not burst. As the Justice Department moved in, Enron melted into bankruptcy in the heat of an accounting fraud.

A whole series of accounting-fraud and securities-violation cases followed: WorldCom, Adelphia Communications, Tyco, ImClone. As 2002 began, New York Attorney General Eliot Spitzer mounted an assault against the Wall Street banks for having inflated stock prices by touting new offerings using biased stock research.[9] Valuations of stocks and bonds began to fall apart as investors lost confidence in the numbers reported to them by managements.

Berkshire's best opportunities always came at times of uncertainty, when others lacked the insight, resources, and fortitude to make the right judgments and commit. *"Cash combined with courage in a crisis is priceless,"* said Buffett. Now his time had come round again. Anyone of normal energy might have been overwhelmed, but Buffett had been waiting for years for the kind of opportunities that sleeted down upon Kiewit Plaza. Every one of his faculties seemed engaged at once. He bought a group of junk bonds, which had become cigar butts, for Berkshire. He bought the underwear maker Fruit of the Loom, quipping, "We cover the asses of the masses."[10] He bought Larson-Juhl, which made picture frames. Berkshire's MidAmerican Energy subsidiary invested in the troubled Williams Companies and bought its Kern River Pipeline.[11] Berkshire bought Garan, the maker of Garanimals children's clothing. It picked up the Northern Natural Gas pipeline from Dynegy, another troubled energy company.[12] Within days, MidAmerican lent more money to Williams Companies.[13] It bought The Pampered Chef, which sold cookware at parties through a salesforce of 70,000 independent "kitchen consultants." It bought farm-equipment maker CTB Industries and teamed with investment bank Lehman Brothers to lend $1.3 billion to struggling Reliant Energy.

Ajit Jain quickly moved into the terrorism-insurance business, filling a sudden vacuum by insuring airlines, Rockefeller Center, the Chrysler Building, a South American oil refinery, a North Sea oil platform, and the Sears Tower in Chicago. Berkshire insured the Winter Olympics in Salt Lake City against a terrorist attack. It insured the FIFA World Cup soccer championship against terrorism.[14] Buffett was handicapping.

Some of Berkshire's businesses struggled in a weak economy. Buffett had always said he'd rather have a lumpy fifteen percent return than a steady ten percent. Most would naturally right themselves over time. NetJets, however, was struggling, not just because of the economy but because the premise for buying it—the uniqueness of its franchise—was looking less unique. Other people who forgot to call the Air-aholic hotline kept setting up businesses to compete with NetJets, even though the economics of the fractional aviation business were unattractive. Buffett now realized that it was testosterone that caused Air-aholism. *"If only women could be CEOs of companies that flew planes,"* he said, *"I think it would be a lot better. It's like sports franchises. If only women could own sports franchises, they'd sell for one-tenth what they sell for now."* He told the shareholders that NetJets would return to profitability and would dominate its market. He did not point out, however, that it might not earn the margin on capital he had hoped, at least not any time soon. After all, NetJets was fun. He knew mountains of minutiae about how the planes were purchased, managed, scheduled, routed, maintained, insured, piloted, and crewed. NetJets was cool. He did a lot of elephant-bumping at NetJets events. He would never sell it, even if the world's other mega-billionaires tried to arm-wrestle him for it.

The more serious, if smaller, problem was Dexter Shoe, the modern equivalent of the textile mill. Buffett would later say it was the worst acquisition he had ever made, quoting Bobby Bare's country song: "I've never gone to bed with an ugly woman, but I've sure woke up with a few."[15] He changed the management. Frank Rooney and Jim Issler, who ran Brown Shoe Company, a more successful operation, eventually shut down Dexter's U.S. operations and moved them overseas.[16] For every dollar they were paying workers in the U.S., it cost a dime to hire employees to make shoes elsewhere.

"I was wrong about the economic future of that one. The people working in the town of Dexter, Maine, were wonderful people who were very good at what they

did. But even if they were twice as good as the Chinese, the Chinese would work for a tenth as much."

Yet even with all this money-spinning activity, Buffett felt that the most important opportunity given him in the aftermath of 9/11 had nothing to do with business. Rather, he now had both the privilege and the responsibility to influence events and ideas. After the bubble of hubris that had enveloped the financial community for the past several years, America had become more sober-minded, and less blind to the corner-cutting in the name of greed that had gone on in the late 1990s. Buffett thought the time was right for him to speak up about the rapacity of the rich and the way it was being validated by fiscal policy.

His sense of justice was particularly inflamed by a proposal that was a centerpiece of President Bush's new budget—a plan to gradually repeal the decades-old federal estate tax, which took for the government a slice of the largest inheritances. Supporters of the plan referred to the estate tax as the "death tax," which had an ominous sound. They cited a proverbial family that would have to sell the family farm to pay the tax when its patriarch died. Undoubtedly, there were some such families. Buffett argued that the suffering of those few was far outweighed by the effect on everybody else.

Buffett used his preacher's pulpit to point out that of the roughly 2.3 million Americans who died each year, fewer than fifty thousand—two percent—paid any estate tax at all. Half of all the estate taxes paid came from fewer than four thousand people—two-tenths of one percent of those who had died.[17] These were the monumentally, colossally rich.

As to the question, it was their money, why shouldn't they be able to do what they wanted with it?—why should they "subsidize" others?—Buffett's answer was that they owed some minimum amount to the society that enabled them to become so rich.

If the estate tax were eliminated, he said, somebody else would have to make up the difference, since the same amount of money would still be required to pay for running the government.

For years a supply-side theory had postulated that cutting taxes would force the government to cut expenses. This theory had an intuitive logic; after all, if people were supposed to live within their income, why not the government? (Of course, by 2002, the populace was busy setting up home-equity lines of credit based on artificially cheap interest rates to avoid living within its income.) Debate over supply-side policy still boiled after twenty years; the taxes the government was collecting usually didn't cover its costs, and it was borrowing to make up the difference. The theory by now looked more dubious. Buffett felt that proposing an estate-tax cut while running the federal budget at a deficit was the height of hypocrisy.[18]

Buffett didn't blame people for acting in their own interests; he even felt pity for the politicians who were chained to the grindstone of endless fund-raising. It was the system that he scorned, in which money bought power.

Shortly after President Bush's inauguration in 2001, Buffett had gone to the LBJ Room in the Capitol Building to speak about political campaign financing to a group of thirty-eight Senators who were part of the Democratic Policy Committee. He said that the campaign finance system was corrupt. The laws were shifting in ways that enhanced the ability of the rich to get ever richer, to keep more of what they made, and to pass more of it along to their heirs. Buffett called this "government by the wealthy, for the wealthy."

He pointed out a growing army of lobbyists whose job was to push for legislation that benefited the rich. He said, however, that nobody lobbied for the other ninety-eight percent of Americans. Lacking their own lobbyists, the best redress for the ninety-eight percent was to understand what was going on and to quit voting for people who enacted laws that took taxes out of the average person's pockets so the rich could pay a lower share.

"I'd have a higher tax at the higher levels of wealth. I wouldn't mind having no tax up to a point and then a hundred percent tax for an estate over a hundred and fifty million dollars.

"The most important thing is to ask, 'And then what?' If you eliminate the twenty billion dollars or so raised by the estate tax, you've got to make the money up by taxing everybody else somehow. It's amazing how hard the American population will fight for the families of those few thousand people who pay large estate taxes and for the whole rest of the country to pay for it out of their own pockets.

"I don't like anything that, in effect, creates a residue of humanity. I don't like a tax system that goes in that direction; I don't like an educational system that goes in that direction. I don't like anything where the bottom twenty percent keep getting a poorer and poorer deal."

But the debate over estate taxes turned shrill and bitter. Buffett was portrayed as a silver-spooned populist who was trying to keep the next generation from bootstrapping its way to success in the classic American entrepreneurial way.[19]

Subtly or not, the estate-tax feud was informed by the issue of Buffett's own money. Some people called rich guys like Buffett tax-dodgers, because they had amassed their money through lightly taxed investments. But to say that

Buffett invested to dodge taxes was like saying that a baby drank its bottle to fill its diapers. Indeed, Buffett was the first to say that the tax on investments was unfairly low. In fact, this was another of his causes; he wanted to raise the tax rate on capital gains. He liked to compare his tax rate to his secretary's, pointing out how unjust it was that she paid a higher tax rate on her income than he did, just because most of his income came from investing.

Having already angered all the plutocrats and would-be plutocrats, but with his credibility at a peak in other quarters, Buffett vowed to carry on the fight against repeal of the estate tax, and would spin on this subject for years. He spoke again on another subject to the Democratic Policy Committee just days before the first shots were fired in the Iraq War in 2003. He said that President Bush's plan to cut taxes on dividends was more "class welfare for the rich." In the *Washington Post,* he wrote about "Dividend Voodoo," noting again that his tax rate was lower than Debbie Bosanek's. The reaction from conservatives against yet another of Buffett's populist manifestos was swift and savage. "Millionaires are seething at Warren Buffett's betrayal of their class," said one.[20]

That, of course, was his point. He felt that the United States of America was never meant to be a country where people with money were a self-perpetuating "class" who constantly gathered more wealth and power unto themselves.

The rich, however, had been getting very rich indeed as the stock market continued its resurgence after 9/11. A dozen new hedge funds seemed to sprout every day. They were cashing in on all the leverage from the low interest rates the Federal Reserve had provided. Billionaires were becoming as common as raccoons around a garbage can. A lot of the quick-bucks wealth of the new economy bothered Buffett because of the way it had been transferred in massive amounts from investors to middlemen without producing anything in return. The average investor was still getting—of course—the average return, but with all of these fees gouged out.

One of Buffett's least favorite ways for the rich to get richer was through stock options—since his famous "no" vote on the pay package at Salomon, no other board had ever asked him to serve on its compensation committee. Coca-Cola had given Doug Daft options on 650,000 shares of its stock in 2001. Daft had originally asked to be compensated with stock options that would pay off only if earnings increased fifteen to twenty percent. The shareholders approved it with Buffett staring at his shoes thinking, Okay, this will never happen. A month later, the compensation committee belatedly realized that too, and back-tracked and bonus-pimped for him, lowering the target to eleven to sixteen percent.[21] That was like moving the finish line in a marathon to the nineteen-mile mark. So far, Daft had not impressed, and Coca-Cola's stock had gone nowhere. Watching trophy-sized option payments proliferate despite rising outrage, Buffett felt he had to seize the opportunity he had been waiting for—to finally kill counterfeit stock-option accounting.

Managers loved stock options because of a quirk of accounting history that said that if companies paid their employees with options instead of cash, they booked no cost. It was as if the stock options did not exist. In the "real" world, a privately owned business would instantly recognize this as a bogus idea. If the butcher, baker, and candlestick maker gave away options for shares worth, say, twenty percent of their businesses, they would be acutely aware that they had just given away a chunk of the profits as well.

But the accounting rules had made stock options into play money. Thus, bonus-pimping on an incredible scale had begun to occur in the late 1990s. CEOs had, on average, been paid forty-two times as much as the average blue-collar worker in 1980. Twenty years later, that ratio had increased to more than four hundred times.[22] The top-earning CEOs got billion-dollar packages. In 2000, Sandy Weill was paid $151 million at Citigroup, Jack Welch $125 million at GE, Larry Ellison $92 million at Oracle. Although Steve Jobs was taking only a $1 salary at Apple for 1997 through 1999, he got a windfall $872 million stock-option grant in 2000—plus a $90 million Gulfstream jet.[23]

When the accountants had tried to change these rules in the early 1990s, corporate America, led by Silicon Valley, stormed the gates of Congress, armed with lobbyists and campaign contributions, begging their representatives to save them from the terrible new accounting rules. Until the bubble finally burst in 2002, they had succeeded in stopping those rules dead in their tracks.

Buffett had been writing about stock options since 1993 but now felt the time was finally ripe for change. He wrote a thundering, influential editorial in the *Washington Post,* "Stock Options and Common Sense."[24]

"*CEOs know what their option grants are worth. That's why they fight for them,*" he wrote, and repeated the questions he had raised before.

"*If options aren't a form of compensation, what are they?*

"*If compensation isn't an expense, what is it?*

"*And if expenses shouldn't go into the calculation of earnings, where in the world should they go?*"

At Sun Valley in July 2002, emotions ran high over stock options. Buffett's loudly expressed view, combined with his influence, hung ominously over the heads of the stock-option lobby. The thermometer hit triple digits, and the sweating celebrities and corporate chiefs headed off in buses to go rafting and escape the heat.

Buffett himself went somewhere else shortly after he arrived, somewhere he needed help to face. Katharine Graham's condominium had been right next to Herbert Allen's, a spot that people passed by often on their way to and from events. The Coca-Cola board would be convening later for a meeting at Allen's, since most of its members were on-site. The purpose was to discuss stock options, and he would not miss this. But first:

"I was with Bill and Melinda, and we went up to the spot where Kay fell. I was shaking, and I couldn't stop. It was like I had the chills or something. And, you know, they were probably embarrassed. I really wasn't. I was just overcome at that point."

Afterward, Buffett was able to perform his ongoing miracle of the bathtub memory, and carried on with composure. The Coca-Cola board made a decision during its meeting and announced in a press release that it would start to book the cost of its employee stock options as an expense, which was currently allowed but not required. Coca-Cola's announcement hit corporate America like a cluster bomb, its force magnified by the venue at which the new policy was proclaimed—the Sun Valley gathering where the press had dug in outside its flowerpot barricades like an encampment. Buffett's thinly veiled hand could be seen behind this announcement. Right after Sun Valley, the Washington Post Company emulated Coca-Cola and announced that it, too, would expense stock options.[25]

Silicon Valley suited up for another fight in Congress. But one by one, other companies began to follow in the footsteps of Coca-Cola and the Washington Post Company, announcing that they, too, would recognize the expense of stock options on their books.

The battle over stock options would continue formally for nearly two years, until the Financial Accounting Standards Board finally made it official. But Coca-Cola's decision had kicked over the domino in a chain of events.

Buffett's momentum as an influential statesman during this period was gathering speed. Although the estate tax was still scheduled to be repealed, he found another target in the accountants who had facilitated the accounting frauds of the past few years. If the auditors had not been sitting in the laps of the CEOs, wagging their tails, he felt, then managements would not have been allowed to loot the shareholders' pockets, transferring vast sums into their own pockets.

Buffett appeared at an SEC roundtable on financial disclosure and oversight, saying that, instead of lapdogs, shareholders needed guard dogs, and directors who served on audit committees and oversaw the auditors must be "Dobermans" who "hold the auditors' feet to the fire."[26]

He said he had a short set of questions for the audit committee at Berkshire Hathaway:

—If the auditor had prepared the financial statements herself (as opposed to their being prepared by the company's management), would they have been prepared the same way?

—If the auditor were an investor, could he understand how the company had performed financially from the way the financial statements were presented and described?

—If the auditor were in charge, would the company follow the same internal audit procedures?

—Did the auditor know about anything the company had done to change the timing of when sales or costs were reported to investors?

"If auditors are put on the spot," Buffett said, *"they will do their duty. If they are not put on the spot... well, we have seen the results of that."*[27]

These simple questions were so obvious, so clearly defining of right and wrong, so self-evidently useful in sorting out the truth and preventing fraud, that at least one or two other companies with directors who had common sense and were concerned about their exposure to liability from lawsuits actually copied Buffett and began to use them.

As Buffett swung his saber with ruthless accuracy, and accountants cowered and compensation committees ducked and muttered about why he publicized their bonus-pimping instead of just shutting up, and as would-be tax-cutters tried to find even nastier terms than the ultimate pejorative, "populist," to throw at him, so encouraged was Buffett by all this newfound authority that in the spring of 2002 he outdid himself and endorsed...a mattress. He let himself be photographed lounging on the "Warren," part of the "Berkshire Collection," sold by the Omaha Bedding Co., as seen on posters of "Buffett and His Bed." Now when he went down to the Nebraska Furniture Mart during the shareholder-meeting weekend, he could lie on his own bed while selling his own mattresses. *"I finally landed the only job I really wanted in life—a mattress tester,"* he said.[28]

The Sage of Omaha, at whom plutocrats railed and tax-cutters shook their fists, before whom accountants quivered and stock-option abusers fled, whom autograph-seekers followed and television lights illuminated, was at heart nothing more than a starstruck little kid, endearingly clueless in many ways about his place in the pantheon. He got excited over and over by fan letters from Z-list celebrities. Every time somebody wrote him to say he was their hero, it was like the first time. When porn star Asia Carrera called him her hero on her Web site, he was thrilled. He was thrilled to be anybody's hero, but being called a hero by a porn star who was a Mensa member had real cachet. His favorite letters were from college students, but when prisoners wrote and said he was their hero, he was proud that his reputation extended to convicts who were trying to turn around their lives. He would much rather be idolized by porn stars and college students and prisoners than by a bunch of rich businessmen.

All this basking in the limelight meant that Debbie Bosanek and Deb Ray had to guard the phone and the door with dogged vigilance. Once, an overexcited woman who flew from Japan to get his autograph arrived in the office. She was so overcome by Buffett's presence that she prostrated herself to "worship" him and had a sort of conniption on the floor. The secretaries hustled her out.

She wrote later that her doctor had given her tranquilizers, and she hoped to be allowed in Buffett's presence again. She sent photographs of herself and wrote letters.

"I *like* being worshipped," Buffett said in a plaintive tone. Nevertheless, the secretaries had their way and the woman wasn't invited back.[29]

57

Oracle

Omaha · April–August 2003

Buffett seemed to thrive like a trumpet vine as he grew larger than life. Yet he remained brilliant at balancing his priorities. As requests for his time grew, his view that commitments are sacred and his natural inclination to conserve energy saved him from succumbing to the flattery of being in demand. If he added something to his schedule, he discarded something else. He never rushed. His friends could pick up the phone and call him whenever they liked. He kept his phone calls warmhearted and short. When he was ready to stop talking, the conversation simply died. The kind of friends he had didn't abuse the privilege. While he had many fond acquaintances, he added true friends only at intervals of years.

Susie added new "friends" at intervals of days or weeks. Kathleen Cole handled a gift list that had grown to literally a thousand people. Susie called herself a "geriatric gypsy" who lived in the sky. She traveled for months on end—visiting grandchildren, caring for the sick and dying, vacationing, traveling on foundation business, seeing Warren and the family.

Not only was Susie a woman who couldn't say no; she was a woman who couldn't be reached. Susie was such a nomad, she was so helpless to limit her attention to anyone, and the number of people who felt they had claim to her time had grown so astoundingly, that by now even her close friends were allowed to contact her only through Kathleen.

Some who loved her grew concerned, although they rarely saw her to say so. "No one can have three or four hundred genuine friendships," argued one. She seemed to run faster all the time. "All this chasing, like chasing your tail," was another friend's reaction. "You can't have friends if you're not around." But "if you're ill," Susie said, "I'll have plenty of time for you." Some felt that her compulsion to serve and please had replaced living life in a straight line toward goals of her own. "She never spoke her own truth," said one. "Her life got heavier and heavier," someone else said. "Stop!" another wanted to tell her. "Get some perspective and nurture yourself." But "it was as if she couldn't slow down, because if she did, something would happen."

Yet many people called her a saint, an angel, and even compared her to Mother Teresa. She gave so much of herself to so many that she seemed fragile now. But isn't that the nature of a saint, mused one friend, to give of herself until nothing was left? Isn't that exactly what Mother Teresa did?[1]

Warren wanted to spend time with Susie so badly that he agreed to go to Africa in the spring of 2007 to celebrate her seventieth birthday. Howie had been planning this trip for eighteen months. "It would have been the eighth wonder of the world to see my father in Africa," he says.[2] The Buffetts would be leaving for Africa a few weeks after their annual trip to New York, which always followed the annual shareholder meeting.

On April 1, 2003, as the shareholder meeting drew near, Berkshire announced the acquisition of a mobile-home manufacturer, Clayton Homes. This deal was like many others Berkshire was making at the time—a natural continuation of buying discount assets in the post-Enron slump.

The Clayton deal had come about because years of low interest rates had given lenders piggy banks full of cheap money, and that had turned them into pigs.[3] Banks were quick to train consumers that low interest rates meant they could buy more stuff for less cash outlay now. Those with equity in houses learned it could be used as a checking account. But whether it was credit cards, houses, or mobile homes, the lenders, in search of growth, increasingly turned to people who were the least able to repay—but wanted to participate in the American dream anyway.[4] In the case of mobile homes, the banks lent money to the manufacturers, who used it to lend money to the buyers. Historically, this process had worked, because if the mobile-home maker made bad loans, it faced the discipline of not getting paid back.

But then the mobile-home makers began to sell their loans, handing off the risk of not getting paid back. That was now somebody else's problem. The "somebody else" who had assumed the problem was an investor. In a process known as "securitization," for some years, Wall Street had neatly packaged loans like these and sold them to investors through a "collateralized debt obligation," or CDO—debt backed by the mortgages. They combined thousands of mortgage loans from all over the U.S. and sliced them into strips called "tranches." The top-tier tranches got first dibs on all the cash flow from a pool of mortgages. The next tranches had second dibs, and so forth down the line.

These tranches paid a rating agency to assign the top AAA rating to the first-dibs tranches, AA ratings to the second-dibs tranches, and so on. The banks sold off the tranches to investors.

As lending standards declined, the quality of the CDOs—even AAA CDOs—got sludgier.[5]

Yet, investing in AAA CDOs now appeared to contain no risk. "When money is free," wrote Charles Morris later, "and lending is costless and riskless, the rational lender will keep on lending until there is no one left to lend to."[6]

If it was pointed out that risk did not disappear, those who participated in the market would explain with a sigh that derivatives "spread" the risk to the far corners of the globe, where it would be absorbed by so many people that it could never hurt anyone.

In his 2002 shareholder letter, Buffett called derivatives "toxic," and said they were "time bombs." At the shareholder meeting that year, Charlie Munger described the accounting incentives to exaggerate profits on derivatives, and concluded, "To say derivative accounting in America is a sewer is an insult to sewage." In his 2003 letter, Buffett wrote of derivatives as "financial weapons of mass destruction."[7] While many people appeared to be participating in a market, in fact a handful of large financial institutions would always tend to dominate it using their leverage. They would also have other assets that seemed uncorrelated with these derivatives but which would actually move in tandem with the derivatives in a collapsing market.

General Re had a derivatives dealer, General Re Securities, which Buffett had shut down, either selling its positions or letting them run off in 2002. He had already turned Gen Re Securities into the cautionary tale of derivatives—writing at length to the shareholders about the expensive and problematic cost of shutting it down. General Re had made Buffett so angry by losing almost $8 billion by now from insurance underwriting that he could barely talk about it. The Scarlet Letter remained posted on the Berkshire Web site, though Ron Ferguson had retired, replaced by Joe Brandon and his number two, Tad Montross. General Re's competitors gleefully told clients that Buffett was going to sell the company or shut it down. Given the example of Salomon, these predictions were not spun from gossamer.

It was going to take billions in profits before General Re groveled its way back into Buffett's good graces. Its derivatives business would have little to do with that, either way. The same was not true for the global economy. By a "low but not insignificant probability," Buffett said, sooner or later—he didn't know when—"derivatives could lead to a major problem." Munger was more blunt. "I'll be amazed," he said, "if we don't have some kind of significant blowup in the next five to ten years." Derivatives were lightly regulated and subject to minimal disclosure. Since the early 1980s, "deregulation" had turned the markets into the financial equivalent of a rugby scrum. The theory was that the market's forces were self-policing. (And yet, the Fed did seem to intervene at times when trouble cropped up.)

By "problem" and "blowup," Buffett and Munger meant that a bubble was brewing in this witch's cauldron of easy credit, lax regulation, and big paydays for the banks and their accomplices. They meant an unsnarlable traffic jam of claims from derivatives leading to financial-institution failures. Large losses at financial institutions could lead to a credit seizure—a global "run on the bank." In a credit seizure, lenders become afraid to make even reasonable loans, and the resulting lack of financing sends the economy spiraling downward. Credit seizures had in the past tipped economies into depressions. But "that's not a prediction, it's a warning," said Buffett. They were giving a "mild wake-up call."

Buffett's "financial weapons of mass destruction" remark was quoted everywhere, often paired with a question about whether he was overreacting.[8]

Even as early as 2002, however, the beginnings of mass destruction could be seen in the mobile-home industry. Stung by bad loans, lenders were cutting off funding or raising interest rates to prohibitive levels.

Buffett began to capitalize on this, first with smaller investments, then with a deal to buy Clayton Homes, which was the class act of the troubled manufactured-housing industry. Even though it was fundamentally sound, its lenders were behaving, as Buffett said, like Mark Twain's cat, who, having once sat on a hot stove, wouldn't sit on a cold one. Buffett felt that Clayton's problem was mainly that its financing was drying up. Clayton stock had fallen with the rest of the industry to as low as $9. The Claytons, like Salomon during its crisis, were starting to run out of funding sources. They were motivated to sell. Buffett called the family in Knoxville and spoke to Jim Clayton's son, Kevin.[9]

Kevin Clayton: "We might entertain an offer in the twenty-dollar range."

Buffett: "Well, it's not likely that we could ever come up with a number that would repay the sweat and time and energy that you and your father have built into this wonderful organization."

Clayton: "Our financing is getting tight. How about if you just lend to us?"

Buffett: "That doesn't work well for Berkshire Hathaway. Why don't you just throw together whatever you have lying around that tells about your company and send it to me someday whenever you have a chance?"

This classic Buffett maneuver, Casting the Line, resulted in the arrival of a massive Federal Express package the next day. The fish had snapped at the bait.

Wall Street valued Clayton at more than all of its competitors combined, and its reputation was deserved: Most of the other mobile-home manufacturers were closing retail stores and losing money. Like most cult stocks, it had a founder with a strong, charismatic personality. Jim Clayton, the company's guitar-picking chairman—a sharecropper's son, who had started the business by refurbishing and selling a single mobile home—thought of his shareholder meetings as "mini-festivals" and had once strolled up the aisle from the rear of the room toward the stage singing "Take Me Home, Country Roads." He delegated the negotiating to Kevin. Kevin, of course, had never heard of Buffetting.

Buffett: "$12.50 bid."

Clayton: "You know, Warren, the board might entertain something in the high teens, more like $17 or $18 a share."

Buffett: "$12.50 bid."

Kevin Clayton got off the phone and went and talked to the board. Even though the stock had recently traded around nine bucks, it was a hard nut to swallow, that the company was worth only $12.50.

Clayton: "The board would consider $15."

Buffett: "$12.50 bid." Although not part of the official record, by this point he had almost certainly applied his other classic maneuver, the Circular Saw, slicing the floor out from under the Claytons by stressing—in a sympathetic way—how weak and vulnerable they were with their funding sources drying up.

The Claytons and their board went through some further processes.

Clayton: "We'd like $13.50."

Buffett: "$12.50 bid."

More discussion.

Clayton: "Okay, we'll take $12.50, on the condition that we get Berkshire stock."

Buffett: "I'm sorry, that's not possible. By the way, I don't participate in auctions. If you want to sell to me, you can't shop this bid against me to any other buyer. You have to sign an exclusive that you won't entertain any other offers."

The Claytons, who perhaps understood the direction that their industry was headed better than most experts did at the time, capitulated.[10]

After Buffetting the Claytons, Warren flew out to Tennessee to meet them, tour the plants, and visit with local Knoxville dignitaries. He had asked Jim Clayton to "pick and sing" with him, and they had rehearsed a couple of songs over the phone, but when the time came, "He forgot all about my guitar on the stand beside him," wrote Clayton later. "Give our new friend Warren a micro-phone and he forgets all about time."[11] Not used to being upstaged, Clayton at least had the consolation of being the guy who brought the famous Warren Buffett to Knoxville.

Yet while the local folks were mostly pleased with the deal, investors in Clayton were not. Buffett's aura worked against him for the first time. Many of the investors knew about Buffetting, even if the Claytons didn't, and they were in no mood to be Buffetted themselves.

Clayton's large investors thought Buffett was buying at the "bottom of the cycle" for mobile homes and had opportunely timed the deal to catch a bounce. At its peak in 1998, the manufactured-housing industry, using aggres-sive lending tactics, had shipped 373,000 homes a year. The outlook for 2003 was a measly 130,000. But surely it would turn. Buffett's history as a savvy trader convinced them that he must have bottom-ticked the price and that they would be suckers if they sold the company now.

That was not what Buffett saw, however. He saw that the mobile-home mar-ket had backed itself into a corner by using easy financing terms to make a large percentage of its sales to people who could not afford to buy a home. Therefore the number of homes sold by the industry was not going to bounce.

But the dissidents were stewing, talking on the phone far away from Omaha.

Unperturbed by shareholder outrage, Buffett reveled in the thought of his future role as a mobile-home impresario. He kind of liked the trailer-park aspect of the thing. And buying a company from a sharecropper's son appealed to the man who ate Dilly Bars at Dairy Queen, still lusted over model-train cat-alogs, and got a huge kick out of having his picture taken with the Fruit of the Loom guys. The P. T. Barnum in him was already beginning to stir. He could picture it so vividly—a giant mobile home installed in the exhibition space down in the basement of Omaha's new Qwest Convention Center at the 2004 shareholder meeting, next to the See's Candies shop maybe. The exhibition space kept adding more vendors and more merchandise for sale every year. The thought of a whole house, right there in the middle of his shareholder meeting, with a lawn even, and shareholders lined up to get into the house, gaping in awe, delighted him. How many mobile homes could you sell at a shareholder meeting? he wondered. None of the guys at Sun Valley ever sold a mobile home at their shareholder meetings.

By the end of the month shareholders jammed every flight into Omaha's airport and filled every hotel room in town for the 2003 shareholders' meeting, to see the man whom popular magazines had been proclaiming the "Comeback Crusader" and "The Oracle of Everything." And there was some surprising news too. The Hong Kong Stock Exchange had disclosed that Berkshire had bought a stake in PetroChina, the giant, mostly state-owned Chinese oil company. It was Buffett's first publicly acknowledged foreign investment in many years.[12] He was notoriously cautious about investing outside the U.S. and had not owned a significant position in a foreign stock since Guinness PLC in 1993.[13]

Reached by reporters hungry for an explanation, Buffett said he knew nothing much about China and had bought it for the oil that was denominated in RMB, the Chinese currency. He was pessimistic about the dollar and optimistic about oil. Buffett had written an article for *Fortune*, "Why I'm Down on the Dollar,"[14] in which he explained his belief that the dollar would decline in value. The reason was something called the trade deficit: Americans were buying more from other countries than they were selling, and at a fast-accelerating rate. They were paying for the difference through borrowing; foreigners were buying Treasury bonds, an I.O.U. from the U.S. government. In short order, the country's "net worth," he said, "is being transferred abroad at an alarming rate."

To hedge the risk of the falling dollar for Berkshire, he had studied Chinese stocks because of China's burgeoning economic power. He had found PetroChina, and gotten comfortable enough to buy it. Although he was able to purchase only $488 million, he said he wished he could have bought more. His endorsement of PetroChina sent investors over the moon. Warren Buffett had bought a foreign stock! PetroChina soared. And so did attendance at the BRK shareholders meeting.

That year, 15,000 people came to Omaha's Woodstock for Capitalists. Buffett's $36 billion fortune was once again exceeded only by Bill Gates's. He had bounced back, almost to the top of the heap.

"What is the ideal business?" a shareholder asked when the questions began. *"The ideal business is one that earns very high returns on capital and that keeps using lots of capital at those high returns. That becomes a compounding machine,"* Buffett said. *"So if you had your choice, if you could put a hundred million dollars into a business that earns twenty percent on that capital—twenty million—ideally, it would be able to earn twenty percent on a hundred twenty million the following year and on a hundred forty-four million the following year and so on. You could keep redeploying capital at [those] same returns over time. But there are very, very, very few businesses like that... we can move that money around from those businesses to buy more businesses."*[15] This was about as clear a lesson on business and investing as he would ever give. It explained why Berkshire was structured as it was. It explained why he was always looking for new businesses to buy, and what he was planning to do with Clayton Homes. He expected to invest part of Berkshire's extra capital in Clayton so that it could survive, take market share away from its bankrupt competitors, and buy and service their portfolios of loans.[16]

On Monday morning at the Berkshire board meeting, Buffett held a little seminar, explaining to the board the things he most wanted to teach them about this year, which consisted of the risk that the dollar would decline against foreign currencies and the problems involved in the financing of mobile homes.

Tom Murphy and Don Keough had just been voted in as directors, joining Charlie Munger, Ron Olson, Walter Scott Jr., Howie, Big Susie, and Kim Chace, the lone representative of the old Hathaway textile family. There had been some grumbling about these appointments, with shareholders making noises about cronyism, and lack of balance and diversity. But the idea of a board of directors overseeing Warren Buffett was ludicrous. A board made up of Barbie dolls would do just as well. When the Berkshire board met, it was to listen to Buffett teach, just as every occasion—from a party to a luncheon to a sing-along with Jim Clayton—turned into an opportunity for Buffett to figuratively stand at the blackboard, fingers dusty with chalk.

The reason shareholders cared about Berkshire corporate governance was not oversight, however, but the question of who would succeed Buffett, who was now almost seventy-three. He had always said there was a "name in an envelope" crowning his successor. But he would not acquiesce to the pressure to reveal the name, because that would tie his hands to one person, and events could change. It would also effectively begin the transition, and he certainly wasn't ready for that.

There was, of course, a guessing game about who this person could possibly be. Most of the managers of the various companies Buffett bought seemed unlikely candidates. Buffett liked managers like Mrs. B—people who shunned the spotlight, who worked as tirelessly as a human anthill—but these people did not manage capital. Where was the capital allocator who could run this thing? The right person had to be willing to sit behind a desk reading financial reports all day long, yet excel at dealing with people in order to retain a bunch of managers who wished they were still working for Warren Buffett.

"I have this complicated procedure I go through every morning," Buffett said, *"which is to look in the mirror and decide what I'm going to do. And I feel at that point, everybody's had their say."*[17] The next CEO would have to be a superb leader—and yet oversized egos need not apply for the job.

As the board meeting ended on Monday, the town emptied of shareholders, and the Buffett family headed to New York for their annual trip. Every year they traditionally attended a dinner with the East Coast members of the Buffett Group, held at Sandy and Ruth Gottesman's house, where Susie would pile into Warren's lap and run her fingers through his hair, and Warren would gaze enraptured at his wife. But this year it seemed obvious that Susie wasn't feeling well. At lunch one day, dressed beautifully in a light wool skirt suit with a wrap-around shawl, she ate only a tiny piece of chicken and some carrots with a glass of milk. She said she was fine but wasn't that convincing.

Within two weeks, shortly before they were to have left for the trip to Africa, Susie was admitted to the hospital with another bowel obstruction. There, the doctors found that she was anemic and had an esophageal ulcer related to her reflux. The Africa trip had to be postponed by a year. Even Warren was dismayed, because he knew how much the trip meant to Susie. But, asked if he was worried, he said, "Oh, no, it would bother Susie if she thought I was worrying about her. She wants to worry about me, not the other way around. She's a lot like Astrid in that sense. I'm not a worrier in general, y'know."

It turned out to be a good thing that Buffett was around that June. As the meeting at which the Clayton shareholders would vote on the merger approached, opposition to the deal swelled like a blister chafed by shareholders' resistance to the price—even to the very idea of selling to Berkshire. Rumors started that another bidder would come in.[18] Some of the shareholders were convinced that the Claytons had sold out to Buffett too cheap in order to keep their jobs and benefit themselves. The potential conflict of interest when the management of a public company wanted to sell the company to Berkshire was about to set off a war.

William Gray of Orbis Investment Management filed a petition with the SEC and a lawsuit with the Chancery Court in Delaware, where Clayton was incorporated; his argument was that the Claytons were heisting the company on behalf of Buffett.[19] After all, said one investor, "if Buffett bids for something, it must by definition be undervalued."[20]

Buffett's reputation, which had been an asset for so many years, had begun to work against him in certain other ways as well. He was such a magnet for publicity that anyone who wanted publicity for themselves or their cause could hijack his shareholder meeting or misappropriate his fame to get it. And so it happened that just before the shareholder meeting and around the time that Berkshire had announced the Clayton deal, Doris Christopher, CEO of The Pampered Chef, called him with just such a problem.

The Pampered Chef sold kitchenware at home parties through independent salespeople, mostly women. After Berkshire's purchase of the company, members of pro-life organizations had begun boycotting their parties. Berkshire's position was that it made no donations to pro-choice or reproductive rights groups, but only acted as a conduit for its shareholders, who through the charitable-contributions program as of now had the right to allocate $18 per share to the charity of their choice. Of the $197 million that had been donated to nonprofit groups of all types, the largest number of recipients were schools and churches, many of them Catholic, and most of the money went to causes not related to abortion. But a significant amount of money had gone to reproductive-rights organizations.[21] As it happened, Warren and Susie's personal share of the contributions—about $9 million in 2002—went to the Buffett Foundation, where it mostly funded reproductive rights. The argument that these contributions were not Berkshire's fell on deaf ears.[22] In 2002, Buffett had tried to square things with one of these groups by showing them how much money went to causes other than family planning. He got a reply from the president of Life Decisions International, saying, "Even if only $1.00 went to Planned Parenthood and $1 billion was donated to pro-life organizations, the former gift would still land Berkshire Hathaway on *The Boycott List*."[23] If the price of filling a parking meter was enough to attract a boycott, that was a pretty clear sign that Berkshire would find little room for compromise.

Doris Christopher had tried to mediate, telling her people that while she personally did not agree with Buffett, "it is not my place to ask or to judge" how he donated money.[24] Still, the boycott was affecting business and hurting the people involved. Christopher called Buffett to tell him the disruption to her business was getting worse.

"She didn't ask me, but I could tell she was hoping I would cancel the program. And you know, I'll do it. I thought we could tough it through, but we can't. It's hurting too many people that I don't want to hurt. It hurts Doris, and these are her flock. They're getting injured, and they're innocent. They're in her office, crying."

In late June, Buffett called Allen Greenberg, his former son-in-law and executive director of the Buffett Foundation, into his office and explained that he had talked to Charlie Munger. Rather than sell The Pampered Chef—one of the options—they had decided to shut down the charitable-contributions program. Greenberg was astounded. The year before, ninety-seven percent of shareholders had defeated a resolution by a pro-life shareholder to cancel the program. He pointed out that the contributions came from individuals, not the corporation. People could still donate on their own. Shutting down the program would accomplish nothing. But Buffett had made up his mind.

Greenberg returned to his office to draft a press release that went out to the news wires right before Sun Valley, over the Fourth of July weekend. The phone rang and rang for several days; the secretaries grew weary from ferrying messages up and down the hall. Life Decisions almost instantly put out its own release dropping Berkshire from its boycott list.

But Buffett's friends, no matter what their views on abortion, mostly reacted the same way: They were stunned. Some were angry. "I was surprised that he gave in on that," one said. "It didn't sound like him to back down so easily. Warren is such a principled person. Was it such a big deal that it had to be done?" asked another.[25]

Buffett said he was worried that such a stance might put The Pampered Chef consultants at risk. And although he didn't say it, not just their livelihoods but their physical welfare might be at stake. Buffett himself was a very big target. Taking a stand might make Berkshire Hathaway, as well as him, a symbol of pro-choice defiance, which was dangerous.[26] He shrank from confrontation anyway; this was something he simply could not do.

Afterward, he never showed any sign of rancor over the criticism or the pro-life victory laps. You can always tell them to go to hell tomorrow, as Murph said. There was never any need to do it today. Over the years he had saved himself a lot of trouble by following this advice. Almost as soon as he got past The Pampered Chef sidebar, he simply stopped thinking about it.

Alas, this did not solve the other problem caused by being the famous Warren Buffett. As the July 16 meeting to vote on the Clayton deal approached, the argument about the industry being at the "bottom of the cycle" gained currency. About thirteen percent of the investors, including respected money managers, said publicly that they would oppose the deal. Kevin Clayton trotted around the country, meeting with investors and pitching the merger, while Orbis and other naysayers worked the phones and the press.

Before Buffett bid, nobody had wanted Clayton. Now the former wallflower suddenly looked prettier to others. At midnight two days before the shareholder meeting, Cerberus Capital faxed a letter to Clayton suggesting that it was likely to make a higher bid. When it came to money, Buffett's attitude was defiant. "Okay, let them," he said. He was certain that Clayton without Berkshire wasn't worth more than $12.50 a share.

And, indeed, by the day of the meeting, it was still a toss-up whether the Claytons had enough votes to win approval of the sale. Jim Clayton faced an hour-long barrage of questions from agitated shareholders who had packed the auditorium where the meeting was held. Manufactured-housing stocks had been on a tear since the deal was announced, making the $12.50 price look even worse by comparison. Some shareholders wanted Cerberus to have a chance to make its offer.

Kevin Clayton left the meeting to call Buffett and ask him to agree to a delay on the vote, to allow Cerberus time to make a bid. Buffett said okay—if they would pay Berkshire $5 million for the delay. Clayton agreed to Buffett's price, reconvened the meeting, and adjourned it before taking a vote.[27]

By now the business press was covering the story as a David and Goliath set piece in which a gang of tiny Davids—the hedge funds that were fighting the deal—tried to defeat the greedy Claytons and the colossus Buffett. The press turned on Buffett. If he was buying something, the price must be too cheap.

The test of whether Buffett was stealing Clayton would be whether another bidder could be found. A week later, when seventy accountants, lawyers, and financial specialists from Cerberus Capital and three other firms descended on Knoxville, the clock began to tick toward the moment of truth. Clayton housed them in its fanciest mobile homes, adjoining the headquarters. Most of the team toured Clayton's plants and pored through rooms full of documents, focusing increasingly on the huge maw of the mortgage unit and the way it sucked down capital.[28]

After a week of digging, the Cerberus people returned to New York and faxed a sheet labeled "for discussion purposes only": "Clayton Recapitalization—Sources & Uses." The sheet was not an offer, but it contained a price: $14 a share. The Claytons' first impression was that Cerberus had beaten Buffett's offer by a healthy margin. However, a closer look revealed that this was a typical leveraged-buyout proposal, in which a company's assets are sold and it takes on debt in order to finance its own sale.[29] The investors would get $9 in cash per share and the recapitalized stock, which was nominally worth $5, but in fact worth much less because it would consist of a piece of a financial company that had piled additional debt on top of a shrunken capital base. Debt was the blood coursing through the veins of mobile-home makers; without it they were dead. Yet lenders were already shying away from the business. How could Clayton take on even more leverage? The Cerberus people had delivered a proposal that was the best that financial engineering could do, but it wasn't financially viable. The Claytons called Cerberus to discuss it and, without any rancor, they agreed to go their separate ways.

CNBC and the financial press were now portraying Buffett as a ruthless financier who had connived with the Claytons to adjourn the shareholder meeting illegally so Buffett could buy the company cheap. The manner in which Buffett's reputation had compounded to the point where it worked against him represented a dramatic reversal of the image of the wise, grandfatherly man who attracted legions of would-be coattail-riders. Large investors were no longer coattail-riding, waiting for his reputation to take prices higher; they wanted to use his reputation against him, to *block* him.

Buffett, however, had never really specialized in buying things that other people wanted at a price that was too cheap. Instead, he bought things that other people didn't want and thought that they were better off without. True, they had often been mistaken about that. Increasingly, since the *Buffalo Evening News,* Berkshire had bought properties that most people really *were* better off without. There weren't many companies that had the balance sheet to look a union in the eye and stare them down, that had the financial wherewithal to finance Clayton's debt, that could make decisions on deals like Long-Term Capital in an hour rather than a week. Berkshire could do all those things, and more. Buffett's real brilliance was not just to spot bargains (though he certainly had done plenty of that) but in having created, over many years, a company that made bargains out of fairly priced businesses.

At the end of July, the adjourned Clayton shareholder meeting finally reconvened. No other bidder had come forward, and Cerberus had declined to make a deal. In the end, 52.3 percent of the shareholders voted for the Berkshire deal, barely enough. Excluding the Claytons, the other shareholders had voted no by a margin of two to one. Buffett sat by the phone until he got the news.

But even then, the battle was not over. As soon as the merger was effective, opponents to the deal won an appeal at the Tennessee Court of Appeals, staying a lower-court ruling that allowed the deal to proceed. That prevented Berkshire from paying out the proceeds. The Court of Appeals gave the lower court a home-work assignment, asking it to rule on a number of issues within two weeks. Lawyers and company people were working almost around the clock.

Kevin Clayton and his wife had just had a baby; she was colicky from a pro-tein allergy. "It took twenty-seven formulas before we found one from London that would work," says Clayton. "Plus, I got shingles right in the middle of it, from stress. I called up my dad and said, 'Dad, this is rough.' And he said, 'Well, son, I had paralysis on the left side of my face when I was your age from stress.' Then I called up Warren, and he said, 'Well, Kevin, when I was younger, I lost a lot of my hair from stress.' I got no sympathy from either one of them."

On August 18, the lower court ordered a trial before a jury. Clayton immedi-ately appealed.

Clayton stock had ceased trading weeks ago, but Berkshire could not pay out the merger proceeds, since the deal marinated in the galley of the appellate court. Forty thousand shareholders awaited their money from Berkshire Hathaway. All $1.7 billion sat in the bank, earning interest for Berkshire.

Buffett got a fax from a couple who were being foreclosed out of their home. They needed the money from the Clayton stock to pay their mortgage. Pay what you can, he told the couple, and just explain the situation. Probably that will be enough to avoid foreclosure.

"It's the Perils of Pauline," he said.

After a series of legal maneuvers—including competing appeals to the Tennessee Supreme Court and the Delaware Chancery Court that did seem like a script from the Perils of Pauline—the legal battle ended with the merger intact.

But soon it became clear that sales of manufactured housing were not going to turn around.[30] Buffett had not bought just as the bounce was coming back. In fact, the downward spiral in manufactured housing had just begun. The price that had looked so cheap was barely reasonable. To help the deal's economics, Buffett had Kevin Clayton begin buying portfolios of distressed loans. It was going to take some mighty fine footwork to make the Clayton deal work out.

58

Buffetted

In September, Buffett was in a state of high excitement. *Fortune* magazine had named him the most powerful person in business. To many oohs and aahs, he had recently auctioned his battered wallet with a stock tip inside for $210,000 to benefit Girls Inc., a nonprofit cause of Susie Jr.'s. Next, he had auctioned himself off on eBay—or, rather, lunch for eight people with him—to benefit Glide Memorial Church in San Francisco, Susie's main cause.[1] According to the highest of fifty bidders on eBay, two hours of Buffett's time and a lunch for eight at Michael's were worth $250,100—that is, more than the stock tip in his wallet. Not only that, the two Susies were scheduled to speak on philanthropy at *Fortune*'s Most Powerful Women Summit the following week, at the beginning of October, before an audience made up of many of the most important women in America, including CEOs, entrepreneurs, and women of stature in many different fields. Buffett was elated at this coronation of his wife and daughter.

On the Friday afternoon before the conference began, Susie called Warren to tell him that she was going to be arriving a day late, because on Monday she was having a biopsy. She had just seen a specialist, five months after a periodontal appointment that had been delayed by her earlier bowel obstructions, esophageal ulcer, and anemia. The periodontist had found some pin-dot-size spots on the floor of her mouth and referred her to a specialist. Two months had passed as Susie tried to work around the specialist's schedule and her own complicated travel itinerary to arrange an appointment.

At the appointment, the doctor had felt around Susie's neck and found swollen lymph nodes on one side. She insisted that Susie see yet another specialist,

Dr. Brian Schmidt, the following Monday for a biopsy. Susie seemed uncon-
cerned about the biopsy. She wanted to delay it in order to avoid missing any
of the *Fortune* conference. Dr. Schmidt refused to postpone the procedure,
however.[2]

Buffett absorbed the news quietly, but was deeply shaken. A few hours after
Susie called, he carried on a long, rambling phone conversation with someone
else, filling the unrelenting minutes after he got home from work. Seconds
before his bridge game was due to begin, he said casually, but in a low, serious
voice, Oh, by the way, Susie's having a biopsy on Monday.

For what?! asked his shocked listener.

Some kind of thing in her mouth, he said. Well, I'll talk to you later. Then he
hung up.

Susie had the biopsy. She went and spoke at the conference, then flew east to
Decatur to visit Howie on the farm, see her grandkids, and ride on the combine
for the harvest before returning to San Francisco. With hindsight, Howie would
think to himself, Gee, she'd always talked about coming out for the harvest, but
she'd never done it before.[3] At the time, however, he noticed nothing unusual,
for she behaved as she always did.[4]

Warren kept his face glued to the computer screen, whether surfing the news
or playing bridge or helicopter. His rising anxiety showed in the usual manner;
he repeated the same questions and statements about a subject over and over
while denying—if asked—that he was concerned.

On Friday, Susie and Kathleen Cole went to learn the biopsy results. Susie
continued to seem oblivious to the potential seriousness of the situation. When
they met with the doctor, he told Susie that she had stage-three oral cancer. She
was stunned by the diagnosis. "It was like somebody shot a thunderbolt through
her," says Cole. She had apparently not even considered this as a possibility.[5]

Susie had her moment of tears. Then, characteristically, by the time they got
into the car she had pulled herself together and started chicken-souping everybody but herself. She called Warren. He did not say much. She called Susie Jr.
and told her, "Call your dad. He's going to be a mess." Then she went home and
talked to Warren again and to Susie Jr., Howie, and Peter.[6] By then, Susie Jr. had
already gone to the Internet to research.[7] She called her father and said, "Don't
read the oral cancer Web site."

An often painless but fast-growing cancer, oral cancer is more deadly than
melanoma, brain cancer, liver cancer, cervical cancer, or Hodgkin's disease.[8] It is
rare, and particularly dangerous because it's usually discovered only after the

primary tumor has spread. The fact that Susie's cancer was stage three meant that it had already spread to at least one lymph node but probably not to more distant sites.

Susie returned to her apartment overlooking the Golden Gate Bridge, every wall covered with a souvenir of a trip, a gift from a friend, or a piece of art that meant something to her. The woman who never let go of anything or anybody started telling people, "I've had a wonderful life. My kids are grown. I've lived to see my grandkids. I love my life, but I've done my job and I'm not really needed anymore."

"If it were up to me," she told Kathleen, "I would go off to a villa in Italy in privacy and just die." She was far more fearful of a protracted, painful death than of dying itself. But if she simply gave up, she would be abandoning people who depended on her. It was really Warren for whom she was going to have the surgery. However, she told Kathleen and others that she hadn't decided whether to do the follow-up radiation that was a standard part of the treatment to reduce the risk of a recurrence, which was high. For some reason, perhaps because she was in a state of shock, she didn't seem to grasp how important it was.[9]

Meanwhile, a stunned Warren paced through his routine, as he invariably did in a crisis. He escorted a very upset Astrid to the Nebraska football game in Lincoln. He flew out to San Francisco the following morning, where he learned that Susie needed major surgery within the next few weeks. She had a fifty percent chance of surviving for five years. The surgery was potentially disfiguring. Susie told Warren little more; she did say she was worried that she would frighten her own grandchildren. They decided she would fly to New York City for a second opinion, although this was largely a formality.

A few days later Susie flew into Omaha with the good news from the second opinion: There was no indication that the cancer had spread. While there she had another episode of crippling pain from her abdominal adhesions. This attack, coming less than five months after the obstruction that had prevented the Buffetts from traveling to Africa the previous May, was disturbing. She had to stay over at Susie Jr.'s, but for once heavy doses of painkillers enabled her to avoid hospitalization, which had always been required before.

Haggard and pasty-faced, Buffett dragged himself to the office, then left in the middle of the week for a Coca-Cola board meeting in Atlanta. By the time he returned, Susie had begun to recover and went to visit Astrid. When she saw Susie, Astrid simply broke down in sobs, and, once again, it was Susie's turn to comfort someone else.

After the weekend, when Susie flew back to San Francisco, Buffett's mood turned dark again, his voice went gravelly, and he was clearly having trouble sleeping. The biennial Buffett Group meeting, which was being held a few days later, weighed on his mind. Susie's doctors didn't want her to travel to the meeting, which was taking place in San Diego. Thus, for the first time since 1969, Warren would be going alone.

Buffett was obviously preoccupied with thoughts of what it would be like to go to this meeting without Susie. For five days he was going to have to answer questions about her and accept sympathy. He would have to perform his role of master of ceremonies without breaking down or striking any false notes of excessive good cheer. Buffett had mastered the art of compartmentalizing to such a degree that these skills were second nature to him—but under the circumstances, it was still going to be a hell of a performance. Once he was back in his hotel room at the end of the evening, he would be alone in the dark with his thoughts and his dreams.

"*I dream a lot,*" he said the day before leaving for San Diego, and the dreams could be disturbing. "*I have a multiplex going on in there. It's a full-time occupation.*" That evening he ate with a visitor in his office, wanting to fill the time until Sharon took over to distract him with a bridge game, then conversation till all hours. At first he struggled through a brittle discussion about business and politics. Eventually, the conversation wound its way to what had been bubbling beneath the surface for days: Susie's surgery.

For the briefest fraction of a second, a look of surprise flickered across his face. Then his face began to crumple, and collapsed into his hands. His shoulders heaved and rocked and he slid forward in his chair, like a tower crumbling in an earthquake. Dry, desolate, heaving sobs, like silent screams, came gasping out of him. There wasn't any consolation for this.

Gradually the wracking sobs spent themselves. Then he began to talk about Susie. He cried quietly, off and on, for about two hours. He was afraid of what she was going to have to suffer through. She was stronger than he; his main concern was the pain she would face. He was even more worried that she might accept death as a natural thing and not fight it as he would. He was terrified of losing her. Assumptions that were part of the very core of his being had been upended. He had always assumed that he would never be alone because she would outlive him. He had always assumed that he could count on her wisdom and judgment to handle any life-and-death decisions that might have to be made. He had always assumed that she would run the foundation after he was gone. She would keep peace within the family if he was not there; she would see to it that Astrid was taken care of; she would resolve any conflicts, soothe any bad feelings. She would handle his funeral and shape the way in which everyone would remember him. Above all, he had been counting on Susie to be there for him at the end, to sit beside him and hold his hand and calm his terror and ease his suffering when death was approaching, just as she had done for so many others. For the first time he had to contemplate that it might not work out this way. But these thoughts were so unbearable that he could only glance at them before shutting them down. He was sure that her doctors would take care of her and that she would live. By the time he left the office for his bridge game, he was in a somber mood but calm and collected.

Buffett was described by friends as subdued but in control while he was in San Diego.[10] He flew from the meeting to San Francisco the day before Susie's surgery. He had been scheduled to attend a NetJets marketing event that day and had made up his mind to go, but Susie Jr., who recognized this as a form of denial, told him he must come to San Francisco instead. Reluctantly, therefore, he joined the family for dinner at Susie's apartment. Everyone behaved in character. Since Susie had no one to care for (but herself), she avoided discussing her feelings about the next day's surgery with the family and busied herself talking on the phone. Warren spent much of the evening playing helicopter, with his eyes leashed to the computer.

Early the next morning, Susie took her daughter into the bathroom and shut the door behind them. She didn't want Warren to hear what she had to say. "Listen," she said, "he is a wuss. *You* need to understand that if they get in there and there's more cancer, don't let them operate. I'm so afraid he's going to tell them to operate even if it's really widespread, because he won't want me to die."

By eight a.m. Susie was in surgery, and the family went to the main surgical lounge, where they awaited word, along with all the other people who were passing the time watching Jerry Springer on television while their loved ones were in the O.R. Warren pretended to read the newspaper. From time to time, he closed the paper, held it up before his face, reached a hand behind to wipe tears from his eyes, then opened it again.

Dr. Isley returned only forty-five minutes later. Although he had found cancer in two lymph nodes, it had not spread from there, which was good news. The surgery would remove only the lower floor of her mouth, the inside of her cheek, and about a third of her tongue. She did not need a bone graft. After Dr. Isley left, Warren began to ask, "Well, now, Sooz, was that what he said would take an hour and a half, or is he going to come back out again? Are you sure? Will they really know?" Each time, Susie Jr. reassured him that they already had the answer, and each time he would wait a few minutes and ask her again. "Well, how did they know so fast?" He kept saying, "I don't think this is good. Maybe he's going to come back out."

Sixteen hours later, Susie was in the intensive-care unit, breathing through a tracheotomy tube.

Warren returned to the hospital the next morning. Susie Jr. told her father, "You need to get really ready for this. It's a shocking thing to see." Warren steeled himself as he walked into Susie's room. He knew he could not allow her to see any spasm on his face that would reveal to Susie how ghastly she appeared. Making a huge effort of will, he managed to sit unflinching with her for a little while. Because Susie's tongue was swollen out of her mouth, a feeding tube had been threaded through her nose into her stomach. She coughed continually, clogging the trach tube, which had to be cleared frequently so that she could breathe.[11] Then Susie Jr. told him and her brothers that they could go home. There was nothing further they could do. After Warren left he says he *"spent two days just crying, basically."*

He went back to San Francisco for the following two weekends. Then, just before Susie was going to leave the hospital and go home, he flew down to Georgia and spoke to a group of students at Georgia Tech. He didn't talk about business much, but he invoked many of his familiar themes. He told them the fable of the genie, and he talked about philanthropy. He said the best investment they could make in life was in themselves. He told them about his hero Ben Graham and said to choose their heroes carefully, because heroes matter in your life. He told them to work for people they admired.

They asked him what had been his greatest success and greatest failure. He didn't tell them about his business mistakes of omission this time. Instead he said:

"Basically, when you get to my age, you'll really measure your success in life by how many of the people you want to have love you actually do love you.

"I know people who have a lot of money, and they get testimonial dinners and they get hospital wings named after them. But the truth is that nobody in the world loves them. If you get to my age in life and nobody thinks well of you, I don't care how big your bank account is, your life is a disaster.

"That's the ultimate test of how you have lived your life. The trouble with love is that you can't buy it. You can buy sex. You can buy testimonial dinners. You can buy

pamphlets that say how wonderful you are. But the only way to get love is to be lovable. It's very irritating if you have a lot of money. You'd like to think you could write a check: I'll buy a million dollars' worth of love. But it doesn't work that way. The more you give love away, the more you get."[12]

Warren continued visiting every weekend after Susie went home to her sunshine-filled apartment overlooking San Francisco Bay. The egg-yolk-yellow rugs were gone, lest their dust clog the trach tube. Chair elevators carried her up the four flights of stairs. The nurses used a rented suction-tracheotomy system. The doctors began to prepare Susie for the six-week course of radiation, which was intended to kill any remaining cancer cells. It would begin in December and continue through the holidays. The radiation, which she had never quite agreed to in the first place, was going to burn her throat. The doctors had told her to bulk up before the surgery because she could expect to lose around fifty pounds over the entire course of the surgery and radiation. That was a lot of weight, but one of the thoughts that had comforted her before the surgery was that she could afford to lose a good bit of it. Now, as the feeding tube came out, the nurses began to feed Susie six units of liquid meal replacement a day. It took her much of the day to get it down, because of the pain.

Under stress, Warren had gained a little weight. He felt that he needed to lose twenty pounds and had decided to diet alongside Susie's liquid meal regimen. "That can't be a lot of fun," he said, "so I won't have any fun either."

Buffett's manner of dieting was as eccentric and unhealthy as the rest of his eating habits. He decided to stick with his usual approach, which was to consume only a thousand calories a day and budget it however he liked. That meant he could spend the thousand calories on licorice, peanut brittle, hamburgers, or whatever else he wanted to eat so long as he didn't exceed the self-imposed limit. The easiest step was to cut back on all the Cherry Coke, replacing it with nothing and thereby dehydrating himself. The idea behind the thousand-calorie starvation regimen was to get the pain of dieting over with fast. He was impatient and cut off debate over the health merits of such a diet. At my height and age, he said, I reckon that I can eat about a million calories a year and maintain my weight. (The nice round, even number of a million calories pleased him.) I can spend those calories however I want. If I want to eat a bunch of hot-fudge sundaes in January and starve the rest of the year, I can do that.

It was completely rational (on the surface) yet totally ludicrous. But since he had never been either seriously overweight or seriously ill, it was pointless to argue with him. (He went on this crash diet every year right before the share-holder meeting; it is possible, however, that all that dehydration may have had nothing to do with his earlier kidney stone.) Regardless, Buffett had a way of winning arguments before they ever occurred.

When Warren was in town, Susie saw no other visitors, only her daughter, her nurses, and a couple of people like Kathleen who were caring for her day to day. Even Jeannie Lipsey Rosenblum and Warren's sister Bertie, who had bought apartments in the same building, were kept away all the time, the feeling being that even a soupçon of attention would be too draining for Susie.

As Warren traveled back and forth to San Francisco every week, he was learn-ing about things he had never known before—medication, radiation, and the ins and outs of dealing with doctors and nurses and hospital equipment. And he was also exploring a new emotional territory—facing Susie's fears as well as his own. When talking about this new world he had just entered, he measured out his words, keeping his feelings private, adjusting how much he shared according to how well he knew his audience. Sometimes he used as a distraction a favorite prop, Arnold Schwarzenegger, a fellow elephant friend whom he had recently endorsed as the Republican candidate in a recall election to unseat Gray Davis, the governor of California. *"My wife had an operation in San Francisco about six weeks ago, and I'll be out there a couple of days every week. (Pause) Well, you know, Arnold, sometimes people can't tell which one is which, when we're next to each other. When we're stripped down, nobody has a chance."*

When someone he knew better called, he struggled to talk about a subject that formerly he would have avoided at all costs.

"Oh, hi, Chuck. Yeah. Well, she's doing better in every respect than people have told us would be the case going in. She doesn't have any energy and it's—it's been an experience like she hasn't had before. But in terms of her mouth healing, in terms of swallowing—everything, it's all going fine. And the people are terrific. Not a lot of pain right now. I think it's psychological more than—I mean, she's not finding life any fun at all at the moment but.

"The annual meeting? Well, I would say this, now with Susie's condition the way it is, I think we're going to skip the music and just—there's no way she'll be singing in this May's meeting, so let's see what happens next year."

From time to time he still talked about Susie being able to sing again, even though that wasn't going to happen. And only with people with whom he was very close, such as his daughter, would he drop the occasional hint that he needed help.

"Hello? Hi. I feel fine. I'm getting two hours of sleep every night. Oh, great. Why don't you come down and swap cars with me? Oh yeah, there's a ham to pick up, incidentally too. It's here.... We will. Maybe tomorrow or something. Okay. Okay? Okay."

Two hours' sleep a night.

"If I'm thinking about something I'm not going to sleep. I slept two hours last night, actually, and I feel fine. It doesn't kill me not to sleep. Susie's going through this thing again about whether she wants the radiation.

"We'll get over it. Her inclination over this was going in a worse direction when I left San Francisco but it's still better than it was when I got there. So.

"The only good thing about Susie having the operation is that this is the first year, in thirty-odd years, that I won't go to Emerald Bay for Christmas. I'm not even sure my house is there anymore."

59

Winter

Susie was still resisting the idea of radiation. Warren's view was that it was a form of handicapping: If radiation improved your odds, why not do it? The surgery, he told her, was the hard part. The radiation wouldn't be nearly as hard. But the radiation oncologist had told Susie, if anyone tells you about their radiation and says it's not that bad, don't believe them. There will be a lot of pain. Susie had already had a lot of pain. She felt she had the right to refuse more pain.

"She's seen a lot of people die, seen people go through more than they needed to go through. We both want control over the end of life. She has no fear of death, but somehow she got the idea that by having radiation, she would lose control and that radiation would increase the chances of a terrible end. We went on for hours and hours, around and around; it's up to her to decide what to do."

To calm her anxiety, every night she went through a bedtime ritual centered around a song by the singer Bono, who had befriended Susie Jr. after meeting Warren at a NetJets event. Now Susie put on U2's *Rattle and Hum* DVD when she was going to bed and fell asleep to "All I Want Is You."

At the NetJets event, Bono had initiated his connection to the Buffetts when he told Warren that he just wanted fifteen minutes of his time.

"I knew nothing of Bono to speak of. So he asked me a few questions, and for some reason we hit it off. When I gave him an idea and he liked it, he'd say, 'That's a melody!' And at the end he said, 'I can't believe it. Four melodies in fifteen minutes.'. . . I love music. But actually U2's music doesn't blow me away. What interests me is that Bono splits the revenue of U2 among four people absolutely equally."

Buffett could at times be brutally rational about the way vast sums of money made a person more attractive, funny, and intelligent. Still, his wonderment had never quite ceased that celebrities of any rank sought him out. No matter how cool he tried to play it, he was flattered that no less a personage than Bono had deemed him smart. When Bono came out to Omaha during his Heartland of America tour, he contacted Buffett and through him met Susie Jr. Susie Jr. in turn was flattered and captivated by the singer's interest in her. Bono had a romantic hipster nobility that appealed to both her and her mother. U2's music spoke of a spiritual longing for love and peace, exactly the kind of thing both Susies would respond to.

Big Susie, however, had never met her daughter's idol. She seemed to feel that she had finished her own personal mission on earth. "Why can't I just lie in bed the rest of my life," she said, "and the grandchildren can come out, and it will be fine." Is she kidding? thought Susie Jr. "You have to get up!" she told her mother. "You can't just lie in bed the rest of your life! You'll do the radiation and you'll get better, and you'll be able to travel again." Big Susie looked surprised. "Do you really think so?" she asked.[1]

Finally Susie was persuaded to go through with the radiation. Some of her friends questioned whether she was once again doing something to please everybody else instead of making her own choices. Nevertheless, she had agreed to thirty-three treatments beginning in mid-December.

Buffett headed out to San Francisco for Christmas, which occurred during the first two weeks of Susie's radiation. Warren and Susie gave each of the kids another six hundred shares of Berkshire stock for their foundations—a complete surprise, which thrilled all of them.[2] With an eye to the future, knowing that they would one day have much larger sums of money to distribute, their parents had decided to give them this gift to train them in philanthropy. Within two years of Warren's or Susie's death, thirty, forty, fifty billion dollars or more—depending on Berkshire's stock price at the time—would sluice into the foundation, and the law required that shortly thereafter the foundation begin giving away five percent each year. But with only a couple of employees, the Buffett Foundation was woefully ill-equipped to ramp up fast enough to give away a billion dollars a year.[3] Warren had been giving this problem a lot of thought, and it occurred to him that one way Susie could choose to deal with it was to turn some of the Buffett Foundation money over to the Gates Foundation. The Bill and Melinda Gates Foundation had grown since its establishment in 2000 to a multibillion-dollar philanthropy. Gates said that 4.2 billion people in the world, most of the earth's population, made less than $2 a day. Yet each of their lives was worth as much as any American's. These people lived in the here and now, not in some generation far in the future.

"*Bill Gates is the most rational guy around in terms of his foundation. He and Melinda are saving more lives in terms of dollars spent than anybody else. They've worked enormously hard on it. He thinks extremely well. He reads thousands of pages a year on philanthropy and health care. You couldn't have two better people running things.*"

Warren was still assuming that Susie ultimately would be the one to make these decisions, however.

"*Susie gets all the money. And she is in total charge of everything. My will just gives it to her, and her will just gives it to me.*"

"*In the first year or two, while they were ramping up on other things, if they just matched what the Gateses did and gave them two billion instead of one billion a year, that'd be perfectly appropriate. Don't get proprietary about it. I'm perfectly willing to let other people do all the work at Berkshire. But they would hate that at the Buffett Foundation. It seems so lacking in imagination and innovativeness. Even though it's terribly logical.*"

"*The normal human institution reacts enormously against that. But that is not a crazy system. It's like doubling your position on a stock.*"

"*He's got people in place. And if we gave some money to him, the last half of the money would be used as intelligently as the first half. There would be very little falloff in utility of the last dollar versus the first dollar. Giving money to other foundations, it's just not what foundations like to do. But there's nothing wrong with copying good people.*"

Coattailing by giving some of the money to the Gates Foundation while the Buffett Foundation was ramping up to give away its tens of billions might be completely logical. What wasn't completely logical was for Warren to assume that Susie would be the one making these decisions, rather than himself or his daughter—and to operate under this scenario without a backup plan. Although maybe he was starting to have the embryo of a backup plan.

Susie was still not well enough to receive any new visitors. Neither of her sons had even seen their mother since the surgery. But Howie, his wife, Devon, and their son, Howie B., finally joined Warren in San Francisco for a couple of days. Howie, still a one-man chorus line of Rockettes when it came to energy, saw Susie "just a touch." But the family was still not allowing other people to visit.

Susie Jr. had instructed everyone around her mother to keep things upbeat. There were things that her mother was unaware of, that had to be kept from her, and which Susie Jr. monitored the fax machine to make sure her mother didn't see. Susie didn't know that Bill Ruane had called Warren to say that he had been diagnosed with lung cancer.

Ruane was doing chemo at Sloan-Kettering, where Susie had gotten her second opinion. Warren got tears in his eyes every time Ruane's name was mentioned. The combination of this and Susie was too much. He had some time ago abandoned the thousand-calorie-a-day diet.

"Susie's weight has been quite stable for the past two weeks. We keep a chart of it. I eat a chocolate sundae, she eats a little bit of the chocolate sundae. And since my diet is naturally fattening, it helps her. I'm gaining weight, and she's stayed stable. She's in no danger of becoming anorexic."

On New Year's Eve, Nancy Munger was throwing Charlie a big eightieth-birthday party. Buffett flew down to Los Angeles for the celebration. He desperately needed the distraction, though it obviously bothered him that he would be attending the party alone, just as it had bothered him to show up at the Buffett Group meeting alone.

He had ordered an oversize cardboard cutout of Benjamin Franklin for a stand-up routine satirizing Munger's fascination with Franklin. He put on a classic performance, which included his singing "What a Friend I Have in Charlie."

Munger closed the festivities with a speech. He began by giving advice to the audience, in the latest iteration of various speeches he had given elsewhere. Charlie's friends and relatives and members of the Buffett Group all had copies of these speeches, now collected into a book, *Poor Charlie's Almanack.*[4] Munger's favorite construct was to invoke Carl Jacobi: "Invert, always invert." Turn a situation or problem upside down. Look at it backward. What's in it for the other guy? What happens if all our plans go wrong? Where don't we want to go, and how do you get there? Instead of looking for success, make a list of how to fail instead—through sloth, envy, resentment, self-pity, entitlement, all the mental habits of self-defeat. Avoid these qualities and you will succeed. Tell me where I'm going to die, that is, so I don't go there.

Munger wandered off on a brief detour to praise his wife for her many wonderful qualities, then returned to giving advice to the audience about the models of life that led to success and happiness. He seemed convinced, however, that he (and Buffett) now lived on some elevated plane. He invoked his independence, and Buffett's, as reasons for their success, but then said it would probably be unwise for others—including his own children—to try to emulate the two of them.

Nancy Munger, who was standing next to Buffett, asked, "How do I get him to stop?"

Charlie started going into his windup. "In the end," he said, "I'm like old Valiant-for-Truth in *The Pilgrim's Progress,* who said, 'My sword I leave to him who can wear it.'" Good Lord, thought some of the Buffett Group members.

Eventually Nancy went out onto the stage and gently led Charlie away.

Buffett went straight back from Charlie's party to San Francisco to see Susie, who had just finished her twelfth treatment.

Susie was spending most of her time in bed. *"It's just amazing how little she is up. She's either asleep, or getting ready to go to sleep, or getting up from being asleep, I would say seventeen or so hours out of twenty-four. We make it a point, no matter what—we walk for six blocks or so every day. The rest of the time, I just hold her, basically."*

The man who had always been on the receiving end was now learning to give. Rather than being taken care of by his wife, he was taking care of her. Buffett, of course, had not become some other person. But by acting out his values—loyalty, stewardship—he seemed, in his own way, to have incorporated some of the lessons of Susie's life into his own.

60

Frozen Coke

Toward the end of her radiation, Susie's mouth was so burned and dry that some days she could not eat or drink. The doctors put her back on the feeding tube because her throat was choked with a thick, dry mucus. She spent most of the time sleeping. But every day, she and her daughter or Kathleen walked a few blocks on Sacramento Street. As spring stole over San Francisco, Susie stayed bundled in a coat, gloves, scarf, and earmuffs to stay warm.

She hated to be alone. "Can't you just sit on the couch and look at magazines while I'm awake?" she asked Susie Jr. Then she scribbled, "WHT," her father's initials, on a piece of paper, a wry reference to the family trait of becoming anxious when alone.

She was cared for by her nurses, Kathleen, her daughter, and John McCabe, her former tennis coach, who, after many years of looking after her once they had both moved to San Francisco, was well-schooled in acting in a one-hundred-percent supportive role. Anyone else, however, was likely to trigger her "giving" impulses and to drain her of energy.[1] On the weekends, when Warren came, he sat with Susie in the TV room watching old episodes of *Frasier,* or simply hung around in his bathrobe, reading the paper. Susie was comfortable with him there; he made her feel secure—but decades of her "giving" and his receiving didn't disappear overnight. Sometimes Susie was so sick from the radiation that even Warren had to leave. But he was doing his best to immerse himself in the day-to-day needs of his family in a way that he had never done before. To give his daughter a break from endless days in Susie's apartment, Warren would take her to Johnny Rockets for a burger. The rest of the time he spent with Sharon.

As Buffett grew more optimistic about Susie's recovery, the business events of the year 2004 began to consume him, in between the trips he made back and forth to San Francisco every weekend. He scribbled away at his letter to shareholders, e-mailing it back and forth to Carol Loomis. He also spent many hours serving as teacher and unpaid father confessor to corporate America. He had become the elder statesman of the business world. CEOs like Jeffrey Immelt of General Electric, Anne Mulcahy of Xerox, and Jamie Dimon of JP Morgan showed up in Omaha to pick his brain.[2] The Internet-search-firm Google was going public that summer, and its cofounders, Sergey Brin and Larry Page, stopped in to see him because they admired his shareholder letters. The previous fall, after her indictment for lying to the government in connection with allegations of insider trading—for which she was never charged—Martha Stewart and her CEO Sharon Patrick had come out to Omaha to visit him. Buffett bought Stewart and Patrick a steak dinner, but couldn't solve Stewart's legal problems.

The environment for prosecution of white-collar fraud was changing rapidly, partly because there was just so much white-collar fraud to prosecute these days. New York Attorney General Eliot Spitzer, who had launched a merciless attack on corruption in business and on Wall Street, now led the SEC and the Department of Justice in a three-legged race to see which agency could prosecute most zealously. Spitzer was diabolically inventive at using the new electronic tools of the Internet—especially e-mail—as evidence, at harnessing an accommodating press as a weapon, and at wielding an arcane New York statute, the Martin Act, which gave him virtually unlimited powers, checked only by his personal—and virtually nonexistent—sense of prosecutorial discretion.

With these tools, he had forced two prominent CEOs to resign—Buffett's business colleague Hank Greenberg, who was now the former CEO of AIG, and his son, Jeffrey Greenberg, the former CEO of insurance broker Marsh & McLennan. A pall of fear hung over corporate America; Spitzer was so successful at execution-by-media that the bitter joke had become that he was saving the government the cost of indictment and trial. Juries that formerly treated white-collar malefactors with deference were now routinely sending them to prison like any other criminal; under new mandatory sentencing guidelines, judges were imposing harsh sentences on them. Some of this mayhem was well-deserved. Greed, hubris, and lack of enforcement had given many people in business the impression that the rules did not apply to them. Just as stock options and the Internet bubble had engorged the senior echelons of business's wallets at an exponential speed, so had the backlash arrived in gargantuan proportions. Buffett—like most of corporate America—had not fully adjusted to this new environment; his view of proportion was shaped by the earlier era: defined by the careful prosecutorial calibrations of former SEC Enforcement Chief Stanley Sporkin and U.S. Attorney Otto Obermaier; by the travails of Salomon, when even Paul Mozer, who nearly brought down the whole financial system after Gutfreund failed to report his crime, had only served four months in prison. His viewpoint would eventually be revised, however, by the outcome of events that had occurred at Berkshire Hathaway itself.

Buffett usually arrived at the airport to pick up his guests personally. He took them on a nerve-racking ride to the office (if, that is, they were not too dazzled by him to notice), spent a couple of hours listening to their issues and throwing out ideas, then usually escorted them to Gorat's and treated them to a T-bone and hash-brown meal. He told them to be plainspoken with shareholders in annual reports, to pay employees in alignment with shareholders, not to run their business according to the whims of Wall Street analysts, to deal with problems forthrightly, not to engage in accounting shenanigans, and to choose good pension-plan advisers. Sometimes people asked how to manage their own money, but while he gave them some basic ideas, he didn't hand out stock tips.

To those who felt the life of a CEO was not what it used to be, Buffett talked about "the ninety-eighth floor" in terms a CEO could understand. People who were looking down from the top at everybody else had to keep things in perspective. So what if they got knocked down a few pegs or lost some of their money? Those who still had their family, their health, and a chance to do something useful for the world should try to count their blessings, not their curses.

"If you go from the first floor to the hundredth floor of a building and then go back to the ninety-eighth, you'll feel worse than if you've just gone from the first to the second, you know. But you've got to fight that feeling, because you're still on the ninety-eighth floor."

He considered himself on the hundredth floor most of the time. However, during the spring, 2004 was definitely shaping up to be a ninety-eighth-floor kind of year. He waited with impatience as Susie suffered through her radiation until the moment later in the spring when her doctors would perform an MRI to determine whether the treatment had knocked out the cancer cells. Business was also problematic on various fronts: Buffett felt that he had "struck out" when it came to bringing home the gingersnaps: new acquisitions and new stocks to buy. Berkshire had around $40 billion in cash or the equivalent, which was "not a happy position."[3]

Still, the challenge of finding new investments wasn't nearly as severe as bird-dogging the ones that Berkshire already had. Coca-Cola was again evolving into a nightmarish preoccupation. Since the death of Goizueta, quarter by quarter, its business had grown steadily worse. New evidence of accounting manipulation appeared; the stock had sunk below $50, from a high in the $80s.

Doug Daft had earned a reputation for volatile moods and byzantine politicking; a number of senior members of management had departed during his tenure.[4] His subtle tweaking of the four main Coke brands had produced unspectacular results.[5] Pepsi had pulled off a huge success with Gatorade after Coca-Cola—partly thanks to Buffett—failed to make a deal with Quaker Oats in 2000. Then, a whistle-blower declared that Coca-Cola rigged a marketing test for a fountain product called Frozen Coke to impress a longtime customer, Burger King. The whistle-blower had also accused Coke of accounting fraud, and the SEC, the FBI, and the U.S. Attorney's office started investigating. The company's stock price shrank to $43. Buffett had had enough of the "managed earnings" that underlay these problems, in which the Wall Street analysts' predictions of what a company would earn enticed managers to dig behind the sofa cushions in order to "make the numbers," thereby meeting or beating "consensus" expectations to please investors.

"I can't tell you how much I hate managed earnings in terms of what they do to people. The nature of managed earnings is that you start out small. It's like stealing five bucks from the cash register and promising yourself you'll pay it back. You never do. You end up the next time stealing ten bucks.... It snowballs. I gave these speeches after we discovered it. I told them, 'Now the monkey's off our back. We don't have to predict anything to the analysts. Let's just give the damn handout showing the results every year, and whatever we earn, we earn.'"[6]

Buffett wanted out of the game. If asked off the record what his worst business mistake was, he no longer listed *"sins of omission"*; instead, he said, *"Serving on boards."* He was weary most of all of the way it tied his hands. Coca-Cola had changed its policy of requiring directors to retire at age seventy-four to one that merely required directors at that age to submit a letter of resignation for the board to consider. Leaving the Coke board would have let him tap-dance off into the sunset. But for the savior of Salomon to snub a company in trouble would be like sticking a dagger in the stock. *"I wouldn't stay on the board, except*

I don't feel like leaving the other guys" to deal with the mess at Coca-Cola, Buffett said. His pro forma letter was, of course, rejected. This was seen externally as a power play to maintain the coziness of a board of cronies. Buffett had no idea what a plateful of misery he had just ordered.

As soon as the proxy statement was filed with Buffett's name listed for election as a director, Institutional Shareholder Services, a powerful organization that consulted on shareholder voting and voted proxies on behalf of institutional investors, told its clients to withhold their votes for him. ISS said that Buffett's independence as a member of the audit committee could be affected by the fact that Berkshire Hathaway companies like Dairy Queen and McLane bought $102 million of Coca-Cola products. After so many scandals, accusations of conflicts of interest and questions of governance were taken with a new seriousness. The cronyism of Coca-Cola's board could have been attacked on other grounds, but ISS lacked any sense of proportion in applying its principles regarding conflict of interest. Its lack of proportion was in keeping with the lack of proportion shown by most who were attacking business at the time (which, to be fair, some in the business world had more than earned)—but nonetheless, disproportionate it was. Since Berkshire's purchases of Coke for its businesses were trivial when compared to Berkshire's ownership stake in Coke, which was huge, how could Buffett's behavior as a member of the audit committee or the board of Coca-Cola be said to be compromised?[7]

The rules of ISS, however, were based on a checklist, with no leeway whatsoever for common sense. CalPERS, the powerful California Public Employees' Retirement System, also decided to withhold support for half of Coke's directors, among them Buffett, in his case because the audit committee on which he sat had approved the auditors to do nonaudit work.[8] While CalPERS was taking a principled stance on auditors, this recommendation was sort of like putting out the candles on a birthday cake with a fire extinguisher.

Buffett made a quasi-joke of it in public, saying that he was paying CalPERS and ISS to rally votes against him as an excuse to get off the board. But in fact he was mad, especially at ISS.

"*If I were a wino off the street, those amounts they're talking about might be significant. But I own eight percent of Coca-Cola. We've got so many more dollars in Coke than anything else. How would I possibly favor Dairy Queen's interests over Coke's when I own so much more of Coke's stock?*"

Herbert Allen sent an emotional letter to the *Wall Street Journal,* citing the Salem witch trials, when "reasonably stupid people accused reasonably smart and gifted people of being witches and casting spells. Then they burned them....Up until the geniuses at ISS said it, nobody knew that Warren was really a witch."[9]

When corporate board members were surveyed, they unanimously thought Buffett was their dream director. "We would come and wash Buffett's car to have him on our board.... There's not a person in the world who wouldn't take him on their board.... CalPERS's action shows the stupidity of corporate governance run amok ... analogous to an NFL coach preferring an unknown quarterback from a Division II college instead of a Super Bowl quarterback...."[10] The *Financial Times* referred to ISS as the Darth Vader of corporate governance, citing a position that "smacked of dogma."[11] With inkwells of backlash spilling all over them, CalPERS and ISS began to look foolish, "somewhere between hideous and self-promoting populists," as one retired CEO put it on the survey. "How could you bring yourself to a position where you would vote against him as a director and think that was a pro-shareholder thing to do? What a ridiculous piece of advice."[12]

Throwing Buffett off the board to improve the audit committee was like firing your doctor because you were still sick. What Coca-Cola needed was more Buffett, not less. But for the Coke board to rail against ISS also lacked a certain credibility and seemliness. Now that Coke's stock was barbecue, its board members could convincingly summon no more than low to middling dudgeon. The accusations of a "crony board" neared the mark. Although it had factions, one faction ruled, or rather misruled; Buffett admitted that he should have done more to try to steer things right at Coke. Indeed, if Coca-Cola had been run by him, assisted only by a six-pack of Cherry Coke, perhaps many of its woes could have been avoided.

Instead, a brew of important people—several of them titanic personalities, and all of them accustomed to being in charge—could not sit back and simply allow themselves to be led by a weak CEO; they had spun into a vortex. That Daft had improved Coca-Cola's profits, sales, and cash flows and had mended poisonous relations with the bottlers was not enough to turn things around for him. In February, Daft suddenly told the board he was resigning.

Daft was unpopular in many quarters, but his announcement set off dismay at the prospect of more bad publicity for Coca-Cola. This time the next guy in line could not be simply plugged into the job. Some board members viewed that as the chance to finally do the job right. In a move that had instantly attracted controversy, however, concurrent with the announcement of Daft's resignation, seventy-seven-year-old Don Keough had joined the board; Keough, who had been sometimes referred to as the "shadow" CEO, became chairman of the search committee. He and Buffett now spent hours on the phone trying to find a leader for Coca-Cola.

The search for a fourth CEO in eight years quickly turned into a spectacle. The board looked at Coca-Cola's president, Steve Heyer, once considered a shoo-in, but the board members split over him, and once outside candidates were proposed, his chances began to fade. Various celebrity CEOs considered then turned down the job. Each rejection fed the media another bit of Schadenfreudenfodder.

Buffett flew to the April 20 board meeting in Wilmington, Delaware, the evening before the Coca-Cola shareholder meeting. The next morning, as he was getting dressed before heading down to the meeting, he reflected on the coming day's events. The Teamsters would already be clogging the street in front of the hotel with their blue tractor-trailer truck parked among the students waving signs that said "Coca-Cola Destroys Lives, Livelihoods, and Communities" and "Killer Cola, Toxic Cola, Racist Cola." He couldn't see from the window, however, whether the Teamsters had brought their twelve-foot-high inflatable rat. The Coke shareholder meeting was becoming a rite of brand-building within the activist community.

Then the phone in his hotel room rang. He picked it up and found the last person he was expecting on the other end of the line—Jesse Jackson. Jackson merely said that he wanted to express his admiration for Buffett. They talked for a minute or two of things of no consequence, and hung up. That's odd, thought Buffett. In fact, it was the first sign that this was going to be the Coca-Cola shareholder meeting to end all shareholder meetings.

Downstairs, protesters in the lobby outnumbered the shareholders. The glassblowers' union handed out bumper stickers to protest the company's purchases of bottles from Mexico.[13] Protesters handed out leaflets accusing Coca-Cola of conspiring with paramilitary groups in Colombia to assassinate labor leaders. Buffett quick-stepped across the lobby to the ballroom, where he was recognized and let inside, along with the rest of the directors. He sat down in the front row. The other attendees picked up credentials, then passed through security, their packages scanned by metal detectors as they surrendered cell phones, cameras, recorders. Coca-Cola put little brochures around the lobby highlighting its community projects and offered a cooler of Coke and Dasani water for people to grab on their way to the stiff-backed shoulder-to-shoulder seats into which the shareholders wedged themselves for the two-hour journey through the Kafka novel that a modern annual meeting had become.

Doug Daft made some brief introductory remarks from the podium between the two long, funereal, white-covered tables behind which the other executives had barricaded themselves. He asked if there was any discussion of the proposal to elect directors. Buffett, seated up front with the rest, turned around when Ray Rogers, president of an agitator-for-hire group that worked mainly for labor unions, stood up and yanked the microphone from the floater who was working the aisles. Rogers started yelling that he had withheld votes "until a number of terrible wrongs are righted by this board." Coca-Cola, he said, was "rife with immorality, corruption, and complicity in gross human rights violations, including murder and torture." Daft was a liar, he screamed, and the company made its money "on the destruction of a lot of communities." As Daft tried to reassert control of the meeting with all the success of a substitute teacher, Rogers continued shouting, shuffling through what appeared to be many pages of text. Daft told him his time was up and asked him to stop speaking, but Rogers carried on. The audio people turned off the microphone's sound, but Rogers's vocal cords were far too well-exercised to be daunted by the mere absence of amplification. Finally, a group of six security guards wrestled him to the floor and carried him away as the audience stared in shock and Daft stood by helplessly, trying to restore order, pleading, "Be gentle, please," to the security guards. Then he muttered audibly to a colleague, "We shouldn't have done that."[14]

The room settled into a jittery hush. Sister Vicky Bergkemp of the Adorers of the Blood of Christ took the microphone next. She gave a short speech about AIDS and asked the management of Coke to inform the stockholders of the business effect of the AIDS pandemic on Coca-Cola. Since AIDS had nothing to do with Coca-Cola's business, management agreeably supported this proposal. Then shareholders introduced other proposals having to do with management's excessive compensation. The company recommended votes against all of these.

At last, the results of the election of directors were reported. This was the moment Buffett had been dreading. "Each of the nominees for election of director have received over ninety-six percent of the votes," said the general counsel, "with the exception of Mr. Buffett. Mr. Buffett received over eighty-four percent of the vote."[15]

Being singled out in public as the least-wanted director at Coca-Cola was humiliating. Never before had a group of shareholders rejected him. Even though CalPERS and ISS accounted for virtually all of the sixteen percent of the votes against him, and institutional investors had for the most part ignored CalPERS and ISS and championed him, it didn't feel like a triumph. Rarely had Buffett regretted serving on boards as much as he did at this moment. However, there was little time for him to dwell on it, because Daft opened the microphone to shareholder questions, and the Reverend Jesse Jackson promptly stood up and hijacked the meeting.

"Mr. Daft, and members of the board," he began in rolling tones, "let me say at the outset... that while many disagreed with the first person making a comment... his violent removal... was beneath... the dignity... of this company. It was... an overreaction.... It was... an excessive use of power.... I ... would like to know," Jackson asked rhetorically, "if there is a person of color... in the mix under consideration for the job" of CEO. The college students' complaints about Coke on campus and accusations that the company had murdered union leaders in Colombia now seemed anticlimactic. Daft struggled to conclude the most disastrous shareholder meeting in Coca-Cola's history, as board members vowed to themselves that the way this meeting had escaped the CEO's control must never be repeated.

After the fiasco, the search for a CEO took on the feeling of an emergency. Steve Heyer, the internal candidate, had been ruled out at the last board meeting and was heading off to pursue other business interests at Starwood Hotels, complete with a huge and controversial severance package that would, once again, embarrass Coca-Cola. Finally, the board reached out to another candidate they had been discussing, sixty-year-old Neville Isdell, who had retired after being clotheslined years before by Doug Ivester. A tall, charismatic Irishman who had been raised in South Africa, Isdell was popular with the board. By then, however, Coca-Cola could do nothing to please its audience. "Bringing in the old guys" was the reaction. "They hired another Daft."[16] Isdell was already presumed a future victim of the board's ax, for the board had earned a fearsome reputation for irksomeness and whimsical behavior.[17]

Yet this was the same board that had sat primly for years as if it were Goizueta's footstool. It was only after Goizueta's untimely death left the leadership in shambles that the board, which for the most part consisted of the same people who had served under Goizueta, had split in two. During the six-year interregnum, a small group of directors had grabbed for the reins of the Real Thing's runaway stagecoach. All the while, the company missed consumer trends and made strategic mistakes. To catch up and correct the problems,

Coca-Cola needed a determined and tough CEO who could tame the faction on the board that became overbearing when deprived of a dominant leader to keep them in line. How long Isdell would survive would depend on how strong a leader he turned out to be.

Buffett gave his speech about managing earnings; Keough started to help Isdell, as he helped every new CEO. Isdell accepted the help, but as it turned out, he wouldn't need all that much.

61

The Seventh Fire

New York City, Sun Valley, Cody • *March–July 2004*

In March, Susie went for her first MRI scan since the surgery. Buffett knew the stakes associated with this event. Susie had said she would have no more surgery.

"She won't go back into the hospital. She won't. I think the odds are reasonably good, but..."

The MRI came back clean. Buffett was overjoyed; he said that Susie's doctors told her that this meant she had the same odds of a recurrence as if she had never had cancer. Susie may have put it this way to Warren because she thought that this was what he needed to believe, but what Dr. Schmidt had actually told her was that she could probably count on one good year. After that, the future was uncertain.[1]

Months of being trapped inside by illness, just as in her childhood, affected Susie predictably. As weak as she was, her pent-up urge to live her life again exploded. "I'm going to see my family," she said. "I want to see everybody. I'm going to do everything I want to do until Dr. Schmidt tells me not to."[2]

The first thing she wanted to do was go to the Laguna house and have the grandchildren come visit. For Warren's sake, she wanted to attend the Berkshire shareholder meeting. She wanted to be strong enough to attend the premiere of Peter's multimedia show, *Spirit—The Seventh Fire*, which was to take place in Omaha in July. She had a long list of other goals as well.

Susie's hair, which had been light-colored for the last few years, was close-cropped now; her youthful face looked a little slimmer but otherwise no different than before. She spoke with a slight lisp, but it was easy to forget what had happened and not notice how little energy she had.

Buffett's preoccupation was whether she would be able to attend the shareholder meeting in May. Susie's presence reassured him; she was not a spectator but part of the show. If she could not attend, it was as though his leading lady would be missing from the stage.

The Buffetts had triangulated the shareholder weekend so that Astrid (who considered the whole thing a bore and was pleased to be excused) accompanied Warren only to the backstage social events, just as she did in real life, while Susie attended the "official" public social events in the role of "wife." She sat in the directors' section at the meeting and sang onstage with Al Oehrle's band in the mall at Borsheim's on Sunday afternoon. Buffett's supporting cast of loyal Daisy Maes had grown larger over time, and made their own appearances. From time to time throughout the weekend, a clanking sound heralded the approach of Carol Loomis wearing her bracelet hung with a collection of twenty-seven matchbook-size gold and enamel charms, facsimiles of the Berkshire Hathaway annual reports—one for each year she had edited Buffett's words. Sharon Osberg became part of the show by taking on any shareholder who wanted to play bridge with a champion on Sunday afternoon in the big white tent outside Borsheim's. Buffett had not yet figured out a way to put his latest Daisy Mae, Devon Spurgeon, to work. Spurgeon, a *Wall Street Journal* reporter who had covered Berkshire for a while, was starting law school in the fall. Buffett had made Spurgeon one of his new people, a great rarity that now occurred only at intervals of years. Buffett had actually suggested that she get married at the meeting, where he would walk her down the long, long center aisle to the front and give her away as a bride. "Imagine how many gifts you would get from Borsheim's," he said. Genuinely touched by his offer—but warily envisioning news stories portraying her nuptials as the Berkshire version of a Moonie wedding—Spurgeon and her fiancé, Kevin Helliker, decided to get married in Italy instead. Buffett had granted her a seat with the managers in their reserved section;[3] Osberg and Loomis, who were de facto family, sat in the section reserved for family and directors.

Everyone else had to scramble to avoid a place in the rafters. This year, so many requests for passes had come in that almost twenty thousand people were expected.

A black market of scalpers had sprung up on eBay, selling meeting credentials for as much as $250 for four passes. Buffett was mildly awestruck. Who ever heard of tickets scalped to a shareholder meeting? The eBay listing said: "Possibly meet in person Warren Buffett or ask him a question at the meeting.... Winning bidder also receives the visitor's guide. The pass also allows you employee pricing at Nebraska Furniture Mart and Borsheim's Jewelry Store.... BBQ party...Cocktail party at Borsheim's...Shareholder party at Buffett's favorite steak house...View displays from many of the Berkshire companies."

As much as the P. T. Buffett loved it, Howard Buffett's son wanted the scalping stopped. He couldn't allow people to be gouged by scalpers just to attend the shareholder meeting. The man who, a year or two earlier, had professed (for good reason) ignorance of technology set up his own e-tailer on eBay, hawking meeting credentials at $5 a pair. People e-mailed anxiously. Would these credentials be "real," or would they look different, stigmatizing the buyer as not a "real" shareholder? The question implied that this would be awful, labeling them as not a member of the "club."

But, no, the credentials would be real, however obtained. And with that, Berkshire Hathaway—once a cozy club made up of rich partners whom Buffett considered friends—suddenly became a fan club. Buffett had opened up the tent and invited *everybody* in.

Omaha's brand-new Qwest Center rose like a great silver circus tent near the Missouri River. Its facade reflected like a mirror on the grimy old Civic Auditorium across town, scene of the last four meetings. Inside, forklifts delivered bales of hay and crates of flowers, lampposts, and tons of mulch that would be landscaped into garden and seating areas in the exhibition hall. Construction crews built neighborhoods of booths to display awnings, air compressors, blocks of knives, encyclopedias, vacuum cleaners, and picture frames.

Buffett bounced around the office like a teenager. His voice grew hoarser as the week wore on and the number of visitors kept increasing. Everyone nagged at him to save his voice for the presentations, but he ignored them, sprayed his throat, and kept talking anyway.

By Friday Buffett's voice sounded like someone recovering from a bad cold. Still, he refused to stop talking. But Buffett never had stopped talking, never once in his life. Since he was a little boy and astonished his parents' friends with his precocity; since he gave his high school teachers advice on stocks; since the Alpha Sigs gathered around to hear him lecture at fraternity parties; since he and Ben Graham held a duet around the conference table at Columbia; since he had sold GEICO as a prescriptionist; since he'd first picked up a stick of chalk and taught investing at night; since he'd bewitched people at cocktail parties in Omaha and dinner parties in New York; from the first meeting of the partners to the last; from the original Berkshire shareholder meeting in Seabury Stanton's old loft to the latest group of students who had shown up at his door—as long as he could be teaching something to somebody, Buffett had never ceased talking.

When the doors opened at seven a.m. on Saturday morning, people ran for the arena and marked out the best seats. By eight-thirty, every seat was filled. When the lights dimmed, talking ceased instantly. Nobody whispered, nobody straggled in late. The audience was waiting, rapt.

Buffett and Munger entered like a couple of graying talk-show hosts and sat down at a white-cloth-covered table. Enormous screens displaying them had been positioned all around the arena, so everybody got a close-up look. Buffett was staring out at a dark arena filled with flashing lights and as many people as would show up in Nebraska to see the Rolling Stones.

Before taking questions, Buffett kicked off the meeting with rapid efficiency to cover a normally perfunctory five-minute business agenda of electing directors, ratifying auditors, and the like. This year, almost immediately, one of the shareholders stood up at a microphone and said in a timid voice that he was withholding his vote; he offered a motion from the floor. He asked that Buffett consider using some of the CEOs of his companies as directors because they were better qualified than Susie and Howie Buffett.

An audible ripple shuddered across the auditorium. The motion, even though presented in a respectful tone, fell like a big wet blot to mar the smooth, engraved surface of the shareholder-meeting agenda. Most of the audience was shocked. Berkshire was now the fourteenth-largest business in the United States, with over 172,000 employees, $64 billion in revenues, and profits of $8 billion a year. But it remained at heart a family corporation; as the largest shareholder, Buffett had the votes to elect a couple of board seats for family members if he wanted. He saw his family's role in Berkshire as similar to the Walton family's at Wal-Mart, a nexus between the Buffett Foundation and the company. Unquestionably, the way he chose his board was purely personal, although some board members happened to be successful businessmen.

"Thank you," said Buffett. "Charlie, do you have any thoughts on that?"

This punting to Munger—no quick comeback or pithy comment—was a measure of Buffett's complete discomfiture. However, it also put Munger on the spot, since anything he said might imply that he had some influence on how Buffett chose his board. He had none whatsoever, so Munger simply said, "I think we should go on to the next item."

Another motion came to the floor. Tom Strobhar, on behalf of Human Life International, one of the organizations that had boycotted Berkshire Hathaway and successfully forced the company to end its charitable-contributions program, gave a speech about abortion that was, as he later wrote, "ostensively [sic]" disguised as a proposal that Berkshire publish a list of its political donations.[4]

Buffett merely said in response that Berkshire hadn't made any political donations. The motion was voted down.

The business section of the meeting had now consumed half an hour instead of its usual five minutes and for the first time had borne a vaguely unpleasant resemblance to the Coca-Cola meeting. All this time, shareholders holding written-out questions had been patiently lined up at the numbered platforms equipped with microphones stationed all around the arena. When Buffett opened the questioning, he used an unrelated query to address the issue that was bothering him: his family as board members. His wife and son, he said, were on the board as "guardians of the culture. They're not there to profit themselves."

It was a remarkable moment. For the first time, he seemed to feel that he had to defend in public the way he ran his company. Afterward, however, nobody else asked anything related to this topic. The shareholders of Berkshire Hathaway seemed to think that Buffett had earned the license to run his company any way he damn well pleased. How was the investing climate? they asked. Our capital is underutilized now, he said. It's a painful condition to be in, but not as painful as doing something stupid.

In the course of answering the many repetitious questions he was asked in between the new and insightful ones, Buffett managed to work many of the items he wanted to discuss into his responses. This year he used the meeting to expound on his "Why I'm Down on the Dollar" theme. The U.S., he said, was like a family that spent more than it earned. Americans were buying huge amounts of products from other countries and didn't have the income to pay for them, because we weren't selling as much to other countries as they were selling to us. To make up the difference, we were borrowing money. Those who were lending it to us might be less willing to do so in the future.

Now, Buffett said, we were spending more than two percent of all our income just to pay the interest on our national debt, and that meant the situation would be hard to turn around. Most likely, he thought, at some point foreign investors would decide they liked our real estate and businesses and other "real assets" better than our paper bonds. We would start selling off pieces of America, like office buildings and companies.

"We think that over time the U.S. dollar is likely to decline in value against some of the major currencies," he said. Therefore, the economy—which had been pretty wonderful over the past twenty years, with both low interest rates and low inflation—could at some point reverse. Interest rates probably would be higher, as would inflation, which would be an unhappy situation. As always when he made predictions, he couldn't say when. In the meantime, however, he had bought $12 billion of foreign currency to hedge Berkshire's dollar risks.

While Buffett and Munger were talking about the perils of debt, people rolled down the ramps and escalators to the shoe department and waited in lines to pull out their credit cards. Fitters from Tony Lama and Justin sold a pair of boots a minute. Over at Borsheim's, on the west side of town, more than a thousand watches and 187 engagement rings were being sold. The Furniture Mart was doing a record $17 million of business.

At the south end of the exhibition hall, rising above the crowd, just as Buffett had pictured it, stood a full-size Clayton Home with a tidy front porch and a real grass lawn and brick foundation bedecked with shrubs. And just as he had fore-seen, a queue snaked back and forth behind a zigzag rope, as if it were Space Mountain at Disneyland.[5]

The black-and-white See's Candies store, conveniently positioned in the middle of the exhibition hall, also had jammed aisles. Many of the customers did not bother to pay. Those taking the five-finger discount hooked huge amounts of candy as well as dozens of pairs of shoes from the shoe store, while, above their heads, Buffett and Munger talked about honesty and the ethical way of life.

As yet unaware of the thievery taking place beneath their feet that might force them to consider installing a Berkyville jail by the bookstore next year, Buffett and Munger ambled on, answering questions and chomping on See's candies, peanut brittle, and Dairy Queen Dilly Bars as they talked their way through the entire six hours.

Any normal person would be exhausted after putting on a six-hour live, unscripted performance, but when the meeting ended, Buffett and Munger went upstairs to a large room and parked themselves at a desk, signing autographs so that shareholders who had come from foreign countries could get closer to them. This was a recent idea of Buffett's. Munger sat through it patiently, but he was getting tired and sometimes talked with bemusement of this circus that Warren had created. He, too, enjoyed being worshipped, but never would have gone to the trouble to stage-manage and encourage it, the way his partner did.

Susie had left to go lie down after the first couple hours of the meeting. She flew to New York with Warren on Monday, but stayed in bed in her hotel room until one in the afternoon, mashing up pills in room-service ice cream. Susie Jr. wanted her mother to limit her outings to one thing a day—one visitor, one shopping trip, one fifteen-minute visit to the hotel lobby.[6]

Susie did attend the traditional dinner party that Sandy and Ruth Gottesman held in their honor every year. Since the mid-1990s, this had become the one time that many of the people in the Buffett Group could count on seeing their old friends during the annual New York trip. Now Susie Jr. said to Ruth Gottesman, "She's going to try to do more than she should. She's going to say she's fine. She's going to lie to you," and she asked for help in protecting her mother. Most of those who gathered at the Gottesmans' had not seen Susie at all during the past year, except perhaps at the shareholder meeting, and then only briefly. She sat in one room and Warren in another, while people came in to greet them and chat. Many people would later recall the event as emotional. Susie declared that she was glad she had gone. But afterward, she was exhausted.

Warren wanted her to do an interview with talk-show host Charlie Rose. Susie said many sentimental and flattering things about her husband, and explained that she gave Warren "unconditional love." She also discussed her move to San Francisco, saying she left, as she told Warren, because "I would like to have a place where I can have a room of my own." On Astrid, "She took care of your man for you?" asked Rose. "She did, and she takes great care of him, and he appreciates it and I appreciate it...she's done me a great favor," Susie said. Perhaps because of the set-up question, this exchange made clear that Susie viewed Astrid as the tool through which she managed Warren—something that Susie may not have intended to reveal quite so bluntly. Afterward, she said to Susie Jr., "Let's go to Bergdorf's."[7] There, she sat on a chair and looked at some things but soon said she was tired and went back to the hotel.

A couple of days later, on Mother's Day, her energy rebounded in time to accept an invitation to meet her daughter's friend Bono at the Tribeca Film Festival. Bono had been faxing her letters during her recovery, which Susie Jr.

would read to her. The letters, according to Susie Jr., "were sort of this giant thing to her." By May, after going to sleep every night listening to Bono sing, she had grown passionately interested in meeting the messianic singer. After their brief encounter, "I just can't even explain to you how excited she was," says Susie Jr.

Susie went to bed and rested for two days. Then Bono and his entourage came over to the Plaza to meet Susie for lunch. For three hours, Susie and Bono sat talking. Then he presented her with a portrait that he had painted from a photograph of her, overwritten with some of the lyrics to the U2 song "One." Susie was overcome. Bono invited her to visit him in France with Susie Jr., who was coming for a meeting of his foundation board.

Susie made up her mind to go to France. She and Susie Jr. started by spending four days at the Ritz in Paris, where Susie recovered from the trip across six time zones. Then they took the TGV bullet train to Nice, to Bono's salmon-colored stucco mansion in Eze Bord de Mer.

In Eze, Susie spent most of her days sleeping, but one afternoon Susie Jr. called her upstairs to a terrace overlooking the water while Bono played music from *How to Dismantle an Atomic Bomb*, U2's unreleased album. That evening they spent four hours talking over dinner, and Bono stood up and toasted her, saying, "I've met my soul mate!"

Her reverence for the charismatic rock star had grown so during the course of getting to know him in person that the next day, on the plane home, Susie stayed awake and played U2 music on her iPod the entire way. "I can't explain the rest I got there," she would later say about Bono's house.[8]

Roughly a week after the two Susies returned from France, most of the family went to Sun Valley, while Peter and Jennifer stayed in Omaha, setting up for the premiere of his show, *Spirit—The Seventh Fire*. After the long year of pain and isolation, Susie was making up for lost time by trying to see everyone and go everywhere. But the feeling of liberation was not unqualified. On the second day, Susie Jr. got a golf cart to take her mother around. When Susie Jr. walked into the condo to pick her mother up, she was shriveled in a little ball on the couch crying, saying, "I can't do it."[9] Even though she spent much of the trip resting, it drained her tiny store of energy.

When the family returned to Omaha, with everybody on hand for the upcoming premiere of Peter's show, Susie took the opportunity to visit her daughter's new knitting shop. Susie Jr. had gotten together with a partner to open String of Purls in a suburban shopping center. Buffett was genuinely excited at his daughter's entrepreneurialism. He could relate to a knitting shop.

He had analyzed its prospects and thought it might gross as much as half a million dollars a year. Once again he could bond with his daughter in a special way.

Peter's multimedia event was nothing like the knitting shop; it was harder for Buffett to comprehend. Based on the PBS special Peter had done earlier, it had consumed four years of effort, during which he focused on improving the execution and experience of the live performances while refining the music and story line. And all of this work would have no certain result—except the satisfaction of the creative act.

Buffett had seen the earlier live performances and knew the show involved Peter on keyboards with a band; a special theater shaped like a tent; lasers, drums, video, and Native American singers and dancers. Warren always gave students advice to pursue their passion, but the examples of passion he used, like becoming backgammon champion of the world, were competitive at their core. Someone driven by an inner fire of artistry, irrespective of the world's rewards, was simply off the map of his reality. That was Susie's territory, the realm of spirit and soul and heart. Nonetheless, his own passion and patience and creativity as he worked with capital resembled Peter's passion and patience and artistic vision with music. Thus, Buffett's genuine wish for Peter's success found its expression in the best and only way he knew—in the marriage between art and commerce. The show's potential for commercial success preoccupied him. *"It gets enthusiastic responses, but what I don't know is just how big the market is. It's not like a Broadway musical, in terms of the depth of the market, so we will find out."*

The Buffett name had worked heavily against Peter when it came to raising money, because people assumed that he had easy access to unlimited funds. People did not take him seriously about not having money until he actually mortgaged his house to fund the show. In a no-lose deal, Warren offered to pay the last ten percent of the cost if Peter could raise the rest. When he had raised two million of the total, his father went ahead and gave him $200,000 of the $300,000 he had promised. Peter then raised the rest of the money himself. From start to finish he struggled against heavy odds to raise funds while trying to stage and produce the show at the same time. His parents, during the same months, waived their "no donations" rule and wrote a $10 million check to Tom Murphy's Save the Children as a gesture of friendship and support.

It seemed a little chilly—even in the name of cultivating self-reliance—to support their son's cause with only two percent of what they gave a family friend. With hindsight, Peter was grateful that his show did not become a vanity project funded by his father—which no one would have taken seriously. He felt that his father had found one of his typically brilliant solutions to complex problems. Peter had his family's endorsement, for which he was grateful, along with the pride of raising most of the three million needed by himself—although he could have used that last hundred thousand dollars.

Spirit—The Seventh Fire was a dazzling story acted by a Native American who told the story of his return from the modern world to reclaim his cultural heritage. Warren did not quite understand his son's fascination with Native Americans. The show's symbolic exploration of stolen identity, and the triumph of man's will in reclaiming what was lost, escaped him. But Warren loved music and was proud of his son, and when he looked at others in the audience at the premiere and saw people clapping and cheering, that told him the show was good. And when the *Omaha World-Herald* called it "poignant, sad, uplifting, thrilling, and powerful," he was delighted. But he also feared, with reason, a hometown bias and waited to see if the show would be well-received elsewhere.

As *Spirit* continued to play in Omaha, Susie went to Laguna with a group of her grandchildren. They were used to Susie indulging their wishes and giving herself to their needs, going here and there with them, the perfect grandmother; she didn't disappoint them now. She took them shopping at the mall, like old times, sitting in a chair and pointing at things around the store, saying, "I'll take one of those, and two of these, and one of those."[10] After this visit, she was exhausted, but began to prepare herself for the annual trip to Herbert Allen's post–Sun Valley gathering.

The wisdom of spending another long weekend with a crowd of people at the high altitude of Cody, Wyoming, so soon after Sun Valley, seemed questionable. Some in the family were strongly against her making this trip. But Susie was doing cartwheels at the sheer joy of living, and Warren wanted to feel that everything was back to normal. Thus, the last week of July, Warren and Susie reunited for a long weekend at Herbert Allen's J—9 ranch.*

Susie struck people as exuberant, elated to be there.[11] At dinner in the great room, where an oversize fireplace took the chill off the high mountain air, she was chatty and outspoken.[12] Afterward, when the table had been cleared and everyone was thinking about dessert and coffee, she stood in the kitchen talk-

---

*Pronounced J-bar-9.

ing.[13] Suddenly, she blinked and said there was something funny going on inside her head.[14] For a split second, Herbert Allen thought she was doing a silly dance step. Then he realized she was going down. As her legs buckled, he and Barbara Oehrle caught her before she hit the floor.[15]

They carried her to a nearby couch, where the yoga teacher Herbert Allen had brought in for the weekend held her. Susie's health had always been so uncertain, and she had pulled through so many other crises, that nobody thought it was that serious. Still, they put through a call for paramedics. Warren called Susie Jr., who was at the Democratic Convention in Boston. He said something about a headache and asked for her doctor's phone number. She gave it to him and he hung up. She wondered briefly if something was wrong, then thought, My mother could have broken her toe and he would be calling for her doctor's number.[16]

Lying on the sofa, Susie was having trouble lifting her arm. She vomited a couple of times and said she was very cold and her head hurt terribly. They wrapped her in blankets. She began drifting in and out of consciousness, at times struggling to speak. As Warren observed Susie's condition, he grew more and more distressed; it was becoming apparent that she had probably had a stroke. The other guests waited, helpless, for the ambulance to arrive. The time passed slowly. After a while they all grew more hopeful when Susie commented that her head felt better and started responding when asked to move her arms and feet. Then the paramedics arrived and did a few tests. They placed her onto the ambulance cot and wheeled her outside, as Warren followed. After they lifted her into the back of the ambulance, Warren got into the front seat and the driver began the thirty-four-mile journey through the winding mountain roads to West Park Hospital in Cody.[17]

As soon as they were in the ambulance, Warren called Susie Jr. "You need to come here," he said. "Something has happened to Mom. I think she's had a stroke." A few minutes later he called again and said, "You need to find your brothers and bring them with you."

Susie Jr. reached Peter in Omaha, where he was in his hotel room preparing for the show.[18] Howie, who was in Africa, was horrified, once reached, to be stranded with no way to get a return flight until the next day.[19]

While Susie Jr. worked on logistics, Herbert Allen and a friend, Western sculptor T. D. Kelsey, followed the ambulance in Allen's car. They grew frustrated at how slowly the ambulance was proceeding; it upset them that Buffett was trapped inside and subjected to the interminable ride. At one point they pulled up alongside the ambulance and Allen shouted at the driver, asking what on earth was going on, but no one answered.

When they finally reached the hospital, the CAT scan revealed that Susie had had a massive cerebral hemorrhage. Warren paced back and forth in the emergency room, and eventually the doctor came out and told him that Susie had little chance of lasting through the night. Tearful and distraught, he went out to the lobby and told this to Kelsey and Allen.[20] Then he walked back upstairs and sat in the room with Susie, waiting. They were alone.

At around four-thirty a.m., the plane carrying Susie Jr. and Peter arrived. After their car pulled into the hospital parking lot, its mountain backdrop much like that at Sun Valley, the first person they saw inside the lobby was Herbert Allen. Susie Jr.'s first thought was "Oh, my God, this feels just like Mrs. Graham."

Upstairs, they found their father sitting next to their mother, holding her hand. A Cherry Coke sat untouched on the table nearby. "I've been here for five hours," he said. Susie was so quiet, you couldn't see her breathing.

Warren went to lie down on the bed in the adjoining room. Peter lay down on the floor, and both fell asleep. Susie Jr. sat down in a chair next to her mother on the bed, touching her.

A little while later, she realized that Susie wasn't breathing. She went and found a nurse. Then she braced herself and woke her father up to tell him.[21]

Warren wept while his children spent the next few hours doing what had to be done. By noon all of them were on the G-IV for the worst flight any of them had ever taken.

After some time in the air, Warren took a deep breath and asked, "Is there a bathroom in the front?" There wasn't. "Walk with your back to the couch," Susie Jr. told him. He inched his way to the back of the plane, his eyes averted from the plane's sofa, where the zippered bag that contained Susie's body lay.[22]

When they landed in Omaha, the family had another surreal experience as the plane taxied straight into the hangar, where a hearse was waiting, rather than stopping on the tarmac, so that they could deboard without having their grief invaded by a band of paparazzi. Warren went straight home, walked upstairs into his bedroom, shut the door, turned off the lights, and got under the covers.

Astrid knew what to do, which was nothing. She made sure he had his sleeping pills and left him alone. Now and then she went over to Susie Jr.'s and cried herself. The rest of the time she stayed at home to take care of Warren.

The next day, Friday, he was still under the covers. Ron Olson, who had some legal obligations under Susie's will and was a close friend and strong influence within the family, particularly with the children, arrived from Los Angeles with his wife, Jane. Warren came downstairs, and the Olsons sat with him for a while. Within an hour, the phone rang. It was Don Graham. "Where are you?" asked Susie Jr. "At the Hilton downtown," he said. He had known to come without being told. Then Susie Jr. drafted a couple of her own friends to join them at the house. Over the next several days, they all sat in the living room to help distract Warren and make sure that he was never alone. At nine-thirty each night, he went up to bed and took his sleeping pill.

A day or two later Warren tried to call a couple of people. When they answered, no words came out; his throat had closed. He gave up trying to talk and heaved with sobs for a few minutes. Then, when the storm of tears passed, he choked out, "I'm sorry," and hung up the phone. They would never have known who it was, except that the sound of Warren sending out an SOS was so unmistakable.

Susie Jr. had already sent for the people who were needed. The following week, Bill Ruane and Carol Loomis arrived to visit for a few hours. Sharon Osberg came. Bill Gates arrived. Kathleen Cole flew in. And Howie finally returned from Africa after "the longest trip home," one that he never wanted to think about again.[23]

Bill and Sharon went ahead with a bridge tournament they had been scheduled to play in—with Warren—that week. He managed to join them for dinner one night at the hotel where the tournament was being held, and he did watch them play for a while, which helped to distract him. Another night they were over at the house, where Warren wanted them to sit with him to watch the Charlie Rose video of Susie's interview. Astrid didn't want to see it, which was just as well, and he was afraid to watch it alone. They put it on the DVD player and it began to play. After a while, Warren was weeping. Bill left the room while Sharon crawled into his lap and rocked him as he cried.[24]

The mere mention of Susie's name sent Warren into tears. As the funeral approached, it became apparent to Susie Jr., who was planning the event, that something else was bothering her father. It dawned on her what this must be. "You don't have to go," she told him.

Warren was overcome with relief. "I can't," he said. To sit there, overwhelmed with thoughts of Susie, in front of everyone, was too much. "I can't go."[25]

Unlike Warren, hundreds of others did want to grieve for Susan Buffett in person, at some sort of memorial service. None was ever held. Only the family, a couple of Susie's closest friends, Bono and his wife, Ali, and Bobby Shriver were invited to the funeral. Susie's musician friend Dave Stryker played the guitar, and the Reverend Cecil Williams from Glide Memorial Church conducted the service. Bono sang "Sometimes You Can't Make It on Your Own." The grandchildren wept.

And for several weeks more, that was all. Warren faced the emptiness. Many people, including Susie herself, had questioned how well he could survive without her. He had never recovered from the death of his father and still could not face the unfinished business of Howard's boxes of papers in the basement. As Sharon put it, he had a tendency to think in the third person. But he suffered this time in the first person, grieving fully, living in the now, even though the now terrified him.

He could not escape from grief, even in sleep. The nightmares haunted him, every night the same. The separation from Susie, the split that he had never been able to contemplate during all the years of their living apart, was happening right before his eyes. He was captive on the endless ride to the hospital in Cody, locked inside the ambulance, helpless to help her, unable to stop the momentum of the wheels. The mountains stood silhouetted against the July stardrift in the thin evening air. Silently the driver picked his way through the winding hills. The road unreeled before them, mile after mile, rows of trees passed like pilgrims climbing to the foothills above. In the back, Susie lay on the cot, pale and still. The sounds in the ambulance faded as the miles went by. Strands of juniper hung like dim moss from the mountainsides while the road ahead stretched thinner in the distance. The stars fell still in the vast black overhead. Time slowed to eternity.

All he had ever asked of her was not to leave him, and she had promised that she never would. No matter how many other people she had cared for and supported, no matter which way her heart had tugged her, through all her travels, no matter how many different directions she had run, Susie had always come back to him. She had never let him down.

Now there was no response. He needed her so much that it was impossible that she would leave him. He would hold on, he would not let go; therefore she must stay with him.

The ambulance crept onward through the darkened mountains. The quiet hum of the oxygen tank mingled with his tears. In the back there was only calm, a bare whisper of breath, no obvious sound of pain.

It was Warren's chest that burned, it was his heart that exploded with each revolution of the wheels. You can't leave me, you can't leave me, please don't leave me.

But Susie was already passing beyond his reach; she was now in other hands. And the force of her withdrawal from his world to the next was tearing him apart.

62

Claim Checks

The first aftershocks of Susie's death occurred at the reading of her will, even though most of its provisions were not unexpected. She left nearly all of her Berkshire stock, worth almost $3 billion, to the newly renamed Susan Thompson Buffett Foundation. Another six hundred shares, worth $50 million at the time, went to each of her children's foundations.

She had been generous to people she cared about, although her husband's influence doubtless dampened her generosity. Her children each received $10 million. A long list of other people received smaller amounts. She had amended her will in the year before her death through a codicil executed by a new lawyer; the codicil gave John McCabe $8 million.[1]

The secret codicil shocked nearly everyone. Susie had never reconciled the divisions within her world and in the end chose to leave them unexplained. The life she lived for others was her legacy; her inner truth would remain forever unspoken. Thus it would be left to others to form their own interpretations.

Warren had long loved his wife as an ideal. She had been the "grounding person who was his connection to the outside world" as well as the "glue that held the family together."[2] After her death, he was never able to look at Susie's photograph without crying. But he did not lapse into a years-long depression, or commit suicide, as Susie had suggested he might. Instead he mourned. For about two months, he seemed deeply depressed. And then, as most people do, he gradually returned to living his life.

Once the dreamlike assumption that "Susie will take care of everything" popped like a soap bubble, Warren began to show a newfound realism. As each month passed, he began to deal more acceptingly with endings and mortality and to connect with his children in a new way. Susie seemed to have willed him some of her strength, a little of her emotional fluency, and a lot of her generosity. Warren seemed to be acquiring unexpected dimensions to his inner life. He reclaimed some of the responsibility for the emotional territory that he had always left to his wife. He became more aware of his children's feelings, of what they were doing and of what mattered to them.

Susie Jr. quickly stepped into the leadership role that her mother had played in philanthropy. She began to hire and to enlarge the foundation's offices to plan for the much larger sums of money it would now be giving away.

Peter was taking *Spirit—The Seventh Fire* to the National Mall in Washington as part of the celebration for the grand opening of the National Museum of the American Indian. One day he called his father to say, Dad, we're setting up the tent! Afterward he realized that he would have once called his mother, who would have told his father. It felt good to have a direct connection.[3] Warren gathered a group of friends and flew to Washington to attend the cocktail party and opening night. With the show, Warren felt a new intimacy with his son— not just because of Peter's success, but through the effort they were making to be part of each other's lives.

When *Spirit* arrived in Philadelphia, it got the kind of recognition that Buffett understood: It was compared to "a Native American version of Philip Glass's dance performance/opera *1,000 Airplanes on the Roof* " with "guitar rolls that would put U2's The Edge to shame."[4] Its costly production, however, meant that even with high ticket prices, *Spirit* was losing money as a touring show. Peter put it on hiatus and began working on a new CD, *Gold Star,* while he considered *Spirit*'s longer-term future.

Howie's business experience had ripened; he now served on two boards. Savvy about money, he had kept his CCE stock and had invested in Berkshire Hathaway stock. This latter gesture bonded him to his father as nothing else could. Warren observed how much his son had settled down and matured in the past ten years. Howie, a "marshmallow" emotionally who had yearned for a warm connection to his father all his life, now saw an opportunity to have a different sort of relationship with him. He and Devon bought a house in Omaha so they could be nearby.

The events following Susie's death affected Astrid deeply. She had lost someone she considered a dear friend, then found out that Susie's life had run on parallel tracks—one of which had always been invisible to her. Years of staying behind the scenes out of deference to Susie and to a marriage that, however unconventional, had been held up to all as some kind of ideal suddenly was revealed as based on a falsehood. She felt betrayed and used. Belatedly, Warren recognized how high a price Astrid had paid for the arrangement he and Susie had worked out, the realities of which they had both avoided facing all these years. He took the blame and went to work setting things right. Gradually, as he passed through the stages of mourning, he brought Astrid more and more into his public life.

In December, Warren sent all of his grandchildren large checks as a Christmas gift. He had always paid for their college tuition, but he had never before given them money without any strings attached.

Buffett made two exceptions to the checks. He did not include Nicole and Erica Buffett, Peter's adopted daughters. Big Susie had loved Erica and Nicole. They had shown up at her funeral dressed in long flowing outfits and wailed like a pair of brunette banshees. Susie had left each of her "adored grandchildren," including Nicole and Erica, $100,000 "as a hug" in her will. But ten days after Susie's funeral, Warren had told Peter, "By the way, I don't consider the girls my grandchildren. I don't want them to expect anything from me in my will." Peter found this inexplicable. "Are you sure you want to do this?" he asked. His father was undeterred. That Susie had given the girls—who had been adopted after their mother's divorce from Peter—money and specified that they had the same status as her other grandchildren in her will seemed to have roused Warren's feelings of possessiveness about money.

Two years later, Nicole participated in Jamie Johnson and Nick Kurzon's documentary *The One Percent,* a story about the children of the rich. In the documentary, Nicole unwisely positioned herself as a spokesman for the unspoiled Buffett way of life. The documentary resulted in follow-up media appearances, including an invitation to appear on an *Oprah* episode about social class in America. Buffett's reaction was harsh; he sent word to Nicole that he didn't consider her his granddaughter, and if asked, would say so. Nicole told Oprah she was "at peace with" not having inherited wealth—apparently a reference to the small amounts that Susie had left her grandchildren—but added, "I do feel that it would be nice to be involved with creating things for others with that money and to be involved in it. I feel completely excluded from it." The "poor little me" aspect of her interview was her second mistake.

Afterward, she sent Buffett a letter asking why he had disavowed her. In a letter marked by a carefully controlled tone,[5] he wrote back and offered her good wishes, told her she had reason to be proud of her accomplishments, and gave her some worthwhile advice. Positioning herself with people as a member of the Buffett family was a mistake, he wrote. *"If you do so, it will become your primary identity with them. People will react to you based on that 'fact' rather than to who you are or what you have accomplished."* But he also wrote, *"I have not legally or emotionally adopted you as a grandchild, nor have the rest of my family adopted you as a niece or cousin. . . . It is simply a fact that just as [your mother] is in no respect my daughter-in-law, her children are not my grandchildren."*

Nicole had wounded him in his most tender spot—his identity and that of his family. In doing so, she ran afoul of what was referred to semi-jokingly in family circles as the "Buffett Name Police," which restricted use of the Buffett name for self-promotional purposes to Warren and, occasionally, his children. The Buffett Name Police enforced its rules by banishment from the family, a punishment that was usually carried out by Susie Jr. and acquiesced to by the rest.

Buffett's unusual decision to banish Nicole personally rather than using a surrogate backfired badly on him. Nicole may have been wrong, but she seemed sincere. Instead of reining her in, the rejection letter sent her off on another round of interviews that made Buffett look like Ebenezer Scrooge; one result was a Page Six story in the *New York Post* (Buffett to Kin: You're Fired!"[6]) portraying him as taking vengeance on her for participating in the documentary. Even four years after Susie's death, their relationship was still not mended. Nicole took the further step of doing an interview with *Marie Claire*[7] in which she provided photographs and letters signed "Grandpa" to prove that Buffett had indeed at one time considered himself her grandfather. To the man who had worked so hard for a lifetime never to alienate anyone, it was a painful irony. It seemed unlikely—though not impossible—that the two would ever reconcile.

Buffett had always had an easier time giving away money to mankind than to his family. He was what is called a "telescope philanthropist." Bill Gates, the most influential philanthropist on earth, was becoming his role model. Their relationship had grown even closer. In late 2004, Buffett overcame some earlier reservations that Gates's powerful personality might dominate the Berkshire board, and invited him to join it. Sharon and Bill had been talking for some time about the challenges that the Buffett Foundation faced. To give away several billion dollars a year after Warren was gone, it would have to change dramatically. No foundation in history had ever succeeded in such a transformation, because no foundation had ever tried. With one exception—the Gates

Foundation—no other philanthropic organization had ever worked with such large sums.

Buffett had also been thinking about the problem. In the fall, he had video-taped a question-and-answer session with his foundation trustees, making sure they understood his wishes. Like Walter Annenberg, he wanted to reduce the chance of being double-crossed after he was dead.

Early in 2005, Osberg "trumped up some pretense" and made a trip to Omaha to speak to Buffett. Given his admiration for Gates, she said, shouldn't he consider leaving his money to the Gates Foundation after he died? Though Buffett reacted noncommittally,[8] he had in fact been considering leaving at least some of the money to the Gateses since well before Susie died.

For a long time Buffett had felt that society was best served if he carried on compounding the money, rather than giving it away. But delaying the gift until his death also amounted to the White Queen's "jam tomorrow"—a postpone-ment in his struggle with endings, with loss, with death, with letting go. Over the years he had gradually evolved from a boy who stole his sister's bicycle and got other people to buy his barbells, from a father who said no to every request for money from his children, to a man who gave them a million dollars every five years on their birthday. Although he still had issues with money, in a profound shift, he was working his way through the problem of whether to serve some of tomorrow's jam today.

That did not mean, however, that the encroachments of time would become easier for him. A year after Susie died, Buffett found himself shocked once again by the impending arrival of another birthday. Could he actually be three-quarters of a century old? He spoke of it with disbelief.

His seventy-fifth birthday party took place at the Marin County home of Sharon Osberg and her husband, David Smith, with Astrid, Bill Gates, and his sister Bertie in attendance. His birthday cake was a white-chocolate replica of a $100 bill. On Saturday morning, Smith had arranged for Buffett to take on Ariel Hsing, a nine-year-old Chinese-American Ping-Pong champion. With the video camera rolling, the little girl crushed him. After a fierce bridge tourna-ment the following morning, an artist whom Osberg and Smith had hired came over to amuse Buffett and Gates by trying to teach them the art of landscape painting. Buffett gamely swiped away with a brush at acrylics, but painting, unlike Ping-Pong, was not rhythmic and repetitious, and he produced a canvas adorned with trees that resembled brown lollipops. Meanwhile, the previous day's Ping-Pong game was fermenting an idea. Why not add the video of him getting trounced by Ariel Hsing to the ever-expanding movie at the shareholders meeting?

Before 2003, Buffett's need for attention had been satisfied by a few interviews a year and the shareholder meeting. He had always been careful and strategic in his cooperation with the media (if not always forthcoming about just how cooperative he had been). But starting around the time of Susie's illness, for whatever reason, he had begun to need the mirror of media attention, television cameras especially, almost like a drug. The intervals he could tolerate without publicity were growing shorter. He cooperated with documentaries, spent hours talking to Charlie Rose, and became such a regular on CNBC that it started to prompt puzzled queries from his friends.

The Buffett who so craved attention contrasted markedly with the Buffett who focused with unaltered intensity on Berkshire Hathaway. To see him flip from one mode into the other in half a second was head-spinning. He remained as focused on investing as he had been as a younger man. That did not mean it was easy for him.

Since the Federal Reserve's dramatic interest rate cuts in the wake of 9/11, the market had steadily recouped its losses until it was nearing bubble-era levels. Buffett wrote in his 2004 letter to shareholders: *"My hope was to make several multibillion dollar acquisitions that would add new and significant streams of earnings to the many we already have. But I struck out. Additionally, I found very few attractive securities to buy. Berkshire therefore ended the year with $43 billion of cash equivalents, not a happy position."*

Buffett used this report to reiterate that he was still down on the dollar, and thought it would decline. Because the dollar had strengthened since his first article, now his view was being widely criticized in the financial press. He had reduced his currency bets in favor of buying foreign stocks, but nothing changed his view. And once again, he decried excessive executive compensation. On derivatives, a topic he now covered every year, Buffett wrote:

"Long ago Mark Twain said: 'A man who tries to carry a cat home by its tail will learn a lesson that can be learned in no other way.'... I dwell on our experiences in derivatives each year for two reasons. One is personal and unpleasant." Here, he wrote about the costly unwinding at General Re.

"The second reason I regularly describe our problems in this area lies in the hope that our experiences may prove instructive for managers, auditors, and regulators. In a sense, we are a canary in this business coal mine and should sing a song of warning as we expire....

*"It could be a different story for others in the future. Imagine, if you will, one or more firms (troubles often spread) with positions that are many multiples of ours attempting to liquidate in chaotic markets and under extreme, and well-publicized pressures. The time to have considered—and improved—the reliability of New Orleans's levees was before [Hurricane] Katrina."*⁹

The general belief, however, continued to be that derivatives spread and reduced risk. In a market shoved upward by cheap debt and derivatives nearly day by day, low interest rates and the "securitization" of mortgages into derivatives were pumping a housing boom that would peak in 2006. By one estimate, total global leverage (debt) had quadrupled in less than a decade.¹⁰ Buffett fretted occasionally that he might never again see the kind of home-run climate for investing that had blessed him in the 1970s. But he never stopped searching, he never stopped delving for ideas.

One day in 2004 he obtained from his broker a thick book, the size of several telephone directories stapled together. Its pages contained listings of Korean stocks. He had been scouring the global economy, looking for a country, a market, that was overlooked and undervalued. He had found it in Korea. Night after night, he leafed through the tome, studying column after column of numbers, page by page by page. But the numbers and their nomenclature puzzled him. He realized that he needed to learn a whole new language of business that described a different culture of commerce. So he got another book and figured out everything important there was to know about Korean accounting. That would reduce the odds of getting hornswoggled by the numbers.

Once he'd mastered the listings, he began sifting and sorting. It felt something like the old days back at Graham-Newman, when he sat next to the ticker machine clad in his cherished gray cotton jacket. He could pick out from hundreds of pages which numbers were important and how they fell into a coherent pattern. Working from a list of several thousand Korean stocks, he quickly pared it down to a workable number; after making some notes on a yellow legal pad he kept going, just as he had when he'd paged through the *Moody's Manual*—until finally he arrived at a much shorter list.

This winnowed-down list was so short that it could be contained on a single piece of legal-size paper. Sitting down with a visitor, he held out the list, which consisted of at most a couple of dozen companies. A few were large—among the largest in the world—but most were very small.

"*Lookit*," he said, "*this is how I do it. They are quoted in won. If you go to the Internet and look them up on the Korean stock exchange, they have numbers instead of ticker symbols, and they all end in zero unless it's a preferred stock, in which case you click in five. If they have a second class of preferred, you don't click in six, you click in seven. Every night you can go on the Internet at a certain time and look up some issues and it'll show you the five brokerage firms that would have been the largest buyers and the five that would have been the largest sellers that day. You have to set up a special account with a bank in Korea. That's not easy to do. I'm learning it as I go along.*

"*It's like finding a new girl to me.*

"*These are good companies, and yet they're cheap. The stocks have gotten cheaper than five years ago, and yet the businesses are more valuable. Half of the companies have names that sound like a porno movie. They make basic products, like steel and cement and flour and electricity, which people will still be buying in ten years. They have a big market share in Korea, which isn't going to change, and some of these companies are exporting to China and Japan too. Yet for some reason, they haven't been noticed. Look, this flour company has more than its market value in cash, and it sells at three times earnings. I couldn't buy very much, but I got a few shares. Here's another one, a dairy. I could end up with nothing but a bunch of Korean securities in my personal portfolio.*

"*Now, I'm no expert on foreign currencies. But I'm comfortable owning these securities denominated in the won right now.*

"*The main risk, and part of why the stocks are cheap, is North Korea. And North Korea is a real threat. If North Korea invaded South Korea, the whole world could go to hell. China, Japan, all of Asia would be drawn into a war. The consequences are almost unimaginable. North Korea is very close to having nuclear weapons. I regard it as one of the world's most dangerous countries. But I would make the bet that the rest of the world, including China and Japan, are simply not going to let the situation get to the point that North Korea makes a nuclear attack on South Korea anytime soon.*

"*When you invest, you have to take some risk. The future is always uncertain. I think a group of these stocks will do very well for several years. Some of them may not do well, but as a group, they should do very well. I could end up owning them for several years.*"

He had found a new game, a new puzzle to figure out. He wanted more of them and kept looking for opportunities with the same eagerness he'd once shown stooping for winning tickets at the racetrack.

In December 2005, in a talk at the Harvard Business School, he was asked about his hopes for the Buffett Foundation's impact on society, since it would someday become the best-funded philanthropy in the world. Buffett responded that his guess was that he was not doing society as great a favor by compounding any more. So he was thinking more these days about giving the money away.

Nobody said anything. Nobody seemed to realize that Buffett had just signaled a total shift in direction.

Later, in the same speech, he talked about the Gates Foundation. He admired Bill and Melinda Gates more than any other philanthropists, he said. Theirs was the most rational and best executed of any foundation policy he had ever seen. And he liked that they didn't want publicity for their philanthropy, did not want their name on any buildings.

By early 2006, his thoughts had begun to crystallize. While he was pleased with the job his kids were doing with their own foundations, the sense of safety and security that Big Susie had given him was not duplicable. This emotional force operated beyond a conscious level. His decision to leave her in charge of the money had never been based on a rational or calculated assessment of her qualifications as a philanthropist. With the accretion of a decades-long relationship, he had simply built up layers of personal trust and comfort in his wife's judgment and wisdom. Now that she was gone, everything was different. He mentioned his change of heart to Tom Murphy at Murphy's daughter's wedding. Out of the blue, he told Sharon Osberg. He was going to give the money away early. But he had only an idea, not a plan.

Charlie Munger had already been encouraging the idea. "It wouldn't surprise me if they had Gates running it eventually," he said shortly after Susie died. "It wouldn't surprise me at all. Warren doesn't like conventional pomposity. Gates is unconventional in the way he thinks, and he's fifty instead of seventy-four."[11]

The plan, which was complicated, took months to work out in detail. The following spring, he started telling the people who were directly affected. "Brace yourself," he said when he sat down with Carol Loomis, one of the Buffett Foundation trustees. "The news was indeed stunning," she wrote.[12]

"I got lots of questions," he said about the conversations in which he made this startling announcement, "and some people had qualms about the plan initially because it was such an abrupt change from what they had been anticipating."[13] His sisters, on the other hand, were instantly enthusiastic when they found out. "This is the best idea you've had," wrote Bertie afterward, "since

you pretended to have asthma to get sent home from Fredericksburg."[14] Doris—
who knew from her own Sunshine Lady Foundation how much work it was to
give money away intelligently—thought it was a brilliant decision.[15]

On June 26, 2006, Buffett announced that he would give away eighty-five
percent of his Berkshire Hathaway stock—worth $37 billion at the time—to a
group of foundations over a number of years. No gift of this size had ever been
made in the history of philanthropy. Five out of every six shares would go to the
Bill and Melinda Gates Foundation, already the largest charity in the world, in a
historic marriage of two fortunes for the betterment of the world.[16] He was
requiring that the money be spent as it was given, so that the foundations could
not perpetuate themselves. To cushion the shock of losing the money that
would someday have made their family foundation the largest in the world,
Buffett divided the remaining shares, worth about $6 billion, among his chil-
dren's individual foundations, each of which would receive shares worth $1 bil-
lion, and the Susan Thompson Buffett Foundation, which would receive shares
worth $3 billion. None of the children had ever expected their personal founda-
tions to reach such an enormous size, especially not while he was alive. At the
date of the gift, the shares handed over in the first year's installment were worth
$1.5 billion to the Gates Foundation, $50 million to each of his children's foundations, and $150 million to the Susan Thompson Buffett Foundation.
Depending on Berkshire's stock price, those values could vary.[17]

The man who was, at the time, the second richest person on earth was giving
away his money without leaving a trace of himself behind. He had spent all his
life rolling up the snowball as if it were an extension of himself; yet he would
establish no Warren Buffett Foundation, no Buffett hospital wing, no college or
university endowment or building with his name on it. To donate the money
without naming something after himself, without controlling personally how it
would be spent—to put the money in the coffers of another foundation that he
had selected for its competence and efficiency, rather than creating a whole new
empire—upended every convention of giving. No major donor had ever done
such a thing before. "It was a historic moment in the field of philanthropy glob-
ally," said Doug Bauer of Rockefeller Philanthropy Advisors. "It's set a bar, a
touchstone, for others."[18]

That Warren Buffett had done this was both surprising and predictable.
An unconventional thinker and problem-solver, he was making a gesture
against philanthropic waste and grandiosity. The Gates Foundation got its
money, but had to spend each installment—and fast. The decision was unusual,

highly personal, a form of teaching by example, and—naturally—enormously attention-getting. Meanwhile, in another sense, this was a classic Buffett no-lose deal. He had stunned the world by giving away almost all of his money by earmarking it, yet got to keep most of it until he actually transferred the shares. Nonetheless, in one stroke he had transformed a lifetime of grasping at money by committing to letting go—and had started to disburse it by the billions. The boy who would not let his family touch the chifforobe where he kept his hoarded coins had finally become a man who could entrust his tens of billions to someone else's hands.

In the announcement speech, Buffett said, "*Just over fifty years ago last month, I sat down with seven people who gave me one hundred and five thousand dollars to manage in a little partnership. And those people made the judgment that I could do a better job in amassing wealth for them than they could do themselves.*

"*Fifty years after that, I sat down and thought about who could do a better job dispensing the wealth than myself. It's really quite logical. People don't often have that second sit-down. They are always saying, Who should handle my money? and they quite willingly turn their money over to people with a certain expertise. But they don't seem to think about doing that very often in the philanthropic world. They pick their old business cronies or whomever to administer wealth after they're gone, at a time when they won't even be able to observe what's happening.*

"*So I got very lucky, because philanthropy is harder than business. You are tackling important problems that people with intellect and money have tackled in the past and had a tough time solving. So the search for talent in philanthropy should be even more important than the search for talent in investments, where the game is not as tough.*"

Buffett then spoke of the Ovarian Lottery. "*I have been very lucky. I was born in the United States in 1930 and won the lottery the day I was born....*

"*All along, I've felt the money was just claim checks that should go back to society. I am not an enthusiast for dynastic wealth, particularly when the alternative is six billion people who've got much poorer hands in life than we have, getting a chance to benefit from the money. And my wife agreed with me.*

"*It was clear that Bill Gates had an outstanding mind with the right goals, focusing intensely with passion and heart on improving the lot of mankind around the world without any regard to gender, religion, color, or geography. He was just doing the most good for the most people. So when the time came to make a decision on where the money would go, it was a simple decision.*"

The Gates Foundation followed a basic creed that Buffett shared: "Guided by the belief that every life has equal value," it worked to "reduce inequities and improve lives around the world" in the areas of global health and education. The Gateses saw themselves as "convenors," who brought together the best minds as advisers to work on permanent solutions to enormous problems.[19]

However much Buffett had changed and grown since Susie's death, he was still very much the same in certain ways. Allen Greenberg, who ran the Buffett Foundation, found out that he would be running not the $45 billion foundation for which he had been preparing, but a $6 billion foundation, by proxy through Allen's new boss and ex-wife, Susie Jr. Warren had been unable to bring himself to confront Greenberg to tell him that all his plans must be downsized. Susie Jr. had to convince Allen that this was in no way a grade on his performance. After his initial explosion over the fact that he hadn't heard the news from the source, he conceded that he would still be administering one of the world's ten largest charitable coffers, and peace ultimately reigned.

All involved had ample reason to behave well. Even though Buffett was giving away a vast sum, the money would be paid out over some years. And the stock he had not yet earmarked as a gift was estimated as worth more than $6 billion at the time. He still had plenty to give away.

The effects of Buffett's announcement were immediate and sizable. Jackie Chan, the Hong Kong actor, announced that he would give away half his wealth. Li Ka-shing, Asia's richest man, pledged a third of his $19 billion to his own charitable foundation. Carlos Slim, the Mexican communications monopolist, ridiculed Buffett and Gates for their philanthropy but, some months later, did a turnabout and announced that he, too, would begin giving money away. And the Gateses set up a new division within their foundation simply to handle people who wanted to make donations to them—such as a seven-year-old girl who sent the Gates Foundation her life savings of $35.

The newly enriched Gates Foundation was having a tectonic impact on the philanthropic world. Its "all-asset approach," which greatly resembled Buffett's ideas about concentration—and, indeed, his investing style—focused resources toward a short, carefully selected list of serious problems. That differed markedly from many other major foundations and community funds, at which a headquarters staff of philanthropoids circled around a series of supplicants, playing "eeny, meeny, miney, moe" as they doled out fragmentary sums. By the end of 2006, certain organizations such as the Rockefeller Foundation had begun modifying their policies to align them more closely with the Gates approach.[20]

Three thousand letters from needy people poured into Buffett's office after the Gates announcement, with more coming every day. They had cataclysmic problems through no fault of their own. They were the losers in the Ovarian Lottery. Warren forwarded the letters to his sister Doris. Over the past ten years her Sunshine Lady Foundation, funded with the proceeds from Howard Buffett's trust, had helped thousands of victims of domestic violence, the severely disadvantaged, and families in crisis. He enclosed $5 million with the letters to help fund Doris's work.[21]

Buffett kept handing out more of his billions. He was already giving $5 million a year to Ted Turner's Nuclear Threat Initiative (NTI), which he considered the most important of the U.S. organizations focused on dealing with the world's nuclear threat, and he was willing to give more. Former Senator Sam Nunn, who ran NTI, had proposed a nuclear-fuel reserve to which countries could turn rather than developing their own nuclear enrichment programs, thereby reducing the likelihood of nuclear proliferation. Buffett felt that this idea had considerable merit, and he pledged $50 million as a matching gift if other funds could be raised. He would make huge amounts of money available to any antinuclear causes that seemed to him able to come up with realistic solutions to the problem.

Astrid was now Warren's official companion at events outside Omaha. She remained virtually unchanged—the same plainspoken, unpretentious person.

Two years after Susie's death, on his seventy-sixth birthday, Warren married Astrid in an unfussy civil ceremony at Susie Jr.'s house with no guests other than family. Astrid wore a simple turquoise blouse and white pants, and Warren wore a business suit. Tears welled from her eyes as he placed a huge diamond solitaire ring on her finger. Afterward, they went to the Bonefish Grill next to Borsheim's for dinner. Then they flew out to San Francisco for a wedding party and a traditional wedding cake at Sharon Osberg and David Smith's. The Gateses joined them for the celebration.

Warren Buffett, the not-simple man of simple tastes, now had the simple life of the man that he had always believed himself to be. He had one wife, drove one car, occupied one house that hadn't been redecorated in years, ran one business, and spent more and more time with his family.[22]

Buffett always said that trees don't grow to the sky. But new saplings form.

The question of who would succeed him had long vexed his shareholders. He sometimes quipped that Berkshire could be run by someone working five hours a week, or by Charlie's bust of Ben Franklin, or by a cardboard cutout. He'd also joked about controlling it after his death: "Well, my backup plan is that I've figured out how to manage the company by séance." No one was fooled by his banter. On other occasions he was just as likely to tell his listeners: "My psyche is all wrapped up in Berkshire." And those who worked for and invested in Berkshire were all wrapped up in Buffett. He was not replaceable. Thanks in part to his television appearances, his image in the public mind was that of America's greatest investor, its wisest thinker on business matters.

Even so, Buffett's adoring club of shareholders had for some time now contained certain rebellious members, some of whom may in fact have joined only to needle him. After the speech about abortion at the fractious 2004 shareholder meeting, Buffett moved the business section of the 2005 meeting to late in the afternoon, both in order to discourage activists and in the hope that if they did appear, the audience would already be on its way to the Furniture Mart or the local bars by the time he had to answer any unpleasant questions.

That year, and the following, no activists appeared to make motions in person. But in 2007, a billboard appeared overlooking a major freeway in Omaha that said, "Will your conscience let you off on a technicality?" The question referred to a proposed resolution to force Berkshire to sell its PetroChina investment; PetroChina's parent company, Chinese National Petroleum Company (CNPC), was implicated in funding Chinese sponsorship of genocide in Darfur. While not required to put the resolution on the ballot, Buffett did so. The supervoting provisions of Berkshire's A shares meant that the resolution could never pass. Thus, it seemed safe to allow a vigorous airing of the Darfur issue at the shareholder meeting, a gesture that would garner praise for transparency.

At the meeting, Buffett stated his position: Since PetroChina was ultimately owned by the Chinese government, it was not responsible for directing how its profits were used. This position met with mixed views; many thought it did amount to a technicality. While Buffett was lauded for his openness, for the most part the resolution generated only bad publicity. Descriptions of Buffett-as-financier-of-genocide competed in the press with the more friendly aspects of the shareholder meeting. Though Buffett downplayed the PetroChina controversy, this was not the finale he was looking for at his "Woodstock for Capitalists"; he cared deeply what his shareholders thought of him and the company. In the end, the question of what to do about the PetroChina shares was mooted when, for reasons that he said were unrelated to Darfur, Buffett sold the PetroChina investment before the 2008 shareholder meeting. The stock had cost Berkshire just under $500 million; the company netted a $3.5 billion profit.

In 2008 and 2009, environmentalists and Native Americans would protest at the meeting, claiming that two of MidAmerican Energy subsidiary PacifiCorp's dams on the Klamath River were killing salmon and causing human health hazards. But by then Buffett had learned his lesson, and understood that it was better to pay as little attention as possible to the activists. For all practical purposes, he ignored the Klamath Dam controversy, and it received far less notice among Berkshire shareholders and the media.

Buffett's long-used technique of criticizing by withholding attention worked as well on activists as it did on everyone else. He directed the media's attention toward anyone and anything he wanted them to focus on, and distracted them— for the most part successfully—from subjects he would rather be ignored.

What Buffett wanted most of all was for investors, shareholders, the media, and, above all, students of business to pay attention to him and to Berkshire Hathaway—his Sistine Chapel, his didactic enterprise, the life's work that spelled out how he thought a business should be managed.

But what would happen to all the capital that Berkshire had accumulated? The question of either a dividend or a huge share repurchase would arise instantly when he was gone. His successor as CEO would have to change some things—for while parts of the Berkshire model should be preserved, other parts should not.

Buffett had addressed the issue of his advancing age partly by adding new directors to the Berkshire board. Before adding Tom Murphy and Don Keough in 2002, he had used his chairman's letter to invite shareholders to nominate themselves for the director position. The letters came pouring in, and Buffett— of course—collected them the way he collected everything. The director nomination stunt revealed the highly personal—bordering on whimsical—style of corporate governance at Berkshire. In response to an SEC request, Berkshire agreed to adopt a formal process for shareholders to nominate directors. After the later additions of Bill Gates and Charlotte Guyman, in 2007 director Malcolm Chace, the last holdover from the old textile mill days, retired. With that, Buffett added Yahoo! chief financial officer Susan Decker to the board, tilting the demographic to a younger average age.

But, along the way, Buffett found that he liked the idea of advertising for people to nominate themselves for jobs. He had always preferred that people ask him for favors. In his 2006 letter to shareholders, prodded by Bill Gates, he had pointed out that Lou Simpson's "top-notch" investing record was at risk (omitting any mention of his own) if anything happened to both Simpson and himself, and advertised for a successor to Simpson. Send in your résumé, Buffett said.

What he did not mention was why Gates was prodding him. Berkshire's big money was always made in times of fear and panic. When others fled a stock and—especially—the whole stock market, Buffett saw that as a cue to buy. In the 1960s he bought American Express; in the 1970s he bought GEICO and the *Washington Post*, and any number of other stocks that positioned Berkshire for its long gallop into the 1990s; in the early 1980s, when investors thought equities were dead, he bought stocks greedily. Later, he bought Coca-Cola when its price war with Pepsi seemed to have eroded the franchise; he scooped up undervalued stocks after the market crash of 1987. He had tried to buy Long-Term Capital Management during the panic its failure created. That he had not succeeded he considered one of the great missed opportunities of his life; Buffett kept the framed offer letter on his office wall.

Buffett reveled in the hard times that terrified most investors. Since the long boom of the 1980s began, he had been waiting for others to become fearful again so that he could become greedy. "*It may not happen in my lifetime,*" he said once. His nagging worry was that after holding Berkshire's powder dry for two decades, he might never get to spend it in a final burst of glory. Who knew how much longer the boom would last? The one thing he did know was that it wouldn't be forever.

Forced to choose someone besides himself who might be in charge of Berkshire's coffers at the time of the next panic—as well as during the speculative investment bubble that would lead up to it—he and Munger were looking for a person who could "*anticipate things that have never happened.*" Seven hundred proposals arrived from all over the world. One person explained, "I am said to be selfish and also ruthless"; many people wrote saying they had no requisite experience, but wanted to be Buffett's apprentice, understudy, or protégé. He collected all these letters in huge boxes in the boardroom before eventually filing them away. In the end he chose four candidates who were already successful and managing money; they waited in the wings to assume the role of being compared to Warren Buffett—ten seconds of omnipotence, fifteen minutes of fame, followed by a marathon endurance test.

Buffett once said that he would be happy if Berkshire was still serving his shareholders thirty years after his death. That was his design. The elegant machine that he had created was built to last more than a generation beyond him. Yet to maintain it would be a remarkable accomplishment; he was the soul of that machine, and without him there would be a vacuum at the center, no matter what. For Buffett was the best there would ever be at the thing that only he could do perfectly, which was to be himself.

No group of shareholders in history had ever missed their CEO as much as Berkshire's shareholders would miss Buffett when he was finally gone. None had ever thought of their CEO as a teacher and a friend the way Buffett's shareholders had thought of him. The man who had made billions had touched thousands of people and had a relationship that felt personal to countless others whom he'd never even met or seen. But oddly enough, no matter how many fan letters Buffett got or how many autographs he signed, he never fully grasped how loved and admired he was. He still got as excited about every letter and request for an autograph as though it were the first.

63

The Crisis

On October 23, 2006, Berkshire Hathaway became the first American stock to trade above $100,000 per share. By the end of 2007, BRK reached $149,200, which gave Berkshire a market value of more than $200 billion. Berkshire was the world's most respected company, according to a *Barron's* survey.[1] Buffett's personal fortune exceeded $60 billion, and only a few months earlier, the Dow had reached its all-time high of 14,164.53.[2] Businesses were posting record earnings; the market, as a discounting machine, built into stock prices the expectation that an even greater and growing stream of money could be coaxed from consumers' pockets.

Buffett dampened his own shareholders' expectations of Berkshire, yet showed no signs of giving up control or competing any less aggressively than before. Even so, a few of Berkshire's longtime shareholders began to sell stock. Some were donating appreciated shares to charity at a recently run-up price. Others cited Buffett's age; he was approaching seventy-eight. And inevitably, the $149,200 price tag for a single share of BRK drew in the sort of new investors who always buy in at the top.

As reflected in Berkshire's stock price, Buffett had been enjoying a period of almost unbroken success since the end of the Internet bubble. Only one episode of any significance marred the record of these six years. This was a legal threat to Buffett and to Berkshire that, at least initially, was as serious as Buffett's earlier encounter with the SEC over Blue Chip, and Salomon's near brush with death. It had to do with General Re, Buffett's onetime problem-child investment, which had—at least financially—undergone a remarkable recovery.

By 2007, the company had become the most successful of Berkshire's long string of insurance turnarounds. After $2.3 billion of cumulative losses related to insurance and reinsurance sold in prior years, and $412 million of charges for the runoff of Gen Re Securities, the company's derivatives unit, General Re was reporting the most profitable results in its history, with $2.2 billion of pretax operating earnings.[3] It had earned back the losses and restored its balance sheet to a better condition than when Buffett bought it; it was operating with nearly one-third fewer employees and the company had been transformed.[4]

General Re had escaped the fate of Salomon and overcome the stigma of its Scarlet Letter. Buffett was finally able to praise it and its senior managers, Joe Brandon and Tad Montross, in some depth in his 2007 shareholder letter, saying *"the luster of the company has been restored"* by *"doing first-class business in a first-class way."*[5]

But at the beginning of 2008, four employees of General Re and one employee of AIG were put on trial in Hartford, Connecticut, on charges of federal criminal conspiracy. For those on trial, the next few months would bring to a climax the years of hell that white-collar criminal investigations impose on their subjects. For Buffett, the trial would mean the beginning of the end to this particularly golden chapter of his life.

The trial came about as a consequence of General Re's last act of ignominy before its change of management in 2001. General Re had created a Salomon-type scandal of its own in which it broke Buffett's rule of not "losing reputation for the firm." This was the event that had, as it unfolded, adjusted Buffett's perception of the new legal-enforcement environment, in which showing extreme contrition and cooperation produced no advantage in how a company was treated by prosecutors. Extreme contrition and cooperation were now the expected minimum standard—in part because of Salomon. Anything short of that—for a company to defend itself or its employees, for example—could be considered grounds for indictment. Trying to exceed the minimum threshold for extreme contrition and cooperation, as Buffett was always inclined to do when confessing any sort of mistake or flaw, could even be a disadvantage now, attracting more attention to a company at a time when the fairness of certain state and federal criminal procedures was being questioned.[6]

General Re had first become entangled in legal and regulatory problems when New York Attorney General Eliot Spitzer started investigating the insurance industry over "finite" reinsurance in 2004. "Finite" reinsurance has been defined in many ways, but, put simply, it is a type of reinsurance used by the client mainly for financial or accounting reasons—either to bolster its capital or to improve the amount or timing of its earnings. While usually legal and sometimes legitimate, finite reinsurance had been subject to such widespread abuse that accounting rulemakers have spent decades trying to rein it in.*

In 2003, both General Re and Ajit Jain's Berkshire Re were condemned in a special investigation for selling finite reinsurance that allegedly contributed to the 2001 collapse of an Australian insurer, HIH.[7] Two years later, General Re was accused by insurance regulators and policyholders of having sold fraudulent reinsurance in the 1990s in connection with the failure of a Virginia medical malpractice insurer, the Reciprocal of America. Though the Department of Justice investigated the allegations extensively, no charges were brought against Gen Re or any of its employees.[8] That same year, Eliot Spitzer's investigation of the insurance industry prompted an additional investigation that concluded that six General Re employees had conspired with one AIG employee to aid and abet an accounting fraud for AIG. Before long, the New York State investigation was joined by the SEC and the Department of Justice.

In June 2005, two of the conspirators, Richard Napier and John Houldsworth, plea-bargained and agreed to testify for the prosecution against General Re's former CEO, Ronald Ferguson; its former chief financial officer, Elizabeth Monrad; its head of finite reinsurance, Christopher Garand; and its general counsel, Robert Graham; as well as Christian Milton, head of reinsurance at AIG, all of whom were indicted on federal conspiracy and fraud charges. At the same time, the SEC and the Department of Justice began pursuing a settlement of some sort with Berkshire Hathaway.

The defendants were tried together as conspirators in a case that began in federal court in Hartford in January 2008 and lasted for several weeks. It was noteworthy for the prosecution's use of numerous e-mails and taped telephone conversations in which several of the defendants had repeatedly discussed the matter in colorful terms. The fraud had been executed through a reinsurance transaction designed to deceive investors and Wall Street analysts by transferring $500 million in reserves to AIG to window-dress AIG's balance sheet. This made AIG appear to have more claim reserves than it actually had, which

---

*Before working on Wall Street, I was one of those trying to rein it in, as a project manager at the Financial Accounting Standards Board, the primary accounting rulemaker. I helped to draft rules that specify how to account for finite reinsurance.

soothed analysts' worries that AIG might be overstating its earnings by failing to record sufficient expenses for claims. In fact, AIG was doing just that.

Spitzer, joined by the SEC and the Department of Justice, had investigated this question, and Munger, Tolles & Olson, led by partner Ron Olson, who sat on Berkshire's board, had conducted a massive internal investigation at Berkshire Hathaway. The investigation, which subsequently expanded to include the AIG deal, focused mainly on General Re and its employees. Munger, Tolles was required to, in effect, act as an arm of the prosecution, and worked with the handicap of representing Berkshire Hathaway, General Re, and Buffett personally as its clients. The conflicts posed by this set of relationships were unusual, although not unheard of in the legal profession. Ordinarily Buffett would not tolerate, much less create, such a conflict-riddled situation, but the investigation terrified him and threatened his deeply ingrained desire for privacy.

Buffett thought of himself and Berkshire as indistinguishable. He had fought like a Rottweiler earlier in his career to escape being named in the consent decree to the Blue Chip fraud case. He was far more invested in his gargantuan reputation now, both psychologically and from a business standpoint. During the months in 2005 and 2006 that the investigation was at full boil, the threat to his reputation from the case obsessed him.

Buffett was put through an awkward investigative process by Munger, Tolles and interviewed by the government, but Spitzer was quick to clear him. In April 2005 (five months after he entered the race for governor of New York), Spitzer told George Stephanopolous on *ABC This Week* that Buffett was "only a witness." He called Buffett an "icon" who had "succeeded in the right way" and who stood for "transparency and accountability." One need not be a cynic to detect that Spitzer might have been angling for an endorsement from the *Buffalo News* in the governors' race.[9]

After New York handed the criminal charges over to the Justice Department for prosecution, Buffett still remained in some jeopardy. If prosecutors could find enough evidence to indict Buffett, they would certainly do so. The question was, what is "enough"?

Contrary to the way they are often portrayed on television, modern prosecutors are not simply on a moral crusade trying to bring the guilty to justice; they are pragmatists who make strategic and tactical decisions. Faced with Warren Buffett, America's icon of business ethics, the prosecutors churned through a unique calculus. There could be no greater prize for a prosecutor than to convict

Warren Buffett; locking up Buffett could put a journeyman attorney on the road to the Supreme Court.

On the other hand, who would take the risk of prosecuting Warren Buffett and failing to convict him? If Buffett had been caught on videotape mugging and snatching a purse from a ninety-year-old lady, there was a pretty good chance a jury would decide that the tape was doctored, she was the mugger, and he deserved a medal—and he would walk. Not only that, prosecutors wanted Buffett as a potential witness because of the star power and credibility he would bring if he testified on their behalf.

In the end, Buffett was omitted from the government's list of unindicted co-conspirators. Some believed that he received kid-glove treatment because of his status as an almost untouchable figure in business. Many in the insurance industry were infuriated because they felt Ferguson and the others were being treated unjustly, especially by comparison. Buffett was left wide open to such perceptions in part because Berkshire did not hire an outside law firm to conduct its internal investigation. Thus no matter how well MTO had performed its responsibilities, the appearance that the investigation was actually not independent was impossible to overcome.

In the trial, the defendants invoked a "Buffett defense," saying that Buffett had approved the outlines of the structured transaction and was involved in setting the fee. The question, however, was not whether Buffett knew about the transaction—he did—but whether he knew it was fraudulent.

General Re's CEO, Joseph Brandon, had been listed among the various unindicted co-conspirators in the case. He had received a "Wells Notice" (of possible civil fraud prosecution) from the SEC, although no civil charges were ever filed. He cooperated with federal prosecutors without asking for immunity. During the trial, Brandon was cited by the defendants' lawyers as having knowledge of the deal; General Re's chief operating officer, Tad Montross, was also named by the defendants as having knowledge of the transaction. In the end, none of the three men—Buffett, Brandon, or Montross—testified in the case.* After weeks in court

---

*I was subpoenaed by the prosecution as both a fact witness and an expert, and testified as an analyst that I would "almost certainly" have not upgraded AIG to a "strong buy" in early 2000 had I known the company's true financial position. Under cross-examination I testified about my acquaintance with all of the defendants. I know some of them better than I do others, but have always had high regard for all of them. I also testified about my relationship with Warren, that I was writing this book, and that Joe Brandon has been a close friend since 1992. I wasn't asked about Tad Montross, but I'm also acquainted with him.

and a short jury deliberation, in February 2008 all five defendants were convicted on all counts in the indictment and were sentenced to terms ranging from a year and a day (Robert Graham) to four years (Chris Milton of AIG). The convicted defendants said they would appeal.

In April 2008, shortly after the trial ended, Brandon resigned as CEO of General Re to help facilitate a settlement between the company and government authorities that has yet to take place. The settlement, when it comes, is likely to include fines, other penalties, and adverse publicity.*

Only a month after the jury reached its verdicts, New York Governor Eliot Spitzer resigned following revelations that he patronized the prostitutes of an escort service called the Emperor's Club.

The Gen Re-AIG case he launched through his investigation was noteworthy in several respects. It is the only U.S. case in which financial reinsurance has resulted in criminal charges and prison sentences, rather than civil settlements. In recent corporate history, no other criminal aiding-and-abetting case has stuck; convictions in a Merrill Lynch case related to Enron were thrown out. For the first time, therefore, employees of one company were held responsible for a fraud committed by another company.

The Gen Re case also was one of the last corporate fraud cases prosecuted under the government policy of compelled waiver of the attorney-client privilege and the attorney work-product doctrine, which was revised after being declared unconstitutional by the U.S. District Court for the Southern District of New York. Thus, the defendants were arguably convicted using evidence that either would not have been available to prosecutors or would have been thrown out if the trial were held today.

Even though he was obsessed during this period with the investigation's potential to harm his reputation, Buffett was able to compartmentalize the way he always did. Whenever a business opportunity presented itself, he'd shift with startling speed from anxious ruminant to hungry great white shark. Buffett was never more himself than when given the chance to invest in something he wanted at a price of his choosing.

With the stock market so expensive, for the past several years Buffett had

---

*Currently I am still under subpoena from former AIG CEO Hank Greenberg in a related case brought against him by the New York Attorney General's office. And at this writing, Berkshire Hathaway has settled with neither the SEC nor the Department of Justice.

continued to buy mostly whole businesses. Berkshire bought Iscar, a highly automated Israeli maker of metal cutting tools, in its first acquisition of a non-U.S. company. For Fruit of the Loom, Buffett bought Russell Athletics. Berkshire took control of Equitas, assuming the old claims of Lloyd's of London in exchange for $7 billion worth of insurance float, and also bought electronics distributor TTI. Buffett invested steadily in the stock of BNSF (Burlington Northern Santa Fe) railroad in 2007, setting off a minor flurry of interest in railroad stocks. His interest in railroads was built on the thesis that U.S. imports from Asia, especially China, would continue to stay high—and the goods would have to be transported to markets all over the United States. Railroads have an advantage over trucking because of their greater fuel efficiency. The level of imports at the time he began buying this stock reflected a relatively weak dollar (compared to what came later) and a boom economy. As these conditions reversed, he stayed true to his long-term strategy; he would eventually increase Berkshire's stake in BNSF to more than twenty percent of the railroad.

One investment that Buffett did not make was in the *Wall Street Journal*. Although it was his favorite newspaper, he had never owned its stock. When press lord Rupert Murdoch offered to buy the paper in 2007, some *Journal* editors and staffers hoped that Buffett would save it in the cause of quality journalism. But he would not pay a premium price for what he considered a rich man's trophy, even to play a potentially historic role in media. Long ago, during the days of the *Washington Monthly,* the unsentimental side of Buffett had divorced his fondness for journalism from his wallet. Nothing had changed that.

In Buffett's lifetime, the rapid "disintermediation" of the entirety of traditional media—that is, the replacement, at varying speeds, of recorded music, movies, newspapers, radio, television, and magazines by a single medium, consisting of the Internet and various hard storage devices such as the personal computer and the iPod—was the greatest change in business that he had ever witnessed in any of the industries he had studied. Even his favorite of Walter Annenberg's "essentialities," the *Daily Racing Form,* had become, for all practical purposes, toast.

Buffett would always love reading newspapers, but his investing was tightly focused on simple businesses that were as close to immortal as possible. Newspapers—in fact, any sort of media—no longer qualified. Candy, on the other hand, was an immortal business, and the economics of the candy business remained predictable.

In 2008, candy maker Mars, Inc. announced that it was buying Wm. Wrigley

Jr. Company for $23 billion. Buffett agreed, through Berkshire, to lend $6.5 billion as part of the deal, in an arrangement facilitated by Byron Trott, his investment banker at Goldman Sachs. Trott had been responsible for several of Berkshire's acquisitions. He understood how Buffett thought, and Buffett said that Trott had Berkshire's interests at heart. Like many of Buffett's investments, the Wrigley deal harkened back to his childhood, when he had refused to sell a single stick of gum to Virginia Macoubrie. "I've been conducting a seventy-year taste test," Buffett said about Wrigley's.

Buffett's first thought after agreeing to make the loan—of course—had been to call Kelly Muchemore Broz and ask her to set aside a little space at the next shareholder meeting, in case Mars and Wrigley wanted to sell products to his shareholders. The 2008 meeting turned into a mini-festival of candy and chewing gum. Attendance set a new record: 31,000 people.

In another deal that year typical of Buffett, Berkshire acquired Marmon Holdings, a small industrial conglomerate with sales of $7 billion. The seller was Chicago's Pritzker family, which had decided to break up its business to settle family squabbling that had broken out after the death of Buffett's old coattailing hero Jay Pritzker in 1999.

Around this time, Buffett had also become more interested in the energy business, even though he had sold the PetroChina stock—for which he had recently taken a lot of heat, because when the price of crude oil peaked in July 2008 at $147 per barrel, six months after the sale, PetroChina's stock kept rising. Buffett's critics didn't hesitate to speak up; he was accused of selling PetroChina too soon. Buffett said that he felt Berkshire had made enough money on the stock. What no one knew at the time was that Buffett was buying a huge slug—66.4 million shares—of ConocoPhillips stock. He was also increasing Berkshire's stake in NRG Energy, Inc.

ConocoPhillips was the cheapest of the major energy stocks, and Buffett was concerned about inflation. Still, it was a surprising move at a time when complaints were proliferating that speculators were manipulating the energy market.

Buffett's next move was equally counterintuitive. He wrote various derivative contracts for Berkshire that amounted to optimistic calls on the stock market in various economies. Some of these were direct bets on the market, and others were indirect bets that tied up some of Berkshire's capital, rendering it unavailable in the event of a market crash.

The direct bets were "put options" on four stock indices—the Euro zone, the United States, the United Kingdom, and Japan—that would expire between

2019 and 2028. Berkshire would pay the buyers if any of the indices were lower at expiration than they had been when the puts were written. The total maximum exposure to these contracts (before taxes, and before $4.9 billion of premiums and the investment income they will earn) was $37.1 billion. Most likely, Berkshire would lose nothing, or a smaller amount. To lose the entire $37.1 billion, all four stock indices would have to fall to zero, in which case the world and whoever is running Berkshire at that time will have far bigger problems to worry about.

In deciding to insure investors against the risk that most of the world (except China) becomes insolvent, Buffett had handicapped the situation the way he would a catastrophe reinsurance contract—by assessing probabilities—and concluded that he liked the price compared to the risk Berkshire was taking. One curious aspect of these deals was their duration. Buffett had entered into contracts worth tens of billions of dollars, which would take up a chunk of Berkshire's capital and whose value would not be known until he was between eighty-nine and ninety-eight years old. It was as if he had staked out a plot of capital within Berkshire, and leased it for this term. For the first time, he seemed to be acting on his determination to match Rose Blumkin's lifespan.

This analysis of Buffett's actions in recent years is constrained by close perspective and lack of hindsight; it is more akin to reporting and should be considered as such—in other words, more subject to revision than other portions of the book. However, it appears that Buffett, the ultimate capital allocator, did not fully understand how much capital he was committing to these deals. Buffett's analysis excluded one other variable. Investors on the other side of Berkshire's equity-index puts needed to hedge their credit risk on Berkshire. Buffett would later acknowledge (at the 2009 shareholders meeting) that he did not realize this. He thought of Berkshire, with its "Fort Knox" balance sheet and triple-A credit rating, as having essentially no credit risk, even though investors looked at it differently—quantitatively. If Berkshire could not pay for any reason, they would lose money. The investors bought credit default swaps (CDSs), a type of derivative that insures against credit risk, to make bets that would pay off if Berkshire stock fell.

The CDS price, or "swap spread," is an indicator of a company's bankruptcy risk. Stocks tend to trade in the reverse direction of their swap spreads. The CDS market has certain flaws, an important one being that a company's bankruptcy risk grows as its stock price falls, and its stock price falls if its perceived bankruptcy risk rises. This self-reinforcing loop means that even companies with strong finances can find their balance sheets encumbered by perceived credit risk if their stock prices fall when their swap spreads rise.

Initially, this feedback loop did not seem important to Berkshire. Its stock price was approaching an all-time high; few people were paying attention to the puts; Berkshire's balance sheet seemed impregnable.

Buffett's sanguine attitude about the market, as displayed in the Conoco-Phillips stock, the derivative deals, and his investing in a pair of Irish banks that were profiting from the booming—some said speculative—Irish economy, was all of a piece with another decision: to maintain large positions in certain stocks, especially financial stocks, but also in the rating agency Moody's and in Coca-Cola, despite record stock valuations and signs of a bursting real estate bubble. In his mind, Buffett could clearly foresee the outlines of a potential financial meltdown. He explained how he wanted Berkshire to be positioned if that happened: *"We want to be the lender of last resort."* Berkshire's balance sheet made it, as Buffett always said, the "Fort Knox of capital."

But it was as if he had never sat down and asked himself: What would Berkshire's balance sheet look like if global stock markets fell by fifty percent? This would later prove an important omission.

Buffett had long preferred to find a great company and own the stock as long as possible. Investors who had watched him over the years had become so accustomed to certain Buffettisms—holding stocks for the equivalent of an investing lifetime, not selling businesses that Berkshire acquired, investing as though there were only twenty punches on your scorecard—that they believed Buffett's investing style was to buy and hold forever.

Buffett had indeed learned through experience that *"when in doubt keep holding"*; he said, *"I've made most of my money sitting on my ass."* He never sold failing businesses unless their economics turned from simply bad to parasitic, for personal reasons: He liked the people, the managers, the business, the simplicity of fewer decisions, and the reputation for loyalty.

Yet during his early, hungry years, he had not hesitated to sell one stock for another when a better opportunity came along. During the 1960s bubble, he moved money into staid AT&T, then shut down his investing partnership completely to protect his partners (and himself) from financial harm. During the 1987 bubble, with no partnership to liquidate and so much capital it had become a struggle to manage, he dumped many stocks in favor of bonds and pared the portfolio—but kept what he called the Inevitables (GEICO, Cap Cities, and the *Washington Post*). Still, by selling stocks, he had at least partly protected his shareholders from the second major market crash of his lifetime.[10]

In the 1990s, more passivity crept into his investing style. By then, Berkshire had far more money than it could use. During the Internet bubble, rather than sell overvalued stocks such as Coca-Cola (another of his Inevitables), Buffett diluted the risk from these stocks to Berkshire's balance sheet by acquiring General Re.

With hindsight, he did say his failure to unload some of those stocks was a mistake. He explained that his role as a board member had gotten in the way of his selling Coca-Cola. Buffett finally stepped down from the board in February 2006, avoiding another referendum on his independence as a board member. Privately, Munger complained that Buffett should have resigned from the Coca-Cola board earlier so that they could have sold the stock. Selling would have pushed down the price, but not by as much as it eventually declined.

"I always used to tell Gates that a ham sandwich could run Coca-Cola. And it was a damn good thing, too, because we had a period there a couple of years ago where, if it hadn't been that great of a business, it might not have survived."

The company—and its stock—did rebound. By 2008, most of its business problems had been largely resolved, and CEO Neville Isdell, who announced his retirement in 2007, had settled the Justice Department investigation and closed a $200 million racial discrimination lawsuit. The new CEO, Muhtar Kent, had led the company's successful push into non-cola drinks, where Coca-Cola had been lagging and was strategically off course.

Still, as of early 2008, Coca-Cola's stock price, at $58, was fifty-six percent above its lowest price, but did not approach its pre-bubble high of more than $87 per share, and couldn't justify Berkshire's having held the stock for a decade. And it would soon turn out that Coca-Cola's stock price was tracking the overall stock market, which would be revealed as part of another speculative bubble, this one buoyed by the ebullient "consumer economy" and driven by cheap credit. Although average wages in the United States had risen only 0.6 percent a year since 1998 and consumer confidence had been declining steadily, GDP had risen 2.6 percent a year. This was an artificial increase—boosted by an $8.6 trillion increase in personal indebtedness and an almost $20 trillion increase in household net worth—that came from rising real estate values and the stock market. In essence, consumer debt had inflated the economy beyond its real size. This economic "growth" was simply borrowed from the future, and would have to be paid back with interest.

The signs of a debt-inflated economy had emerged in the early "noughties" in the subprime lending and real estate markets. Wesco, led by Charlie Munger and with Buffett's wholehearted concurrence, had considered adjustable rate mortgages as early as 1984, recognized the risks that were beginning to creep into the mortgage market from nonstandard terms, and kept its lending standards tight. Thus Wesco would not experience the sort of losses experienced by other mortgage lenders in 2007 through 2009.

By 2004, the giant government-backed mortgage lenders, Federal Home Loan Mortgage Corporation (Freddie Mac) and the Federal National Mortgage Association (Fannie Mae), had bought and guaranteed billions of these subprime mortgages. The Department of Housing and Urban Development required Fannie Mae to devote half its business to low- and moderate-income families, who borrowed through the type of aggressive loans that were fueling the subprime market. Easing the path to these loans, the Federal Reserve had slashed interest rates more than a dozen times and held rates at historically low levels for years. U.S. homeownership peaked at an all-time high of 69.2 percent. Housing prices grew at double-digit rates. Meanwhile, an inventory of unsold homes began to build in overheated markets such as south Florida and Las Vegas.

Berkshire Hathaway, which owned Home Services of America, the nation's second largest real estate broker, collected these statistics, which Buffett monitored with concern. In late 2005 and early 2006, median home prices began to decline in certain areas, as the number of homes for sale rose and the amount of time they remained on the market lengthened. The U.S. home construction index had fallen forty percent by mid-August 2006. By early 2007, mortgage lenders had started setting aside more money for losses as delinquencies rose.

The first piece of serious fallout from the real estate bubble appeared in April 2007, when New Century Financial, the country's largest subprime lender, filed for bankruptcy. Standard & Poor's and Moody's downgraded more than one hundred bonds backed by second-lien subprime mortgages.

As has so often happened with bubbles in the past, despite these ominous signs the Dow hit a new high of 14,000 in July 2007.

The global margin call began in August. Over a period of eight months, the financial world imploded in a credit crisis of historic proportions. Not since the Great Depression had such a severe credit seizure occurred. Not since the Panic of 1907, when old J. P. Morgan himself had personally intervened to orchestrate a solution to the panic, had such extraordinary informal intervention in financial markets taken place as would occur in 2008 and 2009.

The crisis progressed in fits and starts, with weeks and even months of apparent calm followed by shocking convulsions.

"They said all these derivatives made the world safer and spread the risk out. But it didn't spread the risk in terms of how people reacted to a given stimulus. Now, you could argue that it might be way better to have that credit with just five banks, who could all work, than to have it with thousands around the globe, all of whom are going to rush out of it at the same time."

The Federal Reserve cut interest rates once again, and worked with other central banks to activate other emergency sources of financing,[11] yet the reluctance to lend began to show signs of contagion. On October 9, 2007, the Dow reached a high of 14,165, then went into free fall, as with one announcement after another of a huge loss from subprime loans, a fire sale, a bankruptcy, or a collapse, the low rumbling panic grew louder. More people tried to sell assets behind the scenes and found no buyers; more lenders began to call in loans. The CEOs of Merrill Lynch and Citigroup and the president of Morgan Stanley were ousted for subprime-related losses. Central banks began to take coordinated action to provide lending facilities to the major banks, because others were refusing to provide credit. This eased the financial distress temporarily.

MBIA and Ambac, insurers of mortgage-backed bonds, were downgraded by credit rating agencies for being seriously undercapitalized to bear the size of the losses that were emerging. Berkshire Hathaway formed its own bond insurer—Berkshire Hathaway Assurance Co.—to provide triple-A protection for sound municipal bonds that needed insurance. Buffett offered to buy $800 million of municipal bonds from MBIA and Ambac at what he thought was a rich price—$4.5 billion to each. They didn't sell to Berkshire, and, as sizable municipal bond losses began to develop, he would later say he was glad the deal didn't work out.

On Thursday, March 13, 2008, a bank run began on Bear Stearns, the weakest of the investment banks, as its lenders started refusing to roll over its loans. In a near re-creation of the Salomon crisis seventeen years earlier, Bear almost collapsed the following day, Friday, from lack of financing. Asked to bail out Bear, Buffett declined to pour money into a black hole, even for the company run by his old friends Jimmy Cayne and Ace Greenberg. Instead, the Federal Reserve took the unprecedented step of guaranteeing $30 billion of Bear Stearns debt—the first time the Fed had ever bailed out an investment bank. Bear closed at $30 per share on Friday afternoon. Buffett pondered the situation that evening. Long-Term Capital Management's bailout had been a dress rehearsal—on a much smaller scale—for this moment.

"The speed with which fear can spread—nobody has to have an account at Bear Stearns, nobody has to lend them money. It's a version of what I went through at Salomon, where you were just inches away all the time from, in effect, an electronic run on the bank. Banks can't stand runs. The Federal Reserve hasn't bailed out investment banks before, and that was what I was sort of pleading back there in 1991 with Salomon. If Salomon went, who knows what kind of dominoes would set off. I don't have good answers to what the Fed should do. Some parts of the market are pretty close to paralyzed. They don't want contagion to spread to what they would regard as otherwise sound institutions: If Bear fails and two minutes later people worry that Lehman fails, and two minutes after that they worry that Merrill will fail, and it spreads from there."

The rational Buffett tried to unlock the puzzle embedded in the risky choices facing the Federal Reserve. It had no really good options. Either it allowed a financial meltdown or it took actions that would promote inflation by adding to downward pressure on the dollar.

"It could all end on a dime if they flooded the system with enough liquidity, but there are consequences to doing that. If dramatic enough, the consequences would be the immediate expectation of huge inflation. A lot of things would happen that you might not like. The economy is definitely tanking. It's not my game, but if I had to bet one way or another—everybody else says a recession will be short and shallow, but I would say long and deep.

"You absolutely never want to be in a position where tomorrow morning you have to depend on the kindness of strangers in the financial world. I spent a lot of time thinking about that. I never want to have to come up with a billion dollars tomorrow morning. Well, a billion I could. But any significant amount. Because you just cannot be sure of anything. You have to think about things that have never happened before. You always want to have plenty of money around."

All weekend the regulators and bankers toiled, much as they had years earlier on Salomon. This time, however, it was with the almost certain knowledge that the bank's failure would have catastrophic consequences to the global financial system. Whether Bear Stearns deserved its fate was not at issue. Just before the Tokyo markets opened on Sunday, the Federal Reserve announced that it had orchestrated a sale of Bear to investment bank JP Morgan Chase for a pittance.

"It's a weird time. We've gone into a different world, and nobody knows what will happen to the world, but Charlie and I looked at the downside, and nobody else did, very much."

Deleveraging would be a painful process in which banks, hedge funds, financial-services companies, municipalities, the construction and travel industries, consumers, and indeed the whole economy withdrew—fast and painfully or slow and painfully—from the intoxicant of cheap debt. Asset returns could well stay subpar for a long time—what Charlie Munger called a "4 percent return world."

In the midst of all the chaos of the spring of 2008, there sat Buffett, whose thinking about value and risk had not changed in the nearly sixty years of his career. There are always people who say that the rules have changed. But it only looks that way, he said, if the time horizon is too short. Buffett was stooping for cigar butts as if he were a child again.

"We're selling some credit default swaps [insurance against firms going bankrupt] in situations where it is underpriced. I'm sitting here with my newest daily paper that I read, the <u>Bond Buyer</u>, on my lap. Who the hell would have thought that I'd be reading the <u>Bond Buyer</u> every day? The Bond Buyer costs $2,400 a year. I felt like asking for a daily subscription rate. We get these bid lists on failed auctions of tax-exempt money-market funds and other auction rate bonds and have been just picking them off. The same fund will trade at the same time on the same day from the same dealer at interest rates of 5.4 percent and 8.2 percent. Which is crazy, they're the exact same thing, and the underlying loans are perfectly good. There is no reason why it should trade at 820, but we bid 820 and we may get one, while concurrently someone else buys exactly the same issue at 540. If you'd told me ten weeks ago I'd be doing this, I'd have said that's about as likely as me becoming a male stripper. We've put $4 billion into this stuff. It's the most dramatic thing I've seen in my life. If this is an efficient market, dictionaries will have to redefine 'efficient.'"

In exchange for $3.4 billion of premiums, Buffett agreed that Berkshire would pay credit losses on certain companies with a value of $7.9 billion. Buffett would also use derivative contracts to insure municipal bonds at prices that appeared advantageous. Like the credit default swaps, both of these bets would pay off best for Berkshire in an optimistic economic scenario.

Win or lose, these were not things the average person should be doing.

"Stocks are the things to own over time. Productivity will increase and stocks will increase with it. There are only a few things you can do wrong. One is to buy or sell at the wrong time. Paying high fees is the other way to get killed. The best way to avoid both of these is to buy a low-cost index fund, and buy it over time. Be greedy

when others are fearful, and fearful when others are greedy, but don't think you can outsmart the market.

"If a cross-section of American industry is going to do well over time, then why try to pick the little beauties and think you can do better? Very few people should be active investors."

If there is any lesson the life of Warren Buffett has shown, it is the truth of that.

By July 2008, regulators were forced to take other actions in attempts to save the mortgage lending companies Fannie Mae and Freddie Mac from sinking under the weight of the bad loans the government had insisted these companies make. Berkshire was asked to participate in private market bailouts of the mortgage giants, but Buffett suspected this would merely be—as his father might have put it—money down the rathole, and declined.

That same month, Buffett proved again that even though he could envision a financial tsunami with unusual clarity, he did not realize one was actually about to sweep over the world. He agreed to invest $3 billion for Berkshire in convertible preferred stock of Dow Chemical, to finance its merger with Rohm and Haas. The 8.5 percent dividend was modest compared to what Buffett had demanded in other such deals, and would appear paltry in hindsight.

By September, both Fannie Mae and Freddie Mac had failed and were placed under federal conservatorship. Meanwhile, several funds that invested in subprime mortgages also failed. Lehman Brothers put itself up for sale, and investors began betting against the stock, speculating that Lehman's losses might be so heavy (or unquantifiable) that it might not find a buyer.

The weekend of September 13 and 14, in the domino sequence that Buffett had speculated might occur, Lehman continued to search frantically for a buyer, while Merrill Lynch, its stock price melting, struck a deal to sell itself to Bank of America rather than become the next Bear Stearns. Buffett took distress calls that weekend asking him to invest in various deals, among them syndicates to bail out or else buy pieces of insurance giant AIG, which had lost huge amounts on derivatives trades made by its financial products division. Buffett, who was always good at saying no, refused without hesitation, saying that while he couldn't quantify how much money AIG needed, it was far more than Berkshire could supply.

Hanging over all of these stricken companies was the question: What is too big to fail? On Monday morning, September 15, the government delivered the answer. Lehman Brothers entered the largest bankruptcy filing in the history of the United States—$639 billion—after the Federal Reserve failed to organize a rescue for it. The next day the Fed injected an $85 billion emergency loan into AIG,* albeit on terms that amounted to a government takeover of one of the world's largest insurers and essentially wiped out AIG's equity holders.

Lehman, therefore, was not too big to fail, while AIG *was*. Yet Lehman's financial entanglements were so enormous that they nearly took down the entire global financial system. Within days, the Reserve Primary Fund, one of the nation's largest money market funds, failed because it was holding Lehman bonds. Reserve Primary could only pay investors ninety-seven cents on the dollar, setting off a panic in the credit markets and among retail investors by overturning the assumption that a dollar invested in a supposedly safe money market fund was sacrosanct and would always be worth a dollar. Lenders everywhere began to deny each other credit.

This was the nightmare that Buffett had envisioned at Salomon, writ larger because massive growth in the global derivatives market had increased systemic risk over the years. By Thursday, September 18, Morgan Stanley, as the presumed next victim, was trading at midday below $12 per share, versus the previous day's close of $21.75; Goldman Sachs was sliding downward as the next potential casualty in line. The bankers blamed short-sellers, and this was where the government finally drew the line, asking for extraordinary new powers to create an emergency liquidity facility for investment banks that allowed them to convert to bank holding companies in order to access the government's discount window, and issuing an unprecedented, and temporary, ban on short-selling numerous financial and other stocks.† This ban outraged hedge funds, and the SEC was immediately criticized for reducing liquidity and forcing investors to sell more stocks because they could not hedge their positions.

Some investment banks had approached Buffett for aid and were rejected because, he said, the terms weren't rich enough. On September 23, Berkshire invested $5 billion in a preferred stock of Goldman Sachs that paid ten percent nominal interest and included warrants to buy $5 billion of stock for $115 per share. With part of the price assigned to the value of the warrants, the effective yield on the preferred was more than fifteen percent. This kind of loan-shark

---

*Which would later grow to $186 billion.

†I am, at the time of this writing, a senior advisor to Morgan Stanley and owner of Morgan Stanley stock.

interest rate was, at last, what it took to get Buffett to open his wallet and give Goldman his imprimatur, which enabled the firm to raise another $2.5 billion in equity capital. The deal was so rich, he said later, that he couldn't have gotten it a week earlier, or a week later.

Buffett had a longstanding, nostalgic, almost emotional attachment to Goldman, dating from the day his father took him to see Sidney Weinberg when he was ten years old; he liked its management; and, of course, his Goldman banker Byron Trott had helped Berkshire make a lot of money, which Buffett always found endearing. Still, it was astonishing to see Buffett, the critic of Wall Street, once again investing in a conflict-riddled investment bank after his experience with Salomon. The only differences were that he did not have to serve on the board—never again would he take on that responsibility—and that he had gotten better terms—in fact, even better terms than the government was getting on its bailouts.

Within days of Berkshire's investment in Goldman, the House of Representatives rejected the Bush administration's $700 billion bank bailout package. This, combined with the failure of thrift bank Washington Mutual—unprecedented in size—sent the Dow down 777.68 points to 10,365 on September 29, its largest one-day drop in history. Goldman stock swooned, and the blogosphere almost immediately began to call Buffett's investment in Goldman a failure.

Days later, Buffett struck a similar deal with General Electric for both warrants to buy $3 billion worth of common stock, and $3 billion in a perpetual preferred stock, callable by GE within three years, which paid ten percent interest at a price of $22.25 per share. As with the Goldman deal, Buffett's presence as an investor enabled GE to raise money from other investors. The extraordinary terms he could exact were the price of his reputation.

While Buffett was deal-making, he appeared on the television talk show *Charlie Rose* on October 1 to stress the need for confidence in the economy and urge Congress to pass the Treasury's bailout bill. Buffett described the financial crisis as an *"economic Pearl Harbor."* The following day, Congress reversed itself and signed the Emergency Economic Stabilization Act to make $700 billion in emergency funds available to the Treasury. Even if his views were not what had influenced lawmakers (he had the ear of some), Buffett's calming words would soon be cited worldwide. His was probably the most influential expression of confidence during the crisis, at a time when hordes of politicians, pundits, and economists were opining in every possible medium.

Financial institutions were not the only casualties during this phase of the crisis. Another piece of fallout from the Lehman bankruptcy hit Constellation Energy, which saw its stock decline fifty-eight percent in three days. Constellation reached out to a number of parties seeking rescue; Berkshire's MidAmerican Energy made an offer to buy the entire company for $4.7 billion and Constellation accepted. This offer was a classical Buffett no-lose deal: It was priced at less than half the market value of Constellation the previous week; MidAmerican also injected $1 billion of cash—at a fourteen percent interest rate—into Constellation to provide immediate liquidity, and Buffett locked in the deal with an onerous break-up fee. Whether Berkshire bought Constellation or not, it would make a hefty profit.

In December, EDF (Électricité de France SA) offered a far higher competing bid that would pay $4.5 billion for forty-nine percent of Constellation's nuclear energy business. Constellation's management fought to retain the deal with Berkshire, but was ultimately forced to merge with EDF. In exchange for the cancellation, MidAmerican harvested a $917 million gain on its $1 billion investment—plus a $175 million break-up fee.

Yet even this huge profit was smaller than the $2 billion or so that Berkshire netted in the fall and winter of 2008 from a series of casual trades Buffett made buying distressed corporate bonds. This type of investing was easy and automatic for him; he scanned the bond tables and made his choices based on a few mental calculations the way somebody else might fill out a Sudoku puzzle.

As he was picking off bonds, Buffett published a *New York Times* editorial, "Buy American: I Am," in which he said that stocks were cheap enough and that while they might get cheaper, looking for the bottom is a fool's game; that stocks are the best protection against inflation; and that he could be putting all his personal investments into the stock market within the next year. The Dow at the time was trading close to 8,900.* Some investors raced to follow Buffett's advice, and rued doing so when the market soon fell below 7,000. Buffett, who rarely wrote editorials because he was mindful that people followed his lead, blamed the headline, saying, "*I don't write the headline.*"

Investors debated Buffett's sincerity, wondered whether he was grandstanding or genuine, trying to give the country his best opinion or being patriotic. He was accused, as a major owner of financial stocks, of "talking his book" by

---

*It shortly declined below that level and remained there for months, dipping to as low as 6,547 on March 9, 2009.

saying it was time to buy. It was certainly true that Berkshire and Buffett stood to benefit from higher stock prices, but Buffett never risked his reputation for mere money. He only went on the record with a prediction—of any kind—when the odds overwhelmingly favored his being proved right.

In the editorial, he cited inflation as a reason to buy stocks rather than take the risk of staying in cash. Inflation was his ace in the hole; over time, even if the economy did not do well, the nominal earnings of companies would increase significantly if inflation returned, and so would the prices of their stocks. His talk of inflation also shed some light on the economics of the equity-index puts. Even a modest amount of inflation stacked the odds in Berkshire's favor, making it more likely that the indices would be higher at their expiration dates than when Buffett had struck the deals.

These were long-term considerations. For now, incredibly, Buffett—who for years had struggled with having too much money to invest—was out of cash. He had to sell some Johnson & Johnson and Procter & Gamble stock (reluctantly) in order to enter into the GE and Goldman deals. He also sold some ConocoPhillips stock, taking a loss. And Coca-Cola had once again declined to its old territory of $42 a share.

As the stock market fell, and prices of stocks like Coca-Cola, Wells Fargo, U.S. Bancorp, American Express, and Moody's cut a slice into Berkshire's book value, owners of the equity-index puts shorted Berkshire using its credit default swaps. Berkshire's swap spread rose above 475 "basis points" (4.75 percent), several times higher than companies like Travelers and JP Morgan.

About a year after it reached its high price of $149,200, BRK traded between $90,000 and $78,000 per share—around, and at times even less than, its book value.* Unlike in 2000, however, Buffett did not offer to repurchase shares—probably because Berkshire was no longer flush with cash. Along with unrealized investment losses on stocks, Berkshire reported poor third-quarter earnings after hurricane losses in the insurance business and write-downs on derivative bets. The "cigar butt" credit default swaps that Buffett had written around the time Bear Stearns went under were not cigar butts after all. Buffett had turned out not to be skilled enough to price these derivatives with a sufficient margin of safety.

When Berkshire disclosed that Buffett had written these corporate credit and

---

*While writing The Snowball, I never owned Berkshire stock, but I bought some after the book was published and the stock had collapsed.

municipal derivatives, his widespread entry into this market confounded observers who thought of him as a critic of derivatives—Buffett had written in 2002 that they were *"time bombs,"* and in 2003 that they were *"financial weapons of mass destruction."*

But Buffett had never been opposed to the use of derivatives. What he objected to was their almost nonexistent regulation, the lack of disclosure, and an entangled global web of counterparties who owed one another money and, because of opaque valuations, might not be able to pay when claims came due. Without disclosure or oversight, the system was riddled with incentives to overstate the value of derivatives.

Buffett felt he had protected Berkshire from these potential problems because Berkshire was generally getting paid to act as a guarantor—in other words, it would owe its counterparties if a loss occurred. This meant that Berkshire held the money rather than taking the risk that others would not pay. Furthermore, Buffett had declined deals that required Berkshire to put up significant collateral against payment if it appeared likely that a loss might occur in the future.[12]

But this distinction was lost on observers, who suspected Buffett of being a hypocrite for using the very derivatives that he had condemned: The statesman who used simple aphorisms to attack sophisticated financial techniques as chicanery ran into trouble when he tried to use these same techniques in a nuanced way to make money for Berkshire. Even some of Buffett's most ardent supporters thought he should have left the derivatives alone if only for appearance's sake—they were risky and complex, and made him look at best a heedless opportunist, and at worst naive yet still somehow duplicitous.

Above all, they had tied up Berkshire's capital at a time when Buffett needed it.

Formerly, investors would have brushed this off on the assumption that Buffett was more or less infallible and Berkshire would profit in the long run. But some of Buffett's errors seemed inexplicable—or at least he did not offer much of an explanation to the shareholders. The Irish banks had blown up, and ConocoPhillips would prove to be perhaps the worst stock investment, in total financial losses, that Buffett ever made. Meanwhile, the rating agencies, and prudence, now required Berkshire to maintain about a $25 billion cash cushion to support its insurance and other risks. It had become apparent that Berkshire was capital-constrained. And under pressure from the SEC, Buffett agreed to disclose more information about Berkshire's derivative contracts.

Yet in the larger perspective, these troubles were trivial compared to those of most financial services companies. Buffett's more important role—which he had performed magnificently—had been to protect his shareholders from the kind of leverage and uncontrolled risk that had so far brought down Bear Stearns, Lehman, AIG, Fannie, and Freddie; nearly destroyed Merrill Lynch; battered the Swiss banks; almost mortally wounded Morgan Stanley and Goldman Sachs, GE Capital and GMAC; crippled the bond insurers, the life insurers, and even the automakers; destroyed whole business models; and transformed the financial services business so dramatically that the full impact would probably not be understood for years.

Berkshire remained financially healthy, still the "Fort Knox" of capital, still able to invest on highway-robber terms when others were desperately seeking money, able to do deals like Constellation Energy and buy distressed bonds on the cheap. In the long history of Buffett's career, having the foresight to avoid the risky financial instruments that felled so many other companies would rank among his greatest achievements.

It was ironic that, having protected Berkshire so carefully against derivatives by predicting that they would become *"financial weapons of mass destruction,"* even Buffett himself could not anticipate just how right he would be.

The financial crisis expanded late in 2008 and into 2009 with secondary bailouts of automakers (which, characteristically, Buffett showed no interest in participating in, saying understatedly that *"whether they have a sustainable business model is open to question"*) and massive, repeated intervention by central banks around the world. Credit-shocked consumers simply stopped spending money. *"It was like a bell was rung,"* as Buffett put it, sending the U.S. and global economies into a further spasm. Berkshire's high-end retail businesses, especially Borsheim's and NetJets, were most affected. The S&P 500 index closed the year down thirty-eight percent; BRK stock had fallen thirty-two percent.

The "bell-ringing" metaphor was apt for U.S. politics as well. In November 2008, voter outrage over the war in Iraq and the stalled economy gave the Democrats control of the White House for the first time in eight years, with a commanding majority in the House of Representatives and close to a filibuster-proof majority in the Senate.

Buffett's role as a political player in this historic election had placed him in a quandary. For once, he was faced with *two* candidates who were "The Candidate"—politically fresh, running to overturn the established order, and charismatic. This had never happened to him before.

Buffett's tendency to back charismatic candidates dated to the 1970s, but had perhaps reached its apogee in the California gubernatorial-recall election of 2004, when he became the first prominent figure to endorse the actor Arnold Schwarzenegger. His association with Schwarzenegger, the eventual winner, as an economic advisor gave Buffett a heady boost of association with Hollywood power that fed the star-struck side of his personality for at least two years.

Around that time, Senator Barack Obama had cited Buffett's influence in his writing, and Buffett embraced him early in the exploratory stage of the 2008 Democratic primary campaign. Obama was smart and business-savvy, and had views congruent with Buffett's politics; he came across to Buffett as coolheaded yet sincere. He was charismatic, and he was black. He was as perfect a version of "The Candidate" as could be imagined, from Buffett's perspective. Few things could have pleased Buffett more than being associated with the first black president—until Hillary Clinton entered the Democratic primaries.

Clinton's entry into the race presented Buffett with a number of problems. Buffett liked being connected to the Clinton family's political star-power, which had endured through eight years of Republican rule. Buffett had a strong personal attraction to, bordering on a minor obsession with, the reserved Hillary Clinton. He had always been attracted to strong, intellectual women who might figuratively rap his wrist with a ruler if he got out of line; his mother certainly had that style, and he used the term "schoolmarmish" (affectionately) to describe certain women he liked, such as his friend Carol Loomis. Unlike most such women, Hillary Clinton, while friendly, had eluded his efforts to charm her, which made her all the more tantalizingly attractive to Buffett.

Buffett also had a genuinely warm relationship with Bill Clinton. And in seeking sponsors for his foundation, Bill Clinton had cultivated the budding philanthropist Susie Jr., which gave Susie Jr. an entrée into high political circles.

Now, faced with the quandary of saying no to one of two extremely popular candidates, both of whom he liked and who represented minorities, Buffett demurred. He declined to endorse either and said he would be happy if either candidate won. He raised funds for both candidates, giving priority to Clinton early in the race when she was the front-runner, then becoming evenhanded as Obama pulled ahead.

By staying on the sidelines, he had tried to maintain relationships and avoid unpleasant confrontation. He kept his options open to endorse the eventual nominee, Obama. This made some of Buffett's friends grumble about what they considered self-serving calculation or moral cowardice, even though they knew Buffett was incapable of putting himself in a direct path of confrontation.

Because the primary campaign, in the end, was far more hotly contested than the election (which Obama won by a landslide), Buffett in the end wasted his endorsement by holding it back until it became irrelevant. As one observer put it, "Warren only ever wants to back winners. Your real friends are the people who are there for you even though it might cost them something."

During the general election, both Republican candidate John McCain (a longtime friendly political ally of Buffett's on some issues) and Barack Obama said in a debate that they would like Buffett to serve as treasury secretary. Buffett was now so widely seen in the public mind as a steadying influence on the economy that he had become a financial flag for both candidates to wrap around themselves. There was never the slightest chance Buffett would have taken any job that would require him to show up for scheduled meetings, and give up running Berkshire Hathaway. And while Obama might have liked to have Buffett as treasury secretary, Buffett's lengthy withholding of his endorsement also appears to have cost him influence in the White House at a crucial time in American history. Obama had done Buffett a favor by crediting him as a sort of mentor before the campaign; then Buffett failed to reciprocate.

People tended to respond to Buffett's withholding instincts in one of two ways. The more neurotic were stimulated to work harder, often fruitlessly, to win Buffett's approval, favors, and enormous future possible boons that he dangled without necessarily granting.[13] Others, once burned, made sure they were never in his debt and relied on him for nothing so that Buffett lacked anything to withhold. If possible, they arranged it so that Buffett needed something from them instead.

In the end, President Obama named Buffett an economic advisor and Buffett attended a ceremonial meeting—which helped the White House look economically astute—but by all outward signs, he had no special influence on or toehold in the administration.

As the financial crisis evolved, the lame-duck Bush administration and the new Obama administration followed a consistent course under Federal Reserve Chairman Benjamin Bernanke and Treasury Secretary Timothy Geithner, with the Fed injecting trillions of dollars into the U.S. banking system, trying to forestall deflation—chronic falling prices such as occurred in 1932. The still-unfolding crisis revealed its complex brew of causes, including artificially low interest rates, foolish borrowing by businesses and individuals, foolish lending by banks and investors, overreliance by institutions on complex financial instruments, aggressive behavior by derivatives traders, conflicts of interest at the banks being paid as agents to package loans sold to them by originators and resell them to investors, a climate of deregulation, lax oversight and enforcement by regulators, abdication of responsibility by rating agencies, inadequate capitalization of bond insurers, investor indifference—in other words, effects of all the normal dysfunctions that precipitate a bubble.

Of the responsible parties, it was the banks and AIG that earned the public's greatest ire, while Buffett became the public's greatest symbol of financial responsibility.

Treasury yields soon reached zero, but the flood of money failed to open the channels of business lending; credit remained virtually nonexistent. Buffett, who was at the time acting as the economy's greatest cheerleader, lent at interest rates that in some instances bordered on usurious—$150 million of twelve percent notes in Sealed Air; $300 million of Harley-Davidson debt for a fifteen percent interest rate; $300 million of ten-percent contingent convertible senior notes from USG; $250 million of Tiffany bonds at ten percent; and a $2.7 billion, twelve-percent perpetual convertible stake in Swiss Re that would give Berkshire a thirty-percent ownership in the insurance giant.

This latter move baffled insurance industry insiders, including Swiss Re employees. Swiss Re was General Re's biggest competitor; observers concluded that, on any terms, the investment to prop up Swiss Re made no sense because of its negative long-term strategic consequences to Berkshire—unless Buffett ultimately meant to take over Swiss Re and merge it with General Re. In the past, however, Buffett had made opportunistic insurance investments that worked against Berkshire's long-term interests. Challenged on this, he would respond, *"If we don't do it, somebody else will."* Thus it was equally likely that there was no strategy whatsoever behind the deal besides extracting some fast cash from the pockets of the Swiss.

Throughout, Buffett became an even more frequent presence on CNBC and other networks. He filled the role of America's statesman and father figure during the financial crisis, but he had also fallen into the trap of competing for attention instead of trusting that his sterling record would bring it to him. "Dignity, Warren, dignity," counseled one of his friends—but Buffett had never wanted to be dignified; he had never minded looking silly if it would get people to pay attention to him. He was a performer and a showman, and now he feared the show might end. He would keep on giving as many performances as possible while there was time. And indeed, his profile grew and grew in proportion to how often he appeared on the magic medium of television.

All this was not only personally effective—Buffett was his own best publicist—but also understandable for someone his age, until his marathon performances on CNBC resulted in some serious gaffes: criticizing newly elected President Obama's performance, giving advice to the White House (the Shoe Button Complex, something that Buffett had heretofore spent a lifetime avoiding), and a claim that he, like everyone else, had thought housing prices could only go up—an absurdity that raised eyebrows.

When Berkshire finally reported its 2008 earnings, the consequences of some of Buffett's earlier decisions became even clearer. The insurance businesses had suffered large losses from that year's unusually active hurricane season. "Last year was a bad year for a float business," Munger would later say at the shareholder meeting, citing GEICO and the energy and utility businesses as bright spots. Although Buffett referred to Berkshire's *"Gibraltar-like"* balance sheet, the erosion in its financial strength was unmistakable. Because of Berkshire's heavy insurance exposure and its concentration in financial stocks such as American Express, Wells Fargo, and U.S. Bancorp, its book value was down by 9.6 percent—only the second decrease in its history (and the largest). Berkshire had recorded $14.6 billion of accounting losses on its derivative contracts. While many of these losses would probably be reversed in the long run, they had a significant impact on the balance sheet. Nearly all of the decline was due to bets on financial assets that were market-dependent.

Even so, the decrease in Berkshire's book value was insignificant compared to major banks and nonbank lenders, which were technically insolvent or close to it, and receiving hundreds of billions in government aid. Buffett had steered Berkshire to a stellar performance, by that measure. All the work of many years had culminated in this moment: Berkshire standing alone after other businesses crumbled around it.

You would not know this by reading some of the commentary on Buffett. One of his challenges at this late stage of his long career was that he tended to be measured by some observers and journalists against a standard of perfection, as if he had to be infallible to be any good at all.[14] Bloggers and financial writers went wild writing about Buffett's derivatives exposure. Buffett went on the counterattack. That year's shareholder letter contained a lengthy explanation of his reasoning for selling the equity-index puts. Yet by some calculations, under various scenarios Berkshire could indeed lose billions at the expiration dates of these contracts, which were not as well priced as Buffett had apparently thought when he entered into them. Ultimately, the concentration of financial assets and their effect on Berkshire's value was significant enough that first Fitch Ratings, then Moody's, downgraded the credit ratings of Berkshire and its subsidiaries (such as National Indemnity and MidAmerican) by one notch, from AAA or the equivalent.

The top rating had given Berkshire a lower cost of funding and significant advantages in its insurance business, which made it attractive to sellers of businesses. Buffett had displayed quiet satisfaction when Berkshire's two largest insurance competitors lost their triple-A ratings, and had at times said privately that the one thing he would never do was jeopardize Berkshire's triple-A, which he considered one of its most precious assets. In his shareholder letters, he liked to comment that Berkshire was one of only "seven," or whatever the dwindling number was, of the remaining triple-A companies. He considered it unlikely that this rating, once lost, would be reinstated.

Now Berkshire had suffered that blow, which it probably could have avoided by raising (expensive) equity capital, something Buffett chose not to do. At the 2009 shareholder meeting, he downplayed the consequences. He said the derivatives did not impinge on capital and that a triple-A rating only conveyed "*bragging rights.*" "*We're still a triple-A in my mind,*" he said. It was actually possible that Berkshire—in its uniqueness—could get the rating reinstated, but if so, it would be expensive even if Berkshire did not have to raise capital: It would have to reduce its exposures to insurance and equity market risk as a percentage of book value. Buffett probably would choose not to pay that price because its benefit was limited; no other financial institution remained with a triple-A rating.

Thus, the real meaning of the downgrade, in a larger context, was that the crisis had unveiled the true risk inherent in the global financial system—and the rating agencies had responded by increasing the capital threshold for a triple-A rating to a level that meant even the soundest institution found it financially unattractive to qualify.

Buffett also revealed at the 2009 shareholder meeting that to reduce Berkshire's derivative risk, he had renegotiated two of the equity-index put contracts, shortening the terms by eight years in order to lower the price at which Berkshire would have to pay out losses. By then, the values of Wells Fargo, U.S. Bancorp, and American Express had begun to recover, but Wells and U.S. Bancorp had cut their dividends, which would also affect Berkshire's future earnings. Buffett predicted that Wells Fargo would not have to issue stock, a prediction that was almost immediately contradicted when Wells Fargo did just that. He scored better a few weeks later when Berkshire's SEC filings revealed that he had been buying American Express while the stock was on its back.

Thus, during the financial crisis, Buffett made a series of characteristic brilliant moves interspersed with some surprising errors. Above all, he stood pat on existing investments while adding cleverly structured new deals, deals that for the most part were not available to ordinary investors. These opportunities came to Berkshire because of its ready cash and underlying financial strength, and because of Buffett's willingness to rent his well-earned reputation and provide quick, trustworthy handshake dealmaking.

The actions he had taken with deals struck in 2008 and 2009, in accordance with his saying "*Cash combined with courage in a crisis is priceless,*" would enrich Berkshire shareholders for many years to come. At the same time, the crisis—which admittedly had so many episodes of heart-stopping disintegration into near economic collapse that in some ways it eclipsed the events leading to the Great Depression—left Berkshire a weaker company financially. It undercut Buffett's reputation as a nearly infallible manager, and cost the company its top financial rating.

The 2009 shareholder meeting would prove to be both a celebration of Berkshire's success and a chance for Buffett to defend himself. He had changed the meeting format so that half the questions would concern Berkshire and would be submitted through a panel of journalists: Carol Loomis, Becky Quick of CNBC, and Andrew Ross Sorkin of the *New York Times.* A torrent of five thousand questions poured in, many of them tough-minded queries from people who wanted answers but who had not, in the past, been willing to wait hours for a position at the microphone while others asked Buffett about his personal relationship with Jesus Christ and what books he and Munger had read lately.

The new format and the unsteady economy attracted what was said to be a record thirty-five thousand people in attendance despite Berkshire's stock price, which hovered at $90,000 per share. Buffett, who never said anything spontaneous, always seemed to have an answer prepared for every question that could be anticipated. The main difference in 2009 was that shareholders were asking truly challenging questions, rather than flattering him with their gratitude for being able to stand in his presence and receive his wisdom. At his most impressive he rattled off statistics and explained economics with a clarity that people were not hearing from anyone else. But his answers on other questions were more awkward. Buffett liked to deal with confrontation indirectly. Put on the spot, he behaved as he did in private, avoiding direct answers to some questions and meting out unpleasant information through hints and sometimes by omission.

Challenged on his decision not to sell financial stocks in the spring of 2008, he said he only sold when a company's competitive advantage disappeared, he lost faith in management, or he needed cash. He was cutting a fine distinction in trying to separate his criteria for selling stocks when companies' circumstances were changing materially all the time, versus selling whole businesses, which happened only when they became economically unviable or had persistent labor problems. With newspapers folding in cities all over the United States, he also went so far as to raise the possibility of eventually shuttering the *Buffalo News,* but said that as long as the *News* made a little money and had no labor problems, he and Munger would *"keep it going."*

Buffett was questioned sharply about why he did not sell Moody's when its business model was fundamentally compromised after the rating agencies were implicated in causing the financial crisis. He said he thought the odds were that Moody's was still a good business, and that he did not think conflict of interest—rating agencies are paid by the entities they rate—was *"the major cause"* of the problem. (Another conflict of interest, not mentioned, was Berkshire's twenty-percent ownership of Moody's when Moody's rated Berkshire.) Many in the audience had spent years listening to Charlie Munger's often repeated saying, "whose bread I eat, his song I sing," and understood that Buffett was rationalizing as he always did in pursuit of a profit or when he felt backed into a corner—or both.

When Buffett was asked how the four investment managers he had chosen as possible replacements performed during the 2008 market crash, and whether they were still on the list of candidates, he said they *"didn't cover themselves with glory,"* then commented that neither did most investment managers during this period. Buffett did not respond to how these managers did relative to the market or to their relevant benchmarks. He left a vague impression that the list of candidates might change, over time.

What was certain, whichever candidates were chosen, was that the stock market would eventually recover. More important were Berkshire's businesses. Most were among the best in their respective industries. Buffett had built a conglomerate of stable businesses that were likely to be profitable for a long time. Still, the events of 2008 had certainly convinced many shareholders that Berkshire was not a company that could be run by a ham sandwich after Buffett was gone.

At the meeting they grilled Buffett about the question of succession with new intensity. The next CEO's challenges would be keeping Berkshire's managers happy, managing the company's franchise and risks, and investing the cash flow the businesses threw off. Buffett insisted that all the candidates were internal. He said that running a major operating business was the best qualification for the CEO job. He next talked about what he actually did as CEO, which did not involve anything remotely resembling running an operating business (nor had Buffett ever run an operating business; nor could he have, had he been forced to do so).[15] He stated that the operating managers had experience allocating capital—perhaps a necessary rationalization, although nobody truly allocated capital at Berkshire other than Buffett, particularly not in financial services, the heart of the company and the site of Berkshire's recent woes.

The answer revealed that Buffett was publicly introducing a rationale to pave the way for someone like David Sokol, the presumed front-runner who ran MidAmerican Energy. Buffett was also using a selection process that in some ways mirrored his two disastrous experiences at Coca-Cola, one that could someday put the board in an awkward spot.

To be sure, Buffett had already divided executive authority in a way that many outside candidates would not find comfortable—with his son Howie succeeding him as chairman, and Bill Gates taking on the role of de facto lead board member as representative of Berkshire's largest future shareholder, the Bill and Melinda Gates Foundation. This meant that, for better or worse, Berkshire probably would always be run in an unusual manner by unusual people.

The unusual company that Buffett—or Sokol, or possibly even a committee—would be running was stable and successful, and had, because of the financial crisis, gained relative advantage over its rivals in many of the businesses in which it operated, even though as of spring 2009 its results and financial condition also reflected the weakened economy.

As for the future, Buffett said retailing, especially of luxury products, might not recover for years. Companies like Borsheim's and NetJets were going to struggle. He said little more about NetJets; the sparsely populated aisles at Borsheim's on Sunday after the meeting spoke for themselves. On a brighter note, he said that new household formation was the key to recovery of housing-related sales, with 1.3 million new households formed in the United States every year.

He spoke optimistically of the long-term future of the U.S. economy, which had survived two world wars, many panics and depressions, the resignation of a president in disgrace, and civil unrest. At various times, he had discussed what he expected to be inevitable inflation and the declining value of the dollar. Yet it was the "unleashed potential" of the human race that caused economies to grow over time, he said; in other words, productivity. The world's system to increase productivity works naturally and has been working for a long time. Munger waxed enthusiastic over Berkshire's investment in BYD, a Chinese maker of electric cars. We are about to harness the power of the sun, he said, and use more electric energy to preserve hydrocarbon energy for chemicals that are more important. The main technical problem of mankind is about to be fixed, he opined.

Then he and Munger headed off to meet with the international shareholders, and Buffett and Astrid attended another round of parties on Saturday night.

Within days, Buffett would begin planning the 2010 meeting—when he would be almost eighty. He couldn't believe he would be eighty. Every year he attacked the meeting planning as though this year would be his ultimate statement—his greatest show on earth. In 2009, he had shown off an electric car. He would have to find some way to top that in 2010.

Meanwhile, to his slight chagrin, Borsheim's had missed out on one sale in 2009. (Every sale mattered to Buffett.) At 3:00 p.m. during the shareholder meeting, "Alex from Boston" asked Buffett what individuals could do to help the economy. Buffett said, first, to spend money, then repeated that new household formation would be helpful to the economy. With that, "Alex from Boston," who was Buffett's grandnephew Alex Buffett Rozek, asked his girlfriend Mimi Krueger to marry him. Mimi, stunned to be asked in front of thousands of people, said yes, and Alex gave her his grandmother Doris's sapphire-and-diamond ring, which Warren had given his sister for her seventy-fifth birthday.

Buffett the showman had always wanted to have a wedding at the Berkshire shareholder meeting, but had never quite managed to pull that off. He would settle for an engagement instead.

64

The Snowball

Throughout all the ups and downs of the stock market and the economy and his reputation, Buffett never lost his focus on business. But every time he contemplated the ideal way to spend the rest of his life, he was roused by the urge to preach. For some time he had been giving talks to college students around the United States, traveling to their schools, welcoming them to Omaha. He liked talking to students because they were not hardened in their habits, still young enough to take full advantage of what he said.

"I packed my little snowball very early, and if I had packed it ten years later, it would have been way different than where it stands on the hill right now. So I recommend to students that if you start out a little ahead of the game—it doesn't have to be a lot, but it's so much better than starting out behind the game. And credit cards really get you behind the game."

As early as 2002, feeling a sense of urgency, he had begun to pick up speed with his talks to the students. They came from MIT. Northwestern. The University of Iowa. The University of Nebraska. Wesleyan. The University of Chicago. Wayne State. Dartmouth. The University of Indiana. The University of Michigan. Notre Dame. Columbia. Yale. The University of Houston. Harvard/Radcliffe. The University of Missouri. The University of Tennessee. UC Berkeley. Rice. Stanford. Iowa State. The University of Utah. Texas A&M University. Much of his message was that getting rich quick wasn't the worthiest goal in life. Ironically, it was the urge of humankind to worship the rich and famous that made his audience seek him out to hear these words. Like everything else in his life, the visits from students started to snowball.

In 2008, he was crowned the richest man on earth for the first time. By then, the students were coming from Asia, from Latin America, arriving in Omaha in groups of two or three schools at a time, in packs sometimes of more than two hundred, sometimes on several days a month.

Warren's age now weighed on him. It was getting harder for him to read all day long the way he used to, since one of his eyes was getting weak and the other was plagued by a cataract that he was reluctant to have removed. He had finally given in and agreed to wear hearing aids. His voice turned gravelly faster than it once had. He tired more easily. Though he still felt the urge to teach, by the time he reached the age of seventy-nine he was limiting the visits from students to six times a year. But as long as he was able, he would continue to teach.

The students who made the pilgrimage to visit the Sage of Omaha still got the full treatment (excepting only that Buffett did not go to their hotels in person and leave bound volumes of his annual reports for them at the front desk at four-thirty a.m. The Internet now did that job for him.). They toured Rose Blumkin's Nebraska Furniture Mart and roamed the aisles of Borsheim's. Buffett met them in the office. Some days now, he abandoned his gray suits and tight collars, and looked relaxed in casual dress. Their questions often ventured far afield from business. What is the purpose of life? some of them wanted to know. He answered this question the same way he answered the business ones—in mathematical terms.

As he had told the students at Georgia Tech when Susie was in the hospital, recovering from her surgery: *The purpose of life is to be loved by as many people as possible among those you want to have love you.*

How should society be ordered? He told them about the Ovarian Lottery. How do I find the right spouse? Marry up, he said. (He wasn't talking about money.) How do I know what is right? Follow your Inner Scorecard. What should I do about a career? Find something you are passionate about. I only work with people I like. If you go to work every morning with your stomach churning, you're in the wrong business.

He told them about the genie. Treat your body like the only car you'll ever own: Baby that car, garage it every night, buff every dent, and change its oil every week. Then he took them out to lunch or dinner at Gorat's and everyone scarfed down salty T-bones and double hash browns at the scuffed linoleum tables as if the genie had exempted them temporarily from his rules. As they ate, they would leap up, one after another, and jockey to have a picture taken with Warren Buffett. Someday, maybe in forty years, their grandchildren would believe them when they claimed to have talked and sat and dined with the Oracle of Omaha.

What he was teaching were the lessons that had emerged from the unfolding of his own life.

In that unfolding, he admits to ambition, but he denies that there was ever a plan. He finds it hard to acknowledge his own powerful hand as the creator of the sweeping canvas that is his masterpiece. As he tells the story, a series of happy accidents built Berkshire Hathaway; a moneymaking machine sprang up without design. Its elegant structure of true partnership with like-minded shareholders built on what Munger called a "seamless web of deserved trust," with an investment portfolio buried inside an interlocked set of businesses whose capital could be moved at will, all of them turbocharged with "float"—all this had come about, he claims, simply as a reflection of his personality. The final product was a model that could be analyzed and understood, yet few did and, for the most part, nobody coattailed it. What people paid attention to was simply how rich he was. Indeed, as much as he wanted them to study his model, Buffett sometimes inadvertently discouraged it; he also wanted people to believe that he just tap-danced into work every day and had fun.

But that would be the less flattering version.

The truth is this.

When Warren was a little boy fingerprinting nuns and collecting bottle caps, he had no knowledge of what he would someday become. Yet as he rode his bike through Spring Valley, flinging papers day after day, and raced through the halls of The Westchester, pulse pounding, trying to make his deliveries on time, if you had asked him if he wanted to be the richest man on earth—with his whole heart, he would have said, *Yes*.

That passion had led him to study a universe of thousands of stocks. It made him burrow into libraries and basements for records nobody else troubled to get. He sat up nights studying hundreds of thousands of numbers that would glaze anyone else's eyes. He read every word of several newspapers each morning and sucked down the *Wall Street Journal* like his morning Pepsi, then Coke. He dropped in on companies, spending hours talking about barrels with the woman who ran an outpost of Greif Bros. Cooperage or auto insurance with Lorimer Davidson. He read magazines like the *Progressive Grocer* to learn how to stock a meat department. He stuffed the backseat of his car with *Moody's Manuals* and ledgers on his honeymoon. He spent months reading old newspapers dating back a century to learn the cycles of business, the history of Wall

Street, the history of capitalism, the history of the modern corporation. He followed the world of politics intensely and recognized how it affected business. He analyzed economic statistics until he had a deep understanding of what they signified. Since childhood, he had read every biography he could find of people he admired, looking for the lessons he could learn from their lives. He attached himself to everyone who could help him and coattailed anyone he could find who was smart. He ruled out paying attention to almost anything but business—art, literature, science, travel, architecture—so that he could focus on his passion. He defined a circle of competence to avoid making mistakes. To limit risk he never used any significant amount of debt. He never stopped thinking about business: what made a good business, what made a bad business, how they competed, what made customers loyal to one versus another. He had an unusual way of turning problems around in his head, which gave him insights nobody else had. He developed a network of people who—for the sake of his friendship as well as his sagacity—not only helped him but also stayed out of his way when he wanted them to. In hard times or easy, he never stopped thinking about ways to make money. And all of this energy and intensity became the motor that powered his innate intelligence, temperament, and skills.

Warren Buffett was a man who loved money, a man for whom the game of collecting it ran in his veins as his lifeblood. That love kept him going: buying little stocks like National American, selling GEICO to have the money to buy something cheaper, pushing at the boards of companies like Sanborn Map to do the right thing for shareholders. It had made him independent and competitive enough to want his own partnership and say no to the chance to be a junior partner running Ben Graham's old firm. It made him tough enough to shut down Dempster's distribution center and fire Lee Dimon; it gave him the determination to break Seabury Stanton. It had tamed his impatience and made him listen when Charlie Munger insisted that they buy great businesses, even though listening to other people went against his very grain. It stiffened his will to survive the SEC investigation of Blue Chip and to break the strike at the *Buffalo News*. It made him an implacable acquirer. It also led him to lower his standards from time to time when his turf dried up. Yet it saved him from serious losses by keeping him from abandoning his margin of safety.

Warren Buffett was a timid man who shied from confrontation and needed people to cushion him from life's rougher edges. His fears were personal, not financial; he was never timid when it came to money. His passionate yearning to be rich gave him the courage to ride his bicycle past the house with the awful dog and throw those last few newspapers in Spring Valley. It sent him to Columbia, seeking Ben Graham, after Harvard turned him down. It made him put one foot in front of the other, calling on people as a prescriptionist, while they rejected him over and over. It gave him the strength to return to Dale Carnegie after losing his courage the first time. It forced him through the decisions in the Salomon crisis to make his great withdrawal from the Bank of Reputation. It lent him the dignity to face years of almost intolerable criticism without counterattacking during the Internet bubble. He had spent his life contemplating, limiting, and avoiding risk, but in the end he was braver than he realized himself.

Warren Buffett would never call himself courageous; he would cite his energy, focus, and rational temperament. Above all, he would describe himself as a teacher. All his adult life he had sought to live up to the values instilled in him by his father: He said that Howard taught him that the "how" mattered more than the "how much." To hold his ruthlessness in check wasn't an easy lesson for him. It helped that he was fundamentally honest—and that he was possessed by the urge to preach. "He deliberately limited his money," says Munger. "Warren would have made a lot more money if he hadn't been carrying all those shareholders and had maintained the partnership longer, taking an override." Compounded over thirty-three years, the extra money would have been worth many billions—tens of billions—to him.[1] He could have bought and sold the businesses inside Berkshire Hathaway with a cold calculation of their financial return without considering how he felt about the people involved. He could have become a buy-out king. He could have promoted and lent his name to all sorts of ventures. "In the end," says Munger, "he didn't want to do it. He was competitive, but he was never just rawly competitive with no ethics. He wanted to live life a certain way, and it gave him a public record and a public platform. And I would argue that Warren's life has worked out better this way."[2]

It was the will to share what he knew in an act of sheer generosity that made him spend months writing his annual letter to the shareholders; his joy in showmanship that made him want a mobile home at his shareholder meeting; his pixieish sense of fun that led him to endorse a mattress. It was his Inner Scorecard that made him cling to his margin of safety. It was pure love that turned him into what Munger called "a learning machine." It was his handicapping skill that let him use that knowledge to figure out what the future might bring. It was his urge to preach that made him want to warn the world of dangers to come.

He wished he could have the next ten years' worth of newspapers delivered to his doorstep right now. The years ahead weren't endless, but with luck they could be long. Trees don't grow to the sky, but he wasn't scraping the horizon yet. Another new person, another investment, another idea always waited for him. The things left to learn far exceeded what he already knew.

"The snowball just happens if you're in the right kind of snow, and that's what happened with me. I don't just mean compounding money either. It's in terms of understanding the world and what kind of friends you accumulate. You get to select over time, and you've got to be the kind of person that the snow wants to attach itself to. You've got to be your own wet snow, in effect. You'd better be picking up snow as you go along, because you're not going to be getting back up to the top of the hill again. That's the way life works."

The snowball he had created so carefully was enormous by now. Yet his attitude toward it remained the same. However many birthdays lay ahead, he would always be astonished each time the calendar turned, and as long as he lived, he would never stop feeling like a sprout. For he wasn't looking backward to the top of the hill. It was a big world, and he was just starting out.

Notes

Chapter 1: The Less Flattering Version

1. This quote, or its variation, "Behind every great fortune there is a great crime," is cited endlessly without a specific source: for example, in Mario Puzo's *The Godfather* and in commentary on *The Sopranos* and on the Internet bubble. This pithier version condenses what Honoré de Balzac actually wrote in *Father Goriot*: "The secret of a great success for which you are at a loss to account is a crime that has never been found out, because it was properly executed."

Chapter 2: Sun Valley

1. Herbert Allen made an exception for Ken Auletta, the first and only time a writer was allowed to attend and write about Sun Valley. "What I Did at Summer Camp" appeared in the *New Yorker*, July 26, 1999.

2. Interview with Don Keough. Other guests commented on Buffett's role at Sun Valley as well.

3. Except Donald Trump, of course.

4. Dyan Machan, "Herbert Allen and His Merry Dealsters," *Forbes*, July 1, 1996.

5. Elephant herds are matriarchal, and the females eject the males from the herd as soon as they are old enough to become dominant and aggressive. Then the solitary males approach herds of females, trying to mate. However, this isn't exactly the way human elephant-bumping works.

6. Allen & Co. does not release the numbers, but the conference was said to cost around $10 million, more than $36,000 per invited family. Whether $5 or $15 million, that pays for a lot of fly-fishing and golf over the course of a long weekend. Much of the money pays for the conference's exhaustive security and logistics.

7. Buffett likes to tell a joke about having worked his way up to this exalted state: starting from a trailer, then the lodge, then a lesser condo, and so forth.

8. Herbert Allen's son Herbert Jr. is usually referred to as "Herb." However, Buffett refers to Herbert Sr. as "Herb" as a mark of their friendship, as do a few other people.

9. This portrait of Sun Valley and the impact of the dotcom billionaires is drawn from interviews with a number of people, including investment managers with no ax to grind. Most asked not to be named.

10. Allen & Co. and author estimate. This is the total assets under management of money managers who attend the conference, added to the personal fortunes of the guests. It represents their total economic power, not their consumption of wealth. By comparison, the capitalized value of the U.S. stock market at the time was about ten trillion dollars.

11. $340,000 per car in Alaska, Delaware, Hawaii, Montana, New Hampshire, both Dakotas, Vermont, Wyoming, and throw in Washington, D.C., to boot (since the District of Columbia is not a state).

12. Interview with Herbert Allen.

13. Buffett had spoken twice before at the Allen conference, in 1992 and 1995.

14. Buffett and Munger preached plenty to their shareholders at Berkshire Hathaway annual meetings, but this preaching to the choir doesn't count.

15. Al Pagel, "Coca-Cola Turns to the Midlands for Leadership," *Omaha World-Herald*, March 14, 1982.

16. Buffett's remarks have been condensed for readability and length.

17. PowerPoint is the Microsoft program most often used to make the slide presentations so ubiquitous in corporate America.

18. Interview with Bill Gates.

19. Corporate profits at the time were more than 6% of GDP, compared to a long-term average of 4.88%. They later rose to over 9%, far above historic standards.

20. Over long periods the U.S. economy has grown at a real rate of 3% and a nominal rate (after inflation) of 5%. Other than a postwar boom or recovery from severe recession, this level is rarely exceeded.

21. American Motors, smallest of the "Big Four" automakers, sold out to Chrysler in 1987.

22. Buffett is speaking metaphorically here. He admits to investing in things with wings a time or two, and not with good results.

23. Buffett first used this story in his 1985 chairman's letter, citing Ben Graham, who told the story at his tenth lecture in the series Current Problems in Security Analysis at the New York Institute of Finance. The transcripts of these lectures, given between September 1946 and February 1947, can be found at http://www.wiley.com//legacy/products/subject/finance/bgraham/ or in Benjamin Graham and Janet Lowe, *The Rediscovered Benjamin Graham: Selected Writings of the Wall Street Legend.* New York: Wiley, 1999.

24. A condensed and edited version of this speech was published as "Mr. Buffett on the Stock Market," *Fortune*, November 22, 1999.

25. PaineWebber–Gallup poll, July 1999.

26. Fred Schwed Jr., *Where Are the Customers' Yachts? or, A Good Hard Look at Wall Street.* New York, Simon & Schuster, 1940.

27. Interview with Bill Gates.

28. Keynes wrote: "It is dangerous … to apply to the future inductive arguments based on past experience, unless one can distinguish the broad reasons why past experience was what it was," in a book review for Smith's *Common Stocks as Long-Term Investments* in *Nation and Athenaeum* in 1925 that later became the preface for Keynes, *The Collected Writings of John Maynard Keynes. Vol.12, Economic Articles and Correspondence; Investment and Editorial.* Cambridge: Cambridge University Press, 1983.

29. The comedian Mort Sahl used to end his routine by asking, "Is there anyone I haven't offended?"

30. According to a source who overheard them and would rather remain nameless.

31. Interview with Don Keough.

Chapter 3: Creatures of Habit

1. Interview with Charlie Munger.

2. Parts of Munger's explanation are taken from three lectures on the psychology of human misjudgment, and his commencement address to the Harvard School on June 13, 1986, both as found in *Poor Charlie's Almanack, The Wit and Wisdom of Charles T. Munger,* edited by Peter D. Kaufman. Virginia Beach, Va.: Donning Company Publishers, 2005. The rest is from interviews with the author. Remarks have been edited for brevity and clarity.

3. Interview with Charlie Munger.

4. Munger's driving habits are described in Janet Lowe, *Damn Right! Behind the Scenes with Berkshire Hathaway Billionaire Charlie Munger.* New York: John Wiley & Sons, 2000.

5. Required to produce a doctor's note to prove he was blind in one eye and qualified for a special license at the California Department of Motor Vehicles, Munger refused and offered to take out his glass eye instead.

6. Munger's doctor used an older type of surgery that had a higher complication rate. Rather than blame the doctor, Munger claims he should have done more research on doctors and types of surgery himself.

7. Buffett's interest in such products as pig stalls and egg counters is limited; he reviews some of these statistics in a summarized form.

8. Despite the complaints of passengers, Buffett has never, to the author's knowledge, been responsible for an accident, only near heart attacks.

9. Beth Botts, Elizabeth Edwardsen, Bob Jensen, Stephen Kofe, and Richard T. Stout, "The Corn-fed Capitalist," *Regardie's,* February 1986.

Chapter 4: Warren, What's Wrong?

1. Buffett predicted up to 6% growth in the market per year, but gave historical ranges of no growth, and the underlying math suggested that figure could be high. The 6% was a hedged bet.

2. S&P is Standard & Poor's Industrial Average, the most widely used measure of the overall stock market's performance. S&P includes reinvested dividends. Berkshire does not pay a dividend. All numbers are rounded.

3. "Toys 'R' Us vs. eToys, Value vs. Euphoria," Century Management, http://www.centman.com/ Library/Articles/Aug99/ToysRUsvsEtoys.html. In March 2005, Toys "R" Us agreed to a takeover offer from private equity firms Kohlberg Kravis Roberts & Co., Bain Capital, and real estate group Vornado Realty Trust in a deal valued at $6.6 billion.

4. Interview with Sharon Osberg.

5. Buffett, speaking to the Oquirrh Club, "An Evening with Warren Buffett," October 2003.

Chapter 5: The Urge to Preach

1. Warren's sister Doris Buffett, the family genealogist, has done extensive research on the Buffett family tree. This abbreviated account of the early ancestors is drawn from her research.

2. Either Nathaniel or Joseph.

3. This was the largest and finest of the livery stables in town, with seventy horses at its peak, boasting sleighs, buggies, a circus bateau, and even a hearse. It prospered for a number of years but disappeared sometime around the early days of the automobile. "Six Generations Prove That Buffett Family Is Really Here to Remain," *Omaha World-Herald,* June 16, 1950.

4. "Omaha's Most Historic Grocery Store Still at 50th and Underwood," *Dundee and West Omaha Sun,* April 25, 1963.

5. Zebulon Buffett, letter to Sidney Buffett, December 21, 1869.

6. Sidney's store was originally named Sidney H. Buffett and Sons, where both brothers, Ernest and Frank, worked. The store originally sat at 315 South 14th Street downtown, where it stayed until its closing in 1935. Frank took over as sole proprietor after Sidney's death in 1927. In 1915, Ernest opened a branch store, which moved west to 5015 Underwood Avenue in Dundee in 1918. (At the time Dundee was a separate town, eventually annexed by Omaha.)

7. A third child, named Grace, died in 1926. Three more, George, Nellie, and Nettie, died at young ages in the nineteenth century.

8. Warren Buffett quoting Charlie Munger.

9. According to Doris Buffett, she was born Daisy Henrietta Duvall and began to call herself Henrietta (after her mother) rather than Daisy by the time she arrived in Omaha.

10. Charles T. Munger letter to Katharine Graham, November 13, 1974.

11. Ernest Buffett letter to Barnhart & Son, February 12, 1924.

12. Interview with Charlie Munger. His mother told him this story, although, he notes, "she may have been garnishing it just a bit." But others recall the notebook.

13. In letters like one to his son Clarence in January 1931, he analyzed the effect of railroad automation on unemployment and suggested that the best solution for the Great Depression was a great public-works project. It seems ironic that he and his son Howard became such foes of Roosevelt when he initiated the Works Progress Administration after the next election.

14. Ernest Buffett letter to Fred and Katherine Buffett, undated, "ten years after you were married," circa June 1939.

15. He died young, in 1937, in an auto accident in Texas.

16. Coffee with Congress, radio interview with Howard, Leila, Doris, and Roberta Buffett, WRC

Radio, October 18, 1947, Bill Herson, moderator. (Note: This description is based on a tape of the broadcast.)

17. Interview with Doris Buffett.

18. Based primarily on family files.

19. Bryan's "Cross of Gold" speech, delivered on July 9, 1896, has been called the most famous political speech in American history. Bryan is best remembered for opposing the gold standard and for getting involved in the Scopes case, where the famous lawyer Clarence Darrow made him look foolish for testifying against teaching evolution in schools. In fact his interests were broader and less extreme and his contemporary influence greater than he is generally remembered for today.

20. Family files. Bernice blamed her father for marrying into a family with genetic mental defects, begetting children who would suffer the result.

21. Leila was a freshman at Nebraska during the 1923–24 academic year, according to the Cornhusker yearbook, when Howard was a junior. On Coffee with Congress, Howard noted that they met in the fall of 1923, when Leila was 19. Because students usually entered college at 17, this suggests she worked for about two years before starting. She pledged Alpha Chi Omega as a freshman in the 1923–24 school year, but was still classified as a freshman in 1925, suggesting she went home to work on the newspaper and returned in the spring of 1925.

22. Probably in fall 1923.

23. Howard was secretary of the Innocents (*Daily Nebraskan,* September 27, 1923). This group persisted for many more years, until, as Buffett puts it, "the day came when they couldn't find thirteen who were innocent."

24. At Harry A. Koch Co., whose motto was "Pays the Claim First." He made $125 a month.

25. Receipt from Beebe & Runyan, December 21, 1926, annotated by Leila.

26. They were married December 26, 1925.

27. February 12, 1928.

28. Howard became a deacon in 1928 at the age of 25.

29. Address to the American Society of Newspaper Editors, Washington, D.C., January 25, 1925.

Chapter 6: The Bathtub Steeplechase

1. Even so, only three in a hundred Americans owned stocks. Many had borrowed heavily to play the market, entranced by John J. Raskob's article, "Everybody Ought to Be Rich" in the August 1929 *Ladies' Home Journal* and Edgar Lawrence Smith's proof that stocks outperform bonds (*Common Stocks as Long-Term Investments.* New York: The MacMillan Company, 1925).

2. "Stock Prices Slump $14,000,000,000 in Nation-Wide Stampede to Unload; Bankers to Support Market Today," *New York Times,* October 29, 1929; David M. Kennedy, *Freedom from Fear, The American People in Depression and War, 1929–1945.* New York: Oxford University Press, 1999; John Brooks, *Once in Golconda, A True Drama of Wall Street; 1920–1938.* New York: Harper & Row, 1969. Roger Babson's famous warning, "I repeat what I said at this time last year and the year before, that sooner or later a crash is coming," was useless.

3. Kennedy, *Freedom from Fear.* Kennedy notes that interest payment on the national debt rose from $25 million annually in 1914 to $1 billion annually in the 1920s due to World War I, accounting for one-third of the federal budget. The actual budget in 1929 was $3.127 billion a year (*Budget of the U.S. Government, Fiscal Year 1999—Historical Tables,* Table 1.1—Summary of Receipts, Outlays, and Surpluses or Deficits: 1789–2003. Washington, D.C.: Government Printing Office).

4. By the bottom tick on November 13, the market had lost $26 to $30 billion of its roughly $80 billion precrash value (Kennedy, op. cit., Brooks, op. cit.). World War I cost approximately $32 billion (Robert McElvaine, *The Great Depression: America, 1929–1941.* New York: Three Rivers Press, 1993; also Hugh Rockoff, *It's Over, Over There: The U.S. Economy in World War I,* National Bureau of Economic Research Working Paper No. 10580).

5. Charlie Munger reported that all the Buffetts, including those employed elsewhere, worked at the store, in a letter to Katharine Graham dated November 13, 1974.

6. Coffee with Congress.

7. Roger Lowenstein, *Buffett: The Making of an American Capitalist.* New York: Doubleday, 1996.

8. Roger Lowenstein, in *Buffett,* cites Leila Buffett's memoirs for this fact.

9. Ernest Buffett letter to Mr. and Mrs. Clarence Buffett and Marjorie Bailey, August 17, 1931.

10. "Union State Bank Closes Doors Today: Reports Assets in Good Condition; Reopening Planned," *Omaha World-Herald,* August 15, 1931. Characteristically, the story understated the bank's dire situation. It went into reorganization under regulatory supervision and filed for bankruptcy.

11. Howard had borrowed $9,000 to buy $10,000 of stock in the bank. The stock was now worthless. The house and mortgage were in Leila's name. Standard Accident Insurance Company, Howard Homan Buffett application for fidelity bond.

12. "Buffett, Sklenicka and Falk Form New Firm," *Omaha Bee News,* September 8, 1931. Statement of Buffett, Sklenicka & Co. for the month ending September 30, 1931.

13. The wave crested in December 1931 with the failure of the Bank of the United States, an official-sounding institution that had nothing to do with the government. The $286 million collapse broke a record, took down 400,000 depositors, and was understood by everyone—in one sense or another—as a failure of public trust (Kennedy, *Freedom from Fear*). It kicked the quivering legs out from under the banking system and sent the already battered economy into collapse.

14. Although its return on revenues was low, the firm by then was consistently profitable and would remain so, with the exception of a couple of months.

15. By the end of 1932, Howard Buffett was averaging 40–50% more in commissions than in 1931, based on financial statements of Buffett, Sklenicka & Co.

16. Charles Lindbergh Jr., "The Little Eaglet," was kidnapped on March 1, 1932. His body was found on May 12, 1932. Many parents in the 1920s and 1930s were preoccupied with kidnapping, a fear that actually began with the Leopold and Loeb case in 1924 but peaked with the Lindbergh baby. An Omaha country-club groundskeeper claimed he was kidnapped and robbed of $7. In Dallas a minister faked his own kidnapping, trussing himself to his church's electric fan (*Omaha World-Herald,* August 4, 1931, and June 20, 1931).

17. According to Roberta Buffett Bialek, Howard once had rheumatic fever, which may have weakened his heart.

18. Interview with Doris Buffett.

19. Interview with Doris Buffett. Warren also remembers this.

20. Interview with Roberta Buffett Bialek.

21. Interviews with Jack Frost, Norma Thurston-Perna, Stu Erikson, Lou Battistone.

22. The correct clinical term for Leila's condition is unknown, but it may have boiled down to a literal pain in the neck: occipital neuralgia, a chronic pain disorder caused by irritation or injury to the occipital nerve, which is located in the back of the scalp. This disorder causes throbbing, migrainelike pain, which originates at the nape of the neck and spreads up and around the forehead and scalp. Occipital neuralgia can result from physical stress, trauma, or repeated contraction of the neck muscles.

23. Interview with Katie Buffett. This may have been while pregnant with either Warren or Bertie.

24. Interview with Katie Buffett.

25. "Beer Is Back! Omaha to Have Belated Party," *Omaha World-Herald,* August 9, 1933; "Nebraska Would Have Voted Down Ten Commandments, Dry Head Says," *Omaha World-Herald,* November 15, 1944; "Roosevelt Issues Plea for Repeal of Prohibition," Associated Press, July 8, 1933, as printed in *Omaha World-Herald.*

26. U.S. and Nebraska Division of Agricultural Statistics, *Nebraska Agricultural Statistics, Historical Record 1866–1954.* Lincoln: Government Printing Office, 1957; *Almanac for Nebraskans 1939,* The Federal Writers' Project Works Progress Administration, State of Nebraska; Clinton Warne, "Some Effects of the Introduction of the Automobile on Highways and Land Values in Nebraska," *Nebraska History* quarterly, The Nebraska State Historical Society, Vol. 38, Number 1, March 1957, page 4.

27. In Kansas, a banker sent to foreclose on a farm turned up dead, shot full of .22- and .38-caliber bullets and dragged by his own car. "Forecloser on Farm Found Fatally Shot," *Omaha World-Herald,* January 31, 1933. See also "'Nickel Bidders' Halted by Use of Injunctions," *Omaha*

World-Herald, January 27, 1933; "Tax Sales Blocked by 300 Farmers in Council Bluffs," *Omaha World-Herald*, February 27, 1933; "Penny Sale Turned into Real Auction," *Omaha World-Herald*, March 12, 1933; "Neighbors Bid $8.05 at Sale When Man with Son, Ill, Asks Note Money," *Omaha World-Herald*, January 28, 1933, for examples of the mortgage crisis.

28. "The Dust Storm of November 12 and 13, 1933," *Bulletin of the American Meteorological Society*, February 1934; "60 Miles an Hour in Iowa," special to the *New York Times*, November 13, 1933; Waudemar Kaempffert, "The Week in Science: Storms of Dust," *New York Times*, November 19, 1933.

29. Cited from Leila's memoirs in Roger Lowenstein's *Buffett*.

30. From the *Almanac for Nebraskans 1939*. Sponsored by the Nebraska State Historical Society, which also contained some tall tales such as the idea of scouring pots by holding them up to a keyhole.

31. "Hot Weather and the Drought of 1934," *Bulletin of the American Meteorological Society*, June–July 1934.

32. Grasshoppers are the informal state mascot; Nebraska terms itself the "Bugeater State." Long before the Cornhuskers name, the University of Nebraska football team called itself the "Bugeaters" in 1892 in honor of its flying guests. Nebraska football fans still informally call themselves Bugeaters. Grasshoppers love drought conditions and contribute to soil erosion by devouring every living plant down to the black earth. From 1934–1938 the estimated national cost of grasshopper destruction was $315.8 million (about $4.7 billion in 2007 dollars). The region encompassing Nebraska, the Dakotas, Kansas, and Iowa was the epicenter of grasshopper infestation. See *Almanac for Nebraskans 1939*; also Ivan Ray Tannehill, *Drought: Its Causes and Effects*. Princeton: University Press, 1947.

33. "Farmers Harvest Hoppers for Fish Bait," *Omaha World-Herald*, August 1, 1931.

34. As asserted in Franklin Delano Roosevelt's inaugural address (March 4, 1933)—he was speaking, however, of economic paralysis.

35. Lacking electronic security and thoughtful cash controls, banks were more vulnerable to robbery in those days, and an epidemic of bank robberies took place in the 1930s.

36. Several Buffetts, including Howard and Bertie, contracted polio. Another epidemic took place in the mid-1940s. People born after the vaccine became available in the 1950s and '60s may find the chronic anxiety this disease engendered difficult to comprehend, but it was very real at the time.

37. Ted Keitch letter to Warren Buffett, May 29, 2003. Keitch's father worked at the Buffett store.

38. Interview with Doris Buffett.

39. Howard wanted his children to attend Dundee's Benson High School instead of Central, where he had suffered from snobbery.

40. Marion Barber Stahl was a partner in his own firm, Stahl and Updike, and had become counsel to the *New York Daily News*, among other clients. He and his wife, Dorothy, lived on Park Avenue and had no children. Obituary of Marion Stahl, *New York Times*, November 11, 1936.

41. Interview with Roberta Buffett Bialek.

42. Interviews with Roberta Buffett Bialek, Warren Buffett, Doris Buffett.

43. Interview with Doris Buffett.

44. September 9, 1935, at the Columbian School.

45. Interview with Roberta Buffett Bialek as well as Warren Buffett.

Chapter 7: Armistice Day

1. Adults interviewed by the author who attended Rosehill as children recall it as idyllic, yet the year before Warren started first grade, Rosehill parents pleaded for relief from overcrowded rooms and a "mud hole" playground. They were told not to expect help "until the sheriff collects back taxes." "School Plea Proves Vain," *Omaha World-Herald*, January 22, 1935.

2. Interview with Roberta Buffett Bialek.

3. Walt Loomis, the teacher of the boxing lesson, was a big kid, about Doris's age.

4. Interview with Roberta Buffett Bialek.

5. Stella's doctors referred to her as schizophrenic, while noting she suffered annually from predictable periods of agitation and confusion, and indicated that her personality did not deteriorate as expected in schizophrenia. Based on family history and Bernice's statement that other older relatives in addition to Stella's mother, Susan Barber, were "maniacal" and mentally unstable, bipolar disorder may be suspected as the real condition. This disease was barely understood, to say the least, in the 1930s and '40s.

6. From an entry in Leila's "day book."

7. In an interview, one of his classmates, Joan Fugate Martin, recalled Warren showing up on his rounds periodically to "shoot the breeze" in her driveway.

8. Interview with Roberta Buffett Bialek.

9. Interviews with Stu Erickson, Warren Buffett.

10. According to his Rosehill transcript, Warren was promoted to 4B in 1939.

11. Interview with Stu Erickson.

12. *"My appendectomy was the high point of my social life,"* Buffett says.

13. *"I wish one of those nuns had gone bad,"* he says today.

14. Rosco McGowen, "Dodgers Battle Cubs to 19-Inning Tie," *New York Times*, May 18, 1939. (Warren and Ernest did not stay for the entire game.)

15. Ely Culbertson, *Contract Bridge Complete: The New Gold Book of Bidding and Play.* Philadelphia: The John C. Winston Co., 1936.

16. This explanation of bridge was provided by Bob Hamman, eleven-time world champion and #1-ranked bridge player in the world between 1985 and 2004. Hamman appears at the Berkshire shareholders meeting.

Chapter 8: A Thousand Ways

1. Warren bought the gum for three cents a pack from his grandfather.

2. Interviews with Doris Buffett, Roberta Buffett Bialek.

3. Two presidents, Ulysses S. Grant and Theodore Roosevelt, had previously sought election to a third term. Both were defeated.

4. The Trans-Lux Corporation placed the first ticker-tape projection system at the New York Stock Exchange in 1923. The system worked something like a fax machine. Trans-Lux knew a good thing when it saw one: The company's own stock was listed on the American Stock Exchange in 1925, and Trans-Lux remains the oldest listed company on the Amex today.

5. Frank Buffett had reconciled with Ernest on Henrietta's death in 1921 and ran the other Buffett store. John Barber was a real estate agent.

6. Pyramid schemes are frauds that promise investors impossible returns, using cash from later investors to pay off earlier investors and create the appearance of success. To keep going, the scheme has to grow like a pyramid, but their geometrically compounding structure guarantees eventual failure and discovery.

7. Alden Whitman, "Sidney J. Weinberg Dies at 77; 'Mr. Wall Street' of Finance," *New York Times*, July 24, 1969; Lisa Endlich, *Goldman Sachs: The Culture of Success.* New York: Knopf, 1999.

8. That Weinberg cared about his opinion mattered more than the opinion itself; Buffett has no recollection of which stock he recommended to Weinberg.

9. Buffett later said, in an interview, that these were the words that ran through his head—"that's where the money is"—although at the time he was not familiar with the famous quote attributed to bank robber Willie Sutton.

10. Almost a decade later, he would lower the age to 30 while talking to his sister Bertie, who was 14 or 15 at the time. Interview with Roberta Buffett Bialek.

11. Buffett believes he overheard his father talking about the stock, which traded on the "Curb Exchange," where brokers gathered in the street (later organized into the American Stock Exchange).

12. From the records of Buffett, Sklenicka & Co.

Chapter 9: Inky Fingers

1. Leila Buffett letter to Clyde and Edna Buffett, undated but approximately 1964.

2. United States Department of Agriculture and Nebraska Department of Agriculture, *Nebraska Agricultural Statistics (preliminary report) 1930*. Lincoln, Government Printing Office, 1930, p. 3.

3. Buffett's impression of 1940s South Omaha was vivid: "*If you walked around down there in those days, believe me, it was not conducive to eating hot dogs.*"

4. This description of Washington in wartime owes much to David Brinkley's *Washington Goes to War* (New York: Alfred A. Knopf, 1988).

5. Dr. Frank Reichel headed American Viscose.

6. Interviews with Doris Buffett, Roberta Buffett Bialek, Warren Buffett.

7. Buffett is probably embellishing a little here with hindsight.

8. Interview with Roberta Buffett Bialek.

9. Gladys, formerly known as Gussie, changed her name to Mary sometime during this period. Warren vainly pursued a romance with her daughter Carolyn, who later married Buffett's friend Walter Scott.

10. Warren claims it was Byron's idea. Byron claims it was Warren's idea. Stu says he can't remember.

11. Joan Fugate Martin, who remembers the date, in an interview corroborated the story. She called the boys perfect gentlemen, but had nothing to add about their self-confessed awkwardness.

12. Interviews with Stu Erickson and Byron Swanson, who supplied various details of the story.

13. The phone number is from a letter from Mrs. Anna Mae Junno, whose grandfather used to work as a meat cutter.

14. The lowly stock boy was Charlie Munger.

15. Interview with Katie Buffett.

16. Ibid. Leila had a striver's fascination with social hierarchies and upward mobility.

17. "*You might argue that it was working in my grandfather's grocery store that fostered a lot of desire for independence in me,*" Buffett says.

18. This letter, which was at one time one of Buffett's treasured heirlooms, resided in his desk drawer for many years, written on a piece of yellow paper. He can no longer locate it. Through a trade association, Ernest lobbied against chain stores and worked for legislation that would levy special taxes on them—in vain.

19. Interview with Doris Buffett.

20. Warren Buffett letter to Meg Greenfield, June 19, 1984.

21. Sadly, no one in the family can locate a copy of this manuscript today.

22. Spring Valley marketing brochure. The place had its own coat of arms.

23. Alice Deal Junior High School was named after the first junior high principal in Washington, D.C.

24. Buffett is reasonably sure Ms. Allwine was his English teacher and that "*she had good reason*" for her low opinion of him. "*I deserved it,*" he says.

25. Interview with Casper Heindel.

26. "*I'm not sure I paid tax on that either,*" Warren adds.

27. In her memoir, Leila wrote that Warren would not let her touch the money.

28. Roger Bell, who confirms the story in an interview, was saving war-bond stamps until he had enough to buy an actual bond, and cashed them in to fund the trip. "I told my mother we were going, but she didn't believe me," he says.

29. Interview with Roger Bell.

30. From Buffett's 1944 report cards.

31. Based on comments in his report cards.

32. Interview with Norma Thurston-Perna.

33. Queen Wilhelmina owned stock in the Dutch holding company that had bought The Westchester.

34. He collected the bus passes from various routes. *"They were colorful. I collected anything."* Asked if anyone else in his family ever collected anything: *"No. They were more popular."*

35. Customers also discarded old magazines in the stairwells, and Warren would pick them up.

36. While Warren recalls the story, it was Lou Battistone who remembered its fascinating details.

37. Interview with Lou Battistone.

Chapter 10: True Crime Stories

1. This particular prank letter circulated widely in the mid-twentieth century. Where the idea originated and from whom Warren might have gotten a copy is unknown. What makes this fondly recalled prank funny (putting aside whether or how often he actually perpetrated it and upon whom) is how it plays to the commonplace interest in hidden lives and feet of clay. Its essence is a tribute to the power of shame.

2. The impact of Sears, the first department store in Tenleytown, and its unusual rooftop parking lot are described in Judith Beck Helm's *Tenleytown, D.C.: Country Village into City Neighborhood.* Washington, D.C.: Tennally Press, 1981.

3. In an interview, Norma Thurston-Perna substantiates the essential elements of this story, recalls her boyfriend Don Danly "hooking" from Sears with Warren, adds that to some extent this behavior continued into high school, and mentions how annoyed she was to discover that an impressive honeysuckle fragrance and bath powder set given to her by Don as a birthday gift turned out to have been stolen from Sears.

4. A letter from Suzanne M. Armstrong to Warren Buffett, December 20, 2007, recalls a friend of her father's cousin, Jimmy Parsons, stealing golf balls with Buffett while at Woodrow Wilson High School.

5. Hannibal was the antihero of the book and movie *The Silence of the Lambs.*

Chapter 11: Pudgy She Was Not

1. From 1933, when the U.S. went off the gold standard, through 1947, the Consumer Price Index fluctuated wildly, spiking over 18%. The history of the Federal Reserve under inflationary conditions was short and provided little evidence to support an opinion either way.

2. Interview with Roberta Buffett Bialek. The others remember this story.

3. Coffee with Congress.

4. Interview with Katie Buffett. Leila apparently became obsessed with Wallis Warfield Simpson around 1936 during the abdication crisis in England.

5. Woodrow Wilson's terms ran through February and June. Because Warren had skipped half a grade, he started his sophomore year in February.

6. Cartoonist Al Capp created Li'l Abner, who inherited his strength from his mother, the domineering Mammy Yokum, whose knockout "Good night Irene" punch maintained discipline among the Yokum clan.

7. Although most of this information is from *Strength and Health,* Elizabeth McCracken wrote "The Belle of the Barbell," a tribute to Pudgy Stockton, in the *New York Times Magazine,* December 31, 2006.

8. Pudgy was married to Les Stockton, a bodybuilder who had introduced her to weight lifting.

Chapter 12: Silent Sales

1. *"It was never any big success at all ... it did not do well. It did not do terribly either. And it didn't last very long,"* says Buffett.

2. In interviews, Roger Bell and Casper Heindel, as well as Warren Buffett, helped remember details about the farm. Buffett believes he bought this from or through his uncle John Barber, a real estate broker.

3. Interview with Casper Heindel. More than half of all Nebraska land was farmed by tenant farmers. Real property ownership with mortgages was unpopular because unstable crop prices left farmers vulnerable to foreclosure.

4. Interview with Norma Thurston-Perna.

5. In an interview, Lou Battistone observes that he noticed the "two sides" of Buffett's brain in high school—the cool mathematical businessman and the burlesque-watching one—while at the burlesque.

6. Interview with Lou Battistone.

7. Buffett told this story at Harvard Business School in 2005.

8. Carnegie was a salesman for Armour & Co., covering the Omaha territory; the compatibility of his views with Buffett's temperament probably owes something to a shared Midwestern ethos.

9. All text, Dale Carnegie, *How to Win Friends and Influence People.* New York: Simon & Schuster, 1938. Copyright Dale Carnegie & Associates. Courtesy of Dale Carnegie & Associates.

10. Dale Carnegie quoting John Dewey.

11. The average man earned $2,473 a year in 1946, according to the U.S. Department of Commerce, Bureau of the Census, *Historical Statistics of the United States: Colonial Times to 1970, Bicentennial Edition.* Washington, D.C.: Government Printing Office, 1975, Series D-722–727, p. 164.

12. According to Lou Battistone in an interview.

13. According to a newspaper advertisement on July 24, 1931, at early Depression-era prices a dozen years earlier, quality refurbished golf balls cost three for $1.05.

14. Interview with Don Dedrick, a golf teammate from high school.

15. Interview with Lou Battistone.

16. *"We were the only guys that paid the fifty-dollar stamp tax on pinball machines,"* Warren says. *"I'm not sure we would have done it if my dad hadn't been insisting."*

17. Interview with Lou Battistone. The name "Wilson" came from Woodrow Wilson High School.

18. An essay into barbershop food concession ended quickly after the peanut dispenser, filled with five pounds of Spanish nuts, broke and got customers a handful of peanuts mixed with ground glass.

19. Dialogue and expressions used by Buffett in this story came from Lou Battistone, although the facts align with Buffett's recollection.

20. Interview with Don Dedrick.

21. In one version of this story, told by a high school friend of Buffett's who was not present, Kerlin was too smart to fall for it and never made it to the golf course. Whatever happened, Buffett's version is, not surprisingly, funnier.

Chapter 13: The Rules of the Racetrack

1. Interview with Katie Buffett.

2. While this story sounds buffed and polished over the years, the tone of it rings true. Letters from Warren at college to his father a couple of years later have the same breeziness.

3. Interview with Stu Erickson.

4. Interview with Don Dedrick.

5. Interview with Bob Dwyer.

6. According to Gray, Buffett also jokingly dreamed up an idea for a magazine called *Sex Crimes Illustrated* while they were on the train to the Havre de Grace racetrack.

7. Interview with Bill Gray, now Emeritus Professor of Atmospheric Science at Colorado State University and head of the Tropical Meteorology Project.

Chapter 14: The Elephant

1. The class size is approximate because Woodrow Wilson had, in effect, two classes graduating in parallel (February and June graduates); students like Warren could shift from February to the previous June by taking a few extra credits. The school described Buffett's top 50 ranking as falling in the top "one-seventh" of his class.

2. Barbara "Bobby" Weigand, who remembers only the hearse. Doris Buffett recalled the family debate about the hearse.

3. Interviews with Bob Feitler, Ann Beck MacFarlane, Waldo Beck. David Brown became brother-in-law of Waldo Beck, Ann Beck's brother.

4. Interviews with Bob Feitler, Warren Buffett. Note that, because he was using the car for commercial purposes, Buffett would probably have been able to get extra gas coupons at a time when gas was tightly rationed.

5. The term "policy" probably came from the Gaelic *pá lae sámh* (pronounced *paah lay seeh*), which means "easy payday," a nineteenth-century Irish-American gambling term.

6. The bill generated fierce anti-Taft labor reprisals in the Midwest.

7. Interview with Doris Buffett.

8. Estimate based on data supplied by Nancy R. Miller, Public Services Archivist, The University Archives and Record Center, University of Pennsylvania.

9. Jolson, a vaudeville singer, was the most popular stage entertainer of the early twentieth century. He made famous such songs as "You Made Me Love You," "Rock-a-Bye Your Baby with a Dixie Melody," "Swanee," "April Showers," "Toot, Toot, Tootsie, Goodbye," and "California, Here I Come." He performed "My Mammy" in blackface in the 1927 movie *The Jazz Singer,* the first feature film to enjoy widespread commercial success. Jolson was voted "Most Popular Male Vocalist" in a 1948 *Variety* poll on the back of a film about his life, *The Al Jolson Story,* which repopularized him to a younger generation. Performing in blackface would be considered racist today but was ubiquitous and unremarkable at the time.

10. "My Mammy," words by Sam Lewis and Joe Young; music by Walter Donaldson, copyright 1920.

11. Coffee with Congress.

12. Interview with Chuck Peterson.

13. Interview with Clyde Reighard.

14. Interviews with Chuck Peterson, Sharon and Gertrude Martin.

15. Interview with Anthony Vecchione, as quoted in Roger Lowenstein, *Buffett: The Making of an American Capitalist.* New York: Doubleday, 1996.

16. Peterson recalls that he stuck it out all year—or, well, almost.

17. Don Danly, as quoted in Lowenstein, *Buffett.* Danly is deceased.

18. Interview with Barbara Worley Potter.

19. Interview with Clyde Reighard.

20. Beja, as quoted in Lowenstein, *Buffett.* Beja is deceased.

21. Interview with Don Sparks.

22. Shoe-shining was a big thing at Penn; a typical pledge haze was to shine the actives' shoes.

23. In an interview, Reighard recalled the outlines of the story. Buffett became a close friend of the victim Beja's roommate, Jerry Oransky (renamed Orans), who is deceased.

24. Interview with Barbara Worley Potter.

25. Interview with Ann Beck MacFarlane, who thinks the date was engineered by her parents and Leila Buffett.

26. Susan Thompson Buffett described her husband circa 1950 this way.

27. Interview with Clyde Reighard.

28. Interview with Bob Feitler.

29. Interview with Clyde Reighard.

30. Interview with Anthony Vecchione, as quoted in Lowenstein, *Buffett.*

31. Interview with Martin Wiegand.

32. "Buffett Lashes Marshall Plan," *Omaha World-Herald,* January 28, 1948. Buffett campaign literature also describes foreign aid as money down the rat hole.

33. June 5, 1948, dedication of Memorial Park.

34. Last will and testament of Frank D. Buffett, filed February 19, 1949.

35. Approved application to the county court of Douglas County, Nebraska, April 14, 1958. The

bonds were allowed to mature, since the will said proceeds of any property "sold" could only be invested in U.S. bonds. Given the opportunity cost and interest rates, Howard's move was wise.

36. Leila Buffett's day books. "It's Cold—But Remember that Bitter Winter of '48–'49?" *Omaha World-Herald,* January 6, 1959.

37. *Commercial & Financial Chronicle,* May 6, 1948.

38. Interview with Doris Buffett.

39. Interview with Lou Battistone.

40. Interview with Sharon Martin.

Chapter 15: The Interview

1　They would sell 220 dozen balls for a total of $1,200.

2. Warren Buffett letter to Howard Buffett, February 16, 1950.

3. He asked Howard to advance him $1,426 that the broker required him to keep on deposit, signing off, "Yours, for lower auto profits, Warren." Warren Buffett letter to Howard Buffett, February 16, 1950.

4. Warren Buffett letter to Jerry Orans, May 1, 1950, cited in Roger Lowenstein, *Buffett: The Making of an American Capitalist.* New York: Doubleday, 1996.

5. "Bizad Students Win Scholarships," *Daily Nebraskan,* May 19, 1950.

6. Benjamin Graham, *The Intelligent Investor: A Book of Practical Counsel.* New York: Harper & Brothers, 1949.

7. Garfield A. Drew, *New Methods for Profit in the Stock Market.* Boston: The Metcalf Press, 1941.

8. Robert D. Edwards and John McGee, *Technical Analysis of Stock Market Trends.* Springfield, Mass.: Stock Trend Service, 1948.

9. Wood, as cited in Lowenstein, *Buffett.* Wood is deceased. He told Lowenstein he was not sure when this conversation took place—before Buffett was rejected by Harvard or as late as after when he had started at Columbia—but it was apparently before he met Graham himself.

10. According to Buffett, Howard Buffett was acquainted with one of the board members.

11. Columbia University in the City of New York, announcement of the Graduate School of Business for the winter and spring sessions 1950–1951, Columbia University Press.

Chapter 16: Strike One

1. In his memoir, *Man of the House* (New York: Random House, 1987), the late Congressman Tip O'Neill recalled that his pastor, Monsignor Blunt, said it was a sin for Catholics to go to the Protestant-managed YMCA. O'Neill and a Jewish friend stayed at the Sloane House anyway. The regular rate in the 1930s was sixty-five cents a night, but, O'Neill said, "If you signed up for the Episcopal service, it was only thirty-five cents, with breakfast included. We were nobody's fool, so we signed up for the thirty-five-cent deal and figured to duck out after breakfast and before the service. But apparently we weren't the first to think of this brilliant plan, because they locked the doors during breakfast, which meant that we were stuck." By the 1950s, there was no longer a "pray or pay" deal at the Sloane House. "If there had been," Buffett says, "I would have experienced a revelation and embraced whatever denomination offered the greatest discount."

2. Buffett is not certain if the smoking deal applied to all three of the Buffett kids or only his sisters, but they all got the $2,000 on graduation on roughly the same terms.

3. Most of the money was invested in U.S International Securities and Parkersburg Rig & Reel, which he replaced with Tri-Continental Corporation on January 1, 1951. Howard contributed most of the money and Warren contributed the ideas and work, or "sweat equity," to an informal partnership.

4. Benjamin Graham and David L. Dodd, *Security Analysis, Principles and Technique.* New York: McGraw-Hill, 1934.

5. Barbara Dodd Anderson letter to Warren Buffett, April 19, 1989.

6. The Union Pacific Railroad in the nineteenth century was the most scandal-plagued and bankruptcy-riddled of the nation's railroads.

7. William W. Townsend, *Bond Salesmanship*. New York: Henry Holt, 1924. Buffett read this book three or four times.

8. Interview with Jack Alexander.

9. And, according to Buffett, one woman, Maggie Shanks.

10. Interview with Fred Stanback.

11. At $2,600 a year, Schloss as an investor was making less than the average secretary in 1951, who took home $3,060, according to a survey of the National Secretaries Association.

12. Interview with Fred Stanback.

13. Interview with Walter Schloss. Some material is from *The Memoirs of Walter J. Schloss*. New York: September Press, 2003.

14. Stryker & Brown was the "market maker," or principal dealer, in Marshall-Wells stock.

15. Marshall-Wells was the second Graham and Dodd stock he had bought, after Parkersburg Rig & Reel. Stanback confirms the lunch with Green, but can't recall the date.

16. Not, as has been written, from *Who's Who in America*. However, he may have learned it from reading *Moody's*, hearing it from David Dodd or Walter Schloss, or from a newspaper or magazine source.

17. Due to a legal technicality, this divestiture of GEICO stock was required in a consent order with the SEC in 1948. Graham-Newman violated Section 12(d)(2) of the Investment Company Act of 1940, although "in the bona fide, though mistaken, belief that the acquisition might lawfully be consummated." A registered investment company (Graham-Newman was "a diversified management investment company of the open-end type") cannot acquire more than 10% of the total outstanding voting stock of an insurance company if it does not already have 25% ownership.

18. GEICO oral history interview of Lorimer Davidson by Walter Smith, June 19, 1998, and also see William K. Klingaman, *GEICO, The First Forty Years*. Washington, D.C.: GEICO Corporation, 1994, for a condensed version of this story.

19. Making $100,000 in 1929 was equivalent to making $1,212,530 in 2007.

20. By 1951, GEICO was deemphasizing mailings in favor of platoons of friendly telephone operators who answered the phone at regional offices and were trained to quickly screen bad risks.

21. The main problem with tontines was that people were gambling with their life insurance policies instead of using them as protection. Originally a "survivor bet," expulsion from a tontine pool was later based on failure to pay premiums for any reason. "It is a tempting game; but how cruel!" *Papers Relating to Tontine Insurance*, The Connecticut Mutual Life Insurance Company, Hartford, Conn.: 1887.

22. Office Memorandum, Government Employees Insurance Corporation, Buffett-Falk & Co., October 9, 1951.

Chapter 17: Mount Everest

1. Benjamin Graham, *The Memoirs of the Dean of Wall Street*. New York: McGraw-Hill, 1996. Anecdotal material from this source has been verified with Warren Buffett.

2. In 1915, members of the Grossbaum family, like many American Jews, began to anglicize their name to Graham in response to the anti-Semitism that flourished during and after World War I. Ben's family made the change in April 1917. Source: November 15, 2007, speech by Jim Grant to the Center for Jewish History on "My Hero, Benjamin Grossbaum."

3. Graham was born in 1894, the year of one of the biggest financial panics in American history, which was followed by the depression of 1896–97, the panic of 1901, the panic of 1903–04 ("Rich Man's Panic"), the panic of 1907, the war depression of 1913–14, and the postwar depression of 1920–22.

4. Benjamin Graham, *Memoirs*.

5. Ibid.

6. Ibid.

7. Traditionally, people came to Wall Street in one of two ways. Either they entered the family business by following a relative into the job, or, having no such connection, they "came up through

the hawsehole," to use a nautical expression common on Wall Street at the time, starting young as a runner or board boy and working their way up, like Sidney Weinberg, Ben Graham, and Walter Schloss. Attending business school with the conscious intention of working on Wall Street was essentially unheard of until the early 1950s because most areas of finance, and especially the art of security analysis, had not developed as academic disciplines.

8. Details of Graham's early career are from Janet Lowe's *Benjamin Graham on Value Investing: Lessons from the Dean of Wall Street.* Chicago: Dearborn Financial Publishing, 1994.

9. Graham believed that one could be swayed by personality and salesmanship by going to meetings with a company's management, so this was partly a way of remaining dispassionate. But Graham was also not particularly interested in human beings.

10. Interview with Rhoda and Bernie Sarnat.

11. Benjamin Graham, *Memoirs.*

12. Ibid.

13. Interview with Jack Alexander.

14. In *Security Analysis, Principles, and Technique* (New York: McGraw-Hill, 1934), Benjamin Graham and Dodd stressed that there is no single definition of "intrinsic value," which depends on earnings, dividends, assets, capital structure, terms of the security, and "other" factors. Since estimates are always subjective, the main consideration, they wrote—always—is the margin of safety.

15. The apt analogy to Plato's cave was originally made by Patrick Byrne.

16. Often this was because the kind of undervalued stocks he liked were illiquid and could not be purchased in large positions. But Buffett felt that Graham could have followed a bolder strategy.

17. Interview with Jack Alexander.

18. Interview with Bill Ruane.

19. Interviews with Jack Alexander, Bill Ruane.

20. Schloss, in his memoir, wrote with warm affection of his wife, Louise, who "battled depression throughout her entire adult life." They remained married for fifty-three years, until she died in 2000.

21. Interview with Walter Schloss.

Chapter 18: Miss Nebraska

1. Susie's parents were friends of Howard and Leila Buffett, but their children attended different schools, so they did not socialize.

2. Interview with Roberta Buffett Bialek. Susie was born June 15, 1932. Bertie was born November 15, 1933.

3. Earl Wilson was the saloon writer for the *New York Post.* In describing *Newsday* scribe Jimmy Breslin, *Media Life Magazine* defined a saloon writer as the purveyor of "a certain style of journalism that's peculiar to New York, and a bit peculiar in itself, where the writer journeys about the places where ordinary people can be found and writes of their visions of the human condition."

4. A well-known women-only residence still in operation today (at 419 W. 34th Street in New York City).

5. Vanita, in a Valentine letter to Warren, February 1991, poses the possibility that she "never liked cheese sandwiches and that I just ate them to please." (In this letter, as at some other times, she spells her middle name "May" instead of "Mae" as in her youth.)

6. This description came from various letters from Vanita, reminiscing about her dates with Warren—January 1, 1991, February 19, 1991, January 1, 1994, many undated; Buffett agrees.

7. Susan Thompson Buffett, as told to Warren Buffett in 2004. He does not remember this but adds that, of course, he wouldn't.

8. Buffett says that, despite her antics, he was never intimidated by Vanita. "*I wouldn't have had the guts to stick Pudgy in a wastebasket,*" he says. "*I mean, she'd have beaten the hell out of me.*" For her part, Vanita later claimed to Fred Stanback that the incident never happened—although she did have some incentive to downplay the histrionic side of her personality to Fred.

9. As Charlie Munger puts it, Buffett narrowly missed a disastrous marriage when he "escaped the clutches of Vanita."

10. "A Star Is Born?" Associated Press, *Town & Country* magazine, September 24, 1977.

11. Information on William Thompson comes from a variety of sources, including interviews with Warren, Roberta, and Doris Buffett and other family members, and "Presbyterian Minister Reviews Thompson Book," *Omaha World-Herald*, January 5, 1967; "Old 'Prof' Still Feels Optimistic About Younger Generation," *Omaha World-Herald*, March 28, 1970; "W. H. Thompson, Educator, Is Dead," *Omaha World-Herald*, April 7, 1981; "O.U. Alumni Honor Dean," *Omaha World-Herald*, May 15, 1960.

12. As supervisor of the school system's IQ testing, Doc Thompson had access to and, according to Buffett, knew Warren's IQ. Indeed, the IQ test results for the three little Buffetts may have intrigued him, given their remarkably high—and remarkably similar—scores.

13. In an interview, Marge Backhus Turtscher, who attended these services, wondered what on earth motivated Thompson to make the long trip each Sunday to preach at this tiny church. Thompson also once published a book, *The Fool Has Said God Is Dead*. Boston: Christopher Publishing House, 1966.

14. Susan Thompson Buffett told this story to various family members.

15. In many patients, rheumatic fever causes mild to serious heart complications (in Howard Buffett's case, at least moderate complications), but based on her subsequent health history, Susan Thompson appears to have been among the 20–60% who escape significant carditis, or long-term damage to the heart.

16. Warren, Doris Buffett, Roberta Buffett Bialek, Susie Buffett Jr., and other Buffetts talk of this striking film.

17. Interview with Raquel "Rackie" Newman.

18. Interviews with Charlene Moscrey, Sue James Stewart, Marilyn Kaplan Weisberg.

19. According to some high school classmates who asked not to be identified.

20. Interviews with Donna Miller, Inga Swenson. Swenson, who went on to become a professional actress, played Cornelia Otis Skinner opposite Thompson's Emily Kimbrough.

21. A composite taken from interviews with Inga Swenson, Donna Miller, Roberta Buffett Bialek, and John Smith, whose brother Dick Smith took Susie dancing.

22. Interviews with Sue James Stewart, Marilyn Kaplan Weisberg. Stewart, who was Sue Brownlee in high school, had access to a car and drove her best friend Susie to Council Bluffs for dates with Brown.

23. Interviews with Roberta Buffett Bialek, Warren Buffett, Doris Buffett, Marilyn Kaplan Weisberg.

24. The Wildcat Council acted as guides for campus visitors and leaders during New Student Week. Members joined by petitioning the council for membership (Northwestern University Student Handbook, 1950–1951).

25. Interview with Milton Brown, who says he would have depledged had the roles been reversed.

26. Interview with Sue James Stewart. Susie, a self-described "personal theist," flirted with Buddhism, a nontheistic religion, all her life and often referred to Zen or to herself as a "Zen person." It is fair to say she used the terms "Zen" and "theist" loosely.

27. Interview with Roberta Buffett Bialek.

28. Interviews with Chuck Peterson, Doris Buffett.

29. Interview with Charlie Munger.

30. Interview with Sue James Stewart.

31. "*I can see her in those dresses now*," Buffett says, a poignant statement from a man who does not know the color of his own bedroom walls.

32. Warren Buffett letter to Dorothy Stahl, October 6, 1951.

33. Susan Thompson Buffett, as conveyed to Warren Buffett.

34. Interview with Milton Brown.

35. Buffett recalls a literal three-hour lecture. A conversation of such length was almost certainly the result of him working himself up to ask the question while Doc Thompson carried on.

Chapter 19: Stage Fright

1. The net gain on investments was $7,434. He also put $2,500 into the account that he'd saved from his pay working at Buffett-Falk.

2. Delving a little further into Buffett's reasoning about the valuation of an insurance business: *"The stock was trading around forty dollars and therefore the whole company was selling for about seven million. I figured the company would be worth as much as the premium volume, roughly, because they would get the investment income on 'float' that was pretty close to dollar-for-dollar, maybe with the premium income. Plus, they'd have the book value. So I figured it would always be worth at least as much as the premium. Now, all I had to do was get to a billion dollars of premium income and I was going to be a millionaire."*

3. Interview with Margaret Landon, the secretary at Buffett-Falk.

4. According to Walter Schloss in an interview, the Norman family, who were heirs of Julius Rosenwald of Sears, Roebuck, "received GEICO stock because they were big investors in Graham-Newman. When the Normans wanted to put more money with Graham-Newman, they gave Ben Graham the GEICO stock he had distributed to them instead of putting cash in. Warren is out in Omaha, and he's buying GEICO. But Graham didn't know he was selling to Warren, and Warren couldn't figure out why Graham-Newman was selling it." The distribution of GEICO stock by Graham-Newman is also described in Janet Lowe's *Benjamin Graham on Value Investing: Lessons from the Dean of Wall Street*. Chicago: Dearborn Financial Publishing, 1994.

5. Interview with Bob Soener, who called him "Buffie" in those days.

6. As seen in a photograph taken in the classroom.

7. Interview with Lee Seeman.

8. Interview with Margaret Landon. Her memory of him is in this posture, reading.

9. Buffett traded two stocks personally, Carpenter Paper and Fairmont Foods. While astute enough to set the firm up as a market maker and trade the stocks, he was immature (albeit witty) enough to refer to the CEO of Fairmont Foods, D. K. Howe, as "Don't Know Howe."

10. Bill Rosenwald later founded the United Jewish Appeal of New York.

11. Interviews with Doris Buffett, Roberta Buffett Bialek.

12. Brig. Gen. Warren Wood of the 34th National Guard Division.

13. Interview with Byron Swanson.

14. Interview with Fred Stanback.

15. Susie told Sue Brownlee (Sue James Stewart) this the week after she returned from her honeymoon. Interview with Sue James Stewart.

16. Wahoo is best known as the birthplace of movie mogul Darryl F. Zanuck.

17. "Love Only Thing That Stops Guard," *Omaha World-Herald*, April 20, 1952.

Chapter 20: Graham-Newman

1. General Douglas MacArthur made a halfhearted run for the nomination but was eclipsed by Taft. He and his former aide Eisenhower were bitter enemies.

2. This was the same Robert Taft who had cosponsored the Taft-Hartley Act, much favored among businessmen but despised by broad swaths of Americans. In short, Taft represented the extreme end of the party, which made him less likely to capture moderate voters.

3. Ironically, many in this faction promoted tariffs, government farm supports, and tough labor laws desired by their small-business and farm constituents, even though this may have seemed inconsistent with their other views on government. Another famous member of this group was popular Nebraska Senator Ken Wherry, the "merry mortician," famous for malapropisms such as calling Indochina "Indigo China," addressing the chairman as "Mr. Paragraph," and offering his "unanimous opinion." *Time*, June 25, 1951. Wherry died shortly before the election.

4. "Top GOP Rift Closed But Not the Democrats," *New York Times*, September 14, 1952; Elie Abel, "Taft Rallies Aid for GOP Ticket," *New York Times*, October 5, 1952.

5. Howard Buffett wrote to former President Hoover, October 23, 1952: "I have no enthusiasm for Eisenhower, but your decision to support his election is good enough for me." He apparently changed his mind after this letter was written.

6. Interview with Roberta Buffett Bialek.

7. Interview with Katie Buffett, who recalled this conversation and found it amusing. "Warren's probably forgotten he told me that one," she said.

8. Susan Goodwillie Stedman, recalling personal interview with Susan Thompson Buffett conducted November 2001, courtesy of Susan Goodwillie Stedman and Elizabeth Wheeler.

9. Interview with Susan T. Buffett.

10. Interviews with Mary and Dick Holland, Warren Buffett.

11. Interviews with Racquel Newman, Astrid Buffett.

12. The IQ story is a family tale, but since Dr. Thompson was in charge of IQ testing for the whole school system, it has at least some credence. Within the family, Dr. Thompson often tested his daughters and grandchildren while he was creating new psychology and intelligence tests. Whatever her IQ, Dottie was considered no dummy.

13. This story is related in Leila Buffett's diary. Also, Gabe Parks, "Court Has Nomination Vote Vacancy," *Omaha World-Herald,* July 4, 1954.

14. Warren Buffett letter to "Pop" Howard Buffett, dated "Wednesday," presumed August 4, 1954. "Scarsdale G.I. Suicide, Army Reports the Death of Pvt. Newton Graham in France," *New York Times,* August 3, 1954. The entire text of the item read: "Frankfurt, Germany, Aug. 2 (Reuters)—Pvt. Newton Graham of Scarsdale, N.Y., committed suicide at La Rochelle, France, the United States Army announced today." Newton—named after Sir Isaac Newton—was the second of Graham's sons to be named Isaac Newton; the first had died of meningitis at age nine. Noting Newton's increasing mental instability, which he labeled "highly neurotic, even probably schizophrenic," Graham had written letters trying to get him discharged from the Army, but failed. (Benjamin Graham, *The Memoirs of the Dean of Wall Street.* New York: McGraw-Hill, 1996.)

15. Susie Buffett Jr. says she had a crib.

16. Using the term "pay" loosely, since all of the earnings are not actually paid out as a dividend. This distinction was once the subject of heavy academic debate as to the discount that should be imputed to a stock's valuation for earnings that were not paid out. The premium assigned to companies that pay dividends has waned for a number of reasons. See also the reference to "The Frozen Corporation" in Chapter 46, "Rubicon."

17. Interview with Fred Stanback.

18. His personal investment return that year was 144.8%, compared to 50.1% for the DJIA.

19. Union Underwear was the predecessor to Fruit of the Loom.

20. Buffett recalled this classic story in an interview.

21. Interview with Sue James Stewart.

22. Interview with Elizabeth Trumble.

23. Interview with Roxanne Brandt.

24. Buffett's exact quote was *"I can see her pulsing and moaning as she said, 'Tell me more…'"*

Chapter 21: The Side to Play

1. Berkshire Hathaway chairman's letter, 1988.

2. The tax code exemption applied to LIFO inventory liquidations. For tax purposes Rockwood used LIFO accounting, which let it calculate profits using the *most recent* cocoa-bean prices, which minimized taxes. Correspondingly, cocoa beans were carried in inventory at old prices. A large taxable profit would therefore occur if it sold the inventory.

3. Pritzker created a business conglomerate through his investing activities, but is best known as founder of the Hyatt hotel chain.

4. At the onset of the exchange period, Accra cocoa beans, which made up half of Rockwood's 13-million-pound pile, were trading at $0.52 a pound. The price dropped to $0.44 per pound by

the conclusion of the exchange period. The price of these beans had hit a high of $0.73 per pound in August 1954, causing candy companies to shrink the size of their 5¢ candy bars. George Auerbach, "Nickel Candy Bar Wins a Reprieve," *New York Times*, March 26, 1955; "Commodity Cash Prices," *New York Times*, October 4 and 20, 1954.

5. Letter to Stockholders of Rockwood & Co., September 28, 1954.

6. From the 1988 chairman's letter in the Berkshire annual report to shareholders, which contains a brief description of the Rockwood transaction.

7. The speculator's return on the contract also reflects his funding cost. For example, if the speculator broke even on a three-month contract—net of his fee—the contract would actually be unprofitable, considering the speculator's funding cost.

8. In the futures market, the difference between a speculator and a hedger (or "insured") is essentially whether an underlying position in the commodity exists to be hedged.

9. Interviews with Tom Knapp and Walter Schloss, as well as Buffett.

10. Warren Buffett letter to David Elliott, February 5, 1955.

11. Based on its profile in *Moody's Industrial Manual*, Rockwood traded between $14.75 and $85 in 1954 and between $76 and $105 in 1955. Buffett held on to the shares through 1956. Profit on the trade is estimated. Rockwood traded above $80 a share during early 1956, based on the Graham-Newman annual report.

12. In the letter to David Elliott noted above (February 5, 1955), Buffett explains that Rockwood is his second-largest position (after Philadelphia & Reading, which he did not disclose) and writes that Pritzker "has operated quite fast in the past. He bought the Colson Corp. a couple years ago and after selling the bicycle division to Evans Products sold the balance to F. L. Jacobs. He bought Hiller & Hart about a year ago and immediately discontinued the pork-slaughtering business and changed it into a more or less real estate company." Pritzker, he writes, "has about half the stock of Rockwood, which represents about $3 million in cocoa value. I am quite sure he is not happy about sitting with this kind of money in inventory of this type and will be looking for a merger of some sort promptly." He had studied not just the numbers but Jay Pritzker.

13. Initially he had bought the stock from Graham-Newman when he was a stockbroker, after a minor mistake on an order from them caused them to DK ("don't know," or repudiate) the order. Warren kept the stock.

14. Before 2000, investors and analysts routinely sought and received nonpublic information that would be an advantage to them in trading stocks. This gradual flow of information, which benefited some investors at the expense of others, was considered part of the efficient workings of the capital markets and a reward for diligent research. Warren Buffett and his network of investor friends profited significantly from the old state of affairs. Ben Graham was questioned extensively about this practice before Congress in 1955. He commented that "a good deal of information from day to day and month to month naturally comes to the attention of directors and officers. It is not at all feasible to publish every day a report on the progress of the company...on the other hand, as a practical matter, there is no oath of secrecy imposed upon the officers or directors so that they cannot say anything about information that may come to their attention from week to week. The basic point involved is that where there is a matter of major importance it is generally felt that prompt disclosure should be made to all the stockholders so that nobody would get a substantial advantage in knowing that. But there are all degrees of importance, and it is very difficult to determine exactly what kind of information should or must be published and what kind should just go the usual grapevine route." He added that all investors may not be aware of the grapevine, but, "I think that the average experienced person would assume that some people are bound to know more about the company [whose stock they are trading] than he would, and possibly trade on the additional knowledge." Until 2000 that was, in effect, the state of the law.

    While a full discussion of insider trading is beyond the scope of this book, the theory of insider trading was promulgated with SEC Rule 10b-5 in 1942, but "so firmly entrenched was the Wall Street tradition of taking advantage of the investing public," as John Brooks puts it in *The Go-Go Years*, that the rule was not enforced until 1959, and it was not until the 1980s that anyone seriously questioned the duties of people other than insiders under insider-trading laws. Even then, the Supreme Court affirmed, in *Dirks v. SEC*, 463 U.S. 646 (1983), analysts could legitimately tell their clients this type of information, and the Supreme Court also noted in *Chiarella v. United States*, 445 U.S. 222 (1980), that "informational disparity is inevitable in the securities markets." To some extent, there was understood to be some benefit to the market of a gradual leakage of inside information; in fact, how else was the information to get out? The practice of business public relations and conference calls had not developed.

In these 1980s cases, however, the Supreme Court defined a new "misappropriation" theory of insider trading, in which inside information that was misappropriated by a fiduciary could lead to liability if acted upon. Then, largely in response to the Bubble-era proliferation of "meeting and beating consensus" earnings and the "whisper numbers" that companies began to suggest to favored analysts that they were going to earn, in 2000, through Regulation FD (Fair Disclosure), the SEC broadened the misappropriation theory to include analysts who selectively receive and disseminate material nonpublic information from a company's management. With the advent of Reg. FD, the "grapevine" largely ended, and a new era of carefully orchestrated disclosure practices began.

15. He registered the securities in his own name, rather than his brokers', so the checks came straight to his home.

16. Interviews with George Gillespie, Elizabeth Trumble, who heard this story from Madeleine. Warren heard it for the first time at his fiftieth birthday party, from Gillespie. Apparently Susie had never mentioned it to him.

17. More than five decades later, Howie recalls this as his first memory. While that may seem improbable, in "Origins of Autobiographical Memory," Harley and Reese (University of Chicago, *Developmental Psychology*, Vol. 35, No. 5, 1999) study theories of how childhood memories are recalled from the earliest months of life and conclude that this phenomenon does occur. One of the explanations is parents who repeat stories to their children. A gift from Ben Graham—probably significant to Warren—might plausibly be recalled by Howie from infancy because at least one parent helped him imprint it solidly in memory by discussing it so much.

18. Interview with Bernie and Rhoda Sarnat.

19. This story also is cited in Janet Lowe's *Benjamin Graham on Value Investing: Lessons from the Dean of Wall Street.* Chicago: Dearborn Financial Publishing, 1994.

20. Interview with Walter Schloss.

21. Warren Buffett letter to the Hilton Head Group, February 3, 1976.

22. Schloss was starting the partnership with $5,000 of his own capital, a risky arrangement that left him nothing on which to live. Buffett got him help with housing from Dan Cowin. Ben Graham put in $10,000 and had some of his friends do so too; eight of Schloss's friends put in $5,000 each. Schloss charged 25% of profits, "but that's it. If the market went down, we would have to make up the loss until my partners were whole."

23. Knapp was a security analyst at Van Cleef, Jordan & Wood, an investment adviser.

24. Interview with Tom Knapp.

25. Interview with Ed Anderson.

26. Ibid.

27. Graham was born May 9, 1894. He decided to shut down Graham-Newman when he was sixty-one, but the last Graham-Newman shareholder meeting was held on August 20, 1956.

28. Jason Zweig says in a July 2003 *Money* article, "Lessons from the Greatest Investor Ever," that "From 1936 to 1956, at his Graham-Newman mutual fund, he produced an average annual gain of more than 14.7% vs. 12.2% for the overall market—one of the longest and widest margins of outperformance in Wall Street history." This record does not reflect the impressive performance of GEICO, which was distributed to the shareholders in 1948.

Chapter 22: Hidden Splendor

1. At times he had said he wanted to be a millionaire by age thirty.

2. Interview with Ed Anderson.

3. *"Newman and Graham predated A. W. Jones, which everybody thinks is the first hedge fund,"* Buffett says. A. W. Jones is best known as the first promoter of the concept of hedging the risk in stocks with short sales. However, its fee structure, partnership arrangement, and flexible invest-

ing approach—that is, the classic hedge fund as the term is technically defined—were pioneered much earlier, by Graham if not others as well.

4. The first partnership agreement provided: "Each limited partner shall be paid interest at the rate of 4% per annum on the balance of his capital account as of December 31 of the immediately preceding year as shown by the Federal Income Tax Return filed by the partnership applicable to said year's business, said interest payments to be charged as expenses of the partnership business. In lieu of a separate computation of interest for the period ending December 31, 1956, each limited partner shall be paid 2% of his original capital contribution, said payments to be charged as expense of the partnership business for said period. In addition each of the limited partners shall share in the overall net profits of the partnership, that is, the net profits of the partnership from the date of its formation to any given point of time in the proportions set opposite their respective names." The total interest of the partners added up to ²⁴⁄₄₂ or 50% of the total interest in the earnings (Certificate of Limited Partnership, Buffett Associates, Ltd., May 1, 1956). The agreement to share in the losses was an amendment to the partnership agreement on April 1, 1958.

5. According to Joyce Cowin, both Buffett and her own husband, Dan Cowin, who had been introduced to Buffett by Fred Kuhlken, ran money separately for Gottschaldt and Elberfeld.

6. Interview with Chuck Peterson.

7. Some of these remarks were made at a 2003 speech to Georgia Tech students, the rest in interviews with the author.

8. Hartman L. Butler Jr., "An Hour with Mr. Graham," March 6, 1976, interview included in Irving Kahn and Robert Milne, *Benjamin Graham: The Father of Financial Analysis.* Occasional Paper No. 5, The Financial Analysts Research Foundation, 1977.

9. Interview with Tom Knapp.

10. "Tourist Killed Abroad, Portugal-Spain Highway Crash Fatal to Long Island Man," *New York Times,* June 23, 1956. Kuhlken had been on a yearlong trip. The other passenger, Paul Kelting, was listed in critical condition.

11. Sloan Wilson, *The Man in the Gray Flannel Suit.* New York: Simon & Schuster, 1955.

12. Interview with Susie Buffett Jr.

13. Interview with Charlie Munger.

14. Or thereabouts.

15. Interview with Ed Anderson.

16. According to Tom Knapp, one thing Dodge and Buffett had in common was their tightfistedness. Even when he later became one of Buffett's richest partners, Homer Dodge would angle for a free canoe from a canoe maker. He knew every route into New York City from both La Guardia and JFK airports, and took convoluted trips by bus and subway and on foot rather than hire a cab.

17. The Dodges chose a slightly different deal. Buffett's share of the profits would be only 25%, but the amount he could lose was limited to his capital, initially only $100. Certificate of Limited Partnership, Buffett Fund, Ltd., September 1, 1956.

18. Cleary split profits over 4%, while Buffett was exposed to the extent of any arrears. Certificate of Limited Partnership, B-C Ltd., October 1, 1956. In 1961, B-C Ltd. was folded into Underwood Partnership, Ltd.

19. Buffett Partnership files, "Miscellaneous Expense" and "Postage and Insurance Expense," 1956 and 1957.

20. Warren Buffett's first letter to partners, December 27, 1956.

21. During the war, people bought Liberty Bonds, which paid low interest rates, as a patriotic duty. When rates subsequently rose, the bonds traded "below par"—face value. Stock promoters offered shares to Liberty Bond owners in exchange for the par value of the bonds. Thus bondholders thought they were getting $100 worth of stock for a bond selling in the market for, say, $85, when in fact the stock was worth little if anything. Salesmen also promised some buyers board seats, according to Hayden Ahmanson, who told Buffett this.

22. From 1928 to 1954, the manual was published in five volumes annually as *Moody's Manual of Investments,* one volume each for government securities; banks, insurance companies, invest-

ment trusts, real estate, finance and credit companies; industrial securities; railroad securities; and public-utility securities. In 1955, Moody's began publishing *Moody's Bank and Finance Manual* separately.

23. Buffett says Hayden Ahmanson gave him this version of events.

24. Buffett: *"He was my partner in National American insurance. Dan didn't have a lot of money, so he was using his money that he had originally planned to put in the partnership, and borrowed some money too."*

25. Under the Williams Act, passed in 1968, you could not do this today, nor could Howard Ahmanson buy back the stock piecemeal. The act requires buyers to make a "tender offer" that puts all sellers on a level playing field under the same price and terms.

26. According to Fred Stanback, when Buffett had "bought all he could pay for," he also let Stanback start buying.

27. A year later, Buffett sold the National American stock for around $125 (to the best of his memory) to J. M. Kaplan, a New York businessman who had reorganized and headed Welch's Grape Juice in the 1940s and '50s and was later known for his philanthropy. Kaplan eventually sold the stock back to Howard Ahmanson.

28. See, for example, Bill Brown, "The Collecting Mania," *University of Chicago Magazine*, Vol. 94, No. 1., October 2001.

29. Arthur Wiesenberger, *Investment Companies*. New York: Arthur W. Wiesenberger & Co., released annually from 1941.

30. Quote is from Lee Seeman. Buffett confirms the substance of the statement. The intriguing question is who or what prompted Wiesenberger to refer Buffett to Davis.

31. Lee Seeman's recollection in an interview is that Dorothy Davis made the comparison.

32. Buffett, recalling a conversation with Eddie Davis.

33. Dacee resembled the Buffett Fund. Buffett was credited 25% of any profits over a 4% hurdle rate. Certificate of Limited Partnership, Dacee Ltd., August 9, 1957.

34. Congressional records note a Washington, D.C., furniture store was giving away shares of uranium stock with any purchase for a Washington's Birthday sale. (Stock Market Study, Hearings before the Committee on Banking and Currency of the United States Senate, March 1955.)

35. Above a 4% to 6% "bogey." He benchmarked himself against the rate of long-term government bonds, telling his partners that if he could not do better than that, he should not get paid. The wide range of profit-sharing reflected the varying level of risk Warren was taking. In the partnerships that paid him the most, he also had unlimited liability to pay back losses.

36. Buffett was charging 25% of the partnership's appreciation in excess of 6%.

37. Meg Mueller, in an interview, recalls its size relative to other houses on the street at the time.

38. Reynolds was a city councilman. "Sam Reynolds Home Sold to Warren Buffett," *Omaha World-Herald*, February 9, 1958. "Buffett's Folly" was referred to in a letter to Jerry Orans, March 12, 1958, cited in Roger Lowenstein, *Buffett: The Making of an American Capitalist*. New York: Doubleday, 1996.

39. Interview with Susie Buffett Jr.

40. Interview with Howie Buffett.

41. Pyelonephritis, sometimes associated with pregnancy.

42. As quoted in Lowenstein, *Buffett*. Billig is now deceased.

43. Interview with Charlie Munger.

44. Interview with Howie Buffett.

45. Kuhlken had introduced Cowin to Buffett in 1951 on one of Buffett's trips back to New York after his graduation from Columbia.

46. From Joyce Cowin's eulogy for Cowin.

47. Marshall Weinberg, Tom Knapp, Ed Anderson, Sandy Gottesman, Buffett, and others contributed to this portrait of Cowin.

48. *"He lent me unsecured. A dollar of short-term loss offset two dollars of long-term gain for tax purposes, and you could buy a mutual fund that was going to pay a long-term capital-gains dividend and redeem it immediately thereafter to offset a long-term gain going into the end of the year. I bought a combination of long-term gain and short-term loss, which, though equal in amount, had different effects on your tax return. It was all legit then; you can't do it anymore. It probably saved me a thousand dollars. Boy, it was huge,"* says Buffett.

49. Interview with Joyce Cowin.

50. This was an experimental town built to house 1,800 families in low-cost units. Numerous government properties were auctioned off after World War II. "House Passes Bill to Speed Greenbelt Sale," *Washington Post,* April 14, 1949; "U.S. Sells Ohio Town It Built in Depression," *New York Times,* December 7, 1949; "Greenbelt, Md., Sale Extended for 30 Days," *Washington Post,* May 31, 1952.

Chapter 23: The Omaha Club

1. "A. C. Munger, Lawyer, Dies," *Omaha World-Herald,* July 1, 1959.

2. The obituary of Henry A. Homan, son of George W. Homan, in the *Omaha World-Herald,* March 22, 1907, mentions that Homan, who was twelve years older than Judge Munger, was a close friend of the judge. The Homan and Buffett sides of the families, however, were not close.

3. "33 Years a Federal Judge," *Omaha World-Herald,* March 12, 1939.

4. Lowe, *Damn Right!: Behind the Scenes with Berkshire Hathaway Billionaire Charlie Munger.* New York: John Wiley & Sons, 2000. Lowe's biography, which is based on extensive family interviews, was the author's principal source for the Munger family history.

5. Said approvingly in Lowe, *Damn Right!*

6. Interview with Lee Seeman.

7. Interview with Howard Jessen, a friend of the Buffetts'.

8. His grandfather, a prominent Omaha lawyer, was a friend of Dean Roscoe Pound, the dean of Harvard Law School.

9. Munger made no effort to burnish a résumé by, for example, joining the *Law Review.* In an interview, he described himself as relatively aloof.

10. Lowe, *Damn Right!*

11. As quoted in Lowe, *Damn Right!*

12. Munger, as told to Janet Lowe in *Damn Right!*

13. In *Damn Right!,* Munger compared getting married to investing. Nancy said he was "uptight" about showing emotions. His son Charles Jr. said, "There are some things my dad could deal with better if he faced them more" but "he just walks away."

14. Munger, as quoted in Lowe, *Damn Right!*

15. Ibid.

16. In *Damn Right!,* Nancy says that Charlie "was not much of a helpmate around the house." For her seventieth birthday, Buffett says he went to a pawn shop and got her a Purple Heart.

17. Roger Lowenstein, *Buffett: The Making of an American Capitalist.* New York: Doubleday, 1996.

18. Lowe, *Damn Right!*

19. Interview with Charlie Munger.

20. Interview with Lee Seeman.

21. In a year when the Dow was up 38.5%, Warren had managed to beat it, taking minimal risk.

22. In addition to his $100 stake in Buffett Associates, Buffett had later put $100 into each of his other partnerships: Buffett Fund, B-C, Underwood, Dacee, Mo-Buff, and Glenoff.

23. Interview with Lee Seeman.

24. This version differs from some others that have been published. For example, Susie Buffett has said that she was present. Several writers have set the meeting at a dinner at Johnny's Café. Roger Lowenstein, however, also set the meeting at the Omaha Club. Most likely, other versions

are conflations of later events. To the author, Seeman's version is the most detailed yet has the least embellished air.

25. Interview with Charlie Munger. The dinner is reconstructed from interviews with Buffett and Munger, whose memories are hazy. Nancy Munger doesn't remember. The wives were introduced soon after the first meeting, and Johnny's is the most likely location. Buffett recalls Munger's self-intoxication clearly.

Chapter 24: The Locomotive

1. Estimated. Buffett was managing $878,211 at the end of 1958 in six partnerships. The $50,000 Glenoff Partnership was formed in February 1959. By the end of 1959, the partnerships' market value had grown to $1,311,884. His personal funds and Buffett & Buffett increased this total.

2. Sanborn sent its customers paste-over revisions each year showing new construction, changed occupancy, new fire-protection facilities, and changed structural materials. A new map was published every few decades. Buffett took note of the company, as far as he recalls, when a large block of stock came up for sale. The widow of the deceased president was reportedly selling 15,000 shares because her son was leaving the company. Phil Carret owned 12,000 shares.

3. Five or ten shares apiece, forty-six shares in total.

4. Buffett had become friendly with the company's CEO, Parker Herbell, whom he said the rest of the board treated as an "errand boy." Herbell supported the plan to separate the investments from the map business, and had facilitated some of its underpinnings.

5. "It does not make sense to have management, consultants, and major stockholders in complete agreement regarding a course of action but unable to proceed because of directors owning an insignificant amount of stock." Warren Buffett letter to C. P. Herbell, September 25, 1959.

6. As part of the deal, the Buffett partnerships agreed to tender their stock.

7. Interview with Doris Buffett.

8. Interview with Kelsey Flower, a childhood friend of Susie Jr.'s.

9. Interview with Dick and Mary Holland.

10. Interview with Peter Buffett.

11. Interview with Howie Buffett.

12. *Gateway*, May 26, 1961.

13. "Paul Revere's Ride," Henry Wadsworth Longfellow. Listen my children, and you shall hear of the multitudes rescued by Susan Buffett.

14. According to his autobiography, *Stranger to the Game* (written with Lonnie Wheeler, New York: Penguin, 1994), Bob Gibson lived in Omaha in the off season. He talks about playing basketball in Omaha with a white team in 1964, traveling to Iowa for games, and hanging out at a bar on North 30th Street. The bartender wouldn't serve him.

15. Howard Buffett quoted in Paul Williams, "Buffett Tells Why He Joined Birch Society," *Benson Sun*, April 6, 1961.

16. Leila Buffett letter to Dr. Hills, December 10, 1958.

17. Leila Buffett to Mrs. Kray, May 23, 1960.

18. Interview with Susie Buffett Jr. and Howie Buffett. They recall their father's behavior during this period as routine and, with hindsight, as a form of denial.

19. Interview with Howie Buffett.

20. Interview with Chuck Peterson.

21. Interview with Lee Seeman.

22. Interview with Dick Holland.

23. This is how hedge funds are commonly managed to stay within the legal investor limit today.

24. George Payne was also a founding member of this partnership. By then, B-C had been folded into Underwood. Along with the ten partnerships, Warren and his father were still operating Buffett & Buffett.

25. The Dow's results include dividends received. Note that this was the performance for the partnership before Warren's fees.

26. Interview with Chuck Peterson.

27. Interview with Stan Lipsey.

28. Buffett was 31 on January 1, 1962, but his personal investments and gains in the partnership had taken him past the million-dollar mark months earlier, when he was still 30.

29. Interview with Bill Scott.

30. Buffett waived his fee for Scott, one of the two most lucrative arrangements he ever made with an employee. (See Henry Brandt in "Haystacks of Gold" and "Folly" for the other.)

31. He put in everything except his investment in Data Documents, a personal investment in a private company.

32. Letter to partners, July 6, 1962. In the second quarter of 1962, the Dow fell from 723.5 to 561.3, or 23%. In the first half of that year, the partnership saw a loss before payments to partners of 7.5%, compared with a loss of 21.7% including dividends for the Dow—the partners had a 14.2% outperformance.

33. Buffett's phrase is a clever reworking of Graham's original. In *The Intelligent Investor*: "The sovereign virtue of all formula plans lies in the compulsion they bring upon the investor to sell when the crowd is buying and to buy when the crowd lacks confidence" (*Intelligent Investor,* Part I: General Approaches to Investment VI: Portfolio Policy for the Enterprising Investor: The Positive Side, 1949 edition). And in *Security Analysis*: "It would require bond investors to act with especial caution when things are booming and with greater confidence when times are hard" (*Security Analysis,* Part II: Fixed-Value Investments, XI: Specific Standards for Bond Investment, 1940 edition).

Chapter 25: The Windmill War

1. Interview with Verne McKenzie, who says Buffett explained this to him when he hired him. Without a public exit strategy, this is one of only two ways to realize the value of the assets. Buffett had not yet figured out the other one, as the reader will see.

2. Warren Buffett letter to Clyde Dempster, April 11, 1960.

3. Warren Buffett note to Bob Dunn, June 27, 1958: "...has become increasingly less active in the business and it appeared the company was just drifting with him not interested and no one else having the authority to do anything.... We finally got the job accomplished by letting Clyde stay as president." He gave Jack Thomsen, executive vice president, temporary operating authority.

4. Interview with Walter Schloss.

5. At $30.25 per share. Warren Buffett letter to Dempster shareholders, September 7, 1961.

6. Warren Buffett letter to partners, July 22, 1961.

7. "Dempster had earned good money in the past, but was currently only breaking even.

"We continued to buy the stock in small quantities for five years. During most of this period I was a director and was becoming consistently less impressed with the earnings prospects under existing management. However, I also became more familiar with the assets and operations and my evaluation of the quantitative factors remained very favorable," thus leading him to continue buying stock. Letter to partners, January 24, 1962.

8. And water-system parts—as the demand for windmills was waning.

9. "We had parts for windmills and certain farm equipment," says Scott, "where we had a lock on the business and by repricing it could stop losing money down there. And we were successful to some degree."

10. January 18, 1963.

11. "Still a Chance City Can Keep Dempster," *Beatrice Daily Sun,* September 1, 1963; "Drive to Keep Dempster Rolls," *Omaha World-Herald,* September 30, 1963.

12. As Buffett's successor, Dempster's chairman W. B. McCarthy, put it, "We understand, as I am sure you do, that a number of the people in Beatrice do not recognize the fine, necessary job that

you and Harry accomplished with Dempster." W. B. McCarthy letter to Warren Buffett, November 19, 1963.

13. Of the $2.8 million total financing, $1.75 million went to pay the sellers and the remainder to expand the operation. "Launch 11th Hour Effort to Keep Dempster Plant Here," *Beatrice Daily Sun,* August 29, 1963.

14. "Beatrice Raises $500,000," *Lincoln Evening Journal,* September 3, 1963; "Fire Sirens Hail Victory, Beatrice Gets Funds to Keep Dempster," *Omaha World-Herald,* September 4, 1963; "Contracts for Dempster Sale Get Signatures," *Beatrice Daily Sun,* September 12, 1963.

15. The partnership made $2.3 million, almost three times its investment. Buffett changed the name of the holding company to First Beatrice Corp. and moved its headquarters to Kiewit Plaza.

Chapter 26: Haystacks of Gold

1. The speakers appeared as individuals who happened to belong to different groups rather than "representatives" of their races and faiths. All went well, except once, says Doris Buffett, when a Protestant panelist started telling the Catholic and the Jew that they were going to hell.

2. The black workers were squeezed out of jobs as Omaha's packinghouse industry shrank. Marginalized into a ghetto north of downtown called the Near North Side, they lived in dilapidated, aging tenements for which unscrupulous landlords charged high rents. In 1957, the Omaha Plan, a communitywide study, proposed redevelopment of the Near North Side, but bond issues were defeated. A budding civil-rights movement led by college students at Creighton University, the Urban League, and other civic groups had worked to improve black employment and end segregation of teachers in the public schools since 1959.

3. Interview with Susie Buffett Jr., who wondered what good the police whistle was going to do.

4. Interview with Peter Buffett.

5. Interview with Doris Buffett. Viktor E. Frankl, *Man's Search for Meaning.* Boston: Beacon Press, 1962.

6. Interview with Howie Buffett.

7. Howie and Susie Jr. describe themselves and their relationship this way in interviews.

8. This composite picture of the Buffett household is based on interviews with Susie Buffett Jr., Howie Buffett, and Peter Buffett.

9. Interview with Meg Mueller. "My mom has commented on that several times over the years," she says.

10. Interview with Bill Ruane.

11. Interview with Dick Espenshade. One of the founding lawyers, Jamie Wood, joined from another firm.

12. Interview with Ed Anderson.

13. The example has been simplified for ease of understanding the concept of leverage. Obviously the exact return on capital depends on how long it took to make the profit, and on the funding rate.

14. Interview with Rick Guerin in Janet Lowe, *Damn Right!: Behind the Scenes with Berkshire Hathaway Billionaire Charlie Munger.* New York: John Wiley & Sons, 2000.

15. This description is from Ed Anderson.

16. Interview with Ed Anderson.

17. Interviews with Rick Guerin, Ed Anderson.

18. Anderson takes the blame for being too obtuse to read Munger's mind, rather than blaming Munger for not explaining things to him.

19. Interview with Ed Anderson.

20. Along with Munger, Ed Anderson recalls this extraordinary trade. Munger says the story is true in substance. Buffett also recalled the reasoning.

21. Interview with Ed Anderson, who suggested the word "pretender" because, as he put it, "Charlie would never feel like he was an 'apprentice.'"

22. Ira Marshall relates Munger's confusion with names in *Damn Right!*

23. Interview with Ed Anderson. This term was commonly used among Buffett's friends. He referred to "coattail riding" in his partnership letter of January 18, 1963.

24. Charles T. Munger letter to Katharine Graham, December 9, 1974.

25. Ibid.

26. In 1953, Buffett sold copies of this report for $5.

27. Buffett had also let Brandt in on one lucrative private investment, the Mid-Continental Tab Card Company. While Buffett gave up his override on Brandt's money, the deal was a win/win.

28. "There's got to be a warehouse full of these somewhere," said Bill Ruane in an interview, but the author never saw it.

29. Bill Ruane introduced Buffett to Fisher's ideas. Philip A. Fisher, *Common Stocks and Uncommon Profits.* New York, Evanston, and London: Harper & Row, 1958. ("Scuttlebutt" is a nautical term for a barrel with a hole in it used to hold the sailors' drinking water.)

30. The market for soybean oil was not large, a key element in the scheme. It would be impossible for a single individual to amass enough capital to corner the market for, say, oil or treasury bills.

31. Most accounts published about the scandal incorrectly refer to oil floating on top of water in the tanks.

32. Mark I. Weinstein, "Don't Leave Home Without It: Limited Liability and American Express," Working paper, American Law & Economics Association Annual Meetings, Paper 17, *Berkeley Electronic Press,* 2005, p. 14–15, is the source that American Express was certifying more warehouse receipts than the Department of Agriculture said existed in salad oil.

33. The Stock Exchange had closed mid-session on August 4, 1933, due to a tear-gas prank. Some consider the Kennedy assassination closing to be the first "real" closing of the market.

34. H. J. Maidenberg, "Big Board Ends Ban on Williston, Walston and Merrill Lynch Are Instrumental in the Broker's Reinstatement, Haupt Remains Shut, Effect of Move Is Swept Aside by Assassination of President Kennedy," November 24, 1963. The soybean-oil drama, including the American Express role, peaked during a period of about a week following the assassination.

35. American Express at the time was the only major U.S. public company to be capitalized as a joint stock company rather than a limited liability corporation. This meant its shareholders could be assessed for deficiencies in capital. *"So every trust department in the United States panicked,"* recalls Buffett. *"I remember the Continental Bank held over 5 percent of the company, and all of a sudden not only do they see that the trust accounts were going to have stock worth zero, but they could get assessed. The stock just poured out, of course, and the market got slightly inefficient for a short period of time."*

36. The Travelers Cheque was American Express's main product. The company introduced the card defensively when banks developed credit cards as a countermeasure to the Travelers Cheque.

37. Warren Buffett letter to Howard L. Clark, American Express Company, June 16, 1964. Brandt sent Buffett a foot-high stack of material, according to Jim Robinson, former CEO of American Express, who saw it. "I remember seeing Henry's stuff on American Express, just reams of it," said Bill Ruane in an interview.

38. At the end of it all, De Angelis pleaded guilty to four federal counts of fraud and conspiracy, and was sentenced to ten years in prison. "The Man Who Fooled Everybody," *Time,* June 4, 1965.

39. Howard Buffett, August 6, 1953, last will and testament.

40. Interviews with Patricia Dunn, Susie Buffett Jr., Warren Buffett.

41. In *Grand Old Party* (New York: Random House, 2003), Lewis L. Gould describes the way being a Republican became identified with racism in the minds of many people who changed parties during the civil-rights era.

42. Buffett cannot recall whether he initially registered as an independent or a Democrat. His preference would have been to register as an independent, but that would have precluded him from voting in primaries. Either immediately or within a few years, he did register as a Democrat.

43. Interview with Susie Buffett Jr.

44. Susan Goodwillie Stedman, recalling personal interview with Susan T. Buffett conducted November 2001, courtesy of Susan Goodwillie Stedman and Elizabeth Wheeler.

45. Dan Monen as quoted in Roger Lowenstein, *Buffett: The Making of an American Capitalist*. New York: Doubleday, 1996. Monen is now deceased.

46. Warren's inability to deal with Howard's death is the incident most widely cited by family members as indicative of his inner state during this period.

Chapter 27: Folly

1. Warren Buffett letter to Howard L. Clark, American Express Company, June 16, 1964.

2. L. J. Davis, "Buffett Takes Stock," *New York Times*, April 1, 1990.

3. In July 1964, Buffett's letter to partners said, "... our General category now includes three companies where BPL is the largest single stockholder." Readers could infer from this a fairly concentrated portfolio.

4. Letter from Warren Buffett to partners, November 1, 1965.

5. Letter from Warren Buffett to partners, October 9, 1967.

6. Letter from Warren Buffett to partners, January 20, 1966.

7. Interview with John Harding.

8. In 1962, according to an interview with Joyce Cowin.

9. Per capita. According to Everett Allen in *Children of the Light: The Rise and Fall of New Bedford Whaling and the Death of the Arctic Fleet* (Boston: Little, Brown, 1983), yearly income from whaling amounted to $12 million by 1854, making New Bedford probably the richest city per capita in the world before the Civil War.

10. Horatio Hathaway, *A New Bedford Merchant*. Boston: D. B. Updike, the Merrymount Press, 1930.

11. Partnership agreement, Hathaway Manufacturing Company, 1888. Among the other partners was William W. Crapo, a longtime New Bedford associate of Hetty Green's, who also invested $25,000. The total initial capital was $400,000.

12. With a fortune estimated at $100 million.

13. Eric Rauchway, *Murdering McKinley: The Making of Theodore Roosevelt's America*. New York: Hill and Wang, 2003.

14. The North was no workers' paradise, but in the South there were virtually no laws against child labor, excessive work hours, or unsafe work conditions. The mills owned the workers' houses and the stores where they shopped, controlled their water supply, owned their churches, and effectively controlled the state governments and the courts. Machine-gun-bearing state militia prevented strikes. The workers were more like sharecroppers. Nearly ten thousand Northern workers had lost their jobs when the textile industry marched southward to the Carolinas in search of cheaper labor when air-conditioned plants were constructed after World War II.

15. Seabury Stanton, *Berkshire Hathaway Inc., A Saga of Courage*. New York: Newcomen Society of North America, 1962. Stanton made this address to the Newcomen Society in Boston on November 29, 1961.

16. Ibid.

17. In *A Saga of Courage*, Seabury says he conceived of the Stantons as forming part of an "unbroken thread of ownership" that stretched back to Oliver Chace, who had founded New England's textile industry and created Berkshire Fine Spinning's oldest predecessor company in 1806. Chace was a former apprentice of Samuel Slater, who first brought Sir Richard Arkwright's innovative spinning-frame technology to the United States at the end of the eighteenth century.

18. Hathaway Manufacturing Corporation Open House tour brochure, September 1953. Courtesy of Mary Stanton Plowden-Wardlaw.

19. If the goal had been to save jobs, the money to modernize need not have been spent. Roger Lowenstein, in *Buffett: The Making of an American Capitalist* (New York: Doubleday, 1996), quotes Ken Chace (now deceased) as saying that Seabury hadn't the slightest idea of return on investment.

20. Stanton (now deceased) is stated as having these opinions in "Berkshire Hathaway's Brave New World," by Jerome Campbell, *Modern Textiles,* December 1957.

21. Berkshire Hathaway 1994 chairman's letter.

22. Interviews with David S. Gottesman, Marshall Weinberg.

23. Letter to Warren Buffett on May 4, 1990, from James M. Clark Jr. at Tweedy, Browne Co., noting that "Howard Browne gave various accounts code initials."

24. Interview with Ed Anderson.

25. Interviews with Chris Browne, Ed Anderson.

26. According to Ed Anderson, this is how Buffett traded. The author is well acquainted with Buffetting in other contexts.

27. The commission sounds tiny, but at ten cents a share, Buffett later said, it was by far the highest commission he ever paid on a stock.

28. Interviews with Mary Stanton Plowden-Wardlaw, Verne McKenzie.

29. Otis thought Seabury's strategy of trying to bypass the New York "converters"—who turned the company's "gray goods" into finished dyed goods and sold them to customers—was a serious misjudgment.

30. "If you're in a business that can't take a long strike, you're basically playing a game of chicken with your labor unions because they're going to lose their jobs, too, if you close down.... And there's a lot of game theory involved. To some extent, the weaker you are, the better your bargaining position is—because if you're extremely weak, even a very short strike will put you out of business; and the people on the other side of the negotiating table understand that. On the other hand, if you have a fair amount of strength, they can push you harder. But it is no fun being in a business where you can't take a strike." Berkshire Hathaway's Warren Buffett and Charlie Munger, "The Incentives in Hedge Funds Are Awesome, But Don't Expect the Returns to Be Too Swift," *Outstanding Investor Digest,* Vol. XVI, No. 4 & 5, Year End 2001 Edition.

31. Several of the Grahamites swear they saw the room. Buffett swears this story is not true. A former Plaza Hotel employee confirms that the seventeenth floor did have a few exceptionally small rooms, with bad views, and that it was possible to haggle the room prices down, especially later in the evening.

32. Interview with Ken Chace Jr.

33. According to Roger Lowenstein's *Buffett,* Ken Chace was the source. Warren does not recall any of the details, including talking to Jack Stanton, but he says Ken Chace's account is most likely correct.

34. Mary Stanton Plowden-Wardlaw, letter to Warren Buffett, June 3, 1991. Stanley Rubin set it up.

35. Interview with Mary Stanton Plowden-Wardlaw.

36. The detailed version of this story was related in Roger Lowenstein's *Buffett,* with Ken Chace as the source. Buffett recalls sitting on a bench near the Plaza with Chace, eating ice cream.

37. "The Junior League is an organization of women committed to promoting voluntarism, developing the potential of women and improving the community through the effective action and leadership of trained volunteers. Its purpose is exclusively educational and charitable," according to its mission statement. (The author is a member.)

38. He replaced the elderly Abram Berkowitz, who worked for the company's law firm, Ropes & Gray, and had cooperatively decided to step down.

39. Stanton said he "hastened [his] retirement due to a disagreement with regard to policy with certain outside interests which have purchased sufficient stock to control the company." "Seabury Stanton Resigns at Berkshire," *New Bedford Standard-Times,* May 10, 1965.

40. Berkshire Hathaway Board of Directors' minutes, May 10, 1965.

41. "Buffett Means Business," *Daily News Record,* May 20, 1965.

42. Adapted in part from the documentary *Vintage Buffett: Warren Buffett Shares His Wealth* (June 2004) and in part from interviews.

Chapter 28: Dry Tinder

1. Interview with Doris Buffett.

2. Ibid.

3. November 10, 1965.

4. "Riot Duty Troops Gather in Omaha," *New York Times*, July 5, 1966. The governor said the problem was unemployment, which ran triple that of whites. 30% of blacks were unemployed in Omaha.

5. Bertrand Russell, *Has Man a Future?* New York: Simon & Schuster, 1962. This powerful, absolutist book argued that unless something "radical" happened, mankind was eventually doomed by weapons of mass destruction, and predicted the development of mass chemical and biological weapons in the not-distant future.

6. The 1955 Russell-Einstein Manifesto. Russell was president of the Campaign for Nuclear Disarmament in 1958, and was cofounder with Einstein of the Pugwash Conference, a group of scientists concerned about nuclear proliferation.

7. Interview with Dick Holland.

8. Buffett and his chief administrative officer John Harding chose a set of representative large-cap stocks, in effect creating a market index. Buffett did not want to execute the trade through a brokerage firm because the broker kept the proceeds from the sale and paid no interest to him. Harding contacted university endowment funds. Buffett went personally to Chicago to get shares. The idea of lending directly to a short-seller was so novel at the time that most universities passed. However, Harding was able to borrow about $4.6 million of stock.

9. Buffett put $500,000 into treasury bills in the first quarter of 1966.

10. Interview with Susie Buffett Jr., Meg Mueller, Mayrean McDonough.

11. Interview with Kelsey Flower.

12. Interview with Susie Buffett Jr.

13. Interview with Marshall Weinberg.

Chapter 29: What a Worsted Is

1. "The Raggedy Man," by James Whitcomb Riley, a children's poem about a handyman.

2. Interview with Chuck Peterson.

3. Buffett tells the story, which Charlie Heider recalls and found unforgettable. Parsow doesn't recall it.

4. Both Byer-Rolnick and Oxxford were acquired by Koret in 1967.

5. Interview with Sol Parsow.

6. Gottesman worked for Corvine and Company, which, he says, was going out of business. He founded his own firm, First Manhattan Co., in 1964.

7. DRC Offering documents for 8% debentures, December 18, 1967.

8. He gave them the money anyway, and partnered with National City to provide $9 million in short-term financing for the deal. Diversified Retailing Company, Inc., Prospectus, December 18, 1967. According to Gottesman and *Moody's Bank & Finance Manual,* Martin Kohn was on the board of Maryland National Bank.

9. Charles T. Munger testimony, *In the Matter of Blue Chip Stamps, Berkshire Hathaway Incorporated,* HQ-784. Thursday, March 20, 1975, page 187.

10. Interview with Charlie Munger. The company was purchased in April 1967.

11. Diversified Retailing Company, Inc., Prospectus, December 18, 1967.

12. Buffett says Rosner told him he got Aye Simon's consent to sell the business by saying something along the following lines: "And to hell with you. If you're going to second-guess it, you come down and run the store." The relationship was irretrievably broken.

Chapter 30: Jet Jack

1. Including Buffett's stock in Data Documents, a separate investment, the Buffetts' net worth was somewhere between $9.5 and $10 million.

2. Buffett's description, in Patricia E. Bauer's "The Convictions of a Long-Distance Investor," *Channels,* November 1986, was, "One time we had a dog on the roof, and my son called to him and he jumped. It was so awful—the dog that loves you so much that he jumps off the roof . . ."—leaving the reader to wonder how the dog got on the roof.

3. Interview with Hallie Smith.

4. "Haight-Ashbury: The Birth of Hip," CBC Television, March 24, 1968.

5. In 1967, over 2.5 billion shares traded, topping the previous 1966 record by one third. Thomas Mullaney, "Week in Finance: Washington Bullish," *New York Times,* December 31, 1967.

6. But insurers looked undervalued and he thought they would get taken over. He bought Home Insurance and Employers Group Associates.

7. At high rates of return, and paying no tax. If a shareholder had taken $0.06 a share—after paying a tax on the $0.10 dividend—and put it in the market earning 5% on average, he would have about $0.42. If Buffett had kept that $0.10, and compounded it at the 21% he earned over the past forty years, a shareholder, who would have been slightly diluted over the years, would be $135 richer. Looking at it on a larger scale, the tiny dividend "cost" Berkshire shareholders over $200 million as of 2007.

8. Interview with Verne McKenzie.

9. "Requiem for an Industry: Industry Comes Full Circle," *Providence Sunday Journal,* March 3, 1968.

10. Letter to partners, January 25, 1967.

11. By September 30, 1967, the partnership had $14.2 million in treasuries and short-term debt out of a total $83.7 million invested.

12. Interview with Bill Scott.

13. Interview with Charlie Heider.

14. Robert Dorr, "'Unusual Risk' Ringwalt Specialty," *Omaha World-Herald,* March 12, 1967, and Ringwalt's *Tales of National Indemnity and Its Founder* (Omaha: National Indemnity Co., 1990) recount stories of lion tamers, circus performers, and hole-in-one contests. Buffett heard of the burlesque stars from Ringwalt.

15. Berkshire paid Heider a $140,000 fee for the transaction.

16. Interview with Bill Scott.

17. With the company closely held, it took only a week to round up the necessary 80% shareholder approvals.

18. In his book, Ringwalt says he was only driving around looking for a metered place on the street because he refused to pay a parking garage.

19. This was a reason why National Indemnity would not need reinsurance, or protection from other insurers, which both was expensive and would make it a dependent.

20. Ringwalt also was included in the shareholder register of Diversified Retailing in 1976 (he actually sold 3,032 shares back to the company in its tender offer).

Chapter 31: The Scaffold Sways the Future

1. Wead, who declined to be interviewed, was the director of Wesley House, a community improvement organization of the Methodist Church.

2. Interview with Racquel Newman and her son, Tom Newman. A number of other people recalled Susie and Rackie's activities.

3. Interview with Chuck Peterson.

4. Buffett had met Rosenfield through a connection to Hochschild-Kohn.

5. Grinnell's founder, Congregational minister Josiah Grinnell, pastor of the First Congregational church in Washington, D.C., bolted from its doors in 1852 when his Southern congregation took exception to his abolitionist views. It was Grinnell who sought advice from the famous *New York Herald* editor Horace Greeley and who heard the words that every schoolchild in America would subsequently learn without knowing their source: "Go West, young man, go West!" The phrase was originally written by John Soule in the *Terre Haute Express* in 1851.

6. Interview with Waldo "Wally" Walker, Dean of Administration at the time.

7. The luckless George Champion, chairman of the board of Chase Manhattan Bank, followed King on the program, speaking on "Our Obsolete Welfare State."

8. This common paraphrase of Lowell was more eloquent than Lowell's actual words: "Though

her portion be the scaffold, And upon the throne be wrong." James Russell Lowell (1819–1891), "The Present Crisis," 1844.

9. Interview with Hallie Smith.

10. From King's 1963 speech at Western Michigan University. King may have said something like this at the October 1967 Grinnell Convocation, but no transcript exists.

11. King first said this in Cleveland in 1963 and used variations of it in most major speeches thereafter. He called the idea that you can't legislate morality a "half-truth." "It may be true that the law cannot make a man love me," he said, "but it can keep him from lynching me, and I think that is pretty important."

12. Despite flirting briefly with the magic 1,000, it had ended down more than 15%.

13. Letter to partners, January 25, 1967.

14. Letter to partners, January 24, 1968.

15. Galbraith in an interview by Israel Shenker, "Galbraith: '29 Repeats Itself Today," published in the *New York Times* on May 3, 1970. "The explosion in the mutual funds is the counterpart of the old investment trusts. The public has shown extraordinary willingness to believe there are financial geniuses in the hundreds. Financial genius is a rising stock market. Financial chicanery is a falling stock market." Galbraith reiterates this in "The Commitment to Innocent Fraud," *Challenge,* Sept.–Oct. 1999: "In the world of finance, genius is a rising market."

16. "Race Violence Flares in Omaha After Negro Teen-Ager Is Slain," *New York Times,* March 6, 1968; Associated Press, "Disorder, Shooting Trail Wallace Visit"; UPI, "1 Wounded, 16 Held in Omaha Strike," July 8, 1968.

17. He recovered after a lengthy hospital stay. Part of this account is from *The Gate City: A History of Omaha* (Lincoln: The University of Nebraska Press, 1997).

18. In a December 1981 *Playboy* interview, Henry Fonda, an Omaha native, recounts witnessing the same event: "It was an experience I will never forget.... My dad's office looked down on the courthouse square and we went up and watched from the window.... It was so horrifying. When it was all over, we went home. My dad never talked about it, never lectured. He just knew the impression it would have on me."

19. Interview with Racquel Newman.

20. The club was renamed Ironwood in 1999.

21. By coincidence, at the time, Chuck Peterson had also been put up for the Highland. Peterson was eating there a lot with fellow flying enthusiast Bob Levine and thought he ought to join instead of freeloading.

22. Stan Lipsey, another friend of Buffett's, weighed in on behalf of Chuck Peterson. "I got so high-profile because of that," says Lipsey, "that they made me serve on the board next year. No good deed goes unpunished. A golf buddy named Buck Friedman was the chairman. He was very serious, and I'd be trying to crack them up. He didn't like that I'd call him Buckets."

Chapter 32: Easy, Safe, Profitable, and Pleasant

1. Warren Buffett letter to Ben Graham, January 16, 1968.

2. Armon Flenn, "Run for Your Money," *New York Times,* June 3, 1968; "Mutual Interest," *Time,* January 19, 1968; Robert D. Hershey Jr., "Mutual Funds Reaching Further for Investment," *New York Times,* September 29, 1968.

3. In 1929, only about 3% of the population owned stock. In 1968, about 12.5% of the population owned stock or equity mutual funds.

4. Letter to partners, July 11, 1968.

5. The SEC prepared a study stating that the new system, NASDAQ, was "on the horizon" in 1963. NASDAQ went live on February 8, 1971, and traded as much volume as the American Stock Exchange in its first year. Eric J. Weiner, *What Goes Up: The Uncensored History of Modern Wall Street,* New York: Little, Brown, 2005.

6. Warren Buffett letter to the Graham Group, January 16, 1968.

7. Warren Buffett letter to the Graham Group, September 21, 1971.

8. DRC earnings were down overall $400,000, or 17%, in 1968. Associated Cotton Shops earned about 20% on the money employed in the business—an outstanding performance in any year but especially in difficult 1968.

9. Letter to partners, January 24, 1968.

10. Buffett lost money in stocks at times and was quick to cut his losses. The margin of safety didn't prevent losses but shifted the odds away from large losses.

11. The Youth International Party (Yippees), a prankster group of anarchist activists, nominated Pigasus the Pig as their party candidate. Leader Jerry Rubin said, "Why vote for half-pigs like Nixon, Wallace, and Humphrey, when you can have the whole hog?" at a speech to the University of British Columbia Faculty Club (October 24, 1968).

12. Interview with Verne McKenzie, who says that Chace was upset but did not show it. He did what he had to do.

13. The impact of credit cards and a radical change in consumer thinking about consumption is hard to overstate. Savings and layaway—once commonplace in purchasing even items such as clothing—were replaced by debt. Although economists debate measures of household wealth over time, the result has been a world of renters who tithe to financial institutions. The "earthquake risk" is a catastrophic mass deleveraging. (See 2008 credit crisis.)

14. Retailers paid, on average, 2¢ for every dollar of sales for the stamps they gave out and tacked this onto the price of their goods.

15. They priced Blue Chip cheaper, at 1.5¢.

16. Blue Chip had 71% of the trading-stamp business in California at the time. "Safe on Its Own Turf," *Forbes,* July 15, 1968.

17. Sperry & Hutchinson sued Blue Chip when the Alpha Beta and Arden-Mayfair food chains dropped S&H stamps in favor of Blue Chip stamps. Blue Chip paid $6 million to settle this case.

18. Each "package," priced at $101, consisted of $100 face amount of 6.5% ten-year debt plus three shares of $0.333 par common stock. A total of 621,600 Blue Chip shares were included in the offering. Nine retailers who were big Blue Chip customers split another 45%, which went into trusts for ten years. The remaining 10% went to company management (as reported in the *Wall Street Journal,* September 23, 1968).

19. A couple of gas-station chains were still suing, as were a group of small trading-stamp companies in Northern California. Blue Chip Stamps annual report to shareholders, 1969.

20. One of the Graham Group members recalls this.

21. Letter to partners, January 24, 1968.

22. Leslie Berlin, *The Man Behind the Microchip.* New York: Oxford University Press, 2005.

23. Buffett shorted 10,000 shares of Control Data in the third quarter of 1965 in the low $30s—at this point he had over $7 million of his portfolio in shorts. He eventually bought some Control Data for the partnership in 1968, as a "workout," meaning an arbitrage.

24. Interview with Katie Buffett, who said Fred wanted to put in $300 and she "snitched a little" to add another hundred. She thought she would have been better off putting more money in the partnership.

25. In the form of a convertible debenture.

26. Buffett told his partners about the "particularly outstanding performances" of Associated Cotton Shops and National Indemnity Company. But the controlled companies had only a "decent" performance overall; Berkshire and Hochschild-Kohn were dragging down the results.

Chapter 33: The Unwinding

1. A former Kelly girl temporary office worker, Kaiser came to work in January 1967 and stayed until her retirement in 1993.

2. Interview with Donna Walters. Buffett shared Walters with Sol Parsow, the men's haberdasher in the building's lobby.

3. Blue Chip stamps were the closest equivalent.

4. Beginning with "Love Only Thing That Stops Guard," *Omaha World-Herald,* April 20, 1952,

continuing to a cute feature picture of Susie and the kids packing a picnic Thermos, and a story about him buying Sam Reynolds's house.

5. Loomis's recollections are from her memoir in *Fortune*, "My 51 Years (and Counting) at *Fortune*," *Fortune*, September 19, 2005.

6. Loomis wrote an admiring profile of hedge-fund manager A. W. Jones, "The Jones Nobody Keeps Up With," *Fortune*, April 1966, around the time or shortly before she met Buffett. In this article she mentions Buffett in passing. She did not begin to profile him in her writing until "Hard Times Come to the Hedge Funds," *Fortune*, January 1970.

7. Buffett says that he never actually overslept his paper route. This seems to be his version of the common "test-anxiety dream."

8. Interview with Geoffrey Cowan.

9. Buffett put in $32,000 to start.

10. Interview with Charles Peters, with additional condensed comments adapted from Peters's memoir, *Tilting at Windmills*. New York: Addison-Wesley, 1988.

11. Buffett put in another $50,000.

12. After being told that he couldn't donate his investment in the *Washington Monthly* to charity, "I finally let them give the stock to one of the people who worked there, just to get rid of it," says Stanback. "It was worthless."

13. Letter to partners, May 29, 1969.

14. Ibid.

15. Ibid.

16. The Buffetts hired teachers as babysitters, but Howie co-opted the teachers' husbands into becoming his confederates, doubling the degree of lawlessness.

17. Al Pagel, "Susie Sings for More Than Her Supper," *Omaha World-Herald*, April 17, 1977.

18. Interview with Milton Brown.

19. Berkshire Hathaway annual meeting, 2004.

20. Letter to partners, October 9, 1969.

21. John Brooks, *The Go-Go Years*. New York: Ballantine Books, 1973.

22. The stock had "split" so that each share became five, then promptly rose to $25 per share.

23. Blue Chip had called a shareholders meeting to vote on a secondary offering in which shareholders could offer blocks of existing stock to the public.

24. Interview with Wyndham Robertson, who says she could barely understand the code when she first joined the Graham Group two years later in Carmel.

25. Interviews with Marshall Weinberg, Tom Knapp, Fred Stanback, Ruth Scott.

26. Letter from Warren Buffett to Graham Group, September 21, 1971.

27. Interview with Fred Stanback.

28. Interview with Sandy Gottesman, who notes that they basically broke even on the deal; he says that a bit of mythology has arisen around the Hochschild-Kohn deal. "It goes down in history as an enormous mistake," he says. "And I don't think it was as big a mistake as represented . . . it's grown way out of proportion."

29. Supermarkets General bought Hochschild-Kohn in 1969 for $5.05 million cash plus $6.54 million in non-interest-bearing notes with a present value of about $6 million. Effectively, DRC received about $11 million.

30. From the 1969 Diversified Retailing annual report. But if Buffett had been hit by the proverbial bus, under the terms of the debenture, the obligation for mandatory redemption would have ceased. So he was taking the element of random chance out of it.

31. Wilder was not the only doubter. *"Danny [Cowin] thought I was crazy to do it,"* says Buffett.

32. Cited in the 1989 letter to shareholders.

33. "How Omaha Beats Wall Street," *Forbes*, November 1, 1969.

34. The article stated that Buffett had lived in the house since his marriage in 1952, an error later

repeated by other writers. The Farnam house was far from the "starter home" that is implied. Articles often refer to the house as "modest" or some similar term and rarely mention its extensive remodeling. Buffett bought the house in 1958.

35. Evelyn Simpson, "Looking Back: Swivel Neck Needed for Focus Change Today," *Omaha World-Herald*, October 5, 1969.

Chapter 34: Candy Harry

1. Carol Loomis, "Hard Times Come to the Hedge Funds," *Fortune,* January 1970, the first of a series of Loomis articles that showcase Buffett's opinions.

2. Book value. Tangible book value was $43. Warren Buffett letter to partners, October 9, 1969.

3. Ibid.

4. The more inquisitive partners may have discovered that Berkshire Hathaway owned *Sun* Newspapers by reading its 1968 annual report.

5. Letter to partners, October 9, 1969. Buffett explained that he expected stocks to yield about 6½% after tax for the next ten years, roughly the same as a "purely passive investment in tax-free bonds." Even the best managers, he said, were unlikely to do better than 9½% after tax. Compare this to the 17% return he had projected to partners in the early years of the partnership and the 30% average he had actually achieved.

6. Letter to partners, December 5, 1969.

7. According to Buffett, a couple of them never were able to find anyone they trusted to manage their money, and one ended up working as a fortune-teller in San Diego.

8. Letter to partners, December 26, 1969.

9. This statement is intriguing since Buffett had just named Dow Jones as the stock he would like to own on a desert island. However, the *Sun* was not a good investment.

10. Emphasis added by author. By then, a small cult of Buffett-stalkers monitored his holdings, and curiosity about Buffett's intentions was rife among many partners. The importance of a clear statement of his intentions—after more than a decade of obsessive secrecy—should have been unmistakable (at least with hindsight).

11. Buffett indulged in a bit of score-settling with the underwriters in his letter to partners of December 26, 1969, saying that the deal was pitched "with a heavy weight" placed on a comparison to Sperry & Hutchinson, the nearest competitor, but shortly "before the stock was to be offered, with the Dow Jones Industrials much lower but S&H virtually unchanged, they indicated a price far below their former range." (Blue Chip at the time had declined significantly.) "We reluctantly agreed and felt we had a deal but, on the next business day, they stated that our agreed price was not feasible."

12. It was a little unclear what the filling stations' actual beef was. They had given out Blue Chip stamps and made money doing it. If there were five stamp companies in California, they might have given out stamps that cost more, and it isn't clear that they would have made more money—they might have made less.

13. DRC's 1971 annual report discloses $841,042 of notes issued "in exchange for common stock of an affiliated company" due on varying dates, or within twelve months of the death of Warren E. Buffett. DRC continued to issue these notes until 1978, for a total of $1.527 million. During the first year the notes were also payable at the payee's demand. Apparently the notes were reissued with this term eliminated in 1972 (according to the 1972 DRC financial statements).

14. 1970 Annual Statement for Reinsurance Corporation of Nebraska, Berkshire Hathaway, Diversified, and Blue Chip, Forms 10-K and annual reports to shareholders.

15. Interview with Verne McKenzie.

16. Interview with Rhoda and Bernie Sarnat.

17. Interview with Charlie Munger.

18. Through chunks of stock large enough to almost certainly block an unfriendly takeover.

19. Blue Chip sales peaked in 1970 at $132 million.

20. A&P's discounting program, Where Economy Originates, prompted other supermarket chains to adopt discounting in 1972. "The Green Stamp Sings the Blues," *Forbes,* September 1, 1973.

21. From the files of Berkshire Hathaway.

22. Interview with Bill Ramsey. The sale occurred because Laurence A. See, son of Mary See and a founder of the firm, had died, and Charles See, his brother and executor of his estate, mentioned to an attorney acquaintance while on vacation in Hawaii that he might want to sell. The attorney told Bob Flaherty, who worked for Scudder, Stevens, and Clark, and Flaherty talked to Ramsey, who was also a client of the firm.

23. Interview with Ed Anderson.

24. Buffett and Munger paid 11.4x trailing twelve months earnings for See's (i.e., a price equal to over eleven years' worth of the company's earnings—at the past twelve months' earnings rate). This was a remarkably high price/earnings ratio for Buffett, who rarely paid more than ten times earnings. Paying more than book value was also unprecedented. Susie told at least one friend that he "bought it for her," because of her chocolate obsession, which sounds like something he might have said as an endearment.

25. Since 1960.

26. This account is an amalgamation of interviews with Munger and remarks at the Berkshire Hathaway 2003 annual meeting. Warren Buffett and Charlie Munger, "What Makes the Investment Game Great Is You Don't Have to Be Right on *Everything,*" *Outstanding Investor Digest,* Vol. XVIII, Nos. 3 and 4, Year End 2003 Edition.

27. Interviews with Ed Anderson and Chris Browne. Buffett's reasoning in situations like this and Berkshire was that he needed the stock to get control. However, his allies could have kept their stock and voted with him. Indeed, in his younger days when he had less capital, Buffett had arranged such voting blocks.

28. Warren Buffett letter to Chuck Huggins, December 28, 1971.

29. During the early 1970s, the price of sugar increased sixfold. Although most news stories focused on the price of meat, sugar and cocoa were the commodities that experienced the most wrenching price increases.

30. Narrative is based on correspondence among Warren Buffett, Stanley Krum, and Chuck Huggins, 1972. In a letter dated later in 1972, Buffett the teetotaler also says, "Maybe grapes from one little eighty-acre vineyard in France are really the best in the whole world, but I have always had a suspicion that about 99% of it is in the telling and about 1% is in the drinking."

31. This is the lament of a number of the managers.

32. Warren Buffett letter to Chuck Huggins, September 25, 1972.

33. Interviews with Tom Newman, Raquel Newman.

34. Buffett also would have gone on the board of his favorite company, GEICO, had the SEC not concluded that it would be a conflict because Berkshire Hathaway already owned an insurance company, National Indemnity.

35. Interview with Peter Buffett.

36. Each of the advisory-board members invested about $7,000. Control of the bank was retained within the African-American community. Some blacks did not want white investors. "*They just thought we were trying to put something over on them, I guess,*" Buffett says.

37. Interview with John Harding.

38. Interview with Larry Myers. According to Myers, Buffett continued this level of involvement for seventeen years. An advisory board is different from a regular board position and normally requires less time commitment.

39. Roger Lowenstein, *Buffett: The Making of an American Capitalist.* New York: Doubleday, 1996.

40. Interview with Hallie Smith.

41. Interview with Rhoda and Bernie Sarnat. Buffett recalls the story as well.

42. At an anniversary party for the Thompsons a few weeks earlier, the Buffetts' cook served what came to be known throughout Omaha as the "poisoned chicken." Except for a rabbi and his

wife, who ate tuna, everyone present came down with salmonella. By then, Buffett was so well-known that the episode made the *Omaha World-Herald.* Interview with Rabbi Meyer Kripke.

43. As Buffett tells this story he lost the game, but according to Roxanne and Jon Brandt, he was determined not to lose to a six-year-old—and won.

44. According to a friend, Susie began to verbalize this attitude around the late 1960s. She later said these words, as quoted, to Charlie Rose in an interview.

45. Interview with Milton Brown. Several sources confirm that Susie was frequently in contact with Brown during this period.

46. Interviews with Racquel Newman, Tom Newman.

47. His mortgage was $109,000 in 1973.

Chapter 35: The *Sun*

1. "Warming Up for the Big Time: Can John Tunney Make It as a Heavyweight?" Charles T. Powers, *West* magazine *(Los Angeles Times),* December 12, 1971.

2. Interview with Tom Murphy.

3. This version of the story is an amalgamation of Murphy's and Buffett's versions. The stories are identical except for trivial differences in their recollection of the dialogue.

4. The announcement of the sale of the *Fort Worth Star-Telegram* and the area's AM and FM radio stations to Cap Cities for $80 million was on January 6, 1973. However, the closing of the deal was delayed until November 1974.

5. *"I should have done it,"* Buffett says. *"That was really dumb. We would have made a lot of money with that."*

6. According to Boys Town (now renamed Girls and Boys Town), the home opened on December 12, 1917, with about six boys and grew to twenty-five within three weeks. The approximate date and number ("between twenty and thirty") are cited in *Omaha's Own Magazine and Trade Review,* December 1928.

7. Howard Buffett "helped us greatly in securing our own post office for which we were deeply grateful, because he came to us to assist us when we were badly in need of a friend." Patrick J. Norton letter to Warren Buffett, April 24, 1972. The post office was established in 1934 and the village became incorporated in 1936, according to the *Irish Independent,* August 25, 1971. The post office was a key element in the charm of Boys Town's fund-raising appeals.

8. The average contribution at the time of the *Sun*'s story was $1.62. Transcript, Mick Rood interview with Msgr. Nicholas Wegner.

9. Ibid. Robert Dorr, "Hard-Core Delinquent Rarity at Boys Town," *Omaha World-Herald,* April 16, 1972.

10. Paul Williams, *Investigative Reporting and Editing,* Englewood Cliffs, N.J.: Prentice-Hall, 1978. Williams was the editor during the Boys Town investigation.

11. Michael Casey, new director of special projects brought in after the *Sun* story, described the atmosphere as a "minimum-security prison," based on his experience working in prisons and mental hospitals, in "Midlands News" of the *Omaha World-Herald,* March 10, 1974. According to Casey's account, he was forced to resign from Boys Town six months later and stated that reforms were window dressing. Father Hupp says Casey left because his job was done—but Casey was an outspoken ex-convict, which may have made him "too hot."

12. Paul N. Williams, "Boys Town, An Exposé Without Bad Guys," *Columbia Journalism Review,* January/February 1975.

13. The *Sun* had a "four-way" staff that reported stories that would appear in seven editions of the paper. These were the reporters working on the Boys Town story.

14. According to Paul Williams, in *Investigative Reporting and Editing,* Boys Town got school-aid funds and state welfare and gasoline tax funds. While these were "relatively small change" in the context of the overall budget, about $200,000 a year, the discrepancy was real and pointed to other possible problems.

15. Transcript, Mick Rood interview with Msgr. Nicholas Wegner.

16. Paul Williams, *Investigative Reporting and Editing.*

17. Interview with Mick Rood. According to several sources, the "Deep Throat" of Boys Town, a role that required courage in insular Omaha, was Dr. Claude Organ.

18. Jeannie Lipsey Rosenblum described his appearance at that time in an interview.

19. As a religiously affiliated organization, Boys Town was entitled to an exemption for the first two years and could have filed with the archdiocese of Omaha. But it had filed separately anyway.

20. According to Paul Williams, the footwork in Philadelphia was done by Melinda Upp, a Washington reporter whom he previously had tried to hire. Finally, the call came: Are you sure you want this? she asked. The IRS charged a dollar a page and it was 94 pages long. The answer was, Hell, yes.

21. Interview with Randy Brown.

22. In his follow-up columns in the *Sun.*

23. The $25 million is combined fund-raising and investment income.

24. The *Sun* published on Thursdays and worked around its own production schedule while trying to cut off the opportunity for a preemptive response through the *Omaha World-Herald.*

25. Paul Williams, *Investigative Reporting and Editing,* and Craig Tomkinson, "The Weekly Editor: Boys Town Finances Revealed," *Editor & Publisher,* April 15, 1972.

26. Transcript, Mick Rood interview with Msgr. Nicholas Wegner.

27. The reporters interviewed thirteen of the seventeen board members. Two were too old or ill to be interviewed.

28. Msgr. Schmitt, speaking at a press conference on May 22, 1972. Press conference transcript.

29. Interview with Randy Brown.

30. Paul N. Williams, "Boys Town, An Exposé Without Bad Guys."

31. Michael D. LaMontia, director of the State Department of Public Institutions, which oversaw Boys Town, called the *Sun*'s criticisms those of a "vocal minority" that should be ignored in a letter to Wegner, May 25, 1972. The *Sun,* he said, speaks "from a very low profile and is really not heard by many people. The person being attacked can let it die a natural death. . . ." He referred to the reporters as "scavengers" and "professional losers." Possibly Mr. LaMontia was merely being empathetic, but his tone seemed a little more charged-up than that.

32. Paul N. Williams, "Boys Town, An Exposé Without Bad Guys."

33. "Boys Town Bonanza," *Time,* April 10, 1972; "Boys Town's Worth Put at $209 Million," *Los Angeles Times,* March 31, 1972; "Money Machine," *Newsweek,* April 10, 1972; Tomkinson, "The Weekly Editor."

34. "Other Boys Homes Affected by Boys Town Story," *Omaha Sun,* December 14, 1972.

35. Undated two-page letter from Francis P. Schmitt to Boys Town supporters printed on Boys Town stationery; "Boys Town May Take Legal Steps to Initiate New Programs, Policies," *Omaha Sun,* December 14, 1972; correspondence between Paul Williams and the "Irreverent Reverend" Lester Kinsolving of the National Newspaper Syndicate Inc. of America, a muckraking religious columnist widely syndicated through the *San Francisco Chronicle.* Schmitt was angry because, among other things, Boys Town's marketing domicile had backfired: Kinsolving wrote a follow-up story in the *Washington Evening Star,* "Boys Town Money Machine" (November 4, 1972), and datelined it Boys Town, Nebraska. Schmitt (incorrectly) felt that he had no right to do so.

36. Paul Critchlow, "Boys Town Money Isn't Buying Happiness," *Philadelphia Inquirer,* July 20, 1973.

37. The Reverend Monsignor Wegner, letter to a man who said he was an employee of the *San Francisco Examiner* and worked in the composing room, June 1, 1973. The man wrote Lester Kinsolving at the *San Francisco Chronicle* and asked that his name not be used in a story, probably because he was offering it to a competing paper. Kinsolving apparently forwarded this material to Buffett.

38. Warren Buffett letter to Edward Morrow, April 21, 1972.

39. Memo from Paul Williams to Buffett, October 13, 1972, including Buffett's comments.

40. Mick Rood note to personal files, January 19, 1973. Transcript, Mick Rood interview with Msgr. Nicholas Wegner.

41. The award was to "The Sun Newspapers of Omaha, of *The Sun Newspapers of Omaha:* For uncovering the large financial resources of Boys Town, Nebraska, leading to reforms in this charitable organization's solicitation and use of funds contributed by the public." It was the first time a weekly paper won for Local Investigative Specialized Reporting (although according to Pulitzer Center staff, weeklies had won before in categories other than investigative reporting).

42. However, Msgr. Wegner was described as "frail" and had had several recent surgeries. See Paul Critchlow, "Boys Town Money Isn't Buying Happiness."

43. In 1973, Boys Town actually raised more money than in 1972 (over $6 million), according to the *Omaha World-Herald* (March 21, 1973). The main result of the exposé and resulting reforms was increased transparency and accountability over how the money was spent.

44 George Jerome Goodman (writing as "Adam Smith"), *Supermoney.* New York: Random House, 1972. Goodman (known as Jerry) chose his pen name after Adam Smith, the father of market economics.

45. John Brooks, "A Wealth of Notions," *Washington Post,* October 22, 1972.

Chapter 36: Two Drowned Rats

1. Interview with Stan Lipsey. Scripps Howard owned 60% of the paper but had been ordered by the Department of Justice in 1968 to divest it on antitrust grounds because it also owned the *Cincinnati Post & Times-Star,* a competing paper. Blue Chip bought 10% of the *Enquirer*'s stock and tried to get the rest for $29.2 million in February 1971.

2. Scripps would have been interested in selling because it was looking at buying Journal Publishing and Albuquerque Publishing and could not own all three.

3. They had talked to Peter Fleischmann, chairman of the *New Yorker* and a large shareholder, who was willing to sell.

4. Graham thought that the only alternative to going public was to sell one of the company's TV stations, which she did not want to do. To protect the business from an unfriendly bidder, Beebe and family lawyer George Gillespie structured the stock sale in two tiers, with class A shares in the family's hands and class B stock, which carried diluted voting privileges, sold to the public. Katharine Graham, *Personal History.* New York: Alfred A. Knopf, 1997.

5. Graham told this story to Buffett.

6. Katharine Graham, *Personal History.*

7. Katharine Graham letter to Charlie Munger, December 23, 1974.

8. Katharine Graham, *Personal History.*

9. Katharine Graham interview with Charlie Rose, February 5, 1997.

10. Some of the nonvoting B shares went to Kay's brother, Bill, in exchange for an investment in the company. Kay's sisters were not investors in the *Post.* At the time, the unprofitable newspaper was less a financial asset than a public responsibility and a source of prestige.

11. Buffett's former golf coach Bob Dwyer was the office boy who performed this task, in between running copy for the *Post*'s editorial department.

12. Katharine Graham, *Personal History.*

13. These anecdotes are from *Personal History.*

14. C. David Heymann's *The Georgetown Ladies' Social Club* (New York: Atria Books, 2003)—a well-researched account of the most influential Washington hostesses and the private power they wielded—gave examples, such as a black eye, that indicated that on at least some occasions Phil Graham physically abused her.

15. Stories of the women with whom Phil Graham was involved and the allegation that he swapped girlfriends with Kennedy, including the actress-model Noel-Noel, are contained in *The Georgetown Ladies' Social Club.*

16. In her memoir, Graham attributed this partly to the subservience of women in her time and partly to her emotionally abusive upbringing. She seems to have had at least a partial grasp of her own role in enabling Phil's behavior.

17. Katharine Graham interview with Charlie Rose, February 5, 1997.

18. Ibid.

19. Interview with Don Graham.

20. Beebe had been a partner at Cravath, Swaine & Moore in New York and, under the direction of Don Swatland, in 1948 was instrumental in designing the structure that protected the *Post* from a sale outside the family.

21. McNamara later said he commissioned the "History of the United States Decision-Making Process on Vietnam Policy" to "bequeath to scholars the raw material from which they could re-examine the events of the time." Sanford J. Ungar, *The Papers and the Papers: An Account of the Legal and Political Battle over the Pentagon Papers 23-27.* New York: E. P. Dutton, 1972.

22. Dialogue between Graham and Bradlee has been condensed and edited for clarity from *Personal History* and her interview with Charlie Rose. Description of the scene is from *Personal History.*

23. Bob Woodward, "Hands Off, Mind On," *Washington Post,* July 23, 2001.

Chapter 37: Newshound

1. Nixon made explicit threats about the licenses, but a paper trail did not surface to document this until May 1974 (Katharine Graham, *Personal History.* New York: Alfred A. Knopf, 1997). Graham filed an affidavit with the FCC on June 21, 1974, saying the challenge was "part of a White House–inspired effort to injure . . . the company in retaliation for its Watergate coverage." Morton Mintz, "Mrs. Graham Links White House, TV Fights," *Washington Post,* June 27, 1974; David E. Rosenbaum, "Threats by Nixon Reported on Tape Heard by Inquiry," *New York Times,* May 16, 1974.

2. Katharine Graham, *Personal History.*

3. Ibid.

4. All quotes on Meyer are from Cary Reich, *Financier: The Biography of André Meyer: A Story of Money, Power, and the Reshaping of American Business.* New York: William Morrow, 1983.

5. *"The whole company at one point got down to where it was selling for eighty million,"* Buffett says. *"We spent a little less than ten million bucks when all was said and done and paid a price that valued the company on average at a hundred million."*

6. Graham's memoir, which downplays her relationship with Meyer, credits Gillespie and Beebe for the idea of the two-class stock. Meyer's biographer, Cary Reich, credits Meyer for the idea. Given Meyer's talents as a banker, it seems unlikely he had no involvement.

7. Cary Reich used the term "irate" in *Financier.*

8. Interview with Arjay Miller.

9. Katharine Graham, *Personal History.*

10. The company had disclosed in 1971 that the city was interested in buying it.

11. Interview with Bill Ruane.

12. Warren Buffett letter to Malcolm Forbes, August 31, 1973.

13. Interview with Bill Ruane.

14. Katharine Graham, *Personal History.*

15. Patrick Brogan, *The Short Life and Death of the National News Council: A Twentieth Century Fund Paper.* New York: Priority Press Publications, 1985. The Council survived for eleven years before giving up—a decade before the Internet became available—for lack of a viable outlet through which its findings could reach the public.

16. Interview with George Gillespie.

17. Interview with Don Graham.

18. Katharine Graham, *Personal History.*

19. October 20, 1973.

20. Graham more tactfully called him a "delightful and mischievous goad" in *Personal History.*

21. In her book, Graham recalls that "someone" mentioned the amortization of intangibles and that Howard Simons, unprompted, then challenged her to define it. Possibly Graham did not perceive herself as "showing off" when writing what was, after all, her own memoir.

22. Interview with Don Graham.

23. Interview with Liz Hylton.

24. The Dumbarton Oaks Conference; the Dumbarton Oaks Research Library and Collection.

Chapter 38: Spaghetti Western

1. Wattles, confusingly, bore the same name as Gurdon W. Wattles, the "streetcar king" of Omaha, who was no relation.

2. Interviews with Ed Anderson, Marshall Weinberg.

3. Buffett bought American Manufacturing at 40% of what he thought it was worth. "How Omaha Beats Wall Street," *Forbes,* November 1, 1969.

4. It didn't make you huge money unless you picked the shareholders' pockets, as some had done. An unscrupulous operator could milk the subsidiaries for money while saddling the shareholders of the parent company with an unsustainable amount of debt. John S. Tompkins, "Pyramid Devices of 20's Revived," *New York Times,* November 16, 1958.

5. "Fighting the Tape," *Forbes,* April 1, 1973. "I trust this man [Wattles] to do intelligent things," Ruane said. Shareholders had sued over the values in the merger, however, illustrating the conflicts created by the Wattles model.

6. Interview with Charlie Munger.

7. Blue Chip made two purchases totaling 137,700 shares, or 6%, of Wesco on July 11 and July 14, 1972. Between July 1972 and January 1973, Blue Chip bought another 51,300 shares, or 2% of the stock, through open market purchases on twenty different days.

8. "Not Disappointed, Says Analyst As Wesco, FSB Call Off Merger," *California Business,* March 15, 1973.

9. Wesco's equivalent book value per share at the exchange ratio offered was $23, compared to Santa Barbara's $8. Santa Barbara had zero unrestricted capital, whereas Wesco had $7 per equivalent share free net worth. Santa Barbara's earnings per equivalent share after bad debt accruals and deferred taxes were 28.7% lower than Wesco's.

10. A letter from Charlie Munger to Louis Vincenti, February 8, 1973, makes the case that Home Savings' (a California banking giant) cost structure was so low "because it is run like Wesco."

11. Interview with Betty Casper Peters.

12. Charles T. Munger testimony, *In the Matter of Blue Chip Stamps, Berkshire Hathaway Incorporated,* HO-784, Wednesday, March 19, 1975, p. 53. Warren E. Buffett testimony, March 21, 1975, pp. 61–63.

13. Interview with Charlie Munger.

14. "It is awkward," he wrote, "when we want to talk to you about alternatives to be provided by us for Wesco shareholders, to have you sort of prevented from considering anything unless and until released by FSB [Santa Barbara] or actions of ours.... I guess all we can do is have everyone act as best he can as the matter unfolds to an outcome now not entirely clear to us." Charles T. Munger letter to Louis R. Vincenti, February 8, 1973.

15. Charles T. Munger testimony, *In the Matter of Blue Chip Stamps, Berkshire Hathaway Incorporated,* HO-784, Wednesday, March 19, 1975, page 84.

16. Interview with Betty Casper Peters.

17. Minutes of the Special Meeting of Board of Directors of Wesco Financial Corporation, February 13, 1973.

18. Interview with Betty Casper Peters.

19. All analyst commentary from "Not Disappointed, Says Analyst As Wesco, FSB Call Off Merger," *California Business.*

20. Peters was grateful to them, writing to Don Koeppel two months later that the decision to kill the deal looked "heroic" because Santa Barbara's stock price had fallen from over $33 to $15.50.

21. Interview with Charlie Munger.

22. Blue Chip applied to the Federal Savings and Loan Insurance Corporation to buy 50% of Wesco, thereby turning Blue Chip, and potentially its affiliates Berkshire, Diversified, and others, into a savings-and-loan holding company. In the application, the companies said that

Diversified had never considered Blue Chip a subsidiary but Diversified and its affiliates might be deemed to control Blue Chip by view of Buffett's ownership of the stocks of both as well as of Berkshire, which owned 17.1% of Blue Chip at the time.

23. Munger started looking at other California bank stocks and suggested that Wesco might buy a large block of Crocker National Bank.

24. "I have a personal, pronounced prejudice in favor of buying at a material discount from book value stock in extremely entrenched institutions which have earned between 11% and 13% on book value for a decade or more with a history of substantial and ever-increasing dividends. Moreover, I like the idea of diversifying the economic base at Wesco with something like a zero increase in overhead. I also like becoming the largest shareholder in substantial enterprises—on the theory that this adds a possible plus factor to investment performance." Charles T. Munger letter to Lou Vincenti, April 3, 1973.

25. Buffett's trading style that year suggested he might be pessimistic about the economy and was preparing for a downturn. He wrote straight covered-call options on Kennecott Copper and down-and-out options, a more sophisticated type of covered call that limits the downside and upside within a specified range, on several stocks such as Ford Motors, General Motors, and Black & Decker. Selling calls on the latter three economically sensitive stocks was not a market call, but does suggest that he was more pessimistic than optimistic about the economy. Letter from Warren Buffett to Jack Ringwalt, March 9, 1972.

26. At December 31, 1973, his *Post* stock was worth $7.9 million.

27. Catherine Elberfeld letter to Warren Buffett, May 1974.

28. Ben Graham wrote about this Eau Claire, Wisconsin, company in *The Intelligent Investor*.

29. *"I'd have made a hell of a lot more money if I hadn't sold it. I would have made a fortune out of the stock,"* Buffett says. He says he got off quickly when he learned the CEO had different deals with every director about pay. Vornado was under different management and owned discount stores. Today it is a real estate investment trust managed by Steven Roth.

30. Interview with Bob Malott.

31. Buffett says he immediately told Malott that FMC should buy back its own stock, which was cheap. Although FMC considered the idea, it didn't follow through.

32. Mark Trustin, a neighbor, gave Hamilton to the Buffetts.

33. Interview with Susie Buffett Jr., who says she wasn't planning to become a police officer.

34. Interview with Peter Buffett.

35. Interview with Dave Stryker.

36. In the Temptations' world, men are the Daisy Maes: "Since I Lost My Baby," "The Way You Do the Things You Do," "(I Know) I'm Losing You," "I Can't Get Next to You," "Just My Imagination," "Treat Her like a Lady," and, of course, "Ain't Too Proud to Beg."

37. From several sources both close to Susie at the time and who knew her later.

38. Interview with Peter Buffett.

39. His dividends from Blue Chip were also about $160,000 per year before taxes.

40. By having Diversified buy insurance from ("reinsure") National Indemnity through its new subsidiary. The cash was transferred by paying a premium to Diversified. Charles T. Munger testimony, *In the Matter of Blue Chip Stamps, Berkshire Hathaway Incorporated*, HO-784, Thursday, March 20, 1975, pp. 188–194.

41. By year-end 1973, Reinsurance Corp. of Nebraska (renamed Columbia Insurance) had amassed investments of $9 million, which is indicative of its cash flows.

42. Charles T. Munger testimony, *In the Matter of Blue Chip Stamps, Berkshire Hathaway Incorporated*, HO-784, Wednesday, March 19, 1975. Both had previously owned some stock. Munger had bought a block and Gottesman bought stock his partners sold.

43. Charles T. Munger testimony, *In the Matter of Blue Chip Stamps, Berkshire Hathaway Incorporated*, HO-784, Thursday, March 20, 1975, p. 193.

44. Charles T. Munger testimony, *In the Matter of Blue Chip Stamps, Berkshire Hathaway Incorporated*, HO-784, Thursday, March 20, 1975, p. 190.

45. They were reported at the end of the year in DRC's annual report, but few people read it, and it took legwork and initiative to get more timely information from SEC Form 3s and 4s. DRC's 11.2% position was disclosed in BRK's 1973 annual report, as well as the fact that Warren and Susie owned 43% of DRC at the time too.

46. For $1.9 million.

Chapter 39: The Giant

1. From peak to trough in the Depression (September 3, 1929, to July 8, 1932), the Dow fell 89%. From peak to trough in the early 1970s (January 11, 1974, to December 6, 1974), the Dow fell 45%—the two worst bear markets of the century.

2. Robert Redford interview, cited by Graham in *Personal History*. New York: Alfred A. Knopf, 1997.

3. Katharine Graham, *Personal History*.

4. The television stations owned by both would have created a conflict.

5. Katharine Graham, *Personal History*.

6. Interview with Gladys Kaiser.

7. From a letter that Graham wrote Buffett, reprinted in *Personal History*. Don Graham recalls his mother telling him that Susie cooked eggs for her, and Susie and Warren watched Kay eat them and did not eat any themselves.

8. Measured from its peak.

9. Interview with Charlie Munger.

10. The record was 1970: Sequoia 12.11% vs. S&P 20.6%; 1971: Sequoia 13.64% vs. S&P 14.29%; 1972: Sequoia 3.61% vs. S&P 18.98%; 1973: Sequoia (24.8%) vs. S&P (14.72%).

11. Marshall Weinberg as well as Buffett confirmed this in interviews. Malott says he does not recall it.

12. Loomis joined Sandy Gottesman at First Manhattan; Brandt went to work at Abraham & Co.

13. "Look at All Those Beautiful, Scantily Clad Girls Out There!" *Forbes*, November 1, 1974.

14. "*Forbes* didn't use what I considered to be the most significant line," said Buffett in a letter to Pat Ellebracht on October 24, 1974, repeating this quote.

15. Interview with Rod Rathbun; Omni arbitration files of the National Indemnity Company.

16. Compounded over thirty years at 20%, this was perhaps a $2.4 billion investment return forgone. Buffett and Munger have referred to it as the greatest missed opportunity in the history of Berkshire Hathaway. The details are arcane but the essence of the story is as portrayed here.

17. "Why the SEC's Enforcer Is in Over His Head," *BusinessWeek*, October 11, 1976.

18. Interview with Verne McKenzie.

19. Interview with Betty Casper Peters.

20. Interview with Verne McKenzie.

21. Robin Rickershauser, who has often heard this clever trope from her husband, did not realize he originated it until contacted by the author.

22. If true, investors would have been selling without required information about the buyer and his reasons.

23. Charles T. Munger testimony, *In the Matter of Blue Chip Stamps, Berkshire Hathaway Incorporated*, HO-784, Thursday, March 20, 1975, p. 112.

24. The increase in Santa Barbara's price if the deal collapsed would only partially hedge this risk.

25. Charles T. Munger testimony, *In the Matter of Blue Chip Stamps, Berkshire Hathaway Incorporated*, HO-784, Thursday, March 20, 1975, pp. 112–13.

26. Interview with Judge Stanley Sporkin.

27. Ibid. This lawyer was so particularly ferocious that the author was asked not to mention his name.

28. A thick file of documents produced in response to the SEC's February 1975 subpoena illustrates several points: 1) it contained no evidence that Buffett bought on inside information or expect-

ing a takeover; 2) Buffett had become expert on water company regulation and ratemaking, and his interest and expertise in this narrow subject was prodigious; 3) this aspect of the investigation must have been intrusive and an embarrassing form of déjà vù, as it included production of his correspondence with *Forbes* that attempted to clear his name.

29. Partly because of state restrictions on how much stock any one insurance company could hold, the diagram was more complicated than it would have been otherwise. The version shown on pages 352–353 was created by Verne McKenzie and updated through 1977 (i.e., includes the *Buffalo News*). Berkshire was still negotiating with the SEC as late as 1978.

30. During Buffett's testimony, *In the Matter of Blue Chip Stamps, Berkshire Hathaway Incorporated,* HO-784, Friday, March 21, 1975, p. 125, he acknowledged that he and Munger had been buying shares of Wesco in the open market during a tender offer and Rickershauser had advised him to stop, saying that they should use only tender offers to accumulate further shares (which they did). Rickershauser interjected, "I want the record to be clear that I did not tell them it was illegal to do what was done. I told them it would be hard to convince somebody that in hindsight they may not have intended to do what they did. You can swear me in if you want to on that one. I didn't want to be right."

31. Said to a colleague.

32. The SEC apparently considered Buffett, Munger, and Guerin's interests and the companies a controlled group for purposes of tender offers. The combination of Warren (11%), Susie (2%), Munger and his partners (10%), Berkshire Hathaway (26%), and Diversified (16%) controlled 65% of Blue Chip's stock. Warren and Susie owned 36% of Berkshire and 44% of DRC. Munger owned 10% of DRC. DRC owned 15% of BRK and 16% of BC. BC owned 64% of Wesco.

33. The "harm principle" was articulated by scholars such as John Locke, Wilhelm von Humboldt, and John Stuart Mill, who argued that the sole purpose of law was to prevent harm, and the individual's liberty should not be encroached otherwise. The harm principle is the basis for certain portions of the U.S. Constitution.

34. Chuck Rickershauser Jr. letter to Stanley Sporkin, November 19, 1975.

35. Chuck Rickershauser Jr. letter to Stanley Sporkin, December 1, 1975.

36. Warren E. Buffett testimony, *In the Matter of Blue Chip Stamps, Berkshire Hathaway Incorporated,* HO-784, Friday, March 21, 1975, p. 157.

37. Charles T. Munger testimony, *In the Matter of Blue Chip Stamps, Berkshire Hathaway Incorporated,* HO-784, Thursday, March 20, 1975, p. 197.

38. Interview with Judge Stanley Sporkin. Sporkin served as general counsel to the CIA after leaving the SEC in 1981. He became Judge of the U.S. District Court for the District of Columbia in 1985 and served till his retirement in 2000.

39. Ibid. For more on Sporkin see Jack Willoughby, "Strictly Accountable," *Barron's,* April 7, 2003; Peter Brimelow, "Judge Stanley Sporkin? The Former SEC Activist Is Unfit for the Federal Branch," *Barron's,* November 4, 1985; Robert M. Bleiberg, "Sporkin's Swan Song?" *Barron's,* February 2, 1981; "Why the SEC's Enforcer Is in Over His Head," *BusinessWeek,* October 11, 1976.

40. "I bet on a good horse," says Sporkin, "and the horse came in."

41. The company also paid a $115,000 fine. "Consent to Judgment for Permanent Injunction and Other Relief," "Final Judgment for Permanent Injunction and for Other Relief and Mandatory Order and Consent with Respect Thereto," and "Complaint for a Permanent Injunction and Other Relief," *In the Matter of Securities and Exchange Commission vs. Blue Chip Stamps,* June 9, 1976.

42. The SEC Advisory Committee on Corporate Disclosure, July 30, 1976.

Chapter 40: How Not to Run a Public Library

1. Doug Smith, "Solid Buffett Voice Melts Debut Jitters," *Omaha World-Herald,* May 9, 1975.

2. Interview with Charlie Munger.

3. Interviews with Roxanne Brandt, Walter Schloss. Brandt later jokingly admitted this was grounds for divorce.

4. *New York Daily News,* October 30, 1975.

5. As of December 2007, these shares would be worth $747 million.

6. That Buffett, who had never borrowed a significant amount of money in his life, thought it made sense for his sisters to buy Berkshire stock using borrowed money, with only 5% down, speaks volumes about how cheap he thought the stock was and how good its prospects were at the time.

7. Berkshire owned so much *Washington Post* stock and Buffett's position on the board was such that, if it bought a TV station, its ownership would be attributed to the *Washington Post*, pushing it over the limit of five stations that it could own.

8. Howard E. Stark letter to Warren Buffett, June 18, 1975. Also see Lee Smith, "A Small College Scores Big in the Investment Game," *Fortune*, December 18, 1978.

9. Interview with George Gillespie.

10. According to Graham's *Personal History* (New York: Alfred A. Knopf, 1997), this contract would have given the pressmen the highest wages in the nation and security from layoffs. Negotiations broke down in part because the *Post* refused to hire back the workers who had damaged the presses.

11. According to *Personal History*, fifteen former *Post* pressmen pleaded guilty to various misdemeanor charges. Six who had damaged presses and committed more serious crimes were jailed.

12. They sold their interest in Source Capital to its managers.

13. With the press strikes and Watergate affair behind her, Katharine Graham began to focus on growth at the *Washington Post* in the mid-1970s. Up until then, the company didn't have sufficient profits and there was "little more than a hit-or-miss strategy" for growth (*Personal History*). Sales and earnings started to take off in 1976, around the time that they started buying back company stock. Earnings per share were $1.36 in 1976 vs. $0.36 in 1970. Return on equity was 20% compared to 13%. Profit margin grew to 6.5% from 3.2%. And it kept improving from there (Value Line report, March 23, 1979).

14. Charles Munger letter to Katharine Graham, November 13, 1974.

15. Interview with Don Graham.

16. C. David Heymann, *The Georgetown Ladies' Social Club*. New York: Atria Books, 2003.

17. Interview with Don Graham.

18. Interview with Susie Buffett Jr., who credits her parents for not interfering.

19. Interview with Susie Buffett Jr.

20. Interview with Dick and Mary Holland.

21. Interview with Susie Buffett Jr.

22. Interview with Howie Buffett.

23. In an interview Peter Buffett described his routine at this time.

24. According to friends of Susie's who say she blamed Graham for the relationship.

25. Al Pagel, "What Makes Susie Sing?" *Omaha World-Herald,* April 17, 1977.

26. Ibid.

27. This is Jack Byrne's recollection of Davidson's remonstration in an interview. Jack being a colorful guy, it is possible that his recollection is a bit more colorful than what Davidson actually said.

28. Interview with Tony Nicely.

29. Warren Buffett memo to Carol Loomis, July 6, 1988.

30. By 1974, the whole insurance industry was producing what rating agency A. M. Best called "unbearable" losses of $2.5 billion from a vicious price war and inflation of everything from car repairs to lawsuits. (*A.M. Best Company Comment on the State of and Prospects for the Property/Liability Insurance Industry,* June 1975.) The states were also passing "no-fault" insurance legislation, which meant that insurers had to pay for an accident regardless of who caused it. The federal government also slapped price controls on the industry during the Middle East war. Meanwhile, the devastating stock market of 1973–74 had wiped so much value from GEICO's stock portfolio that for every share of stock, investments that had once been worth $3.90 were now worth a dime a share (Leonard Curry, "Policy Renewed: How GEICO Came Back from the Dead," *Regardie's*, October/November 1982).

31. GEICO had $500 million in premiums and would have needed capital of $125 million to meet regulatory and rating agency standards for leverage.

32. Interview with Sam Butler.

33. Interview with Jack Byrne. "The bastards at Travelers had passed me over for president for Ed Budd," recalls Byrne (who likes to tell this story and tells it often). "A million dollars invested with me is now worth a billion, and a million dollars invested with Ed Budd is now worth $750,000. And I used to be pissed, but obviously I'm more mature about it now. Well, I'm still pissed." This story is also recounted in William K. Klingaman, *GEICO, The First Forty Years.* Washington, D.C.: GEICO Corporation,1994.

34. Interview with Jack Byrne.

35. "GEICO's Plans to Stay in the Black," *BusinessWeek,* June 20, 1977. It is Byrne's impression that Wallach did not like him.

36. GEICO had too little capital under regulatory standards to ensure its ability to pay claims on all its policies. By transferring some of its business to competitors, the company would relieve the strain on capital.

37. Interview with Rhoda and Bernie Sarnat.

38. Interview with Lou Simpson.

39. "Leo Goodwin Jr. Is Dead at 63; Headed GEICO Insurance Concern," *New York Times,* January 18, 1978; "Leo Goodwin, Financier, Son of Founder of GEICO," *Washington Post,* January 18, 1978.

40. Interview with Don Graham.

41. Warren Buffett memo to Carol Loomis, July 6, 1988.

42. Blue Chip bought 14% of Pinkerton's in March 1976 and Buffett went on the board, a thrill to the erstwhile boy detective who had also busted open Boys Town's hidden war chest.

43. Interview with Bill Scott.

44. Wallach had invited big insurers to buy up 40% of GEICO's reinsurance treaties, giving them until June 22 to make their decision to participate. Not enough insurers signed up. Wallach was supposed to decide by Friday, June 25, whether to shut GEICO down. He extended the deadline and, in mid-July, revised his rescue plan—requiring only 25% of GEICO's premiums to be taken up by the insurance pool and lowering the amount of capital they needed to raise by year-end to $50 million. Reginald Stuart, "Bankruptcy Threat Fails to Change Status of GEICO," *New York Times,* June 26, 1976; Reginald Stuart, "The GEICO Case Has Landed in His Lap," *New York Times,* July 4, 1976; Matthew L. Wald, "GEICO Plan Is Revised by Wallach," *New York Times,* July 16, 1976.

45. National Indemnity was a specialty company, not yet so large or well-known that it would cause too much push-back on the grounds of helping a competitor. Buffett's other insurers, as will be seen, were struggling.

46. Who knows what General McDermott actually wrote, but any endorsement at all from him would have carried weight among insurers.

47. Some of the people instrumental in making it happen were former GEICO employees, according to Byrne.

48. Interview with Jack Byrne.

49. John Gutfreund quoting Frinquelli in an interview. Frinquelli did not return calls requesting an interview.

50. Interview with Sam Butler.

51. Leonard Curry, "Policy Renewed." According to some sources, Butler also had an instrumental role in convincing Gutfreund to underwrite the deal.

52. Without a doubt it had not. Among other things, GEICO had failed to disclose a change in method of calculating loss reserves, which had enabled it to boost profits by $25 million during the second and third quarters of 1975. "In the Matter of GEICO et al.," October 27, 1976.

53. Leonard Curry, "Policy Renewed."

54. Interview with John Gutfreund.

55. An indication of "aftermarket support" was a principal component in underwriters' assess-

ments of how a stock might trade once it was listed. The presence of aftermarket support helped prevent a "busted deal" in which the underwriter had to buy back the offering with the firm's own capital.

56. Byrne's recollection is that Tom Harnett, the New York superintendent, helped rally the industry to get behind the reinsurance. Harnett, he believes, had an incentive because the New York guaranty fund was prefunded and had invested in Big Mac New York City bonds, which were selling at a fraction of their par value. The insolvency funds in effect had evaporated in the wake of New York City's financial crisis.

57. Byrne has told this story more vividly in times past. In Roger Lowenstein's *Buffett: The Making of an American Capitalist* (New York: Doubleday, 1996), he supposedly said to Sheeran, "Here's your fucking license. We are no longer a citizen of the state of New Jersey." He calls Sheeran "the worst insurance commissioner ever."

58. Disgruntled employees, hearing the news about their jobs, started throwing policies out the top-story window. "Files were floating all around North Jersey in the air," says Byrne. Nobody knew this until GEICO moved the claims office to Philadelphia, "when we went to move the files and they weren't there." Byrne estimates the lost data cost the company as much as $30–40 million in excess claims. GEICO also gave up its license in Massachusetts. It stopped writing business in many other states without surrendering the right to do so in the future. In total, the company nonrenewed 400,000 out of its 2.2 million policyholders.

59. Interview with Jack Byrne. The author first heard this story from a secretary who formerly worked for Byrne.

60. Interview with Jack Byrne.

61. Interview with Tony Nicely.

62. James L. Rowe Jr., "Fireman's Fund Picks Byrne," *Washington Post*, July 24, 1985; Sarah Oates, "Byrne Pulled GEICO Back from Edge of Bankruptcy," *Washington Post*, July 24, 1985.

63. Graham Group members, Buffett friends, and Berkshire employees such as Marshall Weinberg, Wyndham Robertson, Verne McKenzie, Gladys Kaiser, Bob Goldfarb, Tom Bolt, Hallie Smith, Howie Buffett, and Peter Buffett all remember Grossman fondly.

Chapter 41: And Then What?

1. Christopher Ogden, *Legacy, A Biography of Moses and Walter Annenberg*. Boston: Little, Brown, 1999; John Cooney, *The Annenbergs: The Salvaging of a Tainted Dynasty*. New York: Simon & Schuster, 1982.

2. Ogden, in *Legacy*, cites Annenberg as saying he declined to buy the *Washington Times-Herald* from Colonel McCormick and convinced McCormick to sell to the Grahams despite their reservations about Phil Graham's drinking and mental stability. Thus, he felt responsible for putting together the newspaper marriage that made the *Washington Post* what it had become. He felt slighted because the Grahams had never credited him. Buffett says that Annenberg was exaggerating his role and that Graham viewed this notion as ridiculous.

3. Drew Pearson, "Washington Merry-Go-Round: Annenberg Lifts Some British Brows," *Washington Post*, February 24, 1969.

4. In the end, he gave most of his money to the Annenberg Foundation and his art collection to the Metropolitan Museum of Art.

5. Lally Weymouth, "Foundation Woes: The Saga of Henry Ford II, Part II," *New York Times Magazine*, March 12, 1978.

6. Walter Annenberg letter to Warren Buffett, October 1, 1992.

7. Donner was not entirely obliterated. In 1960, seven years after he died at age eighty-nine, the $44 million in assets in his foundation was divided equally—between a newly formed Donner Foundation and the original foundation, which changed its name to the Independence Foundation (www.independencefoundation.org).

8. Walter Annenberg letter to Warren Buffett, October 1, 1992.

9. Said to the author in an interview in 2003—an indicator of the direction of his thoughts at the time.

10. Graham's term, from her autobiography. Liz Smith called Graham Buffett's "frequent hostess"

and Diana McLellan said, "All the way up in New York, they're talking about Kay Graham and Warren Buffet [sic] . . . but oh, so discreetly." Diana McLellan, "The Ear," *Washington Star,* March 12, 1977; Liz Smith, "Mystery Entwined in Cassidy Tragedy," *Chicago Tribune,* March 6, 1977.

11. C. David Heymann, *The Georgetown Ladies' Social Club,* New York: Atria Books, 2003.

12. See, for example, her relationships with Jean Monnet, Adlai Stevenson.

13. The letter was described this way in Lowenstein, *Buffett.*

14. Graham showed Dan Grossman a copy of this letter. Susan Buffett also showed Doris Buffett a copy of this letter. Graham's papers currently are under seal.

15. "Interview with Susan Buffett," *Gateway,* March 5, 1976.

16. Peter Citron, "Seasoning Susie," *Omaha World-Herald,* April 7, 1976.

17. "Buffett Serious," *Omaha World-Herald,* September 14, 1976.

18. Buffett considered buying Alfred Knopf's apartment at 24 West 55th Street, later one of two landmarked Rockefeller apartments.

19. Interview with Susie Buffett Jr.

20. Interview with Al "Bud" Pagel.

21. Denenberg declined to be interviewed.

22. Al Pagel, "What Makes Susie Sing?" *Omaha World-Herald,* April 17, 1977.

23. Ibid.

24. Interview with Al "Bud" Pagel.

25. Ibid.

26. Peter Citron, "Seasoning Susie."

27. Interview with Stan Lipsey. See Leo Litwak, "Joy Is the Prize: A Trip to Esalen Institute," *New York Times Magazine,* December 31, 1967.

28. Steve Millburg, "Williams' Songs Outshine Voice," *Omaha World-Herald,* September 5, 1977.

29. Interview with Astrid Menks Buffett. The sleeping Warren famously did not notice whether Susie was there. In one story related by Racquel Newman, she decided to drive to Dottie's to play music at around ten or eleven at night, ran out of gas in a snowstorm at midnight on her way home, and instead of waking Warren, called a friend and went on an all-night obstacle-filled expedition to a gas station on the interstate, delayed by a tractor-trailer jackknifed on the freeway. She finally got home shortly before dawn. Warren never knew she was gone.

30. Said to a friend of the couple's who believes that Susie was probably sincere, both because she believed Warren really was that dependent on her and because of his preoccupation with suicide, linked to the many suicides among the Stahl family and the Buffetts' friends.

31. Warren Buffett, "How Inflation Swindles the Equity Investor," *Fortune,* May 1977. In a letter to the Graham Group, September 27, 1977, Bill Ruane describes how "This article can well serve as a basis for a discussion of so many things which are central to our economic concerns today. The article not only deals with the central theme of inflation but also with the effects of taxes, rate of return, dividend paying capacity and other elements which are crucial to the appraisal of aggregate values in our economic system."

32. The Buffett Group would take this problem up again and again. Its members were pessimistic about whether the problem could be solved, for they doubted, with good reason, that Congress had the necessary resolve to control the federal budget over the long term.

33. Interview with Marshall Weinberg.

34. The $72 million includes his holdings in BRK, DRC, and Blue Chip Stamps at year-end 1977. Susie added another $6.5 million to this total. This does not include his indirect holdings through the three companies' cross-holdings of each other.

35. Interview with Peter Buffett.

36. Two sources have confirmed this.

37. Interview with Astrid Buffett.

38. Ibid.

39. Interview with Michael Adams.

40. Interview with Astrid Buffett.

41. The 1977 letter contains significantly more "teaching" content than its predecessor. Although Buffett had control of Berkshire for twelve years previously, the 1977 letter was the first to be collected in a bound collection of letters he used to hand out to friends and is the first year featured on Berkshire's Web site.

Chapter 42: Blue Ribbon

1. Interview with Astrid Buffett.

2. From a close friend of the family.

3. Buffett explained in conversation and a letter to the author how he felt, separating his life into two stages with age forty-seven as the turning point.

4. To the end of her life, Estey wrote letters with "Mrs. Benjamin Graham" embossed on her stationery.

5. Interview with the author, 2003.

6. Interview with Stan Lipsey.

7. Interview with Sharon Osberg.

8. Interview with Peter Buffett.

9. The price included $1.5 million in pension liabilities. Blue Chip Stamps Annual Report, 1977. Blue Chip borrowed $30 million from a bank in April 1977 to finance the purchase.

10. Berkshire had assets of $379 million, Blue Chip had $200 million, DRC had $67.5 million at year-end 1977.

11. Warren and Susie personally owned 46% of Berkshire (both directly and indirectly, through their ownership of Blue Chip and Diversified, which owned Berkshire stock), and 35% of Blue Chip (both directly and indirectly).

12. Murray Light, *From Butler to Buffett: The Story Behind the Buffalo News* (Amherst, NY: Prometheus Books, 2004), who notes that only in the face of an inquiry from the Human Rights Commission in the early 1970s did Butler begin publishing wedding photos of African-Americans.

13. The *Evening News* put out a Saturday edition, but its weak ad lineage demonstrated the power of the Sunday edition of the *Courier-Express.*

14. If the trend had continued without the *Evening News* starting a Sunday paper, the logical outcome would have been either a joint operating agreement or outright acquisition of the *Courier-Express* to combine the papers—both expensive alternatives.

15. *Buffalo Courier-Express, Inc., v. Buffalo Evening News, Inc.,* Complaint for Damages and Injunctive Relief for Violation of the Federal Antitrust Laws (October 28, 1977).

16. Chuck Rickershauser had by now left Munger, Tollis to become the head of the Pacific Coast Stock Exchange. His replacement, Ron Olson, was part of a team Munger had assembled from Los Angeles.

17. Interview with Ron Olson.

18. Jonathan R. Laing, "The Collector: Investor Who Piled Up $100 Million in the '60s Piles Up Firms Today," *Wall Street Journal,* March 31, 1977.

19. Testimony of Buffett, *Buffalo Courier-Express, Inc., v. Buffalo Evening News, Inc.,* November 4, 1977.

20. In Roger Lowenstein's *Buffett: The Making of an American Capitalist,* Bob Russell cited Warren as a boy wanting to charge money to people driving by the Russells' house. Buffett does not remember the incident, but if it occurred, most likely he was influenced by the city's efforts to convert the Douglas Street toll bridge—the only passageway over the Missouri River—to a free bridge, one of the most widely reported local news stories during his early youth.

21. The bridge was sold to Marty Maroun in 1979 for $30 million, 30% less than the inflation-adjusted cost of building it thirty years earlier. Maroun parlayed the bridge into an enormous fortune.

22. Findings and Conclusions, Motion for Preliminary Injunction, *Buffalo Courier-Express, Inc., v. Buffalo Evening News, Inc.,* November 9, 1977.

23. Dick Hirsch, "Read All About It," "Bflo Tales" in *Business First,* Winter 1978.

24. In its first full year under Buffett. Murray Light, *From Butler to Buffett.*

25. Interview with Stan Lipsey.

26. Ibid.

27. *Buffalo-Courier Express, Inc., v. Buffalo Evening News, Inc.,* United States Court of Appeals, Second Circuit, 601 F.2d 48, April 16, 1979.

28. Warren Buffett, "You Pay a Very High Price in the Stock Market for a Cheery Consensus," *Forbes,* August 6, 1979.

29. Warren Buffett, "You Pay a Very High Price in the Stock Market..."

30. Blue Chip Stamps 1980 annual report to shareholders.

31. Janet Lowe, *Damn Right!: Behind the Scenes with Berkshire Hathaway's Charlie Munger,* New York: John, Wiley & Sons, 2000.

32. Ibid.

33. Warren Buffett memo to employees, December 2, 1980.

34. At first, management and the unions tried to publish without the drivers (*Buffalo Evening News,* December 2, 1980). The striking union walked out over a pay difference of $41 a week.

35. It was selling 195,000 papers on Sundays, about two-thirds of its rival's sales. From Lowenstein, *Buffett;* Audit Bureau of Circulations figures as of March 1982.

36. The Blue Chip Stamps 1980 annual report to shareholders notes the litigation became "less active and costly" that year.

37. Interview with Ron Olson.

Chapter 43: Pharaoh

1. From $89 million at the end of 1978 to $197 million in August 1980.

2. Interview with Charlotte Danly Jackson.

3. Interview with Verne McKenzie.

4. Affiliated Publications—bought for $3.5 million, jumped to $17 million after nine years. The *Washington Post*—bought for $10.6 million, now worth $103 million. GEICO—bought for $47.1 million, now worth almost seven times that, $310 million. Berkshire's total common stock portfolio was worth double its cost.

5. Buffett and Munger took out a loan of $40 million from Bank of America National Trust and Savings Association for Blue Chip to protect against a rush of redemptions, according to Munger's testimony in the Blue Chip case.

6. In 1976, the U.S. District Court in Los Angeles had said that Blue Chip no longer had to dispose of one third of its business, recognizing that it was impractical after management contacted more than eighty potential buyers and had no serious bids. Sales shrank from $124 million to $9.2 million. The woes of the *Buffalo News,* which Blue Chip owned, made valuing Blue Chip problematic until 1983, given Buffett's proportional interests in the different companies versus other shareholders, principally Munger.

7. Berkshire Hathaway 1983 annual report.

8. In 1984, during a period of relatively high inflation, the union agreed to a wage freeze.

9. The Bank Holding Company Act of 1956 placed restrictions on bank holding companies (those owning more than 25% of two or more banks, i.e., the J. P. Morgans) owning nonbanking interests, in order to avoid monopolistic control in the banking industry. It was amended in 1966 and again in 1970 to further restrict the nonbanking activities of one-bank holding companies (such as Berkshire). In 1982, it was amended to further forbid banks from engaging in insurance underwriting or agency activities. In 1999, the Gramm-Leach-Bliley Act repealed parts of these acts.

10. Interview with Verne McKenzie. According to him and Buffett, Associated was never able to recover from the disintegration of urban centers after the 1960s and adapt to the new culture required to sell discount dresses in shopping malls.

11. Interview with Charlie Munger.

12. Interviews with Dan Grossman, Peter Buffett.

13. Interview with Peter Buffett.

14. Interviews with Marvin Laird, Joel Paley.

15. Interview with Howie Buffett.

16. Ibid. As Susie Jr. says, "When Howie dies, it will be no ordinary death. It will probably be by falling out of a helicopter into a polar bear's mouth."

17. For a four-hundred-acre farm.

18. Interviews with Howie Buffett, Peter Buffett.

19. Peter Kiewit Sons', Inc. was founded by the original Peter Kiewit, a bricklayer of Dutch descent, in 1884. Dave Mack, "Colossus of Roads," *Omaha* magazine, July 1977; Harold B. Meyers, "The Biggest Invisible Builder in the World," *Fortune,* April 1966.

20. When Kiewit died, Buffett got the chance to take an apartment in Kiewit Plaza. He would have loved to do it, but Astrid didn't want to leave her garden. So they stayed on Farnam Street.

21. "Peter Kiewit: 'Time Is Common Denominator,' " *Omaha World-Herald,* undated, approximately November 2, 1979; Robert Dorr, "Kiewit Legacy Remains Significant," *Omaha World-Herald,* November 1, 1999; Harold B. Meyers, "The Biggest Invisible Builder in the World"; interview with Walter Scott Jr., Peter Kiewit's successor, who also had an apartment at Kiewit Plaza.

22. Peter Kiewit died on November 3, 1979. Warren Buffett, "Kiewit Legacy as Unusual as His Life," *Omaha World-Herald,* January 20, 1980.

23. Buffett read Flexner's autobiography three or four times and gave copies to his friends.

24. $38,453 for the year ended June 1980, of which $33,000 went toward colleges, the rest toward local organizations. Five years earlier, in June 1975, the foundation had assets of $400,000, with gifts of $28,498 to similar organizations.

25. Rick Guerin letter to Joe Rosenfield, October 1, 1985.

26. Warren Buffett letter to Shirley Anderson, Bill Ruane, and Katherine (Katie) Buffett, trustees of the Buffett Foundation, May 14, 1969.

27. Richard I. Kirkland Jr., "Should You Leave It All to the Children?" *Fortune,* September 29, 1986.

28. Larry Tisch as quoted by Roger Lowenstein, *Buffett.: The Making of an American Capitalist.* New York Doubleday, 1996. Tisch is deceased.

29. Kirkland, "Should You Leave It All to the Children?"

Chapter 44: Rose

1. *The Dream that Mrs. B Built,* May 21, 1980, Channel 7 KETV. Mrs. Blumkin's quotes have been rearranged and slightly edited for length.

2. Ibid.

3. "The Life and Times of Rose Blumkin, an American Original," *Omaha World-Herald,* December 12, 1993.

4. Ibid.

5. Minsk, near Moscow, is relatively close to the Eastern European border of Russia, which would have been a difficult passage during the war. Her route created a longer trip than traveling between San Francisco and New York by train three times, then winding back to Omaha.

6. This and most of the other details of Mrs. B's journey are from a Blumkin family history.

7. Around 1915, roughly 6,000 Russian Jews lived in Omaha and South Omaha, part of a general migration beginning in the 1880s to escape the pogroms (anti-Jewish riots) that began after the assassination of Czar Alexander II. Most started out as peddlers and small-shop owners, serving the large immigrant working class drawn by the railroads and stockyards. Until 1930, Omaha had the largest percentage of foreign-born residents of any U.S. city. Lawrence H. Larsen and Barbara J. Cottrell, *The Gate City.* Lincoln: University of Nebraska Press, 1997.

8. Interview with Louis Blumkin. His father was comparing the pawnshop to the many banks that failed during this period.

9. *The Dream that Mrs. B Built.*

10. Ibid.

11. Louis Blumkin, who says she sold for $120 coats that cost her $100 and retailed for $200 elsewhere in town.

12. *The Dream that Mrs. B Built.*

13. "The Life and Times of Rose Blumkin, an American Original."

14. Interview with Louis Blumkin.

15. Ibid. They were carving out a piece of their allotments for her.

16. "The Life and Times of Rose Blumkin, an American Original."

17. James A. Fussell, "Nebraska Furniture Legend," *Omaha World-Herald,* August 11, 1988.

18. "The Life and Times of Rose Blumkin, an American Original."

19. Joyce Wadler, "Furnishing a Life," *Washington Post,* May 24, 1984.

20. *The Dream that Mrs. B Built.*

21. "The Life and Times of Rose Blumkin, an American Original."

22. Joyce Wadler, "Blumkin: Sofa, So Good: The First Lady of Furniture, Flourishing at 90," *Washington Post,* May 24, 1984.

23. Buffett, in a letter to Jack Byrne in 1983, noted that Levitz stores averaged about 75% the size of NFM and did 10% the volume of NFM.

24. Frank E. James, "Furniture Czarina," *Wall Street Journal,* May 23, 1984.

25. Speech given at Stanford Law School on March 23, 1990. "Berkshire Hathaway's Warren E. Buffett, Lessons From the Master," *Outstanding Investor Digest,* Vol. V, No. 3., April 18, 1990.

26. Chris Olson, "Mrs. B Uses Home to Eat and Sleep; 'That's About It,'" *Omaha World-Herald,* October, 28, 1984.

27. Joyce Wadler, "Furnishing a Life."

28. Bella Eisenberg letter to Warren Buffett, June 8, 1984.

29. "I can hear my mother [saying it] now," said Louis Blumkin in an interview.

30. In the documentary *The Dream that Mrs. B Built,* Blumkin refers to this incident and said Buffett didn't want to give her the price she wanted and she told him he was too cheap.

31. Possibly it might have had something to do with her early years of sleeping on straw on a bare wood floor.

32. James A. Fussell, "Nebraska Furniture Legend."

33. Berkshire Hathaway 1983 chairman's letter. Initially, Berkshire bought 90% of the business, leaving 10% with the family, and optioning 10% back to certain key young family managers.

34. Robert Dorr, "Furniture Mart Handshake Deal," *Omaha World-Herald,* September 15, 1983.

35. Buffett's sentimental fondness for Mrs. B is notable in light of her similarity to his mother in the sense of her outbursts of abuse toward her family and employees. Only rarely did he take the risk of associating with anyone who could blow up on him.

36. Warren Buffett letter to Rose Blumkin, September 30, 1983.

37. From a retired Berkshire employee (not Verne McKenzie, the star of this anecdote).

38. Interview with Verne McKenzie.

39. Interview with Stan Lipsey.

40. "A Tribute to Mrs. B," *Omaha World-Herald,* May 20, 1984; John Brademas, President, New York University, letter to Rose Blumkin, April 12, 1984.

41. Interview with Louis Blumkin.

42. Joyce Wadler, "Blumkin: Sofa, So Good: The First Lady of Furniture, Flourishing at 90."

43. Interview with Louis Blumkin.

44. Warren Buffett letter to Larry Tisch, May 29, 1984.

45. Beth Botts, Elizabeth Edwardsen, Bob Jensen, Stephen Kofe, and Richard T. Stout, "The Corn-Fed Capitalist," *Regardie's,* February 1986.

46. Robert Dorr, "Son Says No One Wanted Mrs. B to Leave," *Omaha World-Herald,* May 13, 1989.

47. Andrew Kilpatrick, *Of Permanent Value: The Story of Warren Buffett/More in '04* (California edition). Alabama: AKPE, 2004.

48. Robert Dorr, "Son Says No One Wanted Mrs. B to Leave."

49. Sonja Schwarer, "From Wheelchair, Mrs. B Plans Leasing Expansion," *Omaha Metro Update*, February 11, 1990; James Cox, "Furniture Queen Battles Grandsons for Throne," *USA Today*, November 27, 1989.

50. Robert Dorr, "Garage Sale Is Big Success for Mrs. B," *Omaha World-Herald*, July 17, 1989.

51. Andrew Kilpatrick, *Of Permanent Value.*

52. Bob Brown, Joe Pfifferling, "Mrs. B Rides Again: An ABC *20/20* Television News Story," 1990.

53. "A Businessman Speaks His Piece on Mrs. Blumkin," *Furniture Today*, June 4, 1984, Berkshire Hathaway 1984 annual report. Buffett used a line like this with great frequency as a tag to label a person or situation so that other parts of the bathtub could drain.

54. Linda Grant, "The $4-Billion Regular Guy: Junk Bonds, No. Greenmail, Never. Warren Buffett Invests Money the Old-Fashioned Way," *Los Angeles Times*, April 7, 1991.

55. Interview with Louis Blumkin.

56. Harold W. Andersen, "Mrs. B Deserves Our Admiration," *Omaha World-Herald*, September 20, 1987; Robert Dorr, "This Time, Mrs. B Gets Sweet Deal," *Omaha World-Herald*, September 18, 1987.

Chapter 45: Call the Tow Truck

1. Interview with Doris Buffett.

2. Witnessed by a source close to the family who described it in an interview.

3. AIDS had first been discovered among homosexual men in the summer of 1981, but it was reported as pneumonia and as a rare, fatal form of cancer. President Reagan made his first mention of AIDS in September 1985 after his friend, the actor Rock Hudson, announced that he had been diagnosed with the disease.

4. Interview with Marvin Laird and Joel Paley.

5. This story was pieced together from conversations with a number of sources.

6. Alan Levin, "Berkshire Hathaway to Close," *New Bedford Standard-Times*, August 12, 1985.

7. A four-year-old loom that had cost $5,000 went for $26 as scrap. Some of the equipment went to a textile museum.

8. Buffett used the term "disaster" in the 1978 chairman's letter, discussing NICO workers' comp businesses' bad performance, which he laid largely at the door of industry problems.

9. Interviews with Verne McKenzie, Dan Grossman. The man was an agent who allegedly embezzled from Berkshire.

10. Interview with Tom Murphy.

11. Interview with Verne McKenzie.

12. Interview with Dan Grossman.

13. Several reinsurance managers presided during a short-lived interregnum: Brunhilda Hufnagle, Steven Gluckstern, and Michael Palm. For various reasons, none of them stuck.

14. Rob Urban, "Jain, Buffett Pupil, Boosts Berkshire Cash as Succession Looms," *Bloomberg News*, July 11, 2006. While the author has been acquainted with Jain for years, he declined repeated requests to be interviewed.

Chapter 46: Rubicon

1. The Dow was sitting at 875 on the first day of 1982. It had hit that level for the first time back in September 1964.

2. Corporate profits reached what would become the second-lowest point in a fifty-five-year period in 1983 (the lowest was 1992), according to Corporate Reports, Empirical Research Analysis Partners. Data 1952 through 2007.

3. Banks lost their fear of bad credit through the combination of an emerging asset bubble, simple

greed, the advent of securitization, and an eagerness to find toehold ways to fund equity trans-actions, a signal that the wall between commercial and investment banks erected by the Depression-era Glass-Steagall Act was beginning to break down.

4. They started out as investment-grade bonds, but when their issuers cratered, the bonds became so cheap that they paid a higher rate; e.g., a bond that yielded 7% would yield 10% if the price of the bond dropped to 70% of par.

5. See Connie Bruck, *The Predators' Ball: The Inside Story of Drexel Burnham and the Rise of the Junk Bond Raiders.* New York: The American Lawyer: Simon & Schuster, 1988.

6. Typically the deals worked either by giving shareholders who sold a higher price but leaving a much weakened company for those who didn't, or by offering a premium that was only a frac-tion of the value the buyer would create through actions the former management should have taken themselves. Or both.

7. Everyone from Saul Steinberg to Larry Tisch had taken a stake in the company. Meanwhile, management's first-choice buyer was IBM. In the end, Cap Cities proved a strong fit because of the complementary TV license and the minimum divestiture required.

8. Interview with Tom Murphy.

9. Ibid. Details are also recounted in Leonard Goldenson with Marvin J. Wolf, *Beating the Odds.* New York: Charles Scribner's Sons, 1991.

10. Buffett paid sixteen times earnings for Cap Cities, a 60% premium to its recent price, and, on banker Bruce Wasserstein's insistence, threw in warrants that gave the seller a continuing equity stake in ABC. These terms, arguably, are the most lenient Buffett ever struck and suggest how badly he and Murphy wanted to buy ABC. Charlie Munger wrote to the Buffett Group on January 11, 1983, that Tom Murphy at Cap Cities had "compounded the value of his original 1958 investment at 23% per annum for 25 years." Donaldson, Lufkin & Jenrette report February 26, 1980: "Earnings per share growth has compounded at 20% annually over the past decade and this rate has accelerated to 27% over the last five years."

11. Geraldine Fabrikant, "Not Ready for Prime Time?" *New York Times,* April 12, 1987.

12. With 1984 sales of $3.7 billion, ABC earned $195 million, whereas Cap Cities, one third its size, earned $135 million on sales of $940 million. The disparity in profitability was mainly due to the different economics of network affiliate stations versus the network itself but also to Murphy and Burke's management skills.

13. According to "Extortion Charge Thrown Out; Judge Cancels $75,000 Bond," *Omaha World-Herald,* March 19, 1987, charges against Robert J. Cohen were dismissed after the case was referred to the Douglas County Board of Mental Health and Cohen was moved to the Douglas County Hospital from the Douglas County Corrections Center. Terry Hyland, in "Bail Set at $25,000 for Man in Omaha Extortion Case," *Omaha World-Herald,* February 5, 1987, refers to the kidnapping plan.

14. Interview with Gladys Kaiser.

15. Ibid.

16. Ibid.

17. Interviews with Howie Buffett, Peter Buffett, Susie Buffett Jr.

18. Alan Farnham, "The Children of the Rich and Famous," *Fortune,* September 10, 1990.

19. Interview with Howie Buffett.

20. Interview with Peter Buffett.

21. Interviews with Tom Newman, Kathleen Cole.

22. Richard I. Kirkland Jr., "Should You Leave It All to the Children?" *Fortune,* September 29, 1986.

23. Interview with Kathleen Cole.

24. Interview with Ron Parks.

25. Interviews with Verne McKenzie, Malcolm "Kim" Chace III, Don Wurster, Dick and Mary Holland.

26. Interview with George Brumley.

27. Charles Ellis, *Investment Policy: How to Win the Loser's Game.* Illinois: Dow-Jones-Irwin, 1985,

which is based on his article "Winning the Loser's Game" in the July/August 1975 issue of the *Financial Analysts Journal.*

28. Burton Malkiel, *A Random Walk Down Wall Street.* New York: W. W. Norton, 1973.

29. Aside from the *Superinvestors* article, Buffett did not write about EMH directly until the Berkshire 1987 shareholders letter, but he had led up to it with related subjects such as excessive trading turnover since 1979.

30. Transcript of Graham and Dodd 50th Anniversary Seminar. Jensen at the time was professor and director of the Managerial Economics Research Center of the University of Rochester Graduate School of Management. Within a year, he would be at Harvard, where he remains as professor of business administration emeritus.

31. Stanley Perlmeter and the *Washington Post* pension fund. Although, as this book illustrates, Buffett shared ideas with some of these investors in the early days—for example, when he was short on capital—more often the use of similar rules led them to similar veins of ore.

32. One subtle underpinning of EMH was a free-market, quasilibertarian philosophy that aligned with the spirit of deregulation and Reaganomics, under which investors could fend for themselves as free agents in an unfettered self-regulating market. Thus one side effect of EMH was to subtly build support for other types of market deregulation and for government and Federal Reserve actions that arguably contributed to later asset bubbles.

33. In a worst-case scenario, both sides of an arbitrage go the wrong way—the short rises, the long falls. This is the "earthquake risk" of the arbitrageur.

34. Buffett, speaking at the 1994 Berkshire annual shareholders meeting.

35. The model with junk bonds was based on average credit history, not the behavior of the stock or bond market. The two models are not only related, but have the same basic flaw, which is that "earthquake events" are never factored in correctly—because if they were, the model would reveal a prohibitively high cost of capital.

36. With the introduction of equity index futures in 1982, Buffett started trading these instruments as a hedge. Nevertheless, he wrote Congressman John Dingell, chairman of the House Energy and Commerce Committee, warning about their risk, and likewise wrote to Don Graham, "So much for the many claims as to hedge and investment type utilization; in actual practice, virtually all contracts involve short-term highly leveraged gambling—with the brokers taking a bite out of every dollar of public participation." Letter from Warren Buffett to Mr. and Mrs. Don Graham, January 18, 1983.

37. Berkshire Hathaway annual letter, 1985. The deal was $320 million in cash and the rest in assumed debt and other costs. "Scott Fetzer Holders Clear Sale of Company," *Wall Street Journal,* December 30, 1985. In Berkshire's 2000 annual report, Buffett points out that BRK netted $1.03 billion from its net purchase price of $230 million.

38. Interview with Jamie Dimon.

39. Berkshire had $4.44 billion of assets on its books at the end of 1986, including $1.2 billion of unrealized gains on equities. Liquidating before the reform, Berkshire itself could have avoided paying any taxes, with the shareholders paying their 20% tax on the gain, or $244 million. If BRK liquidated after the Tax Reform Act took effect, Berkshire would be paying $414 million in corporate taxes (more than $185 million of which would have accrued to Buffett), before handing over the net proceeds to investors to pay a double tax, adding up to a maximum of a 52.5% tax on the $1.2 billion unrealized appreciation, or $640 million. Thus the total effect was $400 million. See also James D. Gwartney and Randall G. Holcombe, "Optimal Capital Gains Tax Policy: Lessons from the 1970s, 1980s, and 1990s," A Joint Economic Committee Study, United States Congress, June 1997.

40. Berkshire Hathaway annual report, 1986. Notably, Buffett phrases the statement in terms of the costly consequences if Berkshire liquidated after the act, not the huge benefits that would have resulted from liquidating before the act went into effect.

41. A concept of Ben Graham's.

42. This measuring stick has pros and cons, which are covered in investing books. Bottom line, it is a reasonable, conservative measure that can be distorted by acquisitions (something Buffett had discussed; see General Re).

43. Interviews with Walter Scott Jr., Suzanne Scott; also Jonathan R. Laing, "The Other Man From Omaha," *Barron's,* June 17, 1995.

44. Interview with Walter Scott Jr.

45. Jerry Bowyer, in *National Review,* August 11, 2006, wrote that Reagan's "supply-side policies have helped Warren Buffet [sic] amass the world's second-largest pile of wealth, which he routinely uses as a stage on which to stand and denounce the very supply-side measures that helped lift him to incredible prosperity." It is true that like any investor, Buffett has benefited from the supply-side policies that reduce his personal taxes on investment income and capital gains. Notably, much of that benefit is effectively offset by Berkshire Hathaway's taxes. Since the Reagan years, Citizens for Tax Justice and the Institute on Taxation and Economic Policy have been studying the annual reports of the top 250+ companies in the U.S., always coming to the conclusion that they are severely underpaying. See Robert S. McIntyre and T. D. Coo Nguyen, *Corporate Taxes & Corporate Freeloaders* (August 1985), *Corporate Income Taxes in the 1990s* (October 2000), *Corporate Income Taxes in the Bush Years* (September 2004). The top 250 companies in the U.S., while growing profits substantially, have consistently been shown to pay a fraction of the actual corporate tax rate throughout the 1980s, '90s, and today, due to breaks for depreciation, stock options, research, etc. Berkshire, however, has averaged a 30% effective tax rate (net earnings before taxes, divided by the taxes paid currently) since 1986—offsetting Buffett's personal tax benefits. Regardless, Buffett's taxes are irrelevant to whether he is entitled to criticize supply-side policies.

46. Robert Sobel, *Salomon Brothers 1910–1985, Advancing to Leadership,* Salomon Brothers, Inc., 1986.

47. In other words, current partners were paid a premium above their invested capital by Phibro, in which retired partners who had already withdrawn their capital did not share.

48. Anthony Bianco, "The King of Wall Street—How Salomon Brothers Rose to the Top—And How It Wields Its Power," *BusinessWeek,* December 5, 1985.

49. In the "Night of the Long Knives," June 30–July 2, 1934, Hitler executed at least eighty-five perceived enemies of his regime and arrested a thousand others.

50. James Sterngold, "Too Far, Too Fast: Salomon Brothers' John Gutfreund," *New York Times,* January 10, 1988.

51. Paul Keers, "The Last Waltz: He had the power, she craved the position. Life was a ball until he had to resign in disgrace and an era ended," *Toronto Star,* September 1, 1991.

52. Roger Lowenstein, *Buffett: The Making of an American Capitalist.* New York: Doubleday, 1996, who did not identify the executive giving this description.

53. Paul Keers, "The Last Waltz"; Cathy Horyn, "The Rise and Fall of John Gutfreund; For the Salomon Bros. Ex-Head, a High Profile at Work & Play," *Washington Post,* August 19, 1991.

54. Robert Sobel, *Salomon Brothers 1910–1985, Advancing to Leadership.*

55. The combative, powerful banker Bruce Wasserstein, a merger specialist, was supposedly going to run the firm. Gutfreund and his key lieutenants knew they would be instantly replaced by Wasserstein. And Perelman as the largest shareholder might scare clients away.

56. Salomon bought the Minorco block itself at $38, a 19% premium to the stock's $32 market price. It then offered Buffett the stock at the same price. The premium was typical for similar deals at the time (which were also criticized). The stock conveyed 12% voting power in the firm. Perelman offered $42 and said he might raise his stake to 25%.

57. Buffett viewed his investment in Salomon as being like a bond. If he had wonderful stock ideas like GEICO or American Express, he would not be looking at bond equivalents and would not have done this deal.

58. Interview with John Gutfreund.

59. Interviews with John Gutfreund, Donald Feuerstein. Feuerstein's son went to school with one of Perelman's children. He knew Perelman was observant and parlayed for a critical delay past the holiday.

60. According to Graham and Dodd, preferred stocks marry the least attractive features of equity and debt. "As a class," they wrote, "preferred shares are distinctly more vulnerable to adverse developments than are bonds." Benjamin Graham and David L. Dodd, *Security Analysis,*

Principles and Teaching. New York: McGraw-Hill, 1934, Chapter 26. Preferreds are often described as "bonds with a kicker," combining the safety of a bond with the upside of a stock. However, as Graham and Dodd note, this is not really correct. If a company gets in trouble, preferreds lack an enforceable claim to the interest and principal. When things go well, unlike a common stock, the investor has no right to the company's profits. Speaking at the University of Florida in 1998, Buffett said, *"The test of a senior security is whether you are getting an above-average return, after tax, and feel certain of getting your principal back."* Here, the preference to the common was meaningless.

61. Beginning October 31, 1995, in five installments over four years, it was mandatory to either convert into Salomon stock or "put" it back to the company for cash. Perelman offered to beat Buffett's deal—and Gutfreund and several other managers told the board they would quit. He offered a conversion price of $42, much more attractive from Salomon's point of view. He would have owned only 10.9% of Salomon, compared to Buffett's 12%.

62. If a potential buyer for his block of convertible preferred appeared, Buffett was obliged to offer Salomon first refusal. Even if it did not buy back the shares, he was prohibited from selling his entire block to any one purchaser. Berkshire also agreed to limit its investment in Salomon to no more than 20% for seven years.

63. Michael Lewis, *Liar's Poker: Rising Through the Wreckage on Wall Street.* New York: W. W. Norton, 1989.

64. Interview with Paula Orlowski Blair.

Chapter 47: White Nights

1. Berkshire Hathaway letter to shareholders, 1990; Michael Lewis, "The Temptation of St. Warren," *New Republic,* February 17, 1992.

2. At the University of Notre Dame, spring 1991. Cited in Linda Grant, "The $4-Billion Regular Guy: Junk Bonds, No. Greenmail, Never. Warren Buffett Invests Money the Old-Fashioned Way," *Los Angeles Times,* April 7, 1991.

3. In "How to Tame the Casino Economy," *Washington Post,* December 7, 1986, Buffett advocated a 100% confiscatory tax on profits from the sale of stocks or derivative instruments that the holder has owned for less than a year.

4. Linda Grant, "The $4-Billion Regular Guy." Buffett hosannaed Gutfreund in his shareholder letters as well.

5. The principal conflicts inherent in Salomon's business were the undisclosed bid-ask spread that Buffett had objected to while working for his father's firm in Omaha, the conflict between proprietary trades for the firm's account alongside customer trades, the investment banking business built off equity research stock ratings, and the arbitrage department, which could trade on the firm's merger deals. As a board member who made Berkshire's investment decisions, Buffett says he either recused himself from discussions involving deals or did not invest on information he had, yet his board membership did create the appearance of a conflict of interest.

6. The Standard & Poor's 500 index was used as a proxy for the market.

7. In the interest of brevity, the history of portfolio insurance has been shortened considerably. The rout began as the Federal Reserve raised the discount rate over Labor Day weekend 1987. Over the next month, the market wavered and showed signs that investors were nervous. On October 6, the Dow broke a one-day record when it fell 91.55 points. Interest rates continued to climb. The Dow dropped another 108 points on Friday, October 16. Professional money managers spent the weekend pondering. On Black Monday, October 19, many stocks failed to open at all in the early hours of trading and the Dow fell a record-breaking 508 points. The exact cause of the crash remains in dispute. Program trading and equity index futures accelerated the decline, but economic factors, military tensions, comments by Federal Reserve Chairman Alan Greenspan about the dollar, a slowing economy, and other factors have been blamed.

8. Interview with Walter Scott Jr.

9. In this case, the way to be hedged would be to short a broad group or index of stocks.

10. This account is based on both Doris's and Warren's versions of the story.

11. James Sterngold, "Too Far, Too Fast: Salomon Brothers' John Gutfreund," *New York Times,* January 10, 1988.

12. Salomon supplied its clients' debt needs along all points of the maturity ladder. For a bond shop to eliminate its commercial paper department was a baffling decision.

13. Interview with Bob Zeller, chairman of Salomon's compensation committee. Zeller says that Buffett represented the shareholders' interests on the compensation committee with integrity, while trying to determine which employees genuinely deserved reward.

14. John Taylor, "Hard to Be Rich: The Rise and Wobble of the Gutfreunds," *New York,* January 11, 1988.

15. Interviews with John Gutfreund, Gedale Horowitz.

16. Interview with Tom Strauss.

17. While technically the terms of the preferred stock didn't work that way, if Buffett wanted to, he could have found a way to get out.

18. Carol Loomis, "The Inside Story of Warren Buffett," *Fortune,* April 11, 1988. Buffett stated these rumors were false in the article.

19. Robert L. Rose, "We Should All Have an Audience This Receptive Once in Our Lives," *Wall Street Journal,* May 25, 1988.

20. Or 14,172,500 KO shares costing $593 million at an average price of $41.81 (or $5.23 split adjusted for the three 2-for-1 stock splits that occurred between 1988 and 2007). All shares and prices are adjusted for subsequent stock splits.

21. At that point, KO's market value represented 21% of the total market capitalization of Berkshire Hathaway—by far the biggest bet, in dollar terms, that Buffett had ever made on a single stock. Yet in percentage terms, this fit his past pattern.

22. Interview with Howie Buffett.

23. Michael Lewis, *Liar's Poker: Rising Through the Wreckage on Wall Street.* New York: W. W. Norton, 1989.

24. BRK received a 9.25% coupon from the Champion preferred, above the going rate of 7%, and raised debt at 5.5% to fund this $300 million purchase. Champion called the preferred early, but Berkshire was able to convert its shares prior to the call and sell them back to the company at a small discount. Berkshire booked a 19% after-tax capital gain over the six years it held Champion.

25. Linda Sandler, "Heard on the Street: Buffett's Special Role Lands Him Deals Other Holders Can't Get," *Wall Street Journal,* August 14, 1989.

26. From an interview with a friend who said this to Munger.

27. Speech at Terry College of Business, the University of Georgia, July 2001.

28. Interview with John Macfarlane.

29. Interview with Paula Orlowski Blair; Michael Lewis, *Liar's Poker.*

30. Many contracts required posting of collateral or margin, but this did not compensate for the risk of mismarking in the model.

31. Buffett and Munger, 1999 Berkshire Hathaway annual shareholder meeting.

32. Salomon held on for eight years. Phibro sold its share in the JV in 1998. Alan A. Block, "Reflections on resource expropriation and capital flight in the Confederation," *Crime, Law and Social Change,* October 2003.

33. Roger Lowenstein, *When Genius Failed: The Rise and Fall of Long-Term Capital Management.* New York: Random House, 2000.

34. Interview with Eric Rosenfeld.

35. Meriwether characteristically exempted himself from this lucrative deal.

36. Report to the Salomon Inc. Compensation & Employee Benefits Committee, "Securities Segment Proposed 1990, Compensation for Current Managing Directors."

37. This pay deal was still one-sided; the arbs could only break even or win. Buffett's partnership had exposed him to unlimited liability to share in losses if he performed poorly—i.e., his incentives were *truly* aligned with his partners.

38. Michael Siconolfi, "These Days, Biggest Paychecks on Wall Street Don't Go to Chiefs," *Wall Street Journal,* March 26, 1991.

39. Interview with Deryck Maughan.

40. Using different terms. The casino/restaurant analogy was Buffett's. Even if the customer businesses had become profitable, they would have demanded even larger amounts of capital in later years, despite bigger scale and market share, and it is questionable whether their returns would ever have satisfied Buffett.

41. Interview with Eric Rosenfeld.

Chapter 48: Thumb-Sucking, and Its Hollow-Cheeked Result

1. Michael Lewis, *Liar's Poker: Rising Through the Wreckage on Wall Street.* New York: W. W. Norton, 1989.

2. Feuerstein had worked in several senior roles at the SEC, including acting as counsel on Texas Gulf Sulfur, a landmark insider-trading case.

3. Interview with Donald Feuerstein and many others, who confirmed his role and the POD nickname.

4. Interviews with Donald Feuerstein, Tom Strauss, Deryck Maughan, Bill McIntosh, John Macfarlane, Zach Snow, Eric Rosenfeld.

5. Interview with Bill McIntosh.

6. Interview with John Macfarlane.

7. Roger Lowenstein, *Buffett: The Making of an American Capitalist.* New York: Doubleday, 1996, quoting Eric Rosenfeld.

8. Lowenstein, *Buffett,* quoting John McDonough.

9. Interview with Eric Rosenfeld.

10. Interview with Donald Feuerstein.

11. Feuerstein went back into the conference room after talking to Munger and repeated the "thumb-sucking" comment to another lawyer, Zach Snow, without further context. He did not seem to have grasped its significance, according to Snow in an interview. Feuerstein says Munger said, "Warren and I do that all the time." Whatever the wording, neither Feuerstein nor Buffett took alarm at Munger's remark.

12. Interview with Gerald Corrigan.

13. Feuerstein had had breakfast with one director, Gedale Horowitz, and told him much the same story, slightly more informatively, on the morning of August 8. But Horowitz says he also felt misled.

14. Carol Loomis, "Warren Buffett's Wild Ride at Salomon," *Fortune,* October 27, 1997.

15. Munger's later statement that he dragged this out of Feuerstein differs from Feuerstein's recollection. Both agree that Munger was given a clear description. There is no question that Buffett and Munger's overall interpretation of the actions of both Feuerstein and Gutfreund grew harsher as more information came to light.

16. Statement of Salomon Inc., submitted in conjunction with the Testimony of Warren E. Buffett, Chairman and CEO of Salomon, before the Securities Subcommittee, Committee of Banking, Housing and Urban Affairs, U.S. Senate, September 10, 1991.

17. Mercury Asset Management (an affiliate of S.G. Warburg) and the Quantum Fund. When the Federal Reserve contacted Salomon, it was initially because S.G. Warburg had bid in its own name as a primary dealer (Statement of Salomon Inc., September 10, 1991).

18. Charles T. Munger testimony before U.S. Securities & Exchange Commission, "In the Matter of Certain Treasury Notes and Other Government Securities," File No. HO-2513, February 6, 1992.

19. Ibid.

20. Michael Siconolfi, Constance Mitchell, Tom Herman, Michael R. Sesit, David Wessel, "The Big Squeeze: Salomon's Admission of T-Note Infractions Gives Market a Jolt—Firm's Share of One Auction May Have Reached 85%; Investigations Under Way—How Much Did Bosses Know?" *Wall Street Journal,* August 12, 1991.

21. Buffett later said Wachtell, Lipton shared some blame, noting that Wachtell declared effective on August 8 a shelf registration for $5 billion of medium-term notes using a prospectus that was

"purporting to state all material facts about Salomon" as of that date but contained no reference to Mozer's activities or management's inaction. *"If this relaxed position was one that Wachtell, Lipton was conveying to the government and the public through official filings, it is not unlikely that they were conveying something similar to John, although I don't know what,"* Buffett said.

22. Interview with John Macfarlane.

23. Interview with Bob Denham, who discovered this when he moved into Feuerstein's old office.

24. Charles T. Munger testimony before U.S. Securities & Exchange Commission, "In the Matter of Certain Treasury Notes, and Other Government Securities," File No. HO-2513, February 6, 1992.

25. If its lenders failed to renew the firm's loans, Salomon would be forced to liquidate its assets almost overnight. In such a fire sale, assets would sell for a fraction of their carrying value. The apparently invincible balance sheet of Salomon would melt into bankruptcy's black hole immediately.

26. Interview with Bill McIntosh.

27. Interviews with Donald Feuerstein, John Macfarlane.

28. Mozer didn't report an existing net "long," "when-issued" position in Treasury bonds that put it over the limit, and he also submitted another false bid in the name of Tiger Management Company.

29. Mozer denied intentionally manipulating the market. He was suspected of "repo-ing out" the bonds by borrowing cash from customers with the bonds as collateral and making verbal side agreements with these customers that they would not relend the bonds to anyone. That froze the supply of bonds, squeezing the short-sellers. Suspicions of price-fixing dogged Salomon long afterward. There was little doubt that Mozer and his customers had cornered the bonds and created a squeeze. According to Eric Rosenfeld, Salomon's own arb desk was short Treasuries and got burned.

30. Constance Mitchell, "Market Mayhem: Salomon's 'Squeeze' in May Auction Left Many Players Reeling—In St. Louis, One Bond Arb Saw $400,000 Vanish and His Job Go with It—From Confidence to Panic," *Wall Street Journal*, October 31, 1991.

31. Feuerstein didn't find this out right away, even though it was known internally. He blames this omission for his failure to press for a more thorough investigation of the squeeze. Several people, including Meriwether, apparently knew about the "Tiger dinner" (named after one of the hedge-fund customers). However, the "Tiger dinner" did not prove collusion.

32. Interview with John Gutfreund.

33. Or whatever the price was; this is Buffett's general recollection.

34. While this was taking place, Salomon filed a shelf registration statement in connection with a $5 billion senior debt offering, which the directors signed. The filing of a registration statement under these circumstances potentially put the firm in violation of securities laws.

35. Some thought the squeeze may have been simply a matter of timing to make a bet that the Fed was about to ease interest rates, according to Eric Rosenfeld, rather than defiance of the Treasury.

36. Various viewpoints within the firm are drawn from interviews with a number of the principals.

37. Philip Howard, Gutfreund's lawyer, speaking to Ron Insana on CNBC *Inside Opinion*, April 20, 1995.

38. John Gutfreund speaking to Ron Insana, CNBC *Inside Opinion*, April 20, 1995.

39. The auctions of December 27, 1990 (4-year notes), February 7, 1991 (the so-called "billion-dollar practical joke"), and February 21, 1991 (5-year notes) contained false bids. The April 25, 1991, auction included a bid in excess of the amount authorized by a customer. In the May 22, 1991 (2-year-notes) auction, Salomon (Mozer) failed to report a net "long" position to the government, as required, which fueled suspicions of a cover-up of market manipulation, but proof of market manipulation was never found.

40. Interview with Zach Snow, who also testified to this under oath in 1994.

41. Interview with Deryck Maughan.

42. Interview with Jerry Corrigan.

43. Even though he was Mozer's boss, Meriwether did not have the authority to fire him; one managing director could not fire another. Only Gutfreund could do that.

44. Interview with Bill McIntosh.

45. Interviews with John Macfarlane, Deryck Maughan.

46. Spread-widening of ten to twenty basis points only attracted more sellers. As the afternoon wore on, the traders widened the spread until finally they were offering only ninety cents on the dollar for the notes. The price implied a reasonably high probability of default.

47. The firm would still do business as an "agent," which meant it would buy only if it had another buyer in hand to which it could resell the notes.

48. Kurt Eichenwald, "Wall Street Sees a Serious Threat to Salomon Bros.—ILLEGAL BIDDING FALLOUT—High-Level Resignations and Client Defections Feared—Firm's Stock Drops," *New York Times*, August 16, 1991.

49. Interview with Jerry Corrigan.

50. Interview with Jerry Corrigan.

51. Interview with Jerry Corrigan.

52. Interview with Jerry Corrigan. He says that Strauss and Gutfreund had had more than one routine conversation with him between April and June without mentioning anything, and he no longer trusted them.

53. Buffett arrived in New York between 2:30 and 3:00 p.m., during which time the press release would have been drafted and ready to go.

54. From Salomon press release dated August 16, 1991: "In order to give the Salomon Inc., board of directors maximum flexibility, they are prepared to submit their resignations at a special meeting of the board."

55. Interview with Eric Rosenfeld.

56. Interviews with Bill McIntosh, Tom Strauss, Deryck Maughan.

57. Interview with Tom Strauss.

58. Interview with Jerry Corrigan.

59. Interview with Ron Olson.

60. Warren Buffett testimony, "In the Matter of Arbitration Between John H. Gutfreund against Salomon Inc., and Salomon Brothers Inc." Sessions 13 & 14, November 29, 1993.

61. This is Buffett's recollection of Gutfreund's remarks. (From Warren Buffett testimony, "In the Matter of Arbitration Between John H. Gutfreund against Salomon Inc., and Salomon Brothers Inc.," Sessions 13 & 14, November 29, 1993.

62. Interview with Tom Strauss.

63. Carol Loomis, "Warren Buffett's Wild Ride at Salomon."

64. On October 8, 1991, he was displaced when the Walton family, owners of Wal-Mart stock, took over spots 3-7; Buffett became number 8. Entertainment mogul John Kluge and Bill Gates occupied the top two spots.

65. Through a routine letter to Mercury Asset Management when the Treasury Department discovered that Mercury, together with its affiliate S. G. Warburg & Co., had submitted bids for greater than the 35% limit rule for the auction. Mozer had submitted one of these bids without Mercury's authority. Mozer was copied on this letter and covered it up by telling Mercury that Salomon had mistakenly submitted this bid in its name—and was going to correct it, so no need to bother responding to the Treasury. (Statement of Salomon Inc., submitted in conjunction with the Testimony of Warren E. Buffett, Chairman and CEO of Salomon. Before the Securities Subcommittee, Committee of Banking, Housing and Urban Affairs, U.S. Senate, September 10, 1991.)

66. Interview with Deryck Maughan.

67. Speech to students in 1994 at University of North Carolina Kenan-Flagler Business School.

68. The one exception was Stanley Shopkorn, who ran the equities division and, by others' recollections, thought he should get the job.

69. Michael Lewis, *Liar's Poker*.

70. Ibid.

71. Swope fired them all and turned the firm into a radical Black Power, "Truth & Soul" agency.

72. Interview with Deryck Maughan.

73. Interview with Eric Rosenfeld, who says no threats were made. But because Meriwether was not bound by a noncompete, it was obvious that the whole arb team would leave sooner or later.

74. Gutfreund told Buffett that Susan was telling him he was unemployable.

75. Interview with Philip Howard. Warren Buffett testimony, "In the Matter of Arbitration Between John H. Gutfreund against Salomon Inc., and Salomon Brothers Inc.," Sessions 13 & 14, November 29, 1993.

76. Interview with Warren Buffett; Warren Buffett testimony, "In the Matter of Arbitration Between John H. Gutfreund against Salomon Inc., and Salomon Brothers Inc.," Sessions 13 & 14, November 29, 1993, cited this remark as evidence that Gutfreund knew he did not have a deal. (Munger's version of the quote was "I won't let you guys screw me.")

77. Interview with Philip Howard.

78. Warren Buffett testimony, "In the Matter of Arbitration Between John H. Gutfreund against Salomon Inc., and Salomon Brothers Inc.," Sessions 13 & 14.

79. Warren Buffett, Charles T. Munger, testimonies, "In the Matter of Arbitration Between John H. Gutfreund against Salomon Inc., and Salomon Brothers Inc.," Sessions 13 & 14, 33 & 34.

80. Charles T. Munger testimony, "In the Matter of Arbitration Between John H. Gutfreund against Salomon Inc., and Salomon Brothers Inc.," Sessions 33 & 34, December 22, 1993.

81. The Japanese bond market would not open until 7:30 P.M. EST, but Japanese over-the-counter trading would begin as early as 5 P.M., at which point lenders would start selling Salomon's paper, effectively calling its loans.

82. Interview with John Macfarlane.

83. Warren Buffett testimony, "In the Matter of Arbitration Between John H. Gutfreund against Salomon Inc., and Salomon Brothers Inc.," Sessions 13 & 14, November 29, 1993.

84. Interview with Jerry Corrigan.

85. Jerry Corrigan and Paul Volcker contributed insight to this topic.

86. At the time, it was well understood that Buffett had "parlayed his considerable reputation into a partial rescission of the order," although what that meant to him was not obvious. (Saul Hansell, Beth Selby, Henny Sender, "Who Should Run Salomon Brothers?" *Institutional Investor,* Vol. 25, No. 10, September 1, 1991.)

87. Interview with Deryck Maughan.

88. Interview with Charlie Munger.

89. Interview with Deryck Maughan.

90. Hansell, Selby, and Sender, "Who Should Run Salomon?"

91. Ibid.

Chapter 49: The Angry Gods

1. Interview with Paula Orlowski Blair.

2. Interview with Bill McLucas.

3. This is Buffett's recollection of the quote, but Brady's view that Buffett would not leave was corroborated by other regulators.

4. Interview with Paula Orlowski Blair. She thought it funny that her new boss wanted to turn her into a private eye.

5. Interviews with Donald Feuerstein, Bob Denham. Denham says only that they agreed a change was needed.

6. Warren Buffett testified to this in "In the Matter of Arbitration Between John H. Gutfreund against Salomon Inc., and Salomon Brothers Inc.," Sessions 13 & 14, November 29, 1993.

7. During John Gutfreund's arbitration hearing.

8. The firm became Munger, Tolles & Olson in 1986.

9. Law-firm sources and former employees give Buffett all of the credit for this idea, despite the law firm's putative role.

10. Drexel Burnham Lambert had failed after its indictment. Kidder, Peabody was sold to PaineWebber. Salomon's highly leveraged balance sheet put the firm in even greater jeopardy.

11. Interview with Ron Olson.

12. Ibid.

13. Interview with Frank Barron. Rudolph Giuliani, U.S. Attorney for the Southern District of New York, had pressed for Drexel Burnham Lambert to waive the privilege, but the firm did not.

14. Charlie Munger later acknowledged the morally fraught—at best, ambiguous—situation, saying he and Buffett had no choice but to assist in criminal investigation and prosecution of potentially innocent employees. "When the final chapter is written, the behavior evinced by Salomon will be followed in other, similar cases," he said. "People will be smart enough to realize this is the response we want—super-prompt—even if it means cashiering some people who may not deserve it." Lawrie P. Cohen, "Buffett Shows Tough Side to Salomon and Gutfreund," *Wall Street Journal*, November 8, 1991.

15. Warren Buffett letter to Norman Pearlstine, November 18, 1991.

16. Buffett testified to this in "In the Matter of Arbitration Between John H. Gutfreund against Salomon Inc., and Salomon Brothers Inc.," Sessions 13 and 14, November 29, 1993.

17. "I didn't fire them on the spot," said Olson in an interview. "I was a little more subtle than that."

18. House Committee on Energy and Commerce—Telecommunications & Finance Subcommittee, September 4, 1991, regarding securities trading violations by Salomon Brothers and implications for government securities market reform legislation.

19. Maughan had to go back to Washington a few weeks later to testify by himself. "The sea did not part," he says, "and I got thoroughly wet."

20. "Our goal is going to be that stated many decades ago by J. P. Morgan, who wished to see his bank transact 'first-class business in a first-class way.' " Warren Buffett, "SALOMON INC—A report by the Chairman on the Company's Position and Outlook." (This wording was also used in a letter to Salomon Inc. shareholders as reprinted in the *Wall Street Journal*, November 1, 1991.)

21. Senate Subcommittee on Securities Committee on Banking, Housing, and Urban Affairs—Hearing on the Activities of Salomon Brothers Inc., in Treasury Bond Activities, Wednesday, September 11, 1991.

22. At the time, sixty-five lenders had stopped entering into repurchase agreements with Salomon, and the firm's commercial paper balance was falling toward zero. One major counterparty, Security Pacific, was refusing to do daylight foreign-exchange trades without posting of collateral. Buffett says this was his absolute low point. The news media never picked up this story, which, if reported, could have kicked off a panic.

23. Interview with John Macfarlane. The cost of funds motivated traders to run off uneconomic trades. Ultimately the rate went to 400 basis points over Fed Funds rate. The short-term capital-intensive trades like the "carry-trade" (interest arbitrage) ran off.

24. Interview with John Macfarlane.

25. Senate Subcommittee on Securities Committee on Banking, Housing, and Urban Affairs—Hearing on the Activities of Salomon Brothers, Inc., in Treasury Bond Activities, Wednesday, September 11, 1991.

26. By then, many other people, including Denham and Munger, had found out about the Sternlight letter, but they say everybody thought somebody else had told Buffett or that he somehow knew. Buffett and Munger were also incensed to learn that at the June audit committee meeting, with Feuerstein present, Arthur Andersen represented that no events had taken place that were required to be reported to the SEC or the New York Stock Exchange. While Wachtell, Lipton had indeed taken that position, this statement, with hindsight, was manifestly untrue.

27. Employees asked how much Buffett and Munger understood about the workings of Salomon before August 1991, while serving on the board, uniformly said "not much," or words to that

effect, and that information was skillfully meted out to the board so that much of the firm's messiness never surfaced.

28. Lawrie P. Cohen, "Buffett Shows Tough Side to Salomon."

29. Interview with Gladys Kaiser.

30. Buffett cannot remember who did this—although it was neither Astrid, who retires early, nor someone from the office. He thinks it must have been some other local friend or neighbor.

31. Although securities underwriters sell service, price, and expertise, ultimately they are financial guarantors. Salomon's financial-strength ratings had been downgraded. With a criminal indictment and its primary dealership threatened, that the firm managed to retain any banking clients remains one of Wall Street's great survival stories. It did so by giving up lead positions and switching to co-lead, in effect taking on a supporting-cast-member role. Nevertheless, its market share fell from 8% to 2%.

32. The Treasury Department/Fed study also revealed that, over a period beginning in early 1986, Salomon had bought more than half the bonds issued in 30 out of 230 auctions (Louis Uchitelle, Stephen Labaton, "When the Regulators Stood Still," New York Times, September 22, 1991).

33. Warren Buffett testimony, "In the Matter of Arbitration Between John H. Gutfreund against Salomon Inc., and Salomon Brothers Inc.," Session 13 & 14, November 29, 1993.

34. Contracts differ by employee, by company, and by state, and the indemnification provisions use broad wording that is subject to interpretation, but in general, corporate officers accept the legal risk that goes with their position on the condition that their employers pay legal fees unless they are convicted of fraud or other criminal wrongdoing or have engaged in willful misconduct. Salomon's action was highly unusual at the time and remains unusual. In 2005, KPMG's refusal to pay its partners' legal fees became the subject of lawsuits. In July 2007, a U.S. federal judge dismissed a case against thirteen KPMG employees for promoting aggressive tax shelters, because he determined that the government had strong-armed KPMG into denying them legal payments.

35. Interview with Otto Obermaier.

36. Ibid.

37. Interview with Gary Naftalis.

38. Interview with Otto Obermaier.

39. Letter to Salomon Inc. shareholders as reprinted in the Wall Street Journal, November 1, 1991.

40. Interview with Paula Orlowski Blair.

41. Interviews with Gladys Kaiser and Bob Denham.

42. Salomon advertisement in the Wall Street Journal, November 1, 1991. All of Salomon's growth in earnings for several years had been given back to employees. Salomon performed in the bottom third of stocks in its market-cap class. The third-quarter-income statement would have been drenched with red ink had not the lower bonus pool reversed it. The previous "share the wealth" approach subsidized money-losers so that everyone was richly paid. Buffett's biggest change was to link bonuses to individual and division performance. For the five years ending December 31, 1991, Salomon Inc.'s stock ranked 437th in performance among S&P's top 500 stocks. (1991 Salomon Inc., 10K)

43. Interview with Deryck Maughan.

44. For decades, as a partnership, it had—literally—been run for the employees. It was the inherent separation of capital and labor at a publicly owned investment bank that was the problem.

45. Obermaier later wrote "Do the Right Thing: But if a Company Doesn't It Can Limit the Damage," Barron's, December 14, 1992.

46. The same was not true of the May two-year-note squeeze, in which several small firms were bankrupted. Had it ever been proven that Mozer colluded with the hedge funds to corner the market or submitted false bids in that auction, Salomon's and the individuals' penalties doubtless would have been more severe; the whole story might have ended differently.

47. Interviews with Frank Barron and Bill McLucas. McLucas confirms the gist but can't recall the exact words.

48. Mozer served his four months after pleading guilty to lying to the Federal Reserve Bank of New York. The SEC and prosecutors took no action against Feuerstein.

49. Gutfreund was also barred from heading a firm without SEC approval.

50. Interview with Paula Orlowski Blair.

51. In fact, Jerry Corrigan did not lift the full ban on Salomon until August 1992.

52. CNBC *Inside Opinion,* Ron Insana interview with Gutfreund, April 20, 1995.

53. Interview with John Gutfreund.

54. Interview with Charlie Munger.

55. The arbitrators were John J. Curran, Harry Aronsohn, and Matthew J. Tolan.

56. Interview with Frank Barron.

57. Those who have spent any significant amount of time with Munger will instantly recognize the sensation of talking to him when his head is turned off, while something occasionally pierces his band of indifference. *"It's hard to pierce Charlie's band of indifference,"* says Buffett. *"I can tell you that."*

58. Charles T. Munger testimony, "In the Matter of Arbitration Between John H. Gutfreund against Salomon, Inc., and Salomon Brothers, Inc.," Sessions 33 & 34, December 22, 1993.

59. Interviews with Sam Butler, Frank Barron.

60. Interview with Frank Barron.

Chapter 50: The Lottery

1. Michael Lewis, "The Temptation of St. Warren," *New Republic,* February 17, 1992.

2. Ron Suskind, "Legend Revisited: Warren Buffett's Aura as Folksy Sage Masks Tough, Polished Man," *Wall Street Journal,* November 8, 1991.

3. Interview with Bill Gates.

4. Ibid.

5. Grinnell College had made a lot of money from its Intel stock but had already sold it. Noyce died June 3, 1990.

6. Interview with Bill Gates.

7. Interview with Bill Ruane.

8. Interview with Don Graham.

9. Gates was right; Kodak *was* toast. From January 1990 to December 2007, Kodak stock rose a measly 20%, barely more than 1% a year. The S&P over the same period rose 315%. Berkshire Hathaway rose 1,627%. Microsoft rose 6,853%.

10. Interview with Bill Gates.

11. Ibid.

12. Statistics courtesy of Berkshire Hathaway.

13. Interview with Louis Blumkin.

14. A Scott Fetzer product.

15. Interviews with Kathleen Cole, Susie Buffett Jr.

16. Interview with Kathleen Cole.

17. Interview with Howie Buffett.

18. Interview with Susie Buffett Jr.

19. Interview with Bill Gates.

20. Interview with Sharon Osberg.

21. The first week the author started working on this book, she came downstairs to the hotel lobby to find the same package.

22. Interviews with Sharon Osberg and Astrid Buffett, who recalls "Sharon was just beside herself."

23. Interview with Sharon Osberg.

24. Interviews with Astrid Buffett, Dick and Mary Holland.

25. Interview with Dody Waugh-Booth.

26. Carnegie built 2,509 libraries (costing $56 million) and established other public works using over 90% of his $480 million steel-made wealth.

27. Bill Ruane and others recalled this speech.

28. Buffett, characteristically, uses both low and high numbers higher than the current population number (a margin of safety against looking like an alarmist) even though some experts argue that the "carrying capacity" has already been exceeded.

29. Organizations such as the International Humanist and Ethical Union and Planned Parenthood routinely took this position before 1974. See Paige Whaley Eager, *Global Population Policy: From Population Control to Reproductive Rights*. Burlington, Vt.: Ashgate Publishing Ltd., 2004.

30. Garrett Hardin, "The Tragedy of the Commons," *Science*, Vol. 162, No. 3859, December 13, 1968. Hardin's theory was essentially a restatement of the "prisoner's dilemma," which also addresses cooperation and "cheating" as covered in references on that subject. In the 1970s it was assumed that economic progress would accelerate population growth, that population growth would prevent economic progress. The earth's "carrying capacity" was assumed to be essentially fixed, rather than at least somewhat flexible through the use of technology and market forces, incorrect assumptions that caused such forecasts to peg the dates of critical population levels too early.

31. Garrett Hardin, "A Second Sermon on the Mount," from *Perspectives in Biology and Medicine*, 1963.

32. Nevertheless, some remnants of the eugenics movement remained alive, and by the millennial era, developments in genetic, genomic, and reproductive science had raised complicated questions about the idea.

33. The historic linkage between "population control," the eugenics movement, and racism is detailed by Allan Chase in *The Legacy of Malthus: The Social Costs of the New Scientific Racism* (New York: Alfred A. Knopf, 1977). While a full treatment of these issues is beyond the scope of this book, what seems clear, from his change in terminology, steering of the Buffett Foundation, and gradual distancing from the Hardin camp, was Buffett's disenchantment with the Malthusian views of Hardin because of their eugenics implications. (Hardin's personal stationery featured a small U.S. map around the words "Quality of the Population.")

34. In a highly controversial move, the Buffett Foundation had paid half the first-year costs to bring the RU-486 abortion pill to the United States.

35. From Eager's *Global Population Policy: From Population Control to Reproductive Rights*, which chronicles the gradual rejection of neo-Malthusianism and coercive population control methods in favor of voluntary, evolutionary changes in birth rates through economic development, reproductive rights, and an emphasis on women's health.

36. In "Foundation Grows: Buffetts Fund Efforts for Population Control" (*Omaha World-Herald*, January 10, 1988), Bob Dorr quotes Susie as saying, "Warren likes numbers . . . he likes to see concrete results, and you can see them [numbers] change" to explain her husband's interest in groups such as Planned Parenthood and the Population Institute.

37. A similar term, "Ovarian Roulette," was apparently first used by Dr. Reginald Lourie of Children's Hospital, Washington, D.C., at a hearing of the Committee on Government Operations, United States, "Effect of Population Growth on Natural Resources and the Environment," September 15–16, 1969, in a discussion with Garrett Hardin, to describe a mother who takes the risk of an unwanted pregnancy by not using birth control (and the term has since been used by Responsible Wealth). However, it is the second word—"lottery" versus "roulette"—that changes a bad choice to bad luck: from a child who is born unwanted to a woman who trusts to random chance, to a child who is born in cruel circumstances because of random chance.

38. "I Didn't Do It Alone," a report by Chuck Collins's organization, Responsible Wealth.

39. See John Rawls, *A Theory of Justice,* Cambridge: The Belknap Press of Harvard University Press, 1971. The Ovarian Lottery resembles Rawls's view, which is a form of determinism—and assumes that much, though not necessarily all, of what happens to people is *determined* by the present and past, for example, through their genes, or the luck of where they are born and when. The opposite of determinism is free will. From the days of the earliest philosophers, mankind has been debating whether free will exists. Philosophers also debate whether it exists on a scale

or is irreconcilable with determinism. Critic Robert Nozick, in *Anarchy, State, and Utopia*, gives the case for irreconcilability in a critique of Rawls that more or less says that economist Adam Smith's invisible hand gives people what they have earned and deserved (*Anarchy, State and Utopia*. New York: Basic Books, 1974). All true libertarians believe in free will and deny absolutely that determinism exists. Since economic policy is so influenced by these ideas, the topic is worth understanding; for example, it sheds light on the debate over how Alan Greenspan's libertarian leanings influenced Federal Reserve policy that led to recent debt-fueled asset bubbles. Likewise, the debate over eugenics in genomism and reprogenetics resounds with issues of determinism and free will.

40. Interview with Bill Gates.

41. Interview with Bill Gates.

Chapter 51: To Hell with the Bear

1. Anthony Bianco, "The Warren Buffett You Don't Know," *BusinessWeek*, July 5, 1999.

2. In 1993, 707 new issues raised $41.4 billion. In 1994, 608 IPOs raised $28.5 billion, the second-most-productive year in the past quarter century. The third-best year for IPOs had been 1992, when 517 issues raised $24.1 billion. (Securities Data Co. of Newark, N.J.)

3. The Buffetts made other philanthropic gifts using Susie's stock, as well as funding the Buffett Foundation.

4. Berkshire Hathaway press release, February 13, 1996.

5. Interviews with Dana Neuman, Mark Millard.

6. The employees' pay could not really be fully aligned with shareholders. Unlike at the *Buffalo News*, for example, the employees' base pay at a bank is too low to compensate for the labor value of their time that is owed by the shareholders. In effect, much of the bonus is really salary. The reason that a plan that requires employees to work almost for free in a bad year to compensate for "excessive" bonuses in other years cannot succeed is that it transfers some of the risk assumed by capital onto the backs of labor. The bonus structure of Wall Street—without the glue of partnership—is inherently problematic.

7. To be considered an arbitrage, two trades must take place simultaneously to eliminate market risk. Buying a stock and selling it later is not an arbitrage. Buying cocoa beans in Ecuador and selling them in San Diego is not an arbitrage.

8. Interview with Deryck Maughan.

9. Roger Lowenstein, *When Genius Failed: The Rise and Fall of Long-Term Capital Management*. New York: Random House, 2000.

10. In July 1998, Weill shut down Salomon's bond arbitrage unit. One could argue that it was Travelers' subsequent merger with Citicorp—which provided cheap capital—that made the firm a serious competitor in those businesses. Looked at another way, Travelers paid a high price to enter a business with high barriers to entry, and subsequently exploited its capital and scale advantage. Citigroup dropped the Salomon name in 2001.

11. Carol Loomis, "A House Built on Sand," *Fortune*, October 26, 1998.

12. Interview with Charlie Munger.

13. Lowenstein, in *When Genius Failed*, estimated that these returns were achieved through leverage; Long-Term's cash-on-cash return was only about 1%. This low return, multiplied fifty to a hundred times through borrowing, appeared extraordinarily profitable.

14. In *When Genius Failed*, Lowenstein drew this conclusion after extensive interviews with Meriwether's former team.

15. Roger Lowenstein, *When Genius Failed*. Shorting it as a collection of stocks would not work because of a basis mismatch between Berkshire and the offsetting hedgeable positions. Berkshire was a collection of wholly owned businesses fueled by an insurance company that also owned some stocks, not a quasi-mutual fund.

16. Roger Lowenstein, *When Genius Failed*.

17. Stock or merger arbitrage is a bet on whether a merger will close. Merger-arb specialists talk to

lawyers and investment bankers and specialize in scuttlebutt. Their bets are based partly on knowledge about a deal, not just statistics about how typical deals have done.

18. Interview with Eric Rosenfeld; Lowenstein, *When Genius Failed.*

19. Michael Siconolfi, Anita Raghavan, and Mitchell Pacelle, "All Bets Are Off: How Salesmanship and Brainpower Failed at Long-Term Capital," *Wall Street Journal,* November 16, 1998.

20. Interview with Eric Rosenfeld.

21. The Standard & Poor's index was down 19% since July and the NASDAQ down by more than 25%.

22. John Meriwether letter to investors, September 2, 1998.

23. Warren Buffett letter to Ron Ferguson, September 2, 1998.

24. Hence, don't try to make it back the way you lost it.

25. Interview with Joe Brandon.

26. Roger Lowenstein, in *When Genius Failed,* includes, as do other accounts, an interesting sidebar about the role of Goldman Sachs, which, as capital-raiser for the firm, also sent in a mysterious "trader" who spent days downloading Long-Term's positions into a laptop and making mysterious cell-phone calls. Afterward, Long-Term's partners bitterly blamed their demise on predatory behavior by competitors.

27. According to one partner, the lawyer was dubious about the rushed process, saying maybe there was some trickery involved, and wanting to slow things down and take more time to look over the details.

28. Roger Lowenstein, *When Genius Failed.*

29. Michael Lewis, "How the Eggheads Cracked," *New York Times Magazine,* January 24, 1999.

30. Interviews with Fred Gitelman, Sharon Osberg.

31. After three 0.25% interest-rate cuts—September 29, October 15, and October 17—the market leapt 24% from its low on August 31 of 7,539 to an all-time high of 9,374 on October 23.

32. Michael Lewis, "How the Eggheads Cracked."

33. Roger Lowenstein, *When Genius Failed.*

34. Interview with Eric Rosenfeld.

35. The Federal Reserve's instant and dramatic cut of interest rates gave rise to a concept called the "Greenspan Put," the idea that the Federal Reserve would swamp the market with liquidity to bail out investors in a crisis. The Greenspan Put theoretically encourages people to worry less about risk. Greenspan denied there was a Greenspan Put. "It takes a good deal longer for the cycle to expand than for it to contract," he said. "Therefore we are innocent." (Reuters, October 1, 2007, quoting Greenspan speaking in London.)

Chapter 52: Chickenfeed

1. Kurt Eichenwald, *The Informant.* New York: Broadway, 2000. Unbeknownst to Howie, Andreas reportedly made an illegal donation in response to at least one request for a political contribution that Howie had passed along as part of his job, shrugging off the fine as the cost of doing business.

2. Interview with Howie Buffett.

3. Ibid.; Scott Kilman, Thomas M. Burton, and Richard Gibson, "Seeds of Doubt: An Executive Becomes Informant for the FBI, Stunning Giant ADM—Price Fixing in Agribusiness Is Focus of Major Probe; Other Firms Subpoenaed—A Microphone in the Briefcase," *Wall Street Journal,* July 11, 1995; Sharon Walsh, "Tapes Aid U.S. in Archer Daniels Midland Probe; Recordings Made by Executive Acting as FBI Informant Lead to Seizure of Company Files," *Washington Post,* July 11, 1995; Ronald Henkoff and Richard Behar, "Andreas's Mole Problem Is Becoming a Mountain," *Fortune,* August 21, 1995; Mark Whitacre, "My Life as a Corporate Mole for the FBI," *Fortune,* September 4, 1995.

4. Interview with Kathleen Cole.

5. Astrid was going to be well taken care of by Warren, too, although, as he says about the apparent willingness of his fans to buy any article belonging to him—his wallet, his car; *"She's got one of my wisdom teeth. It's the ugliest thing you've ever seen. That's her ace in the hole."*

6. Interview with Bill Gates.

7. Every board member interviewed reached some variation of this conclusion, no matter where they stood on later events.

8. Speaking at the 1998 Berkshire Hathaway shareholder meeting.

9. At the time, NetJets marketed itself both as NetJets and by its legal name, Executive Jet, Inc. It was renamed NetJets in 2002.

10. Interviews with sources; Anthony Bianco, "The Warren Buffett You Don't Know," *BusinessWeek*, July 5, 1999.

11. The business requires a "core fleet" of redundant aircraft, so expensive that running a fractional jet company is by definition unprofitable unless done on a huge scale (or used as a loss-leader by an aircraft manufacturer or other company with a tie-in product).

12. It cost Berkshire over nine times what it paid for the remaining half of GEICO almost three years earlier. The GEICO purchase doubled Berkshire's existing float (to $7.6 billion), while Gen Re tripled that (to $22.7 billion).

13. Interview with Tad Montross.

14. BRK paid approximately three times book value, a premium to prevailing prices at the time. The reinsurance business became more competitive after this acquisition, and multiples have since declined.

15. Berkshire Hathaway 1997 annual shareholders' meeting, May 5, 1997.

16. Shawn Tully, "Stock May Be Surging Toward an Earnings Chasm," *Fortune*, February 1, 1999.

17. At the companies' June 19, 1998, press conference, as quoted in "Is There a Bear on Mr. Buffett's Farm?" *New York Times*, August 9, 1998.

18. Buffett's comments in Anthony Bianco's July 5, 1999, *BusinessWeek* cover story, "The Warren Buffett You Don't Know": " 'Charlie and I don't talk a lot anymore,' acknowledges Buffett, who says he did not even bother to consult his vice-chairman before making the epochal Gen Re acquisition."

19. BRK dropped 4.2% on news of the deal. Over a month later, it was down 15% versus a flat market. Setting an exchange ratio implicitly required a view on equities and interest rates, as well as the underlying businesses' prospects. What investors could not know was the relative weighting of these factors.

20. On August 22, 1997, Wells Fargo stock nosedived after Berkshire Hathaway reclassified it from the publicly filed form 13-F to the confidential disclosure to the SEC, creating the appearance that Buffett had sold his position in Wells Fargo. The SEC announced that it would consider tightening the confidentiality rules. In June 1998, the SEC announced it was tightening its "13F" rule that had allowed Buffett to file confidentially for a year while building large stock positions. Although the SEC did not absolutely rule out confidential filings, Buffett heard the footsteps. Berkshire Hathaway fought an aggressive battle with the SEC over this issue as its confidential filings were denied, and lost. In 1999, Berkshire filed confidentiality requests each quarter along with its regular 13-F forms containing positions that were not confidential. The SEC made a single announcement relating to these three filings that certain of the positions they contained must be publicly disclosed. Buffett's right to make a profit presumably was not part of the SEC's deliberations. The SEC's interest is to protect investors. While the SEC staff had long held that it is desirable to prevent extraordinary fluctuations in stock prices unrelated to fundamental factors so that investors do not profit or suffer as a result, investors' right to know the identity of a company's largest shareholders outweighed that.

21. Interview with Herbert Allen.

22. Ibid.

23. Ivester did not respond to repeated requests for interviews.

24. Betsy Morris and Patricia Sellers, "What Really Happened at Coke," *Fortune*, January 10, 2000.

25. Interview with Sharon Osberg.

26. Betsy Morris, "Doug Is It," *Fortune*, May 25, 1998, and Patricia Sellers, "Crunch Time for Coke," *Fortune*, July 19, 1999.

27. This is Herbert Allen's version of the conversation. Buffett doesn't recall the exact details.

28. "They never sat down, never even removed their overcoats. In tones frostier than the air outside, they told him they had lost confidence in him." Constance L. Hays, *The Real Thing: Truth and Power at the Coca-Cola Company.* New York: Random House, 2004. Buffett and Allen dispute this version and say they sat down and removed their coats. But, they say, it was indeed a very short meeting, with no chitchat.

29. Had the board supported him, it would have left Ivester a weakened CEO. He would also have been gambling that Allen and Buffett would not resign from the board, an instantly fatal blow. Allen and Buffett were also gambling that if Ivester threw himself on the board's mercy and survived, it would not be for long.

30. Interview with James Robinson, former CEO of American Express and Coca-Cola board member.

31. KO stock dropped 14% in two days.

32. Betsy Morris and Patricia Sellers, "What Really Happened at Coke."

33. Martin Sosnoff, "Buffett: What Went Wrong?" *Forbes,* December 31, 1999.

34. Andrew Barry, "What's Wrong, Warren?" *Barron's,* December 27, 1999.

35. Andy Serwer, "The Oracle of Everything," *Fortune,* November 11, 2002.

36. Interview with Kathleen Cole.

37. Interview with Susie Buffett Jr.

38. Interview with Peter Buffett.

39. Interview with Howie Buffett.

40. Interviews with Howie Buffett, Peter Buffett, Susie Buffett Jr.

Chapter 54: Semicolon

1. The expected profit on the deal was 90%; i.e., the premium covered odds that the lottery would hit 1 out of 10 times whereas in fact it was expected to hit less than 1 out of 100 times.

2. Every 10% change in KO was equivalent to 2.5% of BRK (a percentage that is representative over time), but the stocks often traded almost in tandem—especially when there was bad news at Coca-Cola—as if BRK and KO were one and the same.

3. Beth Kwon, "Buffett Health Scrape Illustrates Power—or Myth—of Message Boards," TheStreet .com, February 11, 2000. The story made the *Financial Times* say, "Warren Buffett may not be sick, but his share price is," in the "Lex" column, February 12, 2000. *Financial Times* described the rap on Buffett not buying tech stocks as a "serious charge."

4. Ed Anderson, "Thesis vs. Antithesis: Hegel, Bagels, and Market Theories," *Computer Reseller News,* March 13, 2000.

5. Warren Buffett and Charlie Munger, "We Don't Get Paid for *Activity,* Just for Being *Right.* As to How *Long* We'll Wait, We'll Wait *Indefinitely,*" *Outstanding Investor Digest,* Vol. XIII, Nos. 3 & 4, September 24, 1998, and "We Should All Have Lower Expectations—In Fact, Make That *Dramatically* Lower. . . . ," *Outstanding Investor Digest,* Vol. XIV, Nos. 2 & 3, December 10, 1999.

6. "Focus: Warren Buffett," *Guardian,* March 15, 2000 (emphasis added).

7. E. S. Browning and Aaron Lucchetti, "The New Chips: Conservative Investors Finally Are Saying: Maybe Tech Isn't a Fad," *Wall Street Journal,* March 10, 2000. The *Journal* cited another investor as saying, "It's like when the railroads started up and were changing the whole face of the nation." Yes, it was much like that. Speculation in railroad stocks led directly to the financial panics of 1869, 1873, and 1901. The Erie railroad and Northern Pacific stock corners were only two episodes in the long history of colorful financial chicanery surrounding railroad stocks.

8. Gretchen Morgenson, "If You Think Last Week Was Wild," *New York Times,* March 19, 2000. Another sign that the game was up: On March 20, *Fortune* ran a cover story by Jeremy Garcia and Feliciano Kahn, "Presto Chango: Sales Are HUGE!" accusing many dotcoms of using accounting legerdemain to inflate sales—counting marketing expenses as sales, treating barter revenues as sales, and booking revenues before contracts were signed.

9. Interview with Sue James Stewart.

10. Buffett, who usually dealt with uncomfortable issues by joking about them, ended the 1999

Berkshire annual report (written winter 2000) by saying that he loved running Berkshire, and *"if enjoying life promotes longevity, Methuselah's record is in jeopardy."*

11. This is sort of an inside joke at Berkshire Hathaway.

12. David Henry, "Buffett Still Wary of Tech Stocks—Berkshire Hathaway Chief Happy to Skip 'Manias,'" *USA Today,* May 1, 2000.

13. Buffett measures his performance not by the company's stock price, which he didn't control, but by increase in net worth per share, which he did. There is a link between these two measures over long periods of time. In 1999, book value per share had grown only ½ of 1%. But for the acquisition of General Re, book value per share would have shrunk. Meanwhile, the stock market as a whole was up 21%. Buffett called it a fluke that book value had increased at all, pointing out that in some years it will inevitably decrease. Yet only 4 times in 35 years under Buffett, and not once since 1980, had Berkshire done worse than the market by this measure.

14. James P. Miller, "Buffett Scoffs at Tech Sector's High Valuation," *Wall Street Journal,* May 1, 2000.

15. David Henry, "Buffett Still Wary of Tech Stocks."

16. Interviews with Joseph Brandon, Tad Montross.

17. Interviews with Bill Gates, Sharon Osberg.

18. Amy Kover, "Warren Buffett: Revivalist," *Fortune,* May 29, 2000.

19. Interview with Bill Gates.

20. Berkshire Hathaway press release, June 21, 2000.

Chapter 55: The Last Kay Party

1. Philip J. Kaplan, *F'd Companies: Spectacular Dot-com Flameouts.* New York: Simon & Schuster, 2002.

2. At the end of 2000, Berkshire had spent more than $8 billion buying companies and still had $5.2 billion in cash and cash equivalents, along with $33 billion in fixed maturity securities and $38 billion in stocks.

3. Berkshire Hathaway letter to shareholders, 2000.

4. Interview with Susie Buffett Jr.

5. Interviews with Barry Diller, Don Graham, Susie Buffett Jr.

6. Marcia Vickers, Geoffrey Smith, Peter Coy, Mara Der Hovanseian, "When Wealth Is Blown Away," *BusinessWeek,* March 26, 2001; Allan Sloan, "The Downside of Momentum," *Newsweek,* March 19, 2001.

7. Buffett was not the only one concerned about the implication of this relationship. John Bogle, retired chairman of Vanguard, wrote of it in April 2001. However, he concluded that "some version of reality" had returned to the stock market. What made Buffett's speech noteworthy was not use of this particular metric but rather his pessimistic projection of what it meant.

8. One of Buffett's main points was that companies—many of which had been taking gains from surpluses out of their pension plans—were irresponsibly using unrealistic rates of return assumptions and would have to adjust these to reality, which would show the plans to be less well funded or even underfunded.

9. Vicente Fox worked for Coca-Cola for fifteen years, starting as a route supervisor in 1964, then being promoted ten years later to president of its Mexican, and ultimately its Latin American, operations.

10. Interview with Midge Patzer.

11. Interview with Don Graham.

12. Dr. Griffith R. Harsh, IV, Director, Surgical Neuro-Oncology Program at Stanford University Medical School.

13. Interview with Kathleen Cole.

14. Interviews with Bill Gates, Peter Buffett, Howie Buffett.

15. Interviews with Susie Buffett Jr., Don Graham.

16. Karlyn Barker, "Capacity Crowd Expected at Funeral; Schlesinger, Bradlee, Kissinger, Relatives Among Eulogists," *Washington Post,* July 22, 2001.

17. Paul Farhi, "Close Enough to See: TV Coverage Captures Small, Telling Moments," *Washington Post*, July 24, 2001; Steve Twomey, "A Celebrated Life: Thousands Honor Katharine Graham at the Cathedral," *Washington Post*, July 24, 2001; Mary Leonard, "Thousands Pay Tribute to *Washington Post*'s Katharine Graham," *Boston Globe*, July 24, 2001.

18. Karlyn Barker, "Capacity Crowd Expected at Funeral; Schlesinger, Bradlee, Kissinger, Relatives Among Eulogists."

19. Libby Copeland, "Kay Graham's Last Party: At Her Georgetown Home, A Diverse Group Gathers," *Washington Post*, July 24, 2001.

20. The family sold the house shortly after Graham's death.

Chapter 56: By the Rich, for the Rich

1. Buffett recalled this, and said, "*I think somebody even may have bought a car just because they ran out of rental cars.*"

2. Interview with Bob Nardelli.

3. Interview with Tony Pesavento.

4. Buffett told the author this in 2001, shortly after the terrorist attack.

5. The term "unforeseeable" as an explanation for large losses was virtually universal after 9/11 in the insurance industry.

6. Interview with Susie Buffett Jr.

7. This initial estimate was revised to $2.4 billion in the December 31 annual report.

8. Charles R. Morris, *The Trillion Dollar Meltdown*. New York: Public Affairs, 2008.

9. Leading to reforms such as not allowing analysts to be compensated based on investment-banking work, and setting up "firewalls" between analysts and investment bankers.

10. For $835 million.

11. For just under $1 billion. Kern moved 850 million cubic feet of gas a day from the Rocky Mountains to Las Vegas and California.

12. This pipeline moved 4.3 billion cubic feet of gas per day. Berkshire bought it for $928 million, after Dynegy had gotten it for $1.5 billion when Enron went bankrupt and NNG was being held as collateral (both had assumed $950 million of NNG's debt). After MidAmerican's two pipeline deals in 2002, it transported 8% of the gas in the U.S.

13. Berkshire joined with Lehman and Citigroup to lend $2 billion to Williams at a 20% interest rate.

14. Pre-9/11, Munich Re and AXA struck a derivatives deal valued at $50 million with Berkshire Hathaway Group to reinsure against an earthquake canceling 2002's FIFA World Cup in South Korea and Japan. BRK would pay regardless of the actual cost of the loss, if the tournament was postponed or canceled because of an earthquake of a certain magnitude. Separately, after 9/11, AXA pulled out of insuring the tournament, and on October 30 National Indemnity stepped in to insure it, allowing the World Cup to proceed.

15. Berkshire Hathaway letter to shareholders, 2007.

16. Interview with Frank Rooney.

17. Source: IRS, Statistics of Income Division, March 2007; Joint Committee on Taxation, *Description and Analysis of Present Law and Proposals Relating to Federal Estate and Gift Taxation*, Public Hearing Before the Subcommittee on Taxation and IRS Oversight of the Senate Committee on Finance, March 15, 2001.

18. In 2007, over 8% of the federal budget, or $244 billion, was interest on federal debt. That is almost exactly ten times the amount collected through the estate tax.

19. See, for example, Melik Kaylan, "In Warren Buffett's America . . ." *Wall Street Journal*, March 6, 2001; John Conlin, "Only Individual Freedom Can Transform the World," *Wall Street Journal*, July 26, 2001; Steve Hornig, "The Super-Wealthy Typically Do Not Pay Estate Taxes," *Financial Times*, June 15, 2006; Holman W. Jenkins Jr., "Let's Have More Heirs and Heiresses," *Wall Street Journal*, February 21, 2001.

20. William S. Broeksmit, "Begging to Differ with the Billionaire," *Washington Post*, May 24, 2003.

21. Daft had options to buy 650,000 shares, initially estimated as worth $38.1 million to $112.3 mil-

lion in 2015, depending on how much the stock appreciated. He also got $87.3 million in restricted stock awards, totaling 1.5 million shares. Henry Unger, "If Coca-Cola Chief Daft Fizzles, He'll Lose Millions," *Atlanta Journal-Constitution*, March 3, 2001.

22. The CEO–worker pay gap of 411-to-1 in 2001 was nearly ten times as high as the 1982 ratio of 42-to-1. "If the average annual pay for production workers had grown at the same rate since 1990 as it has for CEOs, their 2001 average annual earnings would have been $101,156 instead of $25,467. If the minimum wage, which stood at $3.80 an hour in 1990, had grown at the same rate as CEO pay, it would have been $21.41 an hour in 2001, rather than the current $5.15 an hour." Scott Klinger, Chris Hartman, Sarah Anderson, and John Cavanagh, "Executive Excess 2002, CEOs Cook the Books, Skewer the Rest of Us, Ninth Annual CEO Compensation Survey." Institute for Policy Studies, United for a Fair Economy, August 26, 2002.

23. Geoffrey Colvin, "The Great CEO Pay Heist," *Fortune,* June 25, 2001. A 2001 option grant later became the subject of controversy in the 2007 stock-option backdating scandal.

24. Warren Buffett, "Stock Options and Common Sense," *Washington Post,* April 9, 2002.

25. Two other companies, Winn-Dixie and Boeing, had earlier started treating stock options as an expense. But they had nothing like Coca-Cola's clout.

26. Warren Buffett, Securities and Exchange Commission's Roundtable on Financial Disclosure and Auditor Oversight, New York, March 4, 2002.

27. Berkshire Hathaway letter to shareholders, 2002.

28. David Perry, "Buffett Rests Easy With Latest Investment," *Furniture Today,* May 6, 2002.

29. He didn't really want her to come back either, although he looked tempted a few times.

Chapter 57: Oracle

1. This portrait of Susie in the late 1990s and early millennial era is based on comments from more than two dozen sources who knew her well but cannot be identified by name.

2. Interview with Howie Buffett.

3. Interest rates, which had been falling since 9/11, hit a low of 1% in June 2003 and remained there until June 2004.

4. This is a shorthand description for investors' limited risk aversion during this period.

5. In "Mortgage Market Needs $1 Trillion, FBR Estimates," Alistair Barr (*MarketWatch,* March 7, 2008) recaps a Friedman, Billings Ramsey research report that estimates that of the total $11 trillion U.S. mortgage market, only $587 billion was backed with equity—meaning that the average U.S. home had scarcely more than 5% equity. Before long, half of all CDOs would be backed by subprime mortgages (David Evans, "Subprime Infects $300 Billion of Money Market Funds," Bloomberg, August 20, 2007).

6. In *The Trillion Dollar Meltdown* (New York: Public Affairs, 2008), Charles Morris explains that because the typical credit hedge fund was leveraged 5:1, the 5% equity was reduced to 1%—a 100:1 leverage ratio, or $1 of capital supporting $100 of debt.

7. He used derivatives himself, but as a borrower, not a lender. Therefore, if things went wrong, he did not have to collect from anyone else.

8. For example, he was called "The Alarmist of Omaha" by Rana Foroohar in *Newsweek* on May 12, 2003.

9. In his memoir, Jim Clayton says people find it hard to believe that he did not return Buffett's call himself. He says it never occurred to him to do so, and he and Buffett have never called each other about business. During the months that the deal was in negotiation and litigation, the author observed that Buffett dealt only with Kevin Clayton.

10. Interview with Kevin Clayton.

11. Jim Clayton, Bill Retherford, *First a Dream.* (Tennessee: FSB Press, 2002.) The 2004 revised edition gives an account of Berkshire Hathaway's fight for Clayton Homes.

12. Buffett had spent only $50 million in April to purchase PetroChina stock, but that brought Berkshire's ownership to $488 million and over the limit that required disclosure to the Hong Kong Stock Exchange.

13. Buffett said he would buy foreign stocks under the right circumstances; e.g., in the United

Kingdom or a newspaper in Hong Kong. However, he did not spend time seriously studying foreign stocks until opportunities in the U.S. began to thin.

14. Warren Buffett, "Why I'm Down on the Dollar," *Fortune*, November 10, 2003.

15. From unpublished coverage of the 2003 Berkshire Hathaway annual meeting, courtesy of *Outstanding Investor Digest*.

16. A major advantage of the deal was Berkshire's access to and low cost of funds. With its AAA credit rating, it could borrow at a far lower rate than any other manufactured-home maker and thus not only survive credit droughts but make money under conditions where Clayton's competitors could not survive.

17. Speaking at the New York Public Library, June 25, 2006.

18. Andrew Ross Sorkin, "Buffett May Face a Competing Bid for Clayton Homes," *New York Times*, July 11, 2003.

19. "Suit Over Sale of Clayton Homes to Buffett," *New York Times*, June 10, 2003. Gray alleged that previous shareholder meetings electing directors had taken place without proper notice. In June the Delaware Chancery Court ruled that Clayton had technically not met the notice requirement, but since the meeting was so well attended by shareholders, the mistake was only technical and results of the meeting would not be overturned.

20. Jennifer Reingold, "The Ballad of Clayton Homes," *Fast Company*, January 2004.

21. At its peak before the death of Susan T. Buffett, the foundation spent $15–$30 million per year in total, mostly on reproductive rights.

22. If Buffett had paid dividends and used them for the donations, the whole point would have been moot.

23. Douglas R. Scott Jr., president, Life Decisions International, letter to Warren Buffett, September 26, 2002.

24. Nicholas Varchaver, "Berkshire Gives Up On Giving: How a Pro-Life Housewife Took On Warren Buffett," *Fortune*, August 11, 2003.

25. Compiled from various interviews.

26. As of 2008, pro-life activists, according to the U.S. National Abortion Federation, had committed 7 murders, attempted 17 other murders, made 388 death threats, kidnapped 4 people, committed 41 bombings, 174 instances of arson, and 128 burglaries, attempted 94 bombings or arsons, made 623 bomb threats, committed 1,306 instances of vandalism, made 656 bioterror threats, and committed 162 instances of assault and battery. These numbers exclude stalking, hoax device/suspect packages, hate mail, harassing phone calls, trespassing, invasion, Internet harassment, and other less serious incidents. The pro-life movement's activities have resulted in 37,715 arrests as of 2007. Most mainstream pro-life organizations reject the terrorist wing of the movement, some vocally.

27. Under Delaware law, only shareholders in attendance were eligible to vote on a recess.

28. Jim Clayton, Bill Retherford, *First a Dream*.

29. Cerberus memorandum, "For Discussion Purposes," reprinted in Jim Clayton, *First a Dream*.

30. By 2006, manufactured-home shipments had fallen to 117,510 units and were still declining at an average rate of 32% in 2007 despite a temporary bump in 2005 from Hurricane Katrina. (Source: Manufactured Housing Institute.)

Chapter 58: Buffetted

1. Buffett participated in two live auctions for Glide before the first eBay auction.

2. Interviews with Kathleen Cole, Susie Buffett Jr.

3. Interview with Howie Buffett.

4. Interviews with Howie Buffett, Susie Buffett Jr.

5. Interview with Kathleen Cole.

6. Ibid.

7. www.oralcancerfoundation.org.

8.   Oral Cancer Foundation.

9.   Interviews with Kathleen Cole, Ron Parks.

10. Interviews with Marshall Weinberg, Walter and Ruth Scott, Lou Simpson, George Gillespie.

11. Interview with Susie Buffett Jr.

12. Adapted from John Dunn, "Georgia Tech Students Quiz Warren Buffett," *Georgia Tech,* Winter 2003.

Chapter 59: Winter

1.   Interview with Susie Buffett Jr.

2.   Interviews with Peter Buffett, Howie Buffett, Susie Buffett Jr.

3.   Generally speaking, federal law governing foundations requires that foundations distribute or use a minimum amount of their assets regularly for their charitable purposes (approximately 5% of the fair market value of the private foundation's investment assets).

4.   Charles T. Munger, edited by Peter Kaufmann, *Poor Charlie's Almanack: The Wit and Wisdom of Charles T. Munger.* New York: Donning Company Publishers, 2005.

Chapter 60: Frozen Coke

1.   Interview with Kathleen Cole.

2.   Interviews with Jamie Dimon, Jeffrey Immelt.

3.   Berkshire Hathaway 2004 chairman's letter, annual report.

4.   Betsy Morris, "The Real Story," *Fortune,* May 31, 2004.

5.   Investors felt that Coke should move aggressively into noncarbonated drinks, but the company insisted that international growth in carbonated beverages—the highest-margin product—was the only way to go. At $50, the stock was also still expensive at 24x earnings and 8.6x book value.

6.   Coca-Cola Enterprises took a $103 million charge for the European recall during Ivester's reign. In 1999, Daft had to report the first loss in a decade and take a total of $1.6 billion of charges. Then, in 1Q2000, Daft reported Coke's second quarterly loss in a row—charges for massive restructuring/layoffs and a write-down of excess bottling capacity in India. In 2000, Coke took more charges and cut its projection for annual worldwide unit case volume growth to 5% to 6%, from 7% to 8%. Coke revised its targets again after 9/11.

7.   Suppose Berkshire demanded a special deal. On $120 million of purchases, this might be worth, say, a dime a share, estimating liberally. Berkshire earned $5,309 per A equivalent share in 2003. (The company doesn't present cents per share in its financial statements.) To a B shareholder, it would be ⁹⁄₁₀ of a penny per share. It's very hard to make a case that an amount so small would incent Buffett to do something so contrary to Coca-Cola's interests as to force it to turn down a big contract with Burger King in order to keep selling Coca-Cola at Dairy Queen. That would be so even if Berkshire owned zero Coca-Cola stock. The problem with the ISS approach was its absolutist checklist approach that applies no reasoning and proportionality.

8.   CalPERS also opposed the election of Herbert Allen, former U.S. Senator Sam Nunn, and Don Keough because of their business relationships with the company.

9.   Herbert Allen, "Conflict-Cola," *Wall Street Journal,* April 15, 2004.

10. Excerpts from a survey of corporate board members conducted by PricewaterhouseCoopers, as reported in *Corporate Board Member,* November/December 2004. PWC identified no comments or sentiment against Buffett.

11. Deborah Brewster, Simon London, "CalPERS Chief Relaxes in the Eye of the Storm," *Financial Times,* June 2, 2004.

12. Interview with Don Graham.

13. The GMP International Union, which also spoke at the meeting.

14. Transcript, Coca-Cola shareholder meeting 2004, courtesy of the Coca-Cola Company; Adam Levy and Steve Matthews, "Coke's World of Woes," *Bloomberg Markets,* July 2004; interviews with several directors and company employees.

15. Transcript, Coca-Cola shareholder meeting 2004, courtesy of the Coca-Cola Company.

16. Adam Levy and Steve Matthews, "Coke's World of Woes." The *New York Times* blasted Coke over severance payments to Heyer and other executives in "Another Coke Classic," June 16, 2004. The criticism was not universal; the *Economist* said Isdell was "welcomed by investors and analysts as a safe pair of hands" ("From Old Bottles," May 8, 2004).

17. For example, Constance L. Hays, in *The Real Thing: Truth and Power at the Coca-Cola Company* (New York: Random House, 2004), makes this inference.

Chapter 61: The Seventh Fire

1. Interview with Kathleen Cole.

2. Ibid.

3. The author, too, has for some years sat in the managers' section, although she is not a shareholder.

4. Tom Strobhar, "Report on B-H Shareholder Meeting," *Human Life International,* May 2004; "Special Report, HLI Embarrasses Warren Buffett in Front of 14,000 Stockholders," July 2004. Mr. Strobhar has a curious history. After serving as a leader in the boycott against Berkshire that resulted in canceling the shareholder-contributions program, he wrote an editorial in the *Wall Street Journal,* "Giving Until It Hurts" (August 1, 2003), criticizing the shareholder-contributions program for being a clandestine way of "paying" Buffett (notwithstanding that Berkshire made no corporate charitable contributions nor paid a dividend). Strobhar identified himself only as the president of an investment firm in Dayton, Ohio, omitting his role in the boycott and the fact that he was chairman of Life Decisions International. Strobhar went on in 2005 to found Citizen Action Now, an organization designed to fight "the homosexual agenda" and for "an America free from the manipulation of homosexual groups." On the Web site of his investment firm, he borrows Buffett's reputation by advertising himself (as of November 2007) as "trained in the tradition of Ben Graham, the 'father of security analysis,' whose students include Warren Buffet [sic], 'the world's greatest investor.' . . . Like Graham and Buffett, Thomas Strobhar's focus is on 'value investing.' "

5. The Omaha Housing Authority bought the house for $89,900.

6. Interview with Susie Buffett Jr.

7. Ibid.

8. Ibid.

9. Ibid.

10. Howard Buffett Jr. (Howie B.), speaking at Susie's funeral.

11. Interview with T. D. Kelsey.

12. Ibid.

13. Interviews with Al Oehrle, Barbara Oehrle.

14. Interview with T. D. Kelsey.

15. Interviews with Herbert Allen, Barbara Oehrle, T. D. Kelsey.

16. Interview with Susie Buffett Jr.

17. Interviews with Herbert Allen, T. D. Kelsey. According to the Oehrles, Herbert Allen, and Barry Diller, the rest of the guests remained in Cody for the weekend and turned the weekend, as best they could, into a sort of tribute to Susie.

18. Interview with Susie Buffett Jr.

19. Interview with Howie Buffett.

20. Interviews with T. D. Kelsey, Herbert Allen.

21. Interviews with Susie Buffett Jr., Peter Buffett.

22. Interviews with Susie Buffett Jr. and Peter Buffett, who both said they found it comforting to have their mother with them in the plane.

23. Interview with Howie Buffett.

24. Interview with Sharon Osberg.

25. Interview with Susie Buffett Jr.

Chapter 62: Claim Checks

1. She left significant amounts of money to Kathleen Cole and Ron Parks, her longtime trusted caretakers and friends. She left her grandchildren and other people modest amounts, from $10,000 to $100,000.

2. Interview with Tom Newman.

3. Interview with Peter Buffett.

4. A. D. Amorosi, "In 'Spirit,' Tradition Is Besieged by Modern Life," *Philadelphia Inquirer,* May 23, 2005.

5. Warren Buffett letter to Nicole Buffett, August 10, 2006.

6. Richard Johnson with Paula Froelich, Chris Wilson, and Bill Hoffmann, "Buffett to Kin: You're Fired!," *New York Post,* September 7, 2006.

7. Leah McGrath Goodman, "The Billionaire's Black Sheep," *Marie Claire,* December 2008.

8. Interview with Sharon Osberg.

9. Berkshire Hathaway annual letter to shareholders, 2005.

10. Charles R. Morris, *The Trillion Dollar Meltdown.* New York: Public Affairs, 2008.

11. Interview with Charlie Munger.

12. Carol Loomis, "Warren Buffett Gives It Away," *Fortune,* July 10, 2006.

13. Ibid.

14. Buffett could not resist: The note that accompanied Bertie's letter containing this comment said, *"She's still smarting about that a little bit."*

15. Interview with Doris Buffett.

16. In installments beginning in 2006, as long as either Bill or Melinda Gates is active in the foundation.

17. The first installment of 602,500 shares declined 5% a year in terms of shares thereafter. Buffett expected, as was reasonable at the time, that the price of Berkshire's stock would increase by at least 5% a year (through modest growth and inflation). Thus, the dollar value of the gifts was likely to remain level or even increase from year to year. During the year between the first gift and the second, Berkshire's stock price went up 17%. The first 602,500-B-share distribution was worth $1.8 billion, compared to the second 572,375-B-share distribution worth $2 billion. In June 2006, BRK was trading at $91,500 (B shares at $3,043).

18. As quoted in "The Life Well Spent: An Evening with Warren Buffett," November 2007.

19. Bill Gates used the term "convenors." This approach differs, for example, from annually funding a vaccine program, which requires a continuing investment without a permanent cure.

20. "The New Powers of Giving," *Economist,* July 6, 2006; Karen DeYoung, "Gates, Rockefeller Charities Join to Fight African Hunger," *Washington Post,* September 13, 2006; Han Wilhelm, "Big Changes at the Rockefeller Foundation," *Chronicle of Philanthropy,* September 8, 2006; Andrew Jack, "Manna from Omaha: A Year of 'Giving While Living' Transforms Philanthropy," *Financial Times,* December 27, 2006.

21. Interview with Doris Buffett. See Sally Beaty, "The Wealth Report: The Other Buffett," *Wall Street Journal,* August 3, 2007.

22. After Susie's death, both of her apartments in San Francisco's Pacific Heights were sold, as was the Buffetts' second house, "the dormitory," in Emerald Bay. Buffett kept the original house in Emerald Bay, which continues to be used by his children and grandchildren. He never goes there.

Chapter 63: The Crisis

1. Michael Santoli, "They've Got Class," *Barron's,* September 10, 2007.

2. On October 9, 2007.

3. This excludes approximately $180 million of imputed investment income on the $5.5 billion of General Re's cash that Buffett had transferred to National Indemnity and Columbia Insurance through intercompany reinsurance agreements. General Re estimated the effect on its return on equity at 150 basis points in each of 2005, 2006, and 2007.

4. The combination of underwriting profits and higher float produced a 20% return on average equity in 2006, compared to losses in earlier years. General Re grew its book value at an average of 12.8% since 2001, bringing its capital to more than $11 billion, compared to $8.6 billion when it was acquired. It made a $526 million profit from underwriting on premiums of about $6 billion—compared to earlier losses of between $1 and $3 billion (depending on the year) on premiums of just under $9 billion. Float had risen from about $15 billion to $23 billion on a 32% decline in premiums.

5. Berkshire Hathaway 2007 letter to shareholders.

6. The Department of Justice was using broad powers under the so-called Thompson Memorandum, which defined what was meant by "cooperation" by a corporation in a criminal investigation, and among other things required companies to compel their employees to waive their Fifth Amendment rights and to deny employees assistance with legal fees, under threat of corporate criminal indictment. The most significant elements of the Thompson Memorandum have since been gutted as unconstitutional.

7. HIH Royal Commission, *The Failure of HIH Insurance*. Australia: National Capital Printing, Canberra Publishing and Printing, 2003.

8. Doug Simpson, "Search for Deep Pockets Widens in Reciprocal of America Case," Unintended Consequences blog (dougsimpson.com/blog), March 3, 2005; Timothy L. O'Brien, "Investigation of Insurance Puts Buffett in Spotlight," *New York Times*, March 28, 2005; Timothy L. O'Brien and Joseph B. Treaster, "The Insurance Scandal Shakes Main Street," *New York Times*, April 17, 2005; Marisa Taylor, "U.S. Dropped Enron-Like Fraud Probe," McClatchy Newspapers, July 23, 2007; Scott Horton, "Corporate Corruption and the Bush Justice Department," *Harper's Magazine*, July 24, 2007.

9. If so, it was unnecessary. The *Buffalo News* undoubtedly would have endorsed Spitzer anyway.

10. In 1986, as the bubble developed, Buffett bought bonds as the *"least objectionable alternative"* (1986 shareholders letter). He kept the *Washington Post*, GEICO, and Cap Cities, which he said would be "permanent" investments. By 1987, therefore, he had made a mental shift toward passive investing in certain public companies.

11. On December 12, 2007, major central banks began to provide funding at terms longer than overnight, and began to auction funding against a broader range of collateral and with a broader set of counterparties. The Federal Reserve activated swap lines to help the other central banks provide liquidity in dollars to their markets.

12. Collateral posted as of March 31, 2009 totaled approximately $1 billion.

13. Buffett especially used his will for this purpose, talking about it in vague terms without making promises, and changing it periodically.

14. The title of a recent book, *Even Buffett Isn't Perfect: What You Can and Can't Learn from the World's Greatest Investor* by Vahan Jinkiqian (New York: Portfolio Hardcover, 2008), says it all about the standard to which Buffett is held.

15. As Berkshire's first-quarter 2009 form 10-Q filed with the SEC stated, "There is minimal involvement by Berkshire's corporate headquarters in the day-to-day business activities of the operating businesses."

Chapter 64: The Snowball

1. Using the return on capital figure he achieved for shareholders through 2007 as a proxy, the author estimates that Buffett (not including Susie's shares) would have been worth between $71 and $111 billion by the end of 2007 had he continued to charge his "partners" fees. Susie's stake would have been worth another $3.7–$5 billion. The difference between the high and low range is the fee structure (Buffett's former 25% plus 6% interest on capital to all partners—the high number—vs. the 2%/20% structure of most hedge funds today—the low number). The calculation assumes that Buffett took out the equivalent of his 6% a year for living expenses, as he typically did while running the partnership. That amounts to $1 million per year by 2007. His and Susie's (really Susie's) living expenses exceeded this by a wide margin; however, Buffett's personal investments—not part of Berkshire—also compounded at an astonishing rate and could (and did) fund Susie's lifestyle without further withdrawals from Berkshire.

2. Interview with Charlie Munger.

A Personal Note About Research

To write *The Snowball*, I spent more than five years interviewing Warren Buffett, both in person and on the phone. For weeks on end I sat in his office or traveled with him observing him work. Some of my most valuable insights came from my own experiences with him. I also interviewed his family, friends, former classmates, business associates, and others—250 people in all. Some of these interviews continued for days and I interviewed many people several times.

Warren gave me virtually unlimited time, and let me roam with surprising freedom among the files and correspondence in his exhaustive collection; it was especially fortunate that he and many of his friends and family members were letter-writers. Berkshire Hathaway's files contained material that helped establish a timeline and flesh out details. I also relied on my own growing understanding of Warren, and at times on my direct knowledge of events. Certain disagreements among sources are aired in the endnotes.

Quotes appear throughout the book to illuminate the narrative. Most quotes are from recorded interviews, and have been edited only for clarity and length. Sources were cited unless the interviewee asked not to be named.

During their interviews, many people recalled remarks from past conversations. Sometimes the events they were describing had taken place decades earlier. It would be naive to assume that all of these quotes are verbatim recollections of every word spoken. Nevertheless, I found them very helpful in conveying the substance of an incident or conversation. Their sources can be found in the endnotes.

In the end, my own extensive experience with Warren and the thousands of jigsaw puzzle pieces given me by so many sources came together in this portrait of a fascinating and deeply complex man.

Photo Credits and Permissions:

Acknowledgments

Without the help of many people this book would never have come into being. If I've succeeded, it's mainly thanks to the generosity of others. First among them, of course, is Warren Buffett. The generosity he showed by giving me so much access to his time, his family, his friends, and his files, and the courage he showed by refraining from meddling with the book for more than five years—right up until the day it went to the printer—are remarkable. His conviction that a smart person can do anything and his gentle but persistent Carnegizing lifted my aspirations as a writer and as a person, and changed my life. His influence on me cannot be described in a paragraph or a couple of pages—but for everything, Warren, I am grateful.

My literary agent, the peerless David Black, gave impeccable guidance. I trust him implicitly—above all to tell me important things that I don't want to hear—the most valuable quality you can have in a friend. He also stunned Warren into a moment of silence at his negotiating skill, not a small achievement.

My great good fortune was that the book was sold to the perceptive Irwyn Applebaum, the president and publisher of Bantam Dell, whose support and wisdom have inspired me throughout. Helping me was Ann Harris, my editor, who elevated *The Snowball* through her encouragement to write the story of a man's life seen in whole, and her editing with a meticulous eye for tone, context, and nuance. Later in the process, Beth Rashbaum unsheathed her red pencil, relentlessly pruning material this first-time author couldn't bear to cut herself, to the immeasurable improvement of the book. *The Snowball* owes much to them and I am grateful to have worked with two such talented editors. Any flaws, of course, are mine alone.

At Bantam I also thank Loren Noveck, who as the book's title administrator oversaw the multiple processes involved in producing a complex book; Virginia Norey, its designer; Ann's assistant Angela Polidoro; and the several others who collaborated in making *The Snowball* happen: deputy publisher Nita Taublib; publishing director Gina Wachtel; attorney Matthew Martin; production experts

Tom Leddy, Maggie Hart, and Margaret Benton; creative marketing director Betsy Hulsebosch and her team; sales marketing director Cynthia Lasky; and publicity director Barb Burg.

I wrote this book while associated with Morgan Stanley as an advisory director, and appreciate my friends' and colleagues' and the firm's support. Lauren Esposito, my researcher, who also came from Morgan Stanley, brought with her a set of financial skills that added immensely to the book, and became adept at locating critical research material. To watch an artist like Marion Ettlinger at work inspired me near the end of the writing, and I thank her for the result.

Doris Buffett, Roberta Buffett Bialek, and Warren Buffett's children Susan, Howard, and Peter, Charlie Munger, Bill Gates, and Don Graham were especially generous with their time and insight, and I am grateful to them for their important contributions.

People trusted by both me and Warren—Sharon Osberg, Vinay Saqi, and Devon Spurgeon—provided various types of assistance throughout, from financial commentary to calming frayed nerves. The love and support of my sister, Elizabeth Davey, and my father, Ken Davey, helped bring the book into being. David Moyer came into my life just in time to learn what it means to live with a writer who is finishing a book on deadline, and kiddingly referred to himself as my "fiancé in exile" while providing a shoulder to lean on, advice, laughter, love, and romance. He, along with Sharon Osberg and Justin Bennett, served as early readers, and *The Snowball* would be far poorer without their comments and advice.

I am indebted to many other people and organizations who helped with research and granted permission to use photographs and copyrighted material, as well as those who gave special help with the project directly or indirectly in various ways. My thanks go to Carol Allen, Herbert Allen, Ed Anderson and Joan Parsons, Jan and Brian Babiak, the Blumkin family, Hal Borthwick, Debbie Bosanek, Betsy Bowen, Joe Brandon, Phil Brooks, Kelly Broz, Jan and John Cleary, Carlon Colker, Robert Conte, Gerald Corrigan, Michael Daly, Leigh Ann Elisio, Stuart Erickson, Paul Fishman, Cynthia George, George Gillespie, Rick Guerin, Marc Hamburg, Carol Hayes, Liz Hylton, Mark Jankowski, Mr. and Mrs. Howard Jessen, Gladys Kaiser, Don Keough, Tom and Virginia Knapp, Margaret Landon, Arthur K. Langlie, David Larabell, Stanford Lipsey, Jack Mayfield, John Macfarlane, Michael McGivney, Verne McKenzie, Charles T. Munger Jr., Molly Munger, Wendy Munger, Tony Nicely, Dorothe Obert, Ron Olson, Chuck Peterson, Susan Raihofer, Rod Rathbun, Deb Ray, Eric Rosenfeld, Neil Rosini, Fred Reinhardt, Mick Rood, Gary Rosenberg, Edith Rubinstein, Michael Ruddell, Richard Santulli, Walter

Schloss, Lou Simpson, Carol Sklenicka, Judge Stanley Sporkin, Mary Stanton Plowden-Wardlaw, Chris Stavrou, Bob Sullivan, Jeffrey Vitale, Marshall Weinberg, Sheila Weitzel, Bruce Whitman, Jackie Wilson, Al Zanner, and those who asked not to be named.

I would also like to express appreciation to the following organizations: the Douglas County Historical Society, GEICO, General Re, Greenwich Emergency Medical Service, Greif Inc., Harvard Business School, Harvard Law School, the Merrick Library, the Martin Luther King Jr. Public Library Washingtoniana Collection, Morgan Stanley, the National Archives, National Indemnity Corporation, the Nebraska Furniture Mart, the New Bedford Free Public Library, the New Bedford Whaling Museum, the New York Public Library, NetJets Inc., the Omaha Press Club, the *Omaha World-Herald, Outstanding Investor Digest,* the Rolls-Royce Foundation, Rosehill School, Ruane Cunniff & Goldfarb Co., The Securities and Exchange Commission, and The Westchester apartments.

Index

PHOTO: © MARION ETTLINGER

Before becoming a full-time writer, Alice Schroeder was a top-ranked Wall Street analyst and managing director at Morgan Stanley. Born in Texas, she earned her undergraduate degree and MBA at the University of Texas at Austin and began her career as a CPA. She now writes a column for Bloomberg News and is a senior advisor to Morgan Stanley. Schroeder lives in Connecticut with her husband.